Masterpieces of American Literature

Masterpieces
of
American Literature

Edited by
Frank N. Magill

HarperCollins*Publishers*

FIRST EDITION

Library of Congress Cataloging-in-Publication Data

Masterpieces of American literature / edited by Frank N. Magill. — 1st ed.
    p.   cm.
  Includes bibliographical references and index.
  ISBN 0-06-270072-3
    1. American literature—Outlines, syllabi, etc. 2. American literature—Stories, plots, etc. 3. Canon (Literature) I. Magill, Frank Northen, 1907-
PS94.M34   1993
810.9—dc20   93-15940
                                                                  CIP

93 94 95 96 97 RRD 10 9 8 7 6 5 4 3 2 1

PREFACE

Masterpieces of American Literature is the companion volume to *Masterpieces of World Literature*, published in 1989, and *Masterpieces of African-American Literature*, published in 1992. This volume surveys the broad range of American achievements in prose and poetry, from Colonial times (the poetry of Anne Bradstreet) to the late twentieth century (Tom Wolfe's *The Bonfire of the Vanities*).

This *Masterpieces* presents 199 standardized articles—162 on classic American works of fiction and nonfiction and 37 general essays about the addresses, essays, poetry, or short stories of notable American writers and thinkers—all arranged alphabetically. Designed primarily for reference, the format allows the reader to find the maximum information in the quickest time. For the works that tell a story—novels, stories, plays, and autobiographies—the contributor was asked to choose the most appropriate format: plot summary or essay-review. For most of these fictional works, the plot-summary format is employed. Each plot digest is preceded by carefully checked reference data that furnish at a glance the type of work, author, type of plot, time of plot, locale, and first publication date. Next, a brief summary of the narrative appears, which can be used either separately or in conjunction with the fuller treatment that follows. Each essay then introduces to the reader the story's principal characters in a list form, including a brief description of each character and his or her relationship to the other characters. The text itself is divided into two sections. "The Story," a well-rounded synopsis, orients the reader to the novel, story, play, or autobiography and refreshes the memory of the reader who is reviewing a book read long ago. Immediately following the plot summary, the "Critical Evaluation" discusses the major critical and analytical approaches to the work, setting the course for formal or informal study.

The remaining works, most of which do not tell a story but impart important thoughts in prose or verse, are presented in the essay-review format. Following the ready-reference data (type of work, author, and publication date, as well as type of plot, time of plot, and locale where applicable), the essay identifies the primary ideas and integrates them with a discussion of the literary merits of the work in a clear, expository style, making accessible to readers many of the ideas that form the American literary and philosophical tradition.

Each of the 199 essays in this edition has been written with an eye to the currency of the ideas presented, requiring an enormous amount of assistance from a carefully selected staff that included scores of English faculty members from universities and colleges throughout the United States. All these contributors deserve recognition; in particular, we would like to acknowledge: Michael Adams, Patrick Adcock, Stanley Archer, Charles Avinger, Gerhard Brand, Thomas J. Cassidy, Patricia Clark, Jeffrey E. Cupp, Bill Delaney, Robert P. Ellis, Thomas L. Erskine, Jean C. Fulton, Leslie Gerber, Jill B. Gidmark, Natalie Harper, Leon Lewis, Janet McCann, Andrew Macdonald, Gina Macdonald, Charles E. May, Laurence W. Mazzeno, Robert A. Morace, Edwin Moses, John M. Muste, George O'Brien, Charles H. Pullen, Rosemary M. Canfield Reisman, Mary Rohrberger, Jill Rollins, Carl Rollyson, Joseph Rosenblum, Robert L. Ross, A. J. Sobczak, Gerald H. Strauss, James Sullivan, James M. Welsh, and Michael Witkoski.

The volume concludes with two indexes to aid the user in locating all works by author (author index) or title (title index).

FRANK N. MAGILL

91176

Acknowledgments

The following plot summaries are used by permission of the publishers and copyright holders.

Absalom, Absalom! by William Faulkner (Random House, Inc., and William Faulkner, 1936).

The Age of Innocence by Edith Wharton (Appleton-Century-Crofts, Inc., 1920; D. Appleton & Co. and Frederic King, 1947).

All the King's Men by Robert Penn Warren (Harcourt, Brace & Co., Inc., 1946).

The Ambassadors by Henry James (Harper & Brothers, 1902, 1903; Henry James, executor, 1930).

An American Tragedy by Theodore Dreiser (Mrs. Theodore Dreiser, The World Publishing Co., and Boni & Liveright, Inc., 1925).

Appointment in Samarra by John O'Hara (Duell, Sloan & Pearce, Inc., and John O'Hara, 1934).

As I Lay Dying by William Faulkner (Random House, Inc., and William Faulkner, 1930).

Babbitt by Sinclair Lewis (Harcourt, Brace & Co., Inc., 1922).

A Bell for Adano by John Hersey (Alfred A. Knopf, Inc., and John Hersey, 1944).

Billy Budd, Foretopman by Herman Melville (Liveright Publishing Corp., 1928).

The Bridge of San Luis Rey by Thornton Wilder (Thornton Wilder and Albert & Charles Boni, Inc., 1927).

The Call of the Wild by Jack London (The Macmillan Co., 1903, 1912, 1931).

The Country of the Pointed Firs by Sarah Orne Jewett (Houghton Mifflin Co. and Sarah Orne Jewett, 1896; Mary R. Jewett, 1924).

Death of a Salesman by Arthur Miller (The Viking Press, Inc., and Arthur Miller, 1949).

Delta Wedding by Eudora Welty (Harcourt, Brace & Co., Inc., and Eudora Welty, 1945, 1946).

Desire Under the Elms by Eugene O'Neill (Random House, Inc., and Boni & Liveright, Inc., 1925).

The Emperor Jones by Eugene O'Neill (Random House, Inc., 1921; Boni & Liveright, Inc., 1948).

A Farewell to Arms by Ernest Hemingway (Charles Scribner's Sons and Ernest Hemingway, 1929).

The Golden Bowl by Henry James (Charles Scribner's Sons, 1904; Henry James, executor, 1932).

The Grapes of Wrath by John Steinbeck (The Viking Press, Inc., and John Steinbeck, 1939).

The Great Gatsby by F. Scott Fitzgerald (Charles Scribner's Sons, 1925).

The Heart Is a Lonely Hunter by Carson McCullers (Carson McCullers, 1940).

The Human Comedy by William Saroyan (William Saroyan and Harcourt, Brace & Co., Inc., 1943).

The Jungle by Upton Sinclair (Upton Sinclair and The Viking Press, Inc., 1905, 1906, 1933, 1946).

The Late George Apley by John P. Marquand (John P. Marquand and Little, Brown & Co., 1937).

Light in August by William Faulkner (William Faulkner and Random House, Inc., 1932).

The Little Foxes by Lillian Hellman (Random House, Inc., and Lillian Hellman, 1939).

Look Homeward, Angel by Thomas Wolfe (Edward C. Aswell, administrator of Thomas Wolfe's estate, and Charles Scribner's Sons, 1929).

McTeague by Frank Norris (Doubleday & Co., Inc., 1899; Jeannette Preston, 1926).

The Maltese Falcon by Dashiell Hammett (Alfred A. Knopf, Inc., 1929, 1930).

The Member of the Wedding by Carson McCullers (Carson McCullers and Houghton Mifflin Co., 1946).

Miss Lonelyhearts by Nathanael West (Farrar, Strauss & Cudahy, Inc., and Nathanael West, 1933).

Mourning Becomes Electra by Eugene O'Neill (Random House, Inc., and Horace Liveright, Inc., 1931).

Murder in the Cathedral by T. S. Eliot (Harcourt, Brace & Co., Inc., 1935).

Mutiny on the Bounty by Charles Nordhoff and James Norman Hall (Mrs. Laura Nordhoff, James Norman Hall, and Little, Brown & Co., 1932).

My Ántonia by Willa Cather (Houghton Mifflin Co. and Willa Cather, 1918; Willa Cather, 1946)

Contents

CONTENTS

CONTENTS

ABSALOM, ABSALOM!

Type of work: Novel
Author: William Faulkner (1897-1962)
Type of plot: Psychological realism
Time of plot: Nineteenth century
Locale: Mississippi
First published: 1936

Instead of his usual sustained interior monologue technique, Faulkner here uses the device of three narrators, each of whom relates the family saga of Thomas Sutpen from his or her unique point of view. This device imparts to Absalom, Absalom!, *which is a metaphor for the rich and chaotic Southern experience, a complexity, a depth of psychological insight, and an emotional intensity that might have been lost in a narrative of more traditional format.*

Principal Characters

Thomas Sutpen, the owner of Sutpen's Hundred in Yoknapatawpha County, Mississippi. Born of a poor white family in the mountains of Western Virginia, he grows up to become an ambitious man of implacable will. After his arrival in Mississippi he thinks he can win his neighbor's respect by building a huge mansion and marrying the daughter of a respectable merchant. When he is not driving his African slaves and a kidnapped French architect to finish the construction of his magnificent house, he seeks relaxation by fighting his most powerful slaves. Wishing to found a family dynasty, he wants, more than anything else, to have a male heir. When one son is killed and the other disappears, Sutpen, now aging, fathers a child by Milly, the granddaughter of Wash Jones, one of his tenants. After learning that the child is a girl, he rejects and insults Milly. Because of his callous rejection, old Wash Jones kills him.

Ellen Coldfield, the wife chosen by Thomas Sutpen because he believes she is "adjunctive" to his design of founding a plantation family. A meek, helpless woman, she is completely dominated by her husband.

Henry Sutpen, the son born to Thomas and Ellen Sutpen. Unlike his sister Judith, he faints when he sees his father fighting with slaves. At first, not knowing that Charles Bon is also Sutpen's son, impressionable Henry idolizes and imitates that suave young man. Later he learns Bon's true identity and kills him, after their return from the Civil War, to keep Judith from marrying her half brother, who is part black.

Charles Bon, Thomas Sutpen's unacknowledged son by his earlier marriage in Haiti. A polished man of the world, he forms a close friendship with the more provincial Henry, whom he meets at college, and he becomes engaged to Judith Sutpen. When the two return from the Civil War, Bon's charming manner does not prevent his being killed by Henry, who has learned that his friend, and the suitor of his sister, is part black.

Judith Sutpen, Thomas Sutpen's daughter. After Charles Bon has been killed and Henry flees, she vows never to marry. She dies of smallpox contracted while nursing Charles Bon's black son by his mistress.

Goodhue Coldfield, a middle-class storekeeper in the town of Jefferson, the father of Ellen and Rosa Coldfield. When the Civil War begins, he locks himself in his attic and disdainfully refuses to have any part in the conflict. Fed by Rosa, who sends him food that he pulls up in a basket, he dies alone in the attic.

Wash Jones, a squatter on Thomas Sutpen's land and, after the Civil War, his drinking companion. While his employer is away during the Civil War, Wash looks after the plantation. Ignorant, unwashed, but more vigorous than others of his type, he serves Sutpen well until the latter rejects Milly and her child by declaring that if she were a mare with a foal he could give her a stall in his stable. Picking up a scythe, a symbol of time and change, Wash beheads Sutpen.

Rosa Coldfield, Goodhue Coldfield's younger daughter. She is an old woman when she tells Quentin Compson that Sutpen, whom she calls a ruthless demon, brought terror and tragedy to all who had dealings with him. A straightlaced person, she recalls the abrupt, insulting fashion in which Sutpen had proposed to her in the hope that she would be able to bear him a son after his wife's death. Never married, she is obsessed by memories of her brother-in-law.

Clytemnestra Sutpen, called **Clytie,** the daughter of

Thomas Sutpen's former slave, who hides Henry Sutpen in the mansion when he returns, old and sick, years after the murder that he committed. Fearing that he will be arrested, she sets fire to the house and burns herself and Henry in the conflagration which destroys that dilapidated monument to Thomas Sutpen's pride and folly.

Milly Jones, the granddaughter of Wash Jones, who has a daughter by Thomas Sutpen. She and her child are killed by Wash after Sutpen's murder.

Charles Étienne de Saint Velery Bon, the son of Charles Bon and his octoroon mistress. He dies of smallpox at Sutpen's Hundred.

Jim Bond (Bon), the half-witted son of Charles Étienne de Saint Velery Bon and a full-blooded black woman. He is the only survivor of Sutpen's family.

Quentin Compson, the anguished son of a decaying Southern family. Moody and morose, he tells the story of the Sutpens to his uncomprehending roommate at Harvard. Driven by personal guilt, he is later to commit suicide. Before leaving for Harvard, he learns about Thomas Sutpen from Rosa Coldfield.

Shrevlin McCannon, called **Shreve,** a Canadian student at Harvard and Quentin Compson's roommate. With great curiosity but without much understanding, he listens to Quentin's strange tale of Southern passions and tragedy leading to decay and ruin.

The Story

In the summer of 1909, when Quentin Compson was preparing to go to Harvard, old Rosa Coldfield insisted upon telling him the whole infamous story of Thomas Sutpen, whom she called a demon. According to Miss Rosa, he had brought terror and tragedy to all who had dealings with him.

In 1833, Thomas Sutpen had come to Jefferson, Mississippi, with a fine horse and two pistols and no known past. He had lived mysteriously for a while among people at the hotel, and after a short time, he had disappeared from the area. He had purchased one hundred square miles of uncleared land from the Chickasaws and had had it recorded at the land office.

When he returned with a wagon load of wild-looking African Americans, a French architect, and a few tools and wagons, he was as uncommunicative as ever. At once, he set about clearing land and building a mansion. For two years he labored, and during all that time he rarely saw or visited his acquaintances in Jefferson. People wondered about the source of his money. Some claimed that he had stolen it somewhere in his mysterious comings and goings. Then, for three years, his house remained unfinished, without windowpanes or furnishings, while Thomas Sutpen busied himself with his crops. Occasionally he invited Jefferson men to his plantation to hunt, entertaining them with liquor, cards, and savage combats between his giant slaves—combats in which he himself sometimes joined for the sport.

At last, he disappeared once more, and when he returned, he had furniture and furnishings elaborate and fine enough to make his great house a splendid showplace. Because of his mysterious actions, sentiment in the village turned against him. This hostility, however, subsided somewhat when Sutpen married Ellen Coldfield, daughter of the highly respected Goodhue Coldfield.

Because Quentin was away in college, many of the things he knew about Sutpen's Hundred had come to him in letters from home. Other details he had learned during talks with his father. He learned of Ellen Sutpen's life as mistress of the strange mansion in the wilderness. He learned how she discovered her husband fighting savagely with one of his slaves. Young Henry Sutpen fainted, but Judith, the daughter, watched from the haymow with interest and delight.

The children grew up. Young Henry, so unlike his father, attended the university at Oxford, Mississippi, and there he met Charles Bon, a rich planter's grandson. Unknown to Henry, Charles was his half brother, Sutpen's son by his first marriage. Unknown to all of Jefferson, Sutpen had gotten his money as the dowry of his earlier marriage to Charles Bon's West Indian mother, a wife he discarded when he learned she was part black.

Charles Bon became engaged to Judith Sutpen. The engagement was suddenly broken off for a period of four years. In the meantime, the Civil War began. Charles and Henry served together. Thomas Sutpen became a colonel.

Goodhue Coldfield took a disdainful stand against the war. He barricaded himself in his attic and his daughter, Rosa, was forced to put his food in a basket let down by a long rope. His store was looted by Confederate soldiers. One night, alone in his attic, he died.

Judith, in the meantime, had waited patiently for her lover. She carried his letter, written at the end of the four-year period, to Quentin's grandmother. Sometime later Wash Jones, a tenant on the Sutpen plantation, came to Miss Rosa's door with the crude announcement that

Charles Bon was dead, killed at the gate of the plantation by his half brother and former friend. Henry fled. Judith buried her lover in the Sutpen family plot on the plantation. Rosa, whose mother had died when she was born, went to Sutpen's Hundred to live with her niece. Ellen was already dead. It was Rosa's conviction that she could help Judith.

Colonel Thomas Sutpen returned. His slaves had been taken away, and he was burdened with new taxes on his overrun land and ruined buildings. He planned to marry Rosa Coldfield, more than ever desiring an heir now that Judith had vowed spinsterhood and Henry had become a fugitive. His son Charles Bon, whom he might, in desperation, have permitted to marry his daughter, was dead.

Rosa, insulted when she understood the true nature of his proposal, returned to her father's ruined house in the village. She was to spend the rest of her miserable life pondering the fearful intensity of Thomas Sutpen, whose nature, in her outraged belief, seemed to partake of the devil himself.

Quentin, during his last vacation, had learned more of the Sutpen tragedy. He now revealed much of the story to Shreve McCannon, his roommate, who listened with all of a Northerner's misunderstanding and indifference.

Quentin and his father had visited the Sutpen graveyard, where they saw a little path and a hole leading into Ellen Sutpen's grave. Generations of opossums lived there. Over her tomb and that of her husband stood a marble monument from Italy. Sutpen himself had died in 1869. In 1867, he had taken young Milly Jones, Wash Jones's granddaughter, to his bed. After she bore a child, a girl, Wash Jones had killed Thomas Sutpen.

Judith and the son of Charles Bon, his child by an octoroon woman who had brought her child to Sutpen's Hundred when he was eleven years old, died in 1884 of smallpox. Before he died, the boy had married a black woman, and they had had an idiot son, James Bond. Rosa Coldfield had placed headstones on their graves, and on Judith's gravestone she had caused to be inscribed a fearful message.

In the summer of 1910, Rosa Coldfield confided to Quentin that she believed that there was still someone living at Sutpen's Hundred. Together the two went there at night and discovered Clytie, the aged daughter of Thomas Sutpen and a slave. More important, they discovered Henry Sutpen himself hiding in the ruined old house. He had returned, he told them, four years before; he had come back to die. The idiot, James Bond, watched Rosa and Quentin as they departed. Rosa returned to her home, and Quentin went back to college.

Quentin's father wrote to tell him the tragic ending of the Sutpen story. Months later, Rosa sent an ambulance out to the ruined plantation house, for she had finally determined to bring her nephew, Henry, into the village to live with her so that he could get decent care. Clytie, seeing the ambulance, was afraid that Henry was to be arrested for the murder of Charles Bon many years before. In desperation, she set fire to the old house, burning herself and Henry Sutpen to death. Only the idiot, James Bond, the last surviving descendant of Thomas Sutpen, escaped. No one knew where he went, for he was never seen again. Miss Rosa took to her bed and died soon afterward, in the winter of 1910.

Quentin told the story to his roommate because it seemed to him, somehow, to be the story of the whole South, a tale of deep passions, tragedy, ruin, and decay.

Critical Evaluation

Absalom, Absalom! is the most involved of William Faulkner's works, for the narrative is revealed by recollections years after the events described have taken place. Experience is related at its fullest expression; its initial import is recollected, and its significance years thereafter is faithfully recorded. The conventional method of storytelling has been discarded. Through his special method, Faulkner is able to re-create human action and human emotion in its own setting. Sensory impressions gained at the moment, family traditions as powerful stimuli, the tragic impulses—these focus truly in the reader's mind so that a tremendous picture of the nineteenth century South, vivid down to the most minute detail, grows slowly in the reader's imagination.

This novel is Faulkner's most comprehensive attempt to come to terms with the full implications of the Southern experience. The structure of the novel, itself an attempt by its various narrators to make some sense of the seemingly chaotic past, is indicative of the multifaceted complexity of that experience, and the various narrators' relationship to the material suggests the difficulty that making order of the past entails. Each narrator has, to begin with, only part of the total picture—and some parts of that hearsay or conjecture—at his or her disposal, and each of their responses is conditioned by their individual experiences and backgrounds. Thus, Miss Rosa's idea of Sutpen depends equally upon her Calvinist background and her failure to guess why Henry Sutpen killed Charles Bon. Quentin's father responds with an ironic detachment, conditioned by his insistence upon viewing the fall of the South as the result of the workings of an inevitable Fate, as in Greek drama. Like Quentin and Shreve, readers must attempt to coordinate these partial views of the Sutpen history into a meaningful whole—with the added irony that they must also deal with Quentin's romanticism. In effect, the reader becomes yet another investigator, but one whose concern is with the entire scope of the novel rather than only with the Sutpen family.

At the very heart of the novel is Thomas Sutpen and his grand design, and the reader's comprehension of the meaning of the work depends upon the discovery of the implications of this design. Unlike the chaos of history that the narrators perceive, Sutpen's design would, by its very nature, reduce human history and experience to a mechanical and passionless process that he could control. The irony of Sutpen's failure lies in the fact that he could not achieve the design precisely because he was unable to exclude such human elements as Charles Bon's need for his father's love and recognition. Faulkner, however, gains more than this irony from his metaphor of design. In effect, Sutpen's design is based upon a formula of the antebellum South that reduces it to essentials. It encompasses the plantation, the slaves, the wife and family—all the external trappings of the plantation aristocracy that Sutpen, as a small boy from the mountains, saw in his first encounter with this foreign world. Sutpen, who never really becomes one of the aristocracy his world tries to mirror, manages, by excluding the human element from his design, to reflect only what is worst in the South. Southern society is starkly revealed to have at its heart the simple fact of possession: of the land, of the slaves, and, in Sutpen's case, even of wives and children. Thus, Faulkner demonstrates here, as he does in his great story "The Bear," that the urge to possess is the fundamental evil from which other evils spring. Sutpen, trying to insulate himself from the pain of rejection that he encountered as a child, is driven almost mad by the need to possess a semblance of the world that denies his humanity, but in his obsession, he loses that humanity.

Once the idea of the design and the principle of possession in *Absalom, Absalom!* is established, Sutpen's treatment both of Charles Bon and Bon's mother is more easily understood. In Sutpen's distorted mind, that which is possessed can also be thrown away if it does not fit the design. Like certain other Faulker characters—Benjy of *The Sound and the Fury* (1929) being the best example—Sutpen is obsessed with the need to establish a perfect order in the world into which he will fit. His first vision of tidewater Virginia, after leaving the timeless anarchy of the mountains, was the sight of perfectly ordered and neatly divided plantations, and, like a chick imprinted by its first contact, Sutpen spends his life trying to create a world that imitates that order and a dynasty that will keep his spirit alive to preserve it. His rejection of Bon is essentially emotionless, mechanical, and even without rancor because Bon's black blood simply excludes him from the design. Similarly, the proposal that Rosa have Sutpen's child to prove herself worthy of marriage and the rejection of Milly when she bears a female child are also responses dictated by the design. Thus Sutpen, and all whose lives touch his, ultimately becomes a victim of the mad design that he has created. Sutpen, however, is not its final victim: The curse of the design lives on into the present in Jim Bond, the last of Sutpen's bloodline.

Sutpen's rejection of Charles Bon and the consequences of that rejection are at the thematic center of *Absalom, Absalom!* In the fact that Charles is rejected for the taint of black blood, Faulkner very clearly points to the particularly Southern implication of his story. Bon must be seen, on one level, to represent the human element within Southern society that cannot be assimilated and will not be ignored. Faulkner implies that the system, which denies the rights and needs of some of its children, dehumanizes all it touches—master and victim alike. In asserting himself to demand the only recognition that he can gain from his father—and that only at second hand through Henry—Charles Bon makes of himself an innocent sacrifice to the sin upon which the South was founded. His death also dramatizes the biblical admonition so relevant to *Absalom, Absalom!*: A house divided against itself cannot stand.

Sutpen's history is a metaphor of the South, and his rise and fall is Southern history written in one individual's experience. The Sutpens, however, are not the only victims in the novel: The narrators too are victims and survivors of the Southern experience, and each of them seeks in Sutpen's history some clue to the meaning of his or her own relationship to the fall of the South. Their narratives seek to discover the designs that will impose some order on the chaos of the past.

THE ADDRESSES OF ABRAHAM LINCOLN

Type of work: Formal speeches
Author: Abraham Lincoln (1809-1865)
First delivered: 1838-1865

Abraham Lincoln, the sixteenth president of the United States and the author of the Gettysburg Address, has come to be recognized as a creative speaker with an individual and appealing style. He had a perceptive sense of humor and an awareness of human dignity and of the tragedy that occurs with the loss of it. His arguments were logically respectable and responsive to the problems of his times. Although he always retained a directness of statement and feeling that reflected the conditions of his boyhood in Kentucky and Indiana, he was by no means a mere homespun speaker or writer; his poetic phrasing and imagery, biblical allusions, and rhetorical devices all testify to the fact that he was a well-educated and intelligent man who could speak to any kind of audience in a manner and with the diction appropriate to the occasion.

Yet Lincoln was not perfect. If it is relevant to state the fact of his imperfection, the reason is that Lincoln's compassion and understanding and his contribution to the creation of American democracy have so impressed his fellow citizens that sometimes romantic legends lead one to believe that he never spoke without winning assent and admiration from those whom he addressed. Yet because he was human and to err is human, and because he was sometimes called upon to speak when there was no great problem to resolve or attack, he was on occasion ineffective in what he said.

Once the legend of Lincoln's perfection is dispelled, the fact of his greatness as an individual, a president, and a speaker emerges. The Gettysburg Address of 1863 was no isolated phenomenon: The ideas, the sentiments, the clear eloquence had all been heard before, but never with such economy and depth.

"The Perpetuation of Our Political Institutions," one of the earliest of Lincoln's speeches, was an address given to the Young Men's Lyceum of Springfield, Illinois, on January 27, 1838. Lincoln began by recalling the political and social legacy bequeathed the American people of the nineteenth century by their parents, and he asked how the task of maintaining the liberties transmitted to them might best be performed. He argued that the danger of loss came not from abroad but only from Americans themselves: "If destruction be our lot, we must ourselves be its author and finisher." Lincoln then referred to several violent instances of mob action and argued that such disregard for law could result in the loss of the legacy of freedom. Although the passion of revolution had helped Americans achieve their liberty, it was necessary to let reason and a reverence for law prevail.

In this early speech, there is ample evidence of Lincoln's power, a power partly literary and partly spiritual. The young speaker reflected his sense of his role, as a citizen, to transmit the American heritage. Like his contemporaries, he placed his faith in reason, law, the orderly processes of government, and a sense of human dignity. He added to this conventional faith, however, his own clear conviction and commitment, applying the principles of democracy to the immediate danger that he found about him. His philosophy of government was conservative; he did not speak for abolition—but what he conserved were the principles needed in critical times. His character, not the particular strain of his politics, was already the most persuasive element in his addresses; the demands of the presidency in a time of civil war were to realize the nobility of that character.

At the close of the Republican State Convention at Springfield, Illinois, on June 16, 1858, Lincoln delivered an acceptance of the senatorial nomination. This speech marked the beginning of the campaign that was to involve him in the series of debates with Stephen A. Douglas. After referring to the increase in slavery agitation, Lincoln declared:

> In my opinion, it will not cease, until a crisis shall have been reached, and passed—
> "A house divided against itself cannot stand."
> I believe this government cannot endure, permanently half slave and half free.
> I do not expect the Union to be dissolved—I do not expect the house to fall—but I do expect it will cease to be divided.
> It will become all one thing, or all the other.

Lincoln went on to discuss the Nebraska Bill, which allowed the people of any state or territory to determine whether slavery was to be allowed in their state or territory, the Dred Scott decision, and the opinions of Senator Douglas. Lincoln maintained that Douglas cared nothing about halting the advance of slavery, and he implied that Douglas' policy tended to divide the Union.

In the first Lincoln-Douglas debate at Ottawa, Illinois, on August 21, 1858, Douglas referred to Lincoln's acceptance speech and quoted Lincoln's remarks concerning the "house divided against itself." He argued that the founders of the nation had believed it possible for the union to exist with both free and slave states, and he suggested that Lincoln could hardly disagree with such men as Washington, Jefferson, Franklin, and Hamilton. He endorsed the Dred Scott decision, declaring that if Lincoln's opinions prevailed "black settlements" would "cover your prairies." "I am in favor of confining citizenship to white men, men of European birth and descent," Douglas asserted, "instead of conferring it upon Negroes, Indians, and other inferior races."

Lincoln replied by correcting a number of misrepresentations made by Senator Douglas, and in order to counter the charge that he was an abolitionist he quoted from a speech he had made at Peoria, Illinois, in 1854. Although he stated that he had no intention of introducing political and social equality between the white and the black races, he added that "notwithstanding all this, there is no reason in the world why the Negro is not entitled to all the natural rights enumerated in the Declaration of Independence—the right to life, liberty, and the pursuit of happiness." Even when, for the sake of politics, Lincoln agreed with Douglas that a black man was not his equal, he qualified his admission: "I agree with Judge Douglas that he [the Negro] is not my equal in many respects—certainly not in color, perhaps not in moral or intellectual endowment." Then, although the "perhaps" made a world of difference, Lincoln closed that particular subject: "But in the right to eat the bread, without the leave of anybody else, which his own hand earns, he is my equal, and the equal of Judge Douglas, and the equal of every living man."

Even now, more than a hundred years after the debates, the speeches by Douglas and Lincoln bring the living man before the imagination. Douglas is the clever, urbane debater, but Lincoln is at least as clever and has the words to reach all minds and to express sentiments that make up the American ideal. In debate, Lincoln was as relentless as his opponent in the attempt to win his points, but he was never vicious, even when he was not as candid as one could be. His homely sense of humor remained an invaluable instrument in his bag of rhetorical devices. Immediately after considering Douglas' charge that he was an abolitionist, Lincoln passed on to the charge of being a grocery-keeper. He said, "I don't know that it would be a great sin if I had been; but he is mistaken. Lincoln never kept a grocery anywhere in the world. It is true that Lincoln did work the latter part of one winter in a little still-house up at the head of a hollow."

At Springfield, Illinois, in his last speech of the campaign of 1858, Lincoln repeated that he admitted the right of the South to reclaim its fugitives and that he denied the right of Congress to interfere with the states. He declared that he had found the campaign painful, particularly because former friends accused him of wishing to destroy the Union. Then he concluded that some had charged him with ambition, but that he would gladly withdraw if he could be assured of "unyielding hostility" to the spread of slavery. The candor and intensity of this brief speech make it one of Lincoln's most moving addresses.

Lincoln's courage became most evident with his address at Cooper Union in New York on February 27, 1860. He took issue with Douglas' claim that the authors of the Constitution understood the "question" as well as the people of his own day. He agreed with Douglas that the framers of the Constitution understood the issue, but he disagreed with Douglas' assertion that they sided with Douglas' view that the Constitution forbids federal control of slavery. Lincoln argued strongly against any interpretation of the Constitution that would have permitted the extension of slavery to the Free States and the territories. He referred to the secessionist threat to destroy the Union if a Republican president were elected, and he urged that the Republicans do their part to maintain peace. He concluded, "Let us have faith that right makes might, and in that faith, let us, to the end, dare to do our duty as we understand it."

Later in the year, in May, Lincoln was nominated for the office of president by the Republican Party; although he had been defeated in his senatorial campaign against Douglas, his speeches had brought him into national prominence. In February, 1861, after having been elected to the presidency in November of the preceding year, Lincoln said farewell to the people of Springfield, Illinois, with a few poignant sentences in which he asked for the assistance of "that Divine Being" who had attended Washington. The Civil War began in April.

Lincoln's inaugural addresses, his message to Congress on July 4, 1861, and his annual messages to Congress presented the facts of the national crisis with clarity and compassion. The Gettysburg Address of November 19, 1863, brought all of Lincoln's sincere idealism into focus and related it to the grief of a nation. His addresses will continue to remain a cherished part of the American heritage and a significant segment of America's literature.

THE ADVENTURES OF AUGIE MARCH

Type of work: Novel
Author: Saul Bellow (1915-   )
Type of plot: Modern picaresque
Time of plot: c. 1920-1950
Locale: Principally Chicago
First published: 1953

This novel, which follows the tradition of the picaresque, tells the story of a young man who refuses to be molded by the society around him. Bellow presents a tragicomic portrait of the Jewish middle classes in the early to mid-twentieth century.

Principal Characters

Augie March, a young man who, having been reared in poverty, embraces materialism and easy morals. Despite the efforts of family members, employers, and girlfriends, Augie refuses to yield to conventional society and thus fails to find satisfaction and purpose in his life.

Simon March, Augie's older brother, who conforms to what is expected of him and earns fortune and respectability as a result. He too tries to convert Augie to middle-class morality and fails.

Georgie March, their feeble-minded younger brother. He learns how to repair shoes, despite his mental handicaps, and serves as a reminder to Augie that having a purpose is valuable.

Mr. and **Mrs. Renling,** shopkeepers who give Augie a job. They want to reform their employee and even adopt him, but Augie is not interested in their wealthy, suburban life-style.

Grandma Lausch, an old woman who has come from Russia and fallen on hard times. She lives with the Marches and attempts to mold Augie's character.

Thea Fenchel, Augie March's sometime mistress. They travel to Mexico together to train a young eaglet to hunt iguanas.

Stella Chesney, Augie's wife.

Saul Bellow's *The Adventures of Augie March*, which won for him his first National Book Award for fiction, is a novel that quickly informs readers that they must be ready to read and understand the book at several levels, each of these being meaningful in itself and yet unmistakably intertwined with the others.

At the simplest and most obvious level of reading, the novel is in the picaresque tradition, telling the adventures, often comic, of a rascal born out of wedlock to a charwoman, reared in the poverty of a down-at-heels Chicago neighborhood, and early addicted to taking life as it comes. Augie March the adult, thus seen, is a ne'er-do-well hanger-on to people of wealth and, at times, a thief, even a would-be smuggler. As a child of poverty, he learned from the adults about him and from his experience that a ready lie told with a glib tongue and an air of innocence is often profitable. Growing older, he learned that many women are of easy virtue and hold the same loose reins on their personal morality as Augie himself. Love (of a kind) and easy money seem, at this

level, to be Augie's goals in life. While he may dream of becoming a teacher, even take a few courses at the University of Chicago and read widely in an informal way, Augie stays on the fringes of the postwar black market, where he finds the easy money that he needs to live in what he regards as style.

When viewed at the literal level, *The Adventures of Augie March*, like Bellow's earlier fiction, is largely in the naturalistic tradition. In his choice of setting, in his pessimistic uses of detail and character, in his use of a wealth of detail, and in the implicit determinism apparent in the careers of Augie March, his relatives, and his friends, one notes similarities to the fiction of Émile Zola, Frank Norris, Theodore Dreiser, and other giants of the naturalistic tradition in literature. One notes also a kinship with the novels of Nelson Algren and James T. Farrell. At times, Augie March seems little more than a Jewish boy from Chicago's Northwest Side who is one part Farrell's Studs Lonigan and one part the same author's Danny O'Neill, from Chicago's South Side Irish neighborhood. With Farrell's characters, Augie March shares immigrant background, a loss of meaning in life, degrading poverty, and a grossly hedonistic view of life.

Unlike many naturalistic novelists, however, Saul Bellow seeks meaning in facts; he is not confined to the principle that the novelist is simply an objective, amoral reporter of life as one finds it, a recorder of life among the lowly, the immoral, the poverty-stricken. Moreover, he does not permit his character Augie March to be merely a creature of environment, molded by forces outside himself, or within himself, over which he has no control. *The Adventures of Augie March* can be read at a deeper level than environmental determinism. Augie is capable of intellectual activity of a relatively high order, of knowing what he is struggling with and struggling for. Throughout his life, he learns that other people want to make him over. Grandma Lausch, an elderly Russian Jew of fallen fortunes who lives with the Marches, tries to form the boy, and he rebels. Later Mr. and Mrs. Renling, well-to-do shopkeepers in a fashionable Chicago suburb and Augie's employers, want to make him over, even adopt him, but he rebels. Augie's brother Simon, who achieves wealth and considerable respectability, tries to make a new man of Augie and finds Augie rebellious. Various women in Augie's life, including Thea Fenchel, Augie's erstwhile mistress (whom he follows to Mexico to hunt iguanas with an eagle), try to recast Augie's nature. They, too, fail, for above all Augie refuses to be molded into someone else's image of what he ought to be.

What does Augie want to be, that he refuses to be cast in any mold suggested by the people about him? He wants to become something, for he is always searching—but he never seriously accepts any goal. He wants always to be independent in act and spirit, and he achieves some sort of independence, empty though it is. He wants to be someone, to achieve all of which he is capable, but he never finds a specific goal or pattern. By refusing to commit himself to anything, he ends up accomplishing virtually nothing. It is a sad fact of his existence that he comes to be a bit envious of his mentally deficient brother Georgie, who has mastered some of the elements of shoe repairing. Bellow seems to be saying through Augie that it is possible to have a fate without a function. Yet, as he presents the character, Bellow shows that without a function no one, including Augie March, can have a fate. The reader cannot be sure whether the irony is intentional.

Another view of the novel that is both logical and fruitful is to regard it at the level of social comment. Most remarkable at this level is the section of American society in which Augie March moves. The fact that Augie is a Jew is literally beaten into him by neighborhood toughs, including those among the Gentiles he thought his friends, while he is a child. As he grows up, takes jobs, finds friends and confidants, and seeks out women to love, Augie moves almost always in the company of Jews. The respectability toward which he is pushed is always the respectability of the Jewish middle classes, particularly that of Jews who have lost their religion and turned to worshiping the quick success in moneymaking, which is mirrored in their passion for fleshy women, flashy cars, and too much rich food. While in one sense Bellow's novel is a novel of an adolescent discovering the world, it is a restricted world in which Augie makes his discoveries. He seems never to understand the vast fabric of American culture that lies about him. If his is a sociological tragedy, and many readers will find it so, it is not an American tragedy in the broad sense. Rather it is the tragedy of a Jewish child who sees only the materialism of Jews who have forsaken their rich tradition and found nothing to replace it.

While some readers will most readily grasp the tragic elements in *The Adventures of Augie March*, others will grasp more readily the comic aspects. Following as it does in some ways the picaresque tradition, the novel is bound to have a wide strain of the comic. Neither Augie nor his creator take some of the character's deviations from conventional standards of conduct very seriously. Augie bounds in and out of crime and sin with scarcely a backward glance. If his loves seem empty, his women unfaithful, Augie accepts the results with comic aplomb. If to be unheroic, to give in with little or no struggle, to be weak and ineffectual is comic (and thus it has long been viewed), Augie is a comic protagonist and the novel a comic work. Nevertheless, the comic spirit is also used traditionally for serious, often satiric, purpose. It is here that the reader well may be puzzled. While the comic elements are undeniably in the novel, adding to the richness of its texture, one wonders at their purpose. The novel seems at times to be offering satiric comment on the foibles of humankind, but such comment seems alien, if not contradictory, in the framework of Bellow's work, unless it is there to show that the creator of Augie March shares the character's belief in the irrational nature of humanity, society, and the universe.

Indeed, Augie seems at times to be a symbol of the irrational; this symbolic value is mirrored by the eaglet that Augie and Thea Fenchel train to hunt. The young bald eagle, fierce in appearance, proved to be an apt pupil; he seemed marvelously equipped, with powerful wings, beak, and claws, to be an instrument of destruction, and he learned well how to attack a piece of meat tendered by his trainers. Yet when a live creature, even a tiny lizard, put up resistance, he turned away from the attack; he refused to do what he was capable of doing, defying his very nature. Like the eagle, Augie March failed as well. Young, handsome, charming, and intelligent, Augie refuses to face life, always seeing it as something someone else wants him to do. When life hit back at him, Augie turned away from what he was prepared to do. He strikes the reader as being left without purpose, like the eagle, to exist, to be looked at, and to be fed. That the character sees this as "living" is perhaps the greatest irony of all. Augie has become an antihero; he is not so much comic as pathetic. As narrator he realizes, however vaguely, that while he has denied the traditional goals that people have held up for him, he has not failed to find a goal for himself that he can regard as worthwhile. In trying to live, he has found little but a meaningless existence.

THE ADVENTURES OF HUCKLEBERRY FINN

Type of work: Novel
Author: Mark Twain (Samuel Langhorne Clemens, 1835-1910)
Type of plot: Humorous satire
Time of plot: Nineteenth century
Locale: Along the Mississippi River
First published: 1884

The title character of this famous novel tells his own story in a straightforward narrative laced with shrewd, sharp comments on human nature. The boy's adventures along the Mississippi form the framework for a series of moral lessons, revelations of a corrupt society, and contrasts of innocence and hypocrisy.

Principal Characters

Huckleberry Finn, a small-town boy living along the banks of the Mississippi in the 1800's before the American Civil War. His adventurous voyage with the African-American slave Jim, when they drift down the Mississippi on a raft, is the trip every child dreams of making, living by adaptable wits and unerring ingenuity. When he contrasts himself with his flamboyant and wildly imaginative friend, Tom Sawyer, Huck feels somewhat inadequate, but deep inside he has a triumphant reliance on the power of common sense. Thus the world of Huck's reality—his capture by and escape from old drunken Pap; the macabre pageant of his townsfolk searching the Mississippi for his supposedly drowned body; his encounters with the King and the Duke, two preposterous swindlers; his stay among the feuding Grangerfords and Shepherdsons; and his defense of the pure, benighted Wilks sisters—is proved to be far more imaginative than Tom Sawyer's imagination. Yet Huck is not some irresponsible wanderer through adolescence. He has a conscience. He knows it is wrong to be harboring a runaway slave, but his friendship with Jim makes him defy the law. His appreciation of the ridiculous allows him to go along with the lies and swindles of the King and the Duke until they seem ready to bring real harm to the Wilks sisters, and he himself will fib and steal to get food and comfort, but his code of boyhood rebels at oppression, injustice, hypocrisy. Mark Twain has created in Huckleberry Finn a magnificent American example of the romanticism that rolled like a great wave across the Atlantic in the nineteenth century.

Jim, the African-American slave of Miss Watson. Believing that he is about to be sold down the river for eight hundred dollars, he runs away and hides on Jackson's Island, where Huck also takes refuge after faking his own murder in order to escape from Pap. Ignorant, superstitious, and gullible, Jim is nevertheless, in Huck's words, "most always right; he had an uncommon level head, for a nigger." He will laugh at everything comical, but he suffers poignantly when he thinks of the family that he has left in bondage. He protects Huck physically and emotionally, believing that the boy is the one white person he can trust and never suspecting that Huck is struggling with his conscience about whether to turn Jim in. When the two companions encounter the King and the Duke, Jim is completely taken in by their fakery, though at one point he asks, "Don't it 'sprise you, de way dem kings carries on, Huck?" Typically, Jim is subservient to and patient with the white man. Even when Tom Sawyer arrives at the Phelpses, where Jim has been caught and held, the slave goes through Tom's complicated and romantic ritual of escape with grumbling good nature. Jim is a sensitive, sincere man who seems to play his half-comic, half-tragic role in life because he is supposed to play it that way.

Tom Sawyer, Huck's friend, who can, with a lively imagination stimulated by excessive reading, turn a raid by his gang on a Sunday-school picnic into the highway robbery of "a whole parcel of Spanish merchants and rich A-rabs . . . with two hundred elephants, and six hundred camels, and over a thousand 'sumter' mules, all loaded down with di'monds. . . ." He is a foil to the practicality of Huck; he is the universal leader in any small town who can sway a gang or friend into any act of fancy, despite grumbling and disbelief. His ritual for the rescue of the captured Jim (who he knows has already been set free by Miss Watson's last will) is a masterful selection of details from all the romantic rescues of fact and fiction.

Pap, Huck's father and the town drunkard. When he learns that Huck has been awarded in trust a share of the money derived from the box of gold found in the robber's cave, he shows up one night to stay in the Widow Douglas' spare room. Finding that Huck's share of the money is legally beyond his reach, Pap kidnaps his son, keeping him prisoner in an old cabin. He then proceeds to go on a classic drunk, followed by a monumental case of delirium tremens. Snakes in abundance crawl all over him and one bites his cheek, though Huck, of course, can see nothing. The boy finally makes his escape from Pap by killing a pig and leaving bloody evidence of a most convincing murder. Jim discovers Pap's dead body in a flooded boat on the Mississippi.

The King and **The Duke,** two rapscallions and confidence men whom Huck and Jim join on their trip down the Mississippi. Their so-called play, "The Royal Nonesuch," finally leads to their just desserts: tarring, feathering, and riding out of town on a rail.

The Widow Douglas and **Miss Watson,** unsuccessful reformers of Huck after he comes into his fortune.

Aunt Polly, Tom Sawyer's relative, who at the end of the story sets straight the by-now complicated identities of Huck and Tom.

The Grangerfords and **The Shepherdsons,** two feuding families. Huck spends some time with the Grangerfords, who renew the feud when a Grangerford daughter elopes with a young Shepherdson.

Mr. and **Mrs. Phelps,** at whose farm the captured Jim is confined until Tom arrives to effect his "rescue."

Mary Jane, Susan, and **Joanna Wilks,** three sisters whom the King and the Duke set out to bilk; Huck thwarts the connivers.

Judge Thatcher, the "law" who protects Huck's interests.

The Story

Tom Sawyer and Huckleberry Finn had found a box of gold in a robber's cave. After Judge Thatcher had taken the money and invested it for the boys, each had a huge allowance of a dollar a day. The Widow Douglas and her sister, Miss Watson, had taken Huck home with them to try to reform him. At first, Huck could not stand living in a tidy house where smoking and swearing were forbidden. Worse, he had to go to school and learn how to read. He did, however, manage to drag himself to school almost every day, except for the times when he sneaked off for a smoke in the woods or to go fishing in the Mississippi.

Life was beginning to become bearable to him when one day he noticed some tracks in the snow. Examining them closely, he realized that they belonged to the worthless father whom Huck had not seen for more than a year. Knowing that his father would be back hunting him when the old man learned about the six thousand dollars, Huck rushed over to Judge Thatcher and persuaded the judge to take the fortune for himself. The judge was puzzled, but he signed some papers, and Huck was satisfied that he no longer had any money for his father to take from him.

Huck's father finally showed up one night in Huck's room at Widow Douglas' home. Complaining that he had been cheated out of his money, the old drunkard took Huck away with him to a cabin in the woods, where he kept the boy a prisoner, beating him periodically and half starving him. Before long, Huck began to wonder why he had ever liked living with the Widow: With his father, he could smoke and swear all he wanted, and his life would have been pleasant if it had not been for the beatings. One night, Huck sneaked away, leaving a bloody trail from a pig that he had killed in the woods. Huck wanted everyone to believe that he was dead. He climbed into a boat and went to Jackson's Island to hide until all the excitement had blown over.

After three days of freedom, Huck wandered to another part of the island, and there he discovered Jim, Miss Watson's slave. Jim told Huck that he had run off because he had overheard Miss Watson planning to sell him down south for eight hundred dollars. Huck swore that he would not report Jim. The two stayed on the island many days, Jim giving Huck an education in superstition. One night, Huck rowed back to the mainland. Disguised as a girl, he called on a house near the shore. There he learned that his father had disappeared shortly after the townspeople had decided that Huck had been murdered. Since Jim's disappearance had occurred just after Huck's alleged death, there was now a three-hundred-dollar reward posted for Jim's capture, as most people believed that Jim had killed Huck.

Fearing that Jackson's Island would be searched, Huck hurried back to Jim, and the two headed down the Mississippi. They planned to leave the raft at Cairo and then go on a steamboat up the Ohio into free territory. Jim told Huck that he would work hard in the North and then buy his wife and children from their masters in the

South. Helping a runaway slave bothered Huck's conscience, but he reasoned that it would bother him more if he betrayed such a good friend as Jim. One night, as they were drifting down the river on their raft, a large boat loomed before them, and Huck and Jim, knowing that the raft would be smashed under the hull of the ship, jumped into the water. Huck swam safely to shore, but Jim disappeared.

Huck found a home with a friendly family named Grangerford. The Grangerfords were feuding with the Shepherdsons, another family living nearby. The Grangerfords left Huck mostly to himself and gave him a young slave to wait on him. One day, the slave asked him to come to the woods to see some snakes. Following the boy, Huck came across Jim, who had been hiding in the woods waiting for an opportunity to send for Huck. Jim had repaired the broken raft. That night, one of the Grangerford daughters eloped with a young Shepherdson, and the feud broke out once more. Huck and Jim ran away during the shooting and set off down the river.

Shortly afterward, Jim and Huck met two men who pretended that they were royalty and made all sorts of nonsensical demands on Huck and Jim. Huck was not taken in, but he reasoned that it would do no harm to humor the two men to prevent quarreling. The Duke and the King were clever schemers. In one of the small river towns, they staged a fake show that lasted long enough to net them a few hundred dollars. Then they ran off before the angered townspeople could catch them.

The Duke and the King overheard some people talking about the death of Peter Wilks, who had left considerable property and some cash to his three daughters. Wilks's two brothers, whom no one in the town had ever seen, were living in England. The King and the Duke went to the three daughters, Mary Jane, Susan, and Joanna, and presented themselves as the two uncles. They took a few thousand dollars of the inheritance and then put up the property for auction and sold the slaves. This high-handed deed caused great grief to the girls, and Huck could not bear to see them so unhappy. He decided to expose the two frauds, but he wanted to ensure Jim's safety first. Jim had been hiding in the woods waiting for his companions to return to him. Employing a series of lies, subterfuges, and maneuverings that were worthy of his ingenious mind, Huck exposed the Duke and King. Huck fled back to Jim, and two escaped on their raft. Just as Jim and Huck thought they were on their way and well rid of their former companions, the Duke and King came rowing down the river toward them.

The whole party set out again with their royal plots to hoodwink the public. In one town where they landed, Jim was captured, and Huck learned that the Duke had turned him in for the reward. Huck had quite a tussle with his conscience. He knew that he ought to help return a slave to the rightful owner, but, on the other hand, he thought of all the fine times that he and Jim had had together and how loyal a friend Jim had been. Finally, Huck decided that he would help Jim to escape.

Learning that Mr. Phelps was holding Jim, he headed for the Phelps farm. There, Mrs. Phelps ran up and hugged him, mistaking him for the nephew whom she had been expecting to come for a visit. Huck wondered how he could keep Mrs. Phelps from learning that he was not her nephew. Then, to his relief, he learned they had mistaken him for Tom Sawyer. Huck rather liked being Tom for a while, and he was able to tell the Phelps all about Tom's Aunt Polly, Tom's half brother Sid, and Mary, Tom's cousin. Huck was feeling proud of himself for keeping up the deception. When Tom Sawyer really did arrive, he told his aunt that he was Sid.

At the first opportunity, Huck told Tom about Jim's capture. To his surprise, Tom offered to help him set Jim free. Huck could not believe that Tom would be a slave stealer, but he kept his feelings to himself. Huck had intended merely to wait until there was a dark night and then break the padlock on the door of the shack where Jim was kept, but Tom said the rescue had to be done according to the books. He laid out a most complicated plan with all kinds of storybook ramifications. It took fully three weeks of plotting, stealing, and deceit to let Jim out of the shack. Then the scheme failed. A chase began after Jim escaped, and Tom was shot in the leg. After Jim had been recaptured, Tom was brought back to Aunt Sally's house to recover from his wound. Then Tom revealed the fact that Miss Watson had died, giving Jim his freedom in her will. Huck was greatly relieved to learn that Tom was not really a slave stealer after all.

To complicate matters still more, Tom's Aunt Polly arrived. She quickly set straight the identities of the two boys. Jim was given his freedom, and Tom gave him forty dollars. Tom told Huck that his money was still safely in the hands of Judge Thatcher, but Huck moaned that his father would likely be back to claim it again. Then Jim told Huck that his father was dead; Jim had seen him lying in an abandoned boat along the river.

Huck was ready to start out again because Aunt Sally said she thought she might adopt him and try to civilize him. Huck thought that he could not go through such a trial again after he had once tried to be civilized under the care of Widow Douglas.

Critical Evaluation

Little could Mark Twain have visualized in 1876 when he began a sequel to capitalize on the success of *The Adventures of Tom Sawyer* that *The Adventures of Huckleberry Finn* would evolve into his masterpiece and one of the most significant works in the development of the American novel. With an unerring instinct for American regional dialects, Twain elected to tell the story in Huck's own words. The skill with which Twain elevated the dialect of an illiterate village boy to the highest levels of poetry established the spoken American idiom as a literary language and earned for Twain his reputation— proclaimed by Ernest Hemingway, William Faulkner, and others—as the father of the modern American novel. Twain also maintained an almost perfect fidelity to Huck's point of view in order to dramatize the conflict between Huck's own innate innocence and natural goodness and the dictates of a corrupt society.

As Huck's own story, the novel revolves around several major themes, including death and rebirth, freedom and bondage, the search for a father, the individual versus society, and the all-pervasive theme of brotherhood. Huck's character reflects a point in Mark Twain's development when he still believed humanity to be innately good but saw social forces as corrupting influences that replaced, with the dictates of a socially determined "conscience," the intuitive sense of right and wrong. This theme is explicitly dramatized through Huck's conflict with his conscience over whether to turn Jim in as a runaway slave. Huck, on the other hand, accepts without question what he has been taught by church and society about slavery. In his own mind, as surely as in that of his Southern contemporaries, aiding an escaped slave was clearly wrong both legally and morally. Thus, Huck's battle with his conscience is a real trauma for him, and his decision to "go to Hell" rather than give Jim up is made with a certainty that such a fate awaits him for breaking one of society's laws. It is ironic that Huck's "sin" against the social establishment affirms the best that is possible in the individual.

Among the many forms of bondage that permeate the novel, ranging from the Widow's attempt to "civilize" Huck to the law of the vendetta that absolutely governs the lives of the Grangerfords and Shepherdsons, slavery provides Twain with his greatest metaphor for both bondage and institutionalized injustice and inhumanity. Written well after the termination of the Civil War, *The Adventures of Huckleberry Finn* is not an antislavery novel in the limited sense that *Uncle Tom's Cabin* is. Rather than simply attacking an institution already legally dead, Twain uses the idea of slavery as a metaphor for all social bondage and injustice. Thus, Jim's search for freedom, like Huck's own need to escape both the Widow and Pap Finn, is as much a metaphorical search for an ideal state of freedom as a mere flight from slavery into free-state sanctuary. Thus, it is largely irrelevant that Twain has Huck and Jim running deeper into the South rather than north toward free soil. Freedom exists neither in the North nor in the South but in the ideal and idyllic world of raft and river.

The special world of raft and river is at the very heart of the novel. In contrast to the restrictive and oppressive social world of the shore, the raft is a veritable Eden where the evils of civilization are escaped. It is here that Jim and Huck can allow their natural bond of love to develop without regard for the question of race. It is here on the raft that Jim can become a surrogate father to Huck, and Huck can develop the depth of feeling for Jim that eventually leads to his decision to "go to Hell." While the developing relationship between Huck and Jim determines the basic shape of the novel, however, the river works in other structural ways as well. The picaresque form of the novel and its structural rhythm are based upon a series of episodes on shore, after each of which Huck and Jim return to the peaceful sanctuary of the raft. It is on shore that Huck encounters the worst excesses of which "the damned human race" is capable, but with each return to the raft comes a renewal of spiritual hope and idealism.

The two major thrusts of Twain's attack on the "civilized" world in *The Adventures of Huckleberry Finn* are against institutionalized religion and the romanticism that he believed characterized the South. The former is easily illustrated by the irony of the Widow's attempt to teach Huck religious principles while she persists in holding slaves. As with her snuff taking—which was acceptable because she did it herself—there seems to be no relationship between a fundamental sense of humanity and justice and her religion. Huck's practical morality makes him more "Christian" than the Widow, though he takes no interest in her lifeless principles. Southern romanticism, which Twain blamed for the fall of the South, is particularly allegorized by the sinking of the *Walter Scott*, but it is also inherent in such episodes as the feud where Twain shows the real horror of the sort of vendetta traditionally glamorized by romantic authors. In both cases, Twain is attacking the mindless acceptance of values that he believed kept the South in its dark ages.

Many critics have argued that the ending hopelessly

flaws *The Adventures of Huckleberry Finn* by reducing its final quarter to literary burlesque. Others have argued that the ending is in perfect accord with Twain's themes. Nevertheless all agree that, flawed or not, the substance of Twain's masterpiece transcends the limits of literary formalism to explore those eternal verities upon which great literature rests. Through the adventures of an escaped slave and a runaway boy, both representatives of the ignorant and lowly of the earth, Twain affirms that true humanity is of people rather than institutions and that everyone can be aristocrats in the kingdom of the heart.

THE ADVENTURES OF TOM SAWYER

Type of work: Novel
Author: Mark Twain (Samuel Langhorne Clemens, 1835-1910)
Type of plot: Adventure romance
Time of plot: Nineteenth century
Locale: St. Petersburg on the Mississippi River
First published: 1876

More than a book for boys, The Adventures of Tom Sawyer, *with its rich native humor and shrewd observations of human character, is an idyll of American village life, of that quieter age that had already vanished when Mark Twain re-created St. Petersburg from memories of his own boyhood.*

Principal Characters

Tom Sawyer, the mischievous ringleader of countless boyish adventures, who almost drives his long-suffering aunt to distraction with his pranks. If not fighting with other village urchins, the indolent boy plans numerous romantic and impractical escapades, many of which cost him hours of conscience-stricken torment. If he is not planning misdemeanors on the high seas, he is looking for buried treasure. Although unthinking, he is not really a bad boy; he is capable of generosity; occasionally, he surprises even himself with magnanimous acts.

Aunt Polly, Tom's warm, tender-hearted aunt. Sometimes this simple scripture-quoting old soul does not understand her mischievous charge. Even though she uses Tom's brother Sid as an example of a model youth, her frequent admonitions, emphasized by repeated thumps on the head with a thimble, fail to have a lasting effect on Tom. Believing herself endowed with subtle guile, she often tries to trap the boy into admitting his pranks. Rarely, however, is she successful. Tom usually manages to outwit her if Sid does not call her attention to certain inexactnesses in Tom's excuses.

Huckleberry Finn, one of Tom's best friends and a social pariah to the village mothers, but not to their sons. In this self-sufficient outcast, the boys see everything that they want to be. They long for his freedom to do as he pleases. Sometimes, to their regret, the other boys try to emulate their individualistic hero. Carefully, they mark the way he smokes strong tobacco in smelly old pipes and sleeps on empty hogsheads. Although he is not accepted by the mothers, Huck, even if he is vulgar, is a decent, honest lad. Happy only when he can sleep and eat where he pleases, Huck feels uncomfortable when the Widow Douglas takes him into her home.

Becky Thatcher, Tom's sweetheart. With her blue eyes, golden hair, and winsome smile, she captures his rather fickle heart at their first meeting. A little coquette, she, like Tom, alternately suffers from and enjoys their innocent love. Tom proves his generosity and love for her when he admits to the schoolteacher a crime that he did not commit, thus astounding the rest of the class with his incredible folly.

Injun Joe, a half-breed. A murderous, sinister figure who lurks mysteriously in the background, the savagely vindictive killer stabs young Dr. Robinson and is subsequently exposed by Tom. In a cave, Injun Joe, who had leaped from the courtroom window during Muff Potter's trial, almost has his revenge against the boy. Finally he pays for his many crimes when he is trapped in the cave and dies of starvation.

Muff Potter, a local ne'er-do-well and, along with Pap Finn, the town drunk. After helping Injun Joe and Dr. Robinson rob a grave, Muff Potter is accused of killing the doctor and almost pays with his worthless life. Had Tom not belatedly intervened, he would have been hanged and Injun Joe would have gone free. When Tom and Huck see a stray dog howling at the newly released Potter, asleep in a drunken stupor, they know that he is still doomed.

Sid, Tom's half brother and considered to be one of the model boys in the community. A quiet, rather calculating child, he exposes Tom's tricks whenever possible. When Tom is presumed drowned, however, Sid manages a few sniffles. To Tom, Sid's behavior is reprehensible; he keeps clean, goes to school regularly, and behaves well in church.

Mary, Tom's cousin. She is a sweet, lovable girl who often irritates him by insisting that he wash and dress carefully for church.

Judge Thatcher, Becky's pompous but kind-hearted father and the local celebrity.

Joe Harper, who runs away with Tom and Huck to Jackson's Island. Pretending to be pirates, they remain there for several days while the townspeople search for their bodies.

The Story

Tom Sawyer lived securely with the knowledge that his Aunt Polly loved him dearly. When she scolded him or whipped him, he knew that inside her breast lurked hidden remorse. Often he deserved the punishment that he received, but there were times when he was the victim of his tale-bearing half brother, Sid. Tom's cousin, Mary, was kinder to him. Her worst duty toward him was to see to it that he washed and put on clean clothes, so that he would look respectable when Aunt Polly took Tom, Sid, and Mary to church on Sunday.

A new family had moved into the neighborhood. Investigating, Tom saw a pretty, blue-eyed girl with lacy pantalets. She was Becky Thatcher. Instantly the fervent love that he had felt for Amy Lawrence was replaced by devotion to this new girl.

Becky was in school the next day, sitting on the girls' side of the room with an empty seat beside her. Tom had come late to school that morning. When the schoolmaster asked Tom why he had been late, that empty seat beside Becky Thatcher caught Tom's eye. Recklessly he confessed he had stopped to talk with Huckleberry Finn, son of the town drunk. Huck wore castoff clothing, never attended school, smoked and fished as often as he pleased, and slept wherever he could. For associating with Huckleberry Finn, Tom was whipped by the schoolmaster and ordered to sit on the girls' side of the room. Amid the snickers of the entire class, he took the empty seat next to Becky Thatcher.

Tom first attracted Becky's attention by a series of drawings on his slate. At length, he wrote the words, "I love you," and Becky blushed. Tom urged her to meet him after school. Sitting with her on a fence, he explained to her the possibilities of an engagement between them. Innocently, she accepted his proposal, which Tom insisted must be sealed by a kiss. In coy resistance, she allowed Tom a brief chase before she yielded to his embrace. Tom's happiness was unbounded. When he mentioned his previous tie with Amy Lawrence, however, the brief romance ended. Becky left her fiancé with a haughty shrug.

That night, Tom heard Huck's whistle below his bedroom window. Sneaking out, Tom joined his friend, and the two went off to the cemetery, Huck dragging a dead cat behind him. They were about to try a new method for curing warts. The gloomy atmosphere of the burial ground filled the boys with apprehension, and their fears increased still more when they spied three figures stealing into the graveyard. They were Injun Joe, Muff Potter, and Dr. Robinson. Evidently they had come to rob a grave. When the two robbers had exhumed the body, they began to quarrel with the doctor about money, and in the quarrel, Potter was knocked out. Then Injun Joe took Potter's knife and killed the doctor. When Potter recovered from his blow, he thought that he had killed Robinson, and Injun Joe allowed the poor old man to believe himself guilty.

Terrified, Tom and Huck slipped away from the scene that they had just witnessed, afraid that if Injun Joe discovered them he would kill them too.

Tom brooded on what he and Huck had seen. Convinced that he was ill, Aunt Polly dosed him with medicine and kept him in bed, but he did not seem to recover. Becky Thatcher had not come to school since she had broken Tom's heart. Rumor around town said that she was also ill. Coupled with this sad news was the fear of Injun Joe. When Becky finally returned to school, she cut Tom coldly. Feeling that there was nothing else for him to do, he decided to run away. He met Joe Harper and Huck Finn. Together they went to Jackson's Island and pretended to be pirates.

For a few days, they stayed happily on the island and learned from Huck how to smoke and swear. One day they heard a boat on the river, firing a cannon over the water. The boys then realized that the townspeople were searching for their bodies. This discovery put a new aspect on their adventure; the people at home thought that they were dead. Gleeful, Tom could not resist the temptation to see how Aunt Polly had reacted to his death. He slipped back to the mainland one night and into his aunt's house, where Mrs. Harper and Aunt Polly were mourning the deaths of their mischievous but good-hearted children. When Tom returned to the island, he found Joe and Huck tired of their game and ready to go home. Tom revealed to them an attractive plan that they immediately decided to carry out.

With a heavy gloom overhanging the town, funeral services were held for the deceased Thomas Sawyer, Joseph Harper, and Huckleberry Finn. The minister pronounced a lengthy eulogy about the respective good characters of the unfortunate boys. When the funeral procession was about to start, Tom, Joe, and Huck marched down the aisle of the church into the arms of the startled mourners.

For a while, Tom was the hero of all the boys in the town. They whispered about him and eyed him with awe in the schoolyard. Becky, however, ignored him until the day she accidentally tore the schoolmaster's book. When the irate teacher demanded to know who had torn his book, Tom confessed. Becky's gratitude and forgiveness were his reward.

After Muff Potter had been put in jail for the murder of the doctor in the graveyard, Tom and Huck had sworn to each other they would never utter a word about what they had seen. Afraid that Injun Joe would murder them for revenge, they furtively sneaked behind the prison and brought Muff food and other cheer. Yet Tom could not let an innocent man be condemned. At the trial, he appeared to tell what he had seen on the night of the murder. While Tom spoke, Injun Joe, a witness at the trial, sprang through the window of the courtroom and escaped. For days Tom worried, certain that Injun Joe would come back to murder him. As time went by and nothing happened, he gradually lost his fears. With Becky looking upon him as a hero, his world was filled with sunshine.

Huck and Tom decided to hunt for pirates' treasures. One night, ransacking an old abandoned house, they watched, unseen, while Injun Joe and a companion unearthed a chest of money buried under the floorboards of the house. The two frightened boys fled before they were discovered. The next day, they began a steady watch for Injun Joe and his accomplice, for Tom and Huck were bent on finding the lost treasure.

When Judge Thatcher gave a picnic for all the young people in town, Becky and Tom were supposed to spend the night with Mrs. Harper. One of the biggest excitements of the merrymaking came when the children went into a cave in the riverbank. The next day, Mrs. Thatcher and Aunt Polly learned that Tom and Becky were missing, for Mrs. Harper said they had not come to spend the night with her. Then everyone remembered that Tom and Becky had not been seen since the picnickers had left the cave. Meanwhile the two, having lost their bearings, had wandered into the cavern. To add to Tom's terror, he discovered that Injun Joe was also in the cave. Miraculously, after spending five days in the dismal cave, Tom found an exit that was five miles from the place where they had entered. Again he was a hero.

Injun Joe starved to death in the cave. After searchers had located his body, Tom and Huck went back into the cavern to look for the chest, which they believed that Injun Joe had hidden there. They found it and the twelve thousand dollars that it contained.

Adopted shortly afterward by the Widow Douglas, Huck planned to retire with an income of a dollar a day for the rest of his life. He never would have stayed with the Widow or consented to learn her prim, tidy ways if Tom had not promised that he would form a pirates' gang and make Huck one of the bold buccaneers.

Critical Evaluation

Beginning his writing career as a frontier humorist and ending it as a bitter satirist, Mark Twain drew from his circus of experiences: as a child in a small Missouri town (who had little formal schooling), a printer's apprentice, a journalist, a roving correspondent, a world traveler, a silver prospector, a Mississippi steamboat pilot, and a lecturer. He was influenced, in turn, by Artemus Ward, Bret Harte, Augustus Baldwin Longstreet, and G. W. Harris. Beginning with the publication of his first short story, "The Celebrated Jumping Frog of Calaveras County," in 1865, and proceeding through his best novels—*Innocents Abroad* (1869); *Roughing It* (1872); *The Gilded Age* (1873), brilliant in concept but a failure in design and execution; *The Adventures of Tom Sawyer* (1876); *Life on the Mississippi* (1883); *The Adventures of Huckleberry Finn* (1885); *A Connecticut Yankee in King Arthur's Court* (1889); and *The American Claimant* (1892)—Twain developed a characteristic style that, though uneven in its productions, made him the most important and most representative nineteenth century American writer. His service as delightful entertainment to generations of American youngsters is equaled only by his influence on such twentieth century admirers as Gertrude Stein, William Faulkner, and Ernest Hemingway.

Twain's generally careful and conscientious style was both a development of the southwestern humor tradition of Longstreet and Harris and a departure from the conventions of nineteenth century literary gentility. It is characterized by the adroit use of exaggeration, stalwart irreverence, deadpan seriousness, droll cynicism, and pungent commentary on the human situation. All of this is masked in an uncomplicated, straightforward narrative distinguished for its wholehearted introduction of the colloquial and vernacular into American fiction, which was to have a profound impact on the development of American writing and also shape the world's view of the United States. Twain, according to Frank Baldanza, had a talent for "paring away the inessential and presenting the bare core of experience with devastating authenticity." The combination of childish rascality and innocence in his earlier writing gave way, in his later and posthumous works, to an ever-darkening vision of humanity that left Twain bitter and disillusioned. This darker vision is hardly present in the three Tom Sawyer books (1876, 1894, 1896) and in his masterpiece, *The Adventures of Huckleberry Finn.*

Twain's lifelong fascination with boyhood play led to the creation of *The Adventures of Tom Sawyer*, a book of nostalgic recollections of his own lost youth that has been dismissed too lightly by some sober-sided academics as "amusing but thin stuff" and taken too analytically and seriously by others who seek in it the complexities—of carefully controlled viewpoint, multiple irony, and social satire—found in *The Adventures of Huckleberry Finn*, begun in the year *The Adventures of Tom Sawyer* was published. Beyond noting that *The Adventures of Tom Sawyer* is a delicate balance of the romantic with the realistic, of humor and pathos, of innocence and evil, one must admit that the book defies analysis. In fact, Twain's opening statement in *The Adventures of Huckleberry Finn* is, ironically, more applicable to *The Adventures of Tom Sawyer*: "Persons attempting to find a motive in this narrative will be prosecuted; persons attempting to find a moral in it will be banished; persons attempting to find a plot in it will be shot." *The Adventures of Tom Sawyer* is purely, simply, and happily "the history of a boy," or as Twain also called it, "simply a hymn, put into prose form to give it a worldly air." It should be read first and last for pleasure, first by children, then by adults.

For *The Adventures of Tom Sawyer* is also, as even Twain admitted, a book for those who have long since passed from boyhood: "It is *not* a boy's book at all. It will be read only by adults. It is written only for adults."

Kenneth S. Lynn explicates the author's preface when he says that *The Adventures of Tom Sawyer* "confirms the profoundest wishes of the heart," as does Christopher Morley, who calls the book "a panorama of happy memory" and who made a special visit to Hannibal because he wanted to see the town and house where Tom lived. During that visit, Morley and friends actually whitewashed Aunt Polly's fence. Certainly there can be no greater testimony to the effectiveness of a literary work than its readers' desire to reenact the exploits of its hero.

Tom is the archetypal all-American boy, defining in himself the very concept of American boyhood, as he passes with equal seriousness from one obsession to another: whistling, glory, spying, sympathy, flirtation, exploration, piracy, shame, fear—always displaying to the utmost the child's ability to concentrate his entire energies on one thing at a time (as when he puts the treasure hunt out of his mind in favor of Becky's picnic). Tom is contrasted to both Sid, the sanctimonious "good boy" informant who loses the reader's sympathies as immediately as Tom gains them, and to Huck. As opposed to Huck's self-reliant, unschooled, parentless existence, his love of profanity, his passive preference for being a follower, and his abhorrence of civilization, Tom is shrewd in the ways of civilization, adventurous and a leader. He comes from the respectable world of Aunt Polly, with a literary mind, a conscious romantic desire for experience and for the hero's part, and insatiable egotism that assists him in his ingenious schematizations of life to achieve his heroic aspirations, and a general love of fame, money, attention, and "glory." The relationship between the two boys may be compared to that between the romantic Don Quixote and the realist Sancho Panza. It was Twain's genius to understand that the games Quixote played out of "madness" were, in fact, those played by children with deadly seriousness. Lionel Trilling summarizes Twain's achievement in this book when he says that "*The Adventures of Tom Sawyer* has the truth of honesty—what it says about things and feelings is never false and always both adequate and beautiful."

THE AGE OF INNOCENCE

Type of work: Novel
Author: Edith Wharton (1862-1937)
Type of plot: Social criticism
Time of plot: Late nineteenth century
Locale: New York City
First published: 1920

This novel is an incisive but oblique attack on the intricate and tyrannous tribal customs of a highly stratified New York society with which the author herself was familiar. The Age of Innocence is a well-made novel, the work of a craftsperson for whom form and method are perfectly welded, and the action results inevitably from the natures of the characters themselves.

Principal Characters

Newland Archer, a young lawyer who is a member of New York's high society. Married to May Welland, a girl from his own class, he falls in love with Ellen Olenska and for a time considers running away with her. He never does so because he is bound by the ties of marriage and convention.

Countess Ellen Olenska, May Welland's cousin. A New York girl of good family, she has married a Polish nobleman but now wishes a divorce from him. Intelligent and beautiful, she comes back to New York, where she tries to fit into the life she had known before her marriage. She falls in love with Newland Archer. When the young attorney, persuaded by her family, urges her not to seek a divorce, she leaves for Europe without him. Years later, Archer's son visits Ellen in Paris.

May Welland Archer, Newland's wife, a typical New York socialite with all the restrictions and forms adopted by that class. She triumphs over Ellen Olenska and saves her marriage with the announcement that she is to become a mother.

Mr. and **Mrs. Welland,** May's parents. Rich, conservative, puritanical, they are somewhat shocked by the discovery that their relative, Ellen, plans to divorce her husband. Clannishly, however, they give in her honor a party at which they announce the engagement of their daughter to Newland Archer.

Mrs. Manson Mingott, May's grandmother, the mother of Mrs. Welland, and a proud old aristocrat who dominates the clan.

Medora Mingott, May's aunt and Ellen's former chaperone. Flighty but good-natured, she brings Ellen back to the family home in New York after Ellen and her husband have separated.

Mr. and **Mrs. van der Luyden,** members of the old, conservative aristocracy. They generously offer to receive Ellen after she has been snubbed by others of her class.

Julius Beaufort, a successful New York businessperson. Married, he carries on affairs on the side. Eventually he goes bankrupt.

Mrs. Beaufort, his wife, a fat, pleasant woman tolerant of her husband's philanderings.

Fanny Beaufort, the daughter of Julius by one of his mistresses. She marries Dallas Archer.

Dallas Archer, the son of May and Newland Archer. He manages to cut the ties of formal society which have held his father captive for so long, marries Fanny Beaufort, and leads a more relaxed and happier life than his father's.

Ned Winsett, one of Newland Archer's friends, a journalist who tries to win Archer over to a less restrictive life.

Reggie and **Mrs. Chivers,** Newland Archer's fashionable but understanding friends. They entertain him when he is trying to have a rendezvous with Ellen.

Jane Archer, Newland's wise and clever little sister. She has an ear for gossip and spends much time talking over tidbits of information with her mother.

Mrs. Archer, Newland's widowed mother. She intercedes for Ellen with the van der Luydens and manages to persuade them to give a dinner party for her after she has been snubbed by the rest of New York society.

Mrs. Lemuel Struthers, a lively, fat woman much interested in musicians and artists. She is considered quite vulgar by the "better" families.

Mr. Letterblau, the senior partner of the law firm for which Newland Archer works. He directs the young attorney to handle the Olenska divorce case.

Lawrence Lefferts, a society friend of the Archers and the Wellands.

The Story

Newland Archer, a handsome and eligible young attorney engaged to lovely May Welland, learned that the engagement would be announced at a party to welcome his fiancée's cousin, Countess Ellen Olenska. This reception for Ellen constituted a heroic sacrifice on the part of the many Welland connections, for her marriage to a ne'er-do-well Polish count had not improved her position so far as rigorous and straitlaced New York society was concerned. The fact that she contemplated a divorce action also made her suspect, and, to cap it all, her rather bohemian way of living did not conform to what her family expected of a woman who had made an unsuccessful marriage.

Newland Archer's engagement to May was announced. At the same party, Archer was greatly attracted to Ellen. Before long, with the excuse that he was making the cousin of his betrothed feel at home, he began to send her flowers and to call on her. To him she seemed a woman who offered sensitivity, beauty, and the promise of a life quite different from that which he could expect after his marriage to May.

Archer found himself defending Ellen when the rest of society was attacking her contemplated divorce action. He did not, however, consider breaking his engagement to May, but constantly sought reasons for justifying what was to the rest of his group an excellent union. With Ellen often in his thoughts, May Welland's cool beauty and correct but unexciting personality began to suffer in Archer's estimation.

Although the clan defended her against all outsiders, Ellen was often treated as a pariah. Her family kept a check on her, trying to prevent her from indulging in too many bohemianisms, such as her strange desire to rent a house in a socially unacceptable part of town. The women of the clan also recognized her as a dangerous rival, and ruthless Julius Beaufort, whose secret dissipations were known by all, including his wife, paid her marked attention. Archer found himself hating Julius Beaufort very much.

Convincing himself that he was seeing too much of Ellen, Archer went to St. Augustine to visit May, who was vacationing there with her mother and her hypochondriac father. In spite of her cool and conventional welcome and her gentle rebuffs to his wooing, her beauty

reawakened in him a kind of affection, and he pleaded with her to advance the date of their wedding. May and her parents refused because their elaborate preparations could not be completed in time.

Archer returned to New York. There, with the aid of the family matriarch, Mrs. Manson Mingott, he achieved his purpose, and the wedding date was advanced. This news came to him in a telegram sent by May to Ellen, which Ellen read to him just as he was attempting to advance the intimacy of their relationship. Archer left Ellen's house and found a similar telegram from May to himself. Telling his sister, Jane, that the wedding would take place within a month, he suddenly realized that he was now protected against Ellen and himself.

The ornate wedding, the conventional European honeymoon which followed, and May's assumption of the role of the proper wife soon disillusioned Archer. He realized that he was trapped, that the mores of his society, helped by his own lack of courage, had prepared him, like a smooth ritual, for a rigid and codified life. There was enough intelligence and insight in Archer, however, to make him resent the trap.

On his return to New York, he continued to see Ellen. The uselessness of his work as junior attorney in an ancient law firm, the stale regimen of his social life, and the passive sweetness of May did not satisfy that part of Archer which set him apart from the rest of his clan.

He proposed to Ellen that they go away together, but Ellen, wise and kind, showed him that such an escape would not be a pleasant one, and she indicated that they could love each other only as long as he did not press for a consummation. Archer agreed. He further capitulated when, urged by her family, he advised Ellen, as her attorney and as a relative, not to get a divorce from Count Olenski. She agreed, and Archer again blamed his own cowardice for his action.

The family faced another crisis when Julius Beaufort's firm, built upon a framework of shady financial transactions, failed, ruining him and his duped customers. The blow caused elderly Mrs. Mingott to have a stroke, and the family rallied around her. She summoned Ellen, a favorite of hers, to her side, and Ellen, who had been living in Washington, D.C., returned to the Mingott house to stay. Archer, who had not met Ellen since he advised her against a divorce, began seeing her again, and certain remarks by Archer's male acquaintances, along with the strained and martyrlike attitude that May had adopted, indicated to him that his intimacy with Ellen was known among his family and friends. The affair came to an end, however, when Ellen left for Paris, after learning that May was to have a baby. It was obvious to all that May had triumphed, and Archer was treated by his family as a prodigal returned. The rebel was conquered. Archer made his peace with society.

Years passed. Archer dabbled in liberal politics and interested himself in civic reforms. His children, Mary and Dallas, were properly reared. May died when Archer was in his fifties. He lamented her passing with genuine grief. He watched society change and saw the old conser-

vative order give way, accepting and rationalizing innovations of a younger, more liberal generation.

One day his son Dallas, about to be married, phoned him and proposed a European tour, their last trip together. In Paris, Dallas revealed to his father that he knew all about Ellen Olenska and had arranged a visit to her apartment. When they arrived, however, Archer sent his son ahead, to pay his respects, while he remained on a park bench outside. A romantic to the end, incapable of acting in any situation that made demands on his emotional resources, he sat and watched the lights in Ellen's apartment until a servant appeared on the balcony and closed the shutters. Then he walked slowly back to his hotel. The past was the past; the present was secure.

Critical Evaluation

Edith Wharton's *The Age of Innocence* is probably one of her most successful books because it offers an inside look at a subject the author knew very well, that is, New York society during the 1870's. That was her milieu, and her pen captures the atmosphere of aristocratic New York as its inhabitants move about in their world of subtleties, innuendoes, and strict adherence to the dictates of fashionable society. Wharton describes those years for herself as "safe, guarded, and monotonous." Her only deviation as a young adult consisted in frequent journeys abroad and summers in Newport. Her marriage to Edward Wharton, a prominent Bostonian, assumed the same character as her own early life until it became apparent that he suffered from mental illness and would have to be hospitalized. During World War I, Edith Wharton worked for the allies and received the French Cross of the Legion of Honor for her work with the Red Cross in Paris. Most critics agree that her best years as a novelist were from 1911 to 1921, during which time she produced *Ethan Frome*, a grim New England study, and *The Age of Innocence*, for which she was awarded the Pulitzer Prize.

Wharton's most successful theme (like that of her friend Henry James) was the plight of the young and innocent in a world that was more complicated than they were prepared for. Newland Archer and Ellen Olenska found the society of New York intricate and demanding and, as such, an impediment to their personal searches for happiness and some degree of freedom. *The Age of Innocence* is a careful blending of a nostalgia for the 1870's with a subtle, but nevertheless inescapable, criticism of its genteel timidities and clever evasions.

With respect to Wharton's style, it can be generalized

that she was not a particularly daring writer, nor an experimenter in form. Rather, she wrote in a comfortable, fixed, formal style that was closely designed. In some instances, her narrative becomes heavy, and the intricate play and counterplay of the characters' motives can lose all but the most diligent reader. The author's presence is never forgotten and the reader feels her control throughout the story, as the narrative view is quickly established from the beginning. Wharton's characters are portrayed through their actions, and the clear lines of the plot are visible. Because *The Age of Innocence* so carefully fits a historical niche, its scope is limited and its direction narrow. That is not to say that drama is limited or lacking. On the contrary, in detailing such a small world, the drama is intense even if it is found beneath a sophisticated, polished surface.

Three figures are projected against the historical background of New York society. May Welland, the beautiful betrothed of Newland Archer, was born and bred in traditions and is completely a product of the system that she seeks to perpetuate. Newland observes, after their marriage, that May and her mother are so much alike that he sees himself being treated and placated just as Mr. Welland is by his wife and daughter. There is no doubt that May will never surprise Newland "by a new idea, a weakness, a cruelty or an emotion."

Ellen Olenska, on the other hand, has freed herself from the restraints of society by her experiences abroad and through her subsequent separation from her husband, the Polish count. Madame Olenska is not only a cosmopolite but also a character of more depth and perception than the other women in the novel. She suggests by her presence, as well as by her past experiences, a tragic and emotionally involved element in the story. Ellen definitely does not conform to the rules of accepted behavior, yet she moves in a cloud of mystery that makes her an intriguing personality to those who observe her, if even only to criticize. As soon as she and Archer are aware of their feelings for each other, Archer tries to persuade Ellen, in a halfhearted way, that one cannot purchase freedom at the expense of another. He has given her an idea by which to live and, in so doing, has unknowingly destroyed his one opportunity to find a new freedom for himself.

Newland Archer is, in many ways, a typical Wharton masculine figure. He is a man set apart from the people he knows by education, intellect, and feeling, but he lacks the initiative and courage to separate himself physically from the securities of the known. The movement of the plot in *The Age of Innocence* is established by the transition from one position to another taken by Archer in his relations with either May or Ellen. Archer's failure to break the barriers of clan convention lead him to an ironic abnegation, for in the last pages of the novel the reader sees Newland retreating from the opportunity to meet with Ellen—an opportunity that his eager son Dallas is quick to arrange. Dallas is anxious to meet Ellen, for he heard from his mother shortly before she died that Archer had given up the thing he had most wanted (namely, Ellen) for her. It is sad to see that Archer, the object of two loves, has never been able to satisfy or be satisfied by either. The tragedy in the novel rests with May, for it is she who appeared to be the most innocent and naïve; yet in the end, she is, perhaps, the most aware of all. She has suffered quietly through the years, knowing that her husband's true desires and passions were elsewhere. Dallas' generation observes the whole situation out of context as "prehistoric." He dismisses the affair rather casually, for his contemporaries have lost that blind adherence to social custom that the Archers and Wellands knew so well.

The Age of Innocence is a novel of manners that delineates a very small world, yet under the surface one sees a world of suffering, denial, and patient resignation—a situation that deserves more attention and reflection than one might give at first reading.

THE AGE OF REASON

Type of work: Theological study
Author: Thomas Paine (1737-1809)
First published: Part I, 1794; Part II, 1796

Although Paine attempted to write a book of profound morality and ethics that criticized institutionalized religion but not God, many readers perceived The Age of Reason *as blasphemy.*

Thomas Paine earned lasting fame as one of history's most powerful and persuasive writers. Born in England as the son of an artisan, and largely self-educated, he wrote robust, plain, emotionally intense English that crystallized thought and galvanized into action the common people of America, Great Britain, and France. Paine, a young English immigrant sponsored by Benjamin Franklin, became beloved in his adopted country after he wrote *Common Sense* (1776), an impelling force in persuading Americans to break their remaining ties with England. His *Crisis* papers, written during the American Revolution, buoyed American spirits, and his *The Rights of Man* (1791-1792), pleading for natural rights and republican principles, won for him admirers throughout the Western world.

Paine placed before the common people the Enlightenment ideas of intellectual circles. He possessed an uncanny ability to translate the abstractions of the well-educated elite into living ideas that moved the masses. He believed that, just as Sir Isaac Newton revealed the natural laws governing the universe, he and others could use reason to uncover the natural rights of individuals, republican principles in politics, or the laws of the marketplace.

While millions of people responded positively to Paine's early writings calling for independence and individual liberty, *The Age of Reason* made him a hated and reviled figure. The once-beloved advocate of humane and gentle treatment of all God's creatures was now presented as a drunkard and moral degenerate—a "filthy little atheist," in the words of Theodore Roosevelt, almost a century after Paine's death.

Although thousands of ministers denounced Paine as an atheist, he clearly stated on the first page of *The Age of Reason* that "I believe in one God, and no more; and I hope for happiness beyond this life." He described his moral principles, those taught by many religious figures: "I believe in the equality of man; and I believe that religious duties consist in doing justice, loving mercy, and endeavoring to make our fellow-creatures happy."

Paine wrote *The Age of Reason* in 1793 in Paris during the French Revolution, which he had promoted and defended. Deeply troubled by the cruel excesses of a minority of revolutionaries, expecting arrest any day, he had seen reason overthrown and monarchy replaced with new despots. Similarly, in religion he saw the spread of atheism as a by-product of attacks on the established church. *The Age of Reason* was a blow against institutionalized religion on the one hand and an antidote to what Paine regarded as the poison of atheism on the other. As his fellow revolutionaries executed the French king and abolished the established church, Paine cautioned them not to dethrone reason, "lest in the general wreck of superstition, of false systems of government and false theology, we lose sight of morality, of humanity and of the theology that is true."

Paine outraged many former admirers not because he rejected God, which he did not do, but because he attacked the Christian church: "I do not believe in the creed professed . . . by any church that I know of. My own mind is my own church." Anticipating Karl Marx, Paine wrote: "All national institutions of churches . . . appear to me no other than human inventions, set up to terrify and enslave mankind, and monopolize power and profit." Government officials propped up the church for the benefit of greedy priests, and in return the church lent legitimacy to government, Paine said. He understood the danger of excess as the church-state edifice toppled, but he believed that reason would free humanity from the despotism of the clerics and protect it from the abyss of amoral anarchism.

Before Paine could present a theology appropriate to an age of reason, he had to strip away the false doctrine of Christianity. All existing religions claimed to be based on revelations from gods, but Paine argued that revelations could only occur between God and those to whom he directly revealed himself. After that, revelations, in the unlikely event that they had occurred, became mere hearsay and had been distorted to protect the position of the clerics.

The Bible was composed of hearsay, not revelation, Paine argued; using what would later be called biblical criticism, he found that many of the Old Testament stories were mere reworkings of ancient pagan tales. God's victory over Satan and the latter's confinement in the pit of fire reminded him of the tale of Jupiter's defeating a giant and confining him under Mount Etna, where he still belches fire. Christian mythologists did not settle the Satan problem so easily, Paine asserted:

> · · · they could not do without him; and after being at the trouble of making him, they bribed him to stay. They promised him ALL the Jews, ALL the Turks by anticipation, nine-tenths of the world beside, and Mahomet into the bargain.

Christian mythologists deified Satan, Paine charged, even forcing God to capitulate to him by surrendering His Son on the Cross.

The Old Testament degraded God by having Him order His people to engage in treachery, murder, and genocide, Paine wrote. It was full of confused chronology and fragments of non-Jewish writing. The books ascribed to Moses, Joshua, Samuel, and others could not have been written by them. That which was not absurd was an obscene history of wickedness. The Book of Job was interesting but was not Hebrew in origin, some of the Psalms properly exalted God but were not superior to other such writings before or since, and the bits of wisdom in the Proverbs were not any wiser than those of Ben Franklin.

Paine then turned to the New Testament. It was not as full of brutality and blood as the Old Testament, but it was even more absurd, he believed. The Gospels of Matthew, Mark, Luke, and John were not revelations but anecdotal hearsay written by unknown figures long after the events they described. The biblical story of Jesus, a modest and humane man whose message was distorted by church mythologists, was an absurdity. The story of his birth was an obscene tale of the violation of a virgin by a ghost. Jesus' death, God dying on a cross, was even more ridiculous: "His historians, having brought him into the world in a supernatural manner, were obliged to take him out again in the same manner, or the first part of the story must have fallen to the ground."

Jesus was a good man, a reformer and revolutionist, who was killed because he posed a threat to greedy priests and power-hungry Romans. Subsequently, the church built myths about him to support and justify a priestly religion of pomp and revenue. It created a false concept of redemption to obscure the fact that all humans at all times occupy the same relation to God, needing no mediation by churches or ministers. The doctrine of redemption served the clerics by turning humans into outcasts living in a dunghill and needing the church to regain the kingdom. The Bible, books of hearsay written centuries after the events they described, was shaped to fit the needs of the church. Church leaders settled by majority vote what would make up the Bible. If the vote had been different, Paine wrote, then Christian belief would be different.

Reason taught a very clear lesson to Paine. All human languages were ambiguous, easily miscopied, or even forged. The word of God would never have been revealed in a human language, a changeable and varying vehicle. The word of God would be revealed in a way that could never be changed or distorted or misunderstood, and it would be revealed to all people in every generation.

"The Word of God IS THE CREATION WE BEHOLD and it is in *this word*, which no human invention can counterfeit or alter, that God speaketh universally to man." In God's creation of the earth and all the universe, one sees His wisdom, power, munificence, and mercy, Paine claimed. The absurdities and creations of the Bible paled beside the workings of the universe in which God placed humanity. The Bible was so inferior to the glory and power of God revealed in His creation that the church had to suppress philosophy and science that would make known the true theology revealed in the creation. Christianity so offended reason that, in order to survive, the church had to suppress freedom of thought.

There was a religious creed suitable for an age of reason, Paine believed: the deistic creed of Ben Franklin and Thomas Jefferson, as well as Voltaire and other European Enlightenment leaders. Paine made his deistic beliefs clear:

> The only idea man can affix to the name of God is that of a *first cause*, the cause of all things. And incomprehensible and difficult as it is for a man to conceive what a first cause is, he arrives at the belief of it from the tenfold greater difficulty of disbelieving it.

People did not need the church and ministers to have access to the mind of God: "It is only by the exercise of reason that man can discover God." The Bible served only to diminish God and to make Him appear cruel and angry.

So Paine ended the first part of *The Age of Reason*. He did not have the leisure to worry about its reception. Maximilien Robespierre and his radical comrades imprisoned Paine and kept him locked up through most of 1794. They probably did not intend to execute him but wanted to keep his pen from being turned against their excesses. He nearly died of illness before James Monroe helped free him. As Paine recovered, he read attacks on the first part of *The Age of Reason*. He had not had access to a Bible in anticlerical France when he wrote the first part. Now he had a Bible at hand and, he wrote, found that it was worse than he remembered.

Paine did not develop new themes in part 2 of *The Age of Reason* but provided more details of biblical criticism to support his argument that Moses, Joshua, Samuel, and others could not have written the books ascribed to them, thus removing any authority that they had as revelation. Paine again hammered at the theme that the Bible reduced God and His holy disciples to barbaric evildoers. Only the Book of Job could be read without indignation and disgust, he said. The New Testament began with the debauchery of Mary and ended with the absurdity of men placing God on a cross. The heart of the New Testament was the often-conflicting Gospels of Matthew, Mark, Luke, and John, each of whom seemed to have known a different Jesus.

Paine reiterated his central message. God's glory and benevolence were not found in the Bible or in churches or in ministers' sermons. Humans did not need mediating institutions to reach God. All people could find God's revelation by looking at His creation, using reason.

Although *The Age of Reason* was a book of profound morality and ethics and a paean to the glories of God, it gained for Paine undying hatred throughout the Christian world. His message was derived from the thought of Isaac Newton and René Descartes. He did not add anything to the deistic thought of Voltaire, Franklin, and Jefferson. Paine's unforgivable sin was to take deistic theology out of the gentlefolk's drawing rooms and to place it in the plain language of the people. His book horrified many of the common people by its seeming blasphemy and frightened the elite by its threat of freeing the masses from religious control. *The Age of Reason* came at the close of the Enlightenment, as reason was being dethroned. A century would pass before Paine's message of political, religious, and economic freedom could again be clearly heard.

ALL THE KING'S MEN

Type of work: Novel
Author: Robert Penn Warren (1905-1989)
Type of plot: Social criticism
Time of plot: Late 1920's and early 1930's
Locale: Southern United States
First published: 1946

Although the rise of Willie Stark is ostensibly the theme of the novel, the real issue is the character of Jack Burden, a caustic-tongued, brilliant journalist whose self-examination becomes the symbol of an era.

Principal Characters

Willie Stark (the Boss), the governor of the state. A relentless, unyielding man, Willie has the capacity and the will to break anyone who opposes him. Often ruthless, he is not entirely bad, but his dictatorial powers grow until he is the leader of a powerful political machine. Nevertheless, he does more for the ordinary people of his state than did his more aristocratic predecessors. By improving schools, roads, and hospitals, he leaves these things behind him as monuments after his death. At last even Jack Burden realizes that there was a streak of greatness in Stark.

Jack Burden, the narrator and Willie Stark's factotum. Although a capable man, Burden has spells he calls the "Great Sleep." During these periods, he becomes completely indifferent to whatever he is doing at the time. While finishing his Ph.D. dissertation, he went into the "Great Sleep"; as a result, the degree was never completed. A very cynical, sometimes negativistic person, he realizes after Willie's death the hidden greatness in the Boss's character. Somehow this realization makes Jack feel better about himself and the rest of humankind.

Anne Stanton, Jack Burden's former sweetheart and the daughter of an earlier governor. After meeting Willie Stark, Anne becomes his mistress, thus bringing destruction to him and to her brother Adam. After Stark's death, she finally marries Jack Burden.

Adam Stanton, Anne's idealistic brother. A famous, dedicated surgeon, Adam represents, in many ways, the aristocratic past. His work is his life; money and fame mean little to him. Feeling that his sister has been ruined by a ruthless dictator, Adam shoots Willie and loses his own life in the process.

Judge Irwin (Monty), Jack Burden's real father. A hawk-visaged, still-handsome old man, he has made one major error in his life. Through bribery, he managed to obtain a high-paying job. In this way he was able to pay off pressing debts, at the same time causing the death of the man whom he replaced. By doing so, he paved the way for his own downfall. When Jack discovers this indiscretion, the seemingly incorruptible old man commits suicide.

Sadie Burke, Governor Stark's hard-bitten, profane secretary. Feeling betrayed by Willie, the jealous woman has Tiny Duffy tell Adam Stanton about Stark's affair with Stanton's sister. No longer able to tolerate Willie's amorous dalliance with other women, she causes the death of two men—Adam and Willie.

Sugar-Boy O'Sheean (Robert), Willie Stark's devoted chauffeur and bodyguard. He causes Jack Burden many uneasy moments because of his fast, though expert, driving. He kills Adam Stanton after the latter shoots Willie.

Tiny Duffy, the shrewd lieutenant governor and Willie Stark's rotund foil. Biding his time, Tiny tells Adam that Anne Stanton is Willie's mistress. In this way, the grossly fat Duffy gets revenge for years of ridicule. Although he becomes governor after Stark's death, Tiny's political future is in doubt.

Sam MacMurfee, Willie Stark's slick political opponent.

Tom Stark, Willie's arrogant, football-playing son, who repays his father's pride with disdain.

Lucy Stark, Willie's long-suffering wife, a former schoolteacher.

Mrs. Ellis Burden, Jack's mother and Judge Irwin's mistress.

Miss Littlepaugh, the sister of the man whose job at the power company Judge Irwin got through bribery, thereby causing the man to commit suicide.

The Story

When Governor Willie Stark tried to intimidate old Judge Irwin of Burden's Landing, the judge stood firm against the demagogue's threats. As a result, Willie ordered Jack Burden to find some scandal in the judge's past that could ruin the elderly man.

Jack had met Willie back in 1922, when Willie, the county treasurer, and Lucy Stark, his schoolteacher wife, were fighting against a corrupt building contractor who was constructing the new schoolhouse. Sent by his newspaper, the *Chronicle*, to investigate, Jack found Willie and Lucy both out of jobs but still fighting against graft. Two years later, the fire escape of the school collapsed during a fire drill and Willie became a hero.

Willie then ran in the Democratic primary race for governor. There were two factions, those of Harrison and MacMurfee. Because it was to be a close election, someone proposed that Willie be used as a dummy candidate to split the rural MacMurfee followers. Tiny Duffy and some other men persuaded Willie that he could save the state. By then, Willie had become a lawyer and politically ambitious man. Jack covered the campaign.

Aiding Willie was Sadie Burke, a clever, energetic woman with political skill. Inadvertently, she revealed Harrison's plan to Willie. Crushed and gloomy at this news, Willie rallied his spirits and offered to campaign for MacMurfee, who was elected.

Willie practiced law for a few years until 1930, when he ran for governor with the assistance of Sadie Burke, who became his mistress, and Tiny Duffy, who was Willie's political jackal.

Meanwhile, Jack had quit his job on the *Chronicle*. Reared by a mother who had remarried because Ellis Burden had deserted her, Jack had become a faithless, homeless cynic whose journalism career meant nothing to him as an ideal. He had, in his youth, played with Anne and Adam Stanton. Adam was now a famous surgeon, and Anne, still unmarried, had become a welfare worker.

Jack was in love with Anne, but time had placed a barrier between him and the girl with whom he had fallen in love during the summer after he had come home to Burden's Landing from college. He had been twenty-one then, she seventeen. Yet Jack's youthful cynicism, which later took possession of him completely, spoiled him in Anne's eyes.

When Jack went to work for Governor Willie Stark, Jack's mother was deeply pained and Judge Irwin was disgusted, but Jack cared little for their opinions.

By 1933, Willie was on the verge of losing his wife,

who could not stand her husband's political maneuvers and his treatment of their son Tom. Willie assured Jack that Lucy knew nothing about Sadie Burke. Lucy remained with Willie through his reelection in 1934 and then retired to her sister's farm. She appeared with Willie in public only for the sake of his reputation.

Jack began to dig into Judge Irwin's past. Delving into the judge's financial transactions during the time when he was attorney general under Governor Stanton, Jack learned that a power company had been sued by the government for a large sum. As a bribe to the attorney general, the company fired one of its men to give a highly paid job to Irwin. Later this man, Littlepaugh, committed suicide after writing the facts in a letter to his sister. Still living, Miss Littlepaugh told Jack the story.

The issue of the Willie Stark six-million-dollar hospital demanded use of this scandal which Jack had uncovered. Willie told Jack that he wanted Adam Stanton to head the new hospital. It would, Jack knew, be a ridiculous offer to the aloof and unworldly young doctor, but he made an effort to persuade Adam to take the post. Adam flatly refused. A few days later, Anne sent for Jack. She wanted Adam to take the position. Jack showed Anne the documents proving Judge Irwin's acceptance of a bribe and Governor Stanton's attempt to cover up for his friend. Knowing that Adam would want to protect his father's good name, Anne showed the evidence to him. He then said he would head the hospital. Later Jack wondered how Anne had known about the plans for the hospital because neither he nor Adam had told her.

Jack's suspicions were confirmed when Sadie Burke, in a torrent of rage, told him that Willie had been betraying her. Jack knew then that Anne Stanton was the cause.

Disillusioned, he packed a suitcase and drove to California. This journey to the West and back completed, Jack, his torment under control, went back to work for Willie.

One of MacMurfee's men tried to bribe Adam to use influence in selecting a man named Larson as the builder of the medical center. When Adam, outraged, decided to resign, Anne phoned Jack for the first time since he had learned of her affair with Willie. Anne and Jack decided to have Adam sign a warrant against the man who had tried to bribe him. Jack also warned Anne that as a witness she would be subject to public scrutiny of her relationship with Willie, but she said she did not care. When Jack asked her why she was associating with Willie, she said that, after what Jack had told her about Governor Stanton's dishonesty in the past, she did not care what happened to her. Later, Jack persuaded Adam not to bring suit.

After Willie's political enemy, MacMurfee, tried to blackmail him because of a scandal concerning Tom Stark, Willie ordered Jack to use his knowledge to make Judge Irwin throw his weight against MacMurfee's blackmail attempt. When Jack went to Burden's Landing to confront Judge Irwin with the evidence that Jack had obtained from Miss Littlepaugh, the old man shot himself.

In the excitement following the suicide, Jack's mother told him that he had caused his father's death. Belatedly, Jack discovered the reason for Ellis Burden's desertion. In his will, Judge Irwin left his estate to his son, Jack Burden.

It seemed that there was only one way left to handle MacMurfee. Willie decided to give the building contract for the hospital to MacMurfee's man, Larson, who in turn would suppress the scandal about Tom. Duffy made the arrangements.

Tom Stark was a football hero. One Saturday during a game, his neck was broken. Adam reported that Tom would remain paralyzed. This news had its effect on Willie. He told Duffy that the hospital deal was off. Turning to Lucy once more, he dismissed Sadie Burke and Anne Stanton.

Duffy, driven too far by Willie, phoned Adam and told him that Anne had been responsible for his appointment. Adam, having known nothing of his sister's relationship with the governor, went to her apartment to denounce her. Then, in the hall of the state building, Adam shot Willie and was killed immediately afterward by Willie's bodyguard.

Piece by piece, the tangled mess of Jack's life began to take new meaning. He separated himself from every particle of his past with the exception of two people: his mother, whose devotion to Judge Irwin over all the years had given her a new personality in Jack's eyes, and Anne Stanton, whom he married.

Critical Evaluation

One of the richest and most powerful of modern American novels is Robert Penn Warren's *All the King's Men*. In its pages, readers can trace a multitude of fascinating subjects, ranging from politics to religion, from sociology to philosophy. They can discover an equally wide scope of thematic questions. Arousing as it does various responses to its complexities—responses that, for example, praise it as Christian or revile it as nihilistic on exactly the same grounds—the book is generally regarded as the masterpiece of a novelist who was also a respected poet, critic, and professor. Warren, a Kentucky native, had a special affinity for the South, and much of his work suggests the traditions and problems of this region. *All the King's Men*, while exploring issues universal as well as regional, also has an unmistakable Southern flavor in areas more vital than mere setting.

An immediate query regarding this Pulitzer Prize-winning book usually touches on a comparison of Willie Stark and Huey Long. Governor of Louisiana from 1928 to 1931, Long led a career parallel to what Warren designs for Stark and presented a similar powerful and paradoxical personality. The product of a poor background, Long nevertheless became a lawyer at twenty-one after completing the three-year Tulane University course in eight months. Aggressive and determined, at twenty-four he sought and won the one state office open at his age— a seat on the Railroad Commission. An unorthodox champion of the common people, Long in his 1924 race for

governor was unsuccessful when he tried to remain moderate on the Ku Klux Klan issue. His 1928 try for the office was a triumph, however, and at thirty-five the outspoken country boy was a governor who ruled the state almost singlehandedly. Using patronage as his lever, Long talked the legislature into a thirty-million-dollar bond issue to finance farm roads, hospitals, free school books, and other programs popular with the poor but infuriating to his opponents. Like Stark, Long soon found himself impeached, charged with bribery, plotting the murder of a senator, misusing state funds, and various other crimes, some of which this strange mixture of demagogue and selfless public servant no doubt committed. Yet his promises and threats kept Long in office when enough senators signed a round-robin promising not to convict him no matter what the evidence.

Long's career, which included the unprecedented move of becoming a United States senator while still serving in effect as governor, as well as plans to seek the presidency, was halted by assassination. In a 1935 scene almost re-created in *All the King's Men*, a man stepped from behind a pillar at the Capitol and shot once, hitting Long. Felled by 61 bullets from Long's bodyguards, the man, Dr. Carl A. Weiss, died within seconds. Thirty hours later, Long, the "Kingfish," was also dead. Weiss's motivations were obscure; speculation said that he was angered when Long's maneuvering cost his father a judgeship.

Despite the overwhelming similarities between Long and Stark, Warren denied that he attempted merely to create a fictional counterpart of a political figure. He claimed, however, that the "line of thinking and feeling" in the book did evolve from the atmosphere of Louisiana that he encountered while he was a teacher at Louisiana State University, an atmosphere dominated and directed by Long's tenure as governor.

Central to the book is the primary theme of humanity's search for knowledge; all other facets are subordinate to and supportive of this theme. Knowledge includes both objective and subjective comprehensions, with the end goal being self-knowledge. "Life is Motion toward Knowledge," one reads in *All the King's Men*. Elsewhere Warren asserts that the right to knowledge is an individual's "right to exist, to be himself, to be a man." Humanity defines itself through knowledge, and the book's pivotal incident demands accumulation of knowledge. Jack, assigned to "dig something up" on the Judge, does indeed uncover the Judge's dishonor, but the information precipitates a far more meaningful understanding.

For each of the characters, it is a lack of knowledge or an incomplete knowledge that constitutes his chief problem, and those who eventually blunder forward do so only when they see what has previously been hidden from them. As the narrator, for example, Jack Burden is allegedly telling Willie Stark's story. Yet one senses that, as he relates the events, Jack is clarifying their meaning mostly for his own benefit. The product of an aristocratic background, Jack in essence eschews knowledge throughout most of the story, for he exists in a vacuum, refusing to be touched or to feel. At moments of crisis, he seeks oblivion in the "Great Sleep" or by adhering to a belief in the "Great Twitch": "Nobody has any responsibility for anything." He is a man of reflection only until those reflections become troublesome.

Seemingly Willie is the book's most knowing character. Yet his knowledge is questioned, at first only occasionally, then fully. Unlike Jack, who drops his idealism for inertia, Stark is always a man of action, action based sometimes on only partial knowledge. His innocence, lost by the "knowledge" that he has been betrayed, is replaced by a willingness to use evil if it is necessary for his purposes. He can justify blackmail or protection of a crook on this basis. For a time, Willie maintains and understands the balance between good and evil, but "obsessed with the evil in human nature and with his power to manipulate it," he is drawn completely onto the side of this dark force.

Jack ignores both ideals and the world, Willie the ideals. The third important character is Adam Stanton, who ignores the world. Make good out of evil, says Willie, for the bad is all that one has. Horrified by such a philosophy, Adam denies that honor, purity, and justice can commingle with blackness. When his preconceptions of the state of the universe prove false, he repudiates not his ideas but the universe. He is a philosopher untainted by fact or action; thus his knowledge is also faulty and weak, a situation that leads him to tragedy.

Through his investigation of the Judge, Jack inadvertently stumbles on the greater truth for himself and for the novel. He learns who he is, in that he discovers his true father. More important, however, he learns what he is as a man: an imperfect being who must accept imperfection in himself and others and lovingly make what he may out of that state. He learns that men cannot be separated from other men, that no action or idea exists alone, and that past, present, and future are entangled in the web. He realizes what Willie initially knew, forgot, and reclaimed at the end of the novel. When he tells Jack that all might have been different, Willie implies that his fate might have been different had he remembered that, although both good and evil exist and influence each other, they are not the same.

Closely aligned with the knowledge theme is the Humpty Dumpty motif. The title hints at multiple meanings, for on one level Willie is the King (the Boss), and the characters "all the king's men." Yet perhaps greater significance arises if one sees Willie as Humpty, for both fall to their doom and cannot be repaired. In this view, the King is God, and the King's "men" are all of God's children. The fall becomes the Fall because Willie ruins himself by his knowledge of evil that is not balanced by a corresponding ability to overcome its effects. One may also view Jack as another Humpty, one whose breakage is not irrevocable because his understanding and knowledge of evil ultimately correspond to an appropriate conception of the nature of good.

THE AMBASSADORS

Type of work: Novel
Author: Henry James (1843-1916)
Type of plot: Psychological realism
Time of plot: About 1900
Locale: Paris, France
First published: 1903

The Ambassadors marks a turning point in James's attitude toward his American characters. This novel contains none of the embarrassment found in many of the earlier works, which portray the author's fellow Americans as slightly barbaric in their inability to appreciate the fineness and subtlety of European culture.

Principal Characters

Lambert Strether, the chief ambassador of Mrs. Newsome, his betrothed, sent to summon her son Chad back from Paris to the family business in Woollett, Massachusetts. A fifty-five-year-old editor of a review, Lambert Strether has all the tact and diplomacy necessary to accomplish his task, but his sensitivity will not allow him either to complete it or to take advantage of Chad's situation to gain his own ends. He sees Chad as immeasurably better off in Paris, himself as somehow changed and strengthened by his sojourn abroad, though he will not allow himself to stay in Europe after having failed his benefactor. His heady experiences renew his earlier impressions, and he forms friendships, visits cathedrals, and lives easily for the first time since his wife died while bearing their son, also dead. His delicacy—in approaching young Newsome and his mistress, Mme de Vionnet; in handling Chad's sister, brother-in-law, and childhood sweetheart; and in breaking off from Maria Gostrey, who loves him—is the more remarkable when one considers that his own hopes of a rich marriage and great influence have been shattered by his actions.

Chadwick Newsome, called **Chad,** the handsome, twenty-eight-year-old successor to a family business on the one hand and the heir to a modest income from another source. Candid and open-hearted, the graying young man has been so improved by his years in Europe, largely under the tutelage of Mme de Vionnet, that no thought of his return can really be harbored by anyone who has seen him. Although he himself is willing to return for a visit and to consider taking over the advertising and sales promotion of the business that he is well equipped to run, his proposed marriage to Mamie Pocock is unthinkable. His greatest triumph comes as the result of his mannerly presentation of his sister's group of ambassadors to his Parisian friends, while his saddest duty is to allow his good friend Lambert Strether to return to face the consequences of a diplomatic failure.

Maria Gostrey, a self-styled introducer and tour director and a chance acquaintance of Lambert Strether. A sensitive, genial, and understanding woman, she proves to be the agent through whom the ambassador discovers the irony of Chad Newsome's situation. Her generosity and devotion to her new friend first touch him and then move him deeply when he sees her loyalty and love unencumbered by desire for personal gain.

Mme Marie de Vionnet the beautiful countess whose religion and social position will not allow her to divorce an unloved and faithless husband. Gravely lovely and charming, she has educated young Chad Newsome in the social graces and has won his heart and soul. Called a virtuous connection by intimate friends, the arrangement seems shabby to Mr. Waymarsh and Mrs. Pocock, typically closed-minded Americans. Through the efforts of good friends, especially those of Lambert Strether, Mme de Vionnet is allowed to retain her younger lover in spite of the fact that they have no future beyond their immediate happiness. Her daughter, who was believed by some to be in love with Chad Newsome, settles on a marriage more reasonable and agreeable to all.

John Little Bilham, called **Little Bilham,** an American expatriate artist and Chad Newsome's close friend. A perceptive, bright young man, Little Bilham becomes the confidant of the ambassadors and, along with a friend, Miss Barrace, their interpreters of social and artistic life in Paris.

Miss Barrace, a shrewd, witty, understanding woman living in Paris. She asks Lambert Strether not to force the issue of Chad Newsome's return home.

Mr. Waymarsh, an American lawyer residing in England, Lambert Strether's friend. He accompanies Strether to Paris and directly involves himself in Chad Newsome's affairs when he writes a letter informing Mrs. Newsome that her ambassador is not fulfilling his mission.

Sarah Newsome Pocock, Chad Newsome's older sister. She, her husband, and her sister-in-law are also dispatched as Mrs. Newsome's ambassadors to make certain that Chad returns to the United States. She and Mr. Waymarsh join forces to separate Chad and Mme de Vionnet.

James Pocock, Sarah's husband, who during Chad Newsome's absence is in control of the Newsome mills. He enjoys his trip to Paris, sympathizes with Chad, and becomes Lambert Strether's tacit ally.

Mamie Pocock, James Pocock's younger sister, the woman that Mrs. Newsome has selected as a suitable wife for her son. Although she accompanies her brother and his wife on their mission to persuade Chad Newsome to return, she loses her personal interest in the young man after meeting John Little Bilham. Little Bilham's announced intention of marrying Mamie helps Chad to solve his own problems of loyalty and love in his affair with Mme de Vionnet.

Jeanne de Vionnet, Mme de Vionnet's daughter. For a time, society assumed that Chad Newsome might be in love with her, but Jeanne becomes engaged to M. de Montbron.

M. Gloriani, a sculptor, Mme de Vionnet's friend. He is famous in the artistic and fashionable circles of Parisian society.

Mme Gloriani, his loving wife.

The Story

Lambert Strether was engaged to marry Mrs. Newsome, a widow. Mrs. Newsome had a son, Chadwick, whom she wanted to return home from Paris and take over the family business in Woollett, Massachusetts. She was especially concerned for his future after she had heard that he was seriously involved with a Frenchwoman. In her anxiety, she asked Strether to go to Paris and persuade her son to return to the respectable life that she had planned for him.

Strether did not look forward to his task, for Chadwick had ignored all of his mother's written requests to return home. Strether also did not know what hold Chadwick's mistress might have over him or what sort of woman she might be. He strongly suspected that she was a young girl of unsavory reputation. Strether realized, however, that his hopes of marrying Mrs. Newsome depended upon his success in bringing Chad back to the United States, where his mother could see him married to Mamie Pocock.

Leaving his ship at Liverpool, Strether journeyed across England to London. On the way, he met Maria Gostrey, a young woman who was acquainted with some of Strether's American friends, and she promised to aid Strether in getting acquainted with Europe before he left for home again. Strether met another old friend, Mr. Waymarsh, an American lawyer living in England, whom he asked to go with him to Paris.

A few days after arriving in Paris, Strether went to Chad's house. The young man was not in Paris, and he had temporarily given the house over to a friend, John Little Bilham. Through Bilham, Strether got in touch with Chad at Cannes. Strether was surprised to learn of his whereabouts, for he knew that Chad would not have dared to take an ordinary mistress to such a fashionable resort.

About a week later, Strether, Miss Gostrey, and Waymarsh went to the theater. Between the acts of the play, the door of their box was opened and Chad entered. He was much changed from the adolescent college boy Strether remembered. He was slightly gray, although only twenty-eight years old.

Both Strether and Chad Newsome were pleased to see each other. Over coffee after the theater, the older man told Chad why he had come to Europe. Chad answered that all he asked was an opportunity to be persuaded that he should return.

A few days later, Chad took Strether and his friends to a tea where they met Mme and Mlle de Vionnet. The former, who had married a French count, turned out to be an old school friend of Miss Gostrey. Strether was at a loss to understand whether Chad was in love with the countess or with her daughter, Jeanne. Since the older woman was only a few years the senior of the young man and as beautiful as her daughter, either was possibly the object of his affections.

As the days slipped by, it became apparent to Strether that he himself wanted to stay in Paris. The French city and its life were much calmer and more beautiful than the provincial existence that he had known in Woollett, and he began to understand why Chad was unwilling to go back to his mother and the Newsome mills.

Strether learned that Chad was in love with Mme de Vionnet, rather than with her daughter. The countess had been separated from her husband for many years, but their position and religion made divorce impossible. Strether, who was often in the company of the Frenchwoman, soon fell under her charm. Miss Gostrey, who had known Mme de Vionnet for many years, had only praise for her and questioned Strether as to the advisability of removing Chad from the woman's continued influence.

One morning Chad announced to Strether that he was ready to return immediately to the United States. The young man was puzzled when Strether replied that he was not sure it was wise for either of them to return and that they should both reconsider whether they would not be better off in Paris than in New England.

When Mrs. Newsome received word of that decision on the part of her ambassador, she immediately sent the Pococks, her daughter and son-in-law, to Paris along with Mamie Pocock, the woman she hoped her son would marry. They were to bring back both Strether and her son.

Mrs. Newsome's daughter and her relatives did not come to Paris with an obvious ill will. Their attitude seemed to be that Chad and Strether had somehow drifted astray, and it was their duty to set them right. At least that was the attitude of Mrs. Pocock. Her husband, however, was not at all interested in having Chad return, for in the young man's absence, Mr. Pocock controlled the Newsome mills. Mr. Pocock further saw that his visit was probably the last opportunity he would have for a spirited time in the European city, and so he was quite willing to spend his holiday going to theaters and cafés. His younger sister, Mamie, seemed to take little interest in the recall of her supposed fiancé, for she had become interested in Chad's friend, Mr. Bilham.

The more Strether saw of Mme de Vionnet after the arrival of the Pococks, the more he was certain that she was both noble and sincere in her attempts to make friends with her lover's family. Mrs. Pocock found it difficult to reconcile Mme de Vionnet's aristocratic background with the fact that she was Chad's mistress.

After several weeks of hints and genteel pleading, the Pococks and Mamie went to Switzerland, leaving Chad to make a decision whether to return to the United States. As for Strether, Mrs. Newsome had advised that he be left alone to make his own decision, for the widow wanted to avoid the appearance of having lost her dignity or her sense of propriety.

While the Pococks were gone, Strether and Chad discussed the course that they should follow. Chad was uncertain of his attitude toward Mamie Pocock. Strether assured him that the woman was already happy with her new love, Mr. Bilham, who had told Strether that he intended to marry the American. His advice was that Chadwick Newsome should remain in France with the countess, despite the fact that the young man could not marry her and would, by remaining in Europe, lose the opportunity to make himself an extremely rich man. Chad decided to take his older friend's counsel.

Waymarsh, who had promised his help in persuading Chad to return to the United States, was outraged at Strether's changed attitude. Miss Gostrey, however, remained loyal, for she had fallen deeply in love with Strether during their time together in Paris. Strether, however, realizing her feelings, told her that he had to go back to the United States alone. His object in Europe had been to return Chad Newsome to his mother. Because he had failed in that mission and would never marry Mrs. Newsome, he could not justify to himself marrying another woman whom he had met on a journey financed by the woman he had at one time intended to marry. Only Mme de Vionnet, he believed, could truly appreciate the irony of his position.

Critical Evaluation

In Henry James's *The Ambassadors*, plot is minimal, as the story line consists simply in Mrs. Newsome sending Lambert Strether to Europe to bring home her son, Chad. The important action is psychological rather than physical; the crucial activities are thought and conversation. The pace of the novel is slow. Events unfold as they do in life: in their own good time.

Because of these qualities, James's work demands certain responses from the reader. One must not expect boisterous action, shocking or violent occurrences, sensational coincidences, quickly mounting suspense, or breathtaking climaxes; these devices have no place in a Henry James novel. Rather, the reader must bring to the work a sensitivity to problems of conscience, an appreciation of the meaning beneath manners, and an awareness of the intricacies of human relationships. Finally, and of the utmost importance, the reader must be patient; the power of a novel like *The Ambassadors* is only revealed quietly and without haste. That is why, perhaps more than any other modern author, James requires rereading—not merely because of the complexity of his style, but because the richly layered texture of his prose contains a multiplicity of meanings, a wealth of subtle shadings.

In *The Ambassadors*, which James considered his mas-

terpiece, this subtlety and complexity is partially the result of his perfection of the technique for handling point
of view. Departing from traditional eighteenth and nineteenth century use of the omniscient narrator, James ex-
perimented extensively with the limited point of view,
exploring the device to discover what advantages it might
have over the older method. He found that what was lost
in panoramic scope and comprehensiveness was more
than compensated for in focus, concentration, and intensity. It was a technique perfectly suited to an author
whose primary concern was with presenting the thoughts,
emotions, and motivations of an intelligent character,
with understanding the psychological makeup of a sensitive mind and charting its growth.

The sensitive and intelligent character through whose
mind all events in the novel are filtered is Lambert Strether.
The reader sees and hears only what Strether sees and
hears; all experiences, perceptions, and judgments are
his. Strictly adhered to, this device proved too restrictive
for James's purpose; therefore, he utilized other characters—called confidants—who enabled him to expand
the scope of his narrative without sacrificing advantages
inherent in the limited point of view. The basic function of these "listening characters" is to expand and enrich Strether's experience. Miss Gostrey, Little Bilham,
Waymarsh, and Miss Barrace—all share with him attitudes and insights arising from their widely diverse backgrounds; they provide him with a wider range of knowledge than he could ever gain from firsthand experience.
Maria Gostrey, Strether's primary confidante, illustrates
the fact that James's listening characters are deep and
memorable personalities in their own right. Miss Gostrey
not only listens to Strether, but she also becomes an important figure in the plot, and as she gradually falls in
love with Strether, she engages the reader's sympathy as
well.

Lambert Strether interacts with and learns from the
environment of Paris as well as from the people he meets
there; thus, the setting is far more than a mere backdrop
against which events in the plot occur. To understand the
significance of Paris as the setting, the reader must appreciate the meaning that the author, throughout his fiction, attached to certain places. James was fascinated by
what he saw as the underlying differences in the cultures
of the United States and Europe and, in particular, in the
opposing values of a booming American factory town
such as Woollett and an ancient European capital such
as Paris. In these two places, very different qualities are
held in esteem. In Woollett, Mrs. Newsome admired practicality, individuality, and enterprise, while in Paris, her
son appreciates good food and expensive wine, conversation with a close circle of friends, and leisure time
quietly spent. Woollett pursues commercialism, higher
social status, and rigid moral codes with untiring vigor;
Paris values the beauty of nature, the pleasure of companionship, and an appreciation of the arts with studied
simplicity. Thus, the implications of a native of Woollett,
such as Lambert Strether, going to Paris at the end of his
life are manifold. It is through his journey that the theme
of the novel is played out.

The theme consists of a question of conscience: Should
Strether, in his capacity as Mrs. Newsome's ambassador,
be faithful to his mission of bringing Chad home, once
he no longer believes in that mission? That he ceases to
believe is the result of his conversion during his stay in
Paris. He is exposed to a side of life that he had not
known previously; furthermore, he finds it to be good.
As a man of noble nature and sensitive conscience, he
cannot ignore or deny, as Sarah Newsome later does, that
life in Paris has vastly improved Chad. Ultimately, therefore, he must oppose rather than promote the young man's
return. The honesty of this action not only destroys his
chance for financial security in marriage to Chad's mother
but also prevents him from returning the love of Maria
Gostrey. Although Strether's discovery of a different set
of values comes too late in life for his own benefit, he
at least can save Chad. The lesson he learns is the one
he passionately seeks to impart to Little Bilham: "Live
all you can; it's a mistake not to. It doesn't so much matter what you do in particular, so long as you have your
life. . . . Don't, at any rate, miss things out of stupidity. . . . Live!"

A reader expecting keenness of observation, insight
into motivations, comprehension of mental processes, and
powerful characterizations from *The Ambassadors* will
not be disappointed. If Henry James demands effort, concentration, and commitment, he also—with his depth
and breadth of vision and the sheer beauty of his craftsmanship—repays the reader a hundredfold.

AN AMERICAN TRAGEDY

Type of work: Novel
Author: Theodore Dreiser (1871-1945)
Type of plot: Social criticism
Time of plot: Early twentieth century
Locale: Kansas City, Chicago, and Lycurgus, New York
First published: 1925

An American Tragedy is probably Dreiser's best novel. The author believed that Clyde Griffiths' downfall was the result of the American economic system, and he presents a strong indictment of that system. His novel is a powerful document on the theme of social inequality and lack of privilege.

Principal Characters

Clyde Griffiths, the tragic hero. The son of itinerant evangelists and reared in poverty and in an atmosphere of narrow-minded religiosity, he has always longed for the things that money can buy.

Roberta Alden, Clyde's mistress. A factory girl and the daughter of poor parents, she falls in love with Clyde, whom she meets at the factory. In spite of her moral scruples, she becomes his mistress. When she finds herself pregnant, she tries to force him to marry her, though she knows that he no longer loves her. This situation leads to her accidental death at Clyde's hands and Clyde's execution.

Titus Alden, Roberta's shiftless father.

Sondra Finchley, a wealthy girl who takes up Clyde to spite his cousin Gilbert. She falls in love with him and is planning to marry him when he is arrested for murder.

Asa Griffiths, Clyde's father, a poverty-stricken itinerant evangelist.

Elvira Griffiths, Clyde's mother, the strongest member of the family.

Hester (Esta) Griffiths, Clyde's sister, who is seduced and abandoned by an actor.

Samuel Griffiths, Clyde's uncle, a rich manufacturer who gives Clyde a job in his factory.

Elizabeth Griffiths, Samuel's wife.

Gilbert Griffiths, their son, a pompous young man who resents Clyde.

Myra and **Bella Griffiths,** daughters of Samuel and Elizabeth.

Hortense Briggs, a crude, mercenary shopgirl whom Clyde tries to seduce. She is interested only in what she can persuade him to spend on her.

Thomas Ratterer, a bellhop who works with Clyde and introduces him to fast life.

Willard Sparser, the boy who steals the car and causes the accident that drives Clyde from Kansas City.

Orville Mason, a ruthless and politically ambitious district attorney who prosecutes Clyde.

Burton Burleigh, Mason's assistant. In the morgue, he threads some of Roberta's hair into Clyde's camera to provide the evidence necessary for conviction.

Alvin Belknap and **Reuben Jephson,** defense attorneys.

Governor Waltham, of New York, who rejects Clyde's plea to commute his sentence.

The Reverend Duncan McMillan, an evangelist. He brings Clyde spiritual comfort just before the execution.

The Story

When Clyde Griffiths was still a child, his religious-minded parents took him and his brothers and sisters around the streets of various cities, where they prayed and sang in public. The family was always very poor, but the fundamentalist faith of the Griffiths was their hope and mainstay throughout the storms and troubles of life.

Young Clyde was never religious, however, and he always felt ashamed of the existence his parents were living. As soon as he was old enough to make decisions for himself, he decided to go his own way. At sixteen, he got a job as a bellhop in a Kansas City hotel. There the salary and the tips that he received astonished him. For the first time in his life, he had money in his pocket, and he could dress well and enjoy himself. Then a tragedy overwhelmed the family: Clyde's sister ran away, supposedly to be married. Her elopement was a great blow to the parents, but Clyde himself did not brood over the matter. Life was too pleasant for him; more and more he enjoyed the luxuries that his job provided. He made friends with the other bellhops and joined them in parties that centered around liquor and women. Clyde soon became familiar with drink and brothels.

One day, he discovered that his sister was back in town. The man with whom she had run away had deserted her, and she was penniless and pregnant. Knowing his sister needed money, Clyde gave his mother a few dollars for her. He promised to give her more; instead, he bought an expensive coat for a girl in the hope that she would yield herself to him. One night, he and his friends went to a party in a car that did not belong to them. Coming back from their outing, they ran over a little girl. In their attempt to escape, they wrecked the car. Clyde fled to Chicago.

In Chicago, he got work at the Union League Club, where he eventually met his wealthy uncle, Samuel Griffiths. The uncle, who owned a factory in Lycurgus, New York, took a fancy to Clyde and offered him work in the factory. Clyde went to Lycurgus. There his cousin, Gilbert, resented this cousin from the Midwest. The whole family, with the exception of his uncle, considered Clyde beneath them socially and would not accept him into their circle. Clyde was given a job at the very bottom of the business, but his uncle soon made him a supervisor.

In the meantime, Sondra Finchley, who disliked Gilbert, began to invite Clyde to the parties that she and her friends often gave. Her main purpose was to annoy Gilbert. Clyde's growing popularity forced the Griffiths to receive him socially, much to Gilbert's disgust.

In the course of his work at the factory, Clyde met Roberta Alden, with whom he soon fell in love. Because it was forbidden for a supervisor to mix socially with an employee, they had to meet secretly. Clyde attempted to persuade Roberta to give herself to him, but she refused. At last, rather than lose him, she consented

and became his mistress.

At the same time, Clyde was becoming fascinated by Sondra. He came to love her and hoped to marry her, thus acquiring the wealth and social position for which he yearned. Gradually, he began breaking dates with Roberta in order to be with Sondra every moment that she could spare him. Roberta began to be suspicious and eventually found out the truth.

By that time, however, Roberta was pregnant. Clyde went to drug stores for medicine that did not work. He attempted to find a doctor of questionable reputation. Roberta went to see one physician who refused to perform an operation. Clyde and Roberta were both becoming desperate, and Clyde saw his possible marriage to Roberta as a dismal ending to all of his hopes for a bright future. He told himself that he did not love Roberta, that it was Sondra whom he wished to marry. Roberta asked him to marry her for the sake of her child, saying that she would go away afterward, if he wished, so that he could be free of her. Clyde would not agree to her proposal and grew more irritable and worried.

One day, he read in the newspaper an item about the accidental drowning of a couple who had gone boating. Slowly, a plan began to form in his mind. He told Roberta that he would marry her and persuaded her to accompany him to an isolated lake resort. There, as though accidentally, he lunged toward her. She was hit by his camera and fell into the water. Clyde escaped, confident that her drowning would look like an accident, even though he had planned it all carefully.

He had been clumsy, however, as letters that he and Roberta had written were found. When her condition became known, he was arrested. His uncle obtained an attorney for him. At his trial, the defense built up an elaborate case in his favor. In spite of his lawyer's efforts, however, he was found guilty and sentenced to be electrocuted. His mother came to see him and urged him to save his soul. A clergyman finally succeeded in getting Clyde to write a statement—a declaration that he repented of his sins. It is doubtful whether he did. He died in the electric chair, a young man tempted by his desire for luxury and wealth.

Critical Evaluation

Few readers claim to like the works of Theodore Dreiser, for his novels are not ones that charm or delight. They are also not clever stories that one explores for their plot. Even his characters are mostly obnoxious beings who fail to appeal in any usual sense. One may then ask

why Dreiser is considered by some to be a genius and why his books are read at all. The answer lies in a strange paradox: Dreiser's very faults are what attract readers again and again. His stumbling and awkward style, his convoluted philosophies, and his pitiable personages com-

bine to present a worldview that, perhaps more successfully than that of any other American writer, conveys a
naturalistic atmosphere. Dreiser's books, like the universe that he seeks to describe, impress and repel by
their very disorder, their mystery, and their powerful demands on comfortable assumptions.

All of Dreiser's characteristics are most clearly reflected in *An American Tragedy*, the masterpiece of an
author who had earlier published three important novels—*Sister Carrie* (1900), *Jennie Gerhardt* (1911), and
The Financier (1912, 1927). In this book, Dreiser the naturalist asserts the doctrine that humans are struggling endlessly to survive in an uncaring world where they are victims of heredity, environment, and chance, leaving them
small room for free choice or action. Dreiser's theory of
life is basically mechanistic, and for *An American Tragedy* he invented the term "chemism" to explain the chemical forces that he believed propelled humanity to act in
a certain way. A human, Dreiser claimed, is a "mechanism, undevised and uncreated and a badly and carelessly driven one at that." Such a poor creature is Clyde
Griffiths, the central character of *An American Tragedy*.
The book, which is full of scientific imagery, shows how
Clyde is driven to his final destruction.

Dreiser chooses to concentrate on the individual's struggle against one particular force: society and its institutions. Clyde, in each of the novel's three sections, strives
against neither a malign God nor a malevolent fate but
against the unyielding structure of his culture. In other
times, people have defined themselves by other touchstones (religion, honor, war), but Clyde can answer his
craving for meaning in only one way. To matter in the
United States means, in the book's terms, to be masterful, to have material goods and status. American culture
tempts him with its powerful businesses, its glittering social affairs, and its promises that anyone who is deserving can share in these riches. That is, of course, a false
promise, for the American tragedy is the gap between
the country's ideals and its reality.

Doomed to failure in his quest, Clyde, whose story has
been called a "parable of our national experience," cannot be blamed for desiring what he sees all about him,
nor can he be criticized for the weaknesses and handicaps that assure his end. Immature and shallow, uneducated and poor, Clyde is willing to compromise in
any necessary fashion in order to become materially successful. Yet his very lack of moral or intellectual distinction, when coupled with the intensity of his desires,
makes him the ideal and innocent representative of a culture in which achievement is gauged by such measure-
ments. In the novel, inspired by a 1906 murder case in-

volving a man named Chester Gillette who killed an in-
conveniently pregnant girlfriend for reasons much like
those in the book, Clyde's attorney calls him a "mental
as well as a moral coward—no more and no less," but
later adds that Clyde cannot help this state. "('After all,
you didn't make yourself, did you?')"

What did "make" Clyde includes poor parents as in-
ept as he is. Impractical and ineffectual, the Griffiths offer him only their God who, as he can plainly see, has
brought them none of the things that he (or they) want.
Religion is one obstacle that Clyde can and does remove
when he ignores their protests and responds instead to
his environment and inner urgings. His adaptability is
exploited in the Arabian Nights atmosphere of the hotels
in which he works, places where luxury alone is vital
and kindness and honesty mere trifles. When in the second part of the novel Clyde finds himself in Lycurgus, he
once again gravitates helplessly toward the surrounding
values. Named after the Spartan who initiated that society's rigid rules, Lycurgus is as tantalizing as the hotels. It is a "walled city" that, as one of the novel's major
symbols, allows outsiders to peek at its glories but rarely
permits them to enter its gates. Clyde, fascinated and
overwhelmed, abandons the simple pleasures that he has
found with Roberta and attempts to climb its walls.

Whenever Clyde struggles free of his environmental
influences, he is frustrated by the accidents and coincidences that haunt him. He unwillingly leaves Kansas
City because of the car accident, and he leaves Chicago
because of a seemingly happy encounter with his uncle.
His chance meeting with Sondra develops their relationship, just as Roberta's unplanned pregnancy so rudely
obstructs his dreams. Even his murder scheme is derived
from a chance newspaper article, and the murder itself is
in a sense self-initiated, for Clyde *allows* rather than
forces Roberta's drowning.

Other characters in the novel are equally victims of the
roles in which they find themselves. While many of them
are compellingly presented, their main importance is to
provide background and stimuli for Clyde. Because he
rarely sees them as people but rather as impediments (his
family, Roberta) or as exciting objects (Sondra), readers
too are interested in them mostly in this respect, and the
book belongs almost entirely to Clyde.

In *An American Tragedy*, Dreiser, a former newspa-
perman and editor of women's publications, watches his
world and its foibles and is moved by humans' shared
helplessness. He shows how useless moral judgment is
in solving such dilemmas and insists, as he does in all
his works, that all one may expect of others is compassion for common plights. Although he offers little en-

couragement, Dreiser does hint that perhaps the human condition may improve. The final scene—"Dusk, of a summer night"—closely resembles the opening. A small boy once again troops reluctantly with a group of street missionaries. Yet Mrs. Griffiths responds to the frustrations of Esta's child as she had never done to Clyde and gives him money for an ice-cream cone. This child, she promises herself, will be different.

APPOINTMENT IN SAMARRA

Type of work: Novel
Author: John O'Hara (1905-1970)
Type of plot: Naturalism
Time of plot: 1930
Locale: Pennsylvania
First published: 1934

In the tradition of the Roaring Twenties, Appointment in Samarra *deals with Prohibition, bootleggers, and easy morals. The novel goes beyond mere pandering to sensationalism, however, in that it sustains a theme of moral judgment. The lives led by these characters can have no fruitful or important end.*

Principal Characters

Julian English, an automobile dealer who drinks too much. He picks fights with his friends and benefactors, gets publicly drunk, drives his wife to seek a divorce, and chases after a bootlegger's woman. When his acts add up and life becomes too complicated for him, he commits suicide.

Caroline English, a woman as superficial as her husband. When she decides to seek a divorce from her husband she acts like a heroine in a melodrama, even to canceling a big party on short notice.

Harry Reilly, a wealthy Irish Catholic who has a highball thrown in his face by a bored Julian English at a party, despite the fact that it is Reilly who has befriended Julian and lent him the money needed to keep his Cadillac agency solvent. Julian seems a bit surprised when Reilly holds a grudge.

Helene Holman, a nightclub singer and a bootlegger's woman. She and Julian get together while drunk at a Christmas celebration. Helene is, as her bootlegger-lover knows, a woman of easy virtue.

Ed Charney, a bootlegger. Though a family man, he keeps Helene as his mistress and is resentful of the favors that she shows other men. He becomes angry at his aide, Al Grecco, for letting Helene become involved with Julian.

Froggy Ogden, Caroline English's one-armed cousin, who tries to goad Julian into a fight after reproaching him for his conduct.

Dr. English, Julian's father, who looks for moral weakness in his son because his own father was an embezzler and a suicide.

Father Creedon, a priest who agrees with Julian that Harry Reilly is a bore and refuses to take the incident of Julian's insulting Reilly seriously.

The Story

Julian English was thirty, a congenial seller of cars, popular with the country club set. He had the right connections with Ed Charney, the local bootlegger, and consequently was always well supplied with liquor. He and Caroline had been married four years. They were both natives of Gibbsville and had an assured social position. They had no children.

Just before Christmas they went to a party at the country club. As usual, Julian had had too much to drink. He sat idly twirling his highball and listening to Harry Reilly's stories. Harry was a rich Irish Catholic and definitely a social climber. Actually, Julian hated Harry, although Harry had lent him twenty thousand dollars the previous

summer to bolster his Cadillac agency. That loan, however, did not give Harry the right to make passes at Caroline, Julian thought darkly.

Harry told stories in paragraphs. He always paused at the right time. Julian kept thinking how fitting it would be if he stopped the stories by throwing his drink in Harry's face. Julian grew bored. On impulse, he did throw his drink in Harry's face. A big lump of ice hit Harry in the eye.

On the way home, Julian and Caroline quarreled furiously. Julian accused his wife of infidelity with Harry, among other people. Caroline said that Julian always drank too much and chased women as well. More important, Harry had a mortgage on the car agency and a good deal of influence with Catholics, and he was a man who could hold a grudge.

Al Grecco was a little man who, as Ed Charney's handyman, had a certain standing in the town. He liked Julian because Julian was the only one of the social set who was really friendly. Al grew up on the wrong side of the tracks. Before he was finally sentenced to a year in prison he had been arrested several times. When he got out he worked in a poolroom for a while until his boss died. The widow wanted Al to stay on as manager, but he went to work for Charney. Now he delivered bootleg booze, ran errands, and kept an eye on the torch singer at the Stage Coach, a country inn owned by Charney. Helene Holman, the singer, was Charney's girl, and if she were not carefully watched, she might out of sheer good-heartedness extend her favors to other men.

On Christmas Day, Julian woke up with a hangover. As was his custom, he quarreled with the cook. At Caroline's suggestion, he went to Harry Reilly's house to apologize. Although Reilly's sister was sympathetic, she brought down word that Harry would not see him; he had a black eye and still nursed a grudge.

Julian's father and mother came for Christmas dinner. The father, a staid, successful surgeon, was suspicious of his son. He always looked for evidence of moral weakness in Julian, for his own father had committed suicide after embezzling a fortune. He was afraid that the English inheritance was stained. Dinner was a trying time.

Caroline and Julian had supper at the club. The usual crowd was there. Julian was unmercifully ribbed in the locker room. In a dismal mood, he sat drinking by himself while he waited for a chance to see Father Creedon and ask him to patch up his affair with Harry. The old priest was sympathetic and made light of the incident. After agreeing that Harry was a bore, he promised to send Julian some good Irish whiskey.

Ed Charney was a good family man who spent Christmas Day with his wife and son. He intended to go out to the Stage Coach only in the evening. Then his son became suddenly ill. It looked as if he would have to stay home. Mindful of Helene's weaknesses, he telephoned Al Grecco to go out to the inn and keep watch on her. It was Christmas night and she would be drinking too much. Al did not care for the assignment, but he dutifully went out to the inn and sat down with Helene.

The country club set began to drift in. Froggy Ogden, who was Caroline's one-armed cousin, was the oldest man there; he seemed to feel a responsibility for Julian, who was still drinking. In a spirit of bravado, Julian danced several times with Helene, even though Al

warned him of Charney's anger. Finally, carried away by the music and too many drinks, Julian and Helene left the dance floor. Caroline and Froggy found Julian in a stupor in the back of a sedan and took him home.

The day after Christmas, Caroline went to her mother and announced her intention to divorce Julian. Her mother found it difficult to listen to her daughter; she believed herself above the foibles of the younger generation. Caroline thought herself a heroine in an old-fashioned melodrama. She was determined not to go back to Julian. After meeting him on the street and quarreling again, she canceled the big party they were to have given that evening.

Al Grecco, as he backed out of the garage with a case of Scotch, had decided to kill Ed Charney. When Charney had phoned him, he had tried to excuse his lack of vigilance: He protested that he had only let Helene dance. In a rage, however, Ed had said some things that Al could not accept.

Determined to look businesslike, Julian went to his office at the auto agency. He sat importantly at his desk and wrote figures on a piece of scratch paper. The only conclusion he could reach was that he needed more money. One of his salespeople came in to try to lay down the law. He asserted that Julian's difficulties were gossiped about strenuously in the little town of Gibbsville. The offense to Charney was particularly grave: He had been a good friend to the agency and had helped them sell cars to other bootleggers.

Julian left the office in no cheerful mood. He wandered into his club for lunch. Because it was the day after Christmas, the dining room was deserted except for some elderly lawyers and Froggy. Avoiding his wife's cousin, Julian sat down in a far corner of the room. After picking up his plate, Froggy followed him and began to reproach him for his conduct with the torch singer. He told Julian that he had always distrusted him and had warned Caroline about his conduct many times. When Froggy invited him outside to fight, Julian refused because he could not hit a one-armed man. Froggy became more insulting, so that the lawyers came to their table to interfere. Julian was intensely angered when they seemed to side with Froggy. Turning quickly, he hit one of the lawyers full in the mouth and dislodged the man's false teeth.

Julian went home and fell asleep. At about ten o'clock, a society reporter awoke him when she came to get a story about the canceled party. After several drinks, he tried to seduce her but with no success. As soon as she left, Julian went to the garage, closed the door, and started the motor. He was pronounced a suicide by the coroner.

Critical Evaluation

John O'Hara was supreme in the art and craft of the short story. Perhaps because of his newspaper background, he was able to condense a tale to its fundamentals and produce tightly crafted and powerful short fiction. With his ear for speech and eye for effect, he was able to bring to life in two or three sentences a character from nearly any walk of life. This gift also gave his novels the primary value that they possess, and perhaps this is especially true of his first novel, *Appointment in Samarra.*

One of O'Hara's shortest and best-structured novels, *Appointment in Samarra* is the story of hubris in a modern setting. It takes place in 1930, after the crash of 1929 but before people understood just how bad the Great Depression was to become. The hero of the novel, Julian English, has status but destroys himself by not living up to it. Julian has two problems—people and alcohol—but both are revealed to be his own inner problems, which ultimately ruin him. There is much discussion in the book of who "belongs" and who does not, of which clubs count in Gibbsville, of what prep schools and colleges matter, and of where one should be seen or not be seen. The laborer, mobster, and society man all think constantly about how they fit into the social ladder. Julian English thinks about it too much.

There is presented in the novel an accurate picture of a broad cross section of Gibbsville society. With the observations of the different kinds of people, from the secretary in the automobile agency to the former convict working for the gangland boss to the society matron, O'Hara achieved a new kind of fictional reporting, in the best sense of the term. The humor and fast pace of the novel and the clean, sure style give it a surface slickness that is almost misleading, for it is not a superficial novel. There is depth behind the meretricious glitter and hard-boiled sensual flavor. The book's racy language and sexual candor continued the groundbreaking trend begun only a short time before by Ernest Hemingway. The characters are concerned with superficialities, but that does not make them superficial characters. O'Hara is able to capture, especially in his dialogue, the nuances of tone that reveal the hidden depths of his many characters.

Julian English, the central figure of the novel, is also the most complex and interesting of the characters. Some individuals seem to burn with a compulsion to self-destruction; Julian English is one of these people. Yet, however drunk he gets, part of his mind warns him when he is about to do something dangerous. Like many intelligent people, he observes himself as he moves through life. Yet he recklessly plunges ahead, throwing the drink in Harry Reilly's face, dancing and going out to the car with Helene Holman at the roadhouse, and getting deliberately drunk so that he will not care what happens. (By the time that he quarrels with Froggy Ogden at the club and fights with the lawyers in the dining room, he has given up all hope—he is as contemptuous of himself as he is of them. Rational action has ceased to have any meaning for him.) Julian English is a direct forerunner of the existential heroes of Jean-Paul Sartre and Albert Camus a decade later—who were influenced by O'Hara and Hemingway and other writers of the American "hard-boiled" school of writing—as he toys with his fate with an almost objective curiosity. "If I do this," he seems to think, "will I get away with it?" Yet he knows somewhere deep inside of him that he will not "get away" with it, that nobody ever gets away with anything. He is filled with "tremendous excitement" when he realizes that "he is in for it." Perhaps, as he contemplates his "unknown, well-deserved punishment," he is even slightly masochistic in his longing for pain and destruction.

Julian English's fatalism, and the fatalism that permeates the novel (and gives it its title), seems to be influenced in part by the novels and stories of Hemingway and F. Scott Fitzgerald. O'Hara, however, while lacking the poetic vision and poetic style of Fitzgerald, also avoids the hard-boiled pose of Hemingway and adds a poignant ruthlessness of his own. With economy and artistry, O'Hara draws the painful and engrossing portrait of a complex, fascinating, and doomed individual.

An inevitable progression, gaining in momentum like a ball rolling down a steep hill, takes over Julian English's fate, until it would take a miracle to halt the inevitable doom that waits for him at the end. As Julian knows, miracles do not happen for people such as him. His death is early foreshadowed by the suicide of his grandfather. His own father frequently expresses fears that Julian's character is as weak as that of his grandfather; Julian, himself, comes to believe in his defective character, and that he is to be doomed by it. This belief numbs him and renders him helpless before the onrush of events.

This novel rises above O'Hara's other long works of fiction because it makes more of an attempt to deal with significant ideas and values. Often, his technique of recording action with the detachment of a photographer fails to establish a moral frame of reference. The reader does not know the author's attitude toward the characters and events. Nevertheless, the character of Julian English lifts *Appointment in Samarra* above the author's other novels.

O'Hara always surrounds his dramatic action with great pieces of historical exposition and discussion, as well as long descriptions of styles of the period, the fashions, the horses and clubs, the automobiles and other transitory items that date a moment in history. In *Appointment in Samarra*, the precise documentation of social strata lends vividness and realism to the story. O'Hara's accuracy with labels and styles had not yet become the excessive mannerism that weighted down his later novels.

O'Hara was born in 1905 in Pottsville, Pennsylvania, the prototype of the Gibbsville of many of his novels and stories. He had a varied career in journalism, as a reporter, critic, and social commentator; later, after his first success as a writer, he became a screenwriter and used much of his Hollywood experience in his fiction. His late work added little to his stature, but his early novels and his stories have shown a remarkable durability.

THE ARMIES OF THE NIGHT: History as a Novel, the Novel as History

Type of work: Novelized autobiography
Author: Norman Mailer (1923-   )
Type of plot: Political, social, and literary history
Time of plot: 1967
Locale: Washington, D.C.
First published: 1968

Mailer describes his involvement in the October, 1967, anti-Vietnam War march on the Pentagon, providing complex insights into social history and his own development as a writer. The author adopts a third-person, wry perspective on his own virtues and foibles that is reminiscent of another American classic, The Education of Henry Adams.

Principal Personages

Norman Mailer, a novelist
Jerry Rubin, an activist

Dwight MacDonald, a critic
Robert Lowell, a poet

The Story

In book 1, "History as a Novel: The Steps of the Pentagon," Mailer introduces himself via an excerpt from a *Time* magazine article describing his drunken, incoherent, scatological speech at the Ambassador Theater in Washington, D.C., the site of the preliminary event for the anti-Vietnam War march on the Pentagon. Noting that Mailer's remarks did even less to explain the war than his recent novel *Why Are We in Vietnam?* (1967), the article reports that Mailer was heckled, that his colleague Dwight MacDonald seemed dismayed at the barroom atmosphere, and that poet Robert Lowell became irritated at shouts that he recite his poems more loudly. By crossing a police line, Mailer did manage to get arrested and jailed during the march, the article concludes, though in the lockup he would find few toilets—the subject of his Ambassador speech was his search for a bathroom—and only coffee. After the excerpt, Mailer comments that now *Time* can be left behind in order to find out what happened.

Mailer begins *The Armies of the Night* with the *Time* piece in order to emphasize the way in which he has often been portrayed: as a lout and buffoon, his public appearances trivialized and the themes of his work obscured. Mailer's intention is to write history—that is, to provide a sober, third-person account of the person (referring to himself as "Mailer") and the event, assessing its origins, development, and impact through a supple, sophisticated sensibility that is aware of its own limi-

tations. Mailer's tone is ironic, as befits a man who is bemused by his own character and who seeks a perspective on it. He treats himself as a character in a novel and his voice is that of a novelist assessing personalities, but his material is history, events that actually happened but that are subject to dispute.

Mailer quickly recounts his reluctant involvement in the march, his preference to stay home and write his novels, and his begrudging then enthusiastic realization that the march on the Pentagon potentially involves thousands of dissenters, an audience that perhaps he will be able to reach with his oratory. When he learns that friends and literary colleagues such as the critic Dwight Macdonald and the distinguished poet Robert Lowell will participate in the event, Mailer looks forward to being counted in their company and to taking his measure among them.

With considerable self-criticism and humor, Mailer supplies his version of the fiasco at the Ambassador, noting his vain pretensions, his desire to dominate the audience, his frustration with the speeches of his fellow writers, and the inebriation that causes him to arrive late to the event and urges him to make up for lost time by trying to bully the audience into his way of thinking.

After this high comedy, Mailer shifts to his role as "the historian," exploring the ambiguity of the march on the Pentagon, describing the ingenious way in which it was organized by Jerry Rubin and other radical activists, and assessing its symbolic significance, the sense in which it spoke for the national mood about the war and the military-industrial complex. Mailer proves here to be a shrewd observer, realizing that this new generation of young people has a kind of civil courage and inventiveness that is quite different from his own youthful experiences as a soldier in the Pacific theater of World War II.

Recalling the march itself, Mailer analyzes his shifting feelings. On the one hand, he is the middle-aged fearful novelist, wondering what the tear gas will do to his weak eyes; on the other hand, he finds himself exhilarated by the camaraderie of the marchers, and later he is impressed by their dogged persistence, especially in the face of the brutality of National Guardsmen who beat the protesters mercilessly. Mailer manages his brief moment of disobedience gracefully when he sprints through a police line and is arrested. He then finds himself in a shouting match with a youthful Nazi who taunts him. This last episode is representative of a narrative that constantly modulates between historical analysis and autobiography, objective and subjective views of the event and of its participants.

Book 2, "The Novel as History: The Battle of the Pentagon," pulls back from Mailer's direct participation in the march and surveys the various accounts of it in newspapers and periodicals, noting discrepancies and biases, assessing the probable size of the demonstration, and commenting on how it was reported. Like a historian, he is critical of his sources, observing how difficult it is to separate the event from the way it was rendered by the mass media. Also like a historian, he seeks what is unique in the event, pointing out that, unlike an earlier generation of the Left schooled in Marxist dialectics and concerned with organized programs, the marchers were by and large not interested in ideology but in spontaneous innovation. They had a theatrical sense of change, thinking that it should be acted out, played as a role, but without a script.

Mailer concentrates on the pivotal role of activist Jerry Rubin, who mapped out the route of the march, met with government officials about various details of the protest, and organized the participation of public figures such as Mailer. Rubin is shown to be an ingenious tactician with a flair for publicity and certainly a match for the bureaucrats who sought to thwart his plans.

Yet the march on the Pentagon was not the product of any single imagination, and Mailer does not pretend to have described the event with complete accuracy; indeed, he believes that a fully reliable and objective history is impossible. Rather, he concludes *The Armies of the Night* by suggesting that the significance of the event resides in the rite of passage it represented for himself and the marchers, who were willing to stake their personal safety and their convictions on an uncertain outcome. Even after the event, Mailer is not sure what its impact has been, except to express the hope that by bearing witness to the atrocity of war the marchers have remitted some portion of its evil.

Critical Evaluation

The Armies of the Night takes its title from a line in a Matthew Arnold poem, "Dover Beach," about ignorant armies clashing by night. The allusion to Arnold suggests Mailer's complex view of history—that in some respects it is impenetrable, a dark record of human struggle that the poet despairs of comprehending. The armies in Mailer's book are the marchers and the National Guardsmen opposing them, and they do clash without much understanding. Yet the triumph of Mailer's book lies in the very effort to understand history, to make as much sense of events as possible while not for a moment forgetting how elusive their meaning is. By implication, Mailer is the Arnoldian poet, lamenting the gaps in understanding but eloquently articulating the absence of knowledge. The analogy with Arnold is strengthened by Mailer's frequent comparisons of himself with Robert Lowell, whom he regards as the United States' premier poet. Mailer yearns for Lowell's eloquence and his easy assumption of the mantel of national bard, reciting the country's history in his verses. Mailer bristles when Lowell refers to him as the country's best journalist, replying to Lowell that on certain days he thinks of himself as the country's greatest writer.

In both his solemnity and his absurdity, Mailer tries to encompass the country's contradictions and diversity. By the end of *The Armies of the Night*, it is clear that the opening comedy of his failure at the Ambassador is meant to dramatize the low end of Mailer's eternal quest to be a national bard and to pose the question of his novel *Why Are We in Vietnam?* It has been his mission in *The Armies of the Night* to make poetry—or as he would have it, a novel of history, insisting that only through his quirky but capacious sensibility can the full measure of the event be taken. The flip *Time* magazine version and even the more thorough accounts of journalists are not commensurate with the mystery and power of the march.

Only a novelist at the full height of his or her powers can hope to capture the profundity of the event, which must include its inscrutable aspects—as Herman Melville includes the unfathomable facets of reality in *Moby Dick: Or, the Whale* (1851), perhaps the work of literature that most influenced Mailer.

The comparison that is most often made, however, is between *The Armies of the Night* and *The Education of Henry Adams* (1907). Like Adams, Mailer scrutinizes himself in the third person as a failure. Like Adams, Mailer presents himself as the struggling historian of his times, a man ambitious to stamp his age with his style and frustrated by his repeated defeats in attempting to move the public to his way of thinking. As Mailer admitted after the publication of *The Armies of the Night*, *The Education of Henry Adams* must have provided him with a model, even though Mailer was not conscious of Adams' influence as he was writing the book. The parallels are undeniable. Mailer not only assumes Adams' ironic attitude toward himself but also writes almost in the cadences of his predecessor, deviating only in the jocularity of some of his remarks—although this aspect of his droll style is reminiscent of Adams' candor about his faults.

The Education of Henry Adams provided Mailer with an example of how to dramatize the individual's intersection with history. Adams worried about the ineffectuality of his individual efforts—a particular burden for a man coming from a family that had produced two presidents—and speculated that the forces of history had become powerful enough to negate anything that an individual might attempt to accomplish. Mailer is no less grim about his own failures, but he leavens them with a romanticism, a stubborn belief in the power of the individual will that proves exhilarating even in the face of the haunting suspicion that he is fooling himself.

Several critics have deemed *The Armies of the Night* to be one of Mailer's finest works because it so exquisitely balances opposites: the individual and the group, fiction and fact, the novel and history, the armies of the Pentagon and the armies of protesters. The book's two-part structure, indicated by the subtitle *History as a Novel, the Novel as History*, suggests the equilibrium that Mailer is seeking to establish. On the one hand, history is as much perception and imagination as it is fact and record. What history means depends very much on how it is interpreted—so the argument goes in book 1. On the other hand, the novel is as much fact and record as it is perception and imagination, Mailer argues in book 2, because the novelist's vision springs from material reality, from events, and from participation in history. To begin to understand, then, what happened in the march on the Pentagon, both the novel and history are needed: One completes the other, and one comments on the other. There is a reciprocal relationship between them, between objectivity and subjectivity, which Mailer views not as wholly separate, self-sustaining categories, but as the halves of a whole explanation.

The Armies of the Night is Mailer's masterpiece because it elegantly establishes the boundaries of two forms of writing, the novel and history, as it simultaneously explores and contains the expression of Mailer's own ego in the events that he witnesses and in which he participates. What makes the book an aesthetic success is the degree of Mailer's control over himself, over the facts, over the events, and over the act of writing itself, showing how every word that he employs is both an expression of self and an interpretation of history.

AS I LAY DYING

Type of work: Novel
Author: William Faulkner (1897-1962)
Type of plot: Psychological realism
Time of plot: Early twentieth century
Locale: Mississippi
First published: 1930

Centering on the effect of Addie Bundren's death and burial on members of her family, this novel has a powerful unity not always found in Faulkner's longer works. Although his method of shifting between the multiple points of view of the different family members binds Faulkner's characters into a homogeneous unit through their common suffering, individual personalities with their special emotions and abnormalities nevertheless emerge.

Principal Characters

Anse Bundren, an ignorant poor white. When Addie, his wife, dies, he is determined to take her body to Jefferson, as he had promised, even though the town is forty miles away. In a rickety old wagon, he and his sons must get across a flooding river that has destroyed most of the nearby bridges. Ostensibly, the shiftless and unlucky man is burying Addie there because of the promise. After a long trip with her unembalmed corpse, now dead more than a week, he arrives in Jefferson, pursued by a flock of buzzards which, like a grim chorus, hang apparently motionless against a sultry Mississippi sky. On reaching Jefferson, his family learns Anse's true reason for the trip: a set of false teeth and the "duck-shaped woman" whom he marries, to the surprise of his children.

Addie Bundren, Anse's overworked wife. Though dying, she wants to see her coffin finished. Anse does not know it, but she has always thought him to be only a man of words—and words, she thinks, are useless. Feeling isolated from him and her children, she has always tried to break through the wall of isolation surrounding her, but despairing, she never finds any meaning in her grinding existence. To her, sexual relationship means only violation, whereas, to Anse, it means love. Before her death, she knows her father's words to be true: "The reason for living was to get ready to stay dead a long time."

Darl Bundren, Anse's strange son, thought by his family to be feebleminded. Unlike the others, he seems to have the gift of second sight. Knowing the true reasons why Anse and the others are going to Jefferson, he tries to burn the barn housing his mother's body. For this act of attempted purification, his family declares him insane, and he is taken to the asylum at Jackson.

Jewel Bundren, Preacher Whitfield's illegitimate son. A violent young man, he loves only his horse, which cost him many long hours of labor at night. Although devoted to the animal, he allows Anse to trade it to Snopes for a badly needed team of mules. Like the rest of the Bundrens, he tenaciously hauls his mother on the long, eventful trip, all the while cursing and raging at his brothers. When Darl tries to burn the corpse, it is Jewel who manages to save her body for burial.

Cash Bundren, Anse's son, a carpenter. While his mother is dying, he busily saws and hammers away at her coffin, just outside her window. Carefully beveling the wood (he hates shoddy work) and showing his mother each board before nailing it in place, he finishes the job shortly after Addie's death. At the flooded river, he desperately tries to save his treasured tools when the wagon overturns. His leg broken on the trip, he stoically endures the pain, even after his father uses cement to plaster the swollen and infected leg.

Vardaman Bundren, Anse's son. Constantly, he repeats to himself, "My mother is a fish."

Dewey Dell Bundren, Anse's daughter. A girl of seventeen, she has a reason for going to Jefferson. She is pregnant and wants to buy drugs that she hopes will cause a miscarriage.

Dr. Peabody, a fat, seventy-year-old country doctor. During his long practice, he has ministered to many poor-white families like the Bundrens. When his unpaid bills reach fifty thousand dollars, he intends to retire.

Vernon Tull, Anse's helpful neighbor. He does what he can to help Bundren on his ghoulish journey.

Cora Tull, Vernon's fundamentalist wife. Constantly praying and singing hymns, she tries to make Addie repent.

Preacher Whitfield, Addie's former lover, the father of Jewel. Hearing of her sickness, this wordy man goes to confess his sin to Anse. On the way, he decides that his fight against the elements, as he crosses the flooding river, helps to expiate his sins. After she dies, he does not believe that a public confession is necessary.

Lafe, a fieldhand, the father of Dewey Dell's unborn child.

Mr. Gillespie, in whose barn Addie's coffin lies when Darl attempts to burn it.

The Story

Addie Bundren was dying. She lay propped up in a bed in the Bundren farmhouse, looking out the window at her son Cash as he built the coffin in which she was to be buried. Obsessed with perfection in carpentry, Cash held up each board for her approval before he nailed it in place. Dewey Dell, Addie's daughter, stood beside the bed, fanning her mother as she lay there in the summer heat. In another room, Anse Bundren, Addie's husband, and two sons, Darl and Jewel, discussed the possibility of the boys making a trip with a wagonload of lumber to earn three dollars for the family. Because Addie's wish was that she be buried in Jefferson, the town where her relatives lay, Anse was afraid the boys might not get back in time to carry her body to the Jefferson graveyard. He finally approved the trip, and Jewel and Darl set out.

Addie died while the two brothers were gone and before Cash could finish the coffin. When it was obvious that she was dying, Dr. Peabody was summoned, but he came too late to help the sick woman. While Dr. Peabody was at the house, Vardaman, the youngest boy, arrived home with a fish he had caught in the river; his mother's death somehow became entangled in his mind with the death of the fish, and because Dr. Peabody was there when she died, Vardaman thought that the doctor had killed her.

Meanwhile, a great rainstorm came up. Jewel and Darl, with their load of lumber, were delayed on the road by a broken wagon wheel. Cash kept working through the rain, trying to finish the coffin. At last it was complete, and Addie was placed in it, but the crazed Vardaman, who once had almost smothered in his crib, tried to let his mother out by boring holes through the top of the coffin.

After Jewel and Darl finally got back with the wagon, neighbors gathered at the Bundren house for the funeral service, which was conducted by Whitfield, the minister. Whitfield had once been a lover of Addie's after her marriage, and Jewel, the son whom she seemed to favor, had been fathered by the minister.

Following the service, Anse, his family, and the dead Addie started for Jefferson, normally one hard day's ride away. The rainstorm, however, had so swollen the river that the bridge had been broken and could not be crossed by wagon. After trying another bridge, which had also been washed out, they drove back to an old ford near the first bridge. Three of the family—Anse, Dewey Dell, and Vardaman, with the assistance of Vernon Tull, a neighboring farmer—got across the river on the ruins of the bridge. Then Darl and Cash attempted to drive the wagon across at the obliterated ford, with Jewel leading the way on his spotted horse. This horse was Jewel's one great possession; he had earned the money to purchase it by working all day at the Bundren farm and then by working all night clearing ground for a neighbor. When the wagon was nearly across, a big log floating downstream upset the wagon. As a result, Cash broke his leg and nearly died; the mules were drowned; the coffin fell out, but was dragged to the bank by Jewel; and Cash's carpenter's tools were scattered in the water and had to be recovered one by one.

Anse refused the loan of anyone's mules, insisting that he must own the team that carried Addie to the grave. He went off to bargain for mules and made a trade in which he offered, without Jewel's consent, to give the spotted horse as partial payment. When Jewel found out what his father had done, he rode off, apparently abandoning the group. Later it turned out that he had put the spotted horse in the barn of Snopes, who was dickering with Anse. Thus, they got their new mules, and the trip continued.

By the time that they arrived in Mottson, a town on the way to Jefferson, Addie had been dead so long that buzzards followed the wagon. In Mottson they stopped to buy cement to strengthen Cash's broken leg. The police and citizens, whose noses were offended, insisted that the wagon move on, but the Bundrens would not budge until they bought the cement and treated the leg. While they were in the town, Dewey Dell left the wagon, went to a drugstore, and tried to buy medicine that would abort the illegitimate child she carried, for she had become pregnant by a man named Lafe, with whom she had worked on the farm. The druggist refused to sell her the medicine.

Addie Bundren had been dead nine days and was still not buried. The family spent the last night before their arrival in Jefferson at the house of Mr. Gillespie, who allowed them to put the odorous coffin in his barn. During the night, Darl, whom the neighbors had always thought to be the least sane of the Bundrens, set fire to the barn. Jewel rescued the coffin by carrying it out on his back. Anse later turned Darl over to the authorities at Jefferson; they sent him to the asylum in Jackson.

Lacking a spade and shovel to dig Addie's grave, Anse stopped at a house in Jefferson and borrowed these tools.

The burial finally took place. Afterward, Dewey Dell again tried to buy medicine at a drugstore. One of the clerks pretended to be a doctor, gave her some innocuous fluid, and told her to come back that night for further treatment. The further treatment took the form of a seduction in the basement of the drugstore.

Cash's broken leg, encased in cement, had by now become so infected that Anse took him to Dr. Peabody, who said Cash might not walk for a year. Before starting on the trip home, Anse bought himself a set of false teeth that he had long needed. He then returned the borrowed tools. When he got back to the wagon, he had acquired not only the new teeth but also a new Mrs. Bundren, the woman who lent him the tools.

Critical Evaluation

Considered by many contemporary critics to be the greatest American fiction writer, William Faulkner was awarded the Nobel Prize in Literature for 1949, after a prolific career that included nineteen novels and two volumes of poetry. Although his formal education was limited, Faulkner read prodigiously in the Greek and Roman classics, the Bible, Shakespeare, the English Romantics, Conrad, Joyce, and Eliot. After relatively undistinguished early attempts in poetry and prose, Faulkner was advised by Sherwood Anderson to concentrate on his "own postage stamp of native soil." This led to the saga of Yoknapatawpha County, a partly true regional history (based on Oxford, Mississippi) merging imperceptibly into a coherent myth, introduced in *Sartoris* (1929) and continued in *The Sound and the Fury* (1929) and *As I Lay Dying*.

In the Yoknapatawpha novels, Faulkner placed himself in the forefront of the avant-garde with his intricate plot organization, his bold experiments in the dislocation of narrative time, and his use of the stream-of-consciousness technique. His stylistic view of times was affected by his sense that past events continue into the present. As he once said, "There is no such thing as *was*; if *was* existed, there would be no grief or sorrow." These stylistic characteristics were undergirded by the development of a complex social structure that enabled Faulkner to explore the inherited guilt of the Southern past, the incapacity of the white aristocracy to cope with modern life, the relations between classes, and the relations between races.

Starkly realistic, poignantly symbolic, grotesquely comic, and immensely complicated as an experiment in point of view, *As I Lay Dying* ranks with Faulkner's greatest novels: *The Sound and the Fury, Sanctuary* (1931), *Light in August* (1932), and *Absalom, Absalom!* (1936). The relative simplicity of its style, characterized by staccato-like sentences and repetitive dialogue, enhances the tragicomic effect. At the same time, the prosaic quality of the narrative often renders to poetry—as when Dewey Dell becomes the symbol of heedless motherhood by wiping everything on her dress, when Darl sees stars first in the bucket and then in his dipper, when Jewel's horse appears "enclosed by a glittering maze of hooves as by an illusion of wings," as when the buzzards accompanying Addie's coffin are juxtaposed suddenly with the sparks that make the stars flow backward for Vardaman, or when Darl, in his visionary fashion, speculates: "It is as though the space between us were time: an irrevocable quality. It is as though time, no longer running straight before us in a diminishing line, now runs parallel between us like a looping string, the distance between the doubling accretion of the thread and not the interval between."

The novel's theme, in the very widest terms, is humanity's absurdly comic distinction between being and not-being. Peabody describes death as "merely a function of the mind—and that of the ones who suffer the bereavement." The theme is stated most clearly in the single chapter narrated from Addie's viewpoint: "I could just remember how my father used to say that the reason for living was to get ready to stay dead a long time." Addie has long since considered Anse dead, because she realizes that he, like most humans, cannot distinguish between the "thin line" of words that float upward into nothingness and the terrible reality of "doing [that] goes along the earth, clinging to it." Her attitude is expressed tersely and succinctly when she comments, after allusively revealing her affair with Whitfield: "Then I found that I had Jewel. When I waked to remember to discover it, he was two months gone."

Nineteen of the fifty-nine chapters are narrated from Darl's viewpoint, making him the primary persona of the novel. His references to his family's conglomerate madness sets the tone: "In sunset we fall into furious attitudes, dead gestures of dolls." The novel proceeds in a jerky, doll-like movement, as the narration passes through the viewpoints of fifteen different characters, not without occasional retrogression and hiatus. Although Darl might be called the primary narrator, whose voice is most representative of the author's own, he is not the only interesting one. Vardaman, with ten chapters, displays a mentality reminiscent of Benjy's in *The Sound and the Fury*, showing readers the crazy events connected with the burial through the eyes of a confused and simpleminded child. The third chapter from his viewpoint consists of a single sentence: "My mother is a fish." Only three chapters present Anse's viewpoint, but that is enough to show that he is a bizarre combination of his sons' characteristics: Darl's imagination, Vardaman's insanity, Cash's stubborn practicality, and Dewey Dell's earthiness (which also sets her in contrast with the bitterness of Addie's outlook on sex and motherhood).

As he does in *The Sound and the Fury*, with Jason's chapter, Faulkner achieves his greatest artistic success with the least intrinsically interesting character, Cash. The first chapter (of five) from Cash's viewpoint is an artistic coup. Until this point, readers have heard, through many different viewpoints, the steady buzzing of Cash's saw preparing his mother's coffin—a sound that provides the thread of continuity through the first half of the novel. Even through the rain and through the night, Cash will not cease his labor: "Yet the motion of the saw has not faltered, as though it and the arm functioned in a tranquil conviction that rain was an illusion of the mind." Finally, his own voice is heard in chapter 18: "I made it on the bevel." After this statement, Cash proceeds to explain what he means as Faulkner presents the carpenter's methodological mind in a straightforward list: beginning with "1. There is more surface for the nails to grip" and ending with "13. It makes a neater job." Cash's second chapter is a nine-line warning to his impatient father and brothers that the coffin "wasn't on a balance" in the wagon. When the tragedy in the river results from their ignoring his warning, Faulkner presents Cash's third chapter in three lines, beginning with, "It wasn't on a balance," and not even mentioning the fact that Cash's leg has been broken. Cash's single-minded craftsmanship and superhuman patience become a reflection of the author's own technique. The final chapter is Cash's.

THE AUTOBIOGRAPHY OF BENJAMIN FRANKLIN

Type of work: Autobiography
Author: Benjamin Franklin (1706-1790)
Time of work: 1706-1757
Locale: Boston, London, and Philadelphia
First published: 1791, as *Mémoires de la vie privée de Benjamin Franklin*

Part diary and part self-help primer, Franklin's autobiography covers the first fifty-one years in the life of this remarkable individual.

Principal Personages

Benjamin Franklin
Josiah Franklin, his father
James Franklin, his brother and first employer
Sir William Keith, the governor of Pennsylvania

Mr. Denham, a merchant
Mr. Meredith, Franklin's partner in the print shop
Alexander Hamilton
Gouverneur Morris

Addressing himself to his "Dear Son," Benjamin Franklin first began in Twyford, England, at the age of sixty-five, to set down reminiscences of his early days. For years he had been collecting data about his ancestors, who had lived in Ecton, Northamptonshire, as far back as 1555, the oldest date of the town records. He thought that his son William Franklin (1731-1813) would someday be interested in the "circumstances" of his father's life, just as Franklin had delighted in anecdotes relating to his family.

The work was composed in installments. The first section, dealing with Franklin's first twenty-four years, was the product of a week of leisure in England in 1771. Then, because of his political activities abroad and at home, he had no further opportunity to continue his task until the urgings of friends persuaded him to resume his writing in 1783. The final section was probably written between November, 1789, and April, 1790. Titled *Mémoires*, it was first printed in France in 1791. No complete text appeared until 1868.

In spite of the lengthy period of composition, only Franklin's life before July, 1757, is covered, with a few comments on his activities in the following year. Yet the failure to complete the *Autobiography* beyond his fifty-first year does not mean that Franklin failed to write of his activities over the next thirty years. Some of his most important diplomatic missions are reported in individual compositions, such as the sample that he showed to Jefferson of the "history of my life" that he said he was preparing. They cover "Negotiations in London for Ef-

fecting a Reconciliation between Great Britain and the American Colonies" and the "Journal of the Negotiations for Peace with Great Britain from March 21st to July 1st, 1782."

In addition, this indefatigable letter writer filled his correspondence (in many ways the most interesting part of his writing) with details and sketches. By combining the correspondence chronologically, a biographer can obtain Franklin's personal reactions to practically everything that happened to him. These letters show Franklin as the first real American who stood apart from European influences.

The Franklin family, whose ancestors had lived in the Northamptonshire village of Ecton from the time they assumed a surname originally signifying a middle-class landowner, was transplanted to Boston about 1682, when Benjamin's father, Josiah, brought his wife and several children to Massachusetts. After his wife's death, the older Franklin remarried. Benjamin, born of the second marriage, was the youngest son of seventeen children.

Fond of study and quickly learning to read, Benjamin was destined for the ministry until his father, a tallow-candler and soap-boiler by trade, began calculating the cost of education and the pitiable salary received by most ministers. Therefore, the boy was taken out of school to learn a trade. After a brief period as his father's assistant, he was, at the age of twelve, apprenticed to his half brother James, a printer. In his brother's shop, he saw his first writing in print: topical ballads written to be sold in the streets.

He continued to read: *The Pilgrim's Progress*, Plutarch's *Parallel Lives*, and essays by Daniel Defoe, Sir Richard Burton, and Cotton Mather. A volume of the *Spectator*, acquired by chance, revealed to him the importance of style, and like Robert Louis Stevenson at a later date, he taught himself by rewriting and comparing sentences. From this printshop came the fifth—Franklin's mistakenly says the second—newspaper in America, the *New England Courant*, to which Franklin became an anonymous contributor.

Fights with his brother eventually sent the seventeen-year-old apprentice to Philadelphia looking for employment. His arrival early in the morning, with three-penny-worth of rolls in his mouth and under his arms as he walked up Market Street past the home of Miss Read, whom he was to marry later, was Philadelphia's first sight of one of its most distinguished citizens.

Neither Bradford nor Keimer, the only printers in Philadelphia, was very advanced. After the boy found a place in Keimer's shop, his wide reading and his ability to talk and to listen brought him many friends. Finally Governor William Keith offered to send him to England to buy type and equipment for a shop of his own. Arriving in London, he learned that Keith, whose credit was not good, had provided nothing but promises. To support himself, Franklin found work in a printing house. After eighteen months, he was happy to accept the offer of a merchant who wanted him to take back to America a consignment of merchandise. Back in Philadelphia, he worked for a time in Keimer's shop; then, finding a partner in Hugh Meredith, he and the Welsh Pennsylvanian set up their own establishment. They prospered and in 1729 Franklin became the sole proprietor, having bought out Meredith, whose drinking habits were distasteful to the temperate, frugal Franklin. He branched out as a stationer. In 1730, he founded the *Pennsylvania Gazette* and also married Miss Read. At this point, the first section of the *Autobiography* ends.

In 1784, in Passy, France, Franklin again began to write his story, this time addressed more generally to the reading public than to his son. With friends interested in scientific and intellectual matters he had in 1743 founded a junto for their mutual exchange of ideas and intellectual improvement; this was later to become the American Philosophical Society. The members sponsored a library for the use of the public.

Now that he had educated himself, Franklin sought moral perfection. He set down twelve virtues, then added a thirteenth: pride, at the suggestion of critical friends. Yet he had reason to be proud. He had learned to speak fluent French, Spanish, and Italian. His civic spirit, born when he was appointed postmaster of Philadelphia, induced him to reorganize the fire department, to start a movement to pave and light the streets, and to establish an academy that later became the University of Pennsylvania. The death of a son from smallpox caused him to argue for inoculation against the disease. He invented an improved form of heating stove and offered it free for general use, only to learn that he had brought wealth to one stove manufacturer. Meanwhile, beginning in 1732, he published *Poor Richard's Almanack*, the usual collection of agricultural and astronomical data to which he added a compendium of practical wisdom and moral maxims. This venture also brought him wealth and enabled him to retire from active business in 1748.

His thoughts about defense caused him to campaign for the establishment of a militia, but this man who so candidly confessed his "errata," or mistakes, was too well acquainted with himself to accept appointment as their colonel. Civic improvements, when initiated by others, needed his approval before his fellow citizens would adopt them. Yale and Harvard universities awarded honorary degrees to this self-taught scholar, and he was elected to membership in cultural and scientific societies at home and abroad.

General Edward Braddock sought Franklin's advice in campaigning against Native American tribes, only to disregard it with disastrous results. After selling out his shop to his foreman, Franklin occupied his time with philosophical concerns and scientific experiments, particularly those relating to electricity. His theories, while ignored or contradicted abroad, led to his experiments with lightning in 1752.

Having represented Pennsylvania at the Albany Congress in 1754, he was chosen to represent it in protests to the English crown. His arrival in England, July 27, 1757, is the last date in his story of himself.

THE AWAKENING

Type of work: Novel
Author: Kate Chopin (1851-1904)
Type of plot: Domestic tragedy
Time of plot: c. 1899
Locale: Grand Isle and New Orleans, Louisiana
First published: 1899

Widely regarded as Chopin's masterpiece, The Awakening *traces Edna Pontellier's growing spiritual and sexual awareness as she discovers the position of women in society and the price that they must pay for freedom.*

Principal Characters

Edna Pontellier, the attractive twenty-eight-year-old wife of a kindly but conventional rich husband. She falls in love with Robert Lebrun, with whom she imagines a life of happiness and independence. He abandons her, shattering her last illusion, and the following day Edna drowns herself in the Gulf of Mexico.

Léonce Pontellier, Edna's husband, twelve years her senior. He loves his wife but regards her as his personal property. Concerned with propriety, he cannot understand what seems to him increasingly bizarre behavior by Edna, and the two drift apart.

Robert Lebrun, who is two years younger than Edna. He enjoys flirting with married women but flees Edna's serious passion.

Adèle Ratignolle, Edna's friend, who embodies all the maternal virtues. The beautiful mother of three, she devotes herself to her family.

Alcée Arobin, a handsome roué who becomes Edna's lover.

Mademoiselle Reisz, a fine pianist who has dedicated her life to her art. She lives alone and has few friends.

Dr. Mandelet, the retired Pontellier family doctor. Better known for his insights into human nature than for his professional skills, he recognizes that Edna is troubled and invites her confidence. He understands the plight of women.

The Story

The Awakening unfolds over the course of nine months, Edna Pontellier's spiritual and sexual transformation corresponding to the pregnancy and delivery of her friend Adèle Ratignolle. Even before the novel opens, Edna has demonstrated occasional signs of rebellion. As a child, she fled her father's Presbyterian church to run in the fields, and she married Léonce Pontellier in part because her father and older sister, Margaret, objected to his Catholicism. Edna's spirit of independence begins to assert itself more fully on Grand Isle, where a number of people from New Orleans have gone for the summer. Edna's first rejection of convention is slight but significant: She has gone bathing in the heat of the day, thus exposing herself to the sun. The action suggests her refusal to remain safely sheltered from experience and passion, her determination to act as she pleases rather than as others, including her husband, expect. Sometime later, she

learns to swim. Her newfound skill at once exhilarates and frightens her. She is proud of her achievement and the freedom that she now has in the water, but when she sees how far she has gone from shore (and safety), she becomes frightened and returns. Her awakening is beginning, though she is still not ready to abandon all conventions. Yet Edna comes back from the sea a changed woman. When her husband finds her lying in the hammock outside, he first asks and then commands her to come inside, but she refuses. She recognizes that previously she would have yielded.

The next day, she goes with Robert Lebrun to church on a nearby island. He is a flirtatious young man with whom she has fallen in love and who, despite himself, has developed a passion for her. As she had run away from the Presbyterian service in her childhood, she now flees Mass. She and Robert spend an idyllic day together, but when they return to Grand Isle that evening, Robert leaves her. He is too traditional to carry on an affair with a married woman, and he soon goes to Mexico, ostensibly on business but actually to get away from Edna.

With the end of summer, the Pontelliers return to New Orleans, where Edna continues her metamorphosis. To her husband's amazement, she gives up her customary Tuesday afternoons "at home." She not only stops receiving company but also fails to return visits from others, clearly violating the social code of her world. In a key episode midway through the book, Edna, alone in her bedroom, removes her wedding band, flings it to the floor, and stamps on it with her boot. Her attitude toward marriage further manifests itself in her refusal to attend the wedding of her younger sister, Janet; Edna remarks that "a wedding is one of the most lamentable spectacles on earth."

Puzzled by and concerned about his wife's behavior, Léonce consults the longtime family physician, Dr. Mandelet. The doctor, too, has noticed a change in Edna. Whether he fully understands what is happening with her or not, he reassures Léonce that Edna is merely moody. Given time, he says, she will return to her former self. Léonce then goes to New York on business, and their two children visit their paternal grandfather in Iberville. Freed from familial responsibilities, Edna feels relieved. As a further sign of independence, she leaves her husband's house for a smaller residence nearby. On the night before she moves, she hosts a party for her friends. Alcée Arobin rightly calls the dinner a coup d'état because it celebrates a new regime of liberation for Edna; she never sees her husband again.

Although Edna loves Robert, she begins a sexual liaison with Alcée, who appeals to her sensually. Despite six years of marriage and two children, Edna has never before experienced true physical passion. The lush landscape of Grand Isle, the Creole women of the region, and Robert Lebrun had begun to arouse Edna. Now, with Alcée Arobin, she feels for the first time the full force of desire. Edna would prefer to make love with Robert, but she has no regrets about her husband, nor is she ashamed of what convention would regard as immorality.

Edna sometimes visits the Ratignolles, whose devotion to family depresses her. She also continues her friendship with the pianist Mademoiselle Reisz, who warns Edna that those who flout social norms must be courageous and strong. Robert corresponds with Mademoiselle Reisz—he never writes to Edna—and one afternoon, seeking her musician friend, Edna finds Robert, newly returned from Mexico. Nothing comes of this encounter, but when they meet again at an outdoor café, Robert goes home with Edna and confesses his love. Before they can consummate their relationship, Celestine, Edna's maid, enters to announce that Madame Ratignolle is in labor and wants Edna's company. Robert asks Edna to remain, but she leaves with the promise of a prompt return. By the time that she gets back, Robert has fled her once more, leaving behind only a short note: "I love you. Good-by—because I love you."

Edna does not sleep that night. The next day, she returns to Grand Isle and the sea. Removing her clothes, the last symbol of restraint and convention, she swims away and drowns in the Gulf of Mexico.

Critical Evaluation

The Awakening has been called the American version of Gustave Flaubert's *Madame Bovary* (1857) or Leo Tolstoy's *Anna Karenina* (1875-1877). For its time, the novel's flavor was decidedly European; its appearance effectively ended Chopin's literary career because thereafter magazines and book publishers refused to print her works. The very publication of the novel in 1899 is somewhat surprising: Two years later, Theodore Dreiser would be unable to find a publisher for *Sister Carrie* (1900).

Though the book is, like its heroine, an anomaly for its time and place, as well as a voice raised against convention, it reflects the naturalistic mood of works such as Stephen Crane's *Maggie: A Girl of the Streets* (1893) that rebelled against the more cheerful realism of William Dean Howells and the local color writers. Chopin

herself has been regarded as a regionalist, and most of her stories are, like *The Awakening*, set in Cajun Louisiana. Her dark vision and insistence on feminist concerns, however, move her beyond most of her contemporaries, and more than sixty years would pass before literary criticism could appreciate her achievement. Only in the 1960's did this novel gain widespread recognition and praise.

Though atypical for its era, the book is the logical culmination of Chopin's writings. A decade earlier, in Chopin's story "Wiser Than a God" (1889), Paula Von Stoltz rejects George Brainard's offer of marriage because she prefers independence and art. In "A Point at Issue!" (1899), Eleanor Gail agrees to marry Charles Faraday, but she, too, retains her individuality; after the couple honeymoon, she remains in Paris while he returns to the United States. In "The Story of an Hour" (1894) and "Athénaïse" (1895), Chopin depicts women who want freedom even though, like Edna, they are married to good men. In "The Storm," which Chopin wrote in 1898 but did not even attempt to publish during her lifetime—it appeared only in 1969—extramarital sex between Calixta and Alcée Laballière provides fulfillment lacking in both marriages and so allows the lovers to be more considerate toward their respective spouses.

Related to such stories as these in its rejection of traditional views about love and marriage, *The Awakening* nevertheless moves beyond them because it implies the impossibility of a woman as gaining freedom in the society of 1899, perhaps in any society. At the beginning of the work, Chopin introduces an anonymous pair of young lovers constantly together and a solitary old woman always praying. Neither the naïve illusions of the former nor the piety of the latter satisfies Edna in her quest for meaning in her life. Adèle Ratignolle provides yet another option. Adèle is one of those "mother-women . . . who idolized their children, worshiped their husbands, and esteemed it a holy privilege to efface themselves as individuals and grow wings as ministering angels." This role, too, fails to content Edna, who wants more than "blind contentment" devoid of "anguish" or "delirium." Mademoiselle Reisz offers another possibility: dedication to some art. Edna has tried writing and shows some promise as a painter, but this path, too, does not satisfy. Perhaps Chopin implies that Edna lacks the strength and courage and talent of Mademoiselle Reisz. As Edna swims away at the end of *The Awakening*, she sees a bird with a broken wing sinking downward to the water. The image may suggest that Edna is too weak to soar on the wings

of art. Perhaps, though, Edna does not want to pay the price of Mademoiselle Reisz, who has never married, has few friends, and seems to have given up even her first name, that sign of sociability, in order to achieve independence. Adèle keeps up her piano playing only for her children; Mademoiselle Reisz has given up having children for her piano. Both, then, may have settled for incomplete lives.

Alone one evening, Edna falls asleep reading the work of Ralph Waldo Emerson. Her suicide may be the ultimate Romantic gesture of independence, or, like her dozing over the Transcendental sage, a rejection of Emersonian optimism that maintains the possibility of freedom. Chopin may be charging that the society of the 1890's did not allow women the full lives that they sought. The bird with the broken wing may, however, connote nature's indifference to suffering and desire. Like the bird, Edna would fly free, but she cannot achieve her goal, not because of society but because of the natural order.

Walking home from Adèle's difficult delivery at the end of the novel, Dr. Mandelet observes to Edna that nature decoys women into becoming mothers. He adds, "Nature takes no account of moral consequences, of arbitrary conditions which we create, and which we feel obliged to maintain at any cost." Robert's desertion hurts Edna, but she does not kill herself simply because he has left her. Her disappointment lies deeper, in the realization that in the natural course of life all passion fades, that absolute freedom is attainable only in death. Robert, who early in the novel taught Edna to swim and first stimulated her sexual revolt, shatters her last unrealistic expectation of happiness. She awakens from her illusions to gain independence and fulfillment in the only way possible for her.

BABBITT

Type of work: Novel
Author: Sinclair Lewis (1885-1951)
Type of plot: Social satire
Time of plot: 1920's
Locale: Zenith, a fictional Midwestern town
First published: 1922

Babbitt is a pungent satire about a man who typifies complacent mediocrity. George F. Babbitt revels in his own popularity, his ability to make money, his fine automobile, and his penny-pinching generosity. Constantly discontented with the life he leads, he is thoroughly satisfied with George F. Babbitt. Because his character is grounded in realism, Babbitt is one of the most convincing creations in American literature.

Principal Characters

George F. Babbitt, a satirically portrayed prosperous real estate dealer in Zenith, a typical American city. He is the standardized product of modern American civilization, a member of the Boosters' Club, hypnotized by all the slogans of success, enthralled by material possessions, envious of those who have more, patronizing toward those who have less, yet dimly aware that his life is unsatisfactory.

Myra Babbitt, his colorless wife, whom he married because he could not bear to hurt her feelings. She lives only for him and the children.

Verona Babbitt, their dumpy daughter. Just out of college, she is a timid intellectual whose mild unconventionality angers her father. He is relieved when she marries Kenneth Escott.

Theodore (Ted) Babbitt, their son. A typical product of the American school system, he hates study and the thought of college. He elopes with Eunice Littlefield, thus winning his father's secret admiration, for he has at least dared to do what he wanted.

Paul Riesling, Babbitt's most intimate friend since college days. With the soul of a musician, he has been trapped into a lifetime of manufacturing tar-roofing and is burdened with a shrewish wife. Goaded to desperation, he shoots her and, though she lives, is sent to prison.

Zilla Riesling, Paul's nagging wife. With a vicious disposition that is made worse by having too much time on her hands, she finally drives Paul to the point of shooting her.

Mrs. Daniel (Tanis) Judique, a widow with whom

Babbitt has a brief affair as a part of his revolt against conventionality.

Seneca Doane, a liberal lawyer, the anathema of all the solid businessmen of Zenith.

William Washington Eathorne, a rich, conservative banker. He represents the real power behind the scene in Zenith.

Charles and **Lucille McKelvey,** wealthy members of Zenith's smart set. The Babbitts are hopeful of being accepted socially by the McKelveys but do not succeed.

Ed and **Mrs. Overbrook,** a down-at-heels couple. They are hopeful of being accepted socially by the Babbitts but do not succeed.

The Reverend Dr. John Jennison Drew, the efficient, high-powered pastor of Babbitt's church.

Vergil Gunch, a successful coal dealer. He is prominent in all the civic organizations to which Babbitt belongs.

T. Cholmondeley (Chum) Frink, a member of Babbitt's social group. He is a popular poet whose work is syndicated throughout the country.

Howard Littlefield, Babbitt's next-door neighbor. An economist for the Zenith Street Traction Company, he can prove to everyone's satisfaction that Zenith is the best of all possible worlds.

Eunice Littlefield, his flapper daughter. She elopes with Ted Babbitt to the public surprise and indignation of both families but to Babbitt's secret delight.

Kenneth Escott, a newspaper reporter. After a tepid courtship, he finally marries Verona Babbitt.

The Story

George F. Babbitt was proud of his house in Floral Heights, one of the most respectable residential districts in Zenith. Its architecture was standardized, its interior decorations were standardized, and its atmosphere was standardized. Therein lay its appeal for Babbitt.

He bustled about in a tile-and-chromium bathroom in his morning ritual of getting ready for another day. When he went down to breakfast, he was as grumpy as usual. It was expected of him. He read the dull real estate page of the newspaper to his patient wife, Myra. Then he commented on the weather, grumbled at his son and daughter, gulped his breakfast, and started for his office.

Babbitt was a real estate broker who knew how to handle business with zip and "zowie." Having closed a deal whereby he forced a poor businessman to buy a piece of property at twice its value, he pocketed part of the money and paid the rest to the man who had suggested the enterprise. Proud of his acumen, he picked up the telephone and called his best friend, Paul Riesling, to ask him to lunch.

Paul Riesling should have been a violinist, but he had gone into the tar-roofing business in order to support his shrewish wife, Zilla. Lately she had made it her practice to infuriate doormen, theater ushers, or taxicab drivers, and then ask Paul to come to her rescue and fight them like a man. Cringing with embarrassment, Paul would pretend he had not noticed the incident. Later, at home, Zilla would accuse him of being a coward and a weakling.

So sad did Paul's affairs seem to Babbitt that he suggested a vacation to Maine together—away from their wives. Paul was skeptical, but with magnificent assurance Babbitt promised to arrange the trip. Paul was humbly grateful.

Back in his office, Babbitt refused a raise for one of his employees. When he got home, he and his wife decided to give a dinner party, with the arrangements taken bodily from the contents of a woman's magazine and everything edible disguised to look like something else.

The party was a great success. Babbitt's friends were exactly like Babbitt. They all became drunk on Prohibition-period gin, were disappointed when the cocktails ran out, stuffed themselves with food, and went home to nurse headaches.

Sometime later, Babbitt and Myra paid a call on the Rieslings. Zilla, trying to enlist their sympathy, berated her husband until he was goaded to fury. Babbitt finally told Zilla that she was a nagging, jealous, sour, and unwholesome wife, and he demanded that she allow Paul to go with him to Maine. Weeping in self-pity, Zilla consented. Myra sat calmly during the scene, but later she criticized Babbitt for bullying Paul's wife. Babbitt told her sharply to mind her own business.

On the train, Babbitt and Paul met numerous businesspeople who loudly agreed with each other that what this country needed was a sound business administration. They deplored the price of motor cars, textiles, wheat, and oil; they swore that they had not an ounce of racial prejudice; and they blamed Communism and socialism for labor unions that got out of hand. Paul soon tired of the discussion and went to bed. Babbitt stayed up late, smoking countless cigars and telling countless stories.

Maine had a soothing effect upon Babbitt. He and Paul fished and hiked in the quiet of the north woods, and Babbitt began to realize that his life in Zenith was not all that it should be. He promised himself a new outlook on life, a more simple, less hurried way of living.

Back in Zenith, Babbitt was asked to make a speech at a convention of real estate people that was to be held in Monarch, a nearby city. He wrote a speech contending that real estate people should be considered professionals and called realtors. At the meeting, he declaimed loudly that real estate was a great profession, that Zenith was God's own country—the best little spot on earth—and to prove his statements quoted countless statistics on waterways, textile production, and lumber manufacture. The speech was such a success that Babbitt instantly won recognition as an orator.

Babbitt was made a precinct leader in the coming election. His duty was to speak to small labor groups about the inadvisability of voting for Seneca Doane, a liberal, in favor of a man named Prout, a solid businessperson who represented the conservative element. Babbitt's speeches helped to defeat Doane. He was very proud of himself for having Vision and Ideals.

On a business trip to Chicago, Babbitt spied Paul Riesling sitting at dinner with a middle-aged but pretty woman. Later, in his hotel room, Babbitt indignantly demanded an explanation for Paul's lack of morality. Paul told Babbitt that he could no longer stand living with Zilla. Babbitt, feeling sorry for his friend, swore that he would keep her husband's secret from Zilla. Privately, Babbitt envied Paul's independence.

Babbitt was made vice president of the Boosters' Club. He was so proud of himself that he bragged loudly when his wife called him at the office. It was a long time before he understood what she was trying to tell him: Paul had shot his wife.

Babbitt's world collapsed about him. Though Zilla was still alive, Paul was in prison. Babbitt began to question his ideas about the power of the dollar. Paul was perhaps the only person Babbitt had ever loved, as Myra had long since become a habit and the children were too full of new ideas to be close to their father. Babbitt felt suddenly alone. He began to criticize the minister's sermons. He no longer visited the Athletic Club and rarely ate lunch with any of his business acquaintances.

One day, a pretty widow, Mrs. Judique, came to his office and asked him to find her a flat. Babbitt joined her circle of bohemian friends. He drank more than he had ever drunk in his life. He spent money wildly. Two of the most powerful men in town requested that he join the Good Citizen's League—or else. Babbitt refused to be bullied. For the first time in his life, he was a human being. He actually made friends with his archenemy, Seneca Doane, and discovered that he liked his liberal ideas. He praised Doane publicly. Babbitt's new outlook on life appealed to his children, who at once began to respect him as they never had before, but Babbitt became un-popular among his business-boosting friends. When he again refused to join the Good Citizen's League, he was snubbed in the streets. Gradually, Babbitt found that he had no real resources within himself. He was miserable.

When Myra became ill, Babbitt suddenly realized that he loved his colorless wife. He broke with Mrs. Judique. He joined the Good Citizen's League. By the time Myra was well again, there was no more active leader in the town of Zenith than George F. Babbitt. Once more, he announced his distrust of Seneca Doane. He became the best Booster the club ever had. His last gesture of revolt was private approval of his son's elopement; outwardly, he conformed.

Critical Evaluation

Zenith, "the Zip City—Zeal, Zest, and Zowie," is Sinclair Lewis' satirical composite picture of the typical progressive American "business city" of the 1920's, and middle-aged, middle-class Midwesterner George F. Babbitt is its average prosperous citizen. Everything about Zenith is modern. A few old buildings, ramshackle witnesses of the city's nineteenth century origins, are embarrassing, discordant notes amid the harmony of newness produced by shining skyscrapers, factories, and railroads. One by one, the old buildings are surrounded and bulldozed. The thrust of all energies in the city is toward growth: One of Zenith's most booming businesses is real estate, and one of its favorite occupations is the religious tallying and charting of population increase.

As Lewis presents his characters, however, the reader discovers that the prosperity and growth of Zenith has been inversely proportional to the intellectual bankruptcy and spiritual stagnation of its inhabitants. Because they subscribe to the values of Zenith's culture, which are all based on the "Dollar Ethic," Lewis' characters think in terms of production and consumption, judge people on the grounds of their purchasing power, and seek happiness in the earning and spending of money. This creed of prosperity permeates every aspect of society. It is evident not only in political and economic beliefs (discussion between Babbitt and his friends about government affairs is limited to the monotonous refrain, "What this country needs is a good, sound business administration") but in moral and religious attitudes as well. Thus, Dr. Drew attracts followers to his "Salvation and Five Percent" church with a combined cross-and-dollar-sign approach. Even more sinister is the facility with which the upright Babbitt carries through crooked deals in his real estate business. In one maneuver, he plots with a speculator to force a struggling grocer to buy the store building (which he has been renting for years) at a scalper's price. The money ethic is so elemental to Babbitt's conscience that he honestly feels nothing but delight and pride when the deal is completed; his only regret is that the speculator carries off nine thousand dollars while Babbitt receives a mere four hundred and fifty dollar commission. At the same time, Babbitt— with no inkling of his hypocrisy—discourses on his virtue to his friend Paul Riesling, touting his own integrity while denigrating the morality of his competitors.

The value placed on money also determines Zenith's aesthetic standards. There is no frivolity about the city's architecture; the most important structures are the strictly functional business buildings. Other structures, such as the Athletic Club—where the businessmen go to "relax" and discuss weighty matters of finance—are gaudy, unabashed copies of past styles; the Club's motley conglomeration includes everything from Roman to Gothic to Chinese. The culmination of literary talent in Zenith is the work of Chum Frink, whose daily newspaper lyrics are indistinguishable from his Zeeco car ads. He comes to Babbitt's dinner party fresh from having written a lyric in praise of drinking water instead of poison booze; with bootleg cocktail in hand, he identifies the American genius as the individual who can run a successful business or write the Prince Albert Tobacco ads.

Most important of all, however, is that the prosperity ethic is at the heart of social norms in Zenith; it is the basis upon which each citizen judges his or her individual worth. Lewis' novel includes caricatures of people in every major field of endeavor: Howard Littlefield is the scholar; T. Cholmondeley Frink, the poet; Mike Monday, the popular preacher; Jake Offut, the politician; Vergil Gunch, the industrialist. Yet despite their various professions, these individuals are identical in their values; they are united in their complacent pride at their own success, and in their scorn for those who have not "made it." People are measured by their incomes and possessions. Thus, Babbitt's car is far more than his means of transportation, and his acquisition of gimmicks such as the nickel-plated cigar cutter more than mere whim; both car and cigar cutter are affirmations of competence and virility. Yet the more Babbitt and his peers strive to distinguish themselves through ownership, the more alike they seem. Thus, the men of Zenith, since they are saturated day after day with the demands of the business life and its values, are even more alike than the women, who are not as immersed in the "rat race" as their husbands.

Mercilessly revealing and minutely detailed as the portrait of Zenith is, however, *Babbitt* would not be the excellent novel that it is if Lewis had stopped at that: In addition to being an exposé of shallowness, the novel is the chronicle of one man's feeble and half-conscious attempt to break out of a meaningless and sterile existence. In the first half of the book, George Babbitt is the Zenithite par excellence; but in the realtor's sporadic bursts of discontent, Lewis plants seeds of the rebellion to come. Babbitt's complacency is occasionally punctured by disturbing questions: Might his wife be right that he bullied Zilla only to strut and show off his strength and virtue? Are his friends really interesting people? Does he really love his wife and enjoy his career?

These nagging questions and the pressures in his life finally build sufficient tension to push Babbitt to the unprecedented step of taking a week's vacation in Maine without his wife and children. The trip relieves his tension and dissolves the questions, and he returns to another year in Zenith with renewed vigor and enthusiasm for Boosters, baseball, dinner parties, and real estate.

It takes the personal tragedy of his friend Paul Riesling to really shock Babbitt out of his routine way of life. Paul's shooting of his wife and consequent imprisonment, which occur approximately midway in the novel, shake Babbitt to his foundations. The Babbitt of the first half of the story is a parody; the Babbitt of the second half is a weak and struggling human being. After Paul goes to prison, Babbitt, to all appearances, throws over his whole previous life-style: He drinks, smokes, curses, frequents wild parties, befriends the city's "bohemian set," adopts radical opinions, and has a love affair. All these things are part of his rebellion against stifling circumstances and his attempt to escape into individuality. The attempt fails because he lacks the inner strength to be independent, and his revolt is ultimately little more than a teapot tempest. Whether preaching the philosophy of the Elks or rebelliously praising the radical politics of Seneca Doane, whether giving a dinner party with his wife or sneaking out to see Mrs. Judique, Babbitt never truly acts on his own.

Thus, by the end of the novel, Babbitt has "returned to the fold," joining the Good Citizen's League and redoubling his zeal in behalf of Zenith Booster activities. Yet even though Babbitt lacks the strength to break out of his mold, Lewis does not imply that he is unchanged by his experience. On the contrary, Babbitt rediscovers his love for his wife and learns something about himself. The Babbitt at the close of the novel has grown in awareness, even if he has proven himself incapable of essentially changing his life. If he has lost his own individuality, he is still able to hope for better things for his son Ted, of whose elopement he secretly approves.

A BELL FOR ADANO

Type of work: Novel
Author: John Hersey (1914-1993)
Type of plot: Social criticism
Time of plot: 1943
Locale: Adano, Italy
First published: 1944

Hersey's novel is one of the outstanding works of fiction to come out of World War II. The author has written realistically and sympathetically of the American invasion troops and of an Italian town and its people, who had lived under Fascist rule for more than twenty years.

Principal Characters

Major Victor Joppolo, the first military governor of Adano after the Americans have retaken Italy in World War II. He is sincerely interested in restoring the dignity of the people there, and consequently he is willing to suffer what many military men would consider a lack of respect for their position. He succeeds in replacing the bell, the town's most prized possession, which the Fascists had taken.

Sergeant Borth, an outspoken aide to Major Joppolo. He is in complete sympathy with what the major is trying to do in the town, if not with the methods he uses.

Captain Purvis, officer in charge of the military police in Adano. Adhering rigidly to military regulations, he is careful to report any infractions of orders, including the major's countermand of General Marvin's order

to keep all carts out of Adano.

General Marvin, the overbearing commander in chief of the American forces in Italy. He cares nothing about the Italian people or their needs and is far too conscious of his own position and the respect he believes is due him.

Giuseppe, Major Joppolo's interpreter, who is quite proud of his position close to the major.

Tomasino, a fisherman. He distrusts all authority and firmly believes in the dignity of the individual.

Gargano, a former Fascist police officer whom Joppolo restores to a position of authority.

Lieutenant Trapani, Captain Purvis' subordinate. He is not afraid of the military and is willing to take some liberty with regulations when the outcome may be helpful.

Colonel Middleton, General Marvin's aide.

The Story

When the American army invaded Sicily, Major Victor Joppolo was placed in command of Adano. He set up his office in the city hall, rehired the janitor, and investigated the records left by the Fascist mayor, who had fled to the hills.

Soon after his arrival, Major Joppolo summoned the leading citizens of the town and asked them, through Giuseppe, his interpreter, what they considered the most important thing to be done. Some answered that the shortage of food was the most pressing problem. Others insisted that what the town needed most was its bell, which had been removed by the Fascists. The bell, it seemed, had a soothing tone. It also regulated the lives of Adano's residents.

The major promised every effort to recover the bell.

Meanwhile, the problem was to obtain food and to have produce brought into the town. In order that his directives would be understood and carried out, the major issued proclamations that the town crier, after being silent for so long, hastened to shout in the village.

On Sunday morning, the major attended mass at one of the churches. There he noticed a blonde girl sitting in front of him. When he later asked Giuseppe about her, the interpreter assumed that the American's interest had nothing to do with official business. Major Joppolo's primary interest, however, was the girl's father, Tomasino, owner of a fishing fleet. The old man refused to take his boats out, and his distrust was contagious. The major had Giuseppe ask Tomasino if he would come to see him. Tomasino, however, distrustful of authority, would not come to headquarters. The major decided to go to Tomasino. He went, followed by practically all the townspeople. The old Italian was defiant, sure that the major had come to arrest him. Finally the Italian was persuaded that the major meant neither to arrest him nor to ask for a cut in the proceeds from the sale of the fish. Tomasino agreed to go out with his fishing fleet, despite the danger of mines.

By that time, the major and his policies had become the subject of much discussion among the people. The Fascist mayor provided them with much amusement. He had come out of hiding and had been paroled into Sergeant Borth's custody. Every morning, the mayor went to Sergeant Borth and publicly confessed a Fascist sin. Giuseppe was astonished to discover that, when the major told him to report for work at seven in the morning, he meant it. Gargano, the former Fascist police officer, learned that he could no longer force the others to make way for him when they stood in line at the bakery.

While driving through Adano one day, General Marvin found the road blocked by a mule cart. The driver, having had his daily quota of wine, was sleeping peacefully.

When the mule refused to budge, the general ordered the vehicle thrown into the ditch. Reluctantly, the soldiers dumped the cart, mule, and sleeping driver. Swearing furiously, the general drove up to the city hall, confronted Major Joppolo, and ordered that the major forbid the entrance of all carts into Adano.

The next day, a group of townspeople besieged the major. The carts, they explained, were essential, for they brought food and water into the town. Major Joppolo countermanded the general's order and telephoned Captain Purvis that he would accept full responsibility. Captain Purvis, anxious to keep out of trouble, ordered Lieutenant Trapani to make a memorandum and to send it to General Marvin. The lieutenant, however, out of regard for Major Joppolo, put the memorandum among Purvis' papers in the hope that the captain, who rarely looked through his files, would never find it.

Major Joppolo's efforts to restore the bell were not successful, for it had been melted down by the Fascists. Nevertheless, a young naval officer, in charge of a nearby station, promised to obtain a ship's bell for him.

In the meantime, Captain Purvis had gone through the papers on his desk and had found the memorandum for General Marvin. He ordered it forwarded at once. Lieutenant Trapani mailed it but addressed it to the wrong person at headquarters in Algiers. From there it was forwarded to the general's aide, Colonel Middleton. Every day, the colonel met with General Marvin and went over important communications. Accordingly, he was halfway through Purvis' letter before he realized what it was. He tried to go on to the next letter, but it was too late. The general had heard Major Joppolo's name and that of Adano, and he remembered both.

The bell arrived in Adano. It was touched, prodded, sounded by the experts, and admired by everybody. When it pealed forth, the townspeople declared that its tone was even better than that of the old bell. The major was a hero. To show their appreciation and affection, the townspeople had him taken to a photographer. From the resulting picture, a local artist painted his portrait.

At the celebration that night, Sergeant Borth was very, very drunk. He refused to take orders from Major Joppolo, saying that the major was no longer in any position to give orders. Captain Purvis, said the sergeant, almost sobbing, had a letter from General Marvin. It ordered Major Joppolo back to Algiers. The next morning, the major said goodbye to Borth, who apologized for his conduct of the previous night. The major asked him to help his successor make the people happy. As he drove away from the town, he heard in the distance the tolling of a bell, the new bell for Adano.

Critical Evaluation

John Hersey's *A Bell for Adano* was popularly regarded as the finest novel to come out of World War II when it first appeared in 1944. The passing of time has removed it from this position, but along with Thomas Heggen's *Mister Roberts* (1946) and Joseph Heller's *Catch-22* (1961), it shows that the war was far better represented in humor than in melodrama. The early appeal of the book was found in the lighthearted episodes of life in a post-liberation Sicilian village, Adano, and in the appeal of the character of the protagonist, Major Joppolo.

To the American public of the postwar period, Joppolo was the embodiment of the "father-husband-brother" figure who was fighting for democracy in a strife-torn world. He was what Americans thought they were: young, sensitive, and good. General Marvin, on the other hand, was the embodiment of a pompous autocrat, thus creating much of the novel's sense of conflict.

Hersey, a war correspondent, was at his best, however, when portraying the common soldier or farmer—ordinary individuals who were caught up in the circumstances of war and were neither all good nor all bad. Early reviewers of the book admitted that they enjoyed reading the book, but its lack of critical character analysis and unity has caused it more and more to be regarded as second-rate literature. Most saw it as a dramatized attempt at nonfiction rather than a novel. Some critics also made mention of the rather "off-color" language of the soldiers in the book. Though rather mild by later standards, some of the words in the book were harsh for the reading public of the middle 1940's. Critics aside, however, it was the American people who made *A Bell for Adano* a best-seller, a hit play on Broadway, and later a popular motion picture.

BENITO CERENO

Type of work: Novella
Author: Herman Melville (1819-1891)
Type of plot: Adventure romance
Time of plot: 1799
Locale: The harbor of St. Maria, off the coast of Chile, and Lima, Peru
First published: 1856

Superficially, this is a story of slavery and mutiny on the high seas, but beneath the adventure-charged plot lies Melville's examination of that subject which so fascinated him: the confrontation of extreme forces of good and evil in the universe. The irony of the tale is that good-hearted, naïve Delano is only victorious in rescuing the victimized Benito because he is too innocent to comprehend the horror and depravity into which he wanders.

Principal Characters

Amasa Delano, an American sea captain. Off the coast of Chile, he sees a ship in distress and sets out with food and water for its company. He finds a Spanish merchant ship carrying slaves. Ship and crew are in deplorable condition, and their captain suffers from what appear to be severe mental disorders. A series of strange and sinister events lead Captain Delano to the knowledge that the Spanish captain is a prisoner of the slaves. He is able to rescue the captive and take him ashore.

Don Benito Cereno, the captain of a Spanish slave ship. His human cargo mutinies and makes him a prisoner, and he is forced to witness horrible atrocities and the murders of the Spanish crew. After his rescue by Captain Delano, he gives testimony concerning the mutiny and dies broken in mind and spirit.

Babo, a mutinous slave. He poses as the devoted servant of Captain Cereno and attempts to deceive Captain Delano concerning his master's true condition. Failing in this attempt, he is captured and hanged on Captain Cereno's testimony.

Don Alexandro Aranda, owner of the cargo of the Spanish slave ship. He is murdered and mutilated by the mutinous slaves.

Raneds, the slave ship's mate, murdered by the mutinous slaves.

The Story

Captain Amasa Delano was commander of an American sealer called *Bachelor's Delight,* which was anchored in the harbor of St. Maria, on an island off the coast of southern Chile. While there, he saw a ship apparently in distress, and thinking it carried a party of monks, he set out in a whaleboat to board the vessel and supply it with food and water. When he came aboard, he found that the ship, the *San Dominick,* was a Spanish merchant ship carrying slaves. The crew was parched and moaning, the ship itself was filthy, and the sails were rotten. Most deplorable of all, the captain, the young Don Benito Cereno, seemed barely able to stand or to talk coherently. Aloof and indifferent, the captain seemed ill both physically (he coughed constantly) and mentally. The captain was attended by Babo, his devoted slave.

Delano sent the whaleboat back to his ship to get additional water, food, and extra sails for the *San Dominick,* while he remained aboard the desolate ship. He tried to talk to Cereno, but the captain's fainting fits kept interrupting the conversation. The Spaniard seemed reserved and sour, in spite of Delano's attempts to assure the man that he was now out of danger. Delano finally assumed that Cereno was suffering from a severe mental disorder. The captain did, with great difficulty and after frequent private talks with Babo, manage to explain that the *San Dominick* had been at sea for 190 days. They had, Cereno explained, started out as a well-manned and smart vessel sailing from Buenos Aires to Lima but had encountered several gales around Cape Horn, lost many officers and men, and then had run into dreadful calms and the ravages of plagues and scurvy. Most of the Spanish officers and all the passengers, including the slave owner, Don Alexandro Aranda, had died of fever. Delano, who knew that the weather in recent months had not been as extreme as Cereno described it, simply concluded that the Spanish officers had been incompetent and had not taken the proper precautions against disease. Cereno continually repeated that only the devotion of his slave, Babo, had kept him alive.

Numerous other circumstances on the *San Dominick* began to make the innocent Delano more suspicious. Although everything was in disorder and Cereno was obviously ill, he was dressed perfectly in a clean uniform. Six black men were sitting in the rigging holding hatchets, although Cereno said that they were only cleaning them. Two were beating up a Spanish boy, but Cereno explained that this deed was simply a form of sport. The slaves were not in chains; Cereno claimed they were so docile that they did not require chains. This notion pleased the humane Delano, although it also surprised him.

Every two hours, as they awaited the expected wind and the arrival of Delano's whaleboat, a large black man in chains was brought before Cereno, who would ask him if he, the captain, could be forgiven. The man would answer, "No," and be led away. At one point, Delano began to fear that Cereno and Babo were plotting against him, for they moved away from him and whispered together. Cereno then asked Delano about his ship, requesting the number of men and the strength of arms aboard the *Bachelor's Delight*. Delano thought that they might be pirates.

Nevertheless, Delano joined Cereno and Babo in Cereno's cabin for dinner. Throughout the meal, Delano alternately gained and lost confidence in Cereno's story. He tried, while discussing a means of getting Cereno new sails, to get Babo to leave the room, but the servant and master were apparently inseparable. After dinner Babo, while shaving his master, cut his cheek slightly despite a warning that had been given. Babo left the room for a

second and returned with his own cheek cut in a curious imitation of his master's. Delano thought this episode curious and sinister, but he finally decided that the man was so devoted to Cereno that he had punished himself for inadvertently cutting his master.

At last, Delano's whaleboat returned with more supplies. Delano, about to leave the *San Dominick*, promised to return with new sails the next day. When he invited Cereno to his own boat, he was surprised at the captain's curt refusal and his failure to escort the visitor to the rail. Delano was offended at the Spaniard's apparent lack of gratitude. As the whaleboat was about to leave, Cereno appeared suddenly at the rail. He expressed his gratitude profusely and then, hastily, jumped into the whaleboat. At first, Delano thought that Cereno was about to kill him; then he saw Babo at the rail brandishing a knife. In a flash, he realized that Babo and the other slaves had been holding Cereno captive. Delano took Cereno back to the *Bachelor's Delight*. Later they pursued the fleeing slaves. The slaves, having no guns, were easily captured by the American ship and brought back to shore.

Cereno later explained that the slaves, having mutinied shortly after the ship set out, had committed horrible atrocities and had killed most of the Spaniards. They had murdered the mate, Raneds, for a trifling offense and had committed atrocities on the dead body of Don Alexandro Aranda, whose skeleton they placed on the masthead.

On his arrival in Lima, Don Benito Cereno submitted a long testimony, recounting all the cruelties that the slaves had committed. Babo was tried and hanged. Cereno felt enormously grateful to Delano, recalling the strange innocence that had somehow kept the slaves from harming him, when they had the chance, aboard the *San Dominick*.

Don Benito Cereno planned to enter a monastery; however, broken in body and spirit, he died three months after he completed his testimony.

Critical Evaluation

Originally serialized in *Putnam's Monthly* in 1855, *Benito Cereno* first appeared, slightly revised, in book form as the first story in Herman Melville's *Piazza Tales* in 1856. It was not reprinted until 1924, when interest was being revived in Melville's writings. Since then, it has often been praised as not only one of Melville's best fictional works but also one of the finest short novels in American literature. In 1964, Robert Lowell adapted *Benito Cereno* into verse-drama as the third act of his play *The Old Glory*.

Benito Cereno is Melville's version of a true story he had read in Amasa Delano's *Narrative of Voyages and Travels in the Northern and Southern Hemispheres* (1817). Melville freely adapted Delano's account to his own fictional purposes. The court depositions, which make up a considerable part of the latter half of *Benito Cereno*, have been shown to be close to those in Delano's account, though Melville omitted some of the court material. In contrast, the creation of atmosphere, the building of suspense, the development of the three main characters—Delano, Cereno, and Babo—and the extended use of symbolism are among Melville's chief contributions to the original story. Also, the thematically important conversation between Delano and Cereno at the end of *Benito Cereno* was added by Melville.

The remarkable third paragraph of *Benito Cereno* illustrates Melville's careful combining of atmospheric detail, color symbolism, and both dramatic and thematic foreshadowing.

> The morning was one peculiar to that coast. Everything was mute and calm; everything grey. The sea, though undulated into long roods of swells, seemed fixed, and was sleeked at the surface like waved lead that has cooled and set in the smelter's mould. The sky seemed a grey surtout. Flights of troubled grey vapours among which they were mixed, skimmed low and fitfully over the waters, as swallows over meadows before storms. Shadows present, foreshadowing deeper shadows to come.

The description, with its repeated use of "grey" and "seemed," is important in setting the scene for a story in which the action will be, as seen through Delano's eyes, ambiguous and deceptive until the light of truth suddenly blazes upon the American captain's mind. Until that time, he will be seeing both action and character through a mist. The grey is symbolically significant also because Delano's clouded vision will cause him to misjudge both the whites and the blacks aboard the *San Dominick*. In the light of the final revelations of the story, the grey has a moral symbolism too, perhaps for Melville and surely for the modern reader, as Cereno and Delano are not morally pure white or good, nor is Babo all black or bad. The Spaniard is a slaver and the American appears to condone the trade, though he is not a part of it; the slave is certainly justified in seeking an escape from captivity for himself and his fellow blacks, though one cannot justify some of the atrocities consciously committed by Babo and his followers. The closing sentence of this mist-shrouded paragraph—"Shadows present, foreshadowing deeper shadows to come"—not only looks forward to the mystery that so long remains veiled but also anticipates the final words of the two captains, words that partly suggest the great difference in their characters. Delano says, "You are saved: what has cast such a shadow upon you?" Cereno replies, "The negro."

In reading *Benito Cereno*, one is caught up in the same mystery that Captain Delano cannot penetrate, and one longs for a final release of the suspense, a solution to the strange puzzle. Melville's hold upon the reader until the flash of illumination in the climax is maintained by his use of Delano's consciousness as the lens through which scene, character, and action are viewed. The revelation is so long delayed because of Delano's being the kind of man he is: "a person of a singularly undistrustful good nature, not liable, except on extraordinary and repeated incentives, and hardly then, to indulge in personal alarms, any way involving the imputation of malign evil in man." His heart is benevolent, but his mind is slow to perceive through the dragging hours from his boarding the *San Dominick* until he is finally shocked into recognition of the truth when Babo prepares to stab Don Benito with the dagger that he had concealed in his hair. At one moment, Delano is repelled by Don Benito's manner and suspicious of his intentions; at the next, he is inclined to acquit Cereno of seeming rudeness because of his frail health and to condemn himself for his suspicions with the excuse that "the poor invalid scarcely knew what he was about."

Just as Melville may have intended to portray Delano as representing a type of American—good-hearted, friendly, and helpful but rather slow-witted and naïve—so he may have delineated Don Benito as emblematic of eighteenth century Spanish aristocracy—proud, enfeebled, and, finally, troubled in conscience over such moral crimes as slave trading. To Delano, he first appears as "a gentlemanly, reserved-looking, and rather young man . . . dressed with singular richness, but bearing plain traces of recent sleepless cares and disquietudes." Later, Don Benito's manner "conveyed a sort of sour and gloomy disdain [which] the American in charity ascribed to the harassing effects of sickness." Further observation leads Delano to conclude that Don Benito's "singular alternations of courtesy and ill-breeding" are the result of either "innocent lunacy, or wicked imposture." He is finally undeceived and apologizes for having suspected villainy in Don Benito toward the end of the danger-filled encounter with the slaves. Delano is lighthearted and eager to dismiss the affair when the danger is over and his suspicions have been erased. Don Benito's mind, however, is of a different cast. He broods on the results in human experience of the confusing of appearance and reality: "You were with me all day," he says to Delano, "stood with me, sat with me, looked at me, ate with me, drank with me, and yet, your last act was to clutch for a monster, not only an innocent man, but the most pitiable of all men. To such degree may malign machinations and deceptions impose. So far may ever the best man err, in judging the conduct of one with the recesses of whose condition he is not acquainted."

The horrors resulting from the slave mutiny, and the tensions and terror that follow Delano's kind offer to aid a ship in apparent distress, leave an already ill man dejected and broken. The shadow of "the negro" has been cast forever upon him. He retires to the monastery on the symbolically named Mount Agonia and, three months later, is released from his sufferings.

Babo, the third major character in *Benito Cereno*, is unforgettable, one of the first important black characters in American fiction (Mrs. Stowe's Uncle Tom had preceded him by only four years). He is one of the most striking of the "masked" characters who appear in Melville's work from beginning to end, hiding their true selves behind the semblance that they present to the world. Captain Delano is completely deceived in his first sight of Babo with Don Benito: "By his side stood a black of small stature, in whose rude face, as occasionally, like a shepherd's dog, he mutely turned it up into the Spaniard's, sorrow and affection were equally blended." His attentiveness makes him seem "less a servant than a devoted companion" to Don Benito. Though he speaks little, his few brief speeches suggest the intelligence that enables him to lead the revolt on the *San Dominick*. He is capable of irony, as

is clear when Benito explains that it is to Babo he owes his preservation and that Babo pacified "his more ignorant brethren, when at intervals tempted to murmurings." "Ah, master," he sighs, " . . . what Babo has done was but duty." The remark is as masked as Babo's bowed face, and the American is so completely taken in that, "As master and man stood before him, the black upholding the white, Captain Delano could not but bethink him of the beauty of that relationship which could present such a spectacle of fidelity on the one hand and confidence on the other."

With its many ironies—an aristocratic Spanish slaver captured by his slaves, a murderous rebel posing as a faithful servant, a naïve American protected from violent death through his own innocence and uncovering villainy by accident—*Benito Cereno* may be read as a magnificently contrived parable of limited, rational, well-ordered humanity struggling against evil in the social and natural universe and achieving at least a partial victory.

BEYOND THE BEDROOM WALL: A Family Album

Type of work: Novel
Author: Larry Woiwode (1941-   )
Type of plot: Family chronicle
Time of plot: Mid-nineteenth century to the mid-twentieth century
Locale: North Dakota, Chicago, and New York
First published: 1975

Originally published as a succession of short stories in The New Yorker *and other magazines, the separate chapters of the five books of* Beyond the Bedroom Wall *have been substantially revised and organized by Woiwode to form a narrative of the Neumiller family over four generations. Individual strands of consciousness coalesce in the novel to form an unfolding vision of human existence.*

Principal Characters

Martin Neumiller, a high-school principal when he is not working as a plumber, plasterer, or insurance salesman. The son of a self-sufficient carpenter, he was reared on a farm in North Dakota and is a warm, decent man who is never quite able to realize his dreams and desires. Martin and his wife, Alpha, rear five children while he attempts to reconcile his various skills and impulses with the circumstances of his family's needs. When his wife dies of uremic poisoning, he tries to handle the responsibilities of the family, partially succeeding with help from other relatives, and then remarries, his life renewed for a short time before Laura, his second wife, dies of cancer. With his children grown, he lives for his expectation of seeing his grandchildren grow toward their future.

Alpha Jones Neumiller, Martin's wife. Trained to be a teacher, she marries and essentially gives up her vocation to become the center of the Neumiller home. She is a thoughtful and intelligent woman whose love for her oldest children gives them a sense of direction and purpose before her death at the age of thirty-four marks their lives with sorrow.

Charles Neumiller (the elder), Martin's father, a man of strong convictions, intense loyalty, high ethical standards, and extraordinary skill as a builder. He is a rock of stability for the family, and his death is an occasion for reflection on the nature of familial love by all members of the Neumiller clan.

Charles Neumiller (the younger), the second son of Martin and Alpha, who is emotional, dramatically effu-

sive, incisive, and sensitive. He becomes a moderately successful actor and carries his mother's spiritual "presence" with him as a kind of guide available during visionary experiences.

Jerome Neumiller, named for Alpha's troubled brother who was drowned in his youth, the oldest son of Martin and Alpha. A taciturn, reserved person, he becomes a dedicated doctor and the guardian of his brother Charles.

Tim Neumiller, Martin and Alpha's middle child, an endlessly inventive, imaginative boy, somewhat of an outcast or outsider, whose intensity and energy lead to eventual success as a runner, a poet, and a teacher. He is the member of the family who is ultimately best suited to manage the complexity of inner relationships that the family engenders.

Ed Jones, Alpha's father, an eloquent maverick and adventurer in his younger days, once a jockey, baseball player, and romantic hustler. He eventually settles into a kind of domestic order with his second wife, but he retains his free-spirited, outspoken manner until his death in his eighties.

Electa Jones, Alpha's mother. She has been charmed by Ed Jones and is now stranded in an uncomfortable situation that thwarts her hopes but to which she responds with a kind of spirited defiance and resilience that expresses her style, her perceptive recognition of her possibilities, and her appreciation of unusual qualities in people, especially her grandson Charles.

The Story

Otto Neumiller, who was born in Germany in 1857, immigrates to the United States, drawn by the promise of "the virgin Dakota plain, limitless as the sea." Through hard work and ingenuity, he becomes a moderately prosperous landowner by 1891, when his son Charles is born. In 1915, he retires from the farm, which he gives to Charles, and becomes involved in a grain elevator cooperative. The Great Depression wipes out his holdings, but he remains as charitable as possible to his neighbors. Eventually, he becomes a recluse with one faithful friend and dies in 1935.

Charles carries his father's motto—"If you're going to do a job, do it right"—as a matter of life principle, and he becomes a master carpenter. His first child, Martin, is born in 1913. A likeable, studious boy, he is offered a college scholarship because of his ability as a pitcher but withdraws from the state university to enter the state teacher's college when the promised financial assistance is withheld. At state college, he becomes friendly with one of his classmates, Alpha Jones, the daughter of an idiosyncratic farm family that is not enthusiastic about Martin's Catholic background. Nevertheless, Martin and Alpha decide to marry when their financial situation permits, each taking a teaching position and keeping in touch with letters and occasional visits. This courtship continues from 1936 to 1938, when Martin and Alpha are married. Martin accepts a position as principal of a school in Hyatt, North Dakota, and during the years of World War II, their sons Jerome, Charles, and Timothy are born. They are followed by a daughter, Marie, just after the war ends.

After Tim's birth, Alpha decides that she wants to convert to Catholicism and begins to study the religion. Martin feels limited by his position and temporarily retires from the educational system, trying to earn a more satisfactory living by working as a plasterer with his brother Jay, as an independent plumber, and as an insurance salesman. He enjoys feeling that he is helping people in each occupation, but he is drawn back to the world of teaching when he is promised a job in Illinois near his father's building business. The family moves to Illinois, but the promised position fails to materialize. They cannot find suitable accommodations and must move in with Martin's parents. The instability and lack of space place considerable stress on Alpha, who has given birth to a daughter, Susan, and is pregnant again. Finally, she is overcome by uremic poisoning and dies.

The shattering circumstance of Alpha's death sends the members of the Neumiller family to separate courses, although they remain intertwined in terms of psychic needs and support. Martin tries to maintain a home for the five children and succeeds to some extent, if frequently overwhelmed by the task of providing love and discipline for all of them. The children spend time on vacations with various relatives, eventually living for extended periods of time in other parts of the country. Martin becomes a physical education teacher in the mid-1950's, a few years after Alpha's death, and Charles and Jerome begin college in the early 1960's. When Martin's father dies, the entire family gathers for his funeral mass, a time for reflection and recollection when the true strength of Charles Neumiller—the foundation rock on which the family's stability has been based—becomes apparent.

Now working again as a principal, Martin meets and becomes friendly with Laura, a widow living in Chicago, and their friendship eventually leads to marriage. She, Martin, and her daughter, Ginny, move in with his daughters in the family home. Jerome is now completing his degree in psychology as a premed student, Charles is very involved in theatrical productions, Tim has become a promising poet and running champion, and Marie and Susan are living with their father and Laura. After graduation, Charles moves to Greenwich Village in New York, living as a bohemian while trying to find work as an actor. He begins a lucrative career doing voiceovers for television commercials.

In the late 1960's, Jerome is studying medicine, while Tim has begun to teach high-school biology. Tim and his wife, Cheri, have had a daughter, Martin's first grandchild. Charles is also married. Marie is majoring in special education, and Susan has dropped out of college after her first year, marrying and moving to a Chicago suburb. Martin is now also living in Chicago, having completed a master's degree at Bradley University, but before he can begin his new job as a guidance counselor, Laura becomes ill. Before a year has passed, she dies from cancer. Stunned by his misfortune, but acting with the characteristic resolution that has carried him through other moments of sadness, Martin gathers his memories and carries his family into the future, the interrelationships among the Neumillers remaining a source of considerable support for all of them.

Critical Evaluation

The epigraph by Erik Erikson that precedes the text of *Beyond the Bedroom Wall* establishes the narrative strategy of what Larry Woiwode calls "a family album" and suggests the philosophical perspective that provides its structural arrangement. "Reality," Erikson observes, "is of course, man's most powerful illusion," and in the course of the five books which constitute the novel, Woiwode gradually develops a constellation of separate realities— the singular components of the individual consciousness of the primary characters—that merge into the greater reality of an interconnected, interactive social construct, a family. Paradoxically, even with the abundance of detail that Woiwode offers, reality for each character remains an elusive, often intangible essence, dependent upon the accumulated particulars of a life placed in memory and available for recall but subject to additional information that can alter and enlarge a previous conception.

Woiwode's essential subject is a very traditional one. The changes in the fortunes of a family in various ways representative of its times—the rise and growth, decline, and then resurgence of successive generations—has been a staple of novelists such as Leo Tolstoy and Charles Dickens. Woiwode presents the Neumillers, an immigrant family living in the American heartland over more than a century of time, as emblematic of a universal familial situation but distinct in the compelling specificity with which he draws each character. The tangible textures of these characters' lives, the incidents and events that form the linked chains of their life patterns, and the dynamics of their individual psychological situations are drawn together in a narrative that establishes the singularity of each primary character while examining their lives in the context of the momentous questions of existence—the great mysteries of Time, Love, and Death.

There is a tendency among some novelists, especially those ruled by the methods of the nineteenth century, to assume that reality is a function of realism, to drown the reader in a mass of material. Woiwode believes that the world of the Neumillers must be evoked in and through minute particulars, but his use of data is selective, his presentation original and effective. Although the story of the Neumillers covers more than a century, from the arrival in the United States of a hopeful immigrant to the dispersal across the country of a fifth generation, Woiwode does not use a strict chronological narrative or a single point of view. Instead, the story moves in overlapping parallel lines, essentially progressing through history but frequently shifting forward or backward from any point of rest. The novel begins with an account of the town of Hyatt, where Martin and Alpha started their family, concentrating on a mental journey along the street where Timothy, the youngest son, lived until he was six. His words are a part of his mental process in a moment of reflection as he lies awake in the early days of his marriage, the book's furthest reach forward in time. Then, there is a transition to an omniscient narrator as Charles

Neumiller prepares his father's body for death in 1935. This is followed by another third-person narration describing the day in January, 1936, when Martin proposed to Alpha; followed by a reproduction of the curriculum vitae that Martin used on his first job application; followed by the diary that Alpha kept from November 9, 1936, until September 15, 1939. These entries conclude the first book of the novel and essentially return it to the street in Hyatt where the Neumillers' first child, Jerome, is born in the early 1940's. Woiwode's technique prevents any character from becoming dominant, although Martin, the grandson of the first Neumiller and the grandfather of the most recent, serves as a kind of primary focus. The effect is to make the family itself the central character-entity. As the narration progresses, the core family is augmented by information on Martin's siblings and is complemented by information on Alpha's family, so that the linear narrative paths seem to advance through surrounding circular courses. The nature of this relationship is expressed by Martin's observation about his kin that "it was impossible to imagine himself existing without their related lives."

While the factual material that Woiwode provides is important in developing an understanding of the circumstances of each character, the language that he uses to convey the ethos of their thoughts and emotions is instrumental in creating the consciousness of each as an individual. In addition, their own self-identity is a function of the manner in which they express themselves, so that Alpha's diary is both a demonstration to the reader of her enthusiasm and eagerness as a young woman and a means of forming the psychological structure of that facet of her personality. Similarly, when Charles Neumiller, Martin's father, uses all of his skills as a master craftsman to fashion his father's coffin, the essence of his being is projected by Woiwode in his dedication to and satisfaction in his task. When Martin's son Charles is engulfed in a delirium of fever from double pneumonia, the Joycean stream-of-consciousness images in his mind not only capture the seriousness of his illness but also reveal the contours of his mental processes so that the complexities of the most introspective of the Neumillers are vividly rendered. Other examples include Woiwode's very deft and accurate rendition of the word games of children at play, particularly Timothy's punning, rhyming, word-creating, and nonsense chanting; the exuberant, explosive, profane, and very colorful speech of Ed Jones; and the rhapsodizing of Charles, overcome with various sensations on a fishing expedition, about the natural world in an echo of Dylan Thomas: "And the strangely colored green of the grass was wavering tales underneath and in front of him."

Each of these episodes of concentrated characterization, in which a unique self emerges in language, serves to anchor or stabilize a person in what remains a vast, daunting universe—the cosmos "beyond the bedroom wall" (the sanctuary, or place of safety) that stretches "beyond North Dakota . . . beyond North and South America" on toward "a vast source of power, God or the sun." Even with all the detail that Woiwode supplies—the accretion of minutiae into the components of consciousness—an individual's identity is still, in many ways, tenuous and fragile, threatened by the crisis points of the narrative. These moments of great change, especially death, call into question the nature of the "reality" that has been gradually and tentatively established. Against this constant sense of uncertainty, Woiwode places rituals of human meaning—the apparatus of religion (here the Catholic church), the practice of craft, the order of work or sport, the consolations of art—as crucial methods for lending value to human life. The entire construc-

tion of *Beyond the Bedroom Wall*, with its shifting temporal patterns and its alternating narrative perspective, is designed to express a flux in which even extraordinary and vivid detail is only a distraction from or temporary stay against chaos. Conrad Jones loves stories from the past, ". . . it doesn't make any difference how many times I go over them. They never grow tiresome." Charles Neumiller, his nephew, finds memory insufficient: "So much has gone over the bridge since then, there's no language that can hold it, at least not for me." Conrad dies in an automobile accident in the course of the novel, while Charles (with his brother Jerome) is the subject of Woiwode's *Born Brothers* (1988) and the last three of the tales collected in *The Neumiller Stories* (1989), written from 1982 to 1989. Yet Conrad also continues as an aspect of Charles's mind, still a member of the family—an abstraction that is part of the most encompassing reality of Woiwode's world.

BILLY BUDD, FORETOPMAN

Type of work: Novel
Author: Herman Melville (1819-1891)
Type of plot: Symbolic tragedy
Time of plot: 1797
Locale: Aboard a British man-of-war
First published: 1924

In this last of Melville's works, published posthumously, the author dramatized the clash between natural goodness and innocence, as personified by Billy Budd, and unprovoked evil, as embodied in Claggart. Captain Vere, as his name suggests, is the upholder of truth and right in the story. When Billy inadvertently kills his antagonizer in a fight, Vere is caught between his love for Billy and his duty to uphold the law and maintain order; he opts for justice over mercy and decides that he must hang the boy.

Principal Characters

Billy Budd, a youthful member of the crew of the merchant ship *Rights-of-Man*, who is impressed into service aboard HMS *Indomitable* during the last decade of the eighteenth century. Billy is twenty-one, "welkin-eyed," and possessed of great masculine beauty. He has no idea who his father and mother were, having been left a foundling in a basket on the doorstep of a "good man" in Bristol, England. Billy was a cheerful, stabilizing influence on the rough crew of the merchant ship; when he is taken aboard the *Indomitable*, he is popular with all the officers and crew except John Claggart, the master-at-arms, who is envious of Billy's almost perfect physique and personality. Honest, refreshing, ingenuous, uncomplaining—each of these adjectives may be applied to Billy Budd, who represents an innocent youth trapped by the brutality of fleet regulations or, perhaps, who represents truth and beauty trapped by the wickedness of the world.

Captain the Honourable Edward Fairfax Vere, of the *Indomitable*. He is known in the fleet as "Starry" Vere to distinguish him from a kinsman and officer of like rank in the navy. The nickname is a misnomer, however, for Captain Vere, a bachelor of about forty, is a quiet, brooding intellectual who reads constantly. He is also a fine commander, but he lacks the flamboyance of the more famous Lord Nelson. He suffers greatly at having to testify before the three-member court against Billy Budd, whom he recognizes as an efficient, attractive, impulsive sailor. He, too, seems trapped by regulations (tightened during the Great Mutiny) which state that strik-

ing an officer is a capital offense. When Claggart comes to Captain Vere with foggy, unsubstantiated charges that Billy is mutinous, the captain summons Billy to his quarters only to prove that Claggart is a false witness.

John Claggart, the master-at-arms of the ship. Because guns have replaced the many small arms used in naval fighting, his duties are mainly to oversee the crew and its work. When Claggart observes Billy Budd, he quickly becomes envious of the personal beauty of the young man. The only basis for the charges that Claggart makes against Billy is that an afterguardsman, a troublemaker, tries to be friendly and confidential with the foretopman. Because he joined the navy for no apparent reason and because he never makes any reference to his previous life ashore, Claggart is a man of mystery about whom many rumors are circulated on the ship.

The Dansker, an old veteran who serves as mainmastman in his watch. He likes Billy from the start and is the one who nicknames him "Baby." When Billy comes to him for counsel and to ask why his petty mistakes are getting him into trouble, the Dansker astutely remarks that "Jimmy Legs" (meaning the master-at-arms) is down on him.

The Afterguardsman, a troublemaking sailor. He approaches Billy and tries to tempt him to join an incipient mutiny. Billy angrily rebuffs him but does not report the incident to any officer.

Lieutenant Ratcliffe, the officer who goes aboard the *Rights-of-Man* and selects Billy to be impressed into his majesty's service.

The Story

In 1797, the British merchant ship *Rights-of-Man*, named after the famous reply of Thomas Paine to Edmund Burke's criticism of the French Revolution, was close to home after a long voyage. As it neared England, the merchant vessel was stopped by a man-of-war, HMS *Indomitable*, and an officer from the warship went aboard the *Rights-of-Man* to impress sailors for military service. This practice was necessary at the time to provide men to work the large number of ships that Great Britain had at sea for protection against the French.

The captain of the *Rights-of-Man* was relieved to have only one sailor taken from his ship, but he was unhappy because the man was his best sailor, Billy Budd. Billy was what his captain called a peacemaker; because of his strength and good looks, he was a natural leader among the other sailors, and he used his influence to keep them contented and hard at work. Billy Budd seemed utterly without guile, a man who tried to promote the welfare of the merchant ship because he liked peace and was willing to work hard to please his superiors. When informed that he was not to return to England but was to head for duty with the fleet in the Mediterranean Sea, he did not appear disturbed; he liked the sea, and he had no family ties. He was an orphan who had been left as a tiny baby in a basket on the doorstep of a family in Bristol.

As the boat from the warship took him away from the merchant ship, Billy called farewell to the *Rights-of-Man* by name, a deed that greatly embarrassed the naval officer who had impressed him. The remark was unwittingly satirical of the treatment to which Billy was being subjected by the navy.

Once aboard the *Indomitable*, Billy quickly made himself at home with the ship and the men with whom he served in the foretop. Because of his good personality and his willingness to work, he soon made a place for himself with his messmates and also won the regard of the officers under whom he served.

At first, the master-at-arms, a petty officer named John Claggart, seemed particularly friendly to Billy—a fortunate circumstance, Billy thought, for the master-at-arms was the equivalent of the chief of police aboard the warship. The young sailor was rather surprised, therefore, when he received reprimands for slight breaches of conduct that were normally overlooked. The reprimands came from the ship's corporals who were Claggart's underlings. Since the reprimands indicated that something was wrong, Billy grew perturbed; he had a deadly fear of being the recipient of a flogging in public. He thought that he could never stand such treatment.

Anxious to discover what was wrong, Billy consulted an old sailor, who told him that Claggart was filled with animosity for the young man. The reason for the animosity was not known, and because the old man could give him no reason, Billy refused to believe that the master-at-arms was his enemy. Claggart had taken a deep dislike to Billy Budd on sight, however, and for no reason except a personal antipathy that the young man's appearance had generated. Sly as he was, Claggart kept, or tried to keep, his feelings to himself. He operated through underlings against Billy.

Not long after he had been warned by the old sailor, Billy spilled a bowl of soup in the path of Claggart as he was inspecting the mess. Even then, Claggart smiled and pretended to treat the incident as a joke, for Billy had done the deed accidentally. A few nights later, however, someone awakened Billy and told him to go to a secluded spot in the ship. Billy went and met a sailor who tried to tempt him into joining a mutiny. The incident bothered Billy, who could not understand why anyone had approached him as a possible conspirator. Such activity was not a part of his personality, and he was disgusted to find it in others.

A few days later, the master-at-arms approached the captain of the ship and reported that he and his corporals had discovered that a mutiny was being fomented by Billy Budd. Captain Vere, a very fair officer, reminded Claggart of the seriousness of the charge and warned the master-at-arms that bearing false witness in such a case called for the death penalty. Because Claggart persisted in his accusations, Captain Vere ended the interview on deck, a place he thought too public, and ordered the master-at-arms and Billy Budd to his cabin. There Captain Vere commanded Claggart to repeat his accusations. When he did, Billy became emotionally so upset that he was tongue-tied. In utter frustration at being unable to reply to the infamous charges, Billy hit the master-at-arms. The petty officer was killed when he fell heavily to the floor.

Captain Vere was filled with consternation, for he, like everyone except the master-at-arms, liked Billy Budd. After the surgeon had pronounced the petty officer dead, the captain immediately convened a court-martial to try Billy for assaulting and murdering a superior officer. Because England was at war, and because two mutinies had already occurred in the British navy that year, action had to be taken immediately. The captain could not afford to overlook the offense.

The court-martial, acting under regulations, found Billy

Budd guilty and sentenced him to be hanged from a yardarm the following morning. Even under the circumstances of Claggart's death, there was no alternative. The only person who could have testified that the charge of mutiny was false was the man who had been killed.

All the ship's company were dismayed when informed of the sentence. Yet Billy bore no animosity for the captain or for the officers who had sentenced him to die. When he was placed beneath the yardarm the following morning, he called out a blessing on Captain Vere, who, he realized, had no other choice in the matter but to hang him. It was quite strange, too, that Billy Budd's calm seemed even to control his corpse. Unlike most hanged men, he never twitched when hauled aloft by the neck. The surgeon's mate, when queried by his messmates, had no answer for this unique behavior.

Some months later, Captain Vere was wounded in action. In the last hours before his death, he was heard to murmur Billy Budd's name over and over again. The common sailors did not forget the hanged man either. For many years, the yardarm from which he had been hanged was kept track of by sailors, who regarded it almost as reverently as Christians might revere the Cross.

Critical Evaluation

According to Harrison Hayford and Merton M. Sealts, Jr., the editors of *Billy Budd, Sailor (An Inside Narrative)* (1962), Herman Melville began the novel in 1886, developed and revised it through several stages, and then left it unpublished when he died in 1891. The Hayford-Sealts text, published in 1963, differs considerably from earlier ones published in 1924 and 1948. Among the noteworthy differences is the change of name for the ship on which the action occurs, from *Indomitable* to *Bellipotent*. The symbolism of the latter name relates it to the emphasis that Melville places in the novel on war, humanity's involvement in it, and the effects of war on the individual.

That Melville did not wish his readers to mistake the nature or the general intent of his novel is clear in his early warning that Billy "is not presented as a conventional hero" and "that the story in which he is the main figure is no romance." The story itself is extremely simple. A young sailor on a British merchant ship is impressed for service on a British warship. He offers no resistance but accepts his new assignment with goodwill and attempts to be an ideal sailor. The ship's master-at-arms takes an immediate and unwarranted dislike to the sailor, plots to cause him trouble, and then accuses him to the captain of having plotted mutiny. The captain summons the sailor, asks him to defend himself, and sees him strike and accidentally kill his accuser. The captain imprisons him, convenes a court-martial, condemns him to death, and has him hanged. This plot is the vehicle for Melville's extended use of moral symbolism throughout the novel.

Billy Budd, Claggart, and Captain Vere are all clearly symbolic characters, and Melville brings out the symbolism through information supplied about their backgrounds, language used to describe them, and authorial comment of moral, theological, and philosophical import.

Melville employs a double symbolism for Billy: He is both a Christ-figure and a representation of innocent or Adamic humanity. Before Billy is removed from the merchant ship, the captain explains to the lieutenant from the warship that Billy has been most useful in quieting the "ratpit of quarrels" that formerly infested his forecastle. "Not that he preached to them or said or did anything in particular; but a virtue went out of him, sugaring the sour ones." The captain's words echo Luke 6:19: "And the whole multitude sought to touch him: for there went virtue out of him, and healed them all." When the lieutenant is adamant about Billy's impressment, the captain's last words to him are: "You are going to take away my peacemaker." Again, there is no mistaking the reference to the Prince of Peace. In describing Billy as he appears to the crew and officers on the warship, Melville mentions "something in the mobile expression, and every chance attitude and movement, something suggestive of a mother eminently favored by Love and the Graces." An officer asks, "Who was your father?" and Billy answers, "God knows, sir." Though Billy explains that he was told he was a foundling, the hint has already been given of divine paternity. Melville drops the Christ symbolism of Billy until the confrontation with Claggart when Billy, unable to reply to Captain Vere's request that he defend himself, shows in his face "an expression which was as a crucifixion to behold." At the hanging, Billy's last words are, "God bless Captain Vere!" and the reader recalls Christ's words on the Cross, "Father, forgive them; for they know not what they do." The symbolism continues with the hanging itself. Captain Vere gives a silent signal and "At the same moment it chanced that the vapory fleece hanging low in the East was shot through with a soft glory as of the fleece of the Lamb of God seen in mystical vision, and simultaneously therewith, watched by the wedged mass of upturned faces, Billy ascended; and, ascending, took the full rose of the dawn." In the final chapter, Melville adds that

> The spar from which the foretopman was suspended was for some few years kept trace of by the bluejackets. . . . To them a chip from it was as a piece of the Cross. . . . They recalled a fresh young image of the Handsome Sailor, that face never deformed by a sneer or subtler vile freak of the heart within. This impression of him was doubtless deepened by the fact that he was gone, and in a measure mysteriously gone.

Even in the verses which close the novel, with Billy's words, "They'll give me a nibble—bit o' biscuit ere I go./ Sure a messmate will reach me the last parting cup," one cannot miss the Last Supper reference.

Yet, though Billy is Christlike, he belongs to humanity, and Melville repeatedly employs him as an archetype. His complete innocence is first suggested in Melville's comment that "Billy in many respects was little more than a sort of upright barbarian, much such perhaps as Adam presumably might have been ere the urbane Serpent wriggled himself into his company." Later, Captain Vere thinks of the handsome sailor as one "who in the nude might have posed for a statue of young Adam before the Fall." Yet innocence will not protect Billy. As Adam's human imperfection led to his fall, so an imperfection in Billy leads to his destruction. In times of stress, Billy stutters or is even speechless and, says Melville, "In this particular Billy was a striking instance that the arch interferer, the envious marplot of Eden, still has more or less to do with every human consignment to this planet of Earth."

The innocence that is his "blinder" causes Billy (or, "Baby," as he is called) to fail to see and be on guard against the evil in Claggart, and his "vocal defect" deprives him of speech when he faces his false accuser. He strikes out as instinctively as a cornered animal, and his enemy dies. Billy did not intend to commit murder but, as Captain Vere tells his officers, "The prisoner's deed—with that alone we have to do." Billy does not live in an animal's instinctive world of nature. His life is bound by social law and particularly by naval law in a time of war. As Captain Vere explains, innocent Billy will be acquitted by God at "the last Assizes," but "We proceed under the law of the Mutiny Act." That act demands death for Billy's deed, and he dies in order that discipline may be maintained in the great navy that must protect Great Britain against its enemies.

As Billy symbolizes innocence, Claggart represents the spirit of evil, the foe of innocence. There is a mystery in Claggart's enmity toward harmless Billy. For, says Melville, "what can more partake of the mysterious than an antipathy spontaneous and profound such as is evoked in certain exceptional mortals by the mere aspect of some other mortal, however harmless he may be, if not called forth by this very harmlessness itself?" Claggart's evil nature was not acquired, "not engendered by vicious training or corrupting books or licentious living, but born with him and innate." He can recognize the good but is "powerless to be it." His energies are self-destructive; his nature is doomed to "act out to the end the part allotted to it." Although he destroys an innocent man, he must himself be destroyed as well.

As Billy at one extreme is Christlike and childishly innocent and Claggart at the other is satanic, Captain Vere represents the kind of officer needed to preserve such an institution as the navy that he serves. He is a man of balance, "mindful of the welfare of his men, but never tolerating an infraction of discipline; thoroughly versed in the science of his profession, and intrepid to the verge of temerity, though never injudiciously so." His reading tastes incline toward "books treating of actual men and events . . . history, biography, and unconventional writers like Montaigne, who, free from cant and convention, honestly and in the spirit of common sense philosophize upon realities." More intellectual than his fellow officers, he seems somewhat "pedantic" to them, and Melville hints that, in reporting Vere's long speech to his junior officers of the drumhead court, he has simplified the phrasing of the argument. Yet elsewhere Captain Vere's speech is simple, brief, and direct.

Although Captain Vere is a thoughtful, reserved man, he is not without feeling. Quickly recognizing Billy's inability to speak when he has been ordered to defend himself, he soothingly says, "There is no hurry, my boy. Take your time, take your time." He is even capable of momentary vehemence as when he surprises the surgeon with the outburst, "Struck dead by an angel of God! Yet the angel must hang!" but he quickly regains control. Melville does not report what Captain Vere says to Billy when he informs him privately of the death sentence, though he suggests that Vere may have shown compassion by catching Billy "to his heart, even as Abraham may have caught young Isaac on the brink of resolutely offering him up." Vere is seemingly overcome after Billy's last words, "God bless Captain Vere!" and the echo from the crew, since "either through stoic self-control or a sort of momentary paralysis induced by emotional shock," he stands "rigidly erect as a musket." The final view of a man whose heart balanced his mind is given in the report of Captain Vere's dying words, "Billy Budd, Billy Budd," spoken not in "the accents of remorse." Though capable of fatherly feeling toward an unfortunate young man, he had caused to be carried out a sentence he believed was needed if the strength of order was to be maintained in the turmoil of war.

Although *Billy Budd* has occasionally been read as a veiled attack on the unjust treatment of a hapless individual by an impersonal, authoritarian state, a close reading of the novel makes it seem more likely that Melville's intent was to show, especially through Captain Vere, that the protection of a state during a time of war must inevitably involve on occasion the sacrifice of an individual.

Melville does include scattered satiric comments on the imperfections of both people and organizations, but his overwhelmingly favorable portrait of Captain Vere as a high-principled and dedicated representative of the state leaves the reader with the final impression that Melville had at last become sadly resigned to the fact that imperfect humanity living in an imperfect world has no guarantee against suffering an unjust fate. That Billy uncomplainingly accepts his end, even asking God's blessing upon the man who is sending him to death, suggests that Melville too had become reconciled to the eternal coexistence of good and evil in the world.

THE BLOOD OF THE LAMB

Type of work: Novel
Author: Peter De Vries (1910-   )
Type of plot: Comic realism
Time of plot: 1920's-1950's
Locale: Chicago, Illinois, and the suburbs of New York City
First published: 1962

The Blood of the Lamb uses a comic approach to present its narrator's search for religious meaning. The characters are typical of De Vries' lighter novels, but this story has an atypically serious message.

Principal Characters

Don Wanderhope, the narrator, the second son of Dutch immigrants. The story begins during his childhood, when he is exposed to an argument concerning the nature or even the existence of God. Later, he struggles with religion in an effort to find meaning in the deaths of several loved ones, including a girlfriend, his mother, his wife, and his daughter.

Ben Wanderhope, Don's father, an intelligent but ill-educated owner of a garbage collection business. Ben's religiosity wavers according to circumstances, and confusion about God's role in the world eventually sends him to a mental hospital.

Greta Wigbaldy, who dates Don and later, after he has returned from treatment for tuberculosis, marries him. She reveals that she had an affair with a married man before marrying Don, and that the affair resulted in a child that Greta gave up for adoption. Her renewed involvement in religion makes Greta begin to doubt her own worth. She is unfaithful to Don, begins drinking, and eventually commits suicide.

Carol Wanderhope, the daughter of Don and Greta who is stricken with leukemia.

Rena Baker, a woman with whom Don falls in love while he is at a sanatorium for treatment of tuberculosis.

The Story

The Blood of the Lamb opens when Don Wanderhope is a child. He listens to an argument about evolution carried on by his father, Ben; his brother, Louie; his uncle Hans; and Dr. Berkenbosch, who has stopped in to check on Don's grandmother. Ben Wanderhope, who wavers in his support of the Dutch Reformed religion, states that he does not believe in hell, throwing more doubts about the literal truth of the Bible into Don's mind. In a private conversation, Don questions Dr. Berkenbosch about claims made by Louie that human fetuses exhibit various stages of evolution in their development. This conversation offers one of many comic moments, as Dr. Berkenbosch, who barely made it through medical school at a time when standards were quite low, misinterprets Don's questions. When asked if he would take a patient with gills and a tail, for example, he states that doctors do not turn patients away—even if they cannot pay.

Louie, a student at the University of Chicago, becomes ill while on a visit home. On his deathbed, his parents question him again about his lack of faith. He assures them that he has no doubts about religion, which they interpret to mean that he has returned to faith. Only Don sees him smile, and only he knows that his parents have completely misinterpreted Louie's statement.

Louie remains a model for Don as the boy grows up. It is in his teenage years that Don shows the cavalier attitudes typical of De Vries' protagonists. He yearns to be a sophisticate and to rise above his background. He begins a series of romantic dalliances. One young woman finally attracts him into a fairly serious relationship, until he discovers to his horror that her father is an organ grinder. Don's social status is anything but enhanced by his father, who runs a garbage collection business and makes collections personally. A comic moment occurs when Ben, with Don as a passenger, accidentally backs his truck too close to the edge of a dump. It slides into the dump. Ben Wanderhope disappears into the garbage, all the while singing the praises of God. Both Wanderhopes eventually escape, but the truck is lost.

Don then befriends Archie Winkler, a fellow college student who lives in a large house and throws extravagant parties. Don thinks that he has fallen in with his desired type of crowd until Archie begins asking for loans, loans that are never paid back. Don breaks with that social set by taking all the money from Archie's wallet while at one of the parties.

Greta Wigbaldy, the daughter of a home builder, draws Don into a relationship. Greta's father discovers the couple in bed at the model home in one of his developments while taking a client on a tour. The moment, which would have been horrifying to the participants, is treated comically. Don is expected to marry Greta, with one of the development homes as a wedding present from Mr. Wigbaldy. Don discovers that Greta hates the idea of the banality of housing developments as much as he does, and that she also dreads the idea of marriage. These discoveries paradoxically draw them closer. Before the marriage can take place, however, Don is diagnosed with tuberculosis.

The diagnosis allows indefinite postponement of his marriage to Greta. It also moves the book into its second of three sections, as Don travels to Denver to undertake a cure at a sanatorium run by the Dutch Reformed church. The first part of the novel shows Don as a carefree young man interested in the pursuit of worldly goods and social status. The second section shows him fighting his own mortality and questioning how God, if there is such a being, could choose to strike down good people. Don is not seriously ill and treats his minor case of tuberculosis as a reprieve from marriage rather than as a cause for concern, and he begins his old pattern of trying to pick up women.

Don falls in love with Rena Baker while at the sanatorium. Rena is both sicker than Don and more devout in her faith. When Rena asks whether Don prays for her, he answers that that would imply that God is a personal being who chooses to make people ill. He says that he would rather believe that people are the victims of chance rather than dignifying any such capricious force with the name of Providence.

Don leaves the sanatorium when he learns that his father shows signs of mental illness. Don finds a mental home for Ben and discovers that Greta Wigbaldy also is a patient there. Her parents lead Don to believe that he is the cause of her depressive state, and he agrees to marry her. The death of Don's mother while all this is going on is treated incidentally, in one sentence.

Afraid to discuss her past with Don, Greta sends him an anonymous note before their wedding. His direct questions allow her to discuss her affair with a married man, an affair that led to a child whom Greta put up for adoption. It was guilt over this affair, rather than regret over sinning with Don, that led her to the mental hospital. Don agrees to marry Greta anyway.

Soon after their marriage, Greta leaves the Dutch Reformed church and joins another. Don refuses to condemn Greta for her sins, as her new evangelist insists. Their religious differences create strains in the marriage, but Greta's pregnancy smooths some of the problems. The pregnancy provides the transition into the third and last section of the novel, involving the family's life in New York. Carol, the Wanderhopes' child, is born, and Don is transferred to the New York branch of the advertising agency at which he works. The family moves to the suburb of Westchester, which Greta finds stultifying. Her emotional state worsens, and she turns to drink and promiscuity. After several years of life in Westchester, Greta commits suicide.

Carol falls ill at the age of eleven and is diagnosed with leukemia. Her illness and treatment compose the remainder of the novel. This is the heart of the book, in which Don has his most serious confrontations with his religious beliefs or lack of them. He alternates between hope and despair as various treatments seem to improve Carol's condition then ultimately fail. Through conversations between Don and other parents at Carol's hospital, the novel confronts the theological issue of why the innocent, especially children, suffer. Don discovers a statue of St. Jude, the patron of hopeless causes, outside a church near Carol's hospital, and prays to it that Carol last just one more year. During Carol's final months, she becomes more mature and thoughtful and provides comfort to her father. She succumbs to her illness, and the blood of the lamb is sacrificed. In a last tragic act of slapstick comedy, Don takes the birthday cake that his daughter never had a chance to taste and hurls it at a Christ figure at the church. Don discovers a tape-recorded message left by Carol in which she explains his religious beliefs to him, using words that he had written for an alumni newspaper. This provides a measure of resolution to his internal debate.

Critical Evaluation

Peter De Vries has been accused of being overly autobiographical in his many novels. His protagonists are often young, rakish characters of immigrant backgrounds, and incidents in his novels often appear to be recollections rather than purely fictitious accounts. This identification with his characters does make for lively, true-to-life stories, even if it makes his novels somewhat repetitive.

The Blood of the Lamb is perhaps De Vries' most serious novel, and it is typically autobiographical. Don Wanderhope is the son of immigrant parents, with a background similar to that of De Vries himself. The focus of this novel, the death of a daughter from leukemia, also comes from De Vries' own life. His own daughter, Emily, died of that disease before adolescence.

De Vries uses comedy to advantage in emphasizing tragedy. Many of the incidents described in the novel are comic because they illustrate the lack of control that people have over their own circumstances. This is the message of the novel, that there is no control, even at the hands of God. There is no deity, Don decides, that can be held responsible for human suffering. God is not responsible for human tragedy, and prayer for the sake of avoiding or alleviating human suffering is pointless.

Each of the many deaths described in the novel reinforces the theme that death often is meaningless. The fact that the narrator describes his own mother's death only in passing, as an event incidental to the story that he tells, illustrates how little there is to be learned from human tragedy. De Vries does not go so far as to make the deaths themselves comic, but he does take a lighthearted approach to near-misses and to otherwise tragic circumstances. His father's sinking into the garbage dump, which would have been harrowing in real life and could have been presented to great dramatic effect, instead comes off as comic. Ben Wanderhope's praising of God as he sinks into the dump also illustrates that some people turn to their religions only when in desperate circumstances. De Vries also turns a birthday party at his daughter's hospital into a tragicomic incident. If one could not laugh at the scene, then one surely would cry. De Vries chooses laughter to make his point that innocents, even children, do suffer, and often capriciously.

The Blood of the Lamb is about the search for meaning on two levels. The first section of the book touches lightly on religion, but it is more concerned with Don's attempts to rise above his middle-class background. This is a common theme in De Vries' novels. This preoccupation with worldly status is interposed nicely with the concern for religious meaning that forms the focus of the third part of the story. Ultimately, De Vries concludes that both of these human quests are pointless, and that life must be treated as a comedy. Those who become too concerned with the search for meaning will, like Ben Wanderhope, end up driving themselves insane.

THE BONFIRE OF THE VANITIES

Type of work: Novel
Author: Tom Wolfe (1931-   )
Type of plot: Realistic tragicomedy
Time of plot: 1980's
Locale: New York City
First published: 1987

In The Bonfire of the Vanities, *Wolfe explores the world of New York City in the 1980's, emphasizing the greed, hatred, racial tensions, crime, class conflict, and hypocrisy of the city and the time. The author seeks to redefine the American novel, creating a social statement out of a combination of fact, fiction, and personal ideology.*

Principal Characters

Sherman McCoy, a phenomenally successful young investment broker who is accidentally involved in injuring an African-American teenager. He becomes embroiled in a criminal trial that inflames the various ethnic groups in New York City.

Judy McCoy, Sherman's beautiful but fading wife, who considers herself an interior decorator and squanders her husband's money on expensive furniture and artwork.

Maria Ruskin, Sherman's sexy, Southern-born mistress, who is actually driving McCoy's car when they run down the teenager.

Peter Fallow, an alcoholic, freeloading British journalist who gets wind of the incident and exaggerates the story in order to salvage his shaky career.

Lawrence Kramer, a young assistant district attorney who hopes to become famous by prosecuting Sherman McCoy.

Thomas Killian, McCoy's streetwise defense attorney in the first trial.

Judge Myron Kovitsky, the feisty Jewish judge who presides at Sherman McCoy's trial for reckless endangerment and who provokes a riot by dismissing the case.

Reverend Reginald Bacon, an African-American minister with questionable credentials. He is making a fortune by misappropriating money donated by well-meaning white liberals to help impoverished African Americans.

The Story

At only thirty-eight years of age, Sherman McCoy is phenomenally successful at selling bonds for a major Wall Street firm. He is married and has a small daughter who attends one of the best private schools. The McCoys live in a Park Avenue co-op apartment valued at close to $3,000,000. Sherman considers himself a "Master of the Universe" yet somehow can hardly manage on his income of one million dollars a year.

Sherman has a mistress who is younger and sexier than his wife, Judy. Maria Ruskin is married to a wealthy old man and is waiting for him to die. One night, while driving Maria home from the airport, Sherman takes a wrong turn and finds himself in the most dangerous part of the Bronx. In his Mercedes sports coupe loaded with Maria's expensive luggage, he is a prime target for a mugging. When he finally comes to a ramp that will take them back onto the expressway, he finds that it has been deliberately barricaded with rubbish. Two African-American teenagers approach as he is trying to remove the obstructions; they are obviously planning to rob him.

Maria panics and gets behind the wheel. As soon as Sherman jumps in beside her, she guns the engine and drives off, but they hear a sound that might be that of the car hitting a human body. Later, they read in the newspaper that a nineteen-year-old African-American youth named Henry Lamb was struck by a hit-and-run driver in that general vicinity and is hospitalized in critical condition. Sherman and Maria decide not to report the incident to the police because they do not want their spouses to learn that they were out together.

Henry Lamb gives his mother a partial license number of Sherman's car before slipping into a coma, but he does not reveal anything else about the incident. Reverend Reginald Bacon, a leader of the African-American community in Harlem, stirs up agitation over the incident because it appears that a rich white man callously ran down a poor ghetto youth and drove off without even bothering to see if he was dead or alive. Peter Fallow, an alcoholic journalist who works for a tabloid that specializes in scandal-mongering, adds fuel to the fire by continuing to publicize what would otherwise be a trivial traffic incident. The police are pressured into making an intensive investigation, which involves interviewing every owner of a Mercedes whose license number resembles that of the vehicle in question.

When the police get around to Sherman, he is all nerves from guilt and apprehension and so clumsy about lying that he arouses their strong suspicions, even though they cannot imagine why an aristocrat living in a Park Avenue apartment would be driving around in the South Bronx. Further investigation reveals such damaging information as the fact that, on the night of the hit-and-run incident, he came home looking shaken and disheveled.

Sherman hires a streetwise lawyer named Thomas Killian to defend him and begins to learn about the sordid realities of the criminal justice system. The district attorney relishes the political advantage involved in prosecuting the "Great White Defendant" instead of the poor, "ignorant" African Americans and Hispanics who flood the criminal courts. Assistant District Attorney Lawrence Kramer hopes to advance his career and is also resentful of people like Sherman who live in multimillion-dollar Park Avenue apartments while he is barely getting by on $30,000 a year.

Eventually, Sherman finds himself given a forced leave of absence because of the unfavorable attention that his troubles are attracting to his prestigious Wall Street firm. Without his big income, Sherman is soon in desperate financial straits and has to sell his co-op apartment. The proceeds are quickly tied up, however, in a civil suit initiated by Reverend Bacon and Henry Lamb's mother. Sherman is thrown into cells with the lowest scum of the city streets and is horrified by his experiences. He has been educated at the best schools and has never before seen the seamy side of New York life.

The irony of the story is that no one really cares about Sherman's alleged crime or the fate of young Henry Lamb, who remains hospitalized in critical condition. Everyone is either concerned with saving face or capitalizing on the incident in one way or another, with the exception of the fair-minded Judge Myron Kovitsky, who still believes in justice and other old-fashioned values.

The exposure to the harsh reality of life in New York City toughens McCoy and turns him into a sort of street warrior crusading for justice. At the end of the story, he has been stripped of all of his money and possessions and is battling the hostile mob with his bare fists while awaiting his third criminal trial, in which he is now charged with manslaughter because of the death of Lamb in the interim.

Critical Evaluation

Tom Wolfe is generally considered the leading spokesperson of the so-called school of new journalism. Members of this school, which includes such prominent writers as Gay Talese, Jimmy Breslin, Norman Mailer, Hunter S. Thompson, and Truman Capote, apply the techniques of fiction to the reporting of actual events. They also interject their own personalities, prejudices, and stylistic idiosyncrasies into their writings, in marked contrast to the traditional style of journalism that calls for scrupulously accurate and dispassionate reporting of the bare facts. *The Bonfire of the Vanities* was Wolfe's first attempt at writing a novel. In a famous and highly controversial article published in *Harper's Magazine* in November, 1989, entitled "Stalking the Billion-Footed Beast: A Literary Manifesto for the New Social Novel," Wolfe explained why he had departed from journalism to write what he described as a realistic novel in the tradition of Honoré de Balzac, Émile Zola, Charles Dickens, and William Makepeace Thackeray:

> To me the idea of writing a novel about this astonishing metropolis, a big novel, cramming as much of New York City between covers as you could, was the most tempting, the most challenging, and the most obvious idea an American writer could possibly have.

He criticized the esoteric literary experimentalism that had dominated fiction for much of the twentieth century and urged American novelists to return to the great tradition of realism to depict the fantastic American culture that was influencing the entire modern world.

Wolfe has a Ph.D. from Yale University in American studies, which partially explains his sociological approach to both journalism and fiction. He is best at describing class behavior. *The Bonfire of the Vanities* does not really represent much of a departure from such insightful works as his well-known essays *Radical Chic and Mau-Mauing the Flak Catchers* (1970), in which he satirizes the self-flagellating upper-class liberals who financed and toadied to the very revolutionaries who wanted to destroy them. Just as many of Wolfe's works are fact with a strong additive of fiction, so *The Bonfire of the Vanities* is fiction with a strong additive of fact.

He believes that novelists have a duty to investigate the world about which they write with as much diligence as journalists, and he praises such writers as Sinclair Lewis, Dickens, and Zola for doing just that. He states in "Stalking the Billion-Footed Beast" that "literary genius, in prose, consists of proportions more on the order of 65 percent material and 35 percent the talent in the sacred crucible."

Wolfe states that his immediate model was Thackeray's *Vanity Fair: A Novel Without a Hero* (1847-1848), that re-creates the city of London at the apogee of the British Empire. *The Bonfire of the Vanities* is Wolfe's attempt to portray modern New York City in all of its intricate and fascinating detail.

Wolfe's characters are all types symbolizing the diverse ethnic mix of the city. He is more interested in capturing the city itself than in creating unique individuals, and for this he was criticized. It was charged that his novel is unimaginative and unadventurous in a creative sense, too much like the colorful and satirical reporting for which he became famous. There may be an element of truth to this accusation, but at the same time, even his harshest critics admitted that Wolfe had written a novel that is not only thought provoking but also almost impossible to put down.

Wolfe's use of fiction rather than reporting makes it possible for him to leave his incendiary thesis implicit rather than spelling it out explicitly. The reader has to assume that Wolfe is implying that New York City is in danger of being destroyed by hordes of ignorant, mostly nonwhite immigrants—"Puerto Ricans, West Indians, Haitians, Dominicans, Cubans, Colombians, Hondurans, Koreans, Chinese, Thais, Vietnamese, Ecuadorians, Panamanians, Filipinos, Albanians, Senegalese, and Afro-Americans!"—who cannot assume the intricate roles played by the educated whites who make it possible for

such a high-technology, capital-intensive, essentially white-collar city as New York to exist at all.

Wolfe scorns white liberalism, believing it is not only hypocritical but suicidal as well. He suggests that the ignorant masses are manipulated by self-seeking demagogues and need to be handled with an iron hand rather than coddled with welfare and other forms of bribery. Above all, he implies that New York is a dog-eat-dog city and that whites are foolish to feel sentimental about the problems of minorities: The members of minority groups feel nothing but hatred for whites and would treat them even worse if their positions were reversed. Many people—especially liberals—disagree vehemently with Wolfe, calling him an elitist, a reactionary, a neofascist, and worse.

The plot of *The Bonfire of the Vanities* owes more to Theodore Dreiser's fatalistic *An American Tragedy* (1925) than to Thackeray. All the legal discussions by the police, the prosecutors, and the defense attorneys sound very much like what occurred in Dreiser's novel after the hero, Clyde Griffiths, was arrested for murdering Roberta Alden. In both novels, no one is really concerned about the victim or the defendant or about "justice" or "truth": All are concerned about making money, winning victories, and advancing their careers. What Wolfe lacks as a fiction writer is obvious if he is compared with Dreiser. Wolfe lacks the human compassion that Dreiser possessed in abundance. Where Dreiser was weak in technical skill, Wolfe is outstanding, but where the unsophisticated Dreiser excelled in conveying simple human emotions, Wolfe is most deficient. Wolfe is essentially a satirist and a student of sociology who writes about people as if they were specimens under his microscope.

No one, however, can fail to be impressed by Wolfe's talent or to admire his fortitude in expressing his conservative convictions in the teeth of the dominant liberal spirit of his time. *The Bonfire of the Vanities* is an important work because it served as a model for "the new social novel" and sought to change the direction of American fiction. It was the first important novel to deal with the most important sociological phenomenon in the United States of the late twentieth century: the disintegration of the white power structure in all the major cities.

THE BOSTONIANS

Type of work: Novel
Author: Henry James (1843-1916)
Type of plot: Psychological realism
Time of plot: Early 1870's
Locale: Boston, Massachusetts, and New York City
First published: 1885-1886

Set in Boston in the early 1870's, The Bostonians *is James's meditation on the American woman and on the women's rights movement as practiced by both misguided reformers and true revolutionaries.*

Principal Characters

Olive Chancellor, the portrait of the Boston lady. She is won over to the cause of the suffragettes but exercises poor taste in attempting to accomplish their goals.

Mrs. Adeline Luna, her sister. She is a worldly woman who does not subscribe to the concept of the "new woman."

Basil Random, her cousin from Mississippi. A lawyer practicing in New York City, he falls in love with Verena Tarrant's voice, if not her ideas, and is able to persuade her to marry him. He believes that people must excel within their appointed stations in society.

Verena Tarrant, Olive's protégée. An attractive young woman, Verena possesses few ideas of her own but is groomed for the cause of the suffragette movement. She is saved from this fate, however, by Basil Random, who carries her off to Mississippi as his bride.

"Doctor" Selah Tarrant, Verena's father, a mesmeric healer who is a fake.

Mrs. Tarrant, Verena's mother. She is the daughter of Boston abolitionists.

Miss Birdseye, the eighty-year-old reformer who is both sincere and ineffectual. James's favorite character, she dies believing that Basil Random has been persuaded of the need for a women's movement.

Dr. Prance, a woman who is a true doctor and who, in her real and practical way, is doing more for the women's rights movement than the suffragettes.

Mrs. Burrage, a New York society hostess.

Henry Burrage, her son, a Harvard undergraduate who courts Verena.

Mrs. Farrinder, a suffragette campaigner who is suspicious of "Doctor" Tarrant.

The Bostonians is the longest of James's novels in an American setting, and in spite of his later dissatisfaction with its middle section or the high promise given to the unfinished *The Ivory Tower* (1917), it is his most important fictive statement on the United States. The name and setting of the novel are significant; two of his other American novels, *The Europeans* (1878) and *Washington Square* (1880), are set in Boston and New York City, respectively. *The Bostonians* begins in Charles Street and ends in the Music Hall in Boston, but its second half begins in New York, which James always claimed as his native city. James had difficulty selecting the title, but when he had settled on *The Bostonians*, he knew it was an exact description of the contents and of his meaning.

The best commentary on the work is found in James's preface to the New York edition; its significance in James's American canon is discussed by F. O. Matthiessen in his introduction to *The American Novels and Stories of Henry James* (1947). James had several times tried to clarify his famous passage, in his life of Nathaniel Hawthorne, on what the United States offered and lacked in respect to the novelist. By his experience, James himself was limited as an American novelist, and *The Bostonians* was his attempt to write on a subject that was at once local and typical, a local manifestation of a national trait. James chose the distinguishing feature of American life known as the "American woman," whose novelty he had presented in Isabel Archer and other heroines. The locality was the Boston he knew of in the early 1870's and the New York he lovingly introduces in the novel. For his purpose, more important than the locale of Boston was its atmosphere of exhausted triumph after abolition and the hectic pursuit of new reform movements, especially that of women's rights. James's general distaste for the reformers if not for their proposals may be sensed in his portraits in the novel.

The "Bostonians" may be variously identified as one, two, or more characters, but the term, used only once, refers to Olive Chancellor and Verena Tarrant. Although James referred to Verena as the "heroine," the true "Bostonian" is Olive, the embodiment of the clash between discriminating and undiscriminating action in Boston of the 1870's. Destined by nature and appearance to be a "New England Nun," she becomes in the very last paragraph of the novel a Boston battler, haranguing a capacity crowd in Boston's largest auditorium in place of Verena, who has in the nick of time been carried away by Basil Ransom to meet her proper destiny as his wife. These three play out an ironic and psychologically penetrating form of the eternal triangle.

James seems to approve Verena's fate, largely because she is unawakened throughout almost the whole novel; she remains a pretty young girl with no mind and of little interest to James. Basil Ransom is a Mississippian trying to revive the family plantation by practicing law in New York; he does not have ideas (until he begins to write reactionary articles) but lives by a code: Everyone must do his or her work well in one's appointed station in life. When he tries to express this idea to Verena as they sit in Central Park, she is horrified and fascinated because there is no "Progress" in his code. In the end, however, Basil and Verena pair off as a fairly normal couple. What Mississippi was to make of Verena would have made a superb sequel to this work, but James did not know the South and treats it simply as the last reservoir of acceptable masculinity from which he plucks his necessary hero.

Olive Chancellor was much more in James's acquaintance. With no other family ties except those to her sister, Mrs. Luna, comfortably settled in Charles Street, she had time, intelligence, taste, and money, which she diffused quietly through twenty committees and reform groups. She is the very portrait of a Boston lady; her tragic flaw is to allow her desire for real action to overrule her taste: She falls in love with Verena's sweet stream of humbug as Basil falls in love with Verena's voice. This is not wholly Olive's fault, as is shown by the gallery of Bostonians introduced at the suffragette party in Miss Birdseye's tasteless apartment at the beginning of the novel. The two male Bostonians are a hack journalist and "Doctor" Selah Tarrant, a mesmeric healer and a fake not only to Basil's eyes but also to those of Dr. Prance, a woman doctor who is truly active in her role of "new woman" and who has little time for talking about the subject. As the real and fake doctors are contrasted, so is Dr. Prance contrasted with the suffragette campaigner

Mrs. Farrinder, who is not a Bostonian and who is also suspicious of Tarrant and his Verena's "inspirational" views. Mrs. Farrinder's weak husband shows what men will amount to and what Basil fights against in the new regime, and Mrs. Farrinder herself, in thinking that talk will achieve the revolution that Dr. Prance quietly demonstrates, shows into what Olive could and possibly does degenerate.

Also ranged about Olive in contrasting positions are the other three Bostonians. Mrs. Luna is completely worldly and contemptuous of any womanly activity but that of the salon. Equally worldly but totally vulgar is Verena's mother, who urges her daughter to accept Olive's impulsive invitation to visit Boston. Verena's visit ends in her staying with Olive and becoming the latter's protégée instead of "Doctor" Tarrant's prodigy: Olive pays the Tarrants to keep away from Verena.

The last and best of the Bostonians is Miss Birdseye, James's favorite creation in the novel. At the age of eighty, she is still a compulsive reformer in a completely selfless and ineffectual manner, which contrasts with the practical Dr. Prance and Mrs. Farrinder and with the worldly creatures of Boston and New York. She appears only three times in the novel: at the initial party that introduces most of the characters; when she plays the part of destiny in giving Ransom Verena's Cambridge address, under the impression he is interested in the movement for women's rights; and at Olive's summer cottage, at Marmion, where she dies happily, mistakenly believing that Verena has enlisted Ransom in the cause. She stands for Boston's true nature, which Olive ignores in trying to achieve a triumph through Verena.

In the second part of the novel, Olive compounds her failure of discrimination by accepting the invitation of Mrs. Burrage, a New York society hostess, to show off Verena in New York; Olive thinks she has triumphed in securing Verena's promise not to marry and in diverting young Henry Burrage's attention from Verena. Olive thus overreaches herself at the same moment and in the same way as Verena: Olive's initial mistake was to invite Ransom to Boston, and Verena invites him to the Burrage evening party, partly as a result of his seeking her out in Cambridge. She thinks she is working for the cause, but she is shown as very slowly awakening to her love for Ransom, which precipitates the catastrophe.

Verena is the fulcrum of the plot, and her affection first for Olive, then for Ransom, is reflected in the structure of the novel. The first twenty chapters contain four scenes: Olive's dinner with Basil, Miss Birdseye's party that night, Basil's call on Olive and Verena the next morning, and some months later a tea party at the Tarrants for

Olive and, as it turns out, Henry Burrage. This first half concentrates on Olive's developing affection for Verena. Yet Verena is incapable of decision or action and in the second half of the novel, as Basil Ransom takes the center of the stage, she gradually falls under his influence. Four principal settings are employed: Cambridge, where Ransom visits Verena; New York, the scene of Mrs. Burrage's party and the discussion between Verena and Basil in Central Park; Marmion, where Olive's cottage is the scene of Miss Birdseye's death and Olive's looming defeat in the suit Basil Ransom presses on Verena; and Boston, where in the anteroom of the Music Hall on the evening of Verena's first public appearance, Basil finally defeats Olive and carries off Verena as most of the remaining cast make a final appearance—the Tarrants, the Burrages, the Farrinders.

Throughout the novel, the characteristic devices of James's late middle style are apparent: lengthening paragraphs, alternating direct and indirect colloquy, the use of idiomatic terms to carry nuances of meaning. More obvious, especially in the dramatic close, is the growing dependence on set scenes to show the stages of the drama. Over all of these is the play of James's irony and pity directed at the latterday Bostonian, Olive Chancellor, the local representation of a national type and the heroine of this distinctly American tragedy.

THE BRIDGE

Type of work: Poem
Author: Hart Crane (1899-1932)
First published: 1930

With The Bridge, *Crane hoped to create a mythology for the United States, a great poem to express his vision of urban America in the 1920's.*

Hart Crane was considered the most promising young poet of the early 1930's. His motivation and central symbol, the sea, he realized brilliantly in his first volume, *White Buildings*, published in 1926. From this source of inspiration and from his vantage point in Brooklyn, in a house once owned by the engineer who designed the famous bridge, Crane conceived a great plan for a poem expressive of his own urban America. A wealthy patron subsidized the volume which, ironically, was written in Cuba and France and first published in Paris. As a result of the reception given *The Bridge*, Crane was awarded the Levinson Prize by *Poetry* and granted a Guggenheim Fellowship. While returning from Mexico, however, where he had chosen to write, he jumped overboard and drowned in the Gulf of Mexico. His short, disordered life has become one of the legends of the "lost generation." *The Bridge*, inspired by the Brooklyn Bridge, has created a view of life that extends its span beyond the 1930's.

Taking his cue from Walt Whitman, the poet he most loved and imitated, Crane wished to establish a mythology for the United States, a country created too late for such a cultural tradition. In "Proem: To Brooklyn 'MSBridge," the poet invokes the genius of this utilitarian work of art to synthesize the chaos of the modern world, for this span joins city, earth, machine, river, sea, and humanity:

> O Sleepless as the river under thee,
> Vaulting the sea, the prairies' dreaming sod,
> Unto us lowliest sometime sweep, descend
> And of the curveship lend a myth to God.

The successive sections of the poem, while unequal in poetic merit and historical significance, extend this symbol from America's discovery to 1930. *Ave Maria*, part 1, is a dedication to Christopher Columbus, the source of the original myth and legend, who seeks to unite his divided world, to sustain his vision of cosmography.

Part 2, *Powhatan's Daughter*, containing several hundred years of American history and legend intermingled, opens on "The Harbor Dawn," in which two lovers awaken to bridge noises and city sights. As an above-ground Dante led by a Beatrice-Pocahontas vision, the poet walks abroad with the fabled past and the strenuous present. In "Van Winkle," the poet's school-day recollections of Pizarro, Cortez, and Priscilla and John Smith combine with his most vivid recollection of Rip Van Winkle. Crane's own boyhood discoveries and tragedies are here synthesized with Van Winkle's, ending on this note of discord for all those who are out of time:

> Macadam, gun-gray as the tunny's belt,
> Leaps from Far Rockaway to Golden Gate. . . .
> Keep hold of that nickel for car-change, Rip,—
> Have you got your *"Times"*—?
> And hurry along, Van Winkle—it's getting late!

"The River," perhaps the best single poem in this spiritual odyssey and anthology, holds the star-spangled jazz beat of Vachel Lindsay coupled with John Dos Passos' itinerary, expanded from coast to coast but centered on the Mississippi River:

> The River, spreading, flows—and spends your dream.
> What are you, lost within this tideless spell?
> You are your father's father, and the stream—
> A liquid theme that floating niggers swell.
>
> Damp tonnage and alluvial march of days—
> Nights turbid, vascular with silted shale
> And roots surrendered down of moraine clays:
> The Mississippi drinks the farthest dale.

Having started from Brooklyn, as did Whitman, and passing by subway to the outer rails and the river with the ghosts of the American past, the poet gives his reason for his Pocahontas theme in "The Dance": the Native American heroine's marriage with a white man gave all Americans a different flesh and blood, a distinct lineage. This unison makes a life dance celebrated vividly in America's childhood and expanded to an idyl, the myth of its Eden. "Indiana," the final poem in this section, envisions another myth, Eldorado, seen through the eyes of a pioneer mother bereft of a son who goes off to sea. Here is suggested the last frontier, possibly symbolizing modern humanity's rootlessness.

In part 3, *Cutty Sark*, the image is jumbled; the vision fades as the poet traverses Manhattan's dark night with a drunken sailor. The loss of Eden, the frontier, makes drink a necessity and distortion a result.

Part 4, *Cape Hatteras*, takes up a different history, the orogeny which lifted the Appalachians above the sea as well as the cosmic eruptions which gave the United States an airplane and a Walt Whitman.

> Dream cancels dream in this new realm of fact
> From which we wake into the dream of act;
> Seeing himself an atom in a shroud—
> Man hears himself an engine in a cloud!
> . . . .
> Walt, tell me, Walt Whitman, if infinity
> Be still the same as when you walked the beach
> Near Paumanok. . . .

Part 5, *Three Songs*, is an interlude in praise of three women—Eve, Magdalene, and Mary—but with satiric overtones. Part 6, *Quaker Hill*, becomes a personal, lyrical celebration of humble pursuits, rural scenes, and seascapes intermingling with the cacophony of the disparate, the distraction of modern life, and death.

In part 7, climactically, the poet returns to the city by air, to *The Tunnel*, the subway, which is the chute to hell. Here Dante-Crane meets Vergil-Poe in what must have been intended as a modern *Inferno*, however fragmented.

> And why do I often meet your visage here,
> Your eyes like agate lanterns—on and on
> Below the toothpaste and the dandruff ads?
> —And did their riding eyes right through your side,
> And did their eyes like unwashed platters ride?
> And Death, aloft,—gigantically down
> Probing through you—toward me, O evermore

The conclusion, *Atlantis*, must then be the *Paradiso*, the bridge the concentric circles. The symbol of Atlantis makes this an earthly-unearthly pilgrimage in time and space.

The final vision is prophetic, possibly, of more spiritual, less materialistic things to come, the eternal bridge to God:

> Always through spiring cordage, pyramids
> Of silver sequel, Deity's young name
> Kinetic of white choiring wings . . . ascends.

THE BRIDGE OF SAN LUIS REY

Type of work: Novel
Author: Thornton Wilder (1897-1975)
Type of plot: Philosophical romance
Time of plot: Early eighteenth century
Locale: Peru
First published: 1927

The Bridge of San Luis Rey *tells a story of Peru in the golden days when it was a Spanish colony. The novel is full of life, of interesting sidelights on an interesting period, and, above all, of excellent character sketches. Wilder has brought together a group of unusual people and made them fit into a narrative pattern in which their individual contrasts stand out more clearly.*

Principal Characters

Brother Juniper, a Spanish friar who tries to prove that the collapse of the bridge of San Luis Rey in Peru is an act showing the wisdom of God, who properly sent five persons to their deaths in the accident. For his book, which is condemned by the Church, the friar is burned at the stake.

The Narrator, who finds a copy of Brother Juniper's eighteenth century book and reconstructs for the reader the lives of the five persons who died when the bridge collapsed.

The Marquesa de Montemayor, an ugly woman with a beautiful daughter. She is highly possessive and selfish, first to her daughter and then to Pepita, her maid. By reading a letter from Pepita to an abbess, the marquesa learns her own nature, becomes contrite, and resolves to be a better woman, only to die the next day when the bridge collapses.

Pepita, the maid for the Marquesa de Montemayor, who also dies when the bridge collapses. She is unhappy when she is sent from her convent by the Abbess Madre María del Pilar, whom she loves, to serve the noblewoman. Her letter confessing her unhappiness reveals to the marquesa the noblewoman's thoughtless and self-centered life.

Uncle Pio, an actor who discovers La Périchole singing in a tavern. He makes a great actress and singer of her, and comes to love her. He is disappointed by the girl, who becomes the mistress of the viceroy and soon is too proud for her own good. Uncle Pio takes her illegitimate child to rear, but the next day he and the child are victims of the collapse of the bridge.

Jaime, the illegitimate son of La Périchole and the viceroy. He dies when the bridge collapses.

Esteban, a young man whose twin brother gives up his love for La Périchole because of the affection between the two brothers, foundlings reared by the Abbess Madre María del Pilar. Manuel dies, and his brother, who becomes a victim of the bridge's collapse, is inconsolable.

La Périchole (Camila), an actress who is overly proud, especially after becoming the viceroy's mistress. Her pride diminishes when smallpox destroys her beauty. She puts her son in the care of Uncle Pio the day before both of them die.

Manuel, the twin brother of Esteban. He hides his love for La Périchole so that he will not hurt his brother's feelings, but in a delirium, close to death, he reveals his secret passion.

The Abbess Madre María del Pilar, who befriends the twin brothers, Esteban and Manuel, as well as Pepita, the girl who becomes the Marquesa de Montemayor's maid. The abbess is a wise and kindly woman.

Doña Clara, the cynical daughter of the Marquesa de Montemayor. She learns too late of her mother's change of heart and inner goodness.

The Story

On Friday, July 20, 1714, the bridge of San Luis Rey, the most famous bridge in Peru, collapsed, hurling five travelers into the deep gorge below. Present at the time of the tragedy was Brother Juniper, who saw in the event a chance to prove, scientifically and accurately, the wisdom of that act of God. He spent all of his time investigating the lives of the five who had died, and he published a book showing that God had had a reason to send each one of them to his death at exactly that moment. The book was condemned by the Church authorities, and Brother Juniper was burned at the stake. He had gone too far in explaining God's ways to humanity. Through a strange quirk of fate, one copy of the book was left undestroyed, and it fell into the hands of the narrator. From it, and from his own knowledge, he reconstructed the lives of the five persons.

The Marquesa de Montemayor had been an ugly child, and she was still homely when she grew up. Because of the wealth of her family, she was fortunately able to marry a noble husband, by whom she had a lovely daughter, Doña Clara. As she grew into a beautiful young woman, the marquesa's daughter became more and more disgusted with her crude and unattractive mother, whose possessive and over-expressive love left Doña Clara cold and uncomfortable. The daughter finally married a man who took her to Spain. Separated from her one joy in life, the marquesa became more eccentric than before and spent her time writing long letters to her daughter in Spain.

In order to free herself of some of her household cares, the marquesa went to the Abbess Madre María del Pilar and asked for a girl from the abbess' school to come and live with her. So Pepita, unhappy that her beloved teacher was sending her away from the school, went to live with the marquesa.

When the marquesa learned by letter that Doña Clara was to have a child, she was filled with concern. She wore charms, bought candles for the saints, said prayers, and wrote all the advice that she could discover to her daughter. As a last gesture, she took Pepita with her to pay a visit to a famous shrine from which she hoped her prayers would surely be heard. On the way, the marquesa happened to read one of Pepita's letters to her old mistress, the abbess. From the letter the marquesa learned just how heartless she had been in her treatment of the girl, how thoughtless and egotistic. She realized that she had been guilty of the worst kind of love toward her daughter, love that was sterile, self-seeking, and false. Aglow with her new understanding, she wrote a letter to her daughter, telling her of the change in her heart, asking for forgiveness, and showing in wonderful language the change that had come over her. She resolved to change her life, to be kind to Pepita, to her household, to everyone. The next day, she and Pepita, while crossing the bridge of San Luis Rey, fell to their deaths.

Esteban and Manuel were twin brothers who had been left as children on the doorstep of the abbess' school. She had brought them up as well as she could, but the strange relation between them was such that she could never make them talk much. When the boys were old enough, they left the school and took many kinds of jobs. At last they settled down as scribes, writing letters for the uncultured people of Lima. One day Manuel, called in to write some letter for La Périchole, fell in love with the charming actress. Never before had anything come between the brothers, for they had always been sufficient in themselves. For his brother's sake, Manuel pretended that he cared little for the actress. Shortly afterward, he cut his leg on a piece of metal and became very sick. In his delirium, he let Esteban know that he really was in love with La Périchole. The infection grew worse, and Manuel died.

Esteban was unable to do anything for weeks after his brother's death, as he could not face life without him. The abbess finally arranged for him to go on a trip with a sea captain who was about to sail around the world. The captain had lost his only daughter and the abbess believed that he would understand Esteban's problem and try to help him. Esteban left to go aboard ship, but on the way he fell with the others when the bridge broke.

Uncle Pio had lived a strange life before he came to Peru. There he had found a young girl singing in a tavern. After years of his coaching and training, she became the most popular actress of the Spanish world. She was called La Périchole, and Uncle Pio's greatest pleasure was to tease her and anger her into giving consistently better performances. All went well until the viceroy took an interest in the vivacious and beautiful young actress. When she became his mistress, she began to feel that the stage was too low for her. After living as a lady and becoming prouder and prouder as time went on, she contracted smallpox. Her beauty was ruined, and she retired to a small farm out of town, there to live a life of misery over her lost loveliness.

Uncle Pio had a true affection for his former protégée and tried time and again to see her. One night, by a ruse, he got her to talk to him. She refused to let him help her, but she allowed him to take Jaime, her illegitimate son, so that he could be educated as a gentleman. The old man and the young boy set off for Lima. On the way, they came to the bridge and died in the fall when it collapsed.

At the cathedral in Lima, a great service was held for the victims. Everyone considered the incident an example of a true act of God, and many reasons were offered for the various deaths. Some months after the funeral, the abbess was visited by Doña Clara, the marquesa's daughter. Doña Clara had finally learned what a wonderful woman her mother had really been. The last letter had taught the cynical daughter all that her mother had so painfully learned. The daughter, too, had learned to see life in a new way. La Périchole also came to see the abbess. She had given up bemoaning her own lost beauty,

and she began a lasting friendship with the abbess. Nothing could positively be said about the reason for the deaths of those five people on the bridge. Too many events were changed by them; one could not number them all. Yet the old abbess believed that the true meaning of the disaster was the lesson of love for those who survived.

Critical Evaluation

The Bridge of San Luis Rey marked the beginning of a key stage in Wilder's development and also revealed the essential dimensions of the artistic program that he would follow. His first novel, *The Cabala* (1926), had viewed the decadent aristocracy of contemporary Rome through the eyes of a young American student. In the tradition of Henry James and Edith Wharton, the highly autobiographical work suffered by comparison and was not praised by the critics. *The Bridge of San Luis Rey*, however, which vividly evoked a forgotten era and a type of society utterly foreign to Wilder's experience, sold three hundred thousand copies in its first year and made its author a celebrity. The description of early eighteenth century Peru was, in Edmund Wilson's estimation, "solid, incandescent, distinct." This success confirmed Wilder's intention to make abundant use of historical materials, and he set his next novel, *The Woman of Andros* (1930), in postclassical Greece. *The Bridge of San Luis Rey* also served notice that a major philosophical and theological writer had entered the literary scene. The engaging simplicity of the book drew its readers toward problems no less recondite than those of the justice of God, the possibility of disinterested love, and the role of memory in human relationships. That Wilder's subsequent works consistently returned to these themes was a surprise to no one, so powerfully had this novel stated them.

The Christianity that inspires and informs *The Bridge of San Luis Rey* is existential and pessimistic. "Only one reader in a thousand notices that I have asserted a denial of the survival of identity after death," Wilder once remarked of the book. He also denies the value of the apologetic task that Brother Juniper undertakes. For even if human reason could "scientifically demonstrate" God's providence—a proposition Wilder rejects—humanity would inevitably employ this knowledge in a self-aggrandizing manner. The inherent mystery of the divine intention is a check to human pride, and pride is Wilder's overriding concern, especially that pride which cloaks itself in the guise of "unselfish love." If there is providence, Wilder suggests, it most clearly operates as

something that exposes the egoistic taint in all love and reveals to lovers their need to be forgiven both by the ones that they love and by the social community.

Despite the ostensible importance of Brother Juniper, Uncle Pio, and Esteban, only Wilder's female characters develop sufficiently to gain awareness of the meaning of the novel's action. The marquesa undergoes the clearest transformation. The maternal love that she cultivates so assiduously is neither spontaneous nor generous. Rather, the marquesa craves her daughter's affection as an antidote to her own insecurity. Her imagination first magnifies the daughter's virtues and prestige; then, to assuage a deep self-loathing, she demands from this "great lady" a meticulous and servile devotion. Aware of her manipulative impulses, the marquesa is nevertheless powerless to conquer them. Moreover, she is not aware of how her distorted passion causes misery to those around her. The revelation of Pepita's agonized loneliness shames and humiliates her, but she thereby gains the strength to eliminate the element of tyranny in the love that she bears for her daughter.

Because La Périchole (Camila) appears in each of the three tales, she is the novel's most real character. Her satirical attack on the marquesa becomes ironic when, later on, her own ugliness and avarice also make her the object of gossip and scorn. Like the marquesa, she does not believe herself to be intrinsically valuable. Yet Uncle Pio, who first treated Camila as something to dominate and take aesthetic delight in, now loves her unconditionally. Her willingness to accept this fact and express her love causes him to suffer and isolates her unnaturally from society. Such a painful yet liberating acceptance is made possible both by Pio's persistence and her love for Jaime. Her grief, and the possibility of disinterested love that it implies, moves her at last to present her disfigured self to society.

Even though her moral insight makes the abbess the standard against which all in the novel are measured, she too must suffer and grow. Unlike the abstract and detached Brother Juniper, she makes herself vulnerable to the pains that love and service involve. Unlike the marquesa, she does not demand instant expressions of servile devotion from those who love her. Yet she does yearn to have her work remembered, to gain that (in Wilder's view, illusory) immortality that comes to those who labor for great causes. Consequently, she manipulates Pepita much as Uncle Pio manipulates Camila. That Pepita died lonely and forsaken reveals to the abbess the results of her misguided passion. Her faith undergoes a purification when she confronts the fact that "Even memory is not necessary for love."

The episode of Esteban and Manuel does not fit neatly into the pattern that Wilder generally establishes. Some critics have suggested that Wilder here meant to deal with homosexual love. This view is partially refuted by the heterosexual activity of both youths and by Esteban's evident unwillingness to stand between Manuel and Camila. One asks, however, whether Esteban unconsciously attempts to retain possession of his brother, communicating his feelings through the uncanny channels of sympathy that bind these twins. Even if this were so, there remains the fact that Manuel also is unable to conceive of a separation. The tale thus seems to constitute a digression, one that serves to underscore the enormous mystery and intensity of all relationships of love. It is linked to the central thematic pattern by Esteban's deep feelings for the abbess, which enable him to reach out to another human being despite his tragic sorrow.

For Wilder, it is almost impossible for human beings to live serenely and faithfully knowing that their personalities will be neither remembered by society nor allowed to survive death in a hereafter. This prospect creates an anxiety that pervades all their efforts to love. They persistently use the beloved to prove themselves worthy and immortal. Then to love are added additional, degrading elements. They never realize, in the abbess' words, that "the love will have been enough." Wilder's views could have led him to enormous sentimentality, but in truth *The Bridge of San Luis Rey* is extraordinarily stark. It is sustained only by the single hope that "all those impulses of love return to the love that made them."

CALL IT SLEEP

Type of work: Novel
Author: Henry Roth (1906-)
Type of plot: Social realism
Time of plot: 1907-1913
Locale: Lower East Side, New York City
First published: 1934

A neglected classic of American literature, Call It Sleep *explores the mind of a young Jewish immigrant who must adjust to life in the United States. Roth, in his only novel, produced a work of insightful lyricism.*

Principal Characters

David Schearl, a young Jewish immigrant boy. Sensitive and fearful, David must learn to cope with a new world that threatens to harm him emotionally and physically. He often finds comfort and strength in sleep.

Genya Schearl, David's mother. She is a beautiful woman who offers safety and love to her young son. She receives much criticism from her husband, but she remains loyal to him.

Albert Schearl, David's father, who is changed by his experiences in the United States. Suspicious and proud, he allows his insecurities to make him what he least wants to be—a fool.

Joe Luter, a print shop foreman and Albert's boss. He pretends to praise Albert so that he can spend time with Genya.

Bertha, Genya's sister and David's aunt. A loud, vulgar woman who frightens David. She marries Nathan Sternowitz, and together they run a candy shop.

Leo Dugovka, a friend of David, he is Christian and cannot believe that David knows nothing of his religion. Leo persuades David to let him seduce the boy's cousin Esther.

Nathan Sternowitz, a widower who marries Aunt Bertha.

Polly and **Esther Sternowitz,** his daughters, whom Leo attempts to seduce. He succeeds with Esther, and Polly tattles.

Rabbi Yidel Pankower, David's tragicomic *cheder* teacher.

Henry Roth's only novel was first published in 1934, a year that produced Scott Fitzgerald's *Tender Is the Night*, Graham Greene's *It's a Battlefield*, John O'Hara's *Appointment in Samarra*, William Saroyan's *The Daring Young Man on the Flying Trapeze*, and Evelyn Waugh's *A Handful of Dust*. The same year saw the publication of forty-three other works considered memorable enough to be listed in the second edition of *Annuals of English Literature* (1961). *Call It Sleep* is not listed, nor is the novel or its author referred to in such compendia as Willard Thorp's *American Writing in the Twentieth Century* (1960) or Max J. Herzberg's *Reader's Encyclopedia of American Literature* (1962).

Nevertheless, the novel survived its early neglect, for *Call It Sleep* is one of those books written in the wrong generation. Just as the poems of Emily Dickinson and the great whale book of Herman Melville waited decades for full appreciation, so Roth's book came to full public attention thirty years after its publication in 1934. One obvious reason for its success in the 1960's is its subject: life in the Jewish ghetto. In the meantime, novelists such as Saul Bellow, Bernard Malamud, and Philip Roth had made the American Jew significant in contemporary literature. It is no wonder that the American public should respond to another book on this popular subject, especially after it has been called one of the most distinguished novels telling of Jewish life in the United States.

The real achievement of the book, however, derives more from technique than from subject. The chief merits of the novel are its harsh but poetic realism, its remarkable power of vivid evocation, and its technical control. Realism implies a picture of life as it is. The life that Henry Roth chooses to portray is that of an Austrian Jewish boy enduring four acutely and painfully formative years in the New York ghettos. Reminiscent of Stephen Crane's *Maggie: A Girl of the Streets* (1893) and of Theodore Dreiser's *Sister Carrie* (1900), *Call It Sleep* portrays the day-to-day existence of David Schearl with a sophisticated accumulation of sensuous detail. One critic, in fact, believes it must be the noisiest novel ever written, so vivid are the sounds of shouts, groans, whispers, insults, streetcars, clocks, feet tramping, and mouths chewing.

Detail for its own sake, however, does not make literature. Roth's success is in the relevance of the detail and in its controlled use to stir and alter emotion in the reader. Aunt Bertha, for example, is a bawdy, loudmouthed woman who exists as a foil to sensitive, fearful David. Through her Roth evokes both the truth of David's uncomfortable life and the necessary sympathy that the reader must have if the novel is to come alive.

Call It Sleep is a masterpiece, and to read it is to be astounded at its neglect. It is difficult to think of another writer who can recall the agonies of childhood with such urgency and immediacy. David Schearl is a child of his race, his time, his environment, but he is all children as well; one experiences something close to discomfort as one's memory is jogged by the universality of David's search for understanding of, and reconciliation with, the world about him.

David's world is presented mainly through a careful documentation of the boy's consciousness, but Roth, in a brilliant stroke, begins with a prologue that creates both the physical and psychological environment with which David will have to struggle. One is taken first to a steamer leaving Ellis Island in 1907. Among the immigrants are David, then about two years old, and his mother, Genya. Albert, the father, had come to the United States earlier and the family is now to be reunited. In Albert's behavior, however, there is a coldness markedly different from the outspoken joy that pervades other such groups around him. His remarks to his wife and son are contemptuous and accusatory; in a gesture full of shame and pathetic pride, he snatches David's old-country hat and hurls it into the river simply because he does not want his boy to look like an immigrant.

The prologue is wonderfully graphic, but it is also important as a source of basic themes and metaphors. First, it establishes the Schearls as people in an alien culture, a circumstance that colors the whole novel. Second, it establishes another and more profound kind of alienation existing between mother and son, on the one hand, and father, on the other. Finally, the prologue suggests a metaphor that underlies the entire work: the voyage that David must take into the alien world of complex experience. In this sense, the sheltering arms of Genya are the old world; David is the immigrant in life who must leave their haven and seek his own meanings in the new cul-

ture of maturity. It is one of the particular triumphs of *Call It Sleep* that these closely related themes lead the reader from the surface of life to the depths of inner experience, and finally into a pattern that lies under the lives of all people.

The stages of David's three-year voyage shape the four books into which the novel is divided. David is six as the narrative begins. His attachment to his mother is profound, not only for herself but also for the shelter that she gives by standing between him and the icy contempt of his father. Critics have pointed out that the mother-son relationship is strongly Oedipal. Irving Howe has had the wisdom also to observe that, through David's observation of the placid and beautiful Genya, the reader is made to relive a relationship that is profoundly touching to most men, whatever its psychiatric implications.

In sharp contrast is the brilliantly realized character of the father: aloof, suspicious, gullible, and eaten away by a tragic pride. Albert is at war with the world. His great fear, induced partly by an awareness of his own foreignness and partly by some deeper insecurity, is that he will be laughed at, cheated, made a fool. Therefore, of course, he is; in an early episode, David's immature but meticulous consciousness records that Albert's foreman, Luter, is flattering Albert only in order to be with Genya.

The first two books are largely concerned with the traumas of David's broadening experience: the Luter episode, a repugnant sexual encounter with a neighborhood girl, a terrible thrashing by Albert. In the second book, David watches the courting of Aunt Bertha by the laconic Nathan Sternowitz and listens in confused fascination to his mother's account of an earlier love affair in Russia. Throughout these chapters, Roth portrays with great skill a young boy's developing awareness of sexuality, particularly his uneasy realization that his mother is also a sexual being.

The third book is centered in the Hebrew school, the *cheder*, where David's intellect is awakened by the rabbi, Yidel Pankower. Pankower is one of the great achievements of the novel, a tragicomic figure of classic proportions. The *cheder* dances to the tunes of his invective. David learns rapidly, but one afternoon a verse from Isaiah puzzles him: It tells how Isaiah saw the Lord seated upon a throne and was afraid. Then a seraph touched a fiery coal to Isaiah's lips, and he heard God speak. David yearns to ask about that coal but does not get the chance. At home, he asks his mother to explain God. He is brighter than day, she says, and He has all power.

On the first day of Passover, there is no school and David wanders toward the East River. He stares at the river, meditating on God's brightness. The experience is almost a mystical trance, but the dazzling contemplation is broken by three boys who come up and taunt him. They can show him magic if he will go to the car tracks and drop a piece of scrap metal in the groove between the tracks. David does so, and suddenly there is a blinding light. David is terrified. His child's mind connects God's power and light with the electrical flash.

David sometimes does not get along with the rough boys of the neighborhood. One day, he discovers the roof of the flat as a place of refuge. From there he sees a boy with blond hair flying a kite. Leo Dugovka is confident and carefree, and he has skates. Leo is surprised to learn that David knows nothing about the Cross or the Mother and Child. David desperately wants Leo to like him.

The next day, David goes on a long walk to Aunt Bertha's candy shop to see if she has any skates that he can use. The living quarters behind the store are cramped, dark, and filthy. Bertha tells him to get Esther and Polly out of bed while she watches the store.

Aunt Bertha has no skates, so David goes to Leo's flat. There he is attracted to a picture of Jesus and to a rosary. Leo is sexually interested in David's two cousins after he hears about them. Leo promises David the rosary if he will take him to see the girls. Though uncomfortable, David agrees. Leo is successful with Esther, but they are caught in the act by Polly. She tattles.

David is terrified; he will be implicated. At *cheder* in the afternoon, he reads nervously before a visiting rabbi. Bursting into tears, he entangles himself in hysterical lies fabricated out of the secret in his mother's past. He says his mother is dead and that his father was a Gentile organist in Europe.

While the puzzled rabbi goes to clear up matters with the Schearls, Nathan Sternowitz is angrily blaming David for what happened to Esther. The rabbi soon learns that David has lied, but the mention of the organist arouses Albert's suspicion. He accuses his wife of unfaithfulness and believes David to be someone else's child. Genya cannot persuade him that he is wrong.

When Bertha and Nathan arrive, David, terrified, runs into the street while his elders argue violently. Images, recollections, and fears spin through his mind. Finding a steel milk-dipper, he desperately decides to produce God again at the car tracks. At first nothing happens as he inserts the dipper; then, suddenly he receives a terrific electric shock that knocks him out. The flash draws a crowd of anxious people, but David has not been hurt seriously. Even his father seems slightly relieved that he is all right.

Soon it is night, and David can go to sleep and forget it all. In sleep, all the images of the past—sights, sounds, feelings—become vivid and alive. While life was painful and terrifying, in sleep he triumphs.

A fundamental aspect of Roth's triumph is his mastery of style. The dialect of a slum street is rendered with unshrinking fidelity; the cultural dilemma of the immigrant is touchingly demonstrated in the disparity between David's American street language and the dignified language of his home, representing a translation of the family's native Yiddish. When the reader enters David's stream of consciousness, language becomes direct experience, and *Call It Sleep* takes its place beside the great lyrical novels of the century.

It would be tempting to summarize Roth's achievement through comparisons. One could say that, as an example of urban naturalism, *Call It Sleep* rivals the best of Dreiser and James T. Farrell; that, in some elements of its stylistic virtuosity, it rivals the work of James Joyce; or that, as a novel of growing up, it must be ranked with *The Adventures of Huckleberry Finn* (1884) and *Look Homeward, Angel* (1929). Yet such comparisons are beside the point. What one most admires about the novel, what must make it survive, is the incomparable richness of its experience re-created in the totality and finality of the work of art.

THE CALL OF THE WILD

Type of work: Novel
Author: Jack London (1876-1916)
Type of plot: Adventure romance
Time of plot: 1897
Locale: Alaska
First published: 1903

The most popular of all Jack London's books, The Call of the Wild *follows the story of the great dog Buck in the Alaskan wilderness. The author obviously had much love for animals and for the country about which he wrote, and he transferred that love into a tale that is filled with adventure and excitement.*

Principal Characters

Buck, a cross between a St. Bernard and a Scottish shepherd. He is the leader of all the dogs on Judge Miller's estate in California until stolen and carted off to the Alaska gold rush. Passed from one owner to another, he finally breaks away to run with a wolf pack.

A Spitz, the bloodthirsty enemy of Buck and the lead dog on the sled until he is killed by Buck.

John Thornton, a prospector who protects Buck from stupid gold seekers. After John is killed by Native Americans, his body is left at the river, to which once a year Buck returns and utters the call of the wild, the howl of a beast for his human friend.

The Story

Buck was the undisputed leader of all the dogs on Judge Miller's estate in California. A crossbreed of St. Bernard and Scottish shepherd, he had inherited the size of the first and the intelligence of the other. Buck could not know that the lust for gold had hit the human beings of the country and that dogs of his breed were much in demand as sled dogs in the frozen North. Consequently, he was not suspicious when one of the workers on the estate took him for a walk one night. The man took Buck to the railroad station, where the dog heard the exchange of money. Then a rope was placed around his neck. When he struggled to get loose, the rope was drawn so tight that it shut off his breath and he lost consciousness.

He recovered in a baggage car. When the train reached Seattle, Buck tried to break out of his cage while he was being unloaded. A man in a red shirt hit him with a club until he was senseless. After that, Buck knew that he could never win a fight against a club. He retained that knowledge for future use.

Buck was put in a pen with other dogs of his type. Each day, some of the dogs went away with strange men who came with money. One day Buck was sold. Two French-Canadians bought him and some other dogs and took them on board a ship sailing for Alaska. The men were fair, though harsh, masters, and Buck respected them. Life on the ship was not particularly enjoyable, but it was a paradise compared to that which awaited Buck when the ship reached Alaska. There he found men and dogs to be little more than savages, with no law but the law of force. The dogs fought like wolves, and when one was downed the pack moved in for the kill. Buck watched one of his shipmates being torn to pieces after losing a fight, and he never forgot the way that one dog in particular, a Spitz, watched sly-eyed as the loser was slashed to ribbons. The Spitz was Buck's enemy from that time on.

Buck and the other dogs were harnessed to sleds on which the two French-Canadians carried mail to prospectors in remote regions. It was a new kind of life to Buck, but not an unpleasant one. The men treated the dogs well, and Buck was intelligent enough to learn quickly those things that made him a good sled dog. He learned to dig under the snow for a warm place to sleep and to keep the traces clear and thus make pulling easier. When he was hungry, he stole food. The instincts of his ancestors came to life in him as the sled went farther and farther north. In some vague manner, he sensed the great cunning of the wolves who had been his ancestors in the wilderness.

Buck's muscles grew firm and taut, his strength greater than ever, but his feet became sore and he had to have moccasins. Occasionally, one of the dogs died or was killed in a fight, and one female dog went mad. The dogs no longer worked as a team, and the two men had to be on guard constantly to prevent fights. One day, Buck saw his chance. He attacked the Spitz, the lead dog on the sled, and killed him. After that, Buck refused to be harnessed until he was given the lead position. He proved his worth by whipping the rebellious dogs into shape, and he became the best lead dog the men had ever seen. The sled made record runs, and Buck was soon famous.

When they reached Skaguay, the two French-Canadians had official orders to turn the team over to a Scottish half-breed. The sled was heavier and the weather bad on the long haul back to Dawson. At night, Buck lay by the fire and dreamed of his wild ancestors. He seemed to hear a faraway call that was like a wolf's cry.

After two days' rest in Dawson, the team started back over the long trail to Skaguay. The dogs were almost exhausted. Some died and had to be replaced. When the team arrived again in Skaguay, the dogs expected to rest, but three days later they were sold to two men and a woman who knew nothing about dogs or sledding conditions in the northern wilderness. Buck and the other dogs started out again, so weary that it was an effort to move. Again and again the gallant dogs stumbled and fell and lay still until the sting of a whip brought them to their feet for a few miles. At last even Buck gave up. The sled had stopped at the cabin of John Thornton, and when the men and the woman were ready to leave, Buck refused to get up. One of the men beat Buck with a club and would have killed him had not Thornton intervened, knocking the man down and ordering him and his companions to leave. They left Buck with Thornton.

As Thornton nursed Buck back to health, a feeling of love and respect grew between them. When Thornton's partners returned to the cabin, they understood this affection and did not attempt to use Buck for any of their heavy work.

Twice Buck saved Thornton's life and was glad that he could repay his friend. In Dawson, Buck won more than a thousand dollars for Thornton on a wager, when the dog broke loose from the ice a sled carrying a thousand-pound load. With the money won on the wager, Thornton and his partners went on a gold-hunting expedition. They traveled far into eastern Alaska, where they found a stream yellow with gold.

In his primitive mind, Buck began to see a hairy man who hunted with a club. He heard the howling of the wolves. Sometimes he wandered off for three or four days at a time, but he always went back to Thornton. At one time, he made friends with a wolf that seemed like a brother to Buck.

Once Buck chased and killed a great bull moose. On his way back to the camp, he sensed that something was wrong. He found several dogs lying dead along the trail. When he reached the camp, he saw Native American warriors dancing around the bodies of the dogs and Thornton's two partners. He followed Thornton's trail to the river, where he found the body of his friend full of arrows. Buck was filled with such a rage that he attacked the band of Native Americans, killing some and scattering the others.

His last tie with humanity broken, he joined the wild wolf packs. The Native Americans thought him a ghost dog, for they seldom saw more than his shadow, so quickly did he move. Had they watched carefully, however, they could have seen him closely. Once each year, Buck returned to the river that held Thornton's body. There the dog stood on the bank and howled, one long, piercing cry that was the tribute of a savage beast to his human friend.

Critical Evaluation

On its simplest, most superficial, and insensitive level, *The Call of the Wild* is just another of Jack London's "dog stories," which also include *White Fang* (1906) and *Jerry of the Islands* (1917). Yet so cavalier a dismissal of *The Call of the Wild*—usually accompanied by contemptuous allegations that the novel is nothing more than a potboiler—is quite unwarranted. Buck's story has far broader implications than the first, hasty reading may reveal. Admittedly, the book's popular success stems largely from its romantic-adventure qualities, yet there is much more to the novel than mere entertainment.

Jack London led a checkered life and had a checkered career; his experiences and knowledge are reflected in his novels and short stories, particularly his sociopolitical and economic views. At best, London's position could be described as eclectic, at worst, vacillating. He admired Herbert Spencer, Charles Darwin, Karl Marx, and Friedrich Wilhelm Nietzsche simultaneously and without much recognition of the contradictions among them. He embraced socialist causes while espousing Nietzschean "superman" theories. It is thus that Buck—under the presumably civilizing influence of John Thornton—becomes a good socialist; that is, Buck works for the common good rather than for his individual advancement. Bereft of Thornton's guidance when his mentor dies, Buck reverts to the Darwinian survival of the fittest and the Nietzschean superman principles for his own protection.

To be sure, the novel has been faulted for Buck's so-called reversion to the wild. Even the most venerable of critics have praised *White Fang* and *Jerry of the Islands* for depicting savagery under civilized control, while disparaging *The Call of the Wild* as a clarion call to brute force. Yet, however such critics deplore the Darwinian-Nietzschean point of view, they seem to ignore the realities of the Marxian position: Peasants and poor peo-

ple—like Buck—can work with their kind of mutual benefit, but without a spirit of cooperation and without leadership or guidance, they must fend for themselves or they will not endure. The cruelties of life are severe for both human and dog. Here the dog Buck is virtually an allegory for Everyman, in the pristine medieval sense, symbolizing the plight of the oppressed and the downtrodden everywhere in their struggle to maintain life. Whatever his intentions or his convictions, and no matter how skewed, London has portrayed, in *The Call of the Wild*, a vivid picture of the dilemma of the disadvantaged, even though he did so by using a dog as his protagonist.

CANTOS

Type of work: Poetry
Author: Ezra Pound (1885-1972)
First published: *A Draft of XVI Cantos*, 1925; *A Draft of the Cantos 17-27*, 1928; *A Draft of XXX Cantos*, 1930; *Eleven New Cantos XXXI-XLI*, 1934; *The Fifth Decad of Cantos*, 1937; *Cantos LII-LXXI*, 1940; *The Pisan Cantos*, 1948; *Section: Rock-Drill 85-95 de los cantares*, 1955; *Thrones: 96-109 de los cantares*, 1959; *Drafts and Fragments of Cantos CX-CXVII*, 1968.

Pound's Cantos, *a sprawling multivolume work on which the poet spent more than forty years of his life, was one of the most fascinating and influential literary experiments of the twentieth century.*

The common conceptions of Ezra Pound's *Cantos*—that they are obscure exhibits in the museum of Pound's prodigious memory rife with references to archaic cultures and unfamiliar languages, or that they are fatally infected with the pox of Pound's Fascist politics—are not entirely without truth but are also oversimplifications which distort the much greater truth that the *Cantos* contain some of the finest poetry and most fascinating and influential literary experiments of the twentieth century. Just as Walt Whitman's *Leaves of Grass* (1855) is a kind of epic of nineteenth century American life and a demonstration of the origins of poetry in American English, the *Cantos* are an epic of modernist thought on American life in the twentieth century and a measure of the growth of American poetic form to the middle of the century.

Building on Whitman's realization that an epic conception of a legendary hero was no longer viable, and acting in accordance with the Romantic emphasis on the creating artist as a cultural exemplar and heroic focus of a song of self, Pound envisioned a work that would record the collision of an evolving poetic sensibility with the crucial historical events of his time. He believed that his essentially self-directed education was sufficient preparation for the project, and he believed as an article of faith that his mental energies were of significant proportions equal to the implicit demand that the mind of an epic poem is a concentration of the voices of history. Both "detesting" and admiring Whitman, he wanted to reach beyond the autobiographical vortex of Whitman's poem so that the convergence of scholarship, cultural theory, and poetic imagery in his own consciousness would range beyond an examination of the self not only to record history and its consequences but also to shape it. As a result, the *Cantos* have an open-ended aspect; Pound, unlike Dante, one of his most important precursors, had no specific charts for the unknown country he was entering.

Yet, even without a definite map in mind, Pound had extensive experience in a variety of poetic forms by the time he started, and he was convinced that structure was possible through, as Hugh Kenner explains, "the electrification of mute experiential filings into a manifestation of form." In addition to what Pound called "a coherent splendor," reachable through a poetic process that stressed the juxtaposition of related images, Pound was intensely aware of the work of painters, composers, and sculptors in Europe whose techniques led him to develop a method akin to what filmmaker Sergey Eisenstein called "ideological montage," in which diverse materials and languages are arranged so as to coalesce into new patterns of meaning. The organizing principle behind Pound's data-collages derived from what Kenneth Rexroth describes as a "radical dissociation and recombination of elements," and while the connections between the various elements sometimes depended on a logic of association inherent in Pound's mind and not clear to anyone outside, from the perspective of an entire sequence of cantos, unifying patterns are clearly discernible. Another method of structural arrangement involves the use of voice—a prophetic voice that is primarily visionary in form and a pedagogic voice that is essentially summary in substance. Among the various insertions of speeches by historical figures, Pound also employs a kind of maverick Yankee dialect to contrast with the staggering erudition of the epic, and in moments of special feeling, what Kenner calls "lyric passages of intoxicated vision." The use of these different voices controls the tone of the poem and permits Pound to modulate mood and develop dramatic tension, another means of establishing structure within an essentially elastic frame.

The first announcement of Pound's intention to begin the *Cantos* came in 1915, when he wrote in a letter, "I am also at work on a cryselephantine poem of immeasurable length which will occupy me for the next four decades." Drafts of the three cantos were published in *Poetry* magazine in 1917, and much of what originally appeared in Canto III was revised into the opening lines of Canto I in the early 1920's. The poem begins with a descent into an *under* or *inner* world patterned after book 11 of Homer's *Odyssey*; the beginning of a mental voyage back into myth to recapitulate literary and cultural sources, which also moves inward toward the center of the poet's subconscious mind, the source of his image-making power. The poet's journey is intersected *in medias res*, specifically in the continuation of a sentence with no preliminary part ("And then went down to the ship . . ."), suggesting a mid-life launching. Canto II introduces key figures in Pound's cultural pantheon (Dionysus), crucial techniques (his use of the ideogrammatic method for fashioning images), and special texts (Ovid's *Metamorphoses*). Canto III deals with the flow of history and visionary moments in time, anticipating other important moments in later cantos, while Canto IV extends this idea by examining the ruins of ancient cities with archaeological insight. Cantos V and VI consider the intersection of sexual power and political action, an important psychological theme, in Renaissance Europe and ancient Greece, while Canto VII establishes an autobiographical connection to the historical material by shifting the focus to the London that Pound and T. S. Eliot knew during the years of World War I. The first six cantos are primarily designed to establish a context and generate an energy field—to place the poet's consciousness into a realm in which an epic assessment of an epoch might become possible.

Pound published Cantos VIII to XI in Eliot's *The Criterion* in 1923 under the title "Maletesta Cantos" after Sigismundo Maletesta, a Renaissance artist and economic planner whose aesthetic integrity and political principles Pound saw as a model for an exceptional individual living amid mundane times and hostile forces. Pound's admiration for Maletesta foreshadows his almost blind obeisance before other people of power and will, but in the poem, his questionable judgment was often balanced by an instinctive interest in figures who provided correction and balance. In Canto XIII, Pound introduced Confucius (Kung-fu-tsu) as another model of reason, insight, and refinement. This canto is one of Pound's clearest, an inventive translation of the Chinese classic *The Great Digest*, in which a just society is carefully and soberly described in stately cadences:

> If a man have not order within him
> He cannot spread order about him
> And if a man have not order within him
> His family will not act with due order;
> And if a prince have not order within him
> He cannot put order in his dominions.

As the canto concludes, Kung warns, "Without character you will be unable to play on that instrument" (in other words, the poet will not be able to write), and he shows some of the consequences of a world in which character is notably absent among social leaders by describing a version of hell that he told his friend Wyndham Lewis was "a portrait of contemporary London." The urban landscape is full of people who represent the worst of the modern world—their names were included in Pound's original manuscript but inked out to avoid libel suits—exploiters, speculators, and avaricious financiers who have produced an economic inferno that Albert Gelpi calls "a fetid, cloacal nightmare of oozing mud, pus, and excrement."

These demons are the first in a long list of "obstructors of distribution" or "liars and loan lice" who have perverted Western economic systems so that commerce is not an extension of a natural process. They are, instead, the promoters of *usura*, Pound's root cause for economic malfunction, and are depicted in a nightmare region, since for Pound usury is "the power of hell." Cantos XV and XVI further illustrate this growing obsession, while Cantos XIII and XVII, which bracket the hellish modern world, offer alternatives. Canto XVII is an elevated vision of Venice, a city presented in positive images of light, air, water, and clean crafted stone, where a dream of utopia enters history, actualized by Venetian artisans who temporarily overcame the usurers who tried to exploit their work. That canto concludes, however, with another return to the course of a history in which usurious oppressors ruin the efforts of craftspeople.

The poem continues with a rough alternation of groups of cantos documenting the effects of usury and groups illustrating heroic resistance to it. Throughout the 1930's, Pound, acting in what he considered to be the spirit of Confucius, celebrated early American politicians (Thomas Jefferson and John Adams in Cantos XXXI and XXXII) who governed with wisdom and direction or those (John Quincy Adams in Canto XXXIV, Andrew Jackson and Martin Van Buren in Canto XXVII) who acted with practical sense, and he described responsible monetary institutions which made credit available to all citizens (the Monte dei Paschi bank in Siena in Cantos XLIII and XLIV).

Paralleling his accounts of heroic action by virtuous individuals, Pound celebrated the powers of light, which he often used as a symbol for the powers of love, in lyric paeans (almost prayers) to Aphrodite or Artemis, and investigated what he believed were both the destructive and the restorative powers of the feminine in passages concentrating on Odysseus and Circe. In one of the most famous sections of the poem, Canto XLV, he delivers a kind of sermon against usury, a rhetorical statement of what Gelpi calls "sustained outrage that usury has corrupted both economic and natural process, both Confucian order and Dionysian creativity." The field of the poem narrows here, as it did in the Kung canto, as it did in future cantos which concentrate energy into very specific concerns. With mounting intensity, Pound chants in bardic indignation:

> with usura the line grows thick
> with usura is no clear demarcation
> and no man can find site for his dwelling.
> Stone cutter is kept from his stone
> weaver is kept from his loom
> WITH USURA

It is CONTRA NATURAM, a plague against the natural order, Pound proclaims. This canto is followed by further examinations of the psychic voyage of Odysseus, as the archetypal explorer seeks knowledge that will permit self-expression through his encounters with Circe (sexual passion) and Tiresias (reflective wisdom). Odysseus continues to be a symbolic figure for Pound, his adventures a reflection of Pound's personal struggles with the artistic, intellectual, and social circumstances of his life.

The first fifty-two cantos move toward a kind of reconciliation, a state of calmness (or still point) in which the processes of the natural world provide the poet with images of visual beauty and psychological truth to be used against destructive external events and disruptive inner forces. In his own life, however, the fracture between the situation of the poem and Pound's personal turmoil as World War II approached prevented him from moving beyond a momentary serenity toward the projected Paradiso that would balance his Inferno. *The Fifth Decad of Cantos* (1937) was followed by three years of almost frantic poetic and political activity as Pound tried to influence the direction of American involvement in the flux of history by arranging an audience with Franklin Roosevelt so that he could explain to the president how to handle events in Europe.

In 1940, Pound published *Cantos LII-LXXI*, ten cantos on Chinese history and ten on John Adams. Drawing on Joseph de Mailla's *Histoire Générale de la Chine* (1777-1785), Pound tried to explain how throughout Chinese history, whenever Confucian order controlled government, the state prospered. When Pound's enemies (militants, merchants, financiers) opposed order, "decadence supervened." In roughly parallel fashion, Pound yoked John Adams to Kung, Adams who left a "line of descendants who have steadily and without break felt their responsibility" and instituted Confucian principles in the American republic. The relatively undistinguished quality of the writing detracted from Pound's attempts to make Adams a pivotal figure in the middle of the entire sequence. The Kung and Adams cantos, though, while not covering new ground, are a kind of attempt to establish a strong historical foundation for the projected paradisiacal conclusion.

By 1940, Pound believed that the poem was essentially complete, lacking only a section that dealt with his spiritual beliefs. At the same time, he had doubts about the unity of his vision, writing, "As to the *form* of *The Cantos*: All I can say or pray is: *wait* till it's there." Yet his determination to persuade Americans not to support capitalist corrupters against Benito Mussolini's new economic order turned, as Gelpi observes, "the prophet into a crank, if not a dupe, if not a crackpot." Pound spent the World War II years in Rapallo, making broadcasts on Rome radio that were considered treasonous by American authorities, and at the conclusion of the war he was incarcerated in a detention camp in Pisa for six months. A psychiatric evaluation in Washington determined that he was not sane enough to stand trial for his actions, and he was placed in St. Elizabeths Hospital for the next thirteen years. During the first three years of his confinement, he wrote *The Pisan Cantos* (1948), in which he stepped out from behind the various literary and historical masks through which he spoke to become the undisguised protagonist of his epic.

The *Cantos* had been derailed by the war. Aside from two unpublished cantos, LXXII and LXXIII, which he wrote in Italy, Pound's literary productivity was subordinated almost entirely to political invective from 1940 to 1945, a period in his life that could accurately be designated by his later term for the entire poem, "a botch." In St. Elizabeths, however, chastened by his treatment and forced to consider the dominant role of his ego in his life, he began to rebuild both his mind and his poetic vision.

In his first descriptions of his life in prison, Pound identified with slaves and criminals, an unprecedented act of humility and compassion. He confronted the need to recognize, admit, and confess his failures and misperceptions, most prominent among which was his inability to offer love unselfishly, and he recognized vanity as a cause for his blindness—an especially adept formulation, considering his previous equation of love with light. As the sequence concluded with Canto LXXXI, in one of his finest passages, Pound offered the wisdom he had drawn from his experiences in a hell he deserved:

>   What thou lovest well remains,
>
>   the rest is dross
>
>   What thou lov'st well shall not be reft from thee
>
>   What thou lov'st well is thy true heritage
>
>   . . . .
>
>   Pull down thy vanity, I say pull down.
>
>   Learn of the green world what can be thy place
>
>   In scaled invention or true artistry,
>
>   Pull down thy vanity,

In accordance with one of his earliest and firmest precepts, the operation of the poet's mind over the material of his life lifts him "out of hell, the pit/ out of dust and glare evil" in the direction of paradise, the early goal of the entire poem.

The next two segments of the *Cantos* were written while Pound was still in prison, and *Section: Rock-Drill* (1955) and *Thrones* (1959) recall his early attempts to outline an ideal society. "I've got to drill it into their beans," Pound wrote to his publisher James Laughlin, and in an unusually explicit explanation of his plans for *Thrones* (Cantos XCVI-CIX), he said, "The thrones in *The Cantos* are an attempt to move out from egoism and to establish some definition of an order possible or at any rate conceivable on earth." Ironically, these two books did not reach out very far, but represented Pound's enclosure within the proscribed bounds of his mind and vast educational experience. The pattern of arcane references and inward-directed linkages tended to seal the material away from easy external scrutiny. Pound may have realized that, and that realization, combined with the other frustrations of his life, may have led to a radically different style in the last cantos, which he called *Drafts and Fragments* and which he did not present for publication until 1968, several years after their completion.

Pound had returned to Europe after his release from confinement, but he found a very different land from the one that he left. "The shock of no longer feeling oneself in the center of something is probably a part of it," he remarked. Combined with his awareness of how conventional critics had misunderstood and dismissed his work and the encroachments of old age, Pound offered the last cantos as hesitant and tentative gestures. "I cannot make it cohere," he lamented in Canto CXVI, and in the 1960's he settled into almost complete (but attentive) silence. Throughout the final, fragmentary poem, a feeling of placidity, of the calm vision of the ancient seer, balances the moods of discouragement. The questions he asks in Canto CXVI—"I have brought the great ball of crystal;/ who can lift it?/ Can you enter the great acorn of light?"— are answered by implication when Pound asserts, "it coheres all right/ even if my notes do not cohere." In other words, even if the poem did not fulfill the epic aim of explaining order on earth, the effort itself leads to a vision of beauty in poetic light. Moments of lyric radiance ("the great acorn of light") exhibit cohering propensity, just as there is a version of unity in "the replacement of paraphraseable plot by rhythmic recurrence," as Kenner comments. The final canto, the shortest of the entire poem, is like a summary prayer of farewell and forgiveness:

>   I have tried to write Paradise
>
>   Do not move
>
>   Let the wind speak
>
>   that is paradise.
>
>   Let the Gods forgive what I
>
>   have made
>
>   Let those I love try to forgive
>
>   what I have made.

CAT ON A HOT TIN ROOF

Type of work: Drama
Author: Tennessee Williams (1911-1983)
Type of plot: Psychological realism
Time of plot: 1950's
Locale: Mississippi Delta
First presented: 1955

Tennessee Williams explores the lies and schemes of a Southern family in one of his greatest plays. The characters of Big Daddy, Brick, and Maggie have become well known in American theater for their frustrated dreams and desperate longings for love.

Principal Characters

Big Daddy, a wealthy Mississippi landowner of humble origins. He does not know that his family and doctors are lying to him about his terminal cancer. Big Daddy uses the occasion of his sixty-fifth birthday party to reach out to his son Brick.

Big Mama, his wife, a simple woman who eventually stands up to her son Gooper about the fate of the family plantation.

Brick, their son, who is loved by Big Daddy. Since the death of his best friend, Skipper, from drink, Brick has become an alcoholic himself. He blames his wife, Margaret, for his rift with Skipper and cannot face anyone sober.

Margaret (Maggie), Brick's wife, who was jealous of his relationship with Skipper. She tries to reconcile with her husband, but he will not listen and refuses to sleep with her. She lies about being pregnant in order to thwart Gooper's plans.

Gooper, the other son of Big Daddy and Big Mama. He has a large family of his own and is attempting to get into Big Daddy's graces before the man dies. He is sometimes called Brother Man.

Mae, his wife, who is sometimes called Sister Woman.

As Williams himself admitted, prior to this play he had been preoccupied with the emotions that tend to make people into prisoners. Believing that all people live in solitary confinement, Williams claimed that everyone can understand the emotions with which he clothed his lonely characters. He endeavored to make his audiences feel not only that they understand his characters but also that they can identify themselves with the persons on the stage. Consequently, the subject matter of his plays lies not in the everyday surface aspects, but in those subjects people do not ordinarily talk about—the hidden, inner concerns of spiritual life or spiritual death. In his plays, however, Tennessee Williams' characters do talk about their problems to such an extent that there is a close rapport between characters and audience, regardless of whether there seems to be a similar closeness between character and character.

Williams' control of his characters is such that, having presented them, they take care of the situations that arise. He seems never to manipulate them; these are no puppets pulled into position by strings. They are, instead, vastly troubled, earthy creatures who speak out their hearts.

The Mississippi Delta family presented in *Cat on a Hot Tin Roof* is not a pretty one. Ruled over by Big Daddy, who emerged as a wealthy landowner after pulling himself up from the position of overseer, each member has gone a separate, lonely way until the time comes to celebrate Big Daddy's sixty-fifth birthday. One son, Gooper, has a brood of five, going on six. The other son, Brick, is an alcoholic whose wife, Margaret, is childless. Big Mama is a hearty, playful, and vacuous creature.

The plot, involving an attempt by Gooper to get possession of the plantation when Big Daddy dies, is as negligible as Gooper himself. Only three characters are the meat of this play. The people who matter are Big Daddy, Brick, and Margaret.

Each has been living a lonely life, but each has put up a front to preserve the social amenities. While they cannot explain themselves to one another, the explanation of their thoughts and feelings comes clearly across the foot-lights in language that is as bold as their thoughts.

Brick and Margaret have been living under a sort of truce since the death of Skipper, whom Margaret had accused of being in love with Brick. Brick accused Margaret of distorting the friendship between himself and Skipper to such an extent that Skipper took to drink and succeeded in blotting himself out. Brick and Skipper had been such a successful pass combination in college football that they could not resist the attraction of a professional team. Margaret, by then married to Brick, believed that the boys refused to grow up but went along with them as an ardent rooter for their team. Before long, they were a jealous triangle. After Skipper drank himself to death, Brick refused to sleep with Margaret and began to drown his own sorrows in alcohol.

This much comes out in the first act, which is really an extended monologue by Margaret. For her, the situation has become so intense that she is merely a cat trying to stay on a hot tin roof as long as possible. She intends to stay, if she can, because she loves Brick.

He is almost oblivious to her, though patient in an impersonal sort of way. Each day, he drinks until he feels a click in his head that promises peace for a while. On this day, Big Daddy's birthday, he has not yet been able to drink enough to feel the click. The night before, he had broken his ankle while trying, in the dark, to jump the hurdles on the high school athletic field, and so he has not attended the birthday dinner. The rest of the family intends to celebrate the cutting of the birthday cake in his room to have him join in the festivities. Impatient and inarticulate, Brick wants nothing to do with any of them, but Margaret persuades him to be as gentle as possible with his father. Big Daddy does not know that the doctors, although assuring him that he suffers only from a spastic colon, have really found him to be fatally ill with cancer.

The second act is again almost a monologue, this time carried on by Big Daddy with Brick as the nearly silent objective, just as he was in the first act with Margaret. After the candles on the cake have been lighted, Big Daddy practically orders the rest of the family out of the room, as he is determined to uncover the reason for Brick's drinking. In an intense scene, Big Daddy pierces through Brick's protective armor by showing that he has had to develop a tolerance for people in spite of their habitual lying and by admitting that he has endured the company of Big Mama and Gooper, although he has hated them for years. It is with love that he reaches through to Brick. When Brick finally explains his reason for drink-ing, Big Daddy finds it incomplete until Brick remembers that, the last time he had talked to Skipper, he had hung up on a telephone call during which Skipper had tried to make a drunken confession. Pointing out that Brick was disgusted with himself for failing to face the truth of the situation, Big Daddy believes that he has found the reason for which he had looked. Brick, however, faces one truth with another and tells his father that the doctors have lied to him. There is only one satisfaction for both men: Neither has ever lied to the other, though they have lived among liars all their lives.

When Tennessee Williams gave this play to Elia Kazan to read, Kazan, who was to direct the play, objected to the third act on three counts: He thought Big Daddy too vivid to be kept off the stage after the second act, he wanted Brick to show some effect of his father's loving insight in the second act, and he wanted Margaret to appear more sympathetic to the audience as the play ended. Williams debated the first suggestion, but a return of Big Daddy could only be an anticlimax after the second act. He thought Brick's paralysis of spirit could not undergo a change so soon after even so revealing a diagnosis. He was willing, however, to make Maggie the Cat as charming to the audience as she had become to him. In the published play, therefore, the reader has a choice of two third acts: the original, as Williams wrote it, and the version used in the Broadway production.

The third act is involved with Gooper's telling Big Mama that her husband really has cancer and suggesting a plan of trusteeship for the plantation after Big Daddy dies. Big Mama will have none of Gooper's plan. Instead, she turns to Big Daddy's favorite, Brick, and suggests that Big Daddy would like best to leave the place to Brick's son if he had one. Aroused by the noise of a family argument inside and a thunderstorm outside the house, Big Daddy comes back. Margaret, telling him she has kept his big birthday present until last, announces that she is carrying Brick's baby. As Big Daddy goes out happily to look over his land, Gooper and his wife pounce on Margaret and declare that she is lying. Brick defies them both. As the play ends, he feels the click of peacefulness and prepares to make Margaret's lie come true.

As is usual with Tennessee Williams' plays, there were mixed reactions among the reviewers following its dramatic presentation. Some found it deep in theme and insight, some found it enjoyable, some thought that Williams had evaded the main issue, and some thought that it had tremendous dramatic impact. All agreed that it had an important place in the Williams canon.

CATCH-22

Type of work: Novel
Author: Joseph Heller (1923-)
Type of plot: Social satire
Time of plot: 1944
Locale: Pianosa, a mythical island eight miles south of Elba, and Rome
First published: 1961

Heller's absurd, horrifying, and bleak look at war and modern society has earned a unique place in American literature. Many critics consider it to be the best novel to come out of World War II.

Principal Characters

Captain John Yossarian, a United States Air Force bombardier who tries to escape World War II by embracing the absurd. He is foiled by the madness and stupidity around him and by the ultimate irony of the rule known as Catch-22: Anyone can be grounded for insanity, but wanting to be grounded means that an individual is sane.

Colonel Cathcart, the group commander, who sends his pilots on increasingly dangerous missions in order to gain fame and a promotion.

Major Major Major, the 256th Squadron commander, who was promoted by a machine.

Lieutenant Milo Mindbinder, the mess officer. He turns his black marketing into a powerful syndicate and is not above aiding the enemy for profit.

Captain Black, the squadron intelligence officer, who constantly requires loyalty oaths from the pilots.

Doc Daneeka, the flight surgeon. He informs Yossarian about the tenets of Catch-22.

Captain R. O. Shipman, the chaplain, who is accused of tampering with the enlisted men's mail.

General Dreedle, the wing commander, who is engaged in a power struggle with General Peckem.

General Peckem, the commander of Special Services. He is more concerned with appearances than with military strategy.

Clevinger, Orr, Kid Sampson, McWatt, Aardvark (Aarfy), Hungry Joe, and **Nately,** members of the 256th Squadron.

The Story

The scenes in *Catch-22* shuttle back and forth between Pianosa, an imaginary Italian island where an American air force bombing group is sweating out the closing months of World War II, and Rome, where the flyers go on leave to stage latter-day Roman orgies in that city of prostitutes. Men who behaved like madmen, as Heller notes, were awarded medals. In a world of madmen at war the maddest—or the sanest—of all is Captain John Yossarian, a bombardier of the 256th Squadron. Having decided that death in war is a matter of circumstance and having no wish to be victimized by any kind of circumstance, he tries by every means he can think of—malingering, defiance, cowardice, irrational behavior—to get out of the war. That was his resolve after the disastrous raid over Avignon, when Snowden, the radio-gunner, was shot almost in two, splashing his blood and entrails over Yossarian's uniform and teaching the bombardier the cold,

simple fact of mortality. For some time after that, Yossarian refused to wear any clothes, and when General Dreedle, the wing commander, arrived to award the bombardier a Distinguished Flying Cross for his heroism, military procedure was upset because Yossarian wore no uniform on which to pin the medal. Yossarian's logic of nonparticipation is so simple that everyone thinks him crazy, especially when he insists that "they" are trying to murder him. His insistence gets him into an argument with Clevinger, who is bright and always has an excuse or an explanation for everything. When Clevinger wants to know who Yossarian thinks is trying to murder him, the bombardier says that everyone of "them" is trying. Clevinger says he has no idea who "they" can be. Yossarian then asks how he knows that "they" are not. Clevinger merely sputters.

Yossarian goes to the hospital complaining of a pain

in his liver. If he has jaundice, then the doctors will discharge him; if not, then they will send him back to duty. Yossarian spends some of his time censoring the enlisted men's letters. To some, he signs Washington Irving's name as censor. On others, he crosses out the letter but adds loving messages signed by the chaplain's name. The hospital would have been a good place to stay in for the rest of the war if it had not been for a talkative Texan and a patient so cased in bandages that Yossarian wondered at times whether there was a real body inside. When he returns to his squadron, he learns that Colonel Cathcart, the group commander, has raised the number of required missions to fifty. Meanwhile, Clevinger had dipped his plane into a cloud one day and never brought it out again. He and his plane simply vanished, and he is not around the officers' club to explain what happened this time.

It is impossible for Yossarian to complete his tour of combat duty because Colonel Cathcart wants, first, to get his own picture in *The Saturday Evening Post* and, second, to become a general. Consequently, he continues to increase the number of required missions for his outfit above those required by 27th Air Force Headquarters. By the time that he has set the number at eighty, Kraft, McWatt, Kid Sampson, and Nately are dead; Clevinger and Orr have disappeared; the chaplain has been disgraced (he is accused of the Washington Irving forgeries); Aarfy has committed a brutal murder; Hungry Joe screams in his sleep night after night; and Yossarian is still looking for new ways to stay alive.

It is also impossible for Yossarian to be sent home on medical relief because of Catch-22. Doc Daneeka, the medical officer, explains that he can ground anyone who is crazy, but anyone who wants to avoid combat duty is not crazy and therefore cannot be grounded. This is Catch-22, the inevitable loophole in the scheme of justice, the self-justification of authority, the irony of eternal circumstance. Catch-22 explains Colonel Cathcart, who continues to raise the number of missions and volunteers his pilots for every dangerous operation in the Mediterranean theater. He also plans to have prayers during every briefing session but gives up that idea when he learns that officers and enlisted men must pray to the same god. It explains the struggle for power between General Dreedle,

who wants a fighting outfit, and General Peckem of Special Services, who wants to see tighter bombing patterns—they look better in aerial photographs—and issues a directive ordering all tents in the Mediterranean theater to be pitched with their fronts facing toward the Washington Monument. It explains Captain Black, the intelligence officer who compels the officers to sign a new loyalty oath each time they get their map cases, flak suits and parachutes, pay checks, haircuts, and meals in the mess.

Above all, Catch-22 explains Lieutenant Milo Mindbinder, the mess officer who parlays petty black market operations into an international syndicate in which everyone, as he says, has a share. By the time that he has his organization on a paying basis, he has been elected mayor of half a dozen Italian cities, Vice-Shah of Oran, Caliph of Baghdad, Imam of Damascus, and Sheik of Araby. Once, he almost makes a mistake by cornering the market on Egyptian cotton, but after some judicious bribery, he unloads it on the United States government. The climax of his career comes when he rents his fleet of private planes to the Germans and from the Pianosa control tower directs the bombing and strafing of his own outfit. Figures of public decency were outraged until Milo opened his books for public inspection and showed the profit that he had made. Then everything was all right: In the writer's strange, mad world, patriotism and profit are indistinguishable. The world lives by Milo's motto, the claim that whatever is good for the syndicate is good for the nation.

Eventually, Yossarian takes off for neutral Sweden, three jumps ahead of the authorities and less than one jump ahead of Nately's whore, who for some reason blames him for her lover's death and tries to kill him. He does not leave, however, before spending a night wandering alone through wartime Rome. This portion of the book is appalling in its picture of greed, lust, and brutality. *Catch-22* is a work reaffirming the ancient ties of cruelty and humor in its vision of everything vicious and absurd in muddled modern society. Heller seems to say that, in this world, people of goodwill must either escape or perish, that if this world is sane, then madness alone makes sense. Without being profound, his novel is a work repudiating the world's values and society's behavior.

Critical Evaluation

In 1961, the publication of *Catch-22* became an occasion for some rather freewheeling critical acclaim. Many reviewers called it the best novel out of World War II, and

at least one proclaimed it the best American novel out of anywhere in years. "Comic," "horrifying," "Rabelaisian," "exhilarating," "devastating," "rowdy," "cruelly sane," "compellingly moving"—these were among the epithets used to describe Joseph Heller's rambunctious first novel. In short, the book got off the ground with all the speed and thrust of jet propulsion.

Some of this acclaim was probably a tribute to the author's daring and prodigality. At a time when most young American writers appeared to be so obsessed by the idea of the well-made novel that their books tended to resemble carefully composed mood studies or tone poems, Heller broke all the rules. Nevertheless, energy and imagination such as he displayed are determinants rather than coordinates in fiction. The simple truth is that *Catch-22* is something less and something more than the conventional novel. As a novel, it is turgid, loose-jointed, and always threatening to break out at the seams. As a piece of writing, however, it is an altogether remarkable performance. Ferociously and bawdily comic in parts, banal in spots, and fantastically gruesome at times, it achieves a lunatic identity and wild inner logic of its own. The book is what one might expect in a collaboration between Franz Kafka and Krazy Kat, to which have been added dialogue passages by a Hemingwayesque master of speech patterns, some scatological scenes suggested by Henry Miller, hallucinated nonsense out of Lewis Carroll, and some chunks of the most undisciplined writing since Thomas Wolfe. It is not, as some have suggested, Mauldin's cartoons in prose or an American version of Jaroslav Hašek's *The Good Soldier: Schweik.* It is a collage of wartime violence, sex, military snafu, black market dealing, hymns of hate, and guffaws of gutty humor.

Despite its obvious flaws, *Catch-22* is brilliant, devastating, and apocalyptic. It has become a pivotal work in contemporary literature of the absurd, sometimes called black humor or bitter comedy. It is not, as in the case of novels out of World War I, a story of initiation. In theme, fable, and mood, it deals with the simple, grim realities of survival in a world with all values reversed by the violence of war. As such, it is an assault, made in hilarious prose, on mechanical, institutionalized, homogenized, and anesthetized society. Black humor has as the objects of its guffawing satire the clichés of thought, feeling, and action that color almost every aspect of modern life, from stereotypes of love, home, religion, and death to the Bomb. If Heller's novel has an underlying purpose, then it is to be found in the writer's apparent belief that a comic vision of experience and a sense of the outrageously absurd in human affairs provide the only possible stance for the rational individual in a world in which the dividing line between graspable reality and wild fantasy has all but disappeared.

THE CATCHER IN THE RYE

Type of work: Novel
Author: J. D. Salinger (1919-   )
Type of plot: Adolescent drama
Time of plot: Late 1940's
Locale: New York City and California
First published: 1951

Salinger's famous and controversial novel The Catcher in the Rye *is a classic study of alienation, the story of a young man who feels completely isolated from the world around him.*

Principal Characters

Holden Caulfield, the novel's teenage protagonist and narrator. After being expelled from school, Holden spends a long weekend wandering the streets of New York City, seeking companionship and understanding from everyone from his little sister and his old girlfriend to taxicab drivers and a prostitute. Yet these encounters provide him no satisfaction; eventually he returns home and has a mental breakdown.

Phoebe Caulfield, Holden's younger sister. Phoebe is the only person to whom Holden believes he can relate; since the death of their brother Allie, she is the only one with whom he feels truly comfortable. Phoebe convinces Holden to return home with her instead of running away.

Ward Stradlater, Holden's roommate at Pencey Prep School. Handsome, popular, aggressive, and self-confident, Ward represents the phoniness that Holden sees in almost everyone around him. Ward's date with Holden's friend Jane Gallagher leads to a fight between Holden and Ward shortly before Holden leaves the school.

Sally Hayes, one of Holden's girlfriends. They meet for a date while he is in New York, but she cannot understand his feelings. After he harshly criticizes her, she cries, and they part.

Mr. Antolini, Holden's former teacher. He offers Holden advice about his problems and invites him to spend the night at his apartment. When Holden awakens to find Mr. Antolini touching his head, he becomes upset and flees.

The Story

By the age of sixteen, Holden Caulfield had been dismissed from three private schools because of academic problems; Pencey Prep School was his fourth such failure. Even more humiliating was his losing the fencing team's equipment on the subway during a trip into New York City. His history teacher, Mr. Spencer, tried to talk with him, expressing concern over Holden's repeated failure, lack of motivation, and nonchalant attitude about his future. Holden, meanwhile, was thinking of the ducks in the lagoon in Central Park, wondering where they went during the winter when the pond froze.

That night, Holden learned that his roommate, Ward Stradlater, had a date with Jane Gallagher, a young woman whom Holden liked and admired. Holden knew Ward's reputation well, and he worried about what might happen to Jane on the date. When Ward returned hours later, Holden got into a fight with him. After Ward left, Hol-

den tried to talk to a neighbor, an unpopular student named Robert Ackley, but all that the usually inquisitive Robert wanted to do was sleep. Instead of waiting the few days before the start of Christmas vacation to go home, Holden impulsively decided to leave the school that night, take a train to New York, and stay in the city by himself until it was time to go home.

Holden took a taxicab from the train station to the Edmont Hotel, where he would stay for several days. He wanted to call his little sister, Phoebe, but was afraid that his parents would find out what he had done; he hesitated to call Jane Gallagher for similar reasons. So he spent his time in bars, but he felt as out of place in the upscale nightclubs as in the cheap hotel lounges. An elevator operator at his hotel persuaded Holden to invite a prostitute to his room, but Holden and the young woman, Sunny, only talked. A dispute over five dollars led the elevator operator, Maurice, to beat Holden while Sunny took the money.

Increasingly depressed, Holden called a girlfriend, Sally Hayes, and they went to a play together. While discussing the play, Holden revealed his deep sense of dissatisfaction and alienation, but Sally could not relate to his feelings. When Holden impulsively suggested running off to New England together, Sally dismissed his idea as ridiculous, failing to understand the feelings of desperation that prompted it. Angered, Holden insulted Sally, who cried before parting from him.

After a meeting with an old schoolmate, Carl Luce, ended in similar disappointment, Holden decided to sneak home to visit Phoebe. Misquoting a Robert Burns poem, Holden told Phoebe that he envisioned himself as "the catcher in the rye"—an imaginary person responsible for catching little children and keeping them from falling off a cliff as they played in a field of rye. Holden gave Phoebe his red hunting hat and slipped out of the apartment when his parents returned home.

Holden accepted an invitation from one of his former teachers, Mr. Antolini, to spend the night at his apartment. They had a long talk in which Antolini expressed many of the same concerns that Mr. Spencer had shared with Holden earlier; Antolini believed that Holden was

"riding for some kind of a terrible, terrible fall." He foresaw Holden growing more bitter and alienated, "dying nobly, one way or another, for some highly unworthy cause." When confronted with this prospect, Holden grew tired and unable to concentrate. He went to bed, and, a short time later, he awakened to find Mr. Antolini stroking his head. Frightened, he fled the apartment and slept on a bench in Grand Central Station.

After experiencing a panic attack while walking down the street, Holden decided to run away: He would fulfill his misanthropic fantasy by living in a cabin in the woods and pretending that he could neither speak nor hear. He met Phoebe one last time. They fought over her wanting to come with him, but they reconciled quickly, and she persuaded him to return home with her. She gave him back his red hunting hat to keep the rain off his head as he watched her ride a carousel, the first gesture of true empathy that he had received or responded to since leaving the school.

After returning home, Holden had an emotional breakdown and was institutionalized. He looked forward to returning to school the following fall, but he displayed as little insight into his problems as he had that final day at Pencey Prep.

Critical Evaluation

The Catcher in the Rye is a popular and controversial novel. Its popularity, especially among young people, attests to the psychological accuracy and insight of Salinger's portrayal of his teenage protagonist, Holden. The controversy has centered primarily on the novel's use of language. Because the novel is written in the first person (the only way that it could be written), character and language are inseparable: Holden's words perfectly reflect and expose his sense of alienation, contempt, and depression.

Holden's sense of alienation is profound. Every incident, conversation, and setting in the novel develops and reinforces this theme. The first-person narrative focuses entirely on Holden, and although other people weave briefly in and out of his path, he is unable to establish real connections with any of them. His short conversations with taxicab drivers, school friends, and women are essentially alike: No one understands (or seems to care about) what Holden is trying to express. No one pauses to ask what is behind his musings about the Central Park ducks; no one considers the extreme sense of loneliness and isolation that would prompt him to invite

taxicab drivers out for drinks or to call acquaintances he has not seen for years. Ward is preoccupied with getting ready for his date (and with persuading Holden to write an English paper for him), Robert only wants to sleep, and Sally can think of nothing but the play and the people she knows in the audience. The places where Holden wanders—a silent dormitory, an empty hotel lobby, deserted city streets—all reinforce his sense of isolation. Yet even in crowded bars Holden feels alone.

Holden reacts by criticizing everyone around him. Except for Phoebe and his brother Allie, whom he idolizes, everyone he knows is a "phony," a "jerk," or a "moron." Salinger reveals Holden's contemptuousness gradually: Holden's initial criticisms of people such as Ward and Robert seem valid, but by the time that he is finding fault with Sir Laurence Olivier and Christ's disciples, the reader realizes that something is definitely wrong. Holden is particularly sensitive to "phoniness," which he finds everywhere—in his teachers, in his friends, in films. Yet Holden is, in a sense, the real "phony": He tells lies for no reason, he gives false names to people he meets, and he pretends to be sexually experienced although he is a virgin. Holden is a study in contradiction. He claims to hate films, but he loves to imitate them, as when he tap dances in the bathroom at Pencey. "I'm quite illiterate, but I read a lot," he says, oblivious to the paradox. Most important, while he obsessively criticizes others, he strenuously resists any critical examination of himself. When Spencer, Antolini, and Phoebe try to make him face his problems, his mind wanders, he cannot concentrate, and he becomes suddenly tired. His resistance is not deliberate, but rather a defensive barricade that his subconscious has set up to shelter him from the pain of self-awareness.

Holden attempts to retreat from a world that he fears and cannot understand—an adult world that includes sex, acceptance of loss, and responsibility for self and others—by adopting an idealized, romantic outlook. He veritably worships Phoebe and Allie (significantly, his younger siblings); he views Jane Gallagher through a hazy mixture of memory and romantic illusion, remembering little more than how she kept her kings on the back row when she played checkers. Fearing change (and, therefore, growth), he takes comfort in museum exhibits that always stay the same, and he is horrified by obscene graffiti scrawled on the walls of Phoebe's school, a brutal intrusion of adult reality into a child's world. Yet Holden's romanticism, like his "catcher in the rye" fantasy, ultimately fails him, resulting in disillusionment and depression. "I don't get hardly anything out of anything," he says. "I'm in bad shape."

Critical reaction to the novel has been mixed, with much of the negative commentary centering on the book's language. Holden's use of phrases such as "don't hardly" has led some critics to question the book's status as "serious literature," and the numerous profanities that pepper Holden's speech have kept the novel on banned or censored book lists across the United States since its publication. Yet Salinger is accurate in his representation of the speech of a sixteen-year-old boy, particularly one as bitter and cynical as Holden. For Holden, everything is "corny," "crumby," or "lousy"; everyone is "dopey," "scraggy," or worse—that is how he views life. It is, in fact, difficult to imagine the book being written any other way.

The Catcher in the Rye is characteristic of much of the literature of the early to mid-1900's. These decades, known in art and literature as the modern period, saw the horrors of World War I and its aftermath, which was not only economic disaster but also a prevailing mood of despair, disillusionment with traditional social institutions, and a profound sense of the meaninglessness of life. Salinger's novel, which was published in 1951 but written over the previous ten years, reflects this worldview. Seen in this light, Holden's story is not a case history of an emotionally disturbed boy but a representative account of modern life. In a world that gave rise to chemical weapons, the Great Depression, and the Nazi death camps, Salinger suggests that the sensitive, intelligent person—the person who sees the world as it is—is doomed, condemned to alienation, paranoia, and anger. The insensitive, self-centered, "phony" people survive and prosper, while the Holden Caulfields remain forever trapped between fragile illusion and overwhelming despair. Holden, who dreams of being the catcher in the rye, is really like one of the children headed for the cliff—and no one is there to catch him and keep him from falling off.

CAT'S CRADLE

Type of work: Novel
Author: Kurt Vonnegut, Jr. (1922-   )
Type of plot: Science-fiction fable
Time of plot: Early 1960's
Locale: Ilium, New York, and the Caribbean republic of San Lorenzo
First published: 1963

One of Vonnegut's four powerful 1960's novels, Cat's Cradle *reflects that era's fear of nuclear annihilation and rejection of Establishment values through the effective use of satirical wit and a lively cast of eccentrics.*

Principal Characters

John, also called **Jonah,** a journalist and the narrator of the novel. His plan to write a book on the events of August 6, 1945, leads him to the Hoenikker family, to *ice-nine,* and finally to an encampment of survivors on the island of San Lorenzo. After the *ice-nine*-generated destruction of the world around them, his initial writing project has become a chronicle of the last days of life on earth. Filtered through the medium of his fervent conversion to the cynical antireligion Bokonism, Jonah's account adopts a tone whose surface sardonic wit only partially conceals his anguish over the coming extinction of life.

Bokonon, alias **Lionel Boyd Johnson,** a Tobagonian adventurer, soldier of fortune, and philosopher. Cast up on San Lorenzo, he devises Bokonism, a cynical antireligion based on lies and deception. The ban against Bokonism provides the *raison d'être* both for San Lorenzo's despotic government and for the furtive devotion of the island's adherents to it. Bokonon is an elusive, powerful presence throughout the story.

Dr. Felix Hoenikker, a father of the atomic bomb and the creator of *ice-nine.* He is a man whose humanity was consumed by his total commitment to scientific curiosity, exploration, and invention. His indifference to his family contributed to his wife's death and the idiosyncrasies of his three children, all as stunted emotionally as his youngest is physically. Hoenikker's last invention, the unique crystals *ice-nine,* caused his own death and drew his children into a conspiracy of power when they divided up the crystals among themselves.

Angela Hoenikker, more than six feet tall, graceless, and possessing only one notable talent: her exquisite clarinet-playing. Condemned by her mother's death to look after her father and younger siblings and held in contempt by a philandering husband whose motive for marriage was to secure the *ice-nine* formula, Angela nevertheless displays tenacious loyalty in all of her relationships. She dies with dignity, putting her *ice-nine*-contaminated clarinet to her lips.

Franklin Hoenikker, the middle child, whose talent for visionary design is belied by his misogyny and his unlovable nature. On the strength of his famous parentage and some luck, Frank at twenty-six is a major-general and "minister of science and progress" to "Papa" Monzano, the tinpot dictator of San Lorenzo. Designated to succeed to the presidency, Frank quickly reveals himself as possessing neither the talent nor the desire for leadership. Instead, he displays a fierce instinct for survival, mirrored in his fascination with a similar instinct that he detects among the ants in his ant farm.

Newton "Newt" Hoenikker, the youngest son of Felix, a midget. Traumatized on the morning of the Hiroshima bombing by his father's one clumsy attempt to play with him, Newt spends his time obsessively painting canvasses showing only variations of the cat's cradle string game that Felix had attempted to show the six-year-old. Newt has an otherwise engaging and gregarious nature, but he is also shrewdly aware of the potential for power contained in his thermos-flasked *ice-nine* crystals.

Philip and Julian Castle, white scions of an American family that established a short-lived sugar business on San Lorenzo. Philip, weary, sad, and cynical, is also San Lorenzo's one luxury-hotel owner, a painter, the island republic's historian, and a steadfast convert to Bokonism. With his father Julian, the founder of the House of Hope and Mercy in the Jungle, Philip represents the disillusionment and alienation of twentieth century rational humanity. No one is saved at Julian's hospital, Philip's mural remains unfinished and his history of San Lorenzo illuminates little. Father and son disappear without a trace after surviving the initial *ice-nine* catastrophe, leaving Jonah with Julian's heartfelt plea ringing in his mind: "For the love of God, *both* of you, *please* keep writing!"

The Story

Jonah sets out to write *The Day the World Ended*, a study of what important Americans were doing on August 6, 1945, when the atomic bomb was dropped on Hiroshima, Japan. His research brings him to Felix Hoenikker, one of the scientists responsible for the bomb's invention. A letter to Hoenikker's youngest son, Newt, elicits a garrulous reply that eventually leads Jonah to the Hoenikkers' hometown of Ilium, a dreary mid-New York State city that belies the glamour of its Trojan namesake. Here, a resentful former colleague of Hoenikker reveals the secret of his last invention, intended originally for military use: *ice-nine*, an ice crystal so formulated that it instantly freezes whatever comes into contact with it. The three Hoenikker siblings—Newt, Angela, and Franklin—have divided between them and preserved the three slivers of the destructive crystals, storing in simple thermos flasks the seeds of the world's annihilation.

A chain of coincidences unites Jonah with Newt and Angela Hoenikker on an airplane to San Lorenzo, a barren rectangular Caribbean island republic that is ruled by the ailing tyrant "Papa" Monzano and Franklin Hoenikker, who had been missing for three years and who is now Papa's right-hand man and scientific adviser. While on the plane trip, Jonah reads San Lorenzo resident Philip Castle's manuscript history of the island republic and encounters the life and "religion" of Bokonon. Jonah's instant conversion to Bokonism is confirmed when he sees the banned religion furtively practiced by the island's native population, especially Papa's exotic and desirable adopted daughter, Mona.

On San Lorenzo, Jonah is drawn into a chain of events that see him designated Papa's reluctant successor and lead him to witness the catastrophic accidental destruction of the dictator's castle fortress, the bizarre release of *ice-nine*, and the instantaneous annihilation of the surrounding landscape and people exposed to the maelstrom of ice. The survivors, whose means of rescue are provided, ironically, by the dungeons and subterranean torture chambers of the ancient fortress, are Frank, Newt, Jonah, and the Crosbys, a couple of stereotypically Ugly American tourist-entrepreneurs. Mona, who has shared shelter for three days with a besotted Jonah, upon their emergence commits suicide by *ice-nine* with the almost vacuous serenity and seeming indifference with which she lived. For her, as for Angela, life without purpose or hope for the future is intolerable.

One other survivor turns out to be Bokonon, whose elusive existence had shaped and directed the dictatorial rule of Papa Monzano. In an anticlimactic encounter between joyous disciple and revered master, Jonah, trying to envisage a post-*ice-nine* future, receives the final response of this cynical messiah: Having completed the books of Bokonon, their author would climb mystical Mount McCabe and commit *ice-nine* suicide, thumbing his nose at God, the universe, and hope. On this note, Jonah's retrospective ends; it appears that he has heralded nothing and that survival must be pursued only for its own sake.

Critical Evaluation

At its publication in 1963, *Cat's Cradle* was not immediately popular. Yet linked with the three other novels that make up Vonnegut's 1960's oeuvre—*Mother Night* (1961); *God Bless You, Mr. Rosewater: Or, Pearls Before Swine* (1965), and especially *Slaughterhouse Five: Or, The Children's Crusade, a Duty-Dance with Death* (1969)—it has provoked much lasting critical discussion about both its style and its themes. *Cat's Cradle* is an iconoclastic, satirical treatment of issues that profoundly affect twentieth century humankind: the loss of religious faith; science as a false god; humankind's deceptive rationale for creativity (*"No damn cat, and no damn cradle,"* observes Newt Hoenikker of the intricate, ancient child's string game that is symbolic of science's smoke-and-mirrors aspect); the unattractiveness of modern reality; a missing sense of human purpose; but finally, affirmation of humanity's will to survive in a meaningful way.

All these themes are explored through narrator Jonah's fatal involvement with the Hoenikker family when he begins research for his intended book, ironically entitled *The Day the World Ended*. Clearly Jonah had planned a stance of moral condemnation, as it was to be "a Christian book," written by a man not yet converted to Bokonism, the informing antireligion of *Cat's Cradle*. Instead, like his Old Testament counterpart, Jonah bears witness to apocalyptic events and heralds an unredemptive Messiah when he rejects Christianity and embraces Bokonism. The novel ends when Jonah finally encounters Bokonon, now a mild-mannered old man who has survived this holocaust with his usual detached aplomb. He is preparing the conclusion both of *The Books of Bokonon*, his antireligion's testament, and his life. He postulates his own death by *ice-nine*, thumbing his nose at "You Know Who." Bokonon's cynical outlook has been taken by some of *Cat's Cradle*'s detractors as Vonnegut's own. Certainly the narrator, Jonah, creates a conundrum by founding his artistic and spiritual odyssey, the novel itself, on Bokonon's paradoxical basic premise—"All of the true things I am about to tell you are shameless lies."—raising critical charges of Vonnegut's flippancy and superficiality. Others have commended the satirical wit with which Vonnegut successfully enlivens the serious themes that he treats.

Cat's Cradle's style generated as much critical discussion as its themes did. Critic James Mellard listed Vonnegut as one of the prime creators of the "exploded" novel form, along with such literary contemporaries as Jack Kerouac, Donald Barthelme, John Barth, and Richard Brautigan. The choppy, fragmented style reflects the twentieth century's anxious preoccupation with alienation, disintegration, even impending annihilation.

The novel has 127 chapters, many as brief as a page. The short, rapid bursts of narrative, delivered mostly in straightforward, unadorned prose, suit the tone taken by the journalist/narrator Jonah: wry, often self-mocking, masking an underlying depth of seriousness. The narrative frequently reads like notes toward a journalistic piece. In vignette after vignette, place, character, event, or mood is strongly evoked; dialogue, often choppy, is lent significance and overtone, even if its subject is trivial; and cliff-hangers or implied logical conclusions tantalize at each chapter's end. The absurd events leading up to the magnificently described cataclysmal destruction by *ice-nine* exemplifies Vonnegut's talent at juxtaposing the trivial and the grand, the silly and the significant, the comic and the terrible that is his (and Bokonon's) view of human existence. Jonah's sense of urgency and mission is emphatic; after all, he is writing *after* the destruction of almost all the world. The fragmentary style best suits his anxious wish to get everything down, for what eventual readers he does not know. Nevertheless, he feels deeply the need to record, to set down, especially as this is his designated task and purpose within the little surviving group that "Mom" Crosby gaily refers to as "the Swiss Family Robinson." The resulting work—*Cat's Cradle*—ultimately achieves an overall coherence and a compelling energy that makes it readable and probably does much to explain the novel's eventual popular appeal, particularly among college students.

By 1963, the younger reading generation, responding in the 1950's to Cold War politics, accelerating materialism, and the more pessimistic premises of existentialism, was turning its attention to the burgeoning Civil Rights movement. If, at *Cat's Cradle*'s publication there was only a small readership for the novel, by the mid-1960's and the acceleration of the anti-Vietnam War movement, it was growing and enthusiastic, receptive to Vonnegut's blend of despair and the comic, of searing-self-doubt and affirmative rejoicing, of his sense of both the meanness and the sublimity of human existence. Above all, as critic William Rodney Allen's study *Understanding Kurt Vonnegut* (1991) makes clear, Vonnegut celebrates humanity's creativity, not so much in the science as in the artistry of life. He affirms human beings' will to survive over their tendency to self-destruction.

CEREMONY IN LONE TREE

Type of work: Novel
Author: Wright Morris (1910-   )
Type of plot: Psychological realism
Time of plot: One day in March, 1957
Locale: Acapulco, Mexico; and Lincoln and Lone Tree, Nebraska
First published: 1960

Using many of his characters from The Field of Vision, *Wright Morris weaves a complex portrait of a group of individuals, both young and old, who must resolve their ties to the past in order to live in the present.*

Principal Characters

Gordon Boyd, a middle-aged writer who acts as a catalyst for other people in finding their true selves. Boyd has always attempted to create a larger-than-life persona.

"Daughter," his young girlfriend, who travels with him to Lone Tree, Nebraska.

Walter McKee, Boyd's boyhood friend. A cattle rancher, he has lived vicariously through Boyd, "witnessing" his acts.

Gordon McKee, Walter's little grandson.

Lois McKee, Walter's wife. Once in love with Boyd, she cannot express her emotions. It is her impetuous act that eventually frees the other characters.

Tom Scanlon, Lois' father, who is to celebrate his ninetieth birthday.

Calvin McKee, Scanlon's great-grandson, who is trapped in his family's frustrated past. He finds love with Etoile.

Etoile Momeyer, Calvin's cousin, a free spirit who revels in her sexuality. She alone is able to discard the past and embrace the future.

Maxine Momeyer, Lois' sister and the mother of Etoile.

Bud Momeyer, Maxine's husband, a mail carrier who shoots animals with a bow and arrow in order to collect bounties.

Lee Roy Momeyer, Bud's nephew, who runs over two bullies.

Charles Munger, a pathological killer. He murders ten innocent people, establishing his identity through violence.

In his first nine novels, Wright Morris processed fragments of a vision that focused on the American Land, Character, and Dream. In *The Field of Vision*, the first novel of a trilogy, these fragments began to cohere. *Ceremony in Lone Tree* is the second novel in the trilogy. Morris' usual method has three phases. First, he describes the scene. Second, he conducts a roundup of the characters. Third, he depicts a kind of ceremony that serves to set up significant relationships and to evoke transient moments of self-knowledge that cause a faint transformation in the characters.

Through a flawed pane of glass in the hotel lobby, old Tom Scanlon gazes upon Lone Tree, Nebraska, a ghost town. His view is to the west over the arid plains, but to the east, the prairie town of Polk prospers. Morris describes "The Scene" in such a way as to suggest his themes and to convey an impression of the spiritual desolation of his characters. The ancestors of the old West-

ern pioneers have now turned eastward again. Having no perspective on the present, Scanlon's point of view is restricted to the wasteland. For the rest of the novel, Morris pushes the old man into the background; during "The Ceremony," he sleeps on a cot behind the stove.

In *Ceremony in Lone Tree*, Morris exhibits most impressively his talent for creating people who illustrate aspects of the American character; if they appear grotesque, they may prove to be similar to the folks next door. In "The Roundup," Morris presents each character in a separate section. Boyd, a self-exiled Nebraska writer, approaches the homeplace from Acapulco, where he has been trying to forget an encounter with his childhood friends, Walter and Lois McKee, at a bullfight in Mexico City. When McKee impulsively invites him to a reunion in honor of Tom Scanlon's ninetieth birthday, Boyd is drawn by perverse nostalgia. To shock the folks back home, he takes with him a woman whom he calls Daughter; audacious, youthful spirit of the present, she sustains him during his journey into the past. Next come the viewpoints of McKee and Lois, who approach Lone Tree from the modern city of Lincoln, Nebraska. McKee has lived his empty life vicariously through Boyd, hoping the hero will fill it with meaning. Lois, the opposite of Daughter, epitomizes the suppression of emotions that make everyone tense and nervous. Characters not presented in *The Field of Vision* appear next. Maxine Momeyer has a difficult life: Her daughter, Etoile, is sexually precocious, and her husband, Bud, has never grown up. When Bud goes off duty as a mail carrier, he collects bounty on stray cats by shooting them with a bow and arrow. Etoile is in love with her stuttering cousin Calvin, who rejects people in favor of horses. Events in the present occur within the frame of a recent incident that shocked the world: the slaughter of ten people by Charles Munger of Lincoln, while his friend, Lee Roy, Bud's nephew, killed two bullies with his hot rod. Jennings, who writes pulp Westerns, is so intrigued by the mystery of life that he has no life of his own. Boyd wonders whether he is drawn to these people because they are so hopeless or so full of hope.

Because there are nine viewpoints, with twenty-eight shifts, unity could have become a problem for Morris. Unity is maintained, however, by a controlling conception, by various patterns of relationship among the characters, and by a consistency of style among the viewpoints—a sophisticated manipulation of the clichés of everyday speech, as filtered through the third person. The tone is comic, but Morris' mingling of the bizarre and the humorous creates a strange atmosphere in which the comedy frightens as it amuses. In the absence of an overt pattern of novelistic action, the relationships among the characters generate suspense and excitement by the controlled development of their many twists and turns, nuances, suppressions, and flare-ups. To common situations, past and present, the characters' differing responses are always active, creating an impressive sense of motion. In ways representative of Morris, character, theme, and motif evolve organically as the novel moves to its climax.

Like a ghost town film set, the Lone Tree Hotel inspires the enactment of an outdated drama, the *personae* of which are Buffalo Bill, Billy the Kid, Santa Claus, Charles Lindbergh, Robin Hood, and Davy Crockett. Shifting from one to another, most of the men play roles whose styles were shaped in the American past; less inclined to play roles, the women lament the failure of the men to make something real happen in the present. Nothing is what it seems because the characters are dis-

posed to see anything suggested to them; what is there (fact) is no more vivid than what the mind can project (fiction). In the rhetoric of magic, the effect is that of "now you see it, now you don't." Just as Bud's attic and basement are full of the junk that he collects from people on his mail route, each character is a repository of cast-off lives; though Lee Roy can make one smoothly running car out of many wrecked ones, a human may break down if he or she is a composite of other people with no strong self-nucleus. Boyd is like a carnival barker, talking about freaks who try, in an exaggerated way, to be what they are not.

Trains, cars, bombs, and guns are other outward, material symbols of the American experience and of the personalities of the characters. The plains are like the sea, and everything seems to move like ships over a metaphysical landscape. Experience has blended, and blurred, fact and fiction, nourishing illusions that aggravate the problem of identity. In Lone Tree, where moonlight illuminates the romance and the nostalgia of the past and real events have an aura of the imaginary, the characters behave as though they are in a motion picture and thus free of responsibility, but they experience disillusionment and nausea in the present. In the foreground, Morris presents a parody of American popular culture, but in the background hovers the image of the atomic bomb. Near the end, past fiction and present fact collide in the lives of the characters and either wake them or lull them to sleep.

To Morris, the suppression of emotion is a trait in the American character; emotion is released vicariously in unconscious parodies of violence. By suddenly expressing their suppressed emotions, Lee Roy and Charles Munger exemplify themes that relate less drastically to the other characters. Though the spirit of the times helped make them what they are, their audacity differs from Boyd's and their violence contrasts with that of the old frontier. In Munger, Morris shows an exaggeration of the nightmare side of the American dream of success: The boy shoots everybody he encounters in order to be somebody. Fear of themselves and of each other, of Munger and his kind, and of atomic annihilation keep the characters tense but responsive to the unexpected.

In quiet, "normal," even prudish people, Morris suggests, there is an inherent wildness. Giving in to impulse by word or act, each character has a moment of truth, audacity, love, or imagination in which wildness and freedom are tasted. Smothered in Maxine, sexuality breathes deeply in Etoile. Boyd's presence stimulates each character to reveal a true self. The reader follows a spontaneous ceremony in which characters rid themselves of the inessentials of the past, improvising upon new personalities. Before the explosion of the bomb (made up of the convergence of lines of tension among the characters), Boyd clowns and indulges in an outburst against the concealment of true feelings. He is made speechless, however, by the behavior of his old witnesses. Ironically, only Boyd and Scanlon, heroes of the past, fail to act audaciously.

The confrontation of the present with past is dramatized in the most highly charged of the concentrated moments of which the novel is composed. When Etoile and Calvin roar into the ghost town in a wagon, a dead showdog in back, shot by Bud with his bow and arrow, Boyd's audacity finally affects Lois; she fires her grandfather's Colt .45 as an impulsive act that rouses her from emotional stultification and sets off a beneficial chain reaction among the other characters. Symbolically, she kills her father and the mythic past represented by his father's pistol. Now the past has come full cycle. Scanlon's birthday is his death day, but it is also the birth of the present for the others. In the wagon in which he was born, old Scanlon is taken to be buried. Yet Morris does not allow this sensational event to jar the primary focus, which is on character consciousness; he goes back to points before the incident and presents it over again through several other points of view.

Ceremony in Lone Tree is a continuation of Morris' exploration of the male-female conflict. Having waited long enough for the men to break up the routine and monotony of their lives, the women act. From a ceremony of death, they try to salvage something for the living. In control, the women will build on the ruins created by the sleeping males.

The relationship between heroes and their witnesses, developed in most of Morris' previous novels, ends in *Ceremony in Lone Tree*. Boyd has always tried, like the United States, to be more than he is, prompted by witnesses who have always hoped for something by which to live. Yet, between the promise of the amateur and the performance of the master, something more than audacity is demanded. Boyd once attempted to walk on water; later he wrote a book about the incident. In his audacity, however, there is no longer an element of spontaneity and surprise, for after Boyd squirts a bull with soda in Mexico, McKee can anticipate the hero's antics. At the end, Boyd, trapped in his own childhood (in a sense he never left the plains), is asleep at the feet of Scanlon, dead embodiment of the heroic past, while McKee, the

disenchanted witness, holds the reins. As they move over a landscape that was once arid plains, McKee gazes over the green wheat of the present, which promises a future unbeguiled by those such as Boyd. The present eludes the hero; only the past has pattern. From childhood, he has, as Lois knows, put the later appreciation before the immediacy of the moment. If the kiss that Boyd gave her on the porch thrilled Lois, then it was the audacity of his own act that charmed Boyd. Lois senses that Boyd's audacity was camouflage, that he was as much afraid of her as McKee was. She sees that Boyd, McKee, and her father have not grown up. Like the country itself, they are still adolescent. Hero Boyd and witness McKee begin to merge, but it is not clear whether the virtues and the faults of the two roles will make an effective blend. Having discovered that it gives off no charge in the present, Boyd is free of the past, but he has as yet no indication of a future.

In the behavior of his characters, Morris depicts a conflict between the American past and present; the future is both promising and ominous. His purpose is to free his characters from the past. Concerned almost entirely with immediate or recent happenings, many seem unaware of their captivity in the distant past. Present and past coexist: A fossil himself, Scanlon recalls the exploration of the Western frontier, while overhead a jet crosses the face of the moon. The past is dead and the present is dying because the United States has failed to realize its promise and now lives in fear of fallout.

The real reason for the reunion is to get Calvin and Etoile together. On the landscape where things began and are now coming to an end, perhaps something can begin for the young lovers. Calvin is trapped in Scanlon's past (which is purely imaginary, for he has confused his father's past with his own uneventful one), but Etoile lives in her own present, eager to precipitate the future. The new generation transforms the past with new forms of audacity. Etoile is Lois' opposite; with Boyd-like audacity, she frees Calvin from the sexual restraint that has prevailed in the past. Because the female seizes the day, Calvin experiences with Etoile what Boyd failed to experience with Lois. In the end, when the past and the present confront each other and explode, it is not clear who gains or loses, but the implication is that the ground is cleared, even though none of the younger generation seems promising material out of which to process a meaningful future.

THE COLOR PURPLE

Type of work: Novel
Author: Alice Walker (1944-   )
Type of plot: Domestic melodrama
Time of plot: Early to mid-twentieth century
Locale: Rural Georgia, Memphis, and Africa
First published: 1982

Walker's story about a young African-American woman in rural Georgia, abused and mistreated by her stepfather and husband and separated from her two children and her beloved sister, made The Color Purple *a critical success and one of her most popular novels.*

Principal Characters

Celie, the narrator and protagonist. She tells the story of her struggle to find an identity through entries written in her diary from the age of fourteen, when she is barely literate, and through letters written to her sister Nettie, from whom she has been separated—a correspondence that continues well into middle age, when the two are finally reunited. She is first schooled by her younger sister Nettie and later by Shug Avery, her husband's mistress, and Sofia, her stepson's wife. Her brutal husband, who drives her sister away, has married her only to have a housekeeper and nurse to care for his children by an earlier marriage. Shug Avery helps her to escape from this abusive and loveless marriage.

Mr.——(Albert), Celie's husband, a farmer and widower with children, whose true love is blues singer Shug Avery. He makes life miserable for Celie and attempts to rape her sister when Nettie comes to live with them; he then sends Nettie away after she refuses his advances. Albert blocks future correspondence between the two sisters after Nettie moves far away by intercepting her letters to Celie. He is a domestic tyrant from whom Celie finally escapes.

Nettie, Celie's sister. She is taken in by Samuel, a minister who becomes a missionary in Africa, and his wife, Corrine, to look after their adopted children, who are in fact Celie's children fathered by her stepfather, Alfonso, who started the pattern of sexual abuse for Celie. Nettie goes with Samuel and Corrine to Africa and lives with them for several years in the village of Olinka. Af-

ter the death of Corrine, Samuel then marries Nettie, who becomes the stepmother of Celie's children. Her story, told through her letters to Celie, constitutes about a third of the novel and serves to teach Celie about her African heritage.

Shug Avery, Albert's mistress, an independent city woman and blues singer. She becomes Celie's most intimate friend and teaches her how to free herself from the dominance of her husband by taking Celie to Memphis, where she encourages Celie to start a business making pants. Shug is tremendously important for the way in which she teaches Celie about love and sexuality.

Sofia Butler, the strong and independent wife of Celie's stepson Harpo. Her life is complicated when she talks back to the white mayor's wife and then strikes out after the mayor slaps her for her insolence. As a consequence, she is first beaten and sent to prison, then paroled to serve as a maid to the mayor. She returns to her family a broken woman, but she is finally healed by her strong spirit. Sofia represents the struggle against Southern racism.

Mary Agnes (Squeak), a parallel figure to Shug Avery, who becomes the mistress of Sofia's husband, Harpo. She manages to get Sofia released on parole from prison by going to the warden, whose brother was her white father. Like Celie, Mary Agnes is influenced by Shug Avery and also becomes a blues singer, going to Memphis and finally running away to Panama with Shug's lover, Grady.

The Story

Celie, a fourteen-year-old African-American girl in rural Georgia, describes her life and troubles by writing letters to God in a diary that she keeps. She has been molested and raped by Alfonso, the man who she thinks is her father but who is in fact her stepfather. Alfonso takes Celie's two children by him, Adam and Olivia, away from her and puts them up for adoption. Celie's mother is sickly and soon dies. Celie lives like a slave, cooking, cleaning, and looking after the other children. She fears that her stepfather will also abuse her younger sister Nettie. A widower, named only Mr.—— (his Christian name is later revealed to be Albert) takes an interest in Nettie and asks for her hand in marriage, but Alfonso refuses consent. Mr.—— then takes Celie for his wife, mainly to rear his children and to keep house. To escape from Alfonso, Nettie comes to live with Celie, but after Albert makes sexual advances toward her that are rejected, Nettie is forced to leave. Thus the sisters are separated, and Albert later intercepts letters that Nettie sends to Celie over the years of separation. For all Celie knows, Nettie may be dead.

Nettie is more fortunate than Celie, however, and is taken in by missionary minister Samuel and his wife, Corrine, to look after their two adopted children, Olivia and Adam, the same children that Celie's stepfather put up for adoption. Nettie travels with this family, first to London and then to the African village of Olinka. Years pass, the children grow up, Corrine falls sick and dies, and Samuel takes Nettie as his second wife. Nettie continues all the while to write letters to Celie that will eventually teach her sister about the wider world and her own African heritage.

Meanwhile, back in Georgia, Celie is beaten, abused, exploited, and humiliated. Albert is openly unfaithful with a blues singer, Shug Avery, the woman whom he truly loves but was forbidden by his father to marry. Eventually, Albert brings Shug, who has taken ill, home for Celie to nurse back to health. A friendship develops between Shug and Celie that is more than close. Celie learns to love Shug, who teaches her how to love. Shug, however, has other lovers, first Grady, with whom she travels on the road, and later Germaine, a young musician.

Celie is also befriended by Sofia Butler, a strong-minded young woman who marries Harpo, Albert's old-est son by his first marriage, and bears him five children. Sofia's independence gets her into trouble. She talks back to the white mayor's wife, who offers her a job in town as her maid. When the mayor himself slaps Sofia and attempts to put her in her place, she hits the mayor and is imprisoned and badly beaten, losing her sight in one eye. These circumstances bring about an eleven-year separation from her husband and children. Harpo, meanwhile, takes a young woman named Mary Agnes, whom he nicknames Squeak because of her high-pitched voice, as his mistress, and she bears his sixth child. Though she had fought with Sofia, who knocked two of her teeth out before the incident in town with the mayor, Mary Agnes is instrumental is getting Sofia released from prison; the white warden happens to be her uncle, though in order to get what she wants, Mary Agnes is forced to submit to the warden sexually. Eventually, Sofia returns home, a broken woman who continues to serve her white masters, but she is able to resume her own family life.

With the help of Shug Avery, Celie discovers the letters written by her sister that Albert has hidden from her. She decides to leave Albert and go to Memphis to live with Shug and Grady. At the same time that Celie declares her independence from Albert, Mary Agnes also announces her intention to leave Albert's son, Harpo, to pursue her own career as a blues singer. In Memphis, an affair develops between Mary Agnes and Grady, who leaves Shug. Celie develops her skills as a seamstress into a business names Folkspants, Unlimited. She discovers that Alfonso, was in fact her stepfather and that her children were not therefore born of incest. When Alfonso dies, Celie inherits his house and land, which had legally passed from her natural father, to her mother, to her. Returning to Georgia, Celie finds Albert a changed man. She will not accept him as her husband again, but she does come to regard him as her friend. A false report reaches Celie that her sister Nettie died on a ship sunk off Gibraltar, but Celie refuses to lose hope. Finally, after more than thirty years of separation, Nettie, Adam, and Olivia return to Georgia and are reunited with Celie.

Critical Evaluation

The Color Purple became a controversial novel because of its strong indictment of the racism and sexism that victimized African-American women in the rural American South. Yet it is also the story of the growth and development of the central character from an ignorant, abused teenager to an accomplished woman who has learned to stand up for herself and cope with her hostile surroundings. The theme is liberation, as brought about by Celie's desire to learn and to improve herself.

In terms of technique, the novel is a throwback to the epistolary style that characterized the first novels in England written by Samuel Richardson during the eighteenth century. One of the advantages of the epistolary style is verisimilitude, as the story is given a strong appearance of truth and seems to provide an actual record of real people. Celie's story is told through letters and journal entries. At first, she is barely literate when she attempts to write letters to God in her diary. Problems of diction and dialect continue to mark Celie's style, which does improve over time as she becomes more mature and better able to understand what is happening to her. After their separation, the more literate Nettie tells her story to Celie through letters written from abroad, letters that are delayed because of the spite and meanness of Celie's husband, Albert. After Celie discovers those letters, the story is resumed through letters that she writes to Nettie. Although the story is often brutal and involves details of sexual abuse, Celie's story is ultimately one of the triumph of the human spirit that describes life as it might have been for a woman of her time and place. The details are often gripping, and the possibility of an eventual reunion between the two sisters creates a sense of dramatic expectation.

Celie's education depends on the letters that she writes and later receives, but she also learns by example, particularly by the examples of Sofia, who marries her stepson Harpo and refuses to be dominated by him or to give in to the white establishment, and Shug, a strong woman who has found financial independence by selling her talents as a blues singer. Shug and Sofia give Celie the strength to stand up to her husband and to leave him. Shug takes Celie to Memphis, where Celie is able to live by her talents as a seamstress, designing and making pants.

This matriarchal novel is about love, hope, and redemption, and despite the controversy surrounding its feminist defense of lesbianism, it won the Pulitzer Prize and the American Book Award for Fiction. The book was later popularized by Steven Spielberg's film adaptation in 1985, starring Whoopi Goldberg as Celie, Danny Glover as her husband, and Oprah Winfrey as Sofia. The film earned eleven Academy Award nominations, but it simplified and sanitized the story and seriously slighted and abridged Nettie's experiences in Africa, concentrating instead on Shug Avery and Sofia in Georgia. The film effectively dramatized part of the story for a mass audience (without emphasizing the intimate relationship between Shug and Celie much beyond a close friendship), but the full power, force, and context of Celie's story can only be found in the novel.

The book touched off many debates because of its criticism of African-American men, represented as tyrannical husbands and fathers. "Man corrupt everything," Celie records as Shug's comment. The controversy was revived and became more heated in 1985 after Spielberg's film version extended Alice Walker's story to a mass audience. Many objected to its image of African-American family life and African-American males who seem, for the most part, to be either brutes or buffoons. The National Association for the Advancement of Colored People (NAACP) protested the way in which Walker stereotypes men as violent and unfeeling. The film was informally boycotted in some cities and picketed by some African Americans when it opened in Los Angeles. Roscoe Nix, the president of the Montgomery County (Maryland) NAACP, pointed out that there is "not a healthy black male in the movie." Such an impression could possibly reinforce white stereotypes concerning African-American family life. Yet it could be argued that the brutality of the novel is no worse than that of rural whites in the Southern Gothic novels of Erskine Caldwell or William Faulkner. Nevertheless, the racial implications made the issue highly sensitive during the mid-1980's.

In this feminist novel, however, as time passes, the men become less brutal. A pattern of oppressive male dominance is established by Old Mr.—— that is passed down to his son Albert and to his grandson Harpo. Men beat their wives into submission and consider themselves above doing menial housework. Celie is victimized by this pattern, and it is so ingrained in her that she even advises Harpo to beat Sofia. The men first seem to be insensitive brutes or clowns, interested only in sex, but some of the men in this novel do improve over time. Harpo is by temperament less a tyrant than his father, and Albert himself improves with age as a result of his life with Celie and feelings of guilt about the way in which he has treated her. After Celie rebels and leaves him, Albert has to put his house in order and is capable enough to do so. By the end of the novel, Albert and Celie are no longer husband and wife, but they are friends. In addition, after his flirtation with Mary Agnes, Harpo is finally reconciled with Sofia after her time in prison. In *The Color Purple*, there is more hope of resolving the issue of sexism than the issue of racism.

The Color Purple is a woman's story about pain, suffering, endurance, and friendship, a story of hardship and hope, of reunion and reconciliation. It is understandable that, ten years later in 1992, Alice Walker returned to characters first introduced in *The Color Purple* when she wrote *Possessing the Secret of Joy*, a novel that traced the further history of Celie's children, Olivia and Adam, as well as of Adam's wife, Tashi, who wants to return to her roots in Olinka in order to seek self-realization.

The title of *The Color Purple* represents Celie's ultimate belief that God is present in all of His creation, in any "blade of grass," in "any scrub of a bush in my yard." As Shug advises, whenever "you trying to pray . . . conjure up flowers, wind, water, a big rock." This joyful and transcendental pantheism sustains Celie in her hope for a better future, one that is well deserved.

A CONNECTICUT YANKEE IN KING ARTHUR'S COURT

Type of work: Novel
Author: Mark Twain (Samuel Langhorne Clemens, 1835-1910)
Type of plot: Social satire
Time of plot: Sixth century
Locale: England
First published: 1889

Buried beneath a layer of wit is the serious social satire of Mark Twain's imaginative chronicle of medieval England. The Connecticut Yankee finds instead of the legendary gallantry a cruel system of feudalism in which the common people are abused and impoverished. The author demonstrates that a government is good only insofar as the bulk of the people benefit from it.

Principal Characters

The Connecticut Yankee (Hank Morgan), an ingenious man struck on the head during a quarrel in a New England arms factory. He awakens in medieval England, in June, 528. About to be burned at the stake on the twenty-first of June, he remembers that history has recorded a solar eclipse for that day. By prophesying the eclipse, he saves his life and discredits Merlin. He gets the name of "The Boss" and determines to raise the status of the common people. He sets up public schools, installs a telephone system, introduces gunpowder, and points out to Arthur the grave injustices of the feudal system while accompanying the king on a tour of his realm. He marries Alisande, and when their little daughter becomes ill, he takes her to the seashore to recuperate. While he is away, the Church orders all his improvements in Camelot destroyed. When he returns, Merlin casts a spell on him that will cause him to sleep for thirteen hundred years.

Clarence, a foppish page who becomes the Boss's chief assistant in his efforts to modernize the land and improve the lot of the common people.

King Arthur, a kind and courageous ruler who does not realize the inequities that exist in the social structure of his kingdom. He is killed in a battle with Sir Lancelot over Queen Guinevere. His death is the signal for the Church to move against and destroy the social progress brought about by the Yankee's democratic innovations.

Sir Kay, who first captures the Yankee.

Sir Sagramor, who challenges the Yankee to a joust and is aided by Merlin.

Merlin, the sorcerer whose magic power cannot match the Yankee's nineteenth century knowledge.

Alisande (Sandy), a damsel in distress whom the Yankee helps and whom he finally marries.

Hello-Central, their daughter, whose illness gives Merlin a chance to unite feudal power and destroy "The Boss."

The Story

Struck on the head during a quarrel in a New England arms factory, Hank Morgan, a skilled mechanic awoke to find himself being prodded by the spear of an armored knight on horseback. The knight was Sir Kay of King Arthur's Round Table and the time was June, A.D. 528 in medieval England, as a foppish young page named Clarence informed the incredulous Yankee, when his captor took him back to white-towered Camelot. The Yankee remembered that there had been a total eclipse of the sun on June 21, 528. If the eclipse took place, he was indeed a lost traveler in time turned backward to the days of chivalry.

At Camelot, the Yankee listened to King Arthur's knights as they bragged of their mighty exploits. The magician, Merlin, told again of Arthur's coming. Finally Sir Kay told of his encounter with the Yankee, and Merlin advised that the prisoner be thrown into a dungeon to await burning at the stake on the twenty-first of June.

In prison, the Yankee thought about the coming eclipse. Merlin, he told Clarence, was a humbug, and he sent the boy to the court with a message that on the day of his death the sun would darken and the kingdom would be destroyed. The eclipse came, and at the right time, for the Yankee was about to be burned when the sky began to dim. Awed, the king ordered the prisoner released. The people shouted that he was a greater magician than Merlin.

The court demanded another display of his powers. With the help of Clarence, the Yankee mined Merlin's tower with some crude explosives he had made and then told everyone he would cause the tower to crumble and fall. When the explosion took place, the Yankee was assured of his place as the new court magician. Merlin was thrown into prison.

The lack of mechanical devices in King Arthur's castle bothered the ingenious New Englander, and the illiteracy of the people hurt his American pride in education. He decided to make the commoners more than slaves to the nobility. He had a title of his own by this time, for the people called him the Boss. As the Boss, he intended to modernize the kingdom.

His first act was to set up schools in small communities throughout the country. He had to work in secret, for he feared the interference of the Church. He trained workers in mechanical arts. Believing that a nation needed a free press, he instructed Clarence in the art of journalism. He had telephone wires stretched between hamlets, haphazardly, however, because there were no maps by which to be guided.

When Sir Sagramor challenged the Boss to a duel, the court decided that he should go upon some knightly quest to prepare himself for the encounter. His mission was to help a young girl named Alisande, whose story he could not get straight. With many misgivings, he put on a burdensome coat of mail and on his heavy charger started off with Sandy, as he called her. Sandy was a talkative companion who told endless tall tales as they traveled through the land. Along the way, the Boss marveled at the pitiable state of the people under the feudal system. Whenever he found a man of unusual spirit, he sent him back to Clarence in Camelot, to be taught reading, writing, and a useful trade. He visited the dungeons of the castles at which he stayed and released prisoners unjustly held by their grim masters.

In the Valley of Holiness, he found another opportunity to prove his magic skill. There a sacred well had gone dry because, according to legend, some sin had been committed. When he arrived, Merlin, now released from prison, was attempting magic to make the spring flow. With much pomp and flourish, the Boss repaired a leak in the masonry at the bottom of the well. As the well filled, Merlin went home in shame.

By chance, the Boss came upon one of his telephone installations in a cave nearby. He talked to Clarence, who told him that King Arthur was on his way to the Valley of Holiness to see the flowing spring. He returned to the spring to find a fake magician assuring the gaping pilgrims that he could tell what anyone was doing at that moment. The Boss asked him about King Arthur. The magician said that he was asleep in his bed at Camelot. The Boss grandly predicted that the king was on his way to the Valley of Holiness. When the king did arrive, the people were again awed by the Boss's magic.

Anxious that King Arthur be convinced of the sufferings of his people, the Boss suggested that he and the king disguise themselves as commoners and travel as pilgrims through the country. The Boss knew that Arthur was not to blame for his social doctrines; he was a victim of his place in society. On their journey, the king proved to be courageous and kind.

Misfortune soon overtook them: They were seized by an earl and sold as slaves, because they were unable to prove themselves free men. The slaves were taken to London, where the Boss picked the lock that held him and escaped. The rest of the slaves were ordered to be hanged after his escape. The Boss located one of his telephones and called Clarence in Camelot, however, ordering him to send Sir Lancelot and an army of knights to London to save their king from hanging.

The Boss came back to Camelot in glory, but not for long. He still had to fight a duel with Sir Sagramor—in reality a battle between Merlin and the Boss. Merlin professed to cover Sir Sagramor with an invisible shield, but the credulous knight was invisible to no one but himself. The Boss wore no armor, and so on the field of the tournament he was able to dodge the charging knight until Sir Sagramor grew tired. Then the Boss lassoed him and pulled him from his horse. When Sir Sagramor returned once again to the field, Merlin stole the Boss's lasso. There was no alternative; the Boss shot Sir Sagramor with his gun. Then he challenged all the knights of the Round Table. He had only twelve shots in his two revolvers, but fortunately, when he had killed nine of the charging knights, the line wavered and gave up.

Three years passed. By this time, the Boss had married Sandy and they had a little girl. He and Clarence were planning to declare a republic after the death of Arthur, for the sixth century kingdom was now a nineteenth century land with schools, trains, factories, newspapers, the telephone, and the telegraph. Although the code of chivalry had been abolished, the knights still insisted on wearing their armor. Then little Hello-Central, the Boss's daughter, became ill, and he and Sandy took the child to the seashore for recuperation. On their return, the Boss found Camelot in a shambles. Only Clarence remained to tell him the story. There had been a battle between King Arthur and Sir Lancelot over Queen Guinevere. The king was dead, and by interdict the Church had destroyed the work of the Boss. Clarence and the Boss built a fortress surrounded by an electrically charged barrier.

In a battle with the surviving chivalry of England, the Boss was stabbed. When an old woman came to the fortress from the enemy lines and offered to nurse him, no one recognized her as Merlin. The magician cast a spell on the Boss and declared that he would sleep for thirteen hundred years. Indeed, the Yankee did awake once more in the nineteenth century.

Critical Evaluation

A Connecticut Yankee in King Arthur's Court should have offered Mark Twain one of his best opportunities to attack the repressive and antidemocratic forces that he saw in the post-Civil War United States, as well as in sixth century England. That the attack becomes in large part an exposé of the very system that Twain sought to vindicate reveals as much the deep division in Twain's own nature as any problem inherent in the material itself. Ironically, though, much of the interest the work holds for contemporary readers is based upon the complications resulting from Twain's inability to set up a neat conflict between the forces of progress and those of repression. The Yankee's visit to King Arthur's court reveals not only the greed and superstition that Twain associates with the aristocracy and the established Church but also some of the weaknesses in humanity that enable these oppressive parasites to exist. One comes to the realization that the industrial Utopia the Yankee tries to establish in old England is nothing more than a hopeless dream.

As a character, Hank Morgan is, in many respects, a worthy successor to his predecessor, Huckleberry Finn. Like Huck, he is representative of the common people, and, at his best, he asserts the ideal qualities that Twain associates with those who escape the corruption of hereditary wealth and power and the conditioning of tradition. Unlike Huck, however, who was largely an observer powerless to change the system, the Yankee is given the opportunity to make his values the basis of a Utopian society. While Huck saw the threat of being "civilized" as an infringement on his individuality and freedom, Hank is, in his own way, fully "civilized" according to the standards of the world that he represents. The pragmatic wit that enabled Huck Finn to survive against all odds becomes for the Yankee the basis of his rise in the industrial system to a position of authority and success. He fully accepts the nineteenth century doctrines of laissez-faire capitalism, progress, and technology as being expressive of the best social and human principles.

Hank represents Twain's vision of technological humanity as a new social ideal: the greatest product of the greatest society.

Twain's choice of Arthur's court as the testing ground for the Yankee's ideas was not accidental. Most immediately, he was offended by Matthew Arnold's attacks upon the American glorification of the common people and the English view of the United States as a kind of cultural desert. Thus, in attacking the golden age of chivalry, Twain simultaneously sought to expose English history, culture, and traditions of aristocratic privilege. At the same time, Twain associates the age of Arthur with the sorts of romantic attitudes he had exposed in *The Adventures of Huckleberry Finn* as the ruin of the American South. Making his spokesperson, Hank Morgan, a product of that society Arnold deplored, Twain mounts a two-pronged attack against Arnold's Europeanism and sophistication and, in his own view, the dangerously reactionary attitudes that asserted the superiority of the "romantic" past over the present.

What begins for Hank, with his prediction of the moment of the eclipse, as a simple expedient for survival quickly becomes open war between Merlin and the Church and the Machine Age represented by the Yankee. Hank sees himself as a Promethean bringer of new knowledge and a new order to the oppressed masses of old England. His humanitarian values are pitted against the selfishness and greed of the aristocracy and Church, and his reason challenges their superstition. Based upon his own and Twain's view of technological humanity as the apex of development, the Yankee naturally assumes that he is the rightful ruler of the world. Twain as well as Hank seems to assume that because he takes up the cause of the oppressed people against their oppressors, he necessarily has, in whatever he does, a moral superiority to those he fights against. Neither the Yankee nor Twain seems to give consideration to the question of ends and means.

It is particularly ironic that Hank, ostensibly the bringer

of light to this benighted people, should rely no less than his archenemy Merlin upon the power of superstition to gain ascendancy over the masses. From the moment he discovers the profound effect that his prediction of the eclipse has upon the audience, the Yankee begins to challenge Merlin to ever-greater miracles. Such episodes as the destruction of Merlin's tower or the restoration of the Holy Well represent Hank's use of technology to create fear and awe like that which Merlin has commanded heretofore. Thus, recognizing that humanity is essentially base and weak, the Yankee, like Merlin, maintains his power through exploitation of ignorance and gullibility.

Thus, it is humanity rather than technology that finally fails Hank. With the exception of the fifty-two young men who have never been exposed to the teachings of the Church, the society that Hank has constructed through his technology reverts to its former state the minute his guard is relaxed. Humans are, as Hank perceives them, no more than conditioned animals, and all his modern miracles cannot change that fact. In the end, the Yankee's technology fails him and his companions. His dream of progress has become a nightmare—a sacrifice to the very ignorance that it would replace. Promethean Hank Morgan, the bringer of light and knowledge, finally only vindicates Twain's pessimistic view of human nature.

The ending of *A Connecticut Yankee in King Arthur's Court* is as bleak as anything Twain was ever to write. The scenes of Hank's Utopia destroyed by perverse human nature, the destruction unleashed by the power of technology, and, finally, the prospect of Hank's forces being overcome by the pollution of the bodies piled in their trenches are frightening to contemplate. Twain, having apparently set out to affirm the nineteenth century doctrine of progress, finally comes full circle to suggest that something permanent within human nature makes such dreams hopeless. Clearly, there is here an anticipation of the later Twain who, having lost hope in the human potential of his Huck Finn, would become a misanthropic voice crying out against the "damned human race."

THE COUNTRY OF THE POINTED FIRS

Type of work: Novel
Author: Sarah Orne Jewett (1849-1909)
Type of plot: Regional romance
Time of plot: Late nineteenth century
Locale: Maine seacoast
First published: 1896

The interest in this novel lies in character portrayal and nature description. Each chapter in Jewett's work can stand alone as a local-color sketch, and the whole explores the deep springs of the New England character.

Principal Characters

The Boarder, a woman writer who comes to Dunnet Landing, Maine, to work in seclusion. Here she meets many people and finds friendly, interesting characters.

Mrs. Almira Todd, a friendly widow who accepts the writer as a boarder. She is also an herb doctor, growing herbs in her garden and searching out others in the fields.

Captain Littlepage, an elderly, retired sea captain who tells the writer a yarn about his own shipwreck and a town of ghosts near the North Pole, where souls await their passage to the next world.

Mrs. Blackett, Mrs. Todd's aged mother. She lives on an island with her son William and does her own housework.

William Blackett, Mrs. Todd's brother, a bashful man. He loves Esther Hight and finally is able to marry her when he is in his fifties.

Mrs. Fosdick, a friend of Mrs. Todd. She comes often to visit with her friend and to tell stories about the local folk.

Mr. Tilley, an old fisherman. He is reserved with strangers, but he accepts the writer as a friend and shows her the house he has kept for eight years just as it was when his wife died.

Esther Hight, a woman loved by William Blackett. She supports herself and her elderly mother by tending sheep. After her mother's death, she is free to marry William.

The Story

A woman writer came one summer to Dunnet Landing, a Maine seacoast town, to find seclusion for her work. She boarded with Mrs. Almira Todd, a friendly widow and the local herb doctor. Besides having a garden full of herbs, Mrs. Todd often roamed far afield for rarer specimens. The boarder sometimes took care of Mrs. Todd's sales of herbs and birch beer when Mrs. Todd was away.

At last the boarder realized that she must get to work on her book and give up the society of Mrs. Todd in the daytime. The boarder found the village schoolhouse a quiet place for her writing, and she spent most of her days there. One morning, she was surprised to have a visit from old Captain Littlepage, a retired sailor who seldom left his house. For a time, he spoke seriously of the great English poets. When he saw that the boarder

did not laugh at him, he launched upon a long narrative. It seemed that he had been shipwrecked upon a small island and had met there another sailor who had been to the North Pole. He told Captain Littlepage of a town of ghosts that he had discovered. It was Captain Littlepage's theory that in this town souls awaited their passage into the next world. The old man's narrative stopped suddenly as his mind returned to the present. The boarder helped him home and told no one about his strange story.

On another day, Mrs. Todd took her boarder out to Green Island, where Mrs. Todd's mother lived. Mrs. Blackett was more than eighty, her daughter past sixty. Mrs. Blackett still did her own work and kept house for her son William, who was past fifty. William was a bashful man, but he found a friend to his liking in the boarder. Mrs. Todd and the boarder gathered some herbs before they left the island, and Mrs. Todd showed her the spot offshore where her husband had gone down in his boat.

Mrs. Fosdick came to visit Mrs. Todd, and the two old ladies and the boarder often spent their evenings together. One night, Mrs. Todd told of her husband's Cousin Joanna, who had lived on Shell-heap Island. Disappointed in love, Joanna went to live alone on the tiny island. Passing fishermen often left presents on the shore for her, but no one ever visited her. Finally, Mrs. Todd and the minister went to see her, for the minister was worried about the state of Joanna's soul. They found Joanna living comfortably but simply. Satisfied with her lonely life, she could not be induced to return to the mainland. Joanna lived out her life on the island and was buried there.

Late in August, Mrs. Todd took her boarder and Mrs. Blackett to the Bowden family reunion. They hired a carriage and drove far inland to the family seat. All the Bowdens for miles around came to the reunion, and Mrs. Blackett was one of the privileged guests because of her age. For once, Mrs. Todd forgot her herbs and spent the entire day in the enjoyment of the society of her friends. William had not come to the gathering because of his bashfulness. Mrs. Blackett treasured every moment of the day, for she knew it was one of the last reunions she would attend.

One day, the boarder stood on the shore below Dunnet Landing. There she met Mr. Tilley, one of the oldest fishermen in the village. Mr. Tilley was reserved toward strangers, but he had at last accepted the boarder as a friend and he invited her to visit him that afternoon. When the boarder arrived, he was knitting some socks. The two friends sat in the kitchen while Mr. Tilley told the boarder about his wife. She had died eight years be-

fore, but her husband had never gotten over his sorrow. He kept the house just as she had left it. Proudly, he showed the boarder the seldom-used parlor and Mrs. Tilley's set of china. The boarder left the cottage feeling the loneliness that surrounded the old fisherman.

When the clear, cool autumn came, it was time for the boarder to leave. Mrs. Todd helped her pack and get her belongings down on the wharf for the steamer. Mrs. Todd took her leave of the boarder before she left the house. From the deck of the steamer, the boarder watched Dunnet Landing fade into the distance. She recalled a day of the past summer when William had come to the mainland. He was going trout fishing in an inland stream. Self-consciously, he asked the boarder to go with him. They caught no fish, but William took her afterward to see Mrs. Hight and her daughter Esther. The boarder stayed to talk to Mrs. Hight, while William went out to speak to Esther, who supported her aged and crippled mother by tending sheep. As William and the boarder left, she realized that William and Esther were lovers.

When the boarder returned to Dunnet Landing in the spring, Mrs. Todd told her that Mrs. Hight had recently died and that Esther and William were to be married immediately. He was to come to the mainland the next day if the weather proved good.

Early in the morning, Mrs. Todd was up to watch for a sail from Green Island. Finally she saw it approaching. Then neighbors began to drop in to inquire why William was coming to the mainland. After the ceremony, William and Esther stopped for a moment at Mrs. Todd's house before returning to the island. Mrs. Todd and the boarder accompanied the pair to the landing to see them off. The older woman expressed no emotion at the leave-taking, but as she and the boarder returned to the house, they walked holding hands all the way.

Critical Evaluation

Willa Cather, when asked to name three American novels "deserving of a long, long life," selected *The Country of the Pointed Firs* to share this honor with *The Scarlet Letter* and *The Adventures of Huckleberry Finn*. One of Sarah Orne Jewett's last works, and probably her highest achievement, the novel is a moving and wise chronicle, unquestionably a genuine and great work of art. The gentle, thoughtful narrative flows with a precision of description worthy of Gustave Flaubert or Ivan Turgenev. The apparently effortless and ever graceful prose is the work of a master craftsperson and a refined and gifted sensibility. The work is rich in symbols that arise natu-

rally from the world about which the author is writing. Perhaps the dominant symbol is that of the great army of pointed firs, darkly cloaked and "standing as if they wait to embark."

The theme of balance is fundamental to the book, as much a part of it as the carefully structured narrative and perfectly poised sentences. One may ask why, for example, the major character, Mrs. Todd, chooses to live in this tiny community. To keep the world balance true, suggests the author, to offset some other, unknown existence. There is always a reason, if one but knows it. Hand in hand with the theme of balance moves that of solitude. Paths are trodden to the shrines of solitude the world over, writes the narrator, whether it be the island of Miss Joanna or the island of Mrs. Todd's mother, or the caves of the saints of the past. The old sea captain's story of the "Waiting Place," the strange, twilight land hovering by the North Pole, again suggests this theme. Perhaps solitude serves humanity as a kind of purgatory, a way station of the soul on its way to paradise. It can be fearful, this uncharted, inner space, but it must be encountered to achieve full humanity. The ship that carried Captain Littlepage to this land was not accidentally named *Minerva*, goddess of wisdom.

The characterizations in *The Country of the Pointed Firs* are among the finest in American literature. Mrs. Todd is perhaps the glory of the book, a creation worthy of Charles Dickens. She might belong to any age, as the narrator says, "like an idyl of Theocritus." With her potions and herbs, however, her Puritan ancestors probably would have burned her as a witch. She is an unlikely classic heroine, yet the narrator cannot resist some flattering comparisons. Mrs. Todd is likened to a grand and architectural caryatid and compared to Antigone standing alone on the Theban plain. Yet it is her language, her way with the Maine way of speaking, that breathes life into her bulky figure. One can taste the salty old expressions as they roll off her tongue.

The past of the whalers, so recently behind the characters, is ever present in the book. Indeed, the past is important on many levels to the characters in the novel. Mrs. Fosdick remarks: "Conversations got to have some root in the past, or else you've got to explain every remark you make. . . ." The rule might be said to apply to all civilized social intercourse. People with no respect for the past are left isolated and hopeless. In the world of Jewett, the present and past enrich each other, and mortals wise enough to accept this are the benefactors.

The Country of the Pointed Firs is a treasure of wisdom and a lesson in the writing of pure, unaffected prose as the highest art. The individuals who stalk through its pages are loners, but they are not unhappy or unloving. Jewett has realized that "in the life of each of us . . . there is a place remote and islanded, and given to endless regret and secret happiness; we are each the uncompanioned hermit and recluse of an hour or a day. . . ." When she writes about her isolated New Englanders on their saltwashed islands, she is writing about all of humanity.

THE CRYING OF LOT 49

Type of work: Novel
Author: Thomas Pynchon (1937-   )
Type of plot: Seriocomic satiric mystery
Time of plot: 1960's
Locale: San Narciso, California (near Los Angeles)
First published: 1966

The Crying of Lot 49, Pynchon's short, critically acclaimed, and popular novel, chronicles Oedipa Maas's search for meaning. Her quest and her inability to determine which of multiple possible interpretations controls her life and the mysteries into which she has been plunged become an absurdist metaphor for the human condition.

Principal Characters

Oedipa Maas, a California housewife, executor of the estate of Pierce Inverarity. Intellectual curiosity and paranoia motivate her quest for meaning.

Wendell ("Mucho") Maas, Oedipa's husband, formerly a used-car salesman, presently a disc jockey who works for station KCUF. He suffers from regular crises of conscience. Drugs and sex become his escape from nightmares about NADA (National Automobile Dealers' Association—"nothing") and of a wasteland reality that he finds daily more unendurable. "Today was another defeat" is his refrain.

Pierce Inverarity, a billionaire California real estate mogul with numerous, tangled assets interlocked with the Yoyodyne company. At one time Oedipa's lover, he may have used his will (initiating her investigation of the Tristero) to play a complex joke on her.

Dr. Hilarius, a former Nazi concentration camp psychiatrist, who experimentally induced insanity at Buchenwald (his hideous "Fu Manchu" face paralyzed viewers) and who now distributes drugs freely to suburban housewives. The police must finally respond to the doctor's guilt-induced fear of an Israeli commando attack, but not before his drugs drive Mucho over the edge and make Oedipa doubt the reality of her senses.

"Baby Igor" Metzger, Inverarity's handsome lawyer, coexecutor of the Inverarity estate, and still a popular child filmstar of television reruns. As Oedipa's present lover, he first mentions the bones that become an important pattern in Oedipa's investigation, reluctantly takes Oedipa to see *The Courier's Tragedy*, and eventually runs away with a fifteen-year-old groupie.

The Paranoids, a youthful teenage rock group with Beatles haircuts and identical mohair suits. Their rock verses add to the comic satire, and their group name sums up Pynchon's theme.

The Story

Oedipa Maas learns that she has been named executrix of the estate of her former lover Pierce Inverarity. The reader follows her activities, pursuits, surmises, and fears. She consults her husband, psychiatrist, and personal lawyer (all in various stages of lunacy) before accepting this challenge. Her coexecutor, "Baby Igor" Metzger, contacts her at the Echo Courts motel, where they watch television reruns of the films that he made as a child star until he seduces her in a hilarious comic sequence.

Oedipa had once tried to escape her humdrum life by having a fling with Inverarity; now she tries to do so again by involving herself in his estate. She is particularly intrigued by his stamp collection, which includes a strange series with black feathers, post horn symbols, peculiar misprints, and other nontraditional, almost menacing, postal oddities. Her investigation of this collection involves her in what seems to be a conspiracy involving a centuries-old, antiestablishment postal service, the Tristero. Mike Fallopian, a Yoyodyne employee, provides her first clue: an oddly timed mail call connected with the symbol of a post horn and the acronym WASTE, which she thereafter spots throughout California, under freeways and in other unlikely spots. Fallopian describes a rebellious, private United States mail delivery service designed to counter the growing power and abuse of the federal post office. Oedipa later learns that WASTE stands for "We Await Silent Tristero's Empire" and that its associate acronym, DEATH, means "Don't Ever Antagonize the Horn."

Metzger's friend Manny Di Presso tells about the bones of a company of GIs taken from the bottom of an Italian lake and used to make cigarette filters, but later connected with the bones of slaughtered mail delivery men from an encounter between the seventeenth century Thurn-Taxis Italian postal monopoly and its counterpart, the Tristero. Oedipa learns about these in a revenge tragedy that Metzger takes her to see: Ralph Wharfinger's *The Courier's Tragedy*. This chilling depiction of murder, incest, and mayhem contains insider allusions to that secret postal group, the Tristero. These make Oedipa see a chilling pattern interlocking past and present, play and real life. Oedipa's later attempts to confirm the existence of lines from the play, however, are continually thwarted. An actor warns that she could waste her life chasing down clues and putting together theses to no avail, for she could never touch the truth. Despite this warning, chasing down clues motivates her action throughout the rest of the novel, as she wonders how accidental her involvement in what appears to be an ancient conspiracy really is and how much of a role Metzger and his employer, Inverarity, have to do with it.

If the Tristero exists, it is a mysterious, underground system employed by the disenfranchised, the antiauthoritarian, the impoverished, the alienated. Oedipa's search for evidence of its existence and involvement in modern life becomes a quest for significance conducted amid a society depicted as bland, moronic, mechanized, and trivial. Communication breaks down, and social relationships disintegrate rapidly. Ultimately, Oedipa searches for one piece of tangible, irrefutable evidence that her perceptions of the world are true, evidence that Pynchon suggests is impossible to attain except through self-delusion. In effect, Oedipa is weaving a tapestry to give meaning and significance to the meaningless and the insignificant, forming patterns and interlocking relationships that may or may not exist anywhere except in the imagination.

She goes from person to person seeking answers: technicians obsessed with theories about entropy; the grandson of a former Pony Express rider with vague memories of a black-feathered country-express service; a stamp collector convinced of an eight-hundred-year-old postal fraud; a member of Inamorati Anonymous, who uses the WASTE mail system to run an Alcoholics Anonymous for those hooked on love; children chanting about Tristero as they jump rope; and revolutionaries and conspirators of every sort, including the Alameda Country Death Cult and the Conjuración de las Insurgentes Anarquistas.

Overwhelmed by such inconclusive but suggestive data, Oedipa checks in on her psychiatrist, Dr. Hilarius, only to find him suffering the paranoid delusion that Israeli commandos are seeking retribution for his Nazi war crimes. After calming him down, she finds that her husband, doing on-the-spot television coverage of the Hilarius story, has himself suffered a total schizophrenic breakdown and believes himself better off as "a whole roomful of people." Back at her hotel, she learns that Metzger has run off with the girlfriend of one of the Paranoids, a rock group. The used bookstore with the Wharfinger edition of the play that alluded to the Tristero has burned down, and the director of the play production that Oedipa viewed has committed suicide. Nevertheless, a librarian interested in rare editions helps her find so many literary allusions to the Tristero (including a pornographic version of *The Courier's Tragedy* in the Vatican) that much of post-Renaissance history seems explicable in terms of the secret connivings of that organization.

With so many tantalizing possibilities and nowhere else to turn, Oedipa decides to attend the auction of the Tristero "forgeries," classified as lot 49. She hopes that a mysterious bidder, perhaps for the Tristero, will attend. "With the courage you have when there is nothing to lose," Oedipa enters a salesroom full of men in black mohair suits and with "pale cruel faces." Oedipa believes that all will be revealed or all will be destroyed, that the auctioneer is an angel of death or an angel of truth. The reader never finds out what happens. One can only guess.

Critical Evaluation

The winner of the Rosenthal Foundation Award for best novel, *The Crying of Lot 49* is an important, controversial second novel, more accessible to the reader than many of Pynchon's other works because of its brief but balanced plot, its quirky but likeable characters, and its unified central focus on an issue basic to the 1960's: paranoia. Pynchon's characters find their vision of reality collapsing around them and begin to fear that outside forces manipulate and control them, themselves powerless to escape. Their personal paranoia reflects their epoch, a time of doubt, distrust, and disenchantment.

The surface nature of this novel is satiric. Pynchon's California is summed up in San Narciso, a stereotypical suburban area, "a grouping of concepts— . . . shopping nuclei, all overlaid with access roads to its own freeway," a narcissistic sprawl of the self-indulgent and the self-deceiving. It reminds Oedipa of a transistor radio circuit, with its "ordered swirl of houses and streets" evoking a deceptive "hieroglyphic sense of concealed meaning." Through the nearby Yoyodyne missile-building complex, San Narciso's biggest source of employment and a giant of the aerospace industry, Pynchon draws an impersonal, dehumanized, *Brave New World* vision of the "organization man." Identical men at identical desks brainwashed into performing indistinguishable tasks—all based on a concept of teamwork and anonymity that stifles creativity and individual initiative. One character finds Yoyodyne "a way to avoid responsibility . . . a symptom of the gutlessness of the whole society." Even the universities take on a group personality of "corduroy, denim, bare legs, blonde hair, hornrims, . . . bookbags" and "posters for undecipherable FSM's, YAF's, VDC's." California's cars and freeways provide further bases for satire. Mucho Maas has nightmares about cars being "motorized, metal extensions" of people, families, and lives, their contents the bubblegum "residue" of lives, the trade-in an endless ritual in which an owner exchanges "a dented, malfunctioning version of himself for another, just as futureless, automotive projection of somebody else's life." Oedipa, in turn, imagines herself "some single melted crystal of urban horse [heroin]" and her road a "hypodermic needle, inserted somewhere ahead into the vein of a freeway" that is in turn "a vein nourishing the mainliner L.A., keeping it happy, coherent, protected from pain." The image is one of people constantly on the go, anesthetized to reality, and sustained by artificial projections, by Tupperware parties, Forest Lawns and "Vesperhavens," John Birchers, endless rows of anonymous motels, Barry Goldwater sweatshirts, Nazi Schutzstaffel (SS) armbands, and endless television reruns. Actors become lawyers, lawyers become actors, and Hollywood images infect word and deed.

This Republican California is set in opposition to an underground world of the disenchanted, the disaffected, and the down-and-out: a world of gay men, drug users, welfare mothers, unemployed veterans, social dropouts, counterrevolutionaries, and American mavericks—a human wasteland more readily contacted in San Francisco and Berkeley. It includes failed suicides, would-be Buddhist monks, youthful delinquents, impoverished minorities, and clandestine Mexican revolutionary groups,

among others. Pynchon sums up their inchoate threat, this alternate reality, through a group that he labels the Tristero (alternately spelled Trystero, perhaps from "tryst" or secret meeting, "triste" or sad, or even vaguely related to "trust") for centuries an alternate postal service in opposition to government-sponsored organizations, an underground alliance in response to the visible wasteland around it. References to the Second Law of Thermodynamics postulate energy loss or entropy as a metaphor for the deterioration of civilization.

Throughout the novel, Pynchon parodies the language and styles of pop artists, "organization men," university types, critics, and so forth with versatility and good humor. In his invented play *The Courier's Tragedy*, which Oedipa views with interest and which plunges her deeper into her investigation of the Tristero, Pynchon parodies both the style and the patterns of the seventeenth century Jacobean revenge tragedy and the literary criticism associated with it. This play (of which the reader has both plot summary and fragments of verse) contains within itself the basic conventions of the genre: disguises, secret messages, in-jokes, incest, violence, dark conspiracies, anticlerical tirades, poisoned relics and other ingenious murder weapons accompanied by agonizing injuries, mutilations, precipitous deaths, and a final, unrelenting bloodbath; at the play's close, there is a lingering sense of the sinister and unresolved. Pynchon depicts the literary criticism about such works as obsessed with trivia, with minor differences in texts, and with technical distinctions—pedantic, pretentious, ignorant of the fundamental historic, social, philosophical, and personal implications of the work studied. It is the violence of this literary piece that makes readers understand Oedipa's paranoid fears that the people disappearing and dying around her are all part of a larger conspiracy that could result in her own destruction and death.

Ultimately, this book is not a simple satire of a particular time, place, and set of mind, but an investigation of the nature of facts and of reality, an epistemological questioning of how one knows what one knows and of whether personal theories are ever more than just that—theories. At the close of her quest for an explanation and understanding of the Tristero, Oedipa is forced to admit to four distinct possibilities. First, she may, like Dr. Hilarius and her schizophrenic husband, be simply insane, and her narration, therefore, deluded ravings. Second, given Dr. Hilarius' contrivances to promote his drug program, she may well have been secretly slipped some exotic, mind-altering drug, so the conspiracies that she encounters are merely hallucinogenic drug projections. Third, an expensive and elaborate plot, a grandiose practical joke (involving forged documents and stamps, bribed librarians, professional actors, and constant surveillance), might have been mounted against her, conceived and financed by her former eccentric and wealthy lover, Pierce Inverarity, and abetted by her more recent seducer, Metzger, perhaps for the sake of revenge, perhaps as a final joke. Fourth, she may have indeed stumbled onto a real alternative to the boring emptiness of daily life, "a secret richness and concealed density of dream . . . a network by which X number of Americans are truly communicating whilst reserving their lies, recitations of routine, arid betrayals of spiritual poverty, for the official government delivery system." Pynchon provides no final answer and no final resolution. When Oedipa enters the auction room for the "crying" (the call for bids for purchases of a particular set of merchandise) of "lot 49" (the revised version of *The Courier's Tragedy*), she postulates a dangerous enemy awaiting her: a Tristero envoy. Yet, whether that enemy really exists or is a product of an unbalanced imagination or a narcotic vision, and whether it will invite her to join the Tristero or destroy her utterly as an uninvited outsider, the reader does not know. The con-

clusions that readers reach and the theories that critics project tell far more about themselves than about Oedipa or Pynchon. Early in the book, Oedipa asks herself, *"Shall I project a world?"* and concludes "Anything might help."

Pynchon's is an absurdist vision of mixed perceptions and alternate realities, a world in which there are no final answers, only a series of disturbing alternatives. His image of the Deaf and Dumb Convention Dance, in which members all move to different rhythms and keys in patterns choreographed in their heads—a silent, gesturing swarm, always on the verge of collision—is a disturbing metaphor for life. So too is Oedipa's description of a painting, *Bordando el Manto Terrestre* (weaving the mantle of the world), displayed in a Mexican art exhibition: frail girls, imprisoned in a circular tower, weaving a tapestry depicting all the cities, forests and peoples of the world, a tapestry that spilled out of the tower into a void that it could never fill. Oedipa muses about whether everyone is a captive maiden in an inescapable tower and about what choices are left if there is no knight of deliverance proof against its magic.

DAISY MILLER

Type of work: Novelette
Author: Henry James (1843-1916)
Type of plot: Psychological realism
Time of plot: Mid-nineteenth century
Locale: Vevey, Switzerland, and Rome, Italy
First published: 1878

In Daisy Miller, *James is interested in a conflict between European and American customs. The crudities and touching innocence of Daisy Miller are revealed against a background of European manners and morals, and both are shown from the point of view of an expatriate American who has lived abroad for too long. This special perspective makes the novel an ironic study of contrasts.*

Principal Characters

Daisy Miller, the charming and unconforming American tourist whose inattention to decorum (she walks unchaperoned with an Italian suitor in the daytime) results in her ostracism by the Europeanized Americans in Rome. In defiance, she visits the Colosseum at night with the same young man and later dies of a fever contracted there.

Frederick Winterbourne, an American expatriate from whose point of view the story is told. At first puzzled by Daisy, he soon becomes convinced that she is immoral. After her death, however, he realizes that her manners indicated only a native American freedom and that he loved her.

Giovanelli, the young Italian whose companionship causes the scandal involving Daisy. An adventurer interested primarily in Daisy's money, he admits to Winterbourne after her death that she never would have consented to marry him.

Mrs. Walker, an American expatriate. Because Daisy rejects Mrs. Walker's efforts to preserve her from scandal, Mrs. Walker cuts her at a party, thus beginning Daisy's complete ostracism.

Randolph Miller, Daisy's young and spoiled brother. His impudence also shocks the American expatriates.

Mrs. Costello, Winterbourne's aunt. She refuses to meet Daisy because she is convinced that the Millers are common.

Eugenio, the Millers' courier and servant. That the Millers treat him almost as a member of the family also causes talk among the American expatriates.

The Story

Frederick Winterbourne was a young American who had lived in Europe for quite a while. He spent much time at Vevey, Switzerland, which was a favorite spot of his aunt, Mrs. Costello. One day, while he was loitering outside the hotel, he was attracted by a young woman who appeared to be related to Randolph Miller, a young American boy with whom he had been talking. After a while, the young woman exchanged a few words with him. Her name was Daisy Miller. The boy was her brother, and they were in Vevey with their mother. They came from Schenectady, New York, Winterbourne learned, and they intended to go next to Italy. Randolph insisted that he wanted to go back home. Winterbourne learned that Daisy hoped to visit the Castle of Chillon. He promised to take her there, for he was quite familiar with the old castle.

Winterbourne asked his aunt, Mrs. Costello, to meet Daisy. Mrs. Costello, however, would not agree because she thought that the Millers were common. That evening, Daisy and Winterbourne planned to go out on the lake, much to the horror of Eugenio, the Millers' traveling companion, who was more like a member of the family than a courier. At the last moment, Daisy changed her mind about the night excursion. A few days later, Winterbourne and Daisy visited the Castle of Chillon. The outing confirmed Mrs. Costello's opinion that Daisy was uncultured and unsophisticated.

Winterbourne made plans to go to Italy. When he

arrived, he went directly to the home of Mrs. Walker, an American whom he had met in Geneva. There he met Daisy and Randolph. Daisy reproved him for not having called to see her. Winterbourne replied that she was unkind, as he had just arrived on the train. Daisy asked Mrs. Walker's permission to bring an Italian friend, Mr. Giovanelli, to a party Mrs. Walker was about to give. Mrs. Walker agreed. Then Daisy said that she and the Italian were going for a walk. Mrs. Walker was shocked, as young unmarried women did not walk the streets of Rome with Italians. Daisy suggested that there would be no objection if Winterbourne would go with her to the spot where she was to meet the Italian and then walk with them.

Winterbourne and Daisy set out and eventually found Giovanelli. They walked together for a while. Then Mrs. Walker's carriage drew alongside the strollers. She beckoned to Winterbourne and implored him to persuade Daisy to enter her carriage. She told him that Daisy had been ruining her reputation by such behavior; she had become familiar with Italians and was quite heedless of the scandal that she was causing. Mrs. Walker said she would never speak to Winterbourne again if he did not ask Daisy to get into the carriage at once. Yet Daisy, refusing the requests of Mrs. Walker and Winterbourne, continued her walk with the Italian.

Mrs. Walker determined to snub Daisy at the party. When Winterbourne arrived, Daisy had not made her appearance. Mrs. Miller arrived more than an hour before Daisy appeared with Giovanelli. Mrs. Walker had a moment of weakness and greeted them politely. As Daisy came to say goodnight, however, Mrs. Walker turned her back upon her. From that time on, Daisy and Giovanelli found all doors shut to them. Winterbourne saw her occasionally, but she was always with the Italian. Everyone thought that they were carrying on an intrigue. When Winterbourne asked her if she were engaged, Daisy said that she was not.

One night, despite the danger from malarial fever, Giovanelli took Daisy to the Colosseum. Winterbourne, encountering them in the ancient arena, reproached the Italian for his thoughtlessness. Giovanelli said that Daisy had insisted upon viewing the ruins by moonlight. Within a few days, Daisy was dangerously ill. During her illness, she sent word to Winterbourne that she had never been engaged to Giovanelli. A week later, she was dead.

As they stood beside Daisy's grave in the Protestant cemetery in Rome, Giovanelli told Winterbourne that Daisy would never have married her Italian suitor, even if she had lived. Then Winterbourne realized that he himself had loved Daisy without knowing his own feelings, that he could have married her had he acted differently. He reasoned, too late, that he had lived in Europe too long, that he had forgotten the freedom of American manners and the complexity of the American character.

Critical Evaluation

In *Daisy Miller*, James represents the conflicts between American innocence and independence and the rigid social conventions characteristic of the American colony in Rome. While Daisy deliberately flaunts convention by her unorthodox behavior, Mrs. Costello and Mrs. Walker make appearance their only basis for moral judgment. Winterbourne, troubled by the ambiguity in Daisy's character, seeks some objective basis for making a judgment.

Daisy realizes that the other Americans have no interest in her as an individual. Living in a world of moral judgments based entirely upon social conventions, they are only concerned to preserve the appearance of morality through "proper" behavior. Determined to be accepted on more meaningful grounds than these, Daisy asserts those freedoms that she would be allowed in the United States, but which are clearly out of place in Rome. Confident in her own innocence, she refuses to conform to the restrictions that her compatriots would place upon her.

Innocence and crudity are the terms characterizing Daisy, and these conflicting qualities are the source of Winterbourne's confusion about her. He, like his aunt and Mrs. Walker, has a tendency to make judgments on the basis of superficial appearances. Daisy, however, seems innocent to him in spite of her unconventional behavior, so he cannot fit her into a neat category as he would like. Yet discovering Daisy in a seemingly compromising position with Giovanelli in the Colosseum gives Winterbourne the evidence he needs, and with some relief he declares Daisy morally corrupt. In so doing, he places himself solidly among the other Americans who, like himself, have lived too long abroad to appreciate the real innocence that underlies Daisy's seeming moral laxity. Too late Winterbourne realizes at the graveside that his formulation of Daisy had been unjust.

DEATH COMES FOR THE ARCHBISHOP

Type of work: Novel
Author: Willa Cather (1873-1947)
Type of plot: Historical chronicle
Time of plot: Last half of the nineteenth century
Locale: New Mexico and Arizona
First published: 1927

Based on the lives of two eminent nineteenth century French clerics, this novel tells of the missionary efforts of the French bishop Jean Latour and his vicar, Father Joseph Vaillant, to establish a diocese in the territory of New Mexico. Besides a skillful reconstruction of these dedicated lives, the novel also provides a vivid picture of a particular region and culture. Tales and legends from Spanish colonial history and from the tribal traditions of the Hopi and Navajo enter the chronicle at many points, creating an effect of density and variety.

Principal Characters

Father Jean Marie Latour, a devout French priest consecrated vicar apostolic of New Mexico and Bishop of Agathonica in Partibus in 1850. With Father Vaillant, his friend and fellow seminarian, he journeys from his old parish on the shores of Lake Ontario to Santa Fe, seat of the new diocese in territory recently acquired from Mexico. In those troubled times, he finds many of the old missions in ruins or abandoned, the Mexican clergy lax and unlearned, and the sacraments corrupted by native superstitions. The travels of these two dedicated missionary priests over a desert region of sand, arroyos, towering mesas, and bleak red hills, the accounts of the labors that they perform and the hardships that they endure to establish the order and authority of the church in a wild land, make up the story of this beautifully told chronicle. Father Latour is an aristocrat by nature and tradition. Intellectual, fastidious, and reserved, he finds the loneliness of his mission redeemed by the cheerfulness and simple-hearted warmth of his old friend and by the simple piety that he often encounters among the humblest of his people; from them, as in the case of old Sada, he learns lessons of humility and grace. For years, he dreams of building a cathedral in Santa Fe, and in time his ambition is realized. By then, he is an archbishop and an old man. In the end, he decides not to return to his native Auvergne, the wet, green country of his youth that he had often remembered with yearning during his years in the hot desert country. He retires to a small farm outside Santa Fe, and when he dies his body rests in state before the altar in the cathedral that he had built. Father Latour's story is based on the life of a historical figure, Jean Baptiste Lamy, the first archbishop of

Santa Fe.

Father Joseph Vaillant, Father Latour's friend and vicar. The son of hardy peasant stock, he is tireless in his missionary labors. If Father Latour is an intellectual aristocrat, then Father Vaillant in his opposite, a hearty man of feeling, able to mix with all kinds of people and to move them as much by his good humor and physical vitality as by his eloquence. Doctrine, he holds, is good enough in its place, but he prefers to put his trust in miracles and the working of faith. When the gold rush begins in Colorado, he is sent to Camp Denver to work among the miners. There he continues his missionary labors, traveling from camp to camp in a covered carriage that is both his sleeping quarters and an improvised chapel. Borrowing and begging wherever he can, he builds for the church and for the future. When he dies as the first bishop of Denver, there is not a building in the city large enough to hold the thousands who come to his funeral. Like Father Latour, Father Vaillant is modeled after a real person, Father Joseph P. Machebeuf.

Padre Antonio José Martinez, the vigorous but arrogant priest at Taos credited with having instigated the revolt of the Taos Native American tribes. A man of violence and sensual passion, he has lived like a dictator too long to accept the authority of Father Latour with meekness or reason. When Father Latour visits him in Taos, he challenges his bishop on the subject of celibacy. After the bishop announces his intention to reform lax practices throughout his diocese, Padre Martinez tells him blandly that he will found his own church if the bishop interferes with him. As good as his promise, he and Padre Lucero defy Father Latour and Rome and try to establish a schism called the Old Holy Catholic Church of Mexico. Until his death a short time later, Padre Martinez carries on his personal and ecclesiastical feud with Father Taladrid, appointed by Father Latour to succeed the old tyrant of Taos.

Padre Marino Lucero, the priest of Arroyo Hondo, who joins Padre Martinez in defying Father Latour's authority. Padre Lucero is said to have a fortune hidden away. After he repents of his heresy and dies reconciled to Rome, buckskin bags containing gold and silver coins valued at almost twenty thousand dollars are found buried under the floor of his house.

Padre Gallegos, the genial, worldly priest at Albuquerque, a lover of whiskey, fandangos, and poker. Although Father Latour likes him as a man, he finds him scandalous and impossible as a priest. As soon as possible, he suspends Padre Gallegos and puts Father Vaillant in charge of the Albuquerque parish.

Manuel Lujon, a wealthy Mexican. During a visit at his ranch, Father Vaillant sees and admires a matched pair of white mules, Contento and Angelica. The priest praises the animals so highly that Lujon, a generous and pious man, decides to give him one of them. Father Vaillant refuses to accept the gift, however, saying that it would not be fitting for him to ride on a fine white mule while his bishop rides a common hack. Resigned, Lujon sends the second mule to Father Latour.

Buck Scales, a gaunt, surly American at whose house Father Latour and his vicar stop on one of their missionary journeys. Warned away by the gestures of his frightened wife, they continue on to the next town. The woman follows them to tell that in the past six years her husband has murdered four travelers as well as the three children she has borne. Scales is arrested and hanged.

Magdalena, the Mexican wife of Buck Scales, a devout woman who reveals her husband's crimes. After her husband's hanging, she lives for a time in the home of Kit Carson. Later Father Latour makes her the housekeeper in the establishment of the Sisters of Loretto in Santa Fe. She attends the old archbishop in his last days.

Kit Carson, the American trapper and scout. He and Father Latour become friends when they meet after the arrest of Buck Scales.

Jacinto, an intelligent young Native American from the Pecos pueblo, often employed as Father Latour's guide on the priest's missionary journeys. On one of these trips, the travelers are overtaken by a sudden snowstorm. Jacinto leads Father Latour into a cave that has obviously been used for ceremonial purposes. Before he builds a fire, Jacinto walls up an opening in the cave. Waking later in the night, Father Latour sees his guide standing guard

over the sealed opening. He realizes that he has been close to some secret ceremonial mystery of the Pecos, possibly connected with snake worship, but he respects Jacinto's confidence and never mentions the matter.

Don Antonio Olivares, a wealthy rancher who has promised to make a large contribution to Father Latour's cathedral fund. He dies suddenly before he can make good his promise, leaving his estate to his wife and daughter for life, after which his property is to go to the church. Two of his brothers contest the will.

Doña Isabella Olivares, the American wife of Father Latour's friend and benefactor. After her husband's death, two of his brothers contest the will on the grounds that Doña Isabella is not old enough to have a daughter of the age of Señorita Inez and that the girl is the child of one of Don Antonio's indiscreet youthful romances, adopted by Doña Isabella for the purpose of defrauding the brothers. Father Vaillant convinces the vain woman that it is her duty to tell the truth about her age in order for her and her daughter to win the case. Much against her will, Doña Isabella confesses in court that she is fifty-three years old and not forty-two, as she has claimed. Later she tells Father Vaillant and Father Latour that she will never forgive them for having made her tell a lie about a matter as serious as a woman's age.

Señorita Inez, the daughter of Doña Isabella and Don Antonio Olivares. Her age and her mother's are questioned when the Olivares brothers try to break Don Antonio's will.

Boyd O'Reilly, a young American lawyer, the manager of Don Antonio Olivares' affairs.

Sada, the wretched slave of a Protestant American family. One December night, she escapes from the stable where she sleeps and takes refuge in the church. Father Latour finds her there, hears her confession, blesses her, and gives her a holy relic and his own warm cloak.

Eusabio, a man of influence among the Navajo. Though he is younger than Father Latour, the priest respects him greatly for his intelligence and sense of honor. Father Latour grieves when the Navajo are forced to leave their country and rejoices that he has been able to live long enough to see them restored to their lands. When the old archbishop dies, Eusabio carries word of his death to the tribe.

Bernard Ducrot, the young priest who looks after Father Latour in his last years. He becomes like a son to the gentle old man.

Padre Jesus de Baca, the white-haired, almost blind priest at Isleta. An old man of great innocence and piety, he lives surrounded by his tame parrots.

Trinidad Lucero, a slovenly young monk in training for the priesthood whom Father Latour meets in the house of Padre Martinez. He passes as Padre Lucero's nephew, but some say he is the son of Padre Martinez. When Padre Martinez and Padre Lucero proclaim their schism, Trinidad acts as a curate for both.

Padre Taladrid, the young Spanish priest whom Father Latour appoints to succeed Padre Martinez at Taos.

The Story

In 1851, Father Jean Marie Latour reached Santa Fe, where he was to become vicar apostolic of New Mexico. His journey from the shores of Lake Ontario had been long and arduous. He had lost his belongings in a shipwreck at Galveston and had suffered painful injury in a wagon accident at San Antonio.

Upon Father Latour's arrival, in company with his good friend Father Joseph Vaillant, the Mexican priests refused to recognize his authority. He had no choice but to ride three thousand miles into Mexico to secure the necessary papers from the bishop of Durango.

On the road, he lost his way in an arid landscape of red hills and gaunt junipers. His thirst created vertigo, and he could blot out his agony only by repeating the cry of the Savior on the Cross. As he was about to give up all hope, he saw a tree growing in the shape of a cross. A short time later, he arrived in the Mexican settlement called *Aqua Secreta*, or Hidden Water. Stopping at the home of Benito, Bishop Latour first performed marriage ceremonies and then baptized all the children.

At Durango, he received the necessary documents and started the long trip back to Santa Fe. Meanwhile Father Vaillant had won over the inhabitants from enmity to amity and had set up the Episcopal residence in an old adobe house. On the first morning after his return to Santa Fe, the bishop heard the unexpected sound of a bell ringing the Angelus. Father Vaillant told him that he had found the bell, bearing the date 1356, in the basement of old San Miguel Church.

On a missionary journey to Albuquerque in March, Father Vaillant acquired as a gift a handsome cream-colored mule and another just like it for his bishop. These mules, Contento and Angelica, served the men in good stead for many years.

On another such trip, the two priests were riding together on their mules. Caught in a sleet storm, they stopped at the rude shack of an American, Buck Scales. His Mexican wife warned the travelers by gestures that their lives were in danger, and they rode on to Mora without spending the night. The next morning, the Mexican woman appeared in town. She told them that her husband had already murdered and robbed four travelers, and that he had killed her three babies. The result was that Scales was brought to justice, and his wife, Magdalena, was sent to the home of Kit Carson, the famous frontier scout. From that time on, Kit Carson was a valuable friend of the bishop and his vicar. Magdalena later became the housekeeper and manager for the kitchens of the Sisters of Loretto.

During his first year at Santa Fe, the bishop was called to a meeting of the Plenary Council at Baltimore. On the return journey, he brought back with him five nuns sent to establish the school of Our Lady of Light. Next, Bishop Latour, attended by the Native American Jacinto as his guide, spent some time visiting his own vicariate. Padre Gallegos, whom he visited at Albuquerque, acted more like a professional gambler than a priest, but because he was very popular with the natives Bishop Latour did not remove him at that time. At last he arrived at his destination, the top of the mesa at Acoma, the end of his long journey. On that trip, he heard the legend of Fray Baltazar, killed during an uprising of the Acomas.

A month after the bishop's visit, Latour suspended Padre Gallegos and put Father Vaillant in charge of the parish at Albuquerque. On a trip to the Pecos Mountains, the vicar fell ill with an attack of the black measles. The bishop, hearing of his illness, set out to nurse his friend. Jacinto again served as guide on the cold, snowy trip. When Bishop Latour reached his friend's bedside, he found that Kit Carson had arrived before him. As soon as the sick man could sit in the saddle, Carson and the bishop took him back to Santa Fe.

Bishop Latour decided to investigate the parish of Taos, where the powerful old priest Antonio José Martinez was the ruler of both spiritual and temporal matters. The following year, the bishop was called to Rome. When he returned, he brought with him four young priests from the seminary of Montferrand and a Spanish priest to replace Padre Martinez at Taos.

Bishop Latour had one great ambition: He wanted to build a cathedral in Santa Fe. In that project, he was assisted by the rich Mexican *rancheros*, but to the greatest extent by his good friend Don Antonio Olivares. When Don Antonio died, his will stated that his estate was left to his wife and daughter during their lives, and after their decease to the church. Don Antonio's brothers contested the will on the grounds that the daughter, Señorita Inez, was too old to be Doña Isabella's daughter, and the bishop and his vicar had to persuade the vain, coquettish widow to swear to her true age of fifty-three, rather than the forty-two years that she claimed. Thus the money was saved for Don Antonio's family and, eventually, the church.

Father Vaillant was sent to Tucson, but after several years Bishop Latour decided to recall him to Santa Fe. When he arrived, the bishop showed him the stone for building the cathedral. About that time, Bishop Latour received a letter from the bishop of Leavenworth. Because of the discovery of gold near Pikes Peak, he asked to have a priest sent there from Father Latour's diocese. Father Vaillant was the obvious choice.

Father Vaillant spent the rest of his life doing good works in Colorado, though he did return to Santa Fe with the papal emissary when Bishop Latour was made an archbishop. Father Vaillant became the first bishop of Colorado. He died there after years of service, and Archbishop Latour attended his impressive funeral services.

After the death of his friend, Father Latour retired to a modest country estate near Santa Fe. He had dreamed during all of his missionary years of the time when he could retire to his fertile green Auvergne in France, but in the end he decided that he could not leave the land of his labors. Memories of the journeys that he and Father Vaillant had made over thousands of miles of desert country became the meaning of his later years. Bernard Ducrot, a young seminarian from France, became like a son to him.

When Father Latour knew that his time had come to die, he asked to be taken into town to spend his last days near the cathedral. On the last day of his life, the church was filled with people who came to pray for him, as word that he was dying spread through the town. He died in the still twilight, and the cathedral bell, tolling in the early darkness, carried to the waiting countryside the news that at last death had come for Father Latour.

Critical Evaluation

When writing of her great predecessor and teacher, Sarah Orne Jewett, Willa Cather expressed her own belief that the quality that gives a work of literature greatness is the "voice" of the author—the sincere, unadorned, and unique vision of a writer coming to grips with material. If any one characteristic can be said to dominate the writings of Cather, it is a true and moving sincerity. She never tried to twist her subject matter to suit a preconceived purpose, and she resisted the temptation to dress up her homely material. She gave herself absolutely to her chosen material, and the result was a series of books both truthful and rich with intimations of the destiny of the American continent. By digging into the roots of her material, she found the greater meanings and expressed them with a deceptive simplicity. Her vision and craftsmanship were seldom more successfully joined than in *Death Comes for the Archbishop*. So completely did Willa Cather merge her voice with her material that some critics have thought that the book is almost too polished, without the sense of struggle necessary in a truly great novel. Yet this opinion, in fact, indicates the magnitude of the author's achievement and the brilliance of her technical skill. *Death Comes for the Archbishop* resonates with the unspoken beliefs of the author and the resolved conflicts that went into its construction. On the surface, it is cleanly wrought and simple, but it is a more complicated and profound book than it appears at first reading. Cather learned well from Jewett the secret of unadorned art, of craftsmanship that disarms by its very simplicity but that is based in a highly sophisticated intelligence.

It is true that this novel is an epic and a regional history, but, much more than either, it is a tale of personal isolation, of one man's life reduced to the painful weariness of his own sensitivities. Father Latour is a hero in the most profound sense of the word, at times almost a romantic hero, with his virtues of courage and determination, but he is also a very modern protagonist, with his doubts and inner conflicts and his philosophical nature. His personality is held up in startling contrast to that of his friend and vicar, Father Vaillant, a more simple, although no less admirable, individual. Cather's austere style perfectly captures the scholarly and urbane religious devotions that compose Father Latour's character. Always in this book, the reader is aware of a sense of the dignity of human life. Cather was not afraid to draw a good man, a man who could stand above others because of his deeds and because of his innate quality. The novel must stand or fall on this character, and it stands superbly.

Although this book is based on a true sequence of events, it is not a novel of plot. It is a chronicle, a character study, and, perhaps more specifically, an interplay of environment and character. Throughout the book, the reader is aware of the reaction of individuals to the land, as well as the reaction of one man to the land that he has chosen. Subtly and deeply, the author suggests that the soul of humanity is profoundly altered by the soul of the land, and Cather never doubts for a moment that the land does possess a soul or that this soul can transform a human being in complex and important ways. Cather was fascinated by the way in which the rough landscape of the Southwest, when reduced to its essences, seemed to take human beings and reduce them to their essences. She abandoned traditional realism in this book, turning toward the directness of symbolism. With stark pictures and vivid styles, she created an imaginary world rooted in realism but transcending realism. The rigid economy with which the book is written forces it to stand with a unique power in the reader's mind long after its reading. The personality of Bishop Latour stands as the greatest symbol, like a windswept crag or precipice in the vast New Mexico landscape, suggesting the nobility of the human spirit despite the inner conflicts against which it must struggle.

The descriptions of place set the emotional tone of the novel. The quality of life is intimately related to the landscape, and the accounts of the journeys and the efforts to survive despite the unfriendliness of the barren land help to create an odd warmth and passion in the narrative. The personalities of Bishop Latour and Father Vaillant establish a definite emotional relationship with the country, and if the other characters in the book are less vividly realized as individuals, perhaps it is because they do not seem to have this relationship with the land. Some of them have become part of the land, worn down by the elements like the rocks and riverbeds, and others have no relationship to it at all. Yet none of them is involved in the intense love-hate relationship with the land with which the two main characters struggle for so many years.

Although the chronology of the book encompasses many years, the novel is essentially static, a series of rich images and thoughtful moments highlighted and captured as by a camera. This quality of the narrative is not a fault; it is a fact of Cather's style. The frozen moments of contemplating, the glimpses into Father Latour's inner world and spiritual loneliness, are the moments that give the book its greatness. Despite the presence of Kit Carson, the novel is not an adventure story any more than it is merely the account of a pair of churchmen attempting to establish their faith in a difficult new terrain. The cathedral becomes the most important symbol in the final part of the book, representing the earthly successes of an individual dedicated to nonworldly ambitions. This conflict between the earthly and the spiritual is at the heart of Bishop Latour's personality and at the heart of the book. Yet the reader understands, at the end, when the bell tolls for Father Latour, that the temptations were never very deep and that the good man was ultimately victorious. The author does not spell out her meaning, but the emotional impact of her narrative brings it home to the reader.

A DEATH IN THE FAMILY

Type of work: Novel
Author: James Agee (1909-1955)
Type of work: Psychological realism
Time of plot: 1915
Locale: Knoxville, Tennessee
First published: 1957

Agee's Pulitzer Prize-winning novel contemplates the nature of love and death, as they affect an average family. When Jay Follet is killed in an automobile accident, his wife, children, and other relatives must pull together in order to cope with the tragedy.

Principal Characters

Rufus Follet, a six-year-old boy who tries to make sense of the world around him, especially after the death of his father.

Mary Follet, his mother. Her husband dies in an accident, and Mary must seek consolation in her religion in order to carry on with her life.

Jay Follet, Rufus' father, who is killed in an automobile accident on his way back from visiting his own sick father. His close relationship with his son makes dealing with Jay's death difficult for the boy.

Catherine, Rufus' young sister, who is not fully aware of what has happened to her father.

Grandfather and **Grandmother Lynch,** Mary's parents. He is an agnostic, and she is deaf.

Andrew and **Amelia,** Mary's brother and sister. Andrew is an opinionated artist.

Great-aunt Hannah, Grandfather Lynch's strong-willed sister, who never married.

Ralph Follet, Jay's brother, an undertaker. Although he is alcoholic and weak, he requests the task of preparing his brother's body for burial as a way of coping with his grief.

For many, *A Death in the Family* restored a world of feeling and moral value to American fiction. A Pulitzer Prize winner for 1957, it is a novel about love that is neither adult lust nor adolescent groping, about death as an inescapable part of the human condition, universal and therefore to be borne. In a very real but almost old-fashioned sense, the book is a celebration of these two great mysteries of experience. Nothing in this novel reveals the originality and power of James Agee more than this ability to suggest the atmosphere of wonder and awe that once surrounded humanity's awareness of being and mortality.

A Death in the Family is a novel of compassion almost overwhelming in its sensitivity, a circumstance not entirely accounted for by its autobiographical theme and the writer's obvious attempt to get at the meaning of the central experience of his own life: the death of his father forty-odd years before. Agee's compassion is for simple, decent people with ordinary lives—the very "ordinariness" of his material is one of the notable features of the novel—in a time of loss and grief. These are matters that he presents with a feeling of shared sorrow and sympathy for what is most personal and yet most general in the human situation.

Agee's sense of experience shared presupposes a universe of social continuity and order, one in which the human effort, in spite of its accumulation of grief, hunger, and waste, becomes meaningful and worthwhile when judged by community values and the idea of moral responsibility. A serious writer, Agee was interested in the nature of good and evil; in his novel, death, the complement of life, is the chink in the armor that gives a small boy his first awareness of evil and threatens with the shock of loss a family in which the ties of kinship have been fulfilled by love. He was able to shape, on a purely domestic level, a fable of compelling tenderness and compassionate insight, achieving within this framework his effects of lyricism, meditative speculation, and drama. James Agee's early death deprived American letters of one of the resourceful and authentic talents of his generation.

Behind this novel, however, lay years of preparation

and apprentice work in a variety of media within the fairly short span of his writing career. Agee was born in Knoxville, the setting of *A Death in the Family*, in 1909, and he died of a heart attack in a New York taxicab in 1955. After schooling at Exeter and Harvard, he had joined the staff of *Fortune* in 1932. His first book was *Permit Me Voyage*, a collection of poems published in the Yale Younger Poets Series in 1934. This verse was rather conventional in form, romantic in its display of strong personal feeling. As poetry written in a period of technical experiment, the book, like *A Death in the Family*, seemed strangely old-fashioned. Later out of an assignment to write a documentary report on the sharecropping system in the South, he produced one of the most original but least-read books of its decade, *Let Us Now Praise Famous Men*, a curious blend of narrative, social history, satire, and philosophy. It is in many ways a youthful book but an impressive one in its praise of the American earth and in its rage against the exploiters of the land and its workers. As a social document, the book is still eloquent and moving, even though the first impression is likely to be one of the tremendous power of language under poor control. Still later, he wrote about motion pictures for *The Nation*, critiques that have become classics of their kind, and reviewed books for *Time*. In 1948, he gave up journalism to devote himself to *A Death in the Family*, but he was constantly being diverted to other tasks: articles for *Life*, scenarios for *The Quiet One* (1949), *The African Queen* (1951), *Face to Face* ("*The Bride Comes to Yellow Sky*" episode, 1952), *The Night of the Hunter* (1955), a documentary on the life of Abraham Lincoln for television, and the novella *The Morning Watch*, published in 1950.

Although Agee came late to fiction, his admirers saw in *The Morning Watch*, a moving study of adolescent confusion against the background of a boy's school, promise of the major work of which he was capable. *A Death in the Family* almost fulfills that promise. When Agee died in 1955, his novel was virtually complete except for the tying of loose ends and the final polishing. In preparing the manuscript for publication, the editors have inserted as thematic interludes several episodes not directly related to the time scheme of the novel and have added as a prologue the sketch entitled "Knoxville: Summer 1915," which had been written some years before. It is safe to say that, if Agee had lived, he would have given his book greater structural unity and might have recast in more dramatic form several sections that remain static in effect. It is doubtful, however, if he could have improved upon the rich contrasts of texture conveyed in characterization, mood, and scene, or refined to greater precision the beautiful clarity of his style.

As an introductory piece, "Knoxville: Summer 1915" creates the mood of affectionate reminiscence within which the novel is embodied. It is a twilight study of a summer evening when children play around the corner lampposts and men in shirt sleeves sprinkle their lawns with water after supper. Later, crickets chirp in the early dark that seems filled with stars as a small boy lies with his father, mother, uncle, and aunt on quilts that have been spread on the grass in the backyard. This is the enchanted world of childhood as it appeared to young Rufus Follet: safe, warm, and secure—a world of protection, understanding, and love.

Rufus and his younger sister, Catherine, are asleep when the telephone rings summoning his father to the country, where his Grandfather Follet has been taken suddenly ill. The ties of family relationships—intimate, trivial, amusing, tender—are evoked as Jay Follet prepares to start out before daybreak and his wife, Mary, gets up to cook his breakfast. Because he expects to be back in time for supper, he leaves without waking the children. They are asleep the next night when the telephone rings again and a stranger's voice tells Mary that her husband has been in an accident. On the way back from the country, the steering mechanism of his car had broken and Jay, thrown clear when the car left the road, had been killed instantly.

This, in outline, is the story of *A Death in the Family*, but not its whole substance. More important is the effect of the death on the people involved. To Mary, it brings the realization that death happens to many people and is very common. In her distress, she turns to her faith for consolation. To Rufus, his father's death is not the maturing experience that it will eventually become, only another baffling circumstance among the mysteries of his young life. These mysteries include his nightmares, his mother's command that he must never mention the color of a black nursemaid's skin, the memory of a visit made a short time before to see his withered great-great-grandmother in the country, or the reason that older boys ask him his name and then break into laughter and run away. Yet he knows that the event gives him some importance that he had never known before: Slowly, to himself, he repeats the fact that his father is dead. Catherine is too young to understand her loss or her mother's sorrow. Beyond these individuals is the widening circle of family: Grandfather Lynch, the agnostic; deaf Grandmother Lynch; Great-aunt Hannah, a tower of strength; Andrew, the sharp-tongued artist uncle, and his sister Amelia; and weak, drunken Uncle Ralph Follet, the undertaker, who asks to prepare his own brother's body for burial.

These people give the novel its texture, establishing the world in which adults and children confront the fact of death while trying to understand its meaning in terms of grief and love.

The novel contains memorable passages in which deep feeling is combined with power and precision of language, as in the account of the relationship between father and son that unfolds as Jay and Rufus walk slowly home after seeing a Charlie Chaplin film; in the scene in which Great-aunt Hannah and Rufus go shopping, and he wears down an adult's reasonable firmness with his small boy's persistence over the purchase of a loud-checked cap; and in the moment when the mourning family seems to sense the dead man's presence in the house. This is also the case in the scene in which young Rufus, eager to display his new cap, runs to his parents' bedroom and sees that his father is not there; instead, he finds his mother propped up on two pillows, looking as if she were sick or tired. James Agee began his career as a poet, and he never lost a poet's eye for the telling detail or the poet's ear. *A Death in the Family* contains passages that, even out of context, show the true quality of a writer to whom literature was a total job of action and feeling, of sights and sounds, of image and meaning, of language and mood. The book is not a perfect novel, but in the universality of its theme and the compassion that it invokes, it uncovers a world of feeling in which all may share. This is more than the truth-telling for which the realist strives; it is truth itself.

DEATH OF A SALESMAN

Type of work: Drama
Author: Arthur Miller (1915-   )
Type of plot: Social criticism
Time of plot: Mid-twentieth century
Locale: New York
First presented: 1949

Death of a Salesman represents a successful attempt to blend the themes of social and personal tragedy within the same dramatic framework. Willy Loman accepts at face value the overpublicized ideals of material success and blatant optimism, and therein lies his tragedy. The playwright's ability to project the story of his lower-middle-class hero into the common experience of so many Americans who sustain themselves with illusions makes this play one of the most significant in the modern American theater.

Principal Characters

Willy Loman, a sixty-three-year-old traveling salesman who has begun to dwell on the past and not to know where he is. In the last two days of his life, his past unrolls before him. He is a father who loves his sons and wants them to have worldly success, although he does not know how to help them achieve it. His last gesture for his son Biff is to commit suicide so that the son can have the insurance money.

Biff Loman, Willy's thirty-four-year-old son, who is still trying to find himself. A high-school athlete, he gets nowhere after graduation. When he is refused a loan to start a business, he steals a cheap fountain pen. Angry and defeated, he curses his father as a fool and a dreamer, though he loves the man.

Happy Loman, Willy's younger son, modestly successful in life as a clerk in a store. He is a woman chaser who seeks pleasure.

Charley, Willy Loman's friend and neighbor. He lends Willy money and offers him a job.

Bernard, Charley's son, a successful lawyer whose own success serves to remind Willy's sons of their inadequacies.

Linda Loman, Willy's wife, a fearful but patient woman who loves her husband despite his failures.

Howard Wagner, Willy's boss's son, who lets Willy know he is finished as a salesman.

Uncle Ben, Willy's brother. He goes out into the jungle and in a few years returns from the diamond mines a rich man. His success contrasts Willy's failure.

The Woman, an unnamed character whom Biff, as a teenager, finds in a hotel room with his father.

The Story

When Willy Loman came home on the same day that he had left on a trip through his New England territory, his wife Linda knew that he was near the breaking point. Lately he had begun to talk to himself about things out of the past. That day he had run off the road two or three times without knowing what he was doing, and he had come home in fear. Willy, sixty-three, had given all his life to the company. He told himself they would just have to make a place for him in the New York home office. Traveling all week and driving futile miles had become too much for him.

Willy had had such hopes before Biff came home from his last job. Biff had always been the favorite, though Happy was the more settled and successful son. Biff was thirty-four now and still had to find himself, but Willy knew he would settle down when the time came. The boy had been the greatest football player his school had ever known. In a game at Ebbets Field, he had been a hero. Three colleges offered him scholarships. Biff had not gone to college, had not done anything but bum around the West, never making more than twenty-eight dollars a week. It was hard to understand him.

During the next two days, Willy's whole life unrolled before him, today's reality intermingled with yesterday's half-forgotten episodes. Broken as it was, the pictures told the story of Willy Loman, salesman.

Perhaps the first mistake was in not following his brother Ben to Alaska—or was it Africa? Ben had wanted Willy to join him, but Willy was a salesman. Some weeks he averaged two hundred dollars. No, that was not quite true; it was nearer seventy. Yet he would make the grade, he told Ben, and so he stayed in New York. Ben went into the jungle a pauper; four years later, he came back from the diamond mines a rich man.

Willy's boys were both well liked; that was important. Bernard, Charley's son, was liked, but not well liked. Bernard had begged to carry Biff's shoulder pads that day at Ebbets Field. Sometimes Willy had worried a little about the boys. Biff stole a football from school, and a whole case of them from the sporting goods store where he worked. He did not mean any harm, Willy knew. Willy even laughed when the boys stole a little lumber from a construction job nearby; no one would miss it. Willy and the boys used it to make the front stoop.

That day at Ebbets Field seemed to be the last great day in Biff's life. Willy had left for Boston after the game, but surely that little Boston affair had not made the difference in the boy. Willy was with a woman when Biff burst in on him. Biff had failed math and could not take one of the scholarships unless Willy talked to the teacher and got him to change the grade. Willy was ready to leave for New York at once, but when Biff saw the woman in Willy's room, he left. Things were never the same afterward.

There was also Happy, who used to stand in Biff's shadow. Happy was a magnificent specimen, just like Biff, and there was not a woman in the world he could not have. An assistant merchandising manager, he would be manager someday, a big man. So would Biff. Biff needed only to find himself.

On the day Willy Loman turned back home, he dreamed his biggest dreams. Biff would go back to that sporting goods store and get a loan from the owner to set himself and Happy up in business. That man had always loved Biff. Willy would go to young Howard Wagner, his boss's son, and demand to be given a place in the New York office. They would celebrate together that night at dinner. Biff and Happy would give Willy a night on the town to celebrate their mutual success.

Biff, however, failed to get the loan. That man who had loved Biff did not even recognize him. To get even, Biff stole a fountain pen and ran down eleven flights with it. Moreover, when Howard heard Willy's story, he told him to turn in his samples and take a rest. Willy realized that he was through. He went to Charley for more money, for he had been borrowing from Charley since he had been put on straight commission months ago. Bernard was in Charley's office. He was on his way to plead a case before the Supreme Court. Willy could not understand it. Charley had never given his life for his boy as Willy had for his. Charley offered Willy a job, but Willy said he was a salesman. They loved him in New England; he would show them yet.

Willy stumbled in to the dinner that they had planned, a failure himself but hoping for good news about Biff. Hearing of Biff's failure, he was completely broken. Happy picked up two girls, and he and Biff left Willy alone.

When Biff and Happy finally came home, Linda ordered them to be out of the house by morning. She was afraid because Willy had tried to kill himself once before. Giving vent to his anger and sense of defeat, Biff cursed Willy for being a fool and a dreamer. He forced himself and Willy to acknowledge that Biff had been only a clerk in that store, not a salesman; that Biff had been jailed in Kansas City for stealing; that Happy was not an assistant manager but a clerk and a philandering, woman-chasing bum; and that Willy had never been a success and never would be. When Biff began to weep, Willy realized for the first time that his son loved him.

Willy, left alone after the others went upstairs, began to see Ben again, to tell him his plan. Willy had twenty thousand in insurance. Biff would be magnificent with twenty thousand. Willy ran out to his car and drove crazily away.

At the funeral, attended only by Linda, the boys, and Charley, Charley tried to tell Biff about his father. He said that a salesman had to dream, that without dreams he was nothing. When the dreams were gone, a salesman was finished. Sobbing quietly, Linda stooped and put flowers on the grave of Willy Loman, salesman.

Critical Evaluation

Born in New York, the city that is the setting for *Death of a Salesman*, Arthur Miller in his earlier plays reacts to the social pressures and fervors of the 1930's (the Great Depression) and 1940's (World War II). *Death of a Salesman*, however, Miller's most famous and most effective play, is also his most complex and is far more than a social document. It is, of course, a very clear attack on at least one aspect of the American success myth or dream, as that dream is defined by Willy Loman. To Willy, success, respect, affection, and authority come to those who are "well liked." Greetings given gladly, doors opened eagerly, sales made readily—these represent the good life to Willy Loman. Yet the dream scarcely suits everyone. It does not suit Willy, despite his great dreams and restless longings. Because, despite constant failure, Willy keeps trying, he ultimately loses sight of his own identity. Biff laments at the end that his father never learned to know himself.

The dream, to Miller, is not only destructive but also amoral. As a boy, Biff is told that, since he is "well liked," he can get away with anything. Disillusioned with his father, Biff, after running away, discovers that he has no direction, no skill, no vocation. The dream proves as destructive to Happy, who is a weak caricature of his father. Nevertheless, the dream's enormous power is shown again and again, particularly at the conclusion of Act I, when Willy, Happy, and Biff grow wildly enthusiastic over the prospect of Biff asking for a business loan from a former employer, an employer whom Biff scarcely knew. When all else fails, Willy can call up the image of his brother, Ben, who represents an earlier get-rich-quick version of the success myth.

The Ben fantasies also suggest another level of the play. They help define an individual whose world is crumbling. His weariness, his suicide efforts, his grumbling as he thinks of the little he has made of his life, his grandiose posturing—all of these are the exterior cracks in a man who is also breaking up inside, as visions and memories out of the past cross and recross the present. The final crack-up is inevitable.

The play was at the center of an interesting controversy: Can a common man be a suitable subject for tragedy? Miller, of course, insisted that he could. Interesting too is the fact that, as his own interests changed, Miller himself announced that Willy was too pathetic for genuine tragic stature. Miller's later plays—*After the Fall* and *The Price*—probe the nature not of society, but of humanity, asserting the individual's own responsibility for his or her life.

THE DEATH SHIP

Type of work: Novel
Author: B. Traven (1890-1969)
Type of plot: Proletarian
Time of plot: 1920's
Locale: Belgium, Holland, France, Spain, and the Mediterranean Sea
First published: 1926, as *Das Totenschiff*

Traven chronicles the experiences of an American sailor in Europe who has lost his passport, and therefore his country. Part proletarian novel and part "tough-guy" fiction, The Death Ship *presents an absurd, uncaring world in which all people are victims of capitalism, nationalism, and, ultimately, fate.*

Principal Characters

Gerard Gales, a young American sailor who is stranded in Europe when his ship leaves without him. He signs on with the *The Yorikke*, a "death ship" that the owners intend to scuttle in order to collect the insurance money. He and fellow sailor Stanislav are shanghaied before *The Yorikke* goes down, however, only to be forced into service on another death ship. The *Empress of Mad-* *agascar* sinks, and Gerard is left clinging to the wreckage, at which point the narrative ends.

Stanislav, Gerard's shipmate and friend. Like Gerard, he works in the furnace room stoking the engines. Stanislav is captured along with his friend to serve aboard the *Empress of Madagascar* and drowns in its destruction when he has a vision of *The Yorikke* and swims after it.

Based on the author's own experiences and written when he was about twenty-four, *The Death Ship* is unique and apparently free of direct influences, just as B. Traven was in some ways unlike any other writer. The book may be classified as a proletarian novel, written in the style of tough-guy fiction. Yet its thesis is not as doctrinaire, as deliberately worked out, as that of a proletarian novel, nor is its style as conscious as that of a tough-guy novel.

For Gerard Gales, the young American narrator, stranded in Antwerp when his ship returns to New Orleans without him, the passport has displaced the sun as the center of the universe. Unable to prove his citizenship, he is a man without a country, and his physical presence is no official proof of his birth. Like Franz Kafka's K. in *Der prozess* (1925; *The Trial*, 1937), he moves through a labyrinth of bureaucracy; officials empowered to dispense passports, certificates, receipts, affidavits, seals, and licenses conduct the Inquisition of the modern age. The war for liberty and democracy has produced a Europe in which to be hungry is human and to lack a passport is inhuman—unless one is rich.

A victim of nationalism, moving among fading echoes of speeches on international brotherhood, Gerard is an individualist. Immigration officials conspire to smuggle him from Belgium into Holland, then back into Belgium, then into France, where he is jailed for riding a train without a ticket and later sentenced to be shot as a suspected spy. Ironically, when he senses the universal animosity toward Americans and pretends to be a German, he is treated royally. In Spain, he is left entirely alone. Politically oppressed, the Spanish seem freer than other peoples, and Gerard loves them. The peasants are so good to him, however, that he feels useless and hates himself; he senses the error in a communist state where the individual is denied the privilege of taking personal risks. Because he is a sailor without a ship, and because he wants to return to his girlfriend, Gerard signs aboard *The Yorikke*.

If he once thought that the world consisted of deckhands and people who made paint, he descends now into a sailor's hell in the stokehold. Its name obscured on the bow, *The Yorikke*, too, appears to lack a proper birth certificate. Although the ship seems ashamed of its name, Gerard exhibits a kind of nationalism himself when he withholds his true name and country and signs on as an Egyptian: No American would sail on such a ship, and he realizes that, despite its many faults, he loves his country and is wretchedly homesick. *The Yorikke* resembles no ship that he has ever seen; it appears to be insane. A model "death ship," it has no life jackets. A death ship is so called because its owners have decided to scuttle it for the insurance. The crew, desperate men called "deads" who are at the end of their tether when they come aboard, do not know when the ship will go down. The sea, Gerard imagines, will probably expel the diseased ship for fear of infection. No supplies—spoons, coffee cups, blankets—are provided; the sailors repeatedly steal a single bar of soap from one another until it has been through every filthy hand; conditions are worse than in a concentration camp. The only thing in ample supply is work, and if a man tries to collect overtime on a ship pathologically committed to profits, he may find himself in a black hold with rats that would terrify a cat. Traven conveys a vivid sense of what "she" means as pronoun for a ship; Gerard constantly describes *The Yorikke* in very intimate and telling female terms.

Gerard admires his mysterious captain, whose intelligence sets him apart from the old-style pirate. He takes care of his men, and they would rather sink with the ship than inform the authorities that it is carrying contraband for the Riffs. *The Yorikke* crew is the filthiest that Gerard has ever seen; the men wear bizarre rags. Some appear to have been shanghaied off the gallows. In the towns, other sailors shun them; men, women, and children fear them; and the police, afraid that they may leave the town in ashes, follow them.

The filthiest member of the gang is the "drag man," who must perform extra and loathsome chores. Work is at the center of this novel—the struggle to get it, and, under extreme conditions, the horror and ultimate beauty of it. Delight in conveying an inside view is a characteristic of tough-guy literature, and Gerard gives all the details of various work routines. One of the most horrific passages in literature is Traven's description of putting back fallen grate bars while the boiler is white-hot. After his first bout at what becomes a daily task, Gerard declares that he is free, unbound, above the gods; he can do what he wishes and curse the gods, because no hell could be greater torture.

Gerard resurrects the freshness of the cliché that humans can become like machines. He feels like a gladiator for Julius Caesar's fight-to-the-death spectacles. Bravery on the battlefield is nothing when compared to the bravery of those who do certain work to keep civilization afloat. No flag drapes the bodies of the ship's casualties; they go like garbage over the fantail. On a death ship, no laws keep a sailor in line; each worker is crucially necessary, and work is a common bond. With no sense of heroics, Gerard helps to save two men and is himself saved. His true countrymen, he discovers, are those workers who are scalded and scorched at the same furnace

with him; he does not desert because his friend Stanislav would then have to work alone. Though Traven appears to show how people can grow accustomed to misery and filth, he insists that nobody really gets used to them; one simply loses the capacity to feel and becomes hard-boiled. Few fictive descriptions of the lives, the hopes, the illusions and attitudes of doomed sailors, their qualities of ingenuity, improvisation, and audacity, are as complete as Traven's.

Ironically, just as Gerard, despite his misery, learns to live and laugh on the ship, he senses *The Yorikke's* imminent doom. A further irony comes when Gerard and Stanislav are shanghaied from *The Yorikke* to serve on the new but disastrously slow *Empress of Madagascar*, which is to be scuttled in a few days. The *Empress* kills its plotting captain, however, and stands like a tower between the rocks before it sinks. Stanislav and Gerard are safely tied to a piece of wreckage, but Stanislav has a hallucination in which he sees *The Yorikke* leaving the dock. Wanting to go with her, he detaches himself and slips into the sea to drown. Not yet rescued, Gerard pays his respects to his comrade in the last lines of the novel.

The style of the story—rough, garrulous, full of completely justified profanity—sounds translated, but it is consistent with Gerard's semiliterate immigrant background. Though these qualities become wearisome in three hundred pages, the sheer energy of the telling achieves a special eloquence. Traven is overly fascinated by the way that words come about; Gerard indulges in figurative rhetoric, but many of his wisecracks seem lame, probably because his slang is dated. Humor, wit, and comedy are interwoven quite naturally among the dark aspects of Traven's narrative. The style provides an amplification of theme through the play of language. Although Traven does not set up satirical situations, his diction and metaphorical pretenses create a satirical distortion in the telling of such episodes as those involving bureaucracy.

No plot, no story line as such holds the novel together; narratively, it seems split in half, but the handling of theme, the picaresque looseness, and the personality of the narrator create an appropriate effect of the material. The static quality is relieved by sudden transitions and by the frequent use of tales and anecdotes, as in Traven's *The Treasure of the Sierra Madre*. Gerard is a storyteller who never tires of retelling a tale. The consulate scenes are repetitious; the reader is offered variations on the same routine, though speeded up and foreshortened sometimes; and toward the end, Stanislav tells Gerard a story about himself that closely resembles Gerard's earlier experiences. Gerard is especially fond of ridiculing popular fiction and film versions of the seafaring life; the difference between living and listening to an experience is discussed in the beginning and at the end. Gerard tells his general story the way a sailor would, commenting with joking metaphors and reflecting constantly on the meaning of events. The reader is visualized as a captive audience for a man who has at last found a way to speak without interruption on various social, political, and economic conditions. The novel has some poignant moments, too, but, as is typical of the tough-guy novel, sentimentality only occasionally intrudes.

Gerard and Stanislav are not to be associated with the victims of modern literature. They are more victims of the nature of things than of conditions that can be reformed. Gerard may gripe with every breath he takes, but he does not whine. He proudly insists that he can do the same work anyone else can do, anywhere. He contemptuously refuses to bow to circumstance. He refuses to blame the shipowners; having failed to take his fate in his own hands by jumping ship, he has no right to refuse to be a slave. Yet he can hope that he will be resurrected from the "deads" by his own will and fortitude. He knows that, for the courageous individual who survives the ordeal of *The Yorikke*, anything is possible. By going to the bottom of agony in his daily task of replacing grate bars, Gerard comes out with a kind of peace, aware of his place in a universe that now has meaning in the slightest thing. His earned romanticism enables him to see beauty in the conventionally ugly.

Although Gerard covers, directly to the reader and in dialogue, almost every grievance of the laborer of the first twenty-five years of the twentieth century, he is not interested in easy working conditions and fringe benefits. Repeatedly, he preaches the gospel of hard work, not because work is good for the soul, which seems less involved than muscle, but because it is good for the human animal. Unlike proletarian writers, Traven achieves a kind of mystique about work. One thinks of Albert Camus' Sisyphus: For his disobedience of the officials, Sisyphus was condemned to the futile task of rolling a huge rock to the top of a mountain, after which it rolled back down to the plain. Camus likened this labor to that of the proletariat. Unintentionally, perhaps, Traven has translated Sisyphus' mythic task into existential reality. The intentions of the novel are uncertain; but at moments it appears to be an allegory about the laboring class. Working unseen at sea, deep in the black hole of an ash pit, these men—who were never born, in a sense, who are without a country—go to their deaths on a ship that does not exist officially. Gerard constantly speaks of the ship metaphorically as being more than five thousand years old. The flag is so dirty that it could represent any country, and thus represents all. Many nationalities are represented among the crew; each nameless person is called, ironically, by the name of the country that he claims but that has denied his existence.

DELTA WEDDING

Type of work: Novel
Author: Eudora Welty (1909-   )
Type of plot: Regional realism
Time of plot: Early 1920's
Locale: Mississippi
First published: 1946

This novel is the chronicle of a remarkable family living in Mississippi in the early 1920's. Although the plot revolves around the preparations for the wedding of one of the Fairchild daughters to a man considered in many ways her inferior, the main theme of the story is actually the portrayal of this unusual family and of a regional way of life.

Principal Characters

Laura McRaven, a cousin to the Fairchilds, a remarkable and close-knit Delta family. At nine, Laura makes her first journey alone. She is going to the Delta to visit her dead mother's people; her cousin Dabney is being married. Laura's chief regret is that she is not to be in the wedding party, but at the last minute, when one of the children falls sick, this wish is granted. After the wedding, Laura's aunt asks her to live with them. Being wanted by the Fairchilds seems wonderful beyond belief, but Laura knows that she must go back to her father.

Dabney Fairchild, Laura's cousin, a bride-to-be. Dabney is marrying the plantation manager, whose social position is inferior. Dabney, before her marriage, feels ambivalent—loving her fiancé, but at the same time afraid of being at all outside her family. After the honeymoon, the couple returns to live at Marmion, an estate owned by the family. Everything now seems right to Dabney.

Battle Fairchild, her father, the owner of Shellmound plantation. The Fairchilds seldom talk as a family but always act as one. Characteristically, Battle is reluctant to let Dabney go, but he cannot even say that he will miss her.

Ellen Fairchild, Dabney's mother. Sharing the Fairchild reticence, which is in fact family loyalty, she expresses only to her husband her anger against her brother-in-law's wife, Robbie, who is making George unhappy.

George Fairchild, Battle's brother, the best loved of all. He married beneath him, and his wife, resentful of George's family, especially after George risked his life to save a feeble-minded cousin, has deserted him. She comes to the Fairchild place and at last, though not in words, George makes her see his love for her.

Robbie Fairchild, George's wife. She believes that the Fairchilds love one another because in doing so they are really loving themselves. Defeated by the family feeling, she wants George to show that he loves her above them.

Shelley Fairchild, the eldest Fairchild daughter. The family disapproves of her plan to become a nun but characteristically does not try to change her mind. Shelley, understanding the family best, knows that George is the best loved because he alone seems to love them all as individuals, not collectively.

Troy Flavin, the manager of Shellmound plantation and Dabney's husband-to-be. His mother sends some beautiful handmade quilts from her mountain shack. Troy is proud, but the Fairchilds are even more ashamed of his background.

The Story

Nine-year-old Laura McRaven made her first journey alone, from Jackson to the Delta, to visit her dead mother's people, the Fairchilds. One of her cousins, Dabney Fairchild, was to be married, and Laura's chief regret was that she could not be in the wedding party because of her mother's recent death. She remembered Shellmound, the Fairchild plantation, and knew that she would have a wonderful time with her exciting cousins and aunts. The Fairchilds were people to whom things happened, exciting, unforgettable things.

At Shellmound, Laura found most of the family assembled for the wedding. Although children her age were her companions, she was aware also of the doings of the grown-ups. It was obvious that the family was not happy about Dabney's marriage. Her husband-to-be was Troy Flavin, the manager of the plantation, whose inferior social position was the main thing against him. Uncle Battle, Dabney's father, was most of all reluctant to let one of his family go from him, but he could not bring himself to say anything to Dabney, not even that he would miss her. In fact, that seemed to Laura to be a strange thing about her cousins. They seldom talked as a united family, but they always acted as one.

There were so many members of the family that it was hard for Laura to keep them straight. Uncle Battle's wife was Aunt Ellen, and their oldest daughter was Shelley, who was going to be a nun. Again the whole family disapproved of her plan, but there was hardly ever any attempt to get her to change her mind. The obvious favorite was Uncle George, Battle's brother. Uncle George had also married beneath himself. He and his wife, Robbie, lived in Memphis, where everyone knew poor Uncle George could never be happy.

When George arrived for the wedding festivities, he was alone and miserable. Robbie had left him, and he had come down alone to see his family. Not wanting to make Dabney unhappy, they did not tell her of Robbie's desertion. The children and the aunts and great-aunts were not told either, although one by one they began to suspect that something was wrong. Ellen could have killed Robbie for making George unhappy, but she kept her feelings to herself except when she was alone with Battle, her husband.

Robbie's anger at her husband began on the afternoon of a family outing. George had risked his life to save one of the cousins, a feeble-minded child caught in the path of a train as they crossed a railroad trestle. After that incident, Robbie was never the same with George. She seemed to want him to prove that he loved her more than he loved his family.

Probably Shelley understood the family best. She knew that they had built a wall against the outside world. She suspected, however, that they were more lonely than self-sufficient. Most people took the family as a group, loving or hating them all together. Only Uncle George seemed to take them one by one, loving and understanding each as an individual. Shelley thought that this was why they all loved Uncle George so much.

Dabney herself seemed to wish for more than she had in her love for Troy. Sometimes she felt left out, as if she were trying to find a lighted window but found only darkness. She loved Troy, but she wanted to feel even more a part of him. She wished also that her family

would try to keep her with them and wanted to be certain of their love.

Preparations for the wedding created a flurry. The dresses had been ordered from Memphis, and when some of the gowns failed to arrive, there was the usual hubbub among the women, a concern that the men could not appreciate. One of the children fell sick at the last minute, so that Laura was made one of the wedding party after all. Troy's mother sent some beautiful handmade quilts from her mountain shack. Troy felt proud, but the Fairchilds were even more self-consciously and unwillingly ashamed of his background.

After their wedding, Dabney and Troy would live at Marmion, an estate owned by the family. Dabney rode over to see the house. Looking at the stately buildings and the beautiful old trees, she knew that best of all she would love being inside it looking out on the rest of the world. That was what she wanted the most, to be inside where she was a part of the light and warmth. That was what marriage must give her.

All the time, unknown to any of the family but Shelley, Robbie was not far away. She had come after George in hopes that he was looking for her. What had almost defeated Robbie was the fear that she had married not George but the whole Fairchild family. It was that fear which had made her angry at the affair on the railroad trestle. Wanting desperately to come first with George, she knew instinctively that he could never set her apart from or above the family. Contrite and humble, she went to Shellmound. The fact that George was not even there at the moment hurt her even more, for she wanted very much for him to be miserable without her. He was, of course, but it was not the Fairchild way to let anyone see his or her true feelings.

Robbie probably hit upon the secret of the family when she said that the Fairchilds loved each other because in so doing they were really loving themselves. Yet of George that fact was not quite true. He was the different one. Because of his gentleness and his ability to love people as individuals, he let Robbie see his love for her without ever saying the words that she had longed to hear.

The wedding was almost an anticlimax, a calm scene following gusty storms of feeling. Troy and Dabney took only a short trip, for Troy was needed to superintend the plantation. While they were gone, Battle worked the hands hard to get Marmion ready for them. Dabney was anxious to move in, but the move was not so necessary after her marriage as it had seemed before; she no longer felt left out of Troy's life. She thought her life before had been like seeing a beautiful river between high banks, with no way to get down. Now she had found the way, and she was at peace. Indeed, the whole family seemed to have righted itself.

When Aunt Ellen asked Laura to live with them at Shellmound, her being wanted by the Fairchilds seemed too wonderful for her belief. Laura knew that she would go back to her father, but feeling that she really belonged to the Fairchilds seemed like a beautiful dream. She clung briefly to Aunt Ellen, as if to hold close that wonderful moment of belonging.

Critical Evaluation

Eudora Welty has created in Shellmound, the home of the Fairchild family in *Delta Wedding*, a world set apart from the rest of Southern plantation society of the 1920's. Shellmound is a haven, isolated from the mainstream of Southern life and unaffected by extremes of grief and suffering. There is no racial tension, no poverty, no war or natural catastrophe, none of the sense of alienation and instability generated by contact with modern urban society, and none of the severe moral deficiencies in the characters that would preclude natural human happiness. The Fairchild estate is thus the perfect stage upon which to play out a drama about the growth of every type of love, from romantic to filial to platonic.

The main focus of the book, therefore, is on the nature of the numerous members of the Fairchild clan and on their relationships; Welty shows how the men are different from the women, how the "insiders" are different from those who have married into the family, how each person relates to the others, and how each person grows individually and privately. In order to explore these various aspects, the author utilizes different narrative voices, thus enabling the reader to view the characters from different perspectives. Aunt Tempe, for example, provides the older generation's point of view. She believes that Delta women have inherited traits that cannot be learned by outsiders, traits that enable them subtly to control their men and the plantations. At the young end of the spectrum is nine-year-old Laura, who comes to live at Shellmound temporarily after her mother's death; she provides the child's viewpoint of events during the hectic wedding preparations. The most objective, wise, and clear-sighted outlook, however, is provided by Aunt Ellen. As an "outsider" (she married Battle Fairchild), she not only sees more accurately than her more involved and subjective relatives but also brings to her judgment insights from the world beyond the plantation.

What distinguishes the Fairchilds most of all is their simultaneous independence from and reliance upon one another; each person is at once intensely caught up in family concerns and fiercely private and separate. The only member who transcends the insular closeness of the circle to achieve a more universal outlook on life is Uncle George. Able to feel and see beyond the limitations of life at Shellmound, he is nevertheless tied to the Fairchilds in his heart. Through the family's constant attempts to study and understand George, and through George's emotional involvement in events at the estate, Welty reveals a group of people at once selfishly exclusive and warmly affectionate, tender, loving and devoted.

DESIRE UNDER THE ELMS

Type of work: Drama
Author: Eugene O'Neill (1888-1953)
Type of plot: Romantic tragedy
Time of plot: 1850
Locale: The Cabot farmhouse in New England
First presented: 1924

Desire Under the Elms *was the last of O'Neill's naturalistic plays and one of his most effective. The playwright's daring reduction of human motives to the simple impulses of love, hate, lust, and greed gives an impression of human nature as convincing and complete as the more complex studies of his later, longer plays.*

Principal Characters

Ephraim Cabot, a greedy, harsh old New England widower. He has taken over his second wife's farm and worked her to death. He has brutalized his three sons, working them like animals on the farm until they hate him bitterly. At the age of seventy-six, he marries thirty-five-year-old Abbie Putnam, a deed intended to cheat his sons of their inheritance. The two older sons have left the farm but Eben, the youngest, remains.

Eben Cabot, Ephraim's son by his second wife. He hates Ephraim for the way that the self-righteous old hypocrite treated his mother. Believing that the farm is really his, Eben buys out the potential claim of his brothers by giving each three hundred dollars from a hoard of gold that his mother had hidden. He bitterly resents the arrival of a young stepmother and he still hates her even after she seduces him and he fathers her child. Neverthe-

less, her final act of love toward him changes his hatred of her to love, and he willingly goes away with her to share her punishment.

Abbie Putnam, Ephraim's third wife who, though half his age, marries him to get a home. Her appearance heightens the hostility that exists between Ephraim and Eben. Abbie seduces Eben in order to get a child who will be Ephraim's heir and who will deprive Eben of his expected inheritance. Though Eben tells her he hates her, Abbie has fallen in love with him and to prove this love she smothers the baby she has tricked him into fathering.

Simeon and **Peter Cabot,** Ephraim's sons and Eben's half brothers. Hating their father and wanting desperately to join the gold rush in California, they accept Eben's offer of three hundred dollars each and renounce all claims to the farm.

The Story

When the news of gold discoveries in California reached New England, Simeon and Peter Cabot, who had spent their lives piling up stones to fence their father's farm, became restless. In the summer of 1850, they were ready to tear down the fences that seemed to hem them in, to rebel against their closefisted old father, and for once in their lives to be free. One day, Ephraim Cabot hitched up his rig and drove off, leaving the farm in charge of his three sons, Sim, Peter, and their younger half brother, Eben. All three sons hated their father because they saw him for what he was: a greedy, self-righteous hypocrite. The older brothers hated old Ephraim for what he had done to them, but Eben had a further grievance. He hated his father because he had stolen the land that had be-

longed to his mother, and had then worked her to death on the farm. Eben believed that the farm belonged to him, and he meant to have it. He had inherited some of old Ephraim's stony implacability, as well as his sensuality, and he gave expression to the latter on his trips down the road to visit Minnie, the local prostitute who had belonged to his father before him.

Realizing that Sim and Peter wanted to go to California, yet had no money to take them there, Eben thought up a plan to get rid of them once and for all. During old Ephraim's absence, he offered them three hundred dollars apiece in gold if they would sign a paper renouncing all claims to the farm. The money had belonged to Eben's mother, and Eben had found it buried beneath the floorboards of the kitchen. The brothers accepted Eben's offer and set off for California.

Shortly afterward, old Ephraim drove home with his third wife. He was seventy-six, and she was thirty-five, but Abbie Putnam had decided that she wanted a home of her own. When old Ephraim offered to marry her, she accepted him at once, and when she moved into the Cabot homestead, she was already determined that whatever happened the farm would be hers someday. She tried unsuccessfully to make friends with Eben. The thought of another woman's coming to take his mother's place and the farm which rightfully belonged to him made him hate Abbie at first.

After a time, Eben began to notice that life on the farm was easier since his stepmother had arrived. Yet the realization that Abbie could influence his father as she desired only strengthened Eben's determination to resist her attempts to conciliate him. Finally, some of his taunts became so pointed that Abbie complained to Ephraim. When she falsely hinted that Eben had been making advances toward her, the old man threatened to kill his son. Realizing that she had gone too far, and that she must take a different approach, Abbie subtly built up in Ephraim's mind the idea that a son and heir who would inherit the farm upon his death would be a better way of getting back at Eben than to kill him outright. The thought that, at the age of seventy-six, he might have a son flattered the old man, and he agreed to let Eben alone.

One night, after Ephraim had gone out to sleep in the barn, Abbie saw her opportunity to make her hold on the farm secure. She managed to lure Eben into his mother's parlor, a room which had not been opened since her death, and there she seduced him, breaking down his scruples with the suggestion that by cuckolding his father he could get revenge for Ephraim's treatment of his mother.

The result of this move on Abbie's part was the son whom Ephraim wanted as an heir. To celebrate the child's birth, Ephraim invited all the neighbors to a dance in the kitchen of the farmhouse. Many of the guests suspected the true circumstances and said so as openly as they dared. Ephraim paid no attention to the insinuations and outdanced them all until even the fiddler dropped from sheer exhaustion.

While the revelry still was going on, the old man stepped outside to cool off. There he and Eben, who had been sulking outside, quarreled over the possession of the farm. Spitefully, Ephraim taunted his son with a revelation of how Abbie had tricked him out of his inheritance. Furious, Eben turned on Abbie, threatening to kill her, and telling her that he hated her and the child he had fathered when she tricked him with her scheme. By this time, however, Abbie was genuinely in love with Eben, and, thinking the child was the obstacle that was keeping them apart, she smothered it in an effort to prove to her lover that it was he and not the child that she wanted. When he discovered what had happened, Eben was both enraged and shocked, and he set off to get the sheriff for Abbie's arrest.

When Ephraim discovered that Abbie had killed the child that was not his, he too was shocked, but his heart filled with contempt at his son's cowardice in giving Abbie over to the law.

On his way to the farm, Eben began to realize how much he loved Abbie, and the great love that she had shown for him in taking the child's life. When the sheriff came to take Abbie away, he confessed that he was an accomplice in the crime. The two were taken off together, both destined for punishment but happy in their love. Ephraim Cabot was left alone with his farm, the best farm in the county. It was, the sheriff told him, a place anybody would want to own.

Critical Evaluation

One of O'Neill's most admired and frequently performed plays, *Desire Under the Elms* provoked enormous controversy during its first stagings. Some audiences were scandalized by what one critic called "distresses" which "range from unholy lust to infanticide, and include drinking, cursing, vengeance, and something approaching incest." In Los Angeles, the cast was arrested for having presented a lewd, obscene, and immoral play. A bizarre trial followed—at one point the entire court witnessed a special private performance. The jury was finally dismissed, having deadlocked with eight members voting for conviction and four for acquittal. It gradually became apparent, however, that O'Neill was aiming at something more than a shocking revelation of unconscious drives and primordial fears. These elements were clearly subordinated to his larger purpose of reintroducing authentic tragic vision to American theater. O'Neill's supporters could point out that the Greek and biblical sources that inspired the play are replete with the very "immoralities" that he depicted.

Euripides' *Hippolytus* and Racine's *Phèdre* served as O'Neill's principal models. These works both draw on the archetypal plot in which a father returns from a journey with a wife who falls in love with her new stepson. This attachment, at first resisted or concealed, results in a struggle between father and son. The father achieves a Pyrrhic victory that costs him both son and spouse. The situation is tragic in that all participants are forced to make conscious choices of evil for the sake of a higher good. It is fate that so structures events as to necessitate the downfall of these essentially noble characters. O'Neill complicates the classic plot by introducing Old Testament motifs: the "hardness" and vengeance of God, the superiority of justice over mercy, and the battle among sons for birthrights and fatherly favor. He also relies on Freudian psychology in treating all sexual relationships.

Critics have questioned whether O'Neill finally succeeds in giving true tragic stature to his characters. There can be no doubt that the drama possesses genuinely tragic aspects, but that the whole deserves the term "tragedy" is doubtful. Three considerations sustain this judgment. First, Eben's basic motivation remains unclear throughout the play, as does the central matter of whether he is the rightful heir to the farm. Second, both Abbie and Eben are far too preoccupied with struggles for possession and revenge; they lack that nobility of purpose that one associates with tragic characters such as Oedipus, Antigone, or Hippolytus. Third, Eben is made to seem so totally a victim of psychological drives that he does not arrive at choices freely. This latter element makes pathos, not tragedy, the dominant quality in *Desire Under the Elms.*

Edgar F. Racey, Jr., has argued persuasively that O'Neill designed his play around a single moral fact: Ephraim Cabot ruined the life of Eben's mother—"murdered her with his hardness," as Eben says—and this sin now cries out for retribution. O'Neill's opening stage directions indicate his intention. The two enormous elms that bend over the farm house are to be expressionistically rendered; they should suggest suffering women and dominate the entire scene with "a sinister maternity." From the beginning, Eben proclaims his monomaniacal desire to take "her vengeance on him—so's she kin rest quiet in her grave." When Abbie enters the parlor, her scheming and erotic tendencies are momentarily subdued by the felt presence of the dead woman's spirit. Eben does not allow himself to be seduced until he is assured that he is doing his mother's will.

The structure of the action reinforces this central theme. In part 1, Eben solidifies his claim to the farm by inducing his half brothers to leave. He uses his mother's money in the process, thus depriving Ephraim of both the fortune and the assistance of his older sons. In part 2,

Eben takes Ephraim's wife from him, begets a son, and sets in motion the process whereby Ephraim is humiliated in the eyes of the community. In part 3, Abbie's killing of the child prevents Ephraim from naming a new heir. Further, the departure of Abbie and Eben dooms Ephraim to that condition of isolation that he has always feared above all. He becomes in effect an exile, living on a farm that now is a curse to him. The pattern of crime and justified punishment has been completed.

Tragic in outline, *Desire Under the Elms* is, however, less than tragic in substance. Quite inexplicably, O'Neill lets the basic issue of Ephraim's persecution of Eben's mother become clouded. Because the audience learns of her suffering only from Eben himself, some skepticism about his truthfulness is engendered. This skepticism grows when two additional factors come into view: Eben's overwhelming Oedipus complex and his deep desire to inherit the farm. That Eben stands to benefit economically by his revenge-taking tends to tarnish his character and to undermine his credibility further. O'Neill intensifies this economic theme both by showing how deeply Peter and Simeon covet the farm and by casting doubt on Eben's claim that he has a clear legal right of ownership. Ephraim discounts this claim completely, and one is inclined to believe that his long work of reclamation gives him at least some moral right to the property.

More important, O'Neill does not seem to realize that the addition of certain Freudian motifs is not compatible with his purpose. For Sigmund Freud, fathers and sons are natural rivals; despite the outward show of paternal and filial love, they both unconsciously desire to monopolize the love and sexual favor of "their" woman. This tendency operates even if the father treats the mother with perfect love and respect. This Ephraim most certainly did not do. Yet the audience wonders how much of Eben's motive is Oedipal and how much is filial devotion. The very fact that such a question can arise demonstrates O'Neill's failure to produce a convincingly tragic work. Had Eben's duty to avenge his mother's suffering run directly counter to his psychological and economic needs, he might have assumed tragic stature. In this respect, the case for *Mourning Becomes Electra* as tragedy is much stronger.

Ironically, the fact that *Desire Under the Elms* is not fully realized tragedy probably accounts partially for its appeal, as does O'Neill's choice of a pastoral, precivilized setting that helps to convey the workings of unconscious forces with astonishing power.

Despite the fact that the outraged protests responsible for such odd and sensational events as the Los Angeles court case came from irate middle-class viewers, such viewers were only a small minority; actually, it was the literate American middle class that formed O'Neill's most avid audience. O'Neill was an iconoclast whose attacks, likened in one of his early poems to torpedoes fired from the submarine of his soul, were directed against middle-class complacency. Much to its credit, however, the audience whose values were under fire responded to plays such as *Desire Under the Elms* with that respect and enthusiasm which springs from recognition of the truth, however disconcerting or uncomfortable that truth may be.

THE EDUCATION OF HENRY ADAMS

Type of work: Novelized autobiography
Author: Henry Adams (1838-1918)
Type of plot: Intellectual and social history
Time of plot: 1838-1905
Locale: The United States, England, and France
First published: 1907

The theme of this autobiography is the process of technological growth and the multiplication of mechanical forces that led, during the author's own lifetime, to a degeneration of moral relationships between people and to the lapsing of their pursuits into money seeking or complete lassitude. The book is a masterpiece of intellectual writing, tracing intimately the author's thought processes and his moral and emotional maturation.

The Story

Henry Brooks Adams was born of the union of two illustrious Massachusetts families, the Brookses and the Adamses, and he was, in addition, the grandson and the great-grandson of presidents. His wealth and social position should have put him among the leaders of his generation.

Although the period of mechanical invention had begun by 1838, Henry Adams was raised in a colonial atmosphere. He remembered that his first serious encounter with his grandfather, John Quincy Adams, occurred when he refused to go to school and that gentleman led him there by the hand. For Henry Adams, the death of the former president marked the end of his eighteenth century environment.

Charles Francis Adams, Henry's father, was instrumental in forming the Free-Soil Party in 1848, and he ran on its ticket with Martin Van Buren. Henry considered that his own education was chiefly a heritage from his father, an inheritance of Puritan morality and interest in politics and literary matters. In later life, looking back on his formal education, he concluded that it had been a failure. Mathematics, French, German, and Spanish were needed in the world in which he found himself an adult, not Latin and Greek.

He had opportunity to observe the use of force in the violence with which the people of Boston treated the antislavery activist Wendell Phillips, and he had seen African-American slaves restored to the South.

Prompted by his teacher, James Russell Lowell, he spent nearly two years abroad after his graduation from college. He enrolled to study civil law in Germany, but finding the lecture system atrocious, Henry instead devoted most of his stay to enjoying the paintings, the op-

era, and the theater in Dresden.

When he returned to Boston in 1860, Henry Adams settled down briefly to read works by Sir William Blackstone. In the elections that year, however, his father became a congressman, and Henry accompanied him to the capital as his secretary. There he met John Hay, who was to become his best friend.

In 1861, President Abraham Lincoln named Charles Francis Adams minister to England. Henry went with his father to Europe. The Adams party had barely disembarked when they were met by bad news. England had recognized the belligerency of the Confederacy. The North was her undeclared enemy. The Battle of Bull Run proved so crushing a blow to American prestige that Charles Francis Adams believed that he was in England on a day-to-day sufferance. The Trent Affair and the Second Battle of Bull Run were equally disastrous abroad. Finally, in 1863, the tide began to turn. Secretary William H. Seward sent Thurlow Weed and William Evarts to woo the English, and they were followed by announcements of victories at Vicksburg and Gettysburg. Charles Francis Adams remained in England until 1868, for Andrew Johnson had too many troubles at home to make many diplomatic changes abroad.

At the end of the war, Henry Adams had no means of earning a livelihood. He had, however, developed some taste as a dilettante in art, and several of his articles had been published in the *North American Review*. On his return to the United States, Henry Adams was impressed by the fact that his fellow Americans, because of the mechanical energy that they had harnessed, were all traveling in the same direction. Europeans, he had thought, were trying to go in several directions at one time. Handicapped by his education and by his long absence from home, he had difficulty in adapting himself to the new industrial America. He achieved some recognition with his articles on legal tender and his essays in the *Edinburgh Review*, and he hoped that he might be offered a government position if Ulysses S. Grant were elected president. Grant, however, a man of action, was not interested in reformers or intellectuals like Henry Adams.

In 1869, Adams went back to Quincy, Massachusetts, to begin his investigation of the scandals of the Grant Administration, among them Jay Gould's attempts to obtain a corner on gold, Senator Charles Sumner's efforts to provoke war with England by compelling her cession of Canada to the United States, and the rivalries of congressmen and cabinet members.

He decided that it would be best to have his article on Gould published in England, to avoid censorship by the powerful financier. Gould's influence was not confined to the United States, however, and Adams was refused by two publications. His essay on Gould was finally published by the *Westminster Review*.

Adams became assistant professor of medieval history at Harvard University and taught in Cambridge for seven years. During that time, he tried to abandon the lecture system by replacing it with individual research. He found his students apt and quick to respond, but he believed that he needed a stone against which to sharpen his wits. He gave up his position in 1871 and went west to Estes Park with a government geological survey. There he met Clarence King, a member of the party with whom he could not help contrasting himself. King had a systematic, scientific education and could have his choice of scientific, political, or literary prizes. Adams sensed his own limitations.

After his flight from Harvard, he made his permanent home in Washington, D.C., where he wrote a series of books on American history. In 1893, he visited the Chicago Exhibition. From his observations of the steamship,

the locomotive, and the newly invented dynamo, he concluded that force was the one unifying factor in American thought. Back in Washington, D.C., he saw the gold standard adopted and concluded that the capitalistic system and American intervention in Cuba offered some signs of the direction in which the country was heading. During another visit to the Exhibition in 1900, Adams formulated an important theory. In observing the dynamo, he decided that history is not merely a series of causes and effects, of individuals acting upon individuals, but the record of forces acting upon individuals. For him, the dynamo became the symbol of force acting upon his own time, as the Virgin had been the symbol of force in the twelfth century.

During the next five years, Henry Adams saw his friends drop away. Clarence King was the first to go. He lost his fortune in the panic of 1893 and died of tuberculosis in 1901. John Hay, under William McKinley, became American minister to England, and then secretary of state. He was not well when he accepted the president's appointments, and the enormous task of bringing England, France, and Germany into accord with the United States and of attempting to keep peace, unsuccessfully, between Russia and Japan caused his death in 1905.

Adams considered that his education was continuous during his lifetime. He had found the tools that he had been given as a youth utterly useless, and he had to spend all of his days forging new ones. As he grew older, he found the moral standards of his father's and grandfather's times disintegrating, so that corruption and greed existed on the highest political levels. According to his calculations, the rate of change, as the result of mechanical force, was accelerating, and the generation of 1900 could rely only on impersonal forces to teach the generation of 2000. He himself could see no end to the multiplicity of forces that were so rapidly dwarfing humankind into insignificance.

Critical Evaluation

"Education" is both the theme and the metaphor of *The Education of Henry Adams*. In the preface, Adams notes that the object of his "study is the garment, not the figure," and he goes on to say that his specific object "is to fit young men, in universities or elsewhere, to be men of the world, equipped for any emergency; and the garment offered to them is meant to show the faults of the patchwork fitted on their fathers." Thus, by recounting the way in which he educated himself, he intends to edu-

cate others—a typical goal of autobiographers such as Benjamin Franklin, St. Augustine, and Jean Jacques Rousseau, all of whom are cited by Adams in his book.

Adopting the voice of a third-person narrator and following a strict chronological order in telling the story, including using parenthetical dates for each chapter title, suggests that this educated man is indeed sharing his knowledge with the uneducated and is doing so with complete objectivity. Yet this apparent objectivity is misleading. The book is more theory than it is narrative, and it does not recount Adams' life with the objectivity that one might expect from the tone and chronological approach. For example, complete silence surrounds all that happened to Adams from 1872 to 1891. He concludes one chapter, entitled "Twenty Years After (1892)," with no explanation of what occurred during that hiatus. Critics have speculated about this silence, suggesting that perhaps Adams simply did not want to write about his marriage and his wife Marian's suicide, or perhaps Adams wanted to emphasize the contrast between what he had been at the age of thirty-three and what he had become by the age of fifty-three. Whatever the reason for the gap, Adams apparently thought that his readers did not need the details to complete their education.

What Adams did give his audience was an autobiography that moves from the self into abstraction, that theorizes about four areas that were critical to his becoming educated: politics, science, nature, and psychology. Each influence helped Adams become a skeptical, observing individual who attempted to educate others.

In addition to showing his family's role in helping him to see the role of politics in his life, Adams devotes an important section of his autobiography to examining President Ulysses S. Grant and the lessons Adams learned from that politician. Adams had hoped for some kind of political office from Grant, but not realizing that goal, he speculates on why that loss was probably his gain and a step toward his being educated. Adams explains how he came to see Grant as a "pre-intellectual, archaic" type, who "would have seemed so even to the cave-dwellers." Though Adams believed that he himself did not suit the twentieth century, he concluded that he possessed what Grant lacked—namely, the ability to think. That quality was one aspect of the educated individual.

Another quality was the ability to live without absolute certainty, the ability to use the scientific method to understand the incompleteness of truth. Describing himself as a Darwinian, he explains that he "was the first in an infinite series to discover and admit to himself that he really did not care whether truth was, or was not, true." In other words, in his educational process, he learned that the process of examination, the inclination to be skeptical about absolutes, was essential.

Equally critical, and related to his understanding of science, was Adams' recognition of what governed na-

ture: chaos. Whereas order was the dream of humanity, chaos, according to Adams, was the order of nature. Thus Adams came to learn that his simplistic notion of an orderly nature needed to be replaced with a more sophisticated sense of the lack of unity and uniformity in nature.

The final influence upon Adams was what he called "the new psychology," which, like Adams' understanding of science and nature, pointed to complexity and a lack of unity. Thus, he pointed to the new psychology as being "convinced that it had actually split personality not only into dualism, but also into complex groups, like telephonic centres and systems, that might be isolated and called up at will." Added to the three other influences, this new way of viewing psychological realities shaped Adams' education, so that he came to realize that his earlier beliefs in unity were being replaced by an awareness of multiplicity.

In coming to this understanding, Adams makes dramatic use of dialectic, emphasizing the tension between opposites. His chapter titles demonstrate this when, for example, he juxtaposes "Quincy" to "Boston," "Political Mortality" to "The Battle of the Rams," and "The Height of Knowledge" to "The Abyss of Ignorance." The most famous of his oppositions occurs in one chapter, "The Dynamo and the Virgin," in which Adams explores the dynamo as the symbol of the twentieth century, contrasted with the Virgin, the symbol of force acting upon medieval times. The chapter in which he explores this particular opposition is actually a condensed version of two books written by Adams in which he carefully explores first unity and then multiplicity. The first book, *Mont-Saint-Michel and Chartres*, is also one of the finest introductions to the Middle Ages, and the second, *The Education of Henry Adams*, continues to be one of the best analyses of twentieth century intellectual history.

In his autobiographical study of opposites and the way in which they contribute to a person's education, Adams determined that the aim of education was the ability to cope, and the aim of education in the twentieth century was the ability to cope with a particularly important phenomenon: multiplicity. As he put it, "The child born in 1900 would, then, be born into a new world which would not be a unity but a multiple." *The Education of Henry Adams* chronicles one man's coming to this realization and his effort to help others become educated as well.

THE EMPEROR JONES

Type of work: Drama
Author: Eugene O'Neill (1888-1953)
Type of plot: Expressionistic melodrama
Time of plot: Early twentieth century
Locale: West Indies
First presented: 1920

O'Neill departed from traditional dramatic writing when he created this play, which concerns itself expressionistically with the forces that shape an individual. In the realm of the stage-actual, Brutus Jones is carried forward in time from his position as emperor to his death from fear. Meanwhile, the action regresses through short, dynamic episodes that symbolize Jones's past and African-American history from 1920 to several hundred years before in the Congo jungle.

Principal Characters

Brutus Jones, an African American who has gained control of a group of superstitious natives on a West Indian island. He flees for his life when he discovers that the natives have finally rebelled against his cruel regime. Jones runs in circles in the jungle all night. As he runs, he encounters apparitions that reveal his story and the history of his race. Jeff, a Pullman porter whom Jones thought he had killed with a razor, is the first wraith. A chain gang, followed by a slave auction, then by the hold of a slave ship, and then by an altarlike arrangement of boulders at which Jones is selected to be a human sacri-

fice, form the subjects that complete the series of ghostly scenes. The natives finally shoot Jones with a silver bullet, the only missile they believe capable of killing him, but the audience understands that Jones actually dies of fear.

Lem, the leader of the rebel force that hunts down Jones.

Henry Smithers, a cockney trader who first suspects that the natives are rebelling. Though he is contemptuous of Jones, he warns him of the danger that he faces.

The Story

Henry Smithers, a cockney adventurer, learned from an African-American woman that the followers of Brutus Jones, the self-styled emperor of a West Indian island, were about to desert their ruler. With Smithers' help, Jones, a former Pullman porter and jail-breaker, had duped the natives into believing that he was a magician. The superstitious natives made him emperor of the island. Smithers disclosed to the emperor the disaffection of his subjects, who had been taxed and cheated by the pair beyond human endurance. Jones had judged that he had six more months of power before the natives caught on to his skulduggery. He had had a silver bullet cast for a good luck charm; besides, the bullet might be useful if he were ever caught by his subjects.

At Smithers' suggestion, Jones rang a bell for his attendants; no one appeared. Jones resigned his position as emperor on the spot and made immediate plans to escape through the jungle to the coast. Drums began to

beat in the hills. The former emperor gave the palace to Smithers, took up his white Panama hat, and walked boldly out the front door.

At the edge of the jungle, Brutus Jones searched unsuccessfully for tinned food he had cached for such an emergency. The drums continued to beat, louder and more insistently. Night fell, and formless fears came out of the jungle to beset Jones. The moon rose. Jones came into a clearing, and there in the moonlight he saw Jeff, a Pullman porter he thought he had killed in a razor duel. Jeff was throwing dice. When the kneeling figure refused to answer him, Jones shot at him. The phantom disappeared. Drums still thudded in the distance. Jones, now sick with fright, plunged into the inky jungle.

After a while, he came upon a road and paused to rest. A chain gang came out of the forest. The guard of the gang motioned to Jones to take his place in the gang and get to work. When the guard whipped him, Jones lifted his shovel to strike him, but he discovered that he actually had no shovel. In his rage of fear and frustration, he fired his revolver at the guard. The road, the guard, and the chain gang disappeared; the jungle closed in. The louder beat of the tom-toms drove Jones on in frantic circles.

Now in tatters, the terrified Jones repented the murders that he had committed and the way that he had cheated the islanders. He came next upon a slave auction attended by whites dressed in the costumes of the 1850's. An auctioneer put Jones on the auction block. Frightened, Jones shattered this apparition by firing one shot at the auctioneer and another at a planter. He dashed into the forest, mad with fear. The drums continued to beat.

At three o'clock, Jones came to a part of the jungle that strangely resembled the hold of a slave ship. He found himself one of a cargo of slaves who were swaying slowly with the motion of the ship. Jones and the other slaves moaned with sorrow at being taken away from their homeland. Having only the silver bullet left in his revolver, Jones saved it and dashed on again into the black of the night.

Next he came upon an altarlike arrangement of boulders near a great river. He sank to his knees as if to worship. A Congo witch doctor appeared from behind a large tree and began a primitive dance. Jones was hypnotized by the ritual. The witch doctor indicated to Jones in pantomime that the former emperor must offer himself as a sacrifice in order to overcome the forces of evil. A great green-eyed crocodile emerged from the river; Jones fired the silver bullet at the monster and the witch doctor disappeared behind a tree, leaving Jones lying on the ground completely overcome by fear.

At dawn Lem, the leader of the rebels, came with Smithers and a group of natives to the edge of the jungle where Jones had entered the night before. Lem had been delayed in pursuing Jones because of the necessity of manufacturing silver bullets, which, Lem believed, were the only means of taking Jones's life. Several of Lem's men entered the jungle. They soon found the prostrate Jones, who had run in circles all the night. One shot him through the chest with a silver bullet. Jones's body was brought back to Lem, who thought that the silver bullet was what had killed Jones. Smithers, however, looking at Brutus Jones's fear-contorted face, knew differently.

Critical Evaluation

By the time that Eugene O'Neill wrote *The Emperor Jones*, he had joined the current of experimental playwrights who were reacting against realism. *The Emperor Jones* employs a technique popularized in Germany called expressionism, a form that employs exaggerated sets and stylized action. It seeks to project feelings and mental states directly, without the intervention of character development and without much concern for the externals of realistic sets, action, and motivation. While a number of such plays were written and produced, few have survived; among the few are *The Emperor Jones* and O'Neill's other completely expressionist play, *The Hairy Ape*. Like Joseph Conrad's *Heart of Darkness*, among other works, *The Emperor Jones* suggests that beneath the surface of civilized existence there is, in each human being, a savagery that marks one's true identity. Public masks versus private realities, identity conflicts, and divisions—these are among O'Neill's central concerns. Furthermore, because Jones moves into and is held and controlled by his past, the play suggests another of O'Neill's major themes: that one cannot escape one's past.

Jones's physical journey through the jungle becomes a symbol of his mental journey into his past, even an entering into his own subconscious. The first two jungle scenes contain Jones's private past; the last three take the audience into his racial past. With each step into the jungle, Jones loses bits and pieces of clothing, his cherished bullets, and his composure—all external marks, not only of the stripping away of his civilized self but of his mental and spiritual reduction as well. Toward the last—on the auction block, in the slave ship, on his knees before the witch doctor—Jones becomes increasingly passive, merging with the scene and thus losing his sense of individual being.

There is very little dialogue in the play. Nevertheless, the throbbing of the tom-toms, the shooting of the gun, and the playing of the lights and shadows of the jungle take the place, quite effectively, of conventional dialogue and action. The play is, in many ways, an exercise in pure theater.

THE ESSAYS OF RALPH WALDO EMERSON

Type of work: Philosophical essays
Author: Ralph Waldo Emerson (1803-1882)
First published: First Series, 1841; Second Series, 1844

Ralph Waldo Emerson's *Essays* proclaim the self-reliance of a man who believed himself representative of all human beings because he believed himself intuitively aware of God's universal truths. He spoke to a nineteenth century that was ready for an emphasis on individualism and responsive to a new optimism that linked God, nature, and humanity into a magnificent cosmos.

Emerson himself spoke as one who had found in Transcendentalism a positive answer to the static Unitarianism of his day. He had been a Unitarian minister for three years at the Old North Church in Boston (1829-1832), but he had resigned because in his view the observance of the Lord's Supper could not be justified in the Unitarian church.

Transcendentalism combined Neoplatonism, a mystical faith in the universality and permanence of value in the universe, with a pervasive moral seriousness akin to the Calvinist conviction and with a Romantic optimism that found evidence of God's love throughout all nature. Derivative from these influences was the faith in humanity's creative power, the belief that individuals, by utilizing God's influence, could continue to improve their understanding and their moral natures. Knowledge could come to one directly, without the need of argument, if only one had the courage to be receptive to God's truth, manifest everywhere.

Through his essays and addresses, Emerson became not only the leading Transcendentalist in the United States but also one of the greatest of American philosophers. The latter accomplishment may be attributed more to the spirit of his philosophy than to its technical excellence, for Emerson had little respect for logic, empiricism, and linguistic analysis—features common to the work of other great American philosophers such as Charles Sanders Peirce, William James, and John Dewey. Emerson also cannot be compared in his method to such a philosopher as Alfred North Whitehead, for Emerson disdained speculative adventures: He believed himself to be affirming what nature told him, and nature spoke directly of God and of God's laws.

Emerson's *Nature* (1836) was the first definitive statement of his philosophical perspective, and within this work may be found most of the characteristic elements of Emerson's thought. The basic idea is that nature is God's idea made apparent to humanity. Thus, "the whole of nature is a metaphor of the human mind." Moreover, "the axioms of physics translate the laws of ethics," and "This relation between the mind and matter is not fancied by some poet, but stands in the will of God, and so is free to be known by all men." Emerson asserted emphatically that "day and night, river and storm, beast and bird, acid and alkali, preexist in necessary Ideas in the mind of God"; hence he agreed with those who supposed that nature reveals spiritual and moral truths. Nature not only reveals truths but also disciplines human beings, rewarding them when nature is used properly and punishing them when it is abused.

One secret of Emerson's charm was his ability to translate metaphysical convictions into vivid images. Having argued that nature is the expression of God's idea, and having concluded that "The moral law lies at the center of nature and radiates to the circumference," he illustrated the moral influence of nature by asking, "Who can guess how much firmness the sea-beaten rock has taught the fishermen?" The danger in Emerson's method, however, was that readers tended to forget that his idealism was philosophically, not merely poetically, intended; he believed literally that only spirit and its ideas are real. He admitted the possibility that nature "outwardly exists"—that is, that physical objects corresponding to his sensations exist—but he pointed out that, because he was not able to test the authenticity of his senses, it made no difference whether such outlying objects existed. All that he could be sure of was his ideas, and these ideas, whether directly or indirectly, came from God. For Emerson, then, idealism was not only a credible philosophy but also the only morally significant one.

If nature is God's idea made apparent to humanity, then it follows that the way to God's truth is not by reason or argument but by simple and reverent attention to the facts of nature, to what humanity perceives in innocence. Emerson criticized science not because it was useless but because more important matters, those having a moral bearing, confronted humanity at every moment in the world of nature; the individual needed only to intuit nature, to see it as it was without twisting it to fit philosophy or science, in order to know God's thoughts. Thus, in the essay "Nature," Emerson wrote that "Nature is the incarnation of a thought, and turns to a thought again. . . . The world is mind precipitated. . . ." He added, with assurance, "Every moment instructs, and every object; for wisdom is infused into every form."

The ideas which Emerson had endorsed in *Nature* found explicit moral application in the address entitled "The American Scholar," delivered before the Phi Beta Kappa Society at the University of Cambridge in 1837. Emerson defined the scholar as "Man Thinking," and he declared that the main influences of the scholar's education are nature, books, and action. The duties of a scholar all involve self-trust; this individual must be both free and brave. The rewards of such freedom and bravery are inspiring: The mind is altered by the truths uncovered, and the whole world will come to honor the independent scholar. It was in this address that Emerson said that "the ancient precept, 'Know thyself,' and the modern precept, 'Study nature,' become at last one maxim."

The essay "Self-Reliance," included in the First Series, emphasizes the importance of that self-trust to which Emerson referred in his Phi Beta Kappa address. It is understandable that this emphasis seemed necessary to Emerson. If nature reveals the moral truths that God intends for humanity's use, then three elements are involved in the critical human situation: nature, humanity, and humanity's attitude toward nature. It is possible to be blind to the truths about one; only the individual who is courageous enough to be willing to be different in his or her search and convictions is likely to discover what is before every individual's eyes. Emerson emphasized self-reliance not because he regarded the self, considered as a separate entity, important, but because he believed that the self is part of the reality of God's being and that in finding truth for oneself, provided one faces nature intuitively, one finds what is true for all people. "To believe your own thought, to believe that what is true for you in your private heart is true for all men—that is genius," Emerson wrote in "Self-Reliance"; he added that it is a kind of genius that is possible for anyone who is willing to acquire it.

Believing that each individual's mind is capable of yielding important truth, Emerson distinguished between goodness and the name of goodness. He urged each person to work and act without being concerned about the mere opinions of others. "Whoso would be a man, must be a nonconformist," and those who would advance in the truth should be willing to contradict themselves, to be inconsistent: "A foolish consistency is the hobgoblin of little minds, adored by little statesmen and philosophers and divines."

That Emerson's philosophy was not an endorsement of selfish behavior is clear from his emphasis upon the use of the mind as an instrument for the intuitive understanding of universal truths and laws, but it is possible to misinterpret "Self-Reliance" as a joyous celebration of individuality. A sobering balance is achieved by the essay "The Over-Soul," in which Emerson subordinates the individual to the whole: "Meantime within man is the soul of the whole . . . the eternal One." Using language reminiscent of Platonism, Emerson wrote that the soul "gives itself, alone, original and pure, to the Lonely, Original and Pure, who, on that condition, gladly inhabits, leads and speaks through it."

Emerson valued the poet because the poet uses imagination to discern the meanings of sensuous facts. The poet sees and expresses the beauty in nature by recognizing the spiritual meaning of events; the poet takes old symbols and gives them new uses, thereby making nature the sign of God. In the essay "The Poet," Emerson wrote that the poet's insight is "a very high sort of seeing," a way of transcending conventional modes of thought in order to attend directly to the forms of things.

It is a misunderstanding of Emerson to regard him as a sentimental mystic, as one who lay on his back and saw divinity in every cloud. Emerson's transcendental insight is more akin to the intelligence of the Platonic philosopher who, having recognized his or her own ignorance, suddenly is able to see the universal in the jumble of particular facts. Emerson may be criticized for never satisfactorily relating the life of contemplation to the life of practical affairs, but he cannot be dismissed as an iconoclastic mystic. For him, the inquiring soul and the heroic soul were one, and the justification of self-reliance and meditation was in terms of the result, in the individual soul, of the effort to recognize the unity of all people. In "Experience," Emerson chose knowing in preference to doing, but it is clear that he was rejecting a thoughtless interest in action and results. In "Character" and again in "Politics," he emphasized the importance of coming to have the character of transcending genius, of spirit that has found moral law in nature and has adapted it for use in the world of mortals. The transforming power of spirit properly educated and employed was something Emerson counted on, and he was concerned to argue that such power is not easily achieved.

Emerson defended democracy as the form of government best fitted for Americans, whose religion and tradition reflect a desire to allow the judgments of citizens to be expressed in the laws of the state. He cautioned, however, that "Every actual State is corrupt," and added,

"Good men must not obey the laws too well." Here the independent spirit, concerned with the laws of God, demands heroism and possibly, as with Henry David Thoreau, civil disobedience.

Scholars have written innumerable articles and books attempting to account for Emerson's influence—which continues to be profound—on American thought. If agreement is ever reached, it seems likely that it will involve acceptance of the claim that Emerson, whatever his value as a philosopher, gave stirring expression to the American faith in the creative capacity of the individual soul.

THE ESSAYS OF EDGAR ALLAN POE

Type of work: Literary criticism
Author: Edgar Allan Poe (1809-1849)
First published: 1835-1850

In his youthful *Essay on Criticism* (1711), Alexander Pope contended that only a demonstrated talent for creative writing gives an individual the right to assess the literary productions of others. The history of criticism, of course, affords some notable exceptions. One is happy to accept the credentials of such distinguished literary critics as Aristotle, Longinus, George Saintsbury, or, to cite a more modern example, I. A. Richards, even though none of them produced a substantial work of creative literature. Sometimes the reverse happens. The critical essays of William Wordsworth, for example, are sometimes dismissed as the left-handed scribblings of a poet whose own practice repudiates his theory. The criticism of Edgar Allan Poe, however, is another matter. For whatever it may be worth, he meets the criterion of Pope; he had produced a number of poems and short stories before turning to criticism in the years that followed 1830. Furthermore, in spite of the fact that his criticism is often vituperative, narrow, derivative, or vague, he writes it with the authority of an accomplished master of composition, and it is here that he has something of value to say.

Most of Poe's critical essays appeared in *The Southern Literary Messenger* and *Graham's Magazine*, both of which he edited for brief periods between 1835 and 1842. Before he began his work as an editor and reviewer, however, he set forth a kind of prospectus of his critical theory in a "Letter" which first appeared as the preface to his *Poems* of 1831 (later published with slight revisions in the *Southern Literary Messenger* for July, 1836). The essay is youthful, impudent, and slight, but it definitely adumbrates the major themes of Poe's maturer criticism. In addition, it is riddled with a number of inconsistencies. Like Pope, Poe begins by asserting that poets alone possess the ability to judge poetry—and shortly after cites a critical opinion of Aristotle. He denounces the reverence paid to foreign writers in preference to American ones, and he delivers a tirade against Wordsworth and Samuel Taylor Coleridge; but he concludes his essay with a definition of poetry that is lifted verbatim, and without acknowledgement, from Coleridge's *Biographia Literaria* (1817). His attack on Wordsworth is spiteful and even sophomoric. At one point, he quotes a passage from Wordsworth's advertisement for the *Lyrical Bal-*

lads of 1798 and embellishes it with jeering, parenthetical interspersions of his own. Nevertheless, in his complaints about the didactic implications of Wordsworth's statements on poetry, he begins to suggest the direction of his own views—that poetry should seek to communicate pleasure rather than truth. He tells the reader also that music is essential to poetry because of its indefiniteness and that poetry is therefore the combination of music with a pleasurable idea.

In the reviews that began with his editorship of the *Southern Literary Messenger* in 1835, Poe exercised his condemnatory energies with considerable gusto, but at the same time he worked toward increasing refinement and precision in his formulation of literary principles. First of all, he sought to persuade the public that criticism of the literary art is a science, founded on the fixed and immutable laws of human reason and emotion, rather than simply an expression of opinion that might include any vague generalization about the work under scrutiny. He denounced especially the chauvinistic tendency of American reviewers, who gave indiscriminate praise to native writers and to books on "American" themes, regardless of their artistic quality, and who instinctively denounced any book with a foreign subject. For his own part, Poe gave no quarter to his fellow Americans. He struck with a scalpel at Theodore S. Fay's *Norman Leslie* (1835), a novel by the influential editor of the *New York Mirror*, mercilessly dissecting its preposterous plot and extravagant language. Yet while the review of *Norman Leslie* is largely an ad hoc exposé of Fay's inadequacies as a novelist, Poe's other reviews are often buttressed by an appeal to critical and literary principles, to considerations that transcend the work in question and that therefore provide a sounder criterion for judgment. His examination of poems by Joseph Drake and Fitz-Greene Halleck in 1836, for example, moves beyond the immediate subject for review into a discussion of poetry in itself. Poetic sentiment, he says, is the sense of the beautiful, the sublime, and the mystical; the only means of evaluating the merits of a poem is by gauging its power to elicit this sentiment in the reader. He introduces, therefore, the principle that becomes a keystone in his poetic and literary theory: A work of creative literature must be analyzed in terms of its total effect.

This principle forms the basis of his critical perspective in all the essays that follow. In a review that appeared in *Graham's Magazine* in April, 1841, he applies it carefully to *Night and Morning* (1841), a novel by Edward Bulwer-Lytton. Poe admires the novel because of its perfection of plot, which he defines as an arrangement of incidents so interdependent that none can be displaced without destroying the fabric of the whole. Bulwer-Lytton, Poe conjectures, has written his story backward, because he has first conceived his denouement and then designed his incidents to act as causes for the final effect. Nevertheless, Poe dislikes the episodic character of the book. He complains that its complexity is too great for the mind to comprehend at one time, so that it does not strike the reader with a single, unified effect. For its failure to produce such an effect, according to Poe, the length of the book is also responsible; this is the reason that he was so dissatisfied with anything long in poetry or fiction. Again and again, he asserted that an over-extended narrative destroys the unity of effect that he thought essential to a literary work.

With his review of Henry Wadsworth Longfellow's *Ballads and Other Poems* (1841) in *Graham's Magazine* of April, 1842, Poe enters the final and most important phase of his career as a critic. In this essay, he explicitly condemns didacticism in literature, specifically the tendency of Longfellow's poems to inculcate a moral. Using terms and categories that he seems to have borrowed from Immanuel Kant by way of Coleridge, he maintains that, just as truth appeals to the intellect and duty to the moral sense, so poetry must appeal to taste alone; taste is the sense that enables humankind to appreciate the beautiful, and especially that which is eternally or supernally beautiful. This is the first of three crucial ingredients in poetry as Poe conceives it. The second is novelty or creativity, and the third—recalling a statement in his early "Letter"—is music, because of its celestial quality. The combination of these ingredients produces the definition to which Poe is finally committed: Poetry is the rhythmical creation of beauty.

The remainder of Poe's essays simply elaborate the principles that he has already announced. In reviewing Nathaniel Hawthorne's *Twice-Told Tales* (1837, 1842) in *Graham's Magazine* of May, 1842, Poe uses the concept of unified effect to formulate his theory of literary composition. He pays tribute to Hawthorne's genius (a generous gesture at the time), but he finds Hawthorne peculiar rather than original, because Hawthorne's stories fail to satisfy the reader's sense of the new. Also, Poe declares that Hawthorne's strain of allegory is objectionable because it interferes with that unity of effect which is absolutely essential to the success of a tale. After these rather perfunctory statements, he proceeds to enunciate his views on the value of brevity in literature. In his review of Bulwer-Lytton's novel, he had criticized the assumption that length has any intrinsic merit; now he contends that, if a poem is to produce the effect of intense excitement, it must be short. Yet it cannot be too short, he says, for it must have sufficient time to build the kind of momentum that makes a powerful impact. In poetry, as in the tale, the writer must have full control over the reader, and extreme length makes such control impossible. It militates against the fulfillment of the single effect that the writer must seek to establish with every word written. That is why Poe believes that a long poem is an impossibility. In his judgment, the hallmark of an effective composition is the evidence of design in every part of it, the ordering of all its aspects to a preestablished end.

Poe demonstrates the practical application of this axiom in what is perhaps the most famous of his critical essays, "The Philosophy of Composition," first published in *Graham's Magazine* of April, 1846. Here he offers a detailed, step-by-step analysis of the process by which he composed "The Raven" (1845). Whatever one may think of this cold-blooded dissection of the creative act, it is very probably true to the spirit (if not the letter) of what actually happened as Poe wrote the poem. In any event, the explication shows exactly how Poe intends a writer to achieve the all-important unity of impression; his composition of "The Raven" is a paradigm of the creative process as he understood it. He began, he reveals, with the intention of creating a single impression, an intense, elevating excitement of the soul. Every piece of the poem was then selected and arranged with this effect in view. First of all, he decided that the poem must be brief. Second, because beauty is the province of poetry, he determined to achieve it with a tone of melancholy, established in a single, sonorous word and continuously repeated for maximum impact. Out of this grew the details of the poem—the refrain of "Nevermore," the raven, the bereaved lover, the dead woman, the chamber at midnight, the antiphonal exchange of questions and answers, and the driving rhythm with its strong alliteration and internal rhymes. All these details were designed to produce a preconceived effect upon the reader, a feeling of beauty tinged with sadness. According to Poe, therefore, the principles of composition are precise, logical, and impersonal, even though the end in view is the evocation of intense psychic excitement. There is no place in the writing of poetry for careless rapture or fine frenzy. Cool and detached, poets construct a formula for the kind of impression that they seek to convey.

In a lecture that he delivered frequently during the last years of his life, Poe summarized the major tenets of his literary theory under the title "The Poetic Principle," and after his death the lecture was published as an essay in *The New York Home Journal* of August 31, 1850. He recapitulates here the points made in the earlier essays, condemning length and didacticism and emphasizing particularly that the value of a poem can be measured only by the effect that it produces. Yet the chief purpose of the essay is to show, by a number of examples from various poems, that the poetic principle itself is the human aspiration for supernal beauty and that the principle is always manifested in an elevating excitement of the soul. Poe thus concludes his literary criticism on a note of majestic vagueness, but he leaves the reader at the same time with a theory of poetry that springs from years of contemplation on his own practice. For all of his generalities, his dogmatism, his vituperative harshness, and his intellectual debts abroad, Poe commands a prominent place in the history of literary criticism in the United States.

THE ESSAYS OF HENRY DAVID THOREAU

Type of work: Philosophical essays
Author: Henry David Thoreau (1817-1862)
First published: From 1842 to after Thoreau's death

To the nonspecialist, Henry David Thoreau's significant works could be numbered on the fingers of one hand. Of these undoubtedly the first to come to mind would be *Walden: Or, Life in the Woods* (1854), his most famous book, and perhaps *A Week on the Concord and Merrimack Rivers* (1849). Yet almost as famous and perhaps even more influential have been several of his essays, which were written on various occasions for different purposes, and generally on rather widely ranging subjects. More than his two famous books, his essays vary in quality from the nearly banal to the profound, from the useless to the useful. To the reader genuinely interested in the life and writings of one of the United States' greatest and most influential writers—as well as perhaps the country's most outstanding true Transcendentalist—all of his works are fascinating. Because many do concern closely related subjects and treat these topics in a similar manner, a selection of the works can give the heart of the essays.

Thoreau's earliest essay, possibly, is one entitled "The Seasons," written when he was only eleven or twelve years old. As would be expected, it is of importance only to the close specialist. There are also in existence at least twenty-eight essays and four book reviews that Thoreau wrote while a student at Harvard University. These, too, are of greater interest to the student interested in the young Harvardian than to the readers looking for the Thoreau of mature ideas and style.

His first published essay was "Natural History of Massachusetts," printed in 1842. This work does more than promise the later adult. It is, in fact, the mature thinker and observer already arrived. Drawn chiefly from entries in his journals, which he had begun to keep after he was graduated from Harvard in 1837, it reveals his characteristics of Transcendentalism and his keen eye for observation, an eye that was to make him acclaimed by many people as one of the United States' best early scientists. It reveals Thoreau's pleasure in viewing the world around him and his detachment from the material world. He believed, for example, that one does not find health in society but in the world of nature. To live and prosper, a person must stand with feet firmly planted in nature. He believed, also, that society is corrupting and is inade-

quate for humanity's spiritual needs; when considered as members of a society, especially a political organization, individuals are "degraded." As a scientist, Thoreau catalogues many aspects of natural phenomena in Massachusetts; he notes, for example, that 280 types of birds live permanently in that state or summer there or visit it passingly.

Among Thoreau's best essays is another early one, "A Winter Walk," published in 1843, the material of which was taken mainly from his journal for 1841. As was generally the case with Thoreau, this essay is lyrical and ecstatic, the lyricism being augmented by the inclusion of various bits of Thoreau's own poetry. Thematically, the essay is strung on a long walk on a winter's day and the observations and meditations of the author as he progresses. Both his observations and his meditations are mature, virtually as vivid and sound as those given in the later *Walden*. His reactions to the physical walk are immediate and sharply detailed. He likes to walk through the "powdery snow," and he feels that humans should live closer to nature in order to appreciate life fully. In a Wordsworthian-pantheistic point of view he believes that plants and animals and human beings, if they would conform, find in nature only a "constant nurse and friend."

Thoreau's most famous essay is "Resistance to Civil Government," published in 1849 and renamed, after Thoreau's death, "Civil Disobedience," the title by which it is known today. As is often the case, this essay grew directly from an experience by the author, this time Thoreau's one-night imprisonment for nonpayment of his taxes—taxes that he claimed would go to finance the Mexican War and that were therefore, in his mind, immoral. The influence of this essay has been profound, far-reaching, and long-lasting. It served Mahatma Gandhi as a guidebook in his campaign to free India from British rule; it also served the British Labour Party in England during its early days. It offered model and hope for the European resistance against Nazi Germany, and it has aided, more recently, the struggle for civil rights in the American South.

The essay is a bristling and defiant reaffirmation of the individualism of humanity, of the moral obligation to restate individualism and to act on it. Government, any government, is at best an expediency. Thoreau heartily accepted the precept, "That government is best which governs least," a thesis which logically leads to the conclusion, "That government is best which governs not at all." Government, however, still exists, but it is not unchangeable: "A single man can bend it to his will." Government, in Thoreau's eyes, was far from pure and beneficent. He thought that he could not have as his government those institutions which enslaved certain races and colors. Therefore, he was compelled to resist his government. He believed that ten individuals—even one—could abolish slavery in the United States if they would allow themselves to go to prison for their belief and practice. People of goodwill must unite, and every good individual must constitute a majority of one to resist tyranny and evil. Democracy may not be the ultimate in systems of government, he concludes, in a ringing statement of humanity's political position: "There will never be a really free and enlightened State, until the State comes to recognize the individual as a higher and independent power, from which all its own power and authority are derived, and treats him accordingly."

One of Thoreau's notable essays is "A Plea for Captain John Brown," published in 1860; it is one of three on the same person, the other two being "After the Death of John Brown," delivered at the Concord memorial services for Brown on the day that the raider of Harpers Ferry was hanged, and "The Last Days of John Brown," written for a memorial service on July 4, 1860. The earliest essay of the three justifies the actions of Brown because, generally, he tried to put Thoreau's convictions into action.

"Walking," published in 1862, was taken from his journal written some ten years earlier and used as material for lectures in the early 1850's. It is an enthusiastic reaction to the joys of walking, "for absolute freedom and wildness," in which Thoreau boasts that the course of progress is always westward, drawn probably from the mere fact, as has been pointed out, that around Concord the best walking country was to the southwest. Extremely lyrical, the essay sometimes surfaces into nonsense, as in the statement that "Above all, we cannot afford not to live in the present. He is blessed over all other mortals who loses no moment of the passing life in remembering the past." Such comments caused a more deeply dedicated thinker, Herman Melville, to react with great scorn

and frequently to satirize Thoreau's easy optimism.

"Life Without Principle," published more than a year after Thoreau's death, in 1864, was likewise drawn from the journals during the author's most powerful decade, in the early 1850's. Delivered in 1854 as "Getting a Living," it is a ringing statement on the dignity and real worth of the individual. It is the voice of the self-reliant person calling all individuals to the assertion of their self-reliance so that they can live fully. Thoreau believed that most people misspend their lives, especially those who are concerned merely with getting money: "The ways by which you may get money almost without exception lead downward. To have done anything by which you earned money *merely* is to have been truly idle or worse." To be born wealthy is disastrous—as he says in one of his pithy statements, it is rather "to be stillborn." The wise cannot be tempted by money. They must be free, as Thoreau was convinced, feeling that their "connection with and obligation to society are still very slight and transient."

The world must be composed of individuals and must live not for the moment but for eternity. "Read not the Times. Read the Eternities." The United States had to reform. "Even if we grant that the American has freed himself from a political tyrant, he is still the slave of an economical and moral tyrant." In other ways, the country had not lived up to its potential; it was not the land of the free. "What is it to be free from King George and continue to be the slaves of King Prejudice? What is it to be born free and not to live free?"

The everyday routines of life are necessary, to be sure, but they should be "unconsciously performed, like the corresponding functions of the physical body" so that the mind—the better parts of human beings—can rise to the greater and noble aspects of living so that they will not discover at death that life has been wasted.

This essay is Thoreau at his best. He is characteristically the Transcendentalist, the individualist, voicing his opinion without reserve, pithily and most tellingly. Thoreau was, perhaps more than any other nineteenth century American writer, circumscribed in his subjects for writing. Therefore, his essays are repetitious. He liked to brag that he was widely traveled in Concord. Yet, though perhaps narrow in breadth, Thoreau's writings are shafts reaching to the essence of being. A half dozen essays represent him truthfully and succinctly.

ETHAN FROME

Type of work: Novel
Author: Edith Wharton (1862-1937)
Type of plot: Domestic tragedy
Time of plot: Late nineteenth century
Locale: Starkfield, a small town in New England
First published: 1911

Unrepresentative though it is of Wharton's works, Ethan Frome *is the most critically acclaimed and most popular. Wharton's terse depiction of Ethan's wasted talents and passions becomes a cynical fable describing the triumph of a trivial, conventional society over the ambitious, creative individual.*

Principal Characters

Ethan Frome, a farmer frustrated in his ambition to become an engineer or a chemist and in his marriage to a nagging, sour, sickly wife. He falls in love with his wife's good and lovely cousin, Mattie Silver, who comes to live with them. When his wife finally drives the girl away, Ethan insists on taking her to the station. Ethan and Mattie decide to take a sleigh ride that they have promised themselves, and, in mutual despair over the impending separation, they resolve to kill themselves by running the sled against a tree. Yet they are not killed, only permanently injured, and Ethan's wife is to look after them for the rest of their lives.

Zenobia Pierce Frome (Zeena), Ethan's wife, a distant cousin who nursed Ethan's mother during a long illness. The marriage between them is loveless, and Zeena is sickly and nagging.

Mattie Silver, Zeena's cousin, who comes to live with the Fromes. She returns Ethan's love. Once when Zeena spends a night away from home, she and Ethan spend a happy evening together, not making love but sitting quietly before the fire, as Ethan imagines happily married couples do. Mattie feels that she would rather die than leave Ethan, but in the crash she suffers not death but a permanent spinal injury. She must submit thereafter to being nursed by Zeena.

Ruth Varnum and **Ned Hale,** a young engaged couple whom Ethan observes stealing a kiss. On his night alone with Mattie, he tells her wistfully about it; it is as close as he comes to making advances.

The Story

Ethan Frome was twenty-one years old when he married Zenobia Pierce, a distant cousin who nursed his sick mother during her last illness. It was a wedding without love. Zenobia, called Zeena, had no home of her own, and Ethan was lonely, so they were married. Zeena's talkativeness, which had been pleasing to Ethan during his mother's illness, quickly subsided, however, and within a year of their marriage Zeena developed the sickliness that was to plague her husband. Ethan became increasingly dissatisfied with his life. He was an intelligent and ambitious young man who had hoped to become an engineer or a chemist, yet he found himself chained to a wife he detested and a farm he could not sell.

The arrival of Mattie Silver brightened the gloomy house considerably. Mattie, Zeena's cousin, had come to Starkfield partly because she had no other place to go and partly because Zeena was in need of a companion around the house. Ethan saw in Mattie's goodness and beauty every fine quality that Zeena lacked.

When Zeena suggested that Ethan help Mattie find a husband, he began to realize how much he was attracted to the girl. When he went to a church social to bring Mattie home and saw her dancing with the son of a rich Irish grocer, he realized that he was jealous. On his way home with her, Ethan felt his love for Mattie more than ever, for on that occasion as on others, she flattered him by asking him questions about astronomy. His dreams of happiness were short-lived, however, for when he reached home, Zeena was her nagging, sour self. The contrast between Zeena and Mattie impressed him more and more. One day, Ethan returned from his morning's work to find Zeena dressed in her traveling clothes. She was going to visit a new doctor in nearby Bettsbridge. Ordinarily, Ethan would have objected to the journey because of the expensive remedies that Zeena was in the habit of buying on such trips. On this occasion, however, he was overjoyed at the news of Zeena's proposed departure, for he realized that he and Mattie would have the house to themselves overnight.

With Zeena out of the way, Ethan became a changed man. Later in the evening, before supper, Ethan and Mattie sat quietly before the fire, just as Ethan imagined happily married couples would do. During supper, the cat broke Zeena's favorite pickle dish, which Mattie had used to brighten the table. In spite of the accident, they spent the rest of the evening happily. They talked about going sledding together, and Ethan told shyly—and perhaps wistfully—how he had seen Ruth Varnum and Ned Hale, a young engaged couple, stealing a kiss earlier in the evening.

In the morning, Ethan was happy, but not because of anything out of the ordinary the night before. In fact, when he went to bed, he remembered sadly that he had not so much as touched Mattie's fingertips or looked into her eyes. He was happy because he could imagine what a wonderful life he would have if he were married to Mattie. He got glue to mend the pickle dish, but Zeena's unexpected return prevented him from repairing it. His spirits were further dampened when Zeena told him that the Bettsbridge doctor considered her quite sick. He had advised her to hire someone to relieve her of all household duties, someone stronger than Mattie. She had already engaged the new girl. Ethan was dumbfounded by this development. In her insistence that Mattie be sent away, Zeena gave the first real hint that she might have

been aware of gossip about her husband and Mattie.

When Ethan told Mattie of Zeena's decision, the girl was as crestfallen as Ethan. Zeena interrupted their lamentations, however, by coming downstairs for something to eat. After supper, she required stomach powders to relieve a case of heartburn. In getting the powders, which she had hidden in a spot supposedly unknown to Mattie, Zeena discovered the broken pickle dish, which had been carefully reassembled in order to give the appearance of being unbroken. Having detected the deception and having learned that Mattie was responsible for the broken dish, Zeena called Mattie insulting names and showed plainly that the girl would be sent away at the earliest possible moment.

Faced with the certainty of Mattie's departure, Ethan thought of running away with her. Yet his poverty, as well as his sense of responsibility to Zeena, offered no solution to his problem, only greater despair. On the morning Mattie was to leave Starkfield, Ethan, against the wishes of his wife, insisted on driving Mattie to the station. The thought of parting was unbearable to both. They decided to take the sleigh ride that Ethan had promised Mattie the night before. Down the hill they went, narrowly missing a large elm tree at the bottom. Mattie, who had told Ethan that she would rather die than leave him, begged until Ethan agreed to take her down the hill a second time and run the sled into the elm. They failed, however, to hit the tree with force sufficient to kill them. The death that they sought became a living death, for in the accident Mattie suffered a permanent spinal injury and Ethan an incurable lameness. The person who then received Mattie into her home, who waited on her, and who cooked for Ethan was Zeena.

Critical Evaluation

When Edith Wharton wrote the introduction to an edition of *Ethan Frome* published in the 1920's, she pointed out that the picture of New England presented in the regional fiction popular a decade earlier "bore little . . . resemblance to the harsh and beautiful land" that she had known from her life in Massachusetts; the "granite" of the landscape had been left out. The attempt to remedy this omission, she goes on to suggest, accounts for the grimness of *Ethan Frome*, a tragic story of thwarted passion, in which the starkness of the natural world and the limited lives of the people who inhabit it are inextricably intertwined.

Certainly, the New England landscape is the most striking feature of Wharton's novella. The "outcroppings of

slate that nuzzled up through the snow like animals pushing out their noses to breathe," the majestic, mute hills that separate small communities from one another, the poor, farmed-over fields where Ethan Frome can barely scratch out a living—all of these suggest a physical and mental terrain that holds little promise for those doomed to spend "too many winters" within its bounds. The blazing blue skies of deep winter and the hard glitter of the snowy hills are beautiful, but they are invariably followed by sunless cold and pitiless storms, which serve to isolate still more the already remote villages and farms. The faint curls of smoke that rise from the chimneys of the scattered frame structures, the only signs of life in winter, suggest that human beings and their affairs are feeble and powerless in the face of nature's indifference and force.

Like Nathaniel Hawthorne and Herman Melville, Wharton depicts a natural world that is profoundly ambiguous. Beautiful as it may seem to the outsider who narrates the story, or to Mattie and Ethan themselves when they wander in the woods together or picnic on a summer day, nature is as treacherous as the elm tree that fails to provide the oblivion that the lovers have chosen. Ethan, trapped in his desolate farmhouse—at first by his mother, then by Zeena, and finally by the momentary impulse that caused him to turn the sled away from the tree at the crucial instant—was doomed from the start by the climate and the land. The contrast that the narrator describes between the farmer's noble, striking head and his twisted body embodies the tragic relationship in this harsh world between human aspirations and the forces that make a mockery of them.

Warmth, color, and passion are equally doomed in this northern place. In Ethan, whose stiff, heroic mien represents an incarnation of the "frozen woe" of the landscape, all sentient response has been buried. He seeks Mattie as a plant seeks sunlight, instinctively. Yet from the beginning, when he stands beside the church, within which the iron flanks of the stove "looked as though they were heaving with volcanic fires," he is an outsider who can only look through barred windows at the source of heat and light. The little study where he spends the last night before Mattie leaves is unheated, and the chill that creeps into him as he contemplates his doomed future is a foretaste of that future.

In a life devoid of sensual resources, individual objects take on symbolic importance. The breaking of Zeena's pickle dish, a pivotal event in the plot, marks a critical step toward the ironic consummation of the lovers' passion. Zeena's anger is clearly a reaction to her accurate perception of the situation between the lovers, yet the event is effective also because of the abject poverty of the senses that it reveals. Zeena is cruel, but she as much as Ethan is a victim of environment; by breaking the garish bit of glass, Mattie has destroyed—and, through her relationship with Ethan, is still destroying—what little Zeena has.

Ethan Frome was written when Wharton's powers as a writer were at their height. Like *The Custom of the Country* (1913) and *The Age of Innocence* (1920), novels that were to follow shortly, *Ethan Frome* displays the author's confident control of her materials and style. The structure of the story, in particular, shows how successfully Wharton had learned the lesson taught by her friend Henry James that the way in which a story is told is at least as important as the story itself. The relatively straightforward tale of the doomed love of Ethan and Mattie is presented to the reader by a narrator who is, the reader is told, basing his story on a superficial observation of town life and a few incomplete conversations with townspeople, who have described to him events of thirty years before. This complex narrative structure enables the writer to present convincingly a story of the interior life of people who would be unlikely to speak of it themselves and who are in fact characterized by their isolation from the outside world. The timeless, legendary quality of the affair is enhanced by Wharton's decision to set it in the past, and the townsfolk, Harmon Gow and Mrs. Hale, not only act as a kind of Greek chorus, interpreting the action to the narrator, but also serve as a bridge to a present time in which power stations and the modern technology they represent will make the kind of isolation that destroyed Ethan and his companions unlikely.

It was when the narrator looked through the doorway into the farmhouse kitchen, he reveals, that he first "began to put together" his vision of Ethan Frome's story. He withholds from the reader the knowledge of what he saw within the dingy kitchen, thereby whetting curiosity. His imaginative reconstruction of the love affair and the accident that led to the scene that he has just witnessed may in fact tell more about him, the narrator, than about the unsympathetic group he is contemplating. He projects his own fantasies and fears onto the dark silences of the community that has remained essentially impenetrable to him as an outsider. What he sees are the twisted remnants of a thwarted passion, enfeebled by poverty and buried beneath the icy reserves of the archetypal New England character. The heat of Ethan and Mattie's brief kisses and the breathless, rushed descent of the sled on the Corbury road are emblematic of the deep eroticism that, denied its natural outlets, twists and destroys its possessors.

Other Wharton novels present their readers with similar visions of denied emotion and unfulfilled passions. Biographers suggest that these had their source in the deep frustrations and isolation of the author's early years, and in the failure of a love affair that had awakened her to the possibilities of the sensual life. Whatever the source, the bleakness and pessimism of Wharton's vision is realized with great power in this New England tale. Although begun in France and finished well after Wharton had become a member of a cosmopolitan and largely expatriate set, *Ethan Frome* is a very American novel. It remains, in the judgment of many readers, one of her simplest and most striking works.

A FAREWELL TO ARMS

Type of work: Novel
Author: Ernest Hemingway (1899-1961)
Type of plot: Impressionistic realism
Time of plot: World War I
Locale: Northern Italy and Switzerland
First published: 1929

This story of a tragic love affair is set on the Italian front during World War I. Hemingway tells his tale with an abundance of realistic detail. Rather than a celebration of the "triumph of victory and the agony of defeat," the author's vision is uncompromisingly disillusioned. Not only is war useless, but efforts to maintain any meaningful relationship with individuals in the modern world are equally doomed.

Principal Characters

Lieutenant Frederic Henry, an American who has volunteered to serve with an Italian ambulance unit during World War I. Like his Italian companions, he enjoys drinking, trying to treat the war as a joke, and (it is implied) visiting brothels. Before the beginning of a big offensive, he meets Catherine Barkley, one of a group of British nurses assigned to staff a hospital unit. Henry begins the prelude to an affair with her but is interrupted by having to go to the front during the offensive; he is wounded, has an operation on his knee, and is sent to recuperate in Milan, where he again meets Miss Barkley, falls in love with her, and sleeps with her in his hospital room. When Henry returns to the front, he knows Catherine is pregnant. In the retreat from Caporetto, Henry is seized at a bridge across the Tagliamento River and, realizing that he is about to be executed for deserting his troops, escapes by swimming the river. At Stresa, he rejoins Catherine and, before he can be arrested for desertion, the two lovers row across Lake Como to Switzerland. For a few months, they live happily at an inn near Montreux—hiking, reading, and discussing American sights (such as Niagara Falls, the stockyards, and the Golden Gate Bridge) that Catherine must see after the war. Catherine is to have her baby in a hospital. Her stillborn son is delivered by cesarean section and that same night Catherine dies. Lieutenant Henry walks back to his hotel through darkness and rain. As developed by Hemingway, Henry is a protagonist who is sensitive to the horrors and beauties of life and war. Many of his reactions are subtly left for the reader to supply. At the end of the novel, for example, Henry feels sorrow and pity for the dead baby strangled by the umbilical cord, but the full, unbearable weight of Catherine's death falls upon the reader.

Catherine Barkley, the nurse whom Frederic Henry nicknames "Cat." She had been engaged to a childhood sweetheart killed at the Somme, but when she falls in love with Henry, she gives herself freely to him. Although they both want to be married, she decides that the ceremony would not be a proper one while she is pregnant; she feels that they are already married. Catherine seems neither a deep thinker nor a very complex person, but she enjoys life, especially good food, drink, and love. She has a premonition that she will die in the rain; the premonition is tragically fulfilled at the hospital in Lausanne.

Lieutenant Rinaldi, Frederic Henry's jokingly cynical friend. Over many bottles they share their experiences and feelings. Although he denies it, Rinaldi is a master of the art of priest-baiting. He is very fond of women, but he teases Henry about Catherine, calling her a "cool goddess."

The Priest, a young man who blushes easily but manages to survive the oaths and obscenities of the soldiers. He hates the war and its horrors.

Piani, a big Italian soldier who sticks by Henry in the retreat from Caporetto after the others in the unit have been killed or have deserted. With other Italian soldiers he can be tough, but with Henry he is gentle and tolerant of what men suffer in wartime.

Helen Ferguson, a Scottish nurse who is Catherine Barkley's companion when Frederic Henry arrives in Stresa. She is harsh with him because of his affair with Catherine.

Count Greffi, ninety-four years old, a contemporary of Metternich and a former diplomat with whom Frederic Henry plays billiards at Stresa. A gentle cynic, he claims that people do not become wise as they grow old; they merely become more careful.

The Story

Lieutenant Frederic Henry was a young American attached to an Italian ambulance unit on the Italian front. An offense was soon to begin, and when Henry returned to the front from leave, he learned from his friend, Lieutenant Rinaldi, that a group of British nurses had arrived in his absence to set up a British hospital unit. Rinaldi introduced him to nurse Catherine Barkley.

Between ambulance trips to evacuation posts at the front, Henry called on Miss Barkley. He liked the frank young Englishwoman in a casual sort of way, but he was not in love with her. Before he left for the front to stand by for an attack, she gave him a St. Anthony medal.

At the front, as Henry and some Italian ambulance drivers were eating in a dugout, an Austrian projectile exploded over them. Henry, badly wounded in the legs, was taken to a field hospital. Later, he was moved to a hospital in Milan.

Before the doctor was able to see Henry in Milan, the nurse prohibited his drinking wine, but he bribed a porter to bring him a supply that he kept hidden behind his bed. Catherine Barkley came to the hospital, and Henry knew then that he was in love with her. The doctors told Henry that he would have to lie in bed six months before they could operate on his knee. Henry insisted on seeing another doctor, who said that the operation could be performed the next day. Meanwhile, Catherine managed to be with Henry constantly.

After his operation, Henry convalesced in Milan with Catherine Barkley as his attendant. Together they dined in out-of-the-way restaurants, and together they rode about the countryside in a carriage. Henry was restless and lonely at nights, and Catherine often came to his hospital room.

Summer passed into autumn. Henry's wound had healed, and he was due to take convalescent leave in October. He and Catherine planned to spend the leave together, but he came down with jaundice before he could leave the hospital. The head nurse accused him of bringing on the jaundice by drink, in order to avoid being sent back to the front. Before he left for the front, Henry and Catherine stayed together in a hotel room; already she had disclosed to him that she was pregnant.

Henry returned to the front with orders to load his three ambulances with hospital equipment and go south

Ettore Moretti, an Italian from San Francisco serving in the Italian army. Much decorated, he is a professional hero whom Frederic Henry dislikes and finds boring.

into the Po valley. Morale was at a low ebb. Rinaldi admired the job that had been done on the knee and observed that Henry acted like a married man. War weariness was all-pervasive. At the front, the Italians, having learned that German divisions had reinforced the Austrians, began their terrible retreat from Caporetto. Henry drove one of the ambulances loaded with hospital supplies. During the retreat south, the ambulance was held up several times by wagons, guns, and trucks that extended in stalled lines for miles. Henry picked up two straggling Italian sergeants. During the night, the retreat was halted in the rain for hours.

At daybreak, Henry cut out of the long line and drove across country in an attempt to reach Udine by side roads. The ambulance got stuck in a muddy side road. The sergeants decided to leave, but Henry asked them to help dislodge the car from the mud. They refused and ran. Henry shot and wounded one; the other escaped across the fields. An Italian ambulance corpsman with Henry shot the wounded sergeant through the back of the head. Henry and his three comrades struck out on foot for Udine. On a bridge, Henry saw a German staff car with German bicycle troops crossing another bridge over the same stream. Within sight of Udine, one of Henry's group was killed by an Italian sniper. The others hid in a barn until it seemed safe to circle around Udine and join the mainstream of the retreat toward the Tagliamento River.

By that time, the Italian army was nothing but a frantic mob. Soldiers were throwing down their arms and officers were cutting insignia of rank from their sleeves. At the end of a long wooden bridge across the Tagliamento, military carabinieri were seizing all officers, giving them drumhead trials, and executing them by the riverbank. Henry was detained, but in the dark of night he broke free, plunged into the river, and escaped on a log. He crossed the Venetian plain on foot, then jumped aboard a freight train and rode to Milan, where he went to the hospital in which he had been a patient. There he learned that the English nurses had gone to Stresa.

During the retreat from Caporetto, Henry had made his farewell to arms. He borrowed civilian clothes from an American friend in Milan and went by train to Stresa, where he met Catherine, who was on leave. The bartender of the hotel in which Henry was staying warned

Henry that authorities were planning to arrest him for desertion the next morning; he offered his boat by means of which Henry and Catherine could escape to Switzerland. Henry rowed all night. By morning, his hands were so raw that he could barely stand to touch the oars. Over his protests, Catherine took a turn at the rowing. They reached Switzerland safely and were arrested. Henry told the police that he was a sportsman who enjoyed rowing and that he had come to Switzerland for the winter sports. The valid passports and the ample funds that Henry and Catherine possessed saved them from serious trouble with the authorities.

During the rest of the fall and winter, the couple stayed at an inn outside Montreux. They discussed marriage, but Catherine would not be married while she was pregnant.

They hiked, read, and talked about what they would do together after the war.

When the time for Catherine's confinement approached, she and Henry went to Lausanne to be near a hospital. They planned to return to Montreux in the spring. At the hospital, Catherine's pains caused the doctor to give her an anesthetic. After hours of suffering, she delivered a dead baby. The nurse sent Henry out to get something to eat. When he went back to the hospital, he learned that Catherine had had a hemorrhage. He went into the room and stayed with her until she died. There was nothing he could do, no one he could talk to, no place he could go. Catherine was dead. He left the hospital and walked back to his hotel in the dark. It was raining.

Critical Evaluation

Ernest Hemingway once referred to *A Farewell to Arms* as his *Romeo and Juliet*. Without insisting on a qualitative comparison, several parallels are obvious. Both works are about "star-crossed" lovers, both show erotic flirtations that rapidly develop into serious, intense, mature love affairs, and both describe the romances against a backdrop of social and political turmoil. Whether *A Farewell to Arms* finally qualifies as tragic is a matter of personal opinion, but it certainly represents, for Hemingway, an attempt to broaden his concerns from the aimless tragicomic problems of the expatriates in *The Sun Also Rises* (1926) to the fundamental question of life's meaning in the face of human mortality.

Frederic Henry begins the affair as a routine wartime seduction, "a game, like bridge, in which you said things instead of playing cards." He feels mildly guilty, especially after learning about Catherine's vulnerability because of the loss of her lover in combat, but he still foresees no complications from the temporary arrangement. It is not until he is wounded and sent to her hospital in Milan that their affair deepens into love—and from that point on, they struggle to free themselves in order to realize it. Yet they are constantly thwarted, first by the impersonal bureaucracy of the military effort, then by the physical separation imposed by the war itself, and, finally, by the biological "accident" that kills Catherine at the point where their "separate peace" at last seems possible.

As Henry's love for Catherine grows, his disillusionment with the war also increases. From the beginning of the book, Henry views the military efforts with ironic detachment, but there is no suggestion that, prior to

his meeting with her, he has had any deep reservations about his involvement. Hemingway's attitude toward war was always an ambiguous one. Like Henry, he thought that "abstract words such as glory, honor, courage, or hallow were obscene." For the individual, however, war could be the necessary test. Facing imminent death in combat, one either demonstrated "grace under pressure" and did the "one right thing" or one did not; one either emerged from the experience as a whole person with self-knowledge and control, or came out of it lost and broken.

There is little heroism in this war as Henry describes it. The hero's disengagement from the fighting is made most vivid in the extended "retreat from Caporetto," generally considered one of the great sequences in modern fiction. The retreat begins in an orderly, disciplined, military manner. Yet as it progresses, authority breaks down, emotions of self-preservation supersede loyalties, and the neat military procession gradually turns into a panicking mob. Henry is caught up in the momentum and carried along with the group in spite of his attempts to keep personal control and fidelity to the small band of survivors with whom he travels. Upon reaching the Tagliamento River, Henry is seized, along with all other identifiable officers, and held for execution. After he escapes by leaping into the river—an act of ritual purification as well as physical survival—he feels that his trial has freed him from any and all further loyalty to the Allied cause.

Henry then rejoins Catherine, and they complete the escape together. In Switzerland, they seem lucky and free at last. Up in the mountains, they hike, ski, make love, prepare for the baby, and plan for their postwar life together. Yet even in their most idyllic times, there are ominous hints. They worry about the baby, Catherine jokes about her narrow hips, and she becomes frightened by a dream of herself "dead in the rain."

Throughout the novel, Hemingway associates the plains and rain with death, disease, and sorrow; the mountains and the snow with life, health, and happiness. Catherine and Frederic are safe and happy in the mountains, but it is impossible to remain there indefinitely. Eventually everyone must return to the plains. When Catherine and Henry descend to the city, it is in fact raining, and she does in fact die.

Like that of Romeo and Juliet, the love between Catherine and Henry is not destroyed by any moral defect in their own characters. Henry muses that Catherine's fate is the price paid for the good nights in Milan, but such a price is absurdly excessive. Moreover, strictly speaking, the war is not responsible for their fate, any more than the Montague-Capulet feud directly provokes the deaths of Shakespeare's lovers. Yet the war and the feud provide the backdrop of violence and the accumulation of pressures that coerce the lovers into actions that contribute to their doom. In the final analysis, both couples are defeated by bad luck—the illness that prevents the friar from delivering Juliet's note to Romeo, the accident of Catherine's anatomy that prevents normal childbearing. Thus, both couples are star-crossed. Yet if a "purpose" can be vaguely ascertained in Shakespeare's version—

the feud is ended by the tragedy—there is no metaphysical justification for Catherine's death; it is, in her own words, "a dirty trick"—and nothing more.

Hemingway does not insist that the old religious meanings are completely invalid but only that they do not work for his people. Henry would like to visit with the priest in his mountain village, but he cannot bring himself to do it. His friend Rinaldi, a combat surgeon, proclaims atheism, hedonism, and work as the only available meanings. Count Greffi, an old billiard player Henry meets in Switzerland, offers good taste, cynicism, and the fact of a long, pleasant life. Catherine and Henry have each other: "You are my religion," she tells him.

All these things fail in the end. Religion is only for others, patriotism is a sham, hedonism becomes boring, culture is a temporary distraction, and work finally fails (the operation on Catherine was "successful"). Even love cannot last; Catherine dies, and both lovers know, although they will not admit it, that the memory of their romance will fade.

All that remains is a stoic acceptance of the above facts with dignity and without bitterness. Life, like war, is absurd. Henry survives because he is lucky; Catherine dies because she is unlucky. There is no guarantee that the luck ever balances out and, because everyone ultimately dies, it probably does not matter. What does matter is the courage, dignity, and style with which one accepts these facts as a basis for life, and, more important, in the face of death.

THE FIELD OF VISION

Type of work: Novel
Author: Wright Morris (1910-   )
Type of plot: Impressionistic realism
Time of plot: Christmas, 1956
Locale: Mexico City, Mexico, and Lone Tree, Nebraska
First published: 1956

Morris uses the drama and violence of a Mexican bullfight to examine the interlocking pasts of several Nebraskans. His characters try to connect with one another, but each has a different perspective, making such communication almost impossible.

Principal Characters

Gordon Boyd, a middle-aged writer who is living in Mexico City. When he encounters his childhood friends from Nebraska, he decides to bring them to a bullfight in order to reawaken his own bold and daring nature.

Walter McKee, Boyd's boyhood friend, a cattle breeder. He has always looked up to Boyd as a role model of audacity. McKee is content to serve as official witness to his friend's attempts at bravery.

Lois McKee, Walter's wife. Almost in spite of herself, she responds to Boyd's boldness, but she realizes that he will never follow up on his foolhardy acts. Lois named her son Gordon because of her love for Boyd.

Tom Scanlon, Lois' father, who is ninety years old.

He tells his great-grandson, also named Gordon, about the experiences of Tom's own father, Tim, on the frontier; he has come to believe that these adventures actually happened to him instead.

Dr. Leopold Lehmann, an amateur psychologist from Austria and a friend of Boyd. He is able to watch the Boyd-McKee-Lois triangle from a distance and to understand their complex relationship.

Gordon McKee, McKee's grandson, who is influenced by Tom and by Boyd.

Paula Kahler, a male transvestite and Lehmann's patient.

In *The Territory Ahead,* a critical book, Wright Morris discusses a particularly American dilemma: the writer's nostalgic immersion, to the point of immolation, in an overflowing reservoir of raw material. In most of his nine novels written before *The Field of Vision*, Morris processed fragments of his own material, searching for a conception that would enable him to achieve the kind of control and coherence that he saw in F. Scott Fitzgerald's *The Great Gatsby* (1925).

In a deliberate act of rediscovery, he took a fresh look at recognizable American artifacts and archetypal American experiences—the young romantic's nomadic wandering away from and nostalgic return to the home place— and presented some of the most authentic Americana of the 1940's. Like William Faulkner, he explored his own special province: the Nebraska plains, where the fertile prairie grass fades into the arid regions. His vision was seriocomic, and his style made imaginative use of Midwestern speech patterns. *The Field of Vision* is Morris'

first major attempt to get the fragments of his raw material into focus, to compress into expressive metaphors his conception of American Land, Dream, and Character.

If both the author and the artist hero of his early novels have become immersed in a nostalgia, unsettled by nausea, and thus need some distance from Lone Tree, Nebraska, what better vantage point than the Mexico City bullring? An external experience has no significance, neither in life nor in literature, Morris believes, until by a deliberate act of consciousness it becomes an internal event. Morris' arrangement of this event is skillfully crafted.

Quite by chance, Gordon Boyd, a failed bohemian writer, encounters Walter McKee, his boyhood friend, and McKee's family in the lobby of a hotel in Mexico City. To shock them, he takes the folks from back home to the bullfight. Seating his characters at the ring, Morris confines the present action to the duration of the bullfight; but in memory, forty years of the past are conjured up. He enters the minds of five of the characters: Boyd; McKee; McKee's wife, Lois; Tom Scanlon, Lois' father; and Dr. Lehmann, Boyd's analyst. Using the third-person point of view, Morris focuses certain external events through each of these characters, one after the other, in a sequence that he repeats five times. Some common focal point, seen from contrasting angles, provides transition from one character's mind to another's. Morris does not go into the minds of two other characters: Paula Kahler, who is traveling with Boyd and Lehmann; and little Gordon, McKee's grandson. Each person provides Morris with a different perspective from which to view the American character.

In the excitement of the accidental reunion and of the bullfight, the characters are charged with the past and the immediate present. The phases of the bullfight and the presence of the others stimulate each character to recall an event in the past in such a way that it is possible for him or her to experience a shock of recognition in the present. The bullfight ritual, with its artistic, spiritual, and brutally physical dimensions, and the technique of shifting points of view provide Morris with a controlling framework that enables him to shuttle back and forth, weaving a tapestry of collective consciousness in which time present and time past form a design. Thus, the reader witnesses a double ceremony. As the torero and his bull move toward the moment of truth, each character comes closer to the horns of his private dilemma. To make the moment of truth possible, the torero must risk being gored; the human mind confronting itself runs a similar risk.

There is a contrast, however, between the action in the ring and the events enacted in the theater of the mind. The events of the past are simple and clichéd; Morris manipulates the clichés of mass culture and language as a witty and humorous function of style working toward insight. McKee, Lois, and Boyd share (though each in the isolation of the mind) the incident on the front porch in Lone Tree when Boyd kissed Lois, McKee's fiancée, and swept her off her feet. Neither Gordon Boyd nor McKee knows that Lois got up that night from her cot on the back porch and, sleepwalking, unlatched the screen to admit her dream lover, Boyd; in the midst of her dream, the cot collapsed. The hero's failure to appear in the flesh persuaded Lois to marry McKee, but she named her firstborn Gordon, who named his own son Gordon.

In another act of audacity, Boyd attempted to "walk on water" at the sand pit outside town; until Boyd went down, McKee believed the hero would succeed. He witnessed a similar bungled act of audacity when Boyd ran onto the field to get a foul ball autographed by base-ball legend Ty Cobb; Boyd dropped the ball but ripped a pocket from Cobb's pants. In the present, parallel audacious gestures are made: For example, a Mexican boy climbs into the ring to make the archetypal amateur confrontation with the bull that has just gored a professional.

In their childhood, Boyd was the hero and McKee was his major witness. He responded to the promise of greatness in Boyd. As opposites, Boyd and McKee are attracted to each other. They illustrate a dichotomy in the American character, two dimensions of the American Dream: the figure of action and the dreamer, the artist and the businessperson, the power of fiction and the authority of fact. At Lone Tree, the land itself, fertile to the east and sterile to the west, exhibits these contrasts.

Through the hero-witness relationship, Morris depicts an element in the American character that frustrates every attempt to realize the dream in a land of promise: the audacity that bewitches rather than transforms both the doer and the observer. To accomplish his limited goals, McKee, like Sancho Panza, must believe that Boyd (Don Quixote) is capable of success somewhere in the realm of possibilities. In *Ceremony in Lone Tree*, however, McKee will escape captivity in the hero-witness relationship, though to no great purpose.

In his youthful enthusiasm, McKee extended this relationship to include Lois, whose own response added a sexual dimension. When Boyd failed to follow up the kiss, Lois (Dulcinea) saw that his foolishness would not end in wisdom. Concluding that most males are hopeless, her father included, she began to suppress her emotions. Ironically, Boyd now regards her as a typical example of the frigid Midwestern housewife. In Mexico, she almost bolts from her situation with a tourist, but he also is a man of mere gestures.

In the American experience, gesture is not often enough followed by the consummate act. Audacious Christopher Columbus, too, walked on water, but he reached the wrong shore; Americans have domesticated a continent but are homeless. The audacious frontier hero survives in people such as Boyd: The boy who once attempted the impossible has become the middle-aged clown who becalms a raging bull by squirting Pepsi Cola into its mouth. With that gesture, Boyd touches bottom. Aware that each of the adults has failed in his or her own way, ways that McKee's grandson may imitate, Boyd makes a desperate attempt to pass the hero's charge on to his namesake, little Gordon. Flinging the boy's phony coonskin cap into the bullring where the beast lies slain by a professional, Boyd lets the boy down into the ring to retrieve his cap and to take the risk that may transform the amateur into the disciplined adult.

Observing the hero-witness relationship between Tom Scanlon and little Gordon, Boyd gets perspective on himself. The old man tells the boy tales of a bygone era of audacity. A fossilized victim of the past, Scanlon is reminded by the gored torero's cry for water of the pioneer trek that his father led across the arid plains. His father, Tim, lying on a bed in a back room of the Lone Tree Hotel, so bemused Tom with stories of the great age of adventure that Tom now believes, in his senility, that it was he who went through the inferno of the desert and witnessed the cannibalism of the survivors upon those who perished. The witness has become the hero, and both are defunct. Trapped himself in Ty Cobb's pocket, which he still carries as a talisman, Boyd knows that the spirit represented by such emblems of the past, including Gordon's coonskin cap, must be repeatedly resurrected in acts of transformation.

A different reflection of each character is offered by every other in the crazy house of mirrors that only Morris, with the complicity of the reader, can focus. As the link between the reader and the characters, Dr. Lehmann, an amateur student of life, is able to view at some distance the triangular Boyd-McKee-Lois relationship. McKee and Lois can see the similarity of the bullring to the porch, the sand pit, the ballpark, and the stage where Boyd's play, depicting those symbolic moments of the past, was performed. Yet while reality imposes correspondences upon the mind, keeping it moving over the surface of things, humanity must will the achievement of insights and concepts. Thus, Lehmann seeks connections. He interprets Boyd's dilemma in terms of Paula Kahler's. Having tasted the ashes of success, Boyd tries to make a success of failure—a typical American enterprise. Unable to cope with human nature, Paula changed

her own, from male to female, from a crippling compassion for people to a safer sympathy for insects and animals. Lehmann discerns the way in which a self-ventriloquism deceives in the realization of the dummy in oneself.

Morris demonstrates Lucifer's perception: "The mind is its own place, and in itself/ Can make a Heav'n of Hell, a Hell of Heav'n." Thus, at the bullring, McKee and Lois are able to see only what they brought with them from Nebraska. The human dilemma is posed in this way: Just as no two people see the same bullfight, despite its element of artistic order, no two characters share the same field of vision. Though they may arrive at similar moments of insight, people communicate in terms of clichés, while the real drama, when it occurs, is an almost unbroken soliloquy. To each character, all the others appear to be mad Hamlets.

These missed connections are at once pathetic, because they foster lives of quiet desperation, and comic, because most of the characters are fools who persist in their folly to a dead end. Morris merely juxtaposes the elements that make perception possible, and while the characters themselves usually miss the connection, the reader is in a position to make it. Morris' art is resolved in the response of the reader, but it is as inaccessible to the inattentive reader as the moment of perception is to the purblind character. Lehmann, however, knows that the accidents and coincidences of a life essentially without design can be patterned by a conscious act of imagination; he also sees the pathos of the human inability to realize those rare moments of truth, those epiphanies. He sees (as does Boyd, though less clearly) that, in such structured experiences, humankind transcends impermanence (as in the bullfight ritual) and enters, if only momentarily, the realm of permanence.

FOUR QUARTETS

Type of work: Poetry
Author: T. S. Eliot (1888-1965)
First published: 1943

Using musical forms such as quartets and sonatas, Eliot fashioned a poetic masterpiece that reflected the maturity and concerns of his later years.

At the age of sixty and already an elder statesman of letters, T. S. Eliot was awarded the British Order of Merit and the Nobel Prize in Literature in 1948, five years after publishing what would be his last masterpiece, *Four Quartets*. Musing on the Nobel Committee's choice, he surmised that they made their selection having considered "the entire corpus" of his work. Although he would go on to write three more plays, several volumes of essays, and some more poetry, *Four Quartets* was to remain the capstone of his career as a poet, the masterpiece of his maturity, very different in style from the masterpiece of his poetic apprenticeship, "The Love Song of J. Alfred Prufrock" (1917), and from his renowned and no longer disputed chef d'oeuvre, *The Waste Land* (1922). Quite simply, some of his poetic concerns had changed, as had his mode of expression.

More seemingly direct and more apparently accessible than Eliot's early work, *Four Quartets* exhibits a certain simplicity of statement that leads into the depth of his thought. The sequence, like some of his earlier poetry, grew incrementally over an eight-year period. "Burnt Norton" (1935), the first of the quartets, was formed from lines originally intended for the verse drama *Murder in the Cathedral* (1935) and contains themes common to the play. Its title refers to a specific country house with a rose garden in the Cotswolds. "East Coker" (1940) invokes the place from which Eliot's forebears emigrated in the seventeenth century; Eliot would be buried in East Coker, Somerset, in 1965. "The Dry Salvages" (1941) is also linked to Eliot's own geography: In his youth his family spent summers in New England, principally in Rockport and Gloucester, Massachusetts, on Cape Ann, near the rocks known as the Dry Salvages (a corruption, Eliot speculates, of *les trois sauvages*). Finally, "Little Gidding" (1942), which some have called Eliot's *Paradiso*, recalls the seventeenth century High Church religious community founded near Huntingdon by Nicholas Ferrar. Each of the poems is a meditation about place or inspired by place; together they form a devotional sequence linked by considerations of time, place, memory, consciousness of the self and of others, transcendence, and the act of writing.

Eliot has endowed the poems, each a quartet, with musical qualities and repetitive motifs. All of Eliot's poetry should be read aloud, and *Four Quartets* in particular should be heard. Walter Pater, to whom Eliot owed many debts that he was eager to conceal, once wrote that "all art continually aspires to the condition of music." In these poems, Eliot's verbal art seems to aspire to that condition, so that in every phrase and sentence that is right, one finds "the complete consort dancing together."

Structurally, the poems follow the five-part plan that Eliot had used in a more startling way in *The Waste Land*. These five movements, patterned on the form of a musical quartet or sonata, concern the varied relationships between time and eternity, the meaning of history, and the experience of Joycean epiphanies. C. K. Stead has provided lengthy and useful analyses of each of the poems by probing each according to a naming of the parts. The first part of each poem is concerned with the movement of time in which fleeting moments of eternity are caught. The second part examines worldly experience, which leads to an inevitable dissatisfaction. In the third part, the speaker seeks purgation in the world and seeks to divest the soul of love for created things. Part 4, the briefest, is a lyric prayer for or affirmation of the need for spiritual intercession. The final part deals with the problems of attaining artistic wholeness, which become analogues for, and blend into, the problems of achieving spiritual health.

"Burnt Norton" begins with two epigraphs from the fragments of the great philosopher of flux, Heraclitus. These are central to the concerns of Eliot as a modern-day poet-philosopher of the Word. Heraclitus' fragments mark him as a profound thinker who assigned the divine attribute of eternity to the universal Logos (word). This Logos Eliot would also find resonating in the later Logos of St. John's Gospel. Heraclitus believed not that the universe began in time but that there exists a perpetual stream of creation in which "all things are an exchange for fire and fire for all things" in a world order that "was, is, and will be everliving fire being kindled in measures and quenched in measures." That for which Heraclitus is generally renowned becomes the more important for Eliot as he reflects, desiderative and expectant, upon his own craft in these poems: Heraclitus was the first Greek writer to explore the nature of discourse and to find an intelligible principle of the universe not only in the Logos but also in the depths of the philosophic soul, depths that deepen even as the soul attempts to fathom them. In particular, Eliot cites two sentences from H. Diels's *Die Fragmente der Vorsokratiker*, likely from the fifth edition of 1934. The first may be loosely translated, "While the Law of Reason (Logos) is common, the majority of people live as though they had an understanding (wisdom) of their own." The second is a paradox fundamental to Eliot's poem: "The way upward and downward are one and the same."

The poem opens with a reflection on the nature of time and leads to the proposition "If all time is eternally present/ All time is unredeemable," a notion that puts in question the need for a redemption and possibly the lack of such a need in a cosmos ruled by the redemptive Logos. The mix of memory and desire leads to the rose garden: Directed by the bird "into our first world," one finds that "the leaves are full of children,/ Hidden excitedly, containing laughter." This, possibly one of those brief encounters with eternity, is ended by the bird: "Go, go, go, said the bird: human kind/ Cannot bear very much reality."

Part 2 focuses upon individual humanity and the tension between an ascending spirit and a descending body. Eliot continues to pit Heraclitean opposites against each other "at the still point of the turning world. . . . Where past and future are gathered." Here is "inner freedom from the practical desire," "release from action and suffering, release from the inner/ And the outer compulsion." The human condition of incompleteness and temporality is an unsatisfactory one. What redeems the time and releases one from it is consciousness, but only in time can memory function. Paradoxically, he concludes, "Only through time time is conquered." Here, as in Heraclitus, the philosophic soul adds to its depths as it seeks to plumb them.

The poem's third part reveals "a place of disaffection," a twilight that has neither the light that turns shadow into transient beauty nor the darkness that purifies the soul. Indeed, spiritual purification is the speaker's goal with his command to "descend lower . . ./ Into the world of perpetual solitude" and his enumeration of necessary negations in abstention to achieve a present "while the world moves/ In appetency, on its metalled ways/ Of time past and time future." The search for purgation reiterates the Heraclitean virtue of desiccation, the "dry soul" approaching the condition of fire.

The short lyric that is part 4 celebrates the darkness in which the soul may be purified and places the speaker in the lower depths, below the sunflower's tendrils and the yew's fingers. Here, in the darkness "the light is still/ At the still point of the turning world." The questions in this section of the poem may hint at the need for intercession, but the mention of the "kingfisher's wing" is a more obvious allusion to the celebrated image that Gerard Manley Hopkins had used for Christ.

In part 5, the speaker muses that "words move, music moves/ Only in time" and continues to meditate on the temporal nature of music, words, silence, ends and beginnings. Here Eliot examines the adequacy and inadequacy of words and moves to consider the Johannine Logos as he reflects that "the word in the desert/ Is most attacked by voices of temptation." In a further contrast between desire (movement) and love (a stillness that impels motion), he finds the latter timeless except for the temporality that is necessary to the difference between unbeing and being. Finally, to draw the sequence full circle to part 1, there is the "hidden laughter/ Of children in the foliage" and a repetition, without attribution, of the bird's directives, and the closing statement, "Ridiculous the waste sad time/ Stretching before and after." The questions of artistic wholeness and spiritual health involve a consideration of words as part of the Word and of love as a timeless present. By association, love participates in Logos; also by association, the laughter of children in the past in the rose garden becomes present and eternal in the remembered words, "Quick now, here, now, always—" and has a connection, however tenuous, with love and Logos.

This type of analysis is only one among many possible approaches to the poem in itself and as part of a sequence. Some have read "Burnt Norton" as the first of a series which features God the Father and concerns the element of air, with "East Coker" focusing on God the Son (earth), "The Dry Salvages" dealing with Mary the Mother of God (water), and "Little Gidding" devoted to God the Spirit (fire). While this scheme offers suggestive possibilities, it presents a somewhat limited view of the poem and the sequence as a whole. What it does reveal is a range of possible interpretations suggested by the text.

To use Stead's fivefold analyses as applied to "Burnt Norton" in considering its three companion pieces is to develop a deep and rich appreciation of the poet at work in exploring his own consciousness. "East Coker" pursues the poet's beginning in his end (part 1), especially in light of family history, and is a much more explicit meditation on the role of the poet as crafter of words (part 5). Like the speaker of Dante's *The Divine Comedy*, he is in the middle way; in his case, he has spent twenty years—"years largely wasted, the years of *l'entre deux guerres*"—trying to learn to use words. "The Dry Salvages" recalls Eliot's youthful life in the United States not only in Massachusetts but also in St. Louis, Missouri, alongside the "strong brown god," the river. This poem, more than the first two, is explicitly concerned with religious thought, with direct references to God and the Annunciation (part 2), Krishna (part 3), and a prayer to the Queen of Heaven, "Figlia del tuo figlio" (daughter of your son). Again, the work of the poet in search of artistic wholeness and spiritual health becomes the clear focus of part 5, as the speaker considers varied attempts to communicate, spiritually and at times fantastically. He does offer a clue to his sense of his own purpose in probing language and time and eternity: "The point of intersection of the timeless/ With time, is an occupation for the saint." It is also an occupation for the poet and for his readers.

The most anthologized poem of the *Four Quartets*, "Little Gidding," contains Eliot's most mature and virtually final poetic statement. Musing on the place Little Gidding and its significance—historically, as a seat of spiritual life in the seventeenth century, and currently, as a source of spiritual strength—he finds "the intersection of the timeless moment/ Is England and nowhere. Never and always." Part 2 describes another sort of spiritual encounter reminiscent of Eliot's earlier dramatic poetry. Here, in Dantean fashion, he encounters the shade "of some dead master" whose burden is a total disillusion expressed in a disclosure of "the gifts reserved for age." He offers these observations as one poet to another, "since our concern was speech, and speech impelled us/ To purify the dialect of the tribe."

Part 3 contains echoes of Dame Julian of Norwich, a fourteenth century mystic, as the speaker reflects upon the inevitability of sin and the mystic knowledge of forgiveness based upon beseeching. The lyrical part 4 combines the "dove" of part 2, which had been a bomber, with the descent of the Spirit at Pentecost and the Heraclitean fire foreshadowed in the epigraph to "Burnt Norton," as the speaker reflects upon love and fire. Finally, in some of his most memorable lines, a paean on poetic practice as a unifying, health-giving activity, Eliot achieves a synthetic vision, summarizes the varied strands of the poem, and ends at an unqualified affirmation. He unifies the sequence in the poem's closing lines by echoing the moments of insight he had revealed in the earlier poems and earlier in this one.

Eliot once wrote that his favorite author, Dante, is "a poet to whom one grows up over a lifetime." Eliot himself has achieved something of that stature: He is a poet to whom one returns without exhausting meaning or the possibility of meaning, especially when one reads his later poetry in light of the earlier work. In particular, *Four Quartets* is a sequence to which a reader may return after few or many years, exploring it anew and coming away with fresh insight.

FRANNY AND ZOOEY

Type of work: Novel
Author: J. D. Salinger (1919-   )
Type of plot: Social satire
Time of plot: November, 1955
Locale: Principally New York City
First published: 1961

Through the eyes of a brother and sister, child prodigies who have become alienated from the rest of society, Salinger examines the meaning of spirituality in the modern world, as well as the process of education.

Principal Characters

Franny Glass, a sensitive college English major and actress. She, like the rest of her siblings, has been reared in an environment of philosophical questioning and advanced scholarship. This upbringing, however, has left her confused and uncertain of her beliefs and values, leading to her nervous breakdown.

Lane Coutell, her pseudointellectual boyfriend at college, who represents the kind of superficiality that has driven Franny to religious fanaticism.

Zooey Glass, Franny's brother, an abrasive television actor. He attempts to help his sister, reexamining their strange childhood and reinforcing her sense of self-worth. Their past has also taken its toll on him, in the form of an ulcer.

Buddy Glass, Franny and Zooey's brother, a writer. Buddy, along with the now-deceased Seymour, was primarily responsible for educating his younger siblings. He functions as the narrator in the second half of the novel.

Bessie Glass, their compassionate mother.

The Story

Franny and Zooey was J. D. Salinger's third book, coming ten years after his novel about adolescence, *The Catcher in the Rye* (1951), was received with acclaim and eight years after *Nine Stories* (1953) further demonstrated his compassion for the sensitive and disturbed, his fine sense of satiric humor, his penchant for discursive first-person narration, and his growing interest in spiritual salvation in the modern world. The two episodes presented in *Franny and Zooey* are parts of a larger design. The characters named in the title are sister and brother, members of a family with whom Salinger had dealt for some time, both before and after his notable success and pursuit of privacy combined to make him one of the most celebrated of contemporary American writers.

Franny and Zooey are the children of Les and Bessie Gallagher Glass, former vaudevillians (Jewish and Irish, respectively) and long-time residents of Manhattan. Franny is a college student, and Zooey is a successful television actor at twenty-five; together, they are the youngest children of a family that once numbered five boys and two girls. Like the rest (most of whom were child quiz-program performers), they are prodigies. More than that, she is beautiful, and he is saved from being dazzlingly handsome only by a slightly protruding ear. Despite these advantages, Zooey has an ulcer, Franny has an incipient nervous breakdown, and both have a sense of profound dissatisfaction with the world, with men, and with themselves. Franny's difficulties, which are the more severe, form the central concern of the book. They are set forth first as one sees her arrival for an Ivy League football game and what proves to be a disastrous and abortive weekend. Her date, Lane Coutell, epitomizes the self-centered pseudointellectual qualities that have caused her to become hypersensitive to those around her, to withdraw from drama and allied activities, and to seek grace and sustenance in the "Jesus Prayer" (from a devotional book called *The Way of a Pilgrim*) consisting of the phrase, "Lord Jesus Christ, have mercy on me." The prayer is ineffectual, however, as she repeats it at the end of the segment bearing her name, while recovering from a fainting spell in the restaurant to which Lane had taken her for lunch.

The "Zooey" section, set on the following Monday in November, 1955, in the Glasses' New York apartment, begins to reveal the fundamental causes of both breakdown and ulcer. The early education of Franny and Zooey had been supervised by the eldest children: Seymour, a Ph.D. in his teens who had committed suicide in 1948 at the age of thirty-one, and Buddy, a self-alleged neurotic serving as writer-in-residence at a women's junior college and as narrator of the "Zooey" section. It had been a program designed to inculcate religious and philosophical knowledge before that of the other disciplines conventionally studied by children. The texts were not only the Testaments but also the Upanishads, the Diamond Sutra, the writings of Zen and Mahayana Buddhism, of Lao-tzu and Ramakrishna, of Master Johannes Eckhart and Søren Kierkegaard. Zooey tells Franny that their training turned them into freaks at an early age, with their standards freakish as well—like the Tattooed Lady who wanted everyone else to look like her. Franny's discontent is objectified in her cry that she is sick and tired of ego—always ego—her own and everyone's. As she sees its manifestations in Lane Coutell and her professors, so Zooey sees them in his television associates. Exhorting Franny, and then telephoning her (on Buddy's telephone in Seymour's old room) with his voice disguised as Buddy's, he tries to show her that detachment is the one thing that matters in religious affairs. Finally, as he restores some measure of her self-confidence and emphasizes the need to give love to others, she achieves a kind of peace resembling the *satori* of Zen and drifts into sleep.

Critical Evaluation

The first section of Salinger's book is the superior of the two. Here he is in control of his material and presents it economically. The second section, however—even granting that it is spoken in the voice of Buddy Glass, brother of the principals, and intimately concerned with their problems—is by contrast prolix and diffuse, at its worst arch and even cute. It demonstrates the consequences of forgetting Henry James's dictum, often repeated to himself: dramatize, always dramatize. When Buddy Glass does render action, it takes the form of conversation— between Zooey and Franny or Zooey and his mother— as in a sixty-eight page passage (surely the longest in modern literature set in a bathroom) between the latter two. James's great contemporary Joseph Conrad wrote that the novelist's primary task was above all to make the reader see. As if striving doubly hard for concrete visual effects in what he argues is not a mystical story or even one mystifying in a religious sense, Salinger includes much description. Yet it is description that often, unhappily, takes the form of a lengthy catalog of the contents of the bathroom medicine chest, Bessie Glass's kimono pockets, the furnishings of the living room, or the aphorisms inscribed on the inside of the door of Buddy's room—two pages' worth being quoted in the text. This looseness of form is also seen in the use of a long footnote and two letters (the letter being, like the diary excerpt, a favorite Salinger device), one of which covers twelve pages.

Early in "Zooey," Buddy writes that the work is not so much a story as a homemade film in prose, and that Bessie, Zooey, and Franny have advised against making it public. One wishes their misgivings had led the author to edit or reshoot some of his "footage." The long letter that Zooey rereads is described by its sender, Buddy, as being seemingly unending, self-indulgent, opinionated, repetitious, patronizing, even embarrassing. It is also, he adds, surfeited with affection. All of the latter comment—and much of the former—applies to "Zooey."

This novel is one of the strongest—one might almost say obsessive—embodiments of Salinger's interest in the individual's quest for spiritual advancement. What the work needs, unrealized in *Raise High the Roof Beam, Carpenters, and Seymour: An Introduction* (1963), is assimilation of the impact upon Salinger's particular sensibility of this subject matter to an extent that will again make possible the subtle control and command that mark his best work in *The Catcher in the Rye* and several of the tales in *Nine Stories*.

THE FRONTIER IN AMERICAN HISTORY

Type of work: History
Author: Frederick Jackson Turner (1861-1932)
Time of work: Early seventeenth century to the 1880's
Locale: American West
First published: 1920

With this revolutionary work, Turner redefined the study of American history and introduced the concept of the frontier, explaining how Americans were influenced by constant expansion and by the promise and allure of the West.

July 12, 1893, is the best known date in American historiography, as distinct from the best known date in American history, July 4, 1776. Yet both saw Declarations of Independence. The scene in 1893 was the annual meeting of the fledgling American Historical Association, held in Chicago to coincide with the Columbia Exposition. The exposition celebrated the four hundredth anniversary of Christopher Columbus; it horribly depressed an Easterner, Henry Adams, but it so excited a Wisconsin native, Hamlin Garland, that he resolved to return from New York and settle in the booming Midwestern city. Another man from Wisconsin got up to deliver a paper before the American Historical Association, and by proposing "The Significance of the Frontier in American History" he read American historians their Declaration of Independence and permanently altered the study of American history in schools and colleges.

Frederick Jackson Turner was the speaker; his paper was often reprinted, but it was not until 1920 that he put together the first full statement of his theory on the frontier by republishing his original paper with twelve supporting articles in *The Frontier in American History*; the second and consequent part of his theory, *The Significance of Sections in American History*, was published in the year he died. His 1893 paper was preceded by his doctoral dissertation on the fur trade in Wisconsin and two articles on history and American history which show the development of his theory of the frontier. Two events precipitated his paper: first, the work of the Italian economist Achille Loria, with its twin suggestions of free land as the key to changes in human society and of America as the best colony in which to test this thesis, came to Turner's notice in the late 1880's and influenced his 1892 paper on "Problems in American History"; second, the superintendent of the 1890 census had recently announced that insufficient free land existed in the United States for the frontier to feature in the census reports as it had done since the first census in 1790. Turner dramatized his paper by opening with this statement; in effect, he was directing his coworkers away from political and diplomatic history, insisting that, no matter what happened in European capitals, American history was made in the hinterland, where the westward movement had been the most important historical phenomenon for Americans. Thus, he opened up the vast frontier of local history to historians in whatever state they might be located. The dramatic setting and occasion for Turner's paper was not at once appreciated, but it played its part in spreading his ideas rapidly.

The initial paper on "The Significance of the Frontier" was constructed in two parts, with an introduction. The first paragraph asserts that American history is the gradual settlement of the West, and this idea is followed by four paragraphs defining the frontier as a moving belt between settled and free land, moving because of the force behind it. Because of the environment into which the frontier moved, its chief characteristic is a process of reversion to savagery followed by a slow recovery of civilization that, because its chief influences have been indigenous, cannot be an imitation of European life and must therefore be American. If the frontier is the maker of Americans, and they are the makers of their history, then the frontier holds the key to that history.

The first part of the paper presents, in rapid survey, the different kinds of frontier in American history and the modes of advance from the time when it began as the frontier of Europe on the Atlantic seaboard in the early seventeenth century to its near completion in the 1880's. The changes are determined by the different geographical boundaries or barriers to the westward advance— Native Americans, farmland, salt supplies, and the like. Here Turner draws several vivid sketches of the succession of different types of settlers who followed one another in any one settlement or who could be imaginatively plotted as a series of different kinds of frontier belts such as hunting, trading, nomadic, grazing, farming, and financing. These stretched back eastward from the most advanced settlement at any given point in American history.

The second part of the paper is a provocative summary of changes enforced by the frontier experience on the regions to the east and in Europe, from whence the frontier impulse came. First, Turner proposes that the frontier is the real melting pot of immigrant nationalities and, without it, the United States would in 1890 resemble those nations of Europe. The next point is the success of the frontier. Although its rate of advance changed, it never faltered, and its increasing distance westward made Americans less dependent on England. Third, the power of the federal government stems from that granted Congress by the Constitution to dispose of the public domain and thus exert federal sway inside the state; without the frontier, the federal government would have had little to legislate and less money. Fourth, the products of the frontier first determined the development of the national economy, maintaining a rural dominance over increasing industrialization in the East. Fifth, the egalitarianism of the frontier kept the United States democratic. Last, in struggles with the economic, religious, and educational power of the East, the West came to have a character of its own, which determined that the distinction of the states would always be a duality of national and sectional interests.

Although the reputation of this paper credits it with causing a revolution in American historiography, it would be truer to say that the paper was so completely in accord with the predilections of American historians in later decades that it both anticipated and supported the predominant social or economic interpretation of American history that came to be preferred to the dynastic—the succession of presidents. This thesis helped to make possible a wholly economic explanation of the causes of the Civil War, for example, and it had the effect of determining Turner's life work. *The Frontier in American History* coped with his first task: to establish the historical outlines of his moving frontier and then to consider the unique character of post-frontier society, the residuum he called "The West." Turner's was, first of all, a new problem in historiography: how to explain that an uninhabited area could affect an inhabited area, a problem unknown in European historiography. He used the term "frontier" as the crossover point between the two areas, and since it was always moving westward, however irregularly, he conceived it imaginatively as altering the physical shape of the inhabited area behind it by leaving successive belts of post-frontier societies, each of which was a "West" and together formed "The West."

Before analyzing his "West," he outlined the westward or moving frontier from Massachusetts to the "Old West" to the "Middle West," where he expanded his outline to closer study of the Ohio and Mississippi valleys. "The Significance of the Mississippi Valley in American History" both completes the moving of the frontier as far as Turner took it and allows him to introduce "The Problem of the West," "Dominant Forces in Western Life," "Contributions of the West to American Democracy," "The West and American Ideals," and "Middle Western Democracy"; this discussion leads him to the large claim that the West is democratic and that "democracy" is another name for "West." Thus the whole meaning of American history is summed up in "The West." At this point, Turner becomes not a narrative historian but a social historian determined to explore "forces," "ideals," and "significances."

In his social history, Turner tends to conclude his work with perorations about the virtue of American democracy and that of the West in producing it, thus showing himself a loyal son of the Middle Border. "The Significance of the Mississippi Valley in American History" concludes that the valley realized the American ideal of democracy and constitutes the heartland of America; it is almost an independent nation and has shed its light on the surrounding feebler nations of the South, the East, and the Far West. Turner developed these ideas during his long tenure at Harvard University and modified them when he took up residence at the Huntington Library in San Marino, California; in turn, they led him to his pioneer work on sections in American history and life. His methods are summarized in his presidential address to the American Historical Association in 1910, "Social Forces in American History," the twelfth chapter of *The Frontier in American History* in which he reads statistics of American growth from 1890 to 1920 as evidence of the force behind the frontier turning to new fields in the development of industrial and federal power. Turner summons his fellow historians to continue the work that he began nearly two decades before by using statistics available from other disciplines, as he did in using the census bulletin in 1893. His embracing view forecasts the development of American studies, and the discipline he hinted at is given meaning by his insistence that the duty of historians is to engage themselves in the life of their nation by continually reinterpreting the immediate past in terms of the present, as he himself had done in Chicago in 1893.

Turner's concluding chapter, "Middle Western Pioneer Democracy," presents his belief that pioneer life gave Americans a chance for a true democracy, personal freedom, and a free society for the individual.

THE GLASS MENAGERIE

Type of work: Drama
Author: Tennessee Williams (1911-1983)
Type of plot: Psychological realism
Time of plot: 1930's
Locale: St. Louis, Missouri
First presented: 1944

Williams' first commercial success, The Glass Menagerie *inspires pathos in the audience by delving into the sad, unfulfilled lives of its main characters. The play examines the danger of romanticism and make-believe while exploding the concept of "Southern charm."*

Principal Characters

Amanda Wingfield, a middle-aged woman and an incurable romantic. Deserted by her husband and forced to live in dreary lower middle-class surroundings, she retreats from reality into the illusory world of her youth. Living for her children, whom she fiercely loves, she nevertheless, by her constant nagging, her endless retelling of romantic stories of her girlhood, and her inability to face life as it is, stifles her daughter, Laura, and drives away her son, Tom.

Tom Wingfield, Amanda's son, through whose memory the story of *The Glass Menagerie* is seen. Professing to literary ambitions, he is trapped by his dreary surroundings, the care of a nagging mother and a crippled sister, and the stifling monotony of a job in a warehouse.

He finally rebels and makes his escape.

Laura Wingfield, the crippled daughter of Amanda Wingfield. So shy that she finds ordinary human relationships almost unbearable, she is totally unequipped for the romantic role in which her mother has cast her. She takes refuge among her glass figurines, the "glass menagerie" that is the symbol of her fragility and her retreat from reality.

Jim O'Connor, a former high school hero whom Laura Wingfield has admired from afar. Working with Tom Wingfield, he is invited to dinner and brings Laura her one moment of confident happiness before the crude but honest Jim tells her that he is engaged to be married.

The Story

This drama of illusion has been much praised for its tenderness, gentleness, and fragile charm. The first of Tennessee Williams' plays to achieve commercial success, it launched him upon a spectacular career in the American theater. Some have claimed that he never again succeeded in regaining the excellence that he attained here and that his subsequent work, popular though it may have been, was anticlimactic.

The action of the drama, involving only four characters, is built around Amanda Wingfield and her effect upon her son and daughter. Infuriating and pathetic by turns, Amanda, an incurable romantic, lives by and for the illusions of her youth, when she was—or thinks she was—the belle of a small Southern town in the Delta region. It is the ghost of this lost past that she constantly conjures up in a pitiful and futile effort to obliterate the grim reality of lower middle-class life in St. Louis. She has been deserted by her husband; she now lives only for her children, for whom she sincerely wants happiness and security. It is the irony of the story, however, that, by her insistent nagging, her endless repetition of anecdotes from her romanticized version of her girlhood, and her inability to face the actualities of her situation, she has crushed her daughter and alienated her son. At one moment, she can envelop herself in exaggerated "Southern charm"; at the next, she can be an unbearable shrew.

Laura, the daughter, is the most pitiable of the three members of the family. A cripple and so abnormally shy that she cannot have even the most ordinary relationships with people, she takes refuge in her "glass menagerie," a collection of small glass animal figurines that symbolizes the fragility of her life and her retreat from reality. She is hopelessly inadequate to play the role of "Southern belle" that her mother wishes her to assume or even to make a marriage that will give her security. She has cared for only one boy during her life—a pompous high school hero. Jim O'Connor is the type, to be found in every school or college, who never in later life measures up to his youthful promise. He is now working in a warehouse, trying hard to "improve himself," but still only a clerk. When Tom, who does not know that his sister had ever known Jim, brings him home to dinner, Laura has her one moment of happiness and her one escape from the world into which she has retreated.

After the dinner that Amanda has produced in a desperate effort to impress him, Jim, in his awkward fashion, does give Laura a flash of self-confidence, enough to enable the audience to see what she might become if she could ever break out of her shell. Too unworldly to handle the situation, she is dazed with happiness when Jim kisses her. Yet Jim, crude as he may be, is fundamentally honest enough to confess that Laura can expect nothing of him, for he is engaged and will be married soon. Therefore, the momentary illusion of happiness collapses around Laura just as the illusion of success collapses around Amanda. It is the final irony of the play that Amanda, who blames the entire catastrophe on her son, drives him from her in their final quarrel with the accusation that he is a dreamer who lives in a world of illusion.

Critical Evaluation

Tom, the frustrated son, is the least successful of the characters, for he is the familiar type of the young man with literary ambitions imprisoned in the deadly monotony of a job in a warehouse. Indeed, with his anguished revolt against his family, his furious outcries against his fate, and his final escape, he seems to have stepped out of a novel by Thomas Wolfe. One can feel desperately sorry for him because he is burdened with the care of a nagging mother and a crippled sister; however, because his inner life and his literary gifts are described rather than seen, he remains unconvincing and shadowy, even though the whole story of the play is seen through his memory.

From the point of view of theatrical technique, the play holds much of interest. Williams uses the long and involved stage directions first made popular by George Bernard Shaw, plus a very elaborate and complicated set of stage devices. The question of the validity of such technical tricks remains an open one. Shaw's use of elaborate stage directions, which all too frequently turned into lengthy and tiresome preachments, succeeded in splitting a play into two aspects: the play as produced, in which these little essays naturally could not appear, and the play as published, in which these comments were extremely important. In the printed version of *The Glass Menagerie*, Williams makes a modified use of this device. His elaborate stage directions comment on the situation as well as give the reader some of the advantages of the spectator.

Williams also employs the device of using Tom as both the narrator of and commentator on the action, somewhat as in the role of a Greek chorus, and as a character in the play. Furthermore, Williams has devised a complicated set of stage effects—rather like the tricks used in a John Dos Passos novel—to point up the mood of his play. The question might well be raised of how legitimate this theatrical sleight of hand may be. Should not dramatists be able to rely on the significance of their fables without calling on so much mechanical ingenuity to get them presented?

Although, in a pantomime scene at the end of the play, Amanda achieves something like dignity as she comforts Laura, it cannot be said that the play reaches the heights of genuine tragedy. The characters, pathetic though they may be, are too shallow, too trivial, to have in them the qualities of tragic greatness. The point has been made that this is a story of "lives of quiet desperation" and that the choice of the 1930's for the setting deliberately contrasts these lives with an increasingly violent world in which illusion can have no place. Perhaps this is part of the human condition of modern times and therefore the only possible subject for a serious dramatist. Yet it remains true that the mood of the play is pathetic, not tragic, and that Williams has created a drama of gentle pathos rather than one of high tragedy.

GO TELL IT ON THE MOUNTAIN

Type of work: Novel
Author: James Baldwin (1924-1987)
Type of plot: Social criticism
Time of plot: March, 1935
Locale: Harlem, New York
First published: 1953

Baldwin examines one day in the life of a young boy—his fourteenth birthday—as well as the pasts, dreams, and obsessions of his mother, his stepfather, and his stepfather's sister. Go Tell It on the Mountain *offers a portrait of religious devotion and shows how it can shape and define identity.*

Principal Characters

John Grimes, a sensitive fourteen-year-old African-American male. John lives in Harlem with his mother, Elizabeth; his stepfather, Gabriel; a half brother, Roy; and two half sisters, Sarah and Ruth. John is consistently oppressed by his self-righteous stepfather. He journeys toward an understanding of self and is initiated into manhood, sex, religion, and the realities of racism in the United States. Physically unattractive and intellectually gifted, John struggles with the preference that his stepfather has for his younger brother, Roy. He has low self-esteem and thinks that he must prove something to the world. John experiences a spiritual awakening and finds direction in his life when he formally dedicates his life to God.

Gabriel Grimes, a former minister and head deacon in the Temple of the Fire Baptized Congregational Church. Gabriel's religious hypocrisy and lustful behavior prove problematic in his early life in the rural South. Gabriel's loveless first marriage is to the barren and undesirable Deborah. Gabriel marries her because of a religious conviction, and his sexual life is unfulfilling; he is led into a series of sexual encounters with Esther. She becomes pregnant with Gabriel's child and migrates north, and she dies shortly after giving birth to her illegitimate son, Royal. Suffering tremendous inner torment, Gabriel does not claim this son, who later dies violently in Chicago. After Deborah's death, Gabriel marries the "hardhearted, stiff-necked, and hard to bend" Elizabeth, John's mother. Gabriel is hardened by his past

life and is inflexible.

Florence, the sixty-year-old sister of Gabriel, Elizabeth's friend. Florence is full of hatred and bitterness for Gabriel. She mocks his ministry and holds him to scorn. Florence believes that her mother always favored the undeserving and sinful Gabriel. Abandoning their mother on her deathbed, Florence leaves the South for New York to start a new life. Her husband, Frank, walks out on her after more than ten years of marriage and exhibits the same sensuality and frailties Gabriel possesses. Florence is tormented by memories of her mother, Gabriel, and Frank; she is also victimized by poor health.

Elizabeth Grimes, Gabriel's wife and the mother of John. She is dark, gentle, and proud, like her father. In her early life, Elizabeth is described as an "unnatural" child. After her mother's death, she is banished from her father at an early age and lives with a strict aunt in Maryland. She never forgives her father for not rescuing her from this oppressive life-style. After meeting and falling in love with Richard, Elizabeth follows him to New York and does menial work to support herself. She is attracted to his nervous courage and has never met a more intelligent man. When Richard is wrongfully accused of a crime, Elizabeth perseveres and finally sees him acquitted, but he commits suicide after experiencing the racism and dehumanization of his life in New York. Devastated by the loss of Richard and already pregnant with John, his son, Elizabeth meets Gabriel, who promises to marry her and to love her and her child.

The Story

Go Tell It on the Mountain portrays the religious conversion of John Grimes and focuses on the prayers of the

"saints"—John's mother, stepfather, and Aunt Florence. The narrative begins with the introduction of the

Grimes family. The young John is oppressed and frustrated by the fire-and-brimstone theology to which his stepfather subscribes. John's religiously structured life-style revolves around serving God and fulfilling his duties to the church. John sees his stepfather as a hypocrite who constantly mistreats and abuses him and does not give love.

It is John's fourteenth birthday, a Saturday, and he is concerned that his day will not be remembered, not even by his mother. John is excited yet reluctant to leave his mother's protection and become fully immersed in the adult world. His stepfather's domination presents a major obstacle in John's spiritual and secular growth. After performing his chores, John is surprised that his mother gives him money for his birthday. With a sense of independence and adventure, John goes to the theater across Sixth Avenue. When John returns home, he discovers that his half brother Roy, Gabriel's favorite, has been injured during a racist gang war. In his fury, Gabriel searches for someone to blame other than Roy. Initially, Gabriel focuses his anger on Elizabeth, and the injured Roy stands up to defend his mother. Gabriel strikes him repeatedly with a belt and, as usual, finds reason to criticize John. John leaves to perform his duties at the church. He meets and confers with Elisha, and during their church service,

John formally dedicates his life to Christ. While the church members begin praying for John, Baldwin recounts the individual supplications by members of John's family.

Florence's prayer begins with memories of her relationship with her mother and her brother Gabriel. She recalls memories of her mother in slavery and her departure from the South in 1900 after her employer had suggested that she become his concubine. Florence conjures memories of her marriage and separation, and she ends with an assessment that God preferred her mother, "the old, black woman," and her brother, "the low black man." Gabriel's prayer painfully depicts his life of struggle against the evils of the flesh. He perseveres as a man of God and demands rigidity in all who profess to be Christians. Gabriel's self-righteousness stems from his struggle with sin. Elizabeth's prayer chronicles rejections of her love by significant others in her life. After losing her father and Richard, she accepts a deplorable existence with Gabriel and dedicates her life to God.

The novel's conclusion provides resolution, as John has been converted before the altar and has hope for salvation. He understands societal pressures and the role that religion plays in his life.

Critical Evaluation

Go Tell It on the Mountain is divided into three sections: "The Seventh Day," "The Prayers of the Saints," and "The Threshing Floor." "The Seventh Day" introduces the Grimes family, highlighting their staunchly religious life-style. "The Prayers of the Saints" presents introspective flashbacks that provide the religious context for John's present situation and relationships. "The Threshing Floor" provides the resolution and presents John's dedication to a life of spiritual faith and commitment.

The historical context for John's quest for identity is also his ancestral past: the life stories of Gabriel, Florence, and Elizabeth. The narrative is a *Bildungsroman*, an explication of John's rites of passage. To proceed in his life, John must confront the humiliation and pain that are a part of his heritage. He must formulate his own secular and religious codes.

Biblical allusions abound and set the stage for the major conflict between John, his father, and the other characters in the novel. *Go Tell It on the Mountain* reveals the schizophrenia of the African-American experience with the Christian religion: Whites utilized it to convert and

enslave African Americans, and it also served as a temporary anesthesia for the masses. Christianity served as a means of keeping African Americans insensitive to the oppressions in their temporal lives and hopeful for an afterlife of joy and freedom.

"The Seventh Day" alludes to the biblical Creation story and to the holiness of the Sabbath in Mosaic law. Most of the names of the characters have biblical significance, and the title of the novel itself evokes the Christian hymn with the same name. Ultimately, it connotes the announcement that Jesus was born to suffer and die for humankind. The numerous allusions in the novel illustrate the universal as well as the African-American condition, suggesting that life's journey is beset with dangers and pitfalls but that salvation is at the end of the journey.

Baldwin's emphasis is on character rather than plot, and his four major characters are psychological case studies. John serves as the emotional center of the novel, for his life is affected by the experiences of all the other characters. John's stepfather is complex; Gabriel had once led revival meetings and had a great reputation, but his reputation had been lost since he left the South. Gabriel becomes only a caretaker, responsible for replacing light-bulbs, caring for hymn books and Bibles, and cleaning the church. He is reduced to a "fill-in speaker or holy handyman."

In "The Prayers of the Saints," Gabriel, Florence, and Elizabeth unsuccessfully attempt to win salvation; Baldwin reveals the human frailties that plague them. Gabriel lacks humility, is self-righteous, and cannot give love to John; Florence cannot forgive Gabriel's sinfulness; and Elizabeth is undone by her love for Richard.

Baldwin's masterful use of metaphors and similes, finely tuned poetic diction and rhythm, juxtaposition of physical and psychological loss, and precisely balanced sentences combine to solidify his brilliant achievement. By the end of the novel, John Grimes has become a man and has confronted the obstacles of his racial and spiritual bondage.

Baldwin's own experiences as a preacher at the Fire-side Pentecostal Assembly form the basis for *Go Tell It on the Mountain.* Clearly autobiographical, the novel addresses Baldwin's discovery that religion was inadequate to solve the problems of African Americans.

The publication of *Go Tell It on the Mountain* when Baldwin was twenty-nine years old marked his emergence as a major American writer and social commentator. Baldwin believed that writing was a public act and that art could effect social change. His artistry documents the dilemma of African Americans in American society.

The reception of *Go Tell It on the Mountain* helped Baldwin to acquire a Guggenheim grant, which he used to begin work on another project. Critics generally received the book as a brilliant first novel, and its publication placed Baldwin in the ranks of the country's best-known African-American writers, alongside Richard Wright, Ralph Ellison, and Langston Hughes. A public-television adaptation of the novel was aired in January, 1985.

THE GOLDEN BOWL

Type of work: Novel
Author: Henry James (1843-1916)
Type of plot: Psychological realism
Time of plot: c. 1900
Locale: England and the Continent
First published: 1904

This novel, which was a forerunner of modern expressionism in literature, chronicles the subtleties of the minds of cultured people. The characters are shut off in a world of their own, a world that will not tolerate crudities.

Principal Characters

Maggie Verver, the motherless daughter of an American millionaire. For a number of years, the Ververs have spent much of their time abroad, where Mr. Verver has devoted himself to acquiring a magnificent art collection for the museum that he plans to build in American City. Sharing her father's quiet tastes and aesthetic interests, Maggie has become his faithful companion, and they have created for themselves a separate, enclosed world of ease, grace, and discriminating appreciation, a connoisseurship of life as well as of art. Even Maggie's marriage to Prince Amerigo, an Italian of ancient family, does not change greatly the pattern of their lives, a pattern that she believes complete when Mr. Verver marries her best friend, Charlotte Stant. What Maggie does not know is the fact that before her marriage the Prince and Charlotte, both moneyless and therefore unable to marry, had been lovers. Several years later the Prince, bored by his position as another item in the Verver collection, and Charlotte, restless because she takes second place beside her elderly husband's interest in art, resume their former intimacy. Maggie finds her happiness threatened when her purchase of a flawed gold-and-crystal bowl leads indirectly to her discovery of the true situation. Her problem is whether to disclose or conceal her knowledge. Deeply in love with her husband and devoted to her father, she decides to remain silent. Her passivity becomes an act of drama because it involves a sense of ethical responsibility and a moral decision; her predicament is the familiar Jamesian spectacle of the innocent American confronting the evil of European morality, in this case complicated by Maggie's realization that she and her father are not without guilt, that they have lived too much for themselves. In the end, her generosity, tact, and love resolve all difficulties. Mr. Verver and his wife leave for the United States, and Maggie regains her husband's love, now unselfishly offered.

Prince Amerigo, a young Italian nobleman, handsome, gallant, sensual, living in England with his American wife. A man of politely easy manners, he is able to mask his real feelings under an appearance of courteous reserve. Though he has loved many women, he has little capacity for lies or deception in his dealings with them; he objects when Charlotte Stant, his former mistress, wishes to purchase a flawed golden bowl as a wedding gift to his wife, for he wants nothing but perfection in his marriage. He and Charlotte are often thrown together after she marries his father-in-law, and they become lovers once more. When his wife learns, through the purchase of the same flawed bowl, the secret of his infidelity, he tries to be loyal to all parties concerned, and he so beautifully preserves the delicate harmony of family relationships that no outsiders except their mutual friends, the Assinghams, know of the situation. Maggie, his wife, is able to save her marriage because his delicacy in the matter of purchased and purchasable partners makes tense situations easier. After Mr. Verver and his wife return to the United States, the Prince shows relief as unselfish as it is sincere; their departure allows him to be a husband and a father in his own right.

Charlotte Stant, the beautiful but impecunious American girl who needs a wealthy husband to provide the fine clothes and beautiful things that she believes necessary for her happiness. Because Prince Amerigo is poor, she becomes his mistress but never considers marrying him. After the Prince's marriage to Maggie Verver, her best friend, Mr. Verver proposes to Charlotte. She accepts him and, though Mr. Verver cannot understand her claim of unworthiness, declares herself prepared to be as devoted as possible, both as a wife and as a stepmother to her good friend. Often left in the Prince's company while Maggie and her father pursue their interest in art, however, she resumes her affair with her former lover. When the truth is finally revealed, Charlotte, determined to prove her loyalties to all concerned, persuades Mr. Verver to return with her to the United States. Her poised and gracious farewell to Maggie and the Prince is more than a demonstration of her ability to keep up appearances; it shows the code of responsibility that she has assumed toward her lover, her friend, and her husband.

Adam Verver, a rich American who has given over the pursuit of money in order to achieve the good life for himself and his daughter, Maggie. In his innocence, he believes that this end may be attained by seeing and collecting the beautiful art objects of Europe. A perfect father, he cannot realize that there is anything selfish in the close tie that exists between himself and his daughter, and he tries to stand in the same relationship with his son-in-law, Prince Amerigo, and Charlotte Stant, his daughter's friend, whom he marries. All he really lives for is to provide for Maggie and his grandson the life of happiness and plenty that he envisions for them. When he finally realizes that the pattern of his life has been a form of make-believe, he sacrifices his own peace of mind and agrees to return with his wife to make the United States his permanent home.

Fanny Assingham, the friend of Maggie and Adam Verver, Prince Amerigo, and Charlotte Stant, and the guardian angel of their secret lives. As one who senses the rightness of things, she helps to bring about both marriages with a sensitive understanding of the needs of all, a delicacy that she will not allow to be disrupted by Maggie's discovery of her husband's infidelity. Her belief is that even wickedness is more to be condoned than wrongness of heart. She helps to resolve the situation between Maggie and Prince Amerigo when she hurls the golden bowl, the symbol of Maggie's flawed marriage and the Prince's guilt, to the floor and smashes it.

Colonel Robert Assingham, called **Bob,** a retired army officer who understands his wife's motives in the interest she takes in the Verver family but who manages to keep himself detached from her complicated dealings with the lives of others.

The Principino, the small son of Prince Amerigo and his wife, Maggie.

The Story

Maggie Verver was the daughter of a wealthy American widower who had devoted all of his life to his daughter. The Ververs lived a lazy life; their time was spent in collecting items to decorate their own existence and to fill a museum that Mr. Adam Verver was giving to his native city back in the United States. They had few friends. Maggie's only confidante was Mrs. Fanny Assingham, the American-born wife of a retired British army officer.

It was Mrs. Assingham who introduced the Ververs to Prince Amerigo, a handsome, quiet young Italian nobleman who struck Maggie's fancy. When she informed her father that she would like to marry the Prince, Mr. Verver provided a handsome dowry so that the wedding might take place.

A few days before the wedding, a painful scene occurred in Mrs. Assingham's home, where the Prince and Charlotte Stant, deeply in love with each other, met to say goodbye. Each was penniless, and a marriage had been out of the question. Since both were friends of Maggie, the present situation was exceptionally difficult for them. As a farewell lark, they spent the last afternoon searching for a wedding present for Charlotte to present to Maggie. In a tiny shop, they discovered a golden bowl that Charlotte wished to purchase as a remembrance for the Prince from her. He refused it because of superstitious fears that a crack in the golden bowl might bring bad luck.

After the wedding of the Prince and Maggie, the lives of the pair coincided with the life that the Ververs had been living for years. Maggie and her father spent much of their time together. The Prince, although he did not complain, was really only a convenience that they had purchased because Maggie had reached the age when she needed to have a husband.

After a year and a half, a baby was born to the Prince and Maggie, but the child made no apparent difference in the relationships between the woman and her father or the woman and her husband. Maggie decided that her father also needed a wife. She went to Mrs. Assingham and told her friend that she planned to have Charlotte Stant marry her father. Charlotte was a quiet person aware of the love between Maggie and her father, and she was the sort of person who would be so thankful to marry a wealthy man that she would cause little trouble. Neither Maggie nor Mrs. Assingham put this aspect into words, but it was tacitly understood.

Mr. Verver, anxious to please his daughter in this as in everything else, married Charlotte a short time later. This second marriage created a strange situation. Maggie and her father both took houses in London, where they could be together much of the time. The association of father and daughter often left the Prince and Charlotte together. Maggie encouraged them to go out and to represent her and her father at balls and dinners. Maggie did not know, however, that her husband and her stepmother had been intimate before her own marriage to the Prince.

Several years went by in this manner, but slowly the fact that there was something strange in the relationships dawned upon Maggie's sensitive feelings. She eventually went to Mrs. Assingham and poured out her suspicions to her. Yet Mrs. Assingham, in full knowledge of the circumstances, decided to keep her silence.

Maggie resolved to say nothing of her suspicions to anyone else. Nevertheless, her attitude of indifference, her insistence in throwing the Prince and Charlotte together, aroused their suspicions that she knew they had been sweethearts, that she suspected them of being lovers after marriage.

Each one of the four speculated at length as to what the other three knew or suspected. Yet their mutual confidence and love prevented each one of them from ever asking anything of the others.

One day, Maggie went shopping for some unusual art object to present to her father on his birthday. She accidentally happened into the same shop where the Prince and Charlotte had gone several years before, and she purchased the golden bowl that they had passed over because of its flaw. The following day, the shopkeeper visited her. The name and address had told him that she was the wife of the prince who had passed up the bowl years before. He knew that the existence of the crack would quickly come to the attention of the Prince, and so he had hastened to inform Maggie of the flaw and to return part of the purchase price. He also told her of the Prince's first visit to the shop and of the young woman who had been with him. Maggie then knew that the Prince and Charlotte had known each other before her marriage and that they had spent an afternoon together the day before she was married. She was upset and again confided in Mrs. Assingham.

Having learned that there was no serious relationship between the Prince and Charlotte, Mrs. Assingham informed Maggie that she was making a great ado over nothing at all. To point up her remark, she raised the bowl above her head and smashed it to the floor, where it broke into several pieces. As she did so, the Prince entered the room and saw the fragments of the bowl. After Mrs. Assingham's departure, he tried to learn how much Maggie knew. Maggie and her husband agreed to say nothing to either Maggie's father or to Charlotte.

Charlotte, too, began to sense that something had disturbed Maggie, and she shrewdly guessed what it was. Then Maggie tried to realign the relationships of the four by proposing that she and Charlotte stay together for awhile and that the Prince and her father go to the Continent to buy art objects. This proposal was gently put forward and as gently rebuffed by the other three.

Maggie and her father began to realize their selfishness in trying to keep up the father-daughter relationship that they had enjoyed before her marriage. Shortly after that selfishness had been brought into the open and discussed by Maggie and Mr. Verver, Charlotte told Maggie that she wished to return to the United States and to take her husband with her. She bluntly informed Maggie that she was afraid that, if Mr. Verver continued to live so close to his daughter, then he would lose interest in his wife. Mr. Verver agreed to accompany Charlotte back to the United States. It was a difficult decision for him to make: He realized that, once he was away, Charlotte would never agree to his coming back to Europe to live.

On an autumn afternoon, Mr. Verver and Charlotte went to have tea with Maggie and the Prince before leaving England. It was almost heartbreaking to Maggie to see her father's carriage take him out of sight and to know that her old way of life was really ended. The only thing that kept her from breaking down completely was the look on the Prince's face as he turned her face away from the direction that her father's carriage had taken. At that moment, seeing his eyes, Maggie knew that she had won her husband for herself and not for her money.

Critical Evaluation

The Golden Bowl, along with *The Wings of the Dove* (1902) and *The Ambassadors* (1903), is one of the novels of the triad of works upon which the high reputation of James's "major phase" rests. In these novels, James's already complex style reaches new levels of sophistication as, increasingly, the writing becomes more and more intricate and convoluted as it tends toward ever-increasingly subtle levels of analysis of character and event. Gradually the "center of consciousness" in the mind of a character, which had been essential to James's earlier works, gives way to an omniscient narrative point of view and to a narrative voice that is James's own. Though it hardly appears so to the eye, James's style of this period is essentially oral—he had developed the habit of dictating his material to a secretary—and reflects his characteristically ponderous manner of speech. Seeming to move endlessly to circle or enfold a subject or an idea without ever touching it directly, James's language and technique in these late novels has been admired highly by critics who place a premium on style, while frequently being disparaged by those who stress content and clarity of thought. For James himself, the art of the novel was everything in writing, and there is little doubt that in *The Golden Bowl* his artistry reached a peak.

With this novel, James continues the subject matter of the "international theme" that had characterized his work from its beginning by dealing with a group of Americans in Europe. Adam Verver, in particular, can be seen as an avatar of the American Adam who recurs in James's fiction, often, as here, in search of European culture that he will take back to his culturally barren homeland. Prince Amerigo is linked by his name to the historic connection between America and Europe, and, by his marriage to Maggie, might be seen as dramatizing a new dependence of the Old World upon the New. Yet, *The Golden Bowl* ultimately is less an international novel than such works as *The American* (1876-1877), *Daisy Miller* (1878), or *The Ambassadors* because its concerns are finally more with individuals than with cultures. Though the Ververs begin in the United States and Adam returns there at the novel's end, neither his experience nor that of Maggie or Charlotte is essentially contingent upon the sort of conflict of cultural values that is at the heart of James's international novels and stories. Rather, the problems of love and marriage at the heart of *The Golden Bowl* are truly universal, with neither their nature nor their solution dependent upon an American perspective.

Like many of James's works, *The Golden Bowl* began in his notebooks with the recording of an anecdote that he had heard concerning a young woman and her widower father, each of whom had taken spouses, who learned that their partners were engaged in an affair. From this scant beginning, James crafted his longest and most elaborate novel not by greatly complicating the essential material of this simple plot, but by scrupulous elaboration of the conflicts and resolutions resulting from the complex relations among his four central characters. By making his characters members of the wealthy leisure class, James frees them from the mundane worries of the world so he can focus his, and their, entire attention on the one particular problem without regard to external complications. Ultimately, the novel seeks to pose moral and philosophical questions that transcend either the psychological or the social levels of the work to confront the basic question of Maggie's adjustment to a less-than-perfect world.

The golden bowl is James's metaphor for the marriage between Amerigo and Maggie, and perhaps, in its larger implications, for life itself. The bowl, not really "golden" but crystal gilded with gold leaf, has the superficial appearance of perfection but is, in fact, cracked. As a symbol of Maggie's "perfect" marriage, the bowl very clearly illustrates the flaw at the heart of the relationship—a flaw that no doubt existed even before the Prince and Charlotte resume their old love affair and that represents a potential threat to the marriage. Both Maggie and her father are guilty of treating the Prince as nothing more than one of the valuable objects that they have come to Europe to purchase—they have bought the perfect marriage for Maggie. Unlike art, however, human relationships are not subject to purchase, nor can they, as in the case of Adam's marriage to Charlotte, be arranged for convenience without regard to the human factors concerned. In fact, both Maggie and her father tend to live in a small, supremely selfish world. Insulated by their money from the actuality of life, they isolate themselves from the real complexities of daily existence. Their world itself is, in effect, more "art" than "life."

The resolution of the novel turns around Maggie's positive act, but in the earlier parts of the novel, she is more passive than active. The marriage itself, for example, seems more of an arrangement between the Prince and Adam Verver than a particular choice of Maggie's: Adam wants the perfect marriage for his daughter, and Prince Amerigo wants access to the Verver millions, so they come to an agreement between themselves. Maggie apparently has little to say about it, and even, judging from her relationship with the Prince throughout most of the novel, no very great interest in the marriage. Her real desire seems to be to continue life with her father as always, rather than to begin an independent life with her husband. Only when confronted with the Prince's infidelity does Maggie recognize that she must confront this reality for all their sakes. In choosing to separate from her father in order to begin making the best of her imperfect marriage, Maggie discovers a latent ability to confront the world as it really is, to rise above the romantic idealism that had characterized her life with her father.

GOLDEN BOY

Type of work: Drama
Author: Clifford Odets (1906-1963)
Type of plot: Social allegory
Time of plot: 1930's
Locale: New York
First presented: 1937

Golden Boy was described by Odets as an allegory, and some of the individual scenes and much of the dialogue represent him at his best. Dealing with a young Italian violinist who becomes a prizefighter in order to gain money and fame, the fable reflects the fight of every individual for a place in the world.

Principal Characters

Joe Bonaparte, a young violinist who becomes a prizefighter. At heart a musician, he has been laughed at and hurt by people against whom he longs to fight back. The fame and money gained in the ring make retaliation possible but brutalize Joe and change his personality. He falls in love with Lorna Moon, who finally persuades him to give up the ring. That night, they are both killed in an automobile accident.

Tom Moody, Joe Bonaparte's fight manager and part owner.

Lorna Moon, Tom Moody's mistress. Asked by Joe Bonaparte's father to help the fighter find himself, she falls in love with Joe but believes that she cannot give up

Tom Moody, whose wife has at last consented to a divorce so that he can marry her. Finally, in Joe's dressing room after a triumphant fight, she tells him again that she loves him and persuades him to leave the ring. She is killed with him that night in an automobile accident.

Mr. Bonaparte, Joe Bonaparte's father. Hoping that Joe will give up fighting and return to music, he refuses the parental blessing on Joe's career until he sorrowfully sees that his son is totally committed to the ring. When Joe is killed, he claims the body and brings the boy home where he belongs.

Eddie Fuseli, a gambler and part owner of Joe Bonaparte.

The Story

Tom Moody, a fight manager, and Lorna Moon, his mistress who wanted to marry him, were having an argument about Tom's wife, who would not give him a divorce. Tom, wanting money for the divorce, needed to find a winning fighter. While they were talking, Joe Bonaparte arrived to tell them that Moody's fighter had broken his hand and could not fight that night. Joe, whom nobody knew, persuaded them to let him substitute, and he won.

Joe, a musician, had always wanted a good violin, and his father had bought him one for his twenty-first birthday. When Joe returned home, his father, who had not been told of the fight, had read of it in the papers and was very much distressed. He tried to persuade Joe to give up fighting and continue his study of music, but Joe wanted to fight. His father, hurt, did not give him the violin.

Joe fought well after that, but there was a serious con-

flict between the sensitive musician that he truly was and the brutal fighter that he had to be. He held back in the ring, fearing that he would ruin his hands for the violin. When Moody tried to persuade him that fame and money would be more important than music, he succeeded only in antagonizing Joe, who threatened to quit. Lorna agreed to try to persuade Joe to reconsider. Joe was basically a musician, but he had been laughed at and hurt by people. Fighting was not a part of his nature, but he wanted to fight back and music could not do that for him. While he was explaining all this to Lorna, he had already decided to remain in the ring.

When Joe was preparing for a fight tour, Mr. Bonaparte asked Lorna to help the young man find himself. When he tried to give Joe the violin, the son refused it. Then he asked for a blessing, which his father refused to give.

Joe's tour was a great success, except for one fight.

He had not fought well on that occasion because he had seen a man with a violin and was reminded of his music. Moody realized that Joe had to be prevented from having any contact with his family and his past.

The fight world changed Joe's personality: Liking the money and the notoriety, he bought a Duesenberg, which he drove recklessly, and became difficult to manage. Eddie Fuseli, a gambler and a gunman, wanted to buy a piece of Joe, and Joe agreed, to Moody's displeasure. He told Lorna to take care of Joe in her own way.

Joe fell in love with Lorna and asked her to give up Moody. She denied loving Joe and said that she could not leave Moody because she felt sorry for him. Joe knew that she was not telling the truth when she began to cry. They talked about their love, and Joe demanded that she tell Moody at once. Lorna said that she would, but when she went to tell him, she learned that his wife had agreed to a divorce and that they could be married in a few months. With this knowledge, she was unable to tell him about her love for Joe. Later, Joe had an argument with Moody and demanded that Lorna tell Moody about their love. Although Lorna denied that there was anything between them, she confessed the truth to Moody when they were alone again.

One night, Mr. Bonaparte came to see Joe fight. Fuseli was disturbed because he did not want Joe to see his father, but Joe saw him anyway. He also saw Moody and Lorna together. Mr. Bonaparte, realizing that Joe had completely changed, finally gave his blessing to his son's career, and Joe cried after his father left. During the fight, Mr. Bonaparte went back into the dressing room rather than see the fighters hurt each other. Joe returned after he had won the fight, but when his trainer attempted to remove the gloves, Joe told him that he would have to cut one of them off. His hand was broken.

Now that he could never be a musician, Joe was all fighter. Moody and Lorna announced that they were getting married in a few days. Because Joe was still in love with Lorna, it was obvious that his unhappiness was hurting his career. While Joe was fighting badly in his most important match, Fuseli blamed Lorna and threatened to kill her. Nevertheless, Joe returned to the dressing room a victor. A few moments later, they were all told that the other fighter had died after being floored by Joe's knockout punch. Everyone left the dressing room except Lorna and Joe. She told him that she loved him and asked him to go back to his music. He showed her his mutilated hands. He decided to give up fighting, however, and he and Lorna went for a wild ride in order to celebrate.

Fuseli, Moody, and the others, not knowing where Joe and Lorna had gone, went to Joe's home and drank and talked while they waited for his return. The telephone rang in the middle of an argument to decide who would own Joe in the future. Joe and Lorna had been killed in an automobile accident. Mr. Bonaparte left to claim Joe's body and to bring him home where he belonged.

Critical Evaluation

Odets is generally regarded as the most talented playwright to emerge from the Depression generation. In his mid-twenties, he became one of the founders of the Group Theatre, the most exciting and innovative American theater of the period, and was its dominating playwright. In the spirit of the times, Odets quickly established himself as a volatile political dramatist with such intense theatrical statements as *Waiting for Lefty* (1935), *Till the Day I Die* (1935), *Awake and Sing!* (1935), and *Paradise Lost* (1935). Although admitting that *Golden Boy* was consciously written "to be a hit" and to shore up the sagging finances of the Group Theatre, Odets insisted that it, too, was an anticapitalistic social play. To a modern audience, however, the personal tragedy of Joe Bonaparte is the most important concern of the drama.

In essence, *Golden Boy* is a variation on the old Faustian theme of a man who sells himself for success and discovers, too late, that he has made a bad bargain. A poor Italian youth coming of age in the middle of the Great Depression, Joe knows that he can find personal satisfaction playing the violin, but the bitterness in his feelings of poverty, coupled with a desire for revenge against people who have scorned him for years, drives him into opting for the fist instead of the fiddle.

At first, he boxes gingerly, trying to protect his hands for his music, but by the end of the first act, he no longer cares. The balance of the play is devoted to showing how this decision corrupts and destroys him. The question of whether it is a social or a personal play probably depends on whether one interprets Joe's decision as resulting from indvidual weakness or social pressure. Once he makes his decision, however, there is no doubt that the ethics of success that he embraces are totally self-destructive.

In the earliest version of the play, Odets subtitled it an allegory, and, as such, it almost resembles a morality play. Embodiments of Good and Evil contend for Joe's "soul," although these other characters are, for the most part, also the victims of conflicting needs and values.

The positive moral forces in the story are represented by old Mr. Bonaparte, a fruit peddler, who encourages Joe's violin playing and is horrified by what he sees in the boxing business; Joe's brother, Frank, a labor organizer, who represents the right kind of militant, one who fights for the things he believes in; and Joe's trainer, Tokio, who, although a part of the fighting business, is a sensitive man who understand's Joe's needs and tries to help him find himself.

Yet Joe cannot take good advice. He must find things out for himself, and when he does, he has gone too far and it is too late. He rejects his real father and accepts Eddie Fuseli, the gangster-gambler, as his model. Joe emulates Fuseli's taste in clothing, goals, and values, and, only at the end of the play, realizes that Fuseli owns him, literally as well as professionally.

Success has done nothing to soften the hatred in Joe, and it is this unleashed hostility that destroys him. He hits his last opponent, the Chocolate Drop, with all his might and kills him. In doing so, Joe finally realizes that he has killed himself as well. No longer able to fight and ruined for the violin, he commits suicide, either consciously or unconsciously, in the most appropriate way: by crashing his Duesenberg, a symbol of materialism and speed, in the company of Lorna Moon, the good-bad girl who shares his confusion of values.

GONE WITH THE WIND

Type of work: Novel
Author: Margaret Mitchell (1900-1949)
Type of plot: Historical romance
Time of plot: 1861-1873
Locale: Atlanta and Tara Plantation, Georgia
First published: 1936

With Scarlett O'Hara, Mitchell created a larger-than-life character that captured the public imagination. Yet, Gone with the Wind *is more than a portrait of one woman or of the South during the Civil War and Reconstruction: The novel dramatizes the universal struggle to survive and the difficulty of coming to grips with the true meanings of love and idealism.*

Principal Characters

Scarlett O'Hara, a Georgia belle. Gently reared on Tara plantation and the wife of Charles Hamilton, she finds herself, through the fortunes of war, a widow and the mistress of a ruined plantation with a family to feed. With an indomitable will to survive and an unquenchable determination to keep Tara, she improves her fortunes with the aid of her own native abilities and opportunistic marriages to Frank Kennedy and Rhett Butler.

Ashley Wilkes, Scarlett O'Hara's sensitive, sophisticated neighbor, with whom she fancies herself in love until, through adversity, he is shorn of the aura of romance with which she has endowed him and shows himself for the weakling that he is.

Rhett Butler, a cynical, wealthy blockade runner, Scarlett O'Hara's third husband. Knowing Scarlett for the unscrupulous materialist that she is, he nevertheless admires her will to survive. He is plagued with a love for her that he finally overcomes just as she discovers that it is he and not Ashley Wilkes that she loves.

Charles Hamilton, Scarlett's first husband, whom she marries for spite.

Frank Kennedy, Scarlett's second husband, whom she marries for money.

Melanie (Hamilton) Wilkes, Ashley Wilkes' reticent, ladylike wife.

Gerald O'Hara and **Ellen O'Hara,** Scarlett's parents.

Bonnie Blue Butler, the daughter of Scarlett O'Hara and Rhett Butler.

Suellen O'Hara, Scarlett's sister.

Miss Pittypat, Melanie Wilkes' aunt.

India Wilkes, Ashley Wilkes' sister.

Mammy, Scarlett's nurse.

Gone with the Wind, one of the best-selling novels of all time, is the story of the subjugation of a proud people by war and the harsh "reconstruction" that followed. Swept along with these events is the beautiful, headstrong daughter of a wealthy plantation owner who, when reduced to poverty and hardship in the wake of General William Tecumseh Sherman's cruel and vicious destruction of the countryside, used her feminine wiles to regain her lost wealth. Having at last attained this goal, she was unable to hold the one man she really loved.

A historical romance of prodigious proportions, this first novel by an unknown author went through twelve printings within two months of publication. Its thousand pages enthralled millions, the sales in a single year exceeding two million copies. The novel has been translated into more than two dozen languages and even after decades, sales continue at a pace brisk enough to please any publisher. The 1939 motion picture adaptation lived up to Hollywood's most studied superlatives.

The unprecedented success of Margaret Mitchell's only novel may be attributed to a combination of the author's style—a sustained narrative power combined with remarkable character delineation—and the universality of her subject, the struggle for survival when the accustomed security of civilized life is abruptly swept away and the human spirit suddenly stands alone. In spite of the fast-moving narrative, one is aware of this underlying thread of universality, this familiarity with human tragedy that all people can understand.

Perhaps the most lasting impression one gets from the novel, however, is the skill with which Mitchell handles her characterizations. Scarlett O'Hara is, without question, one of the memorable characters in fiction. So lifelike did she become in the public mind that the producers of the motion picture preferred not to risk an established actress in the role and be accused of miscasting; they sent to England for a relatively unknown young actress to portray the fire and passion flashing from the tempestuous Scarlett.

The story of Scarlett O'Hara alone would be reason enough for a best-seller; many books have achieved such eminence on far less. This daughter of Irish temper and French sensibilities displays stark and bold emotions that grip the reader. One follows her intense, futile love for Ashley Wilkes, her spiteful marriage to Charles Hamilton, her opportunistic stealing of her sister's fiancé Frank Kennedy, her grasping arrangement of convenience with Rhett Butler. The reader is sometimes appalled at her callous use of her sexuality to gain her ends, looking in vain for some sign of lofty ideals in this woman. Yet, in spite of all this, one finds laudable her will to survive and her contempt for her conquerors.

Three other characters stand out, admirably drawn but not quite inspiring the amount of interest created by Scarlett. Rhett Butler, dissolute son of Charleston blue bloods, is a cynical, materialistic blockade runner who consorts openly with the enemy and scoffs at patriotic ideals. Forceful and masculine, he is accustomed to taking what he wants. His one unfulfilled desire is the love of Scarlett, and this frustration finally breaks his spirit. When at last, after several years of unhappy marriage, he gains her love as Ashley defaults, Rhett, now a bitter, fleshy drunkard, has already reached his decision to leave her.

Ashley Wilkes, the weak-willed object of Scarlett's misguided passion, depicts the impractical idealist dependent on a stronger will to solve life's problems for him. When Scarlett observes his unstable reaction to his wife's death, she is finally able to see him as he really is. Shorn of his cavalier manners and the aura of courtly romance that she had bestowed upon him, he becomes in her eyes an ineffectual weakling, and the sterility of her forbidden love is at last apparent.

Melanie, in a way the winner despite her death at the end of the novel, finds happiness and tranquility in her devotion to her insecure husband. She is reticent, ladylike, saccharine, but intellectually attuned to Ashley; there is never any question that Melanie, not Scarlett, should be Ashley's wife.

High-spirited Scarlett was sixteen when the Civil War began. She fancied herself in love with Ashley Wilkes, the sensitive, sophisticated son at a neighboring plantation, but he did not acknowledge her love. Upon the announcement of his engagement to his soft-spoken cousin Melanie Hamilton, Scarlett impetuously married Melanie's brother Charles, to that surprised young man's pride and delight. Less than a year later Scarlett was a war widow and an unwilling mother.

Here the novel loses the tempo of leisurely plantation life and takes on the urgency of a region at war. Leaving her father's plantation, Tara, Scarlett traveled twenty-five miles to Atlanta to stay with her dead husband's relatives. Later, as Atlanta was besieged by Sherman's troops, Scarlett returned home to Tara through the battle lines at night in a wagon provided by Rhett. With her were Melanie and Ashley's day-old son, whom Scarlett had delivered as guns sounded in the distance.

Approaching Tara through the battle-scarred countryside, she saw that most of the plantation mansions had been looted and burned by the enemy. Tara had been spared as a headquarters, though the outbuildings and baled cotton had been burned and the hogs, cows, and chickens killed. Scarlett's mother, too ill with fever to be moved as the soldiers approached, died with her beloved Tara filled with Yankee conquerors. Her father's mind, unable to stand these shocks, was gone. Now the sheltered Southern belle was faced with the formidable prospect of feeding, from a plantation stripped bare by the ruthless invaders, her father, her child, two sisters, Melanie, and the few servants who remained faithfully behind when the others ran off.

These are the events that helped to shape the character of Scarlett O'Hara, and they explain the hardness, the avarice, that prompted many of her actions. For example, when the carpetbaggers arbitrarily levied an extra three-hundred-dollar tax on Tara with the expectation of taking over the property for unpaid taxes, Scarlett unhesitatingly married storeowner Frank Kennedy, who was engaged to her sister Suellen; he dutifully paid the tax.

The art of Mitchell makes such reprehensible acts seem normal under the circumstances, for the author has skillfully brought her readers along the same harsh road Scarlett has traveled. Being thus exposed to the same experiences, one understands, even condones, Scarlett's responses.

Once Scarlett had learned the law of the jungle, her native abilities came into their own. Borrowing money from Rhett, she bought and operated successfully a sawmill and soon was financially secure. When Frank was killed by occupation troops, she married Rhett, who had amassed half a million dollars during the war as a blockade runner. Yet even the birth of a child, Bonnie Blue, did not bring happiness to this union because of the love for Ashley to which Scarlett absurdly clung. Rhett, always jealous of this will-o'-the-wisp emotion, was unable to cope with what he could not understand. Ironically, Rhett overcame his love for Scarlett just as she was discovering that it was he, not Ashley, whom she loved. When she tried to tell him this, Rhett announced brusquely that she was too late, that he was leaving her forever. There was no mistaking the finality of his words but, characteristically, Scarlett, the self-confident schemer, would not accept them as such.

Gone with the Wind is not a happy book. There are flickers of humor, but for the most part a deadly seriousness pervades the novel. In the end, the callous, grasping cynicism of the leading characters mocks them and, properly, only an empty loneliness remains.

A natural question concerns the position of *Gone with the Wind* and its author in world literature. On the strength of her one novel, Mitchell certainly cannot be called a great author. If her outstanding book ranks as a great novel, however, it is because Scarlett O'Hara continues to convey to readers a certain essence of human behavior.

THE GRAPES OF WRATH

Type of work: Novel
Author: John Steinbeck (1902-1968)
Type of plot: Social criticism
Time of plot: 1930's
Locale: Southwest United States and California
First published: 1939

A bitter chronicle of the exodus of farm families from the Dust Bowl during the 1930's, this work is a harsh indictment of the United States' capitalistic economy. Searching for work in California, the Joads begin their long journey. Treated like enemies by the businessmen along their path, the older members of the family die, and those remaining are herded into migrant camps where the poor help one another to survive.

Principal Characters

Tom Joad, Jr., a former convict. Returning to his home in Oklahoma after serving time in the penitentiary for killing a man in self-defense, he finds the house deserted, the family having been pushed off the land because of dust bowl conditions and in order to make way for more mechanized farming. With Casy, the preacher, he finds his family and makes the trek to California in search of work. During labor difficulties Tom kills another man when his friend Casy, who is trying to help the migrant workers in their labor problems, is brutally killed by deputies representing the law and the owners. He leaves his family because, as a "wanted" man, he is a danger to them, but he leaves with a new understanding which he has learned from Casy; it is no longer the individual that counts but the group. Tom promises to carry on Casy's work of helping the downtrodden.

Tom Joad, Sr., called **Pa,** an Oklahoma farmer who finds it difficult to adjust to new conditions while moving his family to California.

Ma Joad, a large, heavy woman, full of determination and hope, who fights to hold her family together. On the journey to California, she gradually becomes the staying power of the family.

Rose of Sharon Rivers, called **Rosasharn,** the married, teenage daughter of the Joads. Her husband leaves her, and she bears a stillborn baby because of the hardships she endures. As the story ends, she gives her own milk to save the life of a starving man.

Noah, the slow-witted second son of the Joads. He finally wanders off down a river when the pressures of the journey and his hunger become too much.

Al, the third son of the Joads. In his teens, he is interested in girls and automobiles. He idolizes his brother Tom.

Ruthie, the preteen daughter of the Joads.

Winfield, the youngest of the Joads.

Uncle John, the brother of Tom Joad, Sr. He is a lost soul who periodically is flooded with guilt because he let his young wife die by ignoring her illness.

Grampa Joad, who does not want to leave Oklahoma and dies on the way to California. He is buried with little ceremony by the roadside.

Granma Joad, also old and childish. She dies while crossing the desert and receives a pauper's burial.

Jim Casy, the country preacher who has given up the ministry because he no longer believes. He makes the trek to California with the Joads. Casy assumes the blame and goes to jail for the "crime" of a migrant worker who has a family to support. He is killed as a "red" while trying to help the migrant workers organize and strike for a living wage.

Connie Rivers, Rosasharn's young husband, who deserts her after arriving in California.

Floyd Knowles, a young migrant worker with a family, called a "red" because he asks a contractor to guarantee a job and the wages to be paid. He escapes from a deputy sheriff who is attempting to intimidate the workers. Tom Joad trips the deputy, and Jim Casy kicks him in the back of the head.

Muley Graves, a farmer who refuses to leave the land, although his family has gone. He remains, abstracted and lonely, forced to hide, and is hunted and haunted.

Jim Rawley, the kind, patient manager of a government camp for the migrant worker.

Willy Feeley, a former small farmer like the Joads; he takes a job driving a tractor over the land that the Joads farmed.

Ivy Wilson, a migrant who has car trouble on the way to California with his sick wife, Sairy. The Joads help them, and the two families stay together until Sairy becomes too ill to travel.

Sairy Wilson, Ivy's wife. When the Wilsons are forced to stay behind because of her illness, she asks Casy to pray for her.

Timothy Wallace, a migrant who helps Tom Joad find work in California.

Wilkie Wallace, his son.

Aggie Wainwright, the daughter of a family living in a boxcar with the Joads while they work in a cotton field. Al Joad plans to marry her.

Jessie Bullitt, Ella Summers, and **Annie Little-field,** the ladies' committee for Sanitary Unit Number Four of the government camp for migrant workers.

The Story

Tom Joad was released from the Oklahoma state penitentiary where he had served a sentence for killing a man in self-defense. He traveled homeward through a region made barren by drought and dust storms. On the way, he met Jim Casy, a former preacher; the pair went together to the home of Tom's family but found the Joad place deserted. While Tom and Casy were wondering what had happened, Muley Graves, a die-hard tenant farmer, came by and disclosed that all the families in the neighborhood had gone to California or were going. Tom's folks, Muley said, had gone to a relative's place to prepare for going west. Muley was the only sharecropper to stay behind.

All over the southern Midwest states, farmers, no longer able to make a living because of land banks, weather, and machine farming, had sold or were forced out of the farms that they had tenanted. Junk dealers and used-car salesmen profiteered on them. Thousands of families took to the roads leading to the promised land, California.

Tom and Casy found the Joads at Uncle John's place, busy with preparations for their trip to California. Assembled for the trip were Pa and Ma Joad; Noah, their mentally backward son; Al, the adolescent younger brother of Tom and Noah; Rose of Sharon, Tom's sister, and her husband, Connie; the other Joad children, Ruthie and Winfield; and Granma and Grampa Joad. Al had bought an ancient truck to take them west. The family asked Jim Casy to go with them. The night before they started, they killed the pigs that they had left and salted down the meat so that they would have food on the way.

Spurred by handbills which stated that agricultural workers were badly needed in California, the Joads, along with thousands of others, made their tortuous way, in a worn-out vehicle, across the plains toward the mountains. Grampa died of a stroke during their first overnight stop. Later there was a long delay when the truck broke down. Small business people along the way treated the migrants as enemies; and, to add to their misery, returning migrants told the Joads that there was no work to be had in California, that conditions were even worse than they were in Oklahoma. Nevertheless, the dream of a bountiful West Coast urged the Joads onward.

Close to the California line, where the group stopped to bathe in a river, Noah, feeling he was a hindrance to the others, wandered away. It was there that the Joads first heard themselves addressed as "Okies," another word for tramps.

Granma died during the night trip across the desert. After burying her, the group went into a Hooverville, as the migrants' camps were called. There they learned that work was all but impossible to find. A contractor came to the camp to sign up men to pick fruit in another county. When the Okies asked to see his license, the contractor turned the leaders over to a police deputy who had accompanied him to camp. Tom was involved in the fight that followed. He escaped, and Casy gave himself up in Tom's place. Connie, husband of the pregnant Rose of Sharon, suddenly disappeared from the group. The family was breaking up in the face of its hardships. Ma Joad did everything in her power to keep the group together.

Fearing recrimination after the fight, the Joads left the Hooverville and went to a government camp maintained for transient agricultural workers. The camp had sanitary facilities, a local government made up of the transients themselves, and simple organized entertainment. During the Joads' stay at the camp, the Okies successfully defeated an attempt by the local citizens to give the camp a bad name and thus to have it closed to the migrants. For the first time since they had arrived in California, the Joads found themselves treated as human beings.

Circumstances eventually forced them to leave the camp, however, for there was no work in the district. They drove to a large farm where work was being offered. There they found agitators attempting to keep the migrants from taking the work because of unfair wages offered. The Joads, however, thinking only of food, were escorted by motorcycle police into the farm. The entire family picked peaches for five cents a box and earned in a day just enough money to buy food for one meal. Tom, remembering the pickets outside the camp, went out at night to investigate. He found Casy, who was the leader of the agitators. While Tom and Casy were talking, deputies, who had been searching for Casy, closed in on them. The pair fled but were caught. Casy was killed. Tom received a cut on his head, but not before he had felled a deputy with an ax handle. The family concealed Tom in their shack. The rate for a box of peaches dropped, meanwhile, to two-and-a-half cents. Tom's danger and the futility of picking peaches drove the Joads on their way. They hid the injured Tom under the mattresses in the back of the truck, and then they told the suspicious guard at the entrance to the farm that the extra man they had had with them when they came was a hitchhiker who had stayed behind to pick.

The family found at last a migrant crowd encamped in abandoned boxcars along a stream. They joined the camp and soon found temporary jobs picking cotton. Tom, meanwhile, hid in a culvert near the camp. Ruthie innocently disclosed Tom's presence to another little girl. Ma, realizing that Tom was no longer safe, sent him away. Tom promised to carry on Casy's work in trying to improve the lot of the downtrodden everywhere.

The autumn rains began. Soon the stream that ran beside the camp overflowed and water entered the boxcars. Under these all but impossible conditions, Rose of Sharon gave birth to a dead baby. When the rising water made their position no longer bearable, the family moved from the camp on foot; the rains had made their old car useless. They came to a barn, which they shared with a boy and his starving father. Rose of Sharon, bereft of her baby, nourished the famished man with the milk from her breasts. So the poor kept each other alive in the Depression years.

Critical Evaluation

The publication of John Steinbeck's *The Grapes of Wrath* caused a nationwide stir in 1939. This account of the predicament of migrant workers was taken more as social document than as fiction. Some saw it as an exposé of capitalist excesses, others as a distorted call to revolution. Frequently compared to Harriet Beecher Stowe's *Uncle Tom's Cabin* (1852), it was awarded the 1940 Pulitzer Prize in fiction.

Later literary critics, taking a second look at the novel, often lumped it with a number of other dated books of the 1930's as "proletarian fiction." A careful reader, however, recognizes that beneath this outraged account of an outrageous social situation lies a dynamic, carefully structured story that applies not only to one era or society but also to the universal human predicament.

As a social document, the novel presents such a vivid picture of oppression and misery that one tends to doubt its authenticity. Steinbeck, however, had done more than academic research. He had journeyed from Oklahoma to California, lived in a migrant camp, and worked alongside the migrants. (Peter Lisca reports that, after the novel appeared, the workers sent Steinbeck a patchwork dog sewn from scraps of their clothing and wearing a tag labeled "Migrant John.") Before making the 1940 motion picture adaptation, which still stands as one of the great films of the era, Darryl F. Zanuck hired private detectives to verify Steinbeck's story; they reported that conditions were even worse than those depicted in the book. The political situation was a powder keg; Freeman Champney remarked that "it looked as if nothing could avert an all-out battle between revolution and fascism in California's great valleys."

Social injustice was depicted so sharply in the book that Steinbeck himself was accused of being a revolutionary. Certainly, he painted the oppressive economic system in bleak colors. Warren French argued convincingly, however, that Steinbeck was basically a reformer, not a revolutionary; he wanted to change the attitudes and behavior of people—both migrants and economic barons—not overturn the private enterprise system. Indeed, Steinbeck observes that ownership of land is morally edifying.

Steinbeck once declared that the writer must "set down his time as nearly as he can understand it" and that he should "serve as the watchdog of society . . . to satirize its silliness, to attack its injustices, to stigmatize its faults." In *The Grapes of Wrath*, he does all these things, then goes further to interpret events from a distinctly American point of view. Like Walt Whitman, he expresses love for all people and respect for manual labor. Like Thomas Jefferson, he asserts a preference for agrarian society in which individuals retain a close, nourishing tie to the soil: His farmers dwindle psychologically as they are separated from their land, and the California owners become oppressors as they substitute ledgers for direct contact with the soil. Like Ralph Waldo Emerson, Steinbeck demonstrates faith in the common people and in the ideal of self-reliance; he also develops the Emersonian religious concept of an oversoul. The preacher Jim Casy muses ". . . maybe that's the Holy Sperit—the human sperit—the whole shebang. Maybe all men got one big soul ever'body's a part of it." Later, Tom Joad reassures Ma that, even if he isn't physically with her, "Wherever they's a fight so hungry people can eat, I'll be there. Wherever they's a cop beatin' up a guy, I'll be there. . . . I'll be in the way kids laugh when they're hungry an' they know supper's ready. . . ."

This theme, that all people essentially belong together and are a part of one another and of a greater whole that transcends momentary reality, is what removes *The Grapes of Wrath* from the genre of timely proletarian fiction and makes it an allegory for all human beings in all circumstances. Warren French notes that the real story of this novel is not the Joads' search for economic security but their education, which transforms them from self-concern to a recognition of their bond with the whole human race. At first, Tom Joad is intensely individualistic, interest mainly in making his own way; Pa's primary concern is keeping bread on his table; Rose of Sharon dreams only of conventional middle-class success; and Ma, an Earth Mother with a spine of steel, concentrates fiercely upon keeping the "fambly" together. At the end, Tom follows Casy's example in fighting for human rights; Pa, in building the dike, sees the necessity for all people to work together; Rose of Sharon forgets her grief over her stillborn child and unhesitatingly lifts a starving man to her milk-filled breast; and Ma can say

"Use' ta be the fambly was fust. It ain't so now. It's anybody. Worse off we get, the more we got to do." Thus the Joads have overcome that separation that Paul Tillich equated with sin, that alienation from others which existentialists are so fond of describing as the inescapable human condition.

It is interesting to note how much *The Grapes of Wrath*, which sometimes satirizes, sometimes attacks organized Christian religion, reflects the Bible. In structure, as critics have been quick to notice, it parallels the story of the Exodus to a "promised land." Symbolically, as Lisca observed, the initials of Jim Casy are those of Jesus Christ, another itinerant preacher who rebelled against traditional religion, went into the wilderness, discovered his own gospel, and eventually gave his life in service to others.

The novel's language, too, is frequently biblical, especially in the interchapters, which, like a Greek chorus, restate, reinforce, and generalize from the specific happenings of the narrative. The cadences, repetitions, and parallel lines all echo the patterns of the Psalms—Ma Joad's favorite book.

Even the title of the novel is biblical; the exact phrase is poet Julia Ward Howe's, but the reference is to Jeremiah and Revelation. The grapes have been a central symbol throughout the book: first of promise, representing the fertile California valleys, but finally of bitter rage as the midwesterners realize that they have been lured west with false bait and that they will not partake of this fertility. The wrath grows, a fearsome, terrible wrath; but, as several interchapters make clear, better wrath than despair, because wrath moves to action. Steinbeck would have his people act, in concert and in concern for one another—and finally prevail over all forms of injustice.

GRAVITY'S RAINBOW

Type of work: Novel
Author: Thomas Pynchon (1937-)
Type of plot: Comic
Time of plot: 1945
Locale: Western Europe
First published: 1973

Gravity's Rainbow is the most famous novel of the absurdist postmodern school, also called metafiction. Pynchon uses comedy, violence, descriptions of many kinds of sexual behavior, and verbal fireworks to depict the aftermath of World War II.

Principal Characters

Tyrone Slothrop, a young and naïve American officer. His early conditioning makes him vulnerable to being programmed to seek out the A4 rocket that the Germans are reported to be building as World War II nears its end. Slothrop's travels through Western Europe bring him into contact with all kinds of rakish and unusual characters, most of whom are also searching for the A4 rocket.

Ned Pointsman, a psychologist specializing in behaviorism. He is in charge of the White Visitation, the installation where the British are investigating ways of using psychological and parapsychological warfare against the Germans. Pointsman arranges the script by which

Slothrop is directed to search for the A4.

Roger Mexico, a British officer, a mathematician who rejects behaviorist theories and represents a less determinist way of looking at human life. He is opposed to Pointsman's methods and tries to help Slothrop. In the end, he is one of the principal members of the Counterforce, a group of characters who oppose attempts by the powerful to control all aspects of human life.

Colonel Weissmann (Blicero), the German officer in charge of planning and building the A4 rocket. A cruel man who uses any means to carry out his mission, he is also the novel's spokesperson for transcendent values.

The Story

There is no single story in *Gravity's Rainbow*. Rather, numerous plots and subplots revolve around the rocket that the Germans are building, more powerful and deadly than the V-1 and V-2 rockets that terrorized England in the last months of World War II. At the center of one plot is the young and foolish American officer Tyrone Slothrop, whose conditioning as an infant has left him vulnerable to further conditioning. The behaviorist Ned Pointsman concocts an elaborate plan to make use of Slothrop's susceptibility, turning him into a device for locating the missile.

Slothrop's travels take him first to the French Riviera, from there to Switzerland, and then into Germany in the early weeks after the Nazi surrender. He encounters spies, sailors, revolutionaries, willing women, agents for all the Allied nations, and a succession of strange people, most of whom are also looking for the A4 rocket. He has a va-

riety of adventures, from a cruise on a mysterious yacht in the Baltic to a spell as the hero in a village folk festival to a hairbreadth escape from death in the tunnels where the Nazis constructed their rockets. In the end, Slothrop's conditioning wears off. He experiences a kind of enlightenment that shows him he is an ordinary person, not one of the elect, and he disappears from the novel.

Another important plot line is Colonel Weissmann's effort to get the rocket built, a project that involves the double agent Katje Borgesius (later one of Slothrop's lovers), the African tribal leader Enzian, and Weissmann's current lover, the innocent soldier Gottfried. Attached to this plot is the story of Franz Pokler, an engineer, and his wife and daughter, a family that is torn apart by the war. Other plots involve the English officer Roger Mexico, a counterbalance to Pointsman, and Mexico's affair with the beautiful Jessica Swanlake; another British officer,

Pirate Prentice, whose espionage operations are also directed toward finding the A4 rocket; and Enzian's half brother, the Russian agent Tchitcherine, who is less interested in his official duties than in finding and killing Enzian. In the end, no one can be said to have located the rocket, although Enzian's Herero tribesmen have constructed what may be a workable copy of the original.

Perhaps the major subplot has to do with attempts to resist the power of those who control the world for their own purposes, referred to in the novel as "They." Various possible avenues of resistance are tried, from the sexual love of Mexico and Jessica Swanlake to the hope for transcendence through rocketry by Weissmann to the building of an organized Counterforce. None of these approaches can be said to succeed more than briefly; members of the Counterforce have individual triumphs, but their attempt to organize resistance falls victim to bureaucracy and public relations. Only art—music, poetry, film, or any other form—remains a possible means of continuing resistance.

Critical Evaluation

Gravity's Rainbow is less interesting for its rather wild and amorphous plot than for the wealth of information that Pynchon has packed into it and the variety of styles that the author has at his command. The novel includes film scripts; prose versions of comic strips; poems, limericks, and popular songs; long elegiac passages pondering the meaning of the Christmas story and of the mystical experience of one character in the wastes of Siberia; slapstick encounters involving pie-throwing and comic (or sadistic) orgies; violent action involving hairbreadth escapes; lyrical passages involving romantic interludes; and myriad other styles and modes.

The novel's range of knowledge is also overwhelming. In a novel dealing with rocketry, detailed information about that area of modern endeavor can be expected, and Pynchon provides it. In addition, however, he demonstrates thorough knowledge of the chemistry and history of plastics, both German and American film industries (including the chemistry of film), Skinnerian behaviorism and Pavlovian psychology, and what has become known as chaos theory.

Hostile critics have objected to the novel's range of styles and themes, arguing that it is disorderly and unstructured, but other critics have demonstrated that, for all its apparent disorder, *Gravity's Rainbow* is a carefully planned and developed work. One element of this structure is the relative orderliness of the first three of the four sections of the novel, while the fourth section becomes more and more apparently random, the subsections briefer and briefer. This reflects the law of thermodynamics that deals with entropy, a phenomenon that always fascinated Pynchon (his most famous early story is entitled "Entropy"). Entropy means that, in a closed system, movement becomes more random and rapid, giving off increasing heat, as it approaches death or stasis. This definition reflects the idea that the world Pynchon is describing is entering its final phase.

Entropy is one of the concepts that governs *Gravity's Rainbow*. The other is the psychological concept of paranoia, an individual's belief that other people and the world itself are hostile. Pynchon's use of this concept is imaginative and various: A song has the title "Paranoia," there is a series of five "Proverbs for Paranoids" scattered through one of the book's four sections, and the characters are almost all paranoid to one degree or another. Yet the fears of many characters that they are the targets of a hostile plot are very often justified; the most obvious example is that Slothrop is the target of Pointsman's plot to turn him into a kind of guided missile seeking another missile, the A4.

A further example even more closely connected to the book's overwhelming sense of paranoia is the experience of Enzian, the displaced African whose concern is to lead his people back to some semblance of tribal life. Passing through a section of a city devastated by bombs, he has a vision that allows him to see that the destroyed factories are in fact ready to go into operation; the bombing has been intended not to destroy but to clear away older, obsolete machinery to make way for the new wave of technological advances. The official ideologies and their propaganda have been a cover for the real intention of the war, which was to make Europe ready for the next stage of development. Pynchon uses this device to suggest the reasons for the rapid economic recovery of Germany and Japan, in particular, after the end of World War II.

As a major document of metafiction, the absurdist type of novel first popularized in the 1960's, *Gravity's Rainbow* calls attention to the fact that it is fiction, not a representation of reality. The novel's combination of types of narration is one aspect of this approach. Another is the occurrence of fantastic elements, among them the dogfight in the sky between a fighter plane and Slothrop in a hot air balloon, in which the weapons that Slothrop hurls to defeat the enemy are cream pies like those used in a comedy sketch. Pynchon employs the supernatural when Tchitcherine finally encounters Enzian, his African half brother whom he has sworn to kill; knowing that such a killing would destroy both men, Tchitcherine's lover, Geli Tripping, uses magic to prevent him from realizing that the man whom he sees is Enzian.

Gravity's Rainbow advanced Pynchon's career, changing his image from that of a writer who held the interest and admiration of a small group to one who was clearly a leader of the new wave in fiction. The novel itself was not only an achievement for the author but also an important document that validated the whole movement toward metafiction by demonstrating that the mode was capable of producing a major work.

Pynchon's earlier work, including half a dozen short stories (later collected in *Slow Learner*, 1984) and the novels *V.* (1963) and *The Crying of Lot 49* (1966), was clear evidence of an important talent, but *Gravity's Rainbow* elevated Pynchon at once to a status beyond that of such contemporaries as Joseph Heller, Bruce Jay Friedman, William Gaddis, or John Barth. Critics at once recognized that this was a novel that went beyond what this author, or any other, had done before. Yet even *V.* is an amazing work, especially for so young a writer; it is a study of the demoralized generation that was Pynchon's own, set against the backdrop of a century of wars and rumors of wars that led to the passionless search for excitement by a generation that thought of itself (and the world) as doomed. The theme of entropy is a strong element in *V.*, which won the William Faulkner Foundation Award as the best first novel of its year.

The Crying of Lot 49, while much shorter than *V.*, indicated considerable progress in Pynchon's fiction, especially in enunciating the theme of paranoia, which had been present in *V.* but not as the important issue that it was to become in Pynchon's later work. The central figure of *The Crying of Lot 49*, a woman named Oedipa Maas, searches through the world of Silicon Valley and the San Francisco Bay Area for a conspiracy that shows itself only in hints; if it exists, then the conspiracy is a possible means of rebellion against the forces of conformity and technological domination, but Oedipa never finds out whether it is real or only a figment of her imagination. This conspiracy foreshadows the Counterforce that arises toward the end of *Gravity's Rainbow*. Both of these elements also look forward to the underground nature of the lives of most of the characters in Pynchon's fourth novel, *Vineland* (1989).

Gravity's Rainbow was one of the most important novels written by an American in the last third of the twentieth century. Pynchon's range of knowledge, the depth of his critique of contemporary Western culture, and his mastery of styles and command of an immense amount of disparate material made the novel the center of a thriving and contentious critical industry. Books, essays, and reviews continue to analyze the novel and argue about its meaning and value. If these arguments cannot be settled, then their existence is testimony to the power wielded by Pynchon's novel.

THE GREAT GATSBY

Type of work: Novel
Author: F. Scott Fitzgerald (1896-1940)
Type of plot: Social criticism
Time of plot: 1922
Locale: New York City and Long Island
First published: 1925

Jay Gatz changes his name to Gatsby and amasses great wealth by dubious means solely to please Daisy, a socialite. Wooed earlier by the penniless Gatsby, Daisy had rejected him for her social equal, Tom Buchanan. Yet no matter how high Gatsby rises, he is doomed, for the wealthy Buchanans are not worthy of Gatsby's sincerity and innocence. Though Gatsby plans to take the blame for a hit-and-run murder committed by Daisy, Tom Buchanan tells the victim's husband that Gatsby was driving, and the husband murders Gatsby. The Buchanans retreat into the irresponsibility that their wealth allows them.

Principal Characters

Nick Carraway, the narrator. A young midwesterner who, dissatisfied with his life at home, was attracted to New York and now sells bonds there. He is the most honest character of the novel and because of this trait fails to become deeply fascinated by his rich friends on Long Island. He helps Daisy and Jay Gatsby to renew a love that they had known before Daisy's marriage, and he is probably the only person in the novel to have any genuine affection for Gatsby.

Jay Gatsby, a fabulously rich racketeer whose connections outside the law are only hinted at. He is the son of poor parents from the Midwest who has changed his name from James Gatz and who becomes obsessed with a need for making more and more money. Much of his time is spent in trying to impress and become accepted by other rich people. He gives lavish parties for people he knows nothing about and most of whom he never meets. He is genuinely in love with Daisy Buchanan and becomes a sympathetic character when he assumes the blame for her hit-and-run accident. At his death, he has been deserted by everyone except his father and Nick.

Daisy Buchanan, Nick's second cousin. Unhappy in her marriage because of Tom Buchanan's deliberate unfaithfulness, she has the character of a "poor little rich girl." She renews an old love for Jay Gatsby and considers leaving her husband, but she is finally reconciled to him. She kills Tom's mistress in a hit-and-run accident after a quarrel in which she defends both men as Tom accuses Gatsby of trying to steal her from him. Daisy allows Gatsby to take the blame for the accident

and suffers no remorse when he is murdered by the woman's husband.

Tom Buchanan, Daisy's husband. The son of rich midwestern parents, he reached the heights of his career as a college football player. Completely without taste, culture, or sensitivity, he carries on a rather sordid affair with Myrtle Wilson. He pretends to help George Wilson, her husband, but allows him to think that Gatsby was not only her murderer but also her lover.

Myrtle Wilson, Tom Buchanan's mistress. She is a fat, unpleasant woman who is so highly appreciative of the fact that her lover is a rich man that she will suffer almost any degradation for him. While she is with Tom, her pretense that she is rich and highly sophisticated becomes ludicrous.

George Wilson, Myrtle's husband and a rather pathetic figure. He runs an automobile repair shop and believes that Tom Buchanan is really interested in helping him. Aware that his wife has a lover, George never suspects who he really is. His faith in Tom makes him believe what Buchanan says, which, in turns, causes him to murder Gatsby and then commit suicide.

Jordan Baker, a friend of the Buchanans, a golfer. Daisy introduces Jordan to Nick and tries to throw them together, but when Nick realizes that Jordan is a cheat who refuses to assume the elementary responsibility of the individual, he loses all interest in her.

Meyer Wolfshiem, a gambler and underworld associate of Gatsby.

Catherine, Myrtle Wilson's sister, who is obviously

proud of Myrtle's rich connection and unconcerned with the immorality involved.

Mr. and **Mrs. McKee,** a photographer and his wife who try to use Nick and Tom to get a start among the

rich people of Long Island.

Mr. Gatz, Jay Gatsby's father, who, being unaware of the facts of Jay's life, thought his son had been a great man.

The Story

Young Nick Carraway decided to forsake the hardware business of his family in the Midwest in order to sell bonds in New York City. He took a small house in West Egg on Long Island and there became involved in the lives of his neighbors. At a dinner party at the home of Tom Buchanan, he renewed his acquaintance with Tom and Tom's wife, Daisy, a distant cousin, and he met an attractive young woman, Jordan Baker. Almost at once, he learned that Tom and Daisy were not happily married. It appeared that Daisy knew her husband was unfaithful.

Nick soon learned to despise the drive to the city through unkempt slums; particularly, he hated the ash heaps and the huge commercial signs. He was far more interested in the activities of his wealthy neighbors. Near his house lived Jay Gatsby, a mysterious man of great wealth. Gatsby entertained lavishly, but his past was unknown to his neighbors.

One day, Tom Buchanan took Nick to call on his mistress, a dowdy, plump, married woman named Myrtle Wilson, whose husband, George Wilson, operated a second-rate automobile repair shop. Myrtle, Tom, and Nick went to the apartment that Tom kept, and there the three were joined by Myrtle's sister, Catherine, and Mr. and Mrs. McKee. The party settled down to an afternoon of drinking, Nick unsuccessfully doing his best to get away.

A few days later, Nick attended another party, one given by Gatsby for a large number of people famous in speakeasy society. Food and liquor were dispensed lavishly. Most of the guests had never seen their host before.

At the party, Nick met Gatsby for the first time. Gatsby, in his early thirties, looked like a healthy young roughneck. He was offhand, casual, and eager to entertain his guests as extravagantly as possible. Frequently he was called away by long-distance telephone calls. Some of the guests laughed and said that he was trying to impress them with his importance.

That summer, Gatsby gave many parties. Nick went to all of them, enjoying each time the society of people from all walks of life who appeared to take advantage of Gatsby's bounty. From time to time, Nick met Jordan Baker there, and when he heard that she had cheated in an amateur golf match, his interest in her grew.

Gatsby took Nick to lunch one day and introduced him to a man named Meyer Wolfshiem, who seemed to be Gatsby's business partner. Wolfshiem hinted at some dubious business deals that betrayed Gatsby's racketeering activities, and Nick began to identify the sources of some of Gatsby's wealth.

Jordan Baker told Nick the strange story of Daisy's wedding. Before the bridal dinner, Daisy, who seldom drank, became wildly intoxicated and kept reading a letter that she had just received and crying that she had changed her mind. After she had become sober, however, she went through with her wedding to Tom without a murmur. Obviously, the letter was from Jay Gatsby. At the time, Gatsby was poor and unknown; Tom was rich and influential.

Gatsby was still in love with Daisy, however, and he wanted Jordan and Nick to bring Daisy and him together again. It was arranged that Nick should invite Daisy to tea the same day that he invited Gatsby. Gatsby awaited the invitation nervously.

On the eventful day, it rained. Determined that Nick's house should be presentable, Gatsby sent a man to mow the wet grass; he also sent over flowers for decoration. The tea was a strained affair at first, and Gatsby and Daisy were shy and awkward in their reunion. Afterward, they went over to Gatsby's mansion, where he showed them his furniture, clothes, swimming pool, and gardens. Daisy promised to attend his next party. When Daisy disapproved of his guests, Gatsby stopped entertaining. The house was shut up and the bar crowd turned away.

Gatsby informed Nick of his origin. His true name was Gatz, he had been born in the Midwest, and his parents were poor. When he was a boy, he had become the protégé of a wealthy old gold miner and had accompanied him on his travels until the old man died. He had changed his name to Gatsby and was daydreaming of acquiring wealth and position. In World War I, he had distinguished himself. After the war, he had returned penniless to the States, too poor to marry Daisy, whom he had met during the war. Later, he became a partner in a drug business. He had been lucky and had accumulated money rapidly. He told Nick that he had acquired the money for his Long Island residence after three years of hard work.

The Buchanans gave a quiet party for Jordan, Gatsby, and Nick. The group drove into the city and took a room in a hotel. The day was hot and the guests uncomfortable. On the way, Tom, driving Gatsby's new yellow car, stopped at Wilson's garage. Wilson complained because Tom had not helped him in a projected car deal. He said he needed money because he was selling out and taking his wife, whom he knew to be unfaithful, away from the city.

At the hotel, Tom accused Gatsby of trying to steal his wife and also of being dishonest. He seemed to regard Gatsby's low origin with more disfavor than his interest in Daisy. During the argument, Daisy sided with both men. On the ride back to the suburbs, Gatsby drove his own car, accompanied by Daisy, who temporarily would not speak to her husband.

Following them, Nick, Jordan, and Tom stopped to investigate an accident in front of Wilson's garage. They discovered an ambulance picking up the dead body of Myrtle Wilson, struck by a hit-and-run driver in a yellow car. They tried in vain to help Wilson and then went on to Tom's house, convinced that Gatsby had struck Myrtle.

Nick learned that night from Gatsby that Daisy had been driving when the woman was hit. Gatsby, however, was willing to take the blame if the death should be traced to his car. He explained that a woman had rushed out as though she wanted to speak to someone in the yellow car and Daisy, an inexpert driver, had run her down and then collapsed. Gatsby had driven on.

In the meantime, George Wilson, having traced the yellow car to Gatsby, appeared on the Gatsby estate. A few hours later, both he and Gatsby were discovered dead. He had shot Gatsby and then killed himself.

Nick tried to make Gatsby's funeral respectable, but only one among all of Gatsby's former guests attended along with Gatsby's father, who thought his son had been a great man. None of Gatsby's racketeering associates appeared.

Shortly afterward, Nick learned of Tom's part in Gatsby's death. Wilson had visited Tom and had threatened Tom with a revolver, forcing him to reveal the name of the owner of the hit-and-run car. Nick vowed that his friendship with Tom and Daisy was ended. He decided to return to his people in the Midwest.

Critical Evaluation

F. Scott Fitzgerald, the prophet of the Jazz Age, was born in St. Paul, Minnesota, to the daughter of a self-made Irish immigrant millionaire. His father was a ne'er-do-well salesman who had married above his social position. From his mother, Fitzgerald inherited the dream that was America—the promise that young people could become anything that they choose through hard work. From his father, he inherited a propensity for failure. This antithesis pervaded his own life and most of his fiction. Educated in the East, Fitzgerald was overcome with the glamour of New York and Long Island. To him, it was the "stuff of old romance," "the source of infinite possibilities." His fiction focused primarily on the lives of the rich. With the family fortune depleted by his father, Fitzgerald found himself in his early twenties an army officer in love with a Southern belle, Zelda Sayre, who was socially above him. She refused his first proposal of marriage because he was too poor. Fitzgerald was determined to have her. He wrote and published *This Side of Paradise* (1920), on the basis of which Zelda married him.

Their public life for the next ten years epitomized the dizzy spiral of the 1920's—wild parties, wild spending—and, following the national pattern, they crashed spectacularly in the 1930's. Zelda went mad and was committed finally to a sanatorium; Fitzgerald became a functional alcoholic. From his pinnacle in the publishing field during the 1920's, when his short stories commanded as much as fifteen hundred dollars, he fell in the 1930's to writing lukewarm Hollywood scripts. He died in Hollywood in 1940, almost forgotten and with most of his work out of print. Later revived in academic circles, Fitzgerald's reputation in American letters rests primarily on *The Great Gatsby.*

Fitzgerald once said, "America's great promise is that something's going to happen, but it never does. America is the moon that never rose." This indictment of the American Dream could well serve as an epigraph for *The Great Gatsby.* Jay Gatsby pursues his dream of romantic success without ever understanding that it has escaped him. He fails to understand that he cannot recapture the past (his love for Daisy Buchanan) no matter how much money he makes, no matter how much wealth he displays.

The character of Gatsby was never intended by Fitzgerald to be a realistic portrayal; he is a romantic hero, always somewhat unreal, bogus, and absurd. No matter the corrupt sources of his wealth, such as bootlegging and gambling (and these are only hinted at), he stands for hope, for romantic belief—for innocence. He expects more from life than the other characters, who are all more or less cynical. He is an eternal juvenile in a brutal and corrupt world.

To underscore the corruption of the American Dream, Fitzgerald's characters all are finally seen as liars. Buchanan's mistress lies to her husband. Jordan Baker is a pathological liar who cheats in golf tournaments. Tom Buchanan's lie to his mistress Myrtle's husband results in the murder of Gatsby. Daisy, herself, is basically insincere; she lets Gatsby take the blame for her hit-and-run accident. Gatsby's whole life is a lie: He lies about his past and his present, and he lies to himself. Nick Carraway, the midwestern narrator, tells readers that he is the only completely honest person he knows. He panders for Gatsby, however, and in the end, he turns away from Tom Buchanan, unable to force the truth into the open. He knows the truth about Gatsby but is unable to tell the police. His affirmation of Gatsby at the end is complex; he envies Gatsby's romantic selflessness and innocence at the same time that he abhors his lack of self-knowledge.

The Great Gatsby incorporates a number of themes and motifs that unify the novel and contribute to its impact. The initiation theme governs the narrator Nick Carraway, who is a young man come East to make his fortune in stocks and bonds and who returns to the Midwest sadly disillusioned. The frontier theme is also present. Gatsby believes in the "green light," the ever-accessible future in which one can achieve what one has missed in the past. The final paragraphs of the novel state this important theme as well as it has ever been stated. Class issues are very well presented. Tom and Daisy seem accessible, but when their position is threatened, they close the doors, retreating into their wealth and carelessness,

letting others like Gatsby pay the price in hurt and suffering. The carelessness of the rich and their followers is seen in the recurring motif of the bad driver.

Automobile accidents are ubiquitous. At Gatsby's first party, there is a smashup with drunk drivers. Jordan Baker has a near accident after which Nick calls her "a rotten driver." Gatsby is stopped for speeding but is able to fix the ticket by showing the officer a card from the mayor of New York. Finally, Myrtle Wilson is killed by Daisy, who is driving Gatsby's car. Bad driving becomes symbolic of pervasive irresponsibility and self-indulgence.

Settings in the novel are used very well by Fitzgerald, from the splendid mansions of Long Island through the wasteland of the valley of ashes presided over by the eyes of Dr. T. J. Eckleburg on a billboard (where the Wilsons live) to the New York of the Plaza Hotel or Tom and Myrtle Wilson's apartment. Most important, however, is Fitzgerald's use of Nick as a narrator. Like Joseph Conrad before him, Fitzgerald had a romantic sensibility that controlled fictional material best through the lens of a narrator. Like Marlow in Conrad's *Heart of Darkness* (1902), Nick relates the story of an exceptional man who fails in his dream. He is both attracted and repelled by a forceful individual who dares to lead a life he could not sustain. Like Marlow, Nick pays tribute to his hero, who is also his alter ego. Gatsby's tragedy is Nick's education. His return to the Midwest is a moral return to the safer, more solid values of the heartland. Fitzgerald himself was unable to follow such a path, but he clearly believed that the American Dream should be pursued with less frantic, orgiastic, prideful convulsions of energy and spirit.

GRENDEL

Type of work: Novel
Author: John Gardner (1933-1982)
Type of plot: Parodic
Time of plot: Sixth century
Locale: Denmark
First published: 1971

The most frequently taught and discussed of Gardner's novels, Grendel *retells the Anglo-Saxon epic of* Beowulf *from the point of view of a monster whose temperament is decidedly contemporary.*

Principal Characters

Grendel, the monster who narrates his version of the *Beowulf* story. As alienated as any existential antihero, Grendel discovers the absurdity of the world but is also seduced by the affirmative vision embodied in the Shaper's art. Caught between that vision and his perception of the world as it is, Grendel seeks the advice of the Dragon, whose nihilism he largely comes to accept. As in the Anglo-Saxon epic, Grendel will eventually be defeated by the hero Beowulf, which is to say by art and all that it represents.

The Shaper, the Anglo-Saxon scop (poet), teller of the oral tales that embody people's values and legendary history. Blind, as was Homer, the Shaper is a figure for all "true artists," inciting his listeners to enact the ideals that his art affirms.

The Dragon, the Shaper's opposite, a cartoon version of Jean-Paul Sartre, an existentialist who denies everything and affirms nothingness. The Dragon's self-appointed Sartrean "project" is to sit on his hoard of gold and jewels. Upon request, he spouts advice to an uncomprehending Grendel, explaining time and space in words plagiarized from another twentieth century philosopher, Alfred North Whitehead. Content to describe what is, the Dragon has no interest in what might be.

Beowulf, the hero who figures throughout all but the very beginning of *Beowulf*, does not appear in *Grendel* until the last few chapters. He possesses great physical strength, a "cooly murderous tongue," and a vision not entirely different from the Dragon's. Yet, despite his foreknowledge of what will be (as the Dragon says, "Things fade"), Beowulf chooses to act as if the Shaper's visions were indeed possible. It is for this reason that Grendel judges him "insane." The very embodiment of the Shaper's grand vision and of Unferth's definition of the hero, Beowulf represents those values without which human life would be meaningless.

The Story

Narrated in the first person as well as in the present tense, *Grendel* takes place during the twelfth and, as readers of the Anglo-Saxon epic *Beowulf* (c. 1000) already know, last year of Grendel's war with the Danish king Hrothgar. Parts of the story, the early chapters in particular, loop back to the past as Grendel offers his apologia. His is a portrait of the artist as young monster discovering the world beyond his mother's fen and ken. Humans prove his most puzzling discovery. Unlike the bull that attacks him, driven solely by instinct, humans use words to fashion theories to explain their world and their actions in it. The theories are often wrong. The men who come upon Grendel trapped in a tree assume he must be an oak tree spirit that they try first to appease, then to exterminate. Rescued by his mother, Grendel spends the next years observing humans from a safer distance. When a new Shaper arrives to sing Hrothgar's praises, Grendel's interest grows. The theories, now couched in the Shaper's songs, are less about what is and more about what was and especially what will be. Grendel continues to see, as the humans do not, the disparity between their acts (their wasteful, murderous wars in particular) and their flattering visions of themselves. Yet he also sees the positive effect that the Shaper's words have, such as inspiring Hrothgar and his people to build the vast and splendid hall, Heorot, symbol of the king's power and his people's ability to work together for the common good—in short, shaping their lives constructively.

Seduced by the Shaper's sirenlike songs, "converted" to belief in a system that defines him as a monster, a child of Cain forever cursed by God, Grendel arrives at Heorot (with a corpse that he has found in the woods tucked under his huge arm), crying out for mercy, pity, and peace, only to be attacked and turned away. Addicted to a vision that he knows to be a lie, at least in part, and unwilling to return to the darkness and more especially the silence of his mother's world, Grendel visits the Dragon. Sitting atop the treasure that he will only hoard, never use, the Dragon propounds a different, bleaker vision, one based on the existentialist philosophy of Sartre. Although much of the Dragon's explanation is lost on his untutored listener, Grendel comprehends enough to know that he prefers the Shaper's hopeful songs. The gap widens between those songs and the Dragon's seemingly irrefutable but entirely nihilist description of the world as it actually is. The Dragon advises Grendel to seek gold—but not the Dragon's gold—and sit on it (as useful a project as any in an absurd world). Grendel chooses a different Sartrean project: to become the monster of the Shaper's poem.

In attacking Heorot, he teaches Hrothgar and the others the cynical truth of the Dragon's philosophy, that all is indeed waste and all visions lies, as his fight with Unferth seems at first to prove. Unferth, who really is a Cain and whose name means "unpeace," steps forth to kill the monster or die a hero's death trying. Unferth, however, does neither. Instead, Grendel carries the pompous but persistent warrior, now asleep, back to Heorot to live out a life of shame, a hero neither in victory nor in death. " 'Except in the life of a hero,' " Unferth told Grendel, " 'the whole world's meaningless. The hero sees values beyond what's possible. That's the *nature* of a hero. It kills him, of course, ultimately. But it makes the whole struggle of humanity worthwhile.' " Not surprisingly, Grendel sees the life of the hero differently, as simply another way of breaking up the boredom. He follows Hrothgar's army one morning for much the same reason:

Bloodbaths too break up the boredom, as well as confirming the Dragon's version of just how worthwhile "the whole struggle of humanity actually is." This time, Grendel is disappointed. Instead of his blood, the rival king offers his sister Wealtheow, whose name means servant of the common good, to Hrothgar as a wife.

Like the Shaper's songs, Wealtheow proves yet another "wretched violation of the senses." Unwilling to be seduced a second time, Grendel decides to kill the queen, then as suddenly decides not to do so. The latter is not the entirely gratuitous act that Grendel claims it to be, nor is it malicious in intent as his sparing Unferth solely to shame him surely is. Sparing the queen is an act of faith—the proof that Grendel is not entirely lost. He is entirely alone, however, and, except insofar as he continues to play the part of Hrothgar-Wrecker, entirely pointless as well. Grendel does quite literally play the part. He is the monster as actor—or, better, as clown—going so far as self-consciously to parody a variety of poetic styles, mimicking and therefore mocking yet also paying homage to the Shaper, who is his master and, in a way, his maker. On the one hand, Grendel is confirmed in his vision of final waste by the plotting of the king's own nephew, and on the other, he is aroused from his unbelief by Wealtheow and even to a degree by Unferth and the old priest Ork. Similarly, Grendel reacts to news of Beowulf's arrival with glee, not only because Beowulf breaks up the boredom but also because Beowulf is the hero that Unferth described but could not himself be. As in the Anglo-Saxon epic, Beowulf defeats Grendel—by "accident," Gardner's Grendel claims. In the novel, Beowulf does more than simply defeat Grendel (and therefore, although only momentarily, the evil that he embodies). He makes Grendel "sing of walls" and understand that the power by which the hero defeats the monster is the "promise" of renewal, which defeats the Dragon's vision of final and absolute waste. Grendel, standing at the very brink of death and wondering whether it is joy that he feels, ends the novel with words that may be as much blessing as curse: " 'Poor Grendel's had an accident,' I whisper, '*So may you all.*' "

Critical Evaluation

Grendel is a retelling of the Anglo-Saxon epic *Beowulf* from the monster's point of view, and as such, it resembles other texts from the 1960's and early 1970's that retell other similarly canonized works: Donald Barthelme's *Snow White* (1967), Robert Coover's *Pricksongs & Descants* (1969), Ted Hughes's *Crow* (1970), and John

Barth's *Chimera* (1972), to name a few. Such retellings debunk and demystify their sources in large part by drawing them out of the safe sphere of a distant and absolute past and bringing them into the contemporary world of indeterminacy. Employing the techniques of parody and pastiche, these works become verbal collages, what art critic Harold Rosenberg once called "anxious objects." In *Grendel's* case, this effect is compounded by the vast range and high density of intertextual reference, for while Gardner's monster clearly derives from *Beowulf*, he also resembles the Caliban of William Shakespeare's *The Tempest* (1611) and Robert Browning's poem "Caliban upon Setebos," the monster in Mary Wollstonecraft Shelley's *Frankenstein* (1818), Satan in John Milton's *Paradise Lost* (1667, 1674), Holden Caulfield from J. D. Salinger's *The Catcher in the Rye* (1951), Roquentin from Sartre's *La Nausée* (1938; *Nausea*, 1949), and the Beast from Jean Cocteau's film *La Belle et la bête* (1946; *Beauty and the Beast*, 1947). There are as well a host of other, less obvious references, from the poetry of William Blake and William Butler Yeats to the essays of William Gass.

The novel's "thickened texture," to borrow critic Mikhail Bakhtin's term, makes it difficult and perhaps ultimately unwise to read *Grendel* in terms of *Beowulf*. *Beowulf* does, however, provide a point of departure for discussions of Gardner's most popular novel. The writing of *Grendel* grew out of Gardner's teaching of the poem, as did his analysis of *Beowulf* in *The Construction of Christian Poetry in Old English* (1975). In that study, Gardner interprets *Beowulf's* three monsters as perversions of the virtues that the poem extols: wisdom, power, and goodness (that is, the right use of reason, strength, and things). Gardner wrote *Grendel* in part to test the continued viability of those virtues, and to do so, he had to find the monster's modern counterparts. As he explained in the same October, 1970, issue of *Esquire* in which a shortened version of the novel, edited by Rust Hills, appeared, "What *Grendel* does is take, one by one, the great ideals of mankind since the beginning and make a case for these values by setting up alternatives in an ironic set of monster values" centering on Sartrean existentialism.

Gardner was pleased by the attention that *Grendel* received—his first two novels had largely been neglected, while his next three would become best-sellers—but he was also dismayed that so many reviewers read *Grendel* as an endorsement of the very existentialism that Gardner had intended the novel to expose as monstrous. Gardner would articulate his position much more clearly, and narrowly, in *On Moral Fiction* (1978), published seven years after *Grendel* but begun several years before. "True art," Gardner would contend, presents "valid models for imitation, eternal verities worth keeping in mind, and a benevolent vision of the possible which can inspire and incite human beings toward virtue, toward life affirmation as opposed to destruction and indifference." Since then, critics have largely taken Gardner at his word and as a result read *Grendel* in terms of the moral conflict between good art (and artists) and bad: the Shaper and Beowulf on one side, Grendel and the Dragon on the other.

This reading does not entirely depend on the author's extratextual comments in *On Moral Fiction* and in numerous interviews. Unlike the poem, which is structured around the hero's battles with the three monsters, the novel comprises twelve chapters that correspond less to the twelve years of Grendel's war with Hrothgar than to the tradition of the literary epic (divided into either twelve or twenty-four chapters) and more especially the twelve signs of the zodiac, evidence of the cosmic order that Grendel fails to recognize. Ultimately, *Grendel* affirms neither the Shaper's nor the Dragon's vision; it affirms instead, by virtue of its own discontinuity and subjectivity, the ongoing dialogue between the two. Gardner's intended meaning can be "heard" within the text as well as without, but so can the voice of Grendel, a voice that is not only parodic but postmodern and even, however obliquely and unintentionally, postcolonial as well. Speaking in a way that echoes so much of Western literature, from Homer and *Beowulf* to Salinger and Kurt Vonnegut, and speaking a voice that much of that same literary tradition has previously either silenced or spoken for, Grendel proves not so much monstrous as eloquent in his attraction to and simultaneous refutation of the homogeneous "values," "eternal verities," and not so "benevolent vision" that depend upon Grendel's exile and finally his death.

THE HARP-WEAVER AND OTHER POEMS

Type of work: Poetry
Author: Edna St. Vincent Millay (1892-1950)
First published: 1923

The sonnets and ballads of The Harp-Weaver and Other Poems, *which was awarded a Pulitzer Prize, explore Millay's themes of childhood innocence and personal loss.*

Ten years before she was awarded a Pulitzer Prize for *The Harp-Weaver and Other Poems*, Edna St. Vincent Millay's first and best-known poem, "Renascence," appeared in *The Lyric Year*, an anthology of one hundred poems by as many poets. The Vassar undergraduate, Vincent Millay, as her family and friends then called her, scored a signal victory in her contribution to the anthology, the freer form and the liberal spirit of her work standing out against the stilted Victorian verse and sentimentality found in most of the selections.

"All I could see from where I stood," the first line of "Renascence," begins a poem as regular in meter, rhythm, and rhyme as those by her romantic predecessors. Yet the new hedonism and the sharp, almost brittle metaphors based on both landscapes and seascapes create a quite different effect. The pain of omniscience, the poet's burden, is the theme. The imagery is dazzling in its exalted movement to a sensuous climax in which life is celebrated through all the senses.

"Renascence" was a promise of things to come, for the personal lyric was Millay's forte. Her sonnets and her ballads, held in such beautiful balance in *The Harp-Weaver and Other Poems*, are always exact in craftsmanship, capturing at times the innocence of childhood and the sadness of lost ecstasy.

The title poem, "The Ballad of The Harp-Weaver," appearing at the end of the second section, brings into an almost medieval form saddened innocence and lyric tragedy. Written mostly in the traditional four-line ballad stanza with alternating rhymes, the poem varies subtly in meter and end-stopping to include occasional stanzas with a fifth line and shifting rhyme schemes. These last lines create the panic, the pain, and finally the exaltation of deep feeling. The narrative tells in the first person the story of a young boy of the slums living with his widowed mother who can do nothing to make a living and has nothing to sell except "a harp with a woman's head nobody will buy." In a fifth line, "she begins to cry" for the starving boy. This is in the late fall; by the winter, all the furniture has been burned, and the boy can do no more than watch his school companions go by, for he has no clothes to wear. He is disturbed by his mother's attempts to comfort him, to dandle him on her knee while "a-rock-rock-rocking," and to sing to him "in such a daft way." The counterpoint of the harp with a woman's head and "a wind with a wolf's head" suggests the lingering pain after the first panic. The final exaltation, however, is remarkable. A mystical event occurs: The mother weaves clothes for the Christ child, just the size of her own boy, and perishes at the harp, "her hands in the harp strings frozen dead." This odd juxtaposition of the Madonna and the Magi themes with the dance of death demonstrates Millay's versatility and expertness with language.

Part 5 of the volume, "Sonnets from an Ungrafted Tree," creates its effect by quite opposite methods. This sequence concerns a woman who prosaically watches her unloved husband die and then tries to pick up the empty pieces of her own unloving life. He had befriended her in school, when she would have accepted anyone, by flashing a mirror in her eyes; after his death, she has a flash of awareness that he had loved her deeply, though he was in no way remarkable in living or in loving. Whatever heat was in this strange body that had slept and had eaten beside her is now gone, the whole unclassified. The impact of this fact makes of these 238 lines a taut though expressionistic drama in which the unreality of the death is emotionally heightened by the very real, familiar objects that express the widow's desolation.

These macabre themes do not go unrelieved in Millay's book. The opening lyric is the keynote to the first part, and "My Heart, Being Hungry" connects this volume with the earlier "Renascence." The lean heart feeds on "beauty where beauty never stood," and "sweet where no sweet lies," symbolized by the smell of rain on tansy. She continues the theme of the bitter-sweet, light-dark, the opposites of nature that make of the humblest experience something like pain, a pain of sensitive awareness of the tears of things. Always, however, there is pure aesthetic pleasure gained from deep-felt realizations, of

A rock-maple showing red,
Burrs beneath a tree

even in deepest grief, she says in "The Wood Road." In spite of the world's negations, the positive things endure. "The Goose-Girl" summarizes this belief:

> Spring rides no horses down the hill,
> But comes on foot, a goose-girl still.
> And all the loveliest things there be
> Come simply, so, it seems to me.
> If ever I said, in grief or pride,
> I tired of honest things, I lied;
> And should be cursed forevermore
> With love in laces, like a whore
> And neighbors cold, and friends
>   unsteady,
> And Spring on horseback, like a lady!

In the second section, Millay divides her poems between the goose-girl and the lady, the first poem, "Departure," reflecting both. The adolescent girl, busy with her sewing, is pensive, even in despair over half-felt longings:

> It's little I care what path I take,
> And where it leads it's little I care:
> But out of this house, lest my heart
>   break,
> I must go, and off somewhere.

She indulges in the pleasant emotion of self-pity, of her dead body found in a ditch somewhere, an adolescent drama that is interrupted by her mother's friendly query, "Is something the matter, dear?" An old legend retold in "The Pond" presents a suicide who picked a lily before she drowned, a grasp even in death after the beautiful.

The extremely short third section contains all these motifs and some strange new ones. "Never May the Fruit Be Plucked" extends the imagery of "My Heart, Being Hungry" to suggest that "He that would eat of love must eat it where it hangs," and that nothing tangible can be taken away forever. "The Concert" extends the internal monologue of the sewing girl, this time a new departure from rather than toward life and love. "Hyacinth," however, is something new and wonderfully strange:

> I am in love with him to whom a
>   hyacinth is dearer
> Then I shall ever be dear.

> On nights when the field-mice are
>   abroad he cannot sleep:
> He hears their narrow teeth at the
>   bulbs of his hyacinths.
> But the gnawing at my heart he does
>   not hear.

This gnawing at the heart is at least a real emotion, while in "Spring Song" a modern nothingness has replaced the reawakening season. The refrains suggest that modern life has driven out spring with its "Come, move on!" and "No parking here!" The poem ends:

> Anyhow, it's nothing to me.
> I can remember, and so can you.
> (Though we'd better watch out for
>   you-know-who,
> When we sit around remembering
>   Spring).
> We shall hardly notice in a year or
>   two.
> You can get accustomed to anything.

Part 4, the most conventional, is made up of twenty-two unrelated sonnets. These are rather academic in theme and tone, containing as they do echoes of Elizabeth Barrett Browning and John Keats. The first and last illustrate this point, though there are many sonnets in between that point to Millay's individuality. In the first, she prophetically reveals the sadness of life after the loss of a beloved. In the last, she celebrates the glimpse of sheer beauty that was Euclid's in the "blinding hour" when he had his vision

> Of light anatomized. Euclid alone
> He looked on beauty bare. Fortunate
>   they
> Who, though once only and then but
>   far away,
> Have heard her massive sandal set on
>   stone.

The Harp-Weaver and Other Poems presents a poet with vision unclouded by the didacticism that mars some of her later work, for these poems vibrate with an inner fervor that needs no relationship to the political or social scene.

THE HEART IS A LONELY HUNTER

Type of work: Novel
Author: Carson McCullers (1917-1967)
Type of plot: Psychological realism
Time of plot: 1930's
Locale: A Georgia mill town
First published: 1940

To read The Heart Is a Lonely Hunter *as a novel of social criticism is to misinterpret the subtle yet precise art of McCullers. Her true theme in this remarkable first novel is that sense of moral isolation, expressed in terms of loneliness and longing, that is both the social evil of the modern world and the inescapable condition of humanity.*

Principal Characters

John Singer, a tall, immaculate, soberly dressed mute who mysteriously attracts troubled people to him. Mick, Jake, Dr. Copeland, and Biff are all welcome to visit or talk to him. Ironically, he himself longs to talk in sign language to his insane mute friend Spiros in the asylum but cannot penetrate Spiros' apathy and craving for food. Singer shoots himself, leaving his other four friends variously affected by his death.

Mick Kelly, a gangling adolescent girl always dressed in shorts, a shirt, and tennis shoes. A passionate lover of music, she finds relief from her loneliness by talking to Mr. Singer and listening to his radio. After his death, the loneliness returns, along with a feeling that she has been cheated, but by whom she does not know.

Biff Brannon, a café proprietor, a stolid man with a weakness for handicapped and sick people and an interest in human relationships. Having watched Mr. Singer with Jake and Mick, he is left after Singer's death wondering whether love is the answer to the problem of the human struggle.

Jake Blount, a squat man with long, powerful arms. He is a frustrated, idealistic workingman who tries to rouse his fellow workers. He believes that Mr. Singer is the only one who understands him. After Singer's death, Jake joins a free-for-all and later, evading the police, leaves town.

Dr. Benedict Mady Copeland, the only African-American physician in town, an idealistic man devoted to raising the standards of his race. Trying to see the judge about Willie, he is severely beaten by white men and jailed but is released on bail. Still sick from the beating, he broods over Singer's death.

Portia, the doctor's daughter, the Kellys' maid, a devout Presbyterian who worries over her father's and Mick's lack of religious belief.

Willie, Portia's brother, sentenced to hard labor for knifing a man. After brutal punishment for an attempted escape, he loses both feet from gangrene.

Spiros Antonapoulos, Mr. Singer's mute Greek friend, a fat, dreamy, slovenly man who works for his cousin. Spiros is interested in food, sleep, and drink, and sometimes in prayer before sleeping. Becoming insane and a public nuisance as well as a petty thief, he is placed in an asylum.

Charles Parker, Spiros' cousin, a fruit store owner, who has taken an American name. Finally fed up with Spiros' insane actions, he has him committed to the asylum.

Alice, Biff's complaining wife, with whom he has little communication.

Highboy, Portia's husband.

The Story

In a small town in the South, there were two mutes, one a grossly fat Greek named Spiros, the other a tall, immaculate man named Mr. Singer. They had no friends, and they lived together for ten years. After a lingering sickness, the Greek became a changed man. When he began to be obscene in public, the cousin for whom he worked sent him to the state insane asylum. After that, Mr. Singer was desolate.

He took all of his meals at the New York Café owned by Biff Brannon. Biff was a stolid man with a weakness for handicapped and sick people. When Jake Blount, a squat man with long, powerful arms, came to town, he went on a week-long drunk at Biff's expense. Biff had to find out what bothered Jake. Finding Mr. Singer eating at the café, Jake decided that he was the only person who could understand the message that he was trying to deliver. One night, Mr. Singer took Jake home with him. It was not until after he had slept that Jake realized Mr. Singer was a mute. He still believed, however, that the mute could understand him.

Mr. Singer had taken a room at the Kelly's boarding-house, where the daughter Mick, just entering her teens, was a gangly girl, always dressed in shorts, a shirt, and tennis shoes. She loved music and would go anywhere to hear it. Some nights, she went to a big house in town where she could hear symphonic music through the open windows while she crouched in the shrubbery. At home, no one realized what she wanted, until Mr. Singer moved there and let her talk to him when she was lonely.

Mick decided, after entering vocational school, that she had to have some friends. Planning a dance, she invited only high school students. The house was decorated with tinsel. Mick borrowed an evening dress and high-heeled shoes from one of her sisters.

On the night of the party, a throng of teenagers arrived and separated into noisy groups. When Mick handed out the prom cards, the boys went to one side of the room, the girls to the other. Silence descended. No one knew how to start things. A boy finally asked Mick to stroll with him. Outside the house, all the neighborhood children had gathered. While Mick and Harry walked around the block, the neighborhood children joined the party. By the time that Mick got back, the decorations were torn, the refreshments gone, and the invited and the uninvited guests mixed up so badly that the party was bedlam. Everyone congregated on the street to run races and jump ditches, the partygoers forgetful of their nearly grown-up state. Mick finally called off the party after she had been knocked breathless on a jump that she could have made easily in her tennis shoes.

Portia worked for the Kellys. Her father was Dr. Copeland, the only African-American doctor in town. He was an idealistic man who had always worked hard to raise the standards of black people. One dark night, Mr. Singer had stepped up and helped him light a cigarette in the rain. It was the first time that a white man had ever offered Dr. Copeland help or smiled at him. When he told Portia about a deaf-mute boy patient of his, she assured him that Mr. Singer would help the boy.

Jake, who had found a job with a flying-jenny show, tried to rouse the workers. He spent each Sunday with Mr. Singer, explaining that he had first wanted to be an evangelist until he had been made aware of the inequality in the world. He had unintentionally insulted Dr. Copeland twice, but he was one of the first to talk about doing something for Willie, Dr. Copeland's son.

Willie had been sentenced to hard labor for knifing a man. At the prison camp, he and two others tried to run away. They were put in a cold shack for three days with their bare feet hoisted up by a looped rope. Willie lost both feet from gangrene. Dr. Copeland, trying to see the judge about the case, was severely beaten up by a white crowd around the court house and put in jail. Mr. Singer and Portia obtained his release on bail, and Jake went with Mr. Singer to Dr. Copeland's house. There he argued the ethics of the case with the doctor all night, Jake too hysterical to be logical, the doctor too sick.

There was a peacefulness in Mr. Singer's face that attracted Mick. She followed him whenever she could. He bought a radio, which he kept in his room for her to use. Those were hours of deep enjoyment for her. Mick believed that she had music in her that she would have to learn to write down.

She fascinated Biff. After his wife died, he watched Mick begin to grow up, but he seldom spoke to her. He was equally quiet with Mr. Singer when he visited at the Kelly boarding-house. Mr. Singer considered Mick pitiful, Jake crazy, Dr. Copeland noble, and Biff thoughtful, but they were always welcome to his room.

On his vacation, Mr. Singer went to see his Greek friend. He took beautiful presents along with him, but Spiros was petulant over anything but food. Only there did Mr. Singer take his hands out of his pockets; then he wore himself out trying to tell the Greek with his hands everything he had seen and thought since the Greek went away. Although Spiros showed no interest, Mr. Singer tried even harder to entertain him. When he left, the Greek was still impassive.

Mr. Singer's board was the only steady money on which the Kellys could depend. When one sister got sick, the loss of her salary threw the whole family in a quandary. Mick heard that a job was opening at the five-and-ten-cent store. The family in conclave decided that she was too young to work. The fact that they were talking about her welfare for the first time prompted her to apply for the job. She got it, but each night she was too tired for anything but sleep.

It was again time for Mr. Singer to go to see his Greek friend. Laden down with presents, he made the long trip. When he reached the asylum office, the clerk told him that Spiros was dead. Stricken, he found his way back to the town, left his luggage at the station, went to his room, and put a bullet through his chest.

Mr. Singer's death left his four friends confused. Dr. Copeland, still sick, brooded over it. Jake Blount joined in a brawl at the carnival grounds and, after hearing that the police were looking for him, left town. Mick did not sleep well for weeks after the funeral. All that

she had left was Mr. Singer's radio. She felt cheated because there was no time, no money, no feeling anymore for music, but she could never decide who had cheated her. Biff, who had watched Mr. Singer with Jake and Mick, was still puzzling over the relationships he had studied. He questioned whether, in the struggle of humanity, love might be the answer.

Critical Evaluation

All of Carson McCullers' writing turns on the plight of the loving and the lonely, and it is her view of moral and spiritual isolation as the inescapable condition of humanity that makes *The Heart Is a Lonely Hunter* so impressive as a first novel. Although the book shows certain limitations resulting from the author's youth and inexperience, it nevertheless remains a remarkable work for a twenty-two-year-old to write. To read it as a novel of social criticism is to misunderstand the author's subtle art. One character is a fiery white radical and another is a fanatic black Marxist, but their political views are subordinate to the dominant theme of the novel: the loneliness of the individual and the frustrated struggle to communicate with others. Singer, the ironically named mute, is the focal figure in the story. It is to him that the other main characters turn when they wish to unburden themselves, to pour out their views, their ideas, their emotions.

It is ironic that Singer should be the one toward whom the others turn to release the tension and some of the confusion within them, as Singer hears nothing and is really the loneliest person in the story after the removal of his insane mute friend Spiros Antonapoulos to the asylum. With the death of Antonapoulos, Singer has no one to turn to and he shoots himself, while the others, who have given him nothing, continue their own self-centered lives.

Love and hatred struggle for mastery in McCullers'

characters. Jake Blount, itinerant carnival worker, seethes with anger at the injustices that the common people endure in a capitalistic society that permits the rich to prey upon the poor. Dr. Copeland rages also against the inequities of capitalism, but he concentrates his hatred upon the whites who have for so long oppressed his race. Dr. Copeland's intemperance of thought and feeling brings him into conflict both with his family and with Jake, whose own intemperance makes a successful dialogue between himself and Copeland impossible despite their common anger at the political and economic system in which they live.

Mick Kelly is experiencing the pains of adolescence, suffering from self-consciousness, beset by the confusions that accompany her developing sexuality, and indulging in dreams of the future—a future that will be frustrated forever by the economic situation of her family. She is finally embittered by the realization that her Woolworth's job means doom to her hopes.

Biff Brannon, who keeps his café open at night as a haven for lonely people, seeks an understanding of those who come in not only to eat and drink but to talk as well. They are objects for his study, but they also help him to forget the loneliness that he feels when they have gone. He is the last person one sees in the novel—alone, frightened, and awaiting the sun of a new day that will bring customers through the café door.

HENDERSON THE RAIN KING

Type of work: Novel
Author: Saul Bellow (1915-   )
Type of plot: Humorous allegory
Time of plot: 1950's
Locale: Central East Africa
First published: 1959

Bellow presents the archetypal quest for self-fulfillment and identity in Henderson the Rain King. *The character of Henderson, an American millionaire who journeys to Africa in search of himself, is both comic and heroic, allowing readers to identify with his experiences and to find their own truths.*

Principal Characters

Eugene Henderson, an American millionaire. Believing that something is lacking in his life, he travels to East Africa in search of wisdom and purpose. He is comic and larger than life, and his experiences with two very different tribes, the Arnewi and the Wariri, shape his perceptions of himself and his world.

Romilayu, his native guide and companion.

Willatale, the queen of the gentle Arnewi tribe. She realizes that Henderson has a problem with the concepts of life and death.

Mtalba, the queen's sister, who wishes to marry Henderson. He runs away, however, after accidentally destroying the Arnewi's water cistern.

Itelo, the prince of the Arnewi and their champion.

Dahfu, the chief of the warlike Wariri tribe. Having attended missionary school, Dahfu is more enlightened than his subjects and brings Henderson under his tutelage. As head of the tribe's lion cult, he teaches Henderson how to think like a lion, letting him get in touch with his animal side.

Gmilo, a lion superstitiously believed to contain the spirit of Dahfu's father.

Atti, Dahfu's pet lioness, who the tribe fears has bewitched their chief.

Horko and **The Bunam,** the chief's uncle and the high priest of the Wariri. They plot the overthrow of Dahfu, who dies trying to capture a wild lion.

Although the forms and techniques of fiction seem capable of almost endless variation, most novelists have only one main story to tell, and fortunate writers are the ones who find their major themes and fables early in their careers. Saul Bellow found his theme in his first novel, *Dangling Man* (1944): It is the quest, the search for freedom and rest within the fretted human spirit.

For this reason, *Henderson the Rain King* is a messianic novel, like D. H. Lawrence's *The Plumed Serpent* (1926), or William Faulkner's *A Fable* (1954). The pattern that it follows—the outsider in search of the truth, which a local African messiah reveals to him—is as old as Samuel Johnson's *Rasselas, Prince of Abyssinia* (1759). The theme is the achieving of individual identity, of coming into being. To show an individual learning the depths of his or her own nature, Bellow constructs a situation that verges on the fantastic: A middle-aged American millionaire becomes the chief priest of the rain god-

dess for a tribe in a totally isolated region somewhere in East Africa. The identification of the tribe is impossible, the geography is unplaceable, and the realities of travel are ignored. The narrator uses a coarse but effective style; he is what is technically called an "unreliable narrator" who must reveal his character, even when he does not know his identity, in the earlier chapters; the redeemed must act as if he were unredeemed in telling of the events up to his redemption. Unlike Charles Dickens' *Great Expectations* (1860-1861), for example, in which Pip tells the reader all after the close of the action, the narrator employs a continuous past tense so that the narration and the action parallel each other. Thus neither he nor the reader is ever in advance of the final revelation.

Yet the seeker in Bellow's fiction is no Ulysses, Hamlet, Don Quixote, Gulliver, Huck Finn, or Ishmael. He is the philosophical clown, the innocent American and adventurous discoverer of a spiritual quest which begins with the knowledge that "man's character is his fate" and ends with the realization that "man's fate is his character." He is the beggar Joseph in *Dangling Man*, Asa Leventhal in *The Victim* (1947), and Augie in *The Adventures of Augie March* (1953), that free-swinging, irreverent, passionate account of one man's journey on two continents, through the Depression years and a world war, and within the geography of his own soul. All of Bellow's heroes are driven by their desires toward some goal where the beginning of wisdom is often indistinguishable from error and folly. Eugene Henderson, the narrator and central figure of *Henderson the Rain King*, is no exception. In fact, he is the most frantic and grotesque of Bellow's creations.

He is, to begin with, a tremendously comic figure, oversized in physique, great in his appetites, obsessed by the demands of an "I want, I want" that clamors without appeasement within him. He is fifty-five years old when the reader first meets him. A man with a temper as violent as his physical force, he has more money than even his eccentric needs demand, a second wife, and an assorted brood of children. He has turned his home into a pig farm, learned to play the violin, and acquired a reputation for drinking and crude manners. When he tries to sum up his life, it is, as he says, a mess, a fact that he realizes acutely without knowing why.

When he can no longer face himself, his family, or his past, he flees to Africa with dreams of becoming another Dr. Schweitzer. Africa, as Henderson sees it, is an empty and secret land, the last outpost of the prehuman past, a land unmarked by the footprints of history.

With a native guide, Romilayu, he arrives at last in the land of the Arnewi, where he engages in a ritual wrestling bout with Itelo, the champion of the tribe. Yet, in that remote place, he still cannot escape his past; he remains a millionaire, a wanderer, a violent man looking for peace and happiness. The queen of these gentle people tells him that his malady is the *grun-tu-molani*, the will to live instead of dying. Accepted by the Arnewi and courted by the queen's sister, Mtalba, Henderson plans to cleanse the tribe's sacred cistern, which is infested with frogs. His homemade bomb blasts away the wall of the cistern, however, and the water seeps into the parched earth. Rather than face the consequences of this disaster, he runs away.

Henderson next turns up among the Wariri, a more warlike and savage tribe. The king is Dahfu, a ruler considerably more enlightened than his subjects, for he has studied in a missionary school and can speak to Henderson in English. While watching a tribal festival, Henderson is moved to lift the statue of Mummah, goddess of clouds, after several of the Wariri have failed to budge the massive idol. His act of strength, he soon discovers, is sacramental. When a sudden downpour follows, he is acclaimed as the new Sungo, or rain king, of the tribe, and he is compelled to put on the green silk drawers of his office. Yet Henderson, elevated to a post in which he becomes a scapegoat for the capricious rain goddess, is no better off than he was before; he is as much governed by ritual as King Dahfu, who will rule only as long as his powers of procreation last. When they fail, he will be strangled and another ruler will be selected.

In the end, Dahfu is the means of Henderson's salvation. In an underground pit, he keeps a pet lion, Atti, a creature hated and feared by the Wariri because they believe that the beast has bewitched their king. As Dahfu continues to postpone the ritual capture of the wild lion supposed to contain his father's spirit, the chief priest and the king's uncle plot against him. Under Dahfu's tutelage, meanwhile, Henderson learns to romp with the lion and imitate its roars. Dahfu tells him to act the lion's role, to be a beast. Recovery of Henderson's humanity will come later; meanwhile, he is to imitate the lion.

Dahfu's lion cult impresses Henderson. His failure has been his bullish or piggish attempt to alter the world around him, to kick back when he felt kicked by fate. Instead he must alter himself, and in particular cure himself of fear by thinking like a lion, by imagining the lion at the cortex of his brain, and making himself over as a lion. In spite of his crushing failure with the Arnewi, he has learned two things that help him in his daily lion lessons. First, although a person when struck is likely to strike out in revenge (as the Wariri but not the Arnewi do), pure virtue can break the chain of blows. The Arnewi, principally Mtalba, the aunt of Prince Itelo who was once the companion of Dahfu, are virtuous but cowlike because they love their cows; hence their virtue is not for Henderson. Second, he has been confirmed in a sneaking sense of his own worth by Mtalba, who oozed the odor of sanctity and was prepared to marry him. The demanding voice of the "I want, I want" within Henderson becomes the roar of the lion as Dahfu instructs him that humans are still animals, but that it is possible for him to be a lion and not a pig.

The king's final lesson is that of courage in meeting death, which Henderson has always thought the biggest problem of all. When Dahfu is killed, possibly through the chief priest's conniving, while trying to capture a wild lion, Henderson flees the Wariri to avoid becoming the next king, and he returns with a captured lion cub to the United States. One gets a last glimpse of him at the airport in Newfoundland. He is playing with a little boy, who is the child of American parents but who speaks only Persian. Dahfu and his lion have done their work. Henderson's spirit is finally at home in the animal housing of his flesh.

No brief outline of Henderson's story can ever adequately convey the gusty, wild humor, sensuous brilliance, abundant sense of life, or stylistic vigor of Bellow's novel. It is also not profitable to discuss the allegorical or symbolic meanings that it contains, for those are matters that readers must discover for themselves. Call the novel whatever one will—a wild burlesque on all the travel books ever written, a comic extravaganza on modern themes, a melodramatic adventure story, a fantasy, an allegory, or the narrative of a symbolic journey into the dark reaches of the soul—*Henderson the Rain King* allows every reader to find a moment of truth. It is not always the same truth because readers look in different directions, but it is some revelation of the comedy and the tragedy of being. One cannot demand more of any novelist.

HISTORY OF THE CONQUEST OF MEXICO

Type of work: History
Author: William Hickling Prescott (1796-1859)
Time of work: 1519-1525
Locale: Mexico
First published: 1843

The History of the Conquest of Mexico, *Prescott's most brilliant work, describes the subjugation of an entire people by daring conquistadores who played upon the religious superstitions of their victims.*

Principal Personages

Don Diego Velásquez, the governor of Cuba
Hernando Cortés, conqueror of Mexico
Pedro de Alvarado, one of Cortés' lieutenants
Marina, Cortés' Native American mistress

Montezuma, emperor of the Aztecs
Guatemozin, Montezuma's nephew and successor
Cacama, nephew of the emperor
Pánfilo de Narváez, Velásquez' lieutenant

Because William Hickling Prescott deals with his narrative in dramatic terms and with an abundance of background material, particularly on the Aztec civilization, his *History of the Conquest of Mexico* has remained the classic account of the death of a civilization that in many ways rivaled ancient Egypt's. Prescott's observations on the Spanish efforts to convert the Aztecs often betray his rather marked suspicion of the Catholic church, but his personal biases are less pronounced in other matters.

The success of the Spanish conquest was aided by the Aztec legend of Quetzalcoatl, a benevolent god who, once having lived on earth and departed, was expected to return: tall, white-skinned, dark-bearded. When the first Spanish expeditionary party, led by Juan de Grijalva, made a preliminary exploration of the mainland, it encountered an unfriendly reception on landing. When the Aztecs happened to associate the Spaniards with the legend of Quetzalcoatl, however, they sent Grijalva away with rich gifts. As a result, Don Diego Velásquez, governor of Cuba, immediately organized a second expedition, to be led by Hernando Cortés.

Cortés' armada left Cuba on February 10, 1519, and landed on the island of Cozumel. At that time, he acquired two valuable aides: a Spanish soldier named Aguilar, who had been taken captive by the natives of Cozumel during the Grijalva expedition, to serve as an interpreter, and Marina, a girl from the mainland whose mother had sold her on Cozumel. Marina became not only an interpreter but Cortés' mistress as well.

When the Spaniards moved on to the mainland, landing

on Good Friday at what is now Veracruz, they stepped ashore in a Mexico significantly disunited. Montezuma, emperor of the Aztecs, was a good warrior and a just ruler, but he was also superstitious and a lover of pleasure, with numerous enemies. There was in addition to this political unrest a vague feeling among the people that the return of Quetzalcoatl was imminent: Since the days of Christopher Columbus, there had been rumors of the Spaniards, and these rumors had somehow fused with the ancient legend. Dissension among the lesser kingdoms and tribes of Montezuma's empire and the revival of the Quetzalcoatl myth were of great value to the Spaniards in their invasion of Mexico.

Because he sensed mounting resistance to his leadership, Cortés established Veracruz as a civil colony rather than a military base; in this way, he made the expedition responsible only to the crown, not to the governor of Cuba. Later, when Juan Díaz conspired to turn the expedition back to Cuba, Cortés ordered the destruction of his own fleet. With only one small ship left, the men had little to think about but the march forward.

Leaving some soldiers behind to protect the coastal settlement, Cortés began his march toward the capital, Tenochtitlán, now Mexico City. While one of the original purposes of the expedition was the conversion of the local tribes to Catholicism, the expedition, once under way, did not delay for missionary activities. Indeed, Father Olmedo, the expedition's priest, persuaded Cortés not to try to convert all the "heathen" along the route.

The first pronounced resistance to the Spaniards took

place among the Tlascalans, an agricultural people but a nation of warriors as well. Two earlier battles with the Tlascalans were indecisive, but a third, fought on September 5, 1519, was in effect a victory for the Spaniards. The Tlascalan leader, Xicotencatl, continued, however, to threaten and harass the invaders. Cortés forged ahead, his forces plundering as they went, and finally, with Xicotencatl reconciled to submission, the Spaniards arrived at Tlascala itself. In the meantime, Montezuma continued in his policy of sending gifts but barring the Spaniards from Tenochtitlán.

At Cholula, Cortés learned through Marina that the natives were planning a conspiracy with Montezuma's help. Profiting from former enmity between the Cholulans and the Tlascalans, Cortés stationed Tlascalans around the city and proceeded to massacre the treacherous Cholulans.

Suspecting still further hostility, Cortés and his men moved on, passing between the mountains named Iztaccihuatl and Popocatepetl. No further resistance was forthcoming, and the expedition was shortly at a point where the fertile Valley of Mexico lay before them. Confounded by their advance and awed by their power, Montezuma at last sent his nephew Cacama with a message of welcome for the conquistadores. On November 8, 1519, Cortés and his men entered Tenochtitlán, a city built in the middle of a great lake, and Montezuma greeted them with pomp and dignity. Although the Aztecs remained outwardly friendly, Cortés continued to be suspicious of his host because he had received reports from Veracruz of troubles instigated by the emperor. Quauhpopoca, governor of the coastal province, was burned for his part in the disturbances, and Montezuma, taken by surprise, was seized and removed to the fortified quarters occupied by the Spaniards. Although a hostage, Montezuma conducted the business of the country as usual.

In 1520, Montezuma formally announced his subservience to Spain; the nobles concurred, and the legend of Quetzalcoatl was revived among the people. Though conditions appeared to be stable, Cortés ordered the rebuilding of his fleet.

Cortés' relations with Velásquez had now deteriorated to such an extent that the governor outfitted a rival expedition under the leadership of Pánfilo de Narváez. Gonzalo de Sandoval, the governor appointed by Cortés at Villa Rica, maintained a close watch over Narváez's attempts to establish a settlement, but Cortés felt compelled to deal with Narváez personally. Leaving the capital in the care of an aide, Pedro de Alvarado, he marched to the coast with a detachment of troops and Native American allies.

With his band of only 226 men and 5 horses, Cortés surprised Narváez and took him prisoner. In Cortés' absence, revolt broke out in Tenochtitlán. Alvarado, plagued by constant fears of conspiracy, had slaughtered several hundred Aztec nobles during the festival of Huitzilopotchli, the Aztec god of war. Earlier, Cortés had allowed Montezuma's brother, Cuitlahua, to act as the imperial representative during Montezuma's captivity. Bitterly vengeful after the massacre, Cuitlahua led the Aztecs in a retaliatory uprising against the Spaniards.

With his own band reinforced by two thousand Tlascalans, Cortés returned hurriedly to the capital. During the first stages of hostilities following the return of Cortés, Montezuma attempted to intercede and pacify the embattled Aztecs, but his people turned on him, and he was fatally wounded. Broken and in despair, Montezuma died on June 30, 1520.

During the uprising, the Aztecs had destroyed all bridges on causeways leading to the mainland, and the Spanish retreat from the city became chaotic, with heavy losses. On the plains of Otumba, however, the Spaniards and their Tlascalan allies managed to put the Aztecs to flight. The Spaniards retreated into Tlascalan territory, where they could feel safe once more. Yet the troops were restless after their harrowing retreat, and for a time there seemed to be some chance that the Tlascalans might join the Aztecs in common cause against the invaders. Fortunately, the Tlascalans remained friendly; in fact, their chief, before he died of smallpox, became a Christian— the first successfully converted native.

Guatemozin, Montezuma's nephew and successor, had sworn to drive the Spaniards from his country. As Cortés marched back toward the capital, however, he gathered from friendly tribes more Native American auxiliaries to lead against the Aztecs. Welcomed in Tezcuco by the new prince, Ixtlilxochitl, an enemy of Montezuma, Cortés' forces advanced for the final subjugation of the Aztec civilization.

More cohesive than Prescott's companion study on the conquest of Peru, *History of the Conquest of Mexico* is the author's most brilliant work. Though the book may lack profound philosophical insight, it is a vivid portrayal of a fascinating historical fact: the subjugation of a whole people by a mere handful of alien adventurers— cruel, daring intriguers who played upon the religious superstitions of their victims.

THE HOUSE OF THE SEVEN GABLES

Type of work: Novel
Author: Nathaniel Hawthorne (1804-1864)
Type of plot: Psychological romance
Time of plot: 1850
Locale: Salem, Massachusetts
First published: 1851

Woven into the ingenious plot of this novel is the theme that the sins of the parents are passed on to the children in succeeding generations. The book reflects the author's interest in New England history and his doubts about a moribund region that looked backward to past times.

Principal Characters

Colonel Pyncheon, a stern Massachusetts magistrate who, during the famous witchcraft trials of the seventeenth century, sent to his death a man whose property he coveted for himself. Cursed by his innocent victim, the Colonel died on the day that his big new house, the House of the Seven Gables, built on his victim's land, was officially opened to guests.

Matthew Maule, Colonel Pyncheon's victim, who swore that his unjust accuser should drink blood, as Colonel Pyncheon did when he died.

Thomas Maule, the son of Matthew Maule. As the head carpenter building the House of the Seven Gables, young Maule took an opportunity to build a secret recess in which was hidden the deed by which the Pyncheons hoped to claim a vast domain in Maine.

Judge Pyncheon, one of Colonel Pyncheon's nineteenth century descendants and a man like his ancestor in many ways. A judge, a member of Congress at one time, a member of many boards of directors, and an aspirant to the governorship of his state, he is a rich man who through his own efforts has multiplied the fortune that he inherited from his uncle, Jaffrey. Although he tries to present himself in a good light, Judge Pyncheon is a hard man and not entirely honest. He destroyed one of his uncle's wills, which named his cousin Clifford as heir, and he stood by while his cousin was wrongly sent to prison for a murder that he did not commit. Convinced that his wronged cousin knows of additional family wealth hidden by their uncle, the Judge threatens the released but broken man with confinement in an insane asylum if the hiding place of the remaining wealth is not revealed. Fortunately for his cousin, the Judge dies of natural causes induced by emotion while making his threats.

Clifford Pyncheon, the Judge's unfortunate cousin, who serves a thirty-year prison term for allegedly murdering his uncle, who really died of natural causes. A handsome, carefree, beauty-loving man at one time, he emerges from prison three decades later a broken, pale, and emaciated wreck of a human being, content to hide away in the House of the Seven Gables, where he is looked after by his sister Hepzibah and their young cousin Phoebe. Clifford's mind is weakened and his spirit so broken by misfortune that he actually does strange, if harmless, acts, so that the Judge's threat to force Clifford into an asylum could be made good. At the Judge's unexpected death, Clifford feels a great release after having been oppressed by his cousin for so long. Clifford, his sister, and Phoebe inherit the Pyncheon fortune and have the promise of a comfortable life in the future.

Hepzibah Pyncheon, Clifford's sister, who lived alone for many years in shabby gentility in the House of the Seven Gables while her brother was in prison. She has few friends, for she seldom leaves the house, and she is so nearsighted that she always wears a frown, making people think that she is a cross and angry woman. After the return of her brother from prison, she sets up a little shop in her house to try to provide for herself and Clifford, to whom she is devoted. Opening the shop is very difficult for her, as she dislikes meeting people and believes that entering trade is unladylike for a member of the Pyncheon family.

Phoebe Pyncheon, a young, pretty, and lively girl from the country. She comes to live with Hepzibah when her mother, a widow, remarries. Phoebe takes over the little cent-shop and makes it a profitable venture for Hepzibah. Phoebe also brings new life to the House of the Seven Gables by cheering it with her beauty and song, as well as by tending the neglected flowers and doing other homely tasks. She is highly considerate of her elderly cousins and spends much of her time entertaining Clifford.

Mr. Holgrave, a liberal-minded young daguerreotypist who rents a portion of the House of the Seven Gables from Hepzibah. An eager, energetic young man of twenty-two, he falls in love with Phoebe Pyncheon, and they are engaged to be married. When Phoebe inherits a third of the Judge's large fortune, Holgrave decides to become more conservative in his thinking. It is he who reveals the secret recess hiding the now-useless deed to the vast tract of land in Maine. He knows the secret because he is a descendant of Thomas Maule. In fact, his name is Maule, but he hides his true identity by assuming for a time the name of Holgrave.

Uncle Venner, an old handyman befriended by the Pyncheons. He is one of the few persons of the town to accept Hepzibah and Clifford as friends when they are in unfortunate circumstances.

The Story

The House of the Seven Gables was a colonial house built in the English style of half-timber and half-plaster. It stood on Pyncheon Street in quiet Salem, Massachusetts. The house had been built in the seventeenth century by Colonel Pyncheon, who had wrested the desirable site from Matthew Maule, a poor man executed as a warlock. Because Colonel Pyncheon was responsible for the guilty verdict and because he was taking the doomed man's land, Maule, at the moment of his execution, declared that God would give the Pyncheons blood to drink. Despite this grim prophecy, the Colonel had his house, and its builder was Thomas Maule, son of the executed man.

Colonel Pyncheon, dying in his great oak chair just after the house had been completed, choked with blood so that his shirtfront was stained scarlet. Although doctors explained the cause of his death as apoplexy, the townsfolk had not forgotten old Maule's prophecy. The time of the Colonel's death was inauspicious. It was said that he had just completed a treaty by which he had bought huge tracts of land from a Native American tribe, but this deed had not been confirmed by the general court and was never discovered by any of his heirs. Rumor also had it that a man was seen leaving the house about the time that Colonel Pyncheon died.

More recently, another startling event had occurred at the House of the Seven Gables. Jaffrey Pyncheon, a bachelor, had been found dead in the Colonel's great oak armchair, and his nephew, Clifford Pyncheon, had been sentenced to imprisonment after being found guilty of the murder of his uncle.

These events were in the unhappy past, however, and in 1850, the House of the Seven Gables was the home of Miss Hepzibah Pyncheon, an elderly, single woman, who let one wing of the old house to a young man of radical tendencies, a maker of daguerreotypes, whose name was Mr. Holgrave.

Miss Hepzibah was about to open a shop in one of the rooms of her house. Her brother, Clifford, was coming home from the state prison after thirty years, and she had to earn money in some way to support him. On the first day of her venture as a storekeeper, Miss Hepzibah proved to be a failure. The situation was saved, however, by the arrival of young Phoebe Pyncheon from the country. Soon she was operating the shop at a profit.

Clifford arrived from the prison a broken man of childish, querulous ways. Once he tried to throw himself from a big arched window that afforded him almost his only contact with the outside world. He was fond of Phoebe, but Miss Hepzibah irritated him with her sullen scowling. For acquaintances, Clifford had Uncle Venner, a handyman who did odd jobs for the neighborhood, and the tenant of the house, Mr. Holgrave, the daguerreotypist.

The only other relative living in town was the highly respected Judge Pyncheon, another nephew of old Jaffrey Pyncheon, for whose murder Clifford had spent thirty years in prison. He was, in fact, the heir of the murdered man, and he had been somehow involved with Clifford's arrest and imprisonment. For these reasons, Clifford refused to see him when the Judge offered to give Clifford and Hepzibah a home at his countryseat.

Meanwhile, Phoebe had become friendly with Mr. Holgrave. In turn, he thought that she brought light and hope into the gloomy old house, and he missed her greatly when she returned to her home in the country. Her visit was to be a brief one, however, for she had gone only to make some preparations before coming to live permanently with Miss Hepzibah and Clifford.

Before Phoebe returned from the country, Judge Pyncheon visited the House of the Seven Gables and, over Miss Hepzibah's protest, insisted on seeing Clifford, who, he said, knew a family secret that meant great wealth for the Judge. When at last she went out of the room to summon her brother, Judge Pyncheon sat down in the old chair by the fireplace, over which hung the portrait of Colonel Pyncheon, who had built the house. As the Judge sat in the old chair, his ticking watch in his hand, an unusually strong family likeness could be noted between the stern Judge and his Puritan ancestor in the portrait. Unable to find Clifford to deliver the Judge's message, Miss Hepzibah returned. As she approached the door, Clifford appeared from within, laughing and pointing to the chair where the Judge sat dead of apoplexy under the portrait of the old Colonel. His shirtfront was stained with blood. Maule's curse had been fulfilled once more; God had given the Judge blood to drink.

The two helpless old people were so distressed by the sight of the dead man that they crept away from the house without notifying anyone and departed on the train. The dead body of the Judge remained seated in the chair.

It was some time before the body was discovered by Holgrave. When Phoebe returned to the house, he admitted her. He had not yet summoned the police because he wished to protect the old couple as long as possible. While he and Phoebe were alone in the house, Holgrave declared his love for her. They were interrupted by the return of Miss Hepzibah and the now calm Clifford. They had decided that to run away would not solve their problem.

The police attributed the Judge's death to natural causes, and Clifford, Miss Hepzibah, and Phoebe became the heirs to his great fortune. It now seemed certain that Jaffrey Pyncheon had also died of natural causes, not by Clifford's hand, and that the Judge had so arranged the evidence to make Clifford appear a murderer.

In a short time, all the occupants of the House of the Seven Gables were ready to move to the Judge's country estate, which they had inherited. They gathered for the last time in the old room under the dingy portrait of Colonel Pyncheon. Clifford said he had a vague memory of something mysterious connected with the picture. Holgrave offered to explain the mystery and pressed a secret spring near the picture. When he did so, the portrait fell to the floor, disclosing a recess in the wall. From this niche, Holgrave drew out the ancient tribal deed to the lands that the Pyncheons had claimed. Clifford then remembered that he had once found the secret spring. It was this secret that Judge Pyncheon had hoped to learn from Clifford.

Phoebe asked how Holgrave happened to know these facts. The young man explained that his name was not Holgrave, but Maule. He was, he said, a descendant of the accused warlock Matthew Maule and of Thomas Maule, who built the House of the Seven Gables. The knowledge of the hidden deed had been handed down to the descendants of Thomas Maule, who built the compartment behind the portrait and secreted the deed there after the Colonel's death. Holgrave was the last of the Maules, and Phoebe the last of the Pyncheons. Matthew Maule's curse had been expiated.

Critical Evaluation

In reputation, *The House of the Seven Gables* usually stands in the shadow of its predecessor, *The Scarlet Letter*. It is, however, a rich and solid achievement, a Gothic romance whose characters are among Nathaniel Hawthorne's most complex. The author himself thought it, in comparison with the earlier work, "more characteristic of my mind, and more proper and natural for me to write."

In his preface, Hawthorne explicitly states his moral: "The truth, namely that the wrong-doing of one generation lives into the successive ones, and, divesting itself of every temporary advantage, becomes a pure and uncontrollable mischief." This sentiment echoes the biblical adage that "The fathers have eaten sour grapes, and the children's teeth are set on edge." Hawthorne's interest in the heritage of sin was probably whetted by the history of his own family. His first American ancestor, William Hathorne (Nathaniel himself added the *w* to the family name), was a soldier and magistrate who once had a Quaker woman publicly whipped through the streets. William's son John, having, as Nathaniel said, "inherited the persecuting spirit," was a judge at the infamous Salem witch trials, during which a defendant cursed another of the three judges with the cry, "God will give you blood to drink!" Thenceforth, as Hawthorne noted, although the family remained decent, respectable folk, their fortunes began to decline.

The fate of the Pyncheon family of the novel is considerably more dramatic. Matthew Maule's curse on Colonel Pyncheon, who has persecuted him for witchcraft and wrested from him the land on which the seven-gabled house is to be built, is precisely that which Judge John Hathorne had heard in a similar trial. It is apparently fulfilled on the day of the housewarming when Colonel Pyncheon dies of apoplexy, the hemorrhage rising through his throat to stain his white shirt. Hawthorne would have readers believe, however, that one cannot so easily pay for such sins as Pyncheon's. The family occupies the mansion, but misfortune is their constant lot. There are repeated apoplectic deaths, sometimes heralded by an ominous gurgling in the throat; greed leads Judge Pyncheon, like his ancestor, to participate in a trumped-up trial, this time against his own cousin; and years of pride and isolation have thinned the family blood so that, like the scrawny chickens that peck in the Pyncheon garden, they are an unattractive, ineffectual lot. Judge Pyncheon is a monster who hides his avarice and callousness behind a façade of philanthropy and civic service. Clifford, like Hawthorne's Young Goodman Brown, is a sensitive soul who is unmanned by his confrontation with evil; after years of imprisonment, he is poised on the brink of madness. Hepzibah, who has spent most of her life waiting for her brother's release, is virtually helpless either to resolve her precarious financial situation or to deal with her malevolent cousin.

Only young Phoebe possesses both goodness and energy. It is significant that she is the "country cousin" whose father married beneath his rank; Hepzibah observes that the girl's self-reliance must have come from her mother's blood. Thus Hawthorne casts his vote for the energizing effects of a democratic, as opposed to an aristocratic, social system; he has Holgrave, the daguerreotypist, support this view with the comment that families should continually merge into the great mass of humanity, without regard to ancestry.

Holgrave is the other fully vital character in the novel. He is one of Hawthorne's most charming creations: a perceptive, adventurous man who has been, it seems, almost everywhere and done almost everything. His conversations with Phoebe reveal him as a radical who believes that the past "lies upon the Present like a giant's dead body," preventing any generation's true fulfillment—a thesis frequently expressed by Hawthorne's contemporary Ralph Waldo Emerson. Holgrave goes so far as to suggest that institutional buildings should "crumble to ruin once in twenty years, or thereabouts, as a hint to the people to examine into and reform the institutions which they symbolize." He is also a psychologist; his daguerreotypes, which go beyond mere pictorial likeness to expose personality, symbolize his insight into human nature.

At the end of the novel, readers are led to believe that the curse is broken as Phoebe, the last of the Pyncheons, plans to marry Holgrave, who turns out to be a descendant of old Matthew Maule. The curse's effects can all be explained naturally: Holgrave observes that perhaps old Maule's prophecy was founded on knowledge that apoplectic death had been a Pyncheon trait for generations. Avarice and cruelty can certainly be passed on by example, and pride, isolation, and inbreeding can account for the "thin-bloodedness" of the once-aristocratic family. Now that Phoebe, whose blood has already been enriched by plebeian stock, and Holgrave, who has escaped the stifling influence of his own declining family by traveling widely, replace a tradition of hatred with that of love, it seems plausible that the curse may indeed have run its course. Perhaps the chain of ugly events—what Chillingworth of *The Scarlet Letter* termed "dark necessity"—can be terminated by positive acts of goodwill.

The novel is replete with Gothic characteristics: mystery, violence, a curse, gloomy atmosphere, archaic diction, and visits from the spirit world. Yet, though it is not realistic, it demonstrates what Henry James called Hawthorne's "high sense of reality," in that it reveals profound truths about how the effects of the sins of the parents are felt by children for generations to come. The ending discloses that, although he recognized the deterministic effects of heredity, environment, and humanity's predisposition to evil, Hawthorne was essentially a hopeful man who believed that the individual possesses a residuum of will that can cope with and perhaps change "dark necessity."

THE HUMAN COMEDY

Type of work: Novel
Author: William Saroyan (1908-1981)
Type of plot: Sentimental romance
Time of plot: 1940's
Locale: Ithaca, California
First published: 1943

One of the most touching and frankly sentimental of Saroyan's works, The Human Comedy *deals with the family of a soldier who died in World War II. The novel has for its theme the idea that human beings can never die as long as they live on in the hearts of those who loved them.*

Principal Characters

Katey Macauley, a widow who is trying to bring up her family alone. She has imaginary talks with her dead husband, in which she discusses family problems with him. She believes that her husband is not dead as long as he lives in the lives of his children. She accepts Tobey into the family after Marcus is killed.

Homer Macauley, Katey's second oldest son, who takes a night job at the telegraph office. He gets up early every day and exercises so that he will be in shape to run the hurdles at the high school. He finds the telegram that Mr. Grogan has typed out telling Katey that Marcus has been killed.

Marcus Macauley, Katey's oldest son, who goes into the Army and makes friends with Tobey George. Tobey has no family of his own, and so Marcus shares stories of his family with Tobey. Marcus wants Tobey to go to his home and marry his sister, Bess, after the war. Marcus is killed in action.

Mary Arena, Marcus' sweetheart.

Tobey George, an orphan whom Marcus befriends in the army. Tobey is lonely and lives vicariously through Marcus' family. He returns to Marcus' home after the war and, in a sense, takes Marcus' place as a son.

Mr. Grogan, Spangler's assistant in the telegraph office, with whom Homer has long talks concerning the efficacy of war. Mr. Grogan has a weak heart and gets drunk every night. One of Homer's duties is to see that he stays awake. He dies after typing out the message that Marcus has been killed in action.

Thomas Spangler, the manager of the telegraph office.

Bess and **Ulysses Macauley,** Katey's two other children.

Lionel, Ulysses' friend, who takes him to the library and shows him the many books.

The Story

Mr. Macauley was dead, and his wife and children had to take care of themselves. When Marcus went into the Army, Homer, the next oldest son, obtained a job on the night shift in the telegraph office at Ithaca, California. He worked at night because he was still attending school during the day. Little Ulysses watched his family and wondered what was going on, for his baby's mind could not comprehend all the changes that had taken place in his home.

Every morning, Homer arose early and exercised in his room so that he would be physically fit to run the two-twenty low hurdles at the high school. After he and

Bess had eaten their breakfast, Mary Arena, who was in love with Marcus, came from next door, and she and Bess walked to school together.

In the ancient history class, taught by Miss Hicks, Homer and Hubert Ackley the Third insulted each other, and Miss Hicks kept the boys after school. Coach Byfield had picked Hubert to run the two-twenty low hurdles that afternoon, however, and Hubert told Miss Hicks that the principal had asked that he be excused. Indignant at the deceit, Miss Hicks also sent Homer to run the race. Although Hubert was the winner, Homer thought that justice had been done.

Thomas Spangler, was in charge of the telegraph office, and Mr. Grogan, an old man with a weak heart, was his assistant. Because Mr. Grogan got drunk every night, one of Homer's duties was to see to it that Mr. Grogan stayed awake to perform his duties. A problem that had weighed on Homer's mind ever since he had taken his new job and had grown up overnight was whether the war would change anything for people. Mr. Grogan and Homer often talked about the world, Homer declaring that he did not like things as they were. Seeing everyone in the world mixed up and lonely, Homer said, he believed that he had to say and do things to make people laugh.

Mrs. Macauley was happy that her children were so compassionate. Ever since her husband had died, Katey Macauley had pretended to see him and discuss with him problems that arose concerning the rearing of her family. She believed that their father was not dead if he lived again in the lives of his children. One afternoon, she had a premonition of Marcus' death, for she imagined that her husband came to her and told her he was going to bring Marcus with him.

Little Ulysses had a friend, Lionel, who was three years older than he. The older boys chased Lionel away from their games because they said that he was dumb. When Lionel came to Mrs. Macauley to ask her whether he was stupid, the kind woman assured him that he was as good as everyone else. Lionel took Ulysses to the library with him to look at all the many-colored books on the shelves. Ulysses, who spent his time wandering around and watching everything, was pleased with the new experience.

Marcus wrote to Homer from an Army camp somewhere in the South, and Homer took the letter back to the telegraph office with him. The letter told about Marcus' friend, an orphan named Tobey George. Marcus had described his family—Homer, Ulysses, Bess, his mother, and his sweetheart, Mary—to Tobey. Because Tobey had no family of his own, he was grateful to Marcus for bringing to him secondhand the Macauley family. Marcus had told Tobey that, after the war, he wanted Tobey to go to Ithaca and marry Bess. Tobey was not so certain that Bess would want to marry him, but he believed for the first time in his life that he had a family that was almost his own. Marcus had written to Homer, as the new head of the family, to tell him about Tobey George and to ask him to look after his mother and Bess.

Homer was moved by his brother's letter. When he had finished reading it, he told Mr. Grogan that if Marcus should be killed he would spit at the world. Homer could express his love for Marcus in no other way.

The same events repeated themselves many times in Ithaca. Ulysses continued to watch everything with increasing interest. Mary and Bess sang their songs and went for their evening walks. Telegrams came, and Homer delivered them. Soldiers began coming home to Ithaca, to their mothers, and to their families.

Homer had been working at the telegraph office for six months. One Sunday night, while he was walking downtown with Lionel and Ulysses, he saw through the window of the telegraph office that Mr. Grogan was working alone. He sent the two small boys home and went in to see if Mr. Grogan needed him. The old man had suffered one of his heart attacks, and Homer ran to the drugstore to get some medicine for him. Mr. Grogan attempted to type out one more telegram, a message for Katey Macauley telling her that her son Marcus had been killed in action. When Homer returned with the medicine, he found Mr. Grogan slumped over the typed-out message. He was dead. Homer went home with the message that Marcus had been killed.

That night, a soldier had got off the train at Ithaca. He was Tobey George. He walked around for a time before he went to see Marcus' family. When he came to the Macauley porch, he stood and listened to Bess and Mary singing inside the house. Bess came outside and sat next to him while he told her that Marcus had sent him to be a member of the family. When Homer came to the porch with the telegram, Tobey called him aside and told him to tear up the message. Tobey assured him that Marcus was not dead; Marcus could never die. Mrs. Macauley came onto the porch, and Ulysses ran to Tobey and took his hand. For a while, the mother looked at her two remaining sons. Then she smiled at her new son as the family walked into the house.

Critical Evaluation

In *The Human Comedy*, William Saroyan details the life of a small town during World War II. The book is full of vignettes that recall such homey matters as Homer buying day-old pies; Ulysses waving to the train; and Mrs. Macauley comforting her working son with late-night conversations. There is, then, a noticeable mixture of childlike innocence and adult homily in Saroyan's book. The world is seen through the eyes of children, and yet one is always aware of the author, whose presence adds complexity to the experience, just as one is always aware of the fact of war.

While the ordinary problems of human existence, such as school rivalries, adolescent love, and the first experience of evil, are being dealt with by the Widow Macauley and her children, the larger world drives toward cataclysm and challenges the pieties and conventions of innocent, rural America. To be sure Ithaca, an ancient symbol of home itself, comes no closer to actual hostilities than its Greek namesake came to the battlements of Troy, but the arrival and departure of the daily train and the ominous click of the telegraph bring the outside world very close to Ithaca's consciousness.

Saroyan's conclusion is positive, if melodramatic and sentimental. While Homer is conveying the message of Marcus' death in battle to his family, Katey Macauley finds comfort, sustenance, and belief in the continuity of human experience. By the title of the novel itself, Saroyan seems to suggest that all tragedy, finally viewed from a wide enough perspective, dissolves into a comedy of joy and affirmation. If readers are uncomfortable with this philosophy, it may be that they have lost the innocence of faith that Saroyan finds so sustaining in Ithaca.

HUNGER OF MEMORY: The Education of Richard Rodríguez

Type of work: Autobiography
Author: Richard Rodríguez (1944-   )
Time of work: 1950's to the 1970's
Locale: Sacramento and Stanford, California, and London
First published: 1981

This intellectual autobiography describes the author's passage through the American educational system and, in doing so, raises timely questions about race, assimilation, and cultural values in the United States.

Principal Personages

Richard Rodríguez, the youngest son of a Mexican-American family of four. As a child, he shows exceptional scholastic promise, which leads to a successful academic career as a so-called minority student. The more institutional success he earns, however, the more resistant Rodríguez becomes to it. Ultimately, he rejects academic life in favor of the solitary scrutiny of himself and his background in writing.

Victoria Rodríguez, Richard's mother. A kindly, nurturing presence throughout the author's childhood, she is proud of his intellectual achievements while feeling pained by the fact that they are accompanied by feelings of estrangement from the family.

Leopoldo Rodríguez, Richard's father. His son's upwardly mobile career is the antithesis of his own. Years of working at jobs unworthy of his sensitivity and vitality have made him a largely silent and listless presence.

The Story

Richard Rodríguez opens his autobiography, *Hunger of Memory*, with some vignettes from his life as a successful writer and intellectual, and his somewhat sardonic and uncomfortable reaction to these moments. This opening provides a perspective from which the ensuing material is to be appraised. The six chapters that follow form essentially a chronological account of what the book's subtitle identifies as "the education of Richard Rodríguez," though the account is mediated through the author's mature reflections. These chapters take the reader from parochial school in Sacramento, California, where the author grew up, to the reading room of the British Museum in London, where he carried out research for his doctoral thesis on Renaissance English literature.

Such a large cultural transition can hardly have been accomplished without a certain sense of dislocation and an enhanced consciousness of change and its effects, particularly in Rodríguez's case as he is the son of Mexican-American immigrants whose formal educational opportunities were much more limited. It is to a meditation on both these facts of his life—his personal development and the world of his parents that this development overshadows—that Rodríguez devotes *Hunger of Memory*.

The book, therefore, is not a straightforward story in the conventional sense of the word, though it does possess a strong, visible, narrative backbone. It is much more obviously a series of reflective encounters with successive phases of the author's educational progress. Each of these phases has a chronological signature, but its place in time is less important than its cultural and ideological components.

These components are most frequently identified in terms of their verbal content, so much so that it is possible to regard *Hunger of Memory* as the author's inescapable though protracted journey toward the acquisition of his own voice. It is in the public context of education that this journey is made. The story proper begins with tender recollections of the author's childhood home, and the role of Spanish within it. Should the force and validity of the phrase "mother tongue" ever need to be illustrated, material for doing so will be found in abundance in Rodríguez's account of his earliest linguistic experience. Spanish is the author's first language and the language of the home, the family language, the language of intimacy and of the protective aura that intimacy creates. Spanish is also the language of difference, however, as his encounter with English at school makes clear. English, on the other hand, is an instrument to dispel that difference, and the young Rodríguez's desire and ability to erase linguistic and cultural barriers between himself and the world at large results in the eclipse of Spanish in his consciousness. With this eclipse comes that of the environment which familial use of Spanish articulated.

Rodríguez also describes his painful attempts to come to terms with other features of his "foreignness," evident in his skin color and features. The only real means of change at his disposal is his intellectual ability, and to this, with his parents' full support, he devotes his efforts. Thus, change was not only inevitable, as a result of the impact of schooling, but embraced as well, as Rodríguez is anxious and willing to entrust himself completely to an institutional mode of experiencing. To underline his sense of the power of institutions to shape the individual's awareness of the world, and the institution's articulation of that power in distinctively linguistic terms, Rodríguez devotes a chapter to examining his relationship with the Roman Catholic church, whose religion he professes, in the aftermath of liturgical and other changes introduced by the Second Vatican Council. The affirmation of the need of a personal faith within the overall framework of the institution keynotes the ensuing reflections on experiences at places of higher learning.

As Rodríguez's education evolved and he became an undergraduate at Stanford University, he became more aware that, rather than being perceived as an individual, he was being designated as a minority student. His years at Stanford coincided with the introduction of affirmative

action policies in the field of higher education. Much of Rodríguez's evaluation of his undergraduate career has as its focus his complex response to being thought of in racial terms. He believed that it was such terms which his education, and in particular his choice of English as his major, were intended to obviate. His interrogation of the origins and application of affirmative action policies consolidates much of Rodríguez's thinking on the issue, thinking for which he had earned a certain degree of notoriety and status prior to the publication of *Hunger of Memory.*

Rodríguez's pursuit of academic excellence in conventional terms became increasingly linked with a sense of frustration and incipient criticism of the process of acculturation with which he was identified. This painfully paradoxical situation assumed critical proportions when Rodríguez found himself a highly favored applicant for entry-level academic teaching positions. In spite of being assiduously wooed by some of the top English departments in the country, Rodríguez decided not to become an academic. This decision brings the narrative to the point at which it began in the prologue, the author's present. It is at this point that he conveys the estrangement from his parents and from many of the most important, intimate codes of his birth and heritage. The story of Richard Rodríguez's education concludes not with a shared sense of his parents' pride in his achievements but in a sober, understated acknowledgment of how the place in the world that he secured through education inevitably rendered him homeless.

Critical Evaluation

In a number of ways, *Hunger of Memory* is a literary landmark. Despite the vast and diverse experience of assimilation among Americans, there is something of a lack of literary testimony bearing witness to the experience. The warm reception that *Hunger of Memory* received in part was earned by the work's distinctive literary qualities, such as its controlled tone, its eschewal of sentimentality, its essaylike form, and its sophisticated structure. Yet, in part, the praise for Rodríguez's efforts also reflected the overall novelty of his material. Voices with Rodríguez's background, irrespective of the story that they had to tell, were a rarity when *Hunger of Memory* first appeared. The mere fact of the work's existence, quite apart from its assimilation into the documentary mainstream of American experience, makes its presence a culturally noteworthy event.

As a learned, disciplined, and well-read evaluator of texts, sensitive to cultural nuance and to the niceties of interpretation, Rodríguez was presumably aware of his work's cultural significance. It is arguably because of that very awareness that the rendering of experience in *Hunger of Memory* is an intriguing combination of the direct and the inaccessible. The reader may, on the one hand, see Rodríguez's account of his intellectual history as a version of a familiar story concerning such archetypes of social experience as leaving home; developing a sense of values different from, and potentially at odds with, parental and communal ones; being unprepared for encounters with the privileged and intense environments of elite cultural institutions; and eventually attaining the problematical freedom of contemporary individuality. With certain variations of emphasis and context, this is the story of the complex expansion of the middle classes in the United States after World War II, a story that cuts across racial and communal divisions. Moreover, it is a story that articulates a number of the important transitions in postwar American society, such as those from ghetto to suburb, from blue collar to white collar, and particularly from high-school diploma to college degree. In other words, Rodríguez's story is one that exemplifies the extension of what might be termed the cultural and economic franchise to greater numbers of Americans, specifically those whose social reality had hitherto been conceived of in terms of their ethnicity.

Yet, exemplary as Rodríguez's story is from a sociological standpoint, it is also the case that this is the very standpoint that the author of *Hunger of Memory* seeks to repudiate. By doing so, he enriches, through his critique, the culture that has sponsored his attainments. The subsidiary character of this narrative's sociological value is emphasized by Rodríguez's insistence on the primacy of his own experience. Such an emphasis is what his education sought to institutionalize, in effect. His involuntary discovery of his own distinctiveness, and his reluctance for that quality to be reduced through immersion in the American melting pot, confirms both the tendency of education to normalize and to standardize and the necessity to offer a degree of resistance to such a tendency. Rodríguez does not express his resistance for its own sake. Rather, he expresses it for the sake of the American educational system that, at all levels, but particularly at the first and second levels, he believes should evolve a means of reflecting the necessarily complex experiences of those future citizens whom it assumes responsibility for training. The representation of the tense and challenging dialogue between individual history and institutional power—or between what Rodríguez, in the light of his own experience, names the private and public realms of experience—is one of the more noteworthy features of *Hunger of Memory*.

Rodríguez, however, does not have the reputation of a writer whose reflections on the American process of acculturation through education are considered to be revolutionary. On the contrary, those autobiographical and analytical essays based on his educational experience that appeared before *Hunger of Memory*, and upon which the book is to some degree based, were more typically thought of as reactionary. Labels of whatever kind, however illustrative of his experience, are deemed by Rodríguez as irrelevant to his purpose. Nevertheless, his political stance opposing both bilingual education and affirmative action earned for him a certain notoriety, and arguments recapitulating these positions in *Hunger of Memory* did little to dispel the air of controversy that Rodríguez's views attracted. At the same time, however, it is clear from *Hunger of Memory* how such views evolved, and the truth of Rodríguez's experience to which they speak. It might be argued that *Hunger of Memory* needed to be written in order to provide a context for such views, which otherwise might seem glib, if not actually opportunistic. Moreover, the provision of such a context acts as an important reminder that Rodríguez does not profess to be either an educational theorist or the promoter of a minority political agenda.

Such a reminder draws the reader back to the formal discipline of autobiography and to Rodríguez's integrity in adopting it in order to articulate his encounters with culture. By ultimately confining himself to his own story, he continues to take American culture at face value by reposing so much credibility in the worthiness, and in effect the exemplary power (referred to as the public expression) of individual experience. Rodríguez is also aware, however, that his achievement of assimilation is paradoxical and ironic. Through the stylish and brooding expression of that awareness in *Hunger of Memory*, Richard Rodríguez remained faithful to the uncertainty and allure of personal development, as well as to the early sounders of the note of skepticism and loss of innocence that echoes through much American autobiography of the 1980's.

IN COLD BLOOD

Type of work: Nonfiction novel
Author: Truman Capote (1924-1984)
Type of plot: Murder investigation
Time of plot: 1959-1965
Locale: Western Kansas, other parts of the United States, and Mexico
First published: 1966

An outstanding example of new journalism, this "nonfiction novel" uses techniques of fiction to dramatize a real-life murder case, thereby creating a hybrid literary genre that found much popularity.

Principal Characters

Richard Eugene Hickock, a fast-talking, self-styled con artist who conceives the plan to rob and murder the Clutter family. He is thirty-three at the time of his execution.

Perry Edward Smith, his partner in crime. He is a quiet, self-conscious, but potentially explosive youth who lets Hickock do all the thinking and planning. He is thirty-six at the time of his execution.

Alvin Adams Dewey, an agent of the Kansas Bureau of Investigation who is active in the murder investigation

from beginning to end.

Herbert Clutter, an affluent Kansas farmer wrongly thought to have a large sum of money concealed in his isolated home. He is murdered by Hickock and Smith.

Bonnie Clutter, Herbert Clutter's neurotic wife, who is murdered by Hickock and Smith.

Nancy Clutter, their beautiful, popular sixteen-year-old daughter, who is murdered by Hickock and Smith.

Kenyon Clutter, their intelligent, introverted fifteen-year-old son, who is murdered by Hickock and Smith.

The Story

Throughout his novel, Capote uses the device of parallel plots to dramatize the difference between the alienated, amoral killers and the wholesome, religious-minded people of western Kansas. In the opening section, Capote describes the members of the Clutter family, their simple lives, and their orderly environment. These descriptions are interspersed with a dispassionate account of how Richard Eugene Hickock and Perry Edward Smith begin to assemble the tools that they need to commit their planned robbery and multiple murder.

The two paroled convicts have chosen Herbert Clutter's remote farmhouse for their crime because they believe that he keeps ten thousand dollars in an office safe. Hickock got this erroneous information from a cellmate at Kansas State Penitentiary named Floyd Wells, who had worked for the Clutters while drifting from job to job.

Hickock and Smith finally reach Holcomb, Kansas, and enter the Clutters' home, where the doors are never locked because serious crime is unknown in the region. The following day, when Nancy's friends arrive to take her to church, they find that Herb, Bonnie, Nancy, and

Kenyon have all been tied up and hideously murdered with shotgun blasts fired at close range. Capote adroitly avoids telling what actually went on inside the house during the preceding night, instead merely describing the horrible aftermath discovered when law enforcement officials arrive.

In the second section, Capote continues with the parallel plot device, showing how the people of Holcomb react to the tragedy and how the two killers attempt to cover up their tracks. The Clutters' friends and neighbors are stunned. For the first time in memory, people begin locking up their houses at night. Many women are terrified because they believe that the killer is someone in the community. The law enforcement officials are of the same opinion, because of the lack of any apparent struggle and the fact that the killer or killers spent so much time inside the house; furthermore, there is evidence to suggest that the killer or killers knew their way around the premises.

Hickock and Smith drift aimlessly from place to place. They are chronically short of funds, not having obtained any significant sum at the Clutter farm. Hickock is clever at raising money by shoplifting and cashing worthless checks, but he is equally foolish in throwing his money away. Through various devices, the reader learns about the past lives of these two killers. Both had deprived childhoods. Both are intelligent but ignorant. Both have been in prison and have had their antisocial attitudes reinforced by contact with hard-core felons. Both have serious sexual problems: Hickock has a criminal attraction to little girls, and Smith appears to be nearly impotent. Both have unrealistic dreams of fame and fortune, nourished by trashy films and fiction. Hickock and Smith are petty criminals. Neither had ever killed before. They are like two chemicals that are relatively innocuous while separate but volatile when combined. Each becomes a menace to society while trying to prove his toughness and his manhood to the other.

At the beginning of the third section, the plot begins to unravel. Floyd Wells, still in prison, hears about the Clutter murders. He remembers the interest that Hickock had shown in the family and how Hickock had actually told Wells that he was going to enlist the help of his friend Perry Smith to go to the Clutter farm, murder the entire family and anyone else present, and take the cash that Wells believed was kept in a wall safe on the premises. Wells uses his information to obtain a parole and a cash reward.

Law enforcement agencies in seventeen states are alerted that Hickock and Smith are wanted and should be considered armed and dangerous. The only official charge against them, however, is parole violation. Eventually, the two killers are arrested in Las Vegas, Nevada, driving a stolen car. On the way back to Kansas, the cowardly Hickock blurts out a confession and blames all four of the murders on Smith. When Smith learns that his friend has betrayed him, he tells a detailed story of the night of the Clutter murders.

The final section of the book deals with the trial and conviction of the two men, their several appeals and stays of execution, their lives in prison during the next five years, and finally their executions by hanging on the night of April 14, 1965. Alvin Dewey, who has been obsessed with bringing the murderers of the Clutter family to justice, is present at their gruesome hangings and finally believes that he can return to a normal life.

Critical Evaluation

Truman Capote might be accused of exploiting a family's terrible tragedy for personal gain were it not for the fact that he became so emotionally involved in every aspect of that tragedy. It was his intense emotional involvement that made *In Cold Blood* a great book that was eventually translated into twenty-five foreign languages.

For a long time, Capote had been thinking of writing what he called a nonfiction novel: a new type of literary work that involved dramatizing an actual event so that it would read like a work of fiction. Capote spent nearly six years working on his book. His main problem was condensing and organizing his six thousand pages of notes into an artistic whole.

In order to make his book read like a novel, he had to use his creative imagination to describe the feelings of the people involved and to invent dialogue. Although many law enforcement officials were involved in the investigation of the Clutter murders, Capote focused his attention on Dewey in order to provide a protagonist for his story. Capote also used his remarkable literary gifts to color the narration with descriptions of western Kansas and portraits of the people who lived there.

These features—the attribution of emotions to the characters; the invention of dialogue, gestures, and facial expressions; the structuring of the plot as an escalating conflict between protagonist and antagonists; and the evocation of time and place through sensitive description—are what distinguish a nonfiction novel from factual reporting. They are also the characteristic features of most works in the school of the so-called new journalism, of which Capote was a leading member.

Theodore Dreiser's masterpiece *An American Tragedy* (1925) was a naturalistic novel based on an actual crime; however, this work was not at all like Capote's *In Cold Blood*. Dreiser's characters are all imaginary; Capote's are all real. Dreiser invented new incidents to parallel those of an actual murder case; Capote never departs from the true facts. Nevertheless, Dreiser's strong influence can be felt throughout Capote's book. As a novel, *In Cold Blood* belongs to the school of naturalism, which emphasizes the irresistible influence of heredity and environment upon the individual. Hickock and Smith are seen as victims of forces beyond their control and understanding, not unlike Clyde Griffiths, the hero of Dreiser's great naturalistic novel.

The deaths of the Clutter family on the eve of the turbulent 1960's seem to symbolize the death of an innocent American society in which people slept with their doors unlocked. The Clutters were part of the United States' old agrarian tradition, whose values were based on the Bible; their killers represented the new, alienated, proletarianized Americans whose values were shaped by a meretricious pop culture fueled by greed and materialism. Capote maintains an ongoing contrast between the images of settled, hardworking, God-fearing Americans and the image of killers stalking the highways in search of new victims.

It is this vision of the United States that comes through most forcefully. The country is changing. Farm families represent a smaller and smaller percentage of the population as the mechanization of agri-business bulldozes fences and homesteads. *In Cold Blood* is a masterpiece of American literature, not because it describes the deaths of a few individuals, but because it paints a mural of the United States in the midst of a critical period of social transition in the second half of the twentieth century.

In the description of a typical criminal investigation, there is a tendency for the reader's interest to wane because the crime itself, which must occur at the beginning, is the most dramatic incident in the book and tends to make the subsequent investigation, arrest, trial, and punishment seem anticlimactic. In order to sustain interest, Capote deliberately avoids describing the murders until late in the third section of his book, and then quite appropriately describes them from the dispassionate viewpoints of the psychopathic killers who are, after all, the only living witnesses to the night of horror.

In Cold Blood made Capote rich and famous. He became one of the most popular television talk-show personalities until his death in 1984, and people who did not know any other American author by name had heard of Truman Capote. This notoriety naturally enhanced sales of *In Cold Blood* and all of his other books. Yet Capote had paid a heavy emotional price for fame and fortune. He said that he would never go through such an experience again for any amount of money.

Prior to the publication of his best-selling nonfiction crime novel, Capote had been stigmatized as a decadent homosexual whose writing, though sensitive and intelligent, was trivial and effete. Writing about a cold-blooded multiple murder in America's homespun Bible Belt provided the gritty substance that he needed to offset his neurotic hypersensitivity. Capote himself was well aware of his need for such a bitter purge of reality. This diminutive, frail, effeminate aesthete was one of the least likely people in the world to want to attend a double hanging in a cold warehouse on a dark morning, and yet he went through the ordeal out of dedication to his art. He displayed a toughness that belied his delicate appearance.

In structuring his work, Capote relied on the ancient artistic device of contrast to heighten his effects. The combinations of beauty and horror, sanity and psychosis, poetry and brutal fact, give his book a texture lacking in his other works and make it possible for him to be considered an important American author rather than simply another New York freelancer with a genius for obtaining publicity.

In Cold Blood inspired a flood of imitations. After Capote's work, it became commonplace for novelists and journalists to mix fact and fiction. The "true crime novel" became a standard literary genre featuring brilliant works by such authors as Joseph Wambaugh and Norman Mailer. The techniques originally invented by Capote to dramatize an actual crime can be seen imitated by his successors, although few have been as dedicated to their craft.

IN THE AMERICAN GRAIN

Type of work: Historical narratives and essays
Author: William Carlos Williams (1883-1963)
Time of work: Tenth century to the 1860's
Locale: The Americas
First published: 1925

In the American Grain *marks Williams' attempt to meld the approach of a poet to that of an amateur historian as he reorders the American experience.*

Principal Personages

Eric the Red
Christopher Columbus
Hernán Cortés
Juan Ponce de León
Hernando de Soto
Sir Walter Raleigh
Samuel de Champlain
Thomas Morton
Cotton Mather

Père Sebastian Rasles
Daniel Boone
George Washington
Benjamin Franklin
John Paul Jones
Jacataqua
Aaron Burr
Edgar Allan Poe
Abraham Lincoln

History, to paraphrase Corinthians, is many things to many people. It is the record of what really happened and also the story of what people in later times have believed really happened. It is the story of what people thought and felt and did under the pressure and crisis of decisive action. It is concerned with the noble, the foolish, the violent, the base. It is the careful untangling of political, social, and economic motives and forces in the national experience. It is the unvarnished record of fact, and it is also the romantic dream of something that people have believed in and for which they have died. It is a record of truth but never the final truth, for each age interprets the events and personalities of history according to its knowledge or need. Therefore, it becomes almost meaningless to talk about the "lessons" of history or their meanings: History is a story that is never quite finished because it is always open to reappraisal or new conclusions. The many-sided aspects of history provide one reason for the appeal it holds for its writers, professionals and amateurs alike.

In the American Grain, one of the authentic classics of the 1920's, is a poet's venture into historiography. As such, it is unstaled by conventional theory, without debt to academic authority, and as brilliant and idiosyncratic in purpose, insights, and structure as D. H. Lawrence's

Studies in Classic American Literature (1923). Also, like Lawrence's critical essays, it is a book written before its proper period. Only in later decades was it recognized as a revitalizing view of the American past, an original work of considerable magnitude and weight.

At the same time, it was never without influence during the years when it was out of print and neglected by both the critics and the public. One literary debt is found in Hart Crane's *The Bridge* (1930); traces of Williams' insights and idioms run through the poem. The half-title page of "Powhatan's Daughter," for example, requotes a passage from Thomas Morton's *New English Canaan* (1637), and there are obvious likenesses between the vision of Christopher Columbus in the opening "Ave Maria" section of *The Bridge* and Williams' essay entitled "The Discovery of the Indies." Another poet who may have been influenced by *In the American Grain* is Archibald MacLeish in *Conquistador* (1932), especially by Williams' description of the destruction of Tenochtitlán and his accounts of the conquistadores—Hernán Cortés, Juan Ponce de León, and Hernando de Soto. There may be echoes also in the closing paragraphs of F. Scott Fitzgerald's *The Great Gatsby* (1925), in the reference to Henry Hudson and his sailors when they saw for the first time the green shores of the New World and were filled with wonder at the promises that the new continent held for westering dreams. This is not to say that these writers were guilty of plagiarism, only that *In the American Grain* offered to perceptive readers images and impressions to be held in memory and knowledge until they could be released in fresh works of the imagination.

Despite its significance as a seminal work, *In the American Grain* is even more important for the function that it performs. Williams' purpose, briefly, was not to give a new interpretation of history or to consider its uses, but to discover the thing itself, its nature and the conditions under which it took shape. In "Père Sebastian Rasles," he set forth his aim in a discussion with Paul Valéry, who in the essay is called Valéry Larbaud. Impressed by the other man's knowledge of and interest in American history, Williams claims that everything which has happened or been produced in America springs from discoverable roots, resting on ground capable of being explored and mapped. In the face of the other man's urbane probing into Williams' mind and attitude, the poet insists that it is not possible to trust those who have interpreted history previously, from the time of Cotton Mather onward. He will go to the sources, he declares, not to uproot history but to make history reveal itself, to trace to their past beginnings the obscurities and partisan views that oppress him, to uncover in the documents of the time the evidence needed to separate fact from myth.

Williams' reordering of the American experience from the century of the Norseman to the Civil War is symbolic rather than philosophical. Clearly, his task involved more than the retrieving of a usable past from the leveling action of time and from legends growing out of the common imagination, or the attempt to find in the meaning of the past a way out of the unsettled present into the future. Exploratory in nature, the book is first of all an act of discovery and recovery, two aspects of the single process of knowing and understanding. Some events or personalities that most historians gloss over or ignore have been brought into the foreground; others recede from it. Williams is not tracing the development of a society or justifying the culture that it created. To speak of a culture implies an abstraction, a phenomenon of cause and consequence that allows no place within its long perspective for the accidental, the discrete, and the contingent. This view reduces all history to a concept free of all the rich confusion of chance and circumstance that is life itself. Instead, Williams employs what Allen Tate called the "Short View" of history: the particular stories of the particular lives of humans engaged in contemporaneous interactions of place, time, and personality. Believing, like Ralph Waldo Emerson, that history is a record of the

lengthened shadows cast by people on the earth, Williams reveals in this book the same qualities that one finds in his poetry, a strong sense of the "Local"—which is not to be confused with local color—and a ruling passion to express his vision of the world as concisely and concretely as possible. To the poet who declared that there is no reality except in things, no other course was possible.

Williams' experiment in historiography involved also an experiment in style. To give richness of historical content to his book, he borrowed lavishly from his sources. Quotations from letters, chronicles, and journals are scattered through the sketches—passages from Columbus' journals, reports of the Salem witchcraft trials, letters written by Benjamin Franklin and John Paul Jones—to color the prose and give it vitality and the ring of truth. Sometimes this quoted matter complements Williams' own prose; sometimes it clashes with dramatic vigor. One is reminded throughout of one of Williams' statements on the writing of poetry: his declaration that writers take words as they find them but transform them, without destroying their clarity and passion, into an expression of personal feelings and perceptions so presented that they become revelation. It is not what a writer says, he claimed, that is important as a work of art, but the thing that is made with such intensity that it lives by its own force of outward movement and wild inward logic. In the brief narratives and essays making up *In the American Grain*, the writer's historical imagination holds revelation of personality and meaning of situation in delicate but compelling balance, while the language gives the whole resonance and depth.

The book is divided into twenty chapters—dramatic narratives, lyric interludes, brief character sketches— ranging in space and time from the settlement of Greenland through the voyages of Columbus and the exploration of Kentucky to the Civil War, and dealing with such representative or illustrative figures as the conquistadores, Sir Walter Raleigh, Cotton Mather, George Washington, John Paul Jones, Aaron Burr, Edgar Allan Poe, and Abraham Lincoln. The arrangement is chronological, but the scale of values accorded to the personages and events is quite different from that found in the history texts. Franklin, for example, is no longer the wise founding father but the great apostle of catchpenny materialism and opportunism whose face, appropriately, came to decorate the one-cent stamp. Burr, on the other hand, is not the self-seeking man who tried to upset the established order of government because of personal ambition. Williams sees him as a good soldier who brought into politics an element of democratic theory necessary to the times but neglected by others already in power or aspiring to office, a champion of liberty at a time when freedom was subverted to bureaucratic tyranny, a man finally driven to the imprudence and excesses of which his opponents had already accused him.

Two themes run through the book. One is the failure of Americans to create for themselves a sense of place. The early settlers on these shores were already alienated, exiled from European society, and on the new continent their feeling of separation became complete. Settlers saw America not as a place to be sensed and assimilated but as a land to be conquered for selfish ends. The forces motivating them were external circumstances of time and place on the one hand, the opportunity to exploit a vast and rich continent, and on the other inward necessity, the need to justify their own identity as new people in a new land. The first of these drives was public and pragmatic; it hastened the westward movement, created the myth of scientific progress, and laid the foundation for an industrial society and the comforts of an expanding, affluent technical economy, all the while ignoring the cost in terms of individual hardship, economic waste, and the erosion of human values. The other was private and moral. From it, Americans get in part the restlessness, the violence, the communal guilt and shame, the inner fears, the secret loneliness, and desire that agitate modern society. Only at rare intervals, in Williams' view, does history present individuals so complete and so much at ease in their environment that they show themselves capable of acting as Americans, not as transplanted Europeans or aliens in their own society: Daniel Boone as the explorer and settler, Aaron Burr as the politician, Edgar Allan Poe as the artist, Abraham Lincoln as the leader of a divided nation in conflict with itself. This conflict is implicit in the beginnings of American history. Columbus sensed without really understanding the meaning of America and saw with bright vision the possibilities of place and life in the New World. The opposite side of the picture is the story of the Spanish conquerors, the impact of the cross and sword of feudal Spain upon a "pagan" society. Occasionally the exploited land revenged itself on its despoilers; the disappointments of Cortés and the secret river burial of de Soto are in effect payment for the destruction of Tenochtitlán and the rape of Mexico and Peru.

Williams' second theme is the blight of Puritanism over the American land. Like Nathaniel Hawthorne, he viewed the Puritans as "miserable wretches" who possessed strength of purpose and will but not the tolerance of strength or the wisdom of purpose. Puritan bigotry and ignorance were demonstrated in the treatment of Quakers in New England and the Salem witchcraft trials. The abstract ideal of purity and salvation almost entirely excluded from Puritan life the idea of place or a sense of beauty as a concrete, natural thing. Williams finds Cotton Mather niggardly and narrow, a man of great but unassimilated learning whose belief in the supernatural often verged on superstition. Hostile to a flowering of the spirit, the Puritans tried to convert all life into facts and figures, and Benjamin Franklin, as revealed in his maxims, was the inheritor of their materialism and morality. If *In the American Grain* contains a major flaw, it is found in Williams' treatment of the Puritan. Although he does not succumb to the Puritan-baiting popular among intellectuals in the 1920's, he sometimes criticizes Puritanism, or expresses his grudging admiration, for the wrong things. Many critics realize that Puritanism was more than an abstract ideal of an earthly paradise, a theocracy of dogmatic belief and practice; it was also a seedbed of political freedom and independence of mind and spirit.

Because he himself was a poet, perhaps, the true hero of Williams' argument is Poe, whom he calls the first writer to recognize the possibilities of American life in art and to give shape in language to the spirit of place and time. For Poe, culture was not something to be brought into the national experience but something to be revealed because it was already present in the conditions and circumstances of the world around him. In his poems, short stories, and criticism, he tried to find universal meanings in the local, not in setting alone, but in the American psyche, in apocalyptic visions of the American soul. In the end, he was defeated by the forms and forces of culture inherited from the past, and he retreated into a region of grotesques. At best, however, he expressed with originality and vigor the spirit of place, using the creations of his imagination to suggest that literature is a serious business as logical and insightful as science or philosophy. He tried to clear the ground of colonial imitation and the growing belief that material advance was the only possibility offered by American life. His effort was moral as well as aesthetic, and for this reason Williams regards him not as a frustrated genius but as a heroic figure deserving the highest praise.

The book ends with a brief appreciation of Lincoln. The choice is an appropriate one because Lincoln was president in the period of the Civil War, the most deeply felt and possessed experience in American national life, the violent summation of all that had gone before and the adumbration of everything that has happened since. Lincoln is here a symbolic figure, an image of the shortcomings and possibilities in American history, a figure of tragic failure as well as a promise of hope. This impinge-ment of the present upon the past gives *In the American Grain* an added dimension, a deeper relevance in one's understanding of the events and the figures who have shaped American history. This is a poet's book as well as an amateur historian's, a work in which the writer's vision provides new insights into historical truths imag-inatively viewed and passionately re-created in language. In it, the local view strikes deep into the shape and mean-ing of the American past.

INVISIBLE MAN

Type of work: Novel
Author: Ralph Ellison (1914-   )
Type of plot: Social criticism
Time of plot: 1940's and early 1950's
Locale: Deep South and New York City
First published: 1952

In Invisible Man, *an unnamed African-American narrator describes his journey to an understanding of himself and his heritage through his exposure to many different types of people—both black and white.*

Principal Characters

The narrator, the canny, unnamed voice of the story. The narrator looks back on a life begun in the Deep South and brought north to the United States' premier African-American city-within-a-city. In language full of richly oblique double meanings and nuances, he speaks of writing "confession," of ending his "residence underground," and of implying in his own specific case history that of an altogether wider, historic black America.

Dr. A. Herbert Bledsoe, the president of the college that the narrator attends. In one guise, Bledsoe plays the perfect Uncle Tom, fawning and grateful, who dances to the tune of Norton, the white philanthropist. In another, he acts as a despot, the college's presiding tyrant known to students as "Old Bucket-head." His expulsion of the narrator is done in the name of maintaining the image of "Negro" behavior that Bledsoe believes expedient to put before white America.

Mr. Norton, a New England financier and college benefactor. As his name implies, Norton equates with "Northern," a figure of would-be liberal patronage, who sees his destiny as helping African-American students to become dutiful mechanics and agricultural workers. An

encounter with the incestuous Truebloods, however, awakens his own dark longings for his dead daughter.

Brother Jack, the leader of the Brotherhood, a revolutionary group. The white, one-eyed leader of the group's central committee, he takes up the narrator as "the new Booker T. Washington." His is the language of "scientific terminology," "materialism," and other quasi-Marxist argot. He leads a witch-hunt against the narrator, only to have his glass eye pop out, showing him as truly a half-seeing, one-eyed Jack.

Tod Clifton, a Harlem activist. Initially, Clifton operates as a Brotherhood loyalist, a youth organizer pledged to fight African-American joblessness, the color line, and Black Nationalists. Fascinated by the Black Nationalist Ras's Caribbean "Africanness," however, he drops out. When Tod is shot down by a white police officer, his death sparks a long-brewing Harlem riot.

Ras, the Destroyer, a militant, West Indian Rastafarian. Ras advocates, in the style of Marcus Garvey, a back-to-Africa nationalism. He derides the Brotherhood as a white-run fraud serviced by deluded black lackeys.

The Story

Having spoken in the prologue of his need to come out into the light, to surface from a building that has been "rented strictly to whites" and "shut off and forgotten during the nineteenth century," the narrator gives immediate notice that he is telling not a single but a typological, or multiple, story. Everything that has happened to him bears the shadow of prior African-American history. He vows, however, that all past "hibernation," all past "invisibility," must now end. It falls to him to "illumi-

nate"—that is, literally and figuratively to write into being—the history that has at once made both him and black America at large so "black and blue" and yet that has been a triumph of human survival and art.

To that end, he steps back into Dixie and into a "Battle Royal," a brawl in which a group of blindfolded African-American boys fight for the entertainment of whites. The scene gives a crucial point of departure for the novel. In fighting "blind," the boys illustrate an ancestral divide-

and-rule tactic of the white South; the boys' reward is money from an electrified rug. Equally, when a sumptuous white stripper dances before the townsmen, an American flag tattooed between her thighs, the ultimate taboo looms temptingly yet impossibly before the African-American boys. Literally with blood in his throat, the narrator thanks his patrons and leaves, having received a scholarship to a Tuskegee-style college. He thinks, too, of his grandfather's advice, that of a slavery-time veteran of African-American mimicry, who tells him to "overcome 'em with yeses, undermine 'em with grins, agree 'em to death and destruction"—the words of the trickster as seeming "coon" or "good nigra" whose every act of servility in fact derides his white oppressors. The narrator cannot be unmindful of a dream in which mountains of paper contain a single, recurrent message: "Keep this Nigger Boy Running."

At the college, he believes himself to be in a black version of an ideal Dixie. His life, however, undergoes a major reverse when he shows Norton, a white philanthropist, the incestuous "field-nigger" family of the Truebloods, thus reawakening Norton's own sexual hankerings for his recently deceased daughter. In order to find medical help for the overcome Norton, the pair moves on to the Golden Day, an African-American brothel for Army veterans, and there, to his greatest discomfort, the narrator recognizes in the clients as caricatures of the self-same African-American bourgeoisie that he most aspires to join—doctors, teachers, lawyers, and businessmen. His resulting expulsion from the college produces more paper promises, in the form of supposed letters of recommendation to likely employers in New York.

These letters prove false, college president A. Herbert Bledsoe's revenge on a disciple who has strayed from the appointed path. The son of the aptly named Mr. Emerson reveals the deception and guides the narrator to the Liberty Paints factory. Put to work making "Optic White," he inadvertently adds "concentrated remover," as if to insist upon his own blackness within the all-white grid of the United States. He then begins work in the factory's paint process section. The machinery explodes, however,

and in the factory hospital, he overhears himself being talked about as a likely candidate for lobotomy.

Signing a release, he heads back to Harlem, taking part almost by chance in a spontaneous outcry at an eviction. Immediately, the Brotherhood draws him into its ranks, making him their Harlem spokesperson and using him to organize black Manhattan into a political wedge against the ruling order. Yet he also finds himself mythified into a sexual stud by one of the white "sisters." Increasingly, too, he comes up against Ras's fervid Black Nationalism. Most of all, he is held responsible for the disappearance of Tod Clifton, another activist; the narrator later sees Clifton on a street selling Sambo dolls and witnesses his death at the hands of the police. The narrator's trial by the Brotherhood for conspiracy and "petty individualism" follows immediately, a species of witchhunt and black "black comedy" culminating in the spectacle of Brother Jack's glass eye falling out of its socket.

The narrator takes to wearing dark glasses, with the result that a variety of Harlemites mistakenly think him to be Bliss Proteus Rinehart, a numbers man, lover, clergyman, and politician. Yet the impersonation, which he comes to relish, proves inadequate when Harlem erupts. In the melee, he encounters a band of looters who plan to burn their tenement slum building; he then meets Ras himself, in the garb of a black Don Quixote, and finally runs into a pillaging, panic-driven crowd that pushes him underground into a nearby manhole. There, he burns all his past "papers," a briefcase full of false promises and impedimenta, prime among them his high school diploma, one of Clifton's dolls, and the slip that contains his Brotherhood name.

Thus "freed," he endures a massive castration fantasy, and he resolves to abandon his assumed hibernation and to speak—to write down—this "nightmare." If, indeed, *Invisible Man* has been his own story, it has throughout also been that of the African-American community itself. He even suggests still wider human implications, and in such a spirit, "torturing myself to put it down," he bows out by asking in the epilogue: "Who knows but that, on the lower frequencies, I speak for you?"

Critical Evaluation

Invisible Man tells an African-American version of John Bunyan's *The Pilgrim's Progress* (1678-1684), a modern black rite of passage. In part, its story could not be more literal, a South-to-North, Dixie-to-Harlem journey that recalls the movement of African Americans from the postbellum South to the Northern cities. In equal

part, however, the story operates as a kind of fantasia, a "dream" history, that serves as both the narrator's past and that of most of his African-American cocitizenry. As he looks back from his "border area" manhole, lit with 1,369 light bulbs illegally running on electricity from a company named Monopolated Light & Power, he declares himself to be "coming out," no longer either invisible or, as it were, uninscribed and wordless.

In this respect, he offers himself as both an actual man and as a key figure from African-American folklore, a "man of substance, of flesh and bone, fiber and liquids" and a bear whose time of "hibernation" has come to its appointed end. Dipping into blues and jazz, street talk and rap, he promises in the prologue to "irradiate"— that is, in every sense to seek to throw light upon—his own story and that of the larger American black-white encounter. Inevitably, the touchstones involve slavery, Reconstruction, the jazz age, the Great Depression, and interwar Harlem, with hints of the coming 1960's Civil Rights and Black Power movements.

Ellison's narrator in *Invisible Man* ranks as one of the most canny, daring characterizations in modern literature. Every action that he takes, every transition in his life, almost everything that he says, carries a double or emblematic implication without becoming simply or reductively allegorical. His role in the Battle Royal scene calls up the stereotype of the African-American male as pugilist, from slave fighter to Joe Louis. As a student, the narrator might well imagine himself as a would-be Booker T. Washington, but his goals are preset and accommodationist. In Trueblood and the Golden Day, he begins to see the "true" image that white America holds of him and his community, that of either permanent inferior, sexual spectacle, or, at best, token professional.

In the North, equally, he can work at Liberty Paints, but only in the basement, as a support figure for a white, one-color, America. In the Brotherhood, his party membership again rests less in his own gift than in his willingness to follow the committee's dictates, the white-set political line. If he speaks on women's rights, various of the white sisters fantasize him as a sex fiend, a stud. Even in his role as con man, he betrays his true inner self. Finally, forced by the riot to an "underground" self-reckoning, once again both literal and fantastical, he "sees" and in turn demands to be "seen" in a manner beyond myth or stereotype. His own black selfhood and that of his African-American community at last, thereby, emerge on terms undetermined by others.

This same doubling, or multiplication, applies to the other key presences in *Invisible Man*. Bledsoe incarnates a historic past gallery of "separate but equal" leaders, in one face "putt'n on ol' massa" and in another acting the part of mean, self-serving authoritarian. Norton, likewise, imagines himself all good intention, but he is in fact the embodiment of a condescending white liberal racism. In the North, Mr. Emerson proves less the reformer implied in his name than another white betrayer.

Brother Jack, with his "political science," proves as inadequate to the narrator's needs as Ras, with his "Mama Africa" Rastafarian Black Nationalism. Tod Clifton, especially, moves from activist to figure of despair, as sad and ultimately self-destructive as the Sambo dolls that he takes to peddling in the street. These and lesser figures—from Mary Rambo, a warm, transplanted African-American Southern woman who befriends the narrator in Harlem, to Dupre, an arsonist and looter—in Ellison's always inventive fashioning serve as both individuals and types, the one always in a teasing imaginative balance with the other.

Undergirding the whole of *Invisible Man* lie Ellison's organizing metaphors and tropes—invisibility and sight, vision and blindness, blackness and white, underground and above—a complex, supremely adroit creation of texture. If H. G. Wells's science-fiction classic *The Invisible Man* (1897) hovers behind the title, so, equally, do a host of other eclectic sources, from Dante to T. S. Eliot. At the same time, and throughout, Ellison calls upon his intimacy with the treasury of African-American music and folklore. Citing, typically, the old Louis Armstrong version of "What Did I Do to Be So Black and Blue?" the narrator, and Ellison behind him, answers with *Invisible Man*, storytelling with all the feints and improvisational riffs, and at the same time all the overall discipline, of a great jazz composition.

Whether read as "confession" or as "history," the book fuses its high references with those of African-American vernacular culture, both verbal and musical, and its seriousness of purpose with a winning talent for humor and well-taken irony. Best of all, perhaps, it manages to transpose, brilliantly, inventively, the black and white of American society's racial makeup into the black and white of the written page.

Invisible Man quickly gained recognition as a landmark of African-American, and American, literature on its publication in 1952. Together with James Baldwin's *Go Tell It on the Mountain* (1953), it was taken to signal an African-American literary renaissance, a breakthrough from "Negro protest fiction" such as Richard Wright's *Native Son* (1940), Ann Petry's *The Street* (1946), or Chester Himes's *Lonely Crusade* (1947). Supported by writers such as Saul Bellow, as well as by a host of fellow African-American writers, Ellison won, among other major prizes, the National Book Award for *Invisible Man*.

There has long been agreement that the novel represents a pinnacle of African-American literary achievement, with perhaps Jean Toomer's *Cane* (1923), *Native Son*, *Go Tell It on the Mountain*, and Toni Morrison's *Song of Solomon* (1977) as matching companion pieces.

Its rich, startling ventriloquy, command of image, and skillful use of vernacular ensure a rare feast of narration. Such qualities carry over into Ellison's essay work, too, as collected in *Shadow and Act* (1964) and *Going to the Territory* (1986). Occasionally, well-meant talk has arisen of a "School of Ellison," composed, among others, of such writers as Leon Forrest, Morrison, John Edgar Wideman, Clarence Major, Ishmael Reed, and James Alan McPherson. Yet Ellison remains, as always, resolutely his own person, and *Invisible Man* remains the upshot of a uniquely endowed imagination.

THE JUNGLE

Type of work: Novel
Author: Upton Sinclair (1878-1968)
Type of plot: Social criticism
Time of plot: Early twentieth century
Locale: Chicago
First published: 1906

The Jungle is an indignant book, written in anger at the social injustices of the meat-packing industry, and from this anger, the novel derives its power. At the time of publication, the book served its purpose in arousing public sentiment against unfair practices in the meat industry. It remains an honestly told and gripping story.

Principal Characters

Jurgis Rudkus, a Lithuanian peasant immigrant who works in the Chicago stockyards. Victimized, hurt at the plant, and jailed for attacking a man who takes Jurgis' wife to a house of prostitution, he finally hears a Socialist speaker and joins the party because of the rebirth of hope and faith that it offers.

Ona, Jurgis' wife, who sells herself to her boss for money for the family. She dies in childbirth.

Connor, a stockyards boss who is attracted to Ona.

Antanas, Jurgis' baby, who drowns when left unattended.

Elzbieta, Ona's stepmother, and the mother of six.

Stanislovas, the oldest son of Elzbieta, who lies about his age in order to get a job.

Antanas Rudkus, Jurgis' aged father, who kicks back part of his wages in order to keep his job. He dies of tuberculosis.

Jonas, Elzbieta's brother, who works at the stockyards.

Jack Duane, a Chicago safecracker who shows Jurgis how to get quick money.

Marija, Ona's orphan cousin, who loses her job at the stockyards and becomes a prostitute.

The Story

While he was still a peasant boy in Lithuania, Jurgis Rudkus had fallen in love with a gentle girl named Ona. When Ona's father died, Jurgis, planning to marry her as soon as he had enough money, came to the United States with her family. Besides the young lovers, the immigrant party was composed of Antanas, Jurgis' father; Elzbieta, Ona's stepmother; Jonas, Elzbieta's brother; Marija, Ona's orphan cousin; and Elzbieta's six children.

By the time that the family arrived in Chicago, they had very little money. Jonas, Marija, and Jurgis at once got work in the stockyards. Antanas tried to find work, but he was too old. They all decided that it would be cheaper to buy a house on installments than to rent. A crooked agent sold them a ramshackle house that had a fresh coat of paint and told his ignorant customers that it was new.

Jurgis found his job exhausting, but he thought himself lucky to be making forty-five dollars a month. At last Antanas also found work at the plant, but he had to give part of his wages to the foreman in order to keep his job. Jurgis and Ona saved enough money for their wedding feast and were married. Then the family found that they needed more money. Elzbieta lied about the age of her oldest son, Stanislovas, and he too got a job at the plant. Ona had already begun to work in order to help pay for the wedding.

Antanas worked in a moist, cold room, where he developed tuberculosis. When he died, the family had scarcely enough money to bury him. Winter came, and everyone suffered in the flimsy house. When Marija lost her job, the family income diminished. Jurgis joined a union and became an active member. He went to night school to learn to read and speak English.

At last summer came, with its hordes of flies and oppressive heat. Marija found work as a beef trimmer, but at that job the danger of blood poisoning was very great. Ona had a baby, a fine boy whom they called Antanas after his grandfather. Winter came again, and

Jurgis sprained his ankle at the plant. Compelled to stay at home for months, he became moody. Two more of Elzbieta's children left school to sell papers.

When Jurgis was well enough to look for work again, he could find none, because he was no longer the strong man that he had been. Finally he got a job in a fertilizer plant, a last resource, for men lasted only a few years at that work. One of Elzbieta's daughters was now old enough to care for the rest of the children, and Elzbieta also went to work.

Jurgis began to drink. Ona, pregnant again, developed a cough and was often seized with spells of hysteria. Hoping to save the family with the money that she made, she went to a house of prostitution with her boss, Connor. When Jurgis learned what she had done, he attacked Connor and was sentenced to thirty days in jail. Now that he had time to think, Jurgis saw how unjustly he had been treated by society. No longer would he try to be kind, except to his own family. From that time forward, he would recognize society as an enemy rather than as a friend.

After he had served his sentence, Jurgis went to look for his family. He found that they had lost the house because they could not meet the payments and had moved. He found them at last in a rooming house. Ona was in labor with her second child, and Jurgis frantically searched for a midwife. By the time that he found one, Ona and the child had died. Now he had only little Antanas for whom to live. He tried to find work. Blacklisted in the stockyards for his attack on Connor, he finally found a job in a harvesting machine factory. Shortly afterward, he was discharged when his department closed down for a lack of orders.

Next, he went to work in the steel mills. In order to save money, he moved near the mills and came home only on weekends. One weekend, he came home to find that little Antanas had drowned in the street in front of the house. Now that he had no dependents, he hopped a freight train and rode away from Chicago. He became one of the thousands of migratory farm workers; his old strength came back in healthful surroundings.

In the autumn, Jurgis returned to Chicago and got a job digging tunnels under the streets. Then a shoulder injury made him spend weeks in a hospital. Discharged with his arm still in a sling, he became a beggar. By luck, he obtained a hundred-dollar bill from a lavish drunk. When he went to a saloon to get it changed, however, the barkeeper tried to cheat him out of his money. In a rage, Jurgis attacked the man, and he was arrested and sent to jail again. There he met dapper safecracker Jack Duane. After their release, Jurgis joined Duane in several hold-ups and became acquainted with Chicago's underworld. At last he was making money.

Jurgis became a political worker. About that time, the packing plant workers began to demand more rights through their unions. When packinghouse operators would not listen to union demands, there was a general strike. Jurgis went to work in the plant as a scab. One day, he met Connor and attacked him again. Jurgis fled from the district to avoid a penitentiary sentence. On the verge of starvation, he found Marija working as a prostitute. Jurgis was ashamed to think how low he and Marija had fallen since they came to Chicago. She gave him some money so that he might look for a job.

Jurgis was despondent until, one night, he heard a Socialist speak. Jurgis believed that he had found a remedy for the ills of the world. At last he knew how the workers could find self-respect. He found a job in a hotel where the manager was a Socialist. It was the beginning of a new life for Jurgis, the rebirth of hope and faith.

Critical Evaluation

"Here it is at last! The *Uncle Tom's Cabin* of wage slavery! And what *Uncle Tom's Cabin* did for black slaves, *The Jungle* has a large chance to do for the white slaves of today." So wrote Jack London in 1905. His hopes were exaggerated, however, for labor's Magna Carta, the Wagner Act, was not enacted until 1935. Nevertheless, Sinclair's muckraking classic was a singularly important factor leading to the Pure Food and Drug Act.

In *The Jungle*, superb investigative journalism and the art of a master melodramatist combine. Sinclair spent two months gathering his material; he ate in settlement houses, visited workers at home, interviewed strike leaders, and spoke to professional and political leaders who knew "the Yards." On a Sunday stroll, he happened into a Lithuanian wedding and so obtained his characters. At first, publishers balked, so horrifying were Sinclair's revelations. Finally, after verifying key facts, Doubleday sent the book to press. Sinclair was invited to the White House to advise an outraged Theodore Roosevelt on the conduct of a secret presidential investigation. Only the charge that workers who had fallen into lard vats went "out to the world as Durham's Pure Leaf Lard" could not be substantiated.

The effectiveness of Sinclair's story lies in the gradual

and relentless way in which the picture of a terrifyingly oppressive system is revealed. He allows the reader to believe, with Jurgis, that some hope exists in "the American way." Then, even the few positive factors are shown to be related to corruption. The democratic institutions that might have provided a means of change have all been bought off by the "Machine." The opportunity to "rise" causes people to betray their fellow workers.

The Jungle is a naturalistic work: Jurgis' environment forces him into violence and crime; fault lies with "the system," not with him. Yet Sinclair's pessimism is not like that of French novelist Émile Zola: The socialism that Sinclair preached implied a human ability (collectively expressed) to master that system.

THE LAST OF THE MOHICANS: A Narrative of 1757

Type of work: Novel
Author: James Fenimore Cooper (1789-1851)
Type of plot: Historical romance
Time of plot: 1757
Locale: Northern New York State
First published: 1826

This novel remains the most popular of Cooper's Leatherstocking Tales, a classic story of the French and Indian War. The battles and exciting pursuits that constitute the book's plot are rounded out by interesting Native American lore and descriptions of the wilderness.

Principal Characters

Natty Bumppo, called **Hawkeye,** the hardy, noble frontier scout in his prime during the French and Indian Wars. Traveling with his Native American companions, Chingachgook and his son Uncas, in Upper New York, he befriends an English soldier, a Connecticut singing master, and their two female charges, Cora and Alice Munro. When the travelers are ambushed by hostile Huron warriors, he leaves the party to get help, in turn ambushes their captors with the aid of Chingachgook and Uncas, and leads the group to Fort William Henry, besieged by the French. In the massacre of English troops that takes place after the garrison is forced to surrender, the women are captured again by the warriors. Hawkeye assists once more in the escape of Alice; however, a renegade Huron chief, Magua, claims Cora as his reluctant wife. In the ensuing fighting, Cora and Hawkeye's friend, the noble young Uncas, are killed. Hawkeye shoots Magua in return. In the end, he and Chingachgook return sorrowfully to the wilderness.

Chingachgook, a courageous, loyal Mohican chief, Hawkeye's inseparable friend. An implacable enemy of the Hurons, he is decorated as Death. Left to protect the English Colonel Munro after the massacre, he joins the final battle with intense ferocity, only to see his son die. His grief is relieved somewhat by Hawkeye's companionship.

Uncas, Chingachgook's stalwart son, the last of the Mohicans. A young and handsome chieftain, he falls in love with Cora Munro while protecting her and proves invaluable in tracking her after she has been captured. When a Delaware chief awards her to Uncas' rival, Magua, he follows them and is killed avenging her murder.

Major Duncan Heyward, the young English officer in charge of escorting the Munro sisters from Fort Edward to Fort William Henry. Brave, good-looking, and clever, he falls in love with Alice Munro and eventually succeeds in rescuing her from the Hurons. He finally marries her with Colonel Munro's blessing.

Magua, "Le Renard Subtil," the handsome, renegade Huron chief. Both cunning and malicious, he seeks to avenge himself on Colonel Munro by turning his spirited daughter Cora into a servile wife. Twice thwarted by Hawkeye and his companions, he wins Cora by putting his case before Tamenund, a Delaware chieftain. This victory, however, is short lived: Cora is killed by another Huron, and Magua, after killing Uncas, is shot by Hawkeye.

Cora Munro, the colonel's beautiful older daughter, who is part black. She is independent, equal to every situation, and bears up well under the strain of a capture, a massacre, and the threat of marrying Magua. Her love for Uncas, however, is thwarted when she is carried off by Magua and then stabbed.

Alice Munro, the colonel's younger daughter, a pale, immature, but lovely half sister of Cora. Frail and clinging, she excites Heyward's protective feelings during their adventures, and he later marries her.

Colonel Munro, the able but unsuccessful defender of Fort William Henry and the affectionate father of Cora and Alice. After surrendering to the French, he is forced to watch helplessly the slaughter of the men, women, and children from the fort. His sorrow is doubled when Cora is killed.

David Gamut, a mild, ungainly singing master who accompanies Heyward and the Munro sisters. His schoolbook piety contrasts with Hawkeye's natural pantheism. A rather ineffective person, he is nevertheless useful to Hawkeye, for the Hurons believe that David is insane and let him pass without trouble.

The Marquis de Montcalm, the skilled, enterprising general who captures Fort William Henry and then allows the defeated English to be massacred by savage Hurons.

Tamenund, the old Delaware chief who foolishly decides to give Cora to Magua.

Hard Heart, the Delaware chief whom Magua flatters to gain Cora.

General Webb, the incompetent commander of Fort Edward. He refused to aid Colonel Munro.

The Story

Major Duncan Heyward had been ordered to escort Cora and Alice Munro from Fort Edward to Fort William Henry, where Colonel Munro, the father of the sisters, was commandant. In the party was also David Gamut, a Connecticut singing master. On their way to Fort William Henry, they did not follow the military road through the wilderness. Instead, they placed themselves in the hands of a renegade Huron known as Magua, who claimed that he could lead them to their destination by a shorter trail.

It was afternoon when the little party met the woodsman Hawkeye and his Delaware Mohican friends, Chingachgook and his son Uncas. To their dismay, they learned they were but an hour's distance from their starting point. Hawkeye quickly decided Magua had been planning to lead the party into a trap. His Mohican comrades tried to capture the renegade, but Magua took alarm and fled into the woods.

At Heyward's urging, the hunter agreed to guide the travelers to their destination. The horses were tied and hidden among some rocks along a river. Hawkeye produced a hidden canoe from among some bushes and paddled the party to a rock at the foot of Glenn's Falls. There they prepared to spend the night in a cave.

That night, a band of Iroquois led by Magua surprised the party. The fight might have been a victory for Hawkeye if their supply of powder and ball had held out. Unfortunately, their ammunition had been left in the canoe, which was stolen by one of the enemy who had ventured to swim the swirling river. The only hope then lay in the possibility of future rescue, for the capture of the rock and the little group was a certainty. Hawkeye, Chingachgook, and Uncas escaped by floating downstream, leaving the women and Major Heyward to meet the savages.

Captured, Cora and Alice were allowed to ride their horses, but Heyward and David were forced by their captors to walk. Although they took a road paralleling that to Fort William Henry, Heyward could not determine the destination that the band had in mind. Drawing close to Magua, he tried to persuade him to betray his companions and deliver the party safely to Colonel Munro. The Huron agreed, if Cora would come to live with him

among his tribe as his wife. When she refused, the enraged Magua had everyone bound. He was threatening Alice with his tomahawk when Hawkeye and his friends crept silently upon the band and attacked them. The Iroquois fled, leaving several of their dead behind them. The party, under David's guidance, sang a hymn of thanksgiving and then pushed onward.

Toward evening, they stopped at a deserted blockhouse to rest. Many years before, it had been the scene of a fight between the Mohicans and the Mohawks, and a mound still showed where bodies lay buried. While Chingachgook watched, the others slept.

At moonrise, they continued on their way. It was dawn when Hawkeye and his charges drew near Fort William Henry. They were intercepted and challenged by a sentinel of the French under the Marquis de Montcalm, who was about to lay siege to the fort. Heyward was able to answer him in French, and they were allowed to proceed. Chingachgook killed and scalped the French sentinel. Through the fog which had risen from Lake George and through the enemy forces which thronged the plain before the fort, Hawkeye led the way to the gates of the fort.

On the fifth day of the siege, Hawkeye, who had been sent to Fort Edward to seek help, was intercepted on his way back and a letter he carried was captured. Webb, the commander of Fort Edward, refused to come to the aid of Munro.

Under a flag of truce, Montcalm and Munro held a parley. Montcalm showed Webb's letter to Munro and offered honorable terms of surrender. Colonel Munro and his men would be allowed to keep their colors, their arms, and their baggage if they would vacate the fort the next morning. Helpless to do otherwise, Munro accepted these terms. During one of the parleys, Heyward was surprised to see Magua in the camp of the French. He had not been killed during the earlier skirmish.

The following day, the vanquished English started their trip back to Fort Edward. Under the eyes of the French and their tribal allies, they passed across the plain and entered the forest. Suddenly, a Native American warrior grabbed at a brightly colored shawl worn by one of the women. Terrified, she wrapped her child in it. The warrior darted toward her, grabbed the child from her arms, and dashed out its brains on the ground. Then, under the eyes of Montcalm, who did nothing to discourage or hold back his savage allies, a monstrous slaughter began.

Cora and Alice, entrusted to David Gamut's protection, were in the midst of the killing when Magua swooped down upon them and carried Alice away in his arms. Cora ran after her sister, and faithful David dogged her footsteps. They were soon atop a hill, from which they watched the slaughter of the garrison.

Three days later, Hawkeye, leading Heyward, Munro, and his Mohican comrades, tracked the women and David, following a path where they had found Cora's veil caught on a tree. Heyward was particularly concerned for the safety of Alice; the day before the massacre, he had been given her father's permission to court her.

Hawkeye, knowing that hostile Native Americans were on their trail, decided to save time by traveling across the lake in a canoe that he discovered in its hiding place nearby. He was certain that Magua had taken the sisters north, where Magua planned to rejoin his own people. Heading their canoe in that direction, the five men paddled all day, at one point having a close escape from some of their intercepting enemies. They spent that night in the woods and the next day turned west in an effort to find Magua's trail.

After much searching, Uncas found the trail of the captives. That evening, as the party drew near the Huron camp, they met David Gamut wandering about the woods. He told his friends that the tribe thought him crazy because of his habit of breaking into song, and the warriors allowed him to roam the woods unguarded. Alice, he said, was being held at the Huron camp. Cora had been entrusted to the care of a tribe of peaceful Delawares a short distance away.

Heyward went to the Huron camp in an attempt to rescue Alice, while the others set about helping Cora. Heyward was in the camp but a short time, posing as a French doctor, when Uncas was brought in as a captive. Called to treat an ill Huron woman, Heyward found Alice in the cave with his patient. He was able to rescue the woman by wrapping her in a blanket and declaring to the Hurons that she was his patient, whom he was carrying off to the woods for treatment. Hawkeye, attempting to rescue Uncas, entered the camp disguised in a medicine man's bearskin that he had stolen. Uncas was cut loose and given the disguise, while the woodsman borrowed David Gamut's clothes. The singer was left to take Uncas' place while the others escaped, for Hawkeye was certain that the tribe would not harm David because of his supposed mental condition. Uncas and Hawkeye fled to the Delaware camp.

The following day, Magua and a group of his warriors visited the Delawares in search of their prisoners. The chief of that tribe decided that the Hurons had a just claim to Cora because Magua wished to make her his wife.

Under inviolable Native American custom, the Huron was permitted to leave the camp unmolested, but Uncas warned him that in a few hours he and the Delawares would follow his trail.

During a bloody battle, Magua fled with Cora to the top of a cliff. There, pursued by Uncas, he stabbed and killed the young Mohican and was in his turn sent to his death by a bullet from Hawkeye's long rifle. Cora too was killed by a Huron. Amid deep mourning by the Delawares, she and Uncas were laid in their graves in the forest. Colonel Munro and Heyward conducted Alice to English territory and safety. Hawkeye returned to the forest. He had promised to remain with his sorrowing friend Chingachgook forever.

Critical Evaluation

The Last of the Mohicans is the second title published in what was to become a series of five entitled collectively the Leatherstocking Tales. When Cooper published the first of these "romances," as he called them to distinguish them from the somewhat more realistic contemporary novels, he had no plan for a series with a hero whose life would be shown from youth to old age and death. In *The Pioneers* (1823), Natty Bumppo or Leatherstocking is in his early seventies. Responding to a suggestion from his wife, Cooper went back in *The Last of the Mohicans* to Natty's early thirties, when he was called Hawkeye.

The great popularity of *The Last of the Mohicans* led Cooper then to move chronologically beyond *The Pioneers* and to picture in *The Prairie* (1827) the last of Natty's life when he was in his eighties, living as a trapper and finally dying on the Great Plains far from his early home. At the time, Cooper did not intend to revive Natty in further romances. One minor romance of the forest, *The Wept of Wish-Ton-Wish* (1829), was followed by a stream of nautical novels, sociopolitical novels, and nonfictional works of social and political criticism extending until 1840, when Cooper finally answered the pleas of many literary critics and readers and revived the hero whose death he had so touchingly portrayed at the end of *The Prairie*. In *The Pathfinder* (1840), Natty is called Pathfinder, and the action shifts from land to the waters of Lake Ontario and back again. Pleased by the resounding praise that he gained for having brought back his famed hero, Cooper decided to write one final romance about him, in which Natty would be younger than in any of the earlier books. In *The Deerslayer* (1841), Natty is in his early twenties and goes by the nickname Deerslayer. In 1850, Cooper brought out a new edition of all five Leatherstocking Tales arranged according to the order of events in Natty Bumppo's life: *The Deerslayer, The Last of the Mohicans, The Pathfinder, The Pioneers, The Prairie*. For this edition, he wrote a preface in which he remarked (prophetically, as it turned out): "If anything from the pen of the writer of these romances is at all to outlive himself, it is, unquestionably, the series of *The Leather-Stocking Tales*." Despite many complaints from Mark Twain and later critics about Cooper's style, plots, structure, characterization, and dialogue, the Leatherstocking Tales continue to be read, both in the United States and in many foreign countries, and they seem assured of a long life to come.

In Cooper's day, *The Last of the Mohicans* was the most popular of the five tales, and it has continued to be so. Structurally, the novel is superior to the other tales, with three major plot actions and a transitional though bloody interlude (the massacre after the surrender of Fort William Henry). Cooper's action-filled plot, with bad characters chasing good ones or good characters chasing bad ones, has become standard in many action novels, as well as motion pictures and television dramas.

Romantic love was conventional in the plots of novels in Cooper's day. His portrayal of Duncan Heyward and the Munro sisters, Cora and Alice—who carry most of the love interest in *The Last of the Mohicans*—shows no originality. They are all genteel characters who speak in a stiff, formalized manner that seems unreal to present-day readers. Duncan is gentlemanly and the two "females" (as Cooper repeatedly calls them) are ladylike. Cooper contrasts Cora and Alice, as he does the pairs of women who keep turning up in his books. Cora, the dark one, is passionate, independent, and unafraid, even defiant; blonde Alice is timid and easily frightened into faints—she resembles the sentimentalized helpless girls of popular early nineteenth century fiction.

Cooper does much better with his forest characters. Hawkeye is talkative, boastful, superstitious, scornful of the book-learning that he does not possess, and inclined to be sententious at times. Yet he is brave, resourceful, and loyal to his two Mohican friends. His French nickname, La Longue Carabine (the long rifle), attests to his shooting skill. He is religious but sometimes seems more pantheistic than Christian in any formal sense. Hawkeye's arguments with David Gamut oppose his generalized beliefs and Gamut's narrow Calvinism. With his dual background of white birth and early education by Moravian missionaries on the one side and his long experience of living with Native Americans on the other, he is, as Honoré de Balzac called him, "a moral hermaphrodite, a child of savagery and civilization."

Chingachgook and Uncas are idealized representatives of their race. As "good Indians," they are dignified, taciturn, even noble despite their savage ways. Uncas is lithe, strong, and handsome; he reminds the Munro sisters of a Greek statue. Magua is the "bad Indian," sullen, fierce, cunning, and treacherous. His desire for Cora as his wife is motivated by his wish to avenge a whipping ordered by Colonel Munro.

In addition to the love theme, which provides for the marriage of Heyward and Alice, Cooper includes others. Related to the love theme is miscegenation, which Cooper has been accused of evading by killing off both Cora, who is part black, and Uncas, who had wanted to marry her. Another theme is suggested by the title of the romance. Chingachgook is left mourning for his son, the last of the Mohican chiefs. He grieves also because he foresees the eventual vanishing of his race. Both he and Hawkeye despair as they envision the end of their way of life in the great American wilderness, which will gradually disappear.

It is easy to complain of Cooper's faulty style, his verbosity, his heavy-handed humor (with David Gamut), his improbable actions, the insufficient motivation of his characters, and the inconsistency and inaccuracy of his dialogue. Yet many readers willingly suspend their disbelief or modify their critical objections in order to enjoy the rush of action that makes up so much of *The Last of the Mohicans*. They sorrow over the deaths of Cora and Uncas, and their sympathies go out to Chingachgook and Hawkeye in the loss of what had meant so much in their lives. Also, especially in a time when ecologists are fighting to preserve some of the natural beauty of the United States, they enjoy Cooper's respect for nature found in his descriptions of the northeastern wilderness as it was in the eighteenth century.

THE LATE GEORGE APLEY

Type of work: Novel
Author: John P. Marquand (1893-1960)
Type of plot: Simulated biography
Time of plot: Late nineteenth and early twentieth centuries
Locale: Boston
First published: 1937

The satire of this novel is double-edged because of the method of telling the story. Mr. Willing, the supposed biographer of these memoirs, is as much a source of satire as George Apley himself; without the staid, polished, and politely dull narrator, the book would simply be a realistic novel.

Principal Characters

George William Apley, a proper Bostonian carefully trained since childhood to be a respectable member of Boston Brahmin society. Though as a college student he belittled the Brahmin pride of family, he acquired it himself as he matured, and later he attempted to pass it on to his children. Undistinguished academically at Harvard University, he had been active in campus affairs and a member of a select club. Unfit for active business, he derived his income from investments and from his father's substantial legacy. Though he admired Ralph Waldo Emerson's writings, he never became an Emersonian nonconformist; in fact, he believed that the individual in society must submit to the common will. Like his father and his Uncle William, he was a generous giver to worthy causes.

John Apley, his son, who stirred George's heart with pride over his war service, including a wound, and who later married a woman of good family. It was John who requested the writing of his father's life story.

Eleanor Apley, George's daughter. She greatly disappointed George by marrying a journalist.

Catharine Bosworth Apley, George's wife, whose marriage to George was unexciting but successful. According to his sister Amelia, George simply let Catharine and her family dominate him.

Mr. Willing, George Apley's biographer, staid, polished, and politely dull. Like George himself, Mr. Willing is snobbish, for he is also a Brahmin. In accordance

with John's request, he includes along with George's commendable characteristics and actions some derogatory and unsavory details in his life; but he attempts to excuse these as minor aberrations in an essentially admirable man.

Mary Monahan, an attractive woman whose love affair with George ended when George's parents removed him from such a lower-class association.

William Apley, George's uncle, a wealthy businessperson who spent little on himself and scorned ostentation but who was secretly a generous philanthropist. He controlled the Apley mills and opposed labor unions. When over eighty, he shocked the family by marrying his nurse.

Amelia Apley, George's sister. She was more independent and forceful than George.

O'Reilly, a lawyer who tricked George into a scandal.

Horatio Apley, the holder of a diplomatic post in Rome.

Thomas and **Elizabeth Hancock Apley,** George's parents.

Miss Prentiss, the young nurse whom Uncle William married.

Newcomb Simmings, Amelia Apley's husband.

Louise Hogarth Apley, John's wife. She is a divorcée, but when George learns that she is from a fine family, he is satisfied.

William Budd, Eleanor's husband.

The Story

George William Apley was born on Beacon Hill, on January 25, 1866. The Apleys were an old family in Massachusetts. Thomas, known in the old records as Goodman Apley, had emigrated from England to America and settled in Roxbury in 1636. Goodman Apley's son, John, had graduated from Harvard University in 1662. From his time, there had been an Apley in Harvard in each succeeding generation. John Apley's son, Nathaniel, established himself in Boston. A later Apley, Moses, became a shipping master and laid the foundation of the Apley fortune. Moses Apley was George Apley's grandfather.

George Apley grew up in a quiet atmosphere of wealth and social position. He learned his parents' way of living calmly and with fortitude. In an orderly way, he was introduced to the polite world, at first through visits to relatives, later through study at Harvard.

His Harvard days were probably the high point of his life. George was sent to Harvard to shape those qualities of gentlemanly behavior that private grammar school and parents together had tried to encourage. His parents were anxious that he should make friends with the right people. George was carefully instructed in the ways of high-minded gentlemen. His training was indicated by a theme in which he wrote a description of a Boston brothel in terms expressing his repulsion and shock. In the gymnasium, George won distinction as a boxer. Moreover, he became a member of the Board of the Harvard *Lampoon*. He was taken into the Club, an honor his father appreciated greatly. In his junior and senior years, he took part in the musical extravaganzas of the Hasty Pudding Club. In spite of these activities, he never neglected his studies, and he was known as a respectable student with grades placing him in the middle of his class at graduation.

While in college, he fell in love with an impossible woman named Mary Monahan. The affair was cut short by the Apleys and never referred to publicly. Shortly thereafter, his family prescribed a sea voyage for him. When he returned home, he took up the study of law and became a member of the board for the Boston Waifs' Society.

George was instructed in the shrewd businesslike manners and knowledge of the Apleys. He was sent to work with his Uncle William for one summer. William sensed that his nephew would never make a good businessperson, however, and advised that George should be put into law or made a trustee of other people's money, not his own. As a result, George, like many of his friends, never went actively into business.

In February, 1890, George followed his parents' wishes and became engaged to Catharine Bosworth. Both his father-in-law and his own father saw to it that the young couple had a summer cottage and a house for the winter. The two mothers were equally solicitous. George discovered that he had married not only Catharine but also her family.

As the years passed, George devoted his time to charitable groups and learned societies and to writing for his clubs. One of his papers, "Jonas Good and Cow Corner," was said to be among the best papers read before the Browsers in fifty years.

His first child's name was a subject for debate in his own and Catharine's family. The name, John, common to both families, was finally chosen. His second child was a daughter, Eleanor.

Shortly after his sister Amelia's marriage, George's father died of an apoplectic stroke. He left a million dollars to Harvard, other large sums to his charities, and the remainder of his fortune in trust for his family. George had to pay a sum of money to a woman who claimed that she had borne a son to his father. Although he did not believe the charge, he paid rather than cause scandal in the family.

George invested in a place known as Pequod Island, and there he took his friends when he wanted to get away from Boston. On the island, he and his friends condescended to share the campfire with their guides. Planned as a male retreat, the island was soon overrun with literary lights of the times invited by George's wife and sister.

As his son grew up, George noted an increasing desire on the part of the younger generation to be wild and careless with money. Later, George began to realize that he and his generation had let much slip and that Boston was going to the Irish. He gave his name to the "Save Boston Association" as he considered his membership an Apley duty. He also interested himself in bird lore and philosophy and took as much personal concern as possible in the affairs of his children. When his mother died in 1908, George counted her death as one of his most poignant tragedies.

When George's son entered Harvard, George took a new interest in the university and noted many changes that he did not like.

Old Uncle William, now over eighty, still controlled the Apley mills and held out successfully against the new labor unions. One day, the old man shocked his family by marrying his nurse, a Miss Prentiss.

His daughter Eleanor's marriage was completely unsatisfactory to George because she did not induce her husband to give up his job for a position in the Apley mills and to take up residence near her family. Nevertheless, George was proud of his son John for his service at the front. George himself belonged to the Home Guards. When John married a woman of good connections after the war, George was doubly pleased.

At last, George came into opposition with a man named O'Reilly, whom George planned to have brought before criminal court on charges of extortion. O'Reilly, however, tricked George into a scandal. George intended to have the whole case cleared in court, but before the trial he received a note from his one-time sweetheart, Mary Monahan. After an interview with her, he settled the case quietly and bought off his opponents.

In 1928, he became a grandfather. As soon as the baby had been born, George telegraphed the prestigious Groton School to include his grandson's name among the entrance applicants.

In his last years, George took interest in the new novels, condemning those too blatant in their description of sex and fighting against the inclusion of some of them in the Boston libraries. His own copy of D. H. Lawrence's *Lady Chatterly's Lover* (1928) he hid in the silver safe to keep his daughter from seeing it. He defied Prohibition as an abuse of his rights and kept a private bootlegger on principle because he thought it important to help break the Prohibition law.

He thought, too, that the colossal fortunes being gathered by the uneducated should be handed over to the government. In the autumn of 1929, he and his wife made a trip to Rome, where they visited Horatio Apley, recently appointed to a diplomatic post there. George was absent from the United States when the stock market crash came. His financial affairs did not suffer greatly, but, his health breaking, he began to plan his will and his funeral. George Apley died in December, 1933.

Critical Evaluation

The Late George Apley, considered by many to be the best of John P. Marquand's novels, was a turning point in the author's career. For fifteen years prior to its publication, Marquand had, as a "slick" popular writer, enjoyed considerable commercial success but no critical recognition. *The Late George Apley*, however, was immediately recognized as an important book, and its author was promoted by the critics from "popular" to "serious" writer. This elevation was certified when the novel earned for Marquand the Pulitzer Prize in 1938. Throughout the remaining years of his writing career, he confirmed and further consolidated this reputation, although never completely abandoning the commercial marketplace.

The Late George Apley is the first of a trilogy of novels in which Marquand minutely describes and analyzes the social patterns, behaviors, mores, and conflicts in upper-class Boston society during the rapidly changing period between 1880 and 1920. This novel pictures that part of old Boston society with puritanical antecedents and commercial traditions; the second of the books, *Wickford Point* (1939), shows the decline of Bostonians with Transcendentalist ancestors and artistic pretensions; while the last, *H. M. Pulham, Esquire* (1941), examines the life of a Boston businessman in the 1920's and 1930's as he tries to accommodate his geographical and class inheritances to the pressures of the contemporary world.

In each of these books, Marquand explores the ways in which social forms and cultural assumptions left over from the past bind those in the present; how, in short, those environments that evolved to ensure familial and social protection, identity, and continuity become prisons for the individuals who inherit them.

This theme is most obvious in *The Late George Apley*. Actually, the book chronicles three Apley generations. George's father, Thomas, represents the old nineteenth century individualistic businessperson. He is highly intelligent, austere, rigid, hardworking, and uncompromising. His relationship with his son is reserved and formal, almost institutionalized, although he shows concern and, on occasion, affection for the boy. The doubts that are to plague his son are foreign to Thomas. He knows who he is and what his roles are as father, as businessman, as member of the community, and as "Apley." When he and George have their only real public disagreement, the older man emphatically quashes George's fuzzy democratic ideas: "You and I do not stand for the common good. We stand for a small class; but you don't see it. . . . Nobody sees it but me and my contemporaries." Yet Thomas is saved from robber baron status by a sincere Puritan "stewardship" ethic; he truly believes that the Apley position and fortune are signs of godly favor and that the money must be conserved and shared with the community—but only on terms dictated by that "small class" of superior people at the top of the social pyramid.

George Apley envies his father his certainty and strength, but he cannot emulate him personally. Early in his life, he accepts the verdict of his Uncle William, and subsequently Thomas, that he is "not a businessman," that he is "too easy going" and "erratic" and so accepts permanent placement as an investment counselor (of other people's money), lawyer, and civic leader. George assumes from the beginning that his environment is the only one that he "could have survived in," but neither he nor the reader can ever be sure. He is never able to test his well-meaning mediocrity; he is given the opportunity neither to succeed nor to fail, only to fit into a predetermined groove.

In his youth, George makes a few feeble attempts at nonconformity; he chooses some dubious friends, questions a few Apley dogmas, and, most important, has a brief, intense love affair with a middle-class Irish Catholic woman. It is squelched, of course; George is sent on a Grand Tour, and Mary Monahan becomes a sad memory (until the end of the book). Yet, throughout his life, George is plagued by the sense that he is trapped and is living a life filled with activity but devoid of action or meaning. The most important events of his life are family disputes: what to name the baby, how to prevent cousin John from divorcing his wife, where to bury cousin Hattie, and whether to move the rosebushes.

George's few attempts to find even momentary respite from his milieu fail before they begin. He travels abroad but carries Boston with him. "I am a raisin," he says, "in a slice of pie which has been conveyed from one plate to another." He buys an island as a masculine retreat from Bostonian formality and its guardians, the women, and before he knows it, the ladies arrive and "Boston has come to Pequod Island." Throughout his life, he suspects that he cannot escape the "net" (young John's phrase) of an environment that stifles more than it supports, and shortly before his death he acknowledges it. Worst of all, he realizes that it has cost him the one important thing that he might have had from his life—happiness.

As his father before him, George tries to pass the Apley ethic down to his own son, but John rebels more directly and emphatically than his father did. His social and political views baffle and alarm George. John pushes the rebellion further by refusing to join his father's firm, by going to New York City, and by marrying a divorcée. He is much more attuned to the modern world than his father is, and his World War I experiences at the front have matured and sophisticated him. Yet, in the end, John proves to be his father's son; he returns to Boston and sets up housekeeping at Hillcrest, the family estate. George dies secure in the knowledge that the Apley niche in Boston remains filled; the cycle continues.

The Late George Apley, however, is more than a sad story of the environment's tyranny over individuals. For all the bleakness of its conclusions, the novel is most entertaining and amusing. The comedic and satiric center of the novel lies in its narrator, Mr. Willing. Marquand decided to tell the story as "a novel in the form of a memoir" for two reasons: first, to parody the then common subliterary genre of the "collected papers" and, more important, to filter the information about the Apleys through the mind and language of a character even more dogmatically committed to the proper Bostonian vision of life.

Willing understands none of George Apley's incipient rebellions and his son's more blatant social improprieties. Much of the novel's rich humor and gentle satire comes from his fussy, polite, pseudo-literary apologies and rationalizations for the errant Apley behavior. In the end, in spite of Willing's stuffy shortsightedness, the reader gets to know and understand the subject very well, is amused and saddened by his weaknesses and narrowness, but is finally tolerant of, and sympathetic toward, the late George Apley.

LAUGHING BOY

Type of work: Novel
Author: Oliver La Farge (1901-1963)
Type of plot: Romance
Time of plot: Early twentieth century
Locale: American Southwest
First published: 1929

A Pulitzer Prize-winning novel, Laughing Boy *explores the cultural clash between tribal culture and white society and the individual conflicts of two young Native American lovers.*

Principal Characters

Laughing Boy (Sings Before Spears), a young artisan and horse trader who comes from the remote area of the Navajo reservation located in the American Southwest. His efforts to sell his jewelry and horses bring him into contact with the developed white society bordering the reservation's southern boundary. He enjoys competition, native dances, and religious services such as Night Chants. An unspoiled Navajo, he respects tribal customs and ceremonies. His love for Slim Girl brings ecstatic happiness and intense suffering.

Slim Girl (Came with War), a young, beautiful, ambitious, resourceful woman of mixed Navajo and Apache descent. As an orphan child, she was removed from her tribal home and sent to a boarding school run by missionaries, where she found adjustment to white society difficult. Although she genuinely loves Laughing Boy, she views him as a means of returning to her Native American roots on the reservation and from him learns all that she can about Navajo customs. At the same time, she works in order to assure that they can retain some of the security and conveniences found in life off the reservation.

Jesting Squaw's Son, a loyal friend of Laughing Boy who shares his exuberance, high spirits, and competitive activities. His account of disappointment in love foreshadows the tragic end of Laughing Boy's relationship with Slim Girl.

Two Bows, Laughing Boy's father, a Navajo craftsper-

son of middle age. He has taught Laughing Boy the art of making silver-and-turquoise jewelry and has been supportive of his work. A man of dignity, taciturnity, and reserve, he represents the masculine ideal among Native Americans.

Wounded Face, Laughing Boy's blunt, plainspoken uncle, who knows of the reputation of Slim Girl. Sought by Laughing Boy for his advice, he urges the youth not to marry her and seeks to influence other relatives against her.

Red Man, a treacherous, vengeful young Navajo, consumed with passion for Slim Girl. An introverted malcontent and the novel's antagonist, he represents a foil to Laughing Boy's naïve, optimistic, and outgoing nature.

George Hartshorn, a white rancher who lives near the reservation. He continues a long-standing relationship with Slim Girl after her marriage to Laughing Boy, not realizing that she cares only for the money that he gives her. When Laughing Boy accidentally discovers the continuing relationship, he wounds Hartshorn with an arrow.

Yellow Singer, an elderly Navajo who lives in Los Palos, where he has become corrupted through his contact with white society. Although he has become an alcoholic, he still practices Navajo customs and religion and performs the marriage ceremony for Laughing Boy and Slim Girl.

The Story

Attending a four-day ceremonial Navajo dance at Tsé Lani, a village in the southern part of the reservation, Laughing Boy takes part in horse racing and attempts to sell silver jewelry and ornaments he has crafted. There he meets and falls in love with Slim Girl, a beautiful young Navajo whose expensive garments and jewelry add to her romantic appeal. From Red Man, one of her admirers, he wins a wrestling match but acquires a life-long enemy. Despite her disappointment when Laughing Boy gambles away his winnings and other possessions following a successful horse race, Slim Girl agrees to become his wife, for she sees him as a virile man who will take her back to live on the reservation. An orphan with no close relatives, she has known only unhappiness in white society and wishes to return to the land and ways of her people.

Before their marriage, Laughing Boy seeks the approval of his uncle Wounded Face, his father being several days' journey away. Already deeply in love, however, he angrily dismisses his uncle's advice against the marriage and has the proper Navajo ceremony performed. Following the marriage, Slim Girl persuades Laughing Boy to settle in her house in Los Palos, a town on the southern edge of the reservation. Although she desires to return to tribal life, she also wants enough money to protect them from the discomforts and inconveniences found on the reservation. Having seen how Navajo women who tend sheep for a living age prematurely, she wishes to avoid heavy work. Instead, she expects that she and Laughing Boy will earn their living through weaving and jewelry making. In Los Palos, Laughing Boy spends his time raising and selling horses and crafting fine jewelry. After persistent effort marked by failures, Slim Girl learns to weave Navajo blankets. Nevertheless, she continues her relationship with the rancher George Hartshorn by going periodically to his house in Los Palos. She demonstrates resourcefulness in concealing her illicit relationship from Laughing Boy, explaining her absences and the money that she is accumulating by saying that she is working for the wife of a missionary.

On one occasion, she and Laughing Boy travel to his home settlement in Utah, located in the far north of the reservation, to attend a religious ceremony. At this place, Slim Girl meets Laughing Boy's father, Two Bows, and other relatives; though they have heard of her past, they give her a grudging acceptance. During the journey, Slim Girl becomes acquainted with some of the hardships of life on the reservation, including nights in a crowded hogan where others are infested by lice. During intervals between tribal ceremonies, the participants enjoy more worldly activities. At a trading post, Laughing Boy and his friends use their cunning to outwit the proprietor, Narrow Nose. During the return trip, Laughing Boy's friend Jesting Squaw's Son narrates to him the painful episode of his hopeless love for a young woman of his own clan. Although shocked by the revelation of this illicit love, Laughing Boy does his best to console his friend. After he and his wife return to Los Palos, they resume their normal activities of weaving, tending horses, and crafting fine jewelry.

In time, their idyllic relationship becomes inexplicably tense. One day, Laughing Boy pursues an escaped stallion to the other side of town and there discovers Slim Girl at the house of George Hartshorn. Grasping the implication at once, he draws an arrow in his bow and wounds Hartshorn in the shoulder. He then sends another arrow toward Slim Girl with the intent of killing her. Instead, it leaves only a minor wound in her forearm.

Overcome by the grief that follows his rage, Laughing Boy frees his horse and returns slowly to Slim Girl's house, discovering that she has arrived before him. After he has removed the arrow, she narrates the story of her life, which she had previously concealed. After learning how she became a prostitute for a time, Laughing Boy understands and forgives. They gather their belongings and set out for the site on the reservation where they had planned to live, intending to start over.

During the journey, they are sighted by Red Man, who holds a grudge against Laughing Boy. Firing his rifle at Laughing Boy from a great distance, Red Man mortally wounds Slim Girl instead. Laughing Boy agrees to her dying wish that he not seek vengeance for her death. Alone on the desolate landscape, he provides a Navajo ceremonial funeral for her and, after four days of grief, returns to his people.

Critical Evaluation

Trained as an anthropologist, Oliver La Farge devoted much of his life to Native American interests. Among his numerous books concerned with life in the Southwest, only *Laughing Boy* is remembered as a minor classic. The novel attempts to depict the conflicts inherent in tribal life and the plight of Native Americans in their cultural clash with white society. Yet La Farge does not permit his affinity for tribal culture or his sympathetic understanding of Native Americans to obscure the hardships of reservation life. In seeking to present a balanced view, he incorporates as much information as he can about Native American culture and religion.

In a larger context, he is concerned with the disappearance of tribal religion, customs, and ceremonies.

Deliberately, he gives the work a setting nearly a generation before the time in which he wrote, in order to portray Navajo life before the first automobiles arrived on the reservation and greatly increased the rate of change. He attempts to clarify such Navajo concepts as life as a beautiful path or way to be followed. He incorporates within his text a number of Navajo chants and passages of poetry, most in translation but with an occasional Navajo word, and details some of the rituals. In a not entirely successful way, he attempts to show how these rituals relate to the majestic natural setting of the land, with its numerous canyons, wide deserts, towering rock formations, and blue mountains. These natural phenomena are linked to humankind's past when Laughing Boy and Slim Girl pass Anasazi dwellings on their journey into the remote part of the reservation.

Major threats to the Navajo ideal arise from the clash with the dominant culture, as Native Americans attempt to adopt the ways of the whites. They develop cunning and devious methods in their dealing with traders and others who bargain with them, relying heavily on haggling. Many, like Yellow Singer, fall prey to alcoholism and see their lives wrecked. Others alienate themselves from their tribe and become objects of suspicion because they accept some of the white people's ways, like changing their traditional dress. Slim Girl, the most complex character, illustrates how difficult it is for Native Americans to adjust fully to white culture. Educated in a boarding school where she spoke only English, she accepted white values and religion, yet lived to discover that the promised compassion was hollow and unreliable. Thoroughly disillusioned with the dominant society, she sought to recover her essential being through a return to tribal life.

Yet La Farge is too much a realist to portray tribal life as an ideal form of existence. Conflicts and rivalries exist on a large scale, and some of the violent behavior that results from them is exacerbated by the prevalence of alcohol in settlements such as Los Palos. Yet Laughing Boy thinks nothing of attacking a lone Pah-Ute (Paiute) and taking his horses and possessions, simply because members of that tribe are ancient enemies of the Navajos. The novel includes numerous hints of tribal and intratribal feuds and enmities that have been the bane of tribal life throughout history. Furthermore, in an economic sense, life in the remote area of the reservation is depicted as primitive at best. Living in a hogan entails hardships that Laughing Boy and Slim Girl seek to avoid.

In its portrayal of nature and young love, the novel has been called idyllic. The romantic attachment between Laughing Boy and Slim Girl is mirrored by the poignant and hopeless love of Laughing Boy's best friend, Jesting Squaw's Son. Yet the love theme, as critics have pointed out, is the least realistic part of the narrative, for the characters are given values and attitudes alien to Navajo culture. Despite this fact, the love theme contributes to the aesthetic appeal of La Farge's work.

Perhaps it is the aesthetic theme that is paramount, however, for the novel suggests that Navajo tribal values can best be retained by those characters who transform tribal symbols and values into works of art. From his father, Two Bows, Laughing Boy has learned the art of making fine silver-and-turquoise jewelry, and Slim Girl patiently learns the art of weaving beautiful blankets on her loom. Imbued with the Navajo concept of the beautiful way, both intend to earn their living through their artistic abilities. Works of art patiently crafted by dedicated artists both preserve and transmit the values of Navajo culture.

LEAVES OF GRASS

Type of work: Poetry
Author: Walt Whitman (1819-1892)
First published: 1855-1892

From 1855 through the rest of his life, Whitman elaborated and expanded his poetic vision in Leaves of Grass, *his groundbreaking collection of free verse.*

Having been at one time or another an office boy, printer, teacher, newspaper editor and reporter, manager of a printing office and stationery store, and builder of houses, Walt Whitman was thirty-six when his first book of poems, *Leaves of Grass*, was published in July, 1855, a publication for which he himself paid. That same month, he sent a copy of the book of twelve poems to Ralph Waldo Emerson, the famous essayist, poet, and spokesman for Transcendentalism, whom the younger poet had never met but by whose essays he had been greatly influenced. While certainly the gesture of a writer looking for approval from his mentor, Whitman's act also represented his salute to Emerson and Transcendentalism, as well as his gratitude to the great man for showing him the way to his own unprecedented, authentically American kind of poetry.

Whitman's "leaves" would multiply. By the time of his death in 1892, *Leaves of Grass* contained 383 poems, including the magnificent threnody to Abraham Lincoln entitled "When Lilacs Last in the Dooryard Bloom'd," in addition to the great "Out of the Cradle Endlessly Rocking," "Calamus," and "Passage to India." Space limitations preclude discussion of the final 1888 edition of *Leaves of Grass*, but the essence of Whitman's poetic achievement, as well as his historical place and importance in American literature, can be gleaned from the first edition. Even if Whitman had never published any poetry after 1855, his influence would remain apparent in the work of such twentieth century poets as Hart Crane, Robinson Jeffers, Carl Sandburg, Charles Olson, and Allen Ginsberg. His first book of untitled free-verse poems would prove to be not only the single greatest poetic triumph to emerge from Transcendentalism but also the first collection of poetry uniquely American in vision, voice, form, and substance—the kind of poetry that Emerson had envisioned but failed to write.

Emerson was not the first nineteenth century American to note that, after two centuries, America still had not produced poetry uniquely its own. There was Orestes

Brownson who, in 1838, wrote of American writers, "We are now the literary vassals of England, and continue to do homage to the mother country. Our literature is tame and servile, wanting in freshness, freedom, and originality. We write as Englishmen, not as Americans." Even earlier, in 1826, complaining that "rhymes add nothing to poetry, but rather detract from its beauty," Sampson Reed had asserted that "the poet should be free and unshackled as the eagle whose wings, as he soars in the air, seem merely to serve the office of a helm, while he moves on simply by the agency of the will." Whitman would prove himself to be such a "free and unshackled" poet, in the first poem (later titled "Song of Myself") of the 1855 edition of *Leaves of Grass*:

> I fly the flight of the fluid and swallowing soul,
> My course runs below the soundings of plummets.
>
> I help myself to material and immaterial,
> No guard can shut me off, no law can prevent me.
>
> I anchor my ship for a little while only,
> My messengers continually cruise away or bring
> their returns to me.

For those "returns," both "material and immaterial," Whitman's persona in the poems—like the poems themselves—became a crucible for apotheosis, wherein any division between subject and object would be resolved, all categories fused into one; that oneness was to be voiced by the transcendent persona's self. Like Emerson's concept of the human-deifying "transparent eyeball," the self in Whitman's poetry is essentially a transpersonal soul or universal spirit. From childhood to adulthood, the "Walt Whitman" in *Leaves of Grass* has developed his identity through a metaphysical merging with everything around him, as the poet makes clear in the tenth poem (to be titled "There Was a Child Went Forth") of the 1855 edition:

There was a child went forth every day,
And the first object he looked upon and received
    with wonder or pity or love or dread, that
    object he became,
And that object became part of him for the day or
    a certain part of the day. . . . or for many years
    or stretching cycles of years.

Such a "child," whether eight or eighty, "who went forth every day, and who now goes and will always go forth every day," realizes immortality insofar as he slips free of the shackles of personality, of what Emerson calls "mean egotism," enters into a timeless union with all around him and becomes—again Emerson's words— "part or parcel of God."

Besides a healthy irreverence for secondhand customs and beliefs, especially those transplanted to America from England, essential to Transcendentalism was a denunciation by its adherents of institutionalized, traditional religion. Transcendentalists expressed a desire to mend the supposed split between God and humanity, and they insisted that Jesus Christ be seen as a historical personage, a man, and—though wiser—no more or less godlike than other humans. Emerson believed poetry to be the best vehicle for expressing human awareness of the Universal Being, for "poetry was all written before time was, and whenever we are so finely organized that we can penetrate into that region where the air is music, we hear those primal warblings and attempt to write them down." Emerson's attempts at such poetry, however, remained cramped within the traditional prosody adopted from English poets; in 1835, he admitted that, though he was "born a poet," his talent was "of a low class without doubt." Whitman, however, was determined to capture in his poetry "those primal warblings," as he indicates in "Song of Myself": "To me the converging objects of the universe perpetually flow,/ All are written to me, and I must get what the writing means." Later in the poem, he says, "Through me the afflatus surging and surging . . . through me the current and index./ I speak the password primeval." To his readers, Whitman makes an implicit promise: "Stop this day and night with me and you shall possess the origin of all poems./ You shall possess the good of the earth and sun," of the terrestrial and celestial.

"My singing," said Emerson, "is for the most part in prose. Still am I a poet in the sense of a perceiver and dear lover of the harmonies that are in the soul and in matter." Emerson's singing in prose and his remarkable ability as an essayist to articulate what he perceived and conceived inspired Whitman to a feverishly intense responsiveness. In "The American Scholar" (1841), Emerson had asserted that the ideal American scholar-poet, "Man Thinking," should be "the world's eye" and "the world's heart." In "Song of Myself," Whitman is the ideal become real: "With the twirl of my tongue I encompass worlds and volumes of worlds./ Speech is the twin of my vision." Elsewhere (in the fourth poem, later titled "The Sleepers") he asserts, "I dream in my dream all the dreams of other dreamers,/ And I become the other dreamers." Emerson claimed that the "one thing in the world, of value, is the active soul," and that "the soul active sees absolute truth and utters truth, or creates. In this action it is genius. . . . In its essence it is progressive." Whitman responds (in the twelfth poem of the 1855 edition, later titled "Great Are the Myths"): "O truth of the earth! O truth of things! I am determined to press the whole way toward you,/ Sound your voice! I scale mountains or dive in the sea after you." Believing that the world is the "shadow of the soul, or *other* me," as Man Thinking, scholar-poet Emerson claimed to "embrace the common," to "explore and sit at the feet of the familiar, the low." Whitman was equal to such an embrace, exploration, and reverential humility—was in fact the personification of such in his poems, especially in "The Sleepers" and "Song of Myself": "What is commonest and cheapest and nearest and easiest is Me," and in "all people I see myself, none more and not one a barleycorn less."

"We have listened too long to the courtly muses of Europe. The spirit of the American freeman is already suspected to be timid, imitative, tame," Emerson had said in "The American Scholar." Three years later, in "The Poet," he asserted that the ideal American poet would be "representative," that "He stands among partial men for the complete man, and apprises us not of his wealth, but of the common wealth." Eleven years later, he would open *Leaves of Grass* and witness in the first poem the "barbaric yawp" of the actualized ideal: "I am the poet of the woman the same as the man,/ And I say it is as great to be a woman as to be a man." Furthermore, "I am large . . . I contain multitudes," the representative and democratic "I" of Whitman's poems announces. "Neither a servant nor a master am I," he sings in the second poem (to be titled "A Song for Occupations"); "I will be even with you, and you shall be even with me."

Emerson had said in "The American Scholar" that the world is the soul's shadow, and in "The Poet" he claimed that "the Universe is the externization of the soul." Undoubtedly, this would be one of the most salient and liberating Emersonian premises for the younger poet, for it is endlessly all-encompassing, the truths one might discover through it countless and its realm incomprehensibly expansive. In fact, in the 1850's, the United States itself seemed expansive enough to be viewed as "the externization of the soul," and this is how Whitman portrayed it, his persona the embodiment of a harmonious microcosmic and macrocosmic union. He is introduced in "Song of Myself" as "Walt Whitman, an American, one of the roughs, a kosmos,/ Disorderly fleshy and sensual . . . eating drinking and breeding,/ No sentimentalist . . . no stander above men and women or apart from them."

The American poetry that Emerson had envisioned in 1844 would not depend upon meters, he said; rather its form would derive organically from its content, for "a meter-making argument . . . makes a poem,—a thought so passionate and alive that like the spirit of a plant or an animal it has an architecture of its own." He also maintained that, in American poetry, thought should make "everything fit for use. The vocabulary of an omniscient man would embrace words and images excluded from polite conversation." Although Emerson would be incapable of embracing or employing such "words and images" in his poetry, one of the hallmarks of Whitman's is that he did employ them:

> I keep as delicate around the bowels as around the
>   head and heart,
> Copulation is no more rank to me than death is.

I believe in the flesh and the appetites,
Seeing hearing and feeling are miracles, and each
    part and tag of me is a miracle.

Divine am I inside and out, and I make holy
    whatever I touch or am touched from;
The scent of these arm-pits is aroma finer than
    prayer. . . .

Most modern readers would consider the above passage from "Song of Myself" tame in its celebration of the flesh, but in 1855 it was audacious and bold. Nevertheless, Whitman set out to celebrate in poetry what he called, in a letter to Emerson (1856), "the divinity of sex . . . I say that the body of a man or woman, the main matter, is so far quite unexpressed in poems; but that body is to be expressed, and sex is."

As a poet, Whitman proved himself to be the kind of superior student that Emerson had called for in his essays—one who surpasses the teacher. The creator of a revolutionary form of poetry and the uniquely representative American persona of the "barbaric yawp," Whitman was justified in singing, in "Song of Myself," "I am an acme of things accomplished, and I an encloser of things to be."

THE LEFT HAND OF DARKNESS

Type of work: Novel
Author: Ursula K. Le Guin (1929-   )
Type of plot: Science fiction/fantasy
Time of plot: The future
Locale: The planet Gethen
First published: 1969

The brilliance and originality of The Left Hand of Darkness, *in which Le Guin created a planet whose inhabitants are androgynous, made it one of her most acclaimed novels. By telling the story primarily through the eyes of a male alien from earth, the author reveals new truths about sexuality, love, loyalty, patriotism, and political power.*

Principal Characters

Genly Ai, a black male, who has been sent to the planet Gethen as First Envoy to offer its two nations membership in a league of nations called the Ekumen. Although he is befriended by the prime minister of Karhide, Therem Harth rem ir Estraven, Genly Ai does not trust him, but foolishly depends on his own judgments. When he visits Orgoreyn, Karhide's rival, again Genly Ai rejects Estraven's advice, and he is imprisoned. After Estraven rescues him and guides him back to Karhide, Genly Ai comes to accept Estraven as the friend that he is.

Therem Harth rem ir Estraven, the lord of Estre in Kerm and the prime minister of Karhide. A dark, stocky character, "he" is androgynous, like every "normal" person on his planet. A progressive thinker, Estraven favors Karhide's joining the Ekumen. As a result, he is branded a traitor and exiled from Karhide. After rescuing Genly Ai, Estraven once again proves his loyalty to his friend and his country by sacrificing his own life and thus assuring the success of the Genly Ai's mission.

Argaven XV, the king of Karhide. He is arrogant, rude, illogical, and suspicious. Argaven admits that he is governed by fear, evidently the fear of anything or anyone different, and that he uses fear to rule his people. Only his female qualities prevent him from becoming an even more dangerous tyrant than he is.

Estra Pemmer Harge rem ir Tibe, the cousin of King Argaven. Insolent and insincere, Tibe engineers the fall of Estraven and later arranges his death. Tibe is so greedy for power that he is willing to start a war in order to attain it. After the starship lands in Karhide, however, proving the truth of Genly Ai's claims, Tibe is discredited.

Faxe the Weaver, a tall, handsome leader of the Handdara, whom Genly Ai visits at Otherhord. Faxe represents the passive, spiritual life, in contrast to the greed for power that is so evident at court. At the end of the novel, when he sees the starship land, Faxe predicts a new era for his people.

The Story

The Left Hand of Darkness is told as a report from Genly Ai to his superiors in the Ekumen, a loosely organized league of some three thousand states that cooperate by sharing ideas and knowledge with one another. Genly Ai was sent alone to the planet Gethen in order to persuade the nations of Karhide and Orgoreyn to join the Ekumen. The starship from which he had descended continued to remain in the vicinity, but it would not land unless invited to by the local authorities. Thus, the First Envoy was vulnerable and even expendable.

At first, Genly Ai was treated by the residents of Karhide as an honored guest. If he felt any uneasiness, it was toward the powerful prime minister, Therem Harth rem ir Estraven, who professed friendship toward him. Without any specific reason, Genly Ai distrusted Estraven, and he was puzzled as to Estraven's motives in suggesting that he leave Karhide and go to the rival nation of Orgoreyn.

Suddenly, however, the political situation on Karhide changed. Estraven was accused of treason and exiled, and King Argaven XV's cousin, the devious Estra Pemmer Harge rem ir Tibe, became the king's most trusted adviser. Although the king did see Genly Ai and gave him freedom to travel, his attitude was made clear when he fulminated against the "perverted" single sexuality of the Ekumen members and appeared to doubt every statement that the envoy made.

Yet not all the people of Karhide were like the king and the courtiers. At a remote Fastness, Genly Ai met members of a mystical cult called Handdara, including Faxe the Weaver, one of the Foretellers, or prophets. Asking whether Karhide would become a member of Ekumen within five years, Genly Ai was assured that they would. This prediction was the only real hope he had been given that his mission would succeed.

Meanwhile, Estraven had escaped from Karhide and from Tibe's assassins and had been well received in Orgoreyn. There he encountered the First Envoy, who was trying his luck with the Orgota, supposedly the more rational and enlightened of the two peoples. Again Estraven warned him that he might be in personal danger, and again Genly Ai dismissed the warning, trusting instead the professions of factional leaders. This time, it was Genly Ai who suddenly fell out of favor. He was arrested, drugged, interrogated, and sent to a prison camp, from which there was no escape but death. Nevertheless, although he did not realize it, Genly Ai still had one loyal friend. Disguising himself, Estraven managed to rescue Genly Ai and to hide him until the two could decide on a course of action.

The problem was that both were now hunted: Genly Ai would be killed if he remained in Orgoreyn; Estraven would be executed if he returned to Karhide. Yet Genly Ai could not get to Karhide without Estraven's help. The only possible solution was to travel together to Karhide by a circuitous route, avoiding populated areas. After depositing Genly Ai in safety, Estraven would slip back across the border and return to his new home in Orgoreyn.

The story of that arduous, eight-hundred-mile trip through ice and snow is told partly by Genly Ai, partly by Estraven. While this part of the book is a suspenseful tale of survival against the odds, it is also a moving account of the growth of friendship. By the time that they reached Karhide, Estraven and Genly Ai had forged an unbreakable bond—a bond so strong that, when they were betrayed and trapped, Estraven gave his life to save his friend and the mission.

At the end of the novel, both oppressive governments fell; the new governments agreed to become members of the Ekumen; the starship landed; and in the son of Estraven, Genly Ai found another mind ready to question, to venture, and to change society.

Critical Evaluation

Ursula K. Le Guin commented on the genesis of *The Left Hand of Darkness* in an essay entitled "Is Gender Necessary?" Influenced by the feminist movement of the 1960's, Le Guin wrote, she began to think about the relationship between gender and politics, in particular about the possibility that it is male aggressiveness which causes wars. Her speculations led her to imagine a world whose inhabitants are androgynous and then to explore the implications of that fact.

Obviously, Le Guin needed a fictitious foreign observer to comment upon this unusual society. Convinced that a male would feel more threatened in an androgynous society than a female, Le Guin created Genly Ai, a man from Earth, whose observations tell the reader much about Gethenian society but whose reactions also reveal his own gender prejudices. Because the movement of the novel is toward the bonding of the two major characters, however, Le Guin had Genly Ai include in his report two first-person narratives by the androgyne Estraven. By handling point of view in this way, she could emphasize the differences that had to be overcome in the "marriage," as well as tracing the gradual process by which those differences were overcome—primarily through shared hardship that made trust in each other essential.

Ironically, it was not the androgyne Estraven but the more sophisticated First Envoy whose emotional response was initially blocked. In a conversation with Estraven that took place during the long, difficult journey, Genly Ai admitted that he really knew nothing about females. He had certainly never thought of them as equals, he said; in fact, he had never thought much about them at all. As a result of this conversation, Genly Ai finally came to realize why he had felt such uneasiness in the presence of Estraven. Subconsciously, Genly Ai was responding to the female side of Estraven, and according to the standards of Earth, no female could be considered a friend or an equal.

Sadly, even though Genly Ai finally admitted his own prejudices, he was unable to transcend them; during the trip across the ice, when Estraven went into kemmer, or a period of sexual desire, and became a female, Genly Ai could not bring himself to mate with her. Even without a physical union, however, Genly Ai and Estraven did bond. As Estraven muses in his journal, their isolation made that marriage possible: Because they were both aliens in the icy wilderness, they were no longer able to think of their differences from each other. Instead, they came to share their thoughts and feelings, if not their bodies, as they never could have done within the societies into which they had been born.

In *The Left Hand of Darkness*, though important in themselves, gender differences also symbolize the kinds of "otherness" that separate individuals and produce conflict. Certainly the novel does reflect Le Guin's hypothesis that war is caused by masculine aggression. In an androgynous society, where each individual may be at times a female, there are periodic brakes on aggressive tendencies, if only because childbearers and nurturers are too tired for battle. Thus, it is suggested that King Argaven might have been even more tyrannical if he had not been pregnant during Genly Ai's stay in Karhide.

Like single-sex people on Earth, however, the androgynes on Gethen seemed to take pleasure in viewing other individuals as different from themselves. By cultivating this intolerance, they could justify subjugating or annihilating them, as in the death camps of Orgoreyn or in wars motivated by "patriotism," that is, the fear of others. Fear of "otherness" thus became an excuse for aggression.

Yet there was an even more important reason, one that appeared to be rooted in human nature itself. Among the many misjudgments of the First Envoy to Gethen was his evaluation of the differences between the two nations, made when he first arrived in Orgoreyn. Where the people of Karhide were primitive and emotional, those of Orgoreyn, though not particularly interesting, he saw as rational and enlightened. After his arrest and torture, Genly Ai's opinion changed, and he then saw that the leaders of both nations were governed by the same val-

ues. They were all greedy for property, status, and power, and they found their greatest pleasure in snatching these seemingly good things away from others.

The real contrast, then, was not between the people of Karhide and the Orgota, but between those governed by materialistic values and those who had renounced them in favor of spiritual goals. Genly Ai saw this difference clearly after he had spent some time with the Handdara, whose values were the exact opposite of those held by most Gethenians. As their leader Faxe the Weaver explained, the Handdara sought to renounce all desires, even the desire for knowledge. Genly Ai could see the results. Unlike the other people whom he had met, the Handdara had no egotistical need to outdo or outwit others, and therefore they were tolerant, gentle, and generous.

It is significant that Estraven was a member of the Handdara. His spiritual values explain why Estraven consistently put the good of others ahead of his own interests. He lost his own power and property by advising the king to join the Ekumen, he risked his life to rescue Genly Ai from prison, and, finally, he gave his life to save the First Envoy and to ensure the success of his mission.

Critics have had high praise for many of Le Guin's works, such as the politically oriented novel *The Dispossessed: An Ambiguous Utopia* (1974), which won Hugo and Nebula awards, and the highly acclaimed fantasies for young adults called the Earthsea trilogy, consisting of *A Wizard of Earthsea* (1968), *The Tombs of Atuan* (1971), and *The Farthest Shore* (1972). Yet readers and scholars alike find themselves returning to *The Left Hand of Darkness*, drawn by its originality, by its thematic richness, and, perhaps most of all, by the appeal of the two characters who, by learning to love each other, suggest that there may still be hope for human beings on Earth.

"THE LEGEND OF SLEEPY HOLLOW"

Type of work: Tale
Author: Washington Irving (1783-1859)
Type of plot: Regional romance
Time of plot: Eighteenth century
Locale: New York State
First published: 1819-1820

American literature's first great writer, Irving was responsible for two trends in American letters: one toward local color and the legendary tale, the other toward the historical novel. This tale belongs to the first trend and has fascinated and delighted readers for almost two hundred years.

Principal Characters

Ichabod Crane, a schoolmaster of Sleepy Hollow, near Tarrytown on the Hudson. He dreams of a comfortable marriage to Katrina. Because of his belief in ghosts, he is frightened from the area by a ghostly rider.

Gunpowder, Ichabod's gaunt horse.

Katrina Van Tassel, a rosy-cheeked student in Ichabod's singing classes.

Mynheer Van Tassel, her wealthy farmer father.

The Headless Horseman, a legendary apparition, supposedly a Hessian cavalryman whose head was shot off by a cannonball.

Abraham Van Brunt, called **Brom Bones,** who is in love with Katrina. Disguised as the Headless Horseman, he pursues Ichabod and throws a pumpkin at him. Ichabod leaves Sleepy Hollow permanently.

The Story

Near Tarrytown on the Hudson is a little valley that, years ago, was the quietest place in the world. A drowsy influence hung over the place and people so that the region was known as Sleepy Hollow, and the lads were called Sleepy Hollow boys. Some said that the valley was bewitched. It was true that marvelous stories were told there.

The main figure to haunt the valley was a headless horseman. Some said the specter was the apparition of a Hessian horseman who had lost his head from a cannonball, but, whatever it was, it was often seen in the valley and adjacent countryside in the gloom of winter nights. The specter was known to all as the Headless Horseman of Sleepy Hollow.

In the valley, years ago, there lived a schoolteacher called Ichabod Crane. He looked like a scarecrow because of his long, skinny frame and his snipelike nose. As was the custom in that fertile Dutch countryside, he boarded with the parents of his pupils a week at a time. Fortunately for him, the Dutch larders were full and the tables groaning with food, for the schoolmaster had a wonderful appetite. He was always welcome in the coun-

try homes because, in small ways, he made himself useful to the farmers. He was patient with the children, and he loved to spend the long winter nights with the families of his pupils, exchanging tales of ghosts and haunted places while ruddy apples roasted on the hearths.

Ichabod believed heartily in ghosts, and his walks home after an evening of tale-telling were often filled with fear. His only source of courage at those times was his voice, loud and nasal as it made the night resound with many a psalm tune.

The schoolteacher picked up a little odd change by holding singing classes. In one of his classes, he first became aware of a plump and rosy-cheeked girl named Katrina Van Tassel. She was the only child of a very substantial farmer, and that fact added to her charms for the ever-hungry Ichabod. Because she was not only beautiful but also lively, she was a great favorite among the lads in the neighborhood.

Abraham Van Brunt was Katrina's favorite squire. The Dutch first shortened his name to Brom and then called him Brom Bones when he became known for the tall and powerful frame of his body. He was a lively lad with a fine sense of humor and a tremendous amount of energy. When other suitors saw his horse hitched outside Katrina's house on a Sunday night, they went on their way. Brom Bones was a formidable rival for the gaunt and shaggy Ichabod. Brom would have liked to carry the battle into the open, but the schoolteacher knew better than to tangle with him physically. Brom Bones could do little but play practical jokes on lanky Ichabod.

The whole countryside was invited one fall evening to a quilting frolic at Mynheer Van Tassel's. For the occasion, Ichabod borrowed a horse from the farmer with whom he was then living. The horse, called Gunpowder, was as gaunt as Ichabod himself, but the steed still had a fair amount of spirit. The two of them were a sight as they jogged happily along to the party.

Ichabod was well pleased by every prospect he saw on the Van Tassel farm, the most prosperous holding for miles around. Perhaps Ichabod might be able to sell it and, with the proceeds, go farther west. It was a pretty picture he saw as he passed fields full of shocks of corn and pumpkins, granaries stuffed with grain, and meadows and barn-lots filled with sleek cattle and plump fowl.

The party was a merry one with many lively dances. Ichabod was at his best when he danced with Katrina. After a time, he went out on the dark porch with the men and exchanged more Sleepy Hollow ghost stories—but the food was best of all. Ichabod did credit to all the cakes and pies, meats and tea.

After the others left, he tarried to pay court to Katrina, but it was not long before he started home crestfallen on the gaunt Gunpowder. All the stories that he had heard came back to him, and as he rode along in the darkness, he became more dismal. He heard groans as the branches of the famed Major André tree rubbed against one another. He even thought he saw something moving beneath it.

When he came to the bridge over Wiley's Swamp, Gunpowder balked. The harder Ichabod urged him on, the more the horse bucked. Then, on the other side of the marsh, Ichabod saw a huge and misshapen figure.

The figure refused to answer him when he called. Ichabod's hair stood straight on end. Because it was too late to turn back, however, the schoolmaster kept to the road. The stranger—it looked like a headless horseman, but it seemed to hold its head on the pommel—kept pace with him, fast or slow. Ichabod could not stand going slowly, and he whipped Gunpowder to a gallop. As his saddle loosened, he nearly lost his grip, but he hugged the horse around the neck. He could not even sing a psalm tune.

When he reached the church bridge, where by tradition the headless specter would disappear in a flash of fire and brimstone, Ichabod heard the horseman close in on him. As he turned to look, the spirit threw his head at him. Ichabod tried to dodge, but the head tumbled him into the dust.

In the morning, a shattered pumpkin was found near the bridge. Gunpowder was grazing at the farmer's gate nearby. Ichabod, however, was never seen in Sleepy Hollow again. In the valley, they say that Brom Bones, long after he had married the buxom Katrina, laughed heartily whenever the story was told of the horseman who had thrown his head at the schoolteacher during that ghostly midnight pursuit.

Critical Evaluation

Washington Irving was by inclination an amused observer of people and customs. By birth, he was in a position to pursue that inclination. The son of a New York merchant in good financial standing, he was the youngest of eleven children, several of whom helped him to take prolonged trips to Europe for his health and fancy. He was responsible for two trends in American literature: one, toward the legendary tale, steeped in local color; the other, toward the historical novel. "The Legend of Sleepy Hollow" belongs to the first trend.

The two best-known of Irving's stories are "Rip Van Winkle" and "The Legend of Sleepy Hollow," both of which appeared originally in *The Sketch Book of Geoffrey Crayon, Gent.* (1819-1820), a collection of tales and familiar essays. Both stories are based on German folklore, which Irving adapted to a lower New York State setting peopled with Dutch farmers.

In "The Legend of Sleepy Hollow," the Dutch farmers make up most of the folkloric elements, for Ichabod Crane is an outsider, a Yankee schoolmaster among the canny Dutch settlers. As an outsider, and a peculiar-looking one at that, Ichabod Crane becomes the butt of local humor and the natural victim for Brom Bones's practical jokes. Most of the humorous sallies of the Sleepy Hollow boys are in the vein of good-natured ribbing. Yet Brom Bones's practical jokes are somewhat more serious because of the rather unequal rivalry between Brom and Ichabod for the hand of Katrina Van Tassel. It is in the relationship between Brom and Ichabod that the common folk theme of the scapegoat is most clearly seen.

Other folk themes appear in the story as well. Among them is the belief that one can ward off evil spirits with religious symbols; thus, Ichabod sings psalms on his fear-filled homeward treks after evenings of storytelling. The distinction of having a special ghost—one with a definite identity—to haunt a specific locality is a matter of honor and prestige, highly respected as a folkloric theme. Here, the putative Hessian, the Headless Horseman of Sleepy Hollow, fills the role with grace, wit, and style. The character of the comely wench, over whose favors men wrangle, dispute, and plot, is as common a catalyst in folklore as in life; hence, Katrina Van Tassel functions as fulcrum and folk theme in "The Legend of Sleepy Hollow."

These and other themes from folklore and legend appear in "The Legend of Sleepy Hollow" as well as other tales by Washington Irving, for legendary material was one of Irving's two major interests, the other being history, a closely related field. As far as Irving's work is concerned, the two interests seem to feed upon each other to the mutual benefit of both: His historical writings are enlivened by his cultural perceptions, and his stories are made more vivid by his knowledge of history. One of the first professional writers in the United States, and among the first to exercise a significant influence in Great Britain and on the Continent, Irving has been called the founder of American literature.

LET US NOW PRAISE FAMOUS MEN

Type of work: A written and photographic documentary on the Southern cotton tenant farmers
Author: James Agee (1909-1955); Walker Evans (1903-1975), photographer
First published: 1941

Commissioned to create a photographic and written portrait of the typical white sharecropper, Agee and Evans instead produced a radical new document of a time, a place, and a way of life.

In 1936, James Agee, a writer, and Walker Evans, a photographer on leave from the Farm Security Administration, were commissioned by the staff of a magazine to do an article on cotton tenantry that would be a photographic and verbal record of the daily lives of the average white sharecropper. As the two men carried out their assignment, they found it developing into a much larger project than that originally conceived. Ultimately, they were forced to return to their jobs much sooner than they wished, and the work that they had done and assembled was refused publication by those who had commissioned it. Eventually, it found publication on condition that certain words be deleted that were illegal in Massachusetts. By that time, 1941, Agee and Evans envisioned *Let Us Now Praise Famous Men*, complete in itself, as part of a larger whole to be called *Three Tenant Families*. The other part was never done. In its final form, the book consists of sixty-two photographs followed by a lengthy text partly factual, partly imaginative, all extremely detailed. A narrative of fact, a regional study, a moving moral document, a lyric meditation on life and art, and an exercise in style, it was one of the most remarkable books of the twentieth century.

First, as in a playscript, the members of the three families are listed, their ages, relationships, and their farms. In this list, Agee casts himself as a spy, traveling as a journalist, and Evans as a counterspy, traveling as a photographer. Listed also are William Blake, Celine, Ring Lardner, Jesus Christ, and Sigmund Freud, as unpaid agitators.

Many critics considered the book a structural failure. It has no apparent pattern of development. Agee begins by explaining that the project was corrupt, obscene, terrifying, and mysterious. He realized painfully that he was spying into the private misery of these people, that their lives would thus be exposed as passing entertainment to the curious and casual reader, and that he was being paid for doing this. Thus, determined to show the sacredness and dignity of each life down to the smallest detail, he approached his subjects with boundless love and humility.

He records three incidents, called "Late Sunday Morning," "At the Forks," and "Near a Church," so moving to him as to render him almost inarticulate at the time of the event, but about which he writes simply and vividly. In the first, a white foreman intrudes into the African-American community and forces three African Americans to sing for Agee and Evans. At the forks, Agee asks directions of a sick young man, his worn wife, and a mentally retarded older man. Near a church that Evans wished to enter in order to take photographs, Agee frightened a young African-American couple by running up behind them. In each case, he empathized so strongly with each individual that he felt sympathy and understanding for the foreman even though he humiliated the singers, felt sick with joy and gratitude when the wife at the forks showed sufficient confidence in him to smile slightly, and felt the fear of the young couple and the utter impossibility of ever communicating clearly to them his intentions.

A Country Letter, which begins part 1 and which Agee wrote while sitting up late at night, contains some of the most beautiful lyric prose of the entire book. It is unified, developed, and complete in itself. Agee speaks of his tenants specifically, but he places them and their flimsy homes against a backdrop of the earth and the universe so that they and their problems, their joys and sorrows, become representative of all people. The theme running through the entire piece is of aspirations and ideals dulled and lost, worn down by the hard necessities of living, of the flame of life that sinks down almost to an ember as they ask themselves how they were thus caught.

Parts 1 and 2 are primarily factual. The people themselves are introduced, and their complex family relationships are clarified. The order of their rising and their breakfasts are described in detail. Agee explains simply the attempts of the men to find other work during slack times on the farm and the kinds of jobs available to them. The chapter on money is an objective and devastating account of the tenant farmers' financial situation. The section on shelter is almost a hundred pages long.

Agee details the setting of one tenant home, the surrounding fields, the spring, the garden, and the outbuildings, including the contour and quality of the soil, the angle of the path, the flavor of the water, the shape and size of the building, the boards and nails holding them together, and the odds and ends found inside them. Systematically, he examines, as with a microscope, the house itself, its outside structure and materials, the space underneath the house including the dampness, insects living there, the odors; then, inside, the front bedroom, where he himself slept, the rear bedroom, where the family slept, the kitchen and storeroom, and the space beneath the roof. For each room, he describes the walls, floor, placement of furniture, the furniture itself and the contents of each drawer down to bits of dust, the items on the furniture and pinned to the walls, the insects inhabiting the bed, the wasps in the beams of the roof, the textures and odors, and the imagined hopes and feelings of the people whose home it is. His description of the house is of a living thing, flimsy and inadequate, but alive and placed, like the people, against the curve of the earth and sky. He describes the homes of the other two families also, but chiefly to point out their differences from the first. The final part of this section is devoted to the life present other than human: the dogs, cats, cows, mules, pigs, snakes, insects, birds, and trees. These lives too are described with respect and consideration, with humor, and with an appreciation of the beauty to be found in them.

Part 2 is devoted to sections on clothing, education, and work. Agee lists the items of clothing worn by the men and women on Sundays, Saturdays, and workdays. He describes in particular detail a suit of overalls and the shirt worn with them, their cut, pockets, stitching, straps, color, and texture when new, when partly worn out, and when completely worn out, differentiating carefully between the three stages. He makes the clothes almost alive, an outer skin, part of the individual who wears them.

The section on education, termed brilliant by some critics, is an angry analysis of the failure of schools and teachers, not only in the South but also everywhere, properly to educate the young, of society's forcing on them work that has no bearing on their lives and values that are meaningless or harmful.

In "Work," Agee gives a step-by-step description of the raising of cotton, from the preparation of the soil through the sowing, cultivating, and harvesting of the crop. This work is extremely laborious and is done with primitive, inadequate tools. The entire family participates in the labor and in the anxious waiting for harvest, which will determine the meager incomes of the sharecroppers.

The next part of the book, called "Intermission," is illustrative of the confused structure of the book. It deals with a questionnaire sent to writers by *The Partisan Review* and Agee's answer to it.

Part 3, "Inductions," goes back in point of time to the first meetings between Agee and Evans and the three families involved in their work. In particular, the section describes Agee's first night in the Gudgers' home, how he came to be there, what they said and ate, and how they all reacted to the situation.

From that point on, the book consists of short pieces: descriptions of a graveyard, of Squinchy Gudger and his mother, and of Ellen Woods; a poem, the first line of which gives the book its title; and a section entitled "Notes and Appendices" containing various notes, chiefly on Margaret Bourke-White, and a listing of Anglo-Saxon monosyllables.

The concluding piece describes a call, possibly of a small furbearing animal, probably a fox, heard one night from the Gudgers' front porch. The call was answered by another animal, and as the two continued to call back and forth, Agee and his friend speculated on the animals and their locations. Finally, within himself, Agee experienced the joy of hearing the world talk, of nature talking, as well as the grief that comes from the inability to communicate.

The faults of the book arise from its very virtues: Agee's love and compassion for people result not only in vivid, lyric prose but also in verbosity and repetition. When it first appeared, some critics thought Agee's prose arrogant, mannered, precious, and nonsensical; others found it confused and adolescent. Obsessed though the author was with his own complex reactions to his subjects and the rest of the world, and his failure to convey all that he felt, he nevertheless gave a picture of himself and of the tenants and their lives in a way that is vivid and overwhelming. At times, the writer's sensibility would be almost unbearable if it were not of a high moral order. Like Herman Melville's *Moby Dick* (1851) and Henry David Thoreau's *Walden* (1854), *Let Us Now Praise Famous Men* breaks through the limits of reality to convey meanings and insights that are rich and strange in its presentation of personal revelation and moral significance.

LIE DOWN IN DARKNESS

Type of work: Novel
Author: William Styron (1925-   )
Type of plot: Psychological realism
Time of plot: 1945
Locale: Port Warwick, Virginia
First published: 1951

Styron's first novel chronicles the circumstances leading to the suicide of the younger daughter of Milton and Helen Loftis. The author condemns this dysfunctional family—Milton for his pretensions and his uncontrolled appetites and desires, and Helen for her manipulations and abuses.

Principal Characters

Milton Loftis, a lawyer. He is an unlikable, often laughable man who aspires to a poetic soul despite his constant moral lapses.

Helen Loftis, his wife, a hypochondriac. She is a spiteful woman whose jealousies hurt those around her.

Peyton Loftis, their younger daughter. Peyton becomes a pawn in the struggles between her parents—the object of her father's incestuous thoughts and the victim of her mother's vengefulness and paranoia. Her suicide is portrayed as an escape from this trap and as an indictment of Milton and Helen.

Maudie Loftis, their older daughter, who is mentally handicapped. Her mother's devotion to her is another effort at manipulating the other family members.

Ella Swan, the Loftis' African-American maid, a religious woman who preaches to Milton.

La Ruth, her daughter, also a servant.

Dolly Bonner, a socialite who is involved in an adulterous affair with Milton.

Sclater (Pookie) Bonner, her husband.

The Reverend Carey Carr, Helen's confidant.

Harry Miller, Peyton's husband.

Dick Cartwright, Peyton's first lover.

Llewellyn Casper, a mortician.

One may choose to see a paradox not as it reflects back and forth upon itself but rather as it appears in only one of its mirrors. Just such a single-mirrored glimpse of William Styron's first book, *Lie Down in Darkness*, reveals a novel that achieves some success because of an extraordinary failing, one that stems from a startling source: The prose is too good. If the prose were less good, then the book could realize its own harmonic sense and avoid its emergence as a lopsided, Miltonic work that deceives the reader. A proportioned book, however, would also become a lesser work of art.

In this novel, Styron concentrates on the temporal structure of the plot and on language; he uses no central character, for none of the people portrayed warrant his full attention. Yet because its plentiful imagery is clear and accurate, widely gathered and imaginative, both woven into minute detail and scattered among forcible phrases, the language uplifts its paltry players, and they dazzle with a borrowed brilliance. Perhaps one takes them more seriously than they deserve, for they are present in a truth that is not their own. When the writing falters, as it sometimes does (even in a single paragraph can be found excellence sprung from clumsiness), the reader is reminded that Styron is composing on a large scale. At such moments, Milton Loftis and his family declare that their lives are of a particular rather than of a general interest. One pays their torments the same mild attention that a friend might arouse by revealing childhood memories.

The present moment of the novel is a day of burial, a day on which the universe takes no notice of Milton Loftis' tragedy. He awaits the arrival of his daughter's body with pitiful surprise that the world's activity is not suspended in deference to his personal pain. As though to mock him, the hearse is stalled, ships noisily unload their cargoes, and coal gondolas screech and roar about their work. Port Warwick is busy with its everyday concerns.

This is the moment that Styron will use as an anchor post in his game of temporal shifts. Past events spring up to invade the present, and past and present join their voices, one sometimes humming while the other sings.

Yet Styron is always clear about the words; one always knows to whom one is listening.

The story, pieced together from such a clever device, might have been told better in a straightforward narrative, for the ingenious plot construction serves the same fault as does the excellent prose. As told, the story is as complicated as a single event in any person's life usually is. Any readers required to describe their present moment would find themselves gleaning the multifarious moments of the past to shed light on this seemingly simple present. Such explication, however, would be uninteresting except to those personally involved. It is the sign of an artist that the reader becomes personally involved, in some cases throughout a lifetime. Styron's genius makes one deem his characters and their story more worthy of attention than one would allow if they were stripped of his protection. His talents as a novelist do not permit readers to see the characters clearly until they are a safe distance from his deception.

Milton Loftis is a weak individual who, if not actually an alcoholic, is quite dependent upon strong drink. His paternal instincts are adulterated with incestuous stirrings and his connubial duties stained with adulterous conspiracy. Indeed, there is nothing to redeem him, and one can only laugh, as does his wife, Helen, at his political aspirations and at his pretensions to a poetic soul. Yet, so true is Styron's talent that one can sympathize with Loftis and pity his pain, sometimes almost believing him. It is no easy matter to separate the character from the prose, for Styron is not William Faulkner; he uses no Vardaman, of *As I Lay Dying* (1930), to report his own observations.

Although it is Milton whom the reader comes to know best, it is Helen who is least protected by the writer. Her defensive hypochondria and religious fanaticism, her jealousy and abuse of Peyton, her unrelenting nightmares (insisting upon truth), and her neurotic need for her despicable husband all combine in condemnation. Even her devotion to her firstborn, the mentally retarded Maudie, is no virtue in her hands, for she uses it as a weapon against her husband and younger daughter. Yet, she is more sinned against than sinner. Her innocent fault is that she is dull.

As for Peyton Loftis, ironically animated with the vitality of youth, one hardly comes to know her. Mostly, she is seen in the early part of the book through the astigmatic eyes of her parents. They seem vaguely to recognize that her existence is a sign of redemption from the accusing presence of Maudie. To her mother, she is a cunning rival for Milton's affection; to her father, she is a conspirator, almost sibling, against the watchfulness of Helen. By the time that readers enter her mind, they are handling a damaged parcel, diseased by the combination of her inheritance; there is no redemption after all. Peyton's suicide is seen as a relief from the tormented condition of her life, not as a tragedy but rather as an accusation directed against those who are too insignificant in their lives to warrant such infamy.

Styron concludes his book with a mammoth religious meeting among the African-American community of Port Warwick. La Ruth commiserates with Helen while disgusting her, and Ella gently preaches to Loftis. They are superstitious and ignorant, gullibly enmeshed in the corporation of Daddy Faith. Yet, when a child is lost during the baptismal rites, as Peyton had been lost all her life, they care for her and comfort her until her mother arrives.

The same train that brought the reader into Port Warwick at the book's beginning rumbles across the trestle on its return to Richmond, and one hopes that it will come back again, perhaps to tell a more important story.

LIFE ON THE MISSISSIPPI

Type of work: Reminiscence
Author: Mark Twain (Samuel L. Clemens, 1835-1910)
Type of plot: Regional romance
Time of plot: Mid-nineteenth century
Locale: Mississippi River region
First published: 1883

Despite its loose and fragmented structure, Life on the Mississippi *is a vivid, dramatic, and extremely interesting collection of reminiscences. Like the mighty river with which it is concerned, the book has become part of the American tradition.*

The Story

When Mark Twain was a boy, he and his comrades in Hannibal, Missouri, had one great ambition: They hoped to become steamboatmen. They had other ambitions, too, such as joining the circus or becoming pirates, but these soon passed. Only the ambition to be a steamboatman remained, renewed twice each day when the upriver and the downriver boats put in at the rickety wharf and woke the sleepy village to bustling life. Through the years, boy after boy left the river communities, to return later, swaggering in his importance as a worker on a steamboat. Mark Twain saw these boys often, and the fact that some of them had been considered as undeniably damned in the eyes of the pious folk shook Twain's convictions profoundly. He wondered why these boys who flouted Sunday school maxims and ran away from home should win the rewards of adventure and romance that meeker town boys never knew.

Mark Twain, too, had this dream of adventure. His ambition was a lofty one. He determined to become a cub-pilot. While in Cincinnati, he heard that a government expedition was exploring the Amazon. With thirty dollars that he had saved, he took a boat bound for New Orleans. His intention was to travel on the headwaters of the Amazon. The ship was grounded at Louisville, however, and during the delay, Twain came to the attention of Mr. Bixby, the most famous pilot on the Mississippi River. He prevailed upon Bixby to teach him how to navigate.

At first, the adventure was a glorious one, but soon Twain found that the more he knew about the river, the less romantic it seemed. Though he was a dutiful student, he discovered that he could not remember everything Bixby told him, regardless of how important this information seemed to be. Furthermore, to his astonishment and despair, his instructor told him that the river was changing its course continually, that there were no such things as permanent landmarks, and that the river channel was never the same, but always variable. There were times when the young cub-pilot was frightened, especially when he narrowly missed hitting another ship, or trimmed the boat too close to shore. Worse was the experience of piloting in the dead of night, with no landmarks to observe and only deep blackness all around. Bixby claimed the secret of navigation was not to remember landmarks, which changed, but to learn the shape of the river and then to steer by the shape in one's head.

It was undeniably an interesting life. The pilot had to be on the lookout for rafts sailing the river at night without lights. Often a whole family would be on a raft, and they would shout curses at the steamboat that had just barely missed dumping them all into the river. Then there was the fascinating behavior of the river itself. Prosperous towns would be isolated by a new cutoff and reduced to insignificance; towns and islands in one state would be moved up or down and into another state, or, as sometimes happened, into an area that belonged to no state at all.

The river pilot reigned supreme on the boat. The captain was theoretically the master, but as soon as the boat got under way, the pilot was in charge and only a very foolhardy captain would have interfered. The importance of the pilot in river navigation eventually led to the formation of a pilots' association. At first, the idea seemed ridiculous, but the union grew as, one by one, all the good pilots joined. As a result, pilots could make their own terms with the owners. Not only were wages guaranteed but pilots secured better working conditions, pensions, and funds for their widows and orphans as well. Within a few years, the association was the most indestructible monopoly in the country. Nevertheless, its days were numbered. First of all, the railroads came, and river transportation was gradually abandoned in favor of rail traffic. Then, too, the Civil War reduced navigation to a mere trickle and dealt a deathblow to river commerce. The steamboat was no longer an important means of transportation.

From then on, the river was different. It seemed very different to Twain when he returned after many years away from it, and he saw the changes with nostalgic regret. He traveled once more on the Mississippi, but this time as a passenger and under an assumed name. He listened tolerantly to the man who told him wild and improbable stories about the river, and to a fellow traveler who explained, very explicitly, how everything worked.

Twain had decided to search for a large sum of money left by a murderer whom he had met in Germany. He and his companions made plans about the ten thousand dollars soon to be in their possession, and they asked to get off their boat at Napoleon to look for it. Unfortunately, the Arkansas River, years before, had swept the whole town into the Mississippi.

On his return to the river, Twain learned many things that he had not known. He witnessed the vast improvements in navigation and in the construction of the boats, improvements that made navigation easier and safer. He talked to the inhabitants of Vicksburg, who described their life during the bombardment of the town by Union forces. He visited Louisiana and expressed horror at the sham castles that passed for good architecture. He read Southern newspapers and saw in them, as in so many Southern traditions, the romantic sentimentality of Sir Walter Scott, an influence that he regretted, hated, and held responsible for the South's lack of progress. He came in contact with a cheerful and clever gambler; heard about senseless feuds that wiped out entire families; and saw new and large cities that had grown up since he had left the river. He met such well-known writers as Joel Chandler Harris and George W. Cable; had an experience with a spiritualist who grew rich on the credulous and the superstitious; witnessed tragedy, and lost friends in steamboat explosions.

The river would never be the same again. The age of mechanization had arrived to stay. The days of the old river pilots, such as Mr. Bixby, were now a thing of the past. The United States was growing up, and with that growth, the color and romance of the Mississippi had faded forever.

Critical Evaluation

Twain's book is not really a novel or regional romance. Generically, it is beyond classification—unless the reader is willing to be objective (and humorously enough inclined) to see it for what it is: an open-ended reminiscence, as rambling and broad as its subject, the Mississippi River. Readers of *The Adventures of Huckleberry Finn* (1884) will remember the dramatic role of the river in that work; many critics believe that the river is its structural foundation. T. S. Eliot and Lionel Trilling calling the river a "God." It watches over Huck and Jim but also demands wrecked houses and drowned bodies as sacrifices. In *Life on the Mississippi*, the river is seen with the eyes of a comic reporter, not the creative vision of a dramatic and philosophical novelist posing as a juvenile romancer. Nevertheless, the same characteristics that determine the river's symbolic function in *The Adventures of Huckleberry Finn* are singled out and examined here: the dangerous and changing channels, the mud-infested villages, the floods. One way of reading *Life on the Mississippi* is to see it as the objective research from which Twain ultimately fashioned the art of his greatest story. Indeed, *Life on the Mississippi* and *The Adventures of Huckleberry Finn* stand in relation to each other much in the same way as the chapters describing whaling relate to the story of Ahab and his mad hunt in Herman Melville's *Moby Dick* (1851).

The primary quality of the Mississippi River basin is its enormous size. How can such a geographic miracle be contained in a memoir? Twain begins by recalling his youth as an apprentice pilot. Even here, the foreshadowing of Huckleberry Finn is astonishing: Twain learns to pilot down the same river on which Huck effortlessly floats his raft. Twain must master every curve, point, and bar. The feats of memory necessary to perform the skills of the river pilot are almost superhuman. "Nothing short of perfection will do." Just as Twain recalls first the map of the river as his mind mastered it, in *The Adventures of Huckleberry Finn* Twain had to strain his creative memory to bring back the Mississippi of his boyhood.

There is something humbling about the later chapters

in *Life on the Mississippi*. While they are fragmented and often look like padding, there is an undeniable charm in their rambling quality: They seem to attest to Twain's continual deference to the giant and changing river. Although he learned its every curve as a youth, its natural evolution and the effect of social and technological "progress" astonishes him so much that he is reduced to gathering tall tales and newspaper clippings.

LIGHT IN AUGUST

Type of work: Novel
Author: William Faulkner (1897-1962)
Type of plot: Psychological realism
Time of plot: 1930
Locale: Mississippi
First published: 1932

This novel is a study of the race problem in the American South and of this region's psychological obsession with the Civil War. It is a fascinating narrative told with little regard for strict time sequence. Sometimes, Faulkner's sentence structure becomes obscure or the exact meaning of his poetic compression becomes lost, but Light in August *is important in its vivid treatment of a theme of wide social significance.*

Principal Characters

Joe Christmas, a supposed mulatto. Placed in an orphan home by his demented grandfather, he is to lead a tortured life of social isolation, as he belongs neither to the white nor to the black race; in fact, he prefers this kind of existence. After staying with the fanatical Calvin McEachern during his boyhood, Joe knocks his foster father unconscious and strikes out on his own, rejecting any friendly overtures. At last, he is driven to his final desperate act: He kills his benefactress, Joanna Burden, and faces death at the hands of merciless Percy Grimm.

Joanna Burden, Joe Christmas' mistress, the descendant of a New England family. Rejected by many of her neighbors, she is friendly toward African Americans and is interested in improving their lot. In her efforts to make Joe useful to the world, she also tries to possess and dominate him sexually, and so meets her death.

Calvin McEachern, Joe's foster father. A ruthless, unrelenting religious fundamentalist, McEachern, without real animosity, often beats the boy savagely for trifling misdemeanors and tells him to repent. He demands that "the Almighty be as magnanimous as himself."

Eupheus Hines (Doc), Joe Christmas' grandfather. Always a hot-tempered little man, he is often in fights. When he learns that his daughter Milly has a dark-skinned lover, the fiery old man kills him. Later, he allows Milly to die in childbirth, unaided by a doctor. Soon after her death, he places the baby in an orphanage. Years later, learning of Joe's imprisonment, Doc Hines demands that his grandson be lynched. Prior to this time, the old man has devoted much effort to preaching to bemused African Americans about white supremacy.

Gail Hightower, a minister. Most of Hightower's life has been devoted to a dream. Long before, his grandfather had died while serving with a troop of Confederate cavalry. Because of his grandfather, he becomes obsessed with the Civil War. Now an outcast, he has driven his wife to her death because of this obsession; in the process, he is forced from his church by the outraged congregation.

Joe Brown (Lucas Burch), Lena Grove's lover and the unwilling father of her child. A loudmouthed, weak man, he deserts Lena and finds work in another town. After meeting Joe Christmas, he becomes a bootlegger and lives with Joe in a cabin behind Joanna Burden's house. When Christmas is captured, Brown, hoping for a large reward, tells the sheriff that Joe has murdered Burden. Unable to face responsibilities, he hops a freight train in order to avoid Lena.

Lena Grove, a country girl seduced and deserted by Joe Brown. Ostensibly, this simple-hearted young woman pursues her lover because he is the father of her child; actually, she continues looking for him so that she can see different parts of the South.

Milly Hines, Doc Hines' daughter. She dies in childbirth because her enraged father refuses to let a doctor deliver her supposedly mulatto child.

Byron Bunch, a worker at the sawmill. Although he loves Lena, this good man helps her look for Joe Brown.

Mrs. Hines, Joe Christmas' grandmother. Always loving Joe, she tries to get Hightower to say that Joe was elsewhere when the murder was committed.

Mrs. McEachern, Calvin McEachern's long-suffering, patient wife. Like the other women, she is rebuffed when she tries to help Joe Christmas.

Percy Grimm, a brutal National Guard captain. He hunts Joe down after the latter escapes from a deputy. Not satisfied with shooting Christmas, Grimm castrates the injured man.

The Story

Joe Christmas was the illegitimate son of a dark-skinned circus trouper who was thought to be of black blood and a white girl named Milly Hines. Joe's grandfather, old Doc Hines, killed the circus man, let Milly die in childbirth, and put Joe—at Christmastime, hence his last name—into an orphanage, where the children learned to call him "nigger." Doc Hines then arranged to have Joe adopted by a religious and heartless farmer named McEachern, whose cruelties to Joe were met with a matching stubbornness that made of the boy an almost subhuman being.

One day in town, McEachern took Joe to a disreputable restaurant, where he talked to the waitress, Bobbie Allen. McEachern told the adolescent Joe never to patronize the place alone. Nevertheless, Joe went back. He met Bobbie at night and became her lover. Night after night, while the McEacherns were asleep, he would creep out of the house and hurry to meet her in town.

One night, McEachern followed Joe to a country dance and ordered him home. Joe reached for a chair, knocked McEachern unconscious, whispered to Bobbie that he would meet her soon, and raced McEachern's mule home. There he gathered up all the money that he could lay his hands on and went into town. At the house where Bobbie stayed, he encountered the restaurant proprietor and his wife and another man. The two men beat up Joe, took his money, and left for Memphis with the two women.

Joe moved on. Sometimes he worked; more often, he simply lived off the money women would give him. He slept with many women and nearly always told them he was of black blood.

At last, he went to Jefferson, a small town in Mississippi, where he got work shoveling sawdust in a lumber mill. He found lodging in a long-deserted cabin near the country home of Miss Joanna Burden, a spinster of Yankee origin who had few associates in Jefferson because of her zeal for bettering the lot of African Americans. She fed Joe and, when it appeared that he was of black blood, planned to send him to an African-American school. Joe was her lover for three years. Her reactions ranged from sheer animalism to evangelism, in which she tried to make Joe repent his sins and become a Christian.

A young man who called himself Joe Brown came to work at the sawmill, and Joe Christmas invited Brown to share his cabin with him. The two began to sell bootleg whiskey. After a while, Joe told Brown that he was part black; before long, Brown discovered the relations of Joe and Burden. When their bootlegging prospered, they bought a car and gave up their jobs at the lumber mill.

One night, Joe went to Burden's room half-determined to kill her. She attempted to shoot him with an antiquated pistol that did not fire. Joe cut her throat with his razor and ran out of the house. Later in the evening, a fire was discovered in Burden's house. When the townspeople started to go upstairs in the burning house, Brown tried to stop them. They brushed him aside. They found Joanna Burden's body in the bedroom and carried it outside before the house burned to the ground.

Through a letter in the Jefferson bank, the authorities learned of Burden's New Hampshire relatives, whom they notified. Almost at once, word came back offering a thousand dollars reward for the capture of the murderer. Brown tried to tell the story as he knew it, putting the blame on Joe Christmas, so that he could collect the money. Few believed his story, but he was held in custody until Joe Christmas could be found.

Joe Christmas remained at large for several days, but at last with the help of bloodhounds, he was tracked down. Meanwhile, old Doc Hines had learned of his grandson's crime, and he came with his wife to Jefferson. He urged the white people to lynch Joe, but for the most part, his rantings went unheeded.

On the way to face indictment by the grand jury in the courthouse, Joe, handcuffed but not manacled to the deputy, managed to escape. He ran to a cabin and found a gun. Some volunteer guards from the American Legion gave chase and finally found him in the kitchen of the Reverend Gail Hightower. Hightower, a one-time Presbyterian preacher, was an outcast because he had driven his wife into dementia by his obsession with the gallant death of his grandfather in the Civil War. Joe had gone to Hightower at the suggestion of his grandmother, Mrs. Hines, who had had a conference with him in his cell just before he escaped. She had been advised of this possible way out by Byron Bunch, Hightower's only friend in Jefferson. The Legionnaires shot Joe down, and their leader castrated him with a knife.

Brown now claimed his reward. A deputy took him out to the cabin where he had lived with Joe Christmas. On entering the cabin, he saw Mrs. Hines holding a newborn baby. In the bed was a girl, Lena Grove, who had been his lover in a town in Alabama when he was known as Lucas Burch. Lena had started out to find Brown when she knew that she was going to have a baby. Traveling most of the way on foot, she had arrived in Jefferson on the day of the murder and the fire. Directed to the sawmill, she had at once seen that Byron Bunch, to whom she had been sent, was not the same man as

Lucas Burch. Byron, a kindly soul, fell in love with her. From Byron's description, she was sure that, in spite of his new name, Brown was the father of her child. She gave birth to the baby in Brown's cabin, where Byron had made her as comfortable as he could, with the aid of Mrs. Hines.

Brown jumped from a back window and ran away. Byron, torn between a desire to marry Lena and the wish to give her baby its rightful father, tracked Brown to the railroad grade outside town and fought with him.

Brown escaped aboard a freight train.

Three weeks later, Lena and Byron took to the road with the baby, Lena still searching for Brown. A truck driver gave them a lift. Byron was patient, but one night, he tried to compromise her. When she repulsed him, he left the little camp where the truck was parked. The next morning, however, he was waiting at the bend of the road, and he climbed up on the truck as it made its way toward Tennessee.

Critical Evaluation

Faulkner was thirty-five when he wrote *Light in August* as the final explosive creation of the richest part of his artistic career that saw the production of *Sartoris* (1929), *The Sound and the Fury* (1929), *As I Lay Dying* (1930), and *Sanctuary* (1931). Only *Absalom, Absalom!* (1936) would approach again the intensity and splendid richness of this, his tenth book published and the seventh in the serious about Yoknapatawpha County. Armstid, who appears in the novel's first chapter, is the same farmer of *As I Lay Dying*, and Joanna Burden mentions Colonel Sartoris in her account of her own family's bloodspattered history. *Light in August* is Faulkner's longest work, his most varied "in mood and character" (as Richard H. Rovere pointed out), perhaps equalled only by *The Sound and the Fury* as a penetrating and compelling analysis of Southern society.

The style of this novel has often been criticized for its inconsistency, often pointed to as an example of Faulkner's "undisciplined genius." Indeed, its stylistic characteristics are manifold and complex. There are sudden changes of narrative tense, from present to past and back again, as well as abrupt shifts in point of view, ranging from the viewpoints of the major characters to viewpoints of characters who apparently have no part in the main action at all. Faulkner also offers the occasional use of the stream-of-consciousness technique based on the Proustian obsession with key images, or on what James Joyce termed "radiating imagery"; the frequent use, also Joycean, of run-together words such as "womanpinksmelling," "Augusttremulous," "stillwinged," "womanshenegro"; and Joycean epiphanies, as when chapter 16 ends with Hightower's "extended and clenchfisted arms lying full in the pool of light from the shaded lamp" or Joe Christmas caught in the glare of headlamps after the murder. There is the suggestion of T. S. Eliot's emphasis on all the senses ("an odor, an attenuation, an aftertaste"), and the use of Robert Frost's simplicity of im-

agery, mixed with the kind of flamboyant poetic diction characteristic of Wallace Stevens, with the repetition of implicit interrogatives and phrases such as "grown heroic at the instant of vanishment" and the "two inescapable horizons of the implacable earth." There is, in fact, awkwardly repetitive use of manneristic expressions such as "by ordinary," "terrific," and the adverb "quite" (as in "quite calm, quite still") that seem to support the argument that the composition of this admitted masterpiece was at times hurried and even heedless.

Nevertheless, the last two chapters of the novel— Hightower's rambling retrogression into Civil War history, and the resumption of Lena's travels (this time with Byron) as told by the unnamed furniture dealer who has nothing to do with the plot—achieve a sense of openended comprehensiveness that indicates Faulkner's epic concept of his novel. It is the universality of the epic genre that may account for the apparently arbitrary concatenation of stylistic elements. Every angle of insight, every avenue of perspective, every mode of entry is used by the author to compel the reader into the world of the novel—a world complete with its own dimensions, of time as well as of space, of emotions and events. As an epic, *Light in August* falls into the genre of "search epics" that began with Homer's *Odyssey*. Joe is searching for a light that will give meaning to his existence, exploring, in turn, the light of McEachern's "home," the light of his adolescent town, the lamp of Bobbie Allen's room, room lights of nameless African-American ghettoes, the light of Joanna's candle and, finally, the light of the flames of Joanna's burning house. This light is the "light in August" around whose central, sinister radiance all the main characters' lives resolve. That burning light brings their identities into momentary and terrible focus: disillusioning Lena of her dreams of trust and security, forcing Lucas Burch and Gail Hightower to confront their cowardice, coercing Byron Bunch to throw his lot irrevocably with his love, ending Joanna's ambiguously introverted life in perverted horror, and, with supreme irony, ultimately identifying Christmas through the reaction of the outraged town and, through the identification, ending his search in death.

The novel is also epic in its thematic scope, a scope embodied in the ambivalence of Christmas himself who, like Homer's Helen, is tragically made to straddle, through no fault of his own, two worlds—neither of which will accept him because of his relations to the other, neither of which he will accept because of his inherent ability to be singularly defined. The two worlds, as Faulkner steeps them through the very fiber of his novel, may be described as a kind of moveable equation, an equation generally defined by the Jungian distinction between the *anima* and the *animus* and also by the racial distinction between black and white. On one side, Christmas confronts his (possible) black blood, death (as stasis), darkness or artificial light, evil, fire, the female, sleeping, insanity, sin, savageness, violence, secrecy, cunning and deceit, softness, the fugitive state, belief, and passivity. Opposed to these elements, but also mingling and combining with them in unpredictable and unmanageable (for Christmas) patterns, are his white skin, life (as kinesis and fluid movement), light, good, the sun, the male, being awake and aware, control, righteousness, calm, openness, durability and determination, domestic security,

knowing, and activity. "He never acted like either a nigger or a white man," one of his murderers comments at the end. Because Christmas could not find himself on either side of the equation, because his entire life was a confusion between the two sides, his epic quest ends in his own individual death and in the symbolic death of the community of Jefferson.

It is because Faulkner envisioned Christmas as an epic hero that he identified him with Jesus Christ—not only in name but also in his peculiar silences, his master-disciple relationship with Brown, his capture on a Friday, the nurse who offers him a silver-dollar bribe, Joanna's resemblance to both Mary Magdalene and the Virgin Mary, his thirty years of private life (about which the narrator tells of nothing specific), his refusal to complain when beaten at the end, and the town's final comment that "it was as though he had set out and made his plans to passively commit suicide." Yet *Light in August* is Christological only in the sense that it draws upon the Christian myth to complicate and deepen the essentially secular, sociological myth that Faulkner constructs consistently in the saga of Yoknapatawpha County. *Light in August* professes only the religion of humanity, a religion that must function in a world "peopled principally by the dead," as Hightower, the rejected minister, remarks. This is a novel of "mighty compassion."

THE LITTLE FOXES

Type of work: Drama
Author: Lillian Hellman (1905-1984)
Type of plot: Social realism
Time of plot: 1900
Locale: Deep South
First presented: 1939

The Little Foxes is usually considered to be Hellman's major achievement, and many critics place it high on the list of American plays. Her dialogue crackles and her characters convince, and there is no extraneous matter present in the play. Moreover, the trickery of the Hubbard family accurately reflects one aspect of the rise of industrialism in the post-Civil War South.

Principal Characters

Regina Giddens, a conniving and grasping woman who is eager for her share in the profits of a proposed cotton mill. She contrives to get her fatally ill husband, Horace, who is home from the hospital to be manipulated by her family, to supply her share of the needed investment. When he refuses to have anything to do with the project, she cruelly taunts him with her contempt and refuses him his medicine when he feels a fatal attack coming on.

Benjamin and Oscar Hubbard, Regina Giddens' conniving and grasping brothers. Lacking Regina's share of the investment needed for the construction of the cotton mill, they descend on the fatally ill Horace Giddens in an attempt to persuade him to put up the money. When he turns them down, they "borrow" his bonds and complete the deal.

Horace Giddens, Regina Giddens' honest, fatally ill husband. Sick of his scheming wife and her grasping family, he refuses to invest in the projected cotton mill. When he learns of the theft of his bonds by Benjamin and Oscar Hubbard, he ties Regina's hands by planning a will that makes her the beneficiary of the bonds. He dies when she deprives him of his medicine as a heart attack is imminent.

Alexandra, the daughter of Regina and Horace Giddens. Sickened by the treatment given her father by her mother and her uncles, she leaves Regina and the Hubbards after Horace's death.

Birdie Hubbard, Oscar Hubbard's wife, who longs for a return to the refinements of a bygone day.

Leo Hubbard, Oscar Hubbard's son and ally in the theft of Horace Giddens' bonds.

The Story

William Marshall, a Chicago businessman, came South to negotiate with Benjamin and Oscar Hubbard and their sister, the striking Regina Giddens, over matters concerning the construction of a cotton mill. The Hubbard brothers and Regina foresaw a glittering future for them all. No longer would the cotton have to come to the machines; instead, at long last, it would be the other way around. They firmly believed that millions awaited them: The Hubbards would be the richest family in the South. Ben foresaw a stable of race horses, Oscar speculated on a new home, and the hapless Birdie, whom Oscar had married for her father's cotton fields, longed to see Lionnet, her old family home, restored to its former grace and beauty. Birdie continually sought a return to the genteel, refined behavior of earlier days, before the rise of materialistic ruthfulness.

Later, certain difficulties arose. The brothers lacked seventy-five thousand dollars, Regina's third of the sum that the Hubbards were to put up. Presumably this amount would come from Horace, Regina's husband, who lay in a Baltimore hospital with a fatal heart ailment. Though Regina had given Ben and Oscar her promise that Horace would put up the money, no word had yet reached them. Horace, away five months, had failed to acknowledge Regina's demands for his return. Regina suggested, however, that he was possibly holding out for a larger share of the profits; when one's money was badly needed, one should be entitled to a bigger share of the eventual returns. After crafty manipulation, Regina extracted from Ben a promise of a greater share of the profits if she could get Horace home within two weeks. Regina immediately dispatched Alexandra, her daughter, to Baltimore.

When Horace arrived a week later, in response to his daughter's summons, the Hubbards and Regina descended on him. No one in his right mind, the argument ran, would refuse a seventy-five thousand dollar investment that would garner a million. Ben explained how water power would be cheap and how the people of the mountains and small towns would be happy to work for low wages. Thus the profits would be tremendous. Yet Horace, though sourly admitting that the venture was a good deal for the Hubbards, stated that he and Regina had enough money already. The truth was that Horace had had enough of his scheming wife and her equally conniving family, who, having made a sizable sum already through their exploitation of the poor, were now on their way to greater fortune in identical fashion.

Regina protested furiously, but to no avail. Ben and Oscar, however, were not too upset. Oscar's son Leo, through a young banking employee, had discovered that Horace had eighty-eight thousand dollars in bonds in his safe deposit box, securities that he checked only once in six months. Assuming that Horace would never miss them for a few months, Ben had Oscar seize the bonds—more than enough to meet the sum required by Marshall—and leave for Chicago to complete negotiations. Regina, after a fierce argument with Horace, learned that Oscar had gone. Ben now held the upper hand; he simply told Regina that everything had been settled. Horace, an onlooker, was quietly amused. Now, he thought, he would not be a party to the wrecking of the town. He would at least die honestly. To the watching Alexandra's horror, Regina calmly informed him that she hoped he would indeed die as quickly as possible.

Two weeks later, Horace went to his now-estranged wife's part of the house. Knowing that he was to be short lived, he had asked for his deposit box to be brought to him and had discovered the theft. He told Regina of this fact, along with his accurate suspicions as to the thieves' identity. To Regina's surprise, however, he stated that he intended to say nothing unless forced to, and then he would simply call the theft a loan. Horace planned to make a new will, leaving Regina eighty-eight thousand dollars in bonds. Thus she would eventually inherit his bonds, but she would not receive a single cent of the millions that Ben and Oscar prophesied for the Hubbard family. For once, Horace had tied the hands of his cunning wife.

Recalling their unhappy married life, Regina shrewishly revealed her contempt for Horace from the start. Horace, feeling a heart attack coming on, broke his bottle of medicine. Regina, hoping that his efforts to climb the stairs would prove fatal, cruelly refused to go upstairs for his second bottle. Horace staggered from his wheelchair and collapsed on their stair landing.

In an interview with her brothers after Horace was carried to his room, Regina revealed what she had learned from her husband. Should he die, she would blackmail them for a seventy-five percent share of the profits in exchange for the bonds. Soon word came, in the person of the silent Alexandra, that Regina's plan had worked. Horace was dead. Regina then announced her plans for seeing the judge the next day. Any jury would be swayed by a woman whose brothers had stolen from her. Regina also declared that there were not twelve people in the state whom the brothers had not cheated. A philosophical Ben gave in to Regina's demands, but as he left he was wondering what Horace, who had been in a wheelchair, was doing on the landing. Perhaps in the future, he might find out. When he did, he would let Regina know.

Realizing that Alexandra had loved her father very much, Regina tried to be sympathetic. Nevertheless, her saddened, sickened daughter defied her plans for their future in Chicago. Alexandra announced her final departure from Regina and the Hubbards because she believed that her father would have wanted it that way.

Critical Evaluation

Lillian Hellman's play *The Little Foxes* is a story of illusion and sterility set in a small town in the South at the beginning of the twentieth century. The principal characters are all members of the same family, either through association, marriage, or birth. Within the major family are smaller family units, formed by the marriage of one major family member to an "outsider." These marriages serve both to break down the authority of the major family and to enlarge the reduced family by the addition of the husband or wife and any resultant offspring.

The Hubbard family members are marked by their greed

and by the absolute lack of scruples that enables them to fulfill it. Oscar is characterized as a man who hunts daily for sport, having forbidden the town poor to kill game even to supplement their diet. He himself throws away all that he shoots, while depriving the poverty-stricken African Americans of food. He and his brother have made their fortunes through a store that overcharges the town's poor, black and white, for food. A major image in the play is starvation; Hellman makes constant references to hunger and lack of food. Moreover, the image of hunger for love is a powerful counterpoint to the hate-filled reality of the family. Both Oscar and Benjamin are avaricious, as is their sister, Regina. The three of them conspire against one another and against Horace to deprive him of control of his own fortune. Again the author plays on the theme of deprivation and hunger.

Just as the Hubbards conspire to attain power in order to satisfy their insatiable greed, Regina's daughter, Alexandra, suffers from the effects of lack of affection. Her father being absent, her only source of affection is Addie, the African-American house servant. Hellman indicates strongly that of all the play's characters, only Addie, Horace, and Alexandra are capable of feeling a need for love. They are also the only ones capable of giving it, though Horace is not capable of loving Regina. These three are played against the three Hubbards—Regina, Horace and Benjamin. The contrast builds until, by the climax of the play, when Regina has in effect killed Horace, the conflict has become an open battle between love and the death of love. That love wins (barely) is indicated by Alexandra's leaving the sterile household of her mother to go with Addie, who also loves, in search of a better life.

Hellman's characters are made memorable by her sharp portrayal of them; there is an acid bitterness about the play characteristic of her early work, as also seen in *The Children's Hour* (1934). Hellman eventually left behind the anger that pervades her earlier plays, but they are considered to be her strongest work.

LITTLE WOMEN

Type of work: Novel
Author: Louisa May Alcott (1832-1888)
Type of plot: Sentimental romance
Time of plot: Nineteenth century
Locale: A New England village, New York City, and Italy
First published: 1868

Often seen as a sentimental novel for children, Little Women *offers much to the mature reader who can appreciate Alcott's vision of the family as the source of strength. The novel's characters—Jo, Marmee, Amy, Meg, Laurie, and Beth—have become well-loved in American literature.*

Principal Characters

Meg, the oldest of the March girls, a plump governess to unruly neighborhood children. She marries John Brooke.

Jo, a tall, awkward, tomboyish girl who likes to write and to devise plays and entertainments for her sisters. In character and personality, she corresponds to the author. She resents Meg's interest in John but later is happy to have him as a brother-in-law. She writes and sells stories and becomes a governess for Mrs. Kirke in New York. Proposed to by Laurie, she rejects him. She later marries Professor Bhaer, with whom she establishes a boys' school in Plumfield, Aunt March's old home.

Beth, a gentle homebody helpful to Mrs. March in keeping house. She contracts scarlet fever, from which she never fully recovers. She dies during the spring after Jo's return from New York.

Amy, a curly-haired dreamer who aspires to be a famous artist. She is a companion of Aunt Carrol on a European trip. She marries Laurie.

Mrs. March (Marmee), the kindly, understanding, lovable mother of the four March girls.

Mr. March, her husband, an army chaplain in the Civil War who becomes ill while away but who later returns well and happy.

Theodore Lawrence (Laurie), a young neighbor who joins the March family circle. He falls in love with Jo, but after his rejection by her, he transfers his feelings to Amy, whom he marries.

Professor Bhaer, a tutor in love with Jo, whom he marries.

Mr. Lawrence, the wealthy, indulgent grandfather of Laurie.

Aunt March, a wealthy, irascible relative who wills her home to Jo.

John Brooke, Laurie's tutor, who falls in love with and marries Meg.

Aunt Carrol, a relative of the Marches.

Mrs. Kirke, a New York boardinghouse keeper.

Daisy and **Demi,** Meg's children.

The Story

The March family lived in a small house next door to the Lawrence mansion, where young Theodore Lawrence ("Laurie") and his aged grandfather had only each other for company in the great house. Old Mr. Lawrence was wealthy, and he indulged every wish of his grandson, but often Laurie was lonely. When the lamp was lit and the shades were up in the March house, he could see the four March girls with their mother in the center seated around a cheerful fire. He learned to know them by name before he met them, and in his imagination, he almost felt himself a member of the family.

The oldest was plump Meg, who had to earn her living as governess of a group of unruly youngsters in the neighborhood. Next was Jo, awkward, and tomboyish, who spent all her spare time creating plays and entertainments for her sisters. Then there was gentle Beth, content to sit knitting by the fire or to help her mother take care of the house. The youngest was curly-haired Amy, a schoolgirl who dreamed of someday becoming a famous artist like Michelangelo or Leonardo da Vinci.

At Christmastime, the girls were confronted with the problem of what to do with the dollar that Marmee, as they called their mother, had said they might spend. At first, each thought only of her own pleasure, but all ended by buying a gift for Marmee instead. On Christmas morning, they insisted on sharing their breakfast with the Hummels, a poor family in the neighborhood, and for this unselfishness, they were rewarded when rich Mr. Lawrence sent over a surprise Christmas feast consisting of ice cream, bonbons, and four bouquets of flowers for the table.

Many happy days followed, with Laurie, who had met Jo at a fashionable New Year's Eve dance, becoming a part of the March family circle. In November of that same year, however, a telegram brought a message that their father, an army chaplain in the Civil War, was critically ill. Mrs. March did not know what to do. She thought that she should go to her husband at once, but she had barely five dollars in her purse. She was hesitant about going to wealthy, irascible Aunt March for help. Jo solved the problem by selling her beautiful, long, chestnut hair, which was her only vanity, for twenty-five dollars. She made the sacrifice willingly, but that night, after the others had gone to bed, Meg, who thought Jo was asleep, heard her weeping softly. Gently, Meg asked if Jo were crying over her father's illness, and Jo sobbed that it was not her father she was crying for now, but for her hair.

During Marmee's absence, dark days fell upon the little women. Beth, who had never been strong at best, contracted scarlet fever, and for a time it looked as if Jo were going to lose her dearest sister. They sent for Marmee, but by the time she arrived, the crisis had passed and her little daughter was better. By the next Christmas, Beth was her old contented self again. Mr. March surprised them all when he returned home from the front well and happy. The little family was together once more.

Then John Brooke, Laurie's tutor, fell in love with Meg. This fact was disclosed when Mr. Brooke surreptitiously stole one of Meg's gloves and kept it in his pocket as a memento. Laurie discovered the glove and informed Jo. To his great surprise, she was infuriated at the idea that the family circle might be disturbed. Nevertheless, she was quite reconciled when, three years later, Meg became Mrs. Brooke.

In the meantime, Jo herself had grown up. She began to take her writing seriously and even sold a few stories, which helped with the family budget.

Her greatest disappointment came when Aunt Carrol, a relative of the Marches, decided that she needed a companion on a European trip and asked not Jo but the more ladylike Amy to accompany her. Then Jo, with Marmee's permission, decided to go to New York. She took a job as governess for Mrs. Kirke, who ran a large boardinghouse. There she met Professor Bhaer, a lovable and eccentric German tutor, who proved to be a good friend and companion.

Upon her return home, Laurie, who had always loved Jo, asked her to marry him. Jo had imagined that she would always remain an old maid, devoting herself exclusively to her writing. She tried to convince Laurie that they were not made for each other. He persisted, pointing out that his grandfather and her family both expected them to marry. When she made him realize that her refusal was final, he stamped off and shortly afterward went to Europe with his grandfather. In Europe, he saw much of Amy, and the two became close friends, so that Laurie was able to transfer to her younger sister the feeling that he previously had for Jo.

In the meantime, Jo was at home caring for Beth, who had never fully recovered from her first illness. In the spring, Beth died, practically in Jo's arms, and after the loss of her gentle sister, Jo was lonely indeed. She tried to comfort herself with her writing and with Meg's two babies, Daisy and Demi, but not until the return of Amy, now married to Laurie, did she begin to feel her old self again. When Professor Bhaer stopped off on his way to a university appointment in the Midwest, Jo was delighted. One day, under an umbrella that he had supplied to shield her from a pouring rain, he asked her to marry him, and Jo accepted. Within a year, old Aunt March died and willed her home, Plumfield, to Jo, who decided to open a boys' school where she and her professor could devote their lives to instructing the young.

So the little women reached maturity, and on their mother's sixtieth birthday, they all had a great celebration at Plumfield. Around the table, at which there was but one empty chair, sat Marmee, her children, and her grandchildren. When Laurie proposed a toast to her, she replied by stretching out her arms to them all and saying that she could wish nothing better for them than this present happiness for the rest of their lives.

Critical Evaluation

Little Women long has been unfairly characterized as a sentimental children's novel. Actually, it is a surprisingly tough-minded and realistic book dealing with strong and resilient people and their efforts to survive in an often bleak world. In large part, it is concerned with ideals, but these ideals are integrated as part of the lives of the characters. It would have been impossible for the daughter of Bronson Alcott not to incorporate certain ideals of living in her fiction. Yet Louisa May Alcott possessed a much stronger character than her father, and this is evident in her powerful and at times angry picture of the place of women in mid-nineteenth century American life. Any reader who approaches the book objectively will note this continuous theme; the restless Jo, not surprisingly, bears most of its weight. In her later novels, notably in *Jo's Boys* (1886), Alcott was to carry on and intensify her concern with women's rights. The mature Jo, in that later novel, would actively encourage young women to study medicine and other previously unacceptable occupations for women. These aspects of Jo's character and Alcott's radical preoccupations are visible in this early, excellent novel.

The importance of the family unit was vital to all the Alcotts, and this conviction gives *Little Women* much of its power. The family circle is shown as a force that can help individuals survive against all odds—against war, poverty, narrow-minded self-interest, and social change.

Individuals suffer, struggle, and die, but the family endures. At the center of this family unit stands the mother, but Mrs. March is not the saccharine figure that she often is supposed to be. In the novel, she is a tough and courageous woman with a temper that she has had to struggle to control and a character strong enough to hold together her family even when it is divided by war and other trials.

Above all, *Little Women* is a novel rich with fine characterizations. The portraits of Aunt March, Professor Bhaer, old Mr. Lawrence, and so many other individuals, as well as the March clan, have endeared the book to millions of readers. These characters are not sweet, idealized figures, but genuine human beings, with faults and foibles and tremendous vitality. Louisa May Alcott's artistry was so unselfconscious and natural as to seem almost nonexistent, but it was this skill that created such memorable and real characters. *Little Women* has survived the patronizing of many critics and will continue to be a popular and loved book because it is an extraordinary and vigorous piece of writing and because it presents a picture of human endurance that is both touching and inspiring.

LOLITA

Type of work: Novel
Author: Vladimir Nabokov (1899-1977)
Type of plot: Erotic tragedy
Time of plot: Primarily from 1947 to 1952
Locale: New York, New England, and across the United States
First published: 1955

Generally considered to be Nabokov's greatest novel, Lolita *unites farce, pathos, and parody with two powerful, shocking subjects: the passionate feelings of a grown man toward a pubescent girl and the tormentingly complex nature of romantic love.*

Principal Characters

Humbert Humbert, Lolita's lover, born in Paris in 1910, the son of a generally European (Swiss, French, Austrian, Danubean) father and of an English mother. The novel purports to be the manuscript Humbert wrote while awaiting trial for the murder of Clare Quilty, who took from him the teenage "nymphet," Lolita, who is his one and only love.

Lolita (Lo/Lola/Dolly/Dolores) Haze, whom Humbert meets when she is twelve years old, and whose mother he marries solely to have access to the girl during the brief period of her "nymphancy."

Charlotte Haze, Lolita's mother, who becomes Humbert's second wife. She dies, struck by a car, after she has read his diaries, which reveal his love for Lolita.

Clare Quilty, a playwright who enjoys pornography and taking drugs. He takes a passing fancy to Lolita and is tracked down and killed by a vengeful Humbert.

Richard (Dick) Schiller, a mechanic, whom Lolita marries when she is seventeen years old.

Rita, a drunken divorcée twice Lolita's age, with whom Humbert consorts for two years after his loss of Lolita.

The Story

The novel's middle-aged, middle-European narrator "writes" this book as his confession while in a prison cell awaiting trial for murder. He chooses to crouch behind the pseudonym of Humbert Humbert because that double-rumble name, he believes, "expresses the nastiness best." His double-talk name sets the tone of punning parody that pervades the text as various people he encounters address him as Humberg, Herbert, Humbird, Humberger, and Humbug. Humbert was born in France, of mixed European and English parentage. He typically adds, "I am going to pass around in a minute some lovely, glossy-blue picture-postcards." His father owned a luxurious hotel on the Riviera, and it was there, when he was thirteen years old, that he met a little girl his own age named Annabel Leigh.

Humbert traces his sexual obsession for girls between the ages of nine and fourteen—he calls them "nymphets"—to a case of interrupted coitus he suffered when he and Annabel had the beginnings of their first affair

aborted by ribald bathers. The affair itself was terminated by Annabel's death from typhus. Allusions to Poe's poetry, his life, and especially love number at least twenty; many other writers are also alluded to, including William Shakespeare, John Keats, Gustave Flaubert, James Joyce, Marcel Proust and T. S. Eliot. Although he takes a sardonic view of psychoanalysis, Humbert believes that his blighted romance in that kingdom by the sea has made him a "nympholept," sexually and romantically entranced by little girls who exhibit an Annabel-like fey grace and "soul-shattering, insidious charm."

Because society prohibits the expression of such rapture, Humbert settles for a low-comedy marriage to Valeria, a "life-sized" woman in Paris who leaves him for a lover at about the time Humbert learns that a rich uncle in the United States has left him a comfortable income on condition that he move to America. Sailing alone to the United States after divorcing Valeria, he fatefully moves into the sleepy New England town of Ramsdale, as boarder of a widow, Charlotte Haze, who has a twelve-year-young daughter called Lolita, or Lo for short. The girl is an absolute incarnation of Humbert's past Annabel; when he sees Lolita, "The twenty-five years I had lived since then, tapered to a palpitating point, and vanished."

In desperate extremes of desire, Humbert marries Lolita's mother solely to have access to the girl during the brief period of her "nymphancy." This heroic sacrifice— since he finds Charlotte vapid, vulgar, and pretentious— is properly rewarded by the fates. Conveniently for him, Charlotte discovers his pedophilia through reading his diary, runs distractedly out of the house, and is killed by a passing Packard before she can publicize his perversion.

Humbert now undertakes the clumsy comedy of seducing his stepdaughter, to whom he legally stands *in loco parentis*. He decides to ply her with sleeping pills so he can achieve his transport by indirection, out of a scrupulous regard for her presumed purity. To his consternation, however, it is Lolita who seduces him. She already has had sexual experiences, at summer camp, and finds her eager stepfather somewhat maladroit. Humbert is shocked that "My life was handled by little Lo in an energetic, matter-of-fact manner as if it were an insensate gadget unconnected with me."

"Hum" and "Lo" set off on an aimless tour of the continent, encountering a neon-lit landscape of filling stations, motels, juke boxes, billboards, zoos, coffee shops, and highways. Lolita often chews gum, gurgles Coke, reads comic books, and picks her nose while Humbert has his sexual way with her. He finds it difficult to keep up with her moods as she quickly shifts from dreamy childishness to trashy vulgarity, from indifferent acquiescence to whining waywardness. Inevitably there are quarrels, and inevitably Humbert wins them, since Lolita, sobbing, has no place else to go.

Lolita eventually does find somewhere else to go. The couple is shadowed for months by a pornographic playwright, Clare Quilty, who is the author of a drama, *The Enchanted Hunters*, in which Lolita was to have starred at a progressive school before she left it. Quilty spirits the willing Lolita away from Humbert, but, being impotent, cannot achieve carnal connection with her. Against Humbert's perverted but romantic love, Nabokov sets Quilty's perverted but obscene lust. Quilty loses interest in Lolita and discards her when she refuses to engage in the freakish group sex he prefers.

Humbert loses track of Lolita for several years, although he hunts frenziedly for her across the United States. His companion in the search is Rita, an alcoholic divorcée twice Lolita's age, whose doleful but kind company saves his sanity for two years. Then Humbert receives a letter from Lolita, who is now married to a mechanic and pleads for money so her husband can take a promised job in Alaska.

Humbert forsakes the drunken Rita and rushes to Lolita's side. He finds her, at the age of seventeen, worn, plain, pale, and hugely pregnant by her earnest, stolid husband. In a moving episode, Humbert discovers himself in ardently adult love with her, despite her "rope-veined narrow hands" and "unkempt armpits." She refuses to return to him but does give him Quilty's address. He leaves the couple a generous check, then rushes to kill Quilty to avenge the loss of Lolita. He assassinates the playwright, his worst self, in a farcically protracted scene.

The foreword to the novel, by the fictitious "editor," a psychiatrist named John Ray, tells the reader that Lolita died in childbed, while Humbert succumbed to cardiac arrest in the prison to which he was confined after his murder of Quilty. Ray offers *Lolita* as a case history in "potent evils," while Nabokov, in his afterword, counters the didactic Ray with the aesthetic assertion that his novel "has no moral in tow."

Critical Evaluation

The novel is extremely complex, swinging between extreme moods, working on many levels, often shocking readers in one paragraph and then amusing them in the next. It is a remorseless satire of middle-class, immature America, a sociocomic commentary on Continental-American cultural relations. The flight by Humbert and Lolita across the motel-pimpled heartland of the United States is an oddball odyssey that synthesizes many of Nabokov's themes of exile and loss, beauty and brutality, pathos and parody. In the course of showing both the American landscape's natural beauty and its manipulation by advertising's spiels, Nabokov (through Humbert) satirizes American songs, commercials, films, magazines, tourist attractions, summer camps, ranches, hotels, and motels, as well as the Good Housekeeping syndrome and the cant of progressive educationists and child guidance pontificators. Moreover, the ritual of bribe and banter between Humbert and Lolita is a mocking annotation on parental-filial relations.

In one sense, *Lolita* might be considered an extensive

parody of Freudian explanations for psychological aberration. Proclaiming himself "King Sigmund the Second," Humbert mounts a frontal attack on many orthodox Freudian views, making a burlesque of the case study by purposely providing the childhood trauma—the lost child-love Annabel Leigh—that he claims to account for his "nympholepsy." The joke, Humbert insists, is that he is far more perceptive than are his analysts. He leads them on, inventing elaborate dreams and teasing them with faked primal scenes. When he comes in contact with sexual mythists such as the headmistress of Beardsley School, who sees Lolita as shuttling between "the anal and genital zones of development," the reader's laugh is with him and on her.

Lolita remains, more than a generation after its publication, a shocking novel. It conducts an assault on one of the Western world's few remaining sexual prohibitions by relating the violation of the sexual innocence of a girl in her early teens and by virtually condoning this violation. Nabokov often shows Humbert as a poor, sensitive soul, tormented by a love that may seem shameful in most men's hearts and loins but that seems somehow redeemed by his narrative candor, his suffering, his lyric eloquence, and above all his romantic intensity.

To be sure, Humbert is a monster. His treatment of his two wives is calculatingly exploitive, and he enslaves Lolita through deceptiveness, blackmail, and bullying, sometimes cackling triumphantly at his ability to terrorize her despite hearing "her sobs in the night—every night, every night—the moment I feigned sleep." His imprisonment of Lolita denies her a healthy youth.

Humbert's Svengali status is sabotaged by two planes in the novel. One is its frequent comic leverage, which depends on Humbert's ensnaring himself, with his cosmopolitan worldliness, in the eerie vulgarity of materialistic America. He goes to enormous lengths to try to make Lolita happy yet is defeated by her nose-picking indifference and meretriciousness. More significant, he is in the grip of a consuming passion, an intensely romantic rapture. He offers the narrative that this book constitutes as a monument to his love for Lolita.

Lolita is essentially a tale of love, a moving romance in the medieval tradition of courtly adoration, with Humbert Humbert sick with Eros' affliction and displaying his derangement by obsessional devotion and self-pitying masochism. He submits himself to his emotionally unattainable mistress as her slavish servant, even glorying in her cruelly capricious power over him. Andreus Capelanus, in his twelfth century authoritative text on courtly love, distinguishes between married love, governed by socioeconomic concerns and rationally restricted, and adulterous passion-love, ruled by the wild dictates of the heart. Humbert's adoration of Lolita expresses, in its intensity and abjectness, its solemnity and incurable devotion, the imperious absolutism of passion-love. Even when the ravages of time have removed the seventeen-year-old, newly married Lolita beyond the blazes of his lust, Humbert insists that, despite her worn looks and poor hygiene,

> I looked and looked at her, and knew as clearly as I know I am to die, that I loved her more than anything I had ever seen or imagined on earth, or hoped for anywhere else.

Lolita is clearly a complex, ambiguous, and multivalent work, with the ability to rouse uneasiness among readers and throw them off their balance. It is a novel of moral as well as physical mobility, alternately comic, perverse, lyrical, grotesque, and tragic, with these qualities merging to produce an artistic effect that places the book among the twentieth century's masterpieces as Nabokov transforms perversion into literature.

LONESOME DOVE

Type of work: Novel
Author: Larry McMurtry (1936-   )
Type of plot: Western epic
Time of plot: Late nineteenth century
Locale: American West
First published: 1985

Unlike McMurtry's earlier novels, which had contemporary settings, Lonesome Dove *is set in the late nineteenth century and resembles the traditional Western novel. Its epic scope and memorable characters, however, lift it to a level far above that of the usual Western.*

Principal Characters

Augustus (Gus) McCrae, a former captain in the Texas Rangers, an easygoing, talkative man with an eye for women, enjoying life as it comes to him but always ready in any emergency. He is a natural leader, admired by men as well as by women.

Woodrow Call, also a former captain in the Texas Rangers, a hard man who hides his emotions but can display vicious rages. It is his boredom with the quiet life of a livery stable that leads to the decision to make a cattle drive to Montana and try ranching there, a decision that triggers all the further action of the novel.

July Johnson, a sheriff of Fort Smith, Arkansas, sent by his wife to capture a supposed criminal. He, his stepson, and his assistant find their way to the rugged life of the Great Plains, a life for which they are totally unprepared.

Blue Duck, a renegade Comanchero with no apparent human feelings. He captures a woman who is a friend of Gus McCrae and keeps her alive only to sell her to some Kiowas and buffalo hunters. He is casually cruel and kills whoever gets in his way.

The Story

Gus McCrae and Woodrow Call, retired from the Texas Rangers, with whom they had fought Comanches and hunted down criminals, run Hat Creek Stables, a small livery stable and cattle-trading business in a South Texas village called Lonesome Dove. Another former Ranger, Jake Spoon, on the run after a shooting episode in Arkansas, arrives in town and tells Gus and Call about the unspoiled grasslands of Montana, where no one is yet trying to raise cattle. Jake also takes up with Lorie, the beautiful local whore who is desired by most of the cowboys and who is a friend of Gus.

Call's restlessness leads to a decision to run cattle to Montana, and he and Gus gather a crew of cowhands and bring together a herd, partly by purchase, partly by rustling across the border in Mexico. The party sets out, crossing Texas from south to north and going up through Kansas toward Ogallala, Nebraska, where they plan to stop to visit an old love of Gus, Clara Allen. As soon as they set out, however, they begin to run into trouble. The

herd is scattered by a violent storm, and the next day, an inexperienced young cowboy is attacked and horribly killed by cottonmouth snakes in a stream. Jake Spoon has not joined the crew, but he rides nearby with Lorie, who has fallen in love with him. Because of his carelessness, Lorie is left alone briefly and is captured by Blue Duck, a remorseless hater of whites. Gus leaves the cattle drive to find her.

At about the same time, July Johnson's wife, Elmira, a former whore, convinces July to leave Fort Smith, Arkansas, where he is sheriff, to pursue Jake Spoon, who has accidentally shot and killed July's brother. July is reluctant to leave, but Elmira and his brother's widow force him to go, taking along his stepson, Joe. As soon as he is gone, Elmira leaves on a riverboat in search for a former lover; as a result, July's assistant, Roscoe, is sent to Texas to find July and tell him of Elmira's defection. After numerous adventures, July, Joe, and Roscoe eventually connect out on the prairies, but they run into Blue Duck and only July, with Gus McCrae's help, survives.

Meanwhile, Jake Spoon becomes involved with three murderous brothers. Not himself evil but too weak to break away, Jake rides with these men and is implicated in their crimes, which include the murders of some sod-busting farmers and the fatal shooting of Wilbarger, a rancher who had befriended Gus. Once Gus has rescued Lorie and killed the Kiowas and hunters who had held her captive, he and Call go in search of the murderous brothers. When they find them, they hang all three and also, regretfully, Jake Spoon.

July Johnson, after burying Joe and Roscoe, continues his search for Elmira and winds up at a range outside Ogallala where Clara Allen, the woman whom Gus loved and lost, lives with her two daughters and a husband left comatose by an accident. Elmira has been there, given birth to a baby, and gone, leaving behind her infant son. The lover for whom she was searching has been hanged, and she and a buffalo hunter go back east across the plains and are killed by marauding Native Americans. Clara invites July to stay and help her with the ranch while his son is looked after by Clara and her two daughters. He is still there when Gus, Call, and their cowhands arrive with the herd of cattle and with Lorie, who is still traumatized by her experience with Blue Duck and allows no man except Gus to come anywhere near her.

Gus renews his friendship with Clara, who tells Lorie that she could never marry Gus; this information raises Lorie's hopes, as she has fallen in love with him. The men leave for Montana, Lorie staying behind with Clara and July Johnson. The trip becomes even grimmer. The African-American scout, Deets, is killed when his attempt to help a blind child is misunderstood by one of a bedraggled band of Native Americans. Gus and one of the hands, Pea Eye, go on a scouting expedition and are attacked by a local tribe. Pea Eye escapes and, after many hardships, finds his way back across the Wyoming prairies to the herd. Gus, however, has been badly injured. When he reaches Miles City, his wounded legs have turned gangrenous; one is amputated, but he refuses to let the doctor amputate the other. Soon after Call arrives, Gus dies.

Call's lust for adventure has expired. He sets up a ranch and leaves his unacknowledged illegitimate son, Newt, in charge. When spring comes, he takes Gus's body and begins the long trek back to Lonesome Dove, where Gus had wanted to be buried. He stops in Ogallala where Clara, whose husband has finally died, blames Call for the disastrous trip and especially for Gus's death. Clara, who has lost three young sons and a husband to the frontier, now must face the death of Gus, the man whom she really loved. Her bitterness is thoroughly justified. Further south, Call witnesses the death of Blue Duck and later is wounded by Native Americans. He survives to reach Lonesome Dove, where he buries Gus and is left to wonder what he can do with the rest of his life.

Critical Evaluation

In *Lonesome Dove*, Larry McMurtry took the materials of the traditional Western novel and reinvented the genre. The characters are all familiar: Call, the dedicated lawman; Gus, the easygoing hero; Newt, Call's illegitimate son, the naïve youngster who grows up through trouble; Clara, the steadfast widow; Lorie, the whore with a heart of gold; Blue Duck, the vindictive savage; and Deets, the consummate scout. Yet McMurtry has invested each of his characters with motivation and depth, so that they are no longer stock figures but genuine individuals. What happens to them matters.

McMurtry is able to create these three-dimensional figures because the pace of the novel, especially in the early stages, is deliberate, allowing plenty of time for characterization and humor. Much of the humor emanates from Gus, a genuinely amusing man, but other characters are also comic; the scenes leading to Roscoe's unwilling departure from Fort Smith, for example, are almost farcical. Even the episode in which the cowboys raid cat-tle in Mexico, dangerous and frightening as it is, has a humorous side when the raiders stumble upon a couple of young Irish brothers who are lost in the wilderness. The two, who know nothing about cattle or horses, are promptly made part of the crew.

The novel's darker elements, however, begin to dominate once the cattle drive starts. Such new and amusing minor characters as the new cook, Po Campo, continue to appear, and there are still moments of fun and amusing incidents, but McMurtry wants to show that life on the plains was difficult and very dangerous. The cowboys and their leaders go from one violent episode to another, with sympathetic characters joining less pleasant ones in pain, suffering, and violent death. Despite the presence of the comatose husband in a bed upstairs, Clara Allen's home is a much-needed haven from the heat, the bloodshed, and the boredom of a cattle drive. The younger cowboys, allowed to go into town, find drinking and whoring in Ogallala an enlightening experience. Once the drive resumes for its final stages, however, the tone becomes even more bleak and grim.

It is a mark of McMurtry's skill and command of his material that what began as comedy ends in tragedy, and that the novel's changes in tone are entirely appropriate. The successive shocks of Deets's death and Gus's being wounded and dying are in one sense predictable, given the dark turn that the novel has taken. Yet McMurtry does not leave it at that. In Clara's bitter speech to Call, he introduces an entirely new perspective, that of the woman who has lost three sons and a husband to the harsh land and to the desire of men to conquer it. What has seemed to the men a triumph—getting the herd to Montana despite terrible obstacles—is seen by Clara as futile and wasteful, achieving nothing but the satisfying of the male ego. Call, the strong silent hero, is in her view the chief culprit.

Nothing in McMurtry's earlier work suggested that he was capable of a novel such as *Lonesome Dove*. As excellent as *Leaving Cheyenne* (1963), *The Last Picture Show* (1966), and *Terms of Endearment* (1975) are, as well as some of his many other novels, all his previous fictions were based on McMurtry's experiences in North Texas, the Houston area, and California. They showed little interest in the historic past; more important, they did not suggest an ability to present sweeping action or the skill in handling a huge cast of characters that *Lonesome Dove* exhibits. Moreover, when McMurtry went back to the historical past in two later novels that combined real-life Western characters with fictional ones, in *Anything for Billy* (1988) and *Buffalo Girls* (1990), the results were much less impressive. The breadth of vision that informs *Lonesome Dove* and gives it such an impressive scope and power seemed to be unrepeatable.

Furthermore, although McMurtry's earlier fictions contain many sympathetic and interesting female characters, Clara Allen and her point of view are new. Although Call's adventures in getting Gus's body back to Lonesome Dove continue after he leaves Ogallala for the last time, Clara's denunciation of Call and what he represents resonates through the final stages of the book. Nothing that happens to Call and nothing that he does undercuts the truths of what Clara has said to him. The novel that has raised the materials of the classic Western novel to new heights closes with an unanswered challenge to the values of the genre. The need that men have to conquer, to risk their own lives and those of others for ideas or dreams, is finally seen as destructive and mostly pointless.

Lonesome Dove may not be a perfect novel, if such a thing exists. Some of the characters are possibly overdrawn, and there are a few dull patches. It is, however, a novel that sets new and high standards for one of American society's favorite kinds of fiction and that showed abilities in its author that had not been evident previously. The work stands as the classic Western novel.

A LONG AND HAPPY LIFE

Type of work: Novel
Author: Reynolds Price (1933-   )
Type of plot: Regional romance
Time of plot: July to December, 1957
Locale: A North Carolina community
First published: 1962

Price describes the delicate social balance in a small North Carolina community through the eyes of a young woman who must decide her fate. Rosacoke, who finds that she is carrying the child of her boyfriend, Wesley, looks to the women around her to serve as examples for her possible future.

Principal Characters

Rosacoke Mustian, a young woman who has important decisions to make when she discovers that she is pregnant. The father of the child, Wesley, has offered to marry her, but she is afraid of the very thought of childbirth after the death of her friend Mildred Sutton during the birth of Sledge. Rosacoke's participation in the church Christmas pageant as the Virgin Mary reassures her and gives her the strength to determine her future.

Emma Mustian, her mother, who serves as a role model for her daughter as a woman who has survived many ordeals.

Milo and **Horatio (Rato) Mustian,** her brothers. The death of Milo's son Horatio Mustian II also gives Rosacoke pause when she contemplates motherhood.

Wesley Beavers, Rosacoke's boyfriend and the father of the child that she is carrying. Wesley has been seeing Rosacoke for three years, all the while sleeping with other women in Norfolk. It is not until he learns of her pregnancy that he decides to settle down and marry her.

Mildred Sutton, Rosacoke's African-American friend. Like Rosacoke, she is carrying an illegitimate child, and she does not survive the birth of her son Sledge.

Sledge Sutton (or Ransom), Mildred's child, the son of Sammy Ransom.

Mr. Isaac Alston, the oldest member of the community.

Horatio Mustian II, Milo's first child, who dies.

This short lyrical novel tells how Wesley Beavers got Rosacoke Mustian pregnant and was thus reconciled to the marriage that he had been dodging for years. More than the taming of Wesley to a long and happy life, however, the story records the humbling of a determined and self-sufficient young woman, Rosacoke herself. The process of this humbling has been going on for a number of years before the novel opens; the crisis occurs in the last few pages when Rosacoke, having decided to reject Wesley, changes her mind. The instrument of her humbling is the community in which she lives. Although it is connected with the outer world by Wesley's trips to Norfolk, Virginia, 130 miles away, by Rosacoke's daily work as a telephone operator in the nearby town of Warrenton, and by her soldier brother Rato's return for Christmas from Fort Sill, Oklahoma, the locale of the novel is a traditional and self-contained North Carolina community. The long history of the clustered clans that make up the community is seen in the family graves. The speech of the

novel is regional, and the rituals of the community, centering on Delight Baptist Church, provide the incidents and culmination of the plot.

Although the first English edition of the novel carried a note warning the reader to put William Faulkner out of mind, the influence of another Mississippi writer is apparent: Eudora Welty, particularly in *The Ponder Heart* (1953). The technique of the novel is a rapid flow of internal monologue, generally from Rosacoke, broken by exchanges between the characters, all in sharply turned phrases of modified dialect, often highly prescient in meaning. The novel is in three long chapters, broken into shorter passages. Each chapter involves a child: Sledge Sutton (or Ransom), who survives the death of his mother, Mildred, in the first chapter; Horatio Mustian II, who dies at birth in the second; and Frederick Gupton, who plays the Christ child in the Christmas pageant at Delight Baptist Church in the last. The relationship of a long and happy life to a quick death is central to the novel and is indicated in the structure and style; much of the dialogue is about begetting and dying. This contrast is also indicated in the symbols employed, such as the eternal spring, the deer, Mr. Isaac Alston's horehound candy, paregoric, and Wesley's motorcycle. In this meaningfulness of disparate objects, Price also shows a similarity to Welty.

The novel opens with Rosacoke riding pillion with Wesley on his motorcycle to the funeral of Mildred Sutton, Rosacoke's African-American friend who has died in childbirth. Rosacoke's irritation with Wesley seems justified as he weaves in and out of the funeral procession and roars up to the African-American church at Mount Moriah ahead of everyone else. She had met Wesley six years earlier, when he was sixteen and she fourteen; she has been his girl for the past three years on Saturday nights when he comes back from the naval base in Norfolk and takes her dancing. Still, nothing has been decided. Wesley's remoteness (one sometimes learns what he is feeling, but never what he is thinking) is shown in the first encounter six years earlier, when he was resting up in a pecan tree and proved distant and uncommunicative to the girl below him. Nevertheless, he shook down the pecans as Rosacoke demanded. Had she been able to read both the situation and the symbols, Rosacoke might have guessed the only way that she could tame Wesley. Although she knows that he has had affairs with women in Norfolk, she properly rejects all his sexual overtones.

The three chapters of the novel occur at specified intervals in the period from late July to Christmas Eve, when Wesley makes his three visits to Rosacoke, but the events between each principal action are also recorded, often by the time-tested device of letters between Rosacoke and Wesley when he is in Norfolk. The other narrative device is flashback, used when Rosacoke has moments of quiet in her room or on walks in the countryside. The first of these occurs when she arrives at Mount Moriah and waits for the funeral of Mildred Sutton. The fate of Mildred, dead in childbirth, illustrates the tension between Rosacoke and Wesley: He wants what she fears will cut short her long and happy life, as it did Mildred's, and the novel shows how she comes to accept death and to live for life. At Mount Moriah, one of the mourners shouts, "Sweet Jesus," which Rosacoke, sitting inside the church, thinks should bring Wesley to his senses. It does, but not the senses that Rosacoke has in mind. Wesley is busy polishing the motorcycle, an extension of his own powerful physical drive, and the mourner's cry reminds him of the identical ecstatic cries of a woman in his arms at Norfolk. He roars away from the funeral to go home and ready himself for taking Rosacoke to the church picnic later that afternoon.

Rosacoke rejects Wesley's overt advances after the picnic at the lake, but she gives in to him in the second chapter, in early November, when the sight of a deer reminds her of the time that she and Mildred saw one near Mr. Alston's private spring. Rosacoke's thoughts and letters show later in this chapter and the next her confusion when her brother Milo's first baby, Horatio Mustian II, dies at birth and she realizes that she is carrying Wesley's baby. She would have been safer had she given in to Wesley at the picnic. Now she has been caught in the same trap that snared Mildred. Yet her visits to Mildred's baby, Sledge, and to old Mr. Alston—the alpha and omega of the community—to some extent calm her. In addition, when through a series of accidents she must play, under hideously false pretenses, the Virgin Mary at the traditional Christmas pageant that her mother produces at Delight Baptist Church, she reaches her crisis of acceptance. Wesley, still largely a mystery to her and the reader, is glad, he says, to do his duty and marry her at once. This is apparently all that she will get from him, and having to calm eight-month-old Frederick Gupton, a hefty Infant Jesus but soaked with paregoric, allows her to fall in with her lot. Rosacoke's natural fears of childbearing—she is surrounded in the community by breeding mothers—have been allayed by the pageant, the poetry of which is probably necessary to break her will, as happens when she faces the Three Wise Men—Milo, Rato, and Wesley.

The subject of *A Long and Happy Life* is an unusual one for a first novel by a young man, and a considerable triumph of structure and style. It has the merits of brevity and depth. The one comes from the elliptical speech of the community known from childhood, the other from a reading of universal concerns into the daily doings of a community re-created in fiction. The chief achievement of Reynolds Price is that the novel has such a consistent tone that one never thinks of it as a picture of North Carolina country folk. Similarly, there is no temptation to seek an obvious, possibly Lawrencian, message in it. Rosacoke's fearfulness and Wesley's unabashed phallicism are both human characteristics, not typical states. The central theme of "a long and happy life" is first announced in Rosacoke's testimony at Mildred's funeral—she was going to wish these greetings to Mildred on her birthday, when she heard she was dead—and is continued in every character and incident. The most impressive character is Emma Mustian, Rosacoke's mother, who has buried her wreck of a husband and brought up her family and who is on the verge of becoming a grandmother. She is the embodiment of a long, difficult, and happy life.

THE LONG GOODBYE

Type of work: Novel
Author: Raymond Chandler (1888-1959)
Type of plot: Hard-boiled detective story
Time of plot: Early 1950's
Locale: Los Angeles
First published: 1953

In The Long Goodbye, *Philip Marlowe's casual friendship with a charming drunk involves the Los Angeles private eye with a group of troubled rich people, as one murder leads to more violence.*

Principal Characters

Philip Marlowe, a tough private detective. He does a favor for a casual friend, Terry Lennox, driving him to the airport when Lennox must flee the country. A murder investigation involves Marlowe, who is warned away from the case by the police and by the victim's powerful father, as well as by a gangster. Marlowe persists, however, finding links between two cases that seem to be unrelated.

Terry Lennox, a former war hero who is now a charming but idle drunk. When his wife is murdered, he is the chief suspect and asks Marlowe to help him get away. He flies to Mexico and is reported to have committed suicide there in a remote mountain town.

Eileen Wade, an incredibly beautiful Englishwoman married to a writer. She hires Marlowe to solve the problem of her marriage and, later, to find her husband when he has left home. Marlowe finds her behavior inexplicable and resists her attempt to seduce him.

Roger Wade, a highly successful writer who is under pressures that he does not seem to understand. He drinks heavily and leaves home to put himself in the care of a quack doctor. After Marlowe finds him and brings him home, he remains troubled and, after a time, apparently commits suicide.

The Story

An attempt to help a friend, Terry Lennox, involves tough private eye Philip Marlowe with a group of related characters who are wealthy and, for the most part, unpleasant. Lennox's wife, Sylvia, the daughter of the powerful newspaper publisher Harlan Potter, has been cruelly murdered, apparently by Terry Lennox. Although Marlowe had not known of the crime when he took Lennox to the Tijuana airport, he is arrested, beaten by police, and held for several days as a possible accomplice. He is then warned by a district attorney, by a lawyer hired by Harlan Potter, and by a gangster friend of Lennox that he is to stay out of the case. As far as Marlowe knows, there is no reason for him to investigate, especially when Lennox's reported suicide is confirmed by one of Potter's aides, but he never believes that Lennox could have bludgeoned his wife to death.

Marlowe does become involved with the same group of people when he is hired by Eileen Wade, the beautiful wife of writer Roger Wade. Wade has been a highly suc-

cessful author of trashy novels, but he now has a writer's block and an apparent desire to kill himself, without knowing why. Eileen and Wade's publisher try to persuade Marlowe to help Wade. Marlowe refuses, saying that he would not be able to keep a determined man from suicide, but later on, he does agree to try to find Wade when the writer disappears.

Marlowe locates Wade in a dubious drying-out facility and brings him home. Eileen is grateful, but her behavior goes beyond gratitude when, apparently thinking that Marlowe is someone else, she tries to seduce him. He is tempted but manages to resist. Marlowe meets Linda Loring, the sister of Sylvia Lennox, and is attracted to her. She takes him to meet her father, Harlan Potter, who warns Marlowe to stay out of the Lennox case, threatening to have his license revoked if Marlowe does anything that intrudes on Potter's privacy. Marlowe is deeply impressed, but he makes no promises.

Marlowe seems to have dropped out of the case, but a

sober Roger Wade calls and asks him to come to lunch. Eileen is gone for the day, and the servant leaves after fixing sandwiches for the two men. They talk, Wade saying that he has overcome his writer's block and is making good progress on a new novel, Marlowe reminding Wade that he has not faced whatever is bothering him. Wade starts to drink again and passes out; Marlowe goes out on the lawn and watches a water skier on the lake below. The doorbell rings, and Marlowe goes to answer it, admitting Eileen Wade. She says that she has forgotten her keys. In a few minutes, Marlowe goes to check on Roger Wade and finds him dead of a gunshot wound to the head, an apparent suicide.

Marlowe probes more deeply into Terry Lennox's past, establishing that he had served in the British Commandos under another name and had married Eileen before being reported missing in action and presumed dead during World War II. Marlowe, with Roger Wade's publisher as a witness, confronts Eileen with his knowledge and with the fact that she had lied about many small matters. He accuses her of having murdered Sylvia Lennox and of having killed Roger Wade because she thought that he knew of her first crime: Sooner or later, he would have remembered what she had done. Eileen Wade confesses and leaves; that night, she takes an overdose of sleeping pills, leaving a written confession.

Despite the attempts of Harlan Potter and others to kill the story, Marlowe manages to get the confession printed in one of the newspapers. Because there will be no trial, however, Potter takes no revenge, and a gangster friend of Lennox who tries to beat up Marlowe is trapped by the police, using Marlowe as bait. Linda Loring spends a night with Marlowe before leaving for Paris to divorce her husband. Terry Lennox turns up, alive but disguised through plastic surgery; his gangster friends had arranged a fake death and have given him a new identity. Marlowe is glad that Lennox is alive but no longer considers him a friend.

Critical Evaluation

Raymond Chandler's Philip Marlowe, along with Dashiell Hammett's Sam Spade and the Continental Op, was the model for the hard-boiled private detective who replaced the genteel Hercule Poirot-type in popularity. *The Long Goodbye* is the sixth of the seven novels that Chandler wrote in which Marlowe is the central character; it is the longest of these novels and the most intricately plotted. For several reasons, however, critics have not regarded it as highly as two earlier books, *The Big Sleep* (1939) and *Farewell, My Lovely* (1940).

Marlowe's reasons for doing what he does and for taking the cases that he takes are never monetary; in most of his cases, he seems to be underpaid. In the earlier novels, however, he always had a client who paid him for investigating a crime or a disappearance. In *The Long Goodbye*, Marlowe consistently takes action for which he declines to be paid. He refuses to accept money from Terry Lennox for taking him to Tijuana, although Lennox leaves five hundred dollars in a coffee can at Marlowe's house and later sends Marlowe what seems to be a suicide note containing a five-thousand-dollar bill. Marlowe never uses the money, and he also declines to accept money from the Wades. Instead, he acts for reasons of conscience, although he consistently denies that there is anything altruistic about his behavior.

Some critics have found Marlowe's nobility extreme. When the tough cop, Bernie Ohls, points out that Marlowe is not even making expenses for his activities, Marlowe replies with a long speech in which he declares himself to be a romantic. No one else acts from moral principles, but Marlowe says he owes a debt to his friendship with Terry Lennox. That friendship is enough to make him refuse to tell police where Lennox has gone or to cave in to such a powerful figure as Harlan Potter. This attitude, and the several times that Marlowe drinks a gimlet or pours a cup of coffee for his dead friend, amounts to a type of sentimental gesture that the Marlowe of the early novels would have scorned.

Another difference is in Marlowe's relations with women. In none of his earlier novels had he succumbed sexually to any of the temptations that women put in his way. The most characteristic scene occurs in *The Big Sleep*, when he breaks a torrid clinch with a woman to ask her what incriminating information a gangster has on her. In *The Long Goodbye*, however, he practically paws the ground when Eileen Wade smiles at him, and her attempt to seduce him would seemingly have succeeded if a servant had not intervened. Given his expressed opinions of the wealthy, it is odd, at very least, that Marlowe's first consummated relationship with a woman in any of the novels should be with one of Harlan Potter's daughters, a woman who has expressed her disdain for him on several occasions.

Finally, *The Long Goodbye*, unlike the earlier novels, does not send Marlowe down any of the "mean streets" such a detective is supposed to travel, according to Chandler's essay "The Simple Art of Murder." The milieu of the wealthy and casually powerful is one with which Marlowe has been acquainted before, but never so extensively as in this novel. Even the gangsters in *The Long Goodbye* eat in fancy restaurants and wear expensive clothes. It is as if, after five Marlowe novels, Chandler had grown tired of depicting the seamy side of life in Southern California and had decided to give his hero a sex life and a taste of life among the rich.

Despite these problems, *The Long Goodbye* is a considerable achievement. The characters are generally well drawn and interesting. Terry Lennox in particular, a man of great charm but no backbone despite his claims to pride, is an interesting conception, and Marlowe's liking for him is convincing. Credible as well are Lennox's romantic gestures of disappearing and writing a confession to a murder that he did not commit in order to shield a woman whom he had once loved, as well as his sending Marlowe the five-thousand-dollar bill. His reappearance in the novel's final scene is a clever twist, and Marlowe's reaction to him is entirely in character.

Chandler was always a master of creating atmosphere. If the atmosphere in *The Long Goodbye* is less gritty and sordid than that in some of his other novels, it is nevertheless handled very well and made integral to the story. The description of the jail in which Marlowe spends a few days is suitably impersonal and drab, while the sense of the dust and heat of the Southern California summer is strongly conveyed. Chandler also conjures the relief of the valley where Roger Wade and the Lorings live, cooled by ocean breezes and made green by irrigated lawns and gardens. The rough dirt road that discourages tourists from penetrating the valley is a fine touch, and the Wades' cocktail party at which Linda Loring's husband stages a stupid scene is suitably noisy and messy.

Finally, *The Long Goodbye* is more explicit than any of Chandler's other novels in conveying his sense of disappointment at what American society had become after World War II. Bernie Ohls, the sheriff and an old friend of Marlowe, gives vent to some of this disgust in a diatribe on gambling and what it has done to the American character. Marlowe, in an even longer reply, answers that Ohls mistakes effect for cause, arguing that gambling, like Americans' other vices, is the result of their desire for excitement and challenge, a desire that leads to tolerance of lawlessness and corruption. Throughout the novel, Marlowe's feelings of disgust (reflecting Chandler's) with the criminal justice system, with the way in which the rich dictate the terms on which a so-called democracy functions, and with degenerating literary taste are all made a part of the story.

With Chandler's other works, *The Long Goodbye* has been a model for later novels in the hard-boiled manner, including those of such writers as Ross Macdonald, John D. MacDonald, Lawrence Block, Bill Pronzini, and others, and more recently such creators of female private eyes as Sue Grafton, Sarah Paretsky, and Marcia Muller. *The Long Goodbye* is a mature work, showing the skill that Chandler had developed over a long career. It stands as one of the classic examples of the hard-boiled mystery novel.

THE LONG LONELINESS: The Autobiography of Dorothy Day

Type of work: Spiritual autobiography
Author: Dorothy Day (1897-1980)
Time: 1897-1952
Locale: Primarily Chicago and New York City
First published: 1952

In The Long Loneliness, *Day created a unique document. Part autobiography, part religious tract, the book chronicles the author's life, revealing how she turned from radical politics to Catholicism and how she helped to found the Catholic Worker movement.*

Principal Personages

Dorothy Day, a journalist and writer, the cofounder of the Catholic Worker movement.

Peter Maurin, an itinerant French Catholic intellec-

tual whose ideas decisively shaped the movement.

Tamar Teresa Day, Dorothy's only child.

Forster Batterham, Dorothy's common-law husband.

The Story

Dorothy Day's autobiography commences with "Confession," a brief essay about the specific experience of entering the confessional box on a Saturday night. She places her writing in the tradition launched by St. Augustine, one that empowers her to "give an account of the faith that is in me." She asserts that the second part of her life began at the age of twenty-five, when she became a Catholic. Five years later, "I met Peter Maurin and his story must play a great part in this work because he was my master and I was his disciple." Maurin imparted "a way of life and instruction" and helped to found a movement that continues "in the Church throughout the world." She must write about Maurin, but her real subject is her relationship with God, by whom she was haunted until she submitted to Him—out of an abundance of joy, not fear.

Part 1, "Searching," consumes nearly a third of the book and treats the period from 1897 to 1925. Day's father was a sportswriter and horse-racing enthusiast. His jobs kept the family on the move: from New York, to San Francisco, to Chicago. Dorothy and her four siblings were protected from "modern" influences and encouraged to read the Bible and the works of William Shakespeare, Sir Walter Scott, Charles Dickens, Robert Louis Stevenson, and Edgar Allan Poe. This regimen awakened in them a profound love of letters. Indeed, only her sister Della did not have a career in journalism.

At the age of sixteen, Dorothy left home for the Uni-

versity of Illinois. Although she "led a very shiftless life," the two years that she spent in Urbana were pivotal. They were years of intense reading on nonassigned authors: Jack London, Upton Sinclair, Pyotr Kropotkin, Fyodor Dostoevski, Leo Tolstoy. She became consumed by the problem of poverty and joined the Socialist Party. "I was now in love with the masses," she writes. "The poor and oppressed were going to rise up, they were collectively the new Messiah, and they would release the captives." Marxism cut Day away from her religious moorings. Reared in a nonpious Episcopalian family, she had responded profoundly to the New Testament and John Wesley's sermons. Yet, by the time that she took her first job as a reporter for the New York *Call*, a Socialist daily, she had concluded that religion was indeed an opiate of the people. Faith, she thought, was a comfort to the poor and therefore above criticism. For Day personally, however, "Christ no longer walked the streets of this world. He was two thousand years dead and new prophets had risen up in his place."

The years from 1917 to 1925 were remarkable ones for Day. She spent most of them on the Lower East Side, in the world of leftist journalism, socialist and suffragist agitation, ideological wrangling, and artists and intellectuals. She reported on the Industrial Workers of the World (IWW), the Anti-Conscription League, anarchism, and the significance of the Russian Revolution. She knew revolutionary Leon Trotsky, anarchist Alexander Berkman, Communist Party leader Elizabeth Gurley Flynn, and journalist John Reed. In her work with *The Masses* and the *Liberator*, she entered a circle dominated by editors Max Eastman and Floyd Dell and by journalist Mike Gold. Critics Malcolm Cowley and Kenneth Burke, writer Hart Crane, poet Allen Tate, and author Caroline Gordon were her intimate friends.

Imprisoned after a suffragist demonstration in Washington, D.C., Day participated in a ten-day hunger strike—it would be the first in a long series of arrests (including one in 1973). She spent a year as a wartime nurse in a Brooklyn hospital. She formed a close friendship with playwright Eugene O'Neill, one that became the object of much speculation. Her intellectual world was shaped by an early enthusiasm for Sigmund Freud, by Emma Goldman's ideas about sexual emancipation, and by Vladimir Ilich Lenin's views on revolution. Day lived for a time in New Orleans. Her novel *The Eleventh Virgin* was published in 1924, and the motion-picture rights were immediately sold for five thousand dollars. (Later she would spend time in Hollywood as a scriptwriter for films.)

Part 2, "Natural Happiness," consists of only forty pages, but they are among the finest that Day ever wrote. They treat the years from 1925 to 1932, the period of her conversion and political reorientation. For four of these years, she lived a reclusive existence in a beach house on Staten Island. There she wrote and immersed herself in the life "of our small colony"—a melange of émigré Jews and Catholics. Her closest companion was Forster Batterham, to whom she'd been introduced by Kenneth Burke's wife. A war veteran from Asheville, North Carolina, Batterham had roomed with Thomas Wolfe's brother at college.

Day calls her common-law husband an anarchist, but the label does not fit. Forster was deeply antisocial, mistrusting all human institutions and relationships. His passions were fishing, gardening, and the natural world. He was contemptuous of religion, family, and love. "It was hard for me to see at such times why we were together," confessed Day; indeed, "he lived with me as though he were living alone and he never allowed me to forget that this was a comradeship rather than a marriage."

A crisis was inevitable. In the hectic years before Staten Island, Day had increasingly turned to the Catholic church as a source of order and meaning. Her devotion to ordinary working people suggested this move, for many of them were obedient "ethnic" Catholics. Her cities—New York, Chicago, New Orleans, Mexico City, Naples—were very Catholic places; she liked how the rhythms and ceremonies of the liturgical year softened and made sacred harsh secular tendencies. At this point in her life, in the joyous tranquillity of her sequestered life with Forster, her faith deepened: "I was happy but my very happiness made me know that there was a greater happiness to be obtained from life than any I had ever known. I began to think, to weigh things, and it was at this time that I began consciously to pray more."

With the birth of her only child, Tamar Teresa, Dorothy's joy overflowed. She determined that Tamar would have a Catholic baptism, and this meant that she herself must take the final step. Grimly and with no sense of consolation, she entered the Roman Catholic church. She knew she was destroying her relationship with Forster; worse, by uniting herself with (as she then saw it) the most reactionary of institutions, she was sacrificing her radical principles. Yet, for God's sake, she "wanted to die in order to live, to put off the old man and put on Christ." Three years later, immersed in a Catholic world and reconciled to her life as a single mother, she met Peter Maurin. Through him, she could be restored to her radical vocation while remaining a loyal daughter of the church.

Part 3, "Love Is the Measure," celebrates the life and thought of Maurin and traces the development of the Catholic Worker movement. Born in southern France, Maurin was in his mid-fifties when he met Day. Having wandered through a wild variety of occupations and places, he was, in her phrase, a "peasant of the pavements." All the while, he was laboring to develop a comprehensive Catholic social philosophy. That philosophy found utterance in the *Catholic Worker*, which first appeared on May 1, 1933. The one-cent newspaper was intended to compete directly with the Communist *Daily Worker*, offering Party members the vision of a "green revolution" based on the "gentle personalism of traditional Catholicism."

Day traces the early successes of the newspaper and the triumphs and difficulties of the movement: the insistence on pacifism, the mixed success with cooperative farms, and the experiences of living in "houses of hospitality," where lodging and food were provided to the poor. She chronicles her experiences as a single mother and as a traveler to places of chronic unemployment or suffering. The Catholic Worker movement was intent on getting to the level of ordinary people and celebrating the grace of God there. Day shows poignantly what that goal meant on a daily basis. The book ends with a moving account of Maurin's death in 1949 and a lovely postscript on the profundity of community, especially when understood in terms of Eucharist and God's love.

Critical Evaluation

When Dorothy Day published *The Long Loneliness*, she was fifty-five, in good health, and had another third of her life left to live. In many ways, her final three decades were the most interesting and exciting of all. Indeed, in the early 1950's, the Catholic Worker group developed significant positions on international communism, "nuclear pacifism," and the threat of McCarthyism. Also, she was preoccupied with her relationship with the colorful Ammon Hennacy, the "Catholic anarchist" who was then embarked on his famous "one-man revolution" against the United States. Day had already written two intensely autobiographical works: *The Eleventh Virgin* and *From Union Square to Rome* (1938). Some may ask what need there was for a life-writing effort at this point.

The answer is that *The Long Loneliness* is nearly as much a biography of Day's great companion and teacher Peter Maurin as it is an account of her own development. Because Maurin enabled Day to be both a political radical and a devout daughter of the Catholic church, the book should be viewed as the story of how Day arrived at a spiritual conundrum from which only Maurin and the God who sent him could deliver her—or so she finally saw it, through the lens of faith. Thus the autobiography has a plot, and this fact partly explains the work's enduring appeal. As befits any Christian writing, it is a plot whose elements and resolution the reader learns in advance.

The book's satisfactions derive only partly from its well-crafted design. The prose contributes as well, as it is vivid, spare, and specific. The reader immediately trusts Day's strong narrative voice, because she gains her spiritual insights by first engaging the radical particularity of her surroundings. The special odor of a basement in a Chicago tenement building, the look of a row of confessionals, the paraphernalia on a fishing shack, the uninhibited dancing of African-American female prisoners, the way it feels to end a long fast, foulmouthed octogenarians on a hospital ward—she makes such impressions present to the reader in ways that clearly bear Ernest Hemingway's influence.

Day's narrative power can be almost too overwhelming. One finds it tempting to allow her to suppress key facts about her life. For example, Day lost herself totally in a love affair with Lionel Moise, an enigmatic Jewish intellectual who turns up in other accounts of the period, and she conceived a child by him. There was an abortion and an attempt by her to reconstitute the relationship. On the rebound, she married and lived in Europe. None of these facts are shared in *The Long Loneliness*. If one consults William D. Miller's thorough *Dorothy Day: A Biography* (1982), the full extent of Day's omissions can be gauged.

It is to Day's great credit that she does not lose narrative intensity when she brings Maurin into the story. Maurin was thoroughly an intellectual, and she was required to discuss his ideas. She does this in a seemingly effortless way, weaving incident, anecdote, and personal detail into the account. The result is that one learns much about radical Catholic social philosophy while being borne along on a swift tide of narration.

In important ways, Maurin was an early exponent of Liberation Theology, despite his anti-Marxism. In her marvelous chapter entitled "Labor," Day says of the movement: "We felt a respect for the poor and the destitute as those nearest to God, as those chosen by Christ for His compassion." The Incarnation established a permanent alliance between the Creator and the poorest parts of the creation. Thus, "Going to the people is the purest and best act in Christian tradition and is the beginning of world brotherhood."

With this theme as their premise, Catholic Workers developed a position destined to make them a prophetic minority. The movement aimed to "live in accordance with the justice and charity of Jesus Christ" as He is known in Scripture, Catholic teaching (especially the social encyclicals of the popes), and the lives of the saints. The group is "personalist" in three senses. First, the human person is a supremely valuable, free, and rational being whose dignity must not be compromised by parties, states, or economic corporations. Second, the good of persons is inseparable from the common good; it is misguided to glorify self-centered individualism and the competitive society. Third, persons—not agencies, bureaucracies, or "structures"—are responsible for creating the just society.

This understanding of personalism led Catholic Workers to oppose the reliance on the state so prominent in New Deal liberalism, fascism, and communism. They consistently refused to accept any state assistance, eschewing both incorporation and tax-exempt status. Their emphasis on the papal doctrine of "subsidiarity"—as much of society's work as possible must be done by families, communities, and other nonstate bodies—often moved in the direction of philosophical anarchism.

To join Maurin's "green revolution" meant opposing both mainstream American society and much in Catholic public opinion. The movement stood for nonviolence in human relations and pacifism in war. Decentralism and distributionism were key features of Maurin's economic ideal. These positions derived from English Catholics such as writers Vincent McNabb and Hilaire Belloc, who favored the widest possible distribution of private property, a revival of self-sufficient family farms, joint proprietorship in industry, a renaissance of artisanship, cooperatives, and guild structures independent of the state. Maurin expended much energy on conceptualizing new models for farming ventures that combined private and communal property within a parish setting. As a result, the movement gave rise to a number of experiments in agricultural cooperation and rural revival.

Their social vision implied smaller gross national products, but Maurin and Day were unperturbed. They embraced voluntary poverty and manual labor as a way of life. "The mystery of poverty is that by sharing in it, making ourselves poor in giving to others, we increase our knowledge and belief in love," stated the newspaper. Many Catholic Workers carried out voluntary poverty by living in the many "houses of hospitality" established by the movement throughout the urban United States. Here the destitute could find temporary lodging, food, and worship, assisted by people who had abolished income barriers and viewed poverty not as a sign of failure but as an actual calling.

In 1981, activist and priest Daniel Berrigan spoke of how the "work of iconography" concerning Dorothy Day was bound to get underway. This has happened, with the inevitable deflation of the image of one whom that radical priest hailed as "exemplar, mystic, lover of life, fighter of the good fight." Yet many are still prepared to think of her as a saint—or at least a person of the stature of Thomas Merton or Mother Teresa. This much is certain: She bequeathed to Americans a classic work of autobiography. Yet such was not her purpose. The Catholic church was the object of her labors of self-disclosure. It is the place where words like these—they close *The Long Loneliness*—can be spoken: "We cannot love God unless we love each other, and to love we must know each other. We know Him in the breaking of bread, and we know each other in the breaking of bread, and we are not alone any more. Heaven is a banquet and life is a banquet, too, even with a crust, where there is companionship."

LOOK HOMEWARD, ANGEL

Type of work: Novel
Author: Thomas Wolfe (1900-1938)
Type of plot: Impressionistic realism
Time of plot: 1900 to the early 1920's
Locale: North Carolina
First published: 1929

In his novels, Wolfe relied on characters of exceptional brilliance and vitality and portrayed a central character who symbolized the sensitive artist isolated in a hostile world—generally Wolfe himself. In works such as Look Homeward, Angel, *his emotional range is limited to the adolescent and the romantic, but he follows the tradition of American writers who expressed their haunted inner worlds of thought and feeling.*

Principal Characters

Eugene Gant, a shy, imaginative, awkward boy. The youngest child in a tumultuous family, with a wastrel father and a penny-pinching mother, he passes through childhood alone and misunderstood, for there is no family affection. Eugene is precocious, with an insatiable appetite for books. He hates his mother's penuriousness, the family jealousies, and the waste of all their lives, yet he is fascinated by the drunken magniloquence of his father. His salvation is the private school that he is allowed to attend, for the Leonards, who operate it, develop and shape his mania for reading. At fifteen, he enters the state university, where he is considered a freak although he does brilliantly in his studies. He has his first bitter love affair with Laura James during the next summer. In his sophomore year, he becomes something of a campus personality. The great tragedy of these years is the death of his brother Ben, who had loved him in his own strange, abrupt fashion. Just before Eugene leaves for Harvard for graduate study, his brother Luke asks him to sign a release of his future inheritance on the excuse that Eugene has had his share of their parents' estate in extra schooling. Knowing that he is being tricked by his grasping and jealous family, he signs so that he can break away from them forever.

Oliver Gant, his father, a stonecutter from Pennsylvania who has wandered to North Carolina and married there. Hating his wife and her miserly attitude, he is drunken and promiscuous, yet fascinating to his children because of his wild generosities and his alcoholic rhetoric. He is the exact opposite of his wife: She has an overpowering urge to acquire property, and he wants none of it. He will not go with her when she moves to another

house so that she can take in boarders. Their entire marriage has been an unending war, but she wins at last, for his failing health forces him to live with her.

Eliza Gant, Oliver's wife and Eugene's mother, the daughter of a family named Pentland from the mountains. They have all grown prosperous through financial acumen and native thrift. Eliza has an instinctive feeling for the future value of real estate and an almost insane penuriousness; she acquires land until she is a wealthy woman. She alienates Eugene by the stinginess that will never allow her to enjoy the money that she has accumulated. She is rocklike in her immobility, absorbed in her passion for money and her endless, involved reminiscences.

Ben Gant, their son, silent and withdrawn, yet capable of deep affection for Eugene. He dies of pneumonia because his mother will not call a reliable doctor in time. His is a wasted life, for he was endowed with potential that was never realized.

Steve Gant, another son. He is a braggart and wastrel, with all of his father's worst qualities but none of his charm.

Luke Gant, another son. He is a comic figure, stuttering, generous, and ineffectual.

Helen Gant, a daughter. She has her father's expansive nature and takes his side against her mother. She is the only member of the family who can handle Oliver Gant when he is drunk.

Daisy Gant, another daughter. She is a pretty but colorless girl who plays little part in the family drama.

Margaret Leonard, the wife of the principal of the private school that Eugene attends. She directs Eugene's haphazard reading in order to develop the best in his mind; she takes the place of the mother who has had no time for him.

Laura James, a young woman, five years older than Eugene, who is spending the summer at Eliza's board-inghouse. Eugene falls in love with her and she with him. When she returns home, however, she writes that she is to marry a man to whom she has been engaged for a year.

The Story

Eugene, the youngest child in the Gant family, came into the world when Eliza Gant was forty-two years old. His father, Oliver, went on periodic drinking sprees to forget his unfulfilled ambitions and the unsatisfied wanderlust that had brought him to Altamont in the hills of old Catawba. When Eugene was born, his father was asleep in a drunken stupor.

Eliza disapproved of her husband's debauches, but she lacked the imagination to understand their cause. Oliver, who had been raised amid the plenty of a Pennsylvania farm, had no comprehension of the privation and suffering that had existed in the South after the Civil War, the cause of the hoarding and acquisitiveness of his wife and her Pentland relations in the Catawba hill country.

Eliza bore the burden of Oliver's drinking and promiscuousness until Eugene was four years old. Then she departed for St. Louis, taking all the children but the oldest daughter, Daisy, with her. It was 1904, the year of the great St. Louis World's Fair, and Eliza had gone to open a boardinghouse for her visiting fellow townspeople. The idea was abhorrent to Oliver; he stayed in Altamont.

Eliza's sojourn in St. Louis ended abruptly when her twelve-year-old son Grover fell ill of typhoid and died. Stunned, she gathered her remaining children to her and went home.

Young Eugene was a shy, awkward boy with dark, brooding eyes. He was, like his ranting, brawling father, a dreamer. He was not popular with his schoolmates, who sensed instinctively that he was different and made him pay the price. At home, he was the victim of his sisters' and brothers' taunts and torments. His one champion was his brother Ben, though even Ben had been conditioned by the Gants' unemotional family life to give his caresses as cuffs. Yet there was little time for Eugene's childish daydreaming. Eliza believed that early jobs taught her boys manliness and self-reliance. Ben got up at three o'clock every morning to deliver papers. Luke had been an agent for *The Saturday Evening Post* since he was twelve; Eugene was put under his wing. Although the boy loathed the work, he was forced every Thursday to corner customers and keep up a continuous line of chatter until he broke down their sales resistance.

Eugene was not yet eight when his parents separated. Eliza had bought the Dixieland boardinghouse as a good investment. Helen remained at the old house with her father, and Daisy married and left town. Mrs. Gant took Eugene with her, but Ben and Luke were left to shift for themselves, to shuttle back and forth between the two houses. Eugene grew to detest his new home. When the Dixieland was crowded, there was no privacy, and Eliza advertised the Dixieland on printed cards that Eugene had to distribute to customers on his magazine route and to travelers arriving at the Altamont station.

Although life at the boardinghouse was drabness itself, the next four years were the golden days of Eugene's youth, for he was allowed to go to the Leonards' private school. Margaret Leonard, the tubercular wife of the schoolmaster, recognized Eugene's hunger for beauty and love, and she was able to find in literature the words that she herself had not the power to utter. By the time that he was fifteen, Eugene knew the best and the greatest lyrics almost line for line.

Oliver Gant, who had been fifty when his youngest son was born, was beginning to feel his years. Although he was never told, he was slowly dying of cancer.

Eugene was fourteen when World War I broke out. Ben, who wanted to join the Canadian Army, was warned by his doctor that he would be refused because he had weak lungs.

At fifteen, Eugene was sent to the university at Pulpit Hill. It was his father's plan that Eugene should be well on his way toward being a great statesman before the time came for old Oliver to die. Eugene's youth and tremendous height made him a natural target for dormitory horseplay, and his shy, awkward manners were intensified by his ignorance of the school's traditions and rituals. He roomed alone. His only friends were four wastrels, one of whom contributed to Eugene's social education by introducing him to a brothel.

That summer, back at the Dixieland, Eugene met Laura James. Sitting with her on the front porch at night, he was trapped by her quiet smile and clear, candid eyes. He became her lover on a summer afternoon of sunlit green and gold, but Laura went home to visit her parents and wrote Eugene that she was about to marry a boy to whom she had been engaged for nearly a year.

Eugene went back to Pulpit Hill that fall, still determined to go his way alone. Although he had no intimates, he gradually became a campus leader. The commonplace fellows of his world tolerantly made room for the one who was not like them.

In October of the following year, Eugene received an urgent summons to come home. Ben was finally paying the price of his parents' neglect and the drudgery of his life: He was dying of pneumonia. Eliza had neglected to call a competent doctor until it was too late, and Oliver, as he sat at the foot of the dying boy's bed, could think only of the expense the burial would be. As the family kept their vigil through Ben's last night, they were touched with the realization of the greatness of the boy's generous soul. Ben was given, as a final irony, the best funeral that money could buy.

With Ben went the family's last pretenses. When Eugene came back to the Dixieland after graduation, Eliza was in control of Oliver's property and selling it as quickly as she could in order to use the money for further land speculations. She had disposed of their old home. Oliver lived in a back room at the boardinghouse. His children watched each other suspiciously as he wasted away, each concerned for his or her own inheritance. Eugene managed to remain unembroiled in their growing hatred of one another, but he could not avoid being a target for that hatred. Helen, Luke, and Steve had always resented his schooling. In September, before he left for Harvard to begin graduate work, Luke asked Eugene to sign a release saying that he had received his inheritance as tuition and school expenses. Though his father had promised him an education when he was still a child and Eliza was to pay for his first year in the North, Eugene was glad to sign. He was free, and he was never coming back to Altamont.

On his last night at home, he had a vision of his dead brother Ben in the moonlit square at midnight—Ben, the unloved of the Gants and the most lovable. It was for Eugene as well a vision of old, unhappy, unforgotten years, and in his restless imagination, he dreamed of the hidden door through which he would escape forever the mountain-rimmed world of his boyhood.

Critical Evaluation

Essentially plotless, *Look Homeward, Angel* covers roughly the first twenty years of the life of both Thomas Wolfe and his autobiographic hero, Eugene Gant. The three sections of the novel portray the first three stages in Eugene's life: his first twelve years, his four years at the Leonards' school, and his four years at the university. Wolfe's subtitle, *A Story of the Buried Life*, partly suggests the way in which the story is developed. Though there is much external action, talk, and description, the reader is frequently taken into the consciousness of Eugene as well as into that of Ben, Eliza, and Oliver Gant. Eugene's double inheritance, from his rhetoric-spouting, self-pitying, histrionic father and from his more practical and dominating mother, brings him into a series of conflicts with family, school, society, and all that is outside himself. He is the young artist seeking isolation from a world that constantly impinges upon him. Like most highly imaginative and passionately intense young persons, he reacts through both mind and senses to this external world, and his responses are often phrased in a lyrical prose that sweeps the reader emotionally along with Eugene. Young Gant is inclined to take himself very seriously, as when he becomes a hero in his many fantasies. Yet he is capable of self-mockery, particularly as he is growing out of adolescence during his university years.

Stylistically, the novel shows an amazing variety: sensuous, evocative description; symbolism and shifting meanings; realistic, pungent dialogue; bawdy humor; parody and burlesque; satire; fantasy; and dithyrambic passages in which the author becomes intoxicated with the flow of his own words. The shifts of style are often so abrupt that the reader needs a keen awareness to appreciate what Wolfe is doing. *Look Homeward, Angel* is a novel of youth slowly developing into maturity, and perhaps it is best appreciated by readers who can more or less identify with young Eugene. Yet older readers can also lose themselves in it, remembering the turmoil, the joys, and the sorrows of their own maturation.

McTEAGUE

Type of work: Novel
Author: Frank Norris (1870-1902)
Type of plot: Naturalism
Time of plot: 1890's
Locale: San Francisco and Death Valley
First published: 1899

Generally considered the best of Norris' novels, McTeague *falls into the category of naturalism, which employs a hero of much brawn and few brains and displays the influences of heredity and environment upon character. McTeague, Trina, and Marcus are drawn inevitably to catastrophe through their own inherited qualities, acted upon by environmental forces.*

Principal Characters

McTeague (Mac), a massive, slow-witted man with a blond mustache and enormously strong hands. An unlicensed dentist, McTeague sometimes pulls teeth with his bare hands. He snoozes away Sunday afternoons in his dentist's chair until he meets Trina Sieppe, the cousin and fiancée of his friend Marcus Schouler. His friend sees that McTeague and Trina are attracted and with fairly good grace accepts the situation. Many of McTeague's violent and even repulsive qualities are highlighted by incidents in the novel. At an outing, Marcus and McTeague wrestle: Marcus, envious and angry, bites off McTeague's earlobe; the dentist, in turn, breaks Marcus' arm. McTeague's brutality is intensified by drink. Sadistically, he bites his wife's fingers until they are infected and have to be amputated. Adversity can only intensify his desperation, and one is not surprised when he beats his wife to death and then flees the consequences. In the middle of the desert, he is met by his former friend, now a member of the sheriff's posse; again a violent struggle is the only response that McTeague can give. He kills his friend, but not before Marcus has handcuffed them together under the boiling sun. McTeague's death, like his life, is brutish. Readers have considered McTeague's career, as related by Norris, a triumph of realistic description.

Marcus Schouler, who lives above McTeague's dental office. The two men are friends. Smaller than McTeague but gifted with more intelligence, Marcus broods over the loss of his fiancée and her prize money and is petty enough to report McTeague to the authorities for practicing without a license. By fate or by sheer perversity, he binds his enemy to his own dying body with handcuffs; the two face eternity only hours apart.

Trina Sieppe, McTeague's wife, trained to be a thrifty housewife by her Swiss parents. She overdevelops this trait after she wins five thousand dollars in a lottery. She spends every spare moment carving small wooden Noah's ark animals for her uncle's "import" business. Although counting coins is her only joy, she does buy a huge gold tooth as a sign for her husband's dental office. Sexually subservient to her husband's physical strength, she cannot protect herself from his drunken fury when he bites her fingertips. Her character shows only vestigial kindness, and her miserliness leads to her death.

Old Grannis, an aged English bookbinder, comforted each night by the delicate sounds of his neighbor's tea-tray on the opposite side of a partition. The tray belongs to the seamstress next door.

Miss Baker, a genteel dressmaker. She responds with fluttering heart when she hears Grannis and his supper tray. They marry.

Zerkov, a junk dealer.

Maria Macapa, a maid who collects junk for Zerkov. She raves about "gold dishes" once owned by her family. These ravings lead Zerkov to marry Maria. A head blow ends her aberration, however, and in frustration, Zerkov kills her.

Papa and **Mamma Sieppe,** Trina's parents, elderly Swiss immigrants.

The Story

McTeague, born in a small mining town, worked with his unambitious father in the mines, but his mother saw in her son a chance to realize her own dreams. The opportunity to send him away for a better education came a few years after McTeague's father had died. A traveling dentist was prevailed upon to take the boy as an apprentice.

McTeague learned something of dentistry, but he was too stupid to understand much of it. When his mother died and left him a small sum of money, he set up his own practice in an office-bedroom in San Francisco. McTeague was easily satisfied. He had his concertina for amusement and enough money from his practice to keep him well supplied with beer.

In the flat above McTeague lived his friend, Marcus Schouler. Marcus was in love with his own cousin, Trina Sieppe, whom he brought to McTeague for some dental work. While they were waiting for McTeague to finish with a patient, the cleaning woman sold Trina a lottery ticket.

McTeague immediately fell in love with Trina. Marcus, realizing his friend's attachment, rather enjoyed playing the martyr, setting aside his own love in order that McTeague might feel free to court Trina. He invited the dentist to go with him to call on the Sieppe family. From that day on, McTeague was a steady visitor at the Sieppe home. To celebrate their engagement, McTeague took Trina and her family to the theater. Afterward, they returned to McTeague's flat to find the building in an uproar. Trina's lottery ticket had won five thousand dollars.

In preparation for their wedding, Trina was furnishing a flat across from McTeague's office. When she decided to invest her winnings and collect the monthly interest, the dentist was disappointed, for he had hoped to spend the money on something lavish and exciting. Nevertheless, Trina's wishes prevailed. With that income and McTeague's earnings, as well as the little that Trina earned from her hand-carved animals, the McTeagues could be assured of a comfortable life.

Marcus slowly changed in his attitude toward his friend and his cousin. One day, he accused McTeague of stealing Trina's affection for the sake of the five thousand dollars. In his fury, he struck at his old friend with a knife. McTeague was not hurt, but his anger was thoroughly aroused.

In the early months after their wedding, McTeague and Trina were extremely happy. Trina was tactful in the changes that she began to make in her husband. Gradually, she improved his manners and appearance. They both planned for the time when they could afford a home of their own. Because of those plans, however, they had their first real quarrel. McTeague wanted to rent a nearby house, but Trina objected to the high rent. Her thriftiness was slowly turning into miserliness. When McTeague, unknown to her, rented the house, she refused to move or

to contribute to the payment of the first month's rent that the signing of the lease entailed.

Some days later, they went on a picnic to which Marcus was also invited. Outwardly, he and McTeague had settled their differences, but jealousy still rankled in Marcus. When some wrestling matches were held, Marcus and the dentist were the winners in their bouts. It now remained for the two winners to compete. No match for the brute strength of McTeague, Marcus was thrown. Furious, he demanded another match. In that match, Marcus suddenly leaned forward and bit off the lobe of the dentist's ear. McTeague broke Marcus' arm in his anger.

Marcus soon left San Francisco. Shortly thereafter, an order from City Hall disbarred McTeague from his practice because he lacked college training. Marcus had informed the authorities.

Trina and McTeague moved from their flat to a tiny room on the top floor of the building, for the loss of McTeague's practice had made Trina more niggardly than ever. McTeague found a job making dental supplies. Trina devoted almost every waking moment to her animal carvings. She allowed herself and the room to become slovenly, she begrudged every penny they spent, and when McTeague lost his job, she insisted that they move to even cheaper lodgings. McTeague began to drink, and drinking made him vicious. When he was drunk, he would pinch or bite Trina until she gave him money for more whiskey.

The new room into which they moved was filthy and cramped. McTeague grew more and more surly. One morning, he left to go fishing and failed to return. That night, while Trina was searching the streets for him, he broke into her trunk and stole her hoarded savings. After his disappearance, Trina learned that the paint she used on her animals had entered the wounds caused by her husband's bites and had infected her hand. The fingers of her right hand were amputated.

Trina took a job as a scrub woman, and the money that she earned, together with the interest from her five thousand dollars, was sufficient to support her. Now that the hoard of money that she had saved was gone, she missed the thrill of counting over the coins, and so she withdrew the whole of her five thousand dollars from the bank and hid the coins in her room. One evening, there was a tap on her window. McTeague was standing outside, hungry and without a place to sleep. Trina angrily refused to admit him. A few evenings later, drunk and vicious, he broke into a room that she was cleaning. When she refused to give him any money, he beat her until she fell unconscious. She died early the next morning.

McTeague took her money and went back to the mines,

where he fell in with another prospector. Yet McTeague was haunted by the thought that he was being followed. One night, he stole away from his companion and started south across Death Valley. The next day, as he was resting, he was suddenly accosted by a man with a gun. The man was Marcus.

A posse had been searching for McTeague ever since Trina's body had been found, and as soon as Marcus heard about the murder, he volunteered for the manhunt. While the two men stood facing each other in the desert, McTeague's mule ran away, carrying on its back a canteen bag of water. Marcus emptied his gun to kill the animal,

but its dead body fell on the canteen bag and the water was lost. The five thousand dollars was also lashed to the back of the mule. As McTeague went to unfasten it, Marcus seized him. In the struggle, McTeague mortally wounded his enemy with his bare hands. As he slipped to the ground, however, Marcus managed to snap one handcuff to McTeague's wrist, the other to his own. McTeague looked stupidly around, at the hills about a hundred miles away and at the dead body to which he was helplessly chained. He was trapped in the parching inferno of the desert that stretched away on every side.

Critical Evaluation

McTeague presents a unique challenge to the critic. It is a gripping story of human emotions and the relentless pressures of heredity and environment that distort the soul; it is also a melodrama with stereotyped characters, lurid action, and a creaking machinery of symbols that includes everything from dental equipment to snarling dogs. Nevertheless, despite its obvious weaknesses, *McTeague* is exactly what Alfred Kazin said it is: "The first great tragic portrait in America of an acquisitive society." Norris' novel initiates the literary treatment of a theme that eventually informed significant American literary works such as Theodore Dreiser's novel *An American Tragedy* (1925) and Arthur Miller's play *Death of a Salesman* (1949).

McTeague himself is a crude but well-meaning hulk of a man whose gentle temper suggests "the draft horse, immensely strong, stupid, docile, obedient." His brutishness is under control as long as he can putter with his dentistry and sleep off his steam beer in the dental chair. Once he is eroticized by Trina, however, McTeague is sucked into a world of feelings that undermine the self-control that his undisturbed life has made possible. When he and Trina marry, McTeague becomes vulnerable to her avarice and Marcus' jealousy and envy. These destructive emotions, not characteristic of McTeague himself, release the underlying primitiveness of his character. When Marcus bites McTeague's earlobe during the wrestling match at the family picnic, the gentle "draft horse" rises with "the hideous yelling of a hurt beast, the squealing of a wounded elephant. . . . It was something no longer human; it was rather an echo from the jungle." For Norris, a human being is fundamentally an animal, in a world ruled by harsh laws of survival.

McTeague's brutalization is tragic because the humanity that he had achieved was so touching in its vulnera-

bility. Also he is strikingly innocent of avarice. Although the release of McTeague's brutish animal quality results in two slayings, Norris suggests greater dehumanization in the mad greed of Trina counting her gold coins and Zerkov dreaming of Maria's gold plate. McTeague becomes an animal, but the others defy nature itself in the hideousness of their moral and psychological deformity.

It is here that the melodramatic elements of the novel threaten its power. Nevertheless, Norris succeeds in conveying the irony that the nonbrutes in an acquisitive society are more lethal than the brutes, or innocents, who are not conceived in its bowels. McTeague comes from a nonurban world, and it is a testimony to his instincts for self-preservation that he flees back to the mountains after killing Trina. She, Marcus, and Zerkov are all shaped by the city and its acquisitive and artificial environment, and they are all annihilated violently to dramatize the hopelessness of their origins.

Perhaps Norris overdoes the pettiness and petit bourgeois traits of Trina's Swiss family. And his portrait of the psychotic Zerkov hovers close to anti-Semitism. Yet the shallowness of the characterizations serves a larger symbolic purpose. All these people are what they are because their environment is a kind of hell, a swarming, competitive world. If Norris indulges in harsh stereotypes, it is because society produces them. "I never truckled. . . . I told them the truth. They liked it or they didn't like it. What had that to do with me?" This was Norris' literary creed, and he adhered to it relentlessly in other naturalist works of social criticism such as *The Octopus* (1901) and *The Pit* (1903). Even in situations that unobservant readers might dismiss as sentimentalism, Norris preserves his sardonic and tough-minded view of the world. The budding love affair between Old Grannis and Miss Baker, which reads like a contrast to the deteriorating marriage of Mc-

Teague and Trina, is, in reality, a bitter comment on the frustrations of isolation in the congested city. These two old people have conducted their romance through the wall that separates their rooms for so long that their final coming together is a cruelly ironic comment on the life that they have never lived.

The central symbol in *McTeague* is gold: Everyone craves it. Maria, the servant girl, is full of stories about the ancestral gold plate of her family; she captivates Zerkov with descriptions of it and steals gold fillings from McTeague's dental parlor. Trina counts her gold coins into the night, deriving a fiercer erotic joy from this act than from the bearhugs of her husband. Marcus covets Trina's lottery winnings and finally brings about his own death in struggling over the gold with McTeague in the middle of Death Valley. Only McTeague is indifferent to the glitter of gold. For him, it is merely a tool of his trade. When he runs off with Trina's money, he is motivated not by greed, as all critics of the novel agree, but by revenge.

Erich von Stroheim made a famous silent film of *McTeague* and called it *Greed* (1924). He is said to have followed *McTeague* page by page, "never missing a paragraph." Any reader of *McTeague* will agree that Norris moves through his story with what Kenneth Rexroth called "a relentless photographic veracity." Scene after scene unfolds with a visual precision and crispness that leaves an indelible impression on the mind and does much to dispel the reservations that the melodramatic action arouses. There is a relentless and powerful movement in these pictures. From the opening scenes describing McTeague on a Sunday in his cozy dental office slumbering or lazily playing his concertina, to the violent closing scene of the novel in which McTeague and Marcus are locked in a violent death struggle in the middle of the greatest wasteland in the United States, the reader is swept steadily along to increasingly arresting visual involvements. The eye wins over the mind. The environment is rendered with a concreteness that reveals its central power in the novel.

THE MALTESE FALCON

Type of work: Novel
Author: Dashiell Hammett (1894-1961)
Type of plot: Mystery romance
Time of plot: Twentieth century
Locale: San Francisco
First published: 1929-1930

The Maltese Falcon is a detective novel of the hard-boiled school. Its distinction lies in the fact that the detective himself becomes involved in crime through a large bribe. Written in racy, colloquial language, the novel aspires to no more than pure entertainment, but it is a classic example of its genre.

Principal Characters

Sam Spade, a tall, blond, pleasantly satanic-looking, hard-boiled private detective suspected of having killed Thursby and of having also killed Miles Archer in order to marry Iva. He at last discovers how he has been used in the plot to get the Maltese falcon; he discovers the murderers of Miles and Thursby, and he turns Brigid over to the police.

Brigid O'Shaughnessy, his tall, attractive, auburn-haired, deceitful client, who first masquerades as a Miss Wonderly, then shoots Miles, double-crosses her associates, and finally attempts in vain to seduce Sam into letting her go free of a murder charge.

Casper Gutman, her fat, tough employer, who is attempting to get hold of the Maltese falcon. He is shot by Wilmer Cook.

Wilmer Cook, Gutman's young bodyguard, the mur-

derer of Thursby, Jacobi, and Gutman.

Joel Cairo, Gutman's dark-skinned, flashily dressed one-time agent.

Miles Archer, Spade's middle-aged partner, solidly built, wide-shouldered, red-faced. He is shot and killed by Brigid.

Floyd Thursby, Brigid's murdered accomplice.

Iva Archer, Miles's wife, a voluptuous woman in her thirties who is in love with Sam.

Kemidov, a Russian in Constantinople who has substituted a lead imitation for the genuine Maltese falcon.

Jacobi, the captain of the ship *La Paloma*, who is killed by Wilmer.

Effie Perine, Sam's lanky, suntanned secretary.

Rhea Gutman, the daughter of Casper Gutman.

The Story

Brigid O'Shaughnessy went to the office of Sam Spade and Miles Archer, detectives, to ask them to trail Floyd Thursby. Archer, who undertook the job, was killed the first night. About an hour later, Thursby himself was killed in front of his hotel. The police were inclined to suspect Spade of the murder of his partner, for it was known that Iva Archer had been wanting a divorce so that she could marry Spade.

Brigid left word at Spade's office that she wanted to see him. She had changed hotels because she was afraid. She said that she could not tell Spade the whole story, but that she had met Thursby in the Orient and that they had arrived in San Francisco the week before. She said she did not know who killed Thursby.

When Spade returned to his office, Joel Cairo was waiting for him. He asked Spade where the statuette of the black bird was and offered five thousand dollars for the recovery of the ornament. That night, Spade was trailed by a small young man in a gray overcoat and cap. Spade eluded his pursuer long enough to slip into Brigid's hotel unseen. There he learned that Brigid was connected in some way with a mysterious black bird, an image of a falcon. Later, she went with Spade to his apartment, in order to meet Cairo. She told Cairo that she did not have the prize, that he would have to wait possibly a week for its return.

When the police arrived to question Spade about his relations with Iva, they discovered Cairo and Brigid in the apartment. Spade introduced Brigid as an operator in his employ and explained that he had been questioning Cairo about the murders of Archer and Thursby. After Cairo and the police had gone, Brigid told Sam that she did not know what made the falcon so important. She had been hired to get it away from a Russian named Kemidov in Constantinople.

The next morning, before Brigid was awake, Spade went out to get groceries for breakfast and incidentally to search her hotel room for the falcon, which he failed to find. He was certain that Brigid knew where the falcon was. Brigid was afraid of what Cairo might do, however, and Spade arranged for her to stay a few days at the home of Spade's secretary.

Because, in explaining to Cairo how Thursby was killed, Brigid had outlined the letter *G* in the air, Spade knew that there was some special significance attached to the letter. He again saw the young man trailing him in the corridor of a hotel and went up to him. Spade said that someone would have to talk, and "G" might as well know it. Shortly afterward, Casper Gutman called and asked Spade to go see him. Spade told him that Cairo was offering him ten thousand dollars, not five, for the return of the falcon. Gutman laughed derisively; the bird was obviously worth an enormous fortune. Angry because Gutman would tell him no more, Spade left, saying he would give Gutman until five-thirty to talk.

From a taxi driver, Spade learned that Brigid had gone to the Ferry Building and not to his secretary's house and that she had stopped on the way to buy a newspaper. When he returned to Gutman's hotel, he learned that the falcon was an old ornament, made in Malta, encrusted with precious gems and covered with black enamel for protection. Gutman had traced it to the Constantinople home of Kemidov. Now Gutman was wondering where it was.

The next day, Spade searched Cairo's hotel room and found that the ships' schedules had been torn out of a newspaper from the day before. He bought a copy of the paper and saw that the ship *La Paloma* had arrived from Hong Kong. Remembering that Brigid had mentioned the Orient, he associated her going to the Ferry Building with the arrival of the ship. Later he learned that Cairo had checked out of his hotel room. Meanwhile, Spade had gone aboard the *La Paloma* and had learned that Gutman, Cairo, the strange young man, and Brigid had had a long conference with Jacobi, the captain.

While Spade was telling his secretary of his discoveries, a man came in, held out a bundle to Spade, and dropped over dead. Spade opened the package and discovered the falcon. Spade was sure that the man was Jacobi. He had his secretary call the police while he checked the package in a station nearby and mailed the key to his post-office box. He then went to answer a distress call from Brigid, but she was not in her room. Instead, Spade found Gutman's daughter, who sent him to the suburbs on a wild-goose chase. When he returned to his apartment, he met Brigid waiting outside, obviously frightened. Opening the door, he found Gutman, the young man, and Cairo waiting for him.

Spade realized that his wild-goose chase had been planned to get him out of the way long enough to give these people a chance to find Jacobi before he returned. Because they were all together, Spade said he would give them the falcon in return for ten thousand dollars and someone on whom to blame the murders. He suggested the young man, whose name was Wilmer Cook, as the suspect. Spade explained that, if Wilmer were hanged for the murder of Thursby, then the district attorney would drop the case, taking it for granted that Jacobi had been murdered by the same person. Gutman, sure that Thursby had killed Archer, finally consented to make Wilmer the victim.

Gutman produced ten one-thousand-dollar bills. Then Spade called his secretary and asked her to get the claim check from the post office and redeem the falcon. After she had delivered the package to Spade's apartment, Gutman untied it and, to make sure that he had the genuine falcon, began to scratch away the enamel. The falcon was a lead imitation. Kemidov had tricked him. Spade gave back nine thousand dollars. Then he called the police and told them that Wilmer had killed Jacobi and Thursby.

Knowing that Gutman would tell about his and Brigid's part in the plot, Spade made Brigid confess to him that she had drawn Archer into an alley that first night and had killed him with a pistol borrowed from Thursby. He told Brigid that he intended also to turn her over to the police. He had to clear himself of suspicion of killing his partner, and he could not let a woman stand in his way.

Critical Evaluation

The Maltese Falcon introduces the detective Sam Spade, a rough, crude, unassuming, and peculiarly unat- tractive private eye. His appearance is anything but that of a hero's: He lacks a charming smile or an athletic physique. He is an antihero, a negative character cast in a positive role. His success, however, is directly related to his nonheroic qualities. Because his world is the underside of respectability, the seedy areas of San Francisco in which he is usually employed in some sort of marital espionage, Spade must adapt his methods to the environment in order to survive. Indeed, what finally comes clear is that the detective is the only truly sane and perhaps just individual in the novel. He deals with the evil and treacherous, those like the satanic Gutman, as well as with the police, who are for the most part stupid or only intent upon making an arrest, the matter of justice being of no large consequence.

Spade's role as the isolated antihero who brings justice to a corrupt world is a familiar figure in American folklore and literature. *The Maltese Falcon* is in some sense a modern, urban staging of the traditional Western story with Spade as the lone gunman, without credentials, combating the greed of the adventurers in their pursuit of wealth (in the Western, it was gold, here it is the falcon). Notably different, however, is the fact that the heroine in Hammett's novel, Brigid O'Shaughnessy, unlike the Western heroine, is herself treacherous and guilty; and Spade, for all his virtue, is not above dishonest gain. For all the similarities, then, the reader is in a radically different world in *The Maltese Falcon*, one of lost innocence, where heroism is impossible and trust and affection have disappeared. The whole is unsavory and decayed.

THE MEMBER OF THE WEDDING

Type of work: Novel
Author: Carson McCullers (1917-1967)
Type of plot: Impressionistic realism
Time of plot: 1945
Locale: Georgia
First published: 1946

In the story of Frankie Addams, McCullers has reduced the total idea of moral isolation to a fable of simple outlines and a few eloquently dramatic scenes, set against a background of adolescent mood and discovery that is familiar to all. The inescapable loneliness and longing of humankind is reflected in the experiences of this twelve-year-old girl trapped in the confusion of her own adolescence.

Principal Characters

Frances (Frankie) Addams, a twelve-year-old girl. Jealous because she is rejected by other girls and boys in the community, she calls them names, flies into sudden rages against Berenice and John Henry, and bursts into tears when she is ashamed. She worries over her tall, gawky frame and her big feet. She dreams romantically and excitedly of the adventures that she will have with Jarvis and Janice when she accompanies them on their wedding trip, and she fights frantically when she is prevented from going. As the story ends, Frankie appears to be over the worst of her adolescence—she will be Frances from now on.

John Henry West, her six-year-old cousin, a frail child who dies of meningitis. He is Frankie's friend and often her confidant, though he has little understanding of much of what she tells him.

Berenice Sadie Brown, the cook in the Addams household. She is black, short, and broad-shouldered, and her left eye is bright blue glass. She offers kind and motherly comfort, sharp practical advice and criticism, and affectionate understanding to troubled Frankie and little John Henry. Frankie is unaware that Berenice's pity for the motherless, confused, and unhappy girl has kept Bere-

nice from marrying her suitor, T. T. Williams.

Royal Quincy Addams, Frankie's father, a jeweler, kind to his daughter but too busy with his work to pay much attention to her.

Jarvis, Frankie's brother, an army corporal, a handsome blond.

Janice Evans, the fiancée of Jarvis.

Honey Camden Brown, Berenice's light-skinned, mentally weak foster brother, who is jailed for robbing a store while on drugs.

T. T. Williams, Berenice's middle-aged beau, owner of an African-American restaurant.

Aunt Pet and **Uncle Eustace,** John Henry's parents.

Evelyn Owen, Frankie's friend who moves to Florida.

Big Mama, an old African-American palm reader.

Mary Littlejohn, Frankie's best, real friend as she enters her fourteenth year.

Barney MacKean, a boy with whom Frankie once committed a "queer sin" and whom she hates.

Uncle Charles, John Henry's great-uncle, and a very old man who dies the day before the wedding.

Officer Wylie, a police officer who catches Frankie when she tries to run away.

The Story

In the summer of her twelfth year, Frankie Addams believed that she had become an unjoined person. She was a lanky girl with a crew haircut and skinned elbows. Some of the older girls she had played with the year before had a neighborhood club, and there were parties with boys on Saturday nights, but Frankie was not a member. That summer, she got herself into so much trouble

that at last she just stayed home with John Henry West, her little cousin, and Berenice Sadie Brown, the family's African-American cook. Through long, hot afternoons, they would sit in the dingy, sad Addams kitchen and play cards or talk until their words sounded strange, with little meaning.

Berenice Sadie Brown was short and black and the

only mother that Frankie had ever known, her own mother having died when she was born. The cook had been married four times, and during one of her marriages, she had lost an eye while fighting with a worthless husband. Now she owned a blue glass eye, which always interested John Henry West. He was six and wore gold-rimmed glasses. Sometimes Frankie grew tired of him and sent him home. Sometimes she begged him to stay all night. Everything seemed so mixed up that she seldom knew what she did want.

Then, on the last Friday in August, something happened that made life wonderful once more. Frankie's brother Jarvis, a soldier home from Alaska, had come to dinner with Janice Evans, a girl who lived at Winter Hill. They were to be married there on Sunday, and Frankie and her father were going to the wedding. After dinner, Janice and Jarvis returned to Winter Hill, while Mr. Addams went downtown to his jewelry store. Later, while she sat playing cards with Berenice and John Henry, Frankie thought of her brother and his bride. Winter Hill became all mixed up in her mind with snow and icy glaciers in Alaska.

Jarvis and Janice had brought Frankie a doll, but she had no time for dolls anymore. John Henry could have it. She wished her hair were not so short; she looked like one of the freaks from the Chattahoochee Exposition. Suddenly angry, she chased John Henry home. When Berenice teased her, saying that she was jealous of the wedding, Frankie declared that she was going to Winter Hill and never coming back. For a minute she wanted to throw a kitchen knife at the cook. Instead, she hurled it at the stairway door.

Berenice went out with Honey Camden Brown, her foster brother, and T. T. Williams, her beau. Because Honey was not quite right in the head, Berenice was always trying to keep him out of trouble. T. T. owned an African-American restaurant. Frankie did not know that the cook's pity for the unhappy, motherless girl kept her from marrying T. T.

Left alone, Frankie wandered around the block to the house where John Henry lived with Aunt Pet and Uncle Eustace. Somewhere close by, a horn began to play a blues tune. Frankie felt so sad and lonely that she wanted to do something that she had never done before. She thought again of Jarvis and Janice. She was going to be a member of the wedding; after the ceremony, the three of them would go away together. She was not plain Frankie Addams any longer: She would call herself F. Jasmine Addams, and she would never feel lonely or afraid again.

The next morning, with Mr. Addams' grunted permission, Frankie went downtown to buy a new dress and shoes. On the way, she found herself telling everyone she met about the wedding. That was how she happened to go into the Blue Moon, a cheap café where she knew children were not allowed. Yet F. Jasmine Addams was no longer a child, and so she went in to tell the Portuguese proprietor about the wedding. The only other person in the café was a red-headed soldier from a nearby army post. Frankie scarcely noticed him at the time, but she remembered him later when she saw him on the street. By that time, he was drunk and trying to buy an organ-grinder's monkey. The soldier bought Frankie a beer and asked her to meet him that night at the Blue Moon.

When Frankie finally arrived home, she learned that Berenice and John Henry were also to attend the wedding. An aged kinsman of the Wests had died, and Aunt Pet and Uncle Eustace were going to the funeral at Opelika. Berenice, dismayed when she saw the orange silk evening dress, the silver hair ribbon, and the silver slippers that Frankie had bought to wear at the wedding, tried, without much success, to alter the dress for the gawky young girl. Afterward, they began to talk about the dead people they had known. Berenice told about Ludie Freeman, her first husband, whom she had truly loved. The stories about Ludie and the three other husbands made them all feel lonesome and sad. Berenice held the two children on her knees as she tried to explain to them the simple wisdom life had taught her. They began to sing spirituals in the half-dark of the dingy kitchen.

Frankie did meet the soldier that night. First, she went with John Henry to Big Mama's house and had her palm read. Afterward, she told John Henry to go back to her house; she did not want him to know that she was meeting someone at the Blue Moon. The soldier bought two drinks. Frankie was afraid to taste hers. He asked her to go up to his room. Frightened when he tried to pull her down beside him on the bed, she picked up a glass pitcher and hit him over the head. She then climbed down the fire escape and ran all the way home. She was glad to get into bed with no one but John Henry by her side.

The wedding the next day turned into a nightmare for Frankie. Everything was lovely until the time came for the bride and groom to leave. When they carried their bags out to the car, she ran to get her own suitcase. Then they told her, as kindly as possible, that they were going away alone. She grasped the steering wheel and wept until someone dragged her away. Riding home on the bus, she cried all the way. Berenice promised her a bridge party with grown-up refreshments as soon as school opened, but Frankie knew that she would never be happy again. That night, she tried to run away. Not knowing where else to go, she went to the Blue Moon. There a police officer found her and sent for her father.

By November, however, Frankie had almost forgotten the wedding. Other things had happened. John Henry had died of meningitis. Honey Camden Brown, an addict, had tried to hold up a drugstore and was in jail. Mary Littlejohn had become Frankie's best, real friend.

She and her father were leaving the old house and going to live with Aunt Pet and Uncle Eustace in a new suburb. Berenice, waiting to see the last of the furniture taken away, was sad, for she knew that Frankie would depend on her no longer. Frankie—she wanted to be called Frances—was thirteen.

Critical Evaluation

Throughout her kinetic career as a novelist, short-story writer, and playwright, Carson McCullers explored the human condition from several perspectives, but all with the common focus of loneliness and dissatisfaction. *The Heart Is a Lonely Hunter* (1940) reveals a deaf-mute's isolation in a Southern town, and it also draws parallels to the phenomenon of fascism. *Reflections in a Golden Eye* (1941) also takes place in the South, but with *The Member of the Wedding* anxieties are explored in finer detail. Then followed *The Ballad of the Sad Café* in 1951, a collection of short stories including the famous title piece, a novelette dramatized by Edward Albee in 1963. Her last two works were *The Square Root of Wonderful* (1957), a play, and the novel *Clock Without Hands* (1961). McCullers' unpublished works, including some early poetry, appeared posthumously in 1971 under the title *The Mortgaged Heart*.

Although *The Member of the Wedding* certainly deals with themes of loneliness and dissatisfaction, the story is quite interesting as a discussion of the means through which a particular individual attempts to escape these isolating emotions. This psychological novel is enhanced by McCullers' masterful handling of language and point of view. Although the narrative is not in the first person, the language makes it clear that Frankie Addams' viewpoint is of primary concern. The result is that one is able both to observe Frankie objectively and, at the same time, to appreciate her emotions immediately. Frankie's feelings are, in addition, juxtaposed with the intrusion of adult observation (most often from Berenice and Mr. Addams) so that the reader has a realistic synthesis of information. The structural result is triangular: While there is exchange between adults and adolescent, the adult view cannot comprehend the adolescent because it has grown beyond that stage and the adolescent view cannot encompass the adult because it is not yet equipped to do so. The reader completes the triangle, gaining the adolescent view through Frankie and adding the adult view through appreciating the irony of Frankie's observations of adults.

Frankie, Berenice, and John Henry, despite apparent enmities, form a tribunal, sharing experiences and opinions and evaluating them both literally and symbolically, and each is essential in his or her role in the tribunal. Frankie, literally, is the causing factor of the group's existence: Berenice is hired to care for her, and John Henry is present because Frankie wants juvenile companionship to counter that of Berenice. Yet, although she realizes that she is not yet capable of understanding the functionings of the adult world, Frankie, aided by John Henry, symbolizes the almost divine nature often assigned to the child. Frankie *knows* certain truths, as Berenice occasionally confirms in bewilderment, because the girl's mind has not yet been spoiled by realities that obscure those truths. Her almost innate, although selective, knowledge is part of a literary and philosophical ideology most clearly typified by the Wordsworthian view of children. Yet Frankie's strongest understanding is also the most ironic: She realizes that she is incomplete and is terrified by reminders of that fact. In her earnest efforts to belong, to be completed, however, she is driving herself toward adulthood, in which one loses this sort of innate knowledge.

Berenice, one of McCullers' most interesting characters, serves multiple functions. Just as she is employed to care for Frankie in many ways, she is also the pivotal character upon whom the novel depends on several levels of development. In simple terms, she is a counterexample of Frankie's search to belong and to love. Although McCullers' familiar theme of such unending search persists in Berenice, she illustrates that love, even when directed toward a vague objective, has the eventual effect of grace. In addition, she is Frankie's surrogate mother. Frankie is locked into dependence upon Berenice, but it is dependence from a distance; although she longs to be independent of Berenice and all other authority figures, Frankie knows intuitively that she is not old enough to ignore Berenice. She knows that the woman has a function in her life, that Berenice has necessary information to which Frankie has not yet been exposed. She does not want to block Berenice out entirely (while the servant speaks to her, Frankie puts her fingers in her ears—but not far enough to prevent Berenice's voice from reaching her), as Frankie would have to confront life later as an adult without sufficient data. Frankie knows instinctively that ignoring Berenice is only self-defeating. Berenice is, therefore, like an oracle; she comes from the ancient literary tradition of the blind or one-eyed person who speaks the truth clearly because of that missing vision. Berenice has a glass eye ("glass" and "truth" are related etymologically in Latin); therefore, she sees truth through her glass eye, not through her physically functioning one. McCullers is thus able to elevate the group in the kitchen to mythic dimensions: Berenice is the oracle, John Henry is her acolyte, and Frankie is the pilgrim-initiate.

By emphasizing Frankie's progressive learning and by concentrating primarily on the emotions and experiences of only three days in Frankie's life, Carson McCullers achieves the effect of gradually increasing one's expectations. By the end of *The Member of the Wedding*, the reader has been led to believe that the day before the wedding is Frankie's "last afternoon" in town—if not literally, then at least figuratively. Yet this increasing momentum is not followed by a fulfillment of expectation; Frankie is essentially unchanged by the trauma of disappointment. It is suddenly apparent that the initiation of youth into adulthood through artificial, specific rites is a myth. The search for belonging is an unending one; it is simply one's orientation toward that search that can change by the natural process of maturing. In fact, as Berenice's life illustrates, the childlike element of selectively believing in salvation can be concomitantly protective, making both life and the search for social identity not only possible but also bearable.

MISS LONELYHEARTS

Type of work: Novel
Author: Nathanael West (Nathan Weinstein, 1903-1940)
Type of plot: Social satire
Time of plot: Late 1920's
Locale: New York City
First published: 1933

Bitter in its satire, brief, episodic, and unique in its treatment, and ironic and hopeless in its outlook, Miss Lonelyhearts *is not so much a tale of the newspaper business as it is West's grotesque picture of the miserable, monstrous, often disgusting life that humanity has made for itself in its despair.*

Principal Characters

Miss Lonelyhearts, the male writer of advice to the lovelorn on the New York *Post-Dispatch*. The lovelorn column, considered a necessity for the increase in the paper's circulation and regarded by its staff as a joke, becomes an agony to its writer as he sees that the letters he receives are genuine cries for help from the very depths of suffering. In an attempt to escape the pain of the realization that he is the victim of the joke rather than its perpetrator, he turns in vain to drink, to sex, and to a vacation in the country with a girl who loves him. Finally, in the delirium of illness, he imagines himself identified with the Christ whose image has long haunted him. As the crippled Peter Doyle approaches his room, Miss Lonelyhearts runs toward him with arms outstretched to receive him in his healing embrace. His gesture is mistaken for an intended attack, and he is shot.

Willie Shrike, the feature editor, who is Miss Lonelyhearts' boss. He turns the knife in Miss Lonelyhearts'

agony by his unending mockery of the desperate cries for help in the lovelorn letters and of the attempts at escape with which people delude themselves.

Mary Shrike, Willie Shrike's wife, whom Miss Lonelyhearts tries in vain to seduce.

Betty, a girl who is in love with Miss Lonelyhearts. Hoping to cure his despair, she takes him to the country. The attempt fails, as the letters are not forgotten.

Peter Doyle, a handicapped man who consults Miss Lonelyhearts about the meaning of the painful and unremunerative round of his existence. Later, he accuses the columnist of the attempted rape of his wife and shoots him in a struggle following a gesture that the cripple mistakes for an intended attack.

Fay Doyle, Peter Doyle's wife. Dissatisfied with her life with her crippled husband, she seeks out Miss Lonelyhearts and tries to seduce him.

The Story

Miss Lonelyhearts found it hard to write his lovelorn column in the New York *Post-Dispatch:* The letters were not funny—there was no humor as desperate people begged for help. "Sick-of-it-all," for example, with seven children in twelve years, was pregnant again and ill, but being a Catholic she could not consider an abortion and her husband would not let her alone. "Desperate," a sixteen-year-old girl with a good shape and pretty clothes, wanted boyfriends but cried all day because she had no nose (should she commit suicide?). Harold S., fifteen, wrote that his sister Gracie, thirteen, deaf, mute, and not very smart, had something dirty done to her by a man.

Harold could not tell their mother that Gracie was going to have a baby, however, because her mother would beat Gracie up. Shrike, the feature editor and Miss Lonelyhearts' tormentor, was no help at all: Instead of the same old stuff, he said, Miss Lonelyhearts ought to give his readers something new and hopeful.

At Delehanty's speakeasy, where Miss Lonelyhearts went to escape his problems, his boss still belabored him about brooding and told him to forget the Crucifixion and remember the Renaissance. Meanwhile, Shrike was trying to seduce Miss Farkis, a long-legged woman with a childish face. He also taunted the columnist by talking of a Western sect that prayed for a condemned slayer with an adding machine, numbers being their idea of the universal language.

Miss Lonelyhearts' bedroom walls were bare except for an ivory Christ nailed with large spikes, and the religious figure combined in a dream with a snake whose scales were tiny mirrors in which the dead world took on a semblance of life. In the dream, first he was a magician who could not move his audience by tricks or prayer; then he was on a drunken college spree with two friends. Their attempt to sacrifice a lamb before barbecuing it, with Miss Lonelyhearts chanting the name of Christ, miscarried when the blade broke on the altar and the lamb slipped out of their bloodied hands. When the others refused to go back to put the lamb out of its misery, Miss Lonelyhearts returned and crushed its head with a stone.

One day, as he tried to put things in order, everything went against him: Pencils broke, buttons rolled under the bed, shades refused to stay down, and instead of order on the skyline, he found chaos. Miss Lonelyhearts remembered Betty, who could bring order into his world, and he went to her apartment. Yet he realized that her world was not the real world and could never include the readers of his column; his confusion was significant and her order was not. Irritated and fidgety, he could neither talk to her nor caress her, although two months before she had agreed to marry him. When she asked if he were sick, he could only shout at her; when she said that she loved him, he could only reply that he loved her and her smiling through tears. Sobbing that she felt swell before he had arrived and now felt lousy, she asked him to go away.

At Delehanty's, he listened to talk of raping a woman writer, and as he got drunker he heard friends mock Shrike's kidding him, but whiskey made him feel good and dreams of childhood made the world dance. Stepping back from the bar, he collided with a man holding a beer. The man punched him in the mouth. With a lump on his head, a loose tooth, and a cut lip, Miss Lonelyhearts walked in the fresh air with his friend Ned Gates. In a rest room, they met an old man with a terrible cough and no overcoat, who carried a cane and wore gloves because he detested red hands. They forced him to go to an Italian wine cellar. There they told him they were Havelock Ellis and Krafft-Ebing and insultingly mocked him with taunts about homosexuality. When Miss Lonelyhearts twisted the man's arm—imagining it was the arm of "Desperate," "Broken-hearted," or "Sick-of-it-all"—the old man screamed, and someone hit the columnist with a chair.

Next, instead of going to the office after Shrike phoned him, Miss Lonelyhearts went to the speakeasy; he knew that Shrike found him too perfect a butt for his jokes to fire him. Needing a woman, he phoned Mary, Shrike's wife, whom he had never seduced, although she hated her husband and used Miss Lonelyhearts to arouse Shrike. At a nightclub, in a cab, and at her apartment door, Miss Lonelyhearts tried to talk Mary into sleeping with him; but Shrike opened the door, ending that scheme.

The next day, Miss Lonelyhearts received a letter from Fay Doyle, unhappily married to a handicapped man, asking for an appointment. Although he first threw the letter away, he retrieved it, phoned her to meet him in the park, and took her to his apartment. In the intervals of making love, she told of her married life and her child Lucy, whose father was not Doyle.

Physically sick and exhausted in his room for three days, he was comforted by Betty, who tried to persuade him to quit his Lonelyhearts job. He said he had taken the job as a joke, but after several months, the joke had escaped him. Pleas for help had made him examine his values, and then he became the victim of the joke. While Betty suggested that he go to the country with her, Shrike broke into the room, taunted him to escape to the South Seas, hedonism, art, suicide, or drugs, and ended by dictating an imaginary letter from the columnist to Christ.

After he had been ill for a week, Betty finally persuaded Miss Lonelyhearts to go with her to her aunt's Connecticut farm. They camped in the kitchen, sat near a pond to watch frogs, deer, and a fawn, and slept on a mattress on the floor. They walked in the woods, swam in the nude, and made love in the grass.

After several days, they returned to the city. Miss Lonelyhearts knew that Betty had failed to cure him; he could not forget the letters. He vowed to attempt to be humble. In the office, he found a lengthy letter from "Broad Shoulders," telling of her troubles with a crazy husband.

About a week later, while Shrike was pulling the same familiar jokes in Delehanty's, the bartender introduced Miss Lonelyhearts to the crippled Peter Doyle, whose wife wanted the columnist to have dinner at their house. After labored conversation, Doyle gave him a letter about his problems: His job forced him to pull his leg up and down stairs for only $22.50 a week; his wife talked money, money, money; and a doctor prescribed a six months' rest. When their hands touched under the table, they were at first embarrassed, but then held hands in silence.

As they left the speakeasy, very drunk, to go to Doyle's, the man cursed his wife and his foot. Miss Lonelyhearts was happy in his humility. When Mrs. Doyle tried to seduce the columnist, he failed to respond. Meanwhile, her husband called himself a pimp and at his wife's request went out to get gin. Failing to find a message to show Mrs. Doyle that her husband loved her, and disgusted by her obscene attempts to sleep with him, Miss Lonelyhearts struck her again and again before he ran out of the house.

Following a three day illness, Miss Lonelyhearts was awakened by five people, including Shrike and his wife, all drunk, who wanted to take him to a party at the editor's home. Betty was one of the party. Shrike wanted to play a game in which he distributed letters from Miss Lonelyhearts' office file and made taunting comments. When the columnist could stand it no longer, he followed Betty out, dropping unread the letter given him, which Shrike read to the crowd. It was from Doyle, accusing Miss Lonelyhearts of trying to rape his wife.

Miss Lonelyhearts told Betty that he had quit the Lonelyhearts job and was going to look for work in an advertising agency. She told him that she was going to have a baby. Although he persuaded her to marry him and have the baby instead of getting an abortion, by the time he left her he did not feel guilty. In fact, he could no longer feel.

The next morning, he was in a fever. The Christ on his wall was shining, but everything else in the room seemed dead. When the bell rang and he saw Doyle coming up the stairs, he imagined the cripple had come to have Miss Lonelyhearts perform a miracle and make him whole. Misunderstanding the outspread arms, Doyle put his hand in a newspaper-wrapped package as Betty came in the door. In the struggle, the gun that Doyle carried went off and Miss Lonelyhearts fell, dragging Doyle with him.

Critical Evaluation

Nathanael West, born Nathan Weinstein, was graduated from Tufts University in 1924 with a major in philosophy. Immediately upon graduation, he left for Paris, where he remained for two years. On his return from abroad, he took a job as a hotel night clerk, a job for which he was not particularly suited but which enabled him to write. In 1931, his first short novel, *The Dream Life of Balso Snell*, was privately printed; it was remarkably unsuccessful. His next work, *Miss Lonelyhearts*, appeared in 1933; if anything, its lack of success surpassed his first novel—the publisher was forced to declare bankruptcy. In the same year, he went to Hollywood, where he would live until his death. While there, he was acquainted with such prominent authors as William Faulkner and F. Scott Fitzgerald, and there in 1940 he married Eileen McKenney, famous as *My Sister Eileen* (a 1938 book written by Ruth McKenney and later adapted for the stage and screen). He and his wife were killed on December 22, 1940, in an automobile accident.

West was obsessed with the daydreams that people live. Though Jewish, he considered Christ and the Christ-figure the ultimate dream, a concept more comprehensible when one considers that, for West as for many other authors (Miguel de Cervantes is a notable example), the word dream is synonymous with ideal. In *Miss Lonelyhearts*, West explores the modern answers to humanity's

dilemma. Miss Lonelyhearts himself is the central figure of the novel, the observer through whose eyes the reader sees a modern wasteland. The wasteland motif is represented by the letters that Miss Lonelyhearts receives. In each of these letters, sex and the failure of sex are the central conflicts: a woman destroyed by repeated pregnancy, a noseless girl for whom sex is impossible, and a retarded child who has been raped.

Obsessed with the pain of others, Miss Lonelyhearts confuses compassion with identification. He becomes a Christ-figure who embraces his suppliant children with erotic abandon. He renders unto Eros what is Christ's in a confused and tormented ministry. Shrike's taunting remarks all originate in his contempt for Miss Lonelyhearts' original assumption that pure good is a true, human motivation. Determined to make Miss Lonelyhearts confront his own corruption, Shrike taunts him with gibes ridiculing his spiritual vanity. In the end, Miss Lonelyhearts becomes an integral part of the very wasteland that he thought he could redeem. The gospel of Shrike, the Mephistophelian naysayer, is confirmed by the totally ridiculous sacrifice of Miss Lonelyhearts in the arms of Peter Doyle. Miss Lonelyhearts' dream of Christ-like self-sacrifice is parodied in the farcical embrace of seducer and cuckold rolling down the stairs.

MOBY DICK: Or, The Whale

Type of work: Novel
Author: Herman Melville (1819-1891)
Type of plot: Symbolic allegory
Time of plot: Early nineteenth century
Locale: High seas
First published: 1851

Melville brought many disparate elements together in Moby Dick, *a realistic picture of the whaling industry, an adventure-romance of the sea, an epic quest, a Faustian bargain, and metaphysical speculation. Although it is unlikely that any one interpretation of Ahab's obsessive pursuit of the white whale will ever be generally accepted, the depth, sweep, and power of the author's vision guarantees the novel's stature as one of the world's proven masterpieces.*

Principal Characters

Ishmael, a philosophical young schoolmaster and sometime sailor who seeks the sea when he becomes restless, gloomy, and soured on the world. With a new-found friend Queequeg, a harpooner from the South Seas, he signs aboard the whaler *Pequod* as a sailor. Queequeg is the only person on the ship to whom he is emotionally and spiritually close, and this closeness is, after the initial establishment of their friendship, implied rather than described. Otherwise Ishmael does a sailor's work, observes and listens to his shipmates, and keeps his own counsel. Having been reared a Presbyterian (as was Melville), he reflects in much of his thinking the Calvinism out of which Presbyterianism grew, but his thought is also influenced by his knowledge of literature and philosophy. He is a student of cetology. Regarding Ahab's pursuit of Moby Dick, the legendary white whale, and the parts played by himself and others involved, Ishmael dwells on such subjects as free will, predestination, necessity, and damnation. After the destruction of the *Pequod* by Moby Dick, Ishmael, the lone survivor, clings to Queequeg's floating coffin for almost a day and a night before being rescued by the crew of another whaling vessel, the *Rachel.*

Queequeg, Starbuck's veteran harpooner, a tattooed cannibal from Kokovoko, an uncharted South Seas island. Formerly a zealous student of Christianity, he has become disillusioned after living among so-called Christians and, having reverted to paganism, he worships a little black idol, Yojo, that he keeps with him. Although he appears at ease among his Christian shipmates, he keeps himself at the same time apart from them, his only close friend being Ishmael. In pursuit of whales, he is skilled and fearless. When he nearly dies of a fever, he

has the ship's carpenter build him a canoe-shaped coffin that he tries out for size and comfort; then, recovering, he saves it for future use. Ironically it is this coffin on which Ishmael floats after the sinking of the *Pequod* and the drowning of Queequeg.

Captain Ahab, the proud, defiant, megalomaniacal captain of the *Pequod*. He is a grim, bitter, brooding, vengeful madman who has only one goal in life: the killing of the white whale that had deprived him of a leg in an earlier encounter. His most prominent physical peculiarity is a livid scar that begins under the hair of his head and, according to one crewman, extends the entire length of his body. The scar symbolizes the spiritual flaw in the man himself. His missing leg has been replaced by one of whalebone for which a small hole has been bored in the deck. When he stands erect looking out to sea, his face shows the indomitable willfulness of his spirit, and to Ishmael he seems a crucifixion of a "regal overbearing dignity of some mighty woe." Ahab is in complete, strict command of his ship, though he permits Starbuck occasionally to disagree with him. Ahab dies caught, like Fedallah the Parsee, in a fouled harpoon line that loops about his neck and pulls him from a whaleboat.

Starbuck, the first mate, tall, thin, weathered, staid, steadfast, conscientious, and superstitious, a symbol of "mere unaided virtue or right-mindedness." He dares to criticize Ahab's desire for vengeance, but he is as ineffectual as a sailor trying to halt a storm. Ahab once takes his advice about repairing some leaking oil casks, but when Starbuck, during a typhoon off Japan, suggests turning home, Ahab scorns him. Starbuck even thinks of killing or imprisoning Ahab while the captain is asleep, but he cannot. Having failed to dissuade Ahab from the pursuing of Moby Dick, Starbuck submits on the third day to Ahab's will, though feeling that in obeying Ahab he is disobeying God. When he makes one final effort to stop the doomed Ahab, the captain shouts to his boatmen, "Lower away!"

Stubb, the second mate, happy-go-lucky, indifferent to danger, good-humored, easy; he is a constant pipe-smoker and a fatalist.

Flask (King-Post), the young third mate, short, stout, ruddy. He relishes whaling and kills the monsters for the fun of it or as one might get rid of giant rats. In his shipboard actions, Flask is sometimes playful out of Ahab's sight but always abjectly respectful in his presence.

Fedallah, Ahab's tall, diabolical, white-turbaned Parsee servant. He is like the shadow of Ahab, or the two are like opposite sides of a single character. Ahab seems finally to become Fedallah, though retaining his own appearance. The Parsee prophesies that Ahab will have neither hearse nor coffin when he dies. Fedallah dies caught in a fouled harpoon line that is wrapped around Moby Dick.

Moby Dick, a giant albino sperm whale that has become a legend among whalers. It has often been attacked and has crippled or destroyed many men and boats. It is both a real whale and a symbol with many possible meanings. It may represent the universal spirit of evil, God the indestructible, or indifferent Nature, or perhaps it encompasses an ambiguity of meaning adaptable to the individual reader. Whatever its meaning, Moby Dick is one of the most memorable nonhuman characters in all fiction.

Pip, the bright, jolly, genial black cabin boy who, after falling from a boat during a whale chase, is abandoned in midocean by Stubb, who supposes that a following boat will pick him up. When finally taken aboard the *Pequod*, he has become demented from fright.

Tashtego, a Native American, Stubb's harpooner. As the *Pequod* sinks, he nails the flag still higher on the mast and drags a giant seabird, caught between the hammer and the mast, to a watery grave.

Daggoo, a giant African, Flask's harpooner.

Father Mapple, a former whaler, now the minister at the Whaleman's Chapel in New Bedford. He preaches a Calvinistic sermon on Job filled with seafaring terms.

Captain Peleg and **Captain Bildad,** fighting, materialistic Quakers, who are the principal owners of the *Pequod*.

Elijah, a madman who warns Ishmael and Queequeg against shipping with Captain Ahab.

Dough-Boy, the pale, bread-faced, dull-witted steward who, deathly afraid of Queequeg, Tashtego, and Daggoo, does his best to satisfy their enormous appetites.

Fleece, the ship's cook. At Stubb's request, he preaches a sermon to the voracious sharks and ends with a hope that their greed will kill them. He is disgusted also by Stubb's craving for whale meat.

Bulkington, the powerfully built, deeply tanned, sober-minded helmsman of the *Pequod*.

Perth, the ship's elderly blacksmith, who took up whaling after losing his home and family. He makes for Ahab the harpoon intended to be Moby Dick's death dart, which the captain baptizes in the devil's name.

Captain Gardiner, the skipper of the *Rachel* for whose lost son Captain Ahab refuses to search.

The Story

Ishmael was a schoolmaster who often felt the need to leave his quiet existence and go to sea. Much of his life had been spent as a sailor, and his voyages were a means for ridding himself of the restlessness that frequently seized him. One day, he decided that he would sign on a whaling ship, and packing his carpetbag, he left Manhattan and set out, bound for Cape Horn and the Pacific.

On his arrival in New Bedford, he went to the Spouter Inn near the waterfront to spend the night. There he found he could have a bed only if he consented to share it with a harpooner. His strange bedfellow frightened him when he entered the room, for Ishmael was certain that the stranger was a savage cannibal. After a few moments,

however, it became evident that the South Seas native, whose name was Queequeg, was a friendly person, for he presented Ishmael with an embalmed head and offered to share his fortune of thirty dollars. The two men quickly became friends and decided to sign on the same ship.

Eventually they signed on the *Pequod*, a whaler out of Nantucket, Ishmael as a sailor, Queequeg as a harpooner. Although several people seemed dubious about the success of a voyage on a vessel such as the *Pequod*, which was reported to be under so strange a man as Captain Ahab, neither Ishmael nor Queequeg had any intention of giving up their plans. They were, however, curious to see Captain Ahab.

For several days after the vessel had sailed, there was no sign of the captain, as he remained hidden in his cabin. The running of the ship was left to Starbuck and Stubb, two of the mates, and though Ishmael became friendly with them, he learned very little about Ahab. One day, as the ship was sailing southward, the captain strode out on deck. Ishmael was struck by his stern, relentless expression. In particular, he noticed that the captain had lost a leg and that instead of a wooden leg, he now wore one cut from the jawbone of a whale. A livid white scar ran down one side of his face and was lost beneath his collar, so that it seemed as though he were scarred from head to foot.

For several days, the ship continued south looking for the whaling schools. The sailors began to take turns on masthead watches to give the sign when a whale was sighted. Ahab appeared on deck and summoned all of his men around him. He pulled out an ounce gold piece, nailed it to the mast, and declared that the first man to sight the great white whale, known to the sailors as Moby Dick, would have the gold. Everyone expressed enthusiasm for the quest except Starbuck and Stubb, Starbuck especially deploring the madness with which Ahab had directed all of his energies to this one end. He told the captain that he was like a man possessed, for the white whale was a menace to those who would attempt to kill it. Ahab had lost his leg in his last encounter with Moby Dick; he might lose his life in the next meeting. The captain would not listen to the mate's warning. Liquor was brought out, and at the captain's orders, the crew drank to the destruction of Moby Dick.

Ahab, from what he knew of the last reported sighting of the whale, plotted a course for the ship that would bring it into the area where Moby Dick was most likely to be. Near the Cape of Good Hope, the ship came across a school of sperm whales, and the men busied themselves harpooning, stripping, melting, and storing as many as they were able to catch.

When they encountered another whaling vessel at sea, Captain Ahab asked for news about the white whale. The captain of the ship warned him not to attempt to chase Moby Dick, but it was clear that nothing could deflect Ahab from the course that he had chosen.

Another vessel stopped them, and the captain of the ship boarded the *Pequod* to buy some oil for his vessel. Captain Ahab again demanded news of the monster, but the captain knew nothing of the monster. As the captain was returning to his ship, he and his men spotted a school of six whales and started after them in their rowboats. While Starbuck and Stubb rallied their men into the *Pequod*'s boats, their rivals were already far ahead of them.

The two mates, however, urged their crew until they outstripped their rivals in the race, and Queequeg harpooned the largest whale.

Killing the whale was only the beginning of a long and arduous job. After the carcass was dragged to the side of the boat and lashed to it by ropes, the men descended the side and slashed off the blubber. Much of the body was usually eaten by sharks, who swarm around it snapping at the flesh of the whale and at each other. The head of the whale was removed and suspended several feet in the air, above the deck of the ship. After the blubber was cleaned, it was melted in tremendous try-pots and then stored in vats below deck.

The men were kept busy, but their excitement increased as their ship neared the Indian Ocean and the probable sporting grounds of the white whale. Before long, they crossed the path of an English whaling vessel, and Captain Ahab again demanded news of Moby Dick. In answer, the captain of the English ship held out his arm, which from the elbow down consisted of sperm whalebone. Ahab demanded that his boat be lowered at once, and he quickly boarded the deck of the other ship. The captain told him of his encounter and warned Captain Ahab that it was foolhardy to try to pursue Moby Dick. When he told Ahab where he had seen the white whale last, the captain of the *Pequod* waited for no civilities but returned to his own ship to order the course changed to carry him to Moby Dick's new feeding ground.

Starbuck tried to reason with the mad captain, to persuade him to give up this insane pursuit, but Ahab seized a rifle and in his fury ordered the mate out of his cabin.

Meanwhile, Queequeg had fallen ill with a fever. When it seemed almost certain that he would die, he requested that the carpenter make him a coffin in the shape of a canoe, according to the custom of his tribe. The coffin was then placed in the cabin with the sick man, but as yet there was no real need for it. Not long afterward, Queequeg recovered from his illness and rejoined his shipmates. He used his coffin as a sea chest and carved many strange designs upon it.

The sailors had been puzzled by the appearance early in the voyage of the Parsee, Fedallah. His relationship to the captain could not be determined, but that he was highly regarded was evident. Fedallah had prophesied that the captain would die only after he had seen two strange hearses for carrying the dead upon the sea, one not constructed by mortal hands and the other made of wood grown in the United States. He also said that the captain himself would have neither hearse nor coffin for his burial.

A terrible storm arose one night. Lightning struck the

masts so that all three flamed against the blackness of the night, and the men were frightened by this omen. It seemed to them that the hand of God was motioning them to turn from the course to which they had set themselves and return to their homes. Only Captain Ahab was undaunted by the sight. He planted himself at the foot of the mast and challenged the god of evil, which the fire symbolized for him. He vowed once again his determination to find and kill the white whale.

A few days later, a cry rang through the ship. Moby Dick had been spotted. The voice was Captain Ahab's, for none of the sailors, alert as they had been, had been able to sight him before their captain. Then boats were lowered and the chase began, with Captain Ahab's boat in the lead. As he was about to dash his harpoon into the mountain of white, the whale suddenly turned on the boat, dived under it, and split it into pieces. The men were thrown into the sea, and for some time the churning of the whale prevented rescue. At length, Ahab ordered the rescuers to ride into the whale and frighten it away, so he and his men might be picked up. The rest of that day was spent chasing the whale, but to no avail.

The second day, the men started out again. They caught up with the whale and buried three harpoons in its white flanks, but it so turned and churned that the lines became twisted, and the boats were pulled every which way, with no control over their direction. Two of them were splintered, and the men had to be hauled out of the sea, but Ahab's boat had not as yet been touched. Suddenly, Ahab's boat was lifted from the water and thrown high into the air. The captain and the men were quickly picked up, but Fedallah was nowhere to be found.

When the third day of the chase began, Moby Dick seemed tired, and the *Pequod*'s boat soon overtook it. Bound to the whale's back by the coils of rope from the harpoon poles, they saw the body of Fedallah. The first part of his prophecy had been fulfilled. Moby Dick, enraged by its pain, turned on the boats and splintered them. On the *Pequod*, Starbuck watched and turned the ship toward the whale in the hope of saving the captain and some of the crew. The infuriated monster swam directly into the *Pequod*, shattering the ship's timbers. Ahab, seeing the ship founder, cried out that the *Pequod*—made of wood grown in the United States—was the second hearse of Fedallah's prophecy. The third prophecy, Ahab's death by hemp, was fulfilled when rope from Ahab's harpoon coiled around his neck and snatched him from his boat. All except Ishmael perished. He was rescued by a passing ship after clinging for hours to Queequeg's canoe coffin, which had bobbed to the surface as the *Pequod* sank.

Critical Evaluation

Although his early adventure novels—*Typee* (1846), *Omoo* (1847), *Redburn* (1849), and *White Jacket* (1850)—brought Herman Melville a notable amount of popularity and financial success during his lifetime, it was not until nearly fifty years after his death—in the 1920's and 1930's—that he received universal critical recognition as one of the greatest nineteenth century American authors. Melville took part in the first great period of American literature—the period that included Edgar Allan Poe, Ralph Waldo Emerson, Nathaniel Hawthorne, Walt Whitman, and Henry David Thoreau. For complexity, originality, psychological penetration, breadth, and symbolic richness, Melville achieved his greatest artistic expression with the book he wrote when he was thirty, *Moby Dick: Or, The Whale.* Between the time of his birth in New York City and his return there to research and write his masterpiece, Melville had circled the globe of experience—working as a bank messenger, salesman, farmhand, schoolteacher (like his narrator, Ishmael), engineer and surveyor, bowling alley attendant, cabin boy, and whaler in the Pacific on the *Acushnet.* His involvement in a mutinous Pacific voyage, combined with J. N. Reynolds' accounts of a notorious whale called "Mocha Dick" (in *The Knickerbocker Magazine*, 1839), certainly influenced the creation of *Moby Dick.*

The intertangled themes of this mighty novel express the artistic genius of a mind that, according to Hawthorne, "could neither believe nor be comfortable in unbelief." Many of those themes are characteristic of American Romanticism: the "isolated self" and the pain of self-discovery, the insufficiency of conventional practical knowledge in the face of the "power of blackness," the demonic center of the world, the confrontation of evil and innocence, the fundamental imperfection of humanity coupled with Faustian heroism, the search for the ultimate truth, and the inadequacy of human perception. The conflict between faith and doubt was one of the major issues of the nineteenth century, and *Moby Dick*, as Eric Mottram pointed out, is part of "a huge exploration of the historical and psychological origins and development of self, society and the desire to create and destroy gods and heroes." *Moby Dick* is, moreover, a work that eludes classification, combining elements of the psychological and picaresque novel; sea story and allegory; the epic of "literal and metaphorical quest"; the satire of social and religious events; the emotional intensity of the lyric genre, both in diction and metaphor; Cervantian romance; Dantesque mysticism; Rabelaisian humor; Shakespearean drama (both tragedy and comedy), complete with stage directions; journalistic travel book; and scientific treatise on cetology. Melville was inspired by Hawthorne's example to give his story the unifying quality of a moral parable, although his own particular genius refused to allow that parable an unequivocal, single rendering. Both in style and theme, Melville was also influenced by Edmund Spenser, William Shakespeare, Dante, Miguel de Cervantes, Robert Burton, Sir Thomas Browne, Thomas Carlyle, and vastly miscellaneous reading (as witnessed by the two "Etymologies" and the marvelous "Extracts" that precede the text itself, items from the writer's notes and files that he could not bear to discard). It was because they did not know how to respond to its complexities of form and style that the book was "broiled in hell fire" by contemporary readers and critics. Even today, the rich mixture of its verbal texture—an almost euphuistic flamboyance balanced by dry, analytical expository prose—requires a correspondingly receptive range on the part of the reader.

Perhaps the most remarkable thing about the plot of the novel is that Moby Dick does not appear physically until after five hundred pages and is not even mentioned by name until nearly two hundred pages into the novel. Yet whether it be the knowledge of reality, an embodiment of the primitive forces of nature, the deep subconscious energies of humankind, fate or destiny inevitably victorious over illusory free will, or simply the unknown in experience, it is the question of what Moby Dick stands for that tantalizes the reader through the greater part of the novel. In many ways, the great white whale may be compared to Spenser's "blatant beast" (who, in *The Faerie Queene*, also represents the indeterminable elusive quarry, and also escapes at the end to continue haunting the world).

It is not surprising that *Moby Dick* is often considered to be "the American epic." The novel is replete with the elements characteristic of that genre: the piling up of classical, biblical, and historical allusions to provide innumerable parallels and tangents that have the effect of universalizing the scope of action; the narrator's strong sense of the fatefulness of the events that he recounts, and his corresponding awareness of his own singular importance as the narrator of momentous, otherwise unrecorded, events; Queequeg as Ishmael's "heroic companion"; the "folk" flavor provided by countless proverbial statements; the leisurely pace of the narrative, with its frequent digressions and parentheses; the epic confrontation of life and death on a suitably grand stage (the sea), with its consequences for the human city (the *Pequod*); the employment of microcosms to explicate the whole (for example, the painting in the Spouter Inn, the Nantucket pulpit, the crow's nest); epithetical characterization; a cyclic notion of time and events; an epic race of heroes, the Nantucket whalers, with their biblical and exotic names; the mystical power of objects such as Ahab's chair, the doubloon, or the *Pequod* itself; the alienated, sulking hero (Ahab); the use of lists to enhance the impression of an all-inclusive compass. Finally, *Moby Dick* shares the usually didactic purpose of the epic; on one level, its purpose is to teach the reader about whales; on another level, it is to inspire the reader to become a heroic whaler.

All this richness of purpose and presentation is somehow made enticing by Melville's masterly invention of his narrator. Ishmael immediately establishes a comfortable rapport with the reader in the unforgettable opening lines of the novel. He is both an objective observer of and a participant in the events recounted, both spectator and narrator. Yet he is much more than the conventional wanderer/witness. As a schoolmaster and sometime voyager, Ishmael combines book learning with firsthand experience, making him an informed observer and a convincing, moving reporter. Simply by surviving, he transcends the Byronic heroism of Ahab, as the wholesome overcomes the sinister.

MONT-SAINT-MICHEL AND CHARTRES

Type of work: An extended essay delving into architecture, history, and theology
Author: Henry Adams (1838-1918)
Locale: France
First published: 1913; privately printed, 1904

Adams uses a comparison of two medieval buildings, a Norman abbey and a Gothic cathedral, as a springboard to a scholarly and lively discussion of history, architecture, and religion.

On the surface, *Mont-Saint-Michel and Chartres* is the leisurely study of two great medieval buildings, one a Norman abbey, the other a Gothic cathedral. In the author's mind, however, the book had a far wider purpose. It set out to evoke the mood of a whole era in France, the eleventh to the thirteenth century, in all aspects: art, theology, philosophy, and music. Behind this wider purpose was still another. Henry Adams subtitled the book *A Study of Thirteenth Century Unity*, asking that it be read along with his autobiography, *The Education of Henry Adams* (1907), in which he discussed what he called "twentieth century multiplicity."

Adams was a historian, and his two books suggest both a theory of history and an attitude toward history. Western civilization had moved from unity to multiplicity, from a God-centered culture in which faith was the major force to an uncentered culture of competing ideologies and conflicting scientific theories. Adams' attitude was one of quiet regret, and his survey of medieval France is informed by an intellectual's brand of poignant yearning.

This emotional longing for the good order of a medieval culture is more than balanced, however, by the rigorous reasoning that Adams exercises. Translations of old French lyrics, incisive summaries of Thomist theories, detailed analyses of architectural subtleties—these are among Adams' self-imposed duties in the book. Scholars agree that Adams fulfilled his duties with grace and considerable accuracy.

His method is deceptively casual. In the preface, he announces the desired relationship between himself and the reader: An uncle is speaking to a niece, as guide for a summer's study tour of France. Immediately, however, one sees that the genial uncle has planned the course of study quite rigorously. It operates partly in the way that Adams' own mind tended to operate, by emphasizing opposites. Thus Adams concerns himself with contrasts: St. Michel and Chartres, the masculine temperament and the feminine, Norman culture and French culture. All this is within the major contrast of the thirteenth century

and the twentieth. Adams also uses the device of paradox. He insists that his purpose is not to teach. Yet the book is a joy only if the reader's intellect stands alert to follow Adam's careful exposition.

By 1904, when the book was privately printed, Adams had befriended several of the young American scholars who were awakening American universities to the importance of the medieval period. Adams himself had done sporadic writing and study in this realm years earlier. The book can be usefully thought of as an old man's legacy to a new generation, an unpretentious structure of affectionate scholarship, carefully built with some of Adams' finest prose.

Basically, the book contains three parts. The opening chapters deal with Mont-Saint-Michel on the Normandy coast. A transition chapter enables Adams to traverse the necessary route to the cathedral town of Chartres. Here six chapters examine the great cathedral itself, leading the reader to see its full symbolic meaning. The six concluding chapters then attend to history, poetry, theology, and philosophy—the medieval setting in which the jewel of the cathedral shines.

Adams' focus is medieval France, and here his book begins at the offshore sugar-loaf mountain of St. Michel, where the great abbey was built between 1020 and 1135. Instantly, the salient characteristics accumulate, for later contrast with those of Chartres: isolation, height, energy, modest size, utter simplicity, dedication to the archangel St. Michael (representing the Church Militant).

As Mont-Saint-Michel "was one of the most famous shrines of northern Europe," so in French song the *Chanson de Roland* (song of Roland) achieved unequalled eminence. How song and shrine complement each other is Adams' theme in chapter 2. Both represent the militant temper just before the Battle of Hastings; both exalt simplicity, directness, intensity; and both display a certain naïveté. This was France of the eleventh century.

Next it is the early thirteenth century that draws his attention, "the early and perfect period of Gothic art." On the Mount, this period is seen in the ruins of the ancillary buildings (the "Merveille"): great hall, refectory, library, cloisters. The tour of the Mount completed, Adams sums up the meaning of the entire complex, using his key word, "unity": "[I]t expressed the unity of Church and State, God and Man, Peace and War, Life and Death, Good and Bad; it solved the whole problem of the universe."

The uncle goes now to Chartres. As the fenestration of St. Michel's great hall looked ahead to the glass of Chartres, so the choir and façades of Coutances, along the way, prepare one for Chartres, as do Bayeux, Mantes, and Saint-Germain-des-Prés. For Adams, Chartres is the climactic shrine, the central symbol of its age and of his book.

One arrives at Chartres in chapter 5, with a distant glimpse of the two spires. Adams, perhaps at his most genial, explores the façade, especially noting the contrast between the magnificent "old" tower of the twelfth century and the "new" tower completed in 1517. This is a chapter of immense detail perfectly handled, detail that gradually rises into symbolism. Chartres is the church of the Virgin, "the greatest of all queens, but the most womanly of women." It is her palace, the utter opposite of St. Michel: feminine, elaborate, gracious, a building larger and later than the abbey. Minute examination of the portals and porches concludes chapter 5. Only now, anticipation sufficiently stimulated, does Adams permit entry.

Yet, with a bit of the avuncular humor that accounts for the charm of the book, Adams insists on another chapter of delay—"ten minutes to accustom our eyes to the light." This is a ruse. The interior dimness here symbolizes the dim past that Adams' literary art seeks to evoke. This chapter characterizes the Queen of Heaven, who demanded in her church space, light, convenience, and color.

Now follow a full hundred pages that function on several levels. There is narrative, a progressive tour through the church; description, an examination in detail of windows, apses, chapels; evocation, of an era and its art and faith; symbolism, the meaning of the Lady to the architects and worshipers; the meaning of the iconography; and the significance of the age itself. Adams here reaches the high point of his interest and his art, besides demonstrating considerable proficiency as a master of architectural detail.

Next, in his chapter on "The Three Queens," Adams turns to one of his favorite doctrines. He has been posing as one of the Virgin's faithful, so that it is no surprise to see him declaring the doctrine of woman's superiority. The twelfth century held this view, insists Adams: Chartres was built for the Virgin. Secular women of the century held power also. These were Eleanor, queen of France; Mary of Champagne; and Blanche, queen of France. They created the institution of courtly ("courteous") love.

The subject of courtly love leads Adams on to a light-hearted discussion of thirteenth century song, chiefly a synopsis of *Aucassin et Nicolette*, Adam de la Halle's *Le Jeu de Robin et Marion*, and the famous *Roman de la rose*. In his discussion of poetry and architecture, Adams says that in this period "Art leads always to the woman."

Specifically, art leads to the Virgin. Adams now takes up the miracles of the Virgin. They make up a special branch of literature and demonstrate that the sympathetic Virgin "was by essence illogical, unreasonable and feminine"—a pitying "power above law." Here again is the contrast between the Virgin and St. Michael.

Abruptly turning from the "feel" of the Middle Ages, achieved through study of its art, Adams attends to its mind. This subject is introduced by way of Peter Abelard, theologian and dialectician at Notre Dame de Paris. Adams constructs an abstract debate between Abelard and his teacher, William of Champeaux, to bring up the issue of unity versus multiplicity, which will concern him through the rest of the book. The problems of unity and multiplicity were several: How can God be One and yet be a Trinity? How can man in his diversity become one with God?

For the moment, however, the focus is on Abelard, the man who sought God by the force of pure reason. He is the direct opposite of the illogical Virgin and of the equally illogical mystic Francis of Assisi, whom one meets also. Adams thus continues his method of displaying the age by means of its opposites.

Whether such opposites as scholasticism and mysticism could be reconciled is part of Adams' problem in the last chapter. The great reconciler was Thomas Aquinas, whose all-encompassing *Summa theologiae* (1266-1273) Adams elaborately compares to the detail and grandeur of the Gothic cathedral. It was Aquinas who showed how to fuse God's trinity with His unity. Even more important, he showed how God, the One, permeates all being, creating the great multiplicity and diversity of humankind and the universe.

Adams sums up some of the paradoxes and polarities with which he has already dealt. One unusual thing about the Church of the Middle Ages was its multiplicity: It harbored mystics and rationalists, the holy Virgin and the abject sinners whom she pitied. Even greater, however, was its unity. Aquinas demonstrated how God and humanity, Creator and created, formed a grand unity that the age celebrated instinctively in art, architecture, and song. Here was the medieval worldview.

Adams' final point is comparison. The Thomist explanation of God's creativity can be compared usefully to a modern dynamo and its production of energy. The dynamo is the key symbol of *The Education of Henry Adams*, the sequel to *Mont-Saint-Michel and Chartres*. The true subject of the autobiography is the century in which multiplicity won out.

MOURNING BECOMES ELECTRA

Type of work: Drama
Author: Eugene O'Neill (1888-1953)
Type of plot: Romantic tragedy
Time of plot: Shortly after the Civil War
Locale: New England
First presented: 1931

In Mourning Becomes Electra, *a trilogy* (Homecoming, The Hunted, The Haunted) *loosely based on Aeschylus' Oresteia, O'Neill dramatizes his conviction that the Greek concept of fate could be replaced by the modern notion of psychological—especially Freudian—determination. The Mannons are driven to their self-destructive behavior by inner needs and compulsions that they can neither understand nor control. Such, O'Neill believed, was the material of contemporary tragedy.*

Principal Characters

Lavinia Mannon, the daughter of Christine and Ezra Mannon. Tall, flat-breasted, angular, and imperious in manner, Lavinia is fond of her father and fiercely jealous of her mother. While Ezra was fighting in the Civil War, Christine had been having an affair with Captain Adam Brant. An unconscious desire to have Adam for herself leads Lavinia to demand that Christine give up Brant or face a scandal that would ruin the family name. Unable to go on living with a husband whom she despises, Christine plots with Adam to poison Ezra when he returns. Ezra is murdered, and Lavinia discovers her mother's guilt. When her brother Orin returns, wounded and distraught, from the war, Lavinia tries to enlist his aid in avenging their father's death. Orin refuses until Lavinia proves Christine's guilt by a ruse. Blaming Adam for the murder, Orin goes to Adam's ship and shoots him. When Orin reveals to Christine what he has done, she kills herself. Orin and Lavinia then close the Mannon house and voyage to the South Seas. Symbolically liberated from the repressiveness of the New England Puritan tradition, Lavinia blossoms into a duplicate of her voluptuous mother. She plans to marry and start a new life. Yet Orin, hounded by his guilt and going mad, threatens to reveal the Mannons' misdeeds and tries to extort from Lavinia a lover's promise never to leave him. Lavinia agrees but ruthlessly drives Orin to suicide. Now convinced that the Mannon blood is tainted with evil, she resolves to punish herself for the Mannons' guilt. She orders the house shuttered and withdraws into it forever.

Christine Mannon, Lavinia's mother, tall, beautiful, and sensual. Fearing that she will be killed or arrested for her husband's murder, she makes plans with Adam Brant to flee the country and sail for a "happy island." Orin kills Brant. When Orin taunts her with his deed, Christine goes into the Mannon house and shoots herself.

Orin Mannon, Lavinia's brother, a young idealist who has been spiritually destroyed by the war. Progressively degenerating under the burden of his guilt, Orin conceives that Lavinia has taken the place of his beloved mother. Resolved that Lavinia shall never forget what they have done, Orin writes a history of the Mannon family and uses the manuscript to force Lavinia to promise never to leave him.

General Ezra Mannon, Christine's husband, a tall, big-boned, curt, and authoritative aristocrat. Cold, proud, and unconsciously cruel, Ezra always favored Lavinia over Christine and Orin. When he returns from the war, he tries desperately to make Christine love him, but it is too late. She reveals her infidelity, causing Ezra to have a heart attack. When he asks for medicine, she gives him poison.

Captain Adam Brant, Christine's lover, the captain of a clipper ship. The son of Ezra Mannon's uncle and a servant, Marie Brantôme, Adam has sworn to revenge himself on the Mannons, who had allowed his mother to die of poverty and neglect. His first approaches to the Mannon house were motivated by this desire for revenge, but he falls deeply in love with Christine.

Captain Peter Niles, of the U.S. Artillery, a neighbor, Lavinia's intended. Lavinia is forced by Orin to give up her plans to marry Peter and leave behind her the collective guilt of the Mannon family.

Hazel Niles, Peter's sister and Orin's fiancée. She persists in trying to help the erratic Orin lead a normal life. As she becomes aware that Lavinia and Orin share some deep secret, she fears Lavinia will ruin Peter's life and demands of Lavinia that she not marry him.

Seth Beckwith, the Mannons' gardener, a stooped but hearty old man of seventy-five. Seth serves as commentator and chorus throughout the play.

Amos Ames, his wife **Louisa,** and Louisa's cousin **Minnie,** townsfolk who act as the chorus in *Homecoming.*

Josiah Borden, the manager of the shipping company, his wife **Emma,** and **Everett Hills,** a Congregational minister, the chorus in *The Hunted.*

The Chantyman, a drunken sailor who carries on a suspense-building conversation with Adam Brant as Brant waits for Christine to join him on his ship.

Joe Silva, Ira Mackel, and **Abner Small,** the chorus in *The Haunted.*

Avahanni, a Polynesian native with whom Lavinia carried on a flirtation. Lavinia's falsely telling Orin that Avahanni had been her lover helps drive Orin to suicide.

The Story

The Civil War was over, and in their New England home Christine Mannon and her daughter Lavinia awaited the homecoming of old Ezra Mannon and his son, Orin. Lavinia, who adored her father, detested Christine because of Ezra's love for his wife. Christine, on the other hand, jealously guarded Orin's love because she hated her husband and her daughter. In this house of hidden hatred, Seth, the gardener, watched the old mansion and saw that Lavinia also despised Captain Brant, who was a steady caller at the Mannon home.

The Mannons, descended from old New England stock, had their family skeleton. Dave Mannon, Ezra's brother, had run off with a Native American woman named Marie Brantôme. Seth, seeing the antagonism between Lavinia and her mother, disclosed to Lavinia that Captain Brant was the son of Marie and Dave Mannon.

Embittered by her mother's illicit romance with Brant and jealous of Christine's hold on Ezra, Lavinia forced Christine to send her lover away. Christine was too powerful a woman, however, to succumb to her daughter's dominance. She urged the grudge-bearing Brant to send her some poison. It was common knowledge that Ezra had heart trouble, and Christine was planning to rid herself of the husband whom she hated so that she would be free to marry Brant. Lavinia cruelly reminded her mother that her favorite offspring was Orin, who was born while Ezra had been away during the Mexican War.

The family jealousies were obvious by the time that Ezra came home. Ezra, now a kind and just man, realized that Christine shrank from him while she attempted to pretend concern for his health. That night in their bedroom, Ezra and Christine quarreled over their failing marriage. Ezra had a heart attack, and when he gasped for his medicine, Christine gave him the poison instead. As he lay dying in Lavinia's arms, the helpless man feebly but incoherently accused Christine of guilt in his murder. Lavinia had no proof, but she did suspect her mother's part in Ezra's death.

Peter and Hazel Niles, cousins of the Mannons, came to the mansion after Ezra's death. Peter was a rejected suitor of Lavinia, and Hazel was in love with Orin. Lavinia spied upon her mother constantly. When Orin came home, the two women vied for his trust, Lavinia trying to create suspicion against her mother and Christine attempting to regain her son's close affection. Uncomfortable under her daughter's look of silent, sneering accusation, Christine finally realized that Lavinia had found the box of poison. While Hazel, Peter, and Christine tried to make a warm welcome for Orin, Lavinia hovered over the group like a specter of gloom and fatality. Able to get Orin alone before Lavinia could speak to him, Christine told her son about Lavinia's suspicions concerning Captain Brant and Ezra's death, and she tried to convince Orin that Lavinia's distraction over Ezra's death had warped her mind.

Orin, whose affection for his mother had made him dislike Ezra, believed Christine, but the returned soldier swore that, if he ever discovered that the story about Captain Brant were true, he would kill Brant. Desperately, Christine told Lavinia that Orin's trust had been won, that Lavinia need not try to take advantage of his credulity, but Lavinia stared at her mother in silent defiance. Under her daughter's cold stare, Christine's triumphant manner collapsed into a pathetic plea that Lavinia should not endanger Brant's life, for Orin had threatened to kill him.

Lavinia slyly hinted the truth to Orin, and his old childhood trust in his sister led him to believe her story in part—unwillingly, however, for he was still influenced by love for his mother. Lavinia hinted that Christine might run to Brant at the first opportunity. Orin agreed to wait for proof, and if sufficient proof were offered, then to kill Brant. Lavinia instructed Orin to maintain his pretense that he believed her to be mad.

Shortly after Ezra's funeral, Christine did go to Brant. Orin and Lavinia had pretended to be paying a call on a nearby estate, but they followed their mother to Brant's ship, where they overheard the lovers planning to run off together. Although Orin was consumed with jealous hatred of Brant, Lavinia restrained him from impulsive action. When Christine had gone, Orin went into the cabin and shot Brant. Then the brother and sister rifled the ship's cabin and Brant's pockets to make the death appear to have been a robbery and murder.

Orin and Lavinia returned to the Mannon mansion and told Christine what they had done. At the sight of his mother's grief, Orin fell to his knees, pleading with her to forgive him and to give him her love. Fearing that he had lost his mother's affection, the bewildered boy rushed from the room, but Lavinia faced her mother victoriously. Christine went into the house and shot herself. Orin, in a frenzy of grief, accused himself of his mother's murder.

Lavinia took her brother on a long sea trip to help him overcome his feeling of guilt. When they returned, Orin was completely under Lavinia's control, reciting in toneless speech the fact that Christine had been an adulteress and a murderess and that Orin had saved his mother from public hanging. He was changed in appearance and spirit; it was plain that strange thoughts of grief and guilt preyed on his mind. During the trip, Lavinia had grown to look and behave like Christine.

Lavinia was now able to accept Peter's love, but when Orin saw his sister in Peter's embrace, he became angered for a brief moment before he congratulated them.

When Orin became engaged to Hazel, Lavinia was afraid to leave Orin alone with the woman for fear that he would say too much about the past.

Orin began to write a family history, urged by a remorseful desire to leave a record of the family crimes. Becoming jealous of Lavinia's engagement to Peter, he threatened to expose her if she married him. Orin kept hinting to Lavinia that she was planning to poison him as Christine had poisoned the man who held her in bondage. Finally, driven to distraction by Orin's morbid possessive attitude toward her and by his incessant reminding of their guilt, Lavinia suggested to her crazed brother that he kill himself. As Peter held Lavinia in his arms, Orin went to the library to clean his pistol. His death was assumed to have been an accident.

Hazel suspected some vile and sinister fact hidden in Orin's accidental death. She went to Lavinia and pleaded with her not to ruin Peter by marrying him, but Lavinia denied that there was any reason to put off the marriage. While she spoke, however, Lavinia realized that the dead Mannons would always rule her life. The others had been cowards and had died. She would live. She sent Peter away and then ordered Seth the gardener to board up the windows of the mansion. Alone, the last surviving Mannon, Lavinia entered the old house to spend the rest of her life with the dead.

Critical Evaluation

Eugene O'Neill, the first American dramatist to win international recognition, was awarded the Nobel Prize in Literature in 1936. One of the most ambitious playwrights since Aeschylus and William Shakespeare, he introduced the European movements of realism, naturalism, and expressionism to the American stage as devices to express his comprehensive interest in all of life. His plays often make stringent demands on the actors and audience: the long monologues of *Strange Interlude* (1928) and *The Iceman Cometh* (1946), the unrelenting despair of *Long Day's Journey into Night* (1956), and the five-hour production length of *Mourning Becomes Electra.*

O'Neill, of Irish Catholic stock, literally grew up in the theater. He was born in a New York hotel while his father, the famous actor James O'Neill, was starring in *The Count of Monte Cristo.* His mother, suffering from the pains of Eugene's birth, began taking morphine and soon became an addict. Many of O'Neill's plays deal with the intense love-hate relationships and tensions of his mother, father, brother, and himself. The most in-

tensive and explicit of these is the powerful *Long Day's Journey into Night*, published posthumously. Before becoming a playwright, he briefly attended Princeton University, worked as a sailor, and had a bout with tuberculosis. While in the sanatorium, he decided to become a playwright.

O'Neill's plays are bound together by consistent concerns. Embedded in them the reader will find a rejection of Victorian gentility, of materialism and opportunism, and of Puritan beliefs. O'Neill shared the postwar disillusionment with others of his generation who discovered that the Great War to end all wars had been a death trap for young men. His plays exhibit a keen sense of loss of the individual's relationship with family, nation, society's values, nature, and God. Science, materialism, and religion all fail to give O'Neill's protagonists a satisfying meaning for life, or comfort from the fear of death. Still, they engage in often heroic struggles against total alienation. Many of O'Neill's strongest plays center on the question of whether illusions are, after all, the only thing that make reality bearable. He also consistently incorporated popular Freudian psychology in an attempt to project the subconscious levels of his characters. *Mourning Becomes Electra*, a trilogy consisting of *Homecoming*, *The Hunted*, and *The Haunted*, although set at the end of the American Civil War, is an adaptation of the greatest of Aeschylus' trilogies, the *Oresteia*.

Mourning Becomes Electra illustrates the struggle between the life force and death, in which attempts to express natural sensual desires and love of others or even of life itself are overcome by the many forms of death: repression derived from the Puritan religion, death-in-life engendered by society's values, isolation, war, and actual physical death. This struggle is present not only in the plot structure, in which each play culminates in actual death, but also in the setting, the actors' faces, stances, and costumes, and repetitive refrains. Darkness, associated with death, pervades the plays: *Homecoming*, for example, begins with the sunset, moves into twilight, and ends in the dark of night; *The Hunted* takes place during night; *The Haunted* spans two evenings and a late afternoon, indicating the inevitable coming of night, darkness, and death as Lavinia retreats to rejoin the host of dead Mannons.

The Mannon house itself, seen by the audience at the beginning of each play, stands amid the beauty and abundance of nature. It has a white Greek temple portico which, O'Neill directs, should resemble "an incongruous white mask fixed on the house to hide its somber grey ugliness." That the house is an ironic inversion of the affirmation and love of life associated with the Greeks is soon obvious. Christine thinks of the house as a tomb of cold gray stone, and even Ezra compares it to a "white meeting house" of the Puritans, a temple dedicated to duty, to denial of the beauty of life and love—to death. The house itself is not only alienated from nature but also isolated from the community, built on the foundations of pride and hatred and Puritan beliefs. Its cold façade and isolation symbolize the family that lives within it, whose name indicates their spiritual relationship to Satan's chief helper, Mammon. The "curse" of this house stems from the effects of materialism, Puritanism, alienation, and repression of all that is natural—a death-in-life.

The stiff, unnatural bearing of the Mannons and the look of their faces are further evidence that the family is dead in the midst of life. Even the townspeople comment on the Mannons' "secret look." Their dead, masklike faces—in portraits of Orin and Ezra, on Christine's face when she is about to commit suicide, on Lavinia's face after Orin's death—all indicate the Mannons' denial of life, their repression of life, their repression of their sensual natures, and their refusal or inability to communicate with others. The dark costumes of all the family also indicate the hold that death has on them and accentuates the green satin worn first by Christine and later by Lavinia as they struggle to break out of their tomb and reach life.

The instinct of love and life survives strongest in the women, but even they are defeated. The search for pure love through a mother-son relationship is futile, for the Oedipal complex leads beyond the bounds of a pure relationship, as Orin finally realizes. Family love, too, fails, as is evident in the relationships between Christine and Lavinia and Ezra and Orin. Even love between men and women fails to triumph over the alienation and loneliness of the Mannon world, as in the cases of Christine and Ezra and Lavinia and Peter.

The leitmotif of the South Sea islands, symbols of escape from the death cycle of heredity and environment of New England society, is present throughout the three plays. The islands represent a return to nature, a hope of belonging in an environment far removed from Puritan guilt and materialism. Brant has been to these islands, Ezra wishes for one, Orin dreams of being on one with Christine, Christine wants to go to an island, and Orin and Lavinia do finally travel to the islands. They come to realize, however, that they cannot become a permanent part of the island culture; they must return to the society to which they belong by birth and upbringing. As symbols of escape, the islands, too, finally fail.

The Mannons try all avenues of escape from their deathly isolation. David Mannon attempted to escape with Marie Brantôme but finally turned to drinking and suicide. Ezra "escaped" through concentrating on his business and then on the business of death—war—before he realized the trap of death. Christine focuses her attempts to escape first on her son and then on Brant. Orin tries to escape through his mother's love, then through Hazel's, and finally, in desperation, suggests an incestuous relationship with Lavinia. Lavinia does not see the dimensions of the death trap and does not desire escape until her trip to the islands, where she experiences the abundance of guilt-free life. After her return, she is willing to let Orin die, just as Christine let Ezra die, in order to be free to love and live. Then, too late, she feels the curse of the guilt associated with the Puritan beliefs and realizes that she cannot escape. Lavinia learns that Orin was right: Killers kill part of themselves each time they kill, until finally nothing alive is left in them. She underscores this in her last conversation with Peter, remarking, "Always the dead between [us]. . . . The dead are too strong."

Death itself is the only real escape for the alienated, guilt-ridden Mannons.

Compared to its source, Aeschylus' *Oresteia*; O'Neill's themes and characterization seem shallow. Christine, who goads Ezra into a heart attack because of her hatred of his attitude toward their sexual relationship and her love of Brant, is no match for Clytemnestra, who revenges the death of her daughter, her insulted pride, and hatred of Agamemnon with a bloody knife. The weak, neurotic Orin is likewise a lesser character than Orestes, whose strong speech of triumphant justice over his mother's slain body breaks only with his horrified vision of the Furies. Yet Ezra is more human than Agamemnon, and Lavinia's complexities far outstrip Electra's: Her recognition and acceptance of her fate is in the noble tradition of the tragic hero.

The radical difference in the intentions of the two playwrights accounts for some of these disparities. Aeschylus, whose major themes are concerned with the victory of humanity's and the gods' laws, concludes his trilogy with the establishment of justice on earth and the reconciliation of Orestes with society and the gods, affirming that good has come out of evil, order from chaos, and wisdom from suffering. In *Mourning Becomes Electra*, however, the curse is not lifted but is confirmed at the end, as Lavinia gives up her futile struggle against the psychological effects of puritanical guilt. O'Neill's major concerns are with the detrimental effects of materialism; the alienation of human beings from meaningful relationships with one another, nature, and God; the heritage of puritanical beliefs; and the psychological "furies" that drive all people. Although the psychological analysis of these representative members of American society may be oversimplified occasionally, in the hands of a good director and cast *Mourning Becomes Electra* is one of the few works by an American dramatist that can truly be said to evoke the tragic emotions of pity, fear, and perhaps even awe in a modern audience.

THE MOVIEGOER

Type of work: Novel
Author: Walker Percy (1916-1990)
Type of plot: Social commentary
Time of plot: Early 1960's
Locale: New Orleans
First published: 1961

Probably the most successful of Percy's novels, the main attraction of The Moviegoer *is its protagonist, an ordinary but unconventional character who brilliantly captures the search for meaning in modern American urban life.*

Principal Characters

John Bickerson (Binx) Bolling, an aristocratic New Orleanian stockbroker facing his thirtieth birthday and a decision about what to do with his life, whether to fall into what he terms the "despair" of "everydayness" of the unexamined life or whether to engage in a "search" for meaning and purpose. Binx's Aunt Emily Cutrer pushes him to enter medical school in the tradition established by his father, perhaps to do medical research; in fact, Binx has no interest in any profession except that of a rather mystical urban philosopher, a searcher for truth trying to find a way to live in the modern American landscape. Binx escapes into suburban life and dates his lower-middle-class secretaries, but he eventually marries his cousin Kate and accepts a life more conventionally appropriate for his station.

Aunt Emily Cutrer, Binx's great-aunt, who brought him up after his father died. Aunt "Em" represents a passing aristocratic tradition in New Orleans and the old South, and thus tries to make Binx live up to the ideals that she imagines he shares with her.

Sharon Kincaid, Binx's secretary from Eufala, Alabama, a large-boned and good-humored country girl whom Binx takes "spinning along" the Gulf Coast in his sports car. Sharon is one of a series of normal and conventional "girls" Binx has hired as secretaries and then dated.

Mrs. Bolling Smith, Binx's mother. She has remarried after the death of Binx's natural father and lives a determinedly conventional middle-class life as a South Louisiana housewife and mother.

Lonnie Smith, Binx's half brother, afflicted with a crippling disease. He is on a search of his own and shares a secret empathy with Binx.

The Story

Binx Bolling receives a note from his Aunt Emily asking him to lunch, a regular command performance for him. He tells the reader of his conventional life in Gentilly as a very ordinary young stockbroker but also of his love for films, which transform the "everydayness" of life into moments freighted with meaning. Binx explains his "search," an incompletely defined and somewhat mystical attempt to find meaning—and perhaps God—and to avoid "despair," defined in an opening quote by Søren Kierkegaard as being "unaware of despair." This conundrum—that despair entails unawareness of itself—is exemplified by a number of characters Binx runs across: a young honeymooning couple whose anomie is temporarily relieved by a chance meeting with film star William

Holden; Eddie Lovell, an old friend; and Mercer, Aunt Emily's butler. Binx has lunch with his aunt, his uncle Jules, his cousin Kate, and her fiancé, Walter Wade, Binx's college chum. None except Kate shares Binx's sense of wonder at life. After lunch, Binx tries to persuade the reclusive Kate to participate more in social activities and then has a discussion with Aunt Emily, who wishes him to become a medical researcher or to find some direction now that he is almost thirty. Kate and Binx later go to a Mardi Gras parade and then to see Richard Widmark's *Panic in the Streets* (1950), a film set in New Orleans.

Binx next is seen at work in his office in the Gentilly suburbs, helped by his beautiful new secretary, Sharon Kincaid. Binx plots about how to get closer to Sharon and goes to another film with Kate, who comes to visit him a few days later while suffering from one of her regular nervous breakdowns. Binx traps Sharon into driving with him to the beach on Ship Island, off the Mississippi Gulf Coast. A minor car wreck in Binx's sports car leads to Sharon seeing Binx's scar from the Korean War, a wound that caused the shattering of "everydayness" and Binx's search and sense of wonder. Sharon is impressed and becomes very friendly, and on the way home, Binx takes her to his mother's fishing camp at Bayou des Allemands. Unexpectedly, Binx's mother, stepfather, and all his stepbrothers and stepsisters are there, and he and Sharon stay the night, taking his crippled half brother Lonnie to see the film *Fort Dobbs* (1958) at the drive-in.

When Binx finally returns to New Orleans, he meets Sam Yerger, a family friend, who tells him Kate may have attempted suicide. Kate persuades Binx to take her with him to Chicago on a business trip. Binx and Kate leave on the train and make love in her compartment. In Chicago, they visit Harold Graebner, a wartime friend of Binx who saved Binx's life. They see the film *The Young Philadelphians* (1959), and Binx receives a phone call from Aunt Emily, who is furious that he took the unstable Kate with him. Binx and Kate take the bus home to New Orleans, where his aunt accuses him of betraying the aristocratic values of their family. Later, Binx and Kate decide to marry, with Binx taking responsibility for deciding about Kate's most trivial actions. He is reconciled with his aunt and attends medical school. Uncle Jules dies of a heart attack, and Binx's half brother Lonnie dies of complications from his illness. Binx plays the role of good stepbrother to his family and dutiful husband to Kate, who is unable to act without his direction. His search seems to be at an end.

Critical Evaluation

The Moviegoer is both a riveting success and somewhat of a disappointment. The successful elements include the wonderfully drawn figure of Binx Bolling and the precise and persuasively individualized supporting characters, the keen accuracy of the portrait of the New Orleans and South Louisiana setting, and the resonances in the reader's recognition of the true theme of the book. The perception of dislocation and of the absurd about which Binx speaks so calmly is the territory of Jean-Paul Sartre and Albert Camus. The sense of strangeness in the ordinary, of lack of emotional affect, has seldom been rendered more persuasively than in Percy's elegant and balanced prose. The disappointment derives from Binx's failure to provide final answers to the central questions that he raises.

Binx is surely one of the great first-person narrators in modern fiction. He brings readers into his world and introduces them to his philosophical system, one that shocks with the recognition of its place in modernist thinking: despair as the unawareness of being despair; the certification of banal reality provided by film, and by implication, all art, including *The Moviegoer* itself; Binx's wonder at the miracle of life and self-awareness, the miracle of consciousness itself; and Binx's winning combination of enthusiastic carnality and spirituality.

Binx is a seeker of truth in a venerable American literary tradition, but one who is, paradoxically, a creature of setting and yet uniquely individual. He inspires the reader to believe that the search for meaning, for the ultimate, can take place with the Sharons of the world at one's side, in the bland Gentilly suburbs, in fishing camps, and at drive-ins. Society is sunk in "everydayness," and repeated exposures to this environment renders life banal. Some people—the vast majority, according to Binx—embrace this banality, labeling all that they see around them with minimal examination and dismissing it from their thoughts. Binx's wonder at life, begun when he lay wounded in the Korean War, offers an alternative to everydayness, just as films rescue the dull and ordinary by "certifying" them as special and worthy of attention. When William Holden walks through the French Quarter, for example, tourists passing by feel transformed by his presence into something special and valuable. Binx's search for this transformation by maintaining awareness and by, amusingly, dating his provocative young secretaries provides the link between these various themes.

The mixed lot of characters that surrounds Binx ranges from the completely conventional (Sharon) to the bizarrely neurotic (Kate), but are a convincing array of people who might enter the life of any seeker. Aunt Emily and her husband, Jules, as well as an assortment of older wealthy New Orleanians of Binx's social and business acquaintance, suffer from the "malaise" of everydayness in the most extreme form, exacerbated by the weight of their aristocratic past and their rigid codes of conduct. In effect, they fail to perceive the phenomena all around them; they live in the world of ideas that they expect to see. Only Kate escapes this fate, and perhaps at the cost of a suicidal neuroticism. The conventional middle-class characters among whom Binx lives have no awareness at all. Only Lonnie Smith, Binx's half brother, shares Binx's search, and his spirituality seems to come from the crippling disease that kills him.

Yet Binx ultimately lets the reader down, and not simply because Binx the character seems to end his own search at the close of the book, choosing to take responsibility for Kate and to live for others rather than selfishly finding his own meaning. Rather, the concept itself remains tantalizingly incomplete, in the same way that "certification" and "wonder" seem labels as opposed to fully realized philosophies. Some commentators have found a Kierkegaardian search for meaning on the part of Binx through the aesthetic, ethical, and religious realms. Yet, while the philosophical underpinnings are undeni-

ably present, the novel is never explicit about the terms of the "search." One catches an all-too-brief glimpse of Binx's universe but not the instruction in truth-seeking for which Binx makes one yearn. Percy gives readers all the right questions but then leaves them without answers.

It may be churlish to castigate Percy and *The Moviegoer* for not giving the reader the solution to the riddle of life, but that is indeed its subject matter. It is an ambitious project in the confines of a fairly short, very readable book, and for that many readers are grateful. Binx Bolling and Kate are unforgettable characters, and the portrait of a changing New Orleans stands on its own virtues.

MURDER IN THE CATHEDRAL

Type of work: Drama
Author: T. S. Eliot (1888-1965)
Type of plot: Religious chronicle
Time of plot: 1170
Locale: Canterbury, England
First presented: 1935

In this liturgical drama dealing with the assassination of Thomas Becket, Eliot shows the politics, both temporal and churchly, that lay behind the murder. He presents the archbishop as a man torn between acting and suffering. Most of the play is in poetic form, with effective expression by the chorus.

Principal Characters

Thomas Becket, the archbishop of Canterbury. Having just returned from France, where he has gained the support of the pope in his attempt to achieve both temporal and spiritual power in England, he finds a mixed reaction among the people. Although some support him, others would gladly see him dead. He is faced with a dilemma that leaves him no alternative but to sin against his faith. After his murder, he achieves martyrdom and sainthood, which his accusers say he was seeking all along.

Three Priests of the Cathedral, who fear the outcome of Becket's return. They express the pessimism felt by everyone.

The First Tempter, who offers worldly pleasure and success.

The Second Tempter, who offers temporal power through negation of spiritual authority.

The Third Tempter, who offers the support of a faction wishing to overthrow the throne.

The Fourth Tempter, who offers martyrdom and eternal glory. Becket denies all the tempters.

Reginald Fitz Urse, William de Traci, Hugh de Morville, and **Richard Brito,** the knights who murder Becket. They defend their action on the grounds that they will not benefit from their deed, that Becket had refused to acknowledge the king's supremacy, and that he was egotistical to the point of insanity.

The women of Canterbury, who act as the chorus of classical drama.

The Story

The women of Canterbury had been drawn to the cathedral. Instinctively, they knew that they had been drawn there by danger; there was no safety anywhere. They had to come to bear witness. Archbishop Thomas Becket had been gone seven years. He had always been kind to his people, but he really should not return. During the periods when the king and the barons ruled alternately, the poor had suffered all kinds of oppression. Like common people everywhere, the women had tried to keep their households in order and to escape the notice of the various rulers. Now they could only wait and witness.

The priests of the cathedral were well aware of the coming struggle for power. The archbishop had been intriguing in France, where he had enlisted the aid of the pope. Henry of Anjou was a stubborn king, however, and these struggles for power would hurt someone. The priests knew that the strong rule by force, the weak by caprice; the only law was to seize power and hold it.

A herald announced to them that the archbishop was nearing the city. They were to prepare at once for his coming. With great interest, they asked if there would be peace or war, whether the archbishop and the king had been reconciled. The herald was of the opinion that there had been only a hasty compromise. He did not know that, when the archbishop had parted from the king, the prelate had said that King Henry would not see him again in this life.

After the herald left, one priest expressed the pessimism felt by all. When Thomas Becket was chancellor and in temporal power, he had been flattered and fawned on by courtiers, but even then he had felt insecure. It would be better if the king were stronger or if Thomas were weaker. For a time, however, they dispelled their fears; Thomas was returning to lead them. The women thought that the archbishop should return to France. He would still be their spiritual leader, and in France he would be safe. As the priests started to drive out the babbling women, the archbishop arrived and bade them remain.

Thomas Becket told his priests of the difficulties that he had encountered, for rebellious bishops and the barons had sworn to have his head. They had sent spies to him and intercepted his letters. At Sandwich, he had barely escaped with his life. His enemies were waiting to pounce.

The first tempter came to talk with Thomas. When he was chancellor, Thomas had known worldly pleasure and worldly success. Many had been his friends, and at that time he knew how to let friendship oversway principles. To escape his present hard fate, he needed only to relax his severity and dignity, to be friendly, to overlook disagreeable principles. Thomas had the strength to give the tempter a strong refusal.

The second tempter reminded Thomas of his temporal power as chancellor. He could be chancellor again and have lasting power. It was well known that the king only commanded, while the chancellor ruled, and ruled richly. Power was a present attribute; holiness was more useful after death. Real power had to be purchased by wise submission, and his present spiritual authority led only to death. Thomas asked about rebellious bishops whom he had excommunicated and barons whose privileges he had curtailed. The tempter was confident that these dissidents would come to heel if Thomas were chancellor with the king's power behind him. Again Thomas had the strength to say no.

The third tempter was easier to deal with. He represented a clique intent on overthrowing the throne. If Thomas would lead them, they could make the power of the Church supreme. No more would both the barons and the bishops be ruled by a king. Thomas declined the offer to lead the malcontents.

The fourth tempter was unexpected. He showed Thomas how he could have eternal glory. As plain archbishop, the time would come when people would neither respect nor hate him; he would become a fact of history. So it was with temporal power, too: King succeeds king as the wheel of time turns. Shrines are pillaged and thrones totter. Yet, if Thomas would only continue in his present course, he would become a martyr and a saint, to dwell forevermore in the presence of God. Thus the archbishop's dilemma came to him. No matter if he acted or suffered, he would sin against his religion.

Early on Christmas morning, Thomas preached a sermon on peace. Christ left humanity his peace, but not peace as the world thinks of it. Spiritual peace did not necessarily mean England at peace with other countries or the barons at peace with the king.

After Christmas had passed, four knights came to Canterbury on urgent business. Refusing all hospitality, they began to state charges against Thomas, saying that he owed all of his influence to the king. Thomas, they argued, had been ignobly born, and his eminence was attributable solely to King Henry's favor. The knights tried to attack Thomas, but the priests and attendants intervened.

The charges were publicly amplified. Thomas had gone to France to stir up trouble in the dominion and to intrigue with the king of France and the pope. Yet, in his charity, King Henry had permitted Thomas to return to his see. Thomas had repaid that charity by excommunicating the bishops who had crowned the young prince; hence the legality of the coronation was in doubt. The knights then pronounced his sentence: He and his retinue must leave English soil.

Thomas answered firmly. In France, he had been a beggar of foreign charity, and he would never leave England again. He had no dislike for the prince; rather, he had only carried out the pope's orders in excommunicating the bishops. These words availed little. In the cathedral proper, the knights fell on Thomas Becket and slew him.

In turn, the knights gave their reasons for the slaying. It looked like four against one, and the English believed in fair play. Before deciding, however, the people should know the whole story. First, the four knights would not benefit from the murder. The king, for reasons of state, would deplore the incident, and the knights would at least be banished. In addition, it was hard for a good churchgoer to kill an archbishop.

Second, Thomas had been an able chancellor. The king had hoped, in elevating him to the archbishopric, to unite temporal and spiritual rule and to bring order to a troubled kingdom. Yet, as soon as Thomas was elevated, he became more priestly than the priests and refused to follow the king's orders.

Third, he had become an egotistical madman. There was evidence that, before leaving France, he had clearly prophesied his death in England. He was determined to suffer a martyr's fate. In the face of this provocation, the people must conclude that Thomas had committed suicide while of unsound mind.

After the knights left, the priests and populace mourned. Their only solace was that, so long as individuals will die for faith, the Church will be supreme.

Critical Evaluation

Unlike many lesser artists who never seem to change their view of the world or the development of their art, T. S. Eliot grew throughout his career. In his youth, he was primarily a satirist, mocking the conventions of society in poems such as "The Love Song of J. Alfred Prufrock" or "Portrait of a Lady." Later he became a mosaic artist of exquisite sensibility as, fragment by fragment, he pieced together his damning portrait of post-World War I civilization in *The Waste Land* (1922). Still later, finding his ethical pessimism essentially sterile, he climaxed his long interest in philosophy, theology, literary history, and government by becoming a royalist in politics, a classicist in literature, and an Anglo-Catholic in religion. Born in the United States and educated at Harvard University, Eliot early settled in England, soon becoming more English than the English.

Throughout his early career, he had developed more than a casual interest in the play, not merely as an art form in and of itself, but in the theater as a means of instruction. His early fragments such as *Sweeney Agonistes* (1932) tantalize by their incompleteness, but *Murder in the Cathedral* demonstrates Eliot's mastery of the classic tragic form.

In this remarkably effective play, Eliot links devices derived from the Greeks—the chorus, static action, and Aristotelian purgation—with his profound commitment to the Anglo-Catholic liturgy. Thus *Murder in the Cathedral* in many ways resembles a medieval morality play whose purpose is to enlighten as well as to entertain.

Yet *Murder in the Cathedral* is never merely morally instructive. It rises above didacticism because Archbishop Thomas Becket's internal anguish is made extremely personal by its modernity and timeliness. Becket's assassination becomes more real by the contemporary events that it inevitably recalls and by the political and temporal events that it evokes.

Eliot firmly believed that, to be most effective, contemporary drama had to be written in poetry, a belief he shared with William Butler Yeats, his Irish contemporary. Eliot's poetry is moving without being ostentatiously poetic because it reaches the audience on a level that Eliot himself termed "the auditory imagination." Responding from the unconscious, the spectators are drawn deeply into the drama and begin to share Becket's internal agonies by participating in the almost primitive rhythmic manipulations of Eliot's deceptively simple verse.

What makes Eliot's play so timely is that the four allurements offered to Thomas by the tempters are precisely the same ones that the modern audience itself has also faced, whether consciously or unconsciously: worldly pleasure, temporal power, spiritual power, and, finally and most subtly, eternal glory. Thomas refutes all of them quite directly but is entranced for a time by the fourth tempter, who indicates that, if Thomas proceeds on his present course, he may be deliberately courting martyrdom in order to achieve eternal happiness with God. Eventually, Thomas counters the argument with one of the most effective lines in the play: "The last temptation and the greatest treason/ Is to do the right deed for the wrong reason."

Thus Thomas' certainty of the spiritual correctness of his own actions mirrors that of members of the audience, who slowly become aware of their own culpability in acting correctly for insufficient reason in any matter, or even of acting selfishly for a good end. The involvement of the audience so profoundly is another tribute to Eliot's genius.

Eliot works on still another level—that of the conflict of powers, each perhaps justified in its own way. Thomas recognizes that some things are Caesar's, and that the king and the temporal power that he represents have some justification. The king, moreover, had once been Thomas' closest friend and had, in fact, appointed him archbishop. What are the debts to the temporal realm, to friendship, to gratitude? Thomas ponders. Yet, at the same time, he continues to maintain the primacy of the spiritual order over the temporal. If some things are Caesar's, they are Caesar's only because God permitted them to be.

Murder in the Cathedral was first staged in Canterbury Cathedral, that magnificent Gothic antiquity providing a most striking setting. Still often produced in a church edifice, the play gains an immediacy through the verisimilitude achieved by the combination of setting, liturgy, verse, and chorus, as well as the tension created by the opposing forces at work in the play. Eliot, however, in spite of Thomas' brilliant Christmas sermon that opens the second act, does not preach. It is not simply a case of Good versus Evil. Rather, the conflict is one of mystiques, each with a well-developed rationale. The choice appears to be between alternatives, not opposites. Thomas, who fears that he may be a victim of the sin of pride, must nevertheless proceed, to his damnation or to his salvation.

History records that the shrine of St. Thomas Becket at Canterbury was among the most famous of medieval objects of devotion and pilgrimage, and Eliot is always conscious of history. Thus even the justifications of the knights who slew Thomas deserve serious attention, particularly in the modern era. In addition, while the last of the knights attempts to maintain that Thomas' assassination should be viewed as suicide while of unsound mind, more than one modern historical critic has wondered if Thomas were not "hell-bent" on heaven, a question that Thomas himself ponders. If in the end one rejects the justifications of the knights, then one must ask how much of their own conscious rationalizations may be found in one's own unconscious motivations.

Murder in the Cathedral is certainly not theoretical drama, and the themes of faith, justification, power, and internal and external conflict that it celebrates are often themes that recur in the modern world. Thus Eliot has created a timeless work that looks forward to his own profoundly religious and mystical poems known as the *Four Quartets* (1943) and to his later modern treatments of very similar themes in plays such as *The Cocktail Party* (1949) and *The Confidential Clerk* (1953). All of Eliot's later poetry and plays, however, must be read with *Murder in the Cathedral* in mind, for it represents a pivotal achievement in his distinguished career.

MUTINY ON THE BOUNTY

Type of work: Novel
Authors: Charles Nordhoff (1887-1947) and James Norman Hall (1887-1951)
Type of plot: Adventure romance
Time of plot: Late eighteenth century
Locale: South Pacific and Tahiti
First published: 1932

Written in the form of a novel and completely romantic in temper, Mutiny on the Bounty *is a great story of adventure based on actual fact: the voyage of HMS* Bounty, *the mutiny aboard the ship, the exploit of Captain Bligh in piloting a small boat across thirty-six hundred miles of open sea, the trial of some of the mutineers, and the final refuge of others on bleak Pitcairn Island. The authors' free arrangement of their material is designed to give factual narrative the drama and romantic atmosphere of fiction.*

Principal Characters

Lieutenant William Bligh, captain of HMS *Bounty.* Strong, stout, dark-eyed, firm-mouthed, and strong-voiced, he is a fanatical disciplinarian and a grafting exploiter of ship's rationing. He is subject to fits of insane rage.

Roger Byam, the narrator, a retired ship's captain, at the time of the mutiny a young midshipman and student of languages who has been assigned the job of making a dictionary of the native dialects. He becomes quartermaster after the mutiny. He is acquitted of all complicity.

Fletcher Christian, master's mate, leader of the mutiny. He is tall, strong, swarthy, handsome, romantic-looking, resolute, and moody. Unable to bear Captain Bligh's tyranny any longer, he takes charge of the ship, casts off Bligh with a group of loyal men in the ship's launch, and becomes the new acting lieutenant or captain.

George Stewart, a midshipman friend of Byam. A non-mutineer who is appointed master's mate after the mutiny, he drowns when the *Pandora* sinks.

Tehani, a tall, beautiful Tahitian girl, daughter of a high chief. She becomes Byam's wife, bears him a daughter, and dies after he is taken to England.

Sir Joseph Banks, a noted scientist and explorer, president of the Royal Society. He is responsible for Byam's assignment as a dictionary maker.

Hitihiti, a chief and high priest, Byam's *taio* (special friend). He is tall, magnificently proportioned, light-skinned, intelligent, and humorous.

Peggy, a chief's daughter, Stewart's wife.

Maimiti, Christian's sweetheart, Hitihiti's niece, handsome, proud, shy. She goes away with Christian on the *Bounty.*

Robert Tinkler, a midshipman whose testimony saves Byam, Muspratt, and Morrison.

Morrison, boatswain's mate, a non-mutineer. He is pardoned.

Muspratt, an able sailor. As a non-mutineer, he is also pardoned.

Ellison, Burkitt, and **Millward,** able sailors, mutineers who are convicted and hanged.

David Nelson, a botanist in charge of collecting breadfruit trees. He dies at Batavia.

Doctor Hamilton, the kindly doctor on the *Pandora.*

Captain Edwards, captain of the *Pandora.*

The Story

In 1787, Roger Byam accepted Lieutenant William Bligh's offer of a berth as midshipman on HMS *Bounty,* a ship commissioned by the English government to carry the edible breadfruit tree of Tahiti to English possessions in the West Indies, to be used there as a cheap food supply for the black slaves of English planters. Byam's special commission was to work at the task of completing a study of Tahitian dialects for the use of English sailors. After filling the ship's roster and getting favorable weather, the *Bounty* set sail, and Midshipman Byam began to learn the ways of a ship at sea. He also began to learn, when only a few days from England, of the many traits of his captain that were to lead eventually to mutiny. Bligh's fanaticism rested on discipline, which he often enforced at the cost of justice through excessive floggings of the sailors aboard the *Bounty*. The principal objection that the men had, however, was their captain's exploitation of them and their rations for private graft.

When the *Bounty* arrived in Tahiti, the crew was given the freedom that it deserved. Making use of the native custom, each of the men chose for himself a *taio*, or special friend from among the natives, who, during the sailor's stay in Tahiti, would supply him with all the delicacies that the island had to offer.

During the stay at Tahiti, Byam, living ashore, collected information for his language study. Most of the sailors found women with whom they lived and to whom some of them were later married. Master's mate Fletcher Christian chose Maimiti, the daughter of Byam's taio. Midshipman George Stewart chose a Tahitian girl named Peggy. Byam saw Tehani, later his wife, only once during his stay on the island, but from this one appearance he was highly impressed with the beauty of the princess.

Captain Bligh, on the *Bounty*, had continued to practice the cruelties that the men considered not only unfair but also illegal. One practice was the confiscation of gifts that the islanders had brought to the men on ship and that rightfully belonged to those men. He ordered the gifts to be put into the ship's stores. He had further placed the men on salt pork rations, amid all the plentiful fresh fruits of the island. Just before leaving Tahiti, Bligh falsely accused Christian of stealing a coconut.

Collection of the breadfruit trees was finally completed, and the *Bounty* left for England, but not before four of the chagrined crewmen had attempted desertion. They were caught, returned, and flogged before the crew. This was one more incident to worsen the already sullen attitude of the sailors. Feeling continued to run high against Bligh during the early part of the voyage, until that fateful night when a sudden impulse led Christian into mutiny. With his mutineering friends, he gained control of the ship and subsequently set Bligh adrift in the *Bounty's* launch, in the company of as many of the loyal crewmen as that boat would hold. The launch was too small to hold all the loyal hands, and so seven had to stay behind, among them Byam and Stewart, his close friend. The mutiny left the *Bounty* manned by twenty-three sailors, including the seven loyal men.

With Christian in command, the *Bounty* sailed about in the South Seas, the mutineers searching for a suitable island on which to establish a permanent settlement. After several attempts, all blocked by unfriendly natives, Christian returned with the crew to Tahiti. By a show of hands, the crew again split, some of the men continuing with Christian their search for a permanent home, the others, including Byam and Stewart, remaining at Tahiti. They expected eventually to be picked up by an English vessel and returned home to continue their naval careers.

After Christian and his crew had sailed to an unknown destination, Byam and his friend established homes on the island by marrying the native girls with whom they had fallen in love during the first visit there. Byam went to live in the home of Tehani, his wife, and there continued his language studies. During that idyllic year on the island, children were born to the wives of both Byam and Stewart. Then HMS *Pandora* arrived, searching for the lost *Bounty*. Unaware that Bligh, who had miraculously reached England, had not distinguished between mutineer and loyal sailor among the men who remained on the *Bounty*, Byam and Stewart, anxious for some word of home, eagerly met the newly arrived ship. They were promptly placed in irons and imprisoned. They saw their wives only once after imprisonment, and had it not been for the ship's doctor on the *Pandora*, they would have suffered greater hardship than they had experienced on the *Bounty*. The doctor made it possible for Byam to go on with his studies, a task that gave the prisoners something to do and kept them from losing their minds.

The *Pandora* sailed for England with a total of seven prisoners, four of whom were not guilty of mutiny. They suffered many unnecessary hardships, the greatest occurring during a storm in which the *Pandora* was sunk. The captain delayed releasing the men from their irons until the last possible moment, an act that cost the life of Stewart, who was unable to get clear of the sinking *Pandora* and drowned.

The survivors, gathered on a small island, were forced into a decision to try to make the voyage to Timor, in the Dutch East Indies, the nearest island of call. Their experiences in open boats, with little or no water and food, were savagely cruel because of the tropic sun, the madness from lack of water, and the foolish attempts of the *Pandora's* captain to continue to treat the prisoners as prisoners. Eventually, the group reached Timor and there found passage on a Dutch ship bound for England.

Returned to England, the prisoners awaited courtmartial for mutiny. The loyal men, falsely accused, were Byam, Morrison, and Muspratt. Three of the mutineers with them were Ellison, Burkitt, and Millward, sailors who were convicted of their crime and hanged. The evidence concerning the innocent men finally reached a point at which the decision rested upon the testimony of Robert Tinkler, another midshipman on the *Bounty*. Tinkler was believed lost at sea, but he turned up in time to save the lives of Byam, Muspratt, and Morrison.

Byam continued his naval career and eventually became the captain of his own ship. In 1810, he returned to Tahiti. Tehani, his wife, was dead. His daughter he found alive and the image of her mother. In a last romantic gesture, he saw that he could not make himself known to her, and he left Tahiti without telling her that he was her father. To him, that beautiful green island was a place filled with ghosts of younger men, and young Midshipman Byam was one of them.

Critical Evaluation

The first volume of their most commercially successful South Seas trilogy—followed in 1934 by *Men Against the Sea* and *Pitcairn's Island*—*Mutiny on the Bounty* marked the high point of a rare and singularly happy literary collaboration that had begun when Charles Nordhoff and James Norman Hall served in France together prior to the United States' entry in World War I. Their joint books, like their individually written ones, are characterized by straightforward, vividly descriptive narrative that combines journalistic immediacy with historical verisimilitude to produce suspenseful, adventurous, and entertaining reading.

Mutiny on the Bounty is based on an event that occurred in 1789, retaining actual historical characters and detailed background. Like Herman Melville's Ishmael, their narrator had been a midshipman and so combines the roles of participant with objective observer and recorder. Although Hall wrote the English chapters and Nordhoff the Polynesian, the book contains a remarkable consistency of style and characterization. The cruelty of Captain Bligh and the stalwart integrity of Fletcher Christian draw upon a long literary tradition but manage to avoid stereotyping through the authors' realistic portrayals of the two men.

The fascination of a bygone era of seamanship, a wealth of carefully researched detail, and a meticulously constructed true-life plot all work together from the first page of this novel to capture the reader's interest. The authors suggest early the basic personality traits of the main characters, dropping hints to foreshadow their development. Perhaps the characters are too cleanly cut to rank with the greatest of literature, too consistent to type to rise above figures in a romance, but they are successful within the framework of this novel. Nordhoff and Hall allow their story to speak for itself; by choosing an inexperienced young man as their narrator, they deliberately limit the depth of insight into the situation and characters involved. At the same time, the first-person narration increases the sense of immediacy of the tale, and renders it more plausible. The author of *Billy Budd, Foretopman* (1924) and *Moby Dick: Or, the Whale* (1851) undoubtedly would have penetrated far deeper into the minds and hearts of the tormented men trapped on the *Bounty*, particularly into the twisted personality of Bligh; the materials existed for a book of more intense vision and subtle characterization. Nevertheless, *Mutiny on the Bounty*, while not great literature, is a superbly crafted piece of workmanship, a romance that will never cease to please readers.

MY ÁNTONIA

Type of work: Novel
Author: Willa Cather (1873-1947)
Type of plot: Regional chronicle
Time of plot: Late nineteenth and early twentieth centuries
Locale: Nebraska prairie
First published: 1918

My Ántonia is the story of a Bohemian girl whose family came from the Old Country to settle on the open prairies of Nebraska. While she lives on her farm and tills the soil, she is a child of the prairie, but when Ántonia goes to the city, she faces heartbreak, disillusionment, and social ostracism. Only after her return to the land, which is her heritage, does she find peace and meaning in life.

Principal Characters

Ántonia Shimerda, a young immigrant girl of appealing innocence, simple passions, and moral integrity, the daughter of a Bohemian homesteading family in Nebraska. Even as a child, she is the mainstay of her gentle, daydreaming father. She and Jim Burden, the grandson of a neighboring farmer, become friends, and he teaches her English. After her father's death, her crass mother and sly, sullen older brother force her to do a man's work in the fields. Pitying the girl, Jim's grandmother finds work for her as a hired girl in the town of Black Hawk. There her quiet, deep zest for life and the Saturday night dances lead to her ruin. She falls in love with Larry Donovan, a dashing railroad conductor, and goes to Denver to marry him, but he soon deserts her and she comes back to Black Hawk, unwed, to have her child. Twenty years later, Jim Burden, visiting in Nebraska, meets her again. She is now married to Cuzak, a dependable, hardworking farmer, and the mother of a large brood of children. Jim finds her untouched by farm drudgery or village spite. Because of her serenity, strength of spirit, and passion for order and motherhood, she reminds him of stories told about the mothers of ancient races.

James Quayle Burden, called **Jim,** the narrator. Orphaned at the age of ten, he leaves his home in Virginia and goes to live with his grandparents in Nebraska. In that lonely prairie country, his only playmates are the children of immigrant families living nearby, among them Ántonia Shimerda, with whom he shares his first meaningful experiences in his new home. When his grandparents move into Black Hawk, he misses the freedom of life on the prairie. Hating the town, he leaves it to attend the University of Nebraska. There he meets Gaston Cleric, a teacher of Latin who introduces the boy to literature and the greater world of art and culture. From the university, he goes on to study law at Harvard. Aided by a brilliant but incompatible marriage, he becomes the legal counsel for a Western railroad. Successful, rich, but unhappy in his middle years and in the failure of his marriage, he recalls his prairie boyhood and realizes that he and Ántonia Shimerda have in common a past that is all the more precious because it is lost and almost incommunicable, existing only in memories of the bright occasions of their youth.

Mr. Shimerda, a Bohemian farmer unsuited to pioneer life on the prairie. Homesick for the Old World and never happy in his Nebraska surroundings, he finds his loneliness and misery unendurable, lives more and more in the past, and ends by committing suicide.

Mrs. Shimerda, a shrewd, grasping women whose chief concern is to get ahead in the world. She bullies her family, accepts the assistance of her neighbors without grace, and eventually sees her dream of prosperity fulfilled.

Ambrož Shimerda, called **Ambrosch,** the Shimerdas' older son. Like his mother, he is insensitive and mean. Burdened by drought, poor crops, and debt, he clings to the land with peasant tenacity. Even though he repels his neighbors with his surly manner, sly trickery, and petty dishonesties, everyone admits that he is a hard worker and a good farmer.

Yulka Shimerda, Ántonia's younger sister, a mild, obedient girl.

Marek Shimerda, the Shimerdas' youngest child. Tongue-tied and feebleminded, he is eventually committed to an institution.

Mr. Burden, Jim Burden's grandfather, a Virginian who has bought a farm in Nebraska. Deliberate in speech and action, he is a just, generous man; bearded like an ancient prophet, he sometimes speaks like one.

Mrs. Burden, his wife, a brisk, practical woman who

gives selfless love to her orphan grandson. Kindhearted, she gives assistance to the immigrant families of the region, and without her aid the needy Shimerdas would not have survived their first Nebraska winter.

Lena Lingard, the daughter of poor Norwegian parents, from childhood a girl attractive to men. Interested in clothes and possessing a sense of style, she is successful as a designer and later becomes the owner of a dress shop in San Francisco. She and Jim Burden become good friends while he is a student at the University of Nebraska. Her sensuous beauty appeals greatly to his youthful imagination, and he is partly in love with her before he goes to study at Harvard.

Tiny Soderball, a hardworking woman at the hotel in Black Hawk. She moves to Seattle, runs a sailors' boarding house for a time, and then goes to Alaska to open a hotel for miners. After a dying Swede wills her his claim, she makes a fortune from mining. With a comfortable fortune put aside, she goes to live in San Francisco. When Jim Burden meets her there, she tells him the thing that interests her most is making money. Lena Lingard is her only friend.

Wycliffe Cutter, called **Wick,** a miserly moneylender who has grown rich by fleecing his foreign-born neighbors in the vicinity of Black Hawk. Ántonia Shimerda goes to work for him and his suspicious, vulgar wife. Making elaborate plans to seduce Ántonia, he puts some of his valuables in his bedroom and tells her that she is to sleep there, to guard them, while he and his wife are away on a trip. Mrs. Burden sends her grandson to sleep in the Cutter house, and Wick, returning ahead of his wife, is surprised and enraged to find Jim Burden in his bed. Years later, afraid that his wife's family will inherit his money if he should die first, he kills her and then himself.

Mrs. Cutter, a woman as mean and miserly as her husband, whom she nags constantly. He murders her before committing suicide.

Larry Donovan, a railroad conductor and ladies' man. He courts Ántonia Shimerda, promises to marry her if she will join him in Denver, seduces her, and then goes off to Mexico, leaving her pregnant.

Mrs. Steavens, a widow, the tenant on the Burden farm. She tells Jim Burden, home from Harvard, the story of Ántonia Shimerda's betrayal by Larry Donovan.

Otto Fuchs, the Burdens' hired man during their farming years. Born in Austria, he came to the United States as a boy and lived an adventurous life as a cowboy, a stage driver, a miner, and a bartender in the West. After the Burdens rent their farm and move into Black Hawk, he resumes his drifting life.

Jake Marpole, the hired man who travels with young Jim Burden from Virginia to Nebraska. Though a kindhearted man, he has a sharp temper and is violent when angry. He is always deeply ashamed if he swears in front of Mrs. Burden.

Christian Harling, a prosperous, straitlaced grain merchant and cattle buyer, a neighbor of the Burden family in Black Hawk.

Mrs. Harling, his wife, devoted to her family and to music. She takes a motherly interest in Ántonia Shimerda, who works for her as a hired girl for a time, but feels compelled to send her away when the girl begins to go to the Saturday night dances attended by drummers and town boys.

Peter and **Pavel,** Russian neighbors of the Burden family and Mr. Shimerda's friends. Just before he dies, Pavel tells a terrible story of the time in Russia when, to save his own life, he threw a bride and groom from a sleigh to a pack of wolves.

Anton Jelinek, the young Bohemian who makes the coffin for Mr. Shimerda's funeral. He becomes a friend of the Burdens and later a saloon proprietor.

Cuzak, Anton Jelinek's cousin, the sturdy farmer who marries Ántonia Shimerda. Though he has had many reverses in his life, he remains good-natured. Hardworking, dependable, and considerate, he is a good husband to Ántonia.

Rudolph, Anton, Leo, Jan, Anna, Yulka, Nina, and **Lucie,** Ántonia's children by Cuzak.

Martha, Ántonia's daughter by Larry Donovan. She marries a prosperous young farmer.

Gaston Cleric, the young Latin teacher who introduces Jim Burden to the classics and the world of ideas. When he accepts an instructorship at Harvard, he persuades Jim to transfer to that university.

Genevieve Whitney Burden, Jim Burden's wife. Though she does not figure in the novel, her presence in the background helps to explain her husband's present mood and his nostalgia for his early years in Nebraska. Spoiled, restless, temperamental, and independently wealthy, she leads her own life, interests herself in social causes, and acts as a patron to young poets and artists.

The Story

Jim Burden's father and mother died when he was ten years old, and the boy made the long trip from Virginia to his grandparents' farm in Nebraska in the company of Jake Marpole, a hired hand who was to work for Jim's grandfather. Arriving by train late at night in the prairie town of Black Hawk, the boy noticed an immigrant family huddled on the station platform. He and Jake were met by a lanky, scar-faced cowboy named Otto Fuchs, who drove them in a jolting wagon across the empty prairie to the Burden farm.

Jim grew to love the vast expanse of land and sky. One day, Jim's grandmother suggested that the family pay a visit to the Shimerdas, an immigrant family just arrived in the territory. At first, the newcomers impressed Jim unfavorably. The Shimerdas were poor and lived in a dugout cut into the earth. The place was dirty. The children were ragged. Although he could not understand her speech, Jim made friends with the oldest girl, Ántonia.

Jim found himself often at the Shimerda home. He did not like Ántonia's surly brother Ambrosch or her grasping mother, but Ántonia, with her eager smile and great, warm eyes, won an immediate place in Jim's heart. One day, her father, his English dictionary tucked under his arm, cornered Jim and asked him to teach the girl English. She learned rapidly. Jim respected Ántonia's father. He was a tall, thin, sensitive man, a musician in the Old Country. Now he was saddened by poverty and burdened with overwork. He seldom laughed anymore.

Jim and Ántonia passed many happy hours on the prairie. Then tragedy struck the Shimerdas. During a severe winter, Mr. Shimerda, broken and beaten by the prairie, shot himself. Ántonia had loved her father more than any other member of the family, and after his death, she shouldered his share of the farm work. When spring came, she went with Ambrosch into the fields and plowed like a man. The harvest brought money. The Shimerdas soon had a house, and with the money left over, they bought plowshares and cattle.

Because Jim's grandparents were growing too old to keep up their farm, they dismissed Jake and Otto and moved to the town of Black Hawk. There Jim longed for the open prairie land, the gruff and friendly companionship of Jake and Otto, and the warmth of Ántonia's friendship. He suffered at school and spent his idle hours roaming the barren gray streets of Black Hawk.

At Jim's suggestion, his grandmother arranged with a neighbor, Mrs. Harling, to bring Ántonia into town as her hired girl. Ántonia entered into her tasks with enthusiasm. Jim saw a change in her: She was more feminine, she laughed more often, and though she never shirked her duties at the Harling house, she was eager for recreation and gaiety.

Almost every night, she went to a dance pavilion with a group of hired girls. There in new, handmade dresses, the immigrant girls gathered to dance with the village boys. Jim Burden went, too, and the more he saw of the hired girls, the better he liked them. Once or twice, he worried about Ántonia, who was popular and trusting. When she earned a reputation for being a little too fun loving, she lost her position with the Harlings and went to work for a cruel moneylender, Wick Cutter, who had a licentious eye on her.

One night, Ántonia appeared at the Burdens and begged Jim to stay in her bed for the night and let her remain at the Burdens. Wick Cutter was supposed to be out of town, but Ántonia suspected that, with Mrs. Cutter also gone, he might return and harm her. Her fears proved correct, for as Jim lay awake in Ántonia's bed, Wick returned and went to the bedroom where he thought Ántonia was sleeping.

Ántonia returned to work for the Harlings. Jim, eager to go off to college, studied hard during the summer and passed his entrance examinations. In the fall, he left for the state university, and although he found there a whole new world of literature and art, he could not forget his early years under the blazing prairie sun and his friendship with Ántonia. He heard little of Ántonia during those years. One of her friends, Lena Lingard, who had also worked as a hired girl in Black Hawk, visited him one day. He learned from her that Ántonia was engaged to marry a man named Larry Donovan.

Jim went on to Harvard to study law and for years heard nothing of his Nebraska friends. He assumed that Ántonia was married. When he made a trip back to Black Hawk to see his grandparents, he learned that Ántonia, deceived by Larry Donovan, had left Black Hawk in shame and returned to her family. There she worked again in the fields until her baby was born. When Jim went to see her, he found her still the same lovely girl, though her eyes were somber and she had lost her old gaiety. She welcomed him and proudly showed him her baby.

Jim thought that his visit was probably the last time he would see Ántonia. He told her how much a part of him she had become and how sorry he was to leave her again. Ántonia knew that Jim would always be with her, no matter where he went. He reminded her of her beloved father, who, though he had been dead many years, still lived nobly in her heart. She told Jim good-bye and watched him walk back toward town along the familiar road.

It was twenty years before Jim Burden saw Ántonia again. On a Western trip, he found himself not far from Black Hawk and on impulse drove out in an open buggy to the farm where she lived. He found the place swarming with children of all ages. Small boys rushed forward to greet him, then fell back shyly. Ántonia had married well, at last. The grain was high, and the neat farmhouse seemed to be charged with an atmosphere of activity and happiness. Ántonia seemed as unchanged as she was when she and Jim used to whirl over the dance floor together in Black Hawk. Cuzak, her husband, seemed to know Jim before they were introduced, for Ántonia had told all her family about Jim Burden. After a long visit with the Cuzaks, Jim left, promising that he would return the next summer and take two of the Cuzak boys hunting with him.

Critical Evaluation

The character of the pioneer woman Ántonia Shimerda represents a complexity of values, an axis about which *My Ántonia* revolves. The novel in turn illustrates two classical themes of American literature. Written in 1918, it reaches back into the nineteenth century and beyond for its artistic and moral direction.

Willa Cather, the product of a genteel Virginia upbringing, found herself early in life transplanted to the frontier and forced to confront those vast blank spaces over which humans had not yet succeeded in establishing the domination of custom and convention. She saw a few brave settlers confronting the wilderness, meeting the physical challenge as well as the moral one of having to rely on their instincts without benefit of civilized constraints; for her, these people, particularly the women, were a race apart. Ántonia, with her noble simplicity, is among other things a monument to that vigorous race.

She is also an embodiment of a long tradition of fictional heroes of British and American romance. At the time the novel was written, literature and criticism in the United States were undergoing a change of direction. The thrust of literature in the new century owed much to the developing sciences; Sinclair Lewis and Theodore Dreiser appeared on the scene with their sociological novels, signaling the rise of naturalism. Fictional characters would henceforth be viewed as interpreting in their acts the flaws and beauties of laws, institutions, and social structures. *My Ántonia* fits an older mold, a form in which the effects of Colonial Puritanism can be detected. Specifically, the mode demands that the hero overcome or try to overcome the strictures and hazards of a situation by wit, strength, or courage. This convention draws from the very wellspring of American life, the democratic belief in the wholeness and self-sufficiency of the individual, that is, in personal culpability, and in the absolute value of the personal conscience. Cather makes no real indictment of the society that scorns and undervalues Ántonia and the other hired girls; the social conventions are, with the

Waiting in Black Hawk for the train that would take him East, Jim found it hard to realize the long time that had passed since the dark night, years before, when he had seen an immigrant family standing wrapped in their shawls on the same platform. All of his memories of the prairie came back to him. Whatever happened now, whatever they had missed, he and Ántonia had shared precious years between them, years that would never be forgotten.

land, simply the medium through which she fulfills her destiny. It is the peculiarly American sense of starting out brand-new in a new land, that sense of moral isolation, that adds poignance to the struggles of the individual against the vagaries of fortune. This theme of American newness and innocence, which R. B. W. Lewis called "the theme of the American Adam," has as a natural concomitant elements of temptation and fortunate fall. The serpent in Ántonia's story is the town of Black Hawk, where she quarrels with her benefactors and runs afoul of Larry Donovan. Seduced and abandoned, she returns to the land. Yet her experience has made her better able, as she tells Jim Burden, to prepare her children to face the world.

If the town is Ántonia's downfall in terms of one theme, it is the gray backdrop against which she shines in terms of another; in the same way, the prairie is her antagonist in one sense, and the natural force of which she is the flower in another. Jim Burden first finds her, significantly, actually living in the earth. Early on, she begins to take on characteristics of the land: "Her neck came up strongly out of her shoulders, like the bole of a tree out of the turf. . . . But she has such splendid color in her cheeks— like those big dark red plums." She works the land, makes gardens, and nourishes the Harling children with food and stories. Cather insists on Ántonia's connection with the fertile earth. The earth, the virgin land, is in this novel the source of physical vigor and the best resource of the soul. Jim Burden describes his first experience of the land as a feeling of cosmic unity: "Perhaps we feel like that when we die and become part of something entire, whether it is sun and air, or goodness and knowledge. At any rate, that is happiness; to be dissolved into something complete and great." The people who live on the prairie seem to him open and giving like the land; for example, he says of Ántonia that "everything she said seemed to come right out of her heart." By contrast, the life of the town is pinched and ungenerous: "People's speech, their voices, their very glances, became furtive and repressed. Every individual taste, every natural appetite, was bridled by caution."

Ántonia, in all of her acts, shows the naturalness and boundless generosity of the plains; gives freely of her strength and loyalty to her surly brother, to Jim and the Harling children, to Larry Donovan, and to her husband Cuzak; and showers love and nurturance upon her children. She alludes several times to her dislike of towns and cities and to her feeling of familiar friendship with the country. Toward the end of the book, the figure of Ántonia and the infinite fertility of the land come together symbolically in an extremely vivid and moving image. Ántonia and her children have been showing Jim Burden the contents of their fruit cellar, and as they step outside, "[the children] all came running up the steps together, big and little, tow heads and gold heads and brown, and flashing little naked legs; a veritable explosion of life out of the dark cave into the sunlight." The cave might be the apotheosis of Ántonia's first home on the prairie, the latter redeeming the former by its fruitfulness.

Above all, the novel celebrates the early life on the plains of which Jim Burden and Ántonia were a part. The long digressions about Peter and Pavel, the Cutters, and others; the profoundly elegaic descriptions of Jake Marpole and Otto Fuchs; the sharply caught details of farm life, town life, and landscape—these things are bent to the re-creation of a simpler and better time, a hard life now gone beyond recall, but lovingly remembered.

THE NARRATIVE OF ARTHUR GORDON PYM

Type of work: Novella
Author: Edgar Allan Poe (1809-1849)
Type of plot: Adventure romance
Time of plot: Early nineteenth century
Locale: High seas
First published: 1838

Presented as the journal of Arthur Gordon Pym, this story is one of those celebrated literary hoaxes so well suited to Poe's talents and taste. The model of the novella is the Gothic tale of horror, and in its effects of terror and the unbelievable—the eating of human flesh and the discovery of a primitive tribe in the wastes of Antarctica—it equals any other of Poe's tales.

Principal Characters

Arthur Gordon Pym, the narrator, the young son of a Nantucket trader in sea stores. Desirous of adventure, he stows away on a whaling ship, the *Grampus*; helps to overpower and kill the mutineers who seize the ship; becomes briefly a cannibal before he and Dirk Peters are rescued by the *Jane Guy*; survives with Peters after the slaughter of the captain and all of the crew of the *Jane Guy* by natives on an uncharted Antarctic island; and dies of an unexplained accident after most of his story had been prepared for publication. How he managed to travel from the Antarctic to the United States is not revealed, as the last part of his story was lost at his death.

Augustus Barnard, his friend, who aids Pym in hiding aboard the *Grampus* and who shares his experiences and his dangers. He dies from gangrene, the result of an arm wound received in the capture of the ship from the mutineers.

Captain Barnard, Augustus' father, skipper of the *Grampus*. With four loyal sailors, he is set adrift in a rowboat after his ship is seized by the mutineers.

Dirk Peters, a mutineer sailor on the *Grampus*. He is the son of a Native American woman and a white trader. Ferocious-looking and grotesquely misshapen like a dwarf, with huge hands, bowed arms and legs, an immense head, and a ludicrously demonic countenance, he at first joins the mutineers but later turns upon them. He helps Pym and Augustus seize the *Grampus* and becomes a good friend and companion to Pym in all of his later adventures.

Seymour, a black cook, leader of one party of the *Grampus* mutineers.

Hartman Rogers, a mutineer who dies in convulsions after being poisoned by the mate, who leads the other party of mutineers.

Richard Parker, a mutineer who joins Pym, Barnard, and Peters. He is the first to suggest cannibalism for survival, and ironically he draws the short straw and is killed by Peters.

Captain Guy, skipper of the *Jane Guy*, a schooner that rescues Pym and Peters from the battered hulk of the *Grampus*.

Too-Wit, chief of a black-skinned tribe of savages on Tsalal Island in the Antarctic Ocean. Through treachery, the chief and his men entomb, by a landslide, Captain Guy and all the *Jane Guy*'s crew except six men left on board and Pym and Peters, who survive both the landslide and a later attack by the savages.

Nu-Nu, a Tsalal native captured and used as a guide by Pym and Peters in their escape from the island. He dies shortly afterward.

The Story

Arthur Gordon Pym was born the son of a respectable trader at Nantucket. While still young, he attended an academy and there met Augustus Barnard, the son of a sea captain, and the two became close friends. One night after a party, Augustus awoke Pym from his sleep, and together they set off for the harbor. There, Augustus took charge of a small boat, and they headed out to sea.

Before long, Pym, seeing that his companion was unconscious, realized the sad truth of the escapade. Augustus had been drunk, and now in the cold weather was lapsing into insensibility. As a result, their boat was run down by a whaler, and the two narrowly escaped with their lives. They were taken aboard the ship that had run them down and returned to port at Nantucket.

The two friends became even more intimate after this escapade. Captain Barnard was at that time preparing to outfit the *Grampus*, an old sailing hulk, for a voyage on which Augustus was to accompany him. Against his father's wishes, Pym planned to sail with his friend. Because Captain Barnard would not willingly allow Pym to sail without his father's permission, the two boys decided to smuggle Pym aboard and hide him in the hold until the ship should be so far at sea that the captain would not turn back.

At first, everything went according to schedule. Pym was hidden below in a large box with a store of water and food to last him approximately four days. Great was his consternation to discover, at the end of the fourth day, that his way to the main deck was barred. His friend Augustus did not appear to rescue him. In that terrible state, he remained for several days, coming each day closer to starvation or death from thirst.

At last his dog, which had followed Pym aboard the ship, found his way to his master. Tied to the dog's body was a paper containing a strange message concerning blood and a warning to Pym to keep silent if he valued his life.

Pym was sick from hunger and fever when Augustus at last appeared. The story that he had to tell was a terrible one. Shortly after the ship had put to sea, the crew had mutinied, and Captain Barnard had been set adrift in a small boat. Some of the crew had been killed, and Augustus himself was a prisoner of the mutineers. Pym and Augustus located a place of comparative safety where it was agreed Pym should hide.

Pym now began to give his attention to the cargo, which seemed not to have been stowed in accordance with the rules for safety. Dirk Peters, a drunken mutineer, helped both Pym and Augustus and provided them with food.

When the ship ran into a storm, some of the mutineers were washed overboard. Augustus was once more given free run of the ship. Augustus, Pym, and Peters planned to overcome the other mutineers and take possession of the ship. To frighten the mutineers during a drunken brawl, Pym disguised himself to resemble a sailor recently killed. The three killed all the mutineers except a sailor named Richard Parker. Meanwhile a gale had come up, and in a few hours the vessel was reduced to a hulk by the heavy seas. Because the ship's cargo was made up

of empty oil casks, there was no possibility of its sinking from the violence of the heavy seas. When the storm abated, the four survivors found themselves weak and without food or the hope of securing stores from the flooded hold. One day a vessel was sighted, but as it drew near, those aboard the *Grampus* saw that it was adrift and all of its passengers were dead.

Pym tried to go below by diving, but he brought up nothing of worth. His companions were beginning to go mad from strain and hunger. Pym revived them by immersing each of them in the water for awhile. As their agony increased, a ship came near, but it veered away without coming to their rescue.

In desperation, the men considered the possibility of eating one of their number. When they drew lots, Parker was chosen to be eaten. For four days, the other three lived upon his flesh.

At last, they made their way into the stores and secured food. Rain fell, and the supply of fresh water, together with the food, restored their hope. Augustus, who had suffered an arm injury, died. He was devoured by sharks as soon as his body was cast overboard.

A violent lurch of the ship threw Pym overboard, but he regained the ship with Peters' help just in time to be saved from sharks. The floating hulk having overturned at last, the two survivors fed upon barnacles. Finally, when they were nearly dead of thirst, a British ship came to their rescue. It was the *Jane Guy* of Liverpool, bound on a sealing and trading voyage to the South Seas and Pacific.

Peters and Pym began to recover. Within two weeks, they were able to look back upon their horrible experiences with almost the same feeling with which one recollects terrible dreams.

The vessel stopped at Christmas harbor, where some seals and sea elephants were killed for their hides. The captain was anxious to sail his vessel into Antarctica on a voyage of exploration. The weather turned cold. There was an adventure with a huge bear that Peters killed in time to save his companions. Scurvy afflicted the crew. Once the captain decided to turn northward, but later he foolishly took the advice of Pym to continue on. They sailed until they sighted land and encountered some savages, whom they took aboard.

The animals on the island were strange, and the water was of some peculiar composition that Pym could not readily understand. The natives on that strange coast lived in a state of complete savagery. Bartering began, but before the landing party could depart, the sailors were trapped in what seemed to be an earthquake, which shut off their passage back to the shore. Only Pym and Peters escaped, to learn that the natives had caused the tremendous earth slide by pulling great boulders from the top of a towering cliff. The only white men left on the island, they were faced by the problem of evading the natives, who were now preparing to attack the ship. Unable to warn their comrades, Pym and Peters could only watch helplessly while the savages boarded the *Jane Guy* and overcame the six white men who had remained aboard. The ship was almost demolished. The savages brought about their own destruction, however, for in exploring the ship they set off the ammunition and the resulting explosion killed about a thousand of them.

In making their escape from the island Pym and Peters discovered ruins similar in form to those marking the site of Babylon. When they came upon two unguarded canoes, they took possession of one and pushed out to sea. Savages chased them but eventually gave up the pursuit. They began to grow listless and sleepy when their canoe entered a warm sea. Ashy material fell continually around and upon them. At last the boat rushed rapidly into a cataract, and a human figure, much larger than any man and as white as snow, arose in the pathway of the doomed boat. So ended the journal of Arthur Gordon Pym.

Critical Evaluation

Though incomplete and uneven, *The Narrative of Arthur Gordon Pym* is nevertheless one of Poe's most important evocations of the irrational power that ultimately dominates his universe. In this novella, the appearance of reason and order always deceives—the apparently benign is nothing more than a mask over horrors almost too frightening to contemplate. Poe repeatedly demonstrates this as, in the course of the story, an idyllic moonlight cruise leads to near-disaster, Pym's adventurous dream of stowing away becomes the nightmare of being buried alive, and the faithful dog Tiger changes into a raging beast. Human beings are subject to the same forces. Pym, first horrified by the proposal, joins his companions in cannibalizing Parker's body. The "friendly" natives of Tslal prove treacherous savages. Finally, nature itself, as exemplified by the strangely ambiguous white sea (which some critics have seen as suggestive of life-giving milk) flows into the ultimate horror of the metaphysical void.

Arthur Gordon Pym is the archetypal voyager or quester after knowledge whose initiation into the secrets of the universe is the substance of the work. Beginning as the adventurous boy of the opening chapter, he becomes, by the end of the story, the tragic pilgrim who dies a "sudden and distressing death" before he can relate the full extent of his discoveries. Like many of Poe's narrators, Pym represents himself as the epitome of the reasonable individual, and throughout his adventures, he seeks assurances that the universe reflects similar principles. Self-deceived on both counts, Pym seems unaware that his description of the Tslalians as "the most wicked, hypocritical, vindictive, bloodthirsty, and altogether fiendish race of men upon the face of the globe" is equally applicable to himself. Perhaps it is this knowledge to which Pym comes by his look upon the void, and with which he is unable to live.

NARRATIVE OF THE LIFE OF FREDERICK DOUGLASS: An American Slave

Type of work: Autobiography and slave narrative
Author: Frederick Douglass (Frederick Augustus Washington Bailey, 1817?-1895)
Time of work: 1817?-1838
Locale: Maryland and Massachusetts
First published: 1845

Douglass' famous autobiography, published only seven years after he escaped from slavery and fled to the North, chronicles his experiences in bondage and his means of gaining his freedom. The book became a celebrated document in the abolitionist movement and has proved inspirational to many people.

Principal Personages

Frederick Bailey, later **Frederick Douglass,** the narrator. He has inherited his slave status from his mother, Harriet Bailey. Although it is rumored that Frederick's father is white, this does not affect Frederick's social standing: Slavery is matrilineal.

Harriet Bailey, the mother from whom Frederick is separated as an infant. She dies when he is seven years old; before that, he sees her only four or five times.

Betsey Bailey, the grandmother who nurtures Frederick until he is six years old. He remains emotionally attached to her.

Aaron Anthony, Frederick's first master. He is Edward Lloyd's clerk and superintendent and as such is described as the "overseer of the overseers." His beating of Aunt Hester is indelibly etched in Frederick's memory.

Thomas Auld, Aaron Anthony's son-in-law. Frederick becomes his property upon Anthony's death. He proves himself a cruel master, especially after he becomes religious.

Hugh Auld, the brother of Thomas Auld. Frederick is sent to live with Hugh in Baltimore. His home becomes a base for the young slave. Although Frederick leaves on occasion, he always seems to return. Hugh arranges for Frederick to learn the trade of a caulker. Frederick makes his escape to freedom from Hugh Auld's Baltimore home.

The Story

In 1841, three years after Frederick Douglass escaped from slavery, he launched his career as an abolitionist. In Nantucket, Massachusetts, he spoke for the first time about his slave experiences before a white audience. Before that, he had told his story only to African-American gatherings. So impressive was his account that he was hired as a full-time antislavery lecturer by the Massachusetts Anti-Slavery Society.

By 1844, the society was becoming increasingly disturbed that many were doubting Douglass' authenticity. His critics saw him as being too refined and too erudite for a man who had escaped from slavery only six years previously. The leaders of the Anti-Slavery Society, therefore, urged Douglass to write his story.

Narrative of the Life of Frederick Douglass: An American Slave, including a preface by William Lloyd Garrison and a letter from Wendell Phillips, was published in 1845. Its success was immediate. Thousands of copies were sold both in the United States and in Great Britain. The *Narrative* was even translated into French and Dutch.

Just as there were those who doubted Douglass' oral accounts of his experiences in slavery, there were those who declared the written version a hoax. Such an accusation was not as farfetched as it might at first seem. Many slave narratives were not only transcribed but also organized and revised by white abolitionists. The latter, however, were generally careful to indicate the extent of their assistance. They recognized that to do otherwise was to put the whole antislavery movement in jeopardy. The *Narrative,* for its part, is a notable exception. Douglass neither asked for nor received any help from white abolitionists.

Douglass decided to divide the work into two main sections. The first part consists of nine chapters that detail Douglass' experiences in slavery. The second section, with two chapters, is as long as the first and describes Douglass' escape. This organization seems to indicate that the first nine chapters form a kind of prelude to the main action—Douglass' escape from slavery.

Before this escape takes place, the reader is given a graphic account of slavery in pre-Civil War America. Douglass begins his narrative with his birth in Tuckahoe, Talbot County, Maryland. The second sentence states that he does not know his age, followed by other details about which the narrator is unsure. For example, although he knows that Harriet Bailey is his mother, he has very little communication with her. She dies when he is seven years old; he had seen her only four or five times. He lives with his grandmother, Betsey Bailey, on the outskirts of Edward Lloyd's plantation.

The young boy is introduced to the horrors of slavery when he witnesses the beating of his Aunt Hester by their master, Aaron Anthony, soon after Frederick begins living on the plantation. This beating is only the first of many at which the young Frederick is both observer and participant.

Frederick later goes to Baltimore to live with Hugh and Sophia Auld. He considers this move providential, since it sets the stage for his eventual escape from slavery. Sophia Auld begins to teach him to read, and by the time her husband finds out and objects, it is already too late; the young slave has made the connection between literacy and freedom.

There is now no turning back for the city slave. Thus, when Frederick is sent to live with Thomas Auld because of a quarrel between the brothers, Thomas cannot control him. He sends him to Edward Covey, a "nigger-breaker." The stay at Covey's marks another pivotal point in the young slave's journey from bondage to freedom; when Covey attempts to beat Douglass, he defends himself and fights the older man to a standoff.

If Covey is the worst master Frederick has encountered, then his next, William Freeland, is the best. With Freeland, Frederick with his eyes on freedom as never before, teaches a Sabbath school of more than forty slaves. Here, too, he plans an aborted escape. After the failed escape, Frederick is again returned to Hugh Auld in Baltimore. Auld oversees his training as a caulker. With this trade comes increasing independence and a small taste of freedom.

This taste of freedom prepares Douglass for his life after slavery. After a successful escape, Frederick keeps his past shrouded in mystery; he is afraid of unwittingly divulging any information to slaveholders.

Frederick Douglass, having discarded the name given him by the mother he hardly knew, settles in New Bedford, Massachusetts, with his new wife, Anna, and joins the abolitionist cause.

Critical Evaluation

To write an autobiography is to assess the significance of one's life. Douglass' journey from "the peculiar institution" of slavery to freedom has both individual and societal importance. His narrative details the "dehumanizing" and "soul-killing" effects of slavery in language that is both formal and dispassionate.

As others have observed, the first page of the *Narrative* is replete with negatives: The slave narrator does not know his age; he is not allowed to ask about it; all he knows about his father is that he is white. This lack of identifying data is undoubtedly dehumanizing.

The brutality of the slave masters provides other examples of the dehumanization of slavery. The beating of Aunt Hester by Aaron Anthony sets the stage for the many whippings that Douglass will witness. Among the first of these is the incident of the two Barneys, father and son. These slaves take care of Colonel Lloyd's horses, but it is clear that the horses are more valued than they are; their master whips them frequently and arbitrarily. Later, in the incident with Covey, the "nigger-breaker,"

Douglass decides that he has had enough. He fights Covey and declares that the encounter marks "the turning-point in my career as a slave."

The sexual nature of these beatings has been pointed out. In the case of Aunt Hester, this aspect is fairly explicit. Captain Anthony is enraged not so much because Aunt Hester has disobeyed him and gone out in the evening, but rather because she has been with Ned Roberts, another slave. Miscegenation is rife between slaveholders and their female slaves; the slaveholder who is both master and father to his slave is quite common. Conversely, where both beater and beaten are males, homosexuality has been suggested.

While such physical abuse undoubtedly leaves psychological scars, the custom of separating the slave infant from the child's mother is perhaps even more emotionally damaging. Douglass several times refers to this unnatural procedure. In fact, he receives the news of his own mother's death "with much the same emotions I should have probably felt at the death of a stranger."

The narrator, however, is no stranger to religion. References to it become increasingly specific. Early in the *Narrative*, the death of a cruel overseer is "regarded by the slaves as the result of a merciful providence." Similarly, Douglass describes his move to Baltimore as "a special interposition of divine Providence." Later, slaveholders such as Thomas Auld use religion to "sanction and support" their "slaveholding cruelty." Also, the final portion of the *Narrative* concerns itself with the incompatibility of Christianity and slavery. Therefore, by examining one life, Douglass addresses issues that affect society as a whole.

The slave's sense of community is referred to at crucial points in the *Narrative*. Douglass plans his aborted escape with other slaves, and his autobiography ends with the hope that the book will increase awareness about "the American slave system." Such knowledge will, the slave narrator hopes, lead to emancipation. Similarly, when Douglass imagines his grandmother, it is her isolation that pains him most. She has been put out to pasture in utter loneliness.

The passage in which Douglass imagines his grandmother's loneliness is perhaps the most poignant in the book, perhaps because Douglass is angry at himself for not being there when she needs him. Whatever the reason, the passage's tone is unlike that of the rest of the autobiography. "Dispassionate," "matter-of-fact," "detached" are words that come to mind when the tone of the *Narrative* is considered. Such distanced narration could be the detachment of the erudite adult abolitionist looking back; it might also be that the dehumanizing and soul-killing institution has taken its toll. Occasionally in the *Narrative*, Douglass mentions his inability to write down his feelings, and the reader wonders if he is refusing to feel because it is too painful to do so.

Feelings are perhaps not best served by a formal style, and some critics have described Douglass' language as "high-flown." One cannot but admire, however, the language of the apostrophe to the ships on the Chesapeake Bay beginning, "You are loosed from your moorings, and are free; I am fast in my chains, and am a slave!" There is also a wonderful chiasmus as Douglass is about to describe his first confrontation with Covey: "You have seen how a man was made a slave; you shall see how a slave was made a man."

The fight with Covey has symbolic value for Douglass. As Douglass sees it, the slave master who whips him in the future must be prepared to kill him. The autobiographer thus uses one incident to shed light on a larger issue—the brutality of slave masters. The beating of Aunt Hester also addresses this issue symbolically. As the first

of such beatings, it sets the stage for all the rest. In addition, the sexual overtones make the whipping akin to rape and therefore more brutal. The inextricable link between slavery and sexuality cannot be denied.

So pervasive is the emphasis on community that there are critics who regard the *Narrative* not as autobiography but as a personal history of American slavery. That Douglass himself intended the work to be viewed as both is evidenced by the appendix. Here the narrator expands on a theme in the work—the incompatibility of slavery and Christianity—at the same time that he signs his new name with a certain pride and flourish. After all, the individual slave can truly be free only when slavery as an institution is abolished.

Literacy, for Douglass, is the key to the slave's freedom. His epiphany occurs when he witnesses Hugh Auld's anger at his wife's teaching Frederick, now eight years old, to read. By the time that he is twelve, the autobiographer is reading *The Columbian Orator*, with its strong antislavery arguments. He soon learns to write from white children living in the streets. Douglass is aware that true liberation can only be achieved when both body and mind are free.

The actual writing of his autobiography may be regarded as the ultimate freeing of the mind for Douglass. Given the therapeutic nature of the work, therefore, any help from white abolitionists would have been inappropriate. When the former slave signs his new name at the end of the *Narrative*, he is affirming both his literacy and his identity.

Douglass' autobiography is as important to history as it is to literature; it speaks as eloquently to African Americans as it does to whites. Ultimately, the work looks at a timeless theme of inhumanity through the lens of slavery.

Historically, the *Narrative* is a significant document in the pre-Civil War abolitionist movement. In fact, the last sentence of the appendix reminds the reader of the "sacred cause" for which the autobiography was written. Douglass earnestly hopes that his story, detailing the horrors of slavery, will hasten the end of "the peculiar institution."

Douglass' *Narrative* belongs to the genre of slave narratives, a popular literary mode from the end of the eighteenth century to the beginning of the American Civil War. Thousands were written during this period, and many were translated into several languages. Douglass' story epitomizes the best of the genre.

The former slave's story exists in three revised versions: *My Bondage and My Freedom* (1855) and two separate editions of *Life and Times of Frederick Douglass*

(1881 and 1892). The original version, however, received the most critical acclaim. The 1845 rendition has been praised for its narrative skills, succinctness, and clarity.

Although the *Narrative* is Douglass' masterpiece, he was also a publisher and journalist. He launched this career after returning from England, where he had fled upon the publication of the *Narrative* to avoid being re-turned to slavery. His journalistic endeavors included the *North Star, Frederick Douglass Weekly, Frederick Douglass' Paper, Douglass' Monthly,* and the *New National Era.* Despite his prolific journalistic output, Douglass' fame as a writer rests on the *Narrative.* It is a work that will continue to fascinate both the historian and the literary critic.

NATIVE SON

Type of work: Novel
Author: Richard Wright (1908-1960)
Type of plot: Social criticism
Time of plot: 1930's, during the Great Depression
Locale: Chicago
First published: 1940

Wright's intention in Native Son *was to write a book that "no one would weep over." He was successful with this story of an African-American man whose sense of anger and hopelessness leads to his accidental killing of a white woman, his murder of his African-American girlfriend, and his sentence to die in the electric chair.*

Principal Characters

Bigger Thomas, a twenty-year-old African-American from Chicago's South Side. Bigger lives with his mother, brother, and sister in a rat-infested and claustrophobic apartment. His hate and fear of the white world culminate in his accidental killing of Mary Dalton, a white girl. Soon he is forced to murder his girlfriend, Bessie, for the sake of his own survival. Bigger is finally caught and brought to trial. As the novel ends, Bigger is on his way to the electric chair with, at best, a dubious sense of freedom achieved through violence.

Mrs. Thomas, Bigger's mother. Mrs. Thomas has no understanding of her son and is impatient and angry with what she perceives as sheer recalcitrance on his part. She finds solace in religion.

Buddy Thomas, Bigger's younger brother. Buddy admires his older brother, but he does not seem destined to become the rebel that Bigger is. He "stays in his place."

Vera Thomas, Bigger's sister, a timid girl who believes in doing what is expected of her.

Bessie Mears, Bigger's girlfriend. Alcohol is Bessie's mainstay; Bigger gives her liquor in return for sex. Bigger murders her to protect himself.

Mr. Dalton, Bigger's landlord and employer. Although Mr. Dalton gives to African-American charities, he is a slum landlord. He owns the rat-infested tenement in which Bigger and his family lives.

Mrs. Dalton, the blind wife of Mr. Dalton. Her ghostlike appearance in Mary's room causes the panic-stricken Bigger to suffocate Mary.

Mary Dalton, the daughter of Mr. and Mrs. Dalton. Mary is a young, liberal white woman who wants to become friends with African-Americans. Bigger is extremely uncomfortable in her presence; he is used to keeping his distance around whites. Mary's friendliness leads to her death.

Jan Erlone, Mary Dalton's boyfriend, a communist who tries to befriend Bigger. After Bigger has killed Mary, Jan visits him in jail and offers him a lawyer.

Boris Max, Bigger's communist lawyer. His defense of Bigger is eloquent, though not effective. He argues that Bigger is forced to kill because he is the product of slavery and an exploitative and hostile white environment.

The Story

Native Son narrates the life and impending death of Bigger Thomas. The novel opens with the jarring sound of an alarm clock. The family's morning ritual is interrupted by a rat, which Bigger hysterically kills. This act marks the first instance of the fear and rage that pervade the novel.

The planned robbery of Blum's store also elicits fear and rage. Blum is white, and Bigger and his gang are used to preying on other African-Americans. He fights with Gus, a member of his gang, and calls the robbery off.

Bigger gets a job as the Daltons' chauffeur. His first assignment is to take Mary Dalton to the university. She, however, wants to meet her boyfriend, Jan. All three end up at Ernie's Kitchen Shack on the South Side of Chicago, and they get drunk. Mary is so drunk that Bigger has to carry her to her room. As he places her in bed, the ghostlike Mrs. Dalton enters. Panic-stricken, Bigger suffocates Mary with her pillow. He decapitates her so that her body will fit into the blazing furnace and returns home to sleep.

As the investigation into Mary's disappearance begins, Bigger implicates both Bessie and Jan. Mary's bones are eventually found in the furnace, and Bigger must murder Bessie, to whom he has confessed, for his own protection. He kills her with a brick while she is asleep after he has raped her. Bigger flees through abandoned buildings on the South Side of Chicago. He is finally captured atop a water tank and imprisoned.

The third part of the novel—the inquest and trial—is set in Cook County jail and its environs. Bigger faints at the inquest and is taken back to his cell, where he reads newspaper reports of himself as the quintessential "nigger." While in his cell, he is also visited by all those who have influenced his life, including the Reverend Hammond, his mother's minister, who gives Bigger a wooden cross. Back at the inquest, Bigger is represented by Boris Max, his communist lawyer.

Mary's bones and Bigger's signed confession are on display at the inquest. The deputy coroner elicits testimony from Mrs. Dalton and Jan; Max, for his part, questions Mr. Dalton. He points out that Mr. Dalton, as landlord of the rat-infested, one-room tenement in which Bigger and his family live, must bear much of the responsibility for his daughter's death. As testimony continues, Bessie's mutilated corpse is brought in. The jury at the inquest decides that Bigger suffocated and strangled Mary while raping her. He must now be returned to jail to await trial.

Instead of being taken directly to Cook County jail, Bigger is brought to Mary's room at the Daltons' apartment. He is then told to show how he raped and murdered Mary. He insists that he did not rape her and refuses to do anything. As he is being returned to jail, he sees the burning cross of the Ku Klux Klan. On his return, he throws away the wooden cross given him by the Reverend Hammond and is visited by Max. Bigger tells him about his meaningless existence.

Bigger's trial begins. Max focuses on the causes of Bigger's behavior in his defense. Despite Max's eloquence, Bigger is convicted and sentenced to die in the electric chair. An appeal to the governor fails.

Critical Evaluation

Bigger Thomas, as his name suggests, is the stereotypical "nigger." As such, he is destined to end up in jail, and Bigger knows it. Very early in the novel, he admits "that the moment he allowed what his life meant to enter fully into consciousness, he would either kill himself or someone else." Living on Chicago's South Side in the 1930's, Bigger is trapped in a hostile environment. His every action is predicated on his obsessive fear of the white world.

His accidental killing of Mary and his murder of Bessie are both motivated by fear. It is because he is panic-stricken at the thought of Mrs. Dalton finding him in Mary's room that he suffocates Mary. Similarly, he murders Bessie because he is afraid that she will give him up to the police.

After Mary's death, Bigger experiences feelings of power, equality, and freedom. In fact, he might even be said to have acquired an identity. So powerful is he that he no longer needs his knife and his gun. Also, he believes himself the equal of whites because he has destroyed their most prized possession. He can decide how much to tell the police about Mary's disappearance; for a while, the "dumb nigger" is in charge, and Bigger toys with the police. For the first time in his life, he is some-body—a murderer. The word "murderer" is appropriate, as Bigger persuades himself after Mary's accidental killing that he intended to kill her.

Bessie is part of his limited environment, and he kills her because he believes that he must. After he murders Bessie, Bigger's feelings of power, equality, and freedom, as well as his sense of an identity, are all heightened.

In jail, however, Bigger is listless and apathetic. His lawyer becomes his confidant, and Bigger tries to sort out his feelings. His dubious epiphany seems to be that his only viable option is violence. The alternative, as he sees it, is dehumanizing submission to white society.

In Bigger's view, all the other African-Americans in the novel opt for submission to whites. His mother finds solace in religion; his brother unquestioningly accepts the status quo; his sister is excessively timid and believes in the tenets of the "Y"; and Bessie, his girlfriend, turns to alcohol and ultimately does not even find sex satisfying. Bigger's friends, Gus, G. H., and Jack, are not willing to go all the way to rid themselves of white oppression.

The reader sees these characters through Bigger's eyes, and they seem like stereotypes; critics have commented adversely on this aspect of the novel. To some, stereotypical character portrayal is inherently faulty, and these critics find even the portrayal of Bigger unsatisfactory. Others, however, contend that Bigger's character, though stereotypical, is convincingly developed, whereas the other characters are mere stick figures.

Among these stick figures are the whites in the novel. Bigger's blanket response to all whites is fear, hate, rage, and shame, with two exceptions. In the case of Jan, Mary's boyfriend, Bigger's standard response gives way to bewilderment and later reluctant trust. As for Max, Bigger trusts him almost immediately; as a result, some commentators view the Bigger-Max relationship as contrived.

If the theme of trust comes late in the novel and causes skepticism, the same cannot be said of the major theme of fear. The killing of the rat and the fight with Gus not only foreshadow Mary's death but also are motivated by fear. Bigger fights with Gus to cover up his fear of robbing Blum's store. He and his friends are used to preying on other African-Americans, but to rob a white man's store is taboo. Thus, the killing of Mary demonstrates how Bigger's fear and its concomitant emotions of hate, rage, and shame culminate in increasing violence.

On a much larger scale, Wright seems to be saying that the fate of African-Americans is determined by a hostile white environment. Determinism, then, is an important theme in *Native Son*. For the Bigger Thomases growing up on the South Side of Chicago in the 1930's, there is no escape; they will end up in jail. The only question is, for what crime? Other African-Americans are confronted with a Hobson's choice—dehumanizing submission.

Who is to blame for this state of affairs? For most of the novel, Wright seems to be insisting that it is white society that is at fault. As the novel approaches its end, however, the reader gets the sense that Bigger Thomas is the "native son" of all Americans, black and white. If Bigger belongs to all Americans, then he is ultimately responsible for his actions and must be held accountable. By killing, Bigger has carved out an identity for himself; by destroying, he has created. Despite his meager choices, he has chosen violence over submission. Even Bigger recognizes this: "But what I killed for, I am!"

At the end of the novel, the reader is still trying to understand Bigger. The point of view is sympathetic. Wright manages to persuade the reader that this youth who has killed twice and begins to feel only after he has murdered is worthy of understanding and compassion.

Some critics insist that, in the book's concluding section, the pace of the novel slows to a crawl. These critics regard the final section as a major flaw in the novel,

viewing it as contrived and serving only to put forward Wright's communist views. Others concede that, although perhaps too didactic in tone, the concluding section is necessary to show the extent to which Bigger's life is fated. Still others argue that this material should have been integrated into the rest of the novel.

While critics are divided about the effectiveness of Wright's narrative structure, his symbolism is less controversial. The snowfalls and blizzards that occur throughout the novel represent a hostile white society. Similarly, Mrs. Dalton's physical blindness is indicative of the psychological blindness of the other characters. Time, too, has symbolic significance in the novel. Whether it be the cacophonous sound of the alarm clock in the opening line of the novel or the clock ticking at the head of Mary's bed, the references seem to represent Bigger's meaningless existence. Most critics grant a measure of effectiveness to these symbols. The wooden cross, however, does not fare so well. This is the cross that the Reverend Hammond, Bigger's mother's minister, gives Bigger when he visits him in prison. Those who bother to mention it regard it as too obvious. Bigger throws the cross away after seeing the burning cross of the Ku Klux Klan; he cannot absorb the differences between the two symbols. In discarding the wooden cross, however, he is rejecting his mother's religion and, ultimately, his mother.

When first published in 1940, *Native Son* was an immediate success. It was a Book-of-the-Month Club selection, and in three weeks, 215,000 copies were sold.

Richard Wright was a prolific writer, and his other works include *Black Boy: A Record of Childhood and Youth* (1945), *Lawd Today* (written in 1935, but not published until 1963), *Uncle Tom's Children* (1938), and *The Outsider* (1953).

As literature, *Native Son* employs the tenets of naturalism and existentialism to portray Bigger Thomas, the stereotypical "nigger." If, as the naturalist contends, human beings are the products of their environment, then the very title of the novel—*Native Son*—seems to indicate that Bigger responds to environmental forces. In true naturalistic fashion, Bigger does not understand these forces, and hence he cannot control them.

Wright is as true to existential tenets as he is to naturalism. The meaninglessness of Bigger's existence is at one with the existential philosophy. When, at the end of the novel, Bigger says, "But what I killed for, I am!" he is accepting responsibility for his actions—yet another attribute of existentialism.

Native Son is naturalistic and existential not because Wright is intent on adhering to particular philosophical systems but because, as some commentators have observed, he found African-American life in the United States to be both naturalistic and existential.

Since *Native Son* was published in 1940, it has disturbed the complacency of Americans, both black and white. Bigger Thomas' raw rage cannot be ignored; the reader responds either negatively or positively to the novel. Wright kept the promise he made when he dis-covered that "even bankers' daughters could read and weep over and feel good about *Uncle Tom's Children.*" He vowed that his next book would be one that "no one would weep over." In fact, "it would be so hard and deep that they would have to face it without the consolation of tears." In this, Wright succeeded.

NEVER COME MORNING

Type of work: Novel
Author: Nelson Algren (1909-1981)
Type of plot: Naturalism
Time of plot: 1930's
Locale: Chicago
First published: 1942

Algren describes the rise and fall of a young boxer who grapples with his feelings of inadequacy. Trapped in the Polish ghetto of Chicago, he searches for an identity inside a gang and inside the ring, only to be defeated by his own weaknesses.

Principal Characters

Bruno "Lefty" Bicek, a young hoodlum who dreams of emulating his idol, Tiger Pultoric, a former boxing champion. Unwilling to oppose peer pressure, he allows his gang, the Warriors, to rape Steffi Rostenkowski, his girlfriend. His frustration at his weakness, however, prompts him to kill an outsider who also wants Steffi. After serving time in prison on another charge, he returns to the neighborhood and is employed at the brothel where Steffi also works. With her help, he makes a comeback, overcoming the henchmen of the local crime boss and winning a boxing match that would qualify him for a title fight. Shortly after the fight, he is arrested for the murder and states that he knew he would not live to be twenty-one years old.

Steffi Rostenkowski, Bruno's girlfriend and the victim of a gang rape. She subsequently becomes a prostitute and the property of crime boss Bonifacy Konstantine.

Bonifacy Konstantine, the erstwhile barber and crime boss who informs on Bruno.

Casey Benkowski, Bonifacy's henchman and a former boxer whose decline foreshadows Bruno's failure.

"One-Eye" Tenczara, the police captain who eventually arrests Bruno.

Fireball Kodadek, a knife-wielding adversary of Bruno.

Tiger Pultoric, a former boxing champion and Bruno's idol.

The Story

Set in the Polish slums of Chicago, Nelson Algren's novel concerns the fate of boxer Bruno Bicek, whose life is foreshadowed by the knockout of Casey Benkowski, an older version of Bruno. At the urging of neighborhood barber and crime boss Bonifacy Konstantine, Casey enlists Bruno's help in persuading Bruno's gang, the Warriors, to become the Baldheads, thereby lining Bonifacy's pockets. Bruno then visits Steffi Rostenkowski, his girlfriend, who is described as "feigning helplessness to camouflage indolence." After he seduces Steffi, whose situation is symbolized by the fly without wings that Bruno crushes, he basks in his newly gained self-esteem: "Two brief days had brought him from dependence to independence. From boyhood to manhood. From vandalism to hoodlumhood." When he takes Steffi to the amusement park, he rips off the head of the Kewpie doll that he wins for her, thereby foreshadowing his later treatment of her; when he must weigh his "love" for Steffi against peer pressure, he acquiesces to her gang rape. In a rage at his decision, he takes his anger out on an outsider who wants Steffi, and it is the murder of this young Greek man that ultimately destroys Bruno.

Three months later, the police pick up Bruno for the shooting of a drunk in an alley. Despite the intensive interrogation by "One-Eye" Tenczara, Bruno maintains his innocence and does not inform on Casey, who was the killer. In his jail cell, Bruno spends most of his time dreaming about becoming the "Modern" Ketchel (a famous Polish prizefighter) and fantasizing about a relationship with Sylvia Sydney, a film actress. When Sylvia Sydney's face becomes Steffi's face, Bruno must confront his responsibility for his girlfriend's fate. At this point, the significance of the sign in Tenczara's office ("I have only myself to blame for my fall") becomes clear—Bruno cannot escape his guilt, regardless of his attempts to justify his decision by adhering to the "code" and being "regular."

After serving six months in prison on a misdemeanor, Bruno is released and returns to work as a pimp and bouncer at Mama Tomek's brothel, which Bonifacy owns and where Steffi works as a prostitute. Algren suspends the narrative at this point and provides his readers with short character sketches of the prostitutes, who are described as the hunted in Algren's urban wilderness. Steffi, who has become Bonifacy's personal property, and Bruno, who works for Bonifacy, cannot express their feelings for each other. Nevertheless, Bruno is determined to free Steffi and to redeem himself by becoming a prizefighter. With Steffi's help, he wins money from Bonifacy in a card game, and he uses the money to arrange a fight with Honeyboy Tucker, a leading contender. Bonifacy learns that he has been cheated and sends his henchmen, in-

cluding Fireball Kodadek and Tiger Pultoric, to prevent the boxing match. In the ensuing battle, Bruno overcomes Fireball, whose knife he has always feared, and Pultoric, his idol. For the first time in the novel, Bruno seems in control: "Everything was going to be all right after all."

The last chapter of the novel concerns Bruno's boxing match with Tucker, just as the novel had begun with Casey's fight. This fight, however, ends differently; with Casey in his corner, Bruno knocks out Tucker and again sees himself as the "Modern" Ketchel. As he basks in his glory, one of Bonifacy's gangsters enters his dressing room and is followed by Tenczara. It is obvious that Bonifacy has had "witnesses" testify to the police about Bruno's murder of the young Greek man. As he leaves the dressing room with Tenczara, Bruno states that he knew he would "never get t'be twenty-one anyhow." The last words of the novel, "And the bell," not only refer to the bell that signals the end of the next fight but also indicate that Bruno's own fight is over.

Critical Evaluation

Like most of Algren's work, *Never Come Morning* takes place in Chicago, which is depicted as an urban wilderness. *The Neon Wilderness* (1947), Algren's collection of short stories, reflects his view of an urban landscape in which, in Darwinian terms, only the fittest survive. In such a world, conflict is inevitable, and boxing provides Algren with the ideal metaphor for a nature "red in tooth and claw." Yet survival is not enough in the Chicago that serves as a microcosm for the United States. In Algren's work, the American Dream prompts characters to seek fame and fortune, and the media define the dream in icons of success. *Kayo* magazine, matchbook covers with pictures of boxers, Jimmy Cagney films—all promote the images of winners with which losers such as Bruno must identify. Like most of Algren's protagonists, Bruno must compare himself with someone else. He is "Lefty" and "Biceps," in addition to being the "Modern" Ketchel and even the "Great White Hope" in his fight with Honeyboy Tucker.

Bruno's physical prowess masks feelings of inadequacy. Rather than evaluate himself in terms of his own standards, he subjects himself to the opinions of others. He seeks approval from the Baldheads, observes the code of the pack, and finds solace in having been "regular" with his peers, even if that code is incompatible with his feelings toward Steffi. Bruno is also "weak" in terms of his environment, which has produced the code and which val-

ues exploitation and callousness. Unlike his peers, Bruno is both sensitive and human; if he were not, he would not experience guilt over Steffi's fate. Haunted by her image, which replaces Sylvia Sydney's fantasy face, he ponders the words that he heard her speak during the gang rape. For Bruno, the past cannot be undone; he accepts his arrest and impending punishment as his due.

Steffi is also doomed, for no escape is possible for those hunted characters who hope in vain to escape from the hunter or predators, whether they are pimps or members of the vice squad. Like Bruno, she is an inmate of an institution (the brothel), and the images with which she is associated suggest the impossibility of escape. She is a "fly without wings, and her dreams are of vaults, sepulchers, and hunters." He sees her forever "on all fours in the alley behind the poolroom, between the telephone pole and an open refuse can." Algren suggests that Steffi is either an animal or a human whose future is the open, inviting receptacle for the debris of society.

Algren uses animal imagery and stresses the importance of environment. By transforming the city, the center of civilization and technology, into a wilderness, he also suggests that progress is illusory. His characters live in circumscribed worlds and are uncomfortable and inarticulate in the natural world. When he takes Steffi to the lake, Bruno simply cannot express himself. Their urban worlds are even more limited, for Bruno and Steffi do not live in homes, but in institutions (the brothel and jail), in the street, or in the ring, itself an enclosure. Although Algren's world is limited to the Polish-American ghetto, it is a microcosm of the United States. Algren compares both the city and the world to a madhouse, prison, and brothel, an insane, entrapped world where all people—not only Steffi—prostitute themselves.

Like James T. Farrell's *Studs Lonigan: A Trilogy* (1935), with which it is often compared, Algren's novel is a standard city novel. Yet few writers have so captured the essence of a city, not in its realistic detail, but in impressionistic images that reflect the "feel" of Chicago. *Never Come Morning*, however, is also an initiation novel. Like Richard Wright and James Baldwin, whose youthful protagonists' tormented souls and physically afflicted bodies indict their societies, Algren describes the interaction of character and environment. Early in the novel, Bruno, who desires to project maturity and virility, reveals that he nevertheless retains "a wistful longing for the warmth and security of the womb," where "it was always warm." Algren adds, "He could not recall a time when he had not preferred silence and darkness to daylight and struggle." These are unusual sentiments for a young aspiring boxer intent on the limelight, but they reveal Bruno's divided nature and foreshadow his acceptance of his fate and the relief that he seems to feel as he senses his return to night and silence.

Algren's title, *Never Come Morning*, surely is an allusion to this passage. When Bruno emerges from the darkness and subjects himself to the light of the boxing arena, he seems to welcome the struggle and even triumphs over his adversaries, but that moment of glory is analogous to the false dawn that precedes sunrise. His struggles to beat Bonifacy at cards, to defeat his nemesis and idol, to escape obscurity and entrapment—all these efforts bring about Bonifacy's enmity and subsequent informing on Bruno. Like Steffi, Bruno resembles the fly

with no wings: In the Tucker fight, he breaks one of his hands. Even his last words, "Knew I'd never get t'be twenty-one anyhow," refer to his emancipation, as twenty-one is the age at which he would legally have been an independent adult.

In its content, *Never Come Morning* is in the tradition of the American literary naturalism that prevailed at the beginning of the twentieth century. Stephen Crane, in *The Red Badge of Courage* (1895), had depicted a young man's violent struggles and inner conflicts in the Civil War, and Theodore Dreiser updated those struggles as he moved the site of the conflicts from the United States' rural past to its urban present. Algren, with Farrell and Ernest Hemingway, who admired Algren's work, represented the dying strains of that tradition.

In style, Algren is a realist who specializes in "slice-of-life" portraits, liberally augmented by romantic impressions and heavy-handed symbols, much in the style of Frank Norris. By restricting the action to a short period of time, Algren relies on an episodic structure, rather than a carefully crafted plot. Though there is a prizefighting framing device for *Never Come Morning*, the four-part novel chronicles the events that lead to the illusory rise and inevitable fall of Bruno, the protagonist. The narrative, however, is confined to the first and last parts; the second and third parts concern the incarceration of Bruno in jail and Steffi in the brothel. In effect, Algren suspends his plot while he establishes the parallel between the two institutions and develops the idea that prostitution is endemic in a materialistic society. The digressions, though they do reinforce Algren's political theme, interrupt the narrative flow of the novel. Nevertheless, *Never Come Morning* remains a powerful indictment of American society and a moving portrait of a boxer whose humanity paradoxically causes his downfall.

NOTES ON THE STATE OF VIRGINIA

Type of work: Essays on American culture
Author: Thomas Jefferson (1743-1826)
First published: 1784-1785

Jefferson's answer to the French government's skeptical queries about his home state of Virginia takes the form of an ode to the developing culture of the United States just after the American Revolution.

Thomas Jefferson's universality is best evinced in his *Notes on the State of Virginia*, which he began writing in 1780 in answer to inquiries from the French government about conditions in Virginia. Then the governor of that state, Jefferson's far-reaching interests ranged over all of what he called America's empire of liberty. The *Notes* are not restricted, therefore, to the boundaries of Virginia as they existed before 1781, including, in addition to the present commonwealth, the territory now covered by the states of West Virginia, Kentucky, Ohio, Indiana, Illinois, and part of Pennsylvania. The writing of the *Notes* was made easier because Jefferson for some twenty years had collected Colonial maps, legislative journals, newspapers, and explorers' accounts. He had made and continued to make investigations of Virginia's institutions, economy, flora, fauna, fossils, meteorological conditions, and Native American culture. No dry, statistical account, although containing plenty of facts, the *Notes* deal with culture in its widest sense. They include so many of Jefferson's comments about social phenomena that they comprise in capsule his political and social philosophy, his intellectual, scientific, and ethnic beliefs.

The book, with 260 pages of text and appendices, is arranged arbitrarily by the queries of François Marbois, secretary of the French legation in Philadelphia. Jefferson's essays in reply vary in length from one page each on "Sea Ports" and "Marine Force" to the forty-five pages accorded Virginia's "Productions: Mineral, Vegetable, and Animal." Essays between ten and twenty pages consider its "Aborigines," "Constitution," "Laws," and Jefferson's "Draught of a Fundamental Constitution."

Besides writing celebrated descriptions of Harpers Ferry and Natural Bridge, Jefferson speculated on the physical characteristics of beasts and humankind, as well as on the natural resources of his state. He convincingly refuted the contention of the French naturalist Comte de Buffon that there were fewer species of mammals in America than in Europe and that the American ones had degenerated as a result of the inferior climate. With spirit, he contradicted Buffon's disparagement of Native Americans, hailing them as superior to whites in fortitude, as

equal in physical conformation, and as potentially equal in sexual prowess and mental talent. The limitations of Native Americans, insisted Jefferson, were only those that resulted from inadequate diet and a cultural lag that he compared with that of the Gauls before the Roman conquests north of the Alps. In response to the Abbé Raynal's lament that America had produced no good poet, mathematician, or scientist, Jefferson asserted with pride his claims for Benjamin Franklin in physics, for David Rittenhouse in astronomy, for Mark Catesby in ornithology, and for Native American James Logan in eloquence. As for other cultural achievements, Jefferson pleaded for time in which American liberty might achieve what he considered its certain promise.

Although Jefferson did not write a separate essay on the subject of education, he outlined fully his views in the *Notes*. In doing so, he concealed with typical modesty the personal role that he had played in the reform of the College of William and Mary and in proposing a system of primary and grammar school education. Preoccupation with religion at the college was transferred during the American Revolution to emphasis on science; at the same time, Latin and Greek gave ground to modern languages, but interest in mathematics and moral philosophy was continued. Jefferson's schemes for precollege education were not so extreme as is sometimes thought. He did urge free education of all children in the three R's, but only the best student of a school district six miles square would study at the state's expense in an intermediate or grammar school, whose six-year curriculum afforded instruction in Greek, Latin, geography, and mathematics. By the end of the second year of grammar school, the unfit were to have been rigorously pruned. At the end of the sixth year, the upper fifty percent would have been selected by examinations and given scholarships for college. At any stage in this educational pyramid, a prosperous parent could continue his child's education at private expense if the child did not meet the high standards set for state scholars.

Similarly, Jefferson praised the disestablishment of the Colonial church, but he failed to mention his own part in that accomplishment. Reliant on reason, sure that a neighbor's belief in plural gods or in none could hurt no other, he was happy at the increasing sectarian diversity of the Old Dominion, but he urged suspicion of zealots, whom he believed always responsible for persecutions in the name of uniformity. Jefferson's eloquence in the cause of freedom of conscience was later on turned against him, and his enemies twisted his statements in the *Notes* to condemn him as an Antichrist.

The ideal of a simple, frugal, agrarian republic is nowhere better stated than in Jefferson's essay "Manufactures." His conviction that "those who labour in the earth are the chosen people of God" was accompanied by the corollary that "the great mobs of great cities" corrupted both humans and governments. To preserve Virginia's Arcadia, therefore, he discouraged construction of "satanic" mills and factories, saying "let our work-shops remain in Europe." As a scientific farmer, he gleefully asserted that, on the eve of the American Revolution, Virginia had so diversified its economy that wheat almost equaled tobacco as its staple, and he was by no means loath to see its primacy in tobacco pass to more southernly states.

On grounds of republicanism, incentive, and efficiency, Jefferson admonished his fellow citizens that slavery was injurious to both master and slave, and he hoped for a voluntary increase in African-American emancipation and deportation to Africa, whither he would also have consigned African-American criminals at the expense of the state. More than six pages were devoted to consideration of African Americans in his essay "Manufactures," in the course of which Jefferson concluded that they were inferior to the white race when judged on their accomplishments, unlike the white slaves of Greek or Roman times, who had surpassed their masters in that respect. He lamented the lack of study of African Americans as "subjects of natural history," and he advanced the "suspicion only" that blacks were indeed "inferior to the whites in the endowments both of body and of mind." Friendly to the plight of the African American and anxious for emancipation, this future president of that American Colonization Society, which founded Liberia, was adamant on one point: "When freed, he is to be removed beyond the reach of mixture."

Jefferson's policies as president of the United States were also foreshadowed in the *Notes*. Desiring to "cultivate the peace and friendship of every nation," he wished "to throw open the door of commerce to all." With conviction in peaceful progress, he advocated minimum military or naval forces on two grounds: American financial resources could not maintain a force to stand against that

of a European power without bankrupting the country; and the expenditure of such funds would be more beneficially applied to the improving of the arts and handicrafts of America.

In his essay on Virginia's constitution, Jefferson provided a brief historical account of the Old Dominion, for which he also compiled a bibliography of characters and legislative acts. Stressing the continuum of Virginian history, he praised such historians as Captain John Smith and Robert Beverley. Doubtless he considered that he was more factual than a propagandist in insistence on his theme of royal and parliamentary subversion of legislative assemblies and those rights of freeborn Englishmen guaranteed by the ancient charters that he cited. He laid heavy emphasis on the injustice of James I's revocation of the Virginia Company charter, of the diminution of the colony's extent by proprietary grants made by the king out of its domain, and of Parliament's illegal assumption of control over Colonial foreign trade during the 1650's. Indeed, contended Jefferson, the colonists had every right to believe that their capitulation to the Cromwellian military forces in 1651 had secured reaffirmation of ancient boundaries, upon which Maryland impinged, and of freedom in foreign trade. In view of contemporary disputation over Bacon's Rebellion in 1676, it is interesting to observe that Jefferson makes no reference to that event in this formal historical essay. As might be supposed, Jefferson, in bringing the history of the Old Dominion down to his own time, placed the heaviest blame for the wrongs that it suffered on George III and his parliaments. The revolution in 1776 is presented as inevitable, as honorable resistance instead of unconditional submission to tyranny.

Jefferson has been in American history an ideologue claimed by almost all political parties. Unlike much of his profuse personal and official correspondence, his *Notes on the State of Virginia* was a formal, considered work, more important to knowledge of the man, his ideas, and his America than momentary effusions from his pen, such as private letters.

The *Notes* were first published in English at Paris in 1785. During his lifetime, he made corrections, emendations, and addenda to that text with an eye to authorizing the new, corrected, and enlarged edition that was finally published at Richmond in 1853. With good reason, twentieth century scholars looked with renewed interest on the *Notes on the State of Virginia* as one of the first masterpieces of American literature and possibly the most important scientific and political book written by an American before 1785.

OF MICE AND MEN

Type of work: Novel
Author: John Steinbeck (1902-1968)
Type of plot: Sentimental melodrama
Time of plot: Twentieth century
Locale: Salinas Valley, California
First published: 1937

Written as a theatrical melodrama, the compact, tragic story of Of Mice and Men *spins itself out in only three days. The effect of the tightly knit plot is heightened by the naturalness of the setting and the men's talk, as well as by the underlying sympathy that Steinbeck has for all of his creations, even the meanest.*

Principal Characters

Lennie Small, a simpleminded man of great size and strength. His dream is to have a chicken and rabbit farm with his friend George Milton, and to be allowed to feed the rabbits. George tells him about the farm over and over and keeps Lennie in line by threatening not to let him feed the rabbits. The two men are hired to buck barley on a ranch. Lennie crushes the hand of the owner's son, kills a puppy while stroking it, and breaks a woman's neck, all unintentionally.

George Milton, Lennie's friend, a small and wiry man. He assumes responsibility for his simple friend and in the new job does the talking for both. At last, after the unintentional killing by Lennie, George knows that he can no longer save his friend and, after telling him once again of their plan for the farm, he shoots him.

Candy, a swamper on the barley ranch. He makes George and Lennie's dream seem possible, for he has three hundred and fifty dollars and wants to join them.

Curley, the son of the ranch owner. Vain of his ability as a prizefighter and jealous of his slatternly bride, he provokes Lennie into squeezing his hand. Pleased that Curley's hand has been broken, his wife comes to make advances to Lennie, who accidentally kills her.

Slim, the jerkline skinner on the ranch. He gives Lennie the puppy and persuades Curley to say his hand was caught in a machine.

Crooks, the African-American stable hand. Cool to Lennie at first, he is disarmed by Lennie's innocence.

The Story

Late one hot afternoon, two men carrying blanket rolls trudged down the path that led to the bank of the Salinas River. One man—his companion called him George—was small and wiry. The other was a large, lumbering fellow whose arms hung loosely at his sides. After they had drunk at the sluggish water and washed their faces, George sat back with his legs drawn up. His friend Lennie imitated him.

The two men were on their way to a ranch where they had been hired to buck barley. Lennie had cost them their jobs at their last stop in Weed, where he had been attracted by a girl's red dress. Grabbing at her clothes, he had been so frightened by her screaming that George had been forced to hit him over the head to make him let go. They had run away to avoid a lynching.

After George had lectured his companion about let-ting him talk to their new employer when they were interviewed, Lennie begged for a story that he had already heard many times. It was the story of the farm that they would own one day. It would have chickens, rabbits, and a vegetable garden, and Lennie would be allowed to feed the rabbits.

The threat that Lennie would not be allowed to care for the rabbits if he did not obey caused him to keep still when they arrived at the ranch the next day. In spite of George's precautions, their new boss was not easy to handle. He was puzzled because George gave Lennie no chance to talk.

While the men were waiting for the lunch gong, the owner's son, Curley, came in, ostensibly looking for his father, but actually to examine the new men. After he had gone, Candy, the swamper who swept out the bunkhouse, warned them that Curley was a prizefighter who delighted in picking on the men and that he was extremely jealous of his sluttish bride.

Lennie had a foreboding of evil and wanted to leave, but the two men had no money with which to continue their wanderings. By evening, however, Lennie was happy again. The dog belonging to Slim, the jerkline skinner, had given birth to a litter the night before, and Slim had offered one of the puppies to simpleminded Lennie.

Slim was easy to talk to. While George played solitaire that evening, he told his new friend of the incident in Weed. He had just finished his confidence when Lennie came in, hiding his puppy inside his coat. George told Lennie to take the pup back to the barn. He said that Lennie would probably spend the night there with the animal.

The bunkhouse had been deserted by all except old Candy when Lennie asked once more to hear the story of the land that they would buy someday. At its conclusion, the swamper spoke up. He had three hundred and fifty dollars saved, he said, and he knew he would not be able to work many more years. He wanted to join George and Lennie in their plan. George finally agreed, for with Candy's money they would soon be able to buy the farm that they had in mind.

Lennie was still grinning with delighted anticipation when Curley came to the bunkhouse in search of his wife. The men had been taunting him about her wantonness when he spied Lennie's grin. Infuriated with the thought that he was being laughed at, Curley attacked the larger man. Lennie, remembering George's warnings, did nothing to defend himself at first. Finally he grabbed Curley's hand and squeezed. When he let go, every bone had been crushed.

Curley was driven off to town for treatment, with instructions from Slim to say that he had caught his hand in a machine. Slim warned him that the truth would soon be known if he failed to tell a convincing story.

After the others had started to town with Curley, Lennie went to talk to Crooks, the African-American stable hand, who had his quarters in the harness room instead of the bunkhouse. Crooks's coolness quickly melted before Lennie's innocence. While Lennie told the man about the dream of the farm, Candy joined them. They were deep in discussion of the plan when Curley's wife appeared, looking for her husband. The story about her husband and the machine did not deceive her, and she hinted that she was pleased with Lennie for what he had done. Having put an end to the men's talk, she slipped out noiselessly when she heard the others come back from town.

Lennie was in the barn petting his puppy. The other workmen pitched horseshoes outside. Lennie did not realize that the dog was already dead from the mauling that he had innocently given it. As he sat in the straw, Curley's wife came around the corner of the stalls. He would not speak to her at first, afraid that he would not get to feed the rabbits if he did anything wrong, but the girl gradually managed to draw his attention to her and persuaded him to stroke her hair. When she tried to pull her head away, Lennie held on, growing angry as she tried to yell. Finally he shook her violently and broke her neck.

Curley's wife was lying half-buried in the hay when Candy came into the barn in search of Lennie. Finding Lennie gone, he called George, and while the latter went off to get a gun, the swamper spread the alarm. Curley had been looking for the opportunity to catch the murderer. Carrying a loaded shotgun, he started off with the men, George among them.

It was George who found Lennie hiding in the bushes at the edge of a stream. Hurriedly, for the last time, he told his companion the story of the rabbit farm, and when he had finished, Lennie begged that they go at once to look for the farm. Knowing that Lennie could not escape from Curley and the other men who were searching for him, George put the muzzle of his gun to the back of his friend's head and pulled the trigger. Lennie was dead when the others arrived.

Critical Evaluation

Five years before *Of Mice and Men* appeared, Steinbeck showed his interest in what he called "unfinished children of nature," in a collection of short stories entitled *The Pastures of Heaven*. Lennie Small is perhaps the finest expression of the writer's lifelong sympathy for abused common people. Like *Tortilla Flat*, which brought Steinbeck immediate fame in 1935, and *In Dubious Bat-* tle (1936), *Of Mice and Men* is set in the Salinas Valley of California, where the writer himself spent many years as a migrant worker like the characters he depicts. Although he would go on to win the Pulitzer Prize for *The Grapes of Wrath* in 1939, and the Nobel Prize in Literature in 1962, Steinbeck's artistic temperament remained wedded to his concern with working-class problems that developed from his experience in this valley.

Yet *Of Mice and Men* is in no way a political statement. Its simplicity and grace make it a universal metaphor for the inhumanity of the human condition. Lennie—with his "shapeless face," his bearlike movements, his brute gentleness, and his selective forgetfulness—is one of the most sympathetic melodramatic figures of modern fiction (akin to William Faulkner's Benjy, but more immediately accessible). He is not only convincingly childlike but also consciously so—because he knows what will reinforce his relationship with George, the one thing that he values besides all small, soft creatures. Yet, just as Lennie's uncontrollable strength destroys those creatures inevitably, Lennie himself must be destroyed. George destroys him, out of love, because George recognizes that, like Candy's dog, Lennie does not belong in a world that does not protect the innocent from the inhumanity of the selfish. George's tragic action is the last gesture in their extraordinary relationship—a relationship that the others fail to understand because it is based on tenderness rather than on greed.

THE OLD MAN AND THE SEA

Type of work: Novella
Author: Ernest Hemingway (1899-1961)
Type of plot: Symbolic romance
Time of plot: Mid-twentieth century
Locale: Cuba and the Gulf Stream
First published: 1952

On the surface an exciting but tragic adventure story. The Old Man and the Sea *enjoys near-perfection of structure, restraint of treatment, and evocative simplicity of style. On a deeper level, the book is a fable of the unconquerable spirit of humankind, a creature capable of snatching spiritual victory from circumstances of disaster and apparent defeat. On yet another level, it is a religious parable that unobtrusively utilizes Christian symbols and metaphors.*

Principal Characters

Santiago, an old Cuban fisherman. After more than eighty days of fishing without a catch, the old man's patient devotion to his calling is rewarded. He catches a marlin bigger than any ever brought into Havana harbor. Yet the struggle to keep the marauding sharks from the fish is hopeless, and he reaches shore again with only a skeleton, worthless except as a symbol of his victory.

Manolin, a young Cuban boy devoted to Santiago, with whom he fishes until forbidden by his father after Santiago's fortieth luckless day. He begs or steals to make sure that Santiago does not go hungry.

The Story

For eighty-four days, old Santiago had not caught a single fish. At first a young boy, Manolin, had shared his bad fortune, but after the fortieth luckless day, the boy's father told his son to go in another boat. From that time on, Santiago worked alone. Each morning, he rowed his skiff out into the Gulf Stream, where the big fish were. Each evening, he came in empty-handed.

The boy loved the old fisherman and pitied him. If Manolin had no money of his own, he begged or stole to make sure that Santiago had enough to eat and fresh bait for his lines. The old man accepted his kindness with humility that was like a quiet kind of pride. Over their evening meals of rice or black beans, they would talk about the fish that they had taken in luckier times or about American baseball and the great Joe DiMaggio. At night, alone in his shack, Santiago dreamed of lions on the beaches of Africa, where he had gone on a sailing ship years before. He no longer dreamed of his dead wife.

On the eighty-fifth day, Santiago rowed out of the harbor in the cool dark before dawn. After leaving the smell of land behind him, he set his lines. Two of his baits were fresh tunas that young Manolin had given him, as well as sardines to cover his hooks. The lines went straight down into deep dark water.

As the sun rose, he saw other boats in toward shore, which was only a low green line on the sea. A hovering man-o'-war bird showed him where dolphin were chasing some flying fish, but the school was moving too fast and too far away. The bird circled again. This time Santiago saw tuna leaping in the sunlight. A small one took the hook on his stern line. Hauling the quivering fish aboard, the old man thought it a good omen.

Toward noon, a marlin started nibbling at the bait, which was one hundred fathoms down. Gently the old man played the fish, a big one, as he knew from the weight on the line. At last, he struck to settle the hook. The fish did not surface. Instead, it began to tow the skiff to the northwest. The old man braced himself, the line taut across his shoulders. Although he had his skill and knew many tricks, he waited patiently for the fish to tire.

The old man shivered in the cold that came after sunset. When something took one of his remaining baits, he cut the line with his sheath knife. Once the fish lurched suddenly, pulling Santiago forward on his face and cutting his cheek. By dawn, his left hand was stiff and cramped. The fish had headed northward; there was no land in sight. Another strong tug on the line sliced Santiago's right hand. Hungry, he cut strips from the tuna and chewed them slowly while he waited for the sun to warm him and ease his cramped fingers.

That morning the fish jumped. Seeing it leap, Santiago knew he had hooked the biggest marlin he had ever seen. Then the fish went under and turned toward the east. Santiago drank sparingly from his water bottle during the hot afternoon. Trying to forget his cut hand and aching back, he remembered the days when men had called him *El Campéon*, and he had wrestled with a giant black man in the tavern at Cienfuegos. Once an airplane droned overhead on its way to Miami.

Close to nightfall, a dolphin took the small hook that he had rebaited. He lifted the fish aboard, careful not to jerk the line over his shoulder. After he had rested, he cut fillets from the dolphin and also kept the two flying fish he found in its maw. That night he slept. He awoke to feel the line running through his fingers as the fish jumped. Feeding line slowly, he tried to tire the marlin. After the fish slowed its run, he washed his cut hands in seawater and ate one of the flying fish. At sunrise, the marlin began to circle. Faint and dizzy, he worked to bring the big fish nearer with each turn. Almost exhausted, he finally drew his catch alongside and drove in the harpoon. He drank a little water before he lashed the marlin to the bow and stern of his skiff. The fish was two feet longer than the boat. No catch like it had ever been seen in Havana harbor. It would make his fortune, he thought, as he hoisted his patched sails and set his course toward the southwest.

An hour later, he sighted the first shark. It was a fierce Mako, and it came in fast to slash with raking teeth at the dead marlin. With failing might, the old man struck the shark with his harpoon. The Mako rolled and sank, carrying the harpoon with it and leaving the marlin mutilated and bloody. Santiago knew the scent would spread. Watching, he saw two shovel-nosed sharks closing in. He struck at one with his knife lashed to the end of an oar and watched the scavenger sliding down into deep water. He killed the other while it tore at the flesh of the marlin. When the third appeared, he thrust at it with the knife, only to feel the blade snap as the fish rolled. The other sharks came at sunset. At first, he tried to club them with the tiller from the skiff, but his hands were raw and bleeding and there were too many in the pack. In the darkness, as he steered toward the faint glow of Havana against the sky, he heard them hitting the carcass again and again. Yet the old man thought only of his steering and his great tiredness. He had gone out too far, and the sharks had beaten him. He knew they would leave him nothing but the stripped skeleton of his great catch.

All lights were out when he sailed into the little harbor and beached his skiff. In the gloom, he could just make out the white backbone and the upstanding tail of the fish. He started up the shore with the mast and furled sail of his boat. Once he fell under their weight and lay patiently until he could gather his strength. In the shack, he fell on his bed and went to sleep.

There the boy found him later in the morning. Meanwhile other fishermen, gathered about the skiff, marveled at the giant marlin, eighteen feet long from nose to tail. When Manolin returned to Santiago's shack with hot coffee, the old man awoke. The boy, he said, could have the spear of his fish. Manolin told him to rest, to make himself fit for the days of fishing they would have together. All that afternoon, the old man slept, the boy sitting by his bed. Santiago was dreaming of lions.

Critical Evaluation

The Old Man and the Sea is one of the true classics of its generation. The qualities of Ernest Hemingway's short novel are those that readers associate with many great stories of the past: near-perfection of form within the limitations of its subject matter, restraint of treatment, regard for the unities of time and place, and evocative simplicity of style. Also, like most great stories, it can be read on more than one level of meaning. First, it is an exciting but tragic adventure story. On another level, the book is a fable of unconquerable spirit, of the ability to snatch spiritual victory from circumstances of disaster and material defeat. On still another, it is a parable of religious significance, its theme supported by the writer's unobtrusive handling of Christian symbols and metaphors. Like Samuel Taylor Coleridge's Ancient Mariner, Hemingway's Cuban fisherman allows the imagination of his creator to operate simultaneously in two different worlds of meaning and value, the one real and dramatic, the other moral and devotionally symbolic.

Hemingway began his career as a journalist with the *Kansas City Star* in 1917, and later he was a wartime foreign correspondent for the *Toronto Star*. His first important collection of short stories, *In Our Time*, appeared in 1924, to be followed, in 1926, by what many consider to be his finest novel, *The Sun Also Rises.* During his long stay among other American expatriates in Paris, Hemingway was influenced by Gertrude Stein, Ezra Pound, and James Joyce. From their models, from his journalistic background, and from his admiration for Mark Twain, Hemingway developed his own characteristic style. The Hemingway style was further expressed in *A Farewell to Arms* (1929), then gradually sank toward stereotypical stylization in *Death in the Afternoon* (1932), *Green Hills of Africa* (1935), and *For Whom the Bell Tolls* (1940), where it reached its lowest point of self-caricature, undermining his most ambitious novel. This style is marked by consistent elements: understatement created by tersely realistic dialogue; use of everyday speech and simple vocabulary; avoidance of the abstract; straightforward sentence structure and paragraph development; spare and specific imagery; objective, reportorial viewpoint; and emphasis on "the real thing, the sequence of emotion and fact to make the emotion." This last, Wordsworthian, technique accounts for Hemingway's position as the most gifted of the "lost generation" writers.

Accompanying these stylistic traits is a set of consistent thematic concerns that have become known as the Hemingway "code"; obsession with all outdoor pursuits and sports; identification with the primitive; constant confrontation with death; fascination with violence, and with the skillful control of violence; what he calls "holding the purity of line through the maximum of exposure." The typical Hemingway hero, existential in a peculiarly American way, faces the sterility and failure and death of the contemporary world with steady-handed courage and a stoical resistance to pain that allows for a fleeting, but essentially human, nobility and grace.

After a decade of silence, while Hemingway was preoccupied with the turmoil of World War II, he published *Across the River and into the Trees* (1950)—an inferior book that led many to believe his genius had dried up. Two years later, however, drawing from his experiences in Cuba, *The Old Man and the Sea* appeared. It was awarded the Pulitzer Prize and led to a Nobel Prize in Literature in 1954 for his "mastery of the art of modern narration." As a kind of ultimate condensation of the Hemingway code, this short novel attains an austere dignity. Its extreme simplicity of imagery, symbolism, setting, and character stands in stark contrast with the epic sprawl of Herman Melville's masterpiece *Moby Dick* (1851), a work with which it nevertheless has much in common.

Hemingway displays his genius of perception by using, without apology, the most obvious symbolic imagery; in fact, he creates his desired impact by admitting the ordinary (in the way of Robert Frost, whose "An Old Man's Winter's Night" resembles this book). An example is the statement that the old man's furled sail each evening "looked like a flag of permanent defeat." Here the admission of the obvious becomes ironic, since the old man is not, as he himself declares, defeated—although he is "destroyed." Aside from the two overt image-symbols of the lions on the beach and of "the great DiMaggio" ("who does all things perfectly even with the pain of the bone spur in his heel"), the implicit image of Christ stalks through the work until the reader understands that it is not, after all, a religious symbol, but a secular one that affirms that each individual has personal agonies and crucifixion. As for setting, three elements stand out: the sea itself, which the old man regards as feminine and not as an enemy but as the locus in which humanity plays its little part, with security and serenity derived from acceptance of the sea's inevitable capriciousness; the intrusions of the outside world, with the jet plane high overhead and the tourist woman's ignorant comment at the end that shows total insensitivity to the common person's capacity for tragedy; and the sharks, which make "everything wrong" and stand for the heroic absurdity of human endeavors.

The old man's character is revealed in two ways: by the observations of the narrator and by his own monologue. The latter device might seem theatrical and out of place if Hemingway had not taken pains to set up its employment openly: "He did not remember when he had first started to talk aloud when he was by himself." The words he says to no one but himself reveal the old man's mind as clearly as, and even more poignantly than, the narrator's knowledge of his thoughts. He is seen as the unvanquished (whose eyes are as young as the sea); with sufficient pride to allow humility; with unsuspected, though simple, introspection ("I am a strange old man"); with unquestioning trust in his own skills and in the folklore of his trade; with almost superhuman endurance; and with a noble acceptance of the limitations forced upon him by age. Before the drama is over, the old man projects his own qualities onto the fish—his strength, his wisdom—until his initial hunter's indifference turns to pity, and the fish becomes "friend" and "brother." "But I must kill him," the old man says; "I am glad we do not have to try to kill the stars. . . . It is enough to live on the sea and kill our true brothers." Killing with dignity, as it is done also in the bullring, is an accepted part of the human condition. Only the graceless, undignified sharks (like the hyenas in "The Snows of Kilimanjaro") are abhorrent, diminishing the tragic grandeur of the human drama.

The Old Man and the Sea is a direct descendant of

Moby Dick. The size, strength, and mystery of the great marlin recall the presence of the elusive white whale; similarly, the strength, determination (like Ahab, the old man does not bother with eating or sleeping), and strangeness of Hemingway's hero may be compared to the epic qualities of Melville's. Yet the differences are as important as the similarities. In Melville, both the whale and Ahab have sinister, allusive, and unknown connotations that they seem to share between them and that are not revealed clearly to the reader—in the fashion of Romanticism. In contrast, Hemingway's realism does not present the struggle as a pseudosacred cosmic one between forces of darkness but as an everyday confrontation between the strength of an ordinary man and the power of nature. Hemingway's fish is huge, but he is not solitary and unique; the old man is not the oldest or the greatest fisherman. Finally, neither the old man nor the fish is completely victorious. The fish does not kill the old man, neither does the old man become older or wiser; the fish only makes him very tired.

ONE FLEW OVER THE CUCKOO'S NEST

Type of work: Novel
Author: Ken Kesey (1935-)
Type of plot: Symbolic
Time of plot: Mid-twentieth century
Locale: California
First published: 1962

Kesey's well-known and critically acclaimed work describes the dynamics among inmates of a mental hospital, as well as their battle with its head nurse. The author makes use of a variety of image patterns and snippets of pop culture to glorify such values as self-reliance, confidence, egocentricity, and humor among men.

Principal Characters

Bromden, a six-foot-eight-inch half-breed who is pretending he is deaf and mute in order to protect himself from a mental institution and that which it represents to him. Evidently, the hospital has given him numerous shock treatments to control his behavior, causing him to draw a camouflaging mental fog around himself that he believes hides him from officials of the hospital, particularly Nurse Ratched and her African-American hospital attendants. Referred to as Chief Broom, he is the point-of-view character of the novel.

Randall Patrick McMurphy, a swaggering, boastful, gambling man, who gets himself admitted to a mental hospital in order to escape the hard work of a correctional institution. While at the hospital, McMurphy manages to point his fellow inmates toward self-reliance and freedom. He also liberates Bromden, who takes up the gauntlet passed to him by McMurphy.

Nurse Ratched, also called **Big Nurse,** the head nurse of the hospital, whose tightly buttoned and starched uniform appears as a shield protecting her from masculine gazes and desires. The commander of the ward, she enters into a battle to the death with McMurphy and, biding her time, waits for the kill.

Harding, a patient in the hospital, one of the Acutes (as distinguished from the Chronics). A handsome and intelligent man with beautiful, expressive hands that he tries to hide, Harding could be a natural leader if he did not see himself as a victim, a rabbit in a world of wolves.

Billy Bibbitt, Cheswick, Scanlon, and **Colonel Matterson,** other Acutes in the hospital. On the one hand, the Acutes seek shelter from what they consider to be a hostile world, and on the other hand, they cheer on McMurphy in his struggle for their freedom and his own.

Dr. Spivey, the attending physician, as much subject to Nurse Ratched's manipulations as the inmates are.

The Story

Bromden's awareness of the start of a new day is shrouded in what he identifies as fog, a means by which he is able to hide from the hostile world—that of a mental institution—into which he has been cast. Because he has pretended to be deaf and mute and because he is able to handle a broom, he has been privy to some of the secret sessions held by the staff. Because he is often in a fog, the result of an overdose of medication or the after effects of the electroshock treatment used to control his behavior, the world that he sees is the one that he describes. Bromden believes that the hospital is a part of a large combine, a huge organization that attempts to adjust humans to fit their surroundings and also attempts to adjust the outside world in accordance with the organization's vision of a mechanical world put into motion by electricity. The hospital whirrs and hums; Bromden describes microscopic wires, grids, and transistors and speaks of Nurse Ratched as a robot whose use of electroencephalographs is the ultimate means toward "adjustment."

Into this environment swaggers Randall Patrick McMurphy. With a booming voice and a cowboy gait, with a compelling laugh and a gambler's self-confidence, McMurphy introduces himself with a typical folk hero's boast: "My name is McMurphy, buddies, R. P. McMurphy, and I'm a gambling fool." The boast is accompanied by a wink and a song: "whenever I meet with a deck of cards I lays . . . my money . . . down."

McMurphy's approach and manner mesmerize the other men. Before long, with Harding as company leader, they enter the game that McMurphy proposes, the underlying purpose of which is nothing less than to overthrow the present government (Nurse Ratched) and save the people (inmates). It is a battle that is traditional, mock, and epic, led by the folk hero, the Lone Ranger (with sidekick Tonto), Superman, the Grail knight, the Fisher King, the scapegoat savior.

McMurphy's ability to empower the inmates is clear from their responses to his initial overtures. Harding picks up the spirit of the game and enters into it with glee, while the others cheer him on. More significant, however, is Bromden's response. From McMurphy's first touch on his hand, Bromden feels that hand growing, ringing with blood and power.

The novel proceeds by means of a series of episodes, beginning with skirmishes and becoming more serious and dangerous as time passes, acted out by Nurse Ratched and McMurphy. McMurphy explains to Harding the power of a man's laugh in diminishing a woman who is trying to get the best of him. A more effective instrument than the laugh, however, is sex, according to McMurphy. For some moments, McMurphy is daunted by the thought of what a loss in this battle would mean to him, but his cockiness reappears when he learns that Ratched "plays by the rules" and that he can arrange the odds any way that he likes in a bet with fellow inmates, thus coming out ahead on both counts.

As McMurphy becomes more dominant, Bromden stays out of his fog for longer periods, refusing the medication that sustained his hallucinations as well as the nightmare world that revealed unspeakable horrors in the bowels of the combine.

McMurphy's purpose is to rattle Nurse Ratched, to cause her to lose her temper and thus lose face, and he begins his campaign early one morning by singing in the latrine in a voice clear and strong an old folk song: "My wagons are loaded . . . my whip's in my hand . . ." Wearing a cap and a towel around his waist, he emerges from the latrine to badger an attendant for toothpaste before the time that the cabinet is scheduled to be opened. When Nurse Ratched appears, her progress toward the latrine is abruptly halted by the sight of McMurphy's towel. His willingness to drop the towel, as he was breaking a rule by wearing it, causes her even more frustration that quickly moves to anger when she learns that he has

not been issued inmate clothes. Ratched's strength in battle is made clear when she is able to keep her anger focused on the attendant rather than on McMurphy, who continues to taunt her with songs: "Sweet Georgia Brown," followed by another excerpt from "Gambling Man," both explicitly sexual in content.

The first victory is followed by a second as McMurphy persuades Dr. Spivey to arrange for a second day room so that the Acutes can play cards without the constant sound of the radio. Although McMurphy begins to think that winning is a snap, Bromden, with more experience, knows better. The thought that Ratched will eventually conquer throws the big inmate back into a mental fog that becomes so thick that he can hide in it.

There follows a three-day Monopoly game engineered by McMurphy, and then his demand on behalf of the inmates that they be allowed to watch the World Series even though the television is not turned on until the evening hours. During this time, the subject is first broached about how to escape the hospital. McMurphy claims that a control panel is big enough to break through mesh windows constructed to withstand ordinary assault. Yet McMurphy, even though he gives it a mighty try, is unable to lift the panel.

While McMurphy seems in the ascendancy, Bromden falls increasingly into his fog: The more McMurphy points the way to victory, the more Bromden is afraid to face the outside world. Yet, the more Bromden tries to retreat into the darkness, the more he seems to remember about his past life and the reasons for his withdrawal. This conflict within Bromden is resolved when McMurphy's pleas for another vote concerning the World Series are accepted and Bromden is called upon to cast the winning vote. Ratched will not accept his vote, but the inmates turn the defeat into a victory when they refuse to do their daily chores and sit together watching a blank television set.

Bromden's vote clears away his fog, and though he has not yet admitted that he can hear and speak, he is able to look for the first time out of the window at the countryside surrounding the hospital and to watch a dog sniffing squirrel holes. Both sights lead Bromden to recall more of his own past.

About midway through the novel, McMurphy learns two important facts that cause him to stop and reconsider this war against Nurse Ratched. First, he is no longer in jail for a specific period of time; rather, he is committed to a mental institution and cannot get out until authorities release him. Second, most of the Acutes on the ward are self-committed and can leave anytime that they choose. Why then, McMurphy asks himself, should he risk his freedom in an all-out war with Nurse Ratched? For a time, McMurphy is subdued until Billy makes it clear that the Acutes are paralyzed with fear, that they know they are mentally ill. Bromden is of two minds. He will understand if McMurphy gives up (and Bromden thinks he should), but Bromden also wants McMurphy to continue. This desire, once exposed, is simultaneous with McMurphy's resolve to take up the gauntlet again and with Ratched's belief that she has emerged the victor in her battle with McMurphy. She dares to take away from the inmates control of not only their cigarettes but also their use of the tub room for card playing. In answer, McMurphy breaks the glass cabinet to pick up a carton of cigarettes and once again becomes the logger, the gambler, the brawling Irishman, the cowboy out of the television set, meeting a dare.

For a time, it seems that McMurphy is top gun. Spivey even sides with McMurphy about the therapeutic value of a basketball team. McMurphy flaunts his victory at every turn, and the others come to follow his example. Yet Bromden knows that Nurse Ratched is biding her time, waiting for her turn.

The fishing trip that McMurphy sets up is the means to her ends. On the one hand, the trip is immensely liberating for the inmates, allowing them to practice what they value as male prerogative. Yet McMurphy is leading them to his own detriment. As they grow stronger and more self-assured, McMurphy deteriorates until it appears that he has offered himself for the men to feed on. He has paid for their growth with his own body sustenance. Bromden notices how tired and strained, even frantic, McMurphy looks.

Finally, McMurphy gets into the fistfight that he has steadfastly resisted. Such violence leads to numbing medication or bruising shock treatment, which Bromden knows only too well, but he joins McMurphy in the fight and both are sent to shock therapy. Bromden, however, has gained sufficient strength to resist and, using all his strength and determination, pulls himself out of the fog into the light. McMurphy, too, pulls out quickly, but he is subjected to more shocks—four in all—and still he is not defeated. In fact, the longer he stays away from the men, the larger he grows in their eyes. Bromden, forgetting that he is supposed to be deaf and mute, tells them story after story emphasizing McMurphy's heroics, until Ratched realizes what is happening and brings McMurphy back to the ward. The inmates meanwhile plan McMurphy's escape, to take place after the visit of the two prostitutes and the party planned by McMurphy.

The party is a rousing success; Billy proves his manhood, but the inmates oversleep and are unable to carry through with McMurphy's escape. Shamed by Nurse Ratched, Billy commits suicide; McMurphy physically attacks her and is sent for a lobotomy. The self-committed Acutes gradually check out, but Bromden remains waiting to complete an action. When McMurphy does appear, he is a vegetable, and those who are left refuse to recognize him as McMurphy. Soon Bromden figures out his role. Lying atop McMurphy, using all of his strength, Bromden presses a pillow on McMurphy's face, killing him but leaving McMurphy's heroic image intact in the minds of the inmates. Then Bromden lifts the four-hundred-pound panel and breaks out of the hospital, knowing that he is cured and able to face both darkness and light again.

Critical Evaluation

The first-person narrator in *One Flew over the Cuckoo's Nest* is the means by which Ken Kesey is able to portray realistic events in a surrealistic manner. Bromden describes his hallucinations as fact and in so doing provides both the nightmare aspects of the novel and the cartoon-like impressions. Both visions are central to Kesey's apparent purpose—to walk the thin line between the comic and the tragic, joining the images of Captain Slasher, Superman, the Lone Ranger, and the gambling man (common in popular culture) with their transcendental counterparts, such as the Fisher King, the Grail knight, and the scapegoat savior. Thus, the hospital becomes a film set or artist's sketch pad where folk heroes, drawn from a world of moral absolutes, glorify folk values of sexual prowess and energy, humor, shrewdness, individual freedom, and empowerment by means of wealth. At the same time, the hospital is a vast and murky arena where the characters are actors in a replay of mythic proportions, a battle apocalyptic in intent where good confronts evil and wins. The book's shadings, however, question extremes and equivocate meanings.

McMurphy tends to see the world in terms of absolutes; shades and shadows mystify him. His prescription for curing the Acutes is laughter, gaming, and an ample supply of women who will satisfy the sexual needs of men without making other demands on them. McMurphy underestimates Nurse Ratched, thinking that a man can best any woman by laughing at or having sex with her. He overestimates the mental condition of the Acutes, thinking that they can control their own lives by simply walking out of the hospital. Unlike Bromden, McMurphy has had no real experience with the darkness, and it is not until he realizes something of the complexity of motives and needs and makes the inmates' fight his own that he surmounts the world of the comic book and film script and enters a real world of pain, disillusionment, and death. His assumption of the Christ role as scapegoat savior occurs after he experiences the pain of watching an Acute viciously attacked. Realizing his own role in that attack, McMurphy stands up to fight. Although all the men can hear the helpless, cornered despair in McMurphy's voice, they catch him when he is knocked back and push him forward into the fray.

To prevent an unfair fight, Bromden also enters the battle. This action leads to both the "disturbed ward" and shock treatment. At this point in the novel, Christ imagery is abundant: "I wash my hands of the whole deal," "Do I get a crown of thorns?" and "a crucifix-shaped table." These references, together with others to come and with the idea that McMurphy is a fisher of men, establish but one aspect of McMurphy's symbolic role. Another connection is with the Grail knight, who comes to save the kingdom by asking pertinent questions. McMurphy questions authority at every turn and challenges all aspects of ward policy.

The Fisher King can be identified with both McMurphy and Bromden. In fact, Bromden, called Chief, is the chosen one; he saves McMurphy in his savior role by killing him in what is paradoxically both a love and a death embrace. Bromden inherits the kingdom by calling on the strength that he has received from McMurphy. Bromden escapes, carrying the spirit of McMurphy with him. The Fisher King, maimed and impotent, rules over a wasteland. Both Bromden and McMurphy fit this role. Bromden carries a broom about the kingdom and enters into privy sessions. As he gets strength from McMurphy, however, McMurphy loses his own strength until, lobotomized, he becomes the Fisher King as well as the Christ who is sacrificed to save the kingdom. Such archetypal reverberations add depth to the novel, underlining its serious intent.

Critics have disagreed about the identity of the pro-

tagonist of this novel. Some have identified McMurphy as the protagonist involved in a conflict to rid the world of the mechanical, the rigid, the tyrannical. Others have argued that Bromden is the only fully developed character and that the major conflict in the novel is his attempt to get through the darkness to the light in a kind of mythic journey. In this regard, scholars have likened the structure of *One Flew over the Cuckoo's Nest* with that of F. Scott Fitzgerald's *The Great Gatsby* (1925), in which the first-person narrator, Nick, solves his conflict with reference to Jay Gatsby, the exemplum character in the novel.

Other disagreements arise from charges of sexism and racism leveled at Kesey. Some believe that the portrayal of Nurse Ratched represents misogyny at its worst. Big Nurse rules the world with her iron hand, resulting in matriarchal emasculation. Women—who have been seen as the keepers of the house, responsible for the maintenance of the culture, the civilized aspects of society—are rejected by boy-men who attribute more positive values to self-reliance, gaming, fishing, fighting, and lust. Counterarguments have also been given: The novel is basically comic, and the reversal of sexual roles is keyed to that comedy. Thus, Nurse Ratched is said to be cast in a masculine, assertive role and the Acutes in a feminine, submissive role.

A different argument is often made to counter the charges of racism, the result of the depiction of the African-American attendants. The novel makes clear that Nurse Ratched went through a long period of time before she found exactly the right people to act as her attendants. What is left is the result of a long culling out. One would imagine that Nurse Ratched chose her attendants to behave as they do, and not that the behavior of the African-American attendants is stereotypical.

One Flew over the Cuckoo's Nest was an immediate success, bringing Kesey fame and fortune. It was made into a play and film that also enjoyed great popularity. Kesey's second novel, *Sometimes a Great Notion* (1964), did not have the wide success of its predecessor. It is likely that his reputation will rest on his accomplishment in *One Flew over the Cuckoo's Nest*.

THE OREGON TRAIL

Type of work: Record of travel
Author: Francis Parkman (1823-1893)
Type of plot: Travel and adventure sketches
Time of plot: 1846
Locale: The Oregon Trail
First published: 1847-1849

The Oregon Trail is one of the great documents of the West. Parkman wanted to leave a record of the region—the Native American tribes, the trading posts, the mountain men, the great buffalo herds—before it passed into history. He saw in the West something of glamour and interest that, once gone, could never return.

Principal Personages

Francis Parkman, a young man just out of college who decides to see the West and to record his travels.

Quincy Shaw, his friend, who joins Parkman.

Henry Chatillon, their guide, who was married to a Dakota woman.

Deslauriers, their muleteer.

The Whirlwind, a chief of the Dakotas.

Raymond, Parkman's companion on one leg of the journey.

Reynal, a Frenchman who lived with the Dakotas.

Big Crow, a chief of the Dakotas who allows Parkman and his companion to live with him.

The Story

In the spring of 1846, Francis Parkman and his friend Quincy Shaw traveled by railroad from the East to St. Louis. From St. Louis, they went by river steamer up the Missouri River to Kansas, then called "Kanzas," about five hundred miles from the mouth of the river. Their object was a trip to the Rocky Mountains, a very unusual excursion in the 1840's.

Disembarking, the two young men went by wagon to Westport to get horses and guides for their journey. At Westport, they met three acquaintances with whom they agreed to travel: two British army officers and another gentleman, who were planning a hunting expedition on the American prairies. Pleased to have companions on their dangerous journey, the two Easterners were also glad that they did not need to travel with a train of emigrants, for whom Parkman expressed the utmost contempt.

The journey began inauspiciously for the five travelers. The Britishers decided to start by a trail other than the one that had been previously chosen. The result was that the party discovered, after several days of travel, that they had gone far out of their way. The party then rode northward to the Oregon Trail, which they decided to follow to Fort Laramie, seven hundred miles away.

On the twenty-third of May, the party arrived on the Oregon Trail, where they saw the first human being that they had met in eight days of travel. He was a straggler from a caravan of emigrants. At the end of three weeks, Parkman and his companions, the Englishmen and a small group of emigrants who had joined them, reached the Platte River. They were still four hundred miles from Fort Laramie. The journey to the Platte River had been a muddy one, for each night the party was drenched by a terrific thunderstorm. During the day, they also ran into numerous showers as they made their way westward across the uninteresting country east of the Platte, a country almost devoid of any game except for a few birds.

At the Platte, the party entered the buffalo country. Parkman and Shaw were fascinated by the animals, and they slaughtered hundreds, mostly bulls, before their journey ended. When they entered the buffalo country, they also entered the first territory where they were likely to encounter hostile Native American tribes. A few days after crossing the Platte, Parkman, Shaw, and their guide went on a sortie after buffalo. Parkman became separated from his companions and spent several anxious hours before he found his solitary way back to the camp. Shortly after that adventure, the party met the chief of the trading station at Fort Laramie, who was on his way downstream on the Platte with a shipment of skins. He warned them to watch out for Pawnees, in whose country the party was then traveling.

While traveling up the river, the Englishmen made themselves obnoxious to Parkman and his friend by encouraging emigrants to join the party and by camping at any time of the day that they pleased without consulting the Americans. Because Parkman and Shaw had a definite schedule which they wished to keep, they left the Englishmen and pushed on ahead with Henry Chatillon, their guide, and a muleteer named Deslauriers. Not many days afterward, Parkman and his group reached Fort Laramie, at that time a trading outpost and not a military fort.

At Fort Laramie, the travelers introduced themselves and gave the factor in charge a letter that they had brought from his superiors in St. Louis. They were entertained and housed in the best fashion possible at the fort. Parkman and his friend spent the next few days visiting the Native American villages outside the fort, talking with the trappers, and occasionally looking in on emigrant trains that were on their way to the Oregon country. Using a small chest of medical supplies that he carried with him, Shaw gained some little reputation as a medicine man by doctoring a few of the more important Native Americans.

The most decisive news that came to Parkman and Shaw at the fort was that the Dakotas were preparing to make war upon their traditional enemies, the Snake tribe. Parkman and his friend decided that they would accompany the Dakotas on the raid, since their guide, Henry Chatillon, was married to a Dakota squaw and could, through her, promise the Americans protection from the Dakota tribe. The travelers thought that it would be an unusual opportunity to study Native Americans and their customs.

On June twentieth, Parkman's party, now augmented by two traders of Native American and French descent, left Fort Laramie to join the village of a Dakota chief named The Whirlwind. A few days later, reaching a point on Laramie Creek where the tribe would pass, they decided to camp and await the arrival of The Whirlwind and his village. While they waited, two misfortunes broke upon them. Parkman fell seriously ill with dysentery, and word came that Chatillon's wife, who was a member of The Whirlwind's village, was dying. Chatillon went ahead to meet the Dakotas and see his wife before she died. When the Native Americans failed to arrive, Parkman, recovered from his illness, went back to Fort Laramie. There he discovered that the Dakota war spirit had lessened, so that there was some doubt as to whether the tribe would take the war trail.

Parkman and Shaw decided to follow The Whirlwind's village of Dakotas. A day or two after they started, however, they received word that a trader was going to the rendezvous and wished Parkman and Shaw to accompany him. They never did find the trader, but pushed on by themselves to the place where they expected to find the tribe camped before they went on the warpath.

Arriving at the rendezvous, Parkman and Shaw found no one. As Shaw was not particularly interested in studying the Dakotas, Parkman took one man, who was married to a Native American, and set off by himself to find The Whirlwind's village. It was a dangerous undertaking, for there was some risk of bad treatment from all the tribes in the vicinity, both friendly and hostile.

After many days of lonely travel, Parkman and his companion came upon a Dakota village hunting in the foothills of the Rockies. They learned that The Whirlwind had left this village with a few families. A Frenchman named Reynal lived in the village, however, and Parkman gained the protection of Reynal and his squaw's relatives. Without ceremony, Parkman and his man Raymond went to live in the lodge of Chief Big Crow, who was honored that the white men would come to live with him.

Until the first of August, Parkman lived with Big Crow and shared the tribal life of the village. With his host or with other warriors, he went on hunting expeditions after buffalo, antelope, and other game. It was a dangerous life, but Parkman enjoyed it in spite of the many risks.

That summer was a perilous time for the Dakotas. In search of a large herd of buffalo needed to get skins for the repair of their worn tepees, they had deeply penetrated the hunting grounds of their enemies. At last, after a successful hunt, the village turned eastward toward Fort Laramie, to rejoin the other tribe members who had not dared to accompany them. Parkman and his companion traveled part of the way with the tribe. In order to reach Fort Laramie by the date he had set, however, Parkman found that he had to push ahead by himself, for the village traveled too slowly; women, children, and dogs reduced the rate of travel considerably.

Back at Fort Laramie, where he rejoined Shaw, Parkman prepared for the return journey to St. Louis. They left the fort on the fourth of August, accompanied by several traders who had promised to go with them for part of the journey. These men left the party, however, before it reached the Platte. Parkman and Shaw made most of the return journey with only their two hired men. At Bent's Fort, a small trading post, they were joined by a volunteer who had left the army because of sickness.

This man gave them the first news of the Mexican War that Parkman and Shaw had received, for the war had begun after they had left civilization behind them. From that time on, the travelers met many wagon trains and columns of troops on their way westward to fight the Mexicans. Because of the many troop units in the territory, the small party had no difficulty with any of the Native American bands that they encountered.

Early in September, the four men rode into Westport, where they sold their horses and camping equipment. Parkman and Shaw traveled by boat downstream to St. Louis. There they discarded the buckskins that they had been wearing for many weeks.

It had been an amazing vacation. For five months, they had traveled through the heart of Native American country, far from the protection of the government and the Army. They had seen many Native Americans, but without loss of valuables or life. The only casualty had been an old mule that died as a result of a snakebite. The good fortune of Parkman and his friends was pointed up by the hostilities that began shortly after they left the frontier region. Three weeks after their return to civilization, Comanches and Pawnees began raiding the trail over which they had traveled. The raids were so methodical that not a single party passed over the Oregon Trail in the next six months.

Critical Evaluation

When Francis Parkman made the journey to Oregon in 1846, he kept a series of diaries, and these journals were the basis for his first book, *The Oregon Trail.* Unfortunately, the editor found Parkman's notes too crude and earthy for public taste. In their transformation, the writings were watered down.

In the foreword to the first edition, Parkman stated that he was taking the trail to Oregon with his friend Quincy Shaw to study Native Americans, and in this role Parkman proved to be a pioneer literary observer. While he did omit much ethnological material by modern standards, the work is full of data on the Dakota, or Sioux, and other Plains tribes. His compatriots included Henry Chatillon, who already knew much about the tribes, and Parkman acquired information from the mountain man Thomas Fitzpatrick, another "walking encyclopaedia" of information about the West. His treatment of Native Americans while it is most descriptive, reflects unquestionably Parkman's views that they were less than "civilized."

What Parkman learned and accomplished during this adventure would provide the background for his later works on France and England and their role in the New World. Additionally, he called attention to the miracles of this land with all of its environmental blessings: the minerals, soil, timber, and water. Logically, then, *The Oregon Trail* focuses on the relation of humans to the land and weather.

The work first appeared serially in *The Knickerbocker Magazine* beginning with the issue of February, 1847, and running until 1849. The journey that he had undertaken was for Parkman the one great physical test of his life, and he ran some real risks of death. He suffered a nervous breakdown on his return to Boston in October, 1846, but he had accomplished what many modern writers fail to undertake: He had traveled to observe at firsthand the region about which he would write.

This first work of Parkman reflects the attempts of a literary apprentice, for he exhibits a tendency to stress too many facts and is too emphatic in conversations. One who reads his later writings recognizes such formal devices as stereotyping, a flaw that often dilutes the prose in *The Oregon Trail.* Parkman tended to be too melodramatic at times, but he wrote as the events took place and was likely stimulated by the great adventure on which he had embarked. The descriptions thus become functional rather than mere background. A reader can sense that Parkman tried to write a history but strained to use his self-conscious college writing techniques, such as the out-of-place Byronesque epigraphs that appear in both the serial and in the later editions of the work. Such literary formalities, however, did not appear in the original journals.

Nevertheless, Parkman saw the importance of the struggles in the wilderness that made the United States unique. Subsequent historians have recognized this accomplishment. Frederick Jackson Turner, in his classic essay on the closing of the frontier, stressed the validity of Parkman's acute perceptions.

OUR TOWN

Type of work: Drama
Author: Thornton Wilder (1897-1975)
Type of plot: Domestic romance
Time of plot: 1901-1913
Locale: New Hampshire
First presented: 1938

Portraying typical American small-town life, this Pulitzer Prize-winning play employs a minimum of scenery, and The Stage Manager remains informally on the stage to help explain much of the action. With the tender and simple love story of Emily Webb and George Gibbs at its center, Our Town *is an exceptionally fresh retelling of a timeless, nostalgic tale.*

Principal Characters

The Stage Manager, a Chorus who explains and comments upon the action and the characters as the play unfolds.

Emily Webb, a young girl who grows up in Grover's Corners, a small American town. She works hard in school, tries to be cheerful, and falls in love with the town's best baseball player. She dies in childbirth while still young and shyly takes her place among her relatives and friends in the little graveyard. She tries to live over her twelfth birthday, only to discover that to relive is no joy, that the dead can only pity the living who know not what joy they have in life.

George Gibbs, a typical young American boy who loves baseball. He gives up going to college to marry Emily, whom he dearly loves. When his wife dies, he is filled with grief and goes to sob at her grave, not realizing that she pities him for not valuing the life that he still enjoys.

Dr. Gibbs, the local physician and George's father. He is shocked to find that his son wants to marry and become a farmer, but finally realizes that the youth is really no longer a child, any more than the doctor was when he married. Dr. Gibbs is a hardworking man whose hobby is the American Civil War; his idea of a vacation is an excursion to some battlefield of that conflict.

Mrs. Gibbs, George's mother, a hardworking woman who loves her family, even though she does not always understand them. She has found joy in her marriage and hopes that her son will find joy in his.

Rebecca Gibbs, George's sister.

Wally Webb, Emily's brother.

Mr. Webb, Emily's father, the editor-publisher of the local newspaper. He writes editorials every day, yet he cannot bring himself to advise his son-in-law on marriage, though he tries.

Mrs. Webb, Emily's mother, a good-hearted woman. On Emily's wedding day, she finds herself unable to give her daughter advice on marriage, though she had meant to do so.

Simon Stimson, the local choir director. He has become an alcoholic because he cannot find happiness in the small town. Even in death, after committing suicide, he believes that life is ignorance and folly.

Joe Crowell, a newspaper boy.

Howie Newsome, a milkman.

The Story

Early one morning in 1901, Dr. Gibbs returned to his home in Grover's Corners, New Hampshire. He had just been across the tracks to Polish Town to deliver Mrs. Goruslowski's twins. On the street, he met Joe Crowell, the morning paperboy, and Howie Newsome, the milkman. The day's work was beginning in Grover's Corners.

Mrs. Gibbs had breakfast ready when her husband arrived, and she called the children, George and Rebecca, to the table. After breakfast, the children left for school in the company of the Webb children, Wally and Emily, who lived across the way.

After the children had gone, Mrs. Gibbs stepped out to

feed her chickens. Seeing Mrs. Webb stringing beans in her backyard, she crossed over to talk with her. Mrs. Gibbs had been offered three hundred and fifty dollars for some antique furniture; she would sell the furniture, she had decided, if she could get Dr. Gibbs to take a vacation with her. Yet Dr. Gibbs had no wish to take a vacation; if he could visit the Civil War battlegrounds every other year, then he was satisfied.

The warm day passed, and the children began to come home from school. Emily Webb walked home alone pretending she was a great lady. George Gibbs, on his way to play baseball, stopped to talk to Emily and told her how much he admired her success at school. He could not, he insisted, imagine how anyone could spend so much time over homework as she did. Flattered, Emily promised to help George with his algebra. He said that he did not really need schoolwork, because he was going to be a farmer as soon as he was graduated from high school.

When George had gone, Emily ran to her mother and asked if she were pretty enough to make boys notice her. Grudgingly, her mother admitted that she was, but Mrs. Webb tried to turn Emily's mind to other subjects.

That evening, while Mrs. Webb and Mrs. Gibbs were at choir practice, George and Emily sat upstairs studying. Their windows faced each other, and George called to Emily for some advice on his algebra. Emily helped him, but she was more interested in the moonlight. When she called George's attention to the beautiful night, he seemed only mildly interested.

The ladies coming home from choir practice gossiped about their leader, Simon Stimson. He drank most of the time, and for some reason he could not adjust himself to small-town life. The ladies wondered how it would all end. Mr. Webb also wondered. He was the editor of the local paper, and as he came home, he met Simon roaming the deserted streets. When Mr. Webb reached his home, he found Emily still gazing out of her window at the moon—and dreaming.

At the end of his junior year in high school, George was elected president of his class, and Emily was elected secretary-treasurer. When George walked home with Emily after the election, she seemed so cold and indifferent that George asked for an explanation. She told him that all the girls thought him conceited and stuck-up because he cared more for baseball than he did for his friends. She expected men to be perfect, like her father and his.

George said that men could not be perfect, but that women could—like Emily. Then Emily began to cry, insisting that she was far from perfect. George offered to buy her a soda. As they drank their sodas, they found that they had liked each other for a long time. George said he thought he would not go away to agricultural school, after all. When he was graduated from high school, he would start right in working on the farm.

After a time, Dr. and Mrs. Gibbs learned that George wanted to marry Emily as soon as he left high school. At first it was a shock to them, for they could not imagine that George was anything but a child. They wondered how he could provide for a wife, and whether Emily could take care of a house. Then Dr. and Mrs. Gibbs remembered their own first years of married life. They had had troubles, but now they believed that the troubles had been overshadowed by their joys. They decided that George could marry Emily if he wished.

On the morning of his wedding day, George dropped in on Mr. and Mrs. Webb, and Mrs. Webb left the men alone so that her husband could advise George. All that Mr. Webb had to say, however, was that no one could advise anyone else on matters as personal as marriage.

When George had gone, Emily came down to her last breakfast in her parents' home. Both she and Mrs. Webb cried. Mrs. Webb had meant to give her daughter some advice on marriage, but she was unable to bring herself to it.

At the church, just before the ceremony, both Emily and George felt as if they were making a mistake; they did not want to get married. By the time the music started, however, both of them were calm. The wedding ceremony was soon over, and Grover's Corners lost one of its best baseball players.

Nine years passed; it was the summer of 1913. Up in the graveyard above the town, the dead lay resting from the cares of their lives on earth. Now there was a new grave; Emily had died in childbirth, and George was left alone with a four-year-old son.

It was raining as the funeral procession wound its way up the hill to the new grave. Then Emily appeared shyly before the other dead. Solemnly, they welcomed her to her rest. Yet she did not want to rest; she wanted to live over again the joys of her life. It was possible to do so, but the others warned her against trying to relive a day in her mortal life.

Emily chose to live over her twelfth birthday. At first, it was exciting to be young again, but the excitement wore off quickly. The day held no joy, now that Emily knew what was in store for the future. It was unbearably painful to realize how unaware she had been of the meaning and wonder of life while she was alive. Simon Stimson, who had committed suicide, told her that life was like that, a time of ignorance, blindness, and folly. He was still bitter in death.

Emily returned to her resting place. When night had fallen, George approached full of grief and threw himself on Emily's grave. She felt pity for him and for all the rest of the living. She knew how little they really understood of the wonderful gift that is life itself.

Critical Evaluation

Wilder once wrote that *Our Town* was an attempt to place a high value on even the small events of life. Paradoxically, these events can only achieve their pricelessness when they are contrasted with the massive, unimaginable events of history—human, earth, and cosmic. It is only against such a panoramic background that the full individuality and poignancy of personal microcosms become evident. To measure minutiae against the vast infinities of creation need not result in despair so long as the entire continuum inspires wonder.

Both structure and dialogue in *Our Town* convey these awesome contrasts. Emily's youth, marriage, and death—the respective focal points of each act—transpire so swiftly that one wonders whether her life has any significance at all. Wilder reinforces this doubt by having various characters place the play's action in ever-widening contexts. Professor Willard fixes Grover's Corners in geological time; Mr. Webb defines the town in relation to the whole of American society; the Stage Manager speaks of the bank's time capsule, which will be opened in a thousand years; and Rebecca suggests that Emily's ultimate "address" is "the Solar System; the Universe; the Mind of God."

While "belittling" Emily's life, however, Wilder also in effect magnifies it. By showing Emily in all her particularity, by emphasizing the numberless idiosyncrasies that give her own world uniqueness, he creates a character who captures the audience's attention and love. Grover's Corners, partly because it awakens deep nostalgia, also becomes distinctly lovable. Thus Wilder induces a special state of mind—one of fond attachment to utterly "insignificant" things; the fact that humans cherish such things raises them to significance. That this marvelous paradox should be feelingly comprehended by his audience was Wilder's central aim.

Wilder's striking refusal to use traditional stage properties and his reliance on the pantomime techniques of Oriental theater was not only highly innovative but served his thematic purpose as well. By having his audience imagine the paraphernalia of daily life, he required a concentration on and renewed appreciation of this background of minutiae.

THE OX-BOW INCIDENT

Type of work: Novel
Author: Walter Van Tilburg Clark (1909-1971)
Type of plot: Regional realism
Time of plot: 1885
Locale: Nevada
First published: 1940

The Ox-Bow Incident begins as a Western "horse opera," with all the stage settings and characters of a cowboy thriller, but it ends as a saga of human misery. The story rises toward an inevitable climax and, as it does so, states a harsh truth forcibly—the law of survival is linked to an incredible curse of relentless cruelty. Clark has made the Western thriller a novel of art.

Principal Characters

Gil Carter, a wandering ranch hand who drifts into Bridger's Wells looking for Rose Mapen. When she returns to the town with a husband, after having reportedly gone to San Francisco, Gil is furious. He joins a posse, but thinks more of his disappointment in love than of the hanging of three innocent men.

Art Croft, Gil's friend and companion. Though wounded by mistake by a stage driver, he goes on with the posse in search of rustlers.

Rose Mapen, the woman Gil loves and who disappoints him by marrying another man while gone from Bridger's Wells.

Canby, the saloon keeper at Bridger's Wells.

Farnley, a cowboy who assists in hanging the three innocent men. When one of them, Donald Martin, dies too slowly in the hangman's noose, Farnley shoots him.

Kinkaid, Farnley's friend, supposedly killed by rustlers. He turns up alive after three innocent men have been hanged for his murder.

Davies, a storekeeper in the town. He tries to prevent the hanging of innocent men and fails. He takes a ring and a farewell letter to Martin's wife and two children. After the lynching, he comes to believe, erroneously, that the fault was his.

Osgood, a Baptist minister. He tries to help Davies prevent mob action.

Joyce, a young cowboy who goes with Croft to ask Judge Tyler to swear in the posse.

Judge Tyler, the local magistrate. He tries to prevent mob action but ironically stimulates it.

Sheriff Risley, whose absence from town allows the mob to act. He returns too late. He refuses to arrest the members of the posse, claiming lack of evidence.

Mapes, the sheriff's swaggering deputy, who leads the posse he illegally deputizes.

Jenny Grier, called **Ma,** the keeper of a boarding-house. She helps hang the supposed rustlers and murderers.

Tetley, a rancher. He forces his son to participate in the mob's precipitate action. After his son commits suicide, he does as well.

Gerald Tetley, an emotional young man. Horrified by having to participate in the mob killings, he commits suicide.

Donald Martin, a rancher. Wrongly accused of being a rustler, he is hanged unlawfully by the mob.

A Mexican, Martin's rider, also hanged by the mob.

An Old Man, Martin's simpleminded worker, the mob's third victim.

Drew, a rancher. He failed to hand Martin a bill of sale for cattle purchased, thus contributing to the man's death.

The Story

Gil Carter, a cowboy, and his friend Art Croft rode into the little frontier town of Bridger's Wells. At Canby's saloon, they reined in their horses. Canby was alone at the bar, and he served Gil and Croft with silent glumness.

Canby told them that Rose Mapen, the woman Gil

sought, had gone to San Francisco. He also told the two cowboys that all the local cowhands and their employers were on the lookout for rustlers who were raiding the ranches in the valley. More than six hundred head of cattle had been stolen, and the ranchers were even regarding one another with suspicion. Gil and Croft felt suspicion leveled at them when a group of riders and town men came into the bar.

Gil began to play poker and won hand after hand. The stakes and the bad feeling grew higher until finally Gil and a man named Farnley closed in a rough row. Gil downed his opponent but was himself knocked unconscious when Canby hit him over the head with a bottle.

A rider rode up to the saloon with the word that rustlers had killed Kinkaid, Farnley's friend. Farnley did not want to wait for a posse to be formed, but cooler heads prevailed, among them old Davies, a storekeeper, and Osgood, the Baptist minister. Everyone there joined in the argument—some for, some opposed to, immediate action.

Davies sent Croft and a young cowboy named Joyce to ask Judge Tyler to swear in a posse before a lawless manhunt began. The judge was not eager to swear in a posse in the absence of Risley, the sheriff, but Mapes, a loud, swaggering, newly appointed deputy, demanded that he be allowed to lead the posse.

Meanwhile, the tempers of the crowd began to grow sullen. Ma Grier, who kept a boardinghouse, joined the mob. Then Judge Tyler arrived, and his long-winded oration against a posse stirred up the men more than anything else could have done. Davies took over again and almost persuaded the men to disband. At that moment, however, Tetley, a former Confederate officer and an important rancher, rode up with word that his Mexican herder had seen the rustlers.

Mob spirit flared up once more. Mapes deputized the men in spite of Judge Tyler's assertion that a deputy could not deputize others. The mob rode off in the direction of Drew's ranch, where Kinkaid had been killed.

There the riders found the first trace of their quarry. Tracks showed that three riders were driving forty head of cattle toward a pass through the range.

Along the way, Croft talked to Tetley's sullen son, Gerald. Gerald was not cut out to be a rancher, a fact ignored by his stern, domineering father. Croft thought the boy appeared emotional and unmanly.

A stagecoach suddenly appeared over a rise. In the darkness and confusion, the driver thought that the riders were attempting a holdup. He fired, hitting Croft high in the chest. When he learned his mistake, he pulled up his horses and stopped. One of the passengers was Rose

Mapen, the woman Gil had hoped to find in Bridger's Wells. She introduced the man with her as her husband. Gil was furious.

Croft had his wound doctored and continued on with the posse. On a tip from the passengers, the posse headed for the Ox-Bow, a small valley high up in the range.

Snow was falling by the time the riders came to the Ox-Bow. Through the darkness, they saw the flicker of a campfire and heard the sound of cattle. Surrounding the campfire, they surprised the three men sleeping there: an old man, a young, dark-looking man, and a Mexican. The prisoners were seized and tied.

The dark-looking young man insisted there was some mistake. He said that he was Donald Martin and that he had moved into Pike's Hole three days before. One of the members of the posse, however, a man from Pike's Hole, claimed he did not know Martin or anything about him. Martin began to grow desperate. He demanded to be taken to Pike's Hole, where his wife and two children were. The members of the posse were contemptuous.

Only Davies tried to defend Martin, but Mapes soon silenced the old storekeeper. The cattle were proof enough. Besides, Martin had no bill of sale. He claimed that Drew, who had sold him the cattle, had promised to mail a bill of sale later.

The posse was for an immediate hanging. Tetley wanted to force a confession, but most of the riders said it was no kindness to make the three wait to die. Martin told them that the Mexican was only his rider, that he did not know much about him because the man spoke no English. The old man was a simpleminded fellow who had agreed to work for Martin for very little pay.

Martin was permitted to write a letter to his wife. Shortly afterward it was discovered that the Mexican possessed Kinkaid's gun. He began to speak English. He claimed that he had found Kinkaid's gun.

Tetley appointed three of the posse to lead the horses out away from the men, whose necks would then be caught in the nooses of the ropes tied to the overhanging limb of a tree. He insisted that his milksop son was to be one of the three. Farnley was another. Ma Grier was the third.

Martin became bitter and unforgiving. He made Davies promise to look after his wife, and he gave Davies the letter and a ring. A fine snow continued to fall.

The three were executed. The Mexican and the old man died cleanly. Martin, whose horse had been slowly started by Gerald, had to be shot by Farnley. Tetley felled his son with the butt of his pistol for bungling the hanging. Then the posse rode away.

As they rode out of the Ox-Bow, they met Sheriff Risley, Judge Tyler, Drew, and Kinkaid, who was not dead after all. The judge shouted that every member of the posse would be tried for murder. The sheriff, however, said that he could not arrest a single man present for the murders because identity was uncertain in the swirling snow. He asked for ten volunteers to continue the search for the real rustlers.

Only old Davies seemed moved by the affair, more so after he learned that Martin's story was true and that the cattle had been bought from Drew without a bill of sale. Nearly maddened, he gave the ring and letter to Drew,

who promised to look after Martin's widow.

After Croft and Gil had returned to Canby's saloon, Davies began to moan to Croft. Davies now had the idea that he himself had caused the hanging of the three men. Gil got drunk. That day, Gerald Tetley hanged himself. A few hours later, Gerald's father also committed suicide. The cowhands took up a collection for Martin's widow. In their room at Canby's, Gil and Croft could hear Rose laughing and talking in the bar. They decided to leave town.

Critical Evaluation

Clark's *The Ox-Bow Incident* is set against a Nevada landscape in 1885, but its portrayal of mob justice is timeless. The tragedy in the novel does not merely involve the obvious one of innocent people who are wrongly punished. Clark illustrates how unjust and cruel acts can be carried out by intelligent and moral people who allow their sense of social duty to corrupt their greater, if less dominant, sense of human justice.

Bridger's Wells, Nevada, the initial setting for the novel's development, offered its citizens a limited variety of recreational diversions—eating, sleeping, drinking, cards, and fighting. Into that frontier setting stepped Gil Carter and Art Croft to learn that rustlers, who were at once murderers, had provided the place with an exciting alternative. Osgood, the Baptist minister from the only "working church" in town, realized early how tempers could sublimate one's reason and sense of justice. For the minister, however, the timing, if not also the place, was wrong. In times of despair, reason and justice become less attractive when immediate action seems convenient. Bartlett, a rancher who found rustling a particularly vile threat, argued that "justice" often proved ineffective and worked too slowly to guarantee that guilty men would pay the penalties for their crimes. "I say, stretch the bastards." Bartlett proved effective enough to persuade two score townspeople into forming an illegal posse even though none of the men he exhorted owned any cattle, and only two or three even knew the allegedly murdered man. Bartlett, the one rancher, physically weak and unsound though he appeared, had stigmatized any among his listeners who opposed his argument. Davies, the storekeeper, proved unsuccessful in his efforts to delay the manhunt by his words: "True law, the code of justice, the essence of our sensations of right and wrong, is the conscience of society. It has taken thousands of years to develop, and it is the greatest, the most dis-

tinguishing quality which has evolved with mankind." Notwithstanding the thoughtfulness of his argument, a new leader, Tetley, had by then emerged who, capitalizing on his own frustrations as well as on the gullibility of others, effected a peculiar reversal of the "conscience of society" so as to produce, in effect, a new concept of "justice."

Major Tetley's son Gerald, who was forced by his father to take part in the posse, painfully realized the weakness of individuals too afraid to challenge the mob, who persuade themselves that to resist would be to admit weakness, to be the only hunter in a pack to quit. "How many of us do you think are really here because there have been cattle stolen, or because Kinkaid was shot?" he asks. In the absence of Sheriff Risley, who as the legally constituted police authority might have impeded the development toward lynch law, the formation of an illegal posse, the manhunt, and the lynchings, all went ahead with the inevitability of a Shakespearean tragedy.

In the eleventh hour, no gesture that suggested innocence could spare the doomed men. Martin's emotional letter to his wife was to be shared among the posse by Davies in an effort to save the life of a man Davies believed was innocent. The effort was challenged by Martin himself, however, who used the incident to make another point, that even an initial promise to preserve the integrity of his letter would have proved futile among men in whom conscience had long since failed as a measure of just conduct. In a moment where bravery might understandably have failed among men about to be hanged, the Mexican removed a bullet from his own leg, washed the wound and dressed it with a fire-heated knife. He tossed the knife into the ground within an inch of where its owner's foot would have been had he not, in fear, drawn quickly away. The Mexican, who smiled often at the proceedings, did so again, seeing in the posse the absence of the very bravery that they thought they all possessed. All sympathy that Martin's letter and the Mexican's courage might otherwise have created for the three doomed men never materialized, however, because most of the posse had simply made up their minds about the prisoners' fate already, or because they believed that the rest had. Because they believed that fledgling signs of sympathy were wrong and something that had to be concealed, Tetley had his day.

Davies, the one man who had had least to do with the hangings, and perhaps did the most to prevent them, was himself riddled with guilt for the occasion of the crime. "Tetley couldn't help what he did," Davies believed. "Tetley's a beast. . . . But a beast is not to blame." The leader of the posse was successful only to the extent that he was allowed to achieve his goal. Davies, a peaceful man, even thought that he should have resorted to the gun, to violence if necessary, to prevent the illegal executions from taking place. He admitted too, however, that in not having a weapon he was glad his convictions did

not have to be tested. Davies' sense of guilt and his sense of justice made him realize, as no one else could, how little he actually did to prevent the hangings from taking place. "I had everything, justice, pity, . . . and I let those three men hang because I was afraid. The . . . only thing Tetley had, guts, plain guts, and I didn't have it." The sensitive man, lacking the brute convictions of his opposite, is rendered impotent. His final confession is accompanied by laughter in the background.

The Ox-Bow Incident has no hero, yet it cries out for one in a world where the lessons of the Ox-Bow may not be remembered, much less learned. Inasmuch as the novel was written in 1937 and 1938, while Nazism bullied a world into submission, it is not a theme that was then out of step with world developments, and neither, according to Clark, does the story lack American application. "What I wanted to say was 'It can happen here. It has happened here, in minor but sufficiently indicative ways, a great many times.'"

PALE FIRE

Type of work: Novel
Author: Vladimir Nabokov (1899-1977)
Type of plot: Satirical fantasy
Time of plot: Early 1960's
Locale: New Wye, Appalachia, United States, and "Zembla"
First published: 1962

Nabokov cleverly weds the heartfelt examination of the life and literary achievements of a great poet to a satiric portrait of the paranoid and delusionary editor and academician who would interpret that poet's message. The result is a rich, complex novel that is both poetic and comedic.

Principal Characters

John Shade, an American poet. Shade is murdered shortly after the publication of his poem "Pale Fire," which examines his relationships with his wife and daughter and tries to reconcile his daughter's death by apparent suicide.

Sybil Shade, his daughter, who may have committed suicide or who may have drowned accidentally.

Hazel Shade, his wife, whom Shade has loved for forty years.

Dr. Charles Kinbote, the nearly insane editor of Shade's last work. He claims to be from the kingdom of "Zembla" and believes that "Pale Fire" tells the history of his country. Eventually, he comes to believe that he is the last king of Zembla and that Shade was accidentally murdered in his place. Kinbote's attempts at literary interpretation always end in disaster: He misreads references, focuses on irrelevant details, and interjects his own desires and fantasies.

Jacob Gradus, an assassin. It is not known why he murdered Shade, but Kinbote believes that Gradus is an agent of the Extremist Party of Zembla.

Pale Fire is a strikingly successful synthesis of Vladimir Nabokov's peculiar gifts for learning and poetry with his undeniable talent for the novel. The theme of this satiric comedy of criticism is the increasingly familiar idea that the significance of art, and of life, rests not on "text" but on "texture," not upon any supposed integral validity of thoughts, actions, and memories but rather upon the correspondences and coincidences that a civilized human mind can find or create among thoughts, actions, and memories. In its clear and steady focus upon this central theme, the book is almost neoclassically "decorous." Its most recurrent image becomes the mirror, an ideal reflector and agent of coincidence and a paradigm of neoclassical aesthetic theory.

The central characters of Nabokov's *Pale Fire* have a strange relationship between them. As the book opens, John Shade, a distinguished American poet, has just been murdered. The narrator is evidently engaged in editing the last work of Shade and interpreting his life. It appears from the nature of Dr. Charles Kinbote's editorial commentary that he has imposed on the last work of Shade a completely insane superstructure of meaning.

No matter what Shade's poem says, the narrator-editor persists in finding within the poem incredibly minute and esoteric accounts of historical matters. Kinbote is not a native American, but an emigrant from the fictitious kingdom of Zembla, a nation within the Soviet sphere of interest. He believes that the poem "Pale Fire," Shade's last and greatest work, is really a documentary account of the kingdom of Zembla in the late nineteenth and early twentieth centuries.

Kinbote is a parody of that very popular antihero of modern fiction, the professor. Both he and Shade teach at a small college in "New Wye," which is evidently a composite of all the failings of second-rate and private American institutions of learning. The students and the faculty of the college are described with suitable withering sarcasm, and in that respect this is an orthodox campus novel. What makes it different is the lunacy of the narrator and the grotesque mingling of story lines by Nabokov.

One aspect of the story, which traces the recent life of Shade, proceeds on the matter-of-fact biographical level. It is consistently countered by fantasies woven by the editor, who sees in every word of the material he is editing a reference to his own life. This view is further complicated by a typically Nabokovian scheme of interaction, with the result that the historical events so continually alluded to are twisted out of recognizable shape. Professor Kinbote not only believes that the poem "Pale Fire" is about his homeland of Zembla but also is madly convinced that he is in fact the last king of Zembla, and that Shade has died as a result of a murky conspiracy on the part of the Extremist Party of the country.

Rational and moving, appealing to both heart and head, "Pale Fire" is a great poem in its context and at least a good one out of it; Nabokov's skill as a poet makes one accept quite without the usual fideistic strain the notion that John Shade is a genius.

The poem, standing at the heart of the story, serves a double function. Most evidently, it furnishes the straightforward biographical account of Shade's life that is to be confused in the psychotic mind of its editor. In this sense, it is the material of comedy. Yet the poem itself is a statement of considerable feeling about events in the life of the poet that endow it with a deep sense of tragedy. This poem is primarily about the suicide of Shade's daughter, and Nabokov plays the complications of its interpretation off one another. For example, when Shade is being most revealing about the bitterness of his loss, his editor chooses to interpret the lines as referring to personages in Zembla who are not only quite fictitious but whose imaginary character cannot possibly relate to the lines in question. When the poet does refer to a concrete image or a situation that must be treated as purely factual, the editor, in a splendid burst of academic madness, takes up each reference, no matter how trifling or ephemeral, as a personal challenge to his powers of definition. The reader requires not only some sophistication but also much patience.

If the poem mentions the phrase "wood duck," for example, then the psychotic editor embarks on a naturalistic excursus about the ecological condition of the species. He discusses the color of the creature and its habits—in fact a whole biography of the bird. Characteristically, he also adds some quite mad comments that are totally extraneous to the brief appearance of this literary reference. Much of the book, in fact, is devoted to the astonishing non sequiturs of the imagination that Kinbote is capable of achieving. He is, in short, the very figure of the sterile academician, a figure worthy of comparable standing with the mindless professorial puppets of Bernard Malamud, Randall Jarrell, Saul Bellow, and others.

Perhaps the greatest irony of *Pale Fire* is that the poem itself is decidedly a literary achievement. If there is com-

edy to be produced by the conflict between editor and material editorialized, there is also much pathos. The poem tells the familiar story of the American imagination: youth spent in terrible isolation, adulthood as an experience of physical and intellectual awakening, and maturity as a kind of tragedy. Throughout the story, the poem is played against the visions and memories of its doddering editor. If Shade writes of his love for his wife and daughter, exposing this love in language of almost clinical accuracy, the editor adds a subtext of his own. His own story, brought out in the footnotes to Shade's poem, is one of homosexual experiences and desires. When Shade writes of his wife and their forty-year love affair, Kinbote unburdens himself in the sickliest language imaginable of his attraction to young boys. Where Shade abandons himself to remorse over the life and death of his daughter, the editor abandons himself to a series of ambiguous reveries about his life.

Throughout the story, there are allusions to yet another complicated strand of actions. The man who murders Shade is called Jacob Gradus, and at regular intervals in the novel, an account is given of Gradus' wanderings from Zembla to the United States. Gradus is an appallingly ignorant man, scarcely literate in the language of Zembla and hopelessly at a loss in that of any other country. Yet somehow, inexorably, Gradus makes his way west from Zembla and arrives in the United States to accomplish his mission. In the eyes of "New Wye" alone, Gradus appears to be a madman who has killed Shade for reasons accidental. This, in fact, may be the case, yet Nabokov allows another possibility. The narrator, Professor Kinbote, is profoundly convinced that Gradus is an agent of the Extremist Party of Zembla. Kinbote invents a mysterious and complicated history of Gradus. After the death of Shade, shot down on his own lawn, he rejoices that he himself has been spared. Yet the book ends upon an open question. The last "commentaries" of the editor leave unanswered the question of why Shade died: Was it an accident or a conspiracy? The book closes without clear revelation. Kinbote is either a mad professor or a king in disguise, Gradus is either a mindless psychotic or a purposeful assassin, and Shade is either the victim of a ludicrous accident or the man who has taken upon himself the danger of befriending a king. Nabokov does not resolve these issues or the relationship of the poem "Pale Fire" to the events of the story.

This novel appears to have as its point the depiction of ultimate relativism. The events are clouded in mystery, and the characters are finally left without full identities. The reader realizes that the heroine of the poem "Pale Fire" may have killed herself or may have accidentally drowned. One learns that Shade may have been sincerely broken by her death or perhaps only affected in that deepest part of himself, the ego. One discovers that Professor Kinbote is either a royal exile or a psychopath. The book resolves none of these issues. On the contrary, it holds them up for repeated and endless examination. The events take place against a historical background which does not give them any clarity; in this respect, the book is a direct reaction and commentary on the whole course of modern historical fiction.

Working out of a Russian tradition that is unknown to most Americans, working with talents whose scope is almost equally unknown, Nabokov alone was capable of producing a book so sublimely ridiculous, so unridiculously sublime.

PALE HORSE, PALE RIDER: Three Short Novels

Type of work: Novellas
Author: Katherine Anne Porter (1890-1980)
Type of plot: Social chronicles
Time of plot: *Old Mortality*, 1885-1912; *Noon Wine*, 1836-1905; *Pale Horse, Pale Rider*, 1918
Locale: New Orleans, Texas, and Colorado
First published: 1939

This union of three novellas forms a complex statement about the nature of tragedy and love. Old Mortality *deals with the childhood of Maria and Miranda,* Noon Wine *examines the life and suicide of Mr. Thompson, and* Pale Horse, Pale Rider *takes up the story of the adult Miranda with her experiences during and after World War I.*

Pale Horse, Pale Rider is an important book in the literary career of Katherine Anne Porter. Following, as it did, her highly esteemed first collection of short stories, *Flowering Judas and Other Stories* (1930), this collection composed of three short novels marked an advance in technical interest and resources. It demonstrated clearly the artist's ability to handle the expansive complexity of forms larger than the conventional short story and, thus, offered the promise of exploration of the even larger area of the full-length novel, a promise that was finally to be realized with the appearance of *Ship of Fools* in 1962. At the same time, paradoxically, the artistic success of the forms in *Pale Horse, Pale Rider* is so complete that it is hard to imagine, in abstraction from the fact of *Ship of Fools*, what a novel by Porter would be. She matches the weight and density of many fine conventional novels in her shorter form.

For much of the twentieth century, the short story collection was an unwanted and rejected child. The rule was that novelists, those with enough commercial success or literary prestige or both to merit the consideration of their publishers, were permitted to publish a book of stories from time to time, usually after the fact of a novel or occasionally first, in advance, upon the firm promise and possibility of a novel. Therefore, it is quite remarkable that *Pale Horse, Pale Rider* ever appeared. Moreover, the short novel as a form is a rare one in the United States. Magazines have seldom been willing to surrender the space necessary for the long story or short novel. It is a wonder and a triumph that Porter not only created exemplary models of the form but also managed to overcome the publishing odds so that these novellas are a part of the United States' literary heritage.

From the beginning, Katherine Anne Porter was accepted and acknowledged as a master stylist. While this view may have been true, it has certainly been misleading. To call attention to Porter's style is a useful obser-

vation, but it is rather like describing an oak tree exclusively in terms of the shape and color of its leaves. Moreover, emphasis on style tends to imply virtuosity for its own sake and a certain absence of content, with the result that the critic need not come to terms with content at all. In the case of Porter, this habit or cliché of critics is particularly disappointing. She wrote very well indeed, sentence by sentence, but it was the supreme virtue of her style's design not to call attention to itself, but to fit hand in glove the matter and content of her stories, to carry the weight and to suggest the depth of complexity without once interrupting the magic spell that gives fiction its reality. All of her virtuosity was at the service of her story and her characters. It is easy enough for a writer to divert the reader away from content and character by dazzling and intriguing verbal performance. Porter never chose that way. Her method was the more difficult one; clearly the reader is intended to weigh the story in a total and meaningful sense and not to stop short with admiration for its surface and decoration.

The three short novels composing *Pale Horse, Pale Rider* are arranged in an order or structure to make a larger, single statement and effect, and each demonstrates a different way of handling the short novel. The first, *Old Mortality*, is in three separate parts and is, in a sense, a smaller version of the whole book. It is superficially a "romantic" tale of the United States at the beginning of the twentieth century. Part 1 is set in the shifting, complex world of a large family, gossip and the tall tales of the past being its imitative form. The point of view, established but carefully held undifferentiated at this stage, is of the two young sisters, Maria and Miranda, and the real concern is the romance and tragedy of their beautiful Aunt Amy. The whole substance of what might have been a romantic novel of the period is packed into a few pages, filtered through the consciousness of the two young girls. Yet it all seems leisurely, even digressive. Describing the way in which the family passed on its own history, Porter is able at once to give a clue to her own method in this section and to indicate the flaw at the heart of her family's, and American, history, a romantic commitment of the heart and the imagination to the past.

In part 2, Maria and Miranda are young schoolgirls in a New Orleans convent; they are now characterized as quite different, still seeing the world together but reacting differently to it. Here there is a single, central event: their meeting with Uncle Gabriel, the dashing figure of the tragic legend of Aunt Amy, a confrontation with reality. Beautifully executing her chosen point of view, Porter avoids the easy way out, of letting this event have a shattering and instant impact on the two young girls. The impact is implied. One sees what they see and feels what they feel, but one is not invited, as might have been the case in a much more conventional story of youthful disillusionment, to shatter the credible spell of their youth. Moreover, the romantic past is not neatly (and falsely) discredited; it is modified. In part 3, the center of consciousness is Miranda, a young woman now, going home to the funeral of Uncle Gabriel and sharing her train ride by accident with the practical and worldly Cousin Eva, who had always been the antithesis of Aunt Amy. Here Miranda is capable, up to a point, of judging and evaluating the events of the past and able to decide to break with it. Yet the story, which has evolved and emerged as the story of Miranda growing up, is subtly and carefully shown to be incomplete. Porter, unlike many of her contemporaries, was not willing to settle for the simplistic "truth" of young idealism. Miranda's resolution at the end changes nothing as finally as she imagines, yet is in itself an inevitable change.

In *Old Mortality*, certain basic conditions are firmly established that will inform the tenor of the whole book. The subjects, the conflicts, are past and present, "romance" and "reality," a history of how the world changed and became what it is. The larger theme is change and mutability. All these things are shown through the characters, who grow and change credibly and with ever-increasing dimension. The framework is within the terms of the conventional serious story, but these conventions are given renewed vigor and life. Precisely at the point where the conventional response or reaction could end the story and be a solution, the artist gives the story an unexpected resonance by a new tightening of the screw. Her stories do not "end," then, but project a sense of life going on and echo afterward in the readers' mind, an effect that is artistically consistent with her theme and subject of change.

The second of the short novels, the widely known *Noon Wine*, stands in apparently sharp contrast to *Old Mortality*. In time, it parallels the first two parts of the other and, in fact, stands in relation to *Old Mortality* much as the second part of that story does to the first. It is a rural tragedy, plain and harshly realistic, the other side of the coin of the United States' nineteenth century past. Here there are two young people who grow up, too, grubby, small, towheaded, but they are not involved in the consciousness of the story. Apparently omniscient, the story gradually settles into the tragedy of Mr. Thompson, as unlikely a tragic figure as can be imagined, one who for a large part of the story is tagged with characteristics that are conventionally unsympathetic in modern writing. In the end, he changes in the reader's view and estimation, his awful suicide becoming tragic, but not through the usual trick of the revelation of something new or unknown about his character. His character evolves, grows as things happen to him cumulatively, just as the character of Miranda grew and changed in *Old Mortality*, though in a rude and realistic setting and without the benefits of great intelligence or sensibility. Taken together, the two short novels say, "From these roots we the living have grown to maturity." The result is, structurally, to focus attention forward on the final tale, the title story, *Pale Horse, Pale Rider*.

This story combines elements of both the previous stories. There is a real tragic romance, the love of Adam and Miranda, in many ways a parallel of the grand romance of Gabriel and Amy, in part a retelling of the Adam and Eve legend. In addition, there is plenty of the harsh reality of a country at war, in the closing days of World War I, and in the midst of the raging influenza epidemic that marked the end of that war. This sickness takes the life of Adam and almost kills Miranda as well. The story ends with the end of the war and Miranda leaving the hospital, "cured." The final image again projects a future, but now a strangely bleak and bitter one. All things have changed. Part of the subtlety of this story lies in the author's ability to use the war, conventionally, as the end of something of the old order and the loss of something indefinable from the American spirit, and yet to do this within the context of the home front. The raging epidemic, at first as seemingly remote as the bloody fields of France, gradually becomes part of the whole sickness that inflamed the world and destroyed so much. Miranda emerges as much a war casualty as any shell-shocked veteran.

The three short novels of *Pale Horse, Pale Rider* are related and designed to give a rich and complex social history. Porter was not often credited with being a social historian as well as a fine crafter of prose. Perhaps the reason was that she was only indirectly concerned with politics and so those critics whose social vision was conditioned by their political views could not grant the truth of her grand theme. Yet politics is a two-dimensional enterprise, a game of "the image." Porter's fictional art is based upon the flesh and spirit of character, and none of her characters remains an "image" for long. The social history of *Ship of Fools* or *The Leaning Tower and Other Stories* (1944), for example, is evident; it is equally present in *Pale Horse, Pale Rider*. Yet in a larger sense social history was, however complex, merely part of her design. Social history becomes, by the examples of recurring and parallel events, much more than chronology. It becomes a stage where human beings act out their lives. The scenes change, but the human heart and all its mystery does not. Her deepest concern is with people, with character, and in this compassionate and always honest concern she joins the ranks of the very few great artists of fiction. *Pale Horse, Pale Rider*, her three short and related novels, would guarantee her that place among the few had she never written another line.

Something is radically wrong with the working definition of "the novel" if it does not include a book composed and arranged as this one is, able to do more and say more than many weighty works twice the total length. In Porter's rhetoric, there is great respect for the reader. She engages the reader's imagination and lets it work too. The result is a highly condensed fiction that does not seem so because of the richness of echo that she has managed to suggest and evoke. There is nothing small about her work. Its aims are the grandest to which a writer can aspire. Its glory is the remarkable and daring achievement of those aims.

PATERSON

Type of work: Poetry
Author: William Carlos Williams (1883-1963)
First published: 1946-1958

Paterson is Williams' poetic meditation on modern humanity and the nature of urban life, interweaving the story of one man with the larger story of his city.

Anyone who picks up a copy of William Carlos Williams' *Paterson* and gives it a hasty reading may arrive at the end of the poem with a feeling not unlike that of traditional country bumpkins on their first trip to the big city: There are so many different things to look at, in so many different shapes and sizes, and all the people seem to be rushing about so haphazardly, that the poor rustics wind up their day in bemused but happy confusion. Such a reaction to *Paterson* is part of Williams' purpose, for this poem interweaves the story of a city with the story of a man so that the two become interchangeable; and the jumbled kaleidoscope of city life turns and glitters like the conflicting ideas, dreams, loves, and hates that assail the minds of modern humans.

Looked at more closely, however, the poem begins to take on shape, like a city coming out from under a rolling fog or a man walking out of the shadows of trees in a park. Williams unifies his poem by letting the river that flows through the city serve as a symbol of life, both the city's and the man's. That life is like a river flowing somewhere safe to sea is certainly an image as old as poetry itself, but Williams' style and presentation are so fresh, so individual, that he seems to have invented the idea. The poem is divided into four books that correspond to four parts of the river: first, the river above the falls; second, the falls itself; third, the river below the falls; and fourth, the entrance of the river into the sea. Williams opens the first book, called "The Delineaments of the Giants," with these lines:

> Paterson lies in the valley under the
>   Passaic Falls
> its spent waters forming the outline of
>   his back. He
> lies on his right side, head near the
>   thunder
> of the water filling his dreams!

Having quickly presented the blended image of city and man, the poet lets the reader know that there are also symbols for women: a flower, a cliff, the falls. He then introduces one of the main concerns of *Paterson*: the search for a language by which human beings may "redeem" the tragedies of life. To counterbalance this somewhat abstract and nebulous idea, Williams intersperses his poem with many concrete passages, some in prose, that serve as an entrancing documentation of the background of the city and the man. In Book I, for example, historical notes and newspaper clippings tell of the finding of pearls in mussels taken from Notch Brook, near the city; of General Washington's encounter with "a monster in human form"; of the accidental drowning of a Mrs. Cumming at the falls; of the death there of a stuntman named Sam Patch; and of a great catch of eels made by the local people when a lake was drained. Paterson the man is represented by letters written to him, one from a misunderstood female poet. Williams rounds off Book I with a quotation from John Addington Symonds' *Studies of the Greek Poets* (1873-1876). Such diversity of material seems to call for a prestidigitator to make it all seem a part of the whole; Williams does it easily, for he is a master juggler who never quite lets his readers see all the act, making them fill in some of the parts from their own imaginations.

"Sunday in the Park," the title of Book II, concerns itself chiefly with love, including the many kinds of courtship found in a city park, and with poetry, for *Paterson* is as much a tribute to language as it is to a city or a man. Fittingly, this section ends with another long passage from a letter written by the female poet, who is struggling to fit together her work, her life, and her friendship with the "dear doctor" to whom she writes. Book III, "The Library," continues to probe the inarticulateness of tragedy and death, searching for some way that language may assuage, even prevent, those things that one accepts so complacently as a part of existence. In these beautiful lines, Williams has this to say about poetry:

> The province of the poem is the world.
> When the sun rises, it rises in the
>   poem
> and when it sets darkness comes down
> and the poem is dark

Book III also describes a great fire that sweeps the city, destroying the library. The poet continues to insert prose passages, and one of these tells the story of Merselis Van Giesen, whose wife was tormented by a witch that appeared to her nightly in the form of a black cat. In telling the story, Williams throws in a few comments that display his sense of humor, a talent so lacking in many modern poets. When the witch is revealed to be a Mrs. B., "who lived in the gorge in the hill beyond," he comments, "Happy souls! whose devils lived so near." Interspersing the tale with other witty remarks, the poet winds it up by having the husband shoot the cat with a silver bullet made from his cuff links. The shot is a difficult one because the cat is visible only to his wife, who must locate the target for him and direct his aim. He kills the cat and, in the tradition of witch stories, Mrs. B. suffers for some time with a sore on her leg.

Book IV, "The Run to the Sea," which opens with an idyl involving Corydon, Phyllis, and Paterson, also introduces that specter of modern times, the Bomb. The poem concludes when Paterson the man reaches the sea, but he, along with a dog found swimming there, is able to escape from this symbol of death and to head inland.

This poem, which Williams published in sections between 1946 and 1958, has been compared with Walt Whitman's *Leaves of Grass* (1855-1892), Hart Crane's *The Bridge* (1930), and Archibald MacLeish's *Conquistador* (1932). It is certainly as good as anything written by Crane, but it lacks the eloquent brilliance of *Conquistador* and to compare Williams with Whitman is stretching the superlatives until they become tenuous. Whitman writes like a great wind that sweeps readers off their feet, buffeting them with words until they are exhausted; Williams wafts a far gentler breeze. While *Paterson* is a poem filled with variety and surprises, it cannot match the symphonic effect created by Whitman in *Leaves of Grass*. There are times in this poem when Williams turns his kaleidoscope so quickly that one would like to quote from his own work:

> . . . Geeze, Doc, I guess it's all right but what the hell does it mean?

On the other hand, passages of great lyrical beauty occur frequently in *Paterson*, and a careful reading of the poem creates the feeling that one has visited a typical American city and been taken on a tour of it by a man who tells its history as one walks along. More important, one becomes acquainted with the man himself: He is clever, witty, sensitive, wise, and deeply concerned with the people of his city and with their problems. Thus does *Paterson* achieve its purpose; one makes friends with a man and a city, both blended into one of the most fascinating poems of the twentieth century.

THE PEOPLE, YES

Type of work: Poetry
Author: Carl Sandburg (1878-1967)
First published: 1936

With a great love of ordinary Americans, Sandburg celebrates his country—its vibrant colloquialisms, its legends and real-life history, and its heroes both famous and unknown.

For his readers during the Great Depression of the 1930's, the time of breadlines and soup kitchens, it was a pleasure to step suddenly into the bustling sunshine of Carl Sandburg's *The People, Yes.* His strong voice remains cheerful and reassuring. Sandburg does not raise his voice to shout down the pessimists; he hymns America out of no sense of duty. His book arises from a genuine love of the plain people who will somehow survive their blunders, somehow find the answers to "Where to? What next?"

In the opening section of this volume, Sandburg lets these questions be asked by the children of workers who come to build the Tower of Babel and at the end, when the poet looks forward to the "Family of Man" and the time when "brother may yet line up with brother," the questions are still unanswered. In between, the poet makes his tribute to people in general and the American people in particular: Here are the legends, the sayings, the slang, the tall tales, and the dreams of twentieth century American society.

Two of the best (and most quoted) sections of the book are the one on Abraham Lincoln and the one on tall tales, beginning "They have yarns . . ." Sandburg is world famous as an authority on Lincoln; there are his great biography and many poems, speeches, and articles. Yet nowhere is he more successful than in this short poem, which presents the many talents of a great man by asking a series of questions such as "Lincoln? was he a poet?" and "Lincoln? was he a historian?" and then gives the answers from quoted speeches, letters, and conversations of the man himself. The tall-tales poem is an encyclopedia of laughs ranging all the way from the familiar "man who drove a swarm of bees across the Rocky Mountains and the Desert 'and didn't lose a bee'" to the not-so-familiar story of a shipwrecked sailor who has caught hold of a stateroom door and floated in near the coast; when his would-be rescuers tell him he is off New Jersey, he takes a fresh hold on the door and calls back "half-wearily, 'I guess I'll float a little farther.'"

Much of *The People, Yes* is in this same lighthearted tone, for Sandburg loves the American language and the twists that the people give to their sayings. For irony, he quotes from a memorial stone:

> "We, near whose bones you stand,
> were Iroquois.
> The wide land which is now yours,
> was ours.
> Friendly hands have given us back
> enough for a tomb."

For homespun wisdom, he offers this advice: "Sell the buffalo hide after you have killed the buffalo." For unsophistication, he throws in: "The coat and the pants do the work but the vest gets the gravy." There are scores of other wisecracks and jokes, some new and some that wink at the reader like old friends from childhood.

Sandburg has also filled his book with American people—the real, the legendary, and the anonymous. Among the real ones are John Brown, "who was buried deep and didn't stay so"; George Eastman, "the kodak king," who at the age of seventy-seven shot himself to avoid the childishness of senility; and the Wright brothers, who "wanted to fly for the sake of flying." The legends include Mike Fink, John Henry, and, of course, Paul Bunyan, to whom Sandburg devotes a whole section, explaining how the people created this Master Lumberjack, his Seven Axmen, and Benny, his Little Blue Ox. Of the anonymous, there are hundreds, and Sandburg pays tribute to them all, from whoever first said "Wedlock is a padlock" to whoever first remarked, "No peace on earth with the women, no life anywhere without them."

If readers fear that Sandburg will consistently handle the American people with the twin kid gloves of gentleness and affection, they can quickly put their minds at rest. When he feels like it, Sandburg puts on the boxing gloves of a prizefighter (as he had often done since his *Chicago Poems* was first published in 1916) and flails away at what he hates: the liars who do not care what they do to their customers so long as they make a sale; the torturers and the wielders of the rubber hose; the cynics who shrug off the unemployed; the crooked lawyers; the judges who can be bought and those who boast that they can buy them; and, most of all, the mis-leaders who spit out the word "peepul" as if it were scum hocked from their throats.

Of the many books that Sandburg wrote, both prose and poetry, *The People, Yes* came closest to being his coda, his summing up of what he tried to say in a lifetime. As if to indicate as much, he includes echoes from earlier poems. There is the hyacinths-biscuits combination that appeared first in one of his most famous definitions of poetry; he mentions the Unknown Soldier, "the boy nobody knows the name of"; and he includes the refrain from his "Four Preludes on Playthings of the Wind": "We are the greatest city, the greatest people. Nothing like us ever was." Certainly the themes in this book are the same as those that run through all of Sandburg's poetry: his love of the United States and its democracy, the mystery of humankind and where it is going, and the hope that people everywhere will someday blunder through the fogs of injustice, hypocrisy, and skulduggery into a bright world of peace. Sandburg put it all in *The People, Yes* and expressed it perfectly in the fluent style that only he could master. No American poet had a better ear for the right combination of words and certainly none has ever matched his ability at writing dialogue, at putting on paper the way Americans really talk.

As in all books, there are caution signs for the reader to observe. No one should try to read *The People, Yes* at one sitting. It is not a narrative poem with suspense enough to carry one along breathless to the end. Some of the sections are repetitious, and in places the Whitman-esque cataloging drones on monotonously. Perhaps these are flaws that Sandburg might have corrected by devoting more individual sections to the telling of a single story, as in the poems on Lincoln and Paul Bunyan. Sometimes one gets the feeling that over the years the poet kept a gigantic notebook that he crammed with all the jokes and picturesque sayings that he ever heard; then he sat down with notebook beside him and patiently strung them on the strings that are his central themes. Such a feeling can be ameliorated if the reader treats this volume as a sort of reference book without the dryness the word "reference" usually connotes. Here is writing to be dipped into, savored for a time, and put aside, to be taken up again when a sense of humor is drooping, when faith in American democracy is limp and cold.

> The people will live on.
> The learning and blundering people
>   will live on.
>   They will be tricked and sold
>   and again sold
> And go back to the nourishing earth
>   for rootholds . . .
>
> ———
>
> . . . In the darkness with a great bun-
>   dle of grief
>   the people march.
> In the night, and overhead a shovel of
>   stars for
>   keeps, the people march:
>   "Where to? What next?"

PERSONAE: The Collected Poems of Ezra Pound

Type of work: Poetry
Author: Ezra Pound (1885-1972)
First published: 1926

When Personae, *a collection of Pound's shorter poems, was published in 1926, it served as both a summation of his career to date and a promise of great things to come—a promise soon fulfilled by his* Cantos.

From the beginning, Ezra Pound's problem was to re-create what he found meaningful in the past and yet sound modern. He solved the problem partially in *Hugh Selwyn Mauberley* (1920), completely in the *Cantos* (1925-1968). That he did solve it is attested by the enormous influence of his poetry and criticism on the modern idiom, an influence felt even by those who find it difficult to understand him. Yet the solution to what was essentially a problem of form meant, inevitably, any number of false starts that the later Pound would seek, quite humanly, to ignore.

Personae, the 1926 collection of Ezra Pound's shorter poems, notes that it contains all of his poems to date except for the unfinished *Cantos*. The statement is misleading. The volume contains a relatively small selection of the very early Pound, the poet who could, without any difficulty, have two of his poems published in *The Oxford Book of Victorian Verse* ("Ballad for Gloom" and "The Portrait," neither reprinted in *Personae*), and the Pound who smacks so clearly of the pre-Raphaelites, of Algernon Charles Swinburne, of the poetry of the 1890's, of William Butler Yeats, and of Robert Browning. Of the 145 poems printed in Pound's first volumes—*A Lume Spento* (1908), *A Quinzaine for This Yule* (1908), *Personae* (1909), *Exultations* (1909), and *Canzoni* (1911)—only forty-two survive in the *Personae* volume of 1926. Basically, this is the Pound concerned with medieval themes, Provençal forms, and, generally, the tradition of the aesthetes.

In both imagery and idea, "Grace Before Song," from *A Lume Spento*, bespeaks the aesthetic ideal of the 1890's. Concern with fleeting moods, lack of concern with society—these attitudes describe at least one aspect of the decadence. Because the English decadence drew heavily on Swinburne and the pre-Raphaelites, one finds Pound following suit. The medieval atmosphere of the pre-Raphaelite ballad is also to be found in Pound's "Ballad Rosalind."

The pre-Raphaelite ideal of feminine beauty is never absent from these early poems; indeed, it never quite seems to have left Pound. As for the impact of Swinburne, it is defined by Pound himself in the reverential "Salve O Pontifex—for Swinburne; an hemi-chaunt." Of the early Yeats, Pound was almost a disciple. One critic has pointed out that "the Tree" is a compendium of Yeatsian influences. Yeats's opening lines from "He Thinks of His Past Greatness When a Part of the Constellations of Heaven," with their references to the hazel tree and grief for all things known, are clearly echoed in Pound's poem.

The central fact of these early volumes is the tremendous variety of influences and modes. Pound is clearly a seeker who is willing to try anything at least once. In these early volumes, one also discovers Pound's concern with translation as providing both techniques for the developing poet and insight into earlier states of mind. At this point, unfortunately, Pound's translations, mainly from Provençal and early Italian, were colored by pre-Raphaelite diction and turns of phrase. Thus, not only did he fail to "make it new," to quote a favorite phrase of Pound, but the translations are rather obfuscated as well.

Ripostes, published in 1912, is generally taken to mark a turning point in his poetry, but there is still much of the old preciosity in "A Virginal" and "Silet." The best poems (and some of the worst) are translations and adaptations. As always, Pound is never concerned with literal translation, but with a revival of the spirit of the poet and his time; ultimately, the translation is as much Pound's work as the original poet's. The volume contains Pound's famous version of "The Seafarer," for it was inevitable that Pound should attempt at least one example of Anglo-Saxon form. (He repeated it later in "Canto I.") The volume contains also "The Return," modeled on a poem by Henri Régnier.

The poem deals with the return of the Greek gods, who, to Pound, represent eternally recurrent states of mind, the states that are defined again and again in the *Cantos*. It stands as a metaphor of Pound's efforts to make what is still alive in the past speak to and help salvage the present, an effort represented in *Ripostes* by "The Seafarer." It also suggests a shift in allegiance away from the poets of the English decadence to the French Symbolists, who helped Pound, as they helped Eliot and others, learn how to be modern.

By the time he published *Ripostes*, Pound had begun to teach others, becoming a propagandist for the Imagist movement, with its stress on compactness and concreteness. In 1914, he edited the anthology *Des Imagistes*, and in the following year he published what was essentially a set of variations on the Imagist mode in *Cathay*, a book of translations from the Chinese, based on notes left behind him by the expert on Japanese art, Ernest Fenollosa. Inaccurate as they are, these translations are still considered the best introduction to Chinese poetry available to most Westerners. Pound knew not a word of Chinese; clearly his ability to work with Fenollosa's notes was the result of a deeply felt affinity with the nature of Chinese poetry, its avoidance of abstract statement, and its reliance on concrete imagery to suggest mood and idea. Thus, in the famous "River-Merchant's Wife: A Letter," the wife's sense of loss and desire for her absent husband are suggested not by direct assertions, but by indirect description.

In 1916, again working from Fenollosa's notes, Pound, who knew no more Japanese than he did Chinese, published *'Noh' or Accomplishment*. Again inaccurate in many ways, the work made Japanese drama available to the Western mind. In the same year, Pound published *Lustra*, which presented the work of Pound's Imagist period, a Pound free of clutter. Certainly Pound seemed to think so, as one may note in "Salutation the Second."

The sardonic attitude toward his audience is repeated in a number of poems: "Tenzone," "The Condolence," "Salutation," "Causa," "Commission," "Further Instructions," and "Salvationists." It is clear that the satiric muse had taken possession of Pound, and it is employed to pillory many of the states of mind later satirized in the *Cantos* as useless, confused, and uncreative. Among these satiric poems are "The Garden," "Les Millwin," "The Bellaires," and "Our Contemporaries." Seeking hardness and directness, Pound had gone to the Latin and Greek epigrammatists, and a number of the poems reflect this study. Though scarcely Imagistic, the epigrams—"The New Cake of Soap," "Epitaph," "Arides," "The Bath Tub," and a number of others—are concentrated and in this way reflect one of the major concerns of the Imagistic movement. The translations, too, have shed their pre-Raphaelite haze, a fact exhibited in translation from the Provençal of Bertran de Born. Imagistic poems proper, as well as adaptations from the Chinese, appear, including what has become the archetype of the Imagistic poem, "In a Station of the Metro."

The relatively bald statements of the satires, the sharp pictures of the Imagistic poems, are mingled with poems that show the astonishing qualities of Pound's ear: such lyrics as "The Spring," an adaptation of Ibycus, and "Dance Figure," based, apparently, on the mood of "The Song of Songs."

Lustra gives one the impression of an author testing his technical skills in preparation for a major work. It came in 1920 with *Hugh Selwyn Mauberley*, which a number of critics consider Pound's breakthrough, the poem in which he became, finally, modern. Other long poems of the period are the culmination of earlier developments: Translations as a means of re-creating an earlier poetic mood may be seen in "Homage to Sextus Propertius," satire in "Moeurs Contemporaines" and "Villanelle: The Psychological Hour." A sequence rather than a single poem, *Hugh Selwyn Mauberley* is modern in its tight juxtaposition of disparate moods and images, in its containment of a complex of attitudes and experiences, and in its careful, often ironic, control of tone. The poem maintains a duality, a deliberate ambivalence, that can be confusing. It mocks, and bids farewell to, the aesthete in Pound.

Yet if the aesthete is out of step with his time, the time itself is nothing to be proud of, and several poems deal with its pervasive tawdriness. World War I, the ultimate shock to the aesthete, raises the question of the relevance of art and culture in a period of confusion and change. Neither the pre-Raphaelites nor the aesthetes seem to have very much to say in such a time because they fail to reflect the mood of the decade. Successful writers, like "Mr. Nixon," who probably represents Arnold Bennett, are as tawdry as their age. Thus, in the tenth poem of the sequence one is told that, in an age of cheapness and insincerity that is impatient of craftsmanship or indifferent to the heroic example of the artist, the stylist has sought shelter from the world. In the second part of *Hugh Selwyn Mauberley*, the poet drifts toward death, unable to create what "The Age Demanded," and also unable to provide what the age needed: poetry that would relate his private passions to the society around him.

The confrontation of poet and society took place, finally, in the *Cantos*, the long, major poem on which Pound was already at work.

THE PILGRIM HAWK: A Love Story

Type of work: Novel
Author: Glenway Wescott (1901-1987)
Type of plot: Psychological realism
Time of plot: An afternoon in May, 1929
Locale: Chancellet, a town in France
First published: 1940

Wescott explores the nature of love, lust, jealousy, freedom, and captivity in The Pilgrim Hawk. *By focusing on the events of one afternoon as told through the eyes of a writer ten years later, the author can provide a complex tapestry of perceptions, as well as symbols—primary among them the captive hawk of the title.*

Principal Characters

Alwyn Tower, the narrator, a young American novelist. His memories of that afternoon in 1929 when he met the Cullens are filtered through the years and through his artistic viewpoint. Although Tower rarely turns his attention upon himself, the reader is able to discern his character from Tower's interpretations of the events around him.

Madeleine Cullen, a wealthy, middle-aged, attractive Irishwoman. She keeps a trained hawk on her wrist, at the same time keeping her husband in check through games and manipulations.

Larry Cullen, her husband, an Irish aristocrat. Deeply in love with his wife and extremely jealous of other men and of the hawk, he tries to rebel against his situation, futilely pulling a gun on the others.

Alexandra Henry, Tower's friend, a wealthy young American. She discusses the afternoon's occurrences with Tower, concluding that such a display has persuaded her never to marry. Nevertheless, she returns to the United States and marries Tower's brother.

Ricketts, the Cullens' young Cockney chauffeur. He is one of the men who inspires jealousy in Larry Cullen in regard to his wife.

Lucy, the captive hawk, which tries unsuccessfully to gain its freedom when Mr. Cullen releases it.

The Pilgrim Hawk is a tapestry woven of five layers: the hawk's intrinsic or obvious resemblance to the characters; the extrinsic significance imposed by Alwyn Tower as a young man observing the relationship between the Cullens and the hawk; Tower's interpretations ten years later as the middle-aged narrator; the actual intentions of the author (who is very close to Tower); and the reader's own opportunities for seeing symbolic meaning in the hawk. With excellent artistic control, Glenway Wescott conducts the reader in and out of this labyrinth of symbols.

Wescott's strategy is most effective. He draws the reader into Tower's nostalgia for the scene itself by conjuring up the aura of the late 1920's, when Americans lived in romantic self-exile in Europe. In the French town of Chancellet, Tower's friend, Alexandra Henry, has renovated a stable; the interior is ultramodern, with a gigantic picture window that looks out on a wild English-type garden in the back. Having set the stage for the surprise arrival of Madeleine Cullen and her exotic entourage,

Wescott evokes an initial *tableau vivant* that explains Tower's urge to relive, to witness to the reader, the mystery of that afternoon. En route to Budapest in a sleek, dark Daimler, Madeleine Cullen stops off to see her friend Alexandra. A handsome woman with Irish eyes and a London voice, she emerges in fine French clothes and on spectacularly high heels. On her wrist, which is encased in a bloodstained gauntlet, perches a leashed hawk wearing a plumed Dutch hood. Ricketts, a dapper young Cockney chauffeur, and the stout, slightly inebriated Larry Cullen help her over the cobblestones. It is little wonder that Tower is given, even ten years later, to making symbolic connections; at the center of the poetic image, Lucy, the hawk, is an exemplary bird, a many-feathered symbol of love and lust.

Wescott seats his four main characters around the living room and proceeds to satisfy Tower's, Alexandra's, and the reader's curiosity by making Mr. Cullen talkative about falcons and falconry. Later, the four take a walk in the formal garden of a nearby château; the Cullens are diverted by its owner. This tactic gives Wescott a chance to have Alexandra satisfy Tower's and the reader's curiosity about the Cullens. Having left their two wild boys at Cullen Hall in Ireland, they have traveled constantly; become involved with Irish revolutionaries; gone on pig-sticking hunts in Tangier and lion hunts in the jungle. In these activities, Madeleine Cullen is the aggressive one; Larry Cullen merely follows.

Wescott then prepares for the climax of the afternoon's drama. After the ritual feeding of Lucy in the living room, the bird is placed on a bench in the wild garden, while Mrs. Cullen and Alexandra take a rest before dinner. At the chromium bar on the balcony, the drunken Mr. Cullen talks to Tower as he would to a bartender, and one gets more direct information about the Cullens. The husband almost killed an Irish poet out of unjustified jealousy (his wife allows him his own infidelities); compared with his superlative wife, he is a bad horseman, marksman, and sportsman; he loathes travel; and, above all, he despises Lucy who, constantly perched on Madeleine's wrist, prevents him from getting close to his wife. As Cullen's foolishness unveils itself, Tower's malice (the scorn of a captive hawk) increases.

Aware of the symbolic and psychological complexity of his raw material, Wescott imposes control by creating a clear structure of events and a careful series of highly expressive images in a vivid, descriptive style. This control is especially strong in the melodramatic denouement, which comes in three parts: the drunken Mr. Cullen stalks Lucy, removes its hood, and cuts its leash; Mrs. Cullen kicks off her high heels and recaptures the bird; then, just as the Cullens resume their journey and their car heads toward Budapest, Cullen himself tries to achieve liberty by pulling a gun—although it is ambiguous as to whether he intended to shoot the chauffeur (whom he suspects of coveting his wife), Mrs. Cullen, Lucy, or himself. As the bird makes a flapping attempt to hold on, Mrs. Cullen rushes back into the house and out to the garden and throws the revolver into the pond. After the Cullens' final exit, Wescott provides a necessary anticlimax in which Tower, Alexandra, and the reader attempt to see some pattern in the afternoon's events.

Wescott differentiates his characters partly by the degree of awareness with which each plucks the bird of its symbolic resemblances to human nature. Tower and Alexandra (who is normally not curious) are eager to see such correspondences. Sitting erect in a straight kitchen chair, Mrs. Cullen makes swift transitions from hawk to human until she sees that her husband, sunk into a soft easy chair, senses certain comparisons to himself.

Like Nick Carraway in F. Scott Fitzgerald's *The Great*

Gatsby (1925) and Marlow in several Joseph Conrad stories, Tower and his ambiguous responses are almost as interesting and crucial to the story as the romantic characters whose behavior he witnesses. One of the experiences that Wescott creates is the reader's puzzled effort to sift and separate the narrator's reflections and judgments in 1929 from those that he makes in 1940 as he gazes backward. Wescott cunningly keeps Tower's voice out of the dialogue until the end, when he converses with Alexandra; the effect is that one hears his mature voice at some distance, contemplating, musing, shifting back and forth in time and attitude. His tone fluctuates among intense curiosity, intellectual excitement, emotional reserve, repulsion, fascination, sadness, amusement, wit, and irony. The reader may get a little impatient with Tower's constant symbol-mongering, his seizing the least pretext to express insights on love, marriage, drunkenness, the aristocracy, animals as compared with people, sports, and numerous other subjects. Out of all that, however, his character is distilled.

Tower's interest in the Cullens is an extension of his interest in himself. Outdoors people, they are self-centered, non-introspective, strenuous, self-indulgent, and emotionally idle. Tower feels a cool affinity first with Mrs. Cullen (who signals her desire for his understanding), because, like an artist, she is in control of an artificial but satisfying situation that at any moment may revert to the chaos of nature. Then, reluctantly, Tower shifts to Mr. Cullen, for Tower is also a lover and can empathize with the man's predicament: He is a drunken, weak, vain, jealous, dull, mediocre, irritable, boring, conceited, childish fool in love with his wife—who also declares her love for him.

Tower sees that Mrs. Cullen tries to create situations which will allow her husband's masculinity full rein, while she restrains his wildness at the same time. He is a passionate man with streaks of animal ferocity and a desire for the liberty of the wilderness; like the falconer in William Butler Yeats's "The Second Coming," Mrs. Cullen strives to control him, but she is wild herself. She has always wanted a real haggard (trained falcon) to train herself; now she has two. She needs on her pulse an avatar of wildness: Controlling the falcon, she controls herself. When she persuades Tower to take Lucy on his wrist, Mrs. Cullen becomes electric with restlessness.

Like most falcons, Lucy often makes hopeless escape attempts. As a species, birds are free; only individuals are captive. Yet all human beings are captives; each must attempt to gain freedom. Exceptional is the bird that loves captivity; exceptional is the human who truly loves freedom. In captivity, both bird and human require a falconer. The human paradox is seen in the Cullens' relationship: He needs freedom, but she needs a captive; at the same time, he fears freedom, and she is loath to be a captor. Thus, Lucy both humiliates and sublimates Larry Cullen: He frees her to be rid of her and to make a symbolic gesture of escape; he attempts his own actual release when he pulls the gun.

One sees how expert Madeleine Cullen's falconry is when she recaptures the hawk, then the husband. Drink, food, and philandering are to Mr. Cullen what a hood, a pigeon, and Mrs. Cullen's stroking fingers are to Lucy: a tranquilization of the instinct to wildness. Purblind to what she is doing to her husband, Mrs. Cullen, too, is hooded. Both the gun and the hawk are new in the Cullens' life, because in middle age they have exhausted love and are now dependent upon distractions, deceptions, disguises—semblances of love.

Tower tells Alexandra that, given the Cullens as examples, she will never marry. She returns to the United States, however, where she meets and marries Tower's brother; it is Tower who does not marry. Married or not, however, all humans become haggards, spending most of their lives on some perch. Having surrendered to domestication, hawks become scornful of one another; they never breed in captivity. Even wild hawks rarely die of disease, but death by starvation is common. Madeleine has seen people in the Dublin insane asylum whose eyes had an expression similar to those of a starving hawk. Like the lover and the artist, once a hawk loses its tech-

nique, it enters a hopeless cycle of deterioration. The hawk in the sky looks down on its prey; Tower the writer looks down from his tower on human behavior, as when he devours Cullen's story, with the conscious intention of remembering every word and image of that afternoon. Although he occasionally turns his scrutinizing eye upon himself, Tower employs diversionary tactics to avoid the truth. Told the details of the aging hawk's life, he has an intuition of growing old as an artist and a lover. He was failing in 1929; in 1940, he is bitter, nervous, apathetic, full of false pride, bereft of inspiration, and bored.

The concept of vision is one of Wescott's most effective motifs. He describes the hawk's eyes, their function in the hunt, the purpose of the hood; then in various ways he compares the hawk's eyes with those of the other characters. Tower mentions his longsightedness, expresses fear of going blind, and his immediate fear (which he shares with Cullen) that the hawk may attack his eyes. Tower's testimony, with its ambiguous tone and compulsive philosophizing, is a failed artist and lover's means of trying to see while remaining blind to the meaning of that bizarre afternoon. Yet the reader's vision comes into lucid focus. Wescott's use here of the Jamesian point of view is one of the most successful in American literature.

In this manner of handling the parallel between captive hawk and the various forms of human captivity, Wescott controls the flight pattern of the reader as falcon, thus exhibiting the discipline of the artist as falconer.

THE POETRY OF ANNE BRADSTREET

Type of work: Poetry
Author: Anne Bradstreet (1612?-1672)
Principal published works: *The Tenth Muse Lately Sprung Up in America*, 1650; *Several Poems Compiled with Great Variety of Wit and Learning*, 1678.

The astonishing thing about the poetry of Anne Bradstreet is the cultural isolation in which it was composed, for along with her husband, Simon, she belonged to the earliest migration to the Massachusetts Bay Colony. When they arrived on the *Arbella* in 1630, she was around eighteen. The Bay Colony did include educated people. Bradstreet's father, Thomas Dudley, was chosen deputy governor to John Winthrop before the *Arbella* sailed and later became one of the first overseers of Harvard College. He is said to have composed poetry himself, and without a doubt his daughter grew to maturity in a household in which literature mattered. Simon Bradstreet had taken bachelor's and master's degrees at Emmanuel College, Cambridge. These were men of affairs, however— administrators who employed their talents in the multifarious business of the struggling young colony and had little time or opportunity to cultivate the arts in the New World.

Poetry thrives in communities of poets, and England's creative writers were not flocking to Colonial America. Anne Bradstreet must often have felt artistically lonely in Ipswich and Andover, Massachusetts, in the 1630's and 1640's. In England, the poems of John Donne, George Herbert, Ben Jonson, and many other important writers were appearing in print, as was the early work of John Milton. One has only to compare the versification of *The Bay Psalm Book* (1640) with the renderings of the same Psalms that Sir Philip Sidney and his sister Mary, the countess of Pembroke, had made in the 1580's and 1590's to gain a sense of the aesthetic distance between the England from which the Dudleys and Bradstreets migrated and the raw New World. It can be argued that the popular New England book version, far from having any poetical pretensions, was intended instead to serve the purpose of practical devotion, but other scraps of early New England poetry also reflect sensibilities that saw verse principally as a convenient vehicle for commonplaces, usually religious in nature. Bradstreet's volume *The Tenth Muse Lately Sprung Up in America* published, in England incidentally, at mid-century, signals the appearance of the first American settler who can be called, without the necessity of qualifications, a poet.

Bradstreet's brother-in-law John Woodbridge is thought to have conveyed her manuscript to England after having "snatched" it from her, Bradstreet alleges in a later poem, before she had a chance to perfect it, although her protestations may have been a conventional ploy to disarm criticism. She was intensely aware of being not only a poet but a woman poet as well—an unlikely sort of creature even in Europe at the time. She left England in a great age of English poetry, but one in which women practitioners seldom ventured beyond translation, the countess of Pembroke's Psalms being a case in point. That lady's niece, Lady Mary Wroth, composed a prose romance with interspersed poems, *Urania* (1621), an important step in the direction of original female authorship. It is likely that Bradstreet was familiar with these achievements of women who may have been at least distant relatives, for Philip and Mary Sidney's mother had also been a Dudley, though of a more aristocratic branch of the family.

While women poets were uncommon in England, a woman such as the countess of Pembroke, famous as a patron of poetry, was close enough to some of the finest poets in the realm to learn from them, but the only real poet to come to America before or during Bradstreet's time, Sir Walter Raleigh, did not stay. Therefore, Bradstreet had to rely on her knowledge of, and access to, European books of poetry. Fortunately, it was a great age of poetry. Critics have found evidence in her work of familiarity with William Shakespeare's work (and even with that of Geoffrey Chaucer, from a much earlier age), but her acknowledged heroes included two people better known in their time for other achievements but who were poets as well—Sir Philip Sidney and Queen Elizabeth. Bradstreet wrote elegies honoring both of them and another on the French poet Guillaume de Salluste, Seigneur du Bartas, whose biblical epic *La Semaine* (1578) earned the approval of such giants of English poetry as Sidney, Edmund Spenser, and Milton.

Such influences can be traced most readily in her early work, which was bookish and generalized: long poems with titles such as "The Ages of Man" and "The Four Seasons of the Year." Only gradually did she develop the knack of writing specifically about the events and experiences of her life, thereby producing the poems that modern readers find most interesting. Except for "The

Prologue," in which she defends her entry into the masculine stronghold of poetry, her most commonly anthologized poems are products of her forties and fifties composed after *The Tenth Muse Lately Sprung Up in America* first appeared.

Titles such as "To the Memory of My Dear and Ever Honored Father Thomas Dudley Esq. Who Deceased, July 31, 1653, and of His Age 77" and "Here Follows Some Verses upon the Burning of Our House July 10th, 1666," however, suggest how personal and specific her later writing became. She may well have fallen back on such material only because she had exhausted the early ambitious works for which she might hope to be remembered. If so, she belongs to the considerable group of poets who would be surprised to discover what posterity values in their work.

The first half of "The Prologue," a poem of eight heroic sestets, disclaims any capacity for work of epic proportions. She is too "weak," too "mean" a poet to compose in such a vein. The last four stanzas declare her acceptance of the status of minor poet. She will settle for "thyme or parsley wreath" rather than "bays." Interestingly, however, the "bays" or laurel that had come to symbolize poetic as well as heroic accomplishment was botanically just another version of the bay leaves familiar to all good housewives. She hints at the insecurity of a male who would begrudge a female modest poetic competence, and she closes by pointing out that her "unrefined ore" will bring out the "glist'ring gold" of the male poets. A number of readers have accepted her humility as genuine and thoroughgoing, but in acknowledging that men judge her hand as one "a needle better fits" than a pen, it seems likely that she is using her pen as a needle to deflate the pretensions of the poetically dominant sex.

Several love poems to her husband dot the later, expanded edition of her work that appeared in 1678, six years after her death, as *Several Poems Compiled with Great Variety of Wit and Learning.* Simon is, in various poems, her gold mine, her "magazine of earthly store," her sun, her dove, her "turtle" (dove), her deer, her fish. Her poems to him when he was gone, as he frequently was, "upon public employment" can be intense. He is, for example, the "Sun" through whose "heat" she bore "those fruits" who are now nearby to remind her of him. Unlike most male love poets of her era, she offers no expression of the agonies of unrequited love or of the vicissitudes of a love affair. Married as a teenager, she remained married and in love with a man who outlived her by a quarter of a century. Though less intricate, one of her poems to Simon resembles thematically one that

another traveler, John Donne, presumably addressed to his wife, Anne. Donne's "A Valediction: Forbidding Mourning" is a greater poem than "A Letter to Her Husband, Absent upon Public Employment," but the way in which Bradstreet extracts possibilities from her controlling metaphor—Simon as her "Sun" whose heat generated her children, whose absence chills her now and causes her to "mourn in black," whose return to her "zodiac" will set her aglow—entitles it to the honor of acceptance as a first-class "metaphysical" conceit.

Needless to say, her children also are important subjects for this domestically oriented poet, and events such as their births, departures, and deaths occasion poems. "Before the Birth of One of Her Children" conveys her fear that she may not survive. It is addressed to Simon but is probably intended for his eyes only if she does die in childbirth. She surmises the likelihood of his marrying again but hopes that she may somehow continue to "seem thine." She strikes a somewhat discordant but no doubt prudent note in urging him to protect the children from "stepdame's injury."

She survived all lyings-in, however, and on June 23, 1659, she composed a charming tribute to her "eight birds," five of whom have flown away. Of the three boys, one has presumably gone to Europe, one is in the "academy," and one seems to have become a pioneer, while two girls have left with husbands. She deftly addresses them all, reminding them gently of their mother's "care" and "pain," assuring them that she cares and fears for them more than ever, and closing by asserting that their happiness is hers, all the while maintaining the bird imagery. The unpretentiousness and seeming simplicity of this poem notwithstanding, it is a very skillful composition in tetrameter couplets. Although Bradstreet here and in other poems used a high proportion of end-stopped lines, she varies the rhythm deftly to give variety to this ninety-six-line poem.

Her book itself becomes her child in "The Author to Her Book." It is here that she expresses her dismay at the fact of her work being made public too soon "after birth." She is embarrassed that this "rambling brat" (having rambled all the way to England) could call her "mother." The very sight of him is "irksome"; he is full of "defects" that she scarce knows how to "amend." In a pun of the sort that Sir Philip Sidney favored, she refers to the uneven "feet" of her poem, which result in a "hobbling" gait. She concludes by asking her "child" to say that he had no father and that his mother had sent him away from home because she was "poor." Her point is not that she lacks facility at poetry but that her poems were not yet ready for public scrutiny. It is difficult to escape the conclusion, however, that she thoroughly enjoyed the process of condemning her earlier work. As in the case of "The Prologue," the tone here is mock-modest. "The Author to Her Book" achieves its nominal purpose of apologizing for past deficiencies and a subtler one of displaying her keen wit and increasing mastery of her medium.

Several poems of the 1660's commemorate the deaths of grandchildren in early childhood. Reminding the reader of the terrible mortality rate of the seventeenth century, they are competent but conventional. Her grandchild Simon Bradstreet died in November, 1669, at the age of one month and one day: "No sooner came, but gone." He was the third budding Bradstreet flower to perish recently, "Cropped by th' Almighty's hand," in an arresting phrase. She immediately adds "yet is He good," for proper Puritan that she was, she would not permit her contemplation of such an event to decline into bitterness or doubt. Although here and elsewhere in her poetry her need to subdue a potentially rebellious temperament can be sensed, in none of these death poems does she express doubt about a deceased grandchild's heavenly destiny.

Despite the precariousness of life in her time, it seems particularly appropriate that Bradstreet left behind not only her poetry but also numerous surviving progeny, more than a few of them distinguished Americans. From various of her "birds" descended Wendell Phillips, Richard Henry Dana, Jr., and the famous father and son both named Oliver Wendell Holmes. Of American writers descended from Anne Bradstreet, the poet Edwin Arlington Robinson is particularly notable.

One of Bradstreet's finest poems is the thirty-three-stanza "Contemplations," composed considerably later than her other long poems, for otherwise it surely would have found a place in the 1650 volume. Its unusual stanza rhymes *ababccc*; its final line, like that of Edmund Spenser's famous stanza, is one foot longer than the preceding pentameter lines. It has been praised for its celebration of nature, and indeed it evokes the "delectable" leaves and fruits of autumn. Mainly, however, it is a meditation upon the ironic contrast between the mortal fondness of this ephemeral world, with its all-too-obvious mementos of vexation and pain, and humankind's largely submerged immortal longings. As she did in the earlier poems, Bradstreet generalizes to a considerable degree in "Contemplations," and she burdens the poem with some inessential mythological baggage ranging from Phoebus to Philomel, but the poem strikes a personal note nevertheless.

She contemplates the capacity of a woodland stream to flow—unimpeded, it seems—to the ocean that is its destination, in contrast to the obstructions of human life: She wishes that her own "rivulets" could come to rest. Despite human beings' capacity to sense the evanescence of earthly life and their reason to hope in a greater "security" thereafter, they fasten their attention on transitory enjoyments. The reader gains the sense of a thoughtful individual observing the irony of people's general inability to rise above their preoccupation with temporal things, including the benefits of nature, but this perspective is tempered by her humble awareness of the transcendent splendor of nature's author.

In contrast to Edward Taylor, the only other Colonial American poet whose work continues to be widely read and admired, Anne Bradstreet—thanks to her initiative, or that of her kinsman, in publishing her poems—was never lost sight of completely. In fact, Taylor had a copy of her poems in his Westfield, Massachusetts, parsonage. Nevertheless, her work was largely neglected well into the twentieth century. Early histories of American literature tend to ignore her or dismiss her curtly, Moses Coit Tyler near the end of the nineteenth century being for some time a lonely pioneer in appreciating her poetry. The Bradstreet revival owed something to both the feminist upsurge of the 1960's and the burgeoning of interest in social history.

Anne Bradstreet, however, is much more than a person from whose work it is possible to learn something about the life of a Colonial American woman. She is the only American poet before Taylor able to apply the rich Renaissance tradition to New World verse. She capitalized on the restrictions imposed on her as a Colonial housewife and mother by proving that quality poems could be written out of such experiences—paradoxically, at a time when early Restoration England was beginning to lose touch with the personal lyric so much in vogue when she sailed to America. Her work had to wait the better part of three centuries for the recognition that it deserved, but the history of American poetry now begins with this woman, who remains one of the most distinctive feminine poetic voices before Emily Dickinson.

THE POETRY OF E. E. CUMMINGS

Type of work: Poetry
Author: E. E. Cummings (1894-1962)
Principal published works: *Tulips and Chimneys*, 1923; *&*, 1925; *XLI Poems*, 1925; *Is 5*, 1926; *W: Seventy New Poems*, 1931; *No Thanks*, 1933; *1/20 Poems*, 1936; *50 Poems*, 1940; *1 × 1*, 1944; *Xiape*, 1950; *Poems, 1923-1954*, 1954; *95 Poems*, 1958; *73 Poems*, 1963.

The poetry of E. E. Cummings has always appealed to young people. This kinship with youth is no surprise, for even his last poems, the work of a man nearing seventy, celebrate the here and now of being, the eternal present in which limitless future pivots to limited past. It is this moment of aliveness and pure being that youth experiences most fully without regard to the relentless flow of time, and it is that experience which Cummings believed to be living, the only moment of truth.

What *is* is the present, and living fully requires that one expand to fill the moment, to experience it spiritually as well as physically. Cummings was a Romantic and a Transcendentalist, and he believed that the truth that is always here can only be found by love.

E. E. Cummings gave himself in his poetry fully to the life of the now and the love that gives that life its meaning. His thinking is certainly not new; it is as old as thought itself. Poetry is, however, an art of making new, of giving new life to the ideas that have always been, the eternal verities. Cummings set out to refresh his Romantic ideas, to make love itself new. His verbal pyrotechnics and typographical eccentricities are products and tools of that quest. By making language look new on the page, he forces his reader to engage the poem at a new level of concentration and, hopefully, to follow that engagement through to the moment of living that Cummings tried to catch up in the poem.

For example, the first poem in *95 Poems* is a definition of loneliness. Its devices are one metaphor, loneliness as a falling leaf; use of the similarity of the letter *l* to the numeral 1; use of the "one" in "loneliness," a typographical pattern emphasizing the long, narrow numeral 1 and the lone fall of a leaf; and a final definition of loneliness as I-ness. That is all, and yet it does make a simple metaphor into a small poem and demand the reader's involvement in that metaphor, if only to puzzle it out. It is a poem to be read silently on the page, a poem for the eye, but Cummings wrote most of his poems for the ear as well. The cool elegance of the opening of "All in green went my love riding" is an example of this smooth ballad style.

Yet he often went to the other extreme, to the almost unintelligible language of the streets, to the poetry of the very common people, as in the poem "oil tel duh woil doi sez," in the volume titled *W* (pronounced ViVa).

He also changed the language itself, using parts of speech in unexpected ways, forcing verbs to work as nouns, and making new words grow from the everyday words of the language. The poem "so isn't so small one littlest why," in *1 × 1*, for example, is cryptic only until the parts of speech shed their usual functions and take up new ones.

This technique is tricky, like that of so much of the experimental poetry of the 1920's. Of all the experimenters of those years, however, only Cummings found a radically new technical approach which was appropriate to his ideas; only Cummings and William Carlos Williams matched new form to content and wed matter to manner so thoroughly and so well.

The bold technique gave him notoriety and finally fame, but he was not a poet without content, a poet of hollow surfaces. His Romanticism led him on a quest for the truth that shines in the moment but is eternal beyond it, and, like a true Romantic, he scorned those who lived in the material world as if it were the final end of things. He scorned the political world, which he saw as a breeding place for greed and violence. In a poem in *1 × 1*, he defined a politician as an ass that only humans did not ride, and in "THANKSGIVING (1956)," he was overcome by revulsion at the United States' role in the Hungarian uprising. The violence of that poem reflects the hate that is so much a part of the Romantic mind, a hate for the betrayal of an idea and an ideal by practical necessity, of the eternal by the temporal.

Cummings wrote many good political poems, witty and sharply critical of a society that he believed had betrayed its own ideals and its true nature so very often. There are "i sing of Olaf glad and big," "as freedom is a breakfastfood," and "it was a goodly co," and there is "pity this busy monster, manunkind," in which "Progress" is a disease giving comfort to its victims and the only hope seems to lie in leaving the whole mess behind.

There are those poems and the many comic poems about people who fail to live fully and whose spirits are dead, like "the Cambridge ladies who live in furnished souls" and "nobody loses all of the time." Yet the real variety and wonder of Cummings' talent is most clearly figured in his love poetry, the body of poems in which he makes love itself new in the freshness of his eye and voice. He had the personal exuberance and vision to celebrate love both of the flesh and of the spirit in a fashionably existential and disillusioned age. His love sonnets are delicate, controlled, and genuinely lyrical. No puritan, he celebrated at times the honest joy of lust, of purely physical love that achieves the spiritual by making no hypocritical pretense of having it.

There are also love poems of another nature, such as the love poem to his father, "my father moved through dooms of love," or the many loving poems about simple people like "dominic has" in *95 Poems*. These are love poems to humankind, capable of so much love and so much pain; they celebrate the love that has its most intense and moving expression in "Jehovah buried, Satan dead." The spirit of love and the spirit of humanity, in-terwound pure and whole but forever grounded in the world of hate and fear, define Cummings' vision, which is a vision worthy of any true poet.

Like most poets, Cummings had his weaknesses. There are many poems that have become merely cute with the passage of the years, and often he is sentimental rather than tender, nasty rather than angry in spirit. Yet he did capture a young vision of life as a truly vital and growing experience. If one outgrows that view of things, one will have outgrown youth and much of life itself. If E. E. Cummings never offered a poem of the magnitude of T. S. Eliot's *Four Quartets* (1943) or William Carlos Williams' *Paterson* (1946-1958), he did provide lyrics that are truly lyrical, love poems that are truly loving, and poems of the living moment that are truly lively and alive. He taught readers new ways of using words and made them see the old ways anew. He was an honest and passionate poet, and his poems celebrate the honesty of passion and the often painful world redeemed by love.

THE POETRY OF EMILY DICKINSON

Type of work: Poetry
Author: Emily Dickinson (1830-1886)
Principal published works: *The Poems of Emily Dickinson* (edited by Thomas H. Johnson), 1955; *The Complete Poems of Emily Dickinson* (edited by Thomas H. Johnson), 1960.

Few of the United States' great poets waited so long to achieve recognition as did Emily Dickinson. Though she wrote more than 1,775 poems, during her lifetime only seven were published, and those anonymously. When she died, few beyond her circle of family and friends had heard of her, yet nearly seventy years after her death, she was critically acclaimed as one of the leading poets of her time. Along with Walt Whitman, Dickinson is credited with bringing American poetry into the twentieth century, for her highly unusual style and her passion for expressing the truth helped to free nineteenth century verse from its limitations of image, meter, and rhyme.

To neighbors in her hometown of Amherst, Massachusetts, Dickinson was an eccentric figure, the spinster who always dressed in white and who, after her early thirties, never ventured beyond the family home or garden. She rarely received a visitor, and when she did, she would hide upstairs and sometimes send down a note or poem to her guest. Some biographers suggest that the reports of her reclusive life-style may be somewhat exaggerated, but it is nevertheless clear that Dickinson preferred to socialize through letters and to confide her deepest thoughts in her poems. One of Dickinson's long-time correspondents was Thomas Wentworth Higginson, poetry critic for *The Atlantic Monthly*, to whom she initially sent a few poems along with the earnest question whether he found the poems alive. She claimed that his answer that there was life in the poetry had saved her life; yet Higginson, a conventional critic with traditional tastes, was generally lukewarm in his praise. He found her poems strange and unpolished, and his reservations may have contributed to her reluctance to have them published.

After Dickinson's death, her sister discovered hundreds of poems in Emily's room, many hand-sewn into small booklike packets. Lavinia Dickinson persuaded Higginson and a family friend, Mabel Loomis Todd, to publish the poems, which they did in 1890, 1891, and 1896. It is clear, however, that Dickinson's editors had no conception of the value of her work, for they freely made changes to it, smoothing out rhymes and meter, fixing punctuation, and revising diction—in short, making the poems more conventional. Her books sold widely but met with little critical success. Friends and relatives brought

out more editions over the years, but each persisted in the practice of "correcting" her work. It was not until the 1950's, after her estate was given to Harvard University, that a more authentic version finally reached the public through the painstaking scholarship of Thomas H. Johnson. Though some controversy still exists about the dates of composition and Dickinson's final editing choices on some poems, Johnson's edition *The Complete Poems of Emily Dickinson*, along with its system for numbering the poems, is generally accepted as the standard.

Approaching Dickinson's work, what she called her "letter to the World," one should bear in mind the words of the critic Allen Tate: "All pity for Miss Dickinson's 'starved life' is misdirected. Her life was one of the richest and deepest ever lived on this continent." The evidence for this richness and depth is her poems. Though she often wrote about small and common things, her reach was always broad and high, always bringing her to confront, with searching honesty, the larger universal themes: nature, love, death and immortality, and God. What looked unpolished to her contemporaries—the sometimes awkward phrasing, the skewed rhymes, the short staccato bursts set off by dashes rather than the more grammatically polite comma—reveal a passionate thinker, a mind that would not rest, that was continually seeking answers, and for whom poems were not a polite parlor game but rather a lifeline. She searched for truth and knew that the nature of truth made it impossible to nail it down once and for all; one had to nail it down a hundred times. This is why it is difficult to summarize Dickinson's themes, such as her view of death, because for Dickinson, trying to understand death, or love, or God, was a continuous quest.

This passion to understand accounts for the sheer volume of Dickinson's work, as well as its occasional unevenness. Generally it is some uncontrollable feeling, such as the pain of loss, or a mind-numbing despair, or even an ecstatic joy, that tornadolike sets Dickinson's poetic faculties into motion. Often her subject is so volatile that it cannot even be named, a fact reflected in her work by a frequent use of the pronoun "it." Within those poems attempting to define the "it," the argument often proceeds like a riddle, developed with a confusion of imagery. It is as though she gathers words like the flying debris at the outer edge of a storm—mixing her metaphors and throwing words together in unlikely pairs—to give her restless subject at least some shape; or, she mixes words just as various pigments are added to a base of paint, and shaken, to reach an appropriate, exact color. The evidence of Dickinson's various drafts and revisions confirms that word choices that seemed careless to her first critics were actually quite carefully made. The brevity of Dickinson's poems makes them appear simple, but reading them actually requires careful attention, often to what is *not* said. One of Dickinson's strategies is to make an unstated shift in perspective; she will frequently investigate her subject by turning all around it, considering it from differing attitudes and points of view. This approach is manifest in the poems as a sometimes unresolvable tension of opposites, an imbalance, a seeming resolution and then dissolution, a dance between what can and cannot be faced or named. The destination of this process, so turbulently awakened, is always to penetrate to the center of this storm, a place of mastery and calm, where meaning can be distilled. Her passion for meaning is what made this reclusive woman such a literary revolutionary: Dickinson had to bend language and form in order to get at the truth. "Tell all the Truth," she admonished, "but tell it slant."

Dickinson's truth is primarily an inner one. She was one of the first American poets to map carefully the interior landscape of feeling, exploring the terrain of the subconscious before it was "discovered" decades later by Sigmund Freud. Even in those poems that are descriptions of external reality, such as her nature poems, the inner life still carries the greater force. Her well-known "A narrow Fellow in the Grass" (#986) culminates most powerfully when it shifts its focus from the snake, the object observed, to the observer, who with "a tighter breathing" is feeling "Zero at the Bone." "There's a certain Slant of light" (#258), a description of a winter afternoon, projects the poet's despair onto the landscape; in this Dickinson is a forerunner of the twentieth century Imagists, creating imagery that is not ornamental but intrinsic. In poems such as "I felt a Funeral, in my Brain" (#280), Dickinson openly explores the mind, detailing the disturbing loss of reason, when feeling has overtaken sense.

Dickinson's love poems reveal a passion that belies the quiet facts of her biography. They support the speculation that if Dickinson withdrew from society it was not because she was indifferent to it; rather, it was because she felt her attachments to friends and lovers so deeply. There has been much speculation about the identity of the man

for whom Dickinson's unrequited love occasioned an outpouring of poems during her "flood years" of the early 1860's. Many believe it was Charles Wadsworth, a married preacher from Philadelphia who left for California in 1862. Yet knowing about whom Dickinson wrote is ultimately much less significant than the poetry he inspired, poems ranging from the exuberant "Wild Nights—Wild Nights!" (#249) to the despairing "I cannot live with you" (#640).

The subject that holds by far the greatest fascination for Dickinson is death, about which she wrote more than five hundred poems. Sometimes, she considers it from the point of view of the bereaved survivors, as in "The last Night that She lived" (#1100) and "There's been a Death, in the Opposite House" (#389). Other times, she looks at it from the point of view of the person dying, as in "I heard a Fly buzz—when I died" (#465) and "Because I could not stop for Death" (#712). The latter poem's personification of Death as a gentleman caller demonstrates her typically atypical approach. Hers is not so much a morbid fascination as it is an intense and fearless curiosity. At times, she sees death as a horrifying cessation, but at others, it is a blissful release envied by the living. Death is for Dickinson the ultimate punctuation mark, which, appearing at the end of life's sentence, gives it all its meaning. It is a gateway through which one passes to a perhaps even greater type of existence. It is also a mystery about which one can never be completely convinced, which is perhaps why she keeps probing. This restless questioning also characterizes her religious poetry, which vacillates between faith in God and doubt, as when the initial conviction in "I know that He exists" (#338) unravels during the stanzas that follow.

Dickinson also wrote poems about her craft, among them #675, "Essential Oils":

> Essential Oils—are wrung—
> The Attar from the Rose
> Be not expressed by Suns—alone—
> It is the gift of Screws—
>
> The General Rose—decay
> But this—in Lady's Drawer
> Make Summer—When the Lady lie
> In Ceaseless Rosemary—

"Essential Oils" is about poetry, but more specifically, it represents the mastery of a particular question important not only to Dickinson but, in varying degrees, to all poets as well: the choice between the life of the common person, with its sphere of social relationships, and the life of the poet, with its demanding solitude. In "Essential Oils," the choice is distilled, and embodied, in the metaphor of the rose. There is the rose that blooms in a day, whose fragrance is drawn out of it by the attentions of the sun, and the rose that is taken from the garden, so that its essence may be concentrated into an enduring perfume. There is no doubt in the poem about which rose Dickinson prefers. She has passed that stage of the argument, has reached the still center of meaning, and so sustains throughout the conviction that begins the poem.

"Essential Oils," the volatile essence that imparts the characteristic odor of a plant, represents that very nature of a thing, which is incapable of removal without destroying the thing itself or its character. Poems, the volatile essence of the poet, become of life-and-death importance; without them, the poet ceases to be herself. This necessity justifies the process by which they are gotten: They "are wrung," a verb that implies physical and emotional pressure, the process of suffering and pain. This is the poet's secret: Art "is the gift of Screws." As a metaphor for the poetic process, "Screws" is an image of remarkable compression. It suggests not only the flower press but also the pain of the medieval torture device, and as a reference to the tools of the carpenter, it implies discipline and craftsmanship as well. The image also suggests, in its spiral shape narrowing to a point, an emblem for the poet's mind turning around a subject until it reaches its center, until meaning is screwed down. This process is compared to that other one that draws the odor from a bloom, the expressions of "Suns," which for Dickinson is a metaphor for the masculine principle, hence symbolizing the warm attentions of suitors; thus the essence of

the rose becomes an image for a woman's sexual potential. A woman can express her being through a union with a man; but the poet—"alone"—realizes her identity through the creative process.

"The General Rose" is the common rose, different from the rose of the poet. "General" carries the connotation of military ranking, an ironic reference to the command a wife exerts over her household and the social superiority that she may enjoy. In outward form, the first line of this stanza is very similar to the opening line of the first stanza: A modified noun is separated by a dash from its verb. Whereas "Essential" seems to justify and balance the pain in "wrung," however, in this line the emotional scales are tipped, and there is nothing in the "General Rose" to redeem it from "decay," the most negatively charged word in the poem. "But this" redirects the argument to the strength of the poet, her attar, the poems she keeps in her bureau drawer. "Lady's Drawer" as an image of limited space also suggests the artistic isolation and confinement that are necessary to preserving the poet's essence. The scents of poems "Make Summer"—summer for Dickinson being an emblem of fruition, when the potential of nature is realized. This fact masters death for the poet so that it can be described with a gentle euphemism, "When the Lady lie/ In Ceaseless Rosemary." Rosemary has long been associated with the power of memory and was often used to scent coffins. The poet lying in "Ceaseless Rosemary" will not be forgotten after her death; the line is a prophetic description of Dickinson's belated but nevertheless powerful impact on American letters.

THE POETRY OF ROBERT FROST

Type of work: Poetry
Author: Robert Frost (1874-1963)
Principal published works: *A Boy's Will*, 1913; *North of Boston*, 1914; *New Hampshire: A Poem with Notes and Grace Notes*, 1923; *West-Running Brook*, 1928; *A Further Range*, 1936; *A Witness Tree*, 1942; *A Masque of Reason*, 1945; *Steeple Bush*, 1947; *A Masque of Mercy*, 1947; *How Not to be King*, 1951; *In the Clearing*, 1962.

> They would not find me changed from him they knew—
> Only more sure of all I thought was true.

In a sense, this early prediction by Robert Frost is an accurate description of the course of his writing career: Frost's poetry did not change; it simply grew stronger. The dominant characteristics of his work—his impeccable ear for the rhythms of speech; his realistic handling of nature, transcending the ordinary love that one ascribes to poets of the outdoors; his revelation of human character by means of dramatic events; his warm philosophy, which combines the viewpoint of a whimsical poet with that of a dirt farmer—all these qualities were apparent (at least to some readers) early in his career. They were still there at the end, handled with greater precision, displaying more depth.

For an example of this strengthening process, this growth of sapling into tree, one could look first at the little poem "The Pasture," the last stanza of which invites the reader into Frost's *A Boy's Will*:

> I'm going out to fetch the little calf
> That's standing by the mother. It's so young,
> It totters when she licks it with her tongue.
> I sha'n't be gone long—You come too.

The Frost charm is evident in these lines, but there is also a somewhat juvenile quality. When one compares "The Pasture" with "Come In," a much later and firmer treatment of the same general theme, the superior diction is immediately apparent in such magnificent lines as these:

> Far in the pillared dark
> Thrush music went—
> Almost like a call to come in
> To the dark and lament.

Equally apparent is a greater depth of psychological complexity, a stronger suggestion of the "death wish" that John Ciardi discussed in his controversial analysis of "Stopping by Woods on a Snowy Evening," the more famous lyric to which "Come In" is a superb companion piece.

Frost did not change, only grew sure, but there has been an amazing change, down through the years, in the attitude taken toward his poems. At first, his fellow Americans could not see this most American of writers as a poet at all; it was necessary for him to go to England to be hailed for his talent. Then, when the English had pointed him out to his compatriots, Americans cataloged him as another cold New England poet who saw everything in black and white. This astonishing judgment becomes especially egregious when one considers that *A Boy's Will* contains a poem of such warm understanding as "The Tuft of Flowers" and that *North of Boston*, his second volume, includes "The Death of the Hired Man," "Home Burial," and "The Fear," three dramatic poems that are intensely emotional. After Frost's reputation finally became established, the critics forced him into a third stage of his career: He was recognized as a major poet, but one not very interesting to talk or write about because his poetry was thought too simple and because he held aloof from the free-verse poets, whose efforts, he thought, lacked discipline. Near the end of his life, Frost entered a fourth period: His great talents were at last fully recognized, and he came to be regarded as a poet of far more depth and complexity than anyone had previously realized. Two of Frost's poems that are provocative enough to satisfy the most eager analyst are "Directive," with its Grail imagery, and "The Subverted Flower," with its tantalizing psychological horror.

Yet Frost will always be a poet more loved than analyzed. He expresses himself in such an attractive way that his readers identify themselves with a poet; they would like to be Frost. The descriptive lines one finds in "After Apple Picking," for example, have a perfection that seems the only, and inevitable, way of describing the dream that the poet feels coming on. Many other poems by Frost contain this same perfection of word choice. "Two Tramps in Mud Time" is so meticulously written (and yet so effortless, with its touches of the famous Frost wit) that the reader feels surrounded by April weather, and he clearly sees those two hulking tramps who stand around idly, waiting for the poet to hire them to chop his wood.

If Frost had limited his poetry to descriptive and phil-

osophical lyrics, he would still rank as a major poet; fortunately, his poems are also full of people, characters who
are understandable and vividly real. In "The Death of
the Hired Man," four people come alive: Mary, the sympathetic wife; Warren, the practical, somewhat cynical
husband; Harold Wilson, the boy "who studied Latin
like the violin because he liked it"; and Silas, the hired
man who has come "home" to die. Other people are
scattered like old friends throughout the poems: Magoon,
the timid professor, and Lafe, the burly bill collector, in
"A Hundred Collars"; the casual witch in "The Witch of
Coos"; the newlyweds who philosophize so well in "West-
Running Brook"; the old farmer in "The Mountain," who
lives at the foot of a mountain he refuses to climb simply
because he sees no practical reason for doing so; and the
dour farmer in "Brown's Descent," who takes a hilarious
ride down a mountain on a slick crust of snow.

There are others equally memorable, but perhaps the
outstanding character in all the poems is Frost himself.
Everything that he wrote is warmed by his own personality, and he emerges from his volumes as a great and
charming man who felt deeply but who never broke the
restraining tether of good taste. He is emotional but never
overly sentimental, dramatic but never melodramatic, conservative but not reactionary, sometimes pessimistic but
never defeated, and humorous without being flippant.

Trying to summarize the beguiling effect of Frost's
outlook on life is difficult, for his writing personality
is many-sided. Certainly he strikes the reader as a man
who looked at life in a way that was both poetic and
practical. The concluding lines of "Birches" beautifully
illustrate this remarkable blend. In the poem, the speaker
has expressed a desire "to get away from earth awhile"
and then come back for a new start:

> I'd like to go by climbing a birch tree,
> And climb black branches up a snow-white trunk
> *Toward* heaven, till the tree could bear no more,

> But dipped its top and set me down again.
> That would be good both going and coming back.
> One could do worse than be a swinger of birches.

Frost's wise outlook is not always concerned with only
the broad generalities of life; sometimes he becomes specific about the events of his time, as in "To a Thinker,"
which gives advice to a president, and in "U.S. 1946
King's X," which is a mordant piece of irony:

> Having invented a new Holocaust,
> And been the first with it to win a war,
> How they make haste to cry with fingers crossed,
> King's X—no fair to use it any more!

Poets must be more than dramatists, analysts of human
emotion, humorists, and philosophers; they must above
all be poets. Frost meets this difficult test. He wrote in
the rhythms of human speech; sounding as natural as a
man talking to his neighbor, he composed great poetry.
His approach seems casual and disarming, rather like
that of a champion athlete who breaks records without
straining, who never tries too hard.

Yet to claim perfection for anyone—athlete or poet—
is absurd. Frost has his defects. At times, he is like a
kindly teacher whose whimsicality is so sly as to be irritating, whose wisdom sometimes descends to mere crank-
iness. Yet he has written magnificent poetry—simple,
sure, strong. Evidence is this beautiful (but not often
quoted) lyric called "Moon Compasses":

> I stole forth dimly in the dripping pause
> Between two downpours to see what there was.
> And a masked moon had spread down compass rays
> To a cone mountain in the midnight haze,
> As if the final estimate were hers,
> And as it measured in her calipers,
> The mountain stood exalted in its place.
> So love will take between the hands a face.

THE POETRY OF H. D.

Type of work: Poetry
Author: H. D. (Hilda Doolittle, 1886-1961)
Principal published works: *Sea Garden*, 1916; *Hymen*, 1921; *Heliodora and Other Poems*, 1924; *Collected Poems of H. D.*, 1925; *Red Roses for Bronze*, 1931; *The Walls Do Not Fall*, 1944; *Tribute to the Angels*, 1945; *The Flowering of the Rod*, 1946; *By Avon River*, 1949; *Selected Poems of H. D.*, 1957; *Helen in Egypt*, 1961; *Hermetic Definition*, 1972.

The poetry of H. D., as Hilda Doolittle chose to call herself, represents the most Imagistic poems of the school of Imagism. This school of "new" poetry, flourishing during the first two decades of the twentieth century, was finally triumphed over and controlled by Amy Lowell. The proponents had a six-part credo of poetry: the use of common speech; the creation of new rhythms; absolute freedom in subject matter; the use of image; the writing of hard, definite, and clear verse; and the concentration of poetry in its very essence. Although most poets associated with this group later wandered from its narrow statement of beliefs or accomplished little, Doolittle adhered faithfully to the tenets and produced poetry that is very effective.

The first poem in her first collection, called *Sea Garden*, reveals her art and accomplishment. In "Sea Rose," with unemotional words, sharp and hard in their clarity, she describes the desiccated sea rose, stunted and blown with the sand in the wind. Yet, despised and abandoned, it has more real fragrance than another flower, the conventional lovely rose, supposedly more fragrant. The poet's room for maneuver and accomplishment is narrow—she uses sixteen lines and only sixty-four words—but the poem is a fine and delicate cameo chiseled in marble.

Another such poem is "Sea Lily." In this work, H. D. addresses the reed that has been broken and torn by the wind. The scales are torn from its stem and it is cut by sand that is sharp as flint, yet through it all the reed stands lifted up despite all the efforts of enemy elements to cover it.

Such poems are triumphant successes. Many, however, are poignant cries that, because of the author's assiduous use of the credo of the Imagists, somehow fail to come to full development. They suggest and hint, but they are underdeveloped and therefore are generally unsuccessful.

A poem of this kind is "Mid-Day." The poet says that the light and heat are beating her down into nothingness. The wind rattles the seedpods, and her thoughts are scattered like the seeds. In the midst of this dryness, however, she looks up and sees the deep-rooted poplar spreading among the other trees on the hill, and she addressed the poplar, pointing out how much more vital and alive it is on the hill than the writer is, perishing as she is on the rocks.

Another such work is "Pursuit." In it the speaker is following a man whose footsteps are half hidden, interrupted here and there, but distinct enough to be followed. She follows him past the wild hyacinth stalk that he has snapped in passing, through the grass he has brushed, past the forest ledge slopes and the roots that his hand snapped with its weight, on up the hill, then down where he fell, bruising his thigh and thereafter limping. Then the trail is lost and the writer can no longer find any trace of him in the underbrush and the fallen larch cones.

H. D.'s knowledge of Greek was extensive. More than half her work consists of poems on classical subjects and, to a smaller extent, translations of such writers as Euripides. One poem based on a Greek theme is the poignant "Eurydice," which tells how Orpheus descended to Hades, charmed Pluto with his music, and was allowed to lead Eurydice back to earth on the condition that he would not look back until he reached the upper air. The age-old story is, however, told from a different point of view, by Eurydice after she has been condemned to go back to Hades. She blames her fate on the arrogance and ruthlessness of Orpheus. In Hades, she had been forgotten by the world and might have remained in peace, but he came and disturbed her. Time and again, she pathetically asks Orpheus why he turned and looked at her just when their goal was at hand. Because of his actions, she has lost the earth. Yet she consoles herself with the thought that her hell is no worse than his, though he lives on earth with the sun and flowers. In hell, she has more light than he has on earth; she has herself for flowers and her own fervor and her own spirit for a light. She realizes that, before she can be lost, hell must allow the passing of the dead.

In other poems, H. D. passes from Greek mythology to literature, to Homer. Her poem "Helen" paints a death's-head black-and-white portrait of the wife who, by her behavior, caused the war between the Greeks and the Trojans. One of the great sufferers of that conflict, Penelope, is the subject of a powerful poem of passion and pride in "At Ithaca." Penelope, Ulysses' wife, was at home hiding behind her ruse for not marrying any of the suitors who were eating her into poverty: weaving the funeral pall for her father-in-law, Laertes, during the day and unraveling it at night. After years of work, she thought her duty was done, and she longed passionately that one of the suitors would tear her weaving aside and conquer her with a kiss. Yet each time she saw her work in its entirety she was reminded of the greatness of her husband, and in contrast with him all the suitors around her faded into nothingness.

Sometimes, in a single simple sentence, H. D. pours feeling that rends the heart—for example, in "Circe." Circe is alone after Ulysses has thwarted her and gone away. She recalls how easily she bent the other men to her will, changing them into beasts as she chose. Men were easy to conquer because they prayed for a sight of her face or a touch of her hand. She could call men from the corners of the world—all except one, Ulysses. She would give them all up for a glance from him.

The same poignancy enriches the poem "Leda," which concerns itself with the daughter of Thestius and wife of Tyndarus, King of Sparta, seen bathing nude in the river by Zeus, who takes the form of a swan in order to seduce her. This poem is voiced by Leda. She remembers the wonder of love and sighs for the return of the red swan, the soft feathery flutter of his wings, the warmth of his breast.

The poet's same artistic motivations, control, and skill carry over into her translations. There are the same short lines, sometimes only a word, the identical hard, sharp, precise language and images, and the same quite fine artistic triumphs, as in the *Choruses from the Iphigeneia in Aulis and the Hippolytus of Euripides* (1919). The women in the "Chorus of the Women of Chalkis" cross the hills of sand and the sea to see the battleline. To them, Menelaus is golden and Agamemnon is proud; both command the thousand ships of the Greek forces. They are determined to return Helen to Menelaus. The women see Achilles, with the wind strapped about his feet, flying to battle; they are awed by the number and beauty of his ships. The number of Greek vessels is uncountable, and life will no longer be the same. The ships etch the mind.

Doolittle published a considerable bulk of poetry after her *Collected Poems* of 1925. Her play *Hippolytus Temporizes* (1927), although probably a failure as true classical tragedy, is successful as a lyrical development of her thesis that beauty lies in the heart and is inviolable. Increasingly her poetry centered on the ancient world, as in *Red Roses for Bronze*. The escape to the classical world, or perhaps more properly the use of it for present-day problems, is continued in *The Walls Do Not Fall*, which starts in London during World War II but immediately reaches back to an older world, in *Tribute to the Angels*, and in *The Flowering of the Rod*. A departure in subject matter and in style is *By Avon River*, praise in poetry and prose of William Shakespeare and his numerous contemporaries.

The power and thrust of H. D.'s work was quickly recognized. She was one of the Imagists whose accomplishment was solid and whose influence was considerable though short lived, for her later poems did little to broaden her subject matter or to create any momentous changes in style.

THE POETRY OF LANGSTON HUGHES

Type of work: Poetry
Author: Langston Hughes (1902-1967)
Principal published works: *The Weary Blues*, 1926; *Fine Clothes to the Jew*, 1927; *Dear Lovely Death*, 1931; *The Negro Mother*, 1931; *The Dream Keeper and Other Poems*, 1932; *Scottsboro Limited*, 1932; *A New Song*, 1938; *Shakespeare in Harlem*, 1942; *Jim Crow's Last Stand*, 1943; *Lament for Dark Peoples*, 1944; *Fields of Wonder*, 1947; *One Way Ticket*, 1949; *Montage of a Dream Deferred*, 1951; *Selected Poems of Langston Hughes*, 1959; *Ask Your Mama: Or, 12 Moods for Jazz*, 1961; *The Panther and the Lash: Or, Poems of Our Times*, 1967.

James Mercer Langston Hughes was the most versatile, popular, and influential African-American writer of the twentieth century. Hughes published scores of books in his lifetime: two novels, plays, collections of short stories and essays, an autobiography, seven children's books, poetry translations, a number of African-American poetry and fiction anthologies—and fourteen volumes of verse. From the 1920's until his death in May, 1967, Hughes was widely recognized as the unofficial poet laureate of the African-American urban experience, its most dedicated and passionately eloquent voice; his international reputation has only grown over the years since.

Hughes's career as a poet began, rather abruptly, in the spring of 1916. At the age of thirteen, he was elected class poet of his Lincoln, Illinois, grammar school. Even though he had never written a poem, Hughes dutifully produced sixteen poems in praise of his teachers and class, which he read aloud at graduation, to hearty applause. Soon thereafter, Hughes moved to Cleveland, Ohio, with his mother and stepfather. There he attended the city's Central High School and continued to write poetry, both in the free-verse style of Chicago working-class poet Carl Sandburg and in the dialect style of the African-American poet Paul Laurence Dunbar. In the year after his graduation from high school in 1920, Hughes had his first real publications. A number of poems appeared in succeeding issues of *The Brownie's Book*, a junior version of *The Crisis*, the official journal of the National Association for the Advancement of Colored People (NAACP).

Almost immediately, Hughes graduated to the parent journal. The June, 1921, issue of *The Crisis* published "The Negro Speaks of Rivers," Hughes's first great poem. Written a year earlier, on a train crossing the Mississippi, this short lyric (dedicated to NAACP founder W. E. B. Du Bois) proudly affirms the mystical unity of all persons of African descent, regardless of when or where they happen to live. A poem of praise, rendered in plain-spoken free verse, "The Negro Speaks of Rivers" shows the clear influence of Sandburg. Another discernible influence is that of Walt Whitman, whom Hughes regarded as the greatest of American poets. Like Whitman's famous long poem "Song of Myself," Hughes's poem features a first-person speaker, an "I" that refers not only to the poet but also to an entire people he identifies with and, in effect, becomes; when the speaker avers that his "soul has grown deep like the rivers," he assumes the voice of the entire African race throughout history. Finally, in its moving lyricism, "The Negro Speaks of Rivers" harks back to the centuries-old tradition of the African-American spiritual.

That Hughes, at the age of nineteen, had already established a unique and powerful poetic voice became fully evident over the next year and a half as Jessie Fauset, the literary editor of *The Crisis*, published another dozen Hughes poems. Among them were poems that were to be Hughes's most anthologized, such as "The South," "Beggar Boy," "My People," "Mother to Son," and "Negro." "Mother to Son" is a dramatic monologue that displays one of Hughes's signal strengths as a poet: his ability to adopt a convincing persona. The speaker is the mother alluded to in the title, a (presumably) middle-aged African-American woman who recounts her arduous life of poverty and toil in metaphorical terms as the endless climbing of a staircase. The goal at the top of the stair is a freer, more dignified life, not only for herself and her son but for her entire people as well. World-weary but stoic and grimly determined, the mother exhorts her son never to forfeit the struggle by turning back. "Negro" is a free-verse dramatic monologue in much the same vein as "The Negro Speaks of Rivers." The "I" persona that Hughes adopts is, again, universal in scope: that of the black African throughout recorded history. In successive stanzas, the poem's speaker recounts the four basic roles to which he has been relegated throughout the ages: slave, worker, singer, and victim. "Negro" outlines a saga of suffering and sorrow ("The Belgians cut off my hands in the Congo/ They still lynch me in Mississippi"), yet it eschews self-pity. The last stanza, which repeats the first stanza verbatim and thus frames the middle four, ends the poem as it began, on a note of proud and joyous affirmation: "I am a Negro/ Black as the night is black/ Black like the depths of my Africa."

The emphasis on racial pride in "Negro" is typical of Hughes's early poems, many of which are paeans to the dignity, endurance, and inner strengths of African Americans. Hughes's early verse is not, however, monotonously uniform in style and theme. The poems published by *The Crisis* also include protest poems, elegies, miscellaneous lyrics, and formal experiments that were inspired by, and imitative of, jazz and the blues. Indeed, African-American folk music became a major source of inspiration for Hughes after he moved to New York City from the Midwest in the fall of 1921 to attend Columbia University.

The move was a watershed event in Hughes's life, not because of college, which he found uncongenial and quit after his first year, but because it brought him to Harlem. Manhattan's teeming African-American district was the locus for the Harlem Renaissance, a burgeoning cultural revival in which Hughes soon immersed himself. Hughes also explored Harlem's vibrant nightlife. Early evidence of its impact on his sensibilities is "The Weary Blues," a 1923 poem about a piano player performing in a Lenox Avenue nightclub. In "a melancholy tone," the man sings the Weary Blues, a song of thoroughgoing dejection and despair, "far into the night." Yet, ultimately, the blues seem to have a salutary effect. Once he has completely drained off his own anguish through the music, the singer is able to at least escape his plight by going to bed, to sleep "like a rock or a man that's dead." The singer's struggle to master his pain captures the cathartic essence of the blues—and something of the deeper nature of Harlem in the 1920's, which was, despite its hectic cabaret life, a place of considerable poverty and hardship.

"The Weary Blues" was a breakthrough for Hughes; it garnered top prize in a literary contest sponsored by the National Urban League in 1925. The award, in turn, won Hughes the support of a prominent literary critic, Carl Van Vechten, who helped Hughes to publish his first collection of verse, also entitled *The Weary Blues*, in 1926. Yet the poem stirred controversy among Hughes's peers in the Harlem Renaissance, some of whom objected to the award on the grounds that "The Weary Blues" was not "literary" enough. The poem not only unashamedly drew on folk-music traditions, but also featured a blues pianist who sings in dialect such lines as "I's gwine to quit ma frownin'/ And put ma troubles on the shelf." Poetry in the vernacular was deemed politically regressive in some quarters, because it was thought to rein-

force white stereotypes regarding African-American primitivism. Such criticisms, which were also leveled at *The Weary Blues* as a whole, show exactly how Hughes's aesthetic differed from that of the "Talented Tenth," upper-middle-class black intellectuals who tended to value art that promoted respectability and social advancement through integration. Therefore, they had little use for Hughes's blunt realism.

Hughes's second volume of verse, *Fine Clothes to the Jew* (1927), became even more controversial than *The Weary Blues.* The poems in the new book dealt with aspects of everyday life in proletarian Harlem—fundamentalist religion, low-paying jobs, the cabaret, romance, gambling, fights, prostitution, alcohol—and many of them were written in dialect cast in the form of urban folk blues: the ultimate combination of aesthetic sins, according to Hughes's detractors. Not all critics, however, were disdainful of Hughes's choice of form, diction, and subject matter. Critic Alain Locke and a few others understood that, while apparently artless, Hughes's verse was neither simplistic nor vulgar, that the spare effect he achieved was actually crafted with great care and precision, and that Hughes's portrayal of the joys and calamities of the African-American urban masses was executed with honesty and compassion.

The Harlem Renaissance effectively came to an end when the stock market collapsed in October, 1929. The resulting Great Depression, which lasted throughout the 1930's, had a severe impact on the already marginal economy of Harlem. Like much of the rest of the country, Depression-era Harlem was the scene of mass unemployment, bread lines, evictions, and, occasionally, riots. Under such conditions, many leading American artists and intellectuals embraced Marxism as an alternative political philosophy. Hughes was no exception. The five books of verse that he published in the 1930's reveal Hughes as an increasingly militant leftist poet. For example, *Scottsboro Limited* (1932) is a book of four poems and a play in support of the "Scottsboro boys," nine young African-American defendants in an Alabama rape trial who were widely thought to be falsely accused. *A New Song* (1938) is Hughes's only book of verse composed entirely of social-protest poems.

After a decade of world travel, activism, and political poetry, Hughes literally and figuratively returned to Harlem. The result was a collection of verse entitled *Shakespeare in Harlem* (1942), which is superficially similar to *The Weary Blues* and *Fine Clothes to the Jew* in its exclusive focus on Harlem as subject and its preponderant use of folk-music forms. Yet Depression-ravaged Harlem in the early 1940's was a vastly different place than it had been in the 1920's. The colorful exuberance of the Harlem Renaissance had long since given way to bitterness and despair, and Hughes's new book reflected the changed mood in the street. Despite some moments of levity, *Shakespeare in Harlem* was an almost unremittingly bleak portrait of an urban ghetto in steep decline, as a sampling of poem titles suggests: "Cabaret Girl Dies on Welfare Island," "Death Chant," "Ballad of the Pawnbroker," "Down and Out," "Midnight Chippie's Lament," "Evil Morning."

One Way Ticket (1949) and *Montage of a Dream Deferred* (1951), are Hughes's verse sketches of Harlem after World War II. Despite the economic boom of the postwar years, Harlem was still grappling with grinding poverty and its attendant social ills and was perennially frustrated at the lack of improvement. "Harlem," a short lyric from *Montage of a Dream Deferred*, is justly revered as Hughes's most powerful poem of social protest. In a series of rhetorical questions, the poem's speaker asks what happens when the African-American dream of equality of opportunity is endlessly deferred by white society. He conjectures that the dream might "dry up" or "fester" or sag "like a heavy load." Not quite satisfied with these answers, the speaker then asks, "Or does it explode?" The question is a veiled warning that the ghetto may one day erupt in violence. In its brevity, vivid clarity of effect, and moral seriousness, "Harlem" epitomizes Hughes's poetry, which combined consummate artistry with an unflagging social conscience—a relatively rare combination in American literature.

THE POETRY OF ROBINSON JEFFERS

Type of work: Poetry
Author: Robinson Jeffers (1887-1962)
Principal published works: *Flagons and Apples*, 1912; *Californians*, 1916; *Tamar and Other Poems*, 1924; *Roan Stallion, Tamar, and Other Poems*, 1925; *The Woman at Point Sur*, 1927; *Cawdor and Other Poems*, 1928; *Dear Judas and Other Poems*, 1929; *Descent to the Dead*, 1931; *Thurso's Landing and Other Poems*, 1932; *Give Your Heart to the Hawks and Other Poems*, 1933; *Solstice and Other Poems*, 1935; *Such Counsels You Gave to Me and Other Poems*, 1937; *The Selected Poetry of Robinson Jeffers*, 1938; *Be Angry at the Sun and Other Poems*, 1941; *Medea*, 1946; *The Double Axe and Other Poems*, 1948; *Hungerfield and Other Poems*, 1954; *The Beginning and the End*, 1963.

The history of Robinson Jeffers' reputation might be represented diagrammatically by the figure of a sharp, inverted *V*, the apex marked, perhaps, by the year 1933. In 1919, when Jeffers had already published two volumes, Louis Untermeyer did not consider him worthy of inclusion in his famous anthology of American poetry that mirrored the taste of the period as definitely as had Francis Turner Palgrave's *Golden Treasury of the Best Songs and Lyrical Poems in the English Language* in 1861. In 1933, William Rose Benét, in his anthology entitled *Fifty Poets*, spoke of Jeffers as "the Western Titan of our contemporary poetry" and quoted George Sterling's statement that "Jeffers clasps hands with the Great Greeks across Time." In 1950, a critic considered *The Double Axe and Other Poems* beneath critical notice. Decades later, Jeffers is neither well remembered nor widely read.

Two facts of Jeffers' biography seem important to his poetry: first, his study of medicine and, second, his long residence on the coast of California. The first of these gave him the "scientific" point of view, of which much has been made in discussions of the intellectual content of his poems. The second, his home on Carmel Bay—Tor House, which he built in 1914 and occupied until his death—gave him the geographical and scenic background of so many of his poems, the rocky coast that "clasped hands," to repeat Sterling's phrase, with the stony landscape of ancient Greece and its citadels built from the primeval stone. It might almost be maintained that, for Jeffers, there existed only these two worlds: the coasts of Greece and of California.

It was on his long narrative poems—long, that is, by modern standards—contained in his many volumes that Jeffers' reputation was based: "Tamar," "Roan Stallion," "The Loving Shepherdess," "Give Your Heart to the Hawks," "Hungerfield," and others, at least one of them running to a hundred pages. These works were written in a period when it was said that a long poem was impossible. There is another group equally long: Jeffers' rehandling of the Greek myths, although these myths also often stand in the background of his narratives with modern settings. In "The Tower Beyond Tragedy," he rewrote the Orestes legend; "At the Fall of an Age" is a short drama, the climax of which is the death of Helen; and "The Cretan Woman" is based on the *Hippolytus* of Euripides.

A reading of these long narratives, with their setting on the coast of California, or these reworkings of the Greek legends reveals easily the weakness of Jeffers as a poet. His fault was not his utter pessimism, not his utter contempt for humanity. Rather, it was his extremely narrow range, his constant repetition. In this respect, the only modern poet with whom he can be compared is A. E. Housman, who shared Jeffers' tragic view of life and who repeated his theme of the transience of youth and beauty, the peace that comes with death, throughout his two volumes. Yet Housman had the great virtue of compression; his poems were pared down to three or four quatrains, whereas Jeffers stretched out the agony for page after page. It can even be said that to read one of Jeffers' narrative poems is to read them all; they are alike in their preoccupation with drunkenness, lust, incest, and murder. It is not the violence that offends, for violence has become a commonplace in modern literature; it is the sameness, for violence can quite easily become as monotonous as virtuous placidity. One grows weary of drunken, lecherous husbands, of frustrated, rebellious wives, of incestuous relationships. The murders and the incendiarisms pall. The characters do not seem real, so complete is their degradation. One detects in them the same unreality, the same lack of social or moral sense, that T. S. Eliot found in the characters in D. H. Lawrence's fiction. It is not that they are immoral, for immoral characters are perfectly recognizable as human beings; it is that they seem to exist in a world completely devoid of all moral values. Each of these doomed families, although it may live in a perfectly real section of the coast of California and may even have contacts with other families, is shut into a kind of private madhouse where horror is the daily fare. Without indulgence in undue sentimentality, one may say that this state of affairs is not recognizably human.

It is also inaccurate to assume that, because Jeffers depicted such unrelieved tragedy, he was clasping hands with the great Greek writers. To be sure, the Greek myths often stand behind his narrative poems: the Pasiphaë story is discernible in "Roan Stallion," and in "Hungerfield," a woman with the implausible name of Alcmena Hungerfield has a son who wrestles—or thinks he does— with Death, just as the classical Alcmena's son, Herakles, contends with Death in the *Alcestis* of Euripides. Yet to use the great myths of classical antiquity does not make one a Greek. The tragic narratives of Jeffers are not such in the Aristotelian sense of a reversal of fortune—they do not depict the fall of a great figure from the heights of prosperity and happiness to the depths of misery. The characters in these stories have never known happiness; they are drunken, lecherous, cruel, and degraded. Jeffers' real kinship is not with the Greeks but with the late Elizabethans; he "clasps hands" with such men as John Webster and Cyril Tourneur and, beyond them in time, with Seneca. As the tragedy of blood developed on the post-Shakespearean stage, the dramatists piled murder upon murder, horror upon horror, until the spectator was driven either to disgust or to a refusal to take the drama seriously. The complicated story of "Tamar" is as unreal in its sensationally gruesome details as those of Tourneur's *The Revenger's Tragedy* (1607) or *The Atheist's Tragedy* (1611), and it seems as remote from actuality, yet one is asked to accept this nightmare as a story taking place on the California coast in the twentieth century.

In one of his short poems, Jeffers said that the sole purpose of poetry is to feel and completely understand natural beauty; it is in his ability to put into words the wild, primitive loveliness of the area in which he had made his home that Jeffers was at his best as a poet. Despising humanity, he loved nature—the age-old rocks of the California coast, the gulls, and, above all, the hawks. The rock and the hawk were his main symbols: The rock will remain long after humankind has vanished, and the hawk represents power and freedom. To Jeffers, nature was not the guide, philosopher, and kindly nurse that it was to William Wordsworth; it was indifferent to humanity, which is, after all, only an incident in the vast history of the planet. In one of Jeffers' most quoted lines, he said that humankind was the mold from which the world should break away. Again, in writing of the defacing of Carmel Point by a housing development, he added that given time nature knew that what humanity had created would dissolve. The granite of the cliff at Carmel, however, will remain. In "The Tower Beyond Tragedy," he gave voices to the stones of which the citadel is built; they speak to one another of humans as loud, boisterous, and mobile, saying that before the world ends humankind will be gone. According to Jeffers, humans are below the animals, for they are a blight upon the earth. Their empires rise and fall; the United States will fall like the rest, whereas the hawk will still wheel above the cliffs.

Jeffers' medical studies provided him with a certain amount of scientific vocabulary and, perhaps, with his coldly objective view of humanity. One gets the impression of a clinically detached attitude, the attitude of the doctor who has treated so many patients that he can no longer think of them as people. Surely many of the characters in the narrative poems are walking examples from a psychologist's casebook.

Jeffers did not fit into any of the recognized schools or influences of the twentieth century. Superficially, on the printed page, his long, flowing lines resemble those of Walt Whitman, but the rhythm of his verse is very different from that of the older poet. Except for his general reaction against the conventionalities of the late Victorians, Jeffers was unlike anyone else writing during his period, and he apparently exerted no influence on the succeeding generation, as had Ezra Pound and Eliot.

In *Hungerfield and Other Poems*, Jeffers wrote that poets who forget about the agony of life while singing its praises are fools and liars. The statement is certainly true; yet perhaps Jeffers, in an attempt to avoid all false sentiment, went to the other extreme. He was capable of writing beautiful lines, even beautiful short poems. The weakness was that he never varied, never developed; he merely repeated himself. In "To the Stone-Cutters," the poem which in 1933 he considered his best, he said that eventually humankind, the earth, and the sun would die, the sun blind of eye, black to the heart. This grim theme of vision and statement rings throughout all of his work.

THE POETRY OF HENRY WADSWORTH LONGFELLOW

Type of work: Poetry
Author: Henry Wadsworth Longfellow (1807-1882)
Principal published works: *Voices of the Night*, 1839; *Ballads and Other Poems*, 1841; *Evangeline*, 1847; *The Seaside and the Fireside*, 1850; *The Golden Legend*, 1851; *The Song of Hiawatha*, 1855; *The Courtship of Miles Standish*, 1858; *Tales of a Wayside Inn*, 1863; *Kéramos and Other Poems*, 1878.

In the middle of the nineteenth century, Henry Wadsworth Longfellow was regarded as the finest poet that the United States had yet produced. He was recognized and honored as the poetic voice of a new land while such poets as Emily Dickinson and Walt Whitman labored in obscurity or notoriety. The reasons for Longfellow's fame are not hard to find. He was a skilled poet with a gift for the use of unusual meters, he was not an experimental poet but one who kept to the established conventions of poetic form, and he provided the new American nation with a mythology drawn from such sources as the Native American and the Puritan past. The American public could look to Longfellow for a poet who could stand with the greatest British poets of the era, including poet laureate Alfred, Lord Tennyson.

Longfellow's student years were remarkably successful. He attended Bowdoin College in Maine and was judged to be so promising that he was given a fellowship to travel to Europe to learn the modern languages and eventually become a professor at Bowdoin. His remarkable teaching there attracted attention from other institutions, and he was appointed a professor of modern languages at Harvard University. This happy period was marred, however, by the death of his wife, Mary in 1935. Longfellow's extraordinary success as a poet and a professor did not preserve him from a number of family tragedies.

Longfellow's early poems include the familiar "The Village Blacksmith," "The Wreck of the Hesperus," and "Excelsior." Longfellow was a skilled writer of ballads and lyrics that emphasize striving. "Excelsior," for example, describes a young man who seeks the higher ground of the mountain carrying a banner marked Excelsior. He continues on his quest in spite of the warnings of others, and at the end, his body is found while a voice declares, "Excelsior!" In his book of lyric poems *Voices of the Night* (1839), there is another poem of optimistic striving that many have taken as a philosophy by which to live: "The Psalm of Life." The speaker of the poem urges the reader to fight in "the world's broad field of battle," because "the grave is not the goal." The past is to be ruthlessly brushed aside because the emphasis is on acting in the present. The fate of humans is to be heroes, not "dumb cattle." The last stanza is a lifelong program for the active striving reader.

> Let us, then, be up and doing,
> With a heart for any fate;
> Still achieving, still pursuing,
> Learn to labor and to wait.

The last line is curiously quiescent after such strenuous activity; what that activity is, however, Longfellow does not make specific. The poem is a general plan for an active and fruitful life that readers define in their own terms; one unlikely reader who did just that later in the century was Charles Baudelaire. The poem clearly belongs to its own time, and one can find similar calls to activity in the poetry of Robert Browning and Tennyson.

Longfellow did not always write in such an affirmative manner. Another poem in *Voices of the Night* advocates not striving but "rest." The speaker of "The Day Is Done" asks his companion to read a poem in the evening hours as an antidote to the cares of the day and the "sadness and longing" that they create. The poem is not to be one from "the grand old masters" with their "martial music" but by a "humbler poet." Such a poem comes from the heart of the less-honored poet, and it would have the "power to quiet/ The restless pulse of care." At the end of the poem, those cares "that infest the day,/ Shall fold their tents, like the Arabs,/ And as silently steal away." The poem perfectly captures a pensive moment that is the other side of a life of activity in the battlefield of the world.

Longfellow wrote a number of very fine lyric poems describing nature or exploring a mood; there is, however, one poem that is decidedly different, "The Jewish Cemetery at Newport." The poem is an indictment of the hatred and anti-Semitism that forced the Jews to wander the earth. Longfellow is sympathetic to their plight, but he ends the poem by stating that lost nations never rise again. (The creation of the state of Israel in 1948 showed the inaccuracy of that view.)

The first important poem of Longfellow is *Evangeline*, published in 1847. For his source, Longfellow turned to historical accounts of the tragedy of the Acadian people's forced relocation from Nova Scotia to Louisiana. Longfellow added a personal and fictional element, and much sentiment, to this historical account. It is interesting to note that Longfellow did not go to Europe or to the classics but instead to the American past for his subject matter. Indeed, he was to use American history for the subject matter of every one of his major poems. In doing so, he gave Americans an optimistic vision of the history of their country. That vision remained a part of the national mythology until it was replaced by a darker and more accurate view in the twentieth century.

Evangeline was written in the meter of Homer's *Iliad* (c. 800 B.C.) and Vergil's *Aeneid* (c. 29-19 B.C.), dactylic hexameter. The meter is unusual in English; there are few notable successes in adapting the meter of the great epics. Longfellow did add one variation: He ended each dactylic line with a trochaic foot. Longfellow also used, perhaps overused, the Homeric device of the epic simile in the poem; he was not as skilled in using it as he was with the dactyls. It is interesting to note that, with all this epic machinery, Longfellow chose a woman to be the hero of his American epic. This decision is not surprising, however, given that Longfellow's poetic area is not the battlefield but the parlor; his vision is, essentially, domestic and private rather than public.

Evangeline is a long narrative poem that first places the heroine in an idyllic eighteenth century landscape, the land of Acadie. She is soon uprooted by the villainous British colonial power, which claims Acadie to be property of the king. The rest of the poem is a search for the young man to whom she is betrothed, Gabriel. She wanders through nearly all the settled areas of the time, and her travels through America give the poem an epic element. The American landscape is cataloged and described for an American public eager to have a literature of some distinction. Evangeline goes to the Mississippi River, to the "Black Robes" in Native American country, to a Moravian community, and finally to Quaker Philadelphia. At the end of the poem, she finds Gabriel as he is about to die. The question of justice in the world, which was asked earlier in Acadie, is resolved by Evangeline's acceptance of her seemingly cruel and arbitrary fate. Evangeline does not develop as a character in the poem; she retains her optimism from the beginning of the poem until the end. Her gentle acceptance and passivity make her an appropriate heroine for a domestic epic.

Evangeline was a great success and made Longfellow's poetic reputation. (The poem remained an American classic and a text for high-school students until poetic tastes changed and it was banished from the schoolroom in the 1960's.) Longfellow continued to teach at Harvard and to write poems. He married Fanny Appleton in 1843, and they received the Craigie House on Brattle Street in Cambridge, Massachusetts, as a wedding gift. In 1854, Longfellow resigned his professorship at Harvard to devote more time to writing poetry. A year later, he published *The Song of Hiawatha.*

The Song of Hiawatha was another attempt by Longfellow to write an important poem on a typically American subject. The poem, in form a folk epic, uses the Finnish epic *Kalevala* as a structural model in bringing together a number of separate tales into one book. The aim of *The Song of Hiawatha* is to describe the Native American peoples—their history, their religion, and their heroes. The hero of the poem, Hiawatha, brings the tribe such benefits as a staple food source and a written language. There was an historical figure named Hiawatha, and Longfellow seems to have confused him with the legendary Manabozho, but the inaccuracies in the use of sources do not destroy the value of the poem. The poem was written in another distinctive meter: unrhymed trochaic tetrameter. Longfellow handled this meter more easily than the cumbersome hexameters of *Evangeline*, but its insistent rhythm has made it the subject of innumerable parodies.

Hiawatha is as much a prophet as a hero as he is sent to the people to live among them and bring them benefits. For example, Hiawatha defeats Mondamin, the Corn Spirit who has been sent by the gods, in a wrestling contest, buries him, and soon after maize appears; the hero has provided the Ojibwa with their staple food. He also teaches the people how to write so that their history will not be forgotten.

Hiawatha marries Minnehaha, who is a Dakota; by doing so, he brings the two tribes together. He is less a warrior than a peacemaker, as the glory earned by the usual epic hero has little value for Hiawatha. Later, Minnehaha dies during a famine, which shows that Hiawatha does not have the power to overcome natural events; he is not a god. When whites appear, Hiawatha does not quarrel with them, instead seeing the possibility of peace and brotherhood between Native Americans and whites. Nevertheless, he also has a vision of the scattering of his people that the coming of the whites will bring. The destruction of this sympathetically portrayed tribe seems to have little effect on Longfellow's sensibility. He notes the destruction as an historical fact and does not raise a note of protest. Longfellow's ever-present optimism is clearly shown. Before Hiawatha departs, he invites the Black Robes to teach his people Christianity. This touch must have been comforting to Longfellow's readers, although the real history of the tribes and the Jesuits is much more complex and much less sanguine.

The Song of Hiawatha is, for all of its faults, including an absurd optimism, a more successful poem than *Evangeline*. The hero is deftly portrayed, although he does not have the human faults that make other epic heroes so interesting. The idea of a teacher-prophet hero was an effective way to create an epic portraying the Native American people for whites, but epic poems created by some tribes had given Native Americans their own warrior heroes.

In 1858, Longfellow went to the American past once more for material for another major poem; this time, he used the Puritan past of New England for *The Courtship of Miles Standish*. The poem is not an attempt at an American epic, as *Evangeline* and *Hiawatha* had obviously been, and it is written in dactylic hexameters that are far more fluid than those of *Evangeline*. It is a poem that deals with the domestic world, the one poetic area in which Longfellow had few or no rivals. The poem pairs off two character types: Miles Standish is the soldier, and John Alden is the scholar. Standish is a widower, and he wishes to marry Priscilla Mullin because she is "Patient, courageous, and strong." Typically, Standish does not mention her beauty or charm, qualities that enthrall Alden. Because he lacks the right words to woo Priscilla, Standish sends Alden to woo for him. Alden is in love with Priscilla, but he resigns his claim in the name of friendship. Alden's proposal, however, has none of the poetic language that one might expect from him in this situation; he uses a style that is as blunt and direct as that of Miles Standish: "So I have come to you now, with an offer and proffer of marriage/ Made by a good man and true, Miles Standish the Captain of Plymouth." Priscilla immediately rejects the proposal by proxy of an "Old and rough" man. When Alden resumes his attempt to persuade her to marry Standish, Priscilla replies: "Why don't you speak for yourself, John?"

Standish is shocked at the rejection of his proposal and angry at Alden; he thinks that Alden has betrayed their friendship and now wishes to woo Priscilla for himself. Soon the domestic triangle is replaced, however, by the necessity of fighting a local rebellious tribe. As the leader of the expedition, Standish brutally kills the Native American chief, Pecksuot, in the brief war, but he also dies in battle. The domestic problem seems to be resolved, but Alden is haunted by the accusation of betraying Standish's friendship. The couple are united after a short delay, but the ghost of Miles Standish is still over them.

On their wedding day, the ghost of Standish appears, but he comes back to reconcile himself with John Alden and Priscilla Mullin, not to disturb their union. He states that Alden never betrayed his friendship, and the marriage is blessed: "Never so much as now was Miles Standish the friend of John Alden." At the end of the poem, the Puritan town of Plymouth is transformed into the "Garden of Eden," a place of delights that seems a distinctly ahistorical way to describe the harsh and rigid Puritan world.

The Courtship of Miles Standish is one of Longfellow's most successful major poems. The characters are more fully portrayed than the noble and passive Evangeline or the heroic Hiawatha. The style is less insistent than in the two earlier poems, which is helpful in reading a long narrative poem. Longfellow succeeded in making the Puritan world delightful and surprisingly human. Once more, Longfellow went to early America for his subject matter and made that world both elevated and familiar for his readers. These poems provided Americans with a literature that they could call their own. It was written by an American, and it dealt memorably with the American past.

Longfellow's wife, Fanny, died in a fire at Craigie House in 1861, another of those domestic tragedies that seemed to haunt this genial poet. His last years, however, were serene. He received honorary degrees from the Universities of Oxford and Cambridge in 1869. He spent most of his time translating Dante's *La divina commedia* (c. 1320; *The Divine Comedy*) although he did complete *Tales of a Wayside Inn* and published an impressive number of new poems. He died in Cambridge on March 24, 1882. He was seen at that time as the finest poet that his country had produced, and he was honored with a bust in the Poet's Corner at Westminster Abbey.

THE POETRY OF ROBERT LOWELL

Type of work: Poetry
Author: Robert Lowell, Jr. (1917-1977)
Principal published works: *Land of Unlikeness*, 1944; *Lord Weary's Castle*, 1946; *The Mills of the Kavanaughs*, 1951; *Life Studies*, 1959; *Imitations*, 1961; *For the Union Dead*, 1964; *Near the Ocean*, 1967; *Notebook 1967-68*, 1969; *Notebook*, 1971; *The Dolphin*, 1973; *History*, 1973; *For Lizzie and Harriet*, 1973; *Selected Poems*, 1976, 1977; *Day by Day*, 1977.

Of the generation of American poets who came to prominence in the years following World War II, Robert Lowell emerged as the acknowledged master and the most likely candidate for greatness, the odds-on favorite to fill the shoes of the twentieth century's first generation of poets, the generation that included Ezra Pound, T. S. Eliot, William Carlos Williams, Wallace Stevens, and Robert Frost. In the 1960's, Lowell managed to win acceptance and recognition by nearly all cliques and schools of contemporary poetry and by an array of critics at home and abroad. This reputation represented no slight achievement for Lowell and, equally important, seemed to indicate an end to the long and tedious war between "the Academics" and "the Beats." Lowell was recognized as a poet of repute after his *Lord Weary's Castle* was published and won for him the coveted Pulitzer Prize, but for a poet to fulfill his early promise and to gain steadily in stature and popularity as he did is rare, especially during a period of literary conflict, questioning, and change.

Lord Weary's Castle was a powerful and popular introduction to the new formalism that dominated American poetry after World War II interrupted the continuity of American poetry. It is hard, except by going through the books and anthologies of the 1930's, to recapture the prewar literary milieu, but in general the establishment was char acterized by a deep concern for the social problems of the Great Depression and an attempt to employ the vernacular American idiom in poetry, not only for more freedom, richness, and variety in language but also in the hope of reaching out to a larger audience. The underground movement of that period was composed of the Fugitives, who cultivated journalism in verse, together with ambiguity, intellectual and personal complexity, traditionalism, and an apparently aristocratic view of the poet's function. Politically and socially, they called themselves Agrarians, being so at least in their distaste for the excesses wrought by the Industrial Revolution. Regionally, they were Middle Southern, and theologically, they tended to be high church Episcopalians with definite affinities toward Roman Catholicism. They were academics at a time when the relationship between writers and academics was not cozy. Their leader was John Crowe Ransom, and their special hero was T. S. Eliot in England. It is hard to realize the influence that these men and women had on American poetry and fiction. The exemplary amount of either produced by the group was relatively small, but they wrote a great many reviews and much criticism, taking over and breathing life into quiet quarterlies. Moreover, they taught, directly and in a formal context, many of the young people who would, in the years following World War II, move to prominence on the literary scene. One of these young writers was Robert Lowell.

It is possible that Lowell, at least in his early books, was the best pupil that the Fugitives had, and they rallied around him and his work with alacrity and enthusiasm. Yet he seems an unlikely representative of the movement. Coming from a long and distinguished New England tradition, he showed little sympathy for the South or things Southern or, indeed, interest in these things. His heritage was Puritan, yet he rebelled against it and became a convert to Catholicism, with the additional complexity that he was a conscientious objector during World War II, at a time when his newfound church did not recognize that position as legitimate. Neither did the courts, and he was punished by imprisonment for his beliefs. This personal courage and commitment became meaningful to the poets, those who survived to write poems, who came back. Karl Shapiro spoke for many of them when he referred to Lowell as the conscience to which other young poets returned.

There are many conflicts obvious in even this impersonal and casual view of Lowell as a poet, and conflict is the essence of *Lord Weary's Castle*. His personal struggles with his heritage and the present and future of his society are reined in tightly in strict forms, strict rhythms, and solid rhymes. The effect is often that of the moment before an explosion, a highly dramatic moment. The verse is demanding and requires, as was the custom at the time, some notes—ambiguous, allusive, knotty, and what was then called tough-minded. The transitions were swift and almost cinematic in abruptness. Yet the essence of any poetry is voice, the language and especially the verbal texture, that distinguish the work of one poet from another. Lowell showed from the first a good ear for a wide range of language, from the straightforward cadences of the spoken idiom to the high resonance of classical and biblical rhetoric. The texture was as rough and rocky as the New England earth, almost antipoetic in its hardness. There was a "tension"—a word very popular with the Fugitives, who by this time were called the New Critics—between the rugged texture and the smoothness of felicitous metrics and exact rhymes.

The complexity of Lowell's imagery is vaguely reminiscent of Hart Crane, and it may be relevant that Allen Tate, who was Lowell's teacher and friend as well as a friend of Hart Crane, wrote that what prevented Crane from greatness was the lack of an ordered and controlling philosophy or a belief like Roman Catholicism. Finally, it should be noted that Lowell displayed a real affinity toward the Fugitives in his strong dislike for things of modern civilization.

With *Lord Weary's Castle*, Lowell had arrived. Five years later came *The Mills of the Kavanaughs*, described as "a collection of seven dreams, fantasies, and monologues." These were long poems, basically narrative in form, yet combining the strict formality of his earlier work in the longer forms. They sustained and expanded the areas of interest demonstrated in the earlier book: history, his heritage, Catholicism, the classics, and the Bible. There was no diminishment of power, and the poems represent a remarkable achievement of sustained force and energy. They carried certain aspects of Lowell's technique to its limits, almost to the breaking point. This book served to consolidate his reputation, yet at the same time it raised the question of where he would go from there. Eight years later, *Life Studies* appeared, surprising many with its apparent difference and new directions. During those years, the American literary scene had changed somewhat. Those of Lowell's generation, most of them formalists, were now respectable in the academies. Most of them were teaching, and already gifted pupils were turning out good and passable imitations of their work. Meanwhile, another group, equally academic in education and background, was rebelling. These were the so-called Beats. In one sense, they represented a nostalgic return to the prewar poetry. They rejected the rules and idiom of the New Critics. They made an effort to be popular poets, to speak in the vernacular idiom, including obscenity and profanity, to and for a larger audience. They rejected Eliot and set up William Carlos Williams and Ezra Pound as literary heroes. They received much publicity and devoted a large amount of their time, effort, and verse to attacking the Academics. *Life Studies* came as a great relief to many poets and critics on both sides, for they all knew one another and many had been schoolmates. They wanted some form of negotiated peace, and Lowell seemed to supply the answer. The Academics were willing to listen to reason, willing to relax to keep up with the times, and the Beats were realizing that publicity and popular interest did not increase the reading audience of poetry. There remained a limited audience that would have to be shared by both groups. The conditions were ripe for settlement. Robert Lowell was acceptable to both sides. He had proved himself to the formalists. His passion, indignation, and suffering, as well as the widely known vicissitudes of his personal life, qualified him as at least an honorary Beat.

Life Studies is a mixture of things. Part 1 contains a few exciting poems in his earlier manner. Part 2, entitled "91 Revere Street," is a long, personal reminiscence in prose, a kind of short novel. Part 3 is a short collection of literary sketches or snapshots, sometimes using rhyme, but more free and colloquial than anything he had done so far. The final section returns to his personal concerns, his family background and present troubles, but with a significant difference. It is now much more explicitly personal, sometimes openly confessional. The verse is often free in form. The old tough texture and the voice is there, but the form and method seem new. Moreover, this quality of the explicit manifests itself in a direct dealing with social concerns. Lowell speaks out against racial prejudice, injustice, urban blight, and President Eisenhower. In short, *Life Studies*, while compromising none of Lowell's skill and power, manages to make a wedding of the two dominant and established modes of the period.

In the years following *Life Studies*, Lowell devoted himself to translation, to assimilation of those voices in the European tradition that interested him. His free adaptation of *Phaedra* was performed and highly praised, and *Imitations*, a collection of his translations, appeared in 1961, together with an introduction that explained his method of translation and, by implication, his poetry. The book was intended as a special kind of European poetry anthology, in historical time ranging from Homer and Sappho through Boris Pasternak. It was to be called *Imitations* because, in fact, these were original poems, based on the tone and mood of the model in another language and filtered through the consciousness and sensibility of Lowell himself. It is possible that Lowell exaggerated the novelty of his method; this kind of translation by adaptation and imitation has a long history in the English language, and Lowell had already done some similar versions—"War/(After Rimbaud)," "Charles the

Fifth and the Peasant/(After Valery)," "The Shako/(After Rilke)," "Ghost/(After Sextus Propertius)," and others—in *Lord Weary's Castle.*

The significance of an entire book of these imitations, coupled with an assertive and explicit introduction, was twofold. In a personal sense, it was a kind of advertisement for himself—an honest acknowledgment that he had achieved recognition and stature, a boldly open declaration that he was now fully a major poet. Second, though not unrelated to the first effect, it was a further declaration of independence from the so-called Academic school. Some of his peers and colleagues had been translating, a bit more strictly, for some time. Among the very finest of these was Richard Wilbur, whose two very accurate translations of Molière—*Le Misanthrope* and *Tartuffe*, elegantly rendered line by line and rhyme by rhyme, but always with amazing flexibility—had preceded *Phaedra* in performance. In any case, Lowell's method serves to illustrate his deliberate attempt to dissociate himself from what he believed to be a more academic approach to translation. The book not only was a critical success but also sold well. Moreover, the earlier books were brought out again in paperback and sold widely and well. For the first time in many years, a serious poet at the peak of his creative powers had achieved the highest critical praise and at the same time reached a wider audience than either he or his contemporaries had reached before. *Imitations* was at once a breakthrough and a bulwark to Lowell's already secure position.

In 1964, Lowell published his most important collection of poems to date, *For the Union Dead.* This book, containing poems written between 1956 and 1964, is varied and dazzling in its variety. It can also be seen as exemplary of internal peacemaking, for he includes poems in the earlier, taut manner as well as poems as free in form and more so than those in *Life Studies.* In addition, he acknowledged in a "Note" at the beginning that he had gone back to recast or rewrite some of the earlier poems. There is in *For the Union Dead* not only a greater sense and appreciation of the audience but also a firm commitment to poetry as a responsible rhetorical dialogue with that audience. Though the same basic subjects and concerns are there, there is at the same time a greater ease, frankness, and open quality than ever before, a confidence in his place and power. The title poem, a set piece of reminiscence and association based on Augustus Saint-Gaudens' bronze relief of Colonel Robert Gould Shaw and the African-American infantry that he led in the Civil War, becomes the key to the "new" Lowell. In the ever-present conflict of racial integration, he sides proudly, in fact vehemently for a conscientious objector, with the old New England abolitionist tradition, fire-breathing in his condemnation not only of injustice elsewhere but also in his rage and contempt for the indifference of his own townspeople.

At an age when many poets were just beginning to receive the preliminary signs of recognition, Robert Lowell had already earned the appellation "leader of mid-century poetry." As he grew and developed, it seemed that Lowell stood the best chance of any poet of his generation to earn and receive the laurels reserved for the truly great poets. Some critics argue, however, that his poems changed little, except superficially, from the earliest poems. There were slight differences in form, but the concerns and attitudes might or might not have deepened and matured. The matter remains ambiguous and debatable. In later interviews, as well as in the introductory notes to two of his volumes, Lowell showed a disconcerting and dangerously self-conscious concern for ratings on what Robert Frost called "the literary stock-market" and his place in it. It has often proved a fatal mistake to try to write history in advance.

When Lowell's deep personal problems became public property, as he made frank and explicit use of them in his poems, there was, inevitably, a genuine question in the mind of his readers as to whether he had or would overcome some of these problems. They wondered whether these confessional poems were therapeutic and liberating, as Lowell seemed to think, or perhaps symptomatic and ultimately inhibiting. His death of a heart attack in 1977 cut short this debate, perhaps leaving it forever unresolved. Nevertheless, in Lowell the United States had a first-rate poet whose art earned for him a place of honor and distinction.

THE POETRY OF MARIANNE MOORE

Type of work: Poetry
Author: Marianne Moore (1887-1972)
Principal published works: *Poems*, 1921; *Observations*, 1924; *Selected Poems*, 1935; *The Pangolin and Other Verse*, 1936; *What Are Years*, 1941; *Nevertheless*, 1944; *Collected Poems*, 1951; *Selected Fables of La Fontaine*, 1955 (translation); *Like a Bulwark*, 1956; *O to Be a Dragon*, 1959; *Tell Me, Tell Me*, 1966; *The Complete Poems of Marianne Moore*, 1967, 1981.

Marianne Moore, a very individualistic American poet, was "modern" when she was first published in 1921. Although she influenced scores of writers, her poetry is inimitable and unparaphrasable, with an excellence distinctly her own. She was a rare combination of "poet's poet" and advice-giving moralist. As a modern poet in New York in the 1920's, many readers found her poetry esoteric: It was much admired by the select group of modern poets headquartering there, but was almost unintelligible to most readers and certainly did not seem great because most of her topics appeared inconsequential. Her modernism, contrary to writers influenced by T. S. Eliot during the same period, led her away from philosophy; she was never disenchanted by the world around her.

On the contrary, the enchantment that she found is everywhere, even in "business documents and school books." Her fantastic footnotes are from encyclopedias, newspapers, *National Geographic*, documentary films, Tolstoy's diary—everywhere. She seeks to show reality, the genuine.

Moore's favorite "inconsequential topic" is animals. The descriptions of her often exotic menagerie—"The Pangolin," "The Jerboa," "The Frigate Pelican," and monkeys, snakes, mongooses, a buffalo, fish, elephants, a snail—illustrate above all her uncanny accuracy as an observer. The smallest details are included to characterize her animals. In "The Pangolin," her description could be a stage director's explanation of reasons behind actions so that the cast will make their stage movements believable. One could walk like a Pangolin after hearing Moore's instructions.

There are as many examples of minute observation in her poems as there are lines. Perhaps Moore's observations are somewhat difficult to follow; after all, most readers' minds are not as enchanted as hers. The difficulty results, not from inaccuracy, but from her ability to compress so much description into so few unemphasized words. She is, in a way, trying to train her readers to be observers too.

As it often does in Moore's poetry, the title of "The Fish" serves also as the first line. The size of the sea life diminishes as the poem progresses; both order and structure are carefully planned. Like a scientist, Moore works from specifics to generalizations in all of her poems ("The illustration/ is nothing to you without the application"). Her animal poems, more specifically, are like the works of a naturalist interested in animals as animals, not as symbols of people. Nevertheless, Moore is a moralist. Her animal poems, which show what she admires in animals, illustrate what she wants to admire in humans. In fact, most of her animal poems fit into a broader category often termed "essays in verse." She defends the cat, "Peter," for example, by reminding her readers to be true to their own natures.

As animals are imperfect, so are people. Moore admires honestly imperfect efforts because they demand fortitude; "Nevertheless" points out that the most beautiful design comes from "a struggle" in the strawberry plant, and that even the strongest plants must endure hardships. In fact, that is why they are the strongest. She sees beauty and bravery in the simplest things, and in "The Face," she identifies the things that help define her aims as a poet: order, ardor, simplicity, inquiry.

Many of Moore's essays in verse are about the poet and the art of poetry. Her most famous, and her most overt statement about content, is found in the earlier, fuller version of "Poetry." Moore's poems also discuss style. Her own emphasis on compactness is explained in "To a Snail." In "The Labors of Hercules," she speaks to critics of content and style. It is her straightforwardness "like electricity" that controls her metrical individuality.

The strikingly individualistic form of Moore's verse is neither free verse nor accented rhythms. Her model is French: Words are neither accented nor emphasized; neither do they metrically rhyme. Instead, the pattern of syllables per line in each stanza is repeated in the next stanza. This unusual quality and brilliance contribute to the total effect of the previously cited poems.

The conversational effect of unaccented syllabication is consistent with Moore's advice in "Silence," in which she declares that the deepest emotions are always revealed in silence and restraint. The reason for the restraint is given in "The Student," who sometimes appears untouched, not because he is lacking in feeling but because he feels too intensely. The formality of Moore's rigid, yet perfectly controlled, mechanics is indeed formidable until the magic of her tone, some implication of the heart, rescues the reader. Moore never separates intelligence from emotion and sensitivity.

It is Moore's love in her observations that makes her poems, which are so carefully constructed and controlled, so modern and experimental and also so individualistic.

While critics and poets were won over by her mechanical perfections and by her perceptive wit and intelligence, the public appreciated poetry that dismissed the trivial and talks about important things such as real animals, birds, snakes, snails, and toads. Her ability to delight, to record with sensitive perception and appreciation the things of this world, and to convince one of its reality provided the reasons for Moore's popularity and literary reputation among both scholars and general readers. It is just these qualities that make her an individualistic and enchanting part of the American literary tradition.

THE POETRY OF SYLVIA PLATH

Type of work: Poetry
Author: Sylvia Plath (1932-1963)
Principal published works: *The Colossus and Other Poems*, 1960; *Three Women*, 1962; *Ariel*, 1965; *Crossing the Water*, 1971; *Winter Trees*, 1971; *Fiesta Melons*, 1971; *Crystal Gazer*, 1971; *Lyonesse*, 1971; *Pursuit*, 1973; *The Collected Poems*, 1981.

Sylvia Plath is both a cult figure and a solid American poet whose work stands on its own without reference to her biography. The sensational details of her life and death have obscured the value of her work, but, seen on its own, Plath's poetry shows a welding of craft and thought into complex and yet accessible poetry. Her personal anguish and the complex mythology that she devised to express it compel the reader's attention initially, but her subtle rhythms and uncompromising vision repay repeated study.

Plath's work is dominated by feelings of rage and loss, associated with her father's death when she was eight. Otto Plath, a German entomology professor who studied bees, was perceived by his young daughter as remote and demanding. According to her poems, she was never able to win his desperately sought-after affection. Because he died before she could demythologize the father-figure in the ordinary way, Plath became obsessed by the image of her dead father, perceiving him as a demon-god demanding her obedience. In "The Colossus," "Lady Lazarus," and other poems, she attempts to deal with this ominous presence by understanding or by exorcism. She attempted suicide at twenty by taking pills and hiding in her basement. Rescued and hospitalized, she recovered from this depression and charted her suicide attempt and recovery in *The Bell Jar* (1963), her thinly disguised autobiographical novel, as well as in her poetry.

Her marriage to British poet Ted Hughes seemed to raise her spirits, as did her growing success as a poet: The British publisher Methuen published her first book, *The Colossus and Other Poems*, in 1960, and her work was being accepted by the best-known literary journals in the United States and in England. Alfred A. Knopf published a shorter version of *The Colossus* in 1962, fulfilling Plath's dream of placing a book with a major American publisher. Her two children provided new subject material for her work. When Hughes abandoned Plath for another woman, however, she conflated this loss with the earlier loss of her father, plunging into a deep depression that was punctuated by brief episodes of prolific writing. After one such period of anguished poetry, she committed suicide on February 11, 1963.

Plath's poetry falls into two categories that share subjects but diverge in style. Her earlier poems, collected in *The Colossus*, use a variety of traditional and idiosyncratic forms to express death's seductive attraction and a permanent sense of alienation from both self and world. Plath's later work eclipsed the earlier in popularity, but the fine craft of the poems of *The Colossus* emerges in repeated readings. "Point Shirley" expresses the common sentiments of grief for a grandmother's death and pain at nature's indifference to human concerns, but the form and imagery individualize the poem and intensify its impact. Looking at her grandmother's deserted beach home, the speaker describes the violence of the elements: "The shingle booms, bickering under/ The sea's collapse." Alliteration, falling rhythm, and off-rhyme mimic the sounds of the sea. The energy of an individual life seems pointless, dissolvable in the mindless natural cycle. "She is dead,/ Whose laundry snapped and froze here, who/ Kept house against/ What the sluttish, rutted sea could do." Images of the desolate seascape and the sadness of the grown-up child who comes seeking comfort and remembrance build to a negative climax:

> Grandmother, stones are nothing of home
> To that spumiest dove.
> Against both bar and tower the black sea runs.

The black sea, death's undercurrent, dominates even in Plath's first published work. The speaker in these poems tends to be uncentered and displaced, looking at herself through distorting lenses. In "The Colossus," a poem with an Electra theme appropriate to Plath's preoccupations, the speaker is a tiny figure in contrast with the huge destroyed statue that she is trying to reassemble. The giant dead figure, addressed as "father," dwarfs the woman who would piece him together, making a mockery of her attempts. She is nevertheless both possessed by the statue and an inhabitant of it, its dead immensity overwhelming her flickering life: "Nights, I squat in the cornucopia/ Of your left ear," the speaker states, expressing the bizarre disparity. "My hours are married to shadow." Plath distanced herself from the poem in discussing it, claiming that it was a reimagining of Greek myth. In fact, it is Plath's own story, the mythologizing of her life. Much of her work reflects a strenuous effort to piece together the father, to retrieve him so that his malign influence over her can be banished. The father-devil-ghost is summoned to his exorcism.

Early Plath poems include sonnets, villanelles, and syllable-counting forms. Like Emily Dickinson, whose poetic flirtation with death might be said to parallel hers, Plath was a master of off-rhyme. For Plath as for Dickinson, the odd discordant notes served as appropriate background music for a disordered world that provides no clear certainties and no true home. Plath's early poems are dominated by falling rhythms that complement the slant rhyme. The shades of these poems range from gray to black; only occasionally does some gleam of optimism flare, and then this glimmer is notable mostly for its evanescence. An example is "Black Rook in Rainy Weather." The poem asserts that the random gifts of observed beauty, such as the sight of a rook "Ordering its black feathers," can so shock the watcher out of her daily dullness that they can be called miracles: "Miracles occur,/ If you care to call those spasmodic/ Tricks of radiance miracles." Such reprieves from "the dull, ruinous landscape" are rare, sudden, and passing.

"Black Rook in Rainy Weather" has an unusual rhyme scheme, as it consists of eight five-line stanzas that rhyme *abcde*, although the rhymes are casual. (The *e* lines, for example, end with the words "accident," "portent," "incandescent," "inconsequent," "ignorant," "grant," "content," and "descent.") Plath's metrical experimentation is extensive and effective. Her early poems pay minute attention to form, so that metrical form is allied to a logical kind of wit in a way that often suggests a metaphysical sensibility groping in a cosmic darkness. (There are exceptions to this bleakness, such as the playful "Metaphors," a poem about pregnancy in nine lines of nine syllables each.) Plath consulted her dictionary and her thesaurus as she carefully translated her obsessions into image and metaphor.

Plath's later poems, collected in *Ariel*, are violent and obsessive; they burst from her pen. In one of them, she says, "The blood jet is poetry,/ There is no stopping it." Many of these poems were written in the last few months of her life, when she was desperately trying to take care of her two small children alone during a bitterly cold London winter. These works reflect Plath's recent personal disasters. "Burning the Letters" and "For a Fatherless Son" tell of her husband's desertion and its effects on her and the children. Bizarre witchery and moon-magic combine in poems that hover on the edge of reason. Rhymes and rhythms are often ragged. Personal pain

is compared with that of victims of the Holocaust and of Hiroshima—comparisons that seem excessive to some readers, but that reflect the acute suffering she felt. As in earlier work, death and birth merge: "A squeal of brakes./ Or is it a birth cry?" she asks in "Stopped Dead." Wounds fascinate and repel; her life is a wound, gushing blood like the thumb that she slices open in "Cut." The image of hooks recurs, hooks suggesting that attachments to life are painful and limiting. These themes and images are not new to the *Ariel* poems, but they are more insistent and more obvious.

For example, pounding hysteria substitutes for gentle rhythm in "Daddy," a poem with an ironic title that belies its grief and rage. "Daddy" is the repressive and aloof figure who made the speaker feel like a white foot stifled in a black shoe, "Barely daring to breathe or Achoo." In this poem, Plath tears away the mask with which she provided herself in "The Colossus," and she makes direct and explicit the exorcism theme. She rails at the dead father, claiming that she has had enough of his dragging her from life, calling her from the grave: "The black telephone's off at the root,/ The voices just can't worm through." The repeated *oo* sounds at the ends of lines serve as a cry of pain. The frenzy of the poem increases as the speaker describes her earlier attempts to rid herself of this death-bringing ghost through a suicide attempt and through marriage to someone like "daddy":

> I made a model of you,
> A man in black with a Meinkampf look
>
> And a love of the rack and the screw.
> And I said I do, I do.

The speaker claims success in "killing" the father's ghost and the "model" as well, thus freeing herself. When the poem ends with a line of sheer invective, the chant is completed and the exorcism finished.

Plath's obsessive images and uniquely feminine myth outweigh the careful craft in her later poetry. Her bee-myth is developed in one late series; like her entomologist father, she herself kept bees and gathered their honey. Poems such as "Stings," "The Bee Meeting," and "Wintering" use the life cycle of the queen bee and the life of the hive as metaphors to express a preoccupation with a mysterious cycle of death, purification, and rebirth. In "Stings," the male helper distracts the bees and takes the stings, leaving the speaker free to spy and identify with the risen queen:

> Now she is flying
> More terrible than she ever was, red

> Scar in the sky, red comet
> Over the engine that killed her—
> The mausoleum, the wax house.

The red queen, like the reborn red-haired woman who rises from the ashes in another late poem, "Lady Lazarus," is a triumphant assertion of self-affirmation. Yet "Edge," possibly the last poem that Plath wrote, does not triumph in any rebirth. It describes a dead woman, surrounded by two dead children, her posture the conclusion of a ritual. No longer a participant, the woman is observed by a dispassionate moon.

Both early and late Plath poems translate pain into lacerating tropes and images. The anguish is both her own and that of the female artist struggling with the limiting roles of a woman of her era. Plath's world offers few options, and those choices tend to restrict rather than to free. The light of her world is cold, and its communication aborted, as in the final scene of "The Munich Mannequins":

> And the black phones on hooks
>
> Glittering
> Glittering and digesting
>
> Voicelessness. The snow has no voice.

THE POETRY OF EDGAR ALLAN POE

Type of work: Poetry
Author: Edgar Allan Poe (1809-1849)
Principal published works: *Tamerlane and Other Poems*, 1827; *Aaraaf, Tamerlane, and Minor Poems*, 1829; *Poems*, 1831; *The Raven and Other Poems*, 1845.

Of all American writers, perhaps no other has had more conflicting judgments made concerning his work than Edgar Allan Poe. The judgments themselves are remarkable for their variety and, in some ways, for their wit. Poet and essay writer Ralph Waldo Emerson called Poe "the jingle man." James Russell Lowell, an important critic and editor in the late 1800's, claimed in his satirical narrative poem *A Fable for Critics* (1848), that Poe's work was "three-fifths genius and two-fifths sheer fudge."

It is difficult to reconcile such comments with the well-known international appreciation for Poe's work. The great Irish poet William Butler Yeats said of Poe that he was "always and for all lands a great lyric poet." Additionally, Poe was loved and admired by English poets Alfred, Lord Tennyson and Algernon Charles Swinburne, as well as by the French Symbolist poets Charles Baudelaire and Stéphane Mallarmé.

Born in Boston in 1809, Poe was the son of itinerant actors. Perhaps his father had already deserted his mother; regardless, he died a year after Poe's birth. She continued to support Edgar and two other children until her early death when Poe was only three years old. Edgar was taken into the home of a wealthy merchant in Richmond, Virginia, named John Allan. He and Edgar had a complicated, troubled relationship; Edgar was never legally adopted by him and was considerably favored by John Allan's wife, further adding to tension between the two men.

Though Allan had pressed Edgar to prepare for a legal career, Edgar revolted from those pressures and fled to Boston, where he began a career in writing and editing. He worked for a time, for example, for the *Southern Literary Messenger*, helping to increase the magazine's circulation. By 1837, he had published eighty-three reviews, six poems, four essays, and three short stories, and he had written an unpublished tragedy. After taking out a license to marry his young cousin Virginia (aged thirteen), he had married her in 1836. Unsteady employment, health problems, and an addiction to alcohol plagued Poe for all of his life. When his young wife died of tuberculosis, Poe was devastated and never quite recovered his equilibrium.

When Poe's reputation and influence is measured along with the tragic shortness of his life (he died in 1849 at the age of forty), his work can be said to be truly remarkable. A writer in many genres who was especially well known for his fiction (gothic horror tales and early detective stories) and poetry, Poe also wrote some important essays, especially "The Philosophy of Composition" and "The Poetic Principle." Although the number of his enduring poems is small, he nevertheless left an indelible mark on poetry, and not simply American poetry. His poem "The Raven," which was largely responsible for Poe's fame in his time, continues to be memorized and remembered by contemporary readers.

"The Raven," perhaps Poe's most important poem, was first published in 1845 in the *New York Evening Mirror*; it subsequently appeared in a volume in the same year entitled *The Raven and Other Poems*. During Poe's lifetime, the poem was printed in eleven periodicals. "The Raven" consists of eighteen six-line stanzas, five lines of trochaic octameter, and a sixth line of trochaic tetrameter. The poem features a scholarly speaker visited on a stormy, dark night by a visitor who raps at the door. The opening lines of the work immediately establish the sound effects that will predominate throughout the poem:

> Once upon a midnight dreary, while I pondered, weak and weary,
> Over many a quaint and curious volume of forgotten lore—
> While I nodded, nearly napping, suddenly there came a tapping,
> As of some one gently rapping, rapping at my chamber door—
> " 'Tis some visiter," I muttered, "tapping at my chamber door—
>   Only this and nothing more."

Famous for hypnotic sound effects in his poetry, Poe marshalls internal rhyme, onomatopoeia, assonance, and consonance to great effect here. The feeling is eerie, unsettling, and melancholy—exactly the effect that Poe had in mind. Effective as well is the refrain rhyme of "more," varying between "more," "evermore," "nothing more," and "nevermore." The poem's visitor turns out to be an "ebony bird" with the maddening quality of replying "Nevermore" to the scholar's frantic questions. Like many of Poe's other protagonists, the speaker in "The Raven" seems dangerously close to mental breakdown and hysteria. Unable to rid himself of the visitor, the scholar manages an uneasy accommodation of life with the ebony bird. At the end of the poem, the lamplight continues to cast "his shadow on the floor."

Poe's essay "The Philosophy of Composition" claims to be the writer's explanation of the composition process that he went through in writing "The Raven." Though that claim has been disputed by some critics, the essay provides valuable insight into the mind of Poe, especially in the radical split between the writer's rational, mechanical (almost numerical) method of composing the poem and the ethereal and melancholy effect that Poe was trying to create.

"Annabel Lee," another of Poe's truly memorable poems, shares with "The Raven" the situation of a melancholy speaker obsessed with the loss of a beautiful young woman. In "The Raven" the woman, Lenore, is merely one subject that the speaker raises with the eerie bird, whereas in "Annabel Lee" the speaker relates the story of his life with "this maiden" and tells of the cloud that comes, "chilling and killing my Annabel Lee." The poem beautifully evokes young, innocent love and the edenic happiness that the two lovers shared. Again, sound effects are used with power by Poe; repetition and internal rhyme create sound patterns both lovely and hypnotic, imitating the sounds of nature in "this kingdom by the sea."

Much shorter than "The Raven," "Annabel Lee" is a ballad in six stanzas of six lines each, lines that alternate between four and three stresses. Probably Poe's finest poem, "Annabel Lee" appeared posthumously in the New York *Tribune* on October 9, 1849—a mere two days after Poe's death on October 7.

"The Bells" is another of Poe's well-known poems that uses sound effects, especially repetition, in a memorable way. In each of four large sections of "The Bells," Poe appears to be aiming for a different sound quality: first, the sound of sleigh bells; second, the "mellow" sound of wedding bells; third, the shrieking of alarm bells; fourth, the tolling of "Iron bells." Seeming to echo the ages of humanity, the bells take on gothic overtones characteristic of Poe; section 3 is distinctly hysterical at times with its "clang, and clash, and roar." Section 4 is positively funereal with its "tolling, tolling, tolling" sound effects.

Poe was consistent in the aim for his poetry. In his essay "The Poetic Principle," he wrote that this principle came down "strictly and simply, [to] the Human Aspiration for Supernal Beauty." Poe attempted to create that beauty in his carefully crafted, melancholy poems and to a large extent, certainly succeeded.

THE POETRY OF THEODORE ROETHKE

Type of work: Poetry
Author: Theodore Roethke (1908-1963)
Principal published works: *Open House*, 1941; *The Lost Son and Other Poems*, 1948; *Praise to the End!*, 1951; *The Waking: Poems 1933-1953*, 1953; *Words for the Wind*, 1958; *I Am! Says the Lamb*, 1961; *Sequence, Sometimes Metaphysical*, 1963; *The Far Field*, 1964; *The Collected Poems of Theodore Roethke*, 1966.

It used to be commonplace in a discussion of the poetry of Theodore Roethke to emphasize the variety, the differences between his work as he passed through various "phases." It is true that there is variety and there are differences at every stage of his work as he matured as a poet. After his death, however, when it became possible to look at his work as a whole, it was surprising how much of his future work, his interests and the directions that he would later explore, was indicated in *Open House*, mostly written during the decade preceding World War II. (It is to be remembered that, though Roethke was often grouped with Richard Wilbur and Robert Lowell as one of the three leading poets of his generation, he was, in fact, ten years older than both of these poets and much behind them in receiving an equivalent critical recognition.)

It was and is easy to be deceived by the poems of *Open House*. They are short, quiet, rather plainly and strictly formal, evidently subdued and modest. Their artistry is understated, and they blithely ignore some of the critical fiats prevalent at the time. They have a kind of hewn and carved simplicity, with minimal attention paid to the intellectual ambiguity, the forms of irony and wit, that were becoming fashionable. They make frequent and familiar use of abstractions, which had become the equivalent of dirty words to poets and critics who took their standards of judgment at second hand from T. S. Eliot and Ezra Pound. One has to imagine the effect of, for example, the second stanza of the title poem upon the conditioned reader of that period. Except for the poet's obvious use of rhetorical paradox, which was very acceptable at that time, his lines break all the rules. Many critics caught in the web of time have been unable to exercise the necessary self-transcendence to acknowledge the validity of another and different approach. Thus it is not surprising that *Open House*, which turns out to have been the first public statement of a poet of acknowledged greatness, was largely ignored. It was hard then to see the virtues of this work and altogether too easy to label it as the quiet and unassuming verse of an English teacher who was obviously a little too removed from the action, a little out of touch with the exciting center of the literary

scene. Then, also, there was World War II, whose gory clamor drowned all but the loudest voices.

The Lost Son and Other Poems came after the war and after the successes achieved by Lowell in *Lord Weary's Castle* (1946) and Wilbur in *The Beautiful Changes and Other Poems* (1947). Some changes in Roethke's method were immediately evident. The shorter lyric poems shied away from abstraction, coming close at times to the purity of imagism in the exact rendering of the concrete image without regard to generalized comment by the poet. Inevitably, the texture seemed tougher and more conventionally antipoetic. The final stanza of "Cuttings I" is illustrative and shows as well what the poet can do by intense and precise concentration on a single, small action.

A substantial number of the shorter poems in *The Lost Son* are more explicitly personal than before, deriving directly from his experience of growing up around a greenhouse. Some of the titles tell the story: "Root Cellar," "Forcing House," "Weed Puller," "Orchids," "Moss-Gathering," "Old Florist," "Transplanting," "Child on Top of a Greenhouse," "Flower Dump," "Carnations." For the most part, these poems are freer in form than the earlier poems, and when the poet does return to the strictness he had observed—as, for example, in the widely anthologized "My Papa's Waltz"—strict form is used more for humor and irony, which was a more acceptable strategy at that time.

It is possible to view the fine shorter poems of *The Lost Son* as demonstrable proof that Roethke could do what was expected and demanded by his affiliated university and yet in a highly original manner. Yet if Roethke paid the piper and handsomely with the shorter poems, it was the long title poem that made people sit up and take notice. "The Lost Son" was something quite new in American poetry. A long poem, in an original and independent form, it was a kind of dramatic monologue, but an interior one, an objectification of the nearly ineffable drama and history of the psyche—in this case, of a deeply tormented and troubled psyche. To an extent, Roethke availed himself of the techniques of surrealism, and to an extent, he used the resources of primitive arts and forms of expression to create an effect reminiscent of totem objects and cave paintings. More important, he found a logic of images, often fleeting and ghostly images to be sure but always palpable and concrete, to represent the shades and states of being far more complex than other poets had been able to suggest when they started from the outside and evoked the inner drama by hints, clues, and shards. The given setting was the mysterious landscape of consciousness with the unconscious just at the edge of the horizon, all this spelled out in words and images. The effect was ragged, nervous, and raw—a grotesque vision. The poet dared all and risked everything, moving in unknown territory, a realm with more questions than answers. Out of context, he risked the danger that, in his search for meaning and articulation, he would come up only with sheer gibberish. This new method showed difficulty and knotty complexity in a new form and with a new intent, by the articulation of these obscurities to bring light, a poetry that by definition trembled on the verge of madness or mysticism.

This new direction caused a considerable stir in the critical world. Roethke could no longer be labeled. If he could not be identified as a member of a "school" and if, at the same time, he was not setting a new direction for some future school to follow, then he was undeniably an original and attention would have to be paid. "The Lost Son" was, for the poet, the beginning of a remarkable burst of creative energy and inspiration. In 1951, he published *Praise to the End!* with further and deeper explorations of this new mode, including the much praised "The Shape of the Fire," with its opening lines that shocked those as yet unfamiliar with his method.

With *Praise to the End!* and *The Waking*, Roethke established for himself a place. *The Waking* earned him the Pulitzer Prize for 1953, and his literary fortunes had turned for the better. During the 1950's, he became one of the most prolific and widely published American poets, going his own way and marvelously aloof from the struggle between the Beats and the Academics that riddled and cluttered literary journals and little magazines.

Roethke was always much too independent of spirit to be bought and owned by prizes, recognition, or even the knowledge of personal achievement. He pushed himself restlessly to try new and different variations. At the same time that he was writing these profound and knotty psychic monologues, he was writing shorter pieces in a variety of modes: delightful and meaningful children's verse, and some of the finest love lyrics of the twentieth century. His talent was wide and encompassing. He could write, for children of all ages, such delightful poems as "The Cow"; he could write, with sexual gusto, the cele-

brated "I Knew a Woman"; and he could take a shopworn, weary form like the villanelle and make it sing as if he had made it for the first time, as in "The Waking."

It was no wonder that, by the middle of the 1950's, Theodore Roethke seemed to many of the United States' most responsible critics to be the most important poet writing in English.

Words for the Wind, appearing in 1958, won the National Book Award and gave his readers a chance to view Roethke's work as a whole for the first time. It was in fact, more a selected volume than a true collected book, for he dropped and eliminated some poems, revised and rearranged others. Even so, it was a volume of impressive length that few if any of his contemporaries could have equaled, running more than two hundred close-packed pages, illustrating all the variety of his past work, and indicating some of the directions he was following at the time in its concluding section of previously uncollected poems. The book opens with the title poem from *Open House*, and by then only the insentient could fail to recognize how true and how prophetic, how completely stated were the quiet and rigorous lines of the first stanza of that poem. He had said what he was doing and was going to do, had introduced himself and his subject, but no one had listened then. *Words for the Wind* gave them a second chance.

The book brought Roethke immediate recognition. He was then fifty years old, and it had taken almost twenty years for this recognition, but it had happened. Of special interest to his readers were the two long poems, "The Dying Man: In Memoriam: W. B. Yeats" and "Meditations of an Old Woman." "The Dying Man" caught the rhythms and cadences of Yeats, yet assimilated them into the manner and vocabulary of Roethke. It was more than a salute and memorial to a great poet. It demonstrated dramatically the influence of the earlier master on the younger poet and helped the reader to see a certain analogy or affinity between the two poets. Yeats, too, by his Irishness and special interests and concerns, was just outside the literary scene of his own day. It was possible as well to see that Roethke, like Yeats, was more traditional, part of the grand tradition that ignores or transcends fashions if it can, than anyone had realized previously. Finally, there was a wish, a hope to be derived from this deliberate analogy. Yeats alone of the twentieth century's early masters had a career that paralleled his long life. While the others wrote less and less, if at all, standing pat on their finished work, Yeats had written some of his finest poetry as an old man, proving that maturity need not necessarily stifle lyric impulse.

Roethke, after an amazing burst of creativity, had collected his poetry, but, since his powers seemed never stronger, it could be hoped that he might go on to even greater things. "Meditations of an Old Woman," a long and beautifully realized poem in five parts, offered a clue. Here images and pieces from all the early poems, familiar motifs reappeared, but in a new guise. All the intensity of the psychic poems and much of the complexity were present, except that now, through the voice of a fully realized character, there was a difference. There was a difference, too, in the seeming clarity and logic of the poem. Scales of difficulty had fallen away, perhaps partly because the reader was by then familiar with the personal conventions, signs, and symbols of the poet, but even more so because the poet seemed more secure in his knowledge of their wider meanings and, thus, more able to use and to apply rhetorically what had once seemed almost incantatory. Some of his personal ease and security shows itself in his ability to focus the kind of concentrated attention upon details that would not have interested him earlier.

The last poem of the collection is "What Can I Tell My Bones?" It takes as its theme the terror and release of dying, the fear of death and the aspiration of the caged spirit to be free. On the one hand, there is the inexorable logic of the mind, and on the other is the eternal cry of the spirit for deliverance. The poem ends with acceptance and affirmation, the mystical wedding of body (including the mind) and soul, a sense of the peace that passes understanding, utterly credible and at the last confirmed with a quiet summation that might apply as much to the poet as to his dramatic persona.

Ironically, the closing line of this poem, with its emphasis on finality, was to be the last statement in book form that Roethke made in his lifetime. He continued to publish poems in the magazines, but he died suddenly in late summer of 1963, leaving his later poems uncollected. His widow put together these last poems for publication, and *The Far Field*, appearing posthumously, was awarded the National Book Award. *The Far Field* is his finest work, built on the solid foundation of all his earlier ef-

forts. It is divided into four parts: "North American Sequence," "Love Poems," "Mixed Sequence," and "Sequence, Sometimes Metaphysical." The most impressive single piece is "North American Sequence," his longest and most ambitious poem. Here, in a poem as grandly designed in its own way as Hart Crane's *The Bridge* (1930), he goes a giant step beyond the liberty of "Meditations of an Old Woman" by meditating upon the history and meaning of his country. To this meditation he brings the Roethke that the reader knows, with all of himself and all the baggage and burden of himself in his encounter with the staggering fact, half-dreamed and half-realized, of the United States. Time and study will tell to what extent the poet succeeded, but meanwhile there are obvious glories in which to rejoice, such as the variation on the epic catalogue that opens part 3 of the section called "The Rose."

The poems in the other sections are variations on all the forms and subjects with which he had worked, never more eloquently realized. Everything is recapitulated. "The Abyss" is a variation on the earlier psychic mode, the love poems sing and shine as always, and a poem such as "Song" resembles those of *Open House*. With *The Far Field*, one sees, with an inner wince of pathos, another element of Roethke's greatness: Nothing was ever lost. Perhaps he did go through stages—for all individuals do as they grow, learn, and become—but few manage to do so without rejecting what they were and have been. The literary world places a premium on novelty. Roethke was able to come up with something new that neither offended nor isolated the old. His achievement was in part the result of the knowledge, intuitive and marvelous, that he had spent his life trying to communicate in language and within the structure of poetry. This knowledge is at once nakedly simple and as indescribable as a veiled mystery (except in his poems), but he stated it all outright in the concluding lines of "Once More, The Round," saying that everything merges into the final unity, the "One," as humanity dances on and on and on.

THE POETRY OF WALLACE STEVENS

Type of work: Poetry
Author: Wallace Stevens (1879-1955)
Principal published works: *Harmonium*, 1923, 1931; *Ideas of Order*, 1935; *Owl's Clover*, 1936; *The Man with the Blue Guitar and Other Poems*, 1937; *Parts of a World*, 1942; *Notes Toward a Supreme Fiction*, 1942; *Esthétique du Mal*, 1945; *Transport to Summer*, 1947; *Three Academic Pieces*, 1947; *A Primitive Like an Orb*, 1948; *The Auroras of Autumn*, 1950; *Selected Poems*, 1953; *The Collected Poems of Wallace Stevens*, 1954.

Wallace Stevens' poetry has been called both elegant and austere. It has been criticized for "an air of sumptuousness, *chic*, expensiveness, 'conspicuous consumption,'" as well as for bleakness, abstractness, a lack of personal warmth. Neither of these criticisms, however, says much about Stevens, who, according to Northrop Frye, was a rhetorician and therefore expendable, but an essential poet.

Stevens' first and perhaps most elegant, least austere, volume of poems, *Harmonium*, was unlike many first volumes in that it contained statements of all the major themes to appear in his later books. *Harmonium*, in other words, was a mature work, differing from the later volumes largely in manner rather than in meaning. Thus, throughout Stevens' poetry, whether early or late, one observes recurrent elements: a love for precise language resulting in a selection of words at once elegant and austere; a celebration of the imagination and the power of human creativity; a highly abstract, careful examination of different theories of perception and knowledge couched in highly concrete, colorful, often playful language; and a continuing concern for the myth-making capabilities of poetry in a world of defunct myths.

In *Ideas of Order* and *The Man with the Blue Guitar and Other Poems*, Stevens made a perceptible step toward austerity in statement of theme and in technique, although the themes were the same as those in *Harmonium*. Thus, the title poem of the second volume (containing also "Owl's Clover," "A Thought Revolved," and "The Men That Are Falling") consists of a series of thirty-three reevaluations of the position of the artist and the meaning of art in a world of "things as they are," a phrase equivalent to the *"ding an sich"* of the earlier "The Comedian as the Letter C." Instead of Crispin the Comedian's symbolic journey representing the various philosophical metamorphoses of an artist in a world of *"ding an sich,"* however, the guitar player in the later poem plucks out various types of "fictive music" corresponding to varying definitions of poetry. Crispin moves from definition to definition in the course of his journey; the guitar player appears to pose all thirty-three variations of "things as they are" without an exact progression. As in "The Comedian as the Letter C," the guitar player—the artist, the disciplined imagination, the passion for order—is confronted by a world of fact and matter that he tries to transmute on the blue guitar. That fact and matter are changed by the player is known; just how they are changed, and to what degree, becomes the central puzzle in a poem dealing at once with aesthetics, epistemology, and something similar to Samuel Taylor Coleridge's "poetic faith." The general conclusion is the recognition of the importance of poetry as source for "order" and meaning in a world of dazzling, jumbled, apparently purposeless objects—a world without clear meaning. Yet it may be that, given the myth-making importance of poetry in a mythless world, the poet cannot entirely succeed in making fact and matter meaningful.

This is Stevens' central quandary: How can the imagination fulfill humanity's craving for beauty, order, and meaning in a world antipathetic to imagination? Stevens' answers are plural, operating as logical alternatives. Thus, at times, no problem seems to arise at all, for the imagination may be the only thing that is real in an imagined world. This is the possibility or alternative that gives rise to section 25 of "The Man with the Blue Guitar," wherein the hero flings and twirls the world. It is, however, only one possibility, the most playful and optimistic, among thirty-three. Perhaps the simplest statement that can be made about the poem, then, is that its basis is poetry—as is true with all of Stevens' work—"poetry" meaning human perception and creativity (one and the same) rather than words on a page.

Stevens' 1935 volume, *Ideas of Order*, contains no poems of the length of "The Man with the Blue Guitar" but includes a number of excellent short meditative lyrics, such as "Academic Discourse at Havana," "Evening Without Angels," and "The Idea of Order at Key West." Here, Stevens also asks questions leading to an investigation of poetry. Often the form of Stevens' poems becomes a question about the nature of imagination or reality followed by an answer, always tentative or conditional, or series of answers.

Parts of a World continues Stevens' examination of poetry, as the titles of some of the poems therein indicate: "Poetry Is a Destructive Force," or "The Poems of Our Climate." The admired, much-cited "Connoisseur of Chaos" is contained in this volume. The "connoisseur," the poet, seems to live in a world of disorder rather than in the largely historical world that, having the advantages of "order," has also the disadvantage of dogma.

A long, difficult poem entitled "Notes Toward a Supreme Fiction" appeared in the same year as *Parts of a World*. Therein Stevens, in three sections, defines the qualities such a "fiction" must have: "It Must Be Abstract," "It Must Change," and "It Must Give Pleasure." These statements would be simple enough if Stevens were talking about poetry on a page. He is, however, talking about poetry and "fiction" as reality, or poetry as the perception of reality, and consequently "supreme fiction" comes to mean several analogous products of imagination: "the first idea" or "Logos," the created world, the first human, "the idea of man," and, by extension, the imaginative creation that takes place in a human mind. Hence, the qualities that Stevens defines in his three sections are not so much qualities that a poem on a page must have as they are qualities that existence must, and does, have. In this poem, too, appears the conflict that exists between fact and matter. This conflict explains why Stevens, praising poetry, appears to say that poetry gets in the way.

Transport to Summer includes "Notes Toward a Supreme Fiction" and also "Esthétique du Mal," a poem similar to "The Comedian as the Letter C," in which a poet tries to reconcile a comfortable philosophy or "esthetic" with "pain" and the destructiveness symbolized by Mt. Vesuvius. This comfortable philosophy, "his book," is akin to the romantic theory of the sublime and to the "esthétique du mal" nineteenth century style. One shrinks from real pain, the real volcano, and the fact of death. The poet and the poem seek out an "esthétique du mal" that will not shrink or falter, but arrive face to face with *"ding an sich"* and fact and matter as they are, finding a genuine aesthetic merely in living life as it is. All comfortable philosophies and panaceas Stevens counters with *"ding an sich."*

Three Academic Pieces—containing "The Realm of Resemblance," "Someone Puts a Pineapple Together," and "Of Ideal Time and Choice"—deals almost didactically, but always playfully and elegantly, with the nature of poetry. These pieces were included in the later collection of prose and verse lecture-essays, *The Necessary An-*

gel (1951), wherein, with a prose style very much like his poetry, Stevens continues to examine art, the subtitle reading, *Essays on Reality and the Imagination.*

The Auroras of Autumn, which won for Stevens his first National Book Award, includes, besides the title poem, "A Primitive Like an Orb" (published separately in 1948), "An Ordinary Evening in New Haven," and "Things of August." If there is drama in "Ordinary Evening," or in most of Stevens' poetry, it is the drama of thought, of reevaluation and redefinition as in "The Man with the Blue Guitar." The problem, if imagination is the only reality, is solipsism.

The solution—tentative, conditional, and ironic—is poetry. Ironically, in an imagined world, poetry offers reality, the antidote to imagination, "romance," "illusion," and "esthétiques du mal" that do not include all parts of the "sublime." Yet one can question whether poetry is able to dispense with tropisms and offer only a "pure reality." If, finally, poetry is merely the illusion of disillusion, the ultimate and hence least real product of the imagination, then reality is also the ultimate product of the imagination. Therefore, poetry and reality are one— the same dream or the same fact, whatever one may wish to call it. In any case, what one imagines, what one perceives, and what one is do not depend on the implication that reality is an actuality, or on the implication that imagination produces unreality, but only on changing ideas and on facing them directly or indirectly.

The Collected Poems of Wallace Stevens contains most of the poetry that appeared in his previous volumes, with the exception of "Owl's Clover," which Stevens thought unsuccessful, and two poems from *Parts of a World*, "The Woman That Had More Babies than That" and "Life on a Battleship." It also contained a long section, written when he was about seventy, called "The Rock." There, in poems such as "Not Ideas About the Thing but the Thing Itself" and "Reality Is an Activity of the Most August Imagination," Stevens continued his examinations of poetry. There are overtones of the problems of age and death, but such overtones appeared even in *Harmonium*. A reading of Stevens from early to late reveals little change in outlook, though increasing perfection of style and language and perhaps an increasing preference for meditative lyrics, of which "Sunday Morning" is the greatest early example. There followed *Opus Posthumous* (1957), edited by Samuel Morse, drawing together unpublished pieces, Stevens' notebook adages, occasional lectures, and Stevens' early verse plays, "Carlos Among the Candles" and "Three Travellers Watch the Sunrise."

Stevens could write that life is composed of theories about life, and he might also have added that poetry consists of propositions about poetry. Thus Stevens no doubt sounds like the first section of "Notes Toward a Supreme Fiction": "It Must Be Abstract." Yet, while Stevens is "abstract" and does build poetry out of "propositions," his poetry rarely has the dryness of prose philosophy. Stevens' works are among the most exciting, original, and, as Northrop Frye might say, "essential" verse of modern times.

THE POETRY OF RICHARD WILBUR

Type of work: Poetry
Author: Richard Wilbur (1921-   )
Principal published works: *The Beautiful Changes and Other Poems*, 1947; *Ceremony and Other Poems*, 1950; *Things of This World*, 1956; *Poems 1943-1956*, 1957; *Advice to a Prophet and Other Poems*, 1961; *The Poems of Richard Wilbur*, 1963; *Walking to Sleep: New Poems and Translations*, 1969; *Digging for China*, 1970; *The Mind-Reader: New Poems*, 1976; *Seven Poems*, 1981; *New and Collected Poems*, 1988.

It is difficult to assess Richard Wilbur's lyric poetry in terms of a developing career, a linear working-out and discarding of certain ideas, in the way in which one organizes the production of Geoffrey Chaucer's or William Wordsworth's poetry. Wilbur has said that he turned from playful writing to serious poetry because of the experience of potential chaos in World War II, but the war is not overpoweringly present in his first book, *The Beautiful Changes and Other Poems*, although the European Theater seems to loom in the background of many of these poems and the possibility of war remains behind some of his later work.

A comparison of two of the best poems may reveal another kind of development, not of ideas but of poetic power. "On the Eyes of an SS Officer" is one of the few poems in the 1947 volume directly related to the war. The poem is a syllogism in shape; its first two stanzas compare the eyes to ice and glaciers, then to fire and the sun. Clever things happen within the poem. In the first stanza, a metaphor within a metaphor refers to fresh snows at the frozen end of the earth's spit. "Spit" is first a reference to barbecuing, a link to the fire stanza, and then to sputum: It is a clue to the tone of disgust. The second stanza tells of one blinded by the sun. The blind saint is glorified, for he has seen the Platonic truth, but the SS Officer is called mindless. The last stanza concludes the statement and is filled with ambiguity with references to ice, fire, and eyes. The eyes are oases in a wilderness face. The eyes devise their own fire, but the poet asks his God to consign the eyes to hell. This type of ambiguity, however, is too rapid, too quickly understood.

One of Wilbur's best poems is "Advice to a Prophet," the title poem of his 1961 volume. Where in the earlier poem one sees a concern with the problems of tone, problems resolved by apparent syntactic ambiguity and puns, here one sees much larger problems being handled. The advice is offered to a prophet of doom, of the Bomb. The prophet's problem is to find a language by which he can communicate his message. He is evoking God's name to

cause the reader to feel self-pity. The advice is not to speak of the military power of weapons or of the end of the people, for these ideas are inconceivable. Rather, he speaks of the changing world. The loss of nature would destroy humanity; animals and trees are things in which humans themselves are mirrored. They are the ground of human perception and self-knowledge, as well as the elements of language. Language and knowledge have merged; consequently, the poet asks how one can communicate with nature when one can no longer speak. Wilbur's use of concrete image and abstract noun is different. Finally adjectives themselves, bereft of nouns, must function in a bombed or otherwise emptied world.

The first poem solves the problem of how to express hatred in a poem by pressing language to its limits to equate and disequate traditional poetic subjects: ice, fire, eyes. In the second poem, the language of association and the objects of the language are themselves examined. These are the poles of Wilbur's poetry. This is not to say that language in itself is a new interest for Wilbur; his translations reveal him to be an expert in French. The poem "Junk" in *Advice to a Prophet and Other Poems* is written in the style of Old English poetry, in two-stressed half-lines linked by alliteration: The theme is that of the "Lay of the Last Survivor" in *Beowulf*—the transience of artifacts. In Wilbur's *Ceremony and Other Poems*, there is a poem "Beowulf" that interprets the old epic. Unlike the Anglo-Saxon shaper of the poem, Wilbur has momentarily shifted the viewpoint, at the end of the fourth stanza, to inside Beowulf's head in order to comprehend his heroism.

A study of the use of word play in the volumes shows one aspect of Wilbur's poetic maturing. In *The Beautiful Changes*, besides the complex business in "On the Eyes of an SS Officer," there are two poems selected by Wilbur in his collaboration for Louis Untermeyer's anthology of 1955. In one, "Potato," the pun "blind" occurs twice, referring to the potato's eyes. The first line of "Bell Speech" has a phrase playing on the tonguelike clapper of the bell. Both of these puns are based on physiological and colloquial association; neither has a powerfully serious function. The puns are inefficient.

In *Ceremony*, however, the case alters. For example, "Juggler" contains four puns that bear much meaning. The poem is about a juggler who is like God and who balances balls like the planets of the solar system, then hauls his heaven in and returns to earth to balance normal objects, such as tables, brooms, or plates. The problem is that the world falls from human hearts and is forgotten.

Three puns in this poem are "gravity," "lightness," and "sole." Gravity suggests prejugglerian humorlessness, as well as the state of the Newtonian world. Lightness becomes that of objects, of the space around the sun, and of hearts. Sole, is the juggler's loneliness and the soul of worlds, the Neoplatonic, Lucretian soul. The fall of the earth, "fall" being the fourth pun, is overcome by a lighthearted language. In "Still, Citizen Sparrow," there is a picture of a vulture rising over the office described as "rotten." His "office" is both his function as a carrion-eater and a suggestion of the modern office building, leading to the edge of the sky—a skyscraper. The poem is an anti-flyting, taking up the owl's side in the ancient controversy of owl and nightingale, and the inversion is com plete: Contrary to John Keats's vision of his nightingale, it is the owl of this poem, the vulture, who eats death and derides mutability. In the title poem, "Ceremony," there is a line in which those who are familiar with Old or Middle English will recognize a complex series of etymological puns. Another poem, "In the Elegy Season," reverses clichés in the same way that "Advice to a Prophet" does, but this time the cliché is a modern one, the idea of a summer being unremembered in winter.

In Wilbur's next volume, *Things of This World*, there is more play with words. "A Black November Turkey" contains wordplay of the sort that one expects in the newer poems: The hens about the doomed turkey are "clocking," not clucking. They remind one of the bell Great Paul, the ticking of mutability, the winged chariot of Time.

Advice to a Prophet contains few puns in the better poems. In "Shame," a satiric poem, there is a pun that furthers the satire: "Scusi" is the capital city of the humble country, and its name reminds one of "Excuse me" in Romance languages. One of the best poems is "The Aspen and the Stream," in which the characters are the self-effacing, Faustian stream and the aspiring, Shelleyan aspen. Their languages help express their natures, for the aspen makes puns. The aspen tells the stream that he has lost the drift of what was being said. The language of wordplay has been transferred to the peripheries—satire, dialogue—of Wilbur's vision.

Such attention to language on the part of the reader raises the question of why one should pay so much attention to the poem. Analysis too close, too deep, will make anything seem profound. There must be a surface brilliance to attract the attention, to make the reader want to go deeper. Wilbur's method in his best poems is to force the reader's admiration by his sounds. These tonal effects give qualities of excellence to "Tywater," "After the Last Bulletins," "Piazza de Spagna, Early Morning," and "The Undead." The sounds of poems such as these evoke their sense, assuring that such poetry will endure.

THE POETRY OF WILLIAM CARLOS WILLIAMS

Type of work: Poetry
Author: William Carlos Williams (1883-1963)
Principal published works: *Poems*, 1909; *The Tempers*, 1913; *Al Que Quiere!*, 1917; *Kora in Hell: Improvisations*, 1920; *Sour Grapes*, 1921; *Spring and All*, 1923; *Collected Poems, 1921-1931*, 1934; *An Early Martyr and Other Poems*, 1935; *Adam & Eve & the City*, 1936; *The Complete Collected Poems of William Carlos Williams, 1906-1938*, 1938; *The Broken Span*, 1941; *The Wedge*, 1944; *Paterson*, 1946-1958; *Collected Later Poems*, 1950, 1963; *Collected Earlier Poems*, 1951; *The Desert Music and Other Poems*, 1954; *Journey to Love*, 1955; *Pictures from Brueghel*, 1962.

In the headnote to *Paterson*, William Carlos Williams described his view of the function of poetry as a bare-handed answer to Greek and Latin. The deliberate rejection of a received tradition, and reliance on crude native energy of intelligence, are characteristic of a poet who from the start was aggressively American in his poetic themes and techniques. It is not going too far to state that Williams in fact defined himself in his poetic identity by a series of rejections: As early as, 1910, he had thrown over the sonnet and the iamb as dead molds from an English and not an American tradition, and he set out in search of what he would later call the "measure" of the indigenous "American idiom." Inevitably, this search meant the development of new themes and approaches, an intensive reliance on personal sensibility, and the justification of seemingly unpoetic and arbitrary materials—lists of ice-cream prices, the sounds of the elephant seal and of trees in rain—the whole human barnyard that Williams observed daily in his practice as a busy pediatrician in a New Jersey suburb.

A characteristic early poem, "Between Walls," demonstrates Williams' relentlessness in the process of taking up slack, of concentrating his poetic materials. In this short piece, the absence of punctuation, the title entering the very syntax of the poem, and the remarkable pressure exerted on single words all tend to reify language and to deemphasize the distinctions between words and things in poetic description. That ideas are in things is the informal refrain of *Paterson*, the long epic poem in five books in which Williams extends the early discontinuous imagism of a poem like "Between Walls" into a large discourse revolving around the single figure of a man as a city. Late in his career, image and discourse finally come together supremely in this poem on personal and national history, and in the splendid old man's love poem "Asphodel, That Greeny Flower" in the late volume *Journey to Love*. Even in his famous early poem on a red wheelbarrow, Williams had affirmed that much depends on the object under scrutiny, using emotional as well as descriptive language and exploding the restric-

tions of the Imagist school by attempting to unite concepts and objects in a single discourse.

Paterson develops and makes explicit another, related cluster of speculations on the importance of place. This emphasis is implied in such poems as "Dedication for a Plot of Ground," "Franklin Square," and "Nantucket," and indeed it is implied in the anxious descriptive bent of all the early poems, but only in *Paterson* does it become a compelling argument against T. S. Eliot's contention that "place is only place." Like Wallace Stevens, Williams believed that place is all that one has: There is no other place, no other experience, and so the poem will celebrate things for being and happening in themselves, just as it will praise the mind for now and then lighting on something significant. The point is that anyone's experience, however seemingly unpoetic, is universal and valuable to the degree that it is understood in all its relevant detail. Williams accordingly states at the outset of *Paterson*, his long place-poem, that he will attempt to begin with particulars and then make them general. Following this method, the poet is obliged to be a noticer, someone whose vision is at once accurate and clairvoyant.

A detailed sense of place, of community and connection, is all the more important amid the violence and uprooting that Williams observed in the lives of his patients, in the state of the country ("Impromptu: The Suckers" is a bitter attack on the injustice done to Nicola Sacco and Bartolomeo Vanzetti), in the two world wars and in the Great Depression. Anticipating the extended metaphor of divorce in *Paterson*—divorce between lovers, friends, poets and their readers, mind and world, thing and thought—certain earlier poems such as "It Is a Living Coral" and the collection titled *Spring and All* convey an acute sense of debasement.

The need for accurate observation is at one with the need for love in a world without theological sanctions: Energy and the release of energy, the analogies between sexual experience and other modes of knowing such as vision, are at once themes and techniques for Williams, who is one of those post-Romantic poets for whom truth can lie only in the search for truth. In such a scheme, no subject is too low, no juxtaposition too extravagant; the poem "Pastoral" looks, as do so many of the poems early and late, at sparrows, taking their unconscious ingenuousness as emblematic.

"Pastoral" is constructed as a haphazard montage, according to principles that Williams may well have absorbed from his painter friends in Greenwich Village and Paris. According to this technique, the position of images is almost as important as their content. Consecutive images are pulled ahead or back according to the lines of force of the surrounding images. Often Williams enforces a contrast of different orders of experience by such placement, setting emotional statements against descriptive ones, kinetic against static, honesty against pomposity. While Williams' themes remain fairly constant throughout his writing career, these techniques of concentration-by-omission, and of working for speed in the movement of poems, undergo continual change. The effect of simultaneity, analogous to the all-but-instant impact of a painting on a canvas, is something that he early achieves by the montage construction, by forcing attention to new linguistic clusters in the line taken as a unit, and by making extensive use of ellipsis and run-on lines.

In working within the space created by the overarching metaphor of a man as a city, *Paterson* represents a development of the same method of calculated juxtaposition, naturalizing as it does blocks of prose in a poetic setting so as to suggest that the sources of all writing are the same.

Williams abolishes the capital letters at the beginning of each line. This gives the desired effect of placing enormous weight on the punctuation that remains, and the dash, the parenthesis, even the white spacing between words and lines carry a heavy freight of meaning. Thus every poem discovers its own form, a "measure" determined both by the subject at hand and by the breath-rhythm of the poet.

In the process of writing *Paterson*, Williams discovered the three-tier line, which he considered his own contribution to an American measure (he would not call it a formal metric, though he would say it possesses form). His 1955 volume, *Journey to Love*, draws upon and endlessly varies this line, as in "Asphodel, That Greeny Flower."

The condemnation and anger of the early poems turns often, in these later books, to gentleness, a celebration of a small circle of loved people and things. In general, Williams moved from his early concern with objects to a concern with actions, virtues, and broad scenes.

As a strictly secular poet, as a writer who created genuine poems outside traditional metrics, as a theorist of "measure" and a detailed observer (especially in *Paterson*) of the debasement of the American scene, Williams was widely influential: Poets as diverse as Robert Lowell, Charles Olson, and Theodore Roethke pursued Williams' lines of inquiry and technique. The art of immediacy, it seems, is more imitable and available than the hieratic, allusive poetry of a more sophisticated poet such as T. S. Eliot. Future literary historians may well decide that this less "intelligent" poet was in fact more significantly influential than Eliot in directing the course of American poetry.

PORTNOY'S COMPLAINT

Type of work: Novel
Author: Philip Roth (1933-   )
Type of plot: Comic monologue
Time of plot: 1933-1966
Locale: New Jersey, Ohio, New York, Kansas, Washington, D.C., Rome, Athens, and Israel
First published: 1969

Controversial because of its treatment of sex and Jewish life, Portnoy's Complaint *is a darkly humorous look at an American man's obsessions, guilt, and inability to love.*

Principal Characters

Alex Portnoy, a man obsessed by sex and his Jewishness. He grows up suffocated by his mother and seeks escape through fantasies about sex with Gentiles. He becomes a lawyer who fights for the rights of the underprivileged, yet he treats the women in his life as mere appendages who fulfill his sexual needs.

Sophie Portnoy, the archetypal Jewish mother. She confuses Alex by praising his virtues while castigating him for minor transgressions. Sophie considers herself the epitome of self-sacrifice.

Jack Portnoy, Alex's father, an insurance salesman tormented by constipation. He hopes that his son will win honor and respect for the family.

Mary Jane Reed (The Monkey), a semiliterate model. The fulfillment of Alex's sexual fantasies, she longs for a normal life while engaging in acts of depravity.

The Story

Portnoy's Complaint is a lengthy monologue delivered by Alex Portnoy to his psychoanalyst, Dr. Spielvogel, during which the thirty-three-year-old patient reflects upon the people and events that have shaped his unhappy life. As a boy, Alex lives in Jersey City, New Jersey, with his mother, Sophie, his father, Jack, and his older sister, Hannah. When Jack, an insurance agent, is transferred in 1941, the family moves to Newark.

Growing up, Alex is torn by his parents' conflicting views of him as angel and demon and by his mixed feelings about them as well. He considers himself "the nicest little Jewish boy who ever lived" because he worships Tom Paine and Abraham Lincoln, hopes to grow up to be a lawyer fighting for the rights of the underdog, and feels grateful to his parents. Yet while Sophie considers him a second Albert Einstein, she constantly attacks him for his selfishness and thoughtlessness, especially when he eats nonkosher food.

While Sophie thinks of herself as completely virtuous and self-sacrificing, Alex is often embarrassed by her. She is condescending toward their African-American maid, tells her friends about her son's tiny penis, and

sends eleven-year-old Alex out to buy her sanitary napkins. Even at sixty, she hitches up her stockings in front of her adult son.

Preoccupied by chronic constipation, Jack Portnoy too embarrasses Alex, by not knowing how to hold a baseball bat and by ignoring the intellectual magazines that his son wants him to read. Alex, angered by the refusal of his father's employer to give a Jew the decent position that he deserves, also feels pity for his father. Jack idealizes his son, seeing Alex as the family's only opportunity to gain respect.

While Sophie is consumed by her notion of self-sacrifice and Jack by his blocked bowels, Alex is obsessed with sex. Young Alex masturbates constantly, even with a cored apple and a piece of liver that his family will later eat. He masturbates on buses and at a burlesque theater, fantasizing about a romantic gentile ideal that he calls Thereal McCoy. When he goes ice-skating at a park in neighboring Irvington, Alex is enraptured by the blonde goddesses that he encounters. These gentile girls are as exotic to him as creatures from another planet.

When he goes to Antioch College in Ohio, he falls in

love with Kay Campbell, whom Alex thinks of as The Pumpkin because she is slightly overweight. She takes him home to Kansas for Thanksgiving and a glimpse of an ideal gentile life.

Alex goes on to Columbia Law School, where he edits the law review and graduates first in his class. He then joins the staff of a House subcommittee investigating the television quiz scandals of the late 1950's. In Washington, D.C., he has an affair with a more perfect gentile stereotype, Sarah Abbott Maulsby, whom he names The Pilgrim because of her New England pedigree.

After five years with the American Civil Liberties Union, Alex becomes assistant commissioner for the City of New York Commission on Human Opportunity. In Manhattan, he finds the main woman in his life. Mary Jane Reed, a semiliterate model from West Virginia, seems the embodiment of his fantasies about Thereal McCoy. Alex calls her The Monkey because she once ate a banana while watching another couple have intercourse. They act out his fantasies, only for Mary Jane's recriminations to follow. She wants to be sexually liberated but also longs for an ordinary life as wife and mother.

Leaving Mary Jane threatening suicide in an Athens hotel, Alex flees to Israel and quickly falls in love with a young Israeli army lieutenant, Naomi. Alex creates his version of The Monkey's romanticized ideal by wanting to settle down with the first Jewish woman who has attracted him, but Naomi rejects his proposal. When he attempts to force himself upon her, he finds that he is impotent.

Critical Evaluation

Portnoy's Complaint was one of the most controversial novels of its time. It was widely attacked as anti-Semitic, with these critics seeing Philip Roth as Naomi sees Alex: as a self-hating Jew. Many rabbis instructed their congregations not to read the novel. *Portnoy's Complaint* was also strongly censured for its sexual content. The masturbation scenes, the graphic detail of Alex's encounters with The Monkey, and the constant profanity offended some readers.

Most of the charges of anti-Semitism have resulted from Alex's feelings about his mother. Roth employs Sophie to reveal Alex's views toward matters Jewish and as ammunition in his satire of psychoanalytic oversimplifications. Alex acknowledges to Dr. Spielvogel that his relations with Sophie fit the pattern of a classic Oedipus complex while denying that such subconscious feelings exist.

Roth uses Sophie to satirize the excesses of Jewish mothers. Sophie competes with the other Jewish mothers in the Portnoys' apartment building to determine who makes the most sacrifices. She tells anyone who will listen that she is too good and that, because of her virtues, she is always being victimized. Sophie thinks of the most mundane occurrences as high drama because they have happened to her. When Alex is six or seven, she even threatens him with a knife over some triviality—contributing a castration complex to his list of neuroses. Alex blames his father for allowing Sophie to assume the dominant role in the family. She is the one, not Jack, who teaches him to urinate standing up, even tickling his testicles to get him going.

To make certain that Sophie is not perceived as an isolated case, Roth includes the example of Ronald Nimkin, a fifteen-year-old neighbor who hangs himself to escape his domineering mother. A good Jewish boy to the end, Ronald pins a note to his body saying that Mrs. Blumenthal wants his mother to bring her mah-jongg rules to that night's game. Alex cites from Sigmund Freud the image of the giant bird smothering its victim and demands that Jewish mothers "Just leave us alone, God damn it, to pull our little dongs in peace and think our little selfish thoughts."

When visiting the Kansas *goyim*, Alex is most impressed by how quiet and polite everyone is. Yet he does not compare Gentiles favorably to Jews, considering Christianity as ridiculous as his own religion. He is especially appalled by the vulgar rituals surrounding Christmas. Alex is very aware of the sufferings of and intolerance against Jews, seeing his father in particular as unfulfilled because of the irrational prejudices of Gentiles. Yet, while he contemplates how the hatred and disrespect directed toward Jews makes them morally superior to Gentiles, he wonders about the moral implications of Jews hating the *goyim*. One significant aspect of Portnoy's dilemma is his always seeing all sides to an issue even if he, like Sophie, finally interprets matters to reflect best on him.

To Alex, he is less a victim of prejudice than of his family. He rails against Jewish parents for always thinking of their sons as fifteen-year-olds, regardless of their age and accomplishments. He is most angry for finding himself living in the middle of what appears to be a stereotypical Jewish joke but which is hardly humorous to him.

Portnoy's Complaint itself is an extended Jewish joke.

Alex's confession to Dr. Spielvogel resembles the rambling monologue of a stand-up comedian, particularly the routines of Lenny Bruce because of the emphasis on obscenities. Roth makes his awareness of this tradition clear by ending the novel with the psychoanalyst speaking for the first time: "Now vee may perhaps to begin. Yes?" Dr. Spielvogel's comment is appropriately preceded by the label "PUNCH LINE."

Incidents like Ronald Nimkin's suicide contribute to the dark humor of *Portnoy's Complaint* that represented a departure from Roth's work to this point. His previous novels, *Letting Go* (1962) and *When She Was Good* (1967), are realistic, while *Portnoy's Complaint* heralds an excursion into the absurdities and satire associated with black humor that Roth continued in *Our Gang* (1971) and *The Breast* (1972) before returning to a more traditional approach in the Nathan Zuckerman novels.

Adding greatly to the humor of *Portnoy's Complaint* is Roth's treatment of sex. He exaggerates Alex's devotion to masturbation because the subject, normal yet ridiculous and embarrassing, is profoundly comic. For young Alex, it is something much more significant: Masturbation is a search for identity. Smothered as he is by Sophie, he is only truly himself when alone with his penis. Raised to consider anything pleasurable to be unnatural and dangerous, Alex finds the exhilaration of masturbation inevitably followed by guilt.

The adult Alex daydreams about every attractive woman he sees, just as his younger self did. He condemns himself for refusing to control his sexual urges, for thinking about his next conquest while still engaged in the present one. After he and The Monkey pick up a Roman prostitute and engage in three-way sex, he vomits over his depravity. Then he does it again the next day.

Alex is drawn to gentile women for complicated reasons. They represent the feminine ideal that he has grown up seeing in motion pictures. His contempt for the beliefs of *goyim* "is more than neutralized by my adoration of the way they look, the way they move and laugh and speak." Having sex with Gentiles is also a means of getting back at them for their sins against Jews. He considers loving and leaving Sarah Maulsby vengeance for how his father's New England-based employers have treated Jack.

Alex attempts to discover through sex an America that refuses to accept Jews. For Alex, "America is a *shikse* nestling under your arm whispering love love love love love!" Portnoy's problem, however, is that he can receive love but not give it. He drops The Pumpkin when he realizes that she cares more for him than he does for her. He resists The Monkey's plea for a normal life because he is incapable of the affection necessary for such commitment. Mary Jane wants him to rescue her from a life of depravity, yet her depravity is what interests him. Because she fulfills his fantasies, he cannot believe in her humanity. The dehumanizing nickname that he gives her allows him to maintain emotional distance.

Alex begs himself to love Mary Jane and is consumed by guilt when he abandons her. He responds to Naomi because he fears a life of being unloved and unloving. Yet this young Israeli who, ironically, reminds him of Sophie, is more mature than he and rejects him for being what he has feared that he has become: an unhappy baby. Alex's attitude toward sex has not changed since he began masturbating because he has not changed. The novel concludes with his wailing for release from "My endless childhood!"

Despite his selfishness, Alex is finally a sympathetic creation because Roth unfolds his complaint with such comic energy and because the novelist feels more compassion for his protagonist than Alex is capable of himself. Portnoy's alienation is a universal complaint.

THE PORTRAIT OF A LADY

Type of work: Novel
Author: Henry James (1843-1916)
Type of plot: Psychological realism
Time of plot: About 1875
Locale: England, France, and Italy
First published: 1880-1881

In this novel crowded with brilliantly subtle and penetrating character studies, James explores the ramifications of a naïve, young, high-minded American woman's first exposure and gradual acclimatization to the traditions and decadence of an older European culture. The reader follows step by step the mental process of Isabel Archer as she gravitates away from the staunch and stuffy American Caspar Goodwood and her frail, intelligent, and devoted cousin Ralph Touchett, into a marriage with Gilbert Osmond, a worthless, tyrannical dilettante. The Portrait of a Lady is an excellent example of the Jamesian technique of refracting life through the mind and temperament of an individual.

Principal Characters

Isabel Archer, the American heroine of the novel. Orphaned at an early age and an heiress, she uses her freedom to go to Europe to be educated in the arts of life lacking in her own country. She draws the interest and adoration of many people, all of whom believe that they can make a contribution to her growth, or at least can use er. Isabel is somewhat unworldly at the time of her marriage to Gilbert Osmond. After three years of resisting the social mold imposed on her by Osmond and his Roman ménage, Isabel faces a dilemma in which her intelligence and honesty vie with her sense of obligation. Sensitive to her own needs as well as to those of others, she is aware of the complicated future that she faces.

Gilbert Osmond, an American expatriate. He finds in Rome an environment suited to his artistic taste and devotes his time and tastes solely to pleasing himself.

Madame Merle, Isabel's friend. Madame Merle was formerly Osmond's mistress and is the mother of his daughter Pansy. A clever, vigorous woman of considerable shrewdness, she promotes Isabel's marriage to Osmond.

Ralph Touchett, Isabel's ailing cousin. He appreciates the fine qualities of Isabel's nature. Distressed by what he considers her disastrous marriage, he sees to it that his own and his father's estates come to Isabel.

Caspar Goodwood, Isabel's faithful American suitor. He has the simplicity and directness of American insight that Isabel is trying to supplement by her European "education." He does not understand why he fails with Isabel.

Lord Warburton, a friend of Ralph Touchett. Like all the other unsuccessful men in Isabel's life, he deeply admires the young American woman and is distressed by her marriage to Gilbert Osmond.

Henrietta Stackpole, an American journalist and a girlhood friend of Isabel. Henrietta is, in her own right, an amusing picture of the sensation-seeking, uncritical American intelligence ranging over the length and breadth of Europe. She is eager to save Isabel.

Pansy Osmond, the illegitimate daughter of Osmond and Madame Merle. Pansy welcomes Isabel as her stepmother; she believes that in Isabel she has an ally, as indeed she has. Determined to endure gracefully what she must, she feels increasingly the strictures of her father's dictates.

Edward Rosier, a suitor for Pansy's hand. This kind, pleasant man lacks the means sufficient to meet Osmond's demands.

Countess Gemini, Osmond's sister. She is a woman who has been spoiled and corrupted by her European experience, and she finds Isabel's behavior almost boring in its simplicity. Several motives prompt her to tell Isabel about Osmond's first wife and his liaison with Madame Merle. She does not spare Isabel a clear picture of Osmond's lack of humanity.

Mrs. Touchett, Isabel's vigorous and sympathetic aunt. Mrs. Touchett is the one responsible for the invitation that brings Isabel to Europe.

The Story

Isabel Archer, upon the death of her father, had been visited by her aunt, Mrs. Touchett. She proved so attractive to the older woman that Mrs. Touchett decided to give her the advantage of a more cosmopolitan experience, and Isabel was quickly carried off to Europe so that she might see something of the world of culture and fashion.

On the day that the women arrived at the Touchett home in England, Isabel's sickly young cousin, Ralph Touchett, and his father were taking tea in the garden with their friend Lord Warburton. When Isabel appeared, Warburton had been confessing to the two men his boredom and his distaste for his routine existence. The young nobleman was much taken with the American girl's grace and lively manner.

Isabel had barely settled at Gardencourt, her aunt's home, before she received a letter from an American friend, Henrietta Stackpole, a newspaper reporter who was writing a series of articles on the sights of Europe. At Ralph's invitation, Henrietta went to Gardencourt to spend some time with Isabel and to obtain material for her writing.

Soon after Henrietta's arrival, Isabel heard from another American friend. Caspar Goodwood, a would-be suitor, had followed her abroad. Learning her whereabouts from Henrietta, he wrote to ask if he might see her. Isabel was irked by his aggressiveness, and she decided not to answer his letter.

On the day that she received the letter from Goodwood, Lord Warburton proposed to her. Not wishing to seem indifferent to the honor of his proposal, she asked for time to consider it. At last, she decided that she could not marry the young Englishman, for she wished to see considerably more of the world before she married. She was afraid that marriage to Warburton, although he was a model of kindness and thoughtfulness, would prove stifling.

Because Isabel had not seen London on her journey with Mrs. Touchett and because it was on Henrietta Stackpole's itinerary, the two young women, accompanied by Ralph Touchett, went to the capital. Henrietta quickly made the acquaintance of Mr. Bantling, who undertook to escort her around London. When Caspar Goodwood visited Isabel at her hotel, she again refused him, though his persistence made her agree that, if he still wished to ask for her hand, he might visit her again after two years had passed.

While the party was in London, a telegram came from Gardencourt. Old Mr. Touchett was seriously ill with gout, and his wife was much alarmed. Isabel and Ralph left on the afternoon train. Henrietta remained with her new friend.

During the time that Mr. Touchett lay dying and his family was preoccupied, Isabel was forced to amuse herself with a new companion. Madame Merle, an old friend of Mrs. Touchett, had come to Gardencourt to spend a few days. She and Isabel, thrown together, exchanged many confidences. Isabel admired the older woman for her ability to amuse herself; for her skill at needlework, at painting, at the piano; and for her ability to accommodate herself to any social situation. On the other hand, Madame Merle spoke enviously of Isabel's youth and intelligence, lamenting the life that had left her, at middle age, a widow with no children and no visible success in life.

When her uncle died, he left Isabel, at her cousin's instigation, half of his fortune. Ralph, greatly impressed with his young kinswoman's brilliance, had persuaded his father that she should be given the opportunity to fly as far and as high as she might. For himself, he knew that he could not live long because of his pulmonary illness, and his legacy was enough to let him live in comfort.

As quickly as she could. Mrs. Touchett sold her London house and took Isabel to Paris with her. Ralph went south for the winter to preserve what was left of his health. In Paris, the new heiress was introduced to many of her aunt's friends among the American expatriates, but she was not impressed. She thought their indolent lives worthy only of contempt. Meanwhile, Henrietta and Mr. Bantling had arrived in Paris, and Isabel spent much time with them and Edward Rosier. She had known Rosier when they both were children and she was traveling abroad with her father. Rosier was another dilettante, living on the income from his inheritance. He explained to Isabel that he could not return to the United States because there was no occupation there worthy of a gentleman.

In February, Mrs. Touchett and her niece went to the Palazzo Crescentini, the Touchett house in Florence. They stopped on the way to see Ralph, who was staying in San Remo. In Florence, they were joined once more by Madame Merle.

Unknown to Isabel or her aunt, Madame Merle also visited her friend Gilbert Osmond, an American who lived in voluntary exile outside of Florence with his art collection and his young convent-bred daughter, Pansy. Madame Merle told Osmond of Isabel's arrival in Florence, saying that as the heir to a fortune, Isabel would be a valuable addition to Osmond's collection.

The heiress who had rejected two worthy suitors did not refuse the third. She was quickly captivated by the charm of the sheltered life that Gilbert Osmond had created for himself. Her friends were against the match. Henrietta Stackpole, who was inclined to favor Caspar Goodwood, was convinced that Osmond was interested only in Isabel's money, as was Isabel's aunt. Mrs. Touchett had requested Madame Merle, the good friend of both parties, to discover the state of their affections; she was convinced that Madame Merle could have prevented the match. Ralph Touchett was disappointed that his cousin should have fallen in love so quickly. Caspar Goodwood, learning of Isabel's intended marriage when he revisited her two years later as agreed, could not persuade her to reconsider her step. Isabel was indignant when he commented on the fact that she did not even know her intended husband's family background.

After her marriage to Gilbert Osmond, Isabel and her husband established their home in Rome, in a setting completely expressive of Osmond's tastes. Before three years had passed, however, Isabel began to realize that her friends had not been completely wrong in their objections to her marriage. Osmond's exquisite taste had made their home one of the most popular in Rome, but his ceaseless effort to press his wife into a mold, to make her a reflection of his own ideas, had not made their marriage one of the happiest.

He had succeeded in destroying a romance between Pansy and Edward Rosier, who had visited the girl's stepmother and found the daughter attractive. Osmond had not succeeded, however, in contracting the match that he desired between Pansy and Lord Warburton. Warburton had found Pansy as pleasing as Isabel had once been, but he had dropped his suit when he saw that the girl's affections lay with Rosier.

Ralph Touchett, his health growing steadily worse, gave up his wanderings on the Continent and returned to Gardencourt to die. When Isabel received a telegram from his mother telling her that Ralph would like to see her before his death, she believed that it was her duty to go to Gardencourt at once. Osmond reacted to her wish as if it were a personal insult. He expected that, as his wife, Isabel would want to remain at his side and that she would not disobey any of his wishes. He also made it plain that he disliked Ralph.

In a state of turmoil after her conversation with her husband, Isabel met the Countess Gemini, Osmond's sister. The countess, visiting the Osmonds, knew the situation between her brother and Isabel. An honest soul, she felt more sympathy for her sister-in-law than for her brother. To comfort Isabel, she told her the story of Gilbert's past. After his first wife had died, he and Madame Merle had an affair that lasted six or seven years. During that time, Madame Merle, a widow, had borne him a child, Pansy. Changing his residence, Osmond had been able to pretend to his new circle of friends that the original Mrs. Osmond had died in giving birth to the child.

With this news fresh in her mind and still determined to go to England, Isabel stopped to say good-bye to Pansy, who was staying in a convent where her father had sent her to recuperate from her affair with Rosier. There, too, she met Madame Merle. Madame Merle, with her keen perception, had no difficulty realizing that Isabel knew her secret. When she remarked that Isabel would never need to see her again, that she would go to the United States, Isabel was certain that Madame Merle would also find much to her own advantage there.

Isabel was in time to see her cousin before his death. She stayed on briefly at Gardencourt after the funeral, long enough to bid good-bye to Lord Warburton, who had come to offer condolences to her aunt, and to reject a third offer from Caspar Goodwood, who knew of her husband's treatment of her. When she left to start her journey back to Italy, Isabel knew what she must do. Her first duty was not to herself, but to put her house in order.

Critical Evaluation

The Portrait of a Lady first appeared serially in England and the United States (*Macmillan's Magazine*, October, 1880-November, 1881; *Atlantic*, November, 1880-December, 1881); it was published as a book in 1881. Usually regarded as the major achievement of Henry James's early period of fiction writing, *The Portrait of a Lady* is one of the great novels of modern literature. In it, James demonstrates that he has learned well from two European masters of the novel. Ivan Turgenev had taught him how to use a single character who shapes the work and is seen throughout in relationship to various other characters. From George Eliot, he had learned the importance of tightening the structure of the novel and giving the story an architectural or organic form that develops logically from the given materials. He advances in *The Portrait of a Lady* beyond Eliot in minimizing his own authorial comments and analysis and in permitting his heroine to be seen through her own tardily awakening self-realization and also through the consciousness of the men and women who are closest to her. Thus his "portrait" of a lady is one that grows slowly, as touches are added that bring out both highlights and shadows. Isabel Archer stands at the end of the novel as a woman whose experiences have brought her excitement, joy, pain, and knowledge and have given her an enduring beauty and dignity.

Isabel is one of James's finest creations and one of the most memorable women in the history of the novel. A number of sources have been suggested for her. She may have been partly drawn from James's cousin Mary "Minny" Temple, whom he was later to immortalize as Milly Theale in *The Wings of the Dove* (1902). She has been compared to two of Eliot's heroines, Dorothea Brooke in *Middlemarch* (1871-1872) and Gwendolen Harleth in *Daniel Deronda* (1876); to Diana Belfield in an early romantic tale by James entitled "Longstaff's Marriage"; to Bathsheba Everdene in Thomas Hardy's *Far from the Madding Crowd* (1874); and even to James himself, some of whose early experiences closely parallel those of Isabel. James may have drawn from real and fictional people in portraying Isabel Archer, but she possesses her own identity; she grew from James's original "conception of a certain young woman affronting her destiny," as he later wrote in his preface to the novel. He visualized her as "an intelligent but presumptuous girl" who would yet be "complex" and who would be offered a series of opportunities for free choice in facing that destiny. Because of her presumption that she knew more than she did about herself and the world, Isabel was to make mistakes, including the tragic error of misjudging the nature of Gilbert Osmond. Yet her intelligence, though it was not sufficient to save her from suffering, would enable her to achieve a moral triumph in the end.

Of the four men in Isabel's life, three love her, and one uses her innocence to gain for himself what he would not otherwise have had. She refuses marriage to Lord Warburton because, though he offers her a great fortune, a title, an entry into English society, and an agreeable and entertaining personality, she believes she can do better. She turns down Caspar Goodwood, who also offers wealth, because she finds him stiff, and she is frightened by his aggressiveness. Her cousin, Ralph Touchett, does not propose because he does not wish her to be tied to a man who daily faces death. She does not even suspect the extent of his love and adoration until she is almost overwhelmed by learning it just as death takes him from her. She accepts Gilbert Osmond because she is deceived by his calculated charm and because she believes that he deserves what she can offer him: first, a fortune that will make it possible for him to live in idleness but sur-

rounded by the objects of the culture that she believes he represents; and second, a mother's love and care for his supposedly motherless daughter. Half of the novel is given over to Isabel's living with, adjusting to, and, finally, triumphing over the disastrous choice that she has made.

In his preface, James uses an architectural figure to describe *The Portrait of a Lady*. He says the "large building" of the novel "came to be a square and spacious house." Much of what occurs in the novel does so in or near a series of houses, each of which relates significantly to Isabel or to other characters. The action begins at Gardencourt, the tudor English country house of Daniel Touchett that Isabel finds more beautiful than anything she has ever seen. The charm of the house is enhanced by its age and its natural setting beside the Thames above London. It contrasts greatly with the "old house at Albany, a large, square, double house" belonging to her grandmother that Isabel in her childhood had found romantic and in which she had indulged in dreams stimulated by her reading. Mrs. Touchett's taking Isabel from the Albany house to Gardencourt is a first step in her plan to "introduce her to the world." When Isabel visits Lockleigh, Lord Warburton's home, she sees it from the gardens as resembling "a castle in a legend," though inside it has been modernized. She does not view it as a home for herself, or its titled owner as her husband, despite the many advantages that he offers. The front of Gilbert Osmond's house in Florence is "imposing" but of "a somewhat uncommunicative character," a "mask." It symbolizes Osmond, whose mask Isabel does not see through until she has married him. The last of the houses in *The Portrait of a Lady* is the Palazzo Roccanera, the Roman home of the Osmonds, which James first describes as "a kind of domestic fortress . . . which smelt of historic deeds, of crime and craft and violence." When Isabel later broods over it during her night-long meditation in chapter 42, it is "the house of darkness, the house of dumbness, the house of suffocation."

Isabel is first seen at Gardencourt on her visit with Mrs. Touchett, and it is here that she turns down the first of three proposals of marriage. It is fitting that she should be last seen here by turns with each of the three men who have loved her. Asserting the independence on which she has so long prided herself, she has defied her imperious husband by going to England to see the dying Ralph, whose last words tell her that, if she has been hated by Osmond, she has been adored by her cousin. In a brief conversation with Lord Warburton after Ralph's death, Isabel turns down an invitation to visit him and his sisters at Lockleigh. Shortly afterward, a scene six years earlier is reversed. Then she had sat on a rustic bench at

Gardencourt and looked up from reading Caspar Good-wood's letter implying that he would come to England and propose to her—only to see and hear Warburton preparing to offer his own proposal. Now Caspar surprises her by appearing just after she has dismissed Warburton. There follows the one sexually passionate scene in the novel. In it, Isabel has "an immense desire to appear to resist" the force of Caspar's argument that she should leave Osmond and turn to him. She pleads with streaming tears, "As you love me, as you pity me, leave me alone!" Defying her plea, Caspar kisses her:

> His kiss was like white lightning, a flash that spread, and spread again, and stayed; and it was extraordinarily

as if, while she took it, she felt each thing in his hard manhood that had least pleased her, each aggressive fact of his face, his figure, his presence, justified of its intense identity and made one with this act of possession.

Caspar possesses her for a moment only, however, as "when darkness returned she was free." She flees into the house—and thence to Rome, as Caspar learns in the brief scene in London with Henrietta Stackpole that closes the novel.

James leaves the reader to conclude that Isabel's love for Pansy Osmond has principally determined her decision to continue enduring a marriage that she had freely—though so ignorantly and foolishly—chosen.

THE POSTMAN ALWAYS RINGS TWICE

Type of work: Novel
Author: James M. Cain (1892-1977)
Type of plot: Crime
Time of plot: 1933
Locale: Southern California
First published: 1934

Cain's explicit and direct tale of adultery and murder has become a classic novel in the tradition of tough-guy fiction. The Postman Always Rings Twice examines the criminal act—its motives and consequences—without resorting to moral judgments. The tragic triangle of Frank, Cora, and Nick reveals the workings of fate and desire.

Principal Characters

Frank Chambers, a young drifter who seduces the wife of Nick Papadakis and then plans to murder him. He and Cora get away with the killing only to die in accidental circumstances—she in a car accident, he for her supposed murder.

Nick Papadakis, the fat, middle-aged Greek husband of Cora. He inadvertently seals his own fate by conning Frank into operating his service station, unable to foresee the consequences. His murder is avenged by the death of his wife and the execution of Frank.

Cora Papadakis, Nick's young wife, who carries on an affair with drifter Frank Chambers. She tries to leave Frank after they collect the insurance money for Nick's death, but he persuades her to stay with him. She decides to test his love by risking her life swimming out to sea, and he saves her. Nevertheless, she dies immediately afterward in an automobile crash.

Mr. Sackett, the district attorney who tries to solve the case of Nick Papadakis' murder.

Mr. Katz, a lawyer who is very eccentric.

Madge Allen, the owner of an animal farm.

Three related genres that developed in the novel form during the 1930's were the hard-boiled private detective novel (which departed from the genteel English novel of detection), the proletarian novel (which derived from European naturalism and American selective realism), and the tough-guy novel (which derived from the former two). Yet perhaps for the best and most influential work of all three genres "the tough-guy novel" is a good term: Dashiell Hammett's *The Maltese Falcon* (1929-1930) and Raymond Chandler's *The Big Sleep* (1939) in the private detective realm; B. Traven's *The Death Ship*, which appeared in an American edition in 1934, among proletarian novels; and Horace McCoy's *They Shoot Horses, Don't They?* (1935) among the pure tough-guy books are all minor classics in American literature. These and similar novels expressed the mood of American society during the Great Depression, influenced action in motion pictures, affected the tone and attitude of more serious writers, and inspired certain European novelists during the 1940's. The quintessence of all these works is James M. Cain's *The Postman Always Rings Twice.*

Although Frank Chambers, the twenty-four-year-old narrator of Cain's novel, belongs to that legion of unemployed who became tramps of the road, hoboes of the rails, and migrant workers, Cain is not deliberately interested in depicting the social ills of his time; if there is an attack on conditions that produced a man such as Frank, it is only implicit. Frank is an easygoing fellow, remarkably free of bitterness, even when given cause; although he commits murder and pistol-whips a blackmailer, he is not willfully vicious. A spontaneous creature of action whose psychological nature readily accommodates ambivalent attitudes, he can be fond of Nick Papadakis and weep at his funeral, yet seduce his young wife, Cora, and attempt to kill Nick twice.

Although this novel is concerned, as many of Cain's are, with murder and other forms of violence, and although it satisfies momentarily the American craving for details of crime and punishment, it cannot be classified as a detective tale. Cain, like the readers he has in mind, is fascinated by the intricacies of the law and of insurance claims, but his primary interest is in presenting an inside view of the criminal act. Yet Frank is no gangster and Cora is no moll; they are not far removed in status or aspiration from the average anticipated reader of Cain's book.

Frank and Cora lie down in the great American dream-bed of the 1920's, only to wake up in a living nightmare in the 1930's. A lurid decade produced such a lurid relationship and such a lurid tale. When they meet at Nick's Twin Oaks Tavern on a highway outside Los Angeles, Frank has just been thrown off a truck, having sneaked into the back for a ride up from Tijuana, and Cora is washing dishes in the restaurant. To demonstrate the animal impact of their encounter, Cain has them meet on page 5, make love on page 15, and decide to murder her obese, middle-aged Greek husband on page 23. Sharing the dream of getting drunk and making love without hiding, they go on what Cain calls "the Love-Rack." He regards the concept of "the wish that comes true" as a terrifying thing. This terror becomes palpable as soon as Frank and Cora believe that they have gotten away with murder and have acquired money, property, and freedom.

In the background, however, each has another dream that mocks the shared realization of the immediate wish. Cora came to Hollywood from a small town in Iowa bemused by the dream most women of the 1930's cherished: to become a film star. She failed, and Nick rescued her from a hash house. Basically her values are middle class, and above all she wants respectability, even if murder is the prerequisite. An anachronism in the age of technology, though he has a certain skill as a garage mechanic, Frank desires to be always on the move, compelled by something of the spirit of the open road that Whitman celebrated. For a moment, but only for a moment, he shares this romantic, idyllic vision with Cora. After the failure of their first attempt to murder Nick, they set out together for a life of wandering. Thus, in the criminal affair of these lovers, these deliberate outsiders, two central dreams of the American experience—unrestrained mobility and respectable sedentariness—and two views of the American landscape—the open road and the mortgaged house—collide. As the dreams finally betray them, they begin, ironically, to turn on each other, for basically what Frank wants is Cora the sexual dynamo, and what Cora wants is an instrument to be used to gain her ends—money and respectability. Though she may convince herself that the right man, instead of a fat foreigner, is a necessary part of her aspirations, this man would soon wake up in the wrong dream.

While the novel's larger thematic dimensions exist in the background, as a kind of fable of the American experience, giving it a lasting value in the country's literature,

Cain is more immediately concerned with the lovers and with the action that results from their wish. This action keeps in motion certain elements that almost guarantee the reader's interest: illicit love, murder, the smell of tainted money, and sexual violence that verges on the abnormal. In addition, there are strong characterizations of such figures as Sackett, the district attorney; Katz, the eccentric lawyer; and Madge Allen, the pickup who takes Frank to South America to capture jaguars. Cain plays upon the universal wishes of the average American male.

What fascinates serious readers of literature is Cain's technique for manipulating reader response. Not only does he almost automatically achieve certain thematic ironies inherent in his raw material, but the ironies of action are stunningly executed as well. For example, Frank cons Nick out of a free meal, but the con backfires when Nick cons Frank into staying on to operate the service station; as a result, Frank becomes involved in a situation that will leave three people dead. After recovering from what he took to be an accident in the bathtub, Nick searches for Frank and persuades him to return to the roadside restaurant, thus helping to bring about his own death.

Cleared of killing Nick, Frank and Cora collect the insurance. Later, when she is waiting for a taxi in order to leave Frank, Cora sticks a note for him in the cash register; it refers to their having killed Nick for his money. Frank catches her, however, and insists that he loves her; to test his love, Cora, who is now pregnant, swims so far out to sea that Frank will have to help her back. He does help her, but driving back from the beach, they have a wreck and she is killed. The police find the note in the cash register and conclude that Frank has engineered the wreck so that he can have all the money. Because he cannot be tried twice for killing Nick, they execute him for murdering Cora. A careful pattern of minor ironies contributes to the impact of the major ones.

Cain's structural techniques are impressive. The swift execution of the basic situation in the first twenty-three pages has been noted, and each development, each scene, is controlled with the same narrative skill; inherent in each episode is the inevitability of the next. Everything is kept strictly to the essentials. The characters, for example, exist only for the immediate action; there is almost no exposition as such. Cain is the acknowledged master of pace. Violence and sexual passion are thrust forward at a rate that is itself part of the reader's vicarious experience. Contributing to this sense of pace is the swift rhythm of the dialogue, which also manages to keep certain undercurrents flowing. Frank's character justifies the economy of style, the nerve-end adherence to the spine of the action. Albert Camus modeled the style of

L'Étranger (1942; *The Stranger*, 1946) on Cain's novel, and Meursault is cut to the pattern of Frank Chambers. Yet Cain has written what has been called a pure novel, for his deliberate intentions go no further than the immediate experience, brief as a film, as unified in its impression as a poem. Though Frank writes his story on the eve of his execution, Cain does not even suggest the simplest moral that "Crime does not pay." An intense experience that a man tells in such a way as to make it, briefly, the reader's experience, the story is its own reason for being. Camus' novel, however, operates on this premise only in the first half; in the second, he begins to develop a philosophical point of view that affects humanity in every phase of life.

Cain's first novel became a best-seller and went through many editions; Cain also adapted the book to the stage, and it was made into a motion picture in 1946 and again in 1981. The novel continues to be read widely, both as popular entertainment and as a work of art of a very peculiar sort, respected, with severe qualifications, by students of literature.

PRAGMATISM: A New Name for Some Old Ways of Thinking

Type of work: Philosophical essays
Author: William James (1842-1910)
First published: 1907

James's work, consisting of a series of his lectures on the nature of truth and meaning, brought the concept of pragmatism to the forefront of American philosophy.

No more illuminating or entertaining account of pragmatism has ever been written than William James's *Pragmatism: A New Name for Some Old Ways of Thinking.* Yet this is more than a popular exposition prepared for the academic audiences of Lowell Institute and Columbia University during the winter of 1906-1907: It is historic philosophy in the making. Although James was profoundly influenced by Charles Sanders Peirce, who invented the basic statement and name of pragmatism, he was an independent thinker with a distinctive creative direction of his own.

Peirce's essay "How to Make Our Ideas Clear" introduced the pragmatic notion that ideas are clarified by considering what one would expect in the way of experience if one were to act in a certain manner. The whole of one's conception of the "sensible effects" of an object is the whole of one's conception of the object, according to Peirce. This essay, which was clear, radical, and entertaining, appeared in the *Popular Science Monthly* in January, 1878. Professional philosophers, however, were not interested in a theory advanced by a mathematician, particularly when the theory went against the prevailing idealism of American philosophers. It was not until James revived the idea in 1898 with a talk on "Philosophical Conceptions and Practical Results" that the pragmatic philosophy began to stir up controversy. With the lectures on meaning and truth that were published under the titles *Pragmatism* and *The Meaning of Truth*, the former in 1907 and the latter in 1909, James brought pragmatism into the forefront of American thought.

In his first lecture on "The Present Dilemma in Philosophy," James distinguished between the "tender-minded" and the "tough-minded" in temperament, the former inclining toward a philosophy that is rational, religious, dogmatic, idealistic, and optimistic, and the latter inclining toward a philosophy that is empirical, irreligious, skeptical, materialistic, and pessimistic. He then went on to state his conviction that philosophy can satisfy both temperaments by becoming pragmatic.

His lecture on the pragmatic method begins with one of the most entertaining anecdotes in philosophical discourse. James describes a discussion by a group of philosophers on this question: Does a man go around a squirrel that is on a tree trunk if the squirrel keeps moving on the tree so that the trunk is always between himself and the man? Some of the philosophers claimed that the man did not go around the squirrel, while others claimed that he did. James settled the matter by saying "which party is right depends on what you *practically mean* by 'going round' the squirrel." It could be said that the man goes around the squirrel because he passes from the north of the squirrel to the east, south, and west of the squirrel. On the other hand, the man could be said not to go around the squirrel because he is never able to get on the various sides of the squirrel—on the right of him, then behind him, and so forth. "Make the distinction," James said, "and there is no occasion for any further dispute."

James then applied the method to a number of perennial philosophical problems, but only after a careful exposition of the meaning of pragmatism. He described the pragmatic method as a way of interpreting ideas by discovering their practical consequences—that is, the difference that the idea's truth would make in one's experience. He asks, "What difference would it practically make to anyone if this notion rather than that notion were true?" and he replies, "If no practical difference whatever can be traced, then the alternatives mean practically the same thing, and all dispute is idle."

In his lecture, James argued that the pragmatic method was not new; Socrates, Aristotle, John Locke, George Berkeley, and David Hume had used it. What was new, however, was the explicit formulation of the method and a new faith in its power. Yet pragmatism is to be understood not as a set of grand theories but as a method that turns attention away from first principles and absolutes and then directs it to facts, consequences, and results in actual experience.

A bare declaration would hardly have been enough to make pragmatism famous. James devoted a considerable part of his lectures to brief examples of the application of the pragmatic method. He cited with approval Berkeley's analysis of matter as made up of sensations. Sensations, he said, "are the cash-value of the term. The difference matter makes to us by truly being is that we then get such sensations . . ." Similarly, Locke applied the pragmatic method, James claimed, when he discovered that unless by "spirit" one means consciousness, one means nothing by the term.

James wonders whether materialism or theism is true, whether the universe is simply matter acting and interacting or God is involved. James considers this problem pragmatically and reaches a curious result. As far as the past is concerned, he says, it makes no difference. If rival theories are meant to explain what is the case and if it makes no difference in one's experience which theory is true, then the theories do not differ in meaning. If one considers the difference now and in the future, however, then the case is different: "Materialism means simply the denial that the moral order is eternal . . . spiritualism means the affirmation of an eternal moral order and the letting loose of hope."

To this kind of analysis some critics have answered with the charge that James is one of the "tender-minded" philosophers of whom he spoke harshly in his earlier lectures. Yet, throughout the course of this series of lectures and in subsequent books, James continued to use pragmatism as a way of combining the tough and tender temperaments. He extended the use of the term "difference" so that the meaning of an idea or term was to be understood not only in terms of sense experiences, as Peirce had urged, but also in terms of passionate differences, of effects upon human hopes and fears. The essays in *Pragmatism* show this liberalizing tendency hard at work.

The temperate tone of James's suggestions concerning the religious hypothesis is clear in one of his later lectures in the book, "Pragmatism and Religion," in which he writes that "Pragmatism has to postpone dogmatic answer, for we do not yet know certainly which type of religion is going to work best in the long run." He states again that the tough-minded can be satisfied with "the hurly-burly of the sensible facts of nature" and that the tender-minded can take up a monistic form of religion; yet for those who mix temperaments, as James does, a religious synthesis that is moralistic and pluralistic, allowing for human development and creativity in various directions, is to be preferred.

Pragmatism is important not only as a clear statement of the pragmatic method and as an illustration of its application to certain central problems but also as an exposition, although introductory, of James's pragmatic theory of truth. His ideas were developed more fully two years later in *The Meaning of Truth.*

Beginning with the common notion that truth is a property of ideas that agree with reality, James proceeded to ask what was meant by the term "agreement." He decided that the conception of truth as a static relation between an idea and reality was in error, that pragmatic analysis shows that true ideas are those which can eventually be verified, and that an idea is said to be verified when it leads usefully to an anticipated conclusion. Because verification is a process, it becomes appropriate to say that truth "happens to" an idea, and that an idea "*becomes* true, is *made* true by events." A revealing summary statement is this: " 'The true,' to put it very briefly, is only the expedient in the way of our thinking, just as 'the right' is only the expedient in the way of our behaving."

The ambiguity of James's account, an ambiguity that he did not succeed in removing, allows extremes of interpretation. On the one hand, a reader might take the tender-minded route, something in the manner of James himself, and argue that all kinds of beliefs about God, freedom, and immortality are true insofar as they lead people usefully in the course of their lives. On the other hand, a tough-minded reader might be inclined to agree with James that an idea is true if the expectations in terms of which the idea makes sense are expectations that would be met, if one acted—but the reader might reject James's suggestions that this means that many ideas which would ordinarily be regarded as doubtful "become true" when they satisfy the emotional needs of a believer.

One difficulty with which James was forced to deal in his theory of truth resulted not from his idea of truth as the "workableness" of an idea, but from his inadequate analyses of the meanings of certain terms such as "God," "freedom," and "design." James maintained that, pragmatically speaking, these terms all meant the same thing, namely, the presence of "promise" in the world. If this were so, then it would be plausible to suppose that, if the idea that the world is promising works out, the idea is true. Yet if James's analysis is mistaken, if "God" means more than the possibility of things working out for the better, James's claim that beliefs about God are true if they work loses its plausibility.

Whatever its philosophic faults, *Pragmatism* is saved by its philosophic virtues. For the general reader, it offers the rare experience of confronting first-rate ideas by way of a clear and entertaining, even informal, style.

PREJUDICES

Type of work: Essays on social and literary themes
Author: H. L. Mencken (1880-1956)
First published: 1919-1927

With this six-volume work of social criticism, Mencken found a wide and appreciative audience for his brand of gloating iconoclasm.

During the fantastic decade of the 1920's, few literary events were so eagerly awaited as the appearance of a new volume of Mencken's six-part *Prejudices*, so that one might enjoy the spectacle of the Sage of Baltimore as he pulled yet another popular idol down from its moss-covered pedestal and gloated over the fragments. This iconoclasm was accomplished with so much gusto and with such vigorous and picturesque language as to enchant a whole generation that had grown weary of the solemnity of much American writing. The decade badly needed an iconoclast, for it must be remembered that what is now thought of as "the jazz age" was also the era of the Ku Klux Klan and the Anti-Saloon League, of Babbittry and Boosterism.

The essays in these volumes can be divided into two categories: literary criticism and criticism of the American scene as it appeared at the time. Literary criticism Mencken defined as a "catalytic process," with the critic serving as the catalyst. Actually, as a critic Mencken derived mainly from James Huneker, whom he admired enormously and had known personally. Huneker had been familiar with Continental writers, then not too well known in the United States; his criticism was essentially impressionist, often written in breezy, epigrammatic language. Mencken carried certain of these characteristics much further; indeed, his verbal acrobatics became his hallmark. It was a racy, pungent style, very effective for the "debunking" then so popular and deliberately calculated to drive conservative readers into frenzies. His chief target, at which he never grew tired of heaving bricks, was the Puritan tradition in American literature, with its consequent timidity, stuffiness, and narrow-mindedness. As he saw it, the Puritan was afraid of aesthetic emotion and thus could neither create nor enjoy art. This fear had inhibited American literature, he claimed, and had made American criticism equally timid and conventional. Furthermore, criticism had fallen into the hands of the professors, and there was no one—not even a Prohibition agent—that Mencken detested so much as the average American university professor. Hence, such figures as Paul Elmer More, Irving Babbitt, Stuart P. Sherman, and William Lyon Phelps had scorn poured over them for years.

It is ironic that the critical writings of some of these scholars have withstood the passage of time more successfully than have those of Mencken. For, though less a geographical provincial than they, he was more provincial in time and was interested mainly in the contemporary. Of the older native writers, he really admired only Edgar Allan Poe, Mark Twain, and Walt Whitman—the nonconformists. Even among the moderns, his preferences were curiously limited. He had great regard for Joseph Conrad and Theodore Dreiser, but he overlooked much of the talent that was budding during the 1920's. That he should have overpraised some of his contemporaries, James Branch Cabell, for example, should not be held against him; few critics are sufficiently detached to escape this fault. Moreover, Dreiser was an important writer but not the "colossal phenomenon" that Mencken called him. Mencken's greatest failure as a critic, however, was his blindness to poetry. In the third series of *Prejudices*, he included the essay "The Poet and His Art," a study so full of false assumptions, logical fallacies, and plain misstatements of fact that it is a gruesome relic for the critic to have left behind him. In addition, his remarks on Dante stagger belief: Dante's theology was unacceptable to Mencken; therefore, Dante could not actually have believed it, and *The Divine Comedy* was, he said, a satire on the whole Christian doctrine of heaven and hell. Surely no gem that Mencken garnered from the Bible Belt could equal this statement in absurdity.

The essays dealing with the national scene were written in the same slashing manner and naturally infuriated far more readers, as Mencken attacked people, institutions, and ideas more familiar to them. Obviously, many of these pieces retain little significance, for they dealt with situations peculiar to that decade. Some of them, however, continued to be valid: "The Sahara of the Bozart" (second series) was, in some ways, almost as true of the South several decades later as it was in 1920; and his comments on the farmer ("The Husbandman," fourth series) remained even more appropriate. His dissections of such eminent figures as Theodore Roosevelt and Thorstein Veblen are still amusing.

Of Americans in general, Mencken had a low opinion, considering them a mongrel people incapable of high spiritual aspiration. His opinion of democracy was equally low. It was, he believed, merely a scheme to hearten the have-nots in their unending battle with the haves. The inferiority of Americans Mencken attributed to the lack of a genuine aristocracy and to Puritanism. Without an aristocracy, there could be no real leadership, and the vacuum would inevitably be filled by politicians, whom he detested. He also had no faith in reform or reformers.

As for Puritanism, Mencken believed that it had always been the dominant force in his country's history and had left Americans the narrow-minded victims of religious bigotry. The predominance during the 1920's of the more extreme forms of Fundamentalism gave some support to his argument. In his attacks on religion, however, he made the mistake of throwing the baby out with the bathwater; because he was himself a complete skeptic, he simply could not conceive of such a creature as a sincere and yet intelligent Christian. The terms were to him incompatible.

Mencken's enemies were always urging him, in anguished tones, to leave this country if he found it so distasteful. His reply was that nowhere else could so much entertainment be had so cheaply. According to his calculations, it cost him personally only eighty cents a year to maintain Warren Harding in the White House. No better show could be found for the money. In spite of his exaggerations, crudities, and often bad taste, Mencken performed a valuable service. American society always needs a gadfly, and his cynical wit provided the sting at just the right moment.

THE PRINCE AND THE PAUPER

Type of work: Novel
Author: Mark Twain (Samuel Langhorne Clemens, 1835-1910)
Type of plot: Social criticism
Time of plot: Sixteenth century
Locale: England
First published: 1881

In many ways, The Prince and the Pauper *is a companion piece to* A Connecticut Yankee in King Arthur's Court. *Both are historical satires, both deplore the lack of democracy in early England, both scrutinize the past from a viewpoint of modern morality, and both exhibit humor derived from ludicrous situations. The outstanding quality of this novel is the beloved simplicity of the prince himself, his unswerving tenacity to his royal training throughout all of his difficulties, and his final act of clemency.*

Principal Characters

Edward, the Prince of Wales and the son of Henry VIII. When a ragged waif named Tom Canty invades the royal grounds, Edward, curious about life outside the confines of the palace, invites the boy to his quarters. They change clothes as a prank and discover that they are identical in appearance. When the prince appears in the courtyard dressed in Tom's rags, guards mistake him for the intruding waif and throw him into the streets. Protesting time and again that he is the real Prince of Wales, he is ridiculed and thought mad by skeptical London crowds. After many adventures and hardships that reveal to him the harsh lot of the common people, he appears as Tom Canty is about to be crowned king and proves that he himself is the rightful heir by disclosing the location of the Great Seal that his late father had entrusted to him.

King Henry VIII, his ailing father, who has entrusted the Great Seal to Edward.

Mary and **Elizabeth,** daughters of the king. They think that Tom is their brother.

Tom Canty, who was born the same day as the Prince of Wales and is his double in appearance. He trades places with Edward.

John Canty, his father, who treats Tom and Edward cruelly. When Edward becomes king, he wants to hang Canty but cannot locate him.

Miles Hendon, the disinherited son of a baronet. He befriends the homeless Edward.

Hugh Hendon, his brother, who tricks Miles in order to marry Edith.

Edith, who loves Miles but is afraid that Hugh will murder him if she identifies Miles as the true heir of the Hendon estate.

Hugo, a thief who tries to teach Edward his tricks.

The Lord Protector, who identifies the real prince.

The Story

On the same day, in London, Tom Canty and the Prince of Wales were born, the first unwanted and the second long awaited. While the prince, Edward Tudor, lay robed in silks, Tom Canty wallowed in the filth of Offal Court.

Tom's father forced him to beg during the day, and he beat the boy at night; nevertheless, Tom had private dreams of his own. Pretending that he was a prince, he gathered his ragtag court of street urchins around him. One day, hoping to see Prince Edward of England, he invaded the royal precincts, but when he tried to approach the prince he was cuffed by a guard and ordered away. Edward, witnessing the incident, protected Tom and took the young beggar into the palace. There, in the privacy of Edward's chamber, Tom confessed his longing to be a prince. When the two boys exchanged garments, they discovered that they were identical in appearance. Unrecognized as the real prince and mistaken for the beggar boy, Edward was promptly thrown into the streets of London, where he wandered helplessly, mocked by people whom he approached with pleas that they pay homage to him as their rightful prince.

Meanwhile, in the palace, it was thought that the prince had gone mad because he could recall none of the royal matters that he was supposed to know. King Henry VIII issued an edict that no one should discuss the royal lapse of memory, and the princesses Mary and Elizabeth mercifully tried to aid their supposed brother, who by that time was too frightened to confess that he was Tom Canty, a beggar dressed in the prince's clothing.

King Henry, sick in bed, had given the Great Seal of the kingdom to Prince Edward for safekeeping. When Henry demanded the return of his seal, Tom reported that he did not know where it was.

While the Prince of Wales, a homeless waif, wandered the streets under the crowd's mocking raillery, King Henry died. Edward was found by John Canty, Tom's father, and brought to Offal Court during the wild celebration of Tom's ascension to the throne, however, Edward escaped from John Canty. Again tormented by skeptical crowds who laughed at his protests that he was now king of England, Edward was rescued by Miles Hendon, the disinherited son of a baronet. Thinking that Edward was mad, Miles pitied the little waif and pretended to pay him the homage due to a monarch.

Miles had loved a girl named Edith, who was coveted by Miles's brother Hugh. By trickery, Hugh had gained his father's confidence, and Miles was turned away from home. Edward declared that Miles had suffered unjustly and promised the adventurer any favor that he might ask. Recalling the story of John de Courci, who, given a similar opportunity by King John, requested that he and all his descendants might be permitted to wear hats in the presence of the king of England, Miles wisely asked that he be permitted to sit down in Edward's presence, for the young king had been ordering Miles about like any other personal servant.

In the role of king of England, Tom was slowly learning to conduct himself royally. Regarded by his attendants as mad, he was able to display his lack of training, and his failure to recall events familiar to Edward, with no calamitous results. At the same time, his gradual improvement offered hope that his derangement was only temporary.

John Canty lured Edward away from Miles's protection and took the boy to Southwark, there to join a pack of thieves. Still vainly declaring himself king, Edward was again the center of ridicule. One of the thieves, Hugo, undertook to teach Edward the tricks of his trade. Making his escape, Edward wandered to a farmhouse where a kind woman, pitying the poor, insane beggar boy who declared himself king of England, fed him. Edward wandered on to the hut of a hermit who accepted naïvely Edward's claim to royalty. In turn, the hermit revealed to Edward that he was an archangel; the hermit was truly insane. While Edward slept, the hermit brooded over the wrongs done him by King Henry. Believing Edward really to be the king, and planning to murder him, the hermit managed to tie up the boy while he slept. John Canty and Hugo, following the trail of the escaped waif, rescued him and forced him to rejoin the band of rogues. Again he was compelled to aid Hugo in his dishonest trade. At last, Miles found the boy and saved him.

Miles was on his way back to Hendon Hall to claim his heritage and Edith for a wife. Arriving at their destination, they learned that Miles's father was dead and that Hugh, married to Edith, was master of Hendon Hall. Only five of the old servants were still living, and all of them, in addition to Hugh and Edith, pretended not to recognize Miles. Denounced as a pretender, Miles was sentenced to the stocks, where the abuse showered upon him by the mob so enraged Edward that he protested loudly. When the guards decided to whip the boy, Miles offered to bear the flogging instead. Grateful to his friend, Edward dubbed Miles an earl, but the imprisoned man sorrowed at the boy's display of insanity. Upon Miles's release from the stocks, the two set out for London, where they arrived on the day before the coronation of King Edward VI.

In regal splendor, enjoying the adulation of his subjects, Tom Canty rode through the streets of London toward Westminster Abbey. There, just as the crown was about to be set on his head, a voice rang out demanding that the ceremony cease, and the real king, clothed in rags, stepped forth. As the guards moved to seize the troublemaker, Tom, recognizing Edward, ordered them to halt. The Lord Protector solved the mystery by asking the ragged king to locate the Great Seal that had been lost since King Henry's death. Edward, after much dramatic hesitation, managed to remember the exact location of the Seal. Tom admitted that he had innocently used it to crack nuts.

When Miles was brought before the rightful King Edward, he exercised his privilege of sitting in the king's presence. At first, he had doubted that the waif was really the king, but when Edward ordered his outraged guards to permit that disrespectful act, Miles knew that his young friend had not been insane after all. Furthermore, Edward confirmed Miles's title of earl. Hugh was stripped of his titles and land. Later he died, whereupon Miles married Edith, whose earlier refusal to acknowledge his identity had been the result of Hugh's threat to kill his brother.

Tom returned to Offal Court with Edward's promise that he and his family would be honored for the rest of their lives. Edward righted many wrongs he had encountered during his adventures. John Canty, whom he wanted to hang, was never heard from again.

Critical Evaluation

The Prince and the Pauper was Mark Twain's earliest attempt to join his fascination for the romantic past of Europe with his natural bent for satirizing the injustices and social conventions of his own age. He was to do the same later, with far better effect, in *A Connecticut Yankee in King Arthur's Court* (1889) and with less success in *Personal Recollections of Joan of Arc* (1896). It is generally agreed that *The Prince and the Pauper* is a story mainly for children—though if that is wholly true, it must also be said that it is very rewarding for adults.

Twain employs in this novel many of the themes and devices that he may have exercised to better effect in other works, but which are nevertheless used well here. There are, for example, all the usual techniques that he learned so expertly as a teller of tall tales—tongue-in-cheek irony, ridiculous understatement, and exaggeration, to name a few. Miles Hendon's separation from Edward gives Twain the opportunity for soliloquy, a favorite literary device used with great success in *The Adventures of Huckleberry Finn* (1884). The exchange of identities—as in *The Adventures of Huckleberry Finn* and *The Tragedy of Pudd'nhead Wilson* (1894)—is another common occurrence in Twain's works, as is his use of coincidence.

Twain was able in *The Prince and the Pauper* to underscore some of the social follies and injustices of his own age without actually having to attack them directly in the novel. He did this by satirically treating the social and legal conventions of Tudor England, and then assuming that his readers would recognize for themselves the parallels with their own times. Hence, religious intolerance is the target of "In Prison," a chapter in which two women, who have kindly befriended Edward and Miles, are mercilessly burned at the stake because they are Baptists. Tom Canty, as king, labors to change laws that are unduly harsh or blatantly unjust, and Edward himself learns of the unnecessary cruelty of prisons, as well as the nature of the kind of life poor people must endure as a result of their poverty.

Yet Twain's major criticism of society, both Tudor and his own, is of its mistaking the outward appearances of individuals or their circumstances as a final gauge of their true worth. The novel suggests that, under different circumstances, anyone could be a king—just as Tom Canty, given the opportunity, learns to be one. Tom and Edward are equally intelligent and virtuous young boys, but each is born to a different kind of "court." Chance and circumstances alone determine much of one's outward behavior and appearance. For Twain, this was as true for his own times as he believed that it had been for Tudor England.

THE RABBIT SERIES

Type of work: Novels
Author: John Updike (1932-　　)
Type of plot: Realistic tragicomedy
Time of plot: 1959-1989
Locale: Pennsylvania and Florida
First published: *Rabbit, Run*, 1960; *Rabbit Redux*, 1971; *Rabbit Is Rich*, 1981; *Rabbit at Rest*, 1990

Updike examines three decades in the life of Harry "Rabbit" Angstrom, a typical American man struggling with responsibility and relationships. The novels address the issues of sex, death, parenthood, and faith in the 1960's, 1970's, and 1980's.

Principal Characters

Harry "Rabbit" Angstrom, a former basketball star. Frustrated in the early years of his marriage to Janice Springer, he runs away from his responsibilities on more than one occasion. After more than a decade of strained relationships, he and Janice settle down to run the automobile sales business started by her father. Harry achieves some financial prosperity, but his frustrations with his son continually plague him. The good life and a continual disregard for his body cause Harry to develop serious heart trouble, a condition that he virtually ignores until it proves fatal.

Janice Springer Angstrom, Harry's wife, disillusioned with her marriage at times and given to excessive drinking. She is responsible for the death of her young daughter, and the event haunts both her and Harry for the rest of their lives. After a brief affair with a salesman at her father's used car lot, she settles down to be a devoted wife, mother, and eventually grandmother. In later years, she tries to help her son overcome his drug problem and works to save the family business from bankruptcy.

Nelson Angstrom, Harry's only son, a troubled child whose parents' problems affect him greatly. He grows to be an equally troubled adult, forced into a marriage about which he feels uncomfortable. He has a genuine interest in the family business, but his drug habit causes him to steal from the company, eventually driving it to the point of bankruptcy.

Teresa "Pru" Lubell Angstrom, a secretary from a dysfunctional family in Ohio who meets Nelson Angstrom at Kent State University, becomes pregnant, and persuades Nelson to marry her. They move in with the Angstroms in Pennsylvania; Pru provides Harry with two grandchildren, Judy and Roy.

The Story

In *Rabbit, Run*, Harry "Rabbit" Angstrom, a former star of the Mount Judge basketball team, finds himself at twenty-six married, the father of one, and employed as an itinerant salesman. Unable to tolerate the slovenly, alcoholic behavior of his pregnant wife, Janice, Rabbit abandons her and his two-year-old son, Nelson. He takes up residence with Ruth Leonard, a prostitute. When he learns that Janice has gone into labor, Rabbit leaves Ruth and returns to his family. Life at home does not improve much, however, and when Janice refuses the sexual advances of her husband, Rabbit leaves again. In his absence, Janice, in a drunken stupor, drowns their infant daughter. The tragedy brings Rabbit home briefly, but he

cannot stand being blamed for his daughter's death. When Ruth will not take him back, although she is pregnant with his child, he heads out into town, uncertain of his future.

A decade later, in *Rabbit Redux*, Rabbit has settled down with Janice and Nelson in Penn Park, a Brewer suburb. Working as a typesetter for Verity Press, he spends considerable time with Nelson because Janice is away during the day and on many nights, ostensibly because of her job at her father's used car lot, Springer Motors. In reality, she is having an affair with Charlie Stavros, a salesman at the lot. When Rabbit confronts her about the affair, she moves out and settles in with Charlie. Through friends who introduce him to Brewer night life, Rabbit meets Jill Pendleton, a rich runaway who wants to experience the new freedoms of the 1960's. Harry allows Jill to move in with him and Nelson. She soon brings with her Skeeter, an African-American revolutionary who introduces Harry to new ideas about democracy and white supremacy. The trio experiments with drugs and sex. Nelson, too, is allowed to participate on the periphery of their adventures; at the same time, he frequently visits his mother and Charlie.

Neighbors become disenchanted with the unusual lifestyle being displayed at the Angstrom house, and Rabbit receives several threats. On an evening when Rabbit has sought solace in the arms of family friend Peggy Fosnacht, his home is burned, and Jill dies in the fire. Nelson, who has developed a strong affection for Jill, is enraged and blames his father for her death. During the weeks after the fire, Janice and Harry are reunited. They move in with Rabbit's in-laws and resume their rocky married life.

Rabbit Is Rich takes place ten years later. Rabbit has become manager of Springer Motors, which now sells Toyotas. Business has prospered, and the Angstroms have been able to join a local country club—actually a middle-class version of elite establishments of the same name. Much of the novel is given over to the relationships between the Angstroms and other couples who frequent the club.

Clearly there is a strained relationship between Harry and his son. When Nelson returns home from Kent State University for summer break with a girl in tow, Rabbit is suspicious. This young woman is merely a close friend, but there is someone else in Nelson's life: Teresa "Pru" Lubell, a secretary at the university, who eventually joins him at the Springer home, pregnant with Nelson's child. Nelson indicates that he is not interested in finishing college; instead, he wants to work at the car dealership. Harry is reluctant to let him do so, and his son's first ventures in the business drive Harry almost to rage. After Nelson marries Pru, Janice insists that her son be allowed to work at the car lot.

In the fall, after Nelson's wedding, the Angstroms and two other couples take a trip to the Caribbean. There the three wives arrange a night of spouse-swapping. Harry is clearly interested in Cindy Murkett, the young wife of an older friend, but he is paired instead with Thelma Harrison. He learns that Thelma has always loved him, and their one-night reverie begins a long-standing affair. The Angstroms are called away early from their vacation to return to Pennsylvania when Pru goes into labor. They arrive in time for Harry to bask in the glory of having a new granddaughter.

In *Rabbit at Rest*, as the 1980's close, Harry has turned over the management of Springer Motors to Nelson. He and Janice spend half of each year in Florida. Overweight and suffering minor difficulties with his heart, Harry plays golf but eats too much junk food. A Christmastime visit by Nelson and his family causes Harry considerable aggravation, as he has never become totally comfortable with his son. He is especially concerned by information suggesting problems at the car lot. While taking his granddaughter sailfishing, Harry suffers a heart attack and is rushed to the hospital. He recovers and returns in the spring to Pennsylvania, where he confirms that Nelson is stealing from the company to support his drug habit. Top management at Toyota is poised to take over Springer Motors, which is $225,000 in debt.

Nelson, feeling increasingly pressured, finally snaps one evening and strikes his wife. When she calls the Angstroms, Janice insists that Nelson seek help. Harry returns to the lot to set things straight but soon learns that he must have further heart surgery. On the day that he is discharged from the hospital, Janice leaves him with Pru while she goes off to her real-estate course. His daughter-in-law, starved for affection, seduces him on his first night home.

Nelson returns from treatment a fanatic for reform, and he and his mother work hard to restore the company to solvency. Janice suggests selling their home and moving in with Nelson's family; neither Harry nor Pru is pleased, and Pru reveals to mother and son her indiscretion with Harry. Harry bolts for Florida where, alone, he reverts to his bad eating habits and puts further strain on his heart. While out walking, he becomes involved in a one-on-one basketball game, which brings on a fatal heart attack.

Critical Evaluation

Updike's saga of the life and times of Harry "Rabbit" Angstrom offers a chronicle of the United States from the 1950's through the 1980's. A youthful Harry struggles to come to terms with the ironies inherent in the Ameri-can Dream. Later in life, he confronts the revolutions in American society brought on by the Vietnam War, women's liberation, and new attitudes toward sex, drugs, and personal responsibility. He consistently struggles to make his marriage work, in the face of sexual and economic forces that tempt him to stray from his familial responsibilities. As he gets older, Harry finds his life dominated by concerns about money and status. At the same time, he begins to exhibit the physical symptoms common to American men whose careers have focused on achieving the good life: He becomes overweight and develops heart trouble, a condition that eventually kills him. His life is a microcosm of the pattern shared by millions of nameless, unknown Americans who populate cities and towns from Maine to California.

Dominating the landscape in all four novels is the presence of the central character. In the Rabbit novels, Updike offers a hero who epitomizes Middle America. Harry Angstrom is not an intellectual: He has no interest in the arts, and he is an unthinking political conservative. When he turns to reading in middle age, his fare is *Consumer Reports*. Only late in life does he dip into history, and then his interest is merely that of the dilettante. For Harry, the controlling metaphor of his life is sports. Once a star basketball player, he defines success in terms reminiscent of the game that once gave him fame. Like many men, Harry believes that he is the center of the universe, and much of the psychological interest in the novels is generated by the hero's developing awareness of his insignificance amid the plethora of life-forms, human and otherwise, in the universe.

Though these four novels can be read separately, common threads bind them into a seamless fabric held together by the chronicle of Harry Angstrom's progression from youthful ne'er-do-well to middle-aged American businessman. The focus throughout is almost exclusively on the hero's developing sense of his own individuality, defined in his relationships with his wife, his son, his parents and in-laws, and the friends whose lives touch his own. Four issues, common to the novels, give the sequence a sense of proportion bordering on the epic: sex, death, parenthood, and faith.

Updike confronts male sexuality directly, exposing the constant attention paid to matters of sex by ordinary men such as Harry. Most of Rabbit's activity is confined to fantasy, but occasional marital infidelity is part of his life, and Updike presents his hero's sexual encounters with both his wife and his mistresses explicitly. The point that Updike makes throughout the novels is that sex is an inherent part of the American male's life. It is not merely an activity providing moments of ecstasy to individuals;

it is the one guarantee that men have of perpetuating themselves and attaining a form of immortality.

In each of the novels, the specter of death permeates the atmosphere. In the first book, Rabbit's daughter is taken from him in her infancy; in the second, the young Jill Pendleton, toward whom Harry feels alternately a father or a lover, meets a tragic end. Only in *Rabbit Is Rich* is there no death that touches Rabbit directly, but even in this work Harry is reminded of the inevitability of death by the presence of his mother-in-law in his home. The ending lines of the novel, in which Harry celebrates the birth of his granddaughter, are balanced with the sobering thought that her birth is merely another nail in Rabbit's coffin. Finally, in the last novel, Rabbit himself becomes the figure whom death stalks. The work is filled with images of disease and death, so the hero's ultimate demise is wholly expected. Ironically, only in death does Harry find some rest from running both away from and toward his responsibilities.

Making his life more complicated and frustrating is Harry's constant battle with his son, Nelson. To Harry, his offspring's small stature and disdain for athletics makes him an unworthy son. Others see much of Harry in Nelson, however, and readers are made to recognize how much the father really wants to see his son carry on his name and fame. Hence, through this relationship, Updike is able to demonstrate a universal dilemma existing between many fathers and sons: a love-hate relationship caused by the inability of all sons to replicate their fathers.

Finally, in each of the novels Updike subtly introduces matters of religion. Though not a churchgoer, Harry nevertheless is convinced that God exists and that He cares for His creations. Few of the other characters are so naïvely trusting. For Harry, God is personal, not simply a superforce; humans can call on Him for help and expect to be heard. Against the crass materialism that permeates the decades about which he writes, Updike offers readers the sense that Harry is right: His life, and every person's life, has significance, because there is something earned from living one's life well. The concluding paragraphs of *Rabbit Is Rich*, in which Harry's final thoughts are offered for the reader (his family cannot understand him), are an affirmation that all the trouble and turmoil that characterized Rabbit's race through life have been worthwhile.

THE REAL LIFE OF SEBASTIAN KNIGHT

Type of work: Novel
Author: Vladimir Nabokov (1899-1977)
Type of plot: Simulated biography
Time of plot: 1899-1938
Locale: England and Europe
First published: 1941

In The Real Life of Sebastian Knight, *Nabokov addresses the nature of truth and identity through the story of one man's quest to know his late brother. The novel combines near-tragedy with comic absurdity as V. tries to understand the world around him.*

Principal Characters

Sebastian Knight, a writer who has just died. Many people, including his half brother, are trying to pin down who Sebastian really was, to reveal his character and give meaning to his life.

V., Sebastian's half brother, who travels from Russia to England in search of his sibling only to arrive at the hospital the day after Sebastian's death. V. often misinterprets the circumstances that he encounters, convincing himself of certain facts based on intuition alone.

Mr. Goodman, formerly Sebastian's secretary, now his biographer. Goodman's book is written on a superficial level, but even V. finds truth in it.

Clare Bishop, a woman who was loved by Sebastian. V. finds her in the course of his mission but chooses to draw his own conclusions about her relationship with his brother.

Virginia, the mother of Sebastian and V., who died in Roquebrune. Sebastian finds a village by that name and believes that he can almost see the ghost of his mother, only to discover that he is in the wrong town.

The Real Life of Sebastian Knight, written in Paris in 1938 but not published in the United States until 1941, is Vladimir Nabokov's first work in English; previously he had written in Russian. Although this earlier novel does not show quite the same ingenious conjuring with language as *Lolita* (1955) and *Pale Fire* (1962), it is, nevertheless, a brilliant, sometimes comic, and almost perversely complex book.

The novel is written as a biography of Sebastian Knight, a writer who has just died, by his younger half brother, who designates himself only as V. Beginning as an attempt to present the real Sebastian, V.'s biography becomes the quest of V. himself to understand the personality of the man revealed by his search. Two problems, therefore, run as concurrent themes through the novel: first, the problem of communication between writers and their readers, the task of conveying reality with precision, and, second, the greater problem of what this reality is—the multiple views possible of the same thing and the necessarily unsuccessful attempt to capture anything so elusive as personal identity. The novel presents a dazzling series of masks, none of which may be removed completely because knowing more about Sebastian Knight

does not help one to understand him but rather increases his complexity.

Within the novel are three different literary attempts to portray Sebastian. The first is V.'s own earnest, painstaking effort to portray his brother objectively. At the opposite extreme is a slick, superficial biography, already published, by Mr. Goodman, Sebastian's former secretary. Yet V. admits in quoting from it at length that even this book contains elements of truth. Somewhere in the middle are Sebastian's own novels, which reveal obliquely something of the man himself, even though one can never be sure of how much they disclose.

V.'s firsthand knowledge of Sebastian, colored by the adoration of a younger brother for the clever older one and by V.'s nostalgia for Russia, is confined to Sebastian's youth. Sebastian had been born in Russia. His English mother, a restless, romantic woman, deserted her husband and baby; his father remarried. Sebastian left Russia for Cambridge and remained in England, becoming almost a caricature of an Englishman and writing his novels in that country. At this point in his biography, V. must search for people who knew Sebastian, for V. saw almost nothing of him after he left Russia, and their few meetings were cold and strained.

V.'s search for the truth becomes a kind of detective novel, but an enigmatic and paradoxical one. His elaborate quest is continually frustrated—by someone's inability to remember, by his own timidity, and by his willingness to content himself with an intuitive impression, almost as if he does not wish to have any illusions shattered. One is reminded of Sebastian's own first novel, a parody of a detective story; indeed, the quotations from Sebastian's writing provide not only a glimpse of his real self but also an insight into this novel, for one might say of it that he employed parody as a means of achieving effects of serious thought and feeling. This novel of Sebastian's, called *The Prismatic Bezel*, also hints at the many-faceted obliquity of Nabokov's novel.

V.'s quest degenerates into a melodramatic farce. He finds the woman whom Sebastian loved and tricks her into an admission of her identity, but again he contents himself with his own impression of her and his own estimate of the effect that she must have had on his brother. Nabokov weaves parallel situations from Sebastian's novels and from his and the narrator's life into a glittering web that conceals as much as it reveals. One cannot know another person because countless factors of which one is totally unaware intervene. Nabokov's method is the juxtaposition of a series of glimpses, absurd and touching, like a series of sleight-of-hand tricks. One cannot tell what is the trickery of legerdemain and what is not.

Two incidents, one near the beginning and the other at the end of the book, illuminate the novel's meaning. On one of his trips to Europe, Sebastian finds a village called Roquebrune, the town where his mother had died. He finds her house and sits for a long time in the garden, trying to find the mother whom he scarcely knew. At length, he can almost see her figure, like some pastel ghost, gliding up the stairs to the door. Much later, he discovers by accident that the Roquebrune he had found was not even the same town where his mother had lived, but another, many miles away. There is something comic and pathetic in his own deception, something that undercuts and transcends the experience.

The work's meaning is made clearer by the end of the book. V. had been in Marseilles when he received a telegram telling him that Sebastian was seriously ill. After many delays, he finds the hospital, has some difficulties in making the porter understand him, but is eventually shown into the room where the Englishman, still alive, is sleeping. He spends only a few minutes there, but he believes that he can at last express the kinship that he has always felt with his brother, that at last these moments listening to the sound of his breathing have crystallized a whole series of other moments as words could not have done. Yet, on leaving the room, he discovers by chance that this man was not his brother at all, for Sebastian had died the day before. Yet he says that later he found his life transformed by the short time that he spent in the dying man's company. He now believes that the soul—any man's soul—is a way of being rather than a constant state; therefore, souls are constantly in flux and interchangeable. V. believes that he is Sebastian Knight; he wears his mask. Sebastian may even be V., or both may be someone they never knew. In this mood, V. begins to write his brother's biography.

One cannot know another person completely, for one cannot know oneself. The fact that V. goes on to write Sebastian's biography proves that he has understood for only a moment. The existence of a series of masks, however, does not necessarily mean that nothing lies behind them, only that one can penetrate no further.

Nabokov's method is oblique, moving as does the chess knight who must leap in two directions and skip over intervening pieces, because the knowledge of identity must be reached obliquely. This novel is at once a fascinating puzzle and a profound statement, whose depths are disguised as absurdities. It is technically not the tour de force that *Lolita* and *Pale Fire* are, but its discussions of the relationship between writers and their art reveal much about the author's own technique. Its themes are similar to those of Nabokov's other works, as is its deliberate comic view, which approaches within a hair's-breadth of the tragic. This work is at once a witty bit of hocus-pocus and a fine and moving novel.

THE RECTOR OF JUSTIN

Type of work: Novel
Author: Louis Auchincloss (1917-   )
Type of plot: Journal narrative
Time of plot: 1860's to the 1940's
Locale: Eastern Massachusetts
First published: 1964

In The Rector of Justin, *the character of Dr. Francis Prescott, the rector of Justin Martyr Academy, is revealed by the various memoirs and journals about Prescott that are assembled by his disciple Brian Aspinwall.*

Principal Characters

Dr. Francis Prescott, the founder and rector of Justin Martyr Academy, who has dedicated his life to the creation of the ideal boys' church school. The novel begins with Prescott approaching his eightieth year and traces his story back to his earliest days and forward to his retirement and death. At the beginning of the novel, the reader sees Prescott as a revered, aloof, and almost sainted figure. He becomes more faulty and more human, however, through revelations in the various journals.

Brian Aspinwall, a young master at Justin Martyr who worships Dr. Prescott. At first, Dr. Prescott is a feared presence to Brian, but he gains his friendship by reading to and talking with Harriet Prescott, the rector's dying wife. Brian begins a journal that is primarily devoted to recording his impressions and observations of the character of Dr. Prescott. He also acquires the journals or partial biographies of those who have been closest to Prescott. The novel ends with Brian ending his journal and about to begin his biography of Prescott.

David Griscam, a successful New York lawyer who has devoted his life and resources to expanding and supporting Justin Martyr. David is befriended by Dr. Prescott while he is at the school, a friendship which turns his life around. There is, however, a conflict between David's vision of Justin Martyr and Dr. Prescott's. David sees it as an expanding school that would establish its preeminence in New England, while Dr. Prescott continues to see it as a family place.

Horace Havistock, a boyhood friend of Francis Prescott at boarding school. Francis befriends the vulnerable and unpopular Horace. Horace is despised for being both a "new" boy and a very different one, one who dislikes football and loves art. Horace plays a key role in Francis Prescott's marriage. Francis is in love with the beautiful Eliza Dean. When Francis receives a call to become a minister and found a church school for boys, however, Eliza begins to have doubts about her role. Horace advises her to not go through with the marriage because she would never be happy as a headmaster's wife.

The Story

The Rector of Justin is a very unusual novel in the manner of its narration. The central character, the rector or headmaster Dr. Francis Prescott, is seen through a number of journals of different characters in the novel. This multiple view creates not the usual plot but a kaleidoscopic view of the main character. The reader is left to judge the rector's character: Is he a saint of education or a monster who has tortured his students by his bogus rectitude?

The first journal is that of Brian Aspinwall. He describes Justin Martyr Academy, and he notices its architecture and judges the types of students and masters. He has only a dim view, however, of the rector. Brian gets to know the rector by reading to Harriet Prescott, the rector's wife. Brian admires and even loves Harriet for her wit and culture, and the rector begins to understand and like Brian for that perception of his wife. Francis and Harriet Prescott have a conflicted relationship because the rector must give so much to the boys of the school.

Other connections begin to develop between Brian and the rector. Brian wishes to become a minister, but he doubts whether he has the moral and physical strength for the job. Prescott encourages him, although he suggests that Brian should spend another year deciding if the ministry is for him. The other connection is the crucial one: Brian begins to collect notes about the character of Francis Prescott, and he ends up becoming the central narrator of this unusual novel. Brian notices some of Prescott's characteristics, such as his wit, his intelligence, his rectitude, and his occasional arbitrariness. Yet Brian is really only observing the latter end of Prescott's life; he needs some information about Prescott's early life. Fortunately, Prescott's old friend, Horace Havistock, gives Brian his manuscript "The Art of Friendship," which deals with the school years and love life of the young Francis Prescott.

According to Horace's journal, Francis is everything that Horace is not: athletic, popular, righteous. Horace goes to the University of Oxford with Francis and observes him as he goes into business with the Penn Central Railroad. Francis had earlier expressed a desire to become a minister and found a boys' school; however, his religious doubts have interfered with that choice. One day, he feels a "call" to the religious life, which creates a conflict with his fiancée, Eliza Dean. She does not want to play the role of headmaster's wife. Horace resolves the conflict for her by advising Eliza to break off the engagement. Francis does not seem to be exceptionally troubled by this reverse in his emotional life, and he soon finds a substitute for Eliza in Harriet Winslow, who is more fit for the role of headmaster's wife. Prescott's sacrifice is noble, but it also shows something about his ruthless desire to fulfill his ideals. His mission is clearly more important to him than his personal relationship with a wife.

The next journal is that of David Griscam. David entered Justin Martyr in its earliest days and he believes that he owes much to Francis Prescott. The rector advises him not to sink under his father's financial disgrace but to make his own way, so David becomes a supporter of the school. His views of the expansion and enlargement of the school, however, come into conflict with the views of Prescott. David, in essence, wishes to make the school fit his own vision, while Prescott believes that the school is his creation. This disagreement reveals the pride of Prescott and a recognition of his real achievement: Prescott sees that the school is not a physical plant but the sum of his influence upon the boys.

The next journal is that of Cordelia Turnbull, Prescott's third daughter. Cordelia sees her father in psychological terms; she views the boys as rivals for her father's affections. As a result, Cordelia establishes a relationship with one of Prescott's former senior prefects, Charley Strong; they are living together in Paris after World War I. Prescott comes to Paris to help Cordelia, but he realizes that she is beyond hope. His real struggle is for the soul of Charley Strong. Prescott wonders whether Charley will sink into the despair that Cordelia has encouraged or return to the trust in God that the headmaster had instilled in him. After a struggle, Charley dies content with his faith intact; Cordelia has been defeated again by her father.

The greatest challenge to the righteousness of Prescott is contained in the journal of Jules Griscam. Jules is the son of David Griscam, and Prescott gives Jules's journal to Brian so that he might see another side of the headmaster. Jules hates the role that Prescott has played in his father's life and opposes the headmaster in every way that he can. Finally, he is expelled from Justin Martyr, but he is later admitted to Harvard University. There, he continues his vendetta and encourages another student to desecrate Justin Martyr. When Prescott confronts Jules about this act, Jules is not remorseful but blames it on what Prescott has done to him; the headmaster has, according to him, perverted his whole life. Prescott recognizes his failure, and the acknowledgement of that failure suggests much self-awareness.

After Prescott's retirement, he becomes angry at the changes that his successor has made in the school, and he plans to use the diamond jubilee honoring him and the founding of the school as an opportunity to rail against these innovations. The climax of the novel comes not at the jubilee, however, but when David Griscam assembles a group of trustees who are former students from Justin Martyr to talk to Prescott about their lives and their ideas about the school. They see the school only as a good place to have on one's résumé; it helps them to make business and social connections. This meeting dissuades Prescott from giving a speech against the new headmaster, but it also destroys his earlier view of the school. Justin Martyr was to be an ideal place where one learned to be good in a family atmosphere. Now he sees it as just another place to create future stockbrokers. Just before his death, however, Prescott sees that what is important about the school is the fact that he has taught and helped hundreds of boys; he has not created some grand vision, but he has helped his boys to live fuller lives. The book ends with Prescott dying in peace and Brian beginning the biography of the rector of Justin.

Critical Evaluation

The Rector of Justin is a study of a social institution, the New England boys' boarding school. The focus is not, as it is in such novels as John Knowles's *A Separate Peace* (1960), on the formative years of a few boys but on the role of the school itself. The rector, Francis Prescott, founded the school and controlled its development, but the novel asks whether the function of such a school is as a validation of social class or as the best place to frame a boy's moral character. The different narrators in the novel offer conflicting views that are partially but not fully resolved in the peaceful death of the rector.

The setting of the novel is significant, as it takes place in a traditional boys' preparatory school thirty miles west of Boston. The institution grows from an insignificant school of fifty boys in the 1880's to a substantial school with a national reputation. It is also significant that much of the novel takes place during the period of World War II, from 1939 to 1946. By the end of the war, there is a new rector with a very different vision of the nature and function of the school. Prescott struggles against but finally accepts the outward changes, while hoping that the school will continue to perform its higher moral function.

The novel does go against nearly all the trends of its period. It is not an experimental novel, as it instead hearkens back to the early tradition of the English novel in its use of journals. While the novel is not experimental, however, it is complex in its narration. The reader is given various and conflicting views of the main character, and there is no privileged view. Readers must exercise their judgment and sort out and resolve the conflict.

The Rector of Justin might be compared to the novels of Auchincloss' masters, Henry James and Edith Wharton. Auchincloss uses a favorite technique of James, the reflector. The role of the narrators in *The Rector of Justin* is to reflect or illuminate one side of the main character. The style of Auchincloss is not as complex as that of James, but it does retain the formality of diction and tone. There are no low characters, and the style never lapses into the colloquial. Finally, Auchincloss sees his main character, as do James and Wharton, not as an independent being but as one conditioned by and functioning in society. Auchincloss admired Wharton's novels, and he continues her examination of wealth and privilege in the United States.

The Rector of Justin is the novel that made Auchincloss' reputation, and it remains his most typical and sustained performance. It was the first novel that brought him critical recognition and even popularity, causing him to be seen as a serious novelist who probed a specific sphere of American life. *The Rector of Justin* is a most revealing novel about the American social institution of the New England boarding school.

A novel of manners rather than the more common novel of character, *The Rector of Justin* analyzes its characters in the light of the social institutions of its time period—indeed, the book studies the very creation of one of those institutions. The author has been compared to such novelists as John O'Hara and J. P. Marquand, but Auchincloss has a clearer grasp of the social mores of the wealthy. He continues the traditions of the novel that were established by James and Wharton.

THE RED BADGE OF COURAGE: An Episode of the American Civil War

Type of work: Novel
Author: Stephen Crane (1871-1900)
Type of plot: Impressionistic realism
Time of plot: Civil War
Locale: A Civil War battlefield
First published: 1895

Making a dramatic departure from the traditional treatment of war in fiction, this novel ignores powerful generals and historic victories and defeats in favor of probing the personal reactions of unknown foot soldiers fighting unknown enemies in skirmishes of indeterminate outcome. Henry Fleming is motivated not by courage or patriotism but by cowardice, fear, and finally egotism, and events in the novel are all filtered subjectively through his consciousness.

Principal Characters

Henry Fleming, a young recruit under fire for the first time in an unnamed battle of the Civil War, possibly Chancellorsville. A farm boy whose struggle with his emotions might be that of the eternal recruit in any battle of any war, Henry has dreamed of fighting heroically in "Greeklike" battles. Irritated and unnerved by his regiment's inactivity, he tortures himself with the fear that he may run away when the actual firing begins. He does so. Sheepishly rejoining his regiment, he learns that his cowardice is not known to his fellow soldiers. In the next attack, he keeps firing after the others have stopped. When a color-bearer falls, he picks up the flag and carries it forward. Later he hears that the colonel has complimented his fierceness. Henry's psychological battle with himself is now ended; it has gone from fear to cowardice to bravery and, finally, to egotism.

Jim Conklin, "the tall soldier," a veteran who comforts Henry and squabbles with the braggart Wilson. He predicts that the regiment is about to move into battle. When it does so, he is mortally wounded. Henry and "the tattered man" find him stumbling to the rear, still on his feet, fearful of falling under the wheels of an artillery wagon. He wanders into a field, as if it were a place of rendezvous with death. Henry and the tattered man follow him, trying to bring him back. He brushes them off and, with a great convulsion, drops dead.

Wilson, "the loud one." At first he seems confident,

absolutely sure of his courage. As the battle begins, however, he suddenly thinks that he may be killed, and he turns a packet of letters over to Henry Fleming. After the first attack, he asks for the return of the letters. Some of his loudness and swagger is now gone. He and Henry struggle to get the flag from the fallen color-bearer. Henry seizes it, but Wilson aids him in going forward and setting an example for the wavering troops.

"The Tattered Man," a soldier encountered by Henry Fleming just after Fleming has run away. The man embarrasses the recruit by asking where he is wounded. Later he and Henry follow Jim Conklin into the field. The soldier is so impressed by the manner of Jim's death that he calls the dead man a "jim-dandy." Then he cautions Henry to "watch out fer ol' number one."

Lieutenant Hasbrouck, a young officer of Henry Fleming's company. He is shot in the hand in the early part of the battle but is able to drive a fleeing soldier back into the ranks and tries vainly to stop the disorganized retreat. He later compliments Henry and Wilson by calling them "wild cats."

Colonel MacChesnay, the officer who also compliments Henry Fleming and Wilson. He is berated by the general, shortly after Henry's advance with the flag, for not forcing the partial success of the charge to a complete one.

The Story

The tall soldier, Jim Conklin, and the loud soldier, Wilson, argued bitterly over the rumor that the troops were about to move. Henry Fleming was impatient to experience his first battle, and as he listened to the quarreling of the seasoned soldiers he wondered if he would become frightened and run away under gunfire. He questioned Wilson and Conklin, and each man stated that he would stand and fight no matter what happened.

Henry had come from a farm, where he had dreamed of battles and longed for army life. His mother had held him back at first. When she saw that her son was bored with the farm, she packed his woolen clothing and, with a warning that he must not associate with the wicked kind of men who were in the military camps, sent him off to join the Yankee troops.

One gray morning, Henry awoke to find that the regiment was about to move. With a hazy feeling that death would be a relief from dull and meaningless marching, Henry was again disappointed. The troops made only another march. He began to suspect that the generals were stupid fools, but the other men in his raw regiment scoffed at his idea and told him to shut up.

When the fighting suddenly began, there was very little action in it for Henry. He lay on the ground with the other men and watched for signs of the enemy. Some of the men around him were wounded. He could not see what was going on or what the battle was about. Then an attack came. Immediately, Henry forgot all of his former confused thoughts, and he could only fire his rifle over and over; around him, men behaved in their strange individual manner as they were wounded. Henry felt a close comradeship with the men at his side who were firing at the enemy with him.

Suddenly the attack ended. To Henry it seemed strange that the sky above should still be blue after the guns had stopped firing. While the men were recovering from the attack, binding wounds and gathering equipment, another surprise attack was launched from the enemy line. Unprepared and tired from the first fighting, the men retreated in panic. Henry, sharing their sudden terror, ran as well.

When the fearful retreat had ended, the fleeing men learned that the enemy had lost the battle. Now Henry felt a surge of guilt. Dreading to rejoin his companions, he fled into the forest. There he saw a squirrel run away from him in fright. The fleeing animal seemed to vindicate in Henry's mind his own cowardly flight; he had acted according to nature, whose own creatures run from danger. Then seeing a dead man lying in a clearing, Henry hurried back into the retreating column of wounded men. Most were staggering along in helpless bewilderment, and some were being carried on stretchers. Henry realized that he had no wound and that he did not belong in that group of staggering men. There was one pitiful-looking man, covered with dirt and blood, wandering about dazed

and alone. Everyone was staring at him and avoiding him. When Henry approached him, the young man saw the soldier was Jim Conklin. He was horrified at the sight of the tall soldier. Henry tried to help him, but Jim fled into a field and, with a wild motion of despair, fell to the ground dead. Once more, Henry fled.

His conscience was torturing him. He wanted to return to his regiment to finish the fight, but he thought that his fellow soldiers would point to him as a deserter. He envied the dead men who were lying all about him. They were already heroes; he was a coward. Ahead he could hear the rumbling of artillery. As he neared the lines of his regiment, a retreating line of men broke from the trees ahead of him. The men ran fiercely, ignoring him or waving frantically at him as they shouted something that he could not comprehend. He stood among the flying men, not knowing what to do. One man hit him on the head with the butt of a rifle.

Henry went on carefully, the wound on his head hurting him terribly. He walked for a long while until he met another soldier, who led Henry back to his regiment. The first familiar man Henry met was Wilson. Wilson, who had been a terrible braggart before the first battle, had given Henry a packet of letters to keep for him in case he were killed. Now Henry felt superior to Wilson. If the man asked him where he had been, Henry would remind him of the letters. Lost was Henry's feeling of guilt; he felt superior now, his deeds of cowardice almost forgotten. No one knew that he had run off in terror. Yet Wilson had changed. He no longer was the swaggering, boastful man who had annoyed Henry in the beginning. The men in the regiment washed Henry's head wound and told him to get some sleep.

The next morning, Wilson casually asked Henry for the letters. Half sorry that he had to yield them with no taunting remark, Henry returned the letters to his comrade. He felt sorry for Wilson's embarrassment. He felt himself a virtuous and heroic man.

Another battle started. This time, Henry held his position doggedly and kept firing his rifle without thinking. Once he fell down, and for a panicky moment he thought that he had been shot, but he continued to fire his rifle blindly, loading and firing without even seeing the enemy. Finally, someone shouted to him that he must stop shooting, that the battle was over. Then Henry looked up for the first time and saw that there were no enemy troops before him. Now he was a hero. Everyone stared at him when the lieutenant of the regiment complimented his fierce fighting. Henry realized that he had behaved like a demon.

Wilson and Henry, off in the woods looking for water,

overheard two officers discussing the coming battle. They said that Henry's regiment fought like mule drivers, but that they would have to be used anyway. Then one officer said that probably not many of the regiment would live through the day's fighting. Soon after the attack started, the color-bearer was killed and Henry took up the flag, with Wilson at his side. Although the regiment fought bravely, one of the commanding officers of the army said that the men had not gained the ground that they were

expected to take. The same officer had complimented Henry for his courageous fighting. Henry began to believe that he knew the measure of his own courage and endurance.

His outfit fought one more engagement with the enemy. Henry was by that time a veteran, and the fighting held less meaning for him than had the earlier battles. When it was over, he and Wilson marched away with their victorious regiment.

Critical Evaluation

The Red Badge of Courage, Stephen Crane's second novel (*Maggie: A Girl of the Streets* had appeared under a pseudonym in 1893) and his most famous work, has often been considered the first truly modern war novel. The war is the American Civil War, and the battle is presumed to be the one fought at Chancellorsville, though neither the war nor the battle is named in the novel. There is also no mention of Abraham Lincoln or the principal battle generals, Joseph Hooker (Union) and Robert E. Lee and "Stonewall" Jackson (Confederate). This is by design, as Crane was writing a different kind of war novel. He was not concerned with the causes of the war, the political and social implications of the prolonged and bloody conflict, the strategy and tactics of the commanding officers, or even the real outcome of a battle in which the combined losses were nearly thirty thousand men (including "Stonewall" Jackson, mistakenly shot in darkness by one of his own men).

From beginning to end, the short novel focuses upon one Union army volunteer. Though other characters enter the story and reappear intermittently, they are distinctly minor, and they are present primarily to show the relationship of Henry Fleming (usually called only "the youth") to one person, to a small group of soldiers, or to the complex war of which he is such an insignificant part.

Much of the story takes the readers into Henry's consciousness. They share his boyish dreams of glory, his excitement in anticipating battle action, his fear of showing fear, his cowardice and flight, his inner justification of what he has done, his wish for a wound to symbolize a courage that he has not shown (the ironic gaining of his false "red badge"), his secret knowledge of the badge's origin, his "earning" the badge as he later fights fiercely and instinctively, his joy in musing on his own bravery and valiant actions, his anger at an officer who fails to appreciate his soldiery, and his final feeling that "the great death" is, after all, not a thing to be feared so

much. Now, he tells himself, he is a man. In centering the story within the consciousness of an inexperienced youth caught in a war situation whose meaning and complexities he cannot understand, Crane anticipates Ford Madox Ford, Ernest Hemingway, and other later novelists.

Crane has been called a realist, a naturalist, an impressionist, and a symbolist. He is all of these in *The Red Badge of Courage*. Though young Stephen Crane had never seen a battle when he wrote the novel, he had read about the experience of war, talked with veterans, studied history under a Civil War general, and imagined what it would be like to be a frightened young man facing violent death amid the confusion, noise, and turmoil of a conflict that had no clear meaning to him. Intuitively, he wrote so realistically that several early reviewers concluded that only an experienced soldier could have written the book. After Crane had later seen the Greeks and Turks fighting in 1897 (he was a journalist reporting the war), he told Joseph Conrad, "My picture of war was all right! I have found it as I imagined it."

Although naturalistic passages appear in the novel, Crane portrays in Henry Fleming not a helpless ship floating on the indifferent ocean of life but a youth sometimes impelled into action by society or by instinct yet also capable of consciously willed acts. Before the first skirmish, Henry wishes that he could escape from his regiment and considers his plight: ". . . there were iron laws of tradition and law on four sides. He was in a moving box." In the second skirmish, he runs "like a rabbit." When a squirrel in the forest flees after Henry throws a pinecone at him, Henry justifies his own flight: "There was the law, he said. Nature had given him a sign." Yet he is not content to look upon himself as on the squirrel's level. He feels guilt over his cowardice. When he carries the flag in the later skirmishes, he is not a terrified chicken or rabbit or squirrel but a young man motivated by pride, by a sense of belonging to a group, and by a determination to show his courage to an officer who had scornfully called the soldiers in his group a lot of "mule drivers."

From the beginning, critics have both admired and complained about Crane's impressionistic writing and his use of imagery and symbols in *The Red Badge of Courage*. Edward Garnett in 1898 called Crane "the chief impressionist of our day" and praised his "wonderful fervour and freshness of style." Joseph Conrad (himself an impressionist) was struck by Crane's "genuine verbal felicity, welding analysis and description in a continuous fascination of individual style," and Conrad saw Henry as "the symbol of all untried men." By contrast, one American critic in 1898 described the novel as "a mere riot of words" and condemned "the violent straining after effect" and the "absurd similes." Though H. G. Wells liked the book as a whole, he commented on "those chromatic splashes that at times deafen and confuse in the *Red Badge*, those images that astonish rather than enlighten."

Yet judging by the continuing popularity of *The Red Badge of Courage*, most readers are not repelled by Crane's repeated use of color ("blue demonstration," "red eyes," "red animal—war," "red sun") or by his use of images ("dark shadows that moved like monsters," "The dragons were coming," guns that "belched and howled like brass devils guarding a gate"). Only in a few passages does Crane indulge in "arty" writing ("The guns squatted in a row like savage chiefs. They argued with abrupt violence") or drop into the pathetic fallacy ("The flag suddenly sank down as if dying. Its motion as it fell was a gesture of despair"). Usually the impressionistic phrasing is appropriate to the scene or to the emotional state of Henry Fleming at a particular moment, as when, after he has fought, he believes, heroically, the sun shines "now bright and gay in the blue, enameled sky."

A brilliant work of the imagination, *The Red Badge of Courage* will endure as what Crane had intended it to be—"a psychological portrayal of fear."

ROUGHING IT

Type of work: Record of travel
Author: Mark Twain (Samuel Langhorne Clemens, 1835-1910)
Time of work: Mid-nineteenth century
Locale: The West
First published: 1872

Twain's recollections of the still-expanding Western frontier are enlivened by the author's boisterous sense of humor. The book provides excellent eyewitness accounts of Virginia City and the Nevada mining camps, Mormonism, early San Francisco, and the Hawaiian Islands.

Principal Personages

Mark Twain, the famous author of short stories and novels. Before he became a writer, he traveled with his brother to the West and recorded his experiences.

Brigham Young, the Mormon leader, who complains about having too many wives.

Slade the Terrible, a Western desperado who is hanged by a group of vigilantes.

Hank Erickson, a correspondent of Horace Greeley who becomes convinced that Greeley has insulted him.

The Story

When Mark Twain traveled west with his brother, he had no idea that he would stay out there for any long period of time. His brother had been appointed secretary of the Nevada Territory, and Twain went along as his assistant, with no salary. Instead of the three months that he intended to stay, however, he was six years away from home.

The trip itself was exciting. There were many inconveniences, naturally, as well as danger from local Native American tribes and attacks by highwaymen, but Twain saw the country and enjoyed the adventure nevertheless. On the way, he came face to face with Slade the Terrible. Slade was foreman of the stagecoach workers, a man who would kill anyone if crossed and whose reputation ran far and wide. To Twain, however, he seemed very polite, a gentleman, and quite harmless. Yet Slade's days were numbered; the vigilantes were after him. Although he was warned, he was drunk at the time and so was unable to avoid capture. Brought to trial by a vigilante court, he was found guilty and ordered hanged. He died without having seen his wife, probably a fortunate circumstance for the vigilantes. With six-shooters blazing from under her petticoats, she had once rescued Slade from a similar situation.

Twain also met Brigham Young, the Mormon leader, who bemoaned the fact that he had so many wives, as they were jealous and argumentative. Out of curiosity, Twain also read the Mormon Bible.

Twain and two companions set out to prospect for gold in the Nevada mountains. Once they were caught in a snowstorm and seemingly doomed to die. Each of them renounced a particular vice. Twain threw away his pipe, another man his cigarettes, and the third his bottle of whiskey. Yet they did not die. At dawn, they discovered that they had been but a few yards away from an inn. Twain was then sorry that he had thrown away his pipe. He found it in the snow and sneaked behind the barn for a smoke. There he came upon one of his comrades drinking from the whiskey bottle and the other rolling a cigarette.

At first, they had no luck in their search for gold. True, they found places where there was gold, but the operations needed to extract it were too complicated and expensive. Finally, they had real luck. When they found rock that would yield millions of dollars for them, they claimed it and dreamed of spending their lives in luxury. The law specified that some work must be done on each new claim within ten days; otherwise, the claimants lost their right to the claim and anyone else could get control of it. Twain left, having confidence that his partners would work the new claim. Each thought that the other would do the work, however, and so none was done. At the end of ten days, the mine was claimed by others. Twain and his partners were relegated to a common, working existence.

He wandered from place to place, working for newspapers, being fired from them, and moving on. Eventually, he landed in San Francisco and went from there to the Hawaiian Islands, where he visited the spot on which Captain James Cook had been killed by natives. At first, the natives had treated the British explorer kindly. Cook, in turn, had made them believe that he was a god, and he had treated them brutally. One day, injured, he showed his pain. Convinced by his hurt that he was not divine, but a mortal like themselves, the natives killed him— rightly, according to Twain, for he had returned their kindness with cruelty.

Then there was Hank Erickson, the crazy stranger. Erickson had once written a letter to Horace Greeley. A widow had a son who liked turnips, and she wanted to find out if turnips sometimes grew into vines. This was the question that Erickson asked in the letter that he wrote to Greeley. Greeley replied, but the handwriting was so illegible that nothing could be made of it. In fact, every time that Erickson read the letter, it seemed different, but always meaningless. Finally he deciphered it and became convinced that Greeley had insulted him. Erickson wrote to Greeley again. The publisher had a clerk copy the letter, which turned out to be informative and not at all insulting. Twain slyly maintained that he never found out why Erickson was crazy.

Twain decided to try his luck at lecturing. At his first appearance, he was afraid that nobody would laugh at his jokes. He gave free tickets to various people and told them to laugh at the right moments. When he got to the auditorium, the seats were empty. He sat in the wings in sadness. He soon heard the noise of voices, however, and came out of his dream to find that the hall was crowded. His lecture was a great success; people even laughed when his talk was not amusing.

When he returned to San Francisco from Hawaii, Twain planned a trip to Japan. Later he abandoned the idea in order to go back home. He traveled to New York by way of Panama. So ended his Wild West and Hawaiian adventures.

Critical Evaluation

The book begins with an engrossing account, lasting several chapters, of the stage coach trip west from St. Joseph, Missouri. The obvious authenticity of the adventure makes it fascinating even to a modern reader, and in 1872 readers must have found the richness of detail and description of even more interest. The account of the life and career of the desperado Slade reads like a tall tale, yet it is told in a most convincing manner, as are most of the stories that fill the long, but never dull, book.

The Mormons gradually occupy, in the early chapters, an ever-larger place in the narrative. It is obvious that, for the author, they possessed a strange fascination. Brigham Young, the patriarch of the Mormon empire, emerges as a powerful, dynamic individual, a man of integrity and forceful personality who is able to strike the fear of God into his fellow Mormons. At the same time, the chapter dealing with the Mormon leader's problems with his many wives and children is highly amusing. Often Twain's humor is a kind of irony without comment, and all the more effective for the sly manner with which he slips it into the narrative. He uses this device frequently in the section dealing with the Mormons and Brigham Young.

The description of Nevada's capital, Carson City, places it as a rough-and-ready little community. The book is rich in detail; Twain never lost sight of the fact that his descriptions would be new and even startling to his readers. Where a less skillful writer might have merely sketched in a scene, Twain draws a complete picture, yet wastes no words. The scene of the escaped tarantulas in the bunk house at night is a masterpiece of vivid comic writing. The description of unspoiled Lake Tahoe conveys the original beauty of the place with such power that the reader seeing it a century later would feel the tragedy of the change; this is an ironic effect that Twain could not have anticipated when he wrote the book.

The continuing descriptions of prospecting for gold in Nevada, writing for different newspapers in the West, and living in San Francisco are vivid, often exciting, and frequently amusing. The latter part of the narrative, the description of the trip to Hawaii and the long journey home by way of Panama, might not be of as much interest to the more well-traveled modern reader as to Twain's contemporaries, but the account is never dull, and the people Twain meets along the way are often wildly entertaining. Twain's gift for characterization was blossoming here, in portraits such as that of Hank Erickson, and soon he would be branching out into full-fledged fiction writing. *Roughing It*, a book worth reading for its own merits, was also a learning experience for a writer preparing to compose some of the greatest books in American literature.

THE SCARLET LETTER

Type of work: Novel
Author: Nathaniel Hawthorne (1804-1864)
Type of plot: Psychological romance
Time of plot: Early days of the Massachusetts Bay Colony
Locale: Boston
First published: 1850

The Scarlet Letter is Hawthorne's masterpiece and his most profound exploration of sin, alienation, and spiritual regeneration. The novel traces the effects—social, moral, psychological, and spiritual—of Hester Prynne's adulterous relationship with the Reverend Arthur Dimmesdale on four people: the lovers themselves, their daughter Pearl, and Roger Chillingworth, Hester's husband.

Principal Characters

Hester Prynne, an attractive young woman living among the Puritans of Boston during the 1650's. She becomes a martyr because she, presumably a widow, bears a child out of wedlock; this sin results in her being jailed and then publicly exhibited on a pillory for three hours. When she is released from jail, she must wear for a lifetime a scarlet letter *A* upon her bosom. She becomes a seamstress, stitching and embroidering to earn a living for herself and for Pearl, her child. After her one act of sin, Hester behaves with uncanny rectitude in battling against bigotry, the most formidable of antagonists. Hester refuses to name the child's father, who is the Reverend Arthur Dimmesdale, her minister. She does not quail when her supposedly dead husband, Roger Chillingworth, comes from out of the forest to witness her appearance on the pillory. Moreover, without complaint or self-pity, she fights her way back to respectability and the rights of motherhood. Her situation is made more poignant (and heroic) by Dimmesdale's lack of sufficient moral courage to confess that he is Pearl's father. Hester seems to need no partner to share her guilt. Her tale ends in tragedy (as it must) when Dimmesdale dies, but the reader senses that Hester will stoutly and resolutely make her way through life.

The Reverend Arthur Dimmesdale, a minister in Boston. Emotionally he is drawn and halved by the consequences of his sin with Hester, and he is pulled apart by responsibility. His choice is between confessing and thus ruining his career or keeping silent and continuing the great good resulting from his sin-inspired sermons. Outwardly, Dimmesdale is a living man, but inwardly he is the rubble and wreckage resulting from a Puritan con-science. One night, he drags himself (along with Hester and Pearl) up to the pillory, where he feels he should have stood long ago. This confession is a sham, however, for only Roger Chillingworth, hidden in the darkness, observes the trio. Finally, at the end of his Election Day sermon, he takes Hester and Pearl by the hand, ascends the pillory, confesses publicly, and sinks down dead. When his clothing is removed, Puritans see the stigma of an *A* on the skin of his chest.

Roger Chillingworth, Hester's husband, a "physician" who is the personification of evil. Thought to have been killed in a shipwreck, he reenters Hester's life when she first stands on the pillory. Pretending to minister to the physically ailing Dimmesdale, he tries only to confirm his suspicion that the minister is Pearl's father. When Arthur and Hester, in a desperate act of hope, book passage on a ship to England, Chillingworth also signs up for the voyage, and Hester knows that she can never escape him. Although motivated by his wife's bearing another man's child, Chillingworth nevertheless seems chillingly sinister in his revenge. Conniving, sly, monomaniacal, he is more a devilish force than a man.

Pearl, Hester's elfin, unpredictable daughter. She refuses to repeat the catechism for the governor and thus risks being taken from her mother. At a meeting between Hester and Arthur in the forest, she treats the minister as a rival; when he kisses her on the brow, she rushes to a stream and washes away the unwelcome kiss.

Governor Bellingham, of the Massachusetts Bay Colony. He thinks that Hester is unfit to rear Pearl but is persuaded to allow them to remain together by the pleas of Dimmesdale.

The Reverend John Wilson, a stern divine. Early in the story, he exhorts Dimmesdale to force Hester into revealing Pearl's father.

Mistress Higgins, the bitter-tempered sister of the governor; she is simply and literally a witch.

The Story

On a summer morning in Boston, in the early days of the Massachusetts Bay Colony, a throng of curious people had gathered outside the jail in Prison Lane. They were there looking for Hester Prynne, who had been found guilty of adultery by a court of stern Puritan judges. Condemned to wear on the breast of her gown the scarlet letter, the *A* that stood for adulteress, she was to stand on the stocks before the meetinghouse, so that her shame might be a warning and a reproach to all who saw her. The crowd waited to see her ascend the scaffold with her child in her arms, and there for three hours bear her shame alone.

At last, escorted by the town beadle, the woman appeared. She moved serenely to the steps of the scaffold and stood quietly under the staring eyes that watched her public disgrace. It was whispered in the gathering that she had been spared the penalty of death or branding only through the intercession of the Reverend Arthur Dimmesdale, into whose church she had brought her scandalous sin.

While Hester stood on the scaffold, an elderly, almost deformed man appeared from the edge of the forest. When her agitation made it plain that she had recognized him, he put his finger to his lips as a sign of silence.

Hester's story was well known in the community. She was the daughter of an old family of decayed fortune, and when she was young, her family had married her to a husband who had great repute as a scholar. For some years, they had lived in Antwerp. Two years before, the husband had sent his wife alone across the ocean to the Massachusetts Bay Colony, intending to follow her as soon as he could put his affairs in order. There had been news of his departure, but his ship had never been heard of again. Hester, a young, attractive widow, had lived quietly in Boston until the time of her disgrace.

The scaffold of the pillory on which Hester stood was situated next to the balcony of the church where all the dignitaries of the colony sat to watch her humiliation. The ministers of the town called on her to name the man who with herself was equally guilty, and the most eloquent of those who exhorted her was the Reverend Arthur Dimmesdale, her pastor. Still Hester refused to name the father of her child, and she was led back to the prison after her period of public shame had ended.

On her return to prison, Hester was found to be in a state of great nervous excitement. When at last medical aid was called, a man was found who professed knowledge of medicine. His name was Roger Chillingworth, he told the jailer, and he had recently arrived in town after a year of residence among Native Americans. Chillingworth was the stranger who had appeared so suddenly from the forest while Hester stood on the scaffold that afternoon, and she knew him as her husband, the scholar. His ship had been wrecked on the coast, and he had been captive among a local tribe for many months.

He also asked Hester to name the father of her child. When she refused, he stated that he would remain in Boston to practice medicine, swearing at the same time that he would devote the rest of his life to discovering the identity of the man who had dishonored him. He commanded Hester not to betray the relationship between them, and she swore that she would keep his secret.

When Hester's term of imprisonment was over, she found a small house on the outskirts of town, far removed from other habitation. There with her child, whom she had named Pearl, she settled down to earn a living from needlework, an outcast from society and still wearing the scarlet emblem on her breast.

Hester Prynne dressed her child in bright, highly ornamented costumes, in contrast to her own sober dress. As she grew up, Pearl proved to be a capricious, wayward child who was hard to discipline. One day, Hester called on Governor Bellingham to deliver a pair of embroidered gloves. She also wanted to see him about the custody of Pearl, for there was a movement afoot among the strict church members to take the child away from her. In the garden of the governor's mansion, Hester found the governor, Dimmesdale, and old Roger Chillingworth. Because the perverse Pearl would not repeat the catechism, the governor was about to separate the child from her mother. Dimmesdale saved the situation, however, by a persuasive speech that resulted in the decision to let Hester keep Pearl, who seemed to be strangely attracted to the minister.

Roger Chillingworth had become intimately acquainted with Arthur Dimmesdale as both his parishioner and his doctor, for the minister had been in ill health ever since the physician had come to town. As the two men lodged in the same house, the physician came to know Dimmesdale's inmost thoughts and feelings. The minister was much perturbed by thoughts of conscience and guilt, but when he expressed these ideas in generalities to his congregation, the people thought him only the more righteous. Chillingworth, though, was now convinced that Dimmesdale was Pearl's father, and he conjured up for the sick man visions of agony, terror, and remorse.

One night, unable to sleep, Dimmesdale walked to the pillory where Hester Prynne had stood in ignominy. He went up the steps and stood for a long time in the same place. A little later, Hester, who had been watching at a deathbed, came by with little Pearl. The minister called them to the scaffold, saying that they had been there before when he lacked courage to stand beside them. Thus the three stood together, Dimmesdale acknowledging himself as Pearl's father and Hester's partner in sin. This striking tableau was not unobserved. Roger Chillingworth watched them from the shadows.

Hester Prynne was so shocked by Dimmesdale's feeble and unhealthy condition that she was determined to see her former husband and plead with him to free the sick minister from his evil influence.

One day, she met the old physician gathering herbs in the forest and begged him to be merciful to his victim. Chillingworth, however, was inexorable; he would not forgo his revenge on the man who had wronged him. Hester then advised him that she would tell Arthur Dimmesdale their secret and warn him against his physician. A short time later, Hester and Pearl intercepted Dimmesdale in the forest as he was returning from a missionary journey to a local tribe. Hester confessed her true relation with Chillingworth and warned the minister against the physician's evil influence. She and the clergyman decided to leave the colony together in secret, to take passage in a ship then in the harbor, and to return to the Old World. They were to leave four days later, after Dimmesdale had preached the election sermon.

Election Day, on which the new governor was to be installed, was a holiday in Boston, and the port was lively with the unaccustomed presence of sailors from the ship in the harbor. In the crowd was the captain of the vessel, with whom Hester had made arrangements for her own and Dimmesdale's passage. During the morning, the captain informed Hester that Roger Chillingworth had also arranged for passage on the ship. Filled with despair, Hester turned away and went with Pearl to listen to Dimmesdale's sermon.

Unable to find room within the church, she stood at the foot of the scaffold where at least she could hear the sound of his voice. As the procession left the church, everyone had only words of praise for the minister's inspired address. Dimmesdale walked like a man in a dream, and once he tottered and almost fell. When he saw Hester and Pearl at the foot of the scaffold, he stepped out of the procession and called them to him. Then, taking them by the hand, he climbed the steps of the pillory. Almost fainting, but with a voice terrible and majestic, the minister admitted his guilt to the watching people. With a sudden motion, he tore the ministerial band from across his breast and sank dying to the platform. When he thus exposed his breast, witnesses said that the stigma of the scarlet letter *A* was seen imprinted on the flesh above his heart.

Chillingworth, no longer able to wreak his vengeance on Dimmesdale, died within the year, bequeathing his considerable property to Pearl. For a time, Hester disappeared from the colony, but years later, she returned alone to live in her humble thatched cottage and to wear as before the scarlet emblem on her breast. The scarlet letter, which was once her badge of shame, however, became an emblem of her tender mercy and kindness—an object of veneration and reverence to those whose sorrows she alleviated by her deeds. At her death, she directed that the only inscription on her tombstone should be the letter *A*.

Critical Evaluation

Since it was first published in 1850, *The Scarlet Letter* has never been out of print, nor indeed out of favor with literary critics. Considered the best of Nathaniel Hawthorne's writings, it may also be the most typical—the strongest statement of his recurrent themes and an excellent example of his craftsmanship.

The main thematic emphasis in *The Scarlet Letter*, as in most of Hawthorne's work, is on sin and its effects upon both the individual and society. It is frequently noted that Hawthorne's preoccupation with sin springs from the Puritan-rooted culture in which he lived and from his awareness of two of his own ancestors who presided over bloody persecutions during the Salem witchcraft trials. It is difficult for readers from a more permissive era to conceive of the heavy import that seventeenth century New Englanders placed upon transgression of the moral code. As Yvor Winters had pointed out, the Puritans, believing in predestination, viewed the commission of any sin as evidence of the sinner's corruption and pre-ordained damnation. The harsh determinism and moralism of those early years, however, had softened somewhat by Hawthorne's day; furthermore, he had worked out, perhaps during the twelve years that he spent in contemplation and semi-isolation, his own notions about humanity's will and nature. Thus *The Scarlet Letter* proves him closer to Paul Tillich than to Cotton Mather or Jonathan Edwards. Like Tillich, Hawthorne saw sin not as an act but as a state—that which Existentialists refer to as alienation, and which Tillich describes as a threefold separation from God, other humans, and self. This alienation needs no fire and brimstone as consequence; it is in itself a hell.

There is a certain irony in the way in which this concept is worked out in *The Scarlet Letter*. Hester Prynne's pregnancy forces her sin to public view, and she is compelled to wear the scarlet *A* as a symbol of her adultery. Yet, although she is apparently isolated from normal association with "decent" folk, Hester, having come to terms with her sin, is inwardly reconciled to God and self. She ministers to the needy among her townspeople, reconciling herself with others until some observe that her *A* now stands for "Able." On the other hand, Arthur Dimmesdale, her secret lover, and Roger Chillingworth, her secret husband, move freely in society and even enjoy prestige: Dimmesdale as a beloved pastor, Chillingworth as a respected physician. Yet Dimmesdale's secret guilt gnaws so deeply inside him that he views himself with scorn as a hypocrite, and he is unable to make his peace with God or to feel at ease with other people. For his part, Chillingworth has permitted revenge to permeate his spirit to such an extent that his alienation is absolute; he refers to himself as a "fiend," unable to impart forgiveness or change his profoundly evil path. His is the unpardonable sin—unpardonable not because God will not pardon, but because his own nature has become so depraved that he cannot repent or accept forgiveness.

Hawthorne clearly distinguishes between sins of passion and those of principle. Finally, even Dimmesdale, traditional Puritan though he is, becomes aware of the difference:

> We are not, Hester, the worst sinners in the world. There is one worse than even the polluted priest! That old man's revenge has been blacker than my sin. He has violated, in cold blood, the sanctity of a human heart. Thou and I, Hester, never did so.

Always more concerned with the consequences than the cause of sin, Hawthorne anticipated Sigmund Freud's theories of the effects of guilt to a remarkable extent.

Hester, whose guilt is openly known, grows through her suffering into an extraordinarily compassionate and understanding woman, a complete person who is able to come to terms with life—including sin. Dimmesdale, who yearns for the relief of confession but hides his guilt to safeguard his role as pastor, is devoured internally. Again like Freud, Hawthorne recognized that spiritual turmoil may produce physical distress. Dimmesdale's well-being diminishes, and eventually he dies from no apparent cause other than continual emotional stress.

The Scarlet Letter has links with a number of Hawthorne's shorter works. Dimmesdale reminds one of the title character of "Young Goodman Brown," who, having once glimpsed the darker nature of humankind, must forevermore view humanity as corrupt and hypocritical; and of Parson Hooper in "The Minister's Black Veil," who continues to perform the duties of his calling with eloquence and com passion but is forever separated from the company of others by the veil that he wears as a symbol of secret sin. Chillingworth is essentially like the title character of "Ethan Brand," the limeburner who found the unpardonable sin in his own heart: "The sin of an intellect that triumphed over the sense of brotherhood with man and reverence for God, and sacrificed everything to its mighty claims!"

Hawthorne's craftsmanship is splendidly demonstrated in *The Scarlet Letter*. The structure is carefully unified, with three crucial scenes at the beginning, middle, and end of the action taking place on the scaffold. The scarlet *A* itself is entwined into the narrative repeatedly, as a symbol of sin or of shame, as a reminder of Hester's ability with the needle and her ableness with people, and in Dimmesdale's case, as evidence of the searing effects of secret guilt. Several times, there is forewarning or suggestion that is fulfilled later in the book: For example, notice is made that Pearl, the impish child of Hester and Dimmesdale, seems to lack complete humanity, perhaps because she has never known great sorrow. At the end of the story, when Dimmesdale dies, readers are told that "as [Pearl's] tears fell upon her father's cheek, they were the pledge that she would grow up amid human joy and sorrow, nor forever do battle with the world, but be a woman in it."

Hawthorne's skill as a symbolist is fully in evidence. As one critic has noted, there is hardly a concrete object in the book that does not do double duty as a symbol: The scarlet letter, the sunlight that eludes Hester, the scaffold of public notice, the armor in which Hester's shame and Pearl's elfishness are distorted and magnified also serve as central symbols in this greatest allegory of a master allegorist.

THE SEA-WOLF

Type of work: Novel
Author: Jack London (1876-1916)
Type of plot: Adventure romance
Time of plot: 1904
Locale: Pacific Ocean and the Bering Sea
First published: 1904

London began his career as a sailor, and onboard ship, he observed the sea life that he would later describe in his novels and stories. In The Sea-Wolf, *he tells an impossible story with such gusto and fervor that he creates a reality all his own within his limited, specialized world of violent action and masculine interests.*

Principal Characters

Humphrey Van Weyden, called **Hump,** picked up by the sealer *Ghost* after a shipwreck. He has a perilous existence until the crew kill off one another. He and Maud Brewster navigate the crippled ship back to the United States.

Wolf Larsen, called **The Sea-Wolf,** the brutal captain of the *Ghost.* He is buried at sea.

Maud Brewster, the survivor of another wreck, rescued by Wolf and protected from him by Hump.

Death Larsen, the captain of the *Macedonia*, Wolf's brother and enemy. He steals his brother's seal skins.

Johansen, the cruel mate of the *Ghost*, drowned during a mutiny.

Johnson, a sailor beaten by the officers. He tries to desert with Leach but is drowned.

Leach, the former cabin boy, who tries to kill the cook and the captain.

Mugridge, the ship's cook, to whom Hump is assigned. The cook abuses and robs him until Hump turns on him.

Louis, the only crew member friendly to Hump.

The Story

When the ship in which he was a passenger sank in a collision off the coast of California, Humphrey Van Weyden was picked up by the crew of Wolf Larsen's ship, the *Ghost*, a sailing vessel headed for seal hunting ranges in the Bering Sea. Wolf Larsen was a brute. Van Weyden witnessed the inhuman treatment of a sick mate who died shortly afterward. He saw a cabin boy badly beaten. In his own interview with the captain, he fared little better. Instead of promising to help him return to San Francisco, Wolf demanded that Van Weyden sign on as cabin boy and stay with the ship.

The crew set to work taking in the topsails and jibs. From that moment, Hump (as the crew called Van Weyden) learned life the hard way. He had to get his sea legs, and he had to learn the stoical indifference to pain and suffering that the sailors seemed to have mastered already. As cabin boy, he peeled potatoes and washed greasy pots and pans. Mugridge, the cook, abused him and robbed him of his money.

Only one man, Louis, seemed to share Hump's feelings about the captain and his ship. Louis predicted that many deaths would result from this voyage. He said that Wolf Larsen was a violent, dangerous man, that the crew and seal hunters were vicious outcasts. Wolf did seem mad. He varied from moods of wild exultation to spells of extreme depression. In his cabin were classic books of literature, and when he spoke he chose either to use excellent English or the lingo of the sailors. Sometimes he amused himself by arguing with Hump. He claimed that life was without meaning.

During a southeaster, Hump badly dislocated his knee, and Wolf unexpectedly allowed Hump to rest for three days while he talked to him about philosophy and literature. When Hump returned to the galley, the cook was whetting his knife. In return, Hump obtained a knife and began whetting it also. His actions so frightened the cowardly cook that Hump was no longer the victim of his abuse.

Louis talked of the coming season with the seals. Moreover, he hinted that trouble would come if the *Macedo-*

nia, a sealing steamer, came near. Captained by Death Larsen, the brother and enemy of Wolf, the *Macedonia* was a certain menace. As a prelude to things to come, an outbreak of fury took place aboard the *Ghost*. First, Wolf Larsen and the mate beat a sailor named Johnson to a pulp because he complained of ill treatment; then Leach, the former cabin boy, beat the cook. Later, two hunters exchanged shots, severely wounding each other, and Wolf beat them because they had crippled themselves before the hunting season began. Afterward, Wolf suffered from one of his periodic headaches. To Hump, life on board ship was a tremendous experience in human cruelty and viciousness.

A few days later, the men tried to mutiny. In the row that followed, Johansen, the mate, was drowned and Wolf was nearly killed. While Hump dressed Wolf's wounds, Wolf promoted him to mate in Johansen's place. Both Leach and Johnson would have killed Wolf in a second, but he remained too wary for them.

At the seal hunting grounds, a terrific storm cost them the lives of four men. The ship itself was beaten, its sails torn to shreds and portions of the deck swept into the sea.

When Leach and Johnson deserted in a small skiff, Wolf started out in pursuit. On the morning of the third day, an open boat was sighted. The boat contained a young woman and four men, survivors from a sinking steamer. Wolf took them aboard, planning to make sailors of the men as he had of Hump. Shortly afterward, the *Ghost* overtook Johnson and Leach. Refusing to pick them up, Wolf let them struggle to get aboard until their small craft capsized. He watched them drown without comment and then ordered the ship's course set for a return to the seal hunting grounds.

The female survivor was Maud Brewster, a rich woman and a poet, as weak physically for a woman as Hump had been for a man. Wolf resented the intimacy that sprang up at once between Maud and Hump, but he took out his resentment by deciding to give Mugridge the first bath the cook had ever been known to take.

At his orders, Mugridge was thrown into the water with a tow rope slung about his middle. First, however, the cook fled madly about the ship, causing one man to break a leg and another to be injured in a fall. Before Wolf was ready to bring Mugridge back aboard ship, a shark bit off the cook's right foot at the ankle. Dragged aboard, Mugridge in his fury tried to bite Wolf's leg, and the captain almost strangled him. Hump then bandaged the wounded man's leg. Maud looked on, nearly fainting.

The *Macedonia* appeared one day and robbed Wolf's hunters of their day's catch of seals by cutting off the line of approach to the *Ghost*. In revenge, Wolf set his men to work capturing hunters from the *Macedonia*. When the *Macedonia* gave chase, Wolf sailed his ship into a fog bank.

That night, Wolf tried to seize Maud, but Hump, awakening, ran his knife into Wolf's shoulder. At the same time, Wolf was overcome by one of his headaches, this seizure accompanied by blindness. Hump helped him to his bunk, and under cover of darkness, he and Maud made their escape in an open boat. After days of tossing, they came to a small island. Using supplies that they had taken from the *Ghost*, they set about making themselves houses and gathering food for the coming winter.

One morning, Hump saw the wreck of the *Ghost* lying offshore. Going aboard, he discovered Wolf alone, his crew having deserted him to go aboard Death Larsen's ship. Wolf seemed nearly insane, and he had only a sick man's desire to sleep. Hump stole some pistols and food, which he took to the island.

Hump, planning to repair the masts of the *Ghost*, began work on the crippled ship. That night, Wolf undid all of Hump's work and cast the masts off the vessel.

Hump and Maud began anew to refit the ship. One day, Wolf attempted to murder Hump, but during the struggle, he had one of his spasms and fainted. While he was still unconscious, they handcuffed him and shut him in the hold.

Hump and Maud then moved aboard the *Ghost*, and the work of refitting the vessel went forward. Wolf had a stroke that paralyzed the right side of his body.

Hump continued to repair the vessel. At last, it was able to sail. Wolf Larsen finally lost the use of his muscles and lay in a coma. When he died, Hump and Maud buried him at sea. By that time, they were deeply in love. When a United States revenue cutter discovered them one day, they thought that their dangerous odyssey was at an end. They were about to begin another, less perilous journey together.

Critical Evaluation

The Sea-Wolf, published in 1904, is still an exciting yarn; it can also be read as an allegory of the deepest hopes and fears of an age. The hopes were that humankind was becoming more spiritual, that its moral fiber was becoming stronger, its institutions enlightened, and its tastes elevated. The fears were that humanity's animal nature might frustrate these aspirations and that the species might slip backward into a bestial state in which violence, greed, and lust would make a shambles of civilization. Such hopes and fears were a culmination of the preoccupation with the theories of naturalist Charles Darwin (referred to by Wolf and Hump), who had shown man to be a product of evolution and a creature of nature.

Jack London was well prepared to write about this tension between humankind's upward and downward possibilities. Raised in a knockabout way in the San Francisco Bay area, he was on his own at fifteen, an oyster pirate by sixteen, and a crewman on a sealing ship at seventeen. He knew the seamy side of life. He was also an avid reader, a man capable of strong romantic attachments, and a worker for social and economic justice. He aspired to a finer life.

In *The Sea-Wolf*, Wolf Larsen represents the primitive and feral in humanity and Maud Brewster the spiritual. They stand, as Hump observes, at opposite ends of the ladder of evolution; both tug at him. Hump rejects Wolf's philosophy that life is a meaningless and brutal struggle, but he is toughened in body and mind by Wolf's harsh regimen. Maud's beauty and idealism fill Hump with love, tenderness, and chivalric courage. One may conclude that London was hopeful about humanity's future. Amoral Wolf's fierce vitality slowly ebbs. Ethereal Maud, brought at last to safety by Hump, unites with him in a chaste embrace. In this symbolic union, Hump, as a modern human, rejects the cruel and brutish, dedicating himself to what is redeeming and civilized.

THE SEVEN STOREY MOUNTAIN

Type of work: Spiritual autobiography
Author: Thomas Merton (1915-1968)
Time of work: 1915-1942
Locale: France, England, and the United States
First published: 1948

Spanning childhood and early adulthood, Merton's autobiography traces his journey from secular disillusionment to entrance into the Cistercian abbey at Gethsemani. His narrative, intertwined with commentary, suggests that every phase of life has its purpose, a vision that has encouraged a multitude of readers on their own spiritual quests.

Principal Personages

Thomas Merton, a young man who is trying to discover his purpose in life. Merton spends his early adulthood writing poetry, teaching English at a university, and helping the poor of Harlem. Throughout these activities, however, he feels a spiritual emptiness that can only be filled by the life in a monastery. Eventually, he joins a religious order at the abbey at Gethsemani and finds peace at the end of his journey.

Ruth Merton, Thomas' mother, who dies when he is six years old.

Owen Merton, his father, who dies when Thomas is sixteen.

Catherine de Hueck, the woman who runs the Friendship House, which helps poor people in Harlem. She encourages Merton to become a priest.

The Story

Thomas Merton was born January 31, 1915, in Prades in the French Pyrenees. His parents were both artists: Owen Merton, a reflective man from New Zealand, and Ruth Jenkins Merton, an American much interested in social reform and progressive education. The couple moved to Prades to stay, but, Merton says, they stayed "barely long enough for me to be born and get on my small feet" before taking him on his first long journey, setting what seemed to be a pattern of unexpected travel evident throughout Merton's life.

Early in 1916, Owen, Ruth, and young Tom moved to Flushing, Long Island, New York, to live near Ruth's parents. In 1918, a second son was born. In 1921, Ruth died, and Owen, heartsick, took his two small boys to live for a while on Cape Cod in Massachusetts, then to Bermuda. Tom spent the bulk of his time alone, drawing and exploring the seacoasts, though he did attend elementary school sporadically in Bermuda. Periodically, Owen sent the boys back for extended stays with Ruth's parents.

When Tom was ten, his father unexpectedly took him to live in France. The boy attended the Lycée de Montauban, where he found the stern discipline and required religious services disturbing. When he was thirteen, Tom was sent to live in England, under the care of local relatives. There he attended a British preparatory school, then a small but well-respected public school called Oakham, where he was an unruly student. Tom spent his summers with his grandparents in the United States.

When Tom was sixteen, his father died of a brain tumor. At first, the boy was depressed, but soon he reports that he felt a powerful sense of freedom, as if he had been "stripped of everything that impeded the movement of my own will to do as it pleased." During the next few years, Tom immersed himself in daily life, following his own tastes in literature, psychology, and social and political activity. At eighteen, he entered the University of Cambridge in England, but he soon found himself depressed and rebellious, disgusted with the school, with life, and most of all with himself. In November, 1934, on the advice of his guardian, Merton returned to his grandparents in the United States.

Once back in New York, Merton entered Columbia University, where he made a fresh start. His friends were the literary type, and he began to try to publish some of his writing. Merton so enthusiastically embraced the university life of late-night sociability and intellectual fervor that, one day, he collapsed in exhaustion. Merton later called this the occasion of his rescue. It initiated a time of intense inner searching, as well as the seemingly serendipitous discovery of a book that presented an idea of God that Merton could accept intellectually. Reading *L'Esprit de la philosophie médiévale* (1932; *The Spirit of Medieval Philosophy*, 1936), by Étienne Gilson, and other books (both Eastern and Western), Merton found his life taking a different direction—toward the search for meaning and truth.

Merton was graduated from Columbia and entered the master's program there in English. His spiritual vision was significantly influenced by extensive reading of the works of William Blake. By the summer of 1938, Merton says that he became aware that "the only way to live was to live in a world that was charged with the presence and reality of God." He read spiritual books, started attending Catholic Mass, and underwent an experience of conversion while reading about the Jesuit poet Gerard Manley Hopkins. On November 16, 1938, Merton was baptized into the Catholic church.

For about a year, Merton lived peacefully. In February, 1939, he completed his master's degree and decided to continue for his doctorate. He wrote, and spent time with close friends. Yet again Merton sensed a growing futility in his life, and he entered into a period of confusion about what his true direction should be. One morning in September, 1939, while sitting on the floor eating breakfast and listening to records after a late night with his friends, Merton says he had a strong, sweet thought that he would be a priest, a "new and profound and clear sense that this was what I really ought to do." In the spring of 1940, Merton journeyed to Cuba, and in Havana he had one of his deepest spiritual experiences. Something went off inside him like a thunderclap, he says, and he experienced God as a bright, intimate light that neutralized all lesser experiences.

Yet Merton's experiences were not always so encouraging. For example, he tells of trying to clarify his religious vocation during the years that he taught English at St. Bonaventure University in New York, from 1939 to 1941. At one point, Merton was preparing to enter a Franciscan Order when he realized that to do so would

be to deny his own active, romantic nature. Merton began to doubt his fitness to be a priest, and he found himself "once more out in the cold and naked and alone." After much turmoil, he consulted a Franciscan counselor and told the priest about his past. In return, Merton was advised against entering the Order. Merton's response was a resolve to live in the world as if he were a monk, carving for himself a unique spiritual path, and he continued his teaching at St. Bonaventure.

In the spring of 1941, Merton decided to make a one-week retreat at Gethsemani, a Trappist monastery in Kentucky that had been praised by one of his professors at Columbia, Dan Walsh. Merton's experience at Gethsemani stimulated a strong attraction to that life of penance and contemplation, yet he was afraid of being rejected from the priesthood once again. Meanwhile, Merton learned of another way in which he could serve God: working with the poor of Harlem at Friendship House, which was run by Catherine de Hueck. He made a short visit there, decided that he wanted to return permanently, and prepared to leave his teaching job at the end of the year. Yet, people still kept asking if he planned to be a priest, even de Hueck, and this was a question that Merton continued to ask himself. While sitting in a garden one day, Merton finally gained conviction. He says that he heard the bell at Gethsemani calling him in his heart, and he realized that he was free, that he "belonged to God," not to himself. Merton entered into the monastery at Gethsemani on December 10, 1941.

This partial autobiography (covering only the first half of Merton's life) concludes with Merton's entrance into the monastery. He sings euphorically of the life of solitude, extolling the virtues of penance and contemplation. In the short epilogue, Merton reemphasizes the book's main metaphor: life as a journey directed by Divine Grace. Merton tells of hearing God say to him: "I will lead you by the way that you cannot possibly understand, because I want it to be the quickest way." What Merton could not yet understand at the time that he wrote *The Seven Storey Mountain* was the extent to which his life would combine deep solitude with dynamic activity, and the degree to which his prolific written works would give inspiration to other seekers walking the diverse spiritual paths of the world.

Critical Evaluation

Merton was a man of dynamic activity, yet he was drawn to the contemplative life as a man of God. On one level, *The Seven Storey Mountain* is an engrossing narrative of Merton's efforts to resolve the seeming paradoxes of his character and to find his own personal religious identity. Merton is a powerful storyteller, and he re-creates—in great detail—his childhood and young adult years in England, France, and the United States between World War I and World War II.

The chronological autobiography is divided into three sections. Merton begins part 1 by saying that he was born a prisoner of his own selfishness, into a world that was the picture of Hell. He narrates his growing disillusionment and his realization that he is bleeding to death from wounds within him. Part 2 unveils his growing spirituality, culminating in the realization that his call to the priesthood was to answer not a question in his own mind but one that had been prepared "in the infinite depths of an eternal Providence." Before Merton can reach his goal, however, he must take a few side trips, which he tells about in part 3.

The autobiography is deceptive in its simplicity. The title, though not explained in the text, is a reference to Dante's *Purgatorio* from his *La divina commedia* (c. 1320; *The Divine Comedy*), and such critics as Victor Kramer suggest that it implies Merton's belief that, metaphorically, he has reached the stage of purgatory. From such a level, he is looking back at his previous experiences, even as he is simultaneously going beyond the perspectives that he held at that time. On one level, then, *The Seven Story Mountain* details the events of Merton's life. On a deeper level, however, the book is a revelation of Merton's conviction that God's grace is ubiquitous.

The details that he presents, as well as their juxtaposition, are very carefully chosen to this end. Merton interweaves commentary with narrative, and he structures the material so as to help readers become sensitive to the workings of God's grace in their own lives. He presents myriad seemingly unimportant details as they occur, then reveals their significance as stepping-stones on his spiritual path. Readers come to trust that Merton's life is purposeful and, by inference, that the unfolding of their own lives is not random. Merton even suggests that understanding is often best revealed in times of despair, and this pattern reoccurs repeatedly in the narrative: Merton is at first desolate after a loss, then comes to see the results as gain.

Yet, investigating the careful crafting of the autobiography, critics have uncovered discrepancies between the record of *The Seven Storey Mountain* and what Merton wrote in his ongoing journal entries. For example, Merton dramatizes a difficult decision in his autobiography— whether he should leave his teaching at St. Bonaventure to work with the poor in Harlem. Yet critics such as James Baker argue that Merton's journal at that time clearly indicates that he was already more of a monk at heart than his autobiography states, and that even as Mer-

ton was deciding against Harlem, he was already viewing that possibility from quite a distance. It has also been suggested that, in his enthusiasm, Merton idealized the physical hardships endured by the priests at Gethsemani, and Merton himself admitted this to be true in later years.

The constant, reassuring tone of *The Seven Storey Mountain* is not characteristic of Merton's later work. Though always a monk, Merton moved from spiritual solitude to more involvement with the world in the 1950's. He came to understand that the ecstasy from which he wrote when he first entered the monastery was but a step along the way in his ongoing spiritual journey. Merton told an interviewer in 1967, "Life is not as simple as it once looked in *The Seven Storey Mountain.*"

The clear-cut resolution to the autobiography, however, made Merton famous. The book was widely reviewed, and it was enthusiastically praised by the Catholic press. The reaction from secular reviewers was less effusive. One reviewer, for example, complained of what he called sermons scattered throughout the text, suggesting that people liked the book not for its rigid Catholic theology, but in spite of it. Yet, by and large, reviews were positive, and the book was a best-seller.

Merton's other works made it clear that he saw himself primarily as a writer first and a monk second. Yet, in his early days at Gethsemani, Merton was content to give up his writing if that was God's will. It is ironic that the story of his quest for solitude is what brought him to the public's attention, inspiring others on their own spiritual journeys. Merton later explained that writing "is what God has given me in order that I might give it back to Him." Critics suggest that Merton transcended the bonds of individuality in his work by giving up his ambitions as a writer. He detailed his life not for its own sake, but rather as a means to celebrate the mystery of creation as a whole, to highlight the working of God's will in even the most minute aspects of existence.

The Seven Storey Mountain is a combination of colloquial style and more formal expression. It ranges over considerable territory, and Merton suits his language variously to his materials and purposes. He skillfully weaves disparate experiences to create a whole that is greater than the sum of the parts. Underneath the narrative and the commentary, Merton is always the poet, sustained by language even as he offers it to others. The seeming vocational paradox of this writer/monk is in actuality a symbiotic relationship in which Merton's self-referential literary experiences deepened his ability to perceive the reality of life that, in turn, fostered his great power as a writer and spread his influence to seekers around the world.

THE SHORT STORIES OF JOHN CHEEVER

Type of work: Short stories
Author: John Cheever (1912-1982)
Principal published works: *The Way Some People Live*, 1943; *The Enormous Radio and Other Stories*, 1953; *The Housebreaker of Shady Hill and Other Stories*, 1958; *Some People, Places, and Things That Will Not Appear in My Next Novel*, 1961; *The Brigadier and the Golf Widow*, 1964; *The World of Apples*, 1973.

John Cheever was an important short-story writer for a number of reasons, not the least of which was his longevity. His stories appeared over the course of thirty years, a remarkable record of continuous creativity and undiminished quality. Though he won prizes and widespread popular recognition for his novels—such as *The Wapshot Chronicle* (1957), *The Wapshot Scandal* (1964), and *Falconer* (1977)—Cheever was often considered to be a story writer. There were any number of contemporary writers equally well known and distinguished for their work in the short-story form, but none who wrote stories regularly over such a span of time, a time that included portions of at least three separate literary generations. Part of his success must be considered in terms of his long-standing position as one of the stable of contract writers for *The New Yorker*, a magazine that has always encouraged the short story with high payment and the advantages of a large audience with definite expectations and conventions. Yet this fact alone cannot explain how Cheever managed to keep his gift for the short story alive and breathing while other, perhaps equally gifted writers for that magazine, though remembered and honored in short-story anthologies, were not as vigorously productive. It is entirely possible that, weighing everything, John Cheever was the finest story writer of his time to emerge from *The New Yorker*.

To place his work and to understand its development, it is necessary to understand as clearly as possible what a *New Yorker* story was during this period, for the vintage product became to a great degree the accepted model for the modern American short story. Briefly, it was the maximum exploitation of a single, dramatically presented incident while more or less strictly observing the conventional unities of time and place, designed in its condensed form to gain by a richness of implication and by depth of characterization. Plot, in the old-fashioned sense, was absent, and so were the moral dilemmas of the middle class. In setting, the stories were usually regional—the East of suburbia and New York City, the far and uncorrupted West, an updated version of the magnolia South, and foreign lands, aristocratic, and exotic. The stories reflected the general moral views of the magazine and its audience. The moral keystone was a gracious secular humanism coupled with a gentle intellectual skepticism. The virtues celebrated were all civilized virtues, sedentary, sophisticated, and rational, gently draped or camouflaged in veils of irony. The mortal sins were vulgarity without redeeming eccentricity, self-pity, stupidity, hypocrisy, bad manners, complacency, awkward excess of passion, and the absence of good health or physical beauty. In short, *The New Yorker* fiction in this period was a fiction of manners. The political orientation was generally liberal, of the noblesse oblige variety, and as a magazine of manners, the aim was always progressive. No matter how dark the present, how fraught with peril the future, or how quaint the past, the fiction and verse of *The New Yorker* was hand in hand with the plentiful advertisements, the fine cartoons, and "The Talk of the Town," a section of short interviews and observations.

Cheever's stories, within the context of *The New Yorker* milieu, were original and independent. From the beginning with *The Way Some People Live*, his short stories in the magazine exhibited some independence of form. This may have been inevitable, for already the "single event" story was widely anthologized, beginning to be taught in schools, and becoming somewhat less than chic. Cheever's originality manifested itself in subject and treatment. Though part and parcel of the credible and suburban world, stories from *The Way Some People Live* and *The Enormous Radio and Other Stories* occasionally break that orderly universe with the introduction of what used to be called "fantasy," but more accurately might be described as the introduction of some supernatural event or condition into an otherwise perfectly rational and realistic situation. In this sense, his fiction is often analogous to that of Marcel Aymé in France. Technically, the stories range rather freely and widely in time, space, and point of view. They vary even in tense, which is sometimes past, sometimes present, occasionally even future and conditional.

There is often a cheerfully direct and open use of the narrator-writer of the story in Cheever's fiction. He appears in the open like the chorus in an early Elizabethan play. As a narrator, he does his best to establish an air of intimacy and rapport with the reader, and then from time to time he reenters, stopping the action, to point out significant aspects or to make intelligent comment. Like a cultivated and slightly condescending museum guide, this narrator is bright, clever, witty, yet always somehow sympathetic to the reader, perhaps because of his slight but pleasing smile, his habit of ironic self-deprecation, and his wry, worldly-wise shrug. The teller of the tale is always exact and up to date in his references and allusions, his knowledge of the things and habits of this world; he can, when it is necessary, but never without a shared wink of misgiving, summon up a soupçon of the latest slang. The language of the stories is always a model of lucidity and decorum, free from the unrefined excess and extravagance of poetic frenzy.

Clearly, the form went against the grain of the more typical, "dramatic" pattern of *The New Yorker* story, for most of these devices work to call attention to the story not as a happening, but as an artifice. The meaning of this relative freedom of form is equally clear. Cheever wanted to say more, not only about persons, places, and things but also about what these may mean and about the subtle patterns that they make. Even in the earliest stories, for example, Cheever made frequent use of dreams. His characters dream and do so matter-of-factly. He also permits them and the narrator to digress, to reminisce, to imagine. Naturally, this approach makes for a much more inclusive kind of fiction, at once deeper and more complex than the conventional dramatic method of telling a tale. It was one of his special gifts and artistic triumphs to be able to lead his characters and his readers with ease from an apparently "realistic" situation into realms of absurdity, nightmare, and farce. Perhaps this is what one reviewer meant when he tried to describe Cheever's singular qualities. Cheever was deeply interested in character, and he gave his characters depth and dimension, providing veils and layers of experience and being, as well as all the loose ends of living, breathing human beings. Compared with most other contemporary writers, in or out of *The New Yorker*, Cheever had, as a result of his interest in and understanding of character, much more sympathy and compassion for the people he created. It was no mean feat to be a serious and experimental writer and yet at the same time to share without much questioning the standards, rules, laws, and by-laws

of a literary club as exclusive, cozy, and proud as *The New Yorker*.

Cheever's short fiction developed not in stages, in trials and renunciations, but in a fairly straight line. The stories of *The Brigadier and the Golf Widow* differ from the earliest stories only in a slightly freer form, a swifter move toward moral allegory, and a shade more impatience with the rules that he was breaking. The remarkable thing is how little he changed over such a long career. It appears that very early he staked a claim, fenced it, and ever after explored and exploited it. This created an apparent sameness about his work that might have been a disadvantage except that it was balanced against the undeniable appeal of reliability. He did not, like some great writers, hit home runs or strike out. He was marvelously consistent and on a high level. Moreover, he did not, and did not need to, offend the reader. He wrote from conviction, certainty, and a sense of contentment. The effect of his work is at once entertaining and restful. Every sane person is against suffering, pain, hypocrisy, ugliness, and sordid behavior. No one speaks out in favor of sin, and no one, no matter how reactionary, is against progress or reform, though individual definitions may vary widely and deeply and behavior may vary even more.

Cheever's fiction is, therefore, classical in orientation. (It is no wonder that he so frequently employed the great and timeless classical myths to heighten the implications of his stories.) He was a professional writer with an acceptable and decent point of view. If he had a dream, it was a dream of restoration and innocence, not a revolutionary and romantic vision. He conveyed no desire to run for public office or to be accepted as one of the unacknowledged legislators of the world. This attitude was important, for his long and distinguished career and the undeniable artistry of his short fiction gave the lie to the prevalent notion that an artist must be a rebel, an outsider, a boat-rocker to validate a claim to art. After the qualifications were weighed and sifted, John Cheever stood in the front rank, among the best of the short-story writers of his time. When all is said and done, it may be that his humane, graceful, and wistful stories will stand, if not for the best that the United States' writers have been able to achieve, then for the best hopes of its society.

THE SHORT STORIES OF STEPHEN CRANE

Type of work: Short stories
Author: Stephen Crane (1871-1900)
Principal published works: *The Little Regiment*, 1896; *The Open Boat and Other Tales of Adventure*, 1898; *The Monster and Other Stories*, 1899; *Whilomville Stories*, 1900; *Wounds in the Rain*, 1900.

For more than sixty years after Stephen Crane's death, the major problem facing students of his short fiction was access to the texts. Despite the great success, early in his career, of *The Red Badge of Courage* (1895), many of Crane's stories were never collected during his lifetime. (Many, indeed, were ephemeral, slight sketches that are essentially journalistic.) *The Work of Stephen Crane* (1925-1927), a twelve-volume compilation edited by Wilson Follett, was published in a limited edition and never widely available. Anthologies of short stories and of American literature give the impression that Crane's output consisted only of "The Open Boat" (1897), "The Blue Hotel" (1898), and "The Bride Comes to Yellow Sky" (1898). Finally, *Complete Short Stories and Sketches* (1963), edited by Thomas A. Gullason, brought all 112 short fictional pieces together in one volume. It arranges the work chronologically by date of first publication, contains an excellent introduction, and, for anyone interested in more than a superficial sampling of Crane's stories, remains an indispensable text.

Crane's stories fall into four main groups. The stories of life in the New York City slums are reminiscent of the famous novella *Maggie: A Girl of the Streets* (1893). The early war stories, consisting of scenes and revelations from the American Civil War, read like fragments omitted from *The Red Badge of Courage*; later ones draw on his experiences as a war correspondent in Greece and Turkey. The stories of adventure are best exemplified by the three famous anthology pieces. Finally, the late stories of Whilomville—Crane's fictional rendering of Port Jervis, New York, to which the Crane family moved in 1878—represent his closest approach to social realism. Crane did much newspaper work and traveled extensively during his short life. With the single exception of the Civil War stories, all of his fiction draws on scenes and events that, with his sharp reporter's eye, he had closely observed.

Observation transmuted by artistry created work that, far more than that of realists famous in Crane's day, such as Hamlin Garland and William Dean Howells, continues to speak vividly. A typical Crane story is brief; except in *The Red Badge of Courage*, he failed as a novelist. It consists not so much of a conventional plot as a series of sharply sketched episodes out of which emerges—one might better say explodes—psychological and philosophical revelation. The best stories are imbued with a pervasive irony—not merely a sarcastic tone, but an irony arising out of a profound multiplicity of vision. Thus the narrator of "The Open Boat" is at once a character concerned only with survival from moment to moment, and a writer rendering the foibles, pretensions, and ultimate helplessness of humanity. In Crane's universe, everyone is at war. Generally the enemy is human and the cause of the conflict is human blindness: the failure of observation and imagination, leading to an inability to see others as sentient beings capable of suffering. His vision is tragic, complex, at once unsentimental and compassionate, and deeply relevant.

The relevance of "The Men in the Storm" (1894) is strikingly direct, as it is a story of the homeless in the slums of New York. It gives the impression on first reading of being a simple journalistic chronicle: A large and growing group of men waits all afternoon, in a bitter snowstorm, to be admitted to a shelter for the night. The men have no names, no faces, and there is no individual protagonist; the story renders the derelict life of the whole. It works first by darkly ironic contrast, the initial description being of prosperous, well-dressed people hurrying home to dinner, their appetites whetted by weather that to them, as they can get out of it, is exhilarating. To them, as well, the homeless are invisible. A sentimentalist might conjure up a chance meeting leading to a happy ending, but Crane knows, and tells, the truth: Those with a secure economic place in society live in one world, those without in another, and there is no point of connection. The men in the crowd suffer from cold and wet; their grumbling complaints, more resigned than outraged, are heard; and their happy ending, as night falls, is being let into the shelter. That is all, and that is enough. The storm, so tellingly described, is more than just weather: It is a revelation of the frozen hearts of human beings.

"A Dark Brown Dog," published in 1901 but written about 1894, is more typical of Crane's early city fiction, and more like *Maggie* in its depiction of the lives of slum-dwellers. Crane knew in his bones what severe, prolonged economic deprivation did to people, and he never shrank from reality, however harsh. The protagonist of the story, a child of three or four, lives in a world—that of his family, a microcosm of the larger world—that is not merely violent but utterly unpredictable. Everything depends on the moods of his father, which in turn depend on how much he has had to drink. The little boy, a victim of child abuse long before the term was invented, has thus developed the survival skills—essentially, recognizing the danger signals and becoming invisible under the furniture—appropriate to life in the jungle. It is natural that, receiving no affection from his family, he would be drawn to the little brown stray. It is natural too that he would casually abuse it, since that is what he has been taught. The dog, whimsically accepted by the father, in turn develops survival skills (the parallels between child and dog are strongly drawn) that, however, ultimately are not quite sufficient. It is not even anger, but a ghastly perversion of humor—the mood of an ogre in a fairy tale—that causes the father to pitch the dog out the window. The final scene, in which the boy sits beside the body of his friend, is heartbreaking without being sentimental—it is simply true. It is the spirit of his son that the father has killed.

The ironies in "A Mystery of Heroism" (1895), among the most striking of the Civil War stories, are expressed in the two key words of the title. As in *The Red Badge of Courage*, the strategic significance of the action, if it has any, is not known to the soldiers involved and thus not specified. What matters to them as the story opens is not so much survival, as the protagonist's company is sheltered by a bank from heavy artillery fire, but the basic expectations of life in human society. Fred Collins is thirsty; the ordinary response would be to drink, but because humankind is at war, the rules are altered: The only source of water is a well across a meadow wracked by shell-fire. Though no one is close to dying of thirst, Collins at length asks and receives permission to attempt the trip. Against all odds he survives, experiencing terror and exaltation by turns; on the way back, he vainly attempts to give water to a man who is too close to death to drink it. Then when he delivers the water, two young officers, foolishly unaware of its cost, carelessly spill it. At first glance, then, Collins' exploit seems neither mysterious nor heroic. He crosses the meadow on impulse, pushed by the dares of his comrades; the psychology of the men is that of the children in the late Whilomville stories, whose behavior in snowball fights is governed, similarly, by bluster and shame. The irony of a life risked for water spilled is obvious. Yet a mysterious aura surrounds Collins' action: His one-man charge, however

foolhardy, rejects the monstrous absurdity of war and leaves him, in some unknowable way, forever changed.

"Death and the Child" (1898), a late war story set in Greece, is one of Crane's masterpieces. It opens with an unforgettable description of refugees, peasants with their household goods and animals, pouring down a mountain. Walking in the other direction—an early indication that he has no part to play in these lives—is the Greek journalist Peza, the protagonist. His response to what he sees is frantic, unthinking patriotism: He is Greek, he reiterates, and he wants to fight for his country. He falls in with a young officer who promises to lead him to the action; despite the sight of wounded men and the sound of shells passing overhead, however, he retains his innocence. The story then cuts to a child, abandoned by his parents in their panic, playing alone in the dirt outside his mountain shack. In the next scenes, Peza, left alone, continues to seek his destiny; at length, he is offered a rifle and cartridges with which to fight, if only he will remove them from the body of a dead man. Like Henry Fleming in *The Red Badge of Courage*, he runs. Yet while Henry is later redeemed by shallow conventional heroism, dense with irony, Peza's moment of truth is mysterious and profound. The abandoned child by this time is no longer playing the games that, in his imagination, had enabled him to escape. He sits on a boulder, watching the battle that has drawn nearer and suddenly, overcome by fear and strangeness, hunger and loneliness, begins to weep. It is then that Peza reaches the summit and collapses, to be confronted by a simple, calm, devastating question: "Are you a man?" The contrast between the quiet courageous dignity of the child and the blind posturing of the man brings about, for character and reader, an overwhelming initiation into the world of reality.

"The Open Boat," Crane's most famous and arguably finest story, is based on his own experience after the sinking of the *Commodore* off the coast of Florida in January, 1897. Four men in a ten-foot dinghy row up and down, cut off from land and safety by the heavy surf; after a day and a half, they make their way to shore, the boat is swamped, and one of the four is drowned. Yet a summary of the rudimentary plot says little of significance about the story. Life in the open boat teaches the correspondent (the point-of-view character—Crane himself) that humans live on the edge: Six inches of gunwale is all that separates the men from the indifferent wilderness of the sea. The captain cannot so much as shoo away a pesky sea gull for fear of swamping the boat. The correspondent, the only man awake during part of their endless night at sea, learns something of power from the awesome spectacle of a passing shark. Even when they get close enough to wave to people on the shore, they cannot make their need known: They are fundamentally set apart. The surface structure of the story is that of the journey itself, but a deeper movement lies in the rapidly altering perspectives of the men as they experience hope and fear, confidence and despair, anger, puzzlement, and love for one another in the brotherhood of the boat. In the ironic contrast between what humanity is and what it thinks it is, layer after comforting layer of illusion is stripped away. At the story's center lies not the question of who will survive, but the progressively revealed nature of human life.

The characters in "The Blue Hotel" are similarly isolated, in this case in a hotel on the Nebraska prairie during a winter storm. The guests—an Easterner, a cowboy, and a Swede, none of them named—have come to a place that is only superficially a refuge; the quarreling of the proprietor with his family and the infernal power of the stove hint that the storm is more than simply weather. It is the Swede who provides the catalyst. Unable to see the others simply as humans such as himself, he views them as characters in the violent, melodramatic pulp fiction that he has imbibed like strong drink. Thus the violence that erupts, over an accusation of cheating in a card game, is a self-fulfilling prophecy. In a scene full of animal imagery and imbued with primitive power, the Swede and the proprietor's son go out into the storm to fight; the Swede wins, goes to a bar in town, and by his aggressive boastfulness actually does get himself killed. If the story ended here, it would be naturalistic, revealing humans as helpless in the grip of their bestial emotions. A final scene between the Easterner and the cowboy, however, reveals that the Easterner knew that the proprietor's son was cheating at cards but was afraid to speak out and prevent the fight. The others were similarly culpable. Therefore, the story is a powerful tragedy: Because the characters fail to live up to their highest human potential, a man needlessly dies.

In general, the Whilomville stories, of which "His New Mittens" (1898) and "Shame" (1900) are typical, are lighter, at times even humorous, centering as they do on the tribulations of children. As in the darker and greater stories, however, the young heroes are at war, even if with snowballs rather than with bullets; the ironies underlying their illusions, and those of the adults around them, remain. In "The Monster" (1898), Crane uses the small-town setting for an extraordinary dark fable. The opening scenes delineate the daily lives of Jimmie Trescott—the son of one of the leading doctors in town, and the protagonist of several other stories—and Henry Johnson, the doctor's African-American stablehand. The precipitating event is a fire that destroys the Trescotts' house; Jimmie, trapped inside, is rescued by Henry, who takes him out through the doctor's laboratory. In the process, however, Henry is not merely burned but horribly mutilated by acid. His features burned quite away, his mind affected as well, he becomes the monster of the title. The doctor, who feels his obligations deeply and takes them seriously, assumes responsibility for Henry's care. Gradually, through a series of meticulously detailed episodes, it becomes clear that the real monster is society itself; the conventional attitudes of people who, unable to perceive Henry's shared humanity, see "monster" instead of "man." Among the adults, he becomes an object of such acute discomfort—perhaps, as he is a hero, a veiled reproach to them—that they shun the doctor for sheltering him. Among the children, Henry is a half-delectable horror that they dare one another to touch. "The Monster," almost as long as *Maggie*, is too diffuse in places to quite sustain the effects of Crane's finest stories. Nevertheless, it reveals vividly, with dark irony and moral fervor, humankind's inhumanity.

It was Stephen Crane, among the American realists popular in his day, who in his best short fiction made the great leap inward. His concern was to render not merely the surface, but the inner reality of life: what it feels like and what it means. His vision, empowered by a rare gift for the apt and compelling image, was passionately honest and fiercely moral. Whether writing about the slums of New York, the battlefields of Virginia or Greece, the plains of Nebraska, or the deceptively placid landscapes of small-town America, he looked without flinching into the abyss and wrote down what he saw.

THE SHORT STORIES OF F. SCOTT FITZGERALD

Type of work: Short stories
Author: F. Scott Fitzgerald (1896-1940)
Principal published works: *Flappers and Philosophers*, 1920; *Tales of the Jazz Age*, 1922; *All the Sad Young Men*, 1926; *Taps at Reveille*, 1935.

The writings of F. Scott Fitzgerald form a complex, multilayered biography telling the story of an era, an author, and his style. In their content and structure, they are concerned with those most elusive subjects, the human heart and its dreams, and the trajectory that the stories trace rises from wonder to sad understanding. Fitzgerald's characters remained, on the surface, much the same from the start of his relatively brief career to its end, but their inner natures grew and matured, just as the author did, and his unique, distinctive style was the medium that both recorded and evaluated those changes.

Fitzgerald exploded into his literary career as the chronicler of the "jazz age," a term that he popularized but did not, strictly speaking, invent. For too many readers, he remains defined by only that role while he was, in fact, much more. Although not an intellectual, Fitzgerald intuitively recognized that the outward and visible forms of a period, especially one as volatile as the 1920's, are reflections of the dreams and visions of the people who live within that time. On the surface, Fitzgerald often appears concerned merely with recording the social manners of his times, in particular the heady, chaotic spree of the Roaring Twenties and their lingering, decade-long morning after. On closer inspection, however, he is actually analyzing and re-creating the dreams of his characters, revealing how those dreams changed, for better or worse, from contact with reality. In this function, Fitzgerald is a moralist, and his moral vision encompasses not only the characters in his fictions but himself as a man and author as well.

These concerns are shown in his novels—especially in his concentrated, almost perfect creation, *The Great Gatsby* (1925)—but they are revealed even better, because in a briefer and more concentrated compass, in his short stories. In many ways, these stories are an ideal counterpoint to Fitzgerald's novels. Many of them were written during or close to the composition of the novels, some of the stories serving as preliminary sketches, and so approach the same themes and materials in a more distilled fashion. This relationship was recognized, perhaps unconsciously, by Fitzgerald's publishers, who released collections of his stories a year or two after the publication of the novels. Despite the seeming randomness of their composition, and while admitting the varying quality of their worth, Fitzgerald's short stories are actually an integral and valuable part of his body of work, and well worth study in their own right.

The stories deserve such attention despite the fact that they were often written primarily from commercial motives, even to pay off Fitzgerald's debts. In 1925, for example, he wrote eleven stories within a single winter, one of them during an all-night session, to escape a $5,000 burden that he had incurred from parties and riotous living. Fitzgerald could be a quick and facile writer, capable of meeting the demands of popular magazines and the expectations of the casual reader, but it would be a mistake to dismiss his stories as merely commercial fiction. He was too gifted and too serious an artist for that, and although many of the stories may have been produced too quickly and too smoothly, they all show, clearly and unmistakably, indications of Fitzgerald's painstaking craftsmanship and his enduring concerns.

Fitzgerald's key concern was how an individual responds to the demands and expectations of society—that is, other people—and how that response affects the inner, moral nature. Fitzgerald's jazz age flappers and sad young men were linked to Joseph Conrad's Marlow, who believed that each person carried "an ideal concept of one's self," that all actions are judged by how well they accord to that abstract, intangible, but totally real standard. This sense of self carried with it an autobiographical flavor, and many of Fitzgerald's stories reflect or mirror incidents from his own life, while several of his fictional creations embody his own concerns or present aspects of his own personality.

Ultimately, however, it is the literary quality of Fitzgerald's short stories which have caused them to endure, leaving a record of a particular time in American history. Fitzgerald created a body of uniquely American literature at the same time that he recorded a moment of uniquely American history.

At one point early in his career, Fitzgerald had more than one hundred rejection slips for his short stories pinned to his bedroom wall. In 1920, his first novel, *This Side of Paradise*, was published and became a best-seller. Fitzgerald, then famous, found his writing eagerly sought by some of the most popular and high-paying magazines of the day, such as *The Saturday Evening Post*. Almost overnight, Fitzgerald was launched on a career as one of the most successful short-story writers in American literary history.

While the success of *This Side of Paradise* no doubt hastened Fitzgerald's recognition as a short-story writer, the stories themselves stand on their own as solid and craftsmanlike. From the first, they were also particularly attuned to their times, as an early story, "Bernice Bobs Her Hair," illustrates. First published in *The Saturday Evening Post*, the story follows the transformation of Bernice from the dull, visiting cousin to the bright young thing about whom all the boys are crazy. This change is accomplished by the blond charmer Marjorie, with whom Bernice is staying. Marjorie teaches Bernice how to flirt, to be outrageous, and to attract attention by claiming that she will have her long, luxurious hair cut short in a bob. The ploy works all too well, and Bernice wins the attention of all the boys, including Marjorie's. Marjorie then traps Bernice in a situation in which she must have her hair bobbed, a minor but deeply felt humiliation. In revenge, Bernice cuts away her cousin's long blond braids as she sleeps.

On the surface, "Bernice Bobs Her Hair" is a quick-moving, entertaining story, its plot sufficiently familiar to fit into a magazine format, and handled by Fitzgerald with unobtrusive skill. What caused a stir at the time were the actions and attitudes of the characters, especially the "lines" that Marjorie invented for her cousin. Some readers claimed to find these shocking, but what Fitzgerald had done was not simply to invent, but to observe and report. Instead of presenting the traditional two-dimensional figures of popular literature, he was portraying the new generation of the jazz era without criticism or blame. This accuracy in reporting the social mores of his times was to be a recurring concern in Fitzgerald's writings, and few American authors have approached his acuity of vision and honesty of effort.

Social mores and conventions were, for Fitzgerald, a way of registering character traits and moral values. Bernice's actions were not merely about her short hair; they were about an individual finding the self-confidence to be herself. This discovery of the true nature of the self became an almost obsessive theme with Fitzgerald, and he repeated it in a variety of guises in his stories.

Sometimes the self was defined in terms of geography, most often the contrast between North and South, a di-chotomy that fascinated Fitzgerald in part because of his intense, tumultuous relationship with his Southern-born wife, Zelda, whom he once described as "the prettiest girl in Alabama *and* Georgia." Two of his finest stories, "The Ice Palace" and "The Last of the Belles," draw upon this sectional distinction.

The first is the more obvious of the two, relying almost totally on the cultural and social differences between North and South, while the second is a more richly textured piece, encompassing the realization of time's relentless motion and an individual's sense of personal loss. The contrast of these two stories reveals clearly the growth and deepening of Fitzgerald as a writer.

In "The Ice Palace," a Southern girl, Sally Carroll Happner, wants to leave Tarleton, Georgia, so that her life will not, in some mysterious and never defined way, become a failure. She becomes engaged to Harry Bellamy, a Northern boy, and visits him in his parents' home during the town's winter carnival. Her sense of isolation and alienation grows, and Fitzgerald gives her feelings objective reality when Sally ventures into the maze below the festival's Ice Palace only to be lost and nearly frozen in the cold darkness. When the story ends, she has returned to the South and to home, her fear of failure overcome by a sense of identity and belonging.

"The Ice Palace" has a relatively thin story that is redeemed by Fitzgerald's keen observations of his characters. The difference between Northerners and Southerners, in attitude and outlook, is deftly and confidently expressed through Fitzgerald's use of vocabulary, speech patterns, and physical descriptions. Yet, fine as it is, the story does not move beyond these surface perceptions, while "The Last of the Belles" introduces an added dimension of the human experience.

Beautiful and charming Ailie Calhoun captivates all the young officers who meet her in the small Georgia town of Tarleton, where they are training to be pilots in World War I. Andy, the narrator, is drawn to her, as is Earl Schoen, an uncouth Yankee who amuses Ailie, perhaps because he is so alien to everything that she has ever known. In the end, she rejects them all only to find herself rejected by time and the modern world, which leaves her the last of the traditional Southern belles, a memory of what was once youthful and desired. In a sense, Ailie Calhoun has become the failure that Sally Carroll Happner feared she might be.

It is this sense of personal loss, of opportunities wasted, rather than the conflict of simple regional differences, which gives "The Last of the Belles" its power and poignancy. Wistful and elegiac, the story deals strictly with past events and the lost promises that they recall but cannot recapture. Fitzgerald mournfully yet ironically underscores the point in the final scene of the story when Andy returns to Tarleton to visit Ailie; together, they wander through the deserted army camp, "in the knee-deep underbrush, looking for my youth in a clapboard or a strip of roofing or a rusty tomato can."

Even more than sectional differences, Fitzgerald was acutely conscious of social and financial gulfs. "Let me tell you about the very rich," reads one of his most famous lines. "They are different from you and me." To this difference he returned again and again, most notably in *The Great Gatsby,* but nowhere more memorably than in "The Diamond as Big as the Ritz." The story's premise is pure fantasy: A young midwesterner, John Unger, attending an exclusive Eastern school, spends the holidays with a friend, Percy Washington, only to learn that the Washingtons are literally the richest family in the world because they live on a flawless diamond as large as the Ritz-Carlton hotel. The dark side of this private wealth is that the Washingtons have made their estate a prison-fortress where intruders, including visitors such as John Unger, are held captive in a giant cage. In this strange combination of palace and prison, Unger meets and falls in love with Percy's sister Kismine, and together they flee while airplanes guided by an escaped prisoner destroy the estate, the diamond, and the Washington fortune.

The destructive power of great wealth, eluded only through the miracle of true love, is the underlying theme of the story, and the damage that wealth can do to character is a recurring Fitzgerald theme. In many of the tales, wealth is seen as inextricably connected to a loss of talent or moral stature—sometimes, Fitzgerald seems to have compounded the two. These perceptions are found most powerfully in two of his most highly wrought stories, "The Rich Boy" and "Babylon Revisited."

"The Rich Boy" is a subtle and penetrating psychological portrait, a novel in miniature that moves from one significant scene to the next in revealing that its central character, Anson Hunter, is a man without a moral core. "Most of our lives end as a compromise," Fitzgerald writes of Hunter, "it was as a compromise that his life began." Born wealthy, unable to commit himself to another human being, Hunter begins and remains an incomplete person, insulated by his wealth and the unjustified sense of his own superiority. He drifts through a series of unhappy love affairs, wrecks the one true relationship of trust and devotion that his family has, and turns increasingly to alcohol. Yet, ironically, his drinking does not hinder his rise in the superficial world of material wealth.

If, as Fitzgerald wrote, the very rich are "different from you and me," then one crucial difference is that they rely upon others to provide moral and emotional reassurance. Anson Hunter is afraid or unable to invest his emotional capital in another human being, demanding instead that his lovers provide him with the underwriting of his own reality: "I don't think he was ever happy unless some one was in love with him, responding to him like filings to a magnet, helping him to explain himself, promising him something."

The waste of life and promise through wealth was something that Fitzgerald understood both intuitively and through experience. The dissipation of talent through drunken dreams was something he feared that he had lived too frequently. Nowhere is this displayed to more harrowing effect than in "Babylon Revisited." In this story, a reformed alcoholic, Charlie Wales, tries to regain his young daughter and start life anew, but his efforts are destroyed by his past. Wales, who lived through most of the 1920's in an alcoholic mist in Paris, is a widower; he may have caused the death of his wife when, during a drunken rage, he locked her out of their apartment in a snowstorm. Now older, wiser, and sober, he has come to visit his sister-in-law and win custody of his daughter. Just when it seems that he has the suspicious woman convinced of his newfound maturity, old drinking companions appear, ruining his plans and hopes. Rather than relapsing into drink, however, Wales maintains his sobriety, determined to regain his daughter and his sense of self.

This sense of self returns Fitzgerald to the earlier story "Bernice Bobs Her Hair" and emphasizes the way in which themes and concerns intertwine throughout his work. Yet, "Babylon Revisited" is far removed from the earlier story in maturity of plot, style, characters, and vision. Fitzgerald was a writer whose central concern was to tell the story of his particular time as honestly and carefully as he could. He was a consummate craftsman and, perhaps not incidentally, an enormously popular writer who captured the attention and admiration of his readers. The difference between the two stories is found not in a change of Fitzgerald's interest but in the growth and development of his abilities as a writer and in a corresponding expansion of wisdom, tempered by the acceptance of inevitable loss, in himself as a human being. It was this combination and this growth that produced some of American literature's most distinguished achievements in the short story.

THE SHORT STORIES OF NATHANIEL HAWTHORNE

Type of work: Short stories
Author: Nathaniel Hawthorne (1804-1864)
Principal published works: *Twice-Told Tales*, 1837; *Mosses from an Old Manse*, 1846; *The Snow-Image and Other Twice-Told Tales*, 1851.

People have told each other stories since prehistoric times; however, it was not until the nineteenth century that the short story began to be recognized as a distinct literary form. The modern short story is essentially an American creation, and it is the one literary form above all others in which American authors have distinguished themselves.

Two landmark events in the history of the short story were the publication of *Twice-Told Tales* in 1837 and Edgar Allan Poe's review of Nathaniel Hawthorne's book in *Graham's Magazine* in May, 1842. A brief excerpt from that famous review is worth quoting:

> A skillful artist has constructed a tale. He has not fashioned his thoughts to accommodate his incidents, but having deliberately conceived a certain *single effect* to be wrought, he then invents such incidents, he then combines such events, and discusses them in such tone as may best serve him in establishing this preconceived effect. If his very first sentence tend not to the outbringing of this effect, then in his very first step has he committed a blunder. In the whole composition there should be no word written of which the tendency, direct or indirect, is not to the one pre-established design.

Poe also pointed out that many of the selections included in *Twice-Told Tales* were not really tales or stories at all but were actually essays. He identified many of the pieces that are essays masquerading as tales, including "Sights from a Steeple," "Sunday at Home," "Little Annie's Ramble," "A Rill from the Town-Pump," "The Toll-Gatherer's Day," "The Haunted Mind," "The Sister Years," "Snow-Flakes," "Night Sketches," and "Foot-Prints on the Sea-Shore." Poe was perfectly right, and his criticism illustrates the ambiguous condition of the short story or "tale" in the mid-nineteenth century. Either these pieces were not dramatic, were not narratives of events, or were not intended to produce a single effect. Such essays are often called "mood pieces" by modern editors.

Hawthorne's essays or mood pieces in *Twice-Told Tales* and *Mosses from an Old Manse* are well worth reading for a number of reasons. They help the reader to analyze Hawthorne the writer, to understand the literary tastes and popular psychology of his day, and to appreciate the distinctive difference between a short story and a merely descriptive essay. The best-known and most frequently anthologized of these pieces is "The Old Manse," published in a collection entitled *Mosses from an Old Manse.* In that personal essay, Hawthorne describes his home life and provides thumbnail descriptions of some of his distinguished neighbors in Concord, Massachusetts, including the trancendentalists Ralph Waldo Emerson and Henry David Thoreau.

Hawthorne's *Twice-Told Tales* did contain, however, a number of entries that are perfect prototypes of the modern short story. It was these selections that inspired Poe to come up with the definition of the short story that is generally accepted by fiction writers around the world. Thanks largely to Poe and Hawthorne, modern short-story writers generally agree that a short story is a dramatic narrative intended to be read at a single sitting and designed to produce a single effect.

For the student of literature, one of the best ways to approach any short story is by starting at the end and asking, "Does this story produce a single effect, and if it does, what is that effect?" The single effect may be achieved either by a striking climax or by the creation of a mood that permeates the entire piece. Hawthorne's "Wakefield" is an example of a story that creates its effect through an overall mood. Hawthorne deliberately prepares the reader not to expect a shocking or striking ending; he actually tells the whole plot in capsule form in the opening paragraph.

> In some old magazine or newspaper, I recollect a story, told as truth, of a man—let us call him Wakefield—who absented himself for a long time from his wife. . . . The man, under pretence of going a journey, took lodgings in the next street to his own house, and there, unheard of by his wife or friends, and without the shadow of a reason for such self-banishment, dwelt upwards of twenty years. During that period, he beheld his home every day, and frequently the forlorn Mrs. Wakefield. And after so great a gap in his matrimonial felicity—when his death was reckoned certain, his estate settled, his name dismissed from memory, and his wife, long, long ago, resigned to her autumnal widowhood—he entered the door

one evening, quietly, as from a day's absence, and became a loving spouse till death.

Hawthorne gives his whole story away and yet creates a single effect that some readers may remember all of their lives. A single effect in a short story is not necessarily or usually a simple effect. In the case of "Wakefield," it is a complex effect compounded of pity for human folly and terror at the realization of how uncertain a hold one has on one's place in society and even perhaps on one's own personal identities.

Hawthorne, like his great contemporary Poe, was interested in the dark side of human nature. Many of his stories deal with human traits that are normally concealed behind civilized masks. In "Wakefield," there are overtones of insanity, sadism, and sexual perversity. These became common enough themes in stories, novels, plays, and motion pictures in the twentieth century but were shockingly original in Hawthorne's time. The majority of British and American writers believed that it was their duty to be morally uplifting, to promote what the distinguished English critic Matthew Arnold called "sweetness and light."

"Young Goodman Brown" is an excellent example of a story utilizing one of Hawthorne's favorite themes: the repressed or concealed wickedness of humankind. Henry James once said that what appealed most to Hawthorne's imagination was "the old secret of mankind in general . . . the secret that we are really not by any means so good as a well-regulated society requires us to appear." "Young Goodman Brown" is also a good example of a story that obtains its single effect through its surprising ending. The hero, Goodman Brown, leaves his wife on the pretense of going on a business trip (like Wakefield) but plans to attend a devil-worshiping orgy in the forest; he is astonished to discover that his sweet, innocent young wife is one of the devil-worshipers.

"The Minister's Black Veil" also deals with the theme of humankind's hidden wickedness; however, this story is an example of a single effect that is produced by overall mood. The ending has no shock value but is only a fitting culmination to a gloomy story. A minister decides to hide his face behind a veil, creating consternation among his parishioners and distressing his fiancée to such a degree that she breaks off their engagement. The minister never explains why he wears his black veil. Hawthorne creates a very strange effect with this story: He makes it appear that every character in the story is wearing a metaphorical veil and that the minister is exposing their hypocrisy by wearing a real one.

"The Minister's Black Veil" is very similar in theme to that of Hawthorne's novel *The Scarlet Letter* (1850). In that masterpiece, a young woman who bears a child out of wedlock is forced to wear the letter *A* (for adulteress) embroidered on her dress. The reader comes to realize, however, that every citizen of the town, including the feckless minister who fathered her illegitimate child, should be wearing their own letters branding them for their secret sins.

Stories such as "The Minister's Black Veil" helped to give Hawthorne the reputation of being a gloomy, moralistic, puritanical writer, but such was not actually the case. Like Poe, Hawthorne was fascinated with the dark side of human nature and thought that it was a writer's duty to expose this dark side simply because it was there. Hawthorne took the same kind of delight in such subject matter as modern readers take in reading murder mysteries and the horror tales of authors such as Stephen King.

Both Hawthorne and Poe were fascinated with the scientific discoveries of their day. Poe was enthusiastic about scientific progress and wrote some of the earliest science-fiction stories, while Hawthorne mistrusted unrestricted scientific investigation. He could see that science was undermining the authority of the Bible by showing that there was no heaven beyond the stars and no hell below the earth and proving that the cosmos was older by several billion years than the time frame suggested by Genesis. Hawthorne's interest in science was directly related to his interest in sin. Had not Adam and Eve's original sin of eating the forbidden fruit been a kind of scientific experiment? Hawthorne wondered whether there was something inherently sinful about scientific inquiry.

"Dr. Heidegger's Experiment" was one of Hawthorne's first stories dealing with science. The elderly Dr. Heidegger invites three old friends to drink water obtained from the legendary fountain of youth, famous in history as the object of the Spanish conquistador Juan Ponce de León's exploration of Florida in the early years of the sixteenth century. The three elderly subjects, two men and a woman, drink the water and quickly regain the beauty and vitality of their youths. The woman becomes flirtatious, and the two men, inflamed by her charms, become quarrelsome. In their passionate youthful exertions, they knock over the decanter, and the rest of the irreplaceable water is spilled on the floor. This nearly perfect short story, whose single effect is achieved by the surprising climax, leaves the reader with the rueful reflection that "youth is wasted on the young." Implicit in the story is the thesis that humans should not tamper with nature.

"The Birthmark" is another story dealing with the dangers of unbridled intellectual inquiry. The young protagonist has a beautiful wife but is troubled by a tiny birthmark on her cheek and wishes to use his scientific expertise to remove it. The adoring wife unquestioningly drinks the chemical potion that he offers her and eventually dies.

"Rappaccini's Daughter" is Hawthorne's most virulent attack on science. A young man meets a beautiful young woman and falls in love with her, only to discover that she has been turned into a monster by her mad father's scientific experiments. Dr. Rappaccini has been feeding poisons to his daughter all of her life. His intentions are somewhat ambiguous; it would seem that he has been trying to make her immortal but has succeeded only in giving her the power to kill any living creature that she touches.

Not all of Hawthorne's short stories were masterpieces. Hawthorne had a strong tendency to write edifying allegories. His favorite book was John Bunyan's *The Pilgrim's Progress* (1678-1684), which is nothing but a long allegory. Hawthorne is referring to himself when he says of M. de l'Aubépine (*aubépine* is the French word for "hawthorn"), the fictitious author of "Rappaccini's Daughter," "His writings . . . might have won him greater reputation but for an inveterate love of allegory, which is apt to invest his plots and characters with the aspect of scenery and people in the clouds, and to steal away the human warmth out of his conceptions."

Whenever an author's moral or lesson to readers is too conspicuous, the spell is easily broken or never achieved at all; readers fail to become absorbed in the dramatic incidents because they are too conscious of the "meaning," the allegorical references. Such is the case in a story such as "The Artist of the Beautiful," in which the young watchmaker represents all artists, his beloved represents his highest spiritual ideal, her father represents the philistine public, and the blacksmith represents the type of aggressive, unreflective person who is successful in real life.

Just as Hawthorne wrote many essays that he presented as tales, he also wrote many tales that threatened to become essays because they were too heavily laden with allegorical significance. These include such tales as "Ethan Brand," "The Christmas Banquet," and "The Celestial Railroad." All of Hawthorne's works however, are worth reading because of his artistic genius and the exquisite care that he put into every sentence that he wrote.

Hawthorne's stories tend to be slow-moving because they were written for an age in which there were no telephones, radios, television sets, automobiles, or airplanes. He was an avid admirer of Sir Walter Scott, and his fiction is dated, as far as modern readers are concerned, by the same kind of inflated dialogue found in Scott's historical novels. In "Rappaccini's Daughter," Beatrice cries "It is my father's fatal science! No, no, Giovanni; it was not I! Never, never! I dreamed only to love thee, and be with thee a little time, and so to let thee pass away, leaving but thine image in mine heart." Hawthorne's stories tend to contain minute descriptions of nature, of people, and of human habitations. This was partly because of the primitive state of photography and of printing in the nineteenth century. People were not saturated with images as they are today, and they enjoyed the word-pictures provided by gifted authors such as Hawthorne.

Modern readers, who frequently wish not so much to read Hawthorne as to have read him, will miss what is best in the stories unless they force themselves to slow down and savor what is best in this great author's works. Here is a sample from "The Haunted Mind": "Seen through the clear portion of the glass, where the silvery mountain peaks of the frost scenery do not ascend, the most conspicuous object is the steeple; the white spire of which directs you to the wintry lustre of the firmament." The modern reader, in trying to pass quickly through this sensitive, tranquil mood piece will certainly fail to appreciate the image of the warm interior of the bedroom fogging the window and creating rounded silver shapes that resemble mountains. There is no point in reading Hawthorne unless one is willing to read at Hawthorne's pace.

There have been many developments in short-story technique since Hawthorne's time, but no more perfect stories have been created in terms of producing a powerful single effect that encapsulates a profound psychological meaning in an intriguing dramatic narrative.

THE SHORT STORIES OF ERNEST HEMINGWAY

Type of work: Short stories
Author: Ernest Hemingway (1899-1961)
Principal published works: *Three Stories and Ten Poems*, 1923; *In Our Time*, 1924; *Men Without Women*, 1927; *Winner Take Nothing*, 1933; *The Fifth Column and the First Forty-nine Stories*, 1938; *The Snows of Kilimanjaro and Other Stories*, 1961; *The Nick Adams Stories*, 1972.

Ernest Hemingway, who ranks with William Faulkner as an indisputable giant of twentieth century American fiction, wrote more than fifty short stories. Together they constitute probably the greatest, certainly the most widely known and influential, work in this genre during this period. A dozen or so of Hemingway's stories, including "The Snows of Kilimanjaro," "The Short Happy Life of Francis Macomber," "In Another Country," "A Way You'll Never Be," "The Killers," "A Clean, Well-Lighted Place," and "Big Two-Hearted River," seem unsurpassable. Perhaps most at home in this form, which in his case constitutes an unusually large portion of a major writer's work, Hemingway used it for artistic purposes and achievements of the highest order.

Hemingway's first short-story publication of note was *In Our Time*, a collection containing fourteen stories bounded and interspersed by brief interchapters on violence coldly observed at bullfights, in World War I, and especially in the Greco-Turkish War, which Hemingway had recently viewed as a war correspondent. Eight of the stories have for their protagonist Nick Adams—a character Hemingway employed frequently, not only here but also in numerous later stories—and are arranged chronologically, tracing Nick's development from childhood to maturity. Because stories about Nick begin and end the collection, and because the other six stories are placed so that the events in them correspond temporally to stages in Nick's growth, *In Our Time* has a narrative unity similar to that of an episodic novel. As a quasi-novel, the book belongs in a category with James Joyce's *Dubliners* (1914) and Sherwood Anderson's *Winesburg, Ohio* (1919). It belongs there not only because of its narrative organization but also because, like them, it is thematically unified around a concern with what Joyce called paralysis, the spiritual plight of modern humanity. Where Joyce and Anderson chose a specific geographical place, however, Hemingway more ambitiously chose "our time," a vague but readily available temporal location, as the setting for that theme.

Though collected again in multiples of fourteen in *Men Without Women* (1927) and *Winner Take Nothing* (1933), and then finally gathered in a largely complete edition in

The Fifth Column and the First Forty-nine Stories (1938), a collection containing the first three collections plus seven other stories, Hemingway's stories after *In Our Time* are not bound together chronologically and narratively. Yet thematically and stylistically they are, as collections or separate stories, continuations of *In Our Time*. All of his stories—indeed his entire work, nonfiction as well as long and short fiction—are confined to a narrow range that is surveyed repeatedly and thoroughly. That narrowness is evident everywhere in his work, and so in his subject, which Hemingway defined in the introduction to *Men at War* (1942), a collection of war stories and accounts that he edited, where he wrote:

> When you go to war as a boy you have a great illusion of immortality. Other people get killed; not you. It can happen to other people; but not to you. Then when you are badly wounded the first time you lose that illusion and you know it can happen to you. After being severely wounded two weeks before my nineteenth birthday I had a bad time until I figured it out that nothing could happen to me that had not happened to all men before me. Whatever I had to do men had always done. If they had done it then I could do it too and the best thing was not to worry about it.

The wound, that affliction through which humans become aware of their mortality, of their finite limitations, is the definitive encounter with reality upon which all of Hemingway's short stories, and other fiction as well, are closely focused.

In Our Time initiates Hemingway's inquiry into this authentic and authenticating moment. In the first story, "Indian Camp," Nick is present when his father, a doctor, performs a crude cesarean section on a Native American woman who has suffered long, agonizing labor pains. Nick, unable to watch the operation after his first curiosity has passed, rejects its relevance for himself, and instead, after the delivery, while crossing a lake in which he trails his hand, feels sure that he himself will never die. Because *In Our Time* is about love, not war, Nick's war wound is briefly and dryly treated in an interchapter. The more important wounds for him and in the book as a whole are the wounds of love, the pain of its effects and loss. Nick is subjected to the consequences to which love leads for the Native American husband, who, finding his wife's suffering intolerable, cuts his own throat; for Ad Francis, who goes insane when public pressure forces his wife to leave him; and for himself in his own disillusioning affairs with Marge in "An End of Something" and Luz in "A Very Short Story." Nevertheless, Nick marries and gets his wife pregnant. When George, a friend with whom he is skiing in "Cross Country Snow," remarks on the hardship of life in general, Nick says it is not exactly that, though he cannot explain why; he only confesses that that is the way it is. In the last story of the collection, "Big Two-Hearted River," Nick moves through and beyond the burnt-out land to the river, completing a cycle wherein he progresses from innocence through experience via his wounds to self-renewal, from timelessness into time and morality and back to timelessness again. Somewhat paradoxically, in the end he chooses the high ground over the dark, tragic water of the swamp, but in doing so he rejects death—the impersonal, self-obliterating power in the universe. His war and love wounds have thrown him radically back upon himself, defining his conditions as an individual human being, and he accepts those as necessary and even good. His bad times over, he has chosen to live within his human limitations and so has stopped worrying. Like a good soldier, he has learned to hold his imagination at bay and live completely in the present.

In later stories, Hemingway expands upon and clarifies phases in this cycle centering around the wound, with death moving into the foreground and love, when present, into the background. Innocence occurs in its purest form on one later occasion in "The Snows of Kilimanjaro," in which the protagonist's wife, sentimental and preferring illusion to reality like so many women in Hemingway's fiction, fails to recognize the reality of death when her husband dies; and in "The Short Happy Life of Francis Macomber," in which the hero learns not to worry when he assumes his manhood by a sudden act that liberates him from the fear of death. Yet Hemingway's imagination after *In Our Time* is absorbed with the effects resulting from a poignant consciousness of death or a wound received in war. Examples of the former are "A Day's Wait," in which a nine-year-old boy mistakenly waits all day to die, then has a rough time when he realizes that he will live; or "A Clean, Well-Lighted Place, in which an old man and a lonely waiter experience nothingness, the ultimate truth revealed by the wound about a world of death. "A Way You'll Never Be," which elaborates upon Nick's wounding related in an interchapter of *In Our Time*, and *In*

Another Country are Hemingway's subtlest accounts of Nick's bad time resulting from his wound, which spreads its poison throughout his consciousness and destroys all of his illusions—not only those of love and immortality but those of invulnerability, heroism, patriotism, comradeship, security, technology, and rehabilitation as well. The wound eventually strips away all grounds for certainty or hope and bares the reality of inexorable time and change.

"A writer's job," Hemingway repeatedly insisted, "is to write simple true sentences, to tell the truth so purely that it would be truer than anything factual, an absolute truth." This aspiration, inherited from realism and disciplined by his training as a journalist, impelled him to report on the sorrowful loss that lies at the heart of love and death, with precision, economy, and clarity. He sought, above all, like Harold Krebs in "Soldier's Home" of *In Our Time*, to avoid the "nausea" that comes from untruth or exaggeration. He realized that this feeling depended upon his never lying, not to others but most important not to himself, about his own inner fears. The complete truth about himself, about his predicament as a human being, must be faced honestly and without cowardice. His aesthetic aim, the moral and literary values to which he severely committed himself, and his tough and realistic acknowledgement of humanity's deficiencies—coupled with a sane skepticism recognizing both the powers and limits of human intelligence and a sense that the highest, distinctive human enjoyment comes from understanding—makes Hemingway one of the twentieth century's greatest "scientific" writers.

Writing from the heart of his being, which throbbed in unison with the vital currents of Western culture, Hemingway founded his art upon a thoroughly integrated sense of life, so that despite his apparent mannerisms, he has been and remains inimitable. At a time when realism, committed to the dominion of the senses, matter, and environment, held the literary throne, and romanticism, the former royalty, was challenging realism for the renewed supremacy of a passionate consummation with a self-transcendent ideal, Hemingway created the classical short story. A younger contemporary and friend of such foremost modernists as Ezra Pound, James Joyce, and Pablo Picasso, Hemingway learned his intellectualism and classicism from them but then went even further than they toward realizing them. Where their intellectualism and classicism tended to show itself somewhat gaudily in book learning, his was marked by an association of sensibility so subtle as to be seamless. His apparent antiintellectualism actually signifies a completely successful pragmatic interfusion of thought into experience or consciousness. His short stories—unlike realistic ones, which are oppressive with their emphasis on the overwhelming details of the sensory world, and romantic ones, which sob their cries of bitter, futile melancholy born of frustration—exemplify the active mind in quest of essences being nourished by its power to know and abide by the truth. Avoiding the tragic and extremes, the unconscious and romantically ideal, Hemingway wrote stories by and for rational creatures who care about feeling cool and clear inside themselves, who care about a clean, well-lighted place for thought and action within the necessary human limitations. As long as anyone cares for these, the greatness and cogency of Hemingway's short stories will remain undiminished.

THE SHORT STORIES OF O. HENRY

Type of work: Short stories
Author: O. Henry (William Sydney Porter, 1862-1910)
Principal published works: *Cabbages and Kings,* 1904; *The Four Million,* 1906; *Heart of the West,* 1907; *The Trimmed Lamp,* 1907; *The Gentle Grafter,* 1908; *The Voice of the City,* 1908; *Options,* 1909; *Roads of Destiny,* 1909; *Strictly Business,* 1910; *Whirligigs,* 1910; *Sixes and Sevens,* 1911; *Rolling Stones,* 1912; *Waifs and Strays,* 1917.

The once-inflated fame of O. Henry is no more. Today he is not only belittled by most critics of the short story but also practically ignored by writers on American literature in general. Yet his work continues to be widely read. The ingredients that appeal most in the typical O. Henry short story are usually a blend of humor and sentiment or sentimentality. There is no depth of characterization; O. Henry specialized in easily recognizable types. The story is neatly put together and moves rapidly. The style is breezy and slangy. Though the vocabulary may include a number of words unfamiliar to the reader of newspapers and pulp magazines (in which most of O. Henry's stories first appeared), there is enough of the American vernacular to sustain the story on a colloquial level. The unwary reader, in fact, may overlook the many humorous paraphrases from William Shakespeare and other famous authors. The story characters belong either to the great American middle class or to a less exalted level of society. The author is obviously the friend of the "little people" and the enemy of those who would exploit them. There is a plentiful display of local color, especially in the many stories of New York life. In addition, there is a trick or surprise ending, often totally unexpected and illogical, but usually light and amusing. Though the surprise ending may be sentimental or even pathetic, it is never really tragic.

O. Henry has been compared to several of his predecessors and contemporaries from whom he may have learned something about story writing, among them Bret Harte, Guy de Maupassant, Mark Twain, and Frank R. Stockton. Many of the early stories are filled with the easy sentimentality of Harte, as well as his "editorial" remarks about his characters. Maupassant's irony is often imitated, but the master's mordancy is missing, as well as his prevailingly serious view of life. O. Henry uses slang even more than Twain did, but where Twain's is integral, O. Henry's is gratuitous and frequently spoils what might have been some of his best effects. O. Henry is often credited with having introduced the trick ending into the short story, but Stockton had already gained popularity with this type of ending several years before O. Henry's first story was published. Stockton's most famous story—"The Lady or the Tiger?"—did not even have a trick ending; it had none at all, readers being left to supply one for themselves. The reader's-choice ending of O. Henry's "Thimble, Thimble" is reminiscent of Stockton, who is specifically named as a model at the beginning of the story.

These facts show that O. Henry was not so much an originator as a clever practitioner. Far more a craftsperson than an artist, he was a close observer of the surfaces of life and character. In spite of his exaggerations and whimsicality, he remains an effective local colorist in his presentation of life in Bagdad-on-the-Subway, as he called New York, in the first decade of the twentieth century. To read his stories of the metropolis is to enter in imagination a bygone era of gaslights, horse-drawn taxicabs, and rococo decor that was the delight of the rich and the envious dream of shopgirls and ill-paid clerks or sweatshop workers.

Reading "The Furnished Room" in *The Four Million* (1906), one senses how it would feel to be lonely in a gaslit furnished room filled with battered furniture and the scattered, forgotten mementos of former lodgers. One hears the distant, disquieting noises from other rooms and breathes the familiar odors of the dilapidated lodging house. In O. Henry's stories of the metropolis, one joins the strollers in Central Park or on Fifth Avenue, listens to tales told by drinkers in unobtrusive bars, inhales the garlic-rich atmosphere of a small Italian restaurant, or dines on lobster at fabulous Delmonico's.

Among the most famous of O. Henry's New York stories are "The Gift of the Magi," which, though somewhat hackneyed by many reprintings and a filmed version, retains its sentimental appeal; "The Cop and the Anthem," in which Soapy, after vainly trying to get himself jailed for the cold winter, hears church music and vows to reform, only to end with a three-month sentence for vagrancy; "The Romance of a Busy Broker," with the unbelievable revelation at the end that Harvey Maxwell has erred in proposing to his stenographer, because he has forgotten that he married her the evening before; and "The Last Leaf," with its sentimental close that ironically counterbalances the saving of a young girl's life with the death of the kindly old artist who saved it.

Because O. Henry attained his fame while living in New York and because it is the scene of many of his stories, modern readers may forget that the author, like so many of the city dwellers about whom he wrote, was not a native. Born in North Carolina, he grew to adulthood there. He lived for several years in Texas, and he stayed in Honduras for some months after having fled the United States to escape arrest for misappropriating funds from an Austin bank. His life in the South, the Southwest, and Central America provided the backgrounds for numerous stories.

The more than twenty stories set in the Southern states or employing distinctly Southern characters include several of his best. "A Municipal Report" is an excellent story of Nashville, Tennessee, written to answer an offhand comment by the novelist Frank Norris that Nashville was not a "story" city. The despicable Major Caswell of "A Municipal Report" is one of O. Henry's most vividly drawn characters, but he is matched by the very different Major Talbot of "The Duplicity of Hargraves," who romantically personifies the antebellum aristocrats of the columned mansions and great cotton plantations in the storied Old South. The faithfulness of some freed slaves to their former masters is shown in the devotion of Uncle Caesar to Mrs. Caswell in "A Municipal Report" and the solicitude of Uncle Bushrod for the honor of the Weymouth family in "The Guardian of the Accolade." Other Southern stories are "The Whirligig of Life" (Tennessee), "The Rose of Dixie" (Georgia), "Cherchez la Femme" (New Orleans), "A Blackjack Bargainer" (North Carolina), and perhaps the funniest of O. Henry's stories, "The Ransom of Red Chief" (Alabama).

O. Henry's Texas years furnished him with both characters and atmosphere, which he used for narrative purposes in *Heart of the West* (1907) and in scattered stories in other volumes. The leading character of "The Reformation of Calliope" delights in shooting rampages when drunk, like many a villain in Western films. The Cisco Kid of "The Caballero's Way" is said to have been modeled after the notorious Texan killer John Wesley Hardin. "The Passing of Black Eagle" is the story of another Texan desperado. "The Pimienta Pancakes" and "The Hiding of Black Bill" utilize O. Henry's knowledge of ranch life. It should be added, however, that the ludicrously polysyllabic language used by some of the characters in these Texas stories bears little relation to that ever used by any rancher or cowboy, O. Henry included.

For the loosely related series of stories in his first volume, *Cabbages and Kings* (1904), and a few later stories, O. Henry drew upon his stay in Honduras and possibly upon tales that he heard from the train robber Al Jennings and other friends he met there. Though some of these stories have comic-opera overtones, they probably reveal the same closely observed details of actual life that were later to appear in the New York stories.

O. Henry's life was marked by many vicissitudes, but he retained almost to the end a zest for living and a genuine love of people. Because of this fact, and because his writing so frequently shows a humorous virtuosity of language and a facile playing upon the emotions of the readers, O. Henry's fiction seems likely to survive, even without benefit of criticism, for many years to come.

THE SHORT STORIES OF HENRY JAMES

Type of work: Short stories
Author: Henry James (1843-1916)
Principal published works: *An International Episode*, 1878-1879; *The Aspern Papers*, 1888; *The Lesson of the Master*, 1892; *The Better Sort*, 1903; *The Novels and Tales of Henry James*, 1907-1909; *The Complete Tales of Henry James*, 1962-1965.

In a 1919 retrospective article on Henry James for *The New Statesman*, British critic Philip Guedalla divided the writer's work into three metaphorical reigns, those of James I, James II, and the Old Pretender. Later critics, specifically those writing about the Jamesian novels, have agreed with Guedalla's division of the author's style into three distinct periods, the early, middle, and late (or major) phase. Yet the tales of Henry James—some of them true short stories and some novellas—do not present the possibility for such a simple distinction. In addition to the "international theme" common throughout his work, James plays many variations on his stock characters in the tales, including con men (and women), poets, ghosts, and even unscrupulous scholars. By examining five tales from the four major decades of James's career, "An International Episode," "The Aspern Papers," "The Pupil," "The Beast in the Jungle," and "The Jolly Corner," one discovers the major subject of James's writing: the abuse of power and money in human relationships.

"An International Episode," which first appeared in the English *Cornhill Magazine* in 1878, is one of James's best-known early tales, and along with the novella *Daisy Miller* (1878), one of the most controversial. The "episode" is a simple story of the cultural conflict created when an English aristocrat falls in love with a high-minded young American woman. After the portrait of an American woman in *Daisy Miller* was criticized by some of his more jingoistic American readers, James believed that it was only fair to satirize the narrow-minded traits found in the English nobility and upper class. A negative review of the tale in the London *Daily News* brought the only existing letter from James to a reviewer; in it, he states that the characterizations of boring and boorish aristocrats were not meant to be generalizations about the English character. He also noted that the English were often delighted by the less-than-flattering portrayals of Americans in some of his other works. While publicly distancing himself from the charge of unjust criticism, privately James decided that, in the future, he would have to be both more subtle and more cautious. In a letter to his mother, Mary James, Henry stated that he could not afford to continue offending his English audience, a large part of which he thought was made up of vulgar-minded conservatives.

"An International Episode" is divided into two sections, the first set in New York and Newport, the second in England. This displacement allows James to develop his characters by "defamiliarizing" them, and subsequently the reader. A well-known character type is placed in an unfamiliar environment and displays his or her reaction against an exotic backdrop. The conflict in the narrative is one of the prototypic examples of the international theme of American innocence versus European experience. Two English cousins, Lord Lambeth and the barrister Percy Beaumont, come to New York because of a business deal with one of Beaumont's clients. They soon flee to Newport to escape the New York summer heat and to be entertained by Mrs. Kitty Westgate, the wife of a business acquaintance, and her sister Bessie Alden. Bessie Alden, the protagonist of the tale, is the opposite of the flirtatious Daisy Miller; Bessie is an idealistic young woman with a Bostonian education. Lord Lambeth, ill-educated though he is, is impressed by Miss Alden and soon begins to fall in love with her. Beaumont, the first of the experienced characters to try to keep Lambeth away from Bessie Alden, arranges for Lambeth's mother to have her son return to England on a false pretext. The next year, when Mrs. Westgate and Bessie are touring England, Lambeth renews the relationship and begins to court Bessie in a serious and highly public manner. Bessie, however, grows increasingly disenchanted with English snobbery and with Lord Lambeth's cavalier attitude toward his responsibilities as a peer of the realm. When the duchess, Lord Lambeth's mother, and her daughter visit Mrs. Westgate and Miss Alden with the intention of discouraging a marriage between her noble son and a common American, Bessie perceives that she cannot marry into such a family. She refuses Lord Lambeth's proposal when it is offered, deciding instead to visit Paris. By rejecting Lambeth, she represents American independence triumphing over English narrow-mindedness and reaction. Like James himself, Bessie realizes that she admires English culture and history much more than she likes individual Englishmen.

The best Jamesian tale of the decade of the 1880's is "The Aspern Papers." Another of the so-called international theme narratives, "The Aspern Papers" actually deals exclusively with the conduct of Americans living overseas. Based on an anecdote that James heard in 1887, the tale concerns the quest of two unscrupulous American scholars to obtain the private papers of the late American poet Jeffrey Aspern. In order to secure the papers, one of the scholars, the narrator of the story, travels to Venice to the home of Aspern's former mistress, Juliana Bordereau, who lives a secluded life with her niece Tita. The scholar admits early on that hypocrisy and duplicity are his only tactics, and that for the papers he would do still worse. Such a statement leaves the reader unsurprised when the narrator (labeled a "publishing scoundrel" by the elder Bordereau) subsequently attempts to gain the papers by wooing Tita and, more important, by using the Bordereaus' poverty as leverage. He rents a part of their ancient Venetian house and there plots his progress.

Things begin to fall apart for the narrator, however, when he finds that Juliana Bordereau is a shrewd businessperson. She charges an exorbitant rent for the rooms and uses every opportunity to get more money from him. The narrator displays his self-mystifying point of view by stating his disappointment with such vulgar materialism; he cannot get used to the idea that pecuniary profit is the primary motivation of the "divine Juliana." His disapproving attitude is an addition to one of James's favorite subjects: the American double standard, exemplified by Winterbourne in *Daisy Miller*, that everyone but the American male should be disinterested and self-sacrificing. When the narrator is no longer able to wait for the papers to be delivered to him, he searches the old woman's room with the intent of purloining them. Juliana discovers the attempted theft, and the shock of the encounter leads to her fatal illness. After Juliana's death, Tita offers the papers to the narrator if, and only if, he will marry her, but he concludes that the terms of the bargain are too exacting. Several days later, and upon further consideration, the narrator changes his mind and decides that he is ready to pay. Finally, in one of the dialectical twists common to James's fiction, Tita triumphs by telling the narrator to leave and not trouble her again. She has burned the papers, one at a time, and thus saved the privacy of her aunt and Aspern from another attempt at public exposure.

James produced some of his best tales during the 1890's. "The Pupil," first published in 1891, features one of the most despicable families in all of James's fiction. The Moreens, yet another group of transplanted Americans who apparently do nothing but tour the continent of Europe, have adopted a unique mode of living: They either ignore their bills or pay only enough to satisfy their not-too-demanding creditors. Mr. and Mrs. Moreen are the most rascally of the bad parents found in either the novels or the short stories. They enlist Pemberton, a poor, naïve American student studying at the University of Oxford, to serve as a tutor for their youngest son, Morgan. At first, Pemberton is so awed by their style of living that he cannot bring himself to discuss as vulgar a subject as money with so imposing a set of employers. When he does, he is amazed that the Moreens agree to a very liberal salary. He only gradually comes to realize that this ruse has been used previously by the Moreens, that in reality they intend to pay him the absolute minimum wage.

The Moreens eventually recognize and use to their advantage the affection that Pemberton feels for his pupil. They also rely on Pemberton's desire to appear both disinterested and antimaterialistic. At first, they refuse to pay Pemberton the full salary that was promised him, and as times get harder and creditors less generous, they refuse to pay him at all. When Pemberton appeals to Mr. Moreen for back wages, the reply is that Pemberton can have no use for such an extravagant sum of money. On his second attempt at collection, Mrs. Moreen zealously assures him that his real compensation is to be found in his ideal relationship with the gifted child Morgan. In such a situation, the Moreens argue, cash payment would practically be an insult and a degradation. Morgan's reaction to the situation is as precocious as his multilingual speech: "No doubt people had a right to take the line they liked; but why should *his* people have liked the line of pushing and toadying and lying and cheating?" Morgan's hard moral line is not likely to last long in the material world of James's fiction, and like Daisy Miller, Morgan pays the price by dying when his parents offer to give him to Pemberton (although temporarily). Morgan, in his innocence, is so overwhelmed by the proposal that he dies from the joy of such a prospect.

Another tale of fatal devotion is "The Beast in the Jungle" (1903). Representative of the work of the last major decade of James's career, the tale is a moral fable concerned with the main character's fear that some great or even tragic fate awaits him. John Marcher meets May Bartram at the English country estate Weatherend, and he soon recalls that she is the one person in the world to whom he has related the secret of his fate, that some "beast" awaits him in the jungle of his life. Marcher is an egoist on the scale of the Moreens, only much more self-deceiving; like many of the protagonists from James's work of this decade, he lacks the ability to consciously manipulate those around him. It is May, without any prompting from Marcher, who agrees to wait with him until the beast in the jungle appears; much like Pemberton, May receives little compensation for her duties. Marcher visits May regularly after she moves to London and does not even realize that his frequent visits make her the object of vulgar-minded gossip. She eventually confesses to Marcher that she knows what the "beast" is but will not reveal the answer to him. Marcher begins to feel betrayed when May declines in health without revealing the secret. Plagued by loneliness, he thinks that the knowledge of the beast is the cause of May's illness. When May dies, he is still more concerned with the nature of the beast than with her death. Finally, one morning after years of travel, Marcher visits the grave and glimpses the bereavement evident in the face of a mourner at another grave. In a moment of epiphany, Marcher finally comprehends the meaning of the beast—to have lived a life of utter selfishness and detachment. He realizes that he wasted not only his own life but also the selfless love of May Bartram. Even his final act in the tale is questionable: He sees the beast, and flings himself face down on the tomb, but does so only as one last attempt at escape. Having avoided fate all of his life, Marcher still does not have the courage to confront it at the last.

One of the last, and in many ways the most romantic, of James's tales is "The Jolly Corner" (1908). A ghost tale, this primarily psychological investigation is even more introspective than "The Beast in the Jungle." Spencer Brydon, an American who has spent the last thirty-three years in Europe, returns to New York to take care of his inheritance of two properties. Upon his arrival, he meets Alice Staverton, his former love-interest, who is able to tell him of the many changes that have occurred during his absence. Miss Staverton finds his sentimental attachment to New York and the family house on the "jolly" corner ironic when Brydon reveals that the purpose of his visit to New York is to renovate some of his property for rental purposes. While wandering through the family house, Brydon begins to be "haunted" by his alter ego, part of the fourth dimension of history that the German critic Walter Benjamin called "aura." The house, as an architectural remnant of history, represents to Brydon what his American self could have been, how his life might have unfolded if he had stayed at home. Brydon soon discovers that this "aura" appears to him only when he is in the "jolly corner" house. He finally confronts the ghost one night during a search for his other self, but he recoils at its uncanny strangeness and at its face, which is aggressive in its evilness and vulgarity. Brydon faints away after recognizing the otherness of his wealthy, vulgar American self, and he revives to find himself being held by Miss Staverton. Miss Staverton, for her part, has seen the alter ego in a dream and has taken it as a sign that Brydon needed help. Brydon, in his last words in the tale, recognizes the lesson to be learned from the apparition: The ghost has a million dollars a year but does not possess the affection of a faithful partner.

Though the tales of Henry James show a progression from primarily unromantic and antiromantic endings to those of greater self-realization and happiness, the basic subject matter remains the same throughout James's career. The innocent are faced with and are tempted by a system that rewards the wealthy and the experienced. Their response is either to accommodate, becoming part of that world or facing rejection, or, as in the case of Spencer Brydon, to find a self that can achieve at least a truce within those limitations.

THE SHORT STORIES OF BERNARD MALAMUD

Type of work: Short stories
Author: Bernard Malamud (1914-1986)
Principal published works: *The Magic Barrel*, 1958; *Idiots First*, 1963; *Pictures of Fidelman: An Exhibition*, 1969; *Rembrandt's Hat*, 1973; *The Stories of Bernard Malamud*, 1983; *The People and Uncollected Stories*, 1989.

The Stories of Bernard Malamud, published in 1983, is a collection in one volume of short stories previously printed in several volumes appearing at intervals throughout Malamud's writing career. In his introduction to the collected stories, Malamud spoke to his fondness for the short story as a genre: "Somewhere I've said that a short story packs a self in a few pages predicating a lifetime." This comment and others that he made throughout his career indicate that Malamud had a good grasp of the formal characteristics of the genre and understood well not only the kinds of themes most likely to yield successful short stories but also the techniques needed for their crafting.

Notification of his success came early with the awarding of the prestigious National Book Award on the occasion of the publication of his first volume of short stories, *The Magic Barrel*, in 1958. The judges who made that award commented that the stories captured the poetry of human relations at a point where imagination and reality meet. Malamud was certainly influenced by such writers as Isaac Bashevis Singer and Isaac Babel, with their use of the colliding worlds of appearance and reality as expressed in Yiddish folktales. For genre characteristics, however, Malamud needed to go no further than the American literature that he began reading as a young student: Nathaniel Hawthorne's works, for example, or Edgar Allan Poe's, or, making a leap into another century, Sherwood Anderson's or Eudora Welty's, where experiential and transcendental worlds collided and merged. What Hawthorne, Poe, and Welty say about the short story is, not surprisingly, similar to Malamud's comments that the short story "demands form as it teaches it," form is "ultimate necessity," "The best endures in the accomplishment of the masters," and "In a few pages a good story portrays the complexity of a life while producing the surprise and effect of knowledge."

Many of Malamud's own best stories are the ones collected in *The Magic Barrel*, though other stories matching this achievement are to be found in the other volumes—"Idiots First," for example, in the volume of that name and also from that volume, "The Jewbird." Scholars also agree that Malamud's best stories are most often based in Jewish life and thus carry with them a sense of Jewish epic history. At the same time, Malamud provides clear particulars concerning Jews living in New York on the East Side, mostly immigrants or children of immigrants, poor schlemiels (fools), and bumbling innocents living in a corrupt world. All are faced with some moral crisis; everyone an Everyman, regardless of religion, race, or sex.

Usually a Malamud story begins *in medias res*, as do many stories written in the modern mode. A typical Malamud story begins with a sentence identifying character, occupation, and initial problem. Sometimes characters, occupation, and problem are not easily discerned from first sentences but upon further reading are seen to be actually there. Note the first sentence of "The Jewbird": "The window was open so the skinny bird flew in." This sentence seems simply descriptive, but not much later a reader learns that the Jewbird is a real bird named Schwartz who needs a home and food.

Malamud often injects fantasy into a realistic surface, mingling the dream world and the world of fact, and in so doing illuminates dark surfaces with transcendent light. In "Idiots First," the base narrative is simple enough. Mendel, a father, hurries Isaac, his son, through the dark and cold city streets in an attempt to find sufficient money to send Isaac by train to his great-uncle in California. Everything in this story comments on or modifies this base story line. Quickly a reader learns that Mendel is old and ill. He awakes when the clock stops, not when it rings as one would ordinarily expect. For Mendel, the ticks of the clock signify a lack of time, a situation that seems at first tied to his own condition. Mendel's condition is relevant, but just as relevant is Isaac's: His "astonished" mouth is open, he cannot count the peanuts in his hand, and his thick hair is graying on the sides of his head. These facts are revealed one by one as a player would lay out a hand of cards, the additional facts adding dimensions that greatly complicate the action. Isaac must be treated like a small child; Mendel has been saving money for a long time, but still does not have enough; and now time is running out.

Mendel goes from one place to another seeking help, all the time fearing that a man named Ginsberg with black whiskers will show up. The streets are empty; Isaac is hungry and impatient. Mendel pawns his ancient pocketwatch that often stops ticking, and he tries to pawn his coat and hat. Mendel is then off by subway to upper Manhattan to visit Mr. Fishbein, who declares that he never gives to unorganized charity. Outside again, they are buffeted by wind, Isaac moans for food, and Mendel is tired. They stop for a moment by a bench in the park; a stranger who might be Ginsberg greets them and disappears behind a tree. Mendel is terribly frightened and the police officer called to the scene can find nothing, but when Mendel looks again at the tree, it has changed shape and position. Father and son take a trolley to the house of a former friend to discover that he died years ago. Only an elderly rabbi offers help, over the objections of his wife.

With time almost gone, Mendel and Isaac run through the streets and after them, Mendel is sure, runs Ginsberg. When they arrive at the station, it is vast and deserted, and they are too late. The uniformed ticket collector is Ginsberg himself, a bulky bearded man with hairy nostrils and a fishy smell.

By this time, a reader might have noticed a similar descriptor for Ginsberg, Fishbein, and the pawnbroker. Each of them has either eaten fish or smells of fish. Mendel begs the ticket collector to let him through before he realizes that the collector is indeed Ginsberg. Ginsberg tells Mendel that for him the train is gone, that he should have been dead at midnight. Mendel, however, continues to beg for the boy. Ginsberg rejects any responsibility. As Mendel begs for Isaac's life, Ginsberg stands picking his teeth with a matchstick. Mendel lunges at Ginsberg's throat and begins to choke him, asking if he knows what it means to be human.

At this point, the miracle occurs and the worlds collide. In his last agony, Mendel clings to Ginsberg and sees in his eyes the depth of Mendel's own terror. Ginsberg stares into Mendel's eyes and sees mirrored in them the extent of his own awful wrath, and he then beholds a shimmering, starry, blinding light that produces darkness. Evidently having a message from his creator, Ginsberg, now revealed as the Angel of Death, relinquishes Mendel and allows him time enough to take Isaac to the train. Afterward, Mendel goes back to find Ginsberg.

If Ginsberg appears in as many guises as seems likely from the descriptions, the trip through the night is a nightmare journey on which Mendel meets his own impending death time after time. Mendel has carried out his responsibilities as best he can, and he escapes the wrath of God and is redeemed through suffering. Ginsberg also reviews the wrath of God directed toward himself, an angel who did not accept responsibility for an unfortunate

man. The moment that the men look into each other's eyes, revelation occurs and both understand the power of the creator.

Other stories have similar settings and surreal surfaces. "The Death of Me," for example, is set in a crowded tailor's shop that exudes through its walls the angry quarrels of two workers who take proportions larger than the shop itself. The shop belongs to the kindly tailor Marcus, who employs them. The shop's clientele is too large for a one-person operation and too small for the three men who occupy it. The workers—Josip, an overweight, perspiring, crude presser who is a Pole, and Emilio, a thin, dry Sicilian—seem by their very natures doomed to quarrel, perhaps to enact some archetype of battle based on natural antipathies. Marcus comes upon the warring parties as they are caught in a blaze of sunlight, flooding part of the store and blinding poor Marcus, who is appalled by what is happening. The employees are as warriors who have invaded the realm of the rational and the cultured (symbolized by Marcus). The blinding light shocks Marcus into silence, and he has to wait to recover his voice. He cannot understand the reason for the fierce fighting, and neither the presser nor the tailor can explain. The fights do not seem based in territorial claims in the shop or in injury or insults; the fights seem, rather, to be inbred, a natural consequence of their being side by side. Soon the fighting is continuous, day following day, until the demonlike warriors, whom Marcus calls "assassins," succeed in driving Marcus to a heart attack and death.

"Angel Levine" is another story in which surreal elements mix. Manischevitz has been plagued by ill fortune. Overnight, he lost all of his possessions when an accident in his shop, caused by cleaning fluid that exploded, burned his establishment to the ground. Damage suits take the insurance moneys. His son is killed in the war. His daughter runs away with a "lout." He himself begins to have backaches so intense as to keep him from working. Finally, his wife becomes ill with a mysterious ailment. Forced to move to a miserable apartment, his wife confined to a bed with a sagging mattress, he to a chair, Manischevitz prays to God, first wondering what he has done to receive such punishment, then asking only that his wife be well again and he able to walk a few steps without pain.

In this nightmare world, while Manischevitz reads a newspaper in the dim light, he finds himself, without reason, reading for information concerning himself. He then has an intimation that he is not alone. In his living room he finds an angel, an African-American man named Levine. All outward appearances cause Manischevitz to doubt what Levine tells him. Seeing that doubt, Levine leaves disappointed.

Yet the angel's presence, at least for a few minutes, is the reason for the sudden recuperation of Manischevitz and his wife, although Manischevitz does not recognize this fact. A few days pass, and the pains return. In the interval, Manischevitz has considered that Levine might be an angel. Subsequently, Manischevitz goes to Harlem to find Levine. Nightmare imagery intensifies during Manischevitz's visit to Harlem. Not knowing the way, he seems to be walking through darkened mazes with nothing to guide him. Stopping at last at that which is familiar to him, a tailor shop, he is given directions to Bella's Bar, where he finds Levine dancing with Bella. Once again, however, Manischevitz doubts. It is not until his wife is close to death and he is barely able to get about that Manischevitz understands that faith has nothing to do with reason, that acceptance of the rationally impossible is essential to faith. After this realization, he once again can seek out Levine and, finding him, receive the grace that his guardian angel came to give.

This much of the story is easy to discern. A reader also needs to understand that Levine is having his own trials. He comes to this world without wings, and, after rejection by Manischevitz, Levine is drawn more and more into Bella's web until it might seem that he, also, is lost. Manischevitz's acceptance of Levine is instrumental in Levine's "earning of his wings," a pair of strong black ones.

In "The Jewbird," Malamud uses a perfectly realis-tic setting peopled with unremarkable characters into which he introduces only one oddity—a talking bird, a crow, who maintains that he is a Jewbird whose name is Schwartz. The protagonist is not the Jewbird, but the tenant of the apartment that the Jewbird visits. Harry Cohen is a frozen-food salesman who wants the kind of upward mobility that he believes is possible only if he is a fully assimilated American. The presence of the Jewbird will identify Harry as something different from that kind of American. When the Jewbird decides that it is comfortable where it is and desires to stay, Harry objects strenuously, although Harry's wife and son seem pleased. During the ensuing days, the Jewbird takes on qualities characteristic of an elderly parent who is both quarrelsome and helpful. Harry becomes more and more enraged until, one night, he throws the bird out of a window down to its death. When the dead bird is found, the son asks his mother who caused the Jewbird's death. The mother's answer is clear: "Anti-Semeets." The message is also clear: Harry Cohen is anti-Semitic. His antipathy for the Jewbird and what the bird represents is an expression of his rejection of his own parents, very likely immigrants who maintained the customs and behaviors that Harry rejects.

In the best of Malamud's stories, the intrusion of fantasy into matter-of-fact surfaces acts as a unifying device. Elements of the comic and the serious fuse, and metaphysical reality is defined as a combination of the everyday and the transcendental expressed by means of symbol and parable.

THE SHORT STORIES OF FLANNERY O'CONNOR

Type of work: Short stories
Author: Flannery O'Connor (1925-1964)
Principal published works: *A Good Man Is Hard to Find*, 1955; *Everything That Rises Must Converge*, 1965.

In Flannery O'Connor's two novels and two collections of short stories, one recognizes their dramatic power but is repelled by their shocking conclusions. Her nineteen stories would be more comforting if one could narrow their application to the South from whence they come, as with Erskine Caldwell's *Tobacco Road* (1932), for example. They deal, however, wholly with universals and are pervaded by an irony that seems both to involve and to mock, forcing the reader to recognize that O'Connor's vision encompasses the human condition, the naked spectacle of mortality. Flannery O'Connor is reminding readers that their "condition" is fourfold: They are sinners, they shall die, they are equal in the sight of God, and they cannot expect to understand God's mercy but must recognize it in whatever outrageous form it appears, which is the beginning of salvation. Her term for that recognition is the "revelation" of sin, or death, or equality, and the beginning of "redemption." She does not follow the process of redemption, only its initiation through whatever unlikely instrument God chooses. Both O'Connor and her God are ironists, and her readers and all her heroes are willful characters who must be humbled in learning that the will of God must prevail. This is the guiding vision in all of her work.

Most of the titles in *A Good Man Is Hard to Find* are ironically intended and provide a key to the author's meaning. Three of the shortest stories show her intention most clearly: "A Stroke of Good Fortune," "A Late Encounter with the Enemy," and "A Temple of the Holy Ghost." The first describes the progress up four flights of stairs of Ruby Hill, who is terrified of having a baby and gradually realizes as she climbs that she is four months pregnant. This is the "stroke of good fortune" that her palmist foretold; from the most unlikely sources comes the truth about Ruby's "condition." The second story shows how death and truth come to "General" Sash of the Confederacy at the late age of one hundred and four; he is no general, but he is surrounded by false memories of the Confederacy, especially at the Atlanta premiere of *Gone with the Wind* in 1939, and he joins in the pretense. Death, the enemy, did not get him during the Civil War, but eventually he catches up, even with a Confederate general. In the last of the three stories, both a hermaphrodite and a platitudinous nun are shown to be "a temple

of the Holy Ghost"; the outrageous and the comic are also clear signs of the truth for those who can both appreciate the ridiculous and understand its message.

The other stories in the first collection fall into two groups: four independent stories that are related by theme, and three stories that use the same setting and similar cast. The latter group contains "A Circle in the Fire," "Good Country People," and the longest story that O'Connor wrote, "The Displaced Person," which is the culmination of the volume. The common situation is an independent widow running a farm with the help of a succession of tenant farmers and several African Americans. In the first two stories, the tenant farmer's wife acts as cool observer, like the black farmer in *The Violent Bear It Away* (1960) who offers a practical but unacceptable solution to the awkward situation that arises when an intruder arrives at the farm; in the last story, the tenant farmer's wife dies and becomes the motive for the "accidental" death of the "Displaced Person." The meaning of the stories seems to be that, if one embarks on an act of charity, then one must be very sure of one's motives. Mrs. Hopewell, in "Good Country People," may be mistaken in her notions of country folk; certainly her ideas led her educated daughter astray and thus to a realization of the truth about herself, that she is in no way superior to what her mother calls "good country people." The play of ambiguity in these two stories is resolved in the last by identifying Christ as a person displaced from Mrs. McIntyre's heart; when He comes to her in the guise of a Displaced Person she allows Him to be crucified again. It is not sufficient to be "nice"—a theme that recurs whenever this farm setting is used— one must be saved even at the cost of one's life. Mrs. McIntyre, like many of O'Connor's characters, is dying as the result of her revelation, the late reconciliation of word and deed.

The other group of four stories may be distinguished by the death or salvation of the protagonists. The stories are remarkable for the creation of a totally independent universe for each; "The River" and "A Good Man is Hard to Find," contain the contrast between the well-to-do and the poor, and they end in death. The gentle death in the former of the four-year-old child seeking some meaning to his empty life is violently contrasted with the deaths of father, mother, baby, two children, and grandmother in the latter. O'Connor liked to read this story to her audiences, almost as if she were daring her hearers to face the truth in its most hideous manifestation. Solicitude for the family and the niceness of the grandmother notwithstanding, they will all perish at the hands of "The Misfit." The nickname is highly ironic: He is a misfit because he cannot find salvation or meaning to life and he knows his fallen condition. Yet he is not a misfit in a society of misfits who do not know their fallen condition and in turn label him. A "good man" is not merely "hard to find"; without God, he does not exist, and with God, he knows that he is a sinner.

The other two stories in this last group from *A Good Man Is Hard to Find* are "The Life You Save May Be Your Own" and "The Artificial Nigger." In the former, the revelation is accomplished by a road sign that Mr. Shiftlet sees when he abandons his simpleminded bride; both the sign and the "idiot" are common devices in O'Connor's work to represent a truth beneath the surface. The latter story became the title of the English edition of this collection; O'Connor was displeased at the choice because of the inevitable and slipshod references to the South in her work and because, as in all her writing, the ironic meaning of the title belongs in the context of the story. In "The Artificial Nigger," the remark to that effect prompts the reconciliation between old Mr. Head and his estranged grandson, Nelson, whom he has denied. This is probably the happiest story that Flannery O'Connor wrote, and it is important to her work in two ways; Nelson is the forerunner of the heroes of her two novels, and her guiding vision is most succinctly and clearly stated in the next-to-last paragraph, in which Mr. Head sees that God's mercy is not a soothing balm but a burning flame that purifies the sinner.

The stories in the second collection, *Everything That Rises Must Converge*, also fall into three groups. The first group comes early in the collection, and its material, corresponding roughly to the widow-farmer group in the first volume, seems to have come more directly from O'Connor's own experience. This first group includes the title story, "Greenleaf," "The Enduring Chill," and "The Comforts of Home." Each contains a confirmed young bachelor and his mother; the Angel of the Lord appears as a bull, an African-American mother, and a delinquent girl, blasting the complacency of the young man or the mother.

The second group of stories—"A View of the Woods," "Parker's Back," and "Judgment Day"—corresponds roughly to the last group in the first volume. Each story

has a world of its own that is vividly created, though all part of the same countryside, and the characters would seem remote from the writer's experience if one did not know that, like John Millington Synge, O'Connor liked to stand behind the kitchen door and listen to "good country people" spin yarns with her mother. In two stories, the meaning is clear: The saved and fearless soul so profoundly affects the hero's complacency in his way of life that, shaken, he tries to imitate the saved; his revelation is that he must seek his own way to God. In the last story in this group, "Judgment Day," the meaning is less clear; ambiguity plays around the central character and leaves one uncertain whether his way of life is that of salvation. One suspects that it is because his antagonists are the city and a well-to-do daughter, and as far as O'Connor was concerned, both were passports to hell.

Two stories in the second collection so complement each other that their titles seem interchangeable. "The Lame Shall Enter First" is the best example of O'Connor's reworking of a situation, for the story is a rewriting and expansion of the second part of *The Violent Bear It Away*, omitting the preliminary farm and family history and the later return to the country. The infirmities of Rayber, the protagonist of the novel, are tranferred to the protagonist of the short story, Rufus Johnson, a boy with a clubfoot, a bad past, and not a trace of Southern charm. He remains a mystery to Sheppard, the welfare officer determined to rescue the boy's IQ from his circumstances and his religion; the attention is on Sheppard, an indictment of the intellect, or false education, as the chief begetter of complacency and "niceness." Although this view sometimes betrays O'Connor into a glorification of corn pone as the simple true bread of life, this lapse does not occur in "Revelation," a story that draws together many of her materials and states her own vision in that afforded Mrs. Turpin in the sunset by the hog pen. The tenant farmer's wife and the widow-farmer are brought together in Mrs. Turpin (though she is married), and the precocious or educated child becomes the messenger of her revelation in a typically clotted utterance that the protagonist must ponder until it is clarified in an awful moment of truth. Mrs. Turpin has to learn that in certain essentials she is a pig of a woman, less than the trash she so despises, and that the "lame shall enter first" into Heaven, before the "nice" and capable. Mrs. Turpin thus brings up the procession of Flannery O'Connor's characters that began in "A Stroke of Good Fortune." So unified is her vision that the title of the first story discussed could be that of the last.

THE SHORT STORIES OF EDGAR ALLAN POE

Type of work: Short stories
Author: Edgar Allan Poe (1809-1849)
Principal published works: *Tales of the Grotesque and Arabesque*, 1840; *Tales*, 1845.

Although Edgar Allan Poe is often credited by literary historians as being the first self-conscious practitioner of the short-story genre, neither his famous theory about the form nor his well-known stories developed out of a vacuum, but rather grew out of the twin sources of German literary criticism and British gothic romance. Derived primarily from Poe's familiarity with August Wilhelm von Schlegel's *Über dramatische Kunst und Literatur* (1809-1811; *A Course of Lectures on Dramatic Art and Literature*, 1815) and Samuel Taylor Coleridge's *Biographia Literaria* (1817), Poe's theory of totality and unity as expressed in his famous review of Nathaniel Hawthorne's *Twice-Told Tales* (1837) is a relatively simple and straightforward one, but it dominated his thinking and writing from his earliest reviews to his philosophic prose poem *Eureka* (1848).

In his first reference to Schlegel's notion of the importance of "totality of interest" in 1836, Poe argues that, whereas in long works one may be pleased with particular passages, in short pieces the pleasure results from the perception of the oneness and overall unity of the piece based on the adaptation of all the constituent parts. In 1842, Poe uses the word "plot" as synonymous with what he means by "unity," but he is careful to distinguish between the usual notion of plot as merely events that occur one after another and his own definition of plot as an overall unified design. Moreover, Poe insists that only when the reader has an awareness of the "end" of the work, that is, the overall pattern, will seemingly trivial elements become relevant and therefore meaningful.

The 1842 Hawthorne review is the central document for understanding Poe's contribution to the theory of the short story, for it derives from his earlier discussions of the relationship between aesthetic unity and the concept of plot and looks forward to the ultimate implications of pattern and design in *Eureka*. The logic of the argument in the Hawthorne review is quite clear: What is most important in the literary work is unity, but unity can only be achieved in a work that the reader can hold in the mind all at once. After the poem, traditionally the highest of high literary art, Poe says that the short tale has the most potential for being unified. The effect of the tale is synonymous with its overall pattern or design, which is also synonymous with its theme or idea.

Poe took these aesthetic ideas quite seriously. Yet the other source of his thought and art—gothic romance—he did not take so seriously, at least not at first. Indeed, his initial ventures into that form began as simple imitations or comic satires; although he has come to be best known for his more serious gothic horror stories, the largest single grouping of his fiction is in the category of satire, parody, and burlesque. "How to Write a Blackwood Article" is particularly interesting, not only because it is an explicit satire on the gothic tales in *Edinburgh's Blackwood Magazine* that were popular at the time but also because, in the companion piece, "A Predicament," the central character Signora Psyche Zenobia takes the advice in the first story and writes an article in the *Blackwood* manner.

Although the examples that Mr. Blackwood gives Zenobia of the so-called "intensities" typical of *Edinburgh's Blackwood Magazine* are absurd parodies, many of them can be recognized as the basis of Poe's own serious short fiction, such as the requirement that the focus be on an extreme situation that disrupts everyday reality and that the story emphasize a careful attention to detail to persuade the reader of its truth. Because the short story almost always focuses on some breakup of ordinary everyday activity, and because the application of eighteenth century techniques of realism to such breakups constitute one of Poe's central contributions to its development, these are more serious matters than Poe's satiric tone suggests.

Poe's emphasis on aesthetic unity and his familiarity with the gothic romance come together more powerfully in such stories as "The Tell-Tale Heart" and "The Cask of Amontillado," in which the mad, obsessed character typical of the gothic romance creates a tightly unified sense of reality and consequently a tight aesthetic unity. A story unified around a single impression calculated to create a single effect is indeed the artistic equivalent of a psychological obsession. By single effect, Poe does not mean a simple sensational effect, but rather that point at which the mere events of story are transformed into theme or overall pattern. Moreover, in Poe's aesthetic theory, as in an obsession, all irrelevant things are excluded and seemingly trivial things are magnified or transformed into meaningful motifs relevant to the central theme.

The relationship between obsession and unity is clearly illustrated in "The Tell-Tale Heart" and "The Cask of Amontillado," for these two stories are narratives of obsessive acts with no exposition to explain their motives. The first thing that the narrator does in "The Tell-Tale Heart" is to insist that he has no object in killing the old man, no passion; the old man had never wronged him, never insulted him, and the narrator has no desire for his gold. "I think it was its eye!" To try to account for the murder of the old man any other way than in terms of the "eye" is to ignore or avoid Poe's presentation of a motive that is obsessive and metaphoric rather than logical and realistic. To understand motive in terms of metaphor, one cannot refer to a corresponding external reality outside the story. Instead, the reader must determine the identification of the story's unity and the narrator's obsession by analyzing the manifestations of the obsession within the story.

"The Cask of Amontillado" is even more tightly organized than "The Tell-Tale Heart" around an obsession synonymous with the unity of the story itself. The first paragraph of the story announces the problem of motivation, for the first sentence seems to establish the motive for the central dramatic event even as it does not: "The thousand injuries of Fortunato I had borne as I best could, but when he ventured upon insult I vowed revenge." Because readers have no way of knowing what these "thousand injuries" and the mysterious insult are, they can make no judgment on whether Montresor's revenge is justifiable or not.

The most significant and explicit use that Poe makes of the connection between aesthetic unity and the thematic content of his stories can be seen in the subgenre of the form that he developed to its highest degree: the detective story. Indeed, some would argue that no detective story written after Poe goes substantially beyond Poe's own perfection of the form in such stories as "The Murders in the Rue Morgue" and "The Purloined Letter." Poe's detective stories are about discovering patterns. For Poe, the solution to the mystery in the story is synonymous with perceiving the unity of the story itself; it is all a matter of accepting a mystery as a text, a contextual pattern made up of themes or clues that have meaning precisely because of the role that they play within the pattern.

"The Murders in the Rue Morgue," perhaps the first detective story, introduces the key element of the form, the analytical method of the amateur detective, Auguste Dupin. The first indication in the story of Dupin's special analytical ability is when he seems to read the narrator's mind. What seems preternatural, however, is only the result of "method," beginning with observation that presupposes, as the narrator has earlier said, the key element of knowing what to observe. The next step in the method is to create a series of links in a chain, which Dupin achieves by following a process of association in which one idea suggests another.

The next section of "The Murders in the Rue Morgue" primarily comes from newspaper accounts of the deaths of the two women—the key elements of which have to do with conflicting reports about the nature of the language overheard at the scene of the crime. Dupin notes that the problem with the French police is that they often hold things up too close, thus losing sight of the matter as a whole. Dupin's point here is that what must be perceived is indeed the overall pattern, how the objects fit together.

"The Purloined Letter," one of Poe's most important experiments in the creation of the short story, focuses not on what is unknown but on what is known. The only thing that is unknown is the whereabouts of the letter; nothing else in the mystery story is a mystery at all. Moreover, the French prefect of police makes it clear that the one who took the letter is known and that he still has it. Indeed, it is crucial that the owner of the letter knows who has stolen it for the letter to have its blackmailing power. As Dupin says, the power of the robber results from "the robber's knowledge of the loser's knowledge of the robber."

After Dupin gives the letter to the prefect a few months later, the real story begins with Dupin's exposition of the means by which the letter was found. By projecting himself into the intellect of the minister (the thief), Dupin realizes that he would not use ordinary means of hiding the letter, but rather extraordinary ones—by which Dupin means, at least in this case, ordinary means. To hide the letter by putting it in plain sight is to make the ordinary into the extraordinary. The minister, says Dupin, is a poet and a mathematician—a combination of identification and analysis—that makes his reasoning sound; if he has reasoned as a mathematician only, he would have been at the mercy of the prefect. Because the minister is also a poet, Dupin knows that he would have anticipated all the efforts that the police would make to find the letter and would be driven as a matter of course to simplicity as being the most unusual means to hide it. What so fascinates the reader about "The Purloined Letter" is Poe's creation of a story that is about its own explication.

The ultimate implication of Poe's theories of art as the highly unified and patterned creation of a bodiless ideal is the human desire to escape the consequences of being mere body by retreating into the artwork itself. Indeed, two of Poe's best-known stories, "The Masque of the Red Death" and "The Fall of the House of Usher," make this simultaneously irresistible and horrible basic desire their central theme.

"The Masque of the Red Death" is one of Poe's most obviously allegorical stories and thus one of his most straightforward ones, for it seems a clearly delineated parable about the impossibility of humanity's attempt to escape death. As is typical in Poe's work, however, it is not as straightforward as it first appears. The first problem that the reader faces in reading the story allegorically is the fact that the "masque" or mask that represents death is the redness of blood on the face of the victim. Because the redness of blood is a sign of life, Poe's metaphor becomes more complex, it suggests that life is the sign of death.

Prince Prospero's attempts to escape death by retreating into his abbey, "an extensive and magnificent structure, the creation of the prince's own eccentric yet august taste," also complicates a simple allegorical reading of the story. Once all are locked inside, the gates are welded shut to make sure that there is no means of "ingress or egress," and the prince says that "the external world could take care of itself." Furthermore, the prince makes sure that inside he has all the "appliances of pleasure," such as buffoons, improvisatori, ballet dancers, musicians, beauty, and wine. "All these and security were within. Without was the Red Death." Indeed, what Prince Prospero—named for William Shakespeare's imaginative creator of his own world in *The Tempest* (1611)—has done is to create a palace of art by which he attempts to lock life, and thus death, outside.

"The Fall of the House of Usher" is probably Poe's most characteristic story, for it pulls together practically all of his basic themes and innovative techniques. In this small masterpiece, Poe separates the central protagonist, Roderick Usher, the embodiment of obsession and desire, from his observing self. The story begins with the entrance of the narrator into the world of Usher, which is actually Poe's aesthetic universe. It is the house itself, however, that causes the narrator, and the reader, the first difficulties of interpretation. The narrator senses a mysterious feeling of insufferable gloom that the house creates in him, which is not relieved by the poetic sentiment that usually allows one to accept the sternest natural images of the desolate and terrible. He himself poses the basic interpretative question: "what was it that so unnerved me in the contemplation of the House of Usher? It was a mystery all insoluble."

The narrator knows that there are combinations of natural objects that have the power of affecting one in such a way, but he also knows that the "analysis of this power lies among considerations beyond our depth." He considers that perhaps a "different arrangement of the particulars of the scene, of the details of the picture, would be sufficient to modify, or perhaps to annihilate its capacity for sorrowful impression." Thus he tries the experiment of looking at the house from the perspective of its reflection in the tarn, but the inverted reflected image, much like a distorted image in one of Poe's own stories, gives him a shudder more thrilling than the house itself.

Like other Poe protagonists, Usher suffers from a disease characterized by an unusual attentiveness or focus, what the narrator calls "a morbid acuteness of the senses." Yet, for Usher, this acuteness means that he finds all but the most bland food intolerable, can wear garments of only certain textures, finds the odors of flowers oppressive, cannot bear anything but the faintest light, and cannot listen to anything but some peculiar sounds from stringed instruments. It is clear that Usher is the artist who cannot tolerate any sensory input at all, who has indeed cut himself from any stimulus from the external world, much as Prince Prospero wishes to do in "The Masque of the Red Death." Roderick Usher is the ultimate Poe protagonist; living solely within the universe of story, the only end for him is his ultimate dissolution, as both he and the house slip back into the preformulated nothingness of the tarn.

Although Edgar Allan Poe has often been scorned by serious critics as a trivial thinker and the author of a few inconsequential horror stories, a more careful analysis of his theory of aesthetic unity and its relationship to the basic themes of his fiction reveal that Poe made a significant contribution to the development of short fiction that continues to have a powerful effect. His influence on such modern writers as John Barth, Vladimir Nabokov, Jorge Luis Borges, and many others probably exceeds that of any other American nineteenth century writer.

THE SHORT STORIES OF KATHERINE ANNE PORTER

Type of work: Short stories
Author: Katherine Anne Porter (1890-1980)
Principal published works: *Flowering Judas and Other Stories*, 1930; *The Leaning Tower and Other Stories*, 1944; *The Old Order*, 1945; *The Collected Stories of Katherine Anne Porter*, 1965.

As one of the United States' preeminent writers of short fiction, Katherine Anne Porter was widely acclaimed in her long lifetime for a relatively small body of work. *The Collected Stories of Katherine Anne Porter*, published in 1965, comprises twenty-six pieces of varying length published between 1924 and 1944. Her other writings include *Ship of Fools*, a long novel published in 1962, as well as essays, reviews, and miscellaneous pieces, but it is on the stories that Porter's renown securely rests. Praised and admired by literary critics, academics, and other readers, the stories are frequently reprinted in anthologies and college texts, endlessly examined and analyzed by students and scholars, and acknowledged as influential by other writers.

For the locale of most of her stories, Porter used the areas that were especially familiar to her: Louisiana and Texas for the greatest number, as well as Mexico, her "much loved second country," as she wrote in the preface of the *Collected Stories*. Only in a small number of stories are other settings used, such as Denver, Berlin, a farm in Connecticut, or a flat in New York City.

Porter was skillful at creating the atmosphere of a place with only a few cogent details and images. She was not, however, in any sense a regional writer or a local colorist. The settings never constitute the main element of interest in the stories, but they do contribute a rich and vivid quality to the overall effect. It is the characters who claim the most attention, and it is their relationships, their words, and their actions that are responsible for the impact of each story.

The importance of Porter's style cannot be overrated; as much as the skillfully suggested settings and the memorable characters, it is the way in which Porter tells her stories that distinguishes them. Inevitably, her name is often mentioned in the company of such masters of the genre as Guy de Maupassant, Anton Chekhov, Ivan Turgenev, Katherine Mansfield, and Eudora Welty, but it is generally conceded that Porter's position among the great short-story writers is not the result of similarity to any of them or the influence of other practitioners of the art. A Porter story is not like one by any other writer. This uniqueness is not easy to explain, but an examination of some of Porter's best-known and most admired stories

may be helpful in understanding the originality of imagination and the craftsmanship that characterize Porter's work.

As a group, the stories are difficult to classify except in the broadest sense. No one story is like another except in such superficial terms as setting or general human situation, such as romantic love, marriage, family, or childhood. Certain themes and concepts are common to several stories: disappointment, disillusionment, betrayal, loneliness, courage, cruelty. In almost every story, the principal underlying theme is morality, the universal human destiny.

Rejection and negation frequently characterize the emotional climate of the stories; oppression, entrapment, and violence can also be found in many of them. As for characters, the type that appears most often is that of a strong woman, but in many guises—a young Mexican wife, a dying grandmother, a glamorous and romantic belle, a young woman striving to free herself of the past as mythologized by her family. Men are usually the weaker figures, often seen as victims or victimizers.

One group of stories does have a kind of unity; these are commonly called the "Miranda stories." Miranda is the main character in two stories that Porter called short novels: *Old Mortality* and *Pale Horse, Pale Rider*, which were published together with *Noon Wine* in 1939. In addition, Miranda as a child is the principal figure in "The Circus," "The Fig Tree," and "The Grave."

Approaching these stories chronologically, as periods and incidents in Miranda's life, the first shows her as a very young child, allowed to attend her first circus, along with a whole row of cousins, second cousins, her father, her sister, her brother, and the grandmother who also appears in other Miranda stories. Instead of the anticipated pleasure and delight, Miranda experiences only horror and terror. There is no humor for her in the frantic struggles of the tightrope-walking clown or the leering face of a dwarf, who terrifies her when she realizes that he is human. The bold grins of the rough little boys under the stands puzzle her with a premonition of sexual evil that she does not understand but fears nevertheless. "The Circus" delineates the bewilderment and anguish of a very young child's first encounter with evil under the guise of entertainment. Her response is very like the clear-eyed view of Huckleberry Finn, who also did not find the circus amusing.

In "The Fig Tree," Miranda, still very young, experiences the anguish of thinking that she has unintentionally buried a still-living chick when she hears a cheeping from the earth. Again she is surrounded by elders who fail to recognize the agonies of an innocent and sensitive child, until Great-aunt Eliza, an amateur scientist, matter-of-factly explains that the odd chirps that Miranda hears are not the peepings of the buried chick but the sounds of tree frogs signaling rain. This is a short, deceptively simple story that contains the characteristic elements of a Porter story: confusion and fear; the conflict between innocence and knowledge, death and life, youth and age; and most significantly, irony and a point made so subtly and succinctly that it is easy to miss.

In "The Grave," Miranda, now nine years old, and her twelve-year-old brother, Paul, explore the family cemetery from which the coffins have been removed because of the sale of the land in which they were located. The empty graves hold no terror for the children, who are delighted to discover in them buried treasure: a dove that was once a screw head for a coffin and a ring that must have fallen off a bone when the remains were moved. The children then go on a different kind of hunt. Paul shoots a rabbit, skins it expertly, and another discovery is made: The rabbit was pregnant, and the minuscule contents of its womb, barely formed but recognizable, are exposed inside their mother in another sort of grave. Miranda senses that she has seen something that she does not understand, and Paul's caution that she tell no one adds to the troubling nature of the event. Memory then becomes a grave as Miranda forgets all about the incident until twenty years later, when the sight and smell of a street market in a foreign country suddenly recalls to her mind the impressions of corruption and sweetness that she had experienced on that day long ago.

Miranda's story continues in the short novel *Old Mortality*. Miranda is a girl growing up in a large Southern family that perpetuates the romantic myths of the past. Miranda struggles to deal with disillusionment about the family heroine, glamorous Aunt Amy, and a beloved uncle, Gabriel. The central problem of the story is the discrepancy between what is falsely remembered and what is shockingly real. On her way to the funeral of Uncle Gabriel, Miranda encounters an outspoken elderly cousin who gives her a version of the family legend that confirms what Miranda has already discovered. In her struggle to reach the truth through awareness, Miranda rejects what she has been told about the past and vows to know what happens to her without romanticizing—thinking, because of her youth, that she can solve the mystery of the nature of truth.

The title of *Pale Horse, Pale Rider*, another short novel, is a biblical reference to the Book of Revelation by way of a Negro spiritual. It concerns Miranda as a young woman working for a newspaper in Colorado during the last days of World War I, as a plague of influenza is sweeping through the country. She is in love with a handsome young soldier, Adam Barclay, who takes care of her when she succumbs to the disease and, after she is removed to a hospital, returns to his camp. As Miranda suffers the nightmares of fever and pain, the deeper meaning of the story reveals itself. This is not simply an appealing and moving romantic tale, but an exploration of death, and the real plague is seen as a spiritual illness for which the war stands as the controlling force. Miranda recovers but Adam is dead, and she returns, not to life, but to a deeper understanding of mortality, the fragility of love, and the transitory nature of joy.

Death also plays an important role in "The Jilting of Granny Weatherall," a woman whose long, arduous life is epitomized in her name. Here, instead of a pale rider, death is seen as a bridegroom, one who jilted his bride at the altar. The story is told entirely through the waning consciousness of Granny, who confuses the man who did not marry her with the person of Death, equally rejecting and longing for both her long-ago lover and her anticipated one.

Another story of betrayal is told in "María Concepción," Porter's first published story. Drawing on her experiences and observations in Mexico, Porter narrates some events in the life of her young heroine, a strong upright Native American woman. María discovers her young husband making love to a fifteen-year-old girl, María Rosa, the beekeeper. The pair runs off to join a guerilla army, and María Concepción bides her time. When the two lovers, tired of soldiering, return to the village, the wife takes vengeance against the beekeeper, killing her without being caught, protected by the support of her husband and her neighbors. She then takes the newly born child of her husband and his lover and returns home. The story ends as the day ends—quietly, benignly, peacefully.

Other stories set in Mexico are "Flowering Judas," "Virgin Violeta," "The Martyr," "That Tree," and "Hacienda." These stories cover a wide range of concentrated events and dissimilar characters, including a virginal girl's introduction to sexual duplicity, a frightened young woman trying to help revolutionists in prison, an artist absurdly mourning the departure of his lover, a journalist who vengefully awaits the return of his wife, and a film crew at the ranch of a couple suffering an unhappy marriage while one of the serfs is caught in a stupid and pointless murder.

A group of stories that show people struggling to escape a fate determined by their own weak natures includes *Noon Wine*, "He," and "Magic." In the first of these, Mr. Thompson, a lazy but proud farmer, employs an insane fugitive and then kills a bounty hunter seeking the hired hand. "He" is the story of a similar no-account family burdened with a retarded son for whom they can no longer care, and "Magic" tells of a young prostitute who desperately and futilely struggles to escape her cruel life.

"Holiday" is also set in the Southwest, on a Texas farm to which the narrator, seeking to escape unspecified problems, goes for a spring holiday. During the course of her visit, she observes but does not participate in the hardworking lives of the Müller family—the patriarch and his wife, and numerous grown children, their husbands, wives, and young children. The narrator's search for truth and understanding is reminiscent of Miranda's quest, but it goes beyond Miranda's hopeful resolve through an acquaintance with Ottilie, the oldest sister. Horribly disfigured by an accident in her childhood, Ottilie is virtually a slave in the household, ignored and forgotten by the rest of the family, frantically cooking and serving enormous meals without thanks or acknowledgment. The narrator attempts to perform an act of kindness to Ottilie by taking her for a pony-drawn wagon ride. The two characters are beyond each other's reach, however, and the narrator, while realizing what they have in common as fugitives from death, also accepts that there is nothing she can do for the unfortunate servant-sister except take her home to resume her unending labor.

One other story deserves mention, partly because it is quite different in setting and theme from all the others, and partly because it presages the themes and characters of Porter's final work, the long novel *Ship of Fools*. The story, "The Leaning Tower," takes place in Berlin in the days just before World War II. Without a word of authorial comment, Porter shows Charles Upton's disappointment with the city that he has dreamed for years of visiting. Instead of feeling comfortably at home, however, Charles finds himself alienated in a militaristic culture suffering the deprivation and humiliation of the years following World War I.

Although Porter's stories are not equal in quality—some are markedly more successful than others—they all reveal the artistry with which Porter created them. Employing a variety of narrative structures and a broad spectrum of points of view and characters, Porter told her tales with economy and objectivity in a style that is at once elegant, precise, and honest.

In her preface to the *Collected Stories*, Porter bade a happy farewell to her tales, seeing in the publication of that book "a renewal of their life . . . which is what any artist most longs for." Her hope that they would "continue to be read, and remembered" seems certain of fulfillment by those who respect the writer's craft and the ways in which Porter practiced it.

THE SHORT STORIES OF ISAAC BASHEVIS SINGER

Type of work: Short stories
Author: Isaac Bashevis Singer (1904-1991)
Principal published works: *Gimpel the Fool and Other Stories*, 1957; *The Spinoza of Market Street*, 1961; *Short Friday and Other Stories*, 1964; *The Séance and Other Stories*, 1968; *A Friend of Kafka and Other Stories*, 1970; *A Crown of Feathers and Other Stories*, 1973; *Passions and Other Stories*, 1975; *Old Love*, 1979; *The Collected Stories*, 1982; *The Image and Other Stories*, 1985; *The Death of Methuselah and Other Stories*, 1988.

Isaac Bashevis Singer began his literary career as a short-story writer, publishing his first piece in 1925 in *Literarische Bletter*. Saul Bellow's 1953 translation of Singer's "Gimpl Tam" (1945) as "Gimpel the Fool" boosted the reputation that Singer had established with *The Family Moskat* three years earlier, and much of Singer's finest work continued to appear in his short fiction, written first in Yiddish and then translated. In his acceptance speech for his Nobel Prize in Literature, Singer jokingly observed that he chose a dead language because it suits stories about ghosts, which pervade his narratives. On a more serious note, he added that Yiddish is "the wise and humble language of us all." Although he wrote in an idiom familiar to only a small minority of his ultimate readership, and although his settings and characters often derive from a pre-World War II Poland or New York that vanished before many among his audience were born, his fiction retains its appeal because its concerns are universal and timeless: the struggle between good and evil, the search for truth in a silent, mysterious world devoid of revelation.

These themes receive diverse treatment. "The Power of Darkness" and "The Betrayer of Israel" derive from Singer's observations as the young son of a rabbi living at 10 Krochmalna Street in a Jewish section of Warsaw before the outbreak of World War I, and they are told from the perspective of a child. "Zeidlus the Pope" is narrated by Satan and is set in the Lublin, Poland, of the remote past. The events in "The Admirer" occur in an apartment building very much like Singer's own on West 86th Street in New York and seem contemporary with the story's 1975 publication; Singer might be recounting an actual experience. "The Gentleman from Cracow" provides a surrealistic third-person account of life in the Polish village of Frampol in the late seventeenth or early eighteenth century. Despite these differences in setting, point of view, and type of plot, however, an analysis of one story can reveal much about all of them; hence, "A Crown of Feathers" may serve as the epitome of Singer's short fiction.

Like so many of his other works, this is a third-person narrative set in the distant, unspecified Polish past. Nesha, the wife of the rich Reb Naftali Holishitzer, always rejects the men whom the matchmakers choose for her one granddaughter, Akhsa; Nesha continues her criticism even from beyond the grave. Reb Naftali finally insists that Akhsa marry Zemach, a learned but homely young man from another town, but as Akhsa is about to put her name to the marriage contract, her dead grandmother shouts, "Don't sign!" and the girl drops the pen.

Such surrealism, characteristic of Singer, represents one facet of his revolt against classical Yiddish literature, which emphasized the Enlightenment values of rationalism, progress, and benevolence. In the Hasidic stories of Rabbi Nachman of Bratzlav, whose work Singer discovered in his late teens in Bilgoray, supernatural forces appear, but God controls the world and guarantees a happy ending. Such religious certainty and optimism suited Singer no better than its secular counterpart. Moreover, Singer's portraits of the Jews of Krasnobród lack the sentimentality of a Sholem Aleichem or an Isaac Lev Peretz. Zemach is physically and spiritually unattractive; Nesha is overcritical, indeed wicked; and Akhsa isolates herself from her neighbors because their conversation cannot transcend clothes and domesticity. In "The Cafeteria," a Singer-like narrator acknowledges that his readers object to his negative portrayals of Jews. In "Gimpel the Fool," the entire Jewish community delights in deceiving the innocent Gimpel. In "A Quotation from Klopstock," a Jewish woman repeatedly extorts money from a religious uncle by threatening to convert if he does not pay her what she asks; after her death, her family learns that she had become Catholic years earlier.

Already in its opening pages, "A Crown of Feathers" reflects Singer's peculiar blend of the supernatural, with its ghost of Nesha, and realistic depiction of the Jewish community, the refusal to romanticize the past. As the story progresses, it introduces as well a mixture of existential doubt and mysticism that characterizes Singer's fiction.

Akhsa's refusal to marry Zemach shames Reb Naftali, who sickens and dies. While observing the period of mourning for him, Akhsa finds in her grandfather's library a Polish New Testament. The book comforts her, and in a dream Nesha says that it tells the truth, that Christianity is the true religion. Reb Naftali also speaks from beyond the grave to warn Akhsa not to listen to her grandmother. Confused, Akhsa asks for a sign; her grandmother replies that inside her pillow she will find a crown of feathers that no human could make. In the morning, Akhsa rips open the pillow and finds the crown, which is topped with a cross. She converts. As she ages, however, she comes to doubt Christianity as well as Judaism and concludes that Satan had made the crown. Satan visits her in a dream to confirm her suspicions and to tell Akhsa that there is no truth.

For Singer, this denial defines the diabolical. As Rabbi Bainish observes in "Joy," "The wicked live on denials." Affirmation, however, is not easy, and discovering what to affirm is more difficult still because Singer's God is silent. According to the Cabala, in the beginning God occupied all available space. To make the world, He had to contract Himself, to withdraw His presence from the universe to allow it to exist. Because the act of creation required God's absence, evil and folly can flourish. This view informs Singer's writing. As a customer in a bookstore tells Reb Nechemia in "Something Is There," "We have to live without faith and without knowledge." Akhsa's grandmother claims that the crown of feathers proves the truth of Christianity. The devil maintains that it shows that nothing is true. This contradiction leaves the dilemma of how Akhsa, or anyone, can know what to believe.

Akhsa now chooses to listen to the voice of her grandfather; she returns to Judaism and marries Zemach. Her husband imposes terrible penance on both of them, even though Reb Bezalel opposes such harshness. Like so many of Singer's other spiritual leaders, Reb Bezalel is ineffectual. If his is the voice of truth, then it is a voice that goes unheeded and hence becomes irrelevant.

Zemach's harshness kills Akhsa. He represents a fanaticism that, however well intentioned, leads to destruction because it places an abstraction before an individual. The truth may be undefinable, but error is self-evident. On the night before her death, Akhsa again seeks a sign, a revelation, and she hears in her dream that she should tear open her pillow. She finds another crown of feathers, this one bearing the tetragrammaton, the four Hebrew letters

that form God's ineffable name. She realizes, though, that she has been shown nothing. As she asks, "In what way was this crown more a revelation of truth than the other?" She therefore requests another proof, but none is vouchsafed.

The crown's very existence is questionable. When the priest asked Akhsa to bring him the first one that she had found, she could not because the maid had discarded it. The second may be a hallucination, as Akhsa is having strange dreams, and that crown, too, if it existed, is destroyed when a woman from the Burial Society unwittingly steps on it. At the end of the story, Singer emphasizes the ambiguity of truth by observing that the townspeople cannot understand how or why Akhsa tore open her pillow just before she died; they invent diverse explanations, but they never discover the real reason because, as Singer writes, "If there is such a thing as truth it is as intricate and hidden as a crown of feathers."

The absence of revelation is both terrifying and liberating. As Rabbi Bainish of Komarov says in "Joy," "If one knew the truth how could there be freedom? If hell and paradise were in the middle of the marketplace, everyone would be a saint." Meaning may not exist but can be created through sympathy and compassion. If Akhsa is saved—Singer's stories often leave the reader uncertain of the outcome—then her salvation comes not from divine intervention but from her love for Zemach. God's silence imposes a moral imperative: Because He will not prevent evil, people must. Gimpel is saved by rejecting nihilism and vengeance. "The Spinoza of Market Street" demonstrates the revivifying power of love. In "The Unseen," Reb Nathan allows lust to overcome love; both he and his seducer die miserably. Goodness is not necessarily rewarded, but evil proves to be its own punishment. In "The Manuscript," Shibtah avenges betrayal by destroying the manuscript of her unfaithful lover, only to discover that at the same time she has destroyed her ability to love.

Singer emphasized the need for narrative. He claimed that he enjoyed writing for children because they wanted a story, not a moral, and he filled his pages with action and with characters who awaken the reader's interest and sympathy. Always, one wants to know what will happen next. Yet Singer was perpetually a moralist, an advocate for what he called in his Nobel address "frightened and hopeful humanity."

THE SHORT STORIES OF PETER TAYLOR

Type of work: Short stories
Author: Peter Taylor (1917-   )
Principal published works: *A Long Fourth and Other Stories*, 1948; *The Widows of Thornton*, 1954; *Happy Families Are All Alike*, 1959; *Miss Leonora When Last Seen and Fifteen Other Stories*, 1963; *In the Miro District and Other Stories*, 1977; *The Old Forest and Other Stories*, 1985.

Peter Taylor's first published collection of short stories, *A Long Fourth and Other Stories*, was described by Robert Penn Warren as the product of a "disenchanted mind." This cool viewpoint has characterized much of his work. Taylor's literary stature, however, is based chiefly on the skill with which that view is expressed and the flawless technique of his short fiction.

The world that Taylor views, and expresses just short of social satire, is chiefly the modern upper South in its small-town or equivalent suburban setting. His middle-class characters consider themselves a cut above middle class, since on a small-town social scale they are sometimes the next best thing to gentry and are probably charter members of the town's first country club. They have the gentry's adherence to blood, bone, and family, but their plantations are likely to be neat houses on green lawns and their ancestral memories may be conveniently short. The Old South fabric of family is still there, but it is fading and threadbare, in imminent danger of being chopped up by modern scissors and sewed into something for practical usage around the house.

In fact, one might view Taylor's world as an island risen out of Faulknerian seas. The theme of land, that rural hold upon the heart, survives in Taylor, but the reader catches barely a sniff of the barnyard, now safely pushed beyond these city limits. The family, instead of merely falling into ruins, is several generations along and better adjusted to commercialism, or at least it has more muted maladjustments. Tales of aristocracy and historical grief are still told by the old to the young but in a calmer voice. The role of women and African Americans in society remains unsettled, but in Taylor's world, the terms in which each group is discussed have become less simple, less basic, more "civilized." Taylor's characters suspect that there are no easy solutions to find, no such thing as a "woman's role" or the "black person's place." William Faulkner's themes have been updated, dragged forward a few years in time, and there is less despair when the Old Order clashes with the New in Southern society. It has already clashed and does clash, but despair slides over into what Warren called "disenchantment." Taylor's response to his contemporary South is less im-

passioned grief than melancholy, less rage than irony.

Some of these generalizations about Peter Taylor's fictional world were justified in his earliest stories. In "A Long Fourth," the title story of his first book, a son brings into his Southern family household an "intellectual" New York girlfriend. The tensions of their holiday visit are set against the continuing hidden tensions between the mother and her African-American servant. Here is sentiment opposed to youth's embarrassment by sentiment, familiar attachments set against uneasy independence. The author deals almost tenderly with all of his characters, including that generation which has not and never will catch up with the times. He describes Harriet's feeling that her children do not exist any longer; it is as if they died in childhood, never growing up at all.

Other stories that express this tangle of yesterday and today would include "A Spinster's Tale," the story of a motherless girl alienated in an all-male household; "The Scoutmaster," a picture of domestic crisis performed against a backdrop of Southern nobility (this story includes the near-comic creation Uncle Jake, who bears a certain resemblance to Harriet); and "The Fancy Woman."

The latter story is probably Taylor's best-known and most widely anthologized story. Written in 1940, it is the comic, bittersweet, pitiful account of Josie Carlson's weekend stay on a plantation outside Memphis with an oaf named George. The "fancy woman's" visit is interrupted and altered by the arrival of George's two teenage sons and a set of shallow, suburban friends. As one critic has said, this story holds intimations of a society disintegrating and of a tradition that was never wholly perfect or sustaining being replaced by something even less so.

The Taylor countryside, then, is one of Southern change. His characters are either changing or wearing down from their refusal to do so. He picks up the Faulknerian mood several degrees removed from violent upheaval and sets it down in a semi-industrialized, half-accepting, half-reluctant time.

It is not surprising that the style Taylor employs in his short stories should be consistent with their mood and setting. A reader's initial reaction may be almost negative; technically the stories seem at first notable for what they leave out or conceal. Yet the threat of violence and upheaval exists under his smooth surfaces. Most violence and much traditional plot take place offstage. His technical skill in constructing a story, in weaving the rhythm of ordinary speech into narrative, in conveying character through meager but always pertinent bits of dialogue, is such that the technique seems to disappear. He sews up his story with an invisible seam.

One might almost say that Peter Taylor's style is a studied avoidance of style. For example, it is difficult to imagine Taylor parodied, as Ernest Hemingway, Faulkner, Françoise Sagan, or J. D. Salinger lend themselves to parody. There is little to be plucked from his prose as "pure Taylor." This lack of stylistic effect is partly the result of the way in which he casts many of his stories in easy-flowing narrative, the distilled reminiscence of a single character. The narrator may be identified ("Spinster's Tale," "Miss Leonora When Last Seen," "A Strange Story,") or have no formal existence ("Rain in the Heart," "Fancy Woman," "Reservations," "An Overwhelming Question").

If one chooses, however, one can think back and mentally "retell" the story from a specific first-person viewpoint, such as Josie's in "The Fancy Woman" or Helen Ruth's in "A Wife of Nashville." The style of the story itself, on first reading, seems nearly neutral, taking its source from the story and not from a single mind or pair of eyes. Nothing blurs or refracts most of the told events—they are seldom handed out already digested or interpreted. Taylor himself is never spotted onstage adjusting the strings on the puppets. His narrative takes precedence over the language or the temptation to verbal flourishes. The style seems so natural, like conversation and the family tale, that it is clear window glass through which the action is purely seen.

Because there is so little intrusion of the author begging his case, an air of verisimilitude results. The "raisin-colored carpet," for example, simply is that color. The reader is both bemused and convinced by the quiet story told in the quiet parlor.

This apparent lack of effort and the muting of drama work better for Taylor than italics or exclamation points. Such quiet understatement alerts readers, who cast their minds back looking for all those implications woven almost invisibly into the story. When readers do perceive, perhaps by hindsight, the delicate design, they may claim this discovery as some kind of evidence of their own sensitivity.

This method enables Taylor to tell volumes through understatement. "Reservations," subtitled "A Love Story," follows a just-married couple from their bridal reception at the country club to a hotel where they will spend their wedding night. The bride accidentally locks herself in the bathroom and must be rescued by residents of an adjoining room, an embarrassed man and the prostitute he has hired for the evening. Taylor, a serious writer who can be very humorous at times, conveys deftly a case of honeymoon jitters. While Dorothy Parker in "Here We Are" did much the same thing in sharp and witty dialogue, Taylor gives the reader in very little more space a full-length portrait of the nervous bride, her feeling that the prostitute is too familiar, the harsh accusations that she finally screams at the exasperated groom while he struggles with the locked door. Parker wrote of honeymooners; at the end of Taylor's story, the reader knows what the whole marriage will be like. He makes what Hollis Summers once described as the effort to "realize simultaneously the tree and the forest of experience."

There is not a Taylor story that does not fulfill the dictum of short fiction to tell little but suggest much. In "Miss Leonora When Last Seen," Leonora Logan habitually dons dungarees, a cardigan, and a poke bonnet and drives her convertible through an assortment of states, orbiting Tennessee. The last time she drives away, unfortunately, she looks very much like a thousand others seen in small towns and on the highways. She is lost, out of eccentricity and into normality.

Aunt Munsie, in "What You Hear from 'Em?" gives up her hogs and slop wagon, but she also gives up really caring when the two Tolliver boys are coming home to live in Thornton. In "Allegiance," a Tennessee soldier in London goes to call upon an aunt with whom his family has quarreled and during the visit creates the whole microcosm of that family. In "An Overwhelming Question," a bizarre accident at the Hunt and Polo Club prevents the couple from living happily ever after, like a sleeping beauty and a sleeping prince awaking at the same moment in the same place. In these and in other stories, what distinguishes Taylor's fiction is, as Henry James suggested, "the power to guess the unseen from the seen, to trace the implication of things, to judge the whole piece by the pattern."

This is Peter Taylor's special literary talent: to select, unerringly, the small seen moment that is a keyhole to an entire revelation. If the themes are as broad as the changing, contemporary South, Taylor illuminates them with a single pencil-flashlight, and then another, and then another.

The change in one's homeland was expressed by Faulkner in great intensity. Banners were furled and unfurled and armor clanked, so much so that at first it may be hard to see that Taylor's is the same battlefield a few years later, coolly viewed, more quietly described. In literary time, if not chronologically, Peter Taylor is much later than Faulkner; where the Sartoris family bled, there is already a monument. It is useful for the reader to remember, however, that between the older writer and the younger one the issues differ less in substance than in approach, angle, and author's temperament in their presentations of a Southern region and its society.

THE SHORT STORIES OF MARK TWAIN

Type of work: Short stories
Author: Mark Twain (Samuel Langhorne Clemens, 1835-1910)
Principal published works: *The Celebrated Jumping Frog of Calaveras County, and Other Sketches*, 1867; *Mark Twain's Sketches: New and Old*, 1875; *The Stolen White Elephant and Other Stories*, 1882; *The £1,000,000 Bank-Note and Other New Stories*, 1893; *The Man That Corrupted Hadleyburg and Other Stories and Essays*, 1900; *A Double Barrelled Detective Story*, 1902; *King Leopold's Soliloquy: A Defense of His Congo Rule*, 1905; *The $30,000 Bequest and Other Stories*, 1906; *A Horse's Tale*, 1907; *The Curious Republic of Gondour and Other Whimsical Sketches*, 1919; *The Adventures of Thomas Jefferson Snodgrass*, 1926.

Mark Twain's public reputation as a short-story writer is inextricably bound to one early tale, "The Celebrated Jumping Frog of Calaveras County," published in the popular East Coast magazine *Saturday Press* in 1865. The basic story was not original to Twain; variations on it have been seen as far back as the classical periods of Roman and Greek literature, and versions of the same tale were common in the popular press in Twain's time. Yet how Twain told the story made the difference, and it made him an instant, countrywide success after he had been in and out of the newspaper and magazine business for some time. That tale alone is still the best-remembered short story by Twain, and it might be argued that most readers would be hard-pressed to name another, although other short adventures are well known. Next to "The Celebrated Jumping Frog of Calaveras County," Tom Sawyer's success at the fence, his courtship of Becky, and Huck and Jim on the raft are standard memories of Twain's work. These other moments are sections of novels, not short stories, but often these discreet adventures develop lives of their own and are recalled almost as if they were short stories. Part of this effect is caused by the fact that Twain used a picaresque form for his novels, stringing lively, self-enclosed adventures on the longer narrative line, and the best of these incidents are quite legitimately remembered. Not so well remembered are his other short stories, despite the fact that he wrote a considerable number of them.

Part of this lack of knowledge of Twain's stories lies in the power of his novels, and part of it lies in the fact that Twain himself did not clearly distinguish his short stories from his other work, either in form or content. Twain was ambitious and wise enough in his early days of fame to build upon his reputation as a kind of American court jester for the common people. He played the role of the "unlettered" country boy from the West; it was partly true because he was only modestly educated. He was not stupid, however, and his charming turn at country wisdom was as much an act as it was a reality, a romantic celebration of an ordinary man out to make his way in the wide world of international writers. Like Charles Dickens before him, he began as a journalist but never lost the common touch. Moreover, he did not choose to do only one thing. Like Dickens, he was an essayist, and Twain was also a public entertainer, earning huge fees for reading his work in concert halls throughout the United States and Europe. As a result in part of this public demand for something of everything, he did not confine himself, and he did not distinguish the short story as a pure, exclusive art form. It was part of his repertoire as a genial, sometimes wily, but always amusing celebrant of the wild American West at play—not so much as it really was, but as the public wished to see it. That public wanted a bit of fun, a bit of adventure, some folktale, some homespun philosophy, an occasional poke in the ribs at human credulity and hypocrisy, and a rattling good ending. Twain was willing and able to give them a bit of all these things, as often as not wrapped up in the form of a kind of grab bag that could only loosely be called a short story.

Just as Twain's reputation as a novelist depends heavily upon the adventures of Tom Sawyer and Huckleberry Finn, his short-story reputation is circumscribed generally by his skill as a comic chronicler of a sometimes dubiously innocent rural America. Yet that is not the complete story. "The Celebrated Jumping Frog of Calaveras County," a comic masterpiece, contains many of the elements of his short-story skills. Twain often used a genial, informal oral style, and his narrators often adopt aspects of his own public persona: a kind of good-natured, open-minded narrator, sometimes a bit superior to his surroundings and gently patronizing of the rustics with whom he comes into contact. It is an act that worked with considerable flexibility and variation throughout his career as a writer, allowing him to juxtapose the strengths and weaknesses of both the rural and the sophisticated sensibility without prejudicing the reader one way or the other. The voice, seemingly innocent and unbiased, leads to comic insights but restrains any inclination to oversimplification or outright derision. The tonal geniality in which rural stupidity and guile is exposed often is equally able to show up the limitations of worldly-wise experience; each world has its faults. In "The Celebrated Jumping Frog of Calaveras County," the narrator may reveal the comic ignorance and harmless chicanery of the provincial world, but he too is something of a dupe. He only suspects at the end that, for all of his intellectual superiority, he has become a double victim—once of the long-winded bore and also of his friend Ward, who seems to have set him up for the ordeal by asking him to inquire about the Reverend Leonidas W. Smiley.

The narrator is usually the most vital element in Twain's stories. He may sometimes be used simply to frame the tale, but usually his function is more vital. He will provide the point of view that Twain wants to establish; his attitudes and conclusions are often intellectual and moral touchstones. Yet it is important to remember that the narrators are not always reliable and are sometimes themselves part of the problem being explored. For example, the narrator in "The Celebrated Jumping Frog of Calaveras County" is part of the joke, part of the clever construction that distinguished Twain's version of the story from previous attempts and that made it so popular. The story does not seem to be "constructed" at all: It seems to grow out of anecdotal maundering. This style of the casual, rambling tale, disarming and inviting, was to be used by Twain throughout his career, sometimes for modest effects and sometimes for formidable surprise.

Twain, for all of his mock unworldliness, was keenly aware of the fact that he was seen as something of a rough diamond of American literature, but he was also aware of the way in which his seemingly haphazard way of putting a story together could work beyond the comic mode. If his comic tales made him famous and popular, his real ambition lay in taking the form into more ambitious realms of serious comment upon not only the social and political flaws of American society but also the general flaws of humanity, in its psychological makeup and spiritual pride.

Twain tended to use the short story more seriously as he grew older, as is also the case with his novels. Yet, for all of his comic charm on paper or in personal performance, there was a relentless melancholy and deep misanthropy in Twain's work that was hidden in the early years but that started to pervade his work in the late 1880's. As early as 1868, he produced "Extract from Captain Stormfield's Visit to Heaven" but declined to publish it until 1909. It is a corrosively brisk exploration of the Heaven promised to spiritually good human beings

after death—only it is not as good as these sentimental Christians might imagine, or as central to God's Creation as they have been promised. The story is an excellent example of the fecundity of Twain's imagination, even when he is being morose, but the tale was widely withheld at the time of his early popularity because it would surely have done him irreparable harm with the public, especially in the United States.

In 1870, Twain introduced another twist to his skill that is seemingly comic in "How I Edited an Agricultural Paper," a slight work that starts out as fun and turns nasty. The narrator is a seemingly sensible journalist who has been given a temporary job editing an agricultural newspaper while the regular editor takes a short vacation. During his brief tenure, he reveals an astonishingly ignorant attitude toward the rural science, so much so that readers suspect their own sanity as well as his, given the nature of his comments. Watermelons become members of the berry family, and fishermen are advised to play music for oysters because they grow better to music. The regular editor, back from his vacation, attacks his substitute as an irresponsible ignoramus whose articles have a bizarre comic exaggeration that is amusing but are completely useless in a trade publication.

That is the comic part of the tale, and it could have ended there with a lesser writer, but Twain is not finished. The narrator defends himself, proclaiming that, whatever he has done in driving serious readers away, he has increased the circulation immeasurably among the general public, which is amused by the sheer stupidity of the paper. That success, he arrogantly states, is the role of the journalist; truth is irrelevant. Twain never reveals whether the narrator is actually as stupid as his work suggests or is deliberately, cynically debasing the trade. The joke that he has made of the newspaper may have been simply the product of the age-old condition of journalism, often ignorantly bluffing, or it may have been deliberate. It may be a bit of both, reflecting upon the trade and also upon the public, hungry for a new sensation. It is a good, early example of the density that Twain can often get into the simplest story, as well as an indication of his wish to use his literary gift seriously.

Twain's most interesting work in the genre, however, lies with his tales of less-than-comic human frailty. He can, occasionally, show a touch of O. Henry in a tale such as "The £1,000,000 Bank-Note" (1893), which was made into a motion picture in 1954 as *Man with a Million*. It is a simple tale of a young man who is given a bank note of such size that no one can cash it. A bet is made that, despite this liability, he can survive, as society is so susceptible to the influence of riches. Twain proves that money talks even when it is frozen and that human greed will find a way to respect riches. No harm is done, and the young man gets through, managing to make a fortune on the way and gaining the love of a lovely, and very rich, young woman.

A nastier version of the money trap is in "The $30,000 Bequest" of 1906, in which a respectable, hardworking husband and wife are promised a legacy, so long as they do not inquire about it; the money will come if they do nothing. On this occasion, they ruin their lives imagining how they will spend the money, which in the end proves not to be available anyway. They die embittered and blasted by their dreams of avarice.

There are common elements in Twain's short stories that he never abandoned, even when his stories became more complicated and nihilistic. Most of his tales are set in rural areas or small towns, often in the Midwest or on the south coast. Most of his characters are natives of those areas, often undereducated, unworldly, and sometimes superstitious and ignorant. They can be models of generosity and simplicity in the romantic reading of rural life that Twain often celebrated, but they can also be dishonest, violent, and easily misled by fast-talking swindlers. Twain does not allow his characters to be entirely the victims of clever rogues; they too can be greedy when money is involved.

A further aspect of his work was his use of the rural vernacular. Twain admired such writers as Nathaniel Hawthorne or Henry James, with their fastidious use of the English language. Yet he remained committed to an oral style of considerable informality, attempting to reproduce regional dialects as an adjunct to the reality of his tall tales. In addition, the tall tales need not be entirely original; he would use folk material or the rambling tall tale of the mining camps, tailoring it to his needs, and his work often has marks of the fairy tale. The best guide to his stories is the essay "How to Tell a Story" (1900), in which he insists that the secret lies in "the *manner* of the telling." He sees himself as a "humorous" writer, and as such, he rejects the English story (which he calls "comic") and the French tale (which he calls

"witty"); he is an American humorist, and as such he avoids the shaped, pointed conclusions of the European art form. European writers often let it be known that they realize they are comic or witty; Twain creates narrators who do not know that they are amusing, and if the story has a point, then it should be dropped casually. The story, in fact, should look unprofessional and should seem to be told badly, full of error, representing a kind of inarticulate struggle of a sincere man out of his depth.

Most of Twain's later stories are concerned, without much comic relief, with examples of greed, pride, and social hypocrisy; the innocence of Tom Sawyer's world (if shot through with occasional acts of human stupidity and cruelty) is rejected for a mechanistic, meaningless world of grasping, self-interest. The lightness of touch, the deft manipulation of amusing mischief, and the tonal warmth are absent from stories that sometimes take on an unpleasant, bullying aura. The title of "The Man That Corrupted Hadleyburg" (1900) is an indication of the kind of themes that came to interest Twain. The town, inordinately proud of its reputation for honesty, falls into general derision as its leading citizens, tempted by a cache of gold, attempt to "outlie" one another to gain the prize. Even further down the line of pessimism and disgust and humanity is *The Mysterious Stranger*, a novella-length tale, sometimes categorized as a short story, that was not published until six years after Twain's death. In 1916, his publishers allowed it to be printed, and it is easy to see why there was some reluctance to issue it earlier. The story is supposedly set in sixteenth century Austria, but Twain makes little attempt to distinguish the setting or characters from those that he had been finding for years in rural American towns. A group of boys, including the narrator, and an innocent community meet their match in an angel, a nephew of Satan. What he does is bad enough, but what Twain does to the narrator is worse because the conclusion seems to suggest that nothing actually exists. It may be his greatest story. The tale certainly is his most relentlessly cruel one, and it shows how ambitious he was for the medium in his old age.

THE SHORT STORIES OF JOHN UPDIKE

Type of work: Short stories
Author: John Updike (1932-   )
Principal published works: *The Same Door*, 1959; *Pigeon Feathers and Other Stories*, 1962; *Olinger Stories: A Selection*, 1964; *The Music School*, 1966; *Museums and Women and Other Stories*, 1972; *Problems and Other Stories*, 1979; *Too Far to Go: The Maples Stories*, 1979; *Trust Me*, 1987.

By the time that he was in his thirties, John Updike had proved to be a prodigiously talented young writer. He achieved distinction and a very considerable reputation in the first half of the 1960's as a poet, parodist, critic, novelist, and short-story writer. His early career was remarkable, indeed virtually unique among the serious writers of his generation. Perhaps equally remarkable, he gave evidence at such a young age of enough self-transcendence to be aware of the surprising good fortune that attended all of his efforts.

From the first, Updike was a character in that rare thing, a genuine, American, real-life success story. It is the kind of thing that does not happen to most serious American writers. One need only recall the story that Robert Frost used to tell groups of eager young student writers, how a relative had offered him a living for a year, without worry or burden, to determine if he really were a poet. "Give me twenty," was Frost's reply to the astounded relative. Indeed, it took twenty years of hard and lonely labor before Frost was able to persuade a publisher to print his poems. Equally familar and typical is the example of William Faulkner, who wrote professionally for twenty-five years before anyone began to give him or his work any attention or to consider his work worthy of prizes and awards. Contemporary literary history would indicate that Faulkner's career and Frost's are typical—except, perhaps, for the happy endings. John Updike, however, became a "writer" without prolonged struggle or delay.

In a sense, Updike was patronized by two strong and distinguished literary powers—Alfred A. Knopf publishing company and *The New Yorker* magazine—and, thus, given an opportunity to develop his talent under apparently almost ideal circumstances, saved from the simple, mundane, and frequently discouraging conditions that plague most writers. Moreover, his early critical reception was uniformly good. Surely he was one of the most encouraged writers of the 1960's, and he made every effort to justify this extraordinary interest. He was a prodigious worker who did not waste time or fail to make the most of his advantages. There was no doubt that he was a hardworking, highly gifted, and imaginative writer.

There are built-in dangers and disadvantages to this kind of success story. Talent, to be recognized easily and early, must inevitably be based upon precedent, upon a set of existing and accepted standards. For any establishment to offer rewards at the outset, the work of the neophyte must be acceptable to and, indeed, complimentary to the establishment. Looking back in time, one should have no cause to wonder why, for example, Lizette Reese was for so long considered a much better poet than Robert Frost, or why Glenway Wescott was recognized as a literary artist while William Faulkner was not. It is likely that a decently educated and successful young writer would be haunted by the specters of this literary past, troubled by the vague prospect that history may well be repeating itself. The thought might well be inhibiting. Then there are the inhibitions that can so easily come from writing for particular patrons and an already existing audience. If these patrons are essentially conservative in literary matters, one would be disinclined to offend, to bite the hand that feeds. In order to continue to create, a writer would have to believe in these patrons. To question would be crippling, and to rebel might be disastrous. It is, therefore, a tribute to the skill of Updike that, in spite of all these factors, his work continued to grow in stature without the least sign of self-doubt or diminishing integrity.

After his *Rabbit* series—*Rabbit, Run* (1960), *Rabbit Redux* (1971), *Rabbit Is Rich* (1981), and *Rabbit at Rest* (1990)—and his other novels, it is by his short stories that John Updike is best known. It should be observed that chunks and sections of some of his other novels were originally published in somewhat different form as short stories. In this practical sense, Updike's fiction is the short story. *The Same Door* is a collection of sixteen well-wrought stories, for the most part conventionally correct according to the familiar formula of *The New Yorker*; they are careful, restrained, controlled, and unemphatic in the smooth organization of subject, theme, and structure. Though they are not "autobiographical," the stories derive almost exclusively from the author's pragmatic rather than imagined experience, and they modestly do not aspire to extend beyond these self-imposed limitations. There are stories set in Olinger, which he acknowledges in the foreword to *Olinger Stories: A Selection* to be an only lightly disguised reflection of his hometown, Shillington. There are school stories, stories of the pains and pleasures of adolescence, stories set in Oxford, and stories involving young married couples in New York. With the exception of the final story in the book, "The Happiest I've Been," each of these stories is almost a textbook example of *The New Yorker* story of the period—the expanded anecdote, the significant sketch, told in a straightforward and uncomplicated manner, following the accepted convention of the dramatic presentation with a reasonable unity of time and place. Usually, Updike employs third-person narrators for whom, as a result of events, there is likely to be ever-so-slight rearrangements of the structure of their sensibilities.

The stories are fixed, at once precisely and evocatively, in time by the convention of reference to things—the books, fads and fashions, brand names, and popular songs of a particular moment in time. Nevertheless, the essential mood of all the stories, in fact explicitly stated, is memory, unabashed nostalgia—shards dug up, cleaned, polished, and then elegantly displayed against the ruins of time. Time, mutability, the natural process of change, and decay are the principal forces against which the human protagonists must wrestle. It is unfair to point out that this drama is a slight one, for it has a long and honored tradition and great writers have made much of it. It is fair, however, to remark that such a theme allows for only small action and diminutive moral drama. Morality, good and evil, appears only insofar as it relates to the overriding concern of the single perceptive self in time. The moral world is, then, greatly simplified. What is bad is likely to be vulgarity, stupidity, ugliness, the results of imposed conditions rather than active choices.

There is wit and some humor as well in this first book, but basically the stories are extremely serious, at best succeeding in giving a glimpse of the extraordinary mystery at the heart of things, though always in danger, teetering close to the sheer edge of solemnity and the incorrigibly sentimental. It was this seriousness that impressed Updike's enthusiastic critics most uniformly.

Yet none of these things would be enough to lift Updike to official stardom in the established literary firmament. There are a number of qualities that make *The Same Door* more significant than several other and roughly similar collections by young writers. His style and verbal felicity are vitally important to the overall effect. Updike is a poet and a good one. A poet's love of language and the exact shadings and connotations of the right word emerges in sentence after sentence. He displays, as well, a poet's ear, an aptness of dialogue, a breathtaking sense of the

intricate rhythms of prose. Moreover, he demonstrates a superb visual sense—not surprising as he has studied art professionally—an ability to compose a scene or to evoke a person, place, or thing memorably with a few carefully sketched details. The final effect of all these virtues is a haunting quality of evocation, which fits his theme and mood with admirable decorum and, overwhelming all else, leaves a feeling of great richness and beauty, a luminous purity brimming with an inner light.

Pigeon Feathers and Other Stories represented a new and expanded use of Updike's talent. It was another example of the atypical quality of Updike's literary career. Most writers in his time began with experiment and innovation and moved gradually toward the use of a developed style to explore other interests. Typically, *Pigeon Feathers* would be a first collection of stories, though, realistically, it would have been extremely difficult to publish as such. It is important that, with *The Same Door*, Updike passed all the academic tests. With his achievement, he has been able to carry patron and audience with him into more adventurous directions in both form and subject matter. Again his basic theme, stated in a functional epigraph from Franz Kafka, is memory, but now there is a difference. There are the apparently conventional stories, including the title story, but even they are slightly off center when compared to the earlier stories. There are frankly, more explicitly, autobiographical stories, and the first-person narration, used only sparingly in *The Same Door* is here used freely, easily, and often. Most significantly, however, there are varieties and exercises in the form and structure of the short story, which, while hardly new, were very new for Updike and quite new for *The New Yorker*. He has an epistolary story in "Dear Alexandros." He employs the method of dramatic monologue in "A & P," "Archangel," and "Lifeguard." There is a mild story of social consciousness in "The Doctor's Wife."

There are, perhaps most successfully, a group of personal reminiscences that are transmuted into a form of fiction as in "The Crow in the Woods" and the almost essaylike concluding stories—"The Blessed Man of Boston, My Grandmother's Thimble, Fanning Island," and the second, "Packed Dirt, Churchgoing, A Dying Cat, A Traded Car." To make these work as stories required all of his natural and acquired skill and, as well, requires of the reader a more than casual interest not only in the perceptions of the author but also in his life, a rhetorical demand that would be impossible if he were not already known as a writer and a worthy one. To write these stories required great skill and daring, and no little bravado. To do so as a very young man, still at the beginning of his career, was an example of real artistic courage. Yet his experiments were not radical and were, in large part, derivative. Nevertheless, they represented in many cases the first successful popularization of methods and techniques that had been the exclusive domain of the little magazines. Other writers of the short story owe John Updike their gratitude even though he came late to the task. Even if his early artistry was overpraised by his admirers and often praised for the wrong reasons, there is no denying that Updike is a skilled and serious short-story writer.

THE SHORT STORIES OF EUDORA WELTY

Type of work: Short stories
Author: Eudora Welty (1909-   )
Principal published works: *A Curtain of Green and Other Stories*, 1941; *The Wide Net and Other Stories*, 1943; *The Golden Apples*, 1949; *The Bride of the Innisfallen and Other Stories*, 1955; *Moon Lake and Other Stories*, 1980; *Retreat*, 1981.

Eudora Welty is considered one of the best writers of short stories in the twentieth century. A writer of novels as well, her reputation was built upon her short fiction, especially that of her early collections, *A Curtain of Green and Other Stories* and *The Wide Net and Other Stories*. Although somewhat restricted in setting, her short stories have demonstrated a wide variety in subject matter, ranging from the treatment of sideshow freaks in "Keela, the Outcast Indian Maiden" to that of the improvisations of a jazz musician in "Powerhouse." There is also a wide variety in moods, from the broad humor of "Why I Live at the P.O." and "Petrified Man" to the ironic and grim horror of "Flowers for Marjorie," from the fantasy of "Asphodel" to the devastatingly prosaic quality of "No Place for You, My Love." There is also a wide variety in time, for although most of the stories are set in the present, some like "First Love," "A Still Moment," and "The Burning" go back to the times of Aaron Burr, John James Audubon, and the Civil War.

However wide the variety of theme, mood, and time, the first thing that strikes the reader is Welty's absolute control over all of her material. She is a master craftsperson, and when her stories fail, as they sometimes do, it is often because her virtuosity as craftsperson and experimenter overshadows the material on which she is operating. She has an uncanny ability to create a mood and setting for a story in a few sentences. "The Whistle" and "The Key" reveal in their opening paragraphs all there is to know about the story. Nothing is wasted, and all is used to make clearer the inevitable epiphany that occurs in her stories. Perhaps it was her interest in photography and painting that sharpened this gift of observation. Moreover, her ear seems as sharp as her eye; the beauty parlor gossip in "Petrified Man" echoes diction, cadence, and tone brilliantly. The story called "A Memory" is a good illustration of this control, as the girl on the beach seems to be enacting Welty's own creative process. The girl makes frames out of her fingers and observes the world through them. Whereas the girl cannot include the disordered and grotesque in her framing vision, Welty is able to confine and fix all of life in her frame. An order is given to every "still moment" that her artistry captures,

and the purely formal delight that the reader experiences is one of the great pleasures her short stories afford.

Yet there is more than a caught moment in Welty's stories. What gives them their solidity is that there is a caught place as well. Although her stories are mostly set in the present, they cannot really be called contemporary. For example, none of her stories in her first two collections has anything to do with World War II, although they were published at its height. The only sense in which the present is contemporary is that she has chosen to write of the contemporary South, more specifically the region of Mississippi. Only with *The Bride of the Innisfallen and Other Stories* did she move outside the South for her settings. In this volume, however, the stories that are set in the South, such as "Kin" and "No Place for You, My Love," tend to be the better ones. This strong sense of place is closely tied to Welty's artistic control. It is the concrete reality to which her lyrical flights and moves toward fantasy must always return. Welty herself seems aware of the importance of place, and she wrote an article called "Place in Fiction" that throws much light upon her own fictional achievements.

Moving inside this frame of artistic control and place, certain views and themes seem to be characteristic of the stories as a whole. They are often an exploration of what it means to be isolated and set apart. In story after story, the leading character seems set apart or cut off from the world. This isolation is often marked by a peculiar grotesque quality, as if the spiritual and emotional separateness were symbolized by physical abnormality. Her stories are thus peopled with deaf-mutes (Ellie and Albert in "The Key" or Joel Mayes in "First Love"), by the deformed (Keela in "Keela the Outcast Indian Maiden"), by the feebleminded (Lily Daw in "Lily Daw and the Three Ladies"), by the very old and very small (Phoenix Jackson in "A Worn Path" or Solomon in "Livvie"), by the very young and very fat (Gabriella in "Going to Naples"), and by the frustrated and insane (Clytie in "Clytie" and Miss Theo in "The Burning").

Yet those who are isolated are most often people who seem more valuable than the world that isolates them. The reason is that Welty treats their separateness with sympathy and even with love. The isolation is what allows her to get inside her characters; once inside, their shared isolation, with the reader and with the author, becomes a thing of beauty. Welty is very close to Sherwood Anderson in this aspect of her fiction. The "truth" in the grotesque is the special theme of Anderson's *Winesburg, Ohio* (1919), and the beauty, if not the truth, is the very thing on which Welty focuses. Because the abnormality is lovingly handled, the characters are invested with a certain beauty and mystery. Mr. Marblehead has a secret second life, with a second wife and child in another part of town. Ellie and Albert share a speechless communication that sets them apart from the others in the waiting room in "The Key," a communication that moves into love as they discover the key on the floor. This mystery is often connected with a certain ritual, as it is in Phoenix Jackson's long trek along the "worn path" to get medicine for her grandson. Phoenix is as old as the land itself, yet the mysterious force that keeps her going, and over which she seems to have little control, gives her life a singular sort of beauty for those who see her existence in its entirety and not in its isolation. Mystery is closely related to the lyrical quality as well as the ritualistic and almost mythical. As the couple in "The Whistle" silently burn all of their furniture while the whistle that is blown when a freeze threatens is sounding outside, one senses the elegiac beauty created in their wordless act and the beauty revealed as this action enables them to speak with each other.

At times, the beauty is revealed by the fact of isolation. At other times, it comes as a result of the pathos created by the attempt to reach beyond the isolation. In other words, there are those cut off in place and those cut off from place. R. J. Bowman, in Welty's first published story, "Death of a Traveling Salesman," is an example of the latter. An outsider by occupation as well as by nature, Bowman is a rootless salesman who stumbles onto Sonny and his pregnant wife in the middle of nowhere. In their timeless familial bond of love he sees all that his life has not been. Yet, because he sees, he achieves a certain human dignity even as he dies, somewhat ironically, of a heart attack. His heart fails, but also succeeds. The same pathos is achieved in the treatment of Harris, another traveling salesman who, in "The Hitch-Hikers," wishes people would call him "you" rather than "he." Then there is the Eastern businessman in "No Place for You, My Love" who travels south out of New Orleans with another stranger but goes to the end of the road and returns without ever knowing why he went or where.

As opposed to these figures cut off from place, there are those cut off in place, and these are more tragically and also more comically treated. There is, on the comic side, the humorously paranoid narrator of "Why I Live at the P.O." who escapes the isolation of living with her family by going to live at the post office. The tragic statement of the familial sort of isolation is found in the person of Clytie, who is so hounded by her family and the demands that they make on her that she is driven to suicide. There are all the characters living in Morgana in *The Golden Apples* who feel the need to escape but who also know that there is no escape.

Indeed, it can be said that most of these characters who are caught in their isolation are torn by two forces and move toward a tenuous sort of resolution. Most often, it is a movement from innocence to experience, the kind symbolized in "Livvie," in which the young African-American wife whose old husband, Solomon, is on his deathbed, moves from her sheltered existence to the flashy world of Cash McCord, the field hand who offers her all the pleasures of the world. The same conflict and process is present in Jennie in "At the Landing," when her quest for Floyd leads her from her sheltered home to the shack along the river where she is raped by Floyd's fellow fishermen. Yet her innocence seems to prevail, even as she is raped. The innocents are the blessed in Welty's fiction, and if to the world their innocence takes on a grotesque quality, they appear to be normal in the loving world of the inner heart that Welty explores so well.

Closely related to this theme of innocence and experience is the theme and structural device of the dream versus the reality, and the fusion that sometimes remains at the heart of life in general and life in Welty's fiction in particular. Although this is a theme and structural device employed more fully in Welty's later work, especially in "Music from Spain" in *The Golden Apples*, it can be seen in such early stories as "The Purple Hat," "Flowers for Marjorie," "Powerhouse," and "Old Mr. Marblehall." At times when the dream is submitted to the reality there is a shock, as in "Flowers for Marjorie" or "At the Landing." At other times, however, the dream and the reality seem inseparable, as in "The Purple Hat" and "Powerhouse," whose musical improvisations on the theme of his wife's death seem both real and unreal to the reader. What remains true is that most often it is the dream, the lyrical quality in which it is expressed, and the innocence that gives it birth that is beautiful. "Reality" is never beautiful in itself, but is made so by its contact with the dream and the characters who reveal or embody it.

With such emphasis given to humans in their particular environment, there is not much attention given to their place in the universe. Although there is little metaphysical speculation in Welty's stories, the presence of the universe and its reality is sometimes disturbingly felt. When perceived, the universe is at best indifferent and more often than not seemingly malevolent. Humans are sometimes measured by their reaction to it, as in "The Whistle," where the warmth generated by the couple and their fire is equal to the chilling force of the unseasonal weather, but when special attention is drawn from humanity to the universe, humanity stands in a somewhat defeated posture.

SHOSHA

Type of work: Novel
Author: Isaac Bashevis Singer (1904-1991)
Type of plot: Historical realism
Time of plot: 1914-1952
Locale: Warsaw, Poland, and Tel Aviv, Israel
First published: *Neshome Ekspeditsyes*, 1974 (English translation, 1978)

Like many of Singer's novels and short stories, Shosha *is set in the vanished world of pre-World War II Polish Jewry. As Singer explores this microcosm, he raises universal questions about the meaning of life and the existence of God.*

Principal Characters

Aaron Greidinger, the narrator, a struggling writer, in many ways Singer's double. A cynic and a womanizer, he is mysteriously attracted to the childlike Shosha, with whom he had played when they were neighbors. Rejecting Betty Slonim's offer of marriage and asylum in the United States, Aaron marries Shosha and remains in Poland despite the looming Nazi threat. He eventually escapes to the United States, where he becomes a famous author.

Shosha Schuldiener, Aaron's childhood playmate, later his wife. Though physically and mentally immature, she deeply loves Aaron. She dies during the escape from Poland.

Morris Feitelzohn, a writer and Aaron's mentor. An impoverished hedonist and notorious liar, he envisions establishing an academy for soul expeditions (the original title of the novel in Yiddish) and for pleasure. While

hiding from the Nazis, he at last becomes a true philosopher; he dies in 1941.

Dora Stolnitz, a dedicated communist and Aaron's first mistress. Disillusioned by the Stalinist horror, she abandons her plan of going to the Soviet Union. She vanishes during World War II.

Betty Slonim, a Russian-born Jewish actress who has come to Warsaw to resurrect her career. She encourages Aaron to write a play for her, and she falls in love with him. After Aaron rejects her marriage proposal, she moves to the United States; she later commits suicide.

Haiml and **Celia Chentshiner,** rich, intelligent, secular Jews. Celia has affairs with Feitelzohn and Aaron, apparently with the approval of her husband, Haiml. She dies during World War II, and he survives, remarries, and moves to Israel.

The Story

Shosha traces the life of Aaron Greidinger from childhood to middle age. The son of Rabbi Menachem Mendl Greidinger, Aaron lives on Krochmalna Street in Warsaw in an apartment filled with books and prohibitions. For him, the Schuldiener household in the same building provides a refuge from the coarse boys in the street and the restrictions of his parents. Though Aaron is a prodigy of learning and Shosha Schuldiener is such a poor student that she is dismissed from school, the two children enjoy playing together.

In 1914, their youthful idyll ends. In May, the Schuldieners move to another building, and World War I brings hardship to all. The Greidingers leave Warsaw for Old Stykov in Galacia, where Aaron's father and later Aaron's

younger brother, Moishe, earn a meager living as rabbis. Even before this move, Aaron has begun to question traditional Judaism, from which he becomes increasingly alienated. He travels around Poland teaching Hebrew in small villages, eventually returning to Warsaw, where he struggles to live as a writer. He also begins an affair with Dora Stolnitz, an ardent communist, who unsuccessfully tries to convert Aaron to her views.

At the nadir of his fortunes, Aaron meets Betty Slonim and her American lover, Sam Dreiman. Dreiman wants to resurrect Betty's acting career by commissioning a play and renting a Warsaw theater for its production. Aaron has written the first act of a drama based on the life of the Maiden of Ludmir, a nineteenth century girl who wanted to study the Talmud and become a rabbi. Encouraged by Morris Feitelzohn, Betty, and Sam, Aaron agrees to complete the work; Dreiman plies him with advances that allow Aaron to move into a furnished apartment with maid service.

Betty Slonim makes advances of another kind; Aaron becomes her tour guide and lover as well as her playwright. On one of their expeditions, Aaron returns to Krochmalna Street for the first time since his family moved away in 1917, and there he finds Shosha, unchanged despite the passage of time. After that meeting, he visits Shosha daily, though he retains his apartment and the pretense of writing Betty's play.

That work becomes increasingly complex and unactable. Betty and Sam want sex and action; she and other cast members emend the drama, changing the language and adding roles. The Actors' Union wants still more parts for its members. A rehearsal exposes the absurdity of the piece; Aaron, disappointed with himself and disgusted with his former life and associates, returns to

live on Krochmalna Street, sleeping in an alcove of the Schuldiener apartment.

Sam still envisions making Betty a star, but now he intends to do so in the United States. He wants Aaron to join them; he offers to support the young man while he writes a better play and even agrees that Aaron and Betty should marry. Aaron rejects this financial and physical security in order to marry Shosha, even though he has little hope of earning a living and knows that the Nazis will soon invade the country.

An epilogue leaps ahead thirteen years to recount the fates of the various characters. Many of Aaron's associates perish in World War II: Celia Chentshiner, Feitelzohn, Shosha. Dora Stolnitz disappears; Betty Slonim kills herself after Sam's death. Of the prewar world, only Aaron and Haiml Chentshiner survive. Aaron has become a successful writer. On a trip to Israel, he meets Haiml, who has remarried. As the novel ends, the two men discuss the past and ponder the meaning of life.

Critical Evaluation

After rejecting further financial support from Sam Dreiman, Aaron supports himself by writing accounts of various false messiahs: Jacob Frank, Reuveyni, Shlomo Mulkho, Sabbatai Zvi. Singer's own first novel, *Sotan in Goray* (1935; *Satan in Goray*, 1955), deals with the enthusiasm in Poland for Zvi's messianic message in the aftermath of the Cossack pogroms led by Bogdan Chmielnicki from 1648 to 1649. Such autobiographical elements loom large in *Shosha*. Dora Stolnitz is modeled on the ardent communist whom Singer married in the 1920's and who left him to go to the Soviet Union. Aaron's play resembles Singer's story, later to become a 1983 film, about Yentl, the girl who disguises herself as a boy to study the Talmud. Aaron shares with his creator a younger brother named Moishe, a childhood residence at 10 Krochmalna Street, red hair, and vegetarianism. Both Aaron and Singer reject conventional Judaism, yet both remain obsessed with its mysticism and its history, which they seek to preserve in their writing.

Modernists have substituted literature for religion as a stay against time, chance, and mutability. As Aaron observes early in the novel, "I believed that the aim of literature was to prevent time from vanishing." Yet Aaron grows as disenchanted with his new faith as with his old. His books, formerly certain sources of consolation, fail him; the works of Arthur Schopenhauer, Friedrich Wilhelm Nietzsche, and Baruch Spinoza, as well as his own

literary efforts, strike him as hollow. Toward the end of the novel, he believes that he has "thrown away four thousand years of Jewishness and exchanged it for meaningless literature, Yiddishism, Feitelzohnism." He tells Betty, "We are running away and Mount Sinai runs after us. This chase has made us sick and mad."

Moishe, Aaron's younger brother who has succeeded his father as rabbi, has not fled Mount Sinai and appears content, but his faith proves naïve and ineffectual. He maintains that Hitler and Stalin will be punished, but his mother reminds him that, before retribution comes, many innocent people will die. Moishe speaks of the miracles that have saved Jews in the past; Aaron wishes that, for once, the enemies of the Jews would need a miracle. Moishe's mother and wife cannot live together harmoniously, and Moishe's only recourse is emersion in prayer, which does nothing to resolve the conflict.

The history of the search for a messiah is thus the book that Singer, like Aaron, is writing. Secular literature, philosophy, and traditional religion fail, like Jacob Frank or Sabbatai Zvi, to offer salvation. For Dora Stolnitz, the false messiah is communism; even after her closest associates are jailed and executed by Joseph Stalin's regime, she clings to her belief. Feitelzohn trusts to hedonism and spiritualism. The two dybbukim, or wandering souls, that possess Betty Slonim in Aaron's play, a musician and a whore, reflect her two saviors, art and sensuality; her suicide reveals their falsehood.

Singer claims to be a storyteller, not a moralist, but *Shosha* is characteristic of his fiction's exploration of the questions of belief and life. The search for answers that he reveals among the Jews of Warsaw epitomizes the human condition in an existential world where God, if He exists, is silent and where rationalism, the Enlightenment, has failed to unriddle the universe. In Israel, Haiml tells Aaron that, after Celia died, she came to him and told him to marry Genia, and he asks Aaron's opinion of this occurrence. Aaron replies only, "I don't know." Haiml does not know either, and for him the world remains inexplicable: "If God is wisdom, how can there be foolishness? And if God is life, how can there be death? . . . I ask them [God and Satan], 'What need was there for all this?' and I wait for an answer." There Singer leaves his characters, and the reader, still waiting.

No revelation is vouchsafed. Still, Aaron's vegetarianism; Genia's recognition that flies, beetles, and mice are living creatures and so deserving of pity; and Haiml's summary of religion as doing no harm to others reflect Singer's own beliefs. While hiding from the Nazis, Feitelzohn rejects his earlier hedonism for a different faith: If God allows evil, then "we must want righteousness, Hasidism, our own version of grace." Though Haiml and Aaron sit in silent darkness, they sit together. People must provide the love that God denies the world and so create cosmos from chaos. Singer is not so optimistic as to believe that such efforts will always succeed: Celia and Shosha perish, along with Dora Stolnitz and Betty Slonim. Perhaps the best that one can achieve is a personal peace, however uneasy, a version of grace that keeps one from following the false messiahs of fanaticism that lead to isolation and self-destruction.

THE SKIN OF OUR TEETH

Type of work: Drama
Author: Thornton Wilder (1897-1975)
Type of plot: Fantastic parable
Time of plot: All human history
Locale: Excelsior, New Jersey, and the boardwalk at Atlantic City
First presented: 1942

The Skin of Our Teeth is a fantastic parable dealing with humanity's age-old struggle to achieve civilization. The action covers three periods—an ice age, a great flood, and a devastating war—and in each case, humans manage to survive against overwhelming odds.

Principal Characters

George Antrobus, a citizen of the world. He wants to believe in the goodness of humanity and the survival of the race, but often his faith is shaken. A kind and generous man, he insists that starving refugees from the freezing cold enveloping the world be admitted to the house and fed, whereas his practical wife does not want to take them in. A good provider, he obtains a boat in order to save his family during the big flood. After the great war, he decides to try to live in peace with his vicious son, Henry. Striving to regain his confidence in mankind, he takes comfort in his books, his home, and the good people of the world.

Mrs. Antrobus, George's wife. She is a typical middle-class mother who loves her family and willingly sacrifices herself to their needs. Her practical responses enable her to hold onto her husband, survive catastrophes, and perpetuate the race. When she is about to lose George to Sabina, she takes advantage of the coming great flood to bring him back to duty and family. When the great war comes, she finds safety in the basement for herself, her daughter, and, most important, her new grandchild.

Gladys Antrobus, their daughter, a wholesome girl much like her mother. Content to remain within the security of the family circle, she survives the great flood. By hiding in the basement, she and her new baby survive the great war as well.

Henry Antrobus, formerly called **Cain,** the Antrobuses' son, a nonconformist. When he hits his brother with a stone and accidentally kills him, the parents change his name from Cain to Henry and thereafter make every effort to hide his past. In another fit of hate, he kills a neighbor with a stone. In the great war, his aggressive temperament enables him to rise from the rank of corporal to that of general.

Sabina, the maid in the Antrobus household. She is the former mistress of George, who had brought her back from the Sabine rape. She leaves the Antrobuses and, as Miss Lily-Sabina Fairweather, wins a beauty contest at Atlantic City, after which she tries unsuccessfully to win back George.

Moses, a judge; **Homer,** a blind beggar with a guitar; **Miss E. Muse, Miss T. Muse,** and **Miss M. Muse,** refugees from the killing cold, who stop at the Antrobus house for food and warmth.

The Story

A great wall of ice was moving southward over the land, bringing with it an unprecedented cold spell in August. In Hartford, Connecticut, they were burning pianos, and it was impossible to reach Boston by telegraph. The people did nothing but talk about the looming catastrophe. So far, only the extreme cold had reached Excelsior, New Jersey, where Mr. and Mrs. George Antrobus lived in an attractive suburban residence. Their rather commonplace lives were to be greatly changed by the extreme form that the weather had taken.

Mr. Antrobus was a fine man, a sterling example for his community. He had invented the wheel, the alphabet, and the multiplication table. Mrs. Antrobus was the picture of the middle-class mother, with the best interests of her children at heart. Their daughter, Gladys, was much like her mother, but their son was atypical. His name had been Cain until an unfortunate accident occurred in which he hit his brother with a stone and killed him. As the result of that thoughtless action, his name had been changed to Henry, and Mrs. Antrobus went to some pains to keep his past history a secret. Members of the Antrobus household also included Sabina, the maid; a baby dinosaur; and a mammoth.

On this particular day in August, everyone was freezing and even the dogs were sticking to the sidewalk because it was so cold. Sabina was in an agitated state because nothing seemed to be going properly. She had milked the mammoth, but she had let the only fire in the house go out. Her plight was doubly humiliating because her career in the Antrobus house had begun when Mr. Antrobus brought her back from the Sabine rape. He had given her a life of luxury until he tired of her; now she was relegated to the kitchen. She was a canny and observant individual, however, a necessary apex to the age-old triangle.

Sabina was waiting nervously for the return of Mr. Antrobus when a domestic altercation with Mrs. Antrobus prompted her to give a two-week notice. Later, a telegram announcing the arrival of Mr. Antrobus and some salvation from the cold caused her to change her mind for the time being.

When he finally arrived, Mr. Antrobus brought news that most of the outside world was freezing and that there was probably nothing they could do to escape the same fate. When some tramps and refugees from the ice came to the house for warmth and food, Mrs. Antrobus was not in favor of admitting them, but Mr. Antrobus insisted. Mrs. Antrobus agreed, but only after the dinosaur and the mammoth had been evicted. The refugees included a judge named Moses, a blind beggar with a guitar named Homer, and the Misses E., T., and M. Muse. The Antrobus family attempted to keep up some semblance of hope as they gathered around their small fire. When Henry, in another fit of hate, murdered a neighbor with a stone, Mr. Antrobus stamped out the fire. He was cajoled into having faith in humankind again, however, and all, including the audience, were asked to burn their chairs in order to keep the fire going and save the human race from extinction.

That crisis over, Mr. and Mrs. Antrobus went to the Atlantic City convention of the Ancient and Honorable Order of Mammals, Subdivision Humans. Mr. Antrobus, just elected president of the society for the coming year, made a speech of acceptance, which was followed by a few words from Mrs. Antrobus. During an interview immediately afterward, it was learned that Mr. and Mrs. Antrobus would soon celebrate their five thousandth wedding anniversary. Mr. Antrobus had previously judged a beauty contest in which the winner had been the former maid Sabina, now Miss Lily-Sabina Fairweather from the Boardwalk Bingo Parlor. She had decided, as a result of her victory, to take Mr. Antrobus away from his wife; as soon as she could easily do so, she lured him into her beach cabana. During her father's sojourn in the cabana, Gladys bought herself a pair of red stockings, and Henry became involved in an altercation with a boy whom he hit with a stone. When Mr. Antrobus was finally located, he had decided to leave his wife. Told of his intentions, Mrs. Antrobus handled the situation very calmly and maneuvered him into staying with her. She was aided somewhat by a coming storm that made it necessary for the family and a large collection of animals to retreat to a boat in order to survive. Under the directions of a mysterious fortune teller, Mr. Antrobus took them all, including Sabina, off to make a new world.

When the great war came, much of the population of the world and most of Excelsior, New Jersey, were wiped out. The Antrobus household, including Sabina, managed to survive, but not without considerable damage. Mrs. Antrobus, Gladys, and Gladys' new baby had hidden out in the basement. When the war ended, they came out into the world, which in a very short time began to function very much as it had before the war occurred.

Sabina, dressed now as a Napoleonic camp follower, had enjoyed the war. She believed that people were at their best in wartime. Henry, following up his stone-throwing activities, had progressed from a corporal's rating to the rank of a general; he had become the picture of hate, the enemy of humanity. His father ordered that he never come into the house again, or Mr. Antrobus would kill him. When Henry returned, he wanted to kill his father, whom he had hated all these years, and he had brought a gun with which to shoot Mr. Antrobus. When he finally fell asleep from exhaustion, Mrs. Antrobus took the revolver from him. Mr. Antrobus and Henry had an argument during which all the evil in the young man was revealed. Mr. Antrobus, in a fit of self-condemnation, admitted that he would rather fight Henry than try to build a peace with him. His will to survive returned once again, however, and he asked Henry to try to live in peace. Henry agreed, providing he be given a freedom of his own will.

Mr. Antrobus, striving to regain his confidence in humankind, recalled the three things that had always kept him going: the people, his home, and his books. In addition, he remembered the philosophies that he had known and through which he regained his hope for the future.

Critical Evaluation

To American audiences who saw the original production of *The Skin of Our Teeth*, the play seemed mad, incomprehensible, but highly entertaining. Their reaction was understandable, for few American playwrights have employed such bizarre forms to convey serious content. "Dream plays," German expressionism, the comic strip, musical comedy—Wilder once listed these as his sources of dramaturgical inspiration. The play is, however, basically a parody of old-fashioned American stock-company productions and vaudeville. European audiences, for whom the play was performed in bomb-scarred churches and beer halls, had less difficulty in grasping Wilder's message. As the dramatist himself observed, the play "mostly comes alive under conditions of crisis." As depressions, wars, and the threat of ice ages have hardly vanished from the scene, *The Skin of Our Teeth* promises to remain a part of the world's theater experience.

Despite their range and complexity, Wilder's main ideas can be briefly summarized. Indeed, in Sabina's first direct address to the audience, Wilder does this very thing. The play is, she says, "all about the troubles the human race has gone through." Such troubles are of two kinds: those caused by nature and those caused by the human race itself. The Ice Age and the Flood are examples of the first type, though Wilder makes it plain that the real source of catastrophe in act 2 is not the weather but humanity's disordered passions. Depression and war are clearly human creations. The "human race" is not for Wilder a disconnected assemblage of discrete cultures and generations. Rather, it is a being—a living person who experiences, remembers, and matures. The name "Antrobus" expresses this concept, being derived from the Greek word for humanity, *anthropos.*

As one learns from the closing, philosophic quotations, humankind's best hope for "getting by" lies in the species' intellect. Its first priority is to establish order by means of disciplining reason. In doing so, humanity avails itself of a special energy that Aristotle considered divine. This holy energy is ultimately related to the force that created the heavens and the earth. The greatest threat to humanity's survival is not merely its unruly animal nature, which brings disorder to the soul. More seriously, the true threat is an inclination toward evil that infects even rational faculties. To counter this threat, humanity can draw upon its capacity for love, as well as on the accumulated wisdom that history has provided.

This set of ideas shapes all aspects of the drama. Mr. and Mrs. Antrobus stand for Reason, which has masculine and feminine dimensions. Sabina, the maid, represents the passions, especially those which seek erotic pleasure and social power. Henry, their son, claimed Wilder, embodies "strong unreconciled evil." Like Sabina, he resists the rule of law in himself and society, but his murderous nature reveals a far graver sort of wickedness. Like Cain, he despises God and longs to overthrow His order. Yet Wilder's characters are not merely allegorical types. Mr. Antrobus shows himself capable of homicidal intent, and because he loves his theories and machines too much, he is partly to blame for Henry's behavior. Sabina speaks for Wilder when she exclaims, "We're all just as wicked as we can be, and that's God's truth."

No single character symbolizes love in *The Skin of Our Teeth.* Rather this function is fulfilled by the Antrobus family as a whole. In act 1, they share their hearth with the refugees. In act 2, they refuse to enter the ship without Henry. In the final act, they readmit Henry to their circle. Yet, because the Antrobuses are a metaphor for humankind, their gestures have wider significance. The refugees are not strangers, but relatives. So are members of the audience, a fact that the invitation to "Pass up your chairs, everybody" conveys. Wilder symbolizes this condition by making the father of Gladys' beloved baby an anonymous someone, an Everyman. The final acceptance of Henry is the most powerful moment in the play. Despite Henry's evil, Mr. Antrobus grudgingly must acknowledge that "Oh, you're related, all right." Thus Henry may take his place in a family where all belong.

If the human race is actually one, there is finally only one experience and one memory. Wilder dramatizes this concept in a variety of ingenious ways, all of which involve seeing time as an eternal present. Dinosaurs, biblical personages, and figures from Greek mythology crowd into the Antrobus' living room. Because each advance in technology requires a remembering of all previous discoveries, Wilder has the invention of the alphabet "occur" during the era of telegraphic communication. Sabina is, simultaneously, a figure from classical history, a "Napoleonic camp follower," and a contemporary American. The constant interruptions of the action force the audience to dwell in a single time dimension—the present, in which are contained both past and future as well as "real" and "imaginary time."

By these means, Wilder also reinforces the notion that modern humans are what they are because of the experiences of their forebears; or, more exactly, human nature has developed in certain ways because people have inherited certain principles of interpretation. These principles are found in clearest form in the great books of history. Insofar as such principles shape human thought, the thinkers who expressed them live on. Yet people can forget or ignore the education that history has afforded them and become animals again. Thus, books are instruments of humanization. In this sense, Mr. Antrobus is entirely correct when he says to the book-burning Henry, "You are my deadly enemy." Part of Wilder's optimism about humankind's future stems from the mere existence of books and libraries.

The full seriousness and profundity of Wilder's themes tend, unfortunately, to escape most audiences. Indeed, the play's rapid pace and dramaturgical gimmicks draw attention away from its key symbols. Invited to participate on a superficial level, the typical viewer feels puzzled and a bit resentful when, in the third act, the drama suddenly becomes very sombre and too heavily philosophical.

SONG OF SOLOMON

Type of work: Novel
Author: Toni Morrison (1931-   )
Type of plot: Heroic quest
Time of plot: Mid-twentieth century
Locale: Michigan and Virginia
First published: 1977

Song of Solomon is the novel that consolidated Morrison's reputation as one of the most important writers of her generation. Drawing on folklore, recent history, and even details of her own life, Morrison tells the story of Milkman Dead, a young African-American man who locates his identity in his family's roots.

Principal Characters

Macon "Milkman" Dead III, the son of a wealthy African-American landlord and the grandson of the first African-American doctor in town, Dr. Foster, on his mother's side and of a freed slave, Macon Dead the first, on his father's side. The novel begins with Milkman's birth and follows the first thirty-three years of his life, as he grows from a spoiled young boy to a selfish young man to a responsible adult. The novel ends with Milkman leaping across a chasm to confront his childhood friend, Guitar Bains, shortly after Guitar has shot Milkman's aunt, Pilate Dead.

Macon Dead II, Milkman's father, a wealthy African-American landlord in the unnamed Midwestern town in which most of the novel is set.

Pilate Dead, Macon II's sister and Milkman's aunt, a bootlegger but also Milkman's adviser in spiritual matters. It is a blues song that she sings which provides a crucial clue to Milkman's heritage.

Guitar Bains, Milkman's friend for most of his life, a young African-American man from the South who moved north after his father was killed in an accident in a sawmill. Although Guitar and Milkman have always been close, a dispute over gold that they believe Pilate hid years ago turns them into enemies.

Ruth Foster Dead, Milkman's mother and Macon II's wife. She is the daughter of Dr. Foster, an African-American doctor and once the most respected member of the community.

The Story

The opening of *Song of Solomon* is undoubtedly one of the finest first chapters in American literature, but its very complexity can make it hard to follow upon first reading. The novel begins by presenting Milkman Dead's birth the day after Robert Smith, an insurance agent, leaps from the top of Mercy Hospital in an attempt to fly over Lake Superior and into Canada. Present in the crowd that gathers below, but not yet identified as important characters, are Pilate Dead, Guitar Bains, and Ruth Foster Dead, pregnant with Milkman, who goes into labor in front of the hospital. The opening is filled with images of and references to flight, Robert Smith's leap being the most obvious but also including a song that Pilate sings, a reference that she makes to Ruth's unborn baby as a bird, and an offhand comparison that the narrator uses between the crowd that Robert Smith draws and one that

aviator Charles Lindbergh drew several years earlier. Shortly after Milkman is born, one of the first things that the reader is told about him is that, at the age of four, he learned "that only birds and airplanes could fly" and lost all interest in himself. The controlling heroic motif for this novel has been planted: Milkman's birth was announced by flight, and his task will be to learn to fly under his own power.

Part 1 of the novel covers the years from Milkman's birth, in 1931, until he is a young man in his early thirties. In terms of Milkman's growth, the tone of these years is established early in the incident that earns him his nickname. When Freddie, a janitor who sometimes works for Macon, comes by the house in the middle of the day to pay his rent, he finds Ruth nursing the young boy, by now a toddler of four. Freddie dubs him "Milkman" on the spot, and the name sticks; as the novel progresses, the term seems to describe Milkman metaphorically as a man who lives off the milk of his family. He lives at home, where his mother and sisters cook his meals, make his bed, and do his laundry; he works in his father's office; and for many years, he has a long-running sexual affair with his second cousin, Hagar, Pilate's granddaughter. He unceremoniously drops Hagar by sending her a good-bye letter with some cash several days before Christmas, and she dies of grief.

In this first section, Milkman is a selfish character and not the most interesting one that the reader meets. The lives and stories of his friends and family, however, are fascinating. In an important subplot, one slowly learns of Guitar Bains's involvement with a group known as the Seven Days, which is committed to maintaining the ratio between blacks and whites by killing one white person, chosen at random, for every African-American person killed by whites. The most crucial subplot, however, concerns the unveiling of Pilate's and Macon's past, including the story of how their father, the first Macon Dead, a former slave, got the name "Macon Dead" when he registered at the Freedmen's Bureau and how he was murdered when Macon and Pilate were children by men who wanted his land. Macon tells Milkman most of the story in bits and pieces over the years, including the story of how Macon and Pilate hid in a cave after their father's death and Macon killed a man who had been sleeping in the cave near some hidden gold. Their quarrel, when Macon wanted to take this gold and Pilate refused to let him, led to the lifelong hatred that Macon still felt for Pilate when Milkman, as an adult, heard the story of this gold.

By the end of part 1, Milkman is aware how much he has been living in his father's shadow, and he is desperate to move out on his own. His father suggests that Milkman try to find the gold, which Macon is convinced that Pilate hid somewhere. Part 2 of the novel tells of Milkman's quest for this gold, as he retraces Pilate's wanderings from years earlier.

Milkman's search takes him south to Shalimar, Virginia, a town in which everyone seems to claim kinship to a slave called both Shalimar and Solomon. There he hears children singing a blues song that Pilate used to sing, except where she would sing "Sugarman," they sing "Solomon," and they add additional verses that tell of Solomon's legendary flight back to Africa and that list the names of the children he left behind—their ancestors. The youngest of those named in the song is Jake, who Milkman discovers was the man who became the first Macon Dead, his grandfather.

Ebullient to discover that he, who always longed for the power of flight, is descended from a legendary slave who apparently flew back to Africa on his own power, Milkman rushes home to tell Pilate what he has learned. He also wants to tell her that the bag she has been carrying around for years contains the bones of her father, whose body washed downstream after a storm and was left to rot in the same cave where she and her brother had once taken shelter. The two of them travel back to Shalimar, Virginia, to bury the bones on Solomon's Leap, the outcropping of rock in the mountains from which Shalimar is said to have leaped when he flew back to Africa. Guitar, however, who has convinced himself that Milkman has betrayed the Seven Days and who has stationed himself on a nearby outcropping of rock, mistakes Pilate for Milkman and shoots her. Milkman suddenly becomes aware that Pilate has been his unwitting spiritual adviser during his journey in which, by searching for the gold, he has really learned more about himself and more about Pilate. Enraged at her death, Milkman leaps over the edge of the cliff to the opposing outcropping, where Guitar has dropped his gun and is waiting for him. The novel ends with Milkman in midair, knowing "what Shalimar knew: If you surrendered to the air, you could *ride* it."

Critical Evaluation

Song of Solomon was Toni Morrison's third novel. Her first two, *The Bluest Eye* (1970) and *Sula* (1973) had focused on female main characters. *Song of Solomon* was Morrison's first novel to focus specifically on a male protagonist. Furthermore, in both *The Bluest Eye* and *Sula*, Morrison had focused on characters whose identity as African-American women left them marginalized from the mainstream, European currents of American culture. European standards of beauty define Pecola in *The Bluest Eye* as ugly, and they do not allow Sula in *Sula* to develop into the strong, talented woman she shows signs of being in her youth. In *Song of Solomon*, by contrast, Morrison presented an African-American man who, by learning about his heritage, grows into the man he is capable of becoming.

In writing *Song of Solomon*, Morrison drew heavily on African-American culture, most prominently in her use of the story of flying Africans. One version of this tale was collected by Arna Bontemps and Langston Hughes in *The Book of Negro Folklore* (1959), and it tells of an African who was enslaved and brought to America but who spread the secret of flight among his fellow slaves; those who learned the secret would then be able to fly back to Africa. Flight, construed as escape, has been an important motif in African-American literature in general; in slave narratives such as that of Frederick Douglass, in which the flight from slavery is central; and in novels such as Richard Wright's *Native Son* (1940), the middle third of which is entitled "Flight" and tells the story of Bigger Thomas' abortive flight from the law. In *Song of Solomon*, Morrison invokes the power and beauty of the concept of flight, but she tries to transform it into a power to encounter and deal with a situation, rather than to escape it.

Furthermore, Morrison superimposed over Milkman's story details of her own family life. Morrison herself was born February 18, 1931, the date mentioned in the novel as that of Robert Smith's fatal attempt to fly over Lake Superior and the day before Milkman's birthday. While Morrison grew up in Ohio and Milkman grew up in Michigan, both are from the Midwest. Morrison did not create in Milkman a thinly fictionalized version of herself, but rather she created a character who lives through the same times and many of the same tensions as the author. Also, Morrison had a grandfather named Solomon Willis, who lost a farm that he had worked, and a mother named Rahmah, whose name, like the names Pilate and Magdalene and First Corinthians (Milkman's sisters), was chosen at random from the Bible.

Just as Morrison has carefully located her novel within the context of African-American culture, she has been careful to locate it within the cultural constructions of Western European literature. For example, parallels could be drawn between the story of Milkman and that of Sir Parsifal, one of the knights of King Arthur's round table who sets off on his quest for the Holy Grail armed mostly with his own naïveté. More generally, however, this tale can be read as a traditional *Bildungsroman*, as it is the story of the education of a young man who must learn lessons that are of the utmost importance to his community as well as to himself.

Milkman's most important teacher is certainly Pilate, his aunt. Both as a root doctor and as someone who is in contact with the ghost of her dead father, Pilate is a fount of ancestral wisdom, and it is through retracing her steps that Milkman learns to appreciate the value of his own ancestral past. Furthermore, Pilate serves as a strong feminine counterbalance to the dominant masculine presence of Milkman's father. Unlike Macon, who sees people as things and wants to teach Milkman that the secret to happiness is to "Own things. And let the things you own own other things," Pilate's dying words to Milkman are, "I wish I'd a knowed more people. I would of loved 'em all." Where Macon belittles even the people he loves, Pilate wants them to grow.

It is ironic that while *Song of Solomon* won Morrison popular acclaim and prestigious awards, including the National Book Critics Circle Fiction Award, some of the readers and critics who had commended her earlier novels for exploring the violence done to the lives of African-American women through their marginalization in European and American culture greeted *Song of Solomon* only lukewarmly. Many saw in it a novel that makes a hero out of a spoiled young man who thoughtlessly uses the women in his life. The critical consensus that has emerged over time, however, is that *Song of Solomon* is the story of a young man who slowly and painfully learns the value of the people in his life. The most heroic act that Milkman performs is not to leap in the air toward Guitar at the end, but to acknowledge his connection—and the value of that connection—to Pilate, to his dead lover Hagar, to his ancestors, and even to Guitar, his lifelong friend and Pilate's killer.

THE SOT-WEED FACTOR

Type of work: Novel
Author: John Barth (1930-   )
Type of plot: Historical parody
Time of plot: Late seventeenth and early eighteenth centuries
Locale: England and Maryland Province
First published: 1960

With The Sot-Weed Factor, *Barth has created a satire of Colonial America. The author exhibits a tone of cheerful nihilism as he tells the tale of Ebenezer Cooke, an aimless young man who admires only chastity and poetry, and of his journey to Maryland.*

Principal Characters

Ebenezer Cooke, a young would-be poet who is searching for a purpose in life. Holding tight to his chastity, he nevertheless falls in love with a prostitute, whom he then cannot bring himself to hire. Finding a love of poetry, he sets sail for the Maryland Province in America in order to be the supposed poet laureate of this untamed region.

Andrew Cooke, Ebenezer's father, who insists that his son learn a trade and make himself useful. Andrew sends Ebenezer to Maryland so that he can supervise the family's tobacco plantation.

Anna Cooke, Ebenezer's twin sister. Like her brother, she has been greatly influenced by their tutor, Henry Burlingame III.

Henry Burlingame III, an adventurer, tutor, and friend of Ebenezer. He exerts much power over his charge through his unorthodox teaching methods and views of life.

Joan Toast, a prostitute with whom Ebenezer falls deeply in love. At first she scorns his idealism, but she later comes to love him for his purity. Joan follows Ebenezer to America in the hope of settling down with him. She finally does so in the guise of Susan Warren, the wretched swine-tender on a plantation.

John McEvoy, Joan's former pimp, who follows her to the Colonies.

Captain Mitchell, a Maryland planter who employs Joan/Susan.

Bertrand Burton, Ebenezer's valet.

Mary Mungummory, "the Traveling Whore o' Dorset."

The title of this extremely long, wholly outrageous, and cleverly executed novel may strike the reader as curious, and it should be explained before attempting to comprehend the work itself. A sot-weed factor may be defined as a merchant in tobacco. The term not only serves as the title of John Barth's book but also is the title of a satirical poem published in London in 1708 by an actual but obscure Ebenezer Cooke, "Poet & Laureate of the Province of Maryland": *The Sot-Weed Factor: Or, A Voyage to Maryland, A satyr, In which is describ'd the Laws, Government, Courts and Constitutions of the Country; and also the Buildings, Feasts, Frolicks, Entertainments and Drunken Humours of the Inhabitants of that Part of America. By Eben. Cooke, Gent.*

Poetry and innocence drive the principal character in Barth's imaginative, ribald account of Ebenezer Cooke's character and adventures in Colonial America. Twenty-seven years old when he sets out to make his way in the world, Ebenezer simultaneously devotes his life to the twin ideals of chastity and art in an age when many wooed the muse of poetry but very few regarded virtue as a possession to be preserved, and even fewer thought of it as a matter for regret after its loss. His reason for his double dedication, as he frequently explains to unlikely listeners or under strange circumstances, is mystical rather than practical or moral: He has vowed to make purity the essence of his physical as well as his spiritual being. His resolve might have turned him into a prig. Instead, it transforms him into an innocent.

The son of a shrewd man, the planter and trader Andrew Cooke, Ebenezer has suffered in his youth the not uncommon malady of sons of shrewd men. He cannot settle on an occupation; he is adrift. His principal problem is his inability to make up his mind. No one thing seems to appeal to him more than any other; all things are equal in his eyes. His is also the malady of the modern age—an existential vacuum.

Being an awkward fellow, he has failed not only his father's utilitarian goals but also the goals of manhood in his lack of sexual experience. He has pursued scholarship, but cannot achieve it; he has tried business, but is burdened by impracticality. Having been sent by his father to London and apprenticed to a merchant in order to learn the plantation trade, he has frittered away his time and remained a mere clerk on the bottom level of the countinghouse caste. In the meantime, because of his university background and the influence of Henry Burlingame III, his former tutor, he has drifted into the coffeehouse society of the period and become the hanger-on of a pseudo-artistic circle presided over by Ben Oliver, Tom Trent, and Dick Merriweather, drunken poets and low wits. Then he is offered an opportunity to sully his virginity. The offer provides him with impetus into a vocation.

At this point, Barth begins to warm to, and give promise of, the Rabelaisian overtones laced throughout his novel. When, on a wager, Ebenezer is faced with the prospect of having sexual experience thrust upon him, the moment comes in the person of a rare and comely prostitute of the taverns, Joan Toast. He fails to meet the test of his manhood because he falls suddenly and completely in love with the bold young woman. After much confusion, he hurries back to his room. There Mistress Toast pursues him, determined to perform her function in society and collect her rightful fee, only to learn that his love for her will not allow the occasion to be marred by the exchange of money. Either she must have him for his virginity alone or she must leave. In the latter event, he will still adore her, even though his remains an unconsummated love.

Mistress Toast cannot understand this display of idealism, for her experience has conditioned her to complete pragmatism in matters of sex. A dispute follows. After her departure, Ebenezer composes a hymn to chastity and in committing it to paper discovers his true vocation—poetry. Awed by his discovery, he dedicates himself to purity and art.

Meanwhile, Mistress Toast begins to reconsider her reaction to Ebenezer. When she reports to her erstwhile true-love and pimp, John McEvoy, on her unprofitable hour with Ebenezer and McEvoy goes to collect a fee—whether she served Ebenezer carnally has no bearing in the matter; the poet has used her time—she is greatly displeased. Furthermore, when McEvoy fails to collect and as retribution posts a condemning letter to Ebenezer's father, the woman decides in Ebenezer's favor and McEvoy loses her.

McEvoy's letter hastens Ebenezer's departure for Maryland. Angered by the report, Andrew Cooke decides to send his son to Maryland for the purpose of overseeing the family tobacco plantation, Malden, on the Choptank River. Mistress Toast, now fully in love with Ebenezer's purity, vows to follow him. McEvoy himself is destined to be caught up in the web that he has helped to spin, and he ends up in the New World. Ebenezer, unaware of those events, embarks for Maryland after obtaining from Lord Baltimore a commission naming him poet and laureate of the province, a commission that promptly involves the young man in political intrigues and that is eventually revealed as a bogus document devised by Henry Burlingame III.

Because he is the prime mover in the affairs of the novel, Burlingame deserves special attention. Among other things, he is at least part of the reason for Ebenezer's failure as a scholar and a businessman. In the boy's formative years, Andrew Cooke has Burlingame in his employ as a tutor to Ebenezer and his twin sister, Anna. The unorthodox methods of the instruction that they received and the tutor's unusual devotion to the world have left an indelible mark on Ebenezer and Anna. When Ebenezer decided, as a dutiful son, to follow a business career, Burlingame dropped out of the picture, but when the young man launches himself into his new fate by adopting poetry as his soul's profession and virginity as his body's handmaiden, Burlingame is ushered back into the thick of things. From this point on, the author uses Burlingame for everything from scene revitalizer to *deus ex machina*.

The chief story line of *The Sot-Weed Factor* is quite simple. One of the delightful things about the book is that it can be read on several levels at once. It is, on the surface, a bawdy journey through Colonial history and is vastly satisfying on this level as a good tale, well told. It is a farcical tour de force. With a plot more contrived than Henry Fielding's *Tom Jones* (1749), it is an exaggerated burlesque of the picaresque novel. Barth is convinced that the novel is a dying literary form. If it is, *The Sot-Weed Factor* is its grandest requiem.

Implausible coincidence, Rabelaisian romps, and confused identities are all part of the story, as are tales within the tale, much in the manner of Geoffrey Chaucer and Giovanni Boccaccio. The outline is the loss of Malden and the stratagems that bring about its recovery. Ebenezer's disillusionment with the New World is even more vital to his own affairs than the Malden issue, however, as the laureate's rosy vision of writing an epic *Marylandiad* becomes incongruous with the realities of the rough, violent provincial life that he encounters. The book can be read as a moral allegory, tracing the loss of innocence to the realities of life.

Ebenezer's vacillation between the extremes of angel and beast provides an area for the ribald humor that Barth sows throughout his book. The issue of the poet's moral struggle develops ironic perspectives. One example is Joan Toast's career. In trying to change her life's work from that of sinner to that of saint, she is driven by the winds of mischance and paradox further into whoredom, and when Ebenezer meets her again he does not recognize his real love in the person of Susan Warren, the swinetender on Captain Mitchell's plantation. Yet in the end, the author manages to marry her off to Ebenezer. By this development of the plot, the poet loses not only his treasured chastity but also his health, for Mistress Toast has contracted syphilis on her way down the ladder of life.

Burlingame's search for the identity of Burlingame I and II leads to the discovery of the amazing "secret diary" of Captain John Smith. This outrageously comic secret journal details the "true" story of Captain Smith and Pocahontas. The story should set them both twirling in their graves, but it makes for the most boisterously comic reading since Boccaccio.

Barth, in another of his works, has one of his characters remark that only in America can one have cheerful terrorism. This same theme shows up again about halfway through *The Sot-Weed Factor*, when Burlingame answers Ebenezer's question as to what he must do, and where he stands, by saying that humanity's sad lot is to be created by thoughtless man and birthed by thoughtless woman into a thoughtless world. A person is luck's fool, Nature's toy.

Candide had his Pangloss and Gargantua his Ponoc-

rates; Ebenezer has his Burlingame. It is in the role of tutor that Burlingame reveals the real world to Ebenezer. In his many adventures, Ebenezer sees the world as cruel, stupid, intolerant, greedy, savage, selfish, rapacious, and unjust. Barth loves the dark, nightmarish comedy of Colonial history. He even bends history somewhat to suit his story, but it is this aspect of black humor that intrigues him most. In this absurd, meaningless, mechanized society, filled with its catastrophes and atrocities, humanity can only set up a howl of despair that comes out as laughter. Burlingame says at one point that the only things which can save humans from madness are dullness and truth. Truth, being the common one, must be searched after before it can be found. Once it is found, it must be understood and shaped to the finder's will before it can bring about his or her ruin. Why, he asks, does Ebenezer put as much store in poetry and purity, or Burlingame in finding his father or fighting the marplot Goode? One must make and cling to one's soul, choosing what to worship or hate, or go mad. Burlingame knows no other course.

The reader may be left to wonder what justification or direction exists in a world such as the one that this satire exposes. Through *Candide* (1759), Voltaire came to know the blackness of nihilism. Yet Barth's is a cheerful, even an optimistic nihilism. Near the end of the book, Ebenezer explains to Anna that they must hold on to life even though they are searching all the time for a way to escape.

The Sot-Weed Factor in its final meaning is directed toward the ends of the antinovel. Barth has abandoned all allegiance to the novel's form and has shown up its deficiencies by overdoing them. His heroes are antiheroes, his humor is black, and his form is outrageous. His commitment is exploration of the range beyond the novel.

THE SOUND AND THE FURY

Type of work: Novel
Author: William Faulkner (1897-1962)
Type of plot: Psychological realism
Time of plot: 1910-1928
Locale: Mississippi
First published: 1929

The Sound and the Fury, an extremely complex yet rewarding novel, traces from 1910 to 1928 the decline of a once-aristocratic but now degenerated Southern family. Faulkner's method of narration, involving the consciousness of different members and servants of the Compson family, provides four distinct psychological points of view.

Principal Characters

Jason Lycurgus Compson (III), the grandson of a Mississippi governor, the son of a Confederate general, and the father to the last of the Compsons. Like his illustrious ancestors, his name suggested his passion, the classics. Unlike his forebears, he is unable to make a living or to fulfill his deepest ambition, the study of the Greek and Latin epigrammatists, but his stoic philosophy, culled from his reading, stands him in good stead. He speaks wisely, does little, drinks much, and is weary of his complaining wife, his wayward daughter, and his bickering sons.

Caroline Bascomb Compson, his wife, who resents the Compson lineage and feels that hers is more glorious. A neurotic woman with psychosomatic symptoms, she complains constantly of her grievances and ills. Reluctant to face reality and rejoicing that she was not born a Compson, she indulges her fancies and pretends to be an antebellum Southern gentlewoman. Her fortitude in tragedy is even more remarkable for all of her complaining, but she victimizes her children and devoted servants to maintain her resentment and illnesses.

Candace Compson, their only daughter, affectionate, loyal, libido-driven. Called Caddy—a name that results in great confusion for her simpleminded brother whose playground is the pasture sold to a golf course where he hears her name—she herself is doomed, though devoted to her dead brother, her weak-minded brother, her own illegitimate daughter, and her loving father. She is at odds with her mother, her vengeful brother Jason, and several husbands. She is so promiscuous, even urging her sensitive brother Quentin to abortive intercourse, that she does not really know the father of her child. As an adventuress, she travels widely, and in the postlude to the novel appears as the consort of a Nazi officer in Paris.

Quentin Compson, her beloved brother for whom she names her child even before the baby's birth. Obsessed by a sense of guilt, doom, and death, he commits suicide by drowning in June, 1910, two months after his sister's marriage to a man he calls a blackguard. Because he is deeply disturbed by family affairs—the selling of a pasture to pay for his year at Harvard, the loss of his sister's honor, the morbid despair that he feels for his simpleminded brother, his hatred for the family vices of pride and snobbishness—his death is predictable, unalterable.

Jason Compson (IV), the only son to stay on in the old Compson place, loyal to his weak, querulous mother, determined to gain his full share of his patrimony, bitter over his deep failures. His tale is one of petty annoyances, nursed grievances, and egotistic aggressiveness in his ungenerous and self-assertive mastery of his niece and the servants. This descendant of aristocrats is a small-town redneck, wily, canny, cunning, and deceitful. Not without reasons for his bitterness, he finally rids himself of his enervating responsibilities for a dying line by himself remaining a bachelor and having Benjy castrated.

Quentin, the daughter of Candace. Reared by Dilsey, the African-American cook, Quentin is the last of anything resembling life in the old Compson house. As self-assertive as her uncle Jason, she steals money he calls his (but which is rightfully hers) and elopes with a carnival pitchman. Beautiful in the wild way of her mother, she has never had affection from anyone except her morbid old grandmother and a brokenhearted servant. Her father may have been a young man named Dalton Ames.

Dilsey Gibson, the bullying but beloved African-American family retainer, cook, financier (in petty extravagances), and benefactor, who maintains family standards that no longer concern the Compsons. Deeply concerned for them, she babies the thirty-year-old Benjamin, the unfortunate Quentin, and the querulous old "Miss Cahline," though she resists the egocentric Jason. A woman whose wise, understanding nature is beyond limits of race or color, she endures for others and prolongs the lives of those dependent on her shrewdness and strength.

Benjamin Compson, called **Benjy,** at first named Maury after his mother's brother. Mentally handicapped, he observes everything, smells tragedy, loves the old pasture, his sister Caddy, and firelight, but he cannot compose his disordered thoughts into any coherent pattern of life or speech. Castrated by his brother Jason, he moans out his pitiful existence and is finally sent to the state asylum in Jackson, Mississippi.

Maury L. Bascomb, Mrs. Compson's brother. A bachelor, a drunkard, and a philanderer, he is supported by the Compsons. Benjy Compson was christened Maury, after his uncle.

Roskus, the Compsons' African-American coachman when the children were small.

T. P., an African-American servant who helps to look after Benjy Compson. He later goes to Memphis to live.

Luster, a fourteen-year-old African-American boy who is thirty-three-year-old Benjy Compson's caretaker and playmate.

Frony, Dilsey's daughter.

Sydney Herbert Head, a young banker, Caddy Compson's first husband. He divorces her after he realizes that her daughter Quentin is not his child. The divorce ends young Jason Compson's hope of getting a position in Head's bank.

Shreve McCannon, Quentin Compson's Canadian roommate at Harvard.

The Story

The Compson family had once been a good one, but the present generation had done everything possible to ruin the name of Compson for all time. In the little Mississippi town in which they lived, everyone laughed and made slighting remarks when the name Compson was mentioned.

Mrs. Compson had come from what she considered good stock, but she thought she must have sinned terribly in marrying a Compson and was now paying for her sins. For eighteen years, she had been saying that she did not have long to live and would no longer be a burden to her family. Benjy was her greatest cross. He was mentally handicapped and moaned, cried, and slobbered all day long. The only person who could quiet Benjy was Candace, his sister. When they were small, Candace loved Benjy very much and made herself his protector. She saw to it that the other children of the family and the servants did not tease him. As Candace grew up, she continued to love Benjy, but she also loved every man she met, giving herself freely to any man who would have her. Mrs. Compson thought Candace was another cross she had to bear and did very little to force her daughter to have better morals.

Quentin, another son, was a moody, morose boy whose only passion was his sister Candace. He loved her not as a sister but as a woman, and she returned his love. Quentin was sent to school at Harvard. Although she loved Quentin, Candace could not keep away from other men. Sydney Herbert Head was the one serious lover she had. He wanted to marry her. Head, a banker, promised to give her brother Jason a job in his bank after they were married. When Quentin learned that Candace was pregnant, a condition that made her marriage necessary, he became wild. He lied to his father and told him that he had had incestuous relations with Candace and that she must not be allowed to marry. His father did not believe him, and the family went along with their plans for the wedding. At last, Quentin could stand no more. Two months after his sister's wedding, he drowned himself in the Charles River in Cambridge, Massachusetts. Mrs. Compson resigned herself to one more cross.

When Candace had a baby too soon, Head threw her out of his house with her child. Her mother and father and her brother Jason would not let her come home, but they adopted the baby girl, Quentin. Jason believed that Quentin was the child of his brother Quentin and Candace, but the rest of the family refused to face such a possibility and accept it. They preferred to believe, and rightly, that Quentin was the child of some other lover who had deserted Candace. Candace stayed away from the little town for many years.

Quentin was as wild as her mother as she grew up. She, too, gave herself to any man in town and was talked about as her mother had been. Every month, Candace sent money to Mrs. Compson for Quentin's care. At first, Mrs. Compson burned the checks, for she would have none of Candace's ill-gotten money. When Mr. Compson died, Jason became the head of the family. He blamed Quentin for his not getting the job in the bank, for if the child had not been born too soon, Head would not have left Candace and would have given Jason the job. Hating his sister, he wrote checks on another bank and gave those to his mother in place of the checks that Candace sent. The old lady was almost blind and could not see what she burned. Jason then forged her signature on the real checks and cashed them, using the money to gamble on the cotton market.

Quentin hated her uncle Jason as much as he hated her, and the two were always quarreling. He tried to make her go to school and keep away from men, but Mrs. Compson thought he was too cruel to Quentin and took the girl's side.

A show troupe came to town, and Quentin took up with one of the performers. Her grandmother locked her in her room each night, but she climbed out of the window to meet her lover. One morning, she did not answer when old Dilsey, the African-American woman who had cared for the family for years, called her to breakfast. Jason went to her room and found that all of her clothes were gone. He also found that the three thousand dollars he had hidden in his room had been stolen. He tried to get the sheriff to follow the girl and the showman, but the sheriff wanted no part of the Compson family affairs. Jason set out to find the fugitives, but he had to give up his search when a severe headache forced

him to return home for medicine.

Jason felt more than cheated. His money was gone, and he could not find Quentin so that he could punish her for stealing it. He forgot that the money really belonged to Quentin, for he had saved it from the money that Candace had sent for the girl's care. There was nothing left for Jason but blind rage and hatred for everyone. He believed that everyone laughed at him because of his horrible family—because Benjy was a simpleton, Candace a lost woman, Quentin a suicide, and the girl Quentin a village harlot and a thief. He forgot that he, too, was a thief and that he had a mistress. He felt cursed by his family as his mother was cursed.

When he saw Benjy riding through town in a carriage driven by one of the servants, he knocked the black boy down and struck Benjy with all his force, for there was no other way to show his rage. Benjy let out a loud moan and then settled back in the carriage. He very gently petted a wilted flower, and his face assumed a calm, quiet blankness, as if all the strife in the world were over and things were once more serene. It was as if he had understood what old Dilsey meant when she said she had seen the beginning and the end of life. Benjy had seen it all, too, in the pictures he could never understand but which flowed endlessly through his disordered mind.

Critical Evaluation

After early undistinguished efforts in verse (*The Marble Faun*, 1924) and fiction (*Soldier's Pay*, 1926; *Mosquitoes*, 1927), William Faulkner moved suddenly into the forefront of American literature in 1929 with the appearance of *Sartoris* and *The Sound and the Fury*, the first installments in the artistically complex and subtly satirical saga of Yoknapatawpha County that would be spun out further in *As I Lay Dying* (1930), *Light in August* (1932), *Absalom, Absalom!* (1936), *The Unvanquished* (1938), *Go Down, Moses* (1942), *Intruder in the Dust* (1948), the *Hamlet-Town-Mansion* trilogy (1940, 1957, 1959), and *Requiem for a Nun* (1951)—the last an extension of materials in *Sanctuary* (1931). Chiefly in recognition of the monumental literary importance of the Yoknapatawpha saga, Faulkner was awarded the 1949 Nobel Prize in Literature.

The Sound and the Fury marked the beginning of the most fertile period of Faulkner's creativity, when he was in his early thirties. Both for its form and for its thematic significance, this novel may well be considered Faulkner's masterpiece. Never again would his work demonstrate such tight, precise structure, combined with the complex-

ities of syntax and punctuation that became his most characteristic stylistic trait. Furthermore, the themes recorded in his simple but not elegant Nobel Prize speech—"love and honor and pity and pride and compassion and sacrifice"—are already present in this novel with a forcefulness of characterization on which he could hardly improve. It was in this novel that Faulkner found a way of embodying his peculiar view of time in an appropriate style, a style much influenced by Joycean stream of consciousness and by Faulkner's own stated desire ultimately to "put all of human experience between one Cap and one period." That concept of time, most emphatic in Quentin's section, can be summarized by Faulkner's statement that "there is no such thing as *was*; if *was* existed there would be no grief or sorrow." The continuation of the past into the present, as a shaping influence that cannot be avoided, is the larger theme of Faulkner's lifework.

In this novel, that theme is embodied specifically in the history of the decline of the aristocratic Compson family. Nearly twenty years after the original publication of the novel, at the instigation of his publisher Malcolm

Cowley, Faulkner wrote the background history of the Compsons as an "appendix" that appears at the front of the book. The appendix records the noble origins of the Compson land, once the possession of a Chickasaw king named Ikkemotubbe, or "the man." After proceeding through the Compson succession—beginning with Quentin Maclachan Compson, who immigrated from Glasgow, and proceeding to Jason III, the "dipsomaniac" lawyer who could not tear himself away from the Roman classics long enough to preserve the vestiges of his family's good name, Faulkner presents terse but invaluable insights into the chief characters of *The Sound and the Fury*. Candace knew she was doomed and regarded her virginity as no more than a "hangnail," and her promiscuity represents the moral sterility of the family. Quentin III, who "identified family with his sister's membrane," convinced himself that he had committed incest with her. He really loved only death—in his sublimation of emotions into a kind of latter-day courtly love mystique—and found his love in June, 1910, by committing the physical suicide that the destruction of his grandfather's watch symbolized. Benjy, the "idiot" whose "tale" forms the remarkable first section of the novel, "loved three things: the pasture . . . his sister Candace (who 'smelled like trees'), and firelight" and symbolizes both the mental deterioration of the family and, through his castration, its physical sterility. Jason IV, "the first sane Compson since before Culloden and (a childless bachelor) hence the last," commits Benjy to an asylum, sells the house, and displays the pathetically mediocre intelligence that alone is able to cope with the incursions of the modern world as symbolized by the Snopes family.

Quentin IV, the child of Candace, "already doomed to be unwed from the instant the dividing egg determined its sex," is the last Compson and the final burden destined for Mrs. Compson, the personification, to Jason, of all the evil and insanity of his decaying, decadent family.

Benjy's section takes place on April 7, 1928, the day before Quentin IV steals her uncle's money. It is written with incredibly delicate perception, revealing the lucidity of a simpleminded innocence that can yet be accompanied by a terrible sharpness and consistency of memory. In its confusion of his father's funeral with Candace's wedding, in its constant painful reactivation—the sound of the golfers' cry of "caddie" causes him to bellow out his hollow sense of his sister's loss—Benjy's mind becomes the focus of more cruelty, compassion, and love than anyone but Dilsey imagines. Quentin III's section, taking place eighteen years earlier on the day of his suicide at Harvard, is one of the most sustained lyrical passages of twentieth century prose. The concentration of Quentin's stream of consciousness around the broken, handless watch is one of Faulkner's greatest achievements. Just as the leitmotif of Benjy's section was the smell of trees associated with Caddy's loss, the recurring refrain of Quentin's is the desperate rhetorical question, "Did you ever have a sister?" Jason's theme is hate, a hate as pitiful as is the diminution of Compson pride into pathetic vanity; this third section of the novel may be the greatest for its evocation of deep, moving passions from even the most mediocre. The last section is focused on Dilsey, who "seed de first en de last" and who represents, to Faulkner, the only humanity that survives the fall of the house of Compson—the only humanity to endure.

SPOON RIVER ANTHOLOGY

Type of work: Poetry
Author: Edgar Lee Masters (1868-1950)
First published: 1915

With his poetic character sketches of the deceased citizens of Spoon River, Masters presented what some considered to be a sordid portrait of small-town life in the United States.

Like Edward FitzGerald and a few other poets, Edgar Lee Masters established his reputation on the basis of one work, *Spoon River Anthology.* Masters was a prolific writer, producing many volumes of verse, several plays, an autobiography, several biographies, essays, novels, and an attempt to recapture his great success in a sequel, *The New Spoon River* (1924). Except for a handful of individual poems from the other volumes, however, he will be remembered as the creator of a small Middle Western town that he calls Spoon River, but which was probably Lewiston, Illinois, where he studied law in his father's office and practiced for a year before moving on to Chicago.

In form and style, *Spoon River Anthology* is not a work that sprang wholly out of Masters' imagination; it is modeled on *The Greek Anthology*, and the style of the character sketches owes a considerable debt to Robert Browning. Yet Masters composed his book with such an effortless brilliance and freshness that it retains a kind of startling inevitability, as if this were the best and only way to present people in poetry. From their graveyard on the hill, Masters lets more than two hundred of the dead citizens of Spoon River tell the truth about themselves, each person writing what might be his or her own epitaph. The secrets that they reveal are shocking—stories of intrigue, corruption, frustration, adultery. Because of its frankness, mild by later standards, *Spoon River Anthology* provoked howls of protest from disturbed readers who believed that it presented too sordid a picture of American small-town life. Distorted or not, Masters' approach to his subject undoubtedly helped open the way for dozens of novels whose authors seem to use grappling hooks to break that placid surface of life and dredge up secrets from the murk below.

Masters' book, however, is not a novel in verse, and while many of the poems are interrelated and a certain amount of suspense is created by having one character mention a person or incident to be further developed in a later epitaph, the anthology is not centered on a unifying theme. The closest approach to such a theme is the tragic failure of the town's bank, chiefly attributed to

Thomas Rhodes, its president, and his son Ralph, who confesses from the grave.

> All they said was true:
> I wrecked my father's bank with my loans
> To dabble in wheat; but this was true—
> I was buying wheat for him as well,
> Who couldn't margin the deal in his name
> Because of his church relationship.

Many people suffered from the bank's collapse, including the cashier, George Reece, who had the blame placed on him and served a term in prison. A far more corroding effect was the cynicism generated in the citizens when they found that their leaders, the "stalwarts," were weak and culpable.

Masters has pictured many vivid characters in *Spoon River Anthology.* They range all the way from Daisy Fraser, the town harlot, who

> Never was taken before Justice Arnett
> Without contributing ten dollars and costs
> To the school fund of Spoon River!

to Lucinda Matlock, who

> Rambled over the fields where sang the larks,
> And by Spoon River gathering many a shell,
> And many a flower and medicinal weed—
> Shouting to the wooded hills, singing to the
> green valleys.
> At ninety-six I had lived enough, that is all,
> And passed to a sweet repose.

Others are the town physicians, Doc Hill and Doc Myers, both of whose lives are scarred; Petit, the poet whose "faint iambics" rattled on "while Homer and Whitman roared in the pines"; Ann Rutledge, from whose dead bosom the Republic blooms forever; Russian Sonia, a dancer who met old Patrick Hummer, of Spoon River, and went back with him to the town, where the couple lived twenty years in unmarried content; and Chase Henry, the town drunkard, a Catholic who was denied burial in consecrated ground but who won some measure of honor when the Protestants acquired the land where he was buried and interred banker Nicholas and wife beside the old reprobate.

Spoon River Anthology is weighted so heavily on the sordid side—abortions, suicides, adulteries—that the more cheerful and "normal" epitaphs come almost as a relief. Lucinda Matlock and Ann Rutledge fit this category. Others are Hare Drummer, who delights in the memory of a happy childhood; Conrad Siever, content in his grave under an apple tree that he planted, pruned, and tended; and Fiddler Jones, who never could stick to farming and who ended up with "a broken laugh, and a thousand memories,/ And not a single regret."

One especially effective device that Masters makes use of in his collection is the pairing of poems so that the reader gets a startling jolt of irony. Thus when Elsa Wertman, a peasant girl from Germany, confesses that her employer, Thomas Greene, fathered her child and then reared it as his and Mrs. Greene's, one finds in the next poem that Hamilton, the son, attributes his great success as a politician to the "honorable blood" that he inherited from Mr. and Mrs. Greene. There is also Roscoe Purkapile, who ran away from his wife for a year, telling her when he came back that he had been captured by pirates while he was rowing a boat on Lake Michigan. After he told her the story,

> She cried and kissed me, and said it was cruel,
> Outrageous, inhuman!

When Mrs. Purkapile has her say in the next poem, however, she makes it known that she was not taken in by his cock-and-bull story, that she knew he was trysting in the city with Mrs. Williams, the milliner, and that she refused to be drawn into a divorce by a husband "who had merely grown tired of his marital vow and duty."

Masters displays an amazing variety of effects in these short poems. His use of free verse undoubtedly helps to achieve this variety, for a stricter form or forms might make the poems seem too pat, too artificial. Sometimes Masters lets his character's only remembrance of life be a simple, vivid description, as when Bert Kessler tells how he met his death. Out hunting one day, Bert killed a quail, and when he reached down by a stump to pick it up he felt something sting his hand, like the prick of a brier:

> And then, in a second, I spied the rattler—
> The shutters wide in his yellow eyes,
> The head of him arched, sunk back in the rings of him,
> A circle of filth, the color of ashes,
> Or oak leaves bleached under layers of leaves.
> I stood like a stone as he shrank and uncoiled
> And started to crawl beneath the stump,
> When I fell limp in the grass.

Bert tells of his death without comment, but when Harry Williams describes how he was deluded into joining the army to fight in the Spanish-American War, in which he was killed, the poem is full of bitterness, horror, and brutal irony.

To say that every poem in this volume is successful would be as foolish as to contend that each entry in William Shakespeare's sonnet sequence is a masterpiece. Masters frequently strains for an effect; for example, "Sexsmith the Dentist" seems to have been created so that Sexsmith may remark, at the end, that what one considers truth may be a hollow tooth "which must be propped with gold"; and Mrs. Kessler, a washerwoman, was probably included so that she might observe that the face of a dead person always looked to her "like something washed and ironed." There are other poems in which the characters simply do not come alive. One suspects that the poet wrote a number of philosophical lyrics, some of them marred by clichés and cloying rhetoric, and then titled them with names selected at random.

In the main, however, Masters has done a remarkable job in *Spoon River Anthology*. Those readers living in a small town will recognize in these poems the people that they see every day. Though these readers may not like to admit it, when their neighbors die they may carry to the grave secrets as startling and embarrassing as those revealed by the dead of Spoon River.

THE STAND

Type of work: Novel
Author: Stephen King (1947-   )
Type of plot: Epic fantasy
Time of plot: Late twentieth century
Locale: California, Texas, Maine, Nebraska, Colorado, and Las Vegas, Nevada
First published: 1978

One of King's longest works, The Stand *is also one of his most popular. Incorporating elements of science fiction, fantasy, and horror, the novel depicts the world's devastation by a plaguelike virus and the epic battle between the forces of good and evil that follows.*

Principal Characters

Stu Redman, a small-town Texas factory worker, one of the first people to encounter the killer virus, and one of the few who survive it. Stu is a strong, quiet, and brave man. A life of poverty and hard work, as well as the deaths of his parents, brother, and wife, has made him independent, stoic, and tough—qualities necessary for the leadership role that he assumes among the plague survivors in the newly formed society called the Free Zone. Stu falls in love with another survivor, Frannie Goldsmith.

Larry Underwood, a rock star whose overnight success has led to nothing but drug abuse, debt, and desperation. Larry is initially a self-centered man whose romantic relationships and friendships are shallow and painful. Living through the horror of the plague and its aftermath, however, brings Larry's inner strength and decency to the surface, and he eventually sacrifices his life to save the lives of his friends.

Randall Flagg, also called "the dark man" and "the Walkin Dude," the personification of evil. Flagg's identity and history are mysterious; he appears to be human but possesses potent supernatural powers. He attracts the weak, insane, greedy, and cruel plague survivors to Las Vegas, where the forces of evil gather to launch an attack on the Free Zone. He is eventually driven away, though not destroyed, by his own treachery and by the forces of good.

Frannie Goldsmith, a young pregnant woman from Maine. Frannie's love for Stu sparks insane jealousy in a disturbed admirer, Harold Lauder, leading to the deaths of seven people. Frannie's baby becomes the first new life to begin repopulating the world after the plague.

Abigail Freemantle, also called "Mother Abigail," an elderly African-American woman from Nebraska who embodies the forces of goodness and spirituality. Through dreams, Mother Abigail draws the good people among the survivors to her, just as Randall Flagg attracts the evil ones. She offers Stu, Larry, Frannie, and others the wisdom, comfort, strength, and direction necessary for them to battle Flagg for control of the postapocalyptic world.

Nick Andros, a young drifter who cannot hear or speak. Nick is killed in an explosion engineered by Harold Lauder, but his ghost reappears to help his friends.

The Story

An accident at a military installation in California releases a top-secret biological weapon—a constantly mutating strain of a flu-like virus that is 99.4 percent communicable and 100 percent fatal. The virus spreads with frightening speed across the country, leaving only those people with natural immunity untouched. One of these people, Stu Redman, is held captive and studied by government scientists who want to learn the secret of his resistance. After the doctors themselves begin dying, Stu escapes. Government agents carry the virus to other parts of the world, and, in a matter of weeks, only six-tenths of one percent of the world's population remains alive.

As the plague survivors try to adjust to life in their new world of loneliness and death, they begin having strange dreams in which two mysterious figures appear: an elderly African-American woman associated with images of cornfields and a menacing figure whose face cannot be seen but whose very presence is terrifying. Each survivor is drawn to one of these people, who turn out to be real. The people who are basically good seek out Mother Abigail in Nebraska; those who are inherently evil, or merely susceptible to evil influences, find their way to Las Vegas and Randall Flagg.

Under Mother Abigail's influence, Stu, Larry Underwood, Frannie Goldsmith, Nick Andros, a college professor named Glen Bateman, and others gather, relocate to Boulder, Colorado, and form what they call the Free Zone, a small community that attempts to preserve the American ideals of democracy and freedom, if on a small scale. Meanwhile, Randall Flagg sets up a dictatorship in Las Vegas with murderer Lloyd Henreid and pyromaniac Donald Elbert (known as the "Trashcan Man") as his favorites. Mother Abigail is convinced that God has chosen the inhabitants of the Free Zone to be warriors in an Armageddon-like battle with the dark man's forces; Randall Flagg stockpiles weapons for that battle, sending the Trashcan Man to search for ammunition in order to ensure the destruction of the Free Zone.

As Frannie's pregnancy progresses, she and Stu worry that the baby will be born without immunity to the killer virus and will therefore die. Jealous of Frannie and Stu's relationship, Frannie's friend Harold Lauder falls under the influence of Nadine Cross, a Free Zone citizen whose secret allegiance is to Randall Flagg. Nick Andros and six others are killed when Harold's homemade bomb explodes during a meeting of the Free Zone leaders. (Harold dies on the way to Las Vegas; Nadine reaches Las Vegas and becomes the dark man's "bride" before being killed by him in a fit of rage.) Mother Abigail dies later, but first she commands Stu, Larry, Glen, and a fourth man, Ralph Brentner, to go west to confront Randall Flagg and his forces—to make "the stand."

Two spies who were sent from the Free Zone to infiltrate Las Vegas are discovered and killed; a third, Tom Cullen, is able to escape with help from Nick's ghost. Meanwhile, Stu breaks his leg on the journey and must stay behind while Larry, Glen, and Ralph go on to Las Vegas, where they are taken into custody by Flagg's security guards. Lloyd Henreid kills Glen, and then Larry and Ralph are taken out to be publicly executed. When an onlooker protests the executions, Flagg burns him to death with a magical blue flame. At that point, however, the Trashcan Man appears—completely insane and dying of radiation sickness—with a present for Flagg: an atomic warhead stolen from an abandoned military base. Flagg's blue flame, taking on the shape of a gigantic hand, detonates the warhead. Flagg vanishes just before all of Las Vegas is destroyed.

Tom Cullen finds Stu, and they return to the Free Zone. As the remaining citizens begin debating how best to restructure their society, Stu and Frannie, who gives birth to a normal, healthy baby, return to Maine to live by themselves as a family.

Critical Evaluation

The Stand was foreshadowed by a short story entitled "Night Surf" that was published in Stephen King's anthology *Night Shift* (1978). The story deals with a small group of young people in Maine facing eventual death from the virus that later appears in *The Stand*. The novel itself represented a turning point in King's writing. His previous books, *Carrie* (1974), *'Salem's Lot* (1975), and *The Shining* (1977), had been traditional horror stories about vampires, ghosts, and people with supernatural powers. *The Stand* was his first novel to transcend the horror genre, combining elements of science fiction (the human-engineered killer virus) and fantasy (Flagg's magic and the mystical dreams) with his more familiar horrific material. *The Stand* is also the most positive and optimistic of King's early novels. In his previous works, more emphasis was placed on the forces of evil, more scenes were written specifically for horrific effect, and the endings tended to be grim, or at best ambiguous. In *The Stand*, the emphasis is on the forces of good, though some of the characters who have the potential for good, such as Harold Lauder, eventually choose evil. Likewise, the ending is a positive one in spite of all the destruction that has gone before: Stu, Frannie, and their child are the contemporary equivalents of Noah and his family, poised to start the world over again, a world filled with excitement, promise, and hope.

King uses the traditional literary form of the epic to tell his story. One of the oldest types of literature, dating back to Homer's *Odyssey* (c. 800 B.C.) and the Anglo-Saxon poem *Beowulf* (c. sixth century A.D.), the epic is a long narrative depicting a grand, heroic struggle of monumental importance. Epics typically have a vast setting (here, all of the United States, from California to Maine) and center on a heroic quest (in *The Stand*, the four men's journey west to confront Flagg). Whereas the traditional epic focused on one heroic figure (such as Odysseus or Beowulf), King splits the single hero into four (Stu, Larry, Ralph, and Glen). Each has his own role to play in the battle with Flagg, and none is sufficient alone: Larry, Glen, and Ralph must sacrifice their lives to bring about Flagg's destruction, while Stu's inability to complete the quest allows him to return home to play his part in the rebirth of civilization.

The four men's interdependence mirrors one of the book's major themes, the necessity—and difficulty—of individuals joining together to form a society. Reducing the world's population to a tiny fraction of its former size by the device of the killer virus allows King to analyze problems of social interaction microscopically; it also allows him to dismantle existing social structures and examine the process by which a new society is formed. That process, King shows, is both inevitable and fraught with problems. Sociologist Glen Bateman explains why when he describes what happens when people gather in groups: "Give me three and they'll invent that charming thing we call 'society.' . . . Give me five and they'll make one an outcast. Give me six and they'll re-invent prejudice. Give me seven and in seven years they'll re-invent warfare." Individual motivation is no clearer or purer than group motivation: When Stu and Glen discuss forming a governing body in the Free Zone, Glen first emphasizes the need to ratify the Declaration of Independence, the Constitution, and the Bill of Rights, then moments later starts laying plans to elect a handpicked group of leaders. It is also ironic that Flagg's dictatorship is far more politically and technologically efficient than the Free Zone. If society inevitably creates problems, however, it is a preferable alternative—the only alternative—to solitude. Indeed, the first thing that the survivors do is to try desperately to find other living peo-

ple. In a world filled with silence and death, isolation is the ultimate horror.

The Stand is set in the near future, and the time frame varies with each edition of the book. The hardback original, published in 1978, is set in 1980; the paperback was published in 1980, and, to keep the near-future setting, King updated the setting to 1985. The book was his longest to date at more than eight hundred pages, but the original manuscript had been hundreds of pages longer: King was forced to shorten the novel to meet publication requirements. In 1990, a new edition of *The Stand* was released that restored much of the deleted material. The time frame of this uncut version is 1990, making the "near-future" setting even more immediate. Given the book's publication history and setting, it is difficult to avoid seeing parallels between the story of a highly communicable killer virus and the acquired immune deficiency syndrome (AIDS) epidemic that began to spread across the United States only a few years after the book was first published, making the novel grimly prophetic.

King's later novels continued to develop some of the ideas introduced in *The Stand. The Talisman* (1984), which King coauthored with novelist Peter Straub, was another epic fantasy featuring an extended quest and an ongoing struggle between good and evil. Randall Flagg plays a villainous part in *The Eyes of the Dragon* (1984), a children's fantasy, and a Flagg-like character named Leland Gaunt makes an appearance in *Needful Things* (1991), menacing a small Maine town. King also continued to explore science-fiction themes in *The Tommyknockers* (1987). Several of King's later novels exceeded *The Stand* in length, but it seems as though none could exceed it in popularity, both in its original and revised versions.

A STREETCAR NAMED DESIRE

Type of work: Drama
Author: Tennessee Williams (1911-1983)
Type of plot: Psychological realism
Time of plot: 1940's
Locale: New Orleans, Louisiana
First presented: 1947

This Pulitzer Prize-winning play offers some of the most compelling characters of twentieth century American theater. Blanche DuBois, a faded Southern belle with a checkered past, and Stanley Kowalski, a violent and controlling man, are unforgettable figures from Williams' oeuvre.

Principal Characters

Blanche DuBois, a neurotic young woman in her late twenties. A widow, her husband died under mysterious circumstances, and Blanche has a history of seducing teenage boys. When she comes to live with her sister, Blanche has trouble dealing with her brother-in-law, Stanley. When confronted with her past, Blanche turns to alcohol and madness.

Stella Kowalski, Blanche's younger sister. She is married to Stanley, an unpredictable and violent man, but she is enthralled by his manliness. Stella tries to make excuses for her sister's deeds when they come to light, but she refuses to believe that Stanley has raped Blanche.

Stanley Kowalski, Stella's husband, a primitive, brutal man. He sets out to discredit Blanche and send her back to Mississippi by learning of her past indiscretions. He finally rapes Blanche.

Harold Mitchell (Mitch), one of Stanley's poker-playing friends. He courts and proposes to Blanche, unaware of her history. When Stanley reveals the truth about Blanche, Mitch reviles her and even attempts to assault her sexually.

Steve Hubbell and **Pablo Gonzales,** Stanley's other poker partners, who are as violent as he is.

A Streetcar Named Desire was Tennessee Williams' third New York success, winning for its author the 1948 Pulitzer Prize and a second New York Drama Critics Circle Award. Williams won the earlier award for *The Glass Menagerie* in 1945. The play has been successful in a number of translations, notably French, German, Spanish, and Italian. One of its peculiar strengths is the attraction of the role of Blanche for such important actresses as Jessica Tandy and Vivien Leigh. Also, the role of Stanley served to establish the acting career of Marlon Brando.

The Elysian Fields address of the Kowalski family is not really in the French Quarter of New Orleans, although Mitch identifies it as the French Quarter in contradiction to Williams' introductory description. There was, perhaps, a concession to stage designers attracted to fanlight windows and period lampposts. In fact, the set that designer Jo Mielziner produced for this play was one of the glories of his craft. Streetcars, however, do not fit into the small streets of the French Quarter. Possibly Williams envisioned a drearier neighborhood, one with less color and character. The choice of New Orleans as a setting for his play comes from its transplanted Mediterranean character. In the context of D. H. Lawrence and Tennessee Williams, such an atmosphere is a good place to discuss desire.

Two streetcars, one named Desire, the other Cemeteries, bring Blanche on a spring afternoon to the Elysian Fields address of her sister, Stella, whom she has not seen since Stella's marriage to Stanley Kowalski. Blanche, dressed in a fluttering white garden party outfit, jars against the shabbiness and menace of the neighborhood from her first appearance. The blowsy proprietress of the building admits her to the Kowalski apartment some minutes before Stella's return. One of Blanche's primary weaknesses is established in that brief time when, after a successful search for Stanley's whiskey, she drinks half a glass of it neat.

When Stella returns, Blanche makes only a token effort to hide her dismay at her sister's new surroundings. Stella is happy with her wild man and regards Blanche's criticisms with good-humored tolerance. Blanche turns on Stella and defends herself against a fancied accusation that she had allowed Belle Reve, the family mansion, to be lost. When Stanley enters some time later, he greets Blanche brusquely. When he mentions her dead husband, Blanche becomes confused and shaken, and then ill. One of the expressionistic touches in the play is the polka tune that drifts out of the atmosphere like an operatic leitmotif whenever Blanche's husband is mentioned. Later, while Blanche is in the bath, Stanley and Stella are free to discuss the implications of her sudden visit. Stella asks him not to tell Blanche that she is going to have a baby, a request that Stanley disregards.

Stanley is suspicious over the loss of Belle Reve and imagines himself cheated of some property. He tears open Blanche's trunk looking for papers. Blanche enters, makes a pretext to get Stella out of the house, and presents him with legal papers detailing the forfeiture of all the DuBois property. Blanche demonstrates a bewildering variety of moods in this scene; she flirts with Stanley, discusses the legal transactions with calm irony, and becomes abruptly hysterical when Stanley picks up some old love letters written by her dead husband. Her reaction to the news that Stella is going to have a baby is reverent wonderment.

Williams designates the third scene of the play "The Poker Night," a title that he once chose for the entire play. It is Stanley's poker night with two cronies as violent as himself, and a third, Mitch, a large sentimental man who lives with his mother. Stella and Blanche enter after an evening in the French Quarter that they have extended to two-thirty in the morning in order to keep out of the way of the poker game. They cross into the bedroom, separated only by curtains from the living room, and meet Mitch as he leaves the bathroom. Blanche looks after him with some interest as he returns to the game. She begins undressing in a shaft of light through the curtains that she knows will expose her to the men in the next room. She dons a robe in time for Mitch's next trip to the bathroom. Out of the game, he stops to talk to Blanche. During their conversation, she adopts an air of primness and innocence. Not wanting Mitch to see how old she really is, she asks him to cover the naked light bulb with a little Chinese lantern that she bought in the French Quarter. They dance briefly to some music from the radio. When the radio distracts the poker players, however, Stanley becomes violent and throws the radio out of the window, at the same time setting off displays of temperament that involve everyone on stage. Blanche and Stella flee to the upstairs apartment, leaving the men to deal with an outraged Stanley. When Stanley discovers that he is alone, he bellows up the stairway like a lost animal until Stella comes down to him.

The next morning, Blanche persists in regarding as desperate a situation that Stella has long since accepted as pleasantly normal. Blanche remembers an old admirer, Shep Huntleigh, who she thinks will rescue them. When Stella defends Stanley, Blanche retaliates with a long speech describing Stanley as a Stone Age man. The noise of Stanley's entry covered by the sound of a train, he hears the entire speech. To keep them from realizing that he has overheard the conversation, he leaves and enters again. Stella runs into his arms.

Scene 5 opens in the midst of a humid Louisiana summer. Blanche and Mitch have been dating, and she is hoping for a proposal of marriage. Stanley, who has been making investigations into Blanche's conduct in Laurel, Mississippi, torments Blanche with hints of what he has found out. At the end of this scene, Blanche is left alone on the stage. A young man comes to the door to collect for the newspaper. Blanche makes tentative advances to him. Before he leaves, she kisses him very gently on the lips. This scene makes an ambiguous impression in performance, adding one more hint of Blanche's depravity and suggesting with this young man the seventeen-year-old boy she had corrupted while teaching in a high school and the young man who was her husband.

In the following scene, later in the evening, Blanche and Mitch return from a date. He stays on for a talk in which Blanche tells him that she is hardly able to put up with Stanley's boorishness any longer. Mitch almost stops the conversation by asking Blanche how old she is; his mother wants to know. Blanche diverts his attention from her age by telling him about her husband. She and the boy had married when they were very young. One evening, she discovered her husband in a homosexual act with an older man. Later, while they danced to the Varsouviana at a casino outside town, she confronted him with her knowledge. Rushing outside, the young man shot himself. In some way, the mood of this speech prompts the long-awaited proposal from Mitch. Blanche is incoherent with gratitude and relief.

The last section of the play begins in autumn, on Blanche's birthday. Like D. H. Lawrence, Williams was fond of giving zodiacal signs for his characters. Stanley is a Capricorn, Blanche a Virgo—the goat and the virgin. Stella has prepared a birthday dinner for Blanche. Stanley spoils it as effectively as he can. First, he tells Stella that Blanche was a prostitute at a disreputable hotel in Laurel, a hotel that she was asked to leave. She lost her high-school job because of an affair with a seventeen-year-old student. At first, Stella refuses to believe Stanley. Then she defends Blanche's behavior as a reaction to a tragic marriage. Stanley has given the same information to Mitch, who does not appear for the birthday dinner. The evening is a shambles. Stanley climaxes the scene by smashing the dinner dishes on the floor and giving Blanche his birthday present, a bus ticket back to Laurel. At this point, Stella reveals that she is in labor, and Stanley takes her to the hospital.

Much later that same evening, Mitch comes to the Kowalski apartment in an ugly mood. He repeats to Blanche the lurid details of her past that he has learned from Stanley. She admits them angrily and volunteers worse. A symbolic counterpoint to this scene is provided by an old Mexican woman selling her flowers for the dead in the street outside the house. Mitch no longer wants to marry Blanche, but he begins a clumsy sexual assault on her that she repels by screaming, illogically, that the building is on fire.

With the help of Stanley's liquor, Blanche retreats into the safety of madness. When Stanley returns from the hospital, she has decked herself fantastically in scraps of old finery from her trunk. Their long conflict reaches a bizarre resolution: He decides to rape her. Their struggle is underlined by jazz music from a neighboring bar and by a fight between a drunk and a prostitute in the street outside.

In the final scene, Blanche is taken away to an asylum. Stella cannot accept her sister's story that Stanley has raped her; to do so would mean the end of her marriage. (In the 1951 Hollywood film, Stella trundled the baby carriage off down the street in self-righteous indignation.) To persuade Blanche to leave quietly, Stella has told her that Shep Huntleigh has come for her. Another poker game is in progress. When Blanche sees the attendants she is at first frightened, but she quickly responds to their kindness. Her long exit is invested with real tragic import. Mitch rages at Stanley and has to be pulled off him by the other men. Stanley comforts Stella's weeping, and the neighborhood returns to normal, its values undisturbed.

A major difficulty with the play is the problem of identification with Blanche or Stanley. Blanche is psychotic and outside the range of our identification, however one may pity her. If the audience is to be psychologically sophisticated and accept her nymphomania, alcoholism, and exhibitionism as normal behavior, then it is necessary to question the play's assertion that these things were induced by early widowhood, however shocking the circumstances. If Stanley represents the natural man, then his code for judging Blanche seems middle class and harsh rather than primitive. He is most appealing in his sensual exchanges with Stella, but his cruelty antagonizes elsewhere in the play.

Whatever the confusion in point, the work exhibits characters of unusual vividness. The dialogue is natural and frequently eloquent. The events compel our interest and sympathy, and in the theater are often electrifying.

STUDS LONIGAN: A Trilogy

Type of work: Novel
Author: James T. Farrell (1904-1979)
Type of plot: Naturalism
Time of plot: 1916-1931
Locale: Chicago
First published: *Studs Lonigan: A Trilogy*, 1935 (*Young Lonigan: A Boyhood in Chicago Streets*, 1932; *The Young Manhood of Studs Lonigan*, 1934; *Judgment Day*, 1935)

In the course of three novels, Farrell traces the life and death of Studs Lonigan, a young Irish-American tough. The author's use of realistic dialogue and situations shocked many of his readers in the 1930's and after, but his techniques exposed the moral decay of many American neighborhoods.

Principal Characters

William "Studs" Lonigan, a young Chicago Irishman who, growing up in the first three decades of the twentieth century, is a moral failure. He tries to be tough all of his life and succeeds only in leading an empty existence. His thoughts are only of women, drink, and a good time, from his graduation from a parochial grammar school to his sudden death in his thirties.

Patrick Lonigan, Studs's father. He is a man who lives in a world that he understands only from a narrow point of view. He is a painting contractor who provides for his family in a material way and sees nothing more to do. Only his business failure in the 1930's brings him to believe that he has not done well in this world.

Mrs. Lonigan, Studs's mother. She is a woman who wants her children to do well. She always thinks the best of her children, even her half-hoodlum son Studs. She is a possessive woman, not wanting to let go of her influence on her children.

Lucy Scanlan, a pretty neighbor whom Studs loves when they are in their early teens.

Catherine Banahan, a young Irishwoman who loves Studs when he is in his thirties. She becomes his mistress. When he dies suddenly, she is left unmarried to bear his child.

Paulie Haggerty, one of Studs's friends. His early death causes Studs to think of his own mortality.

Weary Reilley, a tough contemporary and sometime friend of Studs. Often in and out of scrapes, he is eventually arrested for raping a woman whom he picks up at a dance.

Frances Lonigan, one of Studs's sisters. She tries to rise out of the intellectual and moral rut of the rest of the family.

Loretta Lonigan, Studs's other sister.

Martin Lonigan, Studs's young brother, who tries to imitate Studs.

Helen Shires, a boyish girl who is Studs's friend when he is young.

Studs Lonigan: A Trilogy, first published in separate volumes from 1932 to 1935, was James T. Farrell's major work, despite the long list of books—novels, collections of short stories, essays, and literary criticism—that followed it. While critics have not always agreed on the merit of Farrell's work, the purposes behind it, or even the nature of the author's craft, they have all admitted that Farrell contributed something of apparent but still unproven value to American fiction written in the twentieth century.

The three volumes about Studs Lonigan portray the disintegration, physical and moral, of a young Chicago Irishman during the period from 1916 to 1931, beginning with the protagonist's graduation from a parochial school on Chicago's South Side and ending with his death. Farrell himself has been explicit in pointing out that *Studs Lonigan* is not a story of the slums, that the tragedy of Studs Lonigan is not rooted in the economics of the community or nation. The trilogy was not intended to illustrate an economic thesis, nor does it. The downfall of Studs is portrayed as the result of spiritual poverty in an Irish-American, lower middle-class neighborhood of Chicago. The elder Lonigan was a painting contractor who was successful enough that his family was not in want. The failure in the world of the Lonigans is a failure of moral sanctions. As Farrell himself stated of that social milieu, there were important institutions that should have played a part in the education of Studs Lonigan and his friends: the home, the family, the church, the school, and the playground. When they failed, the streets and the poolroom took their place. Under these influences, young Lonigan, not an evil young man or a moral cripple, drifted into grim and dismal circumstances. Thus the character of Studs Lonigan is a social manifestation as well as a fictional character.

The story of the growth of the trilogy was told by its creator. While a student at the University of Chicago, Farrell took a course in advanced composition, apparently the only college course which he liked and in which he worked. In that course, he wrote a story entitled "Studs," which, when shown to Professors James Weber Linn and Robert Morss Lovett, won encouragement for its author. Farrell then proceeded to construct a novel, which grew into a trilogy about the character of Studs, who came to be a symbol of the spiritual poverty of his neighborhood, his class, and his times. In a wider social sense, the tragedy of Studs may be also the tragedy of countless young Americans whose drifting, shattered lives have been, and still are, centered about too much sex, too much alcohol, too many empty platitudes, too many empty social dogmas, and too little faith in themselves and human nature, lives ending in alcoholism, drug addiction, delinquency, and crime. Farrell's portrayal of Studs Lonigan, ugly as it is in some respects, may have hit closer to artistic and social truth than the author dreamed of at the time.

Farrell's technique in the *Studs Lonigan* trilogy has been termed both realistic and naturalistic. Neither term, as it is traditionally used, fits Farrell's work, for he has gone beyond conventional categories. The primary reason for not regarding the *Studs Lonigan* trilogy as naturalistic or realistic is that Farrell has used determinism in a different fashion from that of earlier authors such as Frank Norris and Theodore Dreiser. Thus, the character of Studs Lonigan is not molded entirely by his environment; he knows, at least at times, where he is drifting. Farrell intimates in the novel that it was in his character's power not to have failed so entirely. Certainly Danny O'Neill, the hero of a later series of Farrell novels, as well as Farrell himself in real life, did not drift into the

tragedy that becomes Studs Lonigan's lot. Unlike the earlier naturalistic novelists, Farrell did not hold himself aloof, taking an amoral view of his creations. To some extent he asked for reform and improvement, as the traditional naturalistic writer does not.

Another aspect of Farrell's work that has drawn comment is the selection of details and language in *Studs Lonigan*. The story is told in an idiom close enough to the original to be embarrassingly accurate for a person familiar with it, and yet the language is changed sufficiently to admit the expression of wider and deeper concepts than its culturally starved users normally can express or wish to express. Readers who have never experienced this strata of society, however, may honestly feel shocked. Farrell has called his overall technique "social realism," and certainly his language is part of that technique. Part of the objectivity, the realistic portrayal of both character and setting in the trilogy, would have been lost if the writer had employed any other style or selected his details differently. Farrell has chosen not to sentimentalize the world, not to romanticize it or to hide its real character in any other way. It should be noted as well that from early in his career, which he took as seriously as his fictional Danny O'Neill takes his, James T. Farrell had confidence in his materials and in his methods. Many another writer of the same period became the victim of adherence to left-wing brands of determinism in art. Those who did either changed or failed. Farrell did not fail, nor did he have to change, having evaded the trap from the beginning.

To sum up the total significance of the trilogy is difficult. Many readers misunderstand the purposes and the techniques, preferring comfort of illusion to pain of truth. Farrell himself recognized this tendency. In *A Note on Literary Criticism* (1936), he claimed that art must flow from the reality of the writer's experience and that it cannot be better than life. The story of Studs Lonigan shows Farrell practicing what he expressed as his theory. Some critics and others who have admired Farrell's writings have defended the volumes by calling them sociological documents and making of Farrell a student of sociology rather than an artist in fiction. Farrell himself did not stoop to such subterfuge, deeming any such defense unwarranted and unnecessary.

THE SUN ALSO RISES

Type of work: Novel
Author: Ernest Hemingway (1899-1961)
Type of plot: Social criticism
Time of plot: 1920's
Locale: Paris and Pamplona, Spain
First published: 1926

This early Hemingway novel reflects the period following World War I, a period of maladjustment and despair on the part of a war-weary generation for whom life had lost its significance. The Sun Also Rises realistically describes life on the Left Bank in Paris and the color and excitement of a Spanish fiesta.

Principal Characters

Robert Cohn, a Jewish writer living in Paris in the 1920's. He and Jacob Barnes are friends, though Barnes delights in needling him. Cohn seems to mean well, but he has a talent for irritating all of his acquaintances. When Cohn meets Lady Brett Ashley, he immediately brushes off Frances Clyne, his mistress, and spends a few days at San Sebastián with Brett. He now feels that she is his property, though she plans to marry Michael Campbell. Cohn has the temerity to join a group from Paris (including Brett and Michael) going to the fiesta in Pamplona, Spain. When Brett is smitten with a young bullfighter and sleeps with him, Cohn, reputedly once a middle-weight boxing champion at Princeton, gives the bull-fighter a pummeling. Cohn's personality has many contradictions: He is conceited, but is unsure of himself as a writer; he seems both obtuse and sensitive; and he evokes pity from his friends although they all thoroughly dislike him.

Jacob Barnes (Jake), the narrator, an American expatriate also living in Paris, where he works as a correspondent for a newspaper. In World War I, he was wounded in the groin and as a result is sexually impotent. This injury negates the love that he has for Brett and her love for him. Seeming to work very little, Barnes spends much time in cafés, drinking and talking. His greatest problems in life are trying to adjust to the nature of his injury and trying to work out some sort of personal philosophy. Two of his thoughts almost solve the latter problem: "You can't get away from yourself by moving from one place to another" and "Enjoying living was learning to get your money's worth and knowing when you had it." Barnes is a lover of good food and drink, an expert trout fisherman, and an aficionado of the bullfight. Although he drinks as much as the other

characters, some of whom are given to passing out, he has the happy faculty of remaining keen and alert.

Lady Brett Ashley, an Englishwoman separated from her husband. Her first lover died of dysentery during the war, and she is getting a divorce from Lord Ashley. She plans to marry Michael Campbell, but she is actually in love with Barnes—perhaps because she knows he is unattainable, because they can never sexually consummate their love. She is a drunkard and is wildly promiscuous, as is shown by her affairs with Cohn and the young bullfighter Pedro Romero, but she seems as lost in life as Barnes and is appealing. Her successive affairs remind the reader of a little girl trying game after game to keep herself from being bored. In the end, she is determined to settle down with Campbell, even though he is nastily talkative when drunk. In spite of her resolutions, however, Lady Brett seems destined to work her way through life from bed to bed.

Bill Gorton, a witty American friend of Barnes. With Barnes, he fishes for trout in Spain and attends the fiesta in Pamplona.

Michael Campbell, Lady Brett's fiancé. He is pleasant when sober but very frank and blunt when drunk.

Pedro Romero, a young bullfighter of great promise who has an affair with Brett. He is jilted when he says that he wants to marry her and when she realizes that she is not good for him.

Count Mippipopolous, a friend of Brett who would like always to drink champagne from magnums. He is kind to Brett and Jake in Paris.

Montoya, the proprietor of the hotel in Pamplona where the established, truly good bullfighters stay; the hotel thus becomes the headquarters of Barnes's wild vacationers.

The Story

Jake Barnes knew Robert Cohn in Paris shortly after World War I. Somehow Jake always thought that Cohn was typical of the place and the time. Cohn, the son of wealthy Jewish parents, had once been the middleweight boxing champion of Princeton University. He never wanted anyone to forget that fact. After leaving college, he had married and had lived incompatibly with his wife until she ran off with another man. Then in California he met some writers and decided to start an arty review. He also met Frances Clyne, who became his mistress, and when Jake knew Cohn the two were living unhappily in Paris, where Cohn was writing his first novel. Cohn wrote, boxed, and played tennis, and he was always careful not to mix his friendships. A man named Braddocks was his literary friend. Jake Barnes was his tennis friend.

Jake Barnes was an American journalist who had fought with the Italians during the war. His own private tragedy was a war wound that had emasculated him so that he could never marry Lady Brett Ashley, a young English war-widow with whom he was in love. In order not to think too much about himself, Jake spent a lot of time listening to the troubles of his friends and drinking heavily. When he grew tired of Paris, he went on fishing trips to the Basque country or to Spain for the bullfights.

One night, feeling lonely, Jake asked Georgette, a girl of the streets, to join him in a drink at the Café Napolitain. They dined on the Left Bank, where Jake met a party of his friends, including Robert Cohn and Frances Clyne. Later Brett Ashley came in with a group of young men. It was evident that Cohn was attracted to her, and Frances was jealous. Brett refused to dance with Cohn, however, saying that she had a date with Jake in Montmartre. Leaving a fifty-franc note with the café proprietor for Georgette, Jake left in a taxi with Brett for a ride to the Parc Montsouris. They talked for a time about themselves without mentioning what was in both their minds: Jake's injury. At last, Brett asked Jake to drive her to the Café Select.

The next day, Cohn cornered Jake and asked him questions about Brett. Later, after drinking with Harvey Stone, another expatriate, on the terrace of the Café Select, Jake met Cohn and Frances, who announced that her lover was dismissing her by sending her off to London. She abused Cohn scornfully and taunted him with his inferiority complex while he sat quietly without replying. Jake was embarrassed. The same day, Jake received a telegram from his old friend Bill Gorton, announcing his arrival on the *France*. Brett went on a trip to San Sebastián, Spain, with Robert Cohn. She thought the excursion would be good for him.

Jake and Bill Gorton had planned to go to Spain for the trout fishing and the bullfights at Pamplona. Michael Campbell, an Englishman whom Brett was to marry, had also arrived in Paris. He and Brett arranged to join Jake and Bill at Pamplona later. Because Cohn had gone to San Sebastián with Brett and because she was staying now with Mike Campbell, everyone believed that it would be awkward if Cohn accompanied Jake and Bill on their trip. Nevertheless, he decided to join them at Bayonne. The agreement was that Jake and Bill would first go trout fishing at Burguete in the mountains. Later the whole party would meet at the Montoya Hotel in Pamplona for the fiesta.

When Jake and Bill arrived in Bayonne, they found Cohn awaiting them. Hiring a car, they drove on to Pamplona. Montoya, the proprietor of the hotel, was an old friend of Jake because he recognized Jake as a true aficionado who was passionate about the bullfight. The next morning, Bill and Jake left by bus for Burguete, both riding atop the ancient vehicle with several bottles of wine and an assortment of Basque passengers. At Burguete, they enjoyed good fishing in the company of an Englishman named Wilson-Harris.

Once back in Pamplona, the whole party had gathered for the festival of San Fermín. The first night, they went to see the bulls come in, to watch the men let the savage bulls out of the cages one at a time. Much wine freed Mike Campbell's tongue so that he harped constantly on the fact that Cohn had joined the group even though it was obvious that he was not wanted. At noon on Sunday, the fiesta exploded. The carnival continued for seven days. Dancers, parades, religious processions, the bullfights—these and much wine furnished the excitement of that hectic week. Also staying at the Montoya Hotel was Pedro Romero, a bullfighter about twenty years old, who was extremely handsome. At the fights, Romero acquitted himself well, and Brett fell in love with him, a fact that she admitted with embarrassment to Jake. Brett and the young man met at the hotel; Romero soon became interested in her.

Besides the bullfights, the main diversion of the group was drunken progress from one drinking spot to another. While they were in the Café Suizo, Jake told Cohn that Brett had gone with the bullfighter to his room. Cohn swung at both Mike and Jake and knocked them down. After the fight, Cohn apologized, crying all the while. He could not understand how Brett could go off with him to San Sebastián one week and then treat him like a stranger when they met again the next. He planned to leave Pamplona the next morning.

The next morning, Jake learned that after the fight Cohn had gone to Pedro Romero's room, where he found Brett and the bullfighter together. Cohn had beaten Romero badly. In spite of his swollen face and battered body, Romero performed beautifully in the ring, dispatching a bull that had recently killed another torero. That night, after the fights, Brett left Pamplona with Romero. Jake got very drunk.

With the fiesta over, the party dispersed. Bill Gorton went back to Paris, Mike Campbell to Saint-Jean-de-Luz. Jake was in San Sebastián when he received a wire from Brett asking him to come to the Hotel Montana in Ma-

drid. Taking the express, Jake met her the next day. Brett was alone. She had sent Pedro Romero away, she said, because she thought that she was not good for him. Then, without funds, she had sent for Jake. She had decided to go back to Mike, she told Jake, because the Englishman was her own sort.

After dinner, Jake and Brett rode around in a taxi, seeing the sights of Madrid. This, Jake reflected wryly, was one of the few ways that they could ever be alone together—in bars, cafés, and taxis. Both knew the ride was as purposeless as the war-wrecked world in which they lived, as aimless as the drifting generation to which they belonged.

Critical Evaluation

Upon its publication in 1926, *The Sun Also Rises* was instantly accepted as one of the important American novels of the post-World War I period. Part of this recognition was attributable to the superficial fact that sophisticated readers identified current expatriate celebrities among the book's characters; yet, as most of these personages faded into obscurity, this *roman à clef* aspect of the novel soon lost its appeal. A more important reason for the book's immediate success is that it perfectly captured the mood and style of the American artistic and intellectual exiles who drank, loved, and searched for meaning on the Parisian Left Bank in the aftermath of that first world struggle.

The overall theme of *The Sun Also Rises* is indicated by Hemingway's two epigraphs. Gertrude Stein's comment that "you are all a lost generation" suggests the ambiguous and pointless lives of Hemingway's exiles as they aimlessly wander about the Continent drinking, making love, and traveling from place to place and party to party. The quote from Ecclesiastes, which gives the novel its title, implies a larger frame of reference, a sense of permanence, order, and value. If the activities of the characters seem to justify the former quotation, their search for new meanings to replace the old ones—or at least to enable them to deal with that loss—demonstrates their desire to connect with the latter one.

Early in the novel, Jake Barnes declines to kiss Georgette, a prostitute, on the grounds that he is "sick." "Everybody's sick. I'm sick too," she responds. This sickness motif is opposed in another early conversation that Jake has, this one with Count Mippipopolous, a most vivid minor character, who tells him "that is the secret. You must get to know the values." The search for values and the willingness to pay the price, first to acquire them

and then to live by them, are what separate some of Hemingway's exiles from simple, pointless hedonism.

At the center of this search for values is the "Hemingway hero," Jake Barnes. As in all of Hemingway's important works, *The Sun Also Rises* is a novel of "education"—of learning to live with the conditions faced.

Jake's problem is complicated by his war injury. Having been emasculated in combat, Jake's "affair" with Lady Brett Ashley takes on a comical aspect to which he himself freely admits. Yet Hemingway has a very serious intention: Jake's wound is a metaphor for the condition of the entire expatriate group. They have all been damaged in some fundamental way by the war—physically, morally, psychologically, economically—and their aimless existence can be traced back to it. The real symbolic importance of Jake's wound, however, is that it deprives him of the capacity to perform sexually but does not rid him of the desire to do so. The people in *The Sun Also Rises* fervently want meaning and fulfillment, but they lack the ability and the equipment to find it.

The heroes in Hemingway's major works learn the "values" in two ways: through their own actions and by contact with other characters who already know them. These exemplars understand the values either from long, hard experience, like Count Mippipopolous, or intuitively and automatically, like the bullfighter Pedro Romero. Yet such heroes never articulate these values; they only embody them in action. Indeed, once talked about, these virtues become, in the Hemingway lexicon, "spoiled." Jake's education can be most clearly seen in his relationship to three characters: Robert Cohn, Romero, and Brett.

Critics have speculated on why Hemingway begins the novel with a long discussion of Cohn, a relatively minor character. The reason is simple: If it is hard to say exactly what the values are, it is easy to say what they are not. Cohn embodies the old, false, romantic values against which Hemingway is reacting.

In the beginning, Jake feels that Cohn is "nice and awful" but tolerates and pities him as a case of "arrested development." By the end of the book, he thoroughly hates him. Cohn's flaws include a false sense of superiority—reinforced by his pugilistic skills—and a romantic attitude toward himself and his activities that distorts his relationship with everyone around him. To reinforce this false romanticism, Cohn alters reality to suit his preconceptions. Falling "in love" with Brett, he refuses to see her realistically and instead idealizes her. When she spends a weekend with him, because she thinks that it would be "good for him," he treats it as a great affair and demands the rights of a serious lover, striking out at the other men who approach her. In short, Cohn's false perception of reality and his self-romanticization underscore his chief fault, the cardinal sin in Hemingway's view: Cohn refuses to "pay his bill."

Cohn's romantic self-image is finally destroyed by the book's exemplar, the bullfighter Pedro Romero. After being introduced to Brett by Jake, Romero becomes enamored of her. Affronted that Brett has been "taken" from him, Cohn reacts predictably and forces the young man into a prolonged fistfight. Although totally outmatched as a boxer, Romero refuses to give in to Cohn. After absorbing considerable punishment, Romero, by sheer will, courage, and endurance, rallies to defeat and humiliate his opponent. His romantic bubble deflated, Cohn bursts into tears and fades from the novel.

It is appropriate that Cohn's false values be exposed by Pedro Romero, because his example is also central to the educations of both Jake and Brett. As an instinctively great bullfighter, Romero embodies the values in action and especially in the bullring. In a world bereft of religious certainties, Hemingway saw the bullfighter's performance as an aesthetic ceremony that substituted for obsolete religious ritual. Without transcendental meanings, humanity's dignity must come from the manner in which certain destinies are faced; the bullfighter becomes, for Hemingway, the supreme modern hero when performing with skill, precision, and style and without "falsity" (that is, making bullfighting look harder or more dangerous than it really is). Shortly before the bullfight, Jake's group watches the local citizenry run with the bulls down the main street of the town. They see one man gored to death from behind. The following day, that same bull is presented to Romero, and he kills it perfectly by standing directly in front of it as he drives home his sword. This obvious symbolism states in a single image the most important of all the values: the need to confront reality directly and honestly.

Yet it is not only Romero's example that helps to educate Jake but also Jake's involvement in the Brett-Romero affair. His role as intermediary is the result of his would-be romance with her. They have long been in love and deeply frustrated by Jake's "funny-sad" war injury. Despite the impossibility of a meaningful relationship, however, Jake can neither accept Brett as a friend nor cut himself off from her—although he knows that such a procedure would be the wisest course of action. She can, therefore, only be a temptress to him; she is quite accurate when she refers to herself as "Circe."

The only time in the book when Jake feels whole and happy is when he and Bill Gorton go on a fishing trip in Bayonne. There, in a world without women, they fish with skill and precision, drink wine that is naturally chilled in the stream instead of drinking whiskey, relate to the hearty exuberance of the Basque peasantry, and feel serene in the rhythms of nature. Once they return and Jake meets Brett at San Sebastián, however, his serenity is destroyed.

Jake puts his group up at a hotel owned by Montoya, an old friend and the most honored bullfighting patron. Montoya is an admirer and accepts Jake as a true aficionado who understands and appreciates bullfighting not with his intellect but with his whole being. Montoya even trusts Jake to the point of asking advice about the handling of this newest, potentially greatest young bullfighter, Pedro Romero. When Jake presents Brett to Romero, fully understanding the implications of his act, he violates his trust with Montoya. His frustrated love for Brett exposes Romero to her potentially corrupting influence. Jake's realization of his own weakness in betraying Romero, plus the fact that it has cost him his aficionado status, leaves him a sadder, wiser Hemingway hero.

Romero is not destroyed, however, because Brett sends him away before she can do him any damage. Life with Romero held the possibility of wholeness for her—as it held the possibility of dissipation for him. By sending him away, she relinquishes what may be her last chance for health and happiness rather than risk damaging her lover.

Whether Jake's insights and Brett's final moral act give meaning to the lives of these exiles is problematical. During their Bayonne fishing trip, Jake's friend Bill Gorton sings a song about "pity and irony." Those concepts seem to govern the overall tone of the book, and especially of the ending: pity for the personal anguish and aimless searching of these people, but ironic detachment toward characters whose lives and situations are, at best, nearly as comical as they are tragic.

TALES OF SOLDIERS AND CIVILIANS

Type of work: Short stories
Author: Ambrose Bierce (1842-1914?)
First published: 1891

Tales of Soldiers and Civilians is a macabre collection of war tales and mystery stories, each revealing a dark vision in which the only honor is in facing death courageously.

Ambrose Bierce wrote volumes of acid, satirical prose in his long career as a journalist, and he even managed to get a somewhat pretentious twelve-volume edition of his collected works published. Most of it, because of its time-bound nature, was doomed to oblivion as soon as the edition appeared. The work that continues and promises to survive is the collection of short stories entitled *Tales of Soldiers and Civilians*. Bierce's literary reputation rests essentially on this book.

The bland title of this collection stands in ironic contrast to the vision of life that informs the stories themselves. Indeed, Bierce seems to have striven for bland, noncommittal titles to most of his stories. Titles such as "Chickamauga," "An Occurrence at Owl Creek Bridge," and "The Mocking-Bird" tell little of the macabre nature of these tales. Bierce seems to have chosen his mild titles with deliberate irony.

When this volume was reprinted in 1898, it was given the more meaningful title *In the Midst of Life*. The irony is more obvious and more indicative of the true content of the book: In the midst of life is death.

Death is the sole absolute of this book, the common denominator of each story, and the final proposition in a logic of ruthless necessity. Each protagonist is part of a greater logic; each is subordinate to the plot, and each is cursed. Death is separated from life, is raised up as a separate principle antagonistic to life, and becomes an entity in its own right. Death is seen as a hostile specter, rather than a normal process of life. As such, death seeks to conquer life rather than aid it. Death then becomes an inevitable victor who "has all seasons for his own," as Bierce was fond of remarking.

Against such a powerful antagonist, the heroes become victims in a web of cruel necessity, shadow figures drawn into the Valley of the Shadow; as such, they are depicted with sharp, relentless strokes. Bierce's heroes are essentially lonely men who derive their reality from the fear that they experience in their lives. These men are cursed and driven by the logic of their curse. Their strongest motivation is an all-pervasive anxiety that frequently annihilates them. The success of each story depends on its ability to arouse this same fear in the reader.

In consequence, Bierce places a great value on courage in the face of death. He is acute enough to see, however, that courage is not so much fearlessness as it is a greater fear overcoming a lesser fear, in most cases a fear of dishonor overcoming a fear of death. Courage, then, is the faith that one's honor is more important than one's life. Frequently, the heroes Bierce admires court death with an awesome recklessness. His characters are inevitably damned. There is no escape, no transcendence, and no salvation from the macabre situations into which they are drawn. Their doom is an inescapable fact. Yet the measure of their manhood is how they meet death.

Bierce's vision of life is fatalistic, but in a complex manner. Avenging Furies hover about his stories, but they are not the same Furies that haunted Orestes. Bierce is nihilistic, but inevitably there is a macabre humor in his nihilism. The satirical touch that colors the rest of Bierce's work is present here as well. Bierce's Furies are diabolical jesters who love irony more than they love the wretched human spirit. They are divine practical jokers who drum "Dixie" and "John Brown's Body" on the human skull for laughs. One can scarcely tell whether the shriek that one senses in Bierce's prose is that of humor or horror.

Bierce's grotesque wit serves as a relief from the horror of his situations. A related technique that serves the same purpose is his ironic stance, one that removes him from the petty human scene and separates him from the terror of his heroes. Bierce assumes a godlike attitude that determines the objective nature of his prose. He uses a naturalistic style that is precise in diction, spare in depiction, and ironic in narration.

In effect, Bierce takes on the cruel role of the Furies in narrating his stories, and the tone of his prose is frigid, caustic, and inhuman. Yet it is precisely this emotional sterility, this godlike irony, that makes his stories so powerfully chilling. If, for example, Bierce were to sympathize with his heroes, then there would be pathos rather than terror. The very lack of an appropriate emotional response in the narration stimulates to an excessive degree the proper emotional response in the reader. The fact that Bierce himself was caustic, cruel, and sharp, demanding perfection of his fellow human beings, admirably served his limited artistic abilities and enabled him to focus his talent on evoking both terror and humor.

Tales of Soldiers and Civilians is divided into two parts, as the title suggests. There are the war stories and the mystery stories, and each type developed Bierce's vision of life in a different literary direction. The war tales anticipate Ernest Hemingway, while the civilian stories anticipate such horror-tale writers as H. P. Lovecraft.

Beyond a doubt, Bierce reached his artistic peak in the soldier tales. War stories provided the perfect medium for someone of his character and experience. First, Bierce had served in the Civil War, and undoubtedly his stories draw much of their vigor and reality from firsthand experience. His depiction of various battles and their effects have an unmistakable aura of reality. Bierce's description of war is hauntingly vivid and stands in marked contrast to the maudlin accounts given in the vast bulk of Civil War writings.

Second, war tales provided an acceptable outlet for his obsessions with fear, courage, and death. These leitmotifs could be presented naturally in tales of soldiers. Because war abounds in abnormal situations, Bierce could write naturally about a twin killing his twin, about a son killing his father, and about an artillery man killing his wife. In the context of their stories, these plots become necessary accidents, part of some divine causality.

Third, Bierce's naturalistic style was admirably suited to describing the limited vision of the soldier in war, a vision that is not permitted the luxury of feeling pity and that must avoid all contemplation. It is a vision, moreover, that must concentrate on immediate objectives and on carrying out specific orders.

Finally, an army subjugates individuals to the mass. Deeds of fear and courage are the only acts by which a soldier is individualized and judged. Bierce's characters draw their reality from the way in which they face death. Each hero undergoes an ordeal that means death either for him or for someone close to him, and that test deter-

mines his character. Apart from that ordeal, Bierce's characters are lifeless puppets dancing to a meretricious plot.

Bierce's war stories are his best. Nowhere else did he achieve such a perfect fusion of form and content, except perhaps in his aphorisms. In quality, the tales are superior to most of the short fiction that was being written during the nineteenth century in the United States. In many instances, they anticipate or rival Hemingway's stories; many points of comparison can be drawn between Bierce and Hemingway. Both show obsession with fear, courage, and death. Both use a crisp, ironic prose to communicate their vision. Both were to find happy expression in stories of war. Both present characters tested through some ordeal. Both possess a cruel, evocative power that at times gives their fiction a haunting quality as vivid as a nightmare.

Bierce's war tales, particularly "Chickamauga," "An Occurrence at Owl Creek Bridge," "One Kind of Officer," and "Killed at Resaca," are first-rate in what they attempt to do. His civilian stories, however, fall somewhat short of the high standards that he achieved in his war tales.

The reason for this diminished quality is that Bierce attempted to impose on his stories of civilians the same vision of life that pervades his soldier tales, and the grafting was not always successful. Pictures of war provided the perfect literary vehicle for his outlook, as war abounds in pathological situations. When Bierce tried to impose this vision on civilian reality, the imperfections of plot, the implausibilities, and the grotesqueness showed up much more glaringly. The trick endings came off much worse. The characters and plots never matched those of the war stories. To inject a pathological fear into stories about civilians requires great skill.

What Bierce succeeded in doing in these stories was to extend a relatively new prose genre: the short mystery tale. In this lesser genre, Bierce succeeded rather well. His stories continue to hold their own in anthologies. Successful in turning his neuroses into fine artistic stories, Bierce has few equals in suspense, evocative power, clarity, and irony.

TENDER IS THE NIGHT

Type of work: Novel
Author: F. Scott Fitzgerald (1896-1940)
Type of plot: Social criticism
Time of plot: 1920's
Locale: Europe
First published: 1934

The characters of Tender Is the Night, *expatriate Americans wandering from one fashionable place to another in Europe, seem to bear a great resemblance to a common type written about in literature of the 1920's. With Fitzgerald, however, there is a difference in treatment and significance: Dick and Nicole Diver are believable people whose experiences reveal the spiritual disintegration and bankruptcy of an expatriate generation.*

Principal Characters

Dick Diver, a brilliant young psychiatrist who inspires confidence in everyone. As a young man, he met and married a patient of his and devoted most of his time during the next several years to helping her regain a certain normality. In the process of helping his wife, however, he loses his own self-respect, alienates most of his friends, and drowns his brilliance in alcohol. His professional position deteriorates to that of a general practitioner in successively smaller towns across the United States.

Nicole Warren Diver, Dick's wife, a fabulously rich American. As a young girl, she had an incestuous relationship with her father and subsequently suffered a mental breakdown. She marries Dick while still a patient and is content to let him guide her in all things for several years. When he begins to drink heavily and make scenes in public, she tries to stop him; in doing so, she begins to gain some moral strength of her own. In a short time, she no longer needs Dick, has a brief affair, and divorces her husband in order to marry her lover. Apparently aware of her part in Dick's downfall, she continues to be somewhat concerned for him.

Rosemary Hoyt, a beautiful young American film actress. Having fallen in love with Dick, who is several years her senior, on their first meeting, she later has a brief affair with him. When she finally recognizes the decline in him, she is powerless to do anything about it. Although she retains her devotion to both of the Divers, she has never really grown up herself and is incapable of acting positively without direction.

Tommy Barban, a war hero and professional soldier. Typically cold and unfeeling where most people are concerned, he spends much of his time fighting in various wars. He eventually becomes Nicole's lover and then her second husband.

Beth Evan (Baby) Warren, Nicole's older sister. Knowing nothing of the real nature of Nicole's illness, she feels that the family should buy a doctor to marry and care for her. She never fully approves of Dick because her snobbery makes her feel superior to him. After a succession of quiet, well-mannered affairs, she remains without roots or direction in her life.

Mrs. Elsie Speers, Rosemary Hoyt's mother. She devotes her life to making Rosemary a successful actress. She also tries to make her an individual but fails to achieve this goal.

Abe North, an unambitious musician. An early friend of the Divers, he goes consistently downhill and is finally murdered.

Mary North, Abe's wife. She is an ineffectual person while married to Abe; later she makes a more advantageous marriage and fancies herself one of the queens of the international set.

Collis Clay, a young American friend of Rosemary. Fresh from Yale University, he is now studying architecture in Europe and despairs at the thought of having to go back to Georgia to take over the family business.

Franz Gregorovious, a Swiss psychiatrist who becomes Dick Diver's partner in a clinic that they establish with Nicole's money.

Kaethe, the psychiatrist's wife, a tactless woman who is jealous of Americans and their money.

Gausse, the proprietor of a small hotel on the Riviera where the Divers and their friends often spend their summers.

Mr. and **Mrs. McKisco,** an American novelist and

his wife who, after achieving financial success, lose their sense of inferiority and gain the superiority and snobbishness typical of the moneyed Americans in the Divers' set.

Lady Caroline Sibly-Biers, an English friend of Mary North after her second marriage. She typifies the overbearing attitude of her class.

The Story

Rosemary Hoyt was just eighteen, dewy fresh and giving promise of beautiful maturity. In spite of her youth, she was already a famous actress, and her film *Daddy's Girl* was all the rage. She had come to the south of France with her mother for a rest. Rosemary needed relaxation, for she had been very ill after diving repeatedly into a Venetian canal during the shooting of her picture.

At the beach, she met Dick Diver, and suddenly she realized that she was in love. After she became well acquainted with the Divers, she liked Diver's wife, Nicole, too. Nicole was strikingly beautiful, and her two children complemented her nicely. Rosemary's mother also approved of Dick. When Rosemary attended one of the Divers' famous parties, she told Dick outright that she loved him, but he made light of her declaration.

During the party, Mrs. McKisco saw Nicole behaving hysterically in the bathroom, and on the way home she tried to tell about it. Tommy Barban, a war hero, made her keep silent. Resenting Tommy's interference, Mr. McKisco provoked a quarrel with him. The quarrel ended in a duel in which several shots were exchanged but no one was hurt. Rosemary was greatly moved by the occurrence.

Rosemary traveled to Paris with the Divers and went on a round of parties and tours with them. Often she made advances to Dick. He refused, apathetically, until one day a young college boy told of an escapade in which Rosemary had been involved, and then Dick began to desire the young girl. Although their brief love affair was confined to furtive kisses in hallways, Nicole became suspicious.

One night, Abe North, a brawling composer, offended two black men and involved a third in the dispute. While Dick was in Rosemary's hotel room, Abe brought in one of the black men to ask Dick's help in straightening out the mess. While Dick took Abe to his own room, the man stayed in the corridor. The two other black men killed him and laid the body on Rosemary's bed. When the body was found, Dick carried it into the hall and took Rosemary's spread into his bathtub to wash it out. Seeing the bloody spread, Nicole broke down and in an attack of hysteria accused Dick of many infidelities. Her breakdown was like the one that Mrs. McKisco had pre-

viously seen in the bathroom at the party.

Some years before, Dick had been doing research in advanced psychology in Zurich. One day in the clinic, he had met a pathetic patient, beautiful young Nicole Warren. Attracted to her professionally at first, he later learned the cause of her long residence in the clinic.

Nicole came from a wealthy Chicago family. When she was eleven, her mother died, and her father became very close to her. After an incestuous relationship with him, she suffered a breakdown. Her father, too cowardly to kill himself as he had planned, had put her in the clinic at Zurich. For many reasons, Dick became Nicole's tower of strength; with him, she was almost normal. Finally, motivated by pity and love, Dick married her. For a time, he was able to keep her from periodic schizophrenic attacks. The marriage seemed to be a success, aided by the fact that Nicole's family was rich, so rich that Nicole's older sister was able to buy Dick a partnership in the clinic where Dick had first met Nicole.

For some time after the episode involving Rosemary, Nicole was quite calm, but too withdrawn. Then a neurotic woman wrote her a letter accusing Dick of misdeeds with his women patients. The letter was the working of a confused mind, but Nicole believed what the writer claimed and had another relapse. She left her family at a country fair and became hysterical while riding on the ferris wheel.

At one time, Dick had shown great promise as a writer and as a psychologist. His books had become standard, and among his colleagues he was accounted a genius. It seemed, however, that after Nicole's hysterical fit on the ferris wheel he could do little more real work. For one thing, Nicole was growing wealthier all the time; her husband did not have to work. At thirty-eight, he was still a handsome and engaging man, but he began to drink heavily.

On several occasions, Nicole was shamed by her husband's drunken behavior. She did her best to make him stop, and in so doing, she began to gain a little moral strength of her own. For the first time since the long stay at the clinic, she gradually came to have an independent life away from Dick's influence.

Dissatisfied with the life he was leading, Dick decided

to go away by himself for a while. He ran into Tommy Barban, still a reckless, strong, professional soldier. Tommy had just had a romantic escape from the Soviet Union. While still absent from his wife, Dick received word that his father had died.

Going back to the United States was for him a nostalgic experience. His father had been a gentle clergyman, living a narrow life. Yet his father's life had had roots, and he was buried among his ancestors. Dick had been away so long, had lived for so many years a footless, unfettered life, that he almost determined to remain in the United States.

On the way back to meet his family, Dick stopped in Naples. In his hotel, he met Rosemary again. She was making another picture, but she managed to find time to see him. Not so innocent now, she proved an easy conquest. Dick also met Nicole's older sister in Naples.

One night, Dick drank far too much and became embroiled with a swindling taxi driver. When Dick refused to pay an exorbitant fee, a fight broke out and Dick was arrested. The police captain unfairly upheld the taxi driver. Blind with rage, Dick struck a police officer and in return was severely beaten by the Fascist carabinieri. Thinking his eye had been gouged out, Dick got word to Nicole's sister, who brought all of her influence to bear upon the consul to have her brother-in-law released.

Back in Zurich, Dick was busy for a time at the clinic. On a professional visit to Lausanne, he learned to his surprise that Nicole's father was there, very near death. When the dying man expressed a wish to see his daughter again, Dick sent for Nicole. Strangely enough, the weakened father still could not face his daughter. In a despairing frenzy, he escaped from the hospital and disappeared.

Dick continued to go downhill. He always drank too much. A patient, objecting to the liquor on his breath, created a scene. At last, Dick was forced to surrender his partnership in the clinic.

With no job, Dick wandered about restlessly. He and his wife, he realized, had less and less in common. At last, after Dick had disgraced his family many times in drunken scenes, Nicole began to welcome the attentions of Tommy Barban. She confidently looked forward to an independent life with Tommy. She no longer needed Dick.

After the divorce, Dick moved to the United States. Nicole heard of him occasionally. He moved several times to successively smaller towns, an unsuccessful general practitioner.

Critical Evaluation

In all of his literary work, F. Scott Fitzgerald proves to be a retrospective oracle. He describes an age of individuals who came on the scene and burned themselves out even before they were able to conceptualize themselves. His first published novel, *This Side of Paradise* (1920) is autobiographical and describes the early "jazz age," with its vague values of money, beauty, and a distorted sense of social propriety. His masterpiece, *The Great Gatsby*, came in 1925, and *Tender Is the Night* (1934) fictionalizes the personal and social disintegration that followed the success that *The Great Gatsby* brought Fitzgerald.

In addition to the glamor, the excitement, and the frenetic pursuit of the good life between two world wars described in *Tender Is the Night*, the novel also contains a masterful attempt at thematic telescoping. The character of Dick Diver functions in a triple capacity: On the largest scale, he is a contemporary American equivalent of the tragic hero, he also signifies the complex disintegration of the American during this precarious point in time, and, by the close of the novel, the reader's attention is ultimately focused on Diver as a fictional character.

In many ways, Diver's fall follows Aristotle's formula for classical tragedy: He is an isolated hero upon whom an entire community of individuals depends for necessary structure to their lives. He has a tragic flaw, as he is told by a classmate, "That's going to be your trouble—judgment about yourself . . ."; that is, he lacks perspective and introspection. He is a representative individual in that he is a psychiatrist expected to understand human motivation; he is at the mercy of fate, as the precipitating element, Nicole's case, "drifted into his hands"; and his fall is monumental, from an elevated position in life into failure and anonymity. Most significant of all, however, Diver has a true sense of his own tragic importance; he realizes that he is losing his grip on situations, and, even though he recognizes some of the possible consequences of his actions, he is not equipped psychologically to combat them.

Yet Dick Diver is not the strictly tragic figure prescribed in *The Poetics*. Rather, he is at most the sort of tragic hero that American society would allow in the 1920's, and it is in this capacity that Diver serves to describe the gradual disintegration of the American character. Dick is not simply symbolic of Americans; his character is instead individualized to represent what Americans, with their vulnerabilities, could become in a special set of circumstances. Diver and his companions create their own mystique to avoid the realities of a world thrown into, and later extracting itself from, war. Their frenetic rites and the aura in which the compatriots hide ultimately form the confusion that grows larger than Diver, unleashing itself and swallowing him. Diver and the American character at this time are incomplete; each is detrimentally eclectic and at the mercy of the props, such as music, money, and material possessions, upon which it depends for support. Incompleteness nourishes Diver's paternalistic assimilation of portions of the personalities that surround him and depend on him. Yet his need to be needed causes him to assimilate weaknesses more often than strengths, and the organic process is abortive. The American character is a limited one, a possessive one, and there is a sense of something existing beyond Diver's intellectual and emotional reach that could have proved to be his salvation. Fitzgerald emphasizes the eclectic and incomplete nature of the American during this era by interweaving elements of the romantic, the realistic, and the didactic when describing the actions and motivations of his characters. The result presents a severely realistic emotional conflict that sporadically explodes several characters, including Dick Diver, into psychological chaos.

Finally, Diver functions most specifically as the pivotal character of the plot itself. Given the demands of a novel of such scope, Fitzgerald relays Diver's decline quite convincingly. He succeeds by providing the reader subliminally with the correct formula for observing Diver's actions and their consequences. Within the first three chapters of the novel, the reader is taught, through Nicole's example, to appreciate the importance of psychological analysis and to isolate the "precipitating factor" in a character's development, then to consider that factor's influence in subsequent actions. The reader is thereby equipped to transfer these premises to observations of Diver. Throughout the duration of the novel, the reader realizes that Dick Diver's need to be needed leads him increasingly into circumstances that involve him directly, causing him almost voluntarily to allow his energy to be sapped from him.

Tender Is the Night is above all a psychological novel that is more successful than most novels of its type. The device upon which the success of the novel depends is Fitzgerald's handling of time. Here, time serves both a horizontal and a vertical purpose. Horizontally, time is chronological, for chronological observation is an advantage that the reader has—and that Diver does not have—throughout the duration of the novel (this was not the case in earlier drafts of the novel). The reader knows that Diver grows older, that Rosemary matures and finds other interests, and that Nicole eventually recovers from her illness. These are circumstances, however, of which Diver is ignorant. For him, time is merely a psychological abstraction; only major events determine whether one is in stasis. Yet time also functions vertically, making the notion of thematic telescoping possible. Diver is not cognizant of the passing of time until his plunge is in its advanced stages. As Diver's gradual acknowledging of time and of the vast gap between his "heroic period" and his encroaching anonymity becomes increasingly important, one's awareness of Diver's thematic function passes from the purely tragic figure, through the import of the national character, and, toward the close of the novel, rests ultimately on the individual Dick Diver and his acceptance of his situation.

THEIR EYES WERE WATCHING GOD

Type of work: Novel
Author: Zora Neale Hurston (1891-1960)
Type of plot: *Bildungsroman*
Time of plot: Late nineteenth century to the early twentieth century
Locale: Florida
First published: 1937

Their Eyes Were Watching God, *Hurston's most widely read book, tells the story of Janie Crawford's growth and search for identity through three marriages.*

Principal Characters

Janie Crawford, a young woman who is married off to a local farmer, Logan Killicks, by her grandmother. Janie soon runs off with Joe Starks to Eatonville, Florida, where he becomes mayor and she becomes "Mrs. Mayor" in an ultimately unhappy marriage. Janie finally marries Tea Cake Woods, with whom she finds happiness, if only for a short time.

Vergible "Tea Cake" Woods, Janie's third husband, who is several years her junior, a drifter, a gambler, and a migrant worker. Janie is forced to shoot him when he

becomes violent after being bitten by a rabid dog during a hurricane.

Joe Starks, also called **Jody,** Janie's second husband, the mayor and owner of the general store in Eatonville, Florida. As the town's wealthiest resident, he tries to keep Janie distant from the common people of the town, and as a result, their marriage deteriorates over the years.

Pheoby Watson, Janie's closest female friend. Most of the novel is framed by Janie, having returned to Eatonville after Tea Cake's death, telling her story to Pheoby.

The Story

When the novel begins, Janie is returning to Eatonville, Florida, a town in which she has few friends because she was kept separate from most of the townspeople by her second husband, Joe Starks. Because she left with a younger man, Tea Cake Woods, her third husband, and is returning alone, tongues start wagging. Pheoby Watson, however, rushes to greet her friend, and Janie, to explain both her passion for Tea Cake and why she is returning without him, tells Pheoby her life story.

Janie's story begins in the first person but quickly switches to the third when she recalls her first romantic kiss, which was with a young man named Johnny Taylor. When Janie's grandmother, Nanny, sees this event, she quickly arranges a marriage for Janie to Logan Killicks, a local farmer, in the hope of protecting Janie from the threat of rape, which both Nanny and her daughter, Leafy, suffered. Janie, however, has no attraction to Logan, who is a much older man. Nanny, hearing this, prays all night for Janie and then dies shortly thereafter. When Joe Starks, whom Janie calls Jody, comes by on his way to Eatonville, Florida, which he has heard is to be founded as an

African-American community, Janie agrees to join him as his wife.

Janie's marriage to Joe is initially happier than her first marriage, and is certainly longer lasting, but it too ends in frustration. When he arrives in Eatonville, Joe immediately begins asserting himself. He quickly opens a general store, buys and sells real estate, organizes a post office, and gets himself elected mayor. As the town grows, Joe builds the largest house in town for Janie and himself, modeling it after the homes of prosperous white families for which he has worked, right down to the spittoon that he places in the entranceway.

Joe's attachment to creating himself as the patriarch of this town also leads him to keep Janie apart from the townspeople, for whom he has clear contempt, the better to make her into a distant queen figure to them and to make himself the more envied. This separation leads to Janie's increasing sense of isolation, and she begins to identify with an ornery old mule who is the butt of many of the town's jokes. One of the few times that she asserts herself to Joe and to the town is to defend this mule. After the mule dies, she begins to speak up more often and eventually comes into direct conflict with Joe. When Joe puts her down in public, she responds in kind and devastates him. Shortly afterward, Joe becomes sick, and the word around town is that Janie has put a "fix," or a spell, on him. Joe moves into a room separate from Janie and has people come in to feed him, rather than live with her. Eventually, Joe dies of what is diagnosed as kidney failure.

Now a single woman approaching middle age, Janie at first resolves not to wear any of the rags that Joe always had her use to cover her hair, but beyond that, she makes no immediate changes in her life until she meets Vergible "Tea Cake" Woods. A drifter, a gambler, and a man much younger than herself, Tea Cake stops by the store on a day when most of the town is out at a ballgame and teaches Janie how to play checkers. Tea Cake visits several more times, and he and Janie quickly fall in love and get married.

Though their marriage is based on mutual love, they sometimes have a hard time understanding each other. For example, when Tea Cake finds two hundred dollars of Janie's money, he uses it to throw a party without her knowledge, not realizing that he is fulfilling Janie's fears that he really only wanted her for her money. He pays her back with his winnings from gambling, and the couple make their way farther south, doing migrant work. Jealousies do arise, however, when a light-skinned African-American woman named Mrs. Turner, who likes Janie for her light skin but distrusts Tea Cake for his darker

skin, brings her brother to meet Janie. Tea Cake becomes jealous and hits Janie to relieve "that awful fear inside him."

Shortly after this incident, a hurricane erupts; Janie and Tea Cake first try to wait it out and then start running, trying to find high ground to take shelter from the worst effects of the storm. Toward the end of the storm, Janie is blown by a gust of wind into a lake. Seeing a cow struggling with a snarling dog on its back in the water, Janie swims to the cow in order to cling to it. Tea Cake swims out, kills the dog, and rescues Janie, but not before the dog bites him on the cheek.

A few days later, Tea Cake begins to fall sick and is diagnosed with rabies. While the two of them are waiting for a serum to arrive, Tea Cake, in the grips of a fever and sounding a bit like Joe Starks, accuses Janie of ungratefulness and aims a gun at her. In self-defense, Janie fatally shoots Tea Cake.

Janie is tried and acquitted of murder by an all-white jury. The African Americans of the migrant-worker community initially hold her responsible for Tea Cake's death, but they quickly forgive her. With nowhere else to go, she makes her way back to Eatonville, as the narrative circles around to where it began. At the end, Pheoby Watson declares that she has grown ten feet just listening, and she promises that she will try to spread an understanding among the townspeople of what really happened. At the end of the novel, Janie is alone when she is visited by Tea Cake's spirit. She prepares to spend some time reviewing the life that she has lived.

Critical Evaluation

Zora Neale Hurston's work has been called the second beginning of African-American women's literature. For example, although Hurston features a light-skinned African-American woman at the center of *Their Eyes Were Watching God*, Janie does not fit the figure of the tragic mulatto that one sees in such earlier works as Frances E. W. Harper's *Iola Leroy: Or, Shadows Uplifted* (1892) and H. E. Wilson's *Our Nig: Or, Sketches from the Life of a Free Black in a Two-story White House, North* (1859). Something new is clearly happening in Hurston's novel. Just as important, some critical debate exists as to whether the African-American women's writing that existed before Hurston can legitimately be called a tradition. Yet few critical voices doubt that, after Hurston, a definite literary tradition of African-American women writers certainly exists. Among the writers who owe a clear debt to Hurston are Ntozake Shange and Alice Walker.

Their Eyes Were Watching God has fascinated critics with its lively narrative voice, its story of a young woman's need for personal as well as sexual fulfillment, and, not least of all, its apparent aesthetic contradictions. When Hurston wrote *Their Eyes Were Watching God*, writing in black dialect was out of favor among African-American writers, largely because this dialect had often been used by hack writers and vaudevillians to make fun of the African-American community. Hurston was able to use black dialect successfully because her third-person narrator is so clearly in sympathy with her characters. Though she does display the humor in the African-American communities that she describes, she does not make fun of them.

The story of Janie's search for personal and sexual fulfillment also constitutes a crucial aspect of *Their Eyes Were Watching God*. At the time that Hurston wrote her novel, D. H. Lawrence's tale of an upper-class woman's romantic dalliance with a lower-class man, *Lady Chatterley's Lover* (1928), was still banned in the United States. Generally speaking, the rule for novels that featured women being anything less than faithful to one man was that the woman died at the end—as did the title characters in Gustave Flaubert's *Madame Bovary* (1857), Leo Tolstoy's *Anna Karenina* (1875-1877), and Stephen Crane's *Maggie: A Girl of the Streets* (1893). Janie remains loyal to each of her husbands within the bonds of each marriage, but she leaves her first husband, Logan Killicks; symbolically kills her second, Joe Starks, by injuring his pride; and literally kills her third, Tea Cake. With each marriage, Janie must achieve a certain level of self-assertion. In the first two marriages, she has to assert her own right to happiness; in the third, she has to assert her own right to survival. Similarly, her first two marriages are failures because they are sexually and emotionally unsatisfying; by contrast, her marriage to Tea Cake is successful while it lasts, despite the problems that do arise, because it is sexually and emotionally fulfilling.

Their Eyes Were Watching God is a work of seeming contradictions. Among these is the fact that, while the story clearly celebrates the founding of Eatonville as an African-American town, Joe Starks, who is most responsible for creating most of the institutions—the general store, the post office, the town government—is presented as self-centered and authoritarian. Similarly, although the book lingers lovingly on details of the townspeople of Eatonville, the main character of the book, Janie, is not well liked by them and never feels herself one of them. Perhaps most disturbingly, after presenting two unhappy marriages in which Janie must fight to assert her right to an identity, the novel presents a third happy marriage in which Janie seems to relinquish her individual identity willingly. As Mary Helen Washington pointed out in *Invented Lives: Narratives of Black Women, 1860-1960* (1987), Tea Cake early in his marriage to Janie says, "Honey, since you loose me and gimme privilege tuh tell yuh all about myself, Ah'll tell yuh," and from then on, the novel is Tea Cake's story more than Janie's.

Attempting to explain this last contradiction, some critics have seen a symbolic cause-and-effect relationship between Tea Cake's beating of Janie and the hurricane that quickly follows it and that sets off the chain of events forcing Janie to kill him before he kills her. Another point of view praises Hurston for pointing out the sometimes irresolvable complexities and contradictions that arose when an African-American woman in Janie's time and place tried to find an individual identity.

Though *Their Eyes Were Watching God* has been in print continuously since it was first published, it has not always been highly regarded by the literary establishment. For years, Hurston's own very strong personality, which led to public feuds with Langston Hughes and Richard Wright, as well as her politically conservative views (for example, she opposed school desegregation on the grounds that more good could be done by improving African-American schools) overshadowed the considerable merits of her writing. Similarly, writers and critics who viewed the struggle against racism to be the great theme of African-American literature were disappointed in Hurston's masterpiece, which addresses this issue only tangentially. Nevertheless, an important 1977 biography by Robert Hemenway, *Zora Neale Hurston: A Literary Biography*, as well as influential essays by Alice Walker, spurred a revival in interest in this novel and its themes not of the struggle of African Americans against white society, but of African-American women and men who sometimes love and sometimes mistreat one another.

THE THIN MAN

Type of work: Novel
Author: Dashiell Hammett (1894-1961)
Type of plot: Mystery romance
Time of plot: 1930's
Locale: New York
First published: 1934

A classic work of detective fiction, this novel presents a portrait of sophisticated New York life at the end of the Prohibition era. Hammett offers the reader the astute detective, the somewhat obtuse and distrustful police, and the questioning companion. The traditional dropping of clues gives the reader a chance to solve the mystery before the detective provides the final explanation.

Principal Characters

Mimi Jorgensen, Clyde Wynant's former wife, a showy blonde woman in whose arms Julia Wolf dies. She is suspected of Julia's murder.

Dorothy Wynant, Mimi's daughter, a small attractive woman who dislikes her family and who asks Nick to locate Wynant.

Gilbert Wynant, Mimi's son, an odd, extremely inquisitive young man.

Christian Jorgensen, formerly called **Kelterman,** Wynant's former associate who, feeling unfairly treated, breaks with him. Though he already has a wife in Boston, Jorgensen marries Mimi in order to get his hands on the large divorce settlement that Wynant provides for her. Temporarily suspected of Julia's murder, he finally returns to his legal wife in Boston.

Nick Charles, the narrator, a one-time detective, now a lumberman. Humorous, self-possessed, tough, and intelligent, he discovers clues, arranges them, makes deductions, and solves the murders. He then summarizes the whole solution for his admiring Nora.

Nora Charles, his wife, a woman with a well-developed sense of humor who finds Nick fascinating.

Herbert Macaulay, Wynant's thieving attorney, the murderer of Wynant, Julia, and Nunheim. He murders Wynant in order to rob him, Julia to quiet her, and Nunheim because he was a possible witness to Julia's murder.

Shep Morelli, a gangster and former friend of Julia who thinks that Nick knows what happened to her. He shoots Nick and is beaten up by the police, but he is released when Nick does not press charges.

Arthur Nunheim, a former convict who identified Julia's body. He is murdered.

Julia Wolf, a murder victim, Clyde Wynant's secretary and mistress. She plotted with Macaulay to get Wynant's money.

Clyde Wynant, a wealthy, eccentric inventor, once a client of Nick; a tall, thin man murdered by Macaulay.

Guild, a detective.

The Story

Nick Charles, one-time detective and now a California lumberman, arrived in New York with his wife, Nora, for the Christmas holidays. He was drawn into the investigation of a murder case because the dead woman, Julia Wolf, was the secretary of Nick's former client, a lunatic-fringe inventor whose wife had divorced him in order to marry a man named Christian Jorgensen. Clyde Wynant, the inventor, was reported to be out of town, working on some new project. Herbert Macaulay, the attorney for Wynant, had told police that he had not seen Wynant since October, when Wynant had given the lawyer power of attorney.

Suspicion fell on Mimi Jorgensen, just returned from Europe, for she had gone to see Julia on the afternoon of the murder; she had arrived, in fact, in time for Julia to die in her arms. She had wanted, she said, to get her former husband's address, for she needed more money to support his two children, twenty-year-old Dorothy and eighteen-year-old Gilbert, since Jorgensen had run through the large settlement Wynant had made on Mimi at the time of their divorce.

Suspicion fell on Christian Jorgensen, who turned out to be a man formerly known as Kelterman, with whom Wynant had worked several years before. He thought that Wynant had not treated him fairly. Then it was discovered that Jorgensen had a wife living in Boston and that he had married Mimi only to get Wynant's money.

Suspicion fell on Shep Morelli, a gangster who had been fond of Julia. When he learned that Nick was on the case, Morelli went to Nick's apartment and, as the police arrived, shot Nick in the chest, a glancing shot that did not produce a serious wound. Nick told the police that he would not press charges, for the man was apparently in enough trouble. Although the police beat up Morelli, they could find no reason for holding him. He was released the same day.

Suspicion fell on Gil Wynant, as the members of the Wynant family did not have much love for one another. Gil was an odd young man who asked Nick about bizarre subjects such as incest and cannibalism. He was frequently found at keyholes listening to private conversations.

Suspicion fell on Arthur Nunheim, who identified Julia Wolf's body. When Nick went with Guild, a detective, to see Nunheim, they found him living in an extremely untidy apartment with a big, frowzy, blonde woman. In the presence of their callers, Nunheim and the woman insulted each other until the woman left him. Nunheim escaped from Nick through a back window. He was reported murdered a short while later.

Suspicion fell on Clyde Wynant himself, as Macaulay reported that Wynant had made an appointment with him on the day that the murder was committed, but had failed to appear. During the course of the investigation, several people received communications from Wynant that seemed to throw suspicion on Mimi and Jorgensen. One day, Wynant was reported to have attempted suicide in Allentown, Pennsylvania. The report was false, however, as the man was not Wynant.

On First Avenue, Wynant had maintained a shop that the police had given a cursory examination. Nick insisted that they return and tear it apart if necessary, for he felt sure that some clue was to be found there. The police discovered a section of the cement floor newer than the rest. When they tore it up, they found the bones of a dead man, along with a cane, some clothes apparently for a larger man than Wynant, and a key chain bearing the initials D. W. Q.

At last, Nick accused Herbert Macaulay of murdering Wynant, Julia, and Nunheim. He believed that Macaulay and Julia had joined forces to get Wynant's money, that Wynant had gone to Macaulay's house in Scarsdale to accuse Macaulay of the plot, and that Macaulay had killed his client there. Then, Nick reasoned, Macaulay had dismembered the body and brought it back to the workshop, where he buried the body under new cement. The cane, the large-size clothes, and the key chain were intended to prevent identification of the body.

Macaulay, according to Nick, had renewed the lease on the shop and kept it vacant while, with a forged power of attorney and Julia's help, he began to transfer Wynant's fortune to his own accounts. Then Mimi had come back from Europe with her children and had asked for Wynant. When Nick had arrived for his Christmas holiday and had agreed to help Mimi find the missing inventor, Macaulay believed that he would be safer with Julia dead. Later, he sent letters to members of Wynant's family, and even to himself, supposedly from Wynant. Nick thought that Macaulay had killed Nunheim because the former convict had been near Julia's apartment and had probably heard the shots that killed her. When Nunheim had demanded hush money from Macaulay, the lawyer had murdered him to keep him permanently quiet.

So Nick outlined his case. On the day that he made the accusation, however, Gilbert Wynant received a letter, supposedly from his father, telling him to use the enclosed key, go to Julia's apartment, and look for an important paper between the pages of a certain book. Following the instruction in the letter, Gilbert entered the apartment, where a plain-clothesman struck him, fettered him, and took him to police headquarters. The boy showed the officials and Nick the letter that he had received. The book and paper had been invented. When Nick took Gilbert home, he learned from Mimi that Wynant had just been there to leave ten thousand dollars in bonds with Mimi.

As it turned out, Macaulay, knowing that the police would be in Julia's apartment, had sent the letter to Gilbert in an attempt to shift the suspicion back to Wynant once more. Also, Macaulay himself had brought Wynant's bonds to Mimi, making her promise to say that Wynant had brought them and thus give credence to his own story that Wynant was in town. Nick forced Mimi to admit the truth by explaining that Macaulay now had possession of Wynant's fortune and that, if she played his game, she would have to be satisfied with comparatively small sums occasionally. If she were to stop shielding Macaulay, then she would, through her children, have control of her former husband's entire fortune. Jorgensen, meanwhile, had gone back to his legal wife in Boston.

After Nick had explained the whole case to Nora, she could not help feeling that the business of a detective, based as it is on so much probability, is at best unsatisfactory.

Critical Evaluation

The Thin Man was the last and most popular of Hammett's novels. In Nick and Nora Charles, he created probably the most distinctive detective couple in the entire genre. The book not only did very well commercially but also spawned a radio program, television series, and an extremely successful sequence of films starring William Powell and Myrna Loy.

Reasons for the popularity of the novel and its offshoots are not hard to find. It is the most briskly paced of Hammett's books, with an intricate plot that is ingenious and deceptive, although logical and believable. The action takes place among the denizens of New York café society during the Prohibition era, and Hammett portrays this frenzied, colorful world of money, corruption, sex, alcohol, and violence with accuracy and energy.

In addition, his characters are unusually vivid—the most memorable being Nick and Nora Charles themselves. They give the novel qualities seen only occasionally in Hammett's earlier works: verbal wit and situational humor. As a former detective of obvious skill and experience, Nick is adroit enough in dealing with crime solving, but he is no aggressive, hard-boiled Continental Op, Sam Spade, or Ned Beaumont. He has retired from the business to manage Nora's not inconsiderable lumber interests and, at least until his curiosity is aroused, has no desire to get back to his former occupation. Nick reluctantly becomes involved because Nora coaxes and dares him. Nick is a witty, cocky, charming man who would rather party than fight. Nora is equally fun loving. The mystery is, to her, an exciting game—until it gets dangerous. The best scenes in the novel are not those of action and violence, as in previous books, but those featuring witty banter and sexual byplay between Nick and Nora. Nick sums up this attitude at the end of the novel: "Let's stick around for a while. This excitement has put us behind in our drinking."

Yet, for all of its ingenuity and charm, *The Thin Man* is one of Hammett's weakest novels and shows a clear decline in his powers. The picture of New York in the 1920's is realistic and vivid, but superficial and cliché-ridden. The plot is clever and facile, but it has no implications beyond that of an interesting puzzle. The character of Nick Charles, while witty and charming, is relatively shallow and frivolous—and somewhat questionable, morally. He is content to live off Nora's money, indulge her whims, and drift from party to party and city to city. The intense personal morality of the earlier works gives way to a kind of lazy, benevolent hedonism in which nothing is more important than a whiskey-and-soda at three in the morning. In short, the vital ethical and intellectual center seems replaced by slick, entertaining superficiality. In retrospect, it is not surprising that *The Thin Man* was Dashiell Hammett's last novel.

TO KILL A MOCKINGBIRD

Type of work: Novel
Author: (Nelle) Harper Lee (1926-   )
Type of plot: Domestic realism
Time of plot: 1930's
Locale: Maycomb, a fictional town in southern Alabama
First published: 1960

Lee's only published novel, To Kill a Mockingbird, *sold millions of copies, won a Pulitzer Prize for its author, and was made into a classic film. Lee's sensitive story of one just man's influence on his children and his community transcends the limitations of time and region to address the universal need for compassion and understanding.*

Principal Characters

Jean Louise "Scout" Finch, the motherless six-year-old daughter of Atticus Finch. A tomboy by nature, Scout roams freely, despite the periodic attempts of her aunt to make a housebound lady out of her. A more important part of her education, however, is not being neglected: Whenever the opportunity arises, Atticus instructs his children in the difference between right and wrong, tolerance and intolerance, compassion and cruelty. Moreover, he is a role model for them, living according to the principles that he professes. At the end of the novel, Scout has become firmly committed to the code that her father exemplifies.

Jem Finch, Scout's ten-year-old brother. During the course of the novel, Jem learns lessons about compassion, duty, and courage that will enable him to grow into a man worthy to be his father's son.

Atticus Finch, Scout's father, a native of Maycomb County, a respected lawyer, and a gentleman. After the death of his beloved wife, Atticus has devoted himself to the rearing of his two children. Although he feels inadequate to the needs of a daughter, he does his best with Scout, who adores him, and depends on his house-keeper, Calpurnia, to teach her the social niceties that only a woman would know. He is a soft-spoken man with a sense of humor who is respected for his honesty and his bravery.

Arthur "Boo" Radley, a man who for years has been kept isolated from the community, a prisoner in his father's house. Because they do not know him, adults and children alike assume that Boo is some kind of monster. Scout and Jem discover, however, that Boo is a kind person and a loyal friend. It is Boo who saves their lives when they are attacked by Bob Ewell.

Bob Ewell, a coward, a bully, and a ne'er-do-well, who is viewed with contempt by blacks and whites alike. It is his daughter's fear of Ewell that causes her to charge Tom Robinson with rape. After Atticus represents Tom in court, Ewell determines to get revenge upon Atticus by harming his children.

Tom Robinson, the decent African-American man who is falsely accused of raping Mayella Ewell. Despite Atticus' impassioned defense, Tom is found guilty by jury members who know in their hearts that he is innocent. In despair, Tom attempts to escape and is killed.

The Story

To Kill a Mockingbird is narrated in the first person by Jean Louise Finch, nicknamed Scout, who at the beginning of the novel is six years old. The three-year period covered in her account was extremely eventful, both for the children and for the sleepy little Alabama town of Maycomb, where they lived.

The novel is divided into two parts. Although the first section may appear episodic, all the characters and incidents in it are essential to the dramatic events that are related in the second part of the novel. This intricate pattern is suggested by Scout's comment in the first chapter that the explanation of Jem's broken arm must begin with the arrival of Charles Baker "Dill" Harris, of Meridian, Mississippi, to spend the summer with his aunt. It was their new friend Dill who dared the other two children to make their first contact with the mysterious Boo Radley, who was secluded in the house next door.

At school, Scout met another character who was to figure in the plot: Walter Cunningham, the son of a poor but proud farmer. Atticus helped Scout to understand the difference between the upright Cunninghams, victims of the Great Depression, and the morally reprehensible Ewells, who had been poor for generations because of their shiftlessness.

Atticus also helped Scout to see the model of a real lady in the unconventional Miss Maudie Atkinson, who demonstrated her courage and consideration for others the night that her house was destroyed by fire. It was Miss Maudie who explained Atticus' dislike of guns. Although he was the finest marksman in the county, as he demonstrated when he had to shoot a rabid dog, Atticus had decided that a gun gave a man an unfair advantage, and as a gentleman, he could not be a bully.

Although it took some time for Jem and Scout to understand it, Atticus' antipathy to bullying also explained his agreeing to represent Tom Robinson, an African-American man who had been accused of raping a white woman, Mayella Ewell. The prejudice that almost assured Tom's conviction was another case of bullying, and Atticus had to fight it. As he had said when he talked about guns, it was a sin to kill a mockingbird. It would be a sin to convict an innocent man.

Appropriately, the final incident in part 1 taught Jem how wrong it was to prejudge someone. When a nasty old lady, Mrs. Henry Lafayette Dubose, insulted his father, Jem cut off her camellia bushes. At her suggestion, Atticus punished Jem by making him read to her daily for a month. After her death, Atticus told Jem that, because she was determined to die free of her morphine addiction, Mrs. Dubose had been enduring excruciating pain and thus, whatever her other flaws, should be viewed as a model of courage.

In the second part of the novel, it was Atticus who exemplified courage. Despite the disapproval of his sister, who had come to visit, and the remonstrances of his friends, Atticus refused to abandon Robinson. When a lynch mob gathered at the jail, Atticus blocked the door. Ironically, it was Scout's hard-learned manners that broke up the confrontation. Recognizing Mr. Walter Cunningham, she made conversation with him as she had been taught to do, praising young Walter until, touched, Mr. Cunningham led away the mob that had menaced Atticus.

Defying their father's orders, Jem and Scout, accompanied by Dill, slipped into the balcony with the African Americans so that they could see the trial. There they heard their father produce evidence proving his client innocent, such as the fact that Tom's crippled arm would have made the crime impossible; listened to the lies told by the Ewells; and some hours later were horrified when the jury found Tom guilty. They also witnessed the African-American community's homage to their father. As the defeated Atticus was walking down the courthouse aisle, the African-American people in the balcony all rose to honor him.

In the final chapters of *To Kill a Mockingbird*, Jem and Scout assessed what had happened. When Tom Robinson attempted to escape from prison and was killed, it seemed to them that evil had won. Yet both Miss Maudie and Atticus said that there were signs of change in Maycomb, such as the length of time that the jury debated and the outspoken support that Atticus had received from many of the town's leading citizens, including the newspaper editor.

Bob Ewell, however, was still planning revenge. One night, when Jem and Scout were walking home after a Halloween pageant, he attacked them with a knife. When Jem fought back in an attempt to save his sister, Ewell broke Jem's arm. Then Boo Radley intervened and killed Ewell with Ewell's own knife. Even though Boo could not be found guilty of murder (instead becoming a local hero), the sheriff persuaded Atticus just once to conceal the truth, in order to preserve Boo's privacy. As young as she was, Scout understood that to intrude upon it would be like killing a mockingbird.

Critical Evaluation

When Harper Lee won the Pulitzer Prize in 1961, some critics approved of the award, lauding her compassion and her sensitivity to racial injustice, while other critics objected to what they defined as moralizing. Admittedly, Lee has firm ideas about what is right and what is wrong. However, it is not fair to accuse her of sermonizing when she so carefully uses point of view to distance herself from her characters.

First there is the dual point of view of the narrator, Jean Louise Finch, or Scout. It is obvious that Scout is not a nine-year-old narrator telling her story immediately after it has occurred, before she has had time to reflect upon it. Instead, she is a mature adult who can remember her thoughts and her feelings during a formative period in her life. Therefore, like many other stories of initiation, *To Kill a Mockingbird* has the advantage of two points of view, one a child's and one an adult's. In addition, the adult narrator reports the statements of other characters, such as Miss Maudie and Atticus, which were impressed upon her in the same way that the explanations of life voiced by authority figures in one's childhood are usually remembered vividly by adults.

Miss Maudie and Atticus both stated the judgment that is both the title and the theme of the novel: that it is a sin to kill a mockingbird. Miss Maudie explained what Atticus meant by that statement, made after he had given the children air rifles. If something is harmless and beautiful, it should never be destroyed. Later, the symbol is specifically applied to two gentle men, Tom Robinson and Boo Radley. In trying to protect Tom from the brutal Bob Ewell, Atticus was defending a harmless person, who by his kindness and decency brought beauty to his world. Later, by agreeing to keep the fragile Boo Radley's secret, Atticus again wished to prevent harm from coming to a "mockingbird."

As the episode with the rabid dog indicates, however, there is an important corollary to Atticus' rule: Sometimes force must be used to defend the innocent. Thus Atticus' killing of the rabid dog foreshadowed Boo's killing of Bob Ewell. In both cases, weapons were used for good, not evil, purposes, used not to kill mockingbirds, but to protect them, for surely Jem and Scout should be placed in that symbolic category.

Because Lee clearly believes in the opposition of good and evil, the themes of *To Kill a Mockingbird* can also be stated in terms of contrasting values. For example, Tom

Robinson was kind to Mayella Ewell, Boo Radley was kind when he left little gifts for the children, and even Aunt Alexandra meant to be kind when she came to help her brother with Scout. On the other hand, Bob Ewell was cruel to his daughter, to Tom's widow, and to Atticus' children. Similarly, Atticus and Mrs. Dubose both exhibited real courage, which Jem imitated in his defense of his sister, while the venomous Bob Ewell was both a coward and a bully. As far as the community as a whole was concerned, it betrayed the moral values that it professed by accepting the lies of the Ewells and rejecting the truth that Atticus had so clearly shown to them. This action was the result of another evil embraced by too many people in Maycomb—prejudice—which Atticus opposed with his plea for tolerance. Yet prejudice could be seen not only in the community's treatment of Boo Radley and of Tom Robinson but also in Aunt Alexandra's snobbery and in Scout's mockery of young Walter Cunningham.

Although some critics condemned the ending of the book as melodramatic, others have pointed to it as an example of masterful plotting. It brings together not only all the themes of the novel but also the two plot lines, which up to that point have had only thematic connections. Harper Lee's achievement can perhaps best be measured by the fact that each generation seems to be as deeply moved as the previous one both by her novel and by the magnificent film that was made from it in 1962. No matter how distant the story that she relates may be in time and place, its characters and its values have a universal appeal.

TOBACCO ROAD

Type of work: Novel
Author: Erskine Caldwell (1903-1987)
Type of plot: Social melodrama
Time of plot: 1920's
Locale: Georgia
First published: 1932

While Tobacco Road *may appear to be a burlesque on rural life in the South, the book deals truthfully with its characters. In Jeeter Lester, Caldwell gives the world another minor hero, a man whose futile hopelessness attracts the sympathy of the sentimental and the social-minded.*

Principal Characters

Jeeter Lester, a Georgia poor white, the father of seventeen, of whom twelve are surviving and two are still at home. Shiftless but always vaguely hopeful, he makes several halfhearted and futile attempts to feed himself first and afterward his starving family. He burns to death in his shack as a result of a fire that he set to burn the broom sedge grass from his land.

Ada Lester, his wife, who shares his fate.

Dude Lester, his sixteen-year-old son, who is persuaded into marriage with a middle-aged widow by her purchase of a Ford automobile, which subsequently runs over and kills a black man and, later, the Lesters' grand-

mother, both to no one's particular regret.

Bessie Lester, the wife of Dude. She uses her authority as a backwoods evangelist to perform her own marriage ceremony.

Pearl Bensey, Jeeter's fifteen-year-old married daughter. Tied to their bed by her husband, she manages to free herself and run away.

Lov Bensey, Pearl's husband. After Pearl's flight, he is advised by Jeeter to take Ellie May instead.

Ellie May Lester, Jeeter's harelipped daughter, who uses her charms to distract Lov's attention—first from his bag of turnips, later from his marital loss.

The Story

Lov Bensey, the husband of Pearl, the fifteen-year-old daughter of Jeeter Lester, felt low when he stopped by the Lester house on his way home with a bag of turnips. Pearl, he complained, refused to have anything to do with him; she would neither sleep with him nor talk to him.

The Lesters lived in a one-room shack that was falling apart. They had nothing to eat but pork-rind soup. Jeeter was trying to patch an inner tube so that the Lesters' car, a nondescript wreck that had been refused even by the junk dealer, could be used to carry firewood to Augusta. Jeeter's harelipped daughter Ellie May charmed Lov away from his bag of turnips. While she and Lov were dallying in the yard in front of the shack, the other Lesters pounced upon the bag of turnips. Jeeter grabbed it and ran into the scrub woods, followed by his worthless son, Dude. Jeeter ate his fill of turnips. He gave Dude several and even saved a handful for the rest of the family. They returned from the woods to find Lov gone. Sister Bessie,

a woman preacher, had come for a visit. Bessie, middle-aged, and Dude, sixteen, were attracted to each other. Bessie, upon leaving, promised to return to take Dude away to be her husband.

The Lesters were starving. Jeeter had long since been unable to get credit at the local stores in order to buy seed, fertilizer, and food. His land was exhausted, and there was no chance of reclaiming it because of Jeeter's utter laziness. Jeeter and his wife, Ada, had had seventeen children. Twelve of them survived, but all except Ellie May and Dude had left home.

Bessie returned and announced that God had given her permission to marry Dude, but Dude refused to listen until Bessie said that she was planning to buy a new car with some money that her late husband had left her. She and Dude went to town and bought a new Ford, the loud horn of which Dude highly approved. At the county courthouse, over the mild protestations of the clerk because of

Dude's youth, Bessie got a marriage license. Back at the Lesters' shack, Bessie, using her authority as a preacher, married herself to Dude.

The newlyweds went for a ride in their new car; they returned to the tobacco road at sundown with one fender of the car completely ruined. They had run into a farm wagon on the highway and had killed a black man whom they left lying by the roadside.

Jeeter, anxious to get food and snuff, persuaded Bessie and Dude to take him to Augusta with a load of firewood. Their arrival in Augusta was delayed, however, by the breakdown of the car. A gallon and a half of oil poured into the crank case enabled them to get to the city, where Jeeter failed to sell one stick of wood. The trio sold the car's spare tire, for which they could see no use, and bought food. They mistook a house of ill-repute for a hotel; Bessie was absent from Jeeter and her young husband most of the night.

During the return trip to the tobacco road, Jeeter un-loaded the wood beside the highway and set fire to it. He was about to suggest another trip in the car, but Bessie and Dude rode away before he could stop them.

As the car rapidly fell apart, the warmth between Bessie and her young husband cooled. In a fight between Bessie and the Lesters over Jeeter's right to ride in the car again, Dude sided with his wife. After all, the car still ran a little.

Meanwhile Pearl ran away from Lov; she had managed to escape after he had tied her to their bed. Jeeter advised Lov not to look for Pearl, but to take Ellie May in her place. He asked Ellie May to bring back victuals and clothes from Lov's house. The grandmother, who had been run over by Bessie's Ford, died in the yard.

Jeeter anticipated seeding time by burning the broom sedge grass off his land. A wind blew the fire to the house while Jeeter and Ada were asleep. The destitute sharecroppers were burned to death on the land that Jeeter's family had once owned as prosperous farmers.

Critical Evaluation

Tobacco Road, published in the midst of the Great Depression, reflects the social and economic concerns of the 1930's, as well as principles of literary naturalism. During the 1930's, a time of extreme economic hardship, novels such as *Tobacco Road* helped make Americans (and others) aware of the destructive poverty and alienation at the bottom of society.

Naturalism, a significant movement in American literature from just before the beginning of the twentieth century through World War II, stresses the impersonal and powerful forces that shape human destinies. The characters of *Tobacco Road* are caught in the backwaters of industrialization, in the grip of irresistible forces. Unable to farm effectively, yet bound to the land and therefore unable to migrate to the factories, they are trapped from one generation to the next. Jeeter, for example, cannot farm his land, and yet instinct binds him (and, finally, his son) to it.

These characters are also prisoners of other forces, most notably the past and their sexuality. They find mod-ern technology beyond their understanding, and they ruin a new car that Bessie has managed to buy. Unable to use modern farming methods, Jeeter and Ada die trying to burn the fields to clear them for an imaginary cotton crop. Sexuality also operates powerfully on these characters. Bessie's marriage to Dude and Lov's attraction for Ellie May are based entirely on sex. In fact, the reader is left with the impression that the characters of *Tobacco Road* are as little able to cope with sexual forces as with economic forces.

The style of the novel, marked by simple, declarative sentences and catching the rhythms of the dialect used by poor white Southerners, is appropriate for the tragically self-destructive life that Caldwell describes. This plain style, typical of naturalism, corresponds to the basic drives for food, sex, and survival, drives which are not hidden or disguised by the demands of civilization, but which Caldwell lays bare for all to see in the changeless lives of his characters.

TROPIC OF CAPRICORN

Type of work: Autobiographical novel
Author: Henry Miller (1891-1980)
Time: 1920's
Locale: New York City
First published: 1939

With a frank and shocking approach, Miller describes his boyhood experiences and his innumerable sexual exploits in the hope of exploding puritanical notions about sex and work. Miller's tone is one of celebration as he recounts episodes from his extraordinary life.

Principal Personages

Henry Miller, the narrator and principal character of the book. He is determined to make his own rules in life and is obsessed with women.

Gene, his cousin, who participated with Miller in the stoning death of another boy when they were young.

Aunt Caroline, Gene's mother, who provided him and Miller with bread when they returned home from the killing.

Joey Kasselbaum, Stanley, Alfie Betcha, Willie Maine, and **Johnny** and **Joe Gerhardt,** childhood friends of Miller.

Lola Niessen, Miller's piano teacher, who was seduced by the fifteen-year-old Miller.

Dr. McKinney, the local veterinarian in Miller's neighborhood.

Valeska, Pauline Janowski, Mara, Francie, and **Agnes,** some of the women with whom Miller had sexual relationships.

Tropic of Capricorn was the third book of Henry Miller's autobiographical romances. In the first volume, *Tropic of Cancer*, published in 1934, Miller chronicled his lusty days as a pauper in post-World War I Paris; in the second, *Black Spring*, which appeared in 1936, his treatment of his experiences in Paris is interspersed with sections on his boyhood in Brooklyn. *Tropic of Capricorn* deals exclusively with New York, specifically with Miller's childhood, adolescence, and the years of his early manhood, before he took up residence abroad in self-imposed exile. Miller describes his life as a boy in a small neighborhood of Brooklyn, his coming of age and the development of his sexual prowess, his numberless feats of copulation (beginning at the age of fifteen when he seduced his piano teacher, who was nearly twice his age), his exasperatingly hectic job as the employment manager for the "Cosmodemonic Telegraph Company of North America," and the inexhaustible indulgence of his friends, who subsidized his existence for much of the time. Yet *Tropic of Capricorn* is more than a simple recital of facts. It is actually an autobiographical novel, in which Miller reveals the emergence of his deepest, most vital self, and of that characteristically furious optimism with which he celebrates life and humanity in all of its forms.

The book opens in a spirit of violent rebellion and denunciation. Miller recalls his childhood as a time of interior, philosophical reaction to the solidly established Nordic axiom that work, struggle, and effort, fortified by righteousness and cleanliness, are the pillars on which one's life must rest. Against this doctrine Miller set a creed of his own: that he would heed only the law of his personal independence, driven by the spur of caprice rather than the whip of compulsion. In the careful, cautious, foresighted restraint with which his parents labored for an ever-receding "tomorrow," Miller saw nothing but the paralysis of the inner self, the desiccation of life. Consequently, he developed a hatred of work, of conventional goals, of material success, of factories, of everything in the United States that destroys the human personality. He set out deliberately to establish himself as an anomaly, a voice of paradoxical joy and indignation crying out in a wilderness of spiritual death. This is really the key to Miller's "philosophy"—if one can use that term for the violent explosions of his mind. His defiant condemnation of conventional values is balanced by a rhapsodic yea-saying to life, a Whitmanesque celebration of the cosmos in its most primitive, barbaric, and undisciplined variety.

As with *Tropic of Cancer*, however, the value of *Tropic*

of Capricorn lies in the fact that Miller anchors his cosmological speculation to the solid ground of his own rich and intense experience. Early in his life, he claims, he learned to maintain his personal independence by assuming an attitude of sublime indifference toward ordinary tribulations—death, for example. When he was about twelve years old, his best friend died after a long illness. Yet Miller wasted no tears at the young boy's bier; he rejoiced that the boy's death meant the end of suffering, for the boy and for those about him. From this incident, Miller jumps chronologically forward to the years of his early manhood during World War I (a war in which he did not participate), when he spent most of his time searching for a job. In this case, as in that of his boyhood friend, however, Miller looked upon his prospects with a kind of Olympian detachment. He did not care deeply about getting any job in particular, and it was only by the merest twist of chance that he secured a responsible position with the "Cosmodemonic Telegraph Company of North America." He began by applying for a job as a messenger boy, but when the switchboard operator at the company's employment bureau turned him down, he became furious enough to take his case to the company's general manager. The result was an offer of a job as personnel manager, which Miller accepted.

The job turned out to be an almost crushing ordeal of constant chaos. Only about twenty percent of the messenger force was composed of steady workers; the rest were drifters. This state of affairs meant that Miller was forced to hire and fire at a rapid rate; more important, it also meant that he was exposed to an extraordinarily varied collection of men and women from every part of the country and from virtually every part of the world. His applicants ranged from Hindus to prostitutes, from former convicts to Cherokees. Miller treated nearly all of them as human beings in need, hiring with his heart rather than his head and thereby subverting company policy. The company often winced, but did not fire him; in the end, after about five years, it was Miller himself who simply walked out.

After this experience, Miller subsisted principally on the generosity of his friends (who were legion, he says) and of his first wife, who seems to have provided him with little besides money. What becomes important in Miller's universe, therefore, is not so much what he does as what he sees and feels. Many of the experiences recreated in *Tropic of Capricorn* involve the people he meets and the books he reads. A chance encounter with a boyhood friend, just returned from Europe, for example, opened Miller's eyes to the exotic fascination of Capri, Pompeii, Morocco, and Paris, places he would later see for himself but which would always hold a special charm because of the way in which his friend described them. Later in the book, he tells of his response to Henri Bergson's *L'Évolution créatrice* (1907; *Creative Evolution*, 1911), a book which intoxicated him with the excitement of creativity and intensified his own sense of self. It made him feel, he says, as if he had crossed a boundary line into a mysterious new realm, where he felt alone, unknown, and foreign. Yet it gave him also a new sense of order, an ability to understand virtually anything, even total confusion.

Nevertheless, there are more things in heaven and earth than are dreamt of in Bergsonian philosophy, and Miller is principally dedicated in this book to the reality of his own experiences, particularly of his encounters with the men and women who populate his unpredictable world. Needless to say, the women receive the lion's share of Miller's attention, for he is fascinated by them to the point of obsession. The opening chapter of *Tropic of Capricorn* is entitled "On the Ovarian Trolley," and it seems to set the tone for everything that follows. Miller's women wriggle through the pages of his book in a seemingly endless stream: Valeska, the daughter of a prostitute and an anonymous black man, who worked as Miller's secretary at the telegraph company and later committed suicide; Pauline Janowski, a homeless Jewish girl of about sixteen who read the works of Honoré de Balzac and yearned to be a writer; Monica, who came to New York City from Buffalo with the body of her mother; Mara, an Egyptian Jew; Francie, an accommodating Scottish girl whom Miller met in the Catskills; Agnes, her Irish-Catholic friend; and numerous others— whores, derelicts, anonymous ladies of the night. Few of these women assume distinctive personalities, and all tend to merge into the gigantic abstraction of sex, which is Miller's overriding concern. He cares little for their names or faces; he is simply mesmerized by their genitalia, which he describes in exhaustive detail. Miller, however, is more than an ordinary lecher, and there is a kind of metaphysical dimension to his mania for the female organ. Yet, curiously enough for a man with his zest for life, it is not the generative power of the female organ that attracts him. He is fascinated instead with its sheer mystery, and he revels in the freedom and frequency with which he tears away the curtain of conventional reticence about it. It holds for him a kind of mystic significance, which he celebrates with untiring energy. He seems, in fact, to derive as much pleasure from discussing what is normally forbidden or censored as he derives from his own amoral behavior. He luxuriates in the license that permits him to use the great triumvirate of Anglo-Saxon obscenities: the four-letter words for copulation, human excrement, and female genitalia. There is something of the bad boy run wild in Miller, gleefully scrawling his heart out on the lavatory wall.

It would hardly be fair, however, to dismiss the book as simply a lurid catalog of Miller's sexual adventures. Much of it is graphic and vivid evocation of his early years in the Brooklyn neighborhood where he was born as the son of a German tailor and grew up while he watched his environment change. The neighborhood that Miller describes exists now only in his memory, for it was, he says, deteriorating even as he passed his boyhood there; it was being radically altered by the coming of Jewish immigrants. When he returned to it as an adult, to the area of the little street called Fillmore Place that was once his entire world, he could no longer recognize it. The neighborhood that he knew had been obliterated and nullified. It is precisely this feeling, perhaps, that lends a note of nostalgia to his recreation of the past.

Yet there is little of ordinary sentiment in his backward glance. He tells without remorse, for example, how he and his cousin Gene became embroiled in a rock fight when they were less than ten years old and how the two of them stoned another boy to death. Miller recalls the incident without the slightest tremor of guilt; in his account of it, what emerges in boldest relief is not the act of murder but the spontaneous generosity of his Aunt Caroline, who greeted the boys when they returned home with two large slices of sour rye spread with fresh butter and sugar. The gift of the bread was for Miller something like an act of grace—unearned, unmerited, and therefore purer than any bread that he would later gain by the sweat of struggle. In retrospect, the bread assumes a sacramental significance in his mind.

The canvas of these early years is painted with bright if sometimes garish colors. Miller writes of his boyhood chums: of the slow-witted Joey Kasselbaum, whom he and Gene humored in their games of marbles; of Stanley, a Polish boy with a violent temper who would help young Miller to raid Aunt Caroline's icebox; of Alfie Betcha and a crazy boy named Willie Maine, both of whom got drunk at a neighborhood party and fell to biting each other; of a part-Irish youth named Johnny Gerhardt, who beat another boy senseless and then ran away from home; and of Johnny's brother Joe, who distinguished himself by the delicate act of apologizing to the beaten boy. Miller writes too of Dr. McKinney, the local veterinarian who castrated stallions in public and let the blood run into the gutter, and he speaks with bitterness of his father's final illness, induced by his decision to renounce liquor. In the face of impending death, it seems, the old man suddenly acquired an astonishing piety. Yet this effort collapsed upon the departure of the local Congregationalist minister (whom Miller's father had come to worship), and the experience left him a broken, empty, and disillusioned man. The interior life had been drained out of him, and Miller, remembering happier days with a lighthearted father, mourns the loss.

Nevertheless, there is little in his past that Miller mourns. On the whole, his book is an emphatic celebration of life, a paean to vitality. From the sordid sensuality of the Broadway dance hall to the heights of his mystic communion with Bergson, from the spasms of his copulative moments to the depths of his cosmological speculations, Miller was the apostle of the living self.

TRUE GRIT

Type of work: Novel
Author: Charles Portis (1933-   )
Type of plot: Comic adventure
Time of plot: Late 1870's
Locale: Arkansas and the Indian Territory
First published: 1968

True Grit is the tale of an exciting and hazardous mission undertaken by the youthful protagonist and her two unlikely companions. The skillfully rendered border-state atmosphere and dialogue have occasioned favorable comparison with Mark Twain's novels of Missouri.

Principal Characters

Mattie Ross, the narrator-protagonist, a fourteen-year-old but a girl who has been an adult since birth. Mattie is narrating the story fifty years after her grand adventure. She has never married. Her most intimate contact with a man has been her warm, but chaste, relationship with Rooster Cogburn, the grizzled lawman whom she hired to catch her father's killer. Mattie is proud, rigid, and self-righteous. She can also be imperious. More important, however, she is bright, resourceful, tenacious, loyal, and exceedingly brave.

Reuben J. "Rooster" Cogburn, a U.S. deputy marshal for the western district of Arkansas. He has a questionable past, having fought as a guerrilla rather than as a regular soldier during the Civil War. He is approaching middle age, has lost an eye, has grown fat, and drinks too much. Mattie needs a man with grit, however, to run down her father's murderer. Cogburn appears to possess that commodity in abundance, as he has killed twenty-three men in the past four years.

LaBoeuf, a Texas Ranger on detached service, seeking the same quarry as Mattie and Rooster. The fugitive, known by another name in Texas, has killed a state senator in Waco. The senator's family has hired LaBoeuf to find the killer and bring him to justice. Mattie, both as a woman and as an Arkansan, immediately develops a strong prejudice against the swaggering Texan; she finds him flashy, conceited, and condescending.

Tom Chaney, the murderer of Mattie's father, Frank Ross, and (under his original name of Theron Chelmsford) of at least one other man in Texas. After killing Ross in Fort Smith, Chaney flees across the Arkansas River into the Indian Territory. There, he joins Lucky Ned Pepper's band of desperadoes, with whom Mattie, Rooster, and LaBoeuf will eventually have a thrilling confrontation.

The Story

Mattie Ross, the protagonist and narrator, lives on a farm in Yell County, Arkansas, near the river town of Dardanelle. Her father, Frank Ross, travels on business to Fort Smith, a frontier town farther up river. While there, he is shot down and robbed by Tom Chaney, a farmhand who has accompanied him on the trip. Chaney flees into the Indian Territory and joins Lucky Ned Pepper's band of outlaws. Mattie leaves her mother, sister, and brother at home and also travels to Fort Smith. They believe that her purpose is to claim her father's effects, but she does not plan to return to Dardanelle until Tom Chaney has been brought to justice.

Fort Smith is a rough town, the bailiwick of Judge Isaac Parker, the notorious (and historical) "hanging judge." On the very day of Mattie's arrival, she witnesses the public hanging of three miscreants. She learns of the exploits of Reuben J. "Rooster" Cogburn, a federal deputy marshal who has captured and killed many an outlaw. Mattie attempts to hire Rooster to track down Chaney, but he is unwilling to accept the commission without some payment in advance. A livery stable operator named Stonehill had sold Frank Ross four cow ponies and also had stabled his horse, on which Chaney fled following the murder. Mattie browbeats Stonehill into buying back the ponies and paying for her father's horse as well. Then she immediately forces him to sell the best of the ponies, Little Blackie, to her at a price greatly advantageous to the buyer. Armed with the money from these successful transactions, Mattie employs Rooster Cogburn.

The pursuit of Chaney is complicated by the appearance of LaBoeuf (known throughout by his last name only), a Texas Ranger on detached service. Chaney, whose real name is Theron Chelmsford, murdered a state senator in Waco, Texas, and the senator's family hired LaBoeuf in the same way and for the same purpose that Mattie hired Rooster. LaBoeuf intends to take Chaney back to Texas, an outcome that would be completely unsatisfactory to Mattie: She wants him to hang in Arkansas for her father's murder. As Mattie, Rooster, and LaBoeuf cross the Arkansas River into the Indian Territory, they form an uneasy alliance. Mattie and Rooster are irritated by the brash young Texan, whom they take to be representative of his state. Yet, in the moment of crisis, he—like his companions, the priggish Mattie and the boozy Rooster—will show that he has the essential quality of true grit.

Pepper's gang is finally run down when Mattie stumbles onto Tom Chaney just a few yards away from her, across a little creek. She shoots and wounds the outlaw with her father's service revolver (Rooster will later bludgeon him to death with his rifle); then he captures her. While LaBoeuf goes to Mattie's rescue, the fat, middle-aged marshal faces the outlaw gang alone in an exciting shoot-out on horseback. Rooster wounds Lucky Ned Pepper, kills two of his companions, and sends a third fleeing before his big horse, Bo, is shot from under him. He is pinned beneath his horse, and the arm holding his weapon is pinned beneath his body. LaBoeuf saves Rooster's life when he kills Pepper with a magnificent rifle-shot of more than six hundred yards. In the course of this action, Mattie falls into a pit filled with rattlesnakes. She breaks her left arm and is eventually bitten. Rooster pulls her from the pit and races the many miles back toward civilization and medical attention. The gallant pony, Little Blackie, carries the big man and the girl at full gallop until it falls dead. Rooster then carries Mattie on his back. At the Poteau River, he commandeers a wagon and a team of mules at gunpoint. The wild ride saves Mattie's life, although she loses the injured arm just above the elbow.

In the final pages, Mattie summarizes Rooster's decline. The disappearing frontier has greatly lessened the need for quick-triggered lawmen such as Rooster. By the beginning of the twentieth century, he is traveling with Cole Younger and Frank James in a wild West show. He dies suddenly while the show is at Jonesboro, Arkansas. Mattie has her old friend's body exhumed from the Confederate cemetery in Memphis and reburied in the Ross family plot at Dardanelle. She knows that the neighbors consider her behavior eccentric, but she has a will of iron and a disdain for uninformed public opinion.

Critical Evaluation

Charles Portis is a major comic writer. He has mastered the device of the absurd but poignant quest, a device that is at the heart of such comic masterpieces as Miguel de Cervantes' *Don Quixote de la Mancha* (1605, 1615), Henry Fielding's *Tom Jones* (1749), and Voltaire's *Candide* (1759). Portis has been appropriately compared to Mark Twain, whose great novel *The Adventures of Huckleberry Finn* (1884) is also an episodic, picaresque narrative. *True Grit*, Portis' second novel, is most reminiscent of Twain in its characters, setting, and use of period language.

True Grit was successful critically and commercially. It first appeared, in a condensed serialized version, in *The Saturday Evening Post* in May and June of 1968. The full text appeared in book form later that year, and publication in Great Britain followed in 1969. The novel was immediately adapted for the screen, first in 1969 and then in a less satisfying remake some ten years later. In the 1969 adaptation, the veteran film star John Wayne played the role of Deputy Marshal Rooster Cogburn and quickly became identified with the character much as Clark Gable had earlier become Rhett Butler in the public mind. As the one-eyed deputy, Wayne won the Academy Award for Best Actor and went on to reprise the role in *Rooster Cogburn* (1975), a film that merely borrowed the character from *True Grit* and constructed a similar but inferior story around him. Although Portis had no hand in either screenplay, his dialogue was so natural and so necessary a part of the characters that huge chunks of it are used without alteration in the films.

Portis is a regional writer whose works are recognizably in the line of descent from the Southwestern humorists of the 1840's and 1850's. His native state of Arkansas is usually the center of consciousness in his novels. Still, like the best of the regional—usually meaning Southern—writers (such as Twain, William Faulkner, Eudora

Welty, Flannery O'Connor, and Larry McMurtry), he has won a wide audience beyond the region of which he writes.

In *True Grit*, Portis takes the old folktale and song of the Arkansas Traveler and stands it on its head. There, the Traveler is an outsider, attempting to make his way through the wilds of Arkansas, while the indolent native is content to sit at his cabin door, fiddle, and play semantic games with the puzzled stranger. Mattie, who is neither indolent nor playful, leaves a settled life in Arkansas to journey into what she clearly considers a benighted land.

Arkansas, Texas, and Oklahoma (or the Indian Territory, as it was known until 1907) were the westernmost members of the Confederacy, where the Old South met the Old West. Portis uses this clash of cultures and the feelings of state pride and competitiveness to good effect in the novel. Everything about Dardanelle clearly suggests the Old South: Frank Ross fought honorably at the battle of Elkhorn Tavern and was wounded at Chickamauga, his daughter carries his old-fashioned cap-and-ball service revolver into battle against the enemy, and she is initially accompanied to Fort Smith by Yarnell Poindexter, an African-American farm worker. Mattie, writing many years later, says that her first impression of Fort Smith was that it was no city at all compared to Little Rock and that she still feels it should be in Oklahoma instead of Arkansas. She threatens all who oppose her with her Dardanelle lawyer, J. Noble Daggett, for her the embodiment of authority, even of civilization. This Southern girl has left the South behind.

To Mattie, the Indian Territory is the end of the world, a savage and lawless robbers' roost. Portis skillfully incorporates into the dialogue the raillery among Mattie, Rooster, and LaBoeuf. Mattie tells the reader that the latter's name is pronounced "LaBeef," connoting the cowboy culture and the vast plains of his native state and even preparing the reader somewhat for the near-miraculous shot with which he will kill the leader of the outlaw band and silence the criticisms of his Arkansan companions.

In *True Grit*, Portis combines the motifs of the innocent eye and the picaresque, or rogue, hero. Mattie is the former, Rooster the latter. The action of the story is seen through the eyes of the fourteen-year-old Mattie, who is the same age that Huck Finn is supposed to be when he experiences his adventures on the mighty Mississippi River. Mattie's narrative has a maturer tone than Huck's for two reasons: Hers is a memoir composed after Mattie has become an old lady, and in certain ways, she has always been an adult and never a child.

Although Rooster has a certain appeal from his first appearance, it is not until the final pages of the novel that he proves his nickname has been well earned. During the war, he rode with the infamous William Clarke Quantrill, it is rumored that he has killed most of his victims from ambush, and he is drunk so much of the time that Mattie fears he will be of no use when they finally catch up with the outlaws. In the time of trial, however, he shows that he is an old fighting rooster indeed. He also makes manifest the affection that has steadily grown within him for the girl.

True Grit is a fine comedy within both the classical and the contemporary meanings of the term. All ends well, while the comic tone dominates even in the scenes of greatest conflict and danger. While faultlessly choosing incidents and dialogue that range from the amusing to the hilarious, Portis has succeeded in reaffirming his—and perhaps the reader's—belief in a human being's capacity for courage, fidelity, and self-sacrifice.

THE TURN OF THE SCREW

Type of work: Novella
Author: Henry James (1843-1916)
Type of plot: Moral allegory
Time of plot: Mid-nineteenth century
Locale: England
First published: 1898

More than a horrific ghost story, The Turn of the Screw *is an enigmatic and disturbing psychological novel that probes the sources of terror in neurosis and moral degradation.*

Principal Characters

The Governess, from whose point of view the story is told. Employed to look after the orphaned niece and nephew of a man who makes it clear that he does not wish to be bothered about them, she finds herself engaged in a struggle against evil apparitions for the souls of the children. There has been much debate about whether *The Turn of the Screw* is a real ghost story or a study of a neurotic and frustrated woman. Probably both interpretations are true: The apparitions are real, the children are indeed possessed by evil, and the governess is probably neurotic.

Miles, a little boy, one of the governess' charges. At first, he seems to be a remarkably good child, but gradually she learns that he has been mysteriously corrupted by his former governess and his uncle's former valet, whose ghosts now appear to maintain their evil control. Miles dies in the governess' arms during her final strug-

gle to save him from some mysterious evil.

Flora, Miles's sister and feminine counterpart. The governess finally sends her away to her uncle.

Miss Jessel, the former governess, now dead. She appears frequently to the governess and to the children, who refuse to admit the appearances.

Peter Quint, the uncle's former valet, now dead. Drunken and vicious, he was also Miss Jessel's lover. The governess sees his apparition repeatedly.

Mrs. Grose, the housekeeper of the country estate where the story is set. Good-hearted and talkative, she is the source of what little concrete information the governess and the reader get as to the identities and past histories of the evil apparitions. Allied with the governess against the influence of Peter Quint and Miss Jessel, she takes charge of Flora when the child is sent to her uncle.

The Story

It was a pleasant afternoon in June when the governess first arrived at the country estate at Bly, where she was to take charge of Miles, age ten, and Flora, eight. She faced her new position with some trepidation because of the unusual circumstances of her situation. The two children were to be under her complete care, and the uncle who had engaged her had been explicit in the fact that he did not wish to be bothered with his orphaned niece and nephew. Her uneasiness disappeared, however, when she saw her charges, for Flora and Miles seemed incapable of giving the slightest trouble.

The weeks of June passed uneventfully. Then, one evening, while she was walking in the garden at twilight, the governess was startled to see a young man at a dis-

tance. The man looked at her challengingly and disappeared. The incident angered and distressed the young woman, but she decided that the man was a trespasser.

On the following Sunday evening, the young woman was startled to see the same stranger looking in at her through a window. Once again, he stared piercingly at her for a few seconds and then disappeared. This time, the governess realized that the man was looking for someone in particular and that perhaps he boded evil for the children in her care. A few minutes later, the governess told the housekeeper, Mrs. Grose, of the incident and described the appearance of the man. Mrs. Grose told her that it was a perfect description of Peter Quint, the valet to the governess' employer, but that Mr. Quint was dead.

One afternoon shortly afterward, a second apparition appeared. This time, the ghost of Miss Jessel, the former governess, appeared in the garden to both the governess and the little girl, Flora. The strange part of the situation was that the little girl refused to let the governess know that she had seen the figure and knew who it was, though it was obvious that she had understood the appearance fully.

The governess learned from the housekeeper that the two apparitions had been lovers while alive, though the girl had been of a very fine family and the man had been guilty of drunkenness and worse vices. For what evil purpose these two spirits wished to influence the seemingly innocent children, neither the housekeeper nor the governess could guess. The secrecy of the children about seeing the ghosts was maddening to the two women.

They both believed that the boy was continuing to see the two ghosts in private and concealed that fact, just as he had known of the illicit affair between the valet and the former governess in life and had helped them to conceal it. Yet, when in the presence of the children, the governess sometimes thought that it would be impossible for the two children to be influenced into evil.

The third time, the ghost of Quint appeared to the governess inside the house. Unable to sleep, she had sat reading late at night. Hearing someone on the stairs, she went to investigate and saw the ghost, which disappeared when faced by her unflinching gaze. Each night after that, she inspected the stairs, but she never again saw the ghost of the man. Once she glimpsed the apparition of Miss Jessel as it sat dejectedly on the lowest stair. Worse than the appearance of the ghosts was the discovery that the children had left their beds at night to wander on the lawn in communication with the spirits who were leading them to unknown evil. It became apparent to the governess that the children were not good within themselves. In their imaginations, they were living in a world populated by the evil dead restored.

In such an atmosphere, the summer wore away into autumn. In all that time, the children had given no sign of awareness of the apparitions. Knowing that her influence with the children was as tenuous as a thread that would break at the least provocation, the governess did not allude to the ghosts. She herself had seen no more manifestations, but she had often believed from the children's attitude that the apparitions were close at hand. What was worse for the distressed woman was the thought that what Miles and Flora saw were things still more terrible than she imagined, visions that sprang from their association with the evil figures in the past.

One day, Miles went to her and announced his desire to go away to school. The governess realized that it was only proper that he be sent to school, but she feared the results of ghostly influences once he was beyond her care. Later, opening the door of the schoolroom, she again saw the ghost of her predecessor, Miss Jessel. As the apparition faded, the governess realized that her duty was to stay with the children and combat the spirits and their deadly influence. She decided to write immediately to the children's uncle, contrary to his injunction against being bothered on their behalf. That night before she wrote, she went into Miles's room and asked the boy to let her help him in his secret troubles. Suddenly a rush of cold air filled the room, as if the window had been blown open. When the governess relighted the candle blown out by the draft, the window was still closed, and the drawn curtain had not been disturbed.

The following day, Flora disappeared. Mrs. Grose and the governess found her beside the garden pond. The governess, knowing that she had gone there to see the ghost, asked her where Miss Jessel was. The child replied that she only wanted to be left alone. The governess could see the apparition of Miss Jessel standing on the opposite side of the pond.

The governess, afraid that the evil influence had already dominated the little girl, asked the housekeeper to take the child to London and to request the uncle's aid. In place of the lovable angelic Flora, there had suddenly appeared a little child with a filthy mind and filthy speech, which she used in denouncing the governess to the housekeeper. The same afternoon, Mrs. Grose left with the child as the governess had requested.

That evening, immediately after dinner, the governess asked Miles to tell her what was on his mind before he left the dining room. When he refused, she asked him if he had stolen the letter that she had written to his uncle. As she asked the question, she realized that standing outside the window, staring into the room, was the ghost of Peter Quint. She pulled the boy close to her, shielding him from any view of the ghost at the window, while he told her that he had taken the letter. He also informed her that he had already been expelled from one school because of his lewd speech and actions. Noting how close the governess was holding him, he suddenly asked if Miss Jessel were near. The governess, angry and distraught, shrieked at him that it was the ghost of Peter Quint, just outside the window. When Miles turned around, the apparition was gone. With a scream, he fell into the governess' arms. At first, she did not realize that she had lost him forever—that Miles was dead.

Critical Evaluation

One of the world's most famous ghost stories, *The Turn of the Screw* was first published serially in *Colliers' Weekly* from January 27, 1898, to April 16, 1898, and in book form, along with a second story, *Covering End*, late in 1898. In 1908, Henry James discussed at some length the origin and nature of the tale in the preface to volume 12 of *The Novels and Tales of Henry James* (1907-1909). Considerable critical discussion and controversy have been devoted to the story, especially after Edmund Wilson's 1934 essay on "The Ambiguity of Henry James," in which Wilson argues that "the governess who is made to tell the story is a neurotic case of sex repression, and that the ghosts are not real ghosts but hallucinations of the governess." Because many critics have taken issue with Wilson and because Wilson later modified his interpretation, it is important to note briefly what James himself says about his story, his characters, and his theme in the preface. He calls *The Turn of the Screw* "a piece of ingenuity pure and simple, of cold artistic calculation, an *amusette* to catch those not easily caught . . . the jaded, the disillusioned, the fastidious." He terms the governess' account "her record of so many anomalies and obscurities." He comments that he purposely limited his revelation of the governess' character: "We have surely as much of her nature as we can swallow in watching it reflect her anxieties and inductions." He says he presented the ghosts as "real" ones, and he describes them as

> my hovering prowling blighting presences, my pair of abnormal agents . . . [who] would be agents in fact; there would be laid on them the dire duty of causing the situation to reek with the air of Evil. Their desire and their ability to do so, visibly measuring meanwhile their effect, together with the observed and described success—this was exactly my central idea.

Concluding his discussions of "my fable," James explains that he purposely did not specify the evils in which the ghosts either attempt to or actually involve Miles and Flora: "Only make the reader's general vision of evil intense enough, I said to myself . . . and his own experience, his own imagination, his own sympathy (with the children) and horror (of their false friends) will supply him quite sufficiently with all the particulars."

Thus, readers see that James conceived of the tale as one in which the governess, a young woman with limited experience and education but high moral principles, attempts to protect two seemingly innocent children from corruption by the malign ghosts of two former servants who in life were evil persons. His capitalizing of "Evil" and his use of the term "fable" to describe the story suggest a moral as well as an aesthetic intent in writing it. To interpret *The Turn of the Screw* in terms of Freudian psychology, as Wilson and some other critics have done, is to go beyond James and to find what he did not put there—consciously anyway. Admittedly, some of the "anomalies and obscurities" that puzzle and trouble the governess do lead the reader in the direction of a Freudian interpretation. The account is the governess' alone, and there is no proof that anyone else actually saw the ghosts, though she believes that the children saw them and lied to her or tried otherwise to hide the truth from her. Before his reading of the governess' journal, Douglas admits that she was in love with her employer, the children's handsome uncle who showed no personal interest in her. Within the account itself, the reader who hunts may find apparent Freudian symbolism. For example the male ghost, Peter Quint, first appears standing on a tower when the governess has been deeply longing for her employer to appear and approve her care of the children. The female ghost, Miss Jessel, first appears by a lake and watches as little Flora, also watched absorbedly by the governess, plays a childish game:

> She had picked up a small flat piece of wood, Which happened to have in it a little hole that had evidently suggested to her the idea of sticking in another fragment that might figure as a mast and make the thing a boat. This second morsel . . . she was very markedly and intently attempting to tighten in its place.

Ten-year-old Miles's repeated use of the word "dear" in speaking to the governess may suggest a precocious boy's sexual interest in his pretty governess.

One can go on, but it is important to remember that James's story was published in 1898 and that Freud's first significant work explaining psychoanalytic theory did not appear until 1905. Perhaps it is best to regard such details in the story as no more than coincidental, though they may seem suggestive to the post-Freudian reader of *The Turn of the Screw*.

Among the most difficult facts to explain away in developing the theory that the ghosts are mere hallucinations of a sexually frustrated young woman, however, is the governess' detailed description of a man she has never seen or heard of:

> He has no hat. . . . He has red hair, very red, close-curling, and a pale face, long in shape, with straight,

good features and little, rather queer whiskers that are as red as his hair. His eyebrows are, somehow, darker; they look particularly arched. . . . His eyes are sharp— awfully. . . . His mouth's wide, and his lips are thin, and except for his whiskers he's quite clean-shaven.

Mrs. Grose easily identifies him as the dead Peter Quint. She just as easily identifies Miss Jessel when the governess describes the person she later saw: "A figure of quite an unmistakable horror and evil: a woman in black, pale and dreadful—with such an air also, and such a face!—on the other side of the lake." It is difficult to argue convincingly that Peter Quint and Miss Jessel are not "real" ghosts.

The Turn of the Screw will continue to fascinate and to intrigue because James's "cold artistic calculation" has so filled it with suggestiveness and intentional ambiguity that it may be read at different levels and with new revelations at each successive reading. As Leon Edel claimed, "The reader's mind is forced to hold to two levels of awareness: *the story as told*, and *the story to be deduced.*"

UNCLE TOM'S CABIN: Or, Life Among the Lowly

Type of work: Novel
Author: Harriet Beecher Stowe (1811-1896)
Type of plot: Sentimental romance
Time of plot: Mid-nineteenth century
Locale: Kentucky and Mississippi
First published: 1852

A sentimental but powerful document in the controversy over slavery, Uncle Tom's Cabin *is a novel whose political and humanitarian pleading profoundly influenced a nation. The work seems to be linked to two popular traditions: It incorporates all the sentimental elements of the novel of feeling, and in its horror scenes, it suggests Gothic novels.*

Principal Characters

Uncle Tom, an African-American slave. Good and unrebellious, he is sold by his owner. After serving a second kind but improvident master, he comes under the ownership of brutal Simon Legree and dies as a result of his beatings.

Eliza, a slave. Learning that her child is about to be sold away along with Tom, she takes the child and runs away, crossing the Ohio River by leaping from floating ice cake to floating ice cake.

George Harris, her husband, a slave on a neighboring plantation. He too escapes, passing as a Spaniard, and reaches Ohio, where he joins his wife and child. Together, they go to freedom in Canada.

Harry, the child of Eliza and George.

Mr. Shelby, the original owner of Eliza, Harry, and Uncle Tom. Encumbered by debt, he plans to sell a slave to his chief creditor.

Haley, the buyer, a New Orleans slave dealer. He shrewdly selects Uncle Tom and persuades Mr. Shelby to part with Harry in spite of Mr. Shelby's misgivings.

George Shelby, Mr. Shelby's son. He promises to buy Tom back one day but arrives at Legree's plantation as Tom is dying. When his father dies, he frees all of his slaves in Uncle Tom's name.

Mrs. Shelby, Mr. Shelby's wife. She delays the pursuit of Eliza by serving a late breakfast.

Marks and **Loker,** slave catchers hired by Haley to track Eliza through Ohio. Loker, wounded by George Harris in a fight, is given medical treatment by the Quakers who are protecting the runaways.

Augustine St. Clare, the purchaser of Tom after Tom saves his daughter's life. He dies before making arrangements necessary to the freeing of his slaves.

Eva St. Clare, his saintly and frail daughter. Before her death, she asks her father to free his slaves.

Mrs. St. Clare, an imaginary invalid. After her husband's death, she sends Tom to the slave market.

Miss Ophelia, Augustine St. Clare's cousin from the North. She comes to look after Eva and is unused to lavish Southern customs.

Topsy, a pixielike African-American child bought by St. Clare for Miss Ophelia to educate; later, he makes the gift legal.

Simon Legree, the alcoholic and superstitious brute who purchases Tom and kills him. He is a Northerner by birth.

Cassy, Legree's slave. She uses his superstitions to advantage in her escape. Her young daughter, who was sold years ago, proves to be Eliza, and mother and daughter are reunited in Canada.

Emmeline, another of Legree's slaves. She escapes with Cassy.

Madame de Thoux, whom Cassy and Emmeline meet on a northbound riverboat. She proves to be George Harris' sister.

Aunt Chloe, Uncle Tom's wife, left behind in Uncle Tom's cabin on the Shelby plantation.

Senator Bird, in whose house Eliza first finds shelter in Ohio.

Mrs. Bird, his wife.

Simeon and **Rachel Halliday,** who give shelter to the fugitive slaves.

The Story

Because his Kentucky plantation was encumbered by debt, Mr. Shelby made plans to sell one of his slaves to his chief creditor, a New Orleans slave dealer named Haley. The dealer shrewdly selected Uncle Tom as partial payment on Mr. Shelby's debt. While they were discussing the transaction, Eliza's child, Harry, came into the room. Haley wanted to buy Harry too, but at first Shelby was unwilling to part with the child. Eliza listened to enough of the conversation to be frightened. She confided her fears to George Harris, her husband, a slave on an adjoining plantation. George, who was already bitter because his master had put him to work in the fields when he was capable of doing better work, promised that someday he would have his revenge upon his hard masters. Eliza had been brought up more indulgently by the Shelbys, and she begged him not to try anything rash.

After supper in the cabin of Uncle Tom and Aunt Chloe, his wife, the Shelby slaves gathered for a meeting. They sang songs, and young George Shelby, who had eaten his supper there, read from the Bible. In the big house, Mr. Shelby signed the papers making Uncle Tom and little Harry the property of Haley. Eliza, learning her child's fate from some remarks of Mr. Shelby to his wife, fled with her child, hoping to reach Canada and safety. Uncle Tom, hearing of the sale, resigned himself to the wisdom of providence.

The next day, after Haley had discovered his loss, he set out to capture Eliza. She had a good start, however, and Mrs. Shelby purposely delayed the pursuit by serving a late breakfast. When her pursuers came in sight, Eliza escaped across the Ohio River by jumping from one floating ice cake to another, young Harry in her arms.

Haley hired two slave catchers, Marks and Loker, to track Eliza through Ohio. For their trouble, she was to be given to them. They set off that night.

Eliza found shelter in the home of Senator and Mrs. Bird. The senator took her to the house of a man known to aid fugitive slaves. Uncle Tom, however, was not so lucky. Haley made sure that Tom would not escape by shackling his ankles before taking him to the boat bound for New Orleans. When young George Shelby heard that Tom had been sold, he followed Haley on his horse. George gave Tom a dollar as a token of his sympathy and told him that he would buy him back one day.

At the same time, George Harris began his escape. White enough to pass as a Spaniard, he appeared at a tavern as a gentleman and took a room there, hoping to find before long a station on the Underground Railroad.

Eliza was resting at the home of Rachel and Simeon Halliday when George Harris arrived in the same Quaker settlement.

On board the boat bound for New Orleans, Uncle Tom saved the life of young Eva St. Clare, and in gratitude Eva's father purchased the slave. Eva told Tom that he would now have a happy life, for her father was kind to everyone. Augustine St. Clare was married to a woman who imagined herself sick and therefore took no interest in her daughter Eva. He had gone north to bring back his cousin, Miss Ophelia, to provide care for the neglected and delicate Eva. When they arrived at the St. Clare plantation, Tom was made head coachman.

Meanwhile, Loker and Marks were on the trail of Eliza and George. They caught up with the fugitives, and there was a fight in which George wounded Loker. Marks fled, and so the Quakers who were protecting the runaways took Loker along with them and gave him medical treatment.

Unused to lavish southern customs, Miss Ophelia tried to understand the South. Shocked at the extravagance of St. Clare's household, she attempted to bring order out of the chaos, but she received no encouragement because the slaves had been humored too long. Indulgent in all things, St. Clare was indifferent to the affairs of his family and his property. Uncle Tom lived an easy life in the loft over the stable. He and little Eva became close friends with St. Clare's approval. Sometimes, St. Clare had doubts regarding the institution of slavery, and in one of these moods, he bought an odd pixielike child, Topsy, for his prim New England cousin to educate.

Eva grew more frail. Knowing that she was about to die, she asked her father to free his slaves, as he had so often promised. After Eva's death, St. Clare began to read his Bible and to make plans to free all of his slaves. He gave Topsy to Miss Ophelia legally, so that the spinster might rear the child as she wished. Then, one evening, he tried to separate two quarreling men. He received a knife wound in the side and died shortly afterward. Mrs. St. Clare had no intention of freeing the slaves, and she ordered Tom sent to the slave market.

At a public auction, he was sold to a brutal plantation owner named Simon Legree. Legree drank heavily, and his plantation house had fallen to ruin. He kept dogs for the purpose of tracking runaway slaves. At the slave quarters, Tom was given his sack of corn for the week, told to grind it himself and bake the meal into cakes for his supper. At the mill, he aided two women. In return, they baked his cakes for him. He read selections from the Bible to them.

For a few weeks, Tom quietly tried to please his harsh master. One day, he helped a sick woman by putting cotton into her basket. For this act, Legree ordered him to flog the woman. When Tom refused, his master had him flogged until he fainted. A slave named Cassy came to Tom's aid. She told Tom the story of her life with Legree and of a young daughter who had been sold years before. Then she went to Legree's apartment and tormented him. She hated her master, and she had power over him. Legree was superstitious. When she talked, letting her eyes flash over him, he felt as though she were casting an evil spell. Haunted by the secrets of his guilty past, he drank until he fell asleep. Yet he had forgotten his fears by the next morning, and he knocked Tom to the ground with his fist.

Meanwhile, far to the north, George, Eliza, and young Harry were making their way slowly through the stations on the Underground Railroad toward Canada.

Cassy and Emmeline, another slave, determined to make their escape. Knowing the consequences if they should be caught, they tricked Legree into thinking that they were hiding in the swamp. When Legree sent dogs and men after them, they sneaked back into the house and hid in the garret. Legree suspected that Tom knew where the women had gone and decided to beat the truth out of his slave. He had Tom beaten until the old man could neither speak nor stand.

Two days later, George Shelby arrived to buy Tom back, but he came too late. Tom was dying. When George threatened to have Legree tried for murder, Legree mocked him. George struck Legree in the face and knocked him down.

Still hiding in the attic, Cassy and Emmeline pretended that they were ghosts. Frightened, Legree drank harder than ever. George Shelby helped them to escape. Later, on a riverboat headed north, the two women discovered a woman named Madame de Thoux, who said that she was George Harris' sister. With this disclosure, Cassy learned also that Eliza, her daughter, was the Eliza who had married George and with him and her child had escaped safely to Canada.

These relatives were reunited in Canada after many years. In Kentucky, George Shelby freed all of his slaves when his father died. He said that he freed them in the name of Uncle Tom.

Critical Evaluation

It has been suggested that Mark Twain wrote the first book in the American idiom, but surely Harriet Beecher Stowe's powerful novel introduces the reader to an in-depth use of a regional dialect from an earlier period. The author intentionally created the characters of Tom, Legree, Eva, and Topsy, all of whom subsequently became stereotypes, because these features were a part of the conventional wisdom of the antebellum United States. These characters were convenient, effective agencies to warn the Christians of the nation of an impending doom: "Every nation that carries in its bosom great and unredressed injustice has in it the elements of this last convulsion." God would certainly punish such a nation.

First published in book form in 1852, this book attracted millions of readers and came to be required reading in many high schools and colleges. This work will always provide an added dimension to Americans' understanding of the spiritual crisis of pre-Civil War times. The human tragedy in the story symbolizes the moral decay of the country. Simon Legree becomes the epitome of a white America that supported slavery and feared hell, yet was more concerned with the material world.

Tom lost his wife, children, and life to the ravages of the "peculiar institution." The collective guilt of the nation could only be cleansed by the abolition of slavery.

The fate of the nation and the role of Christian churches in perpetuating slavery were topics of great concern to Stowe: "And yet, O my country these things are done under the Shadow of thy laws! O Christ! Thy Church sees them, almost in silence." The author observed and wrote about the crisis that divided Protestantism into sectional churches, a spiritual antecedent of the war. Clearly, the moral regeneration of the individual would lead to the abolition of slavery. Seeking support for her cause, Stowe admonished the reader to pity "those mothers that are constantly made childless by the American slave trade."

The author was a colonizationist, but she believed deeply that white America must first pay reparations to the nation's enslaved blacks. Once freed, the author points out, African Americans needed and desired education and skills. She hoped that her testimony might bring an end to inhumanity. It was little wonder, then, that President Abraham Lincoln, upon meeting Stowe, remarked, "So you're the little lady who started the war."

THE UNDERGROUND MAN

Type of work: Novel
Author: Ross Macdonald (Kenneth Millar, 1915-1983)
Type of plot: Mystery
Time of plot: 1960's
Locale: California
First published: 1971

Representative of Macdonald's works, The Underground Man *has a complex plot with detective Lew Archer as its moral center; the other characters are corrupted or destroyed by their greed, compulsive quests for the truth, or ties to the past.*

Principal Characters

Lew Archer, the narrator, a private detective unlike most in the mystery genre, for he invariably develops a feeling of kinship with clients, fellow sufferers in an imperfect world. A good listener, he gets at the truth not only through his reasoning and instincts but also by learning from those who confide in him. A loner still aching from the trauma of a long-ago divorce, Archer is attracted to women, and they to him. Yet, despite a tender scene at the close of the novel between him and Jean, his client, it is clear that he only wants to help her return to normality as a young widow with a six-year-old son.

Elizabeth Broadhurst, who is seemingly dominated and manipulated by such strong men as Leo Broadhurst and Brian Kilpatrick but who is actually a survivor, shooting her unfaithful husband and living to see Kilpatrick commit suicide rather than confront exposure and ruin. Although her son Stanley has been killed, she has her grandson Ronny, and through the writing of a memoir of her father, she still has a past to shape and control.

Edna Snow, the former Broadhurst housekeeper and a domineering, overprotective mother. In a paranoid way, she clings to her mildly retarded son, Fritz, as the only stable and constant element in her life, even slaying one man in revenge for a false accusation of rape against Fritz and killing two others years later in a futile attempt to keep the first crime a secret.

Jean Broadhurst, the estranged wife of Stanley Broadhurst, who hires Archer to find her son Ronny, presumably kidnapped by his father, Stanley. A young, well-intentioned woman, she is unavoidably caught in a web of intrigue and death whose origins precede her arrival on the scene.

Stanley Broadhurst, who is murdered because his obsessive quest to learn the truth about his father's disappearance threatens to expose other people's secrets. He is only one victim, although the most innocent, of his father's sins.

The Story

While private detective Lew Archer is feeding peanuts to birds outside his West Los Angeles apartment house, he meets six-year-old Ronny Broadhurst, the youngest member of a well-to-do Southern California family that has been rent by marital discord. Fifteen years earlier, his grandfather Leo Broadhurst disappeared, apparently abandoning his wife, Elizabeth, and child for a married woman, Ellen Strome Kilpatrick, but then deserting her as well. Stanley, Leo's son, has been so consumed by his desire to locate his father that his own marriage founders. Although an advertisement that he places in a San Francisco newspaper provides him with vital information, it also dredges up too much of the past for some people and leads to his murder. One of the reward seekers who replies to the advertisement is Albert Sweetner, an escaped convict who had been the foster child of Edna Snow, the onetime Broadhurst housekeeper. His reappearance revives a long-ago scandal in which he and Frederick (Fritz) Snow, then in their teens, were accused of raping Marty Nickerson, also a teenager, who had a child named Susan as a result of that attack. Mrs. Lester Crandall, Marty, and her husband have kept the truth from Susan, who becomes involved with both Stanley Broadhurst and Jerry Kilpatrick. The latter is a rebellious teenager, the son of Brian Kilpatrick and his former wife, Ellen, the sometime mistress of Leo Broadhurst. Jerry and Susan flee with young Ronny in tow, stealing a boat and then a car in the course of a frantic, apparently purposeless odyssey.

Not only is the past closing in upon the Broadhursts and others, but there is also a raging forest fire (symbolic of humanity's self-serving destruction of society and the environment) that Stanley unwittingly begins by carelessly discarding a cigarette while disinterring his father's body, having at last reached the end of his quest. Because the flames of this natural disaster threaten to destroy Archer's evidence, the pressure builds on the detective to solve what unfolds into an increasingly complex mystery that spans three generations and involves several families. Within a few days, he succeeds, discovering that Leo Broadhurst was a womanizer and a rapist and that Elizabeth Broadhurst shot him when she found him in bed with the teenage Marty, whose daughter he had fathered three years earlier. Edna Snow, then Leo's housekeeper, discovered him lying unconscious and stabbed him to death. As she explains her act of vengeance to Archer fifteen years later: "You can't call it murder. He deserved to die. He got Marty Nickerson pregnant and let my boy take the blame. Frederick has never been the same since."

Susan Crandall, who was three years old when she witnessed the tryst between her mother and Broadhurst (her actual father), has been haunted by the affair and the shooting for fifteen years. At the start of the novel, she and Leo's son, Stanley (her half brother), are jointly working at learning about his father's fate through the involved process of piecing together people's recollections,

including hers. After they go their separate ways, Stanley's quest leads him to his parents' mountain retreat, where he thinks that his father may be buried; he borrows a pick and shovel from Fritz Snow, who reports this request to his mother. Because she had made Fritz and Sweetner bury Broadhurst for her fifteen years earlier, Mrs. Snow fears the consequences of Stanley's discovery. Disguising herself as a man, she goes to the Broadhursts' retreat, kills Stanley, and buries him in the hole that he had started to dig. Events, in other words, have moved full circle. Although Stanley solves the mystery of Leo's disappearance, he dies in the process and is interred, ironically, with the father who had abandoned him.

Reviving the past causes other people's deaths as well. Albert Sweetner, who was lured back to his old haunts by Stanley's newspaper reward offer, is killed, also by Mrs. Snow, because she wants to silence him. Brian Kilpatrick commits suicide rather than risk exposure as an unscrupulous wheeler-dealer who had cheated Elizabeth Broadhurst, his real-estate partner. In addition to getting at the truth, however belatedly, and bringing Mrs. Snow to justice, Stanley's quest has other positive aspects: Ellen Kilpatrick Strome is reunited with her son, Jerry; Susan, who will undergo a regimen of psychotherapy for her recurring nightmare, eventually may be able to lead a normal life; the Crandalls, Susan's parents, no longer hiding the truth and living a lie, also can return to normality after many years; and when Ronny grows up, he will not be beset by the sins, obsessions, and secrets of his forebears, as the avenging furies have been purged. Of all the characters, Lew Archer, who as detective has functioned partly as catalyst, alone remains unchanged, and he has not even made much money from his successful efforts.

Critical Evaluation

Traditional detective fiction, starting with Edgar Allan Poe and continuing through Arthur Conan Doyle and generations of successors on both sides of the Atlantic Ocean, is first and foremost a puzzle. It begins with a crime; introduces a detective, usually in private practice, who proceeds to search for a solution; and concludes, sometimes after additional crimes, with the culprit exposed and all aspects of the mystery explained. Any character development usually is stereotypical, as is the standard, recurring theme: Crime does not pay; it is an aberration in a society, and when the perpetrator is exposed, normality is restored. Ross Macdonald's novels

are atypical. Early in his career, he began writing complex studies of the human condition, moving beyond the accepted boundaries of the mystery genre and into the realm of mainstream literature. While mysteries remain central in his fiction, and a private detective is both narrator and prime protagonist, his multilayered novels primarily are carefully constructed studies of the ways in which the past impinges upon the present and how people often are trapped by a heritage of which they may be totally unaware. In *The Underground Man*, more poignantly than in any other Macdonald novel, the characters have "all the years of their lives dragging behind them," and at the end, Archer expresses the hope that Leo Broadhurst's young grandson has "a benign failure of memory." Even Archer himself, nearing the close of the case, feels "shipwrecked on the shores of the past."

Macdonald's twenty-second novel and the seventeenth featuring Lew Archer, *The Underground Man* was published in 1971. It was given more critical attention than detective fiction normally receives, including a *Newsweek* cover story and a laudatory front-page review by novelist Eudora Welty in *The New York Times Book Review*. He thereby was being accepted as a serious novelist and finally was accorded his long-sought recognition as successor to Raymond Chandler and Dashiell Hammett in the hard-boiled school of American detective fiction. As early as 1947, Macdonald had been consciously working in the Chandler-Hammett tradition, and when he created Lew Archer two years later for *The Moving Target* (1949), he named him after Miles Archer, Sam Spade's murdered partner in Hammett's *The Maltese Falcon* (1930). The name notwithstanding, Macdonald says that Archer is "patterned on Raymond Chandler's Marlowe," who is also a "semi-outsider . . . fascinated but not completely taken in by the customs of the natives." Unlike Chandler, however, Macdonald does not think that the detective is the character in a novel who offers the "quality of redemption"; instead, he says, that quality "belongs to the whole work and is not the private property of one. . . . The detective-as-redeemer is a backward step in the direction of sentimental romance, and an oversimplified world of good guys and bad guys."

The Underground Man is not only the breakthrough work for Macdonald but also his major achievement, the novel in which his worldview, especially social commentary on environmental and ecological matters, is given its fullest and most memorable expression. In this book, more memorably than anywhere else, Archer's pursuit of the truth exposes the venality behind the façade of propriety. The title of the novel, recalling as it does Fyodor Dostoevski's *Zapiski iz podpolya* (1864; *Notes from the Underground*, 1918), leads the reader beyond the literal reference to the buried Leo or Stanley and to the Russian novelist's focus upon the themes of guilt and suffering.

The quest and Oedipal motifs that are central to the story of the Broadhursts and their milieu are developed most fully in the character of Stanley, whose love-hate relationship with his father is the motivating and inevitably destructive force of his life. Jean, Stanley's wife, says that "he's angry at his father for abandoning him; at the same time he misses and loves him." The Oedipal theme also is obvious in the Snows. A domineering mother, Mrs. Snow clings to her thirty-five-year-old son as the

one constant element in her life, killing three people to avenge and protect him, and Fritz heeds her will, having been convinced of his own dependence. Although she has endured and survived largely because of an inner strength, Archer sees her as "one of those paranoid souls who kept her conscience clear by blaming everything on other people. Her violence and malice appeared to her as emanations from the external world." Like so many others in the book, she is trapped and ultimately destroyed by the past.

Macdonald's attitude toward the past is expressed in a letter that the Reverend Riceyman sends to Stanley: "*The past can do very little for us—no more than it has already done, for good or ill—except in the end to release us. We must seek and accept release, and give release.*" Archer thinks that this is good advice and regrets that Stanley had not taken it; perhaps he simply did not live long enough. Elizabeth Broadhurst, however, lives long enough to see the secrets of her husband's past exposed and laid to rest. Wiser and more emotionally restrained than Edna Snow, Mrs. Broadhurst finds refuge from Leo's shame by writing a memoir of her father, thereby reshaping his life by idealizing him in her manuscript as "a god come down to earth in human guise."

Another theme that pervades Macdonald's novel is humanity's alienation from itself and from nature. This concept is presented by means of the forest fire, a leitmotif through much of the book, consuming everything in its path in the same wantonly destructive manner that the characters pursue their dreams or rebel against their nightmares. Macdonald served in the Pacific theater of operations during World War II, and war imagery is common in his novels. Archer's first reaction to the forest fire evokes war, the ultimate destructive act of humanity: "Under and through the smoke I caught glimpses of fire like the flashes of guns too far away to be heard. The illusion of war was completed by an old two-engine bomber, which flew in low over the mountain's shoulder." When he comes to the Broadhurst ranch, Archer sees fire-scorched fruit, which "hung down from their branches like green hand grenades."

Squabbling jays open the novel, and a fire spreads through the course of it. At the end, however, rain is quenching the threatening blaze and, as Archer says, "washing the detritus of summer downhill toward the sea." Evil has been purged, and there is a promise of renewal on the horizon. Macdonald follows this pattern elsewhere, but echoes notwithstanding, *The Underground Man* has a distinctive quality and combines perfectly themes that are both timeless and timely.

U.S.A.

Type of work: Novel
Author: John Dos Passos (1896-1970)
Type of plot: Social chronicle
Time of plot: 1900-1935
Locale: The United States
First published: 1937 (*The 42nd Parallel*, 1930; *1919*, 1932; *The Big Money*, 1936)

The trilogy U.S.A. offers a great variety of characters, each moving upon a different social level but all presented within the limits of a single world. The result is a complete cross section of American life covering the political, social, and economic history of the United States from the beginning of the twentieth century to the Depression-ridden, war-threatened 1930's. In addition to the life stories of his characters, Dos Passos provides "Newsreels" (quotations from newspapers, speeches, and popular songs), "The Camera Eye" (brief impressionistic sketches from the author's own life), and "Biographies" (portraits of such public figures as radicals, inventors, and politicians).

Principal Characters

Fenian O'Hara McCreary, called **Mac,** a young Irishman who learns the printing trade from an uncle, whose bankruptcy puts McCreary out of a job and makes a tramp of him. Because of his skill as a printer, McCreary is able to find work here and there, one with a shoddy outfit called the Truthseeker Literary Distributing Co., and he travels from place to place, usually riding on freight trains. In his travels, he falls in with members of the International Workers of the World (IWW) and becomes an earnest worker in that labor movement. He marries Maisie Spencer, but eventually they quarrel. He leaves his family in California when he goes to become a labor organizer in Mexico. There, he lives a free and easy life.

Maisie Spencer, a shopgirl who marries Mac McCreary. She is unable to share his radical views, and they part.

Janey Williams, a woman who wants a career in business. She becomes a stenographer and, through her luck and skill, is hired as secretary to J. Ward Moorehouse, a prominent man in public relations. She becomes an efficient, if sour, woman who makes a place for herself in business. Her great embarrassment is her brother Joe, a sailor who shows up periodically in her life with presents for her.

Joe Williams, Janey Williams' brother, a young man who cannot accept discipline. He loves life at sea and becomes a merchant sailor after deserting from the Navy. Although he is in and out of scrapes all the time, he manages to qualify as a second officer during World War I. His life ends when a Senegalese man hits him over the head with a bottle in a brawl over a woman in the port of Saint-Nazaire.

Della Williams, Joe Williams' wife. Although she is cold to her husband and claims that she is modest, she comes to believe during World War I that it is her patriotic duty to entertain men in uniform all she can, much to her husband's chagrin.

J. Ward Moorehouse, an opportunist who becomes a leading public relations and advertising executive. He is anxious to succeed in life and to have a hand in many activities. His first wife is Annabelle Strang, a wealthy, promiscuous woman; his second is Gertrude Staple, who helps him in his career. Though he succeeds as a businessperson, he is unhappy in his domestic life, to which he gives too little time because he prefers a whole series of women to his wife. A heart attack finally persuades him that the life he leads is not a fruitful one.

Annabelle Strang, the wealthy, amoral woman who becomes J. Ward Moorehouse's first wife.

Gertrude Staple, J. Ward Moorehouse's second wife, a wealthy young woman whose family and fortune help her husband become established as a public relations counselor. She becomes mentally ill and spends many years in a sanatorium.

Eleanor Stoddard, a poor girl from Chicago. Gifted with artistic talent, she sets herself up as an interior decorator and succeeds professionally. She becomes a hard, shallow, but attractive woman. While serving as a Red Cross worker in Europe, she becomes J. Ward Moorehouse's mistress for a time. Always climbing socially, she becomes engaged to an exiled Russian nobleman in New York after World War I.

Eveline Hutchins, the daughter of a liberal clergyman. She becomes Eleanor Stoddard's erstwhile business partner. A young woman who spends her life seeking pleasure and escape from boredom, her life is a series of rather sordid love affairs, both before and after marriage. She finally commits suicide.

Paul Johnson, Eveline Hutchins' shy and colorless soldier husband, whom she meets in France while doing Red Cross work.

Charley Anderson, a not very promising youth who becomes famous as an aviator during World War I. He cashes in on his wartime reputation and makes much money, both as an inventor and as a trader on the stock market. His loose sexual morality and his heavy drinking lose him his wife, his jobs, his fortune, and finally his life. He dies as the result of an automobile accident that happens while he is drunk. He has a brief love affair with Eveline Hutchins.

Margo Dowling, the daughter of a ne'er-do-well drunkard. Through her beauty and talent, she makes her own way in the world and becomes a film star after many amatory adventures. For a time, she is Charley Anderson's mistress.

Agnes Mandeville, Margo Dowling's stepmother, friend, and financial adviser. She is shrewd with money.

Frank Mandeville, a broken-down vaudeville actor and Agnes' husband. A lost man after the advent of motion pictures, he spends much of his time trying to seduce Margo Dowling and eventually rapes her.

Tony de Carrida, Margo Dowling's first husband, an effeminate Cuban musician who is finally reduced to being Margo's uniformed chauffeur.

Sam Margolies, a peculiar but successful film producer who "discovers" Margo Dowling and makes her a star. He becomes her second husband.

Richard Ellsworth Savage, called **Dick,** a bright young man and a Harvard graduate who wishes to become a poet. He meets J. Ward Moorehouse and ends up as a junior partner in Moorehouse's firm. He is Anne Elizabeth Trent's lover for a time.

Anne Elizabeth Trent, called **Daughter,** a wild young girl from Texas who makes the wrong friends. In Europe, as a relief worker after World War I, she falls in love with Richard Ellsworth Savage and becomes pregnant by him. She goes for an airplane ride with a drunken French aviator and dies when the plane crashes.

Mary French, a bright young Vassar graduate interested in social work. She becomes a radical and a worker for various labor movements sponsored by communists. She loses her lover, Don Stevens, who returns from a visit in Moscow with a wife assigned to him by the Party.

Don Stevens, a communist organizer who for a time is Mary French's lover. In Moscow, he marries a wife of whom the Party approves.

Benny Compton, a Jewish boy from New York who drifts into labor work and becomes a highly successful labor organizer and agitator. He turns communist and gives all of his energy to work for the Party. Sentenced to the penitentiary in Atlanta for his activities, he is released after World War I. He lives for a time with Mary French.

Webb Cruthers, a young anarchist who for a brief period is Anne Elizabeth Trent's lover.

The Story

The Spanish-American War was over. Politicians with mustaches said that the United States was now ready to lead the world.

Mac McCreary was a printer for a fly-by-night publisher in Chicago. Later he worked his way to the West Coast. There he got work as a printer in Sacramento and married Maisie Spencer, who could never understand his radical views. They quarreled, and he went to Mexico to work in the revolutionary movement there.

Janey Williams, growing up in Washington, D.C., became a stenographer. She was always ashamed when her sailor brother, Joe, showed up, and even more ashamed of him after she became secretary to J. Ward Moorehouse. Of all Moorehouse's female acquaintances, she was the only one who never became his mistress.

J. Ward Moorehouse's boyish manner and blue eyes were the secret of his success. They attracted Annabelle Strang, the wealthy nymphomaniac he later divorced. Gertrude Staple, his second wife, helped to make him a prominent public relations expert. His shrewdness made him an ideal man for government service in France during World War I. After the war, he became one of the nation's leading advertising executives.

Because Eleanor Stoddard hated the sordid environment of her childhood, her delicate, arty tastes led her naturally into partnership with Eveline Hutchins in the decorating business, and eventually to New York and acquaintanceship with J. Ward Moorehouse. In Europe with the Red Cross during the war, she lived with Moorehouse. Back in New York in the 1920's, she used her connections in shrewd fashion and became engaged to a member of the Russian nobility.

Charley Anderson had been an aviator in the war. A successful invention and astute opportunism made him a wealthy airplane manufacturer. He married a woman who had little sympathy for his interest in mechanics. In Florida, after a plane crash, he met Margo Dowling, an actress. Charley Anderson's series of drinking binges ended in a grade crossing accident.

Joe Williams was a sailor who had been on the beach in Buenos Aires. In Norfolk, Virginia, he met Della, who urged him to give up seafaring and settle down. Unable to hold a job, he shipped out again and almost lost his life when the ship he was on was sunk by a German submarine. When Joe got his third mate's license, he and Della were married. He was ill in the East Indies, arrested in New York for not carrying a draft card, and torpedoed once more off Spain. Della was unfaithful to him. Treated coldly the few times he looked up his sister Janey, he shipped out for Europe once more. One night in Saint-Nazaire he attacked a huge Senegalese man who was dancing with a woman he knew. Joe's skull was crushed when he was hit over the head with a bottle.

Teachers encouraged Dick Savage in his literary talents. During his teens, he worked at a summer hotel and there slept with a minister's wife who shared his taste in poetry. A government official paid his way through Harvard University where Dick cultivated his estheticism and mild snobbery before he joined the Norton-Harjes ambulance service and went to Europe. There some of his letters about the war came to the attention of censorship officials, and he was shipped back to the United States. His former sponsor got him an officer's commission, and he returned to France. In Italy, he met a relief worker named Anne Elizabeth Trent, who was his mistress for a time. When he returned to the United States, he became an idea man for Moorehouse's advertising agency.

Eveline Hutchins, who had some artistic talent, became Eleanor Stoddard's partner in a decorating establishment in New York. All of her life she tried to escape boredom through sensation. Beginning with the Mexican artist who was her first lover, she had a succession of affairs. In France, where she was Eleanor's assistant in the Red Cross, she married a shy young soldier named Paul Johnson. Later she had a brief affair with Charley Anderson. Dissatisfied, she decided at last that life was too dull to endure and died from an overdose of sleeping pills.

Anne Elizabeth Trent, known as Daughter, was the child of moderately wealthy Texans. In New York, she met Webb Cruthers, a young anarchist. One day, seeing a police officer kick a female picketer in the face, Daughter attacked him with her fists. Her night in jail disturbed her father so much that she returned to Texas and worked in Red Cross canteens. Later she went overseas. There she met Dick Savage. Pregnant, she learned that he had no intention of marrying her. In Paris, she went on a drunken spree with a French aviator and died with him in a plane crash.

Benny Compton was the son of Jewish immigrants. After six months in jail for making radical speeches, he worked his way west through Canada. In Seattle, he and other agitators were beaten by deputies. Benny returned East. One day, police broke up a meeting where he was speaking. On his twenty-third birthday, Benny went to Atlanta to serve a ten-year sentence. Released after the war, he lived for a time with Mary French, a fellow traveler in the Communist Party.

Mary French spent her childhood in Trinidad, where her father, a physician, did charity work among the native miners. Mary, planning to become a social worker, spent her summers at Jane Addams' Hull-House. She went to Washington, D.C., as secretary to a union official, and later worked as a union organizer in New York City. There she took care of Ben Compton after his release from Atlanta. While working with the Sacco-Vanzetti Committee, she fell in love with Don Stevens, a fellow Communist Party member. Summoned to Moscow with a group of Party leaders, Stevens returned to New York with a wife assigned to him by the Party. Mary went back to her committee work for worker's relief.

Margo Dowling grew up in a run-down house in Rockaway, Long Island, with her drunken father and Agnes, her father's mistress. At last, Agnes left her lover and took Margo with her. In New York, Agnes became the common-law wife of an actor named Frank Mandeville. One day, while drunk, Mandeville raped the girl. Margo ran off to Cuba with Tony, an effeminate Cuban guitar player, whom she later deserted. She was a cheerful companion for Charley Anderson, who gave her a check for five thousand dollars on his deathbed. In Hollywood, she met Sam Margolies, a successful producer, who made a star of her.

Jobless and hungry, a young hitchhiker stood by the roadside. Overhead droned a plane in which people with the big money rode the skyways. Below, the hitchhiker with an empty belly thumbed cars speeding by him. The haves and the have-nots—that was the United States in the Great Depression of the 1930's.

Critical Evaluation

John Dos Passos' statement at the beginning of *U.S.A.* that the country is, more than anything else, the sounds of its many voices, offers several insights into the style and content of the trilogy. The style, for example, reflects the author's attempt to capture some sense of characteristically American "voices," not only in the idiomatic narration of the chronicles (or novel sections) but in the "Newsreels," "Biographies," and "The Camera Eye" as well. While these sections reflect, respectively, the public voice of the media and popular culture, the oratorical and eulogistic voice of the biographies, and the personal and private voice of the artist, the most important voices in the trilogy are those of the chronicles in which Dos Passos introduces a cross section of American voices ranging from the blue-collar worker to the professional and managerial classes, and representing a variety of regional and ethnic backgrounds. Like Walt Whitman, who profoundly influenced him, Dos Passos takes all the nation as his subject matter as he tries to capture the meaning of *U.S.A.* through the sounds of the many voices that characterize its people and institutions.

Many people have associated the social, political, and economic views expressed in *U.S.A.* with Marxism—leftists in the 1930's liked to believe this important author made common cause with them—but it is really the American economist Thorstein Veblen, rather than Karl Marx, who seems to have shaped Dos Passos' thinking about the economic and political situation in the United States during the first quarter of the twentieth century. Dos Passos had read Veblen's *The Theory of the Leisure Class* (1899), *The Theory of Business Enterprise* (1904), and other writings, and it was from these sources that his attack on the American business economy stems. In *The Big Money*, Dos Passos offers a "Biography" of Veblen in which he summarizes this economist's theories of the domination of society by monopoly capitalism and the sabotage of the workers' human rights by business interests dominated by the profit motive. According to Dos Passos, the alternatives that Veblen saw were either a society strangled and its workers destroyed by the capitalists' insatiable greed for profit or a society in which the needs of those who do the work would be the prime consideration. Veblen, writing just at the beginning of the twentieth century, still held out hope that the workers might yet take control of the means of production before monopoly capitalism could plunge the world into a new dark age. Dos Passos goes on to develop the idea that any such hope died with World War I and that the American dream of democracy was dead from that time forward.

Against the background of Veblen's ideas, *U.S.A.* can be seen as a documentary chronicling the growing exploitation of the American worker by the capitalist system, as well as a lamentation of the lost hope of Veblen's dream of a society that would make producers the prime beneficiaries of their own labor. The best characterization of the blue-collar worker is Mac McCreary, a rootless laborer constantly searching for some outlet for his idealistic hope of restoring power to the worker. Certainly one of the most sympathetic characters in *U.S.A.*, Mac dramatizes the isolation and frustration of modern workers, who are only human cogs in the industrial machine, unable either to take pride in their work or finally to profit significantly by it. Other characters as well fit within the pattern of the capitalist system as Veblen described it, or else, like Mac, revolt against the injustice of the system. There are the exploiters and the exploited, and there are a few, such as Mary French and Ben Compton, who make opposition to the system a way of life. Equally prevalent are those characters who dramatize Veblen's theory of conspicuous consumption by serving as playthings (Margo Dowling), lackeys (Dick Savage), or promoters (J. Ward Moorehouse) for those who control the wealth and power.

Throughout the trilogy, the essential conflict is that between the business interests who control the wealth, and the workers who produce it. Yet Dos Passos is almost equally concerned with the way in which the system of monopoly capitalism exploits and destroys even those of the managerial class who seem to profit most immediately from it. Dick Savage, for example, starts out as a talented young writer only to be corrupted by the system. Charley Anderson, who early could be seen as typifying the American dream of success through ingenuity and imagination, dies as much a victim of the system as any of its workers. J. Ward Moorehouse, on the other hand, makes nothing and produces nothing, but his is the talent that can parlay nothing into a fortune and the mentality that can survive in the world of *U.S.A.*

The two national historical events to which Dos Passos gives most attention are World War I and the execution of the anarchists Nicola Sacco and Bartolomeo Vanzetti. As Dos Passos saw it, the war, under the pretense of making the world safe for democracy, gave the capitalists the opportunity that they needed to solidify their power by actually crushing the democratic spirit. For Dos Passos, democracy had died in the United States with World War I, and the Sacco and Vanzetti case proved it. The death of these two immigrant Italian radicals on a trumped-up charge of murder was, in Dos Passos' eyes, the ultimate demonstration of the fact that Americans' traditional freedoms were lost and that monopoly capitalism had usurped power. When, in his later and more conservative years, John Dos Passos was accused of having deserted the liberal positions of his youth, he maintained that his views had not shifted from those he argued in *U.S.A.* The evidence of the novel would seem to bear him out. The *U.S.A.* trilogy is a more nostalgic than revolutionary work, and it looks back to that point in American history before the options were lost, rather than forward to a socialist revolution. His finest work shows Dos Passos as a democratic idealist rather than as a socialist revolutionary.

THE VIRGINIAN

Type of work: Novel
Author: Owen Wister (1860-1938)
Type of plot: Regional romance
Time of plot: Late nineteenth century
Locale: Wyoming
First published: 1902

This novel is one of the classic works about the American West. Wister, who was familiar with Wyoming and the cowboys who worked there, saw that, although the mountains and the plains would remain, the picturesque cowboy was rapidly disappearing. The Virginian *seeks to preserve the myth of this heroic, colorful figure.*

Principal Characters

The Virginian, a cowboy in Wyoming who is one of nature's gentlemen. He can perform his duties well and hold his own in practical jokes, drinking bouts, and poker games. When given an opportunity, he proves to be an apt leader and a successful ranch foreman. He falls in love with a young schoolteacher from the East and by his manly behavior proves his worth to her. She finally marries him, even though he is a rough-and-ready man by her standards. The Virginian believes in law and order, even if violence is required to maintain them; one of his most difficult experiences is the hanging of a friend who has turned cattle rustler.

Molly Wood, a very feminine but efficient young woman from Vermont who comes to Wyoming to teach in the grade school at Bear Creek. She entrances the Virginian, who almost immediately falls in love when he rescues her from a stagecoach marooned by high water. Molly acts the coquette at first with the cowboy, but she falls in love with him, even risking her life to attend to him when he is wounded by hostile Native Americans. She tries to keep him from a gunfight by threatening not

to marry him, but when he emerges from the duel unscathed, she is too happy that he is alive to make good her threat.

Trampas, a cowboy who becomes the Virginian's enemy when the latter accuses him of cheating at cards and faces him down without a fight. Trampas turns cattle rustler and becomes an outlaw, even killing a fellow rustler in order to save his own life. He is finally killed by the Virginian in a gunfight.

Steve, a cowboy, one of the Virginian's close friends. He becomes a cattle rustler and is hanged by a posse of which the Virginian is a member. When caught, Steve refuses to speak to his friend, who feels badly about the death of Steve, outlaw or not.

Judge Henry, owner of a cattle ranch at Sunk Creek, Wyoming, where the Virginian works. Judge Henry is impressed by the Virginian and makes him his foreman.

Shorty, a cowboy who becomes one of Trampas' fellow rustlers. He is killed by Trampas when his death will allow the other outlaw to escape justice.

The Story

The Virginian had been sent by his employer to meet an Eastern guest at Medicine Bow, Wyoming, and escort him the two hundred and sixty miles from the town to Sunk Creek Ranch. While the Virginian and the guest were awaiting the arrival of the Easterner's trunk on the following westbound train, the cowboy entered into a poker game. One of the players, a cowboy named Trampas, accused the Virginian of cheating. The man backed down, however, before the gun of the cowboy from Sunk

Creek. It was apparent to everyone that the Virginian had made an implacable enemy.

A few months later, in the fall, a schoolmistress came West from Vermont to teach in the new school at Bear Creek, Wyoming. All the single men, and there were many of them in the territory, anxiously awaited the arrival of the new teacher, Molly Wood. The Virginian was fortunate in his first meeting with her. A drunken stagecoach driver tried to ford a creek in high water and marooned his coach and passenger. The Virginian, passing by, rode to the stagecoach, lifted out the young woman, and deposited her safely on the bank of the stream. After he had ridden away, Molly missed her handkerchief and realized that the young cowboy had somehow contrived to take it.

The next time that the Virginian saw Molly, she was a guest at a barbecue. The cowboy had ridden his horse for two days for an opportunity to see her, but she coquettishly refused to notice him. The Virginian and another cowboy, piqued by her attitude, got drunk and played a prank on all the people who had brought their children to the barbecue. They switched the babies and their clothing, so that when the barbecue was over many of the mothers carried off the wrong babies. Before he left for Sunk Creek, the Virginian warned Molly that she was going to love him eventually, no matter what she thought of him then.

During the next year, the Virginian began to read books for the first time since he had left school in the sixth grade. He borrowed the books from Molly in order to ride to Bear Creek to see her at intervals. In the meantime, he had risen high in the estimation of his employer. Judge Henry put him in charge of a party of men who were to escort two trainloads of steers to the Chicago market.

On the trip back to the ranch, the Virginian's men threatened to desert the train to go prospecting for gold, which had been discovered in the Black Hills. The ringleader of the insurgents was Trampas.

The Virginian saw that the best way to win over the men was to make a fool of Trampas. His chance came when the train stopped near a bridge that was being repaired. Because there was no food on the train, the Virginian went out and gathered a sackful of frogs to cook. Then he began a story about frogs, a tall story by which Trampas was completely taken in. As soon as the rest of the cowboys saw how foolish Trampas appeared, they were willing to return to the ranch, much to the discomfiture of their ringleader.

Back at Sunk Creek, the Virginian found a pleasant surprise awaiting him. The foreman of the ranch had been forced to leave because of an invalid wife, and the judge had made the Virginian his foreman.

Trampas had expected to be discharged from his job as soon as the Virginian became foreman at the Sunk Creek Ranch. The Virginian, however, decided it was better to have his enemy in sight, and so Trampas stayed on, sullen and defiant in his behavior.

The following spring, the Virginian made a trip to a neighboring ranch. On the way back, he was attacked by a local tribe and severely wounded. He managed to escape and make his way to a spring. There he was found, half dead, by Molly Wood. She stayed with him at the risk of her life, for the attackers were still in the vicinity. She then bound his wounds, took him back to her cabin, and called a doctor.

Molly, meanwhile, had packed her possessions, for she was preparing to leave for her home in the East. By the time that the Virginian had recovered sufficiently to go back to work, she had decided not to leave Wyoming. She was sure by then that she was in love with the cowboy foreman. When the Virginian left her cabin for Sunk Creek, Molly had promised to marry him.

Upon returning to work the Virginian found that his enemy, Trampas, had disappeared, taking another of the cowboys, Shorty, with him. About the same time, the ranches in that territory began to lose cattle to rustlers, and a posse was formed to track down the cattle thieves. After several weeks of searching, two of the thieves were caught. Because the rustlers had somehow managed to gain control of the local courts and had already been freed on one charge, the posse hanged both of them. It was a terrible experience for the Virginian, because one of the men, Steve, had been a close friend. The Virginian hated to think that he had hanged his friend, and the hurt was made worse by the fact that the condemned man had refused to say a word to his former companion.

On his way back to Sunk Creek, the Virginian came across the trail of the other two rustlers. They were Trampas and Shorty. Because they had only one horse between them, Trampas murdered Shorty in order to escape.

When Molly Wood heard of the lynching and the Virginian's part in it, she refused to marry him. After a conversation with Judge Henry, however, she realized that the Virginian had done no more than his duty. She and the Virginian were reconciled, and a date was set for their wedding.

On the day before their wedding, Molly and the Virginian started to ride to Medicine Bow. On the way, they met Trampas, who galloped ahead of them into the town. Molly questioned the Virginian about the man and discovered the enmity between the two. When they arrived in town, they were warned that Trampas had said he would shoot the Virginian if he were not out of town by sunset. Molly told him that she could never marry him if he fought with Trampas and killed him. The Virginian, knowing that his honor was at stake, left her in the hotel and went out to face his enemy. Trampas fired first and missed. Then the Virginian fired and killed Trampas.

When the Virginian returned to the hotel, Molly was

too glad to see him alive to remember her threat. Hearing the shots, she had been afraid that the Virginian had been killed. They were married the following day, as they had planned, and spent two months of their honeymoon high in the Rocky Mountains where no other humans ever went.

Critical Evaluation

This book appeared in 1902, some ten years after the closing of the frontier and shortly after Frederick Jackson Turner explained in his famous "safety-valve" thesis the function that the frontier had performed in American history. Perhaps *The Virginian* is an expression of the need, once the frontier was gone, to experience a frontier that never was. This book is one of the first serious novelistic treatments of the American cowboy, if one excludes the dime novels that had dismayed parents for the previous fifty years. When the open range was gone, the cowboy came into his own as a literary figure, and there seems to be more than coincidence in the two facts. The end of the frontier era and the beginning of the cowboy novel meld too closely for there to be much accident about it.

This book is not set in the American West so much as in a country called Cattle Land, where men are men and possess all the virtues and characteristics popularly associated with Horatio Alger. Wister associates one more element to the mythical character about which he is writing—primal humanity. Wister very often describes the Virginian as "wild" or "natural," and the two words are seemingly interchangeable. The East is decadent, and the American virtues have their last home in the West.

Tied up with this idea of primal innocence is the concept of an Americanism that is itself primal, free of the decadence of Europe. Yet decadence has swept westward, as Wister sees it, and has pushed Americanism in front of it. The only Vermonter, back in Molly's home state, to approve of her new husband is the great-aunt who sees in the Virginian the spirit of her own husband, a general in the revolutionary war. This theme of Americanism being a primal, Adamic innocence and being found only in the West is brought out most forcefully when Judge Henry tries to explain to Molly why the Virginian and others had to lynch a cattle rustler. Molly objects that they took the law into their own hands. The judge's reply is that the law came originally from people who delegated this responsibility to their representatives; in turn, they established in the Constitution machinery for administering the law. In Wyoming, however, the hands of the law were weak and could not do the job that had been delegated to them. Therefore, the Virginian had only been taking back what had been his own. The delegates to the constitutional convention, then, were in spirit to be found in the far West, ironically at a Wyoming lynching party.

This is Wister's world, one which, as he wrote in his foreword to the novel, no longer exists. He was wrong when he said this in 1902, for people like the Virginian, although less romantic when seen in the flesh, are still spread over the country. They seem to be part of a dying breed. Many Americans would agree with much that the Virginian says and represents, and in that respect the cowboy has not vanished from the land any more than the belief in the primal innocence of the United States has lessened.

WALDEN: Or, Life in the Woods

Type of work: Autobiography and nature notes
Author: Henry David Thoreau (1817-1862)
Time of work: 1845-1847
Locale: Walden Pond, near Concord, Massachusetts
First published: 1854

More than a naturalist's record of finely observed phenomena, Walden *is a major philosophical statement on the American character, the uses of a life of simple toil, and the values of rugged independence.*

The Story

Early in the summer of 1845, Henry David Thoreau left his family home in the village of Concord, Massachusetts, to live for two years by himself in a rude house that he had constructed beside Walden Pond, in a far corner of Concord township. While there, he wrote in his journal about many of the things he did and thought. He was not the owner of the land on which he settled, but he had received the owner's permission to build his house and to live there. His objective was really to live simply and think and write; in addition, he proved to himself that the necessities of food, clothing, shelter, and fuel could be rather simply obtained for a man who desired only what he needed.

As early as March, 1845, Thoreau went out to Walden Pond and cut the timber that he needed for the framework of his house, doing all the labor himself. When that was done and the framing in place, Thoreau bought a shanty from an Irish railroad worker. He then tore down the shanty and used the boards for the sidings of the house, even making use of many of the nails already in the boards. By July, then, the house was ready for his occupancy. Before the advent of cold weather the following fall, Thoreau also built himself a fireplace and a chimney for cooking and heating purposes. He lathed and plastered the interior of the one-room house, in order that it would be warm and comfortable during the cold New England winter.

Having done all the work himself, and having used native materials wherever possible, he had built the house for the absurdly low cost of twenty-eight dollars. In addition to providing himself with a place to live, Thoreau believed that he had taught himself a great lesson in the art of living. He was also vastly pleased that he had provided himself with a place to live for less than a year's lodging had cost him as a student at Harvard College.

In order to get the money needed to build the house, Thoreau had planted about two and a half acres of beans, peas, potatoes, corn, and turnips, which he sold at harvest time. The land on which they were grown was lent by a neighbor who believed, along with everyone else, that the land was good for nothing. In addition to selling enough produce to pay his building expenses, Thoreau had enough yield left from his gardening to provide himself with food. Yet he did not spend all of his time working on the house or in the garden. One of his purposes in living at Walden Pond was to live so simply that he might have plenty of time to think, to write, and to observe nature; therefore, he spent only as much time in other labors as he had to. He had little respect for possessions and material things. He believed, for example, that most people were really possessed by their belongings, and that such a literary work as the *Bhagavadgītā* was worth more than all the towers and temples of the Orient.

Thoreau was quite proud of how little money he needed to live comfortably while at Walden Pond. The first eight months that he was there, he spent only slightly more than a dollar a month for food. In addition to some twenty-odd dollars he received for the vegetables that he raised, his income, within which he lived, was slightly more than thirteen dollars. His food consisted almost entirely of rye and Indian meal bread, potatoes, rice, a little salt pork, molasses, and salt. His drink was water. Seldom did he eat large portions of meat, and he never hunted. His interest in the animals that lived in the woods and fields near Walden Pond was the interest of a naturalist. Although he spent some time fishing, he believed that the time he had was too valuable to spend in catching fish to feed himself.

For the small amounts of cash that he needed, Thoreau worked with his hands at many occupations, working only so long as was necessary to provide himself with the money that his meager wants required. He kept as much time as possible free for thinking and studying. His study consisted more of humanity and nature than of books, although he kept a few well-selected volumes about him at all times.

While at Walden Pond, summer and winter, Thoreau lived independent of time: He refused to acknowledge days of the week or month. When he wished to spend some time observing certain birds or animals, or even the progress of the weather, he felt free to do so. About the only thing to remind him that people were rushing pell-mell to keep a schedule was the whistle of the Fitchburg Railway trains, which passed within a mile or so of his dwelling. He did not dislike the railroad: In fact, he thought it a marvel of ingenuity, and he was fascinated by the cargoes that the trains carried from place to place. Yet he was glad that he was not chained to the commerce that those cargoes represented. As much as he sometimes enjoyed the sound of the train, he enjoyed far more the sounds of the birds and animals, most of which he knew, not only as a country dweller knows them but as the naturalist knows them as well. The loons, the owls, the squirrels, the various kinds of fish in Walden Pond, the migratory birds—all of these were part of his conscious existence and environment.

People often dropped in to visit with Thoreau, who frankly confessed that he did not consider people very important. He failed, in fact, to tell who his most frequent visitors were. He preferred only one visitor at a time if the individual was an intelligent conversationalist. Whenever he had more visitors than could be accommodated in his small house, with its three chairs, he took them into his larger drawing room—the pine woods that surrounded his home. Few people, it seems, came to visit him, perhaps because he was a crusty kind of host, one who, if he had nothing better to do, was willing to talk, but who usually had more to occupy him than ordinary conversation.

During the winter months, Thoreau continued to live comfortably at Walden Pond, though his activities changed. He spent more time at the pond itself, making a survey of its bottom, studying the ice conditions, and observing the animal life that centered about the pond, which had some open water throughout the year.

After two years of life at Walden, Thoreau left the pond. He felt no regret for having stayed there or for leaving; his attitude was that he had many lives to live and that he had finished with living at the pond. He had learned many lessons there, had had time to think and study, and had proved what he had set out to prove twenty-six months before: that living could be extremely simple and yet fulfill the individual.

Critical Evaluation

Few contemporaries of Henry David Thoreau would have predicted the enormous popularity that his small volume, *Walden*, would win in the twentieth century. Author and work were virtually neglected during Thoreau's lifetime. Locally, he was considered the village eccentric; even his great friend and mentor Ralph Waldo Emerson was disappointed because his young disciple seemingly frittered away his talent instead of "engineering for all America." After Thoreau's death in 1862, his works attracted serious critical attention, but unfavorable reviews by James Russell Lowell and others severely damaged his reputation. Toward the beginning of the twentieth century, he began to win favorable attention again, mainly in Great Britain. During the Great Depression of the 1930's, when most people were forced to cut the frills from their lives, *Walden*—whose author admonished readers voluntarily to "Simplify, simplify, simplify!"—became something of a fad. In the 1960's, with new awareness of environment and emphasis on nonconformity, Thoreau was exalted as a prophet and *Walden* as the bible of individualists.

Walden can be approached in several different ways. Obviously, it is an excellent nature book. During the Romantic era, many writers—William Wordsworth, Lord Byron, Percy Bysshe Shelley, Emerson, and Walt Whitman, to name a few—paid tribute to nature. Yet Thoreau went beyond simply rhapsodizing natural wonders. He was a serious student of the natural world, one who would spend hours observing a woodchuck or tribes of battling ants, who meticulously mapped Walden Pond, and who enjoyed a hilarious game of tag with a loon. Like Emerson, he saw nature as a master teacher. In his observations of nature, Thoreau was a scientist; in his descriptions, a poet; and, in his interpretations, a philosopher and psychologist. He was an ecologist in his insistence on humanity's place in (not over) the natural universe, as well as on humanity's need for daily contact with the earth.

Walden may also be considered as a handbook for the simplification of life. As such, it becomes a commentary upon the sophistication or "refinement" of frequently distorted values and devotion to things of civilized society. Thoreau admits the necessities of food, shelter, clothing, and fuel, "for not till we have secured these are we prepared to entertain the true problems of life with freedom and a prospect of success." He then illustrates how one may strip these necessities to essentials for survival and health, ignoring the dictates of fashion or the yearning for luxury. "Most of the luxuries, and many of the so-called comforts of life," he asserts, "are not only not indispensable, but positive hindrances to the elevation of mankind." With relentless logic, he points out how making a living has come to take precedence over living itself; how people mortgage themselves to pay for more land and fancier clothing and food than they really require; how they refuse to walk to a neighboring city because it will take too long—but then must work longer than the walk would take in order to pay for a train ticket. He questions the dedication to "progress," noting that it is technological, not spiritual: "We are in great haste to construct a magnetic telegraph from Maine to Texas; but Maine and Texas, it may be, have nothing important to communicate."

Perhaps the most serious purpose of *Walden* and its most powerful message is to call people to freedom as individuals. One looks at nature in order to learn about oneself, one simplifies one's life in order to have time to develop that self fully, and one must honor one's uniqueness if one is to know full self-realization. It is this emphasis on nonconformity that has so endeared Thoreau to the young, who adopt as their call to life these words from the final chapter of *Walden:* "If a man does not keep pace with his companions, perhaps it is because he hears a different drummer. Let him step to the music which he hears, however measured or far away."

There is an ease, a clarity, a concreteness to Thoreau's prose that separates it from the more abstract, eloquent, and frequently intricate styles of his contemporaries. The ease and seeming spontaneity are deceptive. Thoreau revised the book meticulously during the five years that it took to find a publisher; there are five complete drafts that demonstrate how consciously he organized not only the general outline but every chapter and paragraph as well. For an overall pattern, he condensed the two years of his actual Walden experience into one fictional year, beginning and concluding with spring—the time of rebirth.

The pace and tone are also carefully controlled. Thoreau's sentences and paragraphs flow smoothly. The reader is frequently surprised to discover that sentences occasionally run to more than half a page, paragraphs to a page or more; syntax is so skillfully handled that one never feels tangled in verbiage. The tone varies from matter-of-fact to poetic to inspirational and is spiced with humor—usually some well-placed satire—at all levels. Even the most abstract topics are handled in concrete terms; Thoreau's ready use of images and figurative language prepares one for twentieth century Imagist poetry.

Taken as a whole, *Walden* is a first-rate example of organic writing, with organization, style, and content fused to form a work that continues to be as readable and perhaps even more timely than when it was written. In *Walden*, Thoreau reaches across the years to continue to "brag as lustily as Chanticleer . . . to wake my neighbors up."

THE WASTE LAND

Type of work: Poem
Author: T. S. Eliot (1888-1965)
First published: 1922

Eliot's mastery of the Symbolist poem, his virtuosity with language, and his use of literary and historical allusions mark The Waste Land *as a singular achievement in English poetry of the twentieth century.*

By the time that T. S. Eliot startled the literary world in 1922 with the publication of *The Waste Land* in *The Criterion* and *The Dial*, he had already achieved considerable recognition as an innovative and prolific essayist and reviewer and a highly original poet of considerable depth and complexity. His earlier poems, particularly "The Love Song of J. Alfred Prufrock" (1917), "Portrait of a Lady" (1917), and "Gerontion" (1920), contain arresting images, dramatic situations and monologues, highly allusive language, and linguistic virtuosity reminiscent of the work of John Donne and Robert Browning. They also serve as preludes to the most famous poem of the twentieth century, one that has engendered more commentaries, exegeses, and speculations than any other, *The Waste Land.* Indeed, Eliot considered "Gerontion" to be a prologue to the longer work. It is useful, then, for readers coming to Eliot's work for the first time to read *The Waste Land* in the context of his earlier poetry, as those poems contain the seeds of the later work and, in many respects, introduce it. Thematically, they anticipate *The Waste Land's* examination of aridity, the burden of history, the use of memory (personal history), a larger economy of spiritual dimensions, the problems raised by sexuality and love, and the quest to find meaning by ordering and reordering personal, historical, and mythic experience. Technically, they are of a piece with it in that they employ a stream of consciousness centered in various characters, an approach that owes much to Eliot's admiration for French Symbolist poetry, especially the poetry of Jules Laforgue and others that he had found revealed to him in Arthur Symons' *The Symbolist Movement in Literature* (1899).

The Waste Land is a series of five poems that together form one poem. Each is separable, but all are joined together by the vision of the blind Tiresias, into whom Gerontion (the little old man) has been transformed. When he published the poem in book form, also in 1922, Eliot added some fifty notes to it, only some of which are helpful to reading the poem as a poem rather than as a compendium of literary and cultural allusions. One note (to line 218) helps readers to focus on the unified nature of the work by claiming that "what Tiresias *sees*, in fact, is the substance of the poem." Tiresias, he has noted, is the poem's "most important personage, uniting all the rest." The male characters, he suggests, melt into one another and are not wholly distinct from each other; likewise, "all the women are one woman, and the two sexes meet in Tiresias," the androgynous seer. Following Eliot's clue, the reader may enter into the vision of the ancient Theban, his vision of the future that is the poet's present and the reader's present and past. The vision is both temporal and timeless, linked to the post-World War I era of disillusion and transcending it in its universality and visionary quality.

This latter, dreamlike aspect is important to bear in mind when attempting to make sense of one's own experience of the poem. If one considers the work as a Symbolist poem, many of its historical and cultural elements diminish in importance. The archetypal elements of infertility, the barren land and the sterile sexuality, ritual death and rebirth are played out symbolically within the dreamscape in fragmented fashion. Indeed, a key to understanding the nature of the poem lies near its end (line 431): "These fragments I have shored against my ruins." The fragments of speech, action, thought, and emotion are the very words of the poem, shored up against the ruins of culture or of an individual sense of its dilapidation that the reader is invited to share.

The poem's title, epigraph, and dedication merit attention. *The Waste Land* is a phrase common to the varied medieval tellings of the Grail quest, a tale rooted in earlier myths of Indo-European culture. The land is a waste as a result of some grievous wrong that can be righted only by a naïve and sometimes reluctant adventurer (reader), who must ask the right question of its wounded ruler, the Fisher King, to free the land from its curse. Eliot refers to Jessie L. Weston's *From Ritual to Romance* (1920) as a clue to understanding the poem's title and to Sir James Frazer's *The Golden Bough* (1890-1915) for its detailed study of vegetation myths and rituals. The epigraph, in Latin and Greek, about the Cumean Sibyl, a seer who was granted immortality but not eternal youth, points to the necessity of inquiry (the boy asks what the Sibyl wants), the impossibility of her wish (to die), and the prophetic nature of the poem. The dedication, to Ezra Pound, "the better craftsman," directs the reader to Pound's poetry as a way of thanking the poet who "discovered" Eliot in 1914 and who had a principal hand in editing the poem. More important, the dedication points to Pound's innovative work as a context for reading and thinking about Eliot's poem. Thus, before reading the first line of the poem the reader is conditioned to think of ancient myths and modernist poetry.

Part 1, "The Burial of the Dead," presents the reader with a perplexing wealth of images; allusions in English, German, and French; the arcana of the tarot; and varied voices mixing memory and desire in the paradoxical season of rebirth in which burial is remembered and reenacted. The speakers range from Marie to a biblical seer to Madame Sosostris, "famous clairvoyante," to Stetson and his acquaintance. The profusion of images, particularly those of water, vegetation, growth, aridity, decay, decomposition, and rebirth, imitates dream sequences and promotes a confusion of time and place, of incidents and meanings. Part 1 also foreshadows events of subsequent sections (such as the heap of broken images and death by water) and instills in the reader a disquietude. Familiar acts such as the rush-hour walk over London Bridge take on an aspect of Dantean menace, and the commonplace errand of delivering a horoscope becomes a dangerous business: "One must be so careful these days." Its concluding line, from Charles Baudelaire's *Les Fleurs du mal* (1957; *Flowers of Evil*, 1931), serves to startle the reader, now directly addressed as a reader who is both hypocrite and friend, into a sharp and eager observation and reflection on the lines preceding it. The keynotes of the section, as Bernard Bergonzi observed, are movement in time across day, season, year, and centuries, and change from youth to age, from motion to stillness in death, and reluctant rebirth. These give the reader an emotional sense of the poem but not necessarily a rational sense of logical connections between the stanzas or verse paragraphs.

"A Game of Chess" (part 2) continues to meld the mythic with the banal, joining the story of Philomel and the tale of Lil, both of which involve unsatisfactory sexuality, while the entire sequence presents a disenchantment with worldly experience at both ends of the social spectrum. The sequence opens with evocations of royalty in the richly ornate, overwrought boudoir and proceeds to depict the emptiness of luxury and the means by which the speakers choose to while away their time. The scene shifts from mindless opulence to a gossipy late evening in a pub at closing time. Here one learns of Albert and Lil in a catty postwar monologue punctuated by the barman's call, which, for want of an apostrophe, becomes a plea for the advent of some long-awaited event: "HURRY UP PLEASE ITS TIME."

The title of the poem's third part, "The Fire Sermon," refers to a refining fire of purgation. This section introduces Tiresias as one among many voices, including those of the Fisher King, the three Thames-daughters, Saint Augustine, and the Buddha. The ordinary but sordid sexual encounters along the Thames, in a flat, in a canoe, in the heralded tryst of Sweeney and Mrs. Porter, and in Mr. Engenides' proposition conspire to equate sexuality with seaminess and to present it as a mindless and emotionless, automatic and animal impulse. Over against this view of the body is the exaltation of the soul, as Eastern and Western spirituality join at the end of the sequence in a burning away of the physical to free the spirit. As the omniscient narrator who foresees all, Tiresias subsumes the other voices; thus the unifying technique of the poem begins to work.

In the briefest, ten-line part of the poem, part 4, "Death by Water," the reader considers the drowned Phlebas the Phoenician and recalls the cards dealt by Madame Sosostris earlier with the warning to "fear death by water" (line 55). Phlebas serves as an appropriate memento mori and possibly as something of a model in the liberation of the soul: Two weeks dead, he "forgot" the usual concerns as he passed, in reverse, "the stages of his age and youth" and entered the whirlpool. In counterpoint to the burning of "The Fire Sermon," here "a current under sea/ Picked his bones in whispers" as water becomes a cleansing agent.

In part 5, "What the Thunder Said," the waste land, still parched, is haunted by a "dry sterile thunder without rain" until "a damp gust/ Bringing rain" arrives. The thunder speaks in the words of the Upanishads, "datta, dayadhvam, damyata" (give, sympathize, control). The thunder's words bring revitalizing rain and a wisdom that allows for the possibility of revivification. As Eliot had blended the journey of Jesus' disheartened disciples to Emmaus, the approach to the Chapel Perilous, and "the present decay of eastern Europe" in the beginning of this final part of the poem, so he introduces a more ancient spiritual element to begin to change the present state of spiritual decay and to retrieve the land from waste. How he does so is, characteristically, with words—words the thunder speaks, words presumably still reported by Tiresias, words the poet, after all, writes. The quest for spiritual health is, the poem suggests, achieved through the recovery of artistic wholeness.

Elsewhere, Eliot has written about seeing the end in the beginning and the beginning in the end. At the end of *The Waste Land*, one finds the possibility for beginning the poem anew, for reading it anew with the knowledge gleaned from Tiresias and with a sense of direction. In the last stanza, for example, the Fisher King, no longer fishing in the dull canal behind the gashouse as he did in part 3, has the arid plain behind him and is fishing on the shore. He poses himself a healing question that seems to precipitate a multivocal and multilingual chorus in the poem's concluding lines. If the Fisher King can contemplate "at least" setting his lands in order, this notion implies his ability to do so, and the words of the thunder seem to have had some effect. Immediately after the question is posed, as is so often the case in the Grail quest narratives, the king and the land revive. The next line of the poem borrows from the children's nursery rhyme "London Bridge Is Falling Down" and heralds the destruction of the pathway to the burial of the dead (part 1). It is followed by a citation from Dante's *Purgatory* (c. 1320) in which the lustful Arnaut Daniel leaps voluntarily into the refining fire (possibly glossing "The Fire Sermon"). Next, a phrase from the poem *Pervigliam Veneris* and the song of the nightingale (which in the Latin poem sadly silences the speaker) serve to recall Philomel (parts 1 and 2). An allusion to Gérard de Nerval's "El desdichado" suggests yet another approach to yet another tower,

reinforcing the quest motif. The line that follows, as already noted, highlights the poet's act of shoring up verbal fragments against his ruins, just as the Fisher King shores up fragments to set his lands in order and Tiresias shores up fragmented visions into a continuous discourse. Eliot's citation from Thomas Kyd's *The Spanish Tragedy* (c. 1586) may also be self-referential, as the mad Hieronymo proposes to "fit" together a play using poetic fragments in several languages. The penultimate line's repetition of what the thunder said reinforces the ostensibly salvific effect of these words, as the poem concludes with the repetition of "Shantih"—the formal ending, Eliot's note explains, to an Upanishad, equivalent to the phrase "the peace which passeth understanding." The journey from the cruelest month to this peace, while foreseen by Tiresias, is one which the reader may wish to undertake again with Tiresias as guide.

Eliot's mastery of the Symbolist poem and his virtuosity in the use of language mark *The Waste Land* as a singular achievement in English poetry of the twentieth century. His multiple allusions, suggesting a place in world literature and cultural traditions for his work, serve to make it, indeed, part of those traditions while adding to them. As is the case with the best poetry, *The Waste Land* is a poem to which readers return, to contemplate and to find a newly familiar voice of considerable relevance to succeeding generations.

WHO'S AFRAID OF VIRGINIA WOOLF?

Type of work: Drama
Author: Edward Albee (1928-   )
Type of plot: Psychological realism
Time of plot: Sunday morning, the early 1960's
Locale: The living room of a house on the campus of a small New England college
First presented: 1962

Albee's play, which takes place one morning after a party, chronicles the games of power and cruelty between George and Martha as they draw Nick and Honey into their desperate and mean-spirited world. The revelations about these two couples are dominated by sex and by the hope or fear of having children.

Principal Characters

Martha, a large, boisterous woman who trades cruel barbs with her husband, George. She is obsessed with her inability to have children, and she and George create a detailed imaginary child in order to assuage their sense of emptiness.

George, her husband, a thin, graying man. He can match his wife in game-playing and humiliation, and it is he who decides to "kill" their imaginary child in order to hurt Martha.

Nick, a blond, good-looking new teacher at the college. At first, he refuses to participate in George and Martha's games, but eventually he shows himself to be just as capable of their insensitivity and need for control.

Honey, his wife, who is young and rather plain. She does not want to have children, and so she has been taking pills to abort her fetuses. It seems that Honey is not very bright and that many of the implications of the conversation go by her.

"Who's afraid of Virginia Woolf?" Edward Albee and his characters ask several times in the play. After witnessing a marathon verbal and psychological massacre, the reader may answer, along with Martha, the casualty most maimed, "I am."

George, a history professor, and Martha arrive home at two in the morning after a cocktail party given by Martha's father, the president of the college, to enable old and new teachers to get to know one another, an innocuous phrase that soon takes on lethal significance. Martha informs her weary husband that she has asked Nick, a handsome new teacher, and his wife, Honey, to an after-party party, because her father has asked her and George to be nice to them.

Six years older than George, Martha was once married to a beautiful boy who ran a power mower. Although her father annulled the marriage, Martha still loves and admires him, as she clearly reveals in a maudlin monologue at the beginning of act 3. George loathes him. Early in the play, George charges Martha with a "braying" sociability and excessive drinking. Martha lashes back, calling him a blank nonentity and saying that if he really existed as a person she would divorce him. Later George tells Nick that he and Martha have nothing in

common, that they are merely perambulating the remnants of their wits.

For these frequent insults, they take revenge on each other in the form of "Fun and Games," the title of act 1. They have created quite naturally a somewhat socially acceptable ritual for the release of their bitterness, perversities, self-loathing, sexual frustrations, and hate, as well as grudging love and affection. "Fun and Games," characteristic of clever, educated, supposedly uninhibited moderns who seldom communicate in anything but "in"-sounding jokes, witticisms, and puns, enable George and Martha to turn their insides out, to move easily at critical moments from one stance to another, all in the name of good clean fun. Birth is a joke that sets off a chain reaction, making life one monstrous gag.

These games, requiring a kind of *commedia dell'arte* pace and readiness of wit, involve a profusion of sex, drinking, and cursing. Many are spontaneously improvised upon ordinary moments: the opening of a door, going to the bathroom, the conventions of getting acquainted. Others are habitual, personal games with rigid rules. The games are both an occasion for and a relief from the spew of insults, taunts, teasings, and abusive names in which George and Martha and, later, Nick indulge. George tells Nick that he and Martha are like children viciously playing sad games. The characters slip in and out of these games so subtly that it is difficult for both reader and characters to mark the frequent shifts from mood to mood, as the blend of "fun" and seriousness is ambiguous. They charge one another with not knowing the difference between illusion and reality. When Nick says disgustedly that he cannot tell whether George and Martha are lying, George insists that they must behave as though they themselves knew the differences. Nevertheless, he himself has stopped caring.

Honey and Martha complement each other. Martha is vulgarly and boisterously sexual; Honey is vapidly and "maidenly" sensual. Martha is an alcoholic; Honey gets drunk on occasion. Martha desperately wants a child; Honey takes abortion pills. While Honey is friendly in her simpleminded way, Nick is grimly polite. Hard, cold, introspective, private, and ambitious, Nick does not like games. As George makes a relentless assault on his stone front, viciously mocking him at first subtly and then openly, Nick becomes increasingly annoyed; he drops his solicitous manner with his wife and snaps at her. Eventually, however, he reveals himself to George. He married Honey, a childhood friend, because she was pregnant, but it proved to be a hysterical pregnancy. Money is another factor in their marriage. While it would appear to have been money and position, passion was the real basis of George's own marriage. To George, Nick represents the younger generation. There is symbolic truth in George's joking pretense, in the final act, that Nick is his son. When Nick, going along with one of George's games, outlines his strategy for climbing up in the college by playing "musical beds" among the faculty wives, including Martha, George indicates that Nick is more serious than he himself realizes. George tries to warn and advise him, but Nick answers contemptuously. It seems to George that Nick's retort is a fitting peroration to the development of Western civilization as it enters its decline. A biochemist, Nick is engaged in research that will enable scientists to control birth and gene distribution. Such research, as George argues, will spawn a race of test-tube men who will all resemble Nick. Also, it will be necessary to cut the sperm tubes of many men. Albee suggests that, emotionally, this castration has already occurred: Martha unmans both George and Nick, and Honey emasculates Nick. Against scientific determinism, George opposes historical inevitability, with its acceptance of human nature, its prolonged woes and brief joys.

After an act of "Fun and Games," Nick probably reflects the sentiments of a large segment of readers when he tells George that he cannot see why others should be subjected to such marital violence. These people are so unlikable, so lacking in the familiar characteristics or situation tags that most playwrights use to engage an audience (even Samuel Beckett's bums are "fun," reminiscent as they are of clowns), that empathy would seem impossible. Certainly, at one time or other, most people talk to one another in a mercilessly sadistic way, but this is a side that one renounces, and one might sympathize with characters who show this tendency if they soon reveal an admirable trait. Fascinated though one may be by the sheer ferocity of George and Martha's witty, vibrant dialogue, a besieged reader is kept at a distance by a profound conscious reluctance to identify with the characters and thus associate oneself with the orgiastic flux of emotions.

Simultaneously, the way for identification is being opened by the reader's empathy with Honey and Nick, especially the latter. As soon as Nick allows himself to play this quasi-real game, for the sadistic fun of it (the play appeals to the sadist in everyone), he and the reader are hooked, and the game grows deadly serious. More resistant readers may identify with Honey, who does not seem to know what is going on but whose actions signify that the process of suggestion has caused a subconscious eruption; certain readers will enjoy the sadistic interplay of emotions without seeing, but certainly feeling, their significance. In this dynamic relationship to the play, a psychic tension is generated in the reader and sustained after the book is closed. The acting out of George and Martha's own nightmares becomes very suggestive to the younger couple; turned inside out by their emotional exhibitionism, they become mirrors in whom Nick and Honey may see reflections of their own inner selves and perhaps take heed.

Three of the four major games, links in the spine of the play, are played in act 2, entitled *"Walpurgisnacht."* The first, begun in act 1, is Humiliate the Host, and George is "it." In search of an "heir apparent" to her father's great achievement, the building of the college, Martha found George. Detailing his career, she lashes him into a crying fury. At the height of an argument about their son, she returns to the subject of George's failures and reveals that her father forced him to withdraw his novel. When Martha tells the story of the novel, which was very autobiographical, Nick recognizes it because previously George had told it to him in the guise of an anecdote about a school friend. The boy accidentally killed his mother with a shotgun; the following summer, while learning to drive with his father, he swerved to avoid a porcupine and hit a tree, and his father was killed, with the result that for the past thirty years he has not uttered a sound. In a sense, of course, George's verbal amplitude has been expended upon saying nothing. When Martha refuses to relent, George chokes her. Subdued by Nick, George suggests a game of Get the Guests.

Pretending now to tell the plot of his second novel, George relates the story of Nick and Honey as told to him by Nick when the women were out of the room. Martha and Nick protest, but Honey is at first too drunk to understand. Then she says that, knowing the people, she dislikes the story. Nick pleads with George to stop. Honey rages at Nick for telling an outsider about their marriage and runs out to be ill for the second time. Nick threatens to get even. Martha charges George with having taken advantage of "pigmies." He reminds her that she has certainly cut *him* to pieces tonight. Her reply shocks him. He claims that it is she who is sick; he has tried to go along with her all these years in her bloody games. Concluding that tonight their whole arrangement for maintaining some kind of surface on which to stand has collapsed, they declare total war on each other.

While Honey lies on the bathroom floor sucking her thumb, and while George reads a book about the decline of the West, feigning indifference, Martha gets revenge by having sex with Nick in the kitchen. While this game of Hump the Hostess is going on, Honey emerges from the bathroom, crying that she does not want children, and George realizes that she has been killing her embryos with pills. As a final triumph over Martha, George decides to tell her that a messenger has come with the news that their son, expected home that day for his birthday, is dead. Later, Martha taunts Nick for his sexual failure, which he blames on alcohol, and treats him like a houseboy. She has passed her life in meaningless infidelities with men such as Nick. George, she tells him, was the only man who ever satisfied her; she is punishing him for the "sin" of loving her, and she realizes that one night she will go too far and break him. At one point, Martha and George gang up on Nick; with Honey's indirect help, they make him over into a potential George.

The last game, Bringing up Baby, is played in act 3, "The Exorcism." Apprehensive, Martha pleads that they play no more games. George assures her that it will soon be over; like a surgical operation, using the scalpel of the tongue, the layers of skin, even the bones, have been removed, and the marrow is next. At this point, they have all indeed got to know one another, for Honey decides that she does not remember anything, suggesting that she and George, also, have had sex. George gives Martha her cue and prompts her in the one game that they always played, until tonight, alone. Perhaps they are more public tonight because, having reached their limits, they recog-

nize in this couple duplicates of themselves as they were in the beginning. Almost weeping, Martha goes through the ritual by rote, according to rules evolved over the years. There are moments of weird lyricism in the recitation describing their feelings for the son. Honey screams that she wants a child. Toward the end, George accompanies Martha with a litany in Latin. Sensing that he has led her to some kind of precipice, Martha stops. George declares that Martha needs her son because her father does not care whether she lives or dies; she has used their son as a club to dominate George. Martha declares that the one person she has tried to protect and redeem in this disastrous marriage is their son. George finally announces that their son died in a car wreck, with his driver's permit on his person. Thus, the parents kill their children before they are born, George and Honey directly, motivated differently, Martha and Nick indirectly.

With rage and loss, Martha screams that George cannot decide for himself that their son is dead, as they created him together. Horrified, Nick understands now. The son is imaginary; it was not possible for them to have children, they tell him, communally. The rules were that if either told a stranger, the other, like God the Creator, could kill the son. The death of the son is the price of surrender to the need to exhibit emotional turmoil before strangers. Just as God sent Christ to comfort the suffering, they created their son.

Albee sounds the deepest level of marital discord in his depiction of this familial mayhem, in which every psychological weapon within the resources of sick, near-psychotic people is used. People reach such a dismal state sometimes that the only way any contact can be made is through the grotesque exaggerations of fun and games; these finally culminate in a *Walpurgisnacht* in which illusion and reality are so dynamically fused that the charged emotions of two human beings who are in one sense dead to each other may become humanly engaged. Thus, Martha congratulates George on his performance in the game Get the Guests. They are hollow people, but in their clashings, they utter the only human sounds such people can hope to make. Albee is probably not saying that emotional violence and moral anarchy are good. Yet in contrast to the bland surface of most lives, constituted of lies, illusions, subterfuge, avoidance, and pale conventions, such experiences may be the means of exorcising some of the lies that one is most reluctant to relinquish.

Their son—as real, in a sense, as any "real" child— was born of a mutual, profound need. Fun and games provided a means of keeping the illusion alive, but by the nature of fun and games, this final, unendurable exposure and desecration became inevitable. While exposing every personal truth about each other, they had to nurture together this illusory parenthood; but in taking revenge upon each other, they kill the one illusion upon which their sanity of cohesiveness as husband and wife has depended. Like Godot, the son is a human-made savior, and reliance on him is foredoomed.

In the last four pages, the submerged pathos the reader has almost grudgingly sensed emerges. George sends his "children" out into the world; Nick and Honey are perhaps beginning the cycle that the older couple has just completed. Thrown back upon each other now, plunged to the bottom of despair, where Søren Kierkegaard believed that humanity finds either salvation or suicide, they see each other completely naked of any decent life rooted in reality, any consoling illusions. The vacuum that they share seems the womb of love. The death of their imaginary son may make love possible: not a great love, not a "healthy" love, but something. Now Martha is afraid of Virginia Woolf, for the "wolf" that each person creates has been unleashed within her.

Albee's absurd perspective on modern humanity's psychological predicament is expressed with meaningful exaggeration. One may question the naturalistic, excruciatingly meticulous conversational detail. Albee pushes naturalism just beyond its limits, achieving an expressionistic effect: The reader is overwhelmed with one lucid image of a psychological and spiritual condition. This dynamic image could be forged perhaps only within limitations of situation, set, and character. Albee is not interested in realism; he does not even describe the set. The reader is transported into a realm as unrepresentational as that in which Beckett's *En attendant Godot* (1952; *Waiting for Godot*, 1954) is set, a realm where intuitive truths, painfully revelatory and blinding in the same instant, are perceived. Cramped in the core of nowhere, reduced to the lowest level of existence and human relationship, Beckett's bums scrape the barrel of hu-

man resources for ingenious ways to pass the time while waiting for Godot. They comprise Everyman—stripped. Here Albee places two well-to-do couples in a comfortable home and presents them in the very act of stripping themselves. His expressionistic technique was already taking shape in *The Zoo Story* and *The Death of Bessie Smith* (first performed in Berlin in 1959 and 1960, respectively) and in *The Sandbox* (1960) and *The American Dream* (1961), all quickly written, one-act, autobiographical plays in which people talk to one another with a vicious frankness seldom sparked in life, but presented in an authentic manner. It seems absurd that emotions that appear so real and yet lack the kind of careful preparation necessary to most emotionally devastating plays could generate such heat.

In this play, although he claims to write a black brand of humor, Albee takes one to the depths of the ridiculous instead. The bond among other well-known playwrights of the American Theater of the Absurd is reputed to be humor. To label Albee's special vision "humor" distracts rather than illuminates. Even as sick comedy that sees humor in hate, it is too prolonged, too vicious, too inhumane to function as humor. Almost every line has a semblance of humor, but lines that in moderation, in appropriate contexts, would be comic or witty have, when taken together, a noncomedic effect. The exaggerated indulgence of Albee's characters in witty quarreling is the major expressionistic projection of their inner sickness. Yet this is humor as symptom, not as reader participation. Audience laughter at this play must be a rather frightening display of group therapy and catharsis. The label "humor" lends a spurious respectability to sickness. As undraped sickness, on the other hand, the play provides some alarming insights. Albee is serious in a way that few writers are, for it is a serious matter when the plight of human beings can be viewed in this horribly humorous light.

WINESBURG, OHIO

Type of work: Novel
Author: Sherwood Anderson (1876-1941)
Type of plot: Psychological realism
Time of plot: Late nineteenth century
Locale: Winesburg, Ohio
First published: 1919

In simple though highly skillful and powerful language, Anderson tells the story of a small town and the lonely and frustrated people who live there. In a novel that is at once beautiful and tragic, realistic and poetic, the author succeeds in interpreting the inner compulsions and loneliness of the American psyche with a high degree of accuracy and emotional impact.

Principal Characters

George Willard, the young reporter who learns about life from the confessions and observations of people in his small town. The son of an insensitive man and a sensitive mother, young Willard accepts the practical help of his father but follows the inclinations of his mother in accepting his job. Living as he does in the family hotel, which has seen better days, he runs alone and thinks long thoughts. Something about him draws the weak, the insecure, and the hopeless, as well as the clever and strong, but his loyalties to those who give him their confidences are unflinching. He sleeps with a lonely farm girl, but only at her insistence, and then secretly. On the other hand, he has an exaggerated sense of chivalry concerning the girl whom he has long admired. He is searching for the truth. This search finally, after his mother's death, takes him away from the town that formed him.

Elizabeth Willard, his mother, whose hotel and life savings never benefit anyone, but whose spirit serves as a bond and inspiration to two men. Promiscuous in her youth, though in search of spirituality, Mrs. Willard had married on the hearsay of village wives expressing contentment. Never in love with her husband, she cherishes a beautiful memory of a lover who murmured to her, "Oh, the dear, the dear, the lovely dear." The two who loved her most, her son and Dr. Reefy, repeat these words to her dead but seemingly young and uncorrupted body. She lives and dies in quiet desperation and in search of loveliness.

Dr. Reefy, the poet of obscurity who writes great truths on scraps of paper that he throws away in wads and with a laugh. True to a vision of greatness, the doctor loved twice in his life. One love was a pregnant girl who miscarried, then married the understanding doctor and died, leaving him a comfortable income. The other, Elizabeth Willard, he befriends in her last days of a ravaging disease, but he was never her lover.

Helen White, the banker's daughter with a college complexity but a small-town disposition. Lovely and gracious, Helen is an inspiration to three Winesburg boys, though only George Willard arouses a like response in her. Like the other main characters, she is unconsciously in quest of beauty and truth.

Kate Swift, the schoolteacher who burns inwardly with a deep desire to live and to pass along the passion of living. Attracted as she is to her former student George Willard, Kate cannot finally cast aside her small-town prudery. Always confusing the physical and the spiritual in her effort to awaken her protégé, spinsterish Kate is secretly worshiped in a like way by the Presbyterian minister, who considers her a messiah of sorts (having seen her naked and praying from his clerical window).

The Reverend Curtis Hartman, the Presbyterian minister, Kate's admirer.

Wing Biddlebaum, a fugitive teacher who ran from unfair accusations of homosexuality to become the restless berry picker and handyman of the town. Only once in the many years of his hiding out in Winesburg does Wing attempt to pass along his fervor for knowledge that made him a great teacher. George is on the verge of discovering Wing's tragic secret and is moved by the aging man's eloquence.

Jesse Bentley, Louise Hardy, his daughter, and **David Hardy,** his grandson. These people reveal the deterioration of the pioneering spirit in northern Ohio. Jesse, the lone surviving brother of a farm family, turns from the ministry to farm management with religious zeal. He neglects his frail wife, who dies in childbirth, and he resents the daughter who should have been his son David. When his neurotic but brilliant daughter turns to a village boy and has a son by him, the old man takes this birth as his omen and names the son David. In a moment

of fright when the obsessed old man is about to offer up a lamb as a sacrifice to God, the boy strikes his grandfather, leaves him for dead, and runs away, never again to see the old man, his mother, or the town.

The Story

Young George Willard was the only child of Elizabeth and Tom Willard. His father, a dull, conventional, insensitive man, owned the local hotel. His mother had once been a popular young belle. She had never loved Tom Willard, but the young married women of the town seemed to her so happy, so satisfied, that she married him in the hope that marriage would somehow change her own life for the better. Before long, she realized that she was caught in the dull life of Winesburg, her dreams turned to drab realities by her life with Tom Willard.

The only person who ever understood her was Dr. Reefy. Only in his small, untidy office did she feel free; only there did she achieve some measure of self-expression. Their relationship, doomed from the start, was nevertheless beautiful, a meeting of two lonely and sensitive people. Dr. Reefy, too, had his sorrows. Once, years ago, a young girl, pregnant and unmarried, had come to his office, and shortly afterward he had married her. The following spring, she had died, and from then on Dr. Reefy went around making little paper pills and stuffing his pockets with them. On the pieces of paper he had scribbled his thoughts about the beauty and strangeness of life.

Through her son George, Elizabeth Willard hoped to express herself, for she saw in him the fulfillment of her own hopes and desires. More than anything, she feared that George would settle down in Winesburg. When she learned that he wanted to be a writer, she was glad. Unknown to her husband, she had put away money enough to give her son a start. Before she could realize her ambition, however, Elizabeth Willard died. Lying on her bed, she did not seem dead to either George or Dr. Reefy. To both she was extremely beautiful. To George, she did not seem like his mother at all. To Dr. Reefy, she was the woman he had loved, now the symbol of another lost illusion.

Many people of the town sought out George Willard; they told him of their lives, of their compulsions, of their failures. Old Wing Biddlebaum, the berry picker, years before had been a schoolteacher. He had loved the boys in his charge, and he had been, in fact, one of those few teachers who understand young people. One of his pupils, however, having conceived a strong affection for his teacher, had accused him of homosexuality. Wing Biddlebaum, though innocent, was driven out of town. In Winesburg, he became the best berry picker in the region. Yet always the same hands that earned his livelihood were a source of wonder and fear to him. When George Willard encountered him in the berry field, Wing's hands went forward as if to caress the youth, but a wave of horror swept over him and he hurriedly thrust them into his pockets. To George, also, Wing's hands seemed odd, mysterious.

Kate Swift, once George's teacher, saw in him a future writer. She tried to tell him what writing was, what it meant. George did not understand exactly, but he understood that Kate was speaking, not as his teacher, but as a woman. One night, in her house, she embraced him, for George was now a young man with whom she had fallen in love. On another night, when all of Winesburg seemed asleep, she went to his room. Yet just as she was on the point of yielding to him, she struck him and ran away, leaving George lonely and frustrated.

Kate lived across the street from the Presbyterian church. The pastor, Reverend Curtis Hartman, accidentally had learned that he could see into Kate's room from his study in the bell tower of the church. Night after night, he looked through the window at Kate in her bed. He wanted at first to prove his faith, but his flesh was weak. One night, the same night that Kate had fled from George Willard, he saw her come into her room. He watched her. Naked, she threw herself on the bed and furiously pounded the pillows. Then she arose, knelt, and began to pray. With a cry, the minister got up from his chair, swept the Bible to the floor, smashed the glass in the window, and dashed out into the darkness. Running to the newspaper office, he burst in upon George. Wild-eyed, his fist dripping blood, he told the astonished young man that God had appeared to him in the person of a naked woman, that Kate Swift was the instrument of the Almighty, and that he was saved.

Besides Kate Swift, there were other women in George's life. There was Helen White, the banker's daughter. One night, George and Helen went out together. At first they laughed and kissed, but then a strange new maturity overcame them and kept them apart. Louise Trunnion, a farm girl, wrote to George, saying that she was his if he wanted her. After dark, he went out to the farm, and they went for a walk. There, in a berry field, George Willard enjoyed the love that Helen White had refused him.

Like Louise Trunnion, Louise Bentley also wanted love. Before going to live in Winesburg, Louise had lived on a farm, forgotten and unloved by a greedy, fanatical father who had desired a boy instead of a daughter. In Winesburg, she lived with the Hardy family while she went to school. She was a good student, praised by her teachers, but she was resented by the two Hardy girls, who believed that Louise was always showing off. More than ever, she wanted someone to love. One day, she sent young John Hardy a note, and a few weeks later she slept with him. When it became clear that she was pregnant, Louise and John were married.

John reproached her for cruelty toward their son, David. She would not nurse her child, and for long periods of time she would ignore him. Because she had never really loved her husband, nor he her, the marriage was not a happy one. At last, she and John separated, and shortly afterward her father took young David to live with him on the farm.

Old Jesse Bentley was convinced that God had manifested Himself in his grandchild, that the young David, like the biblical hero, would be a savior, the conqueror of the Philistines who owned the land that Jesse Bentley wanted for himself. One day, the old man took the boy into the fields with him. Young David had brought along a little lamb, and the grandfather prepared to offer the animal as a sacrifice to the Almighty. The youngster, terrified, struck his grandfather and ran away, never to return to Winesburg.

The time came when George Willard had to choose between staying in Winesburg and starting out on his career as a writer. Shortly after his mother's death, George got up early one morning and walked to the railroad station. There he boarded the train and left Winesburg behind him.

Critical Evaluation

Using young George Willard both as protagonist and observer, Sherwood Anderson creates in *Winesburg, Ohio* a probing psychological portrait of small-town America. Though his characters outwardly seem dull and commonplace, Anderson is acutely tuned to the tensions between their psychological and emotional needs and the restrictions placed upon their lives by the small-town atmosphere of Winesburg. Though not scientific, Anderson's work probes deeply into the psychic lives of these "grotesques" to discover the emotional wounds that have been inflicted by the Puritan attitudes of the midwestern village. Though Anderson may not have been directly influenced by Sigmund Freud or Carl Jung, his interests clearly parallel those of the psychoanalysis that became popular with American intellectuals during the first quarter of the twentieth century. In this respect, Anderson can legitimately be called the United States' first psychological novelist.

Anderson believed that the traditional forms of the novel were too restrictive and formal to adapt well to his American subject matter, so *Winesburg, Ohio* represents in part an experiment in form. Rather than unifying his work through a plot in the usual sense, Anderson uses patterns of imagery, tone, character, and theme to achieve a sense of wholeness. It is, however, George Willard's narrative voice and presence as either observer or protagonist in the stories that ultimately unify them. As a small-town reporter, Willard can credibly serve as a confidant for his townspeople; he is a kind of professional observer recording the surface lives of his people for the newspaper. At the same time, one must see him as the budding artist who is interested in discovering the deeper and more meaningful truths of people's lives than those seen at the surface. Eventually, George must make his own choice as to which of these roles he will elect, but meantime his function as the central consciousness of the book is vital to its aesthetic success.

Winesburg, Ohio also follows the classic pattern of the *Bildungsroman* or "portrait of the artist as a young man" as it traces George Willard's growth from adolescence to maturity. Central to this aspect of the novel is George's relationship with his mother, whose death eventually frees him to escape from Winesburg. Elizabeth Willard is the first person to see, in George's ambition to write, a potential release for her own inarticulate suffering, so she encourages his ambition partly to fill her own needs. As George comes into contact with other characters in the novel, they too see in him a way to make their voices heard. Therefore, they tell him their stories so that he might write them down.

Part of George's growing maturity results from the understanding that he finds as a result of his willingness to listen, but this passive development is paralleled by more overt experience. In particular, sexual initiation is an essential part of George's learning and growth, as is his coming to understand something of the nature of love in its various aspects. Through this combination of active and passive experiences, George eventually comes to the realization that isolation is an essential part of the human condition. People, George realizes in the sketch called "Sophistication," must learn to live with the limited relationships possible in a world that must isolate them, and they must develop the strength not to be destroyed by loneliness. This knowledge gives George the maturity that he needs to break with Winesburg and face the future as an adult and an artist. In "Departure," the final sketch, he goes toward that responsibility.

Anderson's introduction to *Winesburg, Ohio*, called "The Book of the Grotesque," suggests yet another way in which this work is unified. Conceived as a whole within which the sketches and stories are pulled together by the idea of the "grotesques," the work can be seen as a group of stories connected by a central thematic concern. Anderson defined his grotesques as people who had seized upon some aspect of the truth that so dominates their lives as to distort their entire beings. This definition, however, only loosely fits the characters that one actually encounters in the novel. Rather, the failure in some way of emotional life seems to account for the twists of character that lead Winesburg's citizens to their universal sense of failure and isolation. In spite of apparent differences, virtually all of Anderson's figures suffer from a deep sense of failure—frequently of material as well as emotional failure—and from a frustrating inability to express their pain and rage in a meaningful way.

Essentially, they are emotional cripples who must turn to George Willard in search of a voice to articulate their suffering.

Paralleling that level of *Winesburg, Ohio* which is concerned with individual psychology is a general reaction against the American small town and its atmosphere of puritanical repression. Though Anderson is not without some nostalgia for the small-town life that was already passing from the American scene when *Winesburg, Ohio* was published in 1919, he does not allow his sentiment to stand in the way of a powerful condemnation of the cultural and spiritual sterility characteristic of this small-town life. While other writers were mourning the passing of the nation's innocent youth by sentimentalizing the small agrarian community, Anderson revealed its dark underside of destroyed lives, thwarted ambitions, and crippled souls—all of which resulted in part from the repressive atmosphere of towns such as Winesburg. Thus, even while *Winesburg, Ohio* marks the end of an era of agrarian order in the United States, it raises the very real possibility that this innocent past had been less of a paradise than the sentimentalist would have one believe.

Studies of the modern American novel tradition often begin with *Winesburg, Ohio*. By its pioneering of new techniques, introduction of new subject matter, and development of new attitudes and ideas, as well as a new frankness, this novel changed the course of American literary history. Moreover, Anderson's generous help to such younger writers as Ernest Hemingway and William Faulkner, who would continue to shape the course of the American novel, further justifies his title as the founder of the modern American novel.

WISE BLOOD

Type of work: Novel
Author: Flannery O'Connor (1925-1964)
Type of plot: Gothic
Time of plot: Early 1950's
Locale: Taulkinham, a Southern city
First published: 1952

Wise Blood *constitutes an extended religious discussion that is both poignant and comic. O'Connor traces the life and death of Hazel Motes, a young man who is trying to come to terms with his Christianity in an atmosphere of sin and falsehood. It is the author's intention that Hazel's fate be seen as ironic in its tragedy and redemption.*

Principal Characters

Hazel Motes, a twenty-two-year-old man who is searching for spiritual answers to the questions in his life. He must deal with several setbacks and false prophets before he finds his own truth in martyrdom.

Enoch Emery, an eighteen-year-old zoo attendant. He is one of the false prophets, as he preaches the guidance of one's "wise blood" and worships a mummified man.

Asa Hawks, the second false prophet who tries to lead Hazel astray. He is an itinerant preacher and beggar who claims that he blinded himself in order to see the true path to redemption.

Sabbath Lily Hawks, his daughter, who knows that she is damned but does not care. She adopts the mummified man.

Hoover Shoats, also known as **Onnie Jay Holy,** a religious racketeer who hires Solace Layfield to dress like Hazel and preach an imitation Church of Christ Without Christ.

Mrs. Flood, Hazel's landlady in the city. She cheats him and leads to his death at the hands of two police officers, but she does find some enlightenment from Hazel's actions.

Mrs. Leora Watts, a prostitute who sleeps with Hazel upon his return from the Army.

Solace Layfield, a preacher who is hired by Hoover Shoats to double for Hazel Motes and offer a false message to the people under the name the True Prophet; Hazel kills him.

The directions for reading this novel are given in the short, dryly ironic note that Flannery O'Connor prefaced to the second edition. Like the directions for getting places in Lewis Carroll's *Through the Looking-Glass and What Alice Found There* (1871), they warn readers that they must cope with the opposite to whatever they expect in fiction; what in life may appear tragic is here comical triumph—Hazel Motes's self-blinding—and the hero, like every character in the book, is a most unattractive person. Where Hazel Motes is not laughable he is pitiable. The novel is thus a comic and wholly serious presentation of the painful inevitability of becoming a Christian in the absolute sense that O'Connor intends, however much one is offended by the lack of humanity in the characters and their creator. Hazel achieves the integrity and hence the dignity of the human soul by giving up the struggle to escape redemption by Christ, and for most of the time that he wriggles on the hook of his destiny he looks undignified.

The novel is simply constructed of fourteen chapters, most of them episodes in Hazel Motes's unwilling quest for the true Jesus through an assortment of false prophets. The complexity of the novel comes from the novelist's intention. Flannery O'Connor is herself a prophet warning by lurid exempla of the wrath to come. Hazel Motes is surrounded by people who think that they act reasonably, especially in allowing a comfortable religious feeling as a small part of their existence; operators such as Hoover Shoats and Mrs. Flood do not know that they are swine about to be deluged. They are in hell and do not know it, unlike the damned—Sabbath Lily Hawks— who do know it and do not care. Hazel thinks that he has shaken off any fooling about with the religion of his grandfather and mother and is thus clean of hypocrisy; he can sleep nights with a prostitute, Mrs. Leora Watts, and not imperil his soul. He learns better by the end of the novel, and it is, as it must be, an agonizing experience. He has to blind himself with quicklime before he can see clearly his redemption by Christ. The irony of the novel consists in showing that every step Hazel thinks will take him farther from Christ simply brings him closer to his Redeemer.

Such irony would be objectionable if it were possible to treat Hazel Motes as contemptible in his madness or, remembering Christian charity, as deserving of sympathy, a welfare check, and a course of analysis. Yet Motes is eventually superior in humanity's only proper business of holy living and holy dying, and a martyr for the reader's edification. One also senses that O'Connor has martyred him in mortification of her own ego. This novel could stand as her New Testament to the necessity of forgetting self in the service of God, even to mutilation if that is necessary, just as her second novel, *The Violent Bear It Away* (1960), seems to recover for her the meaning of the Old Testament.

Hazel Motes is either repulsively or ludicrously grotesque from his first entrance in the train on his way to the city; he has just been discharged from Army service at the age of twenty-two and has kept himself clean all that time. He returns to Eastrod, Tennessee, only to find that dwindling hamlet vanished. He is now free of his Christian past and proceeds to the city—where else?—to sin, which he accomplishes with Mrs. Watts. He buys a car as well and thus joins the gallery of O'Connor's characters for whom the city and the automobile are symbols of corruption.

In the third chapter, Hazel meets the false prophets: Asa Hawks, who says that he has blinded himself for his belief in redemption by Christ, and Enoch Emery, the young man of eighteen, country-bred like Hazel, who lives by the "wise blood" that he inherits from his daddy. Thereafter, Hazel becomes more involved with both these prophets of a false way of life and has to shake himself free of each. It is not until four events happen that he is freed from the false trail that he is following, summarized in the novel as the Church of Christ Without Christ that he preaches before film houses: He sees that Asa Hawks is not blind; he rejects the false god (a mummified man) that Enoch worships and Sabbath Lily Hawks adopts; he kills the look-alike Solace Layfield or the True Prophet, whom Hoover Shoats has hired to preach the false or imitation Church of Christ Without Christ; and his car is deliberately wrecked by a police officer. The last two episodes probably repel the reader more than the fantastic doings of Enoch, Asa, and Lily. Someone, one believes, should bring the police officer to justice for smashing the boy's car, even if Hazel did not have a driver's license; at the same time, someone should charge Hazel with murder.

Another justice, however, is at work here: the swift and terrible speed of mercy. Hazel Motes has been mercifully delivered by God from his false prophets, and he proceeds to blind himself in accordance with the police officer's dictum that those who have no license need no car: Those who have a "mote" in their eye must cast it out; they that have no eyes for the true God need no sight. Hazel spends his last days in the hands of Mrs. Flood, who is indirectly responsible for his murder by two casual police officers, until he is at last composed in death. In the final paragraph of the novel, Mrs. Flood glimpses the vision that Hazel's actions are governed by a secret that could be the light of her life. Her tentative achievement of this diminutive revelation could be the meaning of Hazel's life and death.

The possessor of the "wise blood," Enoch Emery, plays a subordinate but integral role in the novel; in the fifth, eighth, and eleventh chapters, his story is told independently and then related to that of Hazel Motes. Although O'Connor began in the third chapter by letting Enoch tell his history to Hazel, in the later chapters she lets Enoch go his own way, guided by the "wise blood" which tells him that Hazel is important to him. This intuition is confirmed when Hazel seeks him out before he begins to preach the Church of Christ Without Christ, and Enoch shows Hazel the mummified man that fascinates him in the run-down museum attached to the zoo, places which are symbolic of humankind's animal nature and dead past.

When Enoch hears Hazel preaching, he determines to steal the mummified man and give the figure to Hazel as his new "Christ." After doing so, however, his "wise blood" takes charge again and leads him to seize the gorilla suit of a fake "gorilla" film star, Gonga, and try to make friends in this costume. The whole of the twelfth chapter is devoted to this episode, which leaves "Gonga" Emery alone and puzzled on the highway. It contains some of O'Connor's most comic writing, partly verbal, partly comedy of situation, and at the same time profoundly meaningful. This is a human as a "bare, forked animal" thinking that he can be a success in life by following his "wise blood." Enoch is thus a more direct contrast to Hazel than Asa Hawks or Hoover Shoats ("Onnie Jay Holy"), who simply use religion to make money and thus confirm Hazel's disgust with institutional or evangelical Christianity. Theirs is a false way to salvation, but Enoch's is equally profitless in his determination to get on in the world at all costs, and his is the more prevalent code.

The many minor characters are not all condemned by O'Connor, as is shown by their treatment of Hazel Motes. Those who cheat him—the car salesman, the hat salesman, Mrs. Flood—are clearly vicious, though the way that they gull poor simple Hazel is richly comic. On at least three occasions, however, someone tries to tell Hazel the truth about his Essex car, but he will not listen, leading to its destruction at the hands of the police officer. Swift sketches of the physical appearance and nature of the minor characters, such as the woman at the swimming pool, reveal O'Connor's remarkable gift for caricature.

Striking similes and other tricks of style—elliptical country speech, in which so much is left unsaid, and the rapid succession of events in the narrative—carry the story along at a fast pace. The narrative is brief and the meaning clear. Granted the initial stance of high irony in which everything is at once itself and its opposite, there is no difficulty in seeing that Hazel Motes and O'Connor are preaching the Church of Christ *with* Christ.

The writer's gifts amply ensure an understanding of the story's meaning, but there may remain a final hesitation for those readers whose Christ is a tender and loving spirit. When Hazel's mother reminds him that Christ died to redeem him from sin, he replies that he did not ask Christ to do that. There is no freedom for the individual in this novel because, as Flannery O'Connor suggests in her introductory note, humanity's free will is simply a conflict of many wills or desires; this conflict is resolved only when one abandons these desires and accedes to the will of God, allowing it to be imposed on one. This is the "jealous" God of the Old Testament who in the New Testament sent His Son to be crucified for humanity. One must expect to be equally crucified in turn, as Hazel Motes is in this novel.

THE WOMAN WARRIOR: Memories of a Girlhood Among Ghosts

Type of work: Novelized autobiography
Author: Maxine Hong Kingston (1940-   )
Type of plot: Chinese mythology and personal narrative
Time of plot: 1924-1974
Locale: China and Stockton, California
First published: 1976

This book, which is at once autobiographical and mythical, has two central themes: the generational bonding and conflict among women, and the tug and pull of Chinese and American cultures in forging a personal identity and art. The book is a lyrical tour de force, complex, multilayered, and highly inventive, showing how rich Asian cultural elements are transformed by a new American world.

Principal Personages

Maxine Hong Kingston, the author, a young Chinese-American woman.

Brave Orchid, her mother, who is strong-willed.

Moon Orchid, Brave Orchid's sister, who is timid.

No Name Woman, another sister, who committed suicide after she gave birth to an illegitimate child.

The Story

Maxine Hong Kingston's autobiography centers on her female ancestors and their impact on her life. Five narrative segments are used to illustrate the dynamics of revelation and suppression between mothers and daughters as they "talk story." Although the overall movement of the book is chronological, it has no single, unified plot in a conventional sense. Stories of Kingston's female relatives are told in the first, third, and fourth sections, while the second and fifth ones explore Kingston's own life.

In the first section, "No Name Woman," family shame and secrecy conceal the truth about Kingston's deceased aunt. Kingston's mother, Brave Orchid, tells her that, years after the aunt's husband left China for the United States, this "No Name Woman" became pregnant. On the night that the baby was born, angry villagers raided the house, slaughtered livestock, and destroyed the aunt's belongings. The aunt gave birth alone in a pigsty, then drowned the child and herself in the family well. Family shame was so deep that the aunt was never mentioned again. Kingston's mother conveys the bare outlines of the incident to her when she reaches puberty as a warning not to humiliate the family in the same way. Kingston wants to know more, however, especially her aunt's state of mind when she conceived the child: Had she been raped, was she a promiscuous woman, or was she truly in love with another man? The author also longs for in-

formation about her aunt's personality and preferences, but she knows that her mother will reveal nothing more. Brave Orchid's "talking story" has transferred to her daughter all the "useful parts" of the incident; adultery is a despicable "extravagance" that dare not be explored. Kingston knows that the family's necessary secrecy is a way of redeeming themselves from guilt and that she must remain unsatisfied and unsettled. She will never know exactly how and where her aunt's life branches into her own; that part of her genetic heritage and history is effectively blocked from her.

In the second section, "White Tigers," ancient Chinese mythology and Kingston's personal life coalesce. The frame for the myth about the Chinese swordswoman heroine Fa Mu Lan is Kingston's mother telling her bedtime stories when she is nine years old. In giving her the story and its chants, Brave Orchid also symbolically empowers her with the inspiration, the desire, and the expectation to grow up a "warrior woman."

As the telling of the myth begins, fantasy and reality blend as the narrative voice at once belongs to both Kingston and Fa Mu Lan. The warrior woman at age seven follows a black-winged bird into the mountains to the home of an old man and an old woman. The couple rear her for fifteen years, teaching her "tiger ways" and "dragon ways" so that she will be powerful enough to avenge her ancestral village. After her training, Fa Mu Lan returns home, where her parents carve words of vengeance upon her back. She marries and bears a child. With an army of soldiers, she slays a giant and the emperor who has oppressed her village.

Fa Mu Lan's legendary status and her mother's unspoken charge to her to emulate it momentarily confound Kingston, who is confused about the relevance of the myth to her own life. In excelling academically and eschewing kitchen tasks, she defies the traditional, submissive Chinese expectation for women. Significantly, she discovers that she can be a woman warrior by being a woman writer, empowered by language (the words upon her back) and by her mother's storytelling.

In "Shaman," Kingston looks directly at the personal history of her mother, Brave Orchid. It is the story of a heroine in China and an ordinary woman in the United States, confident in one sphere and confused in the other. Kingston weaves two story lines to tell her mother's life, implying that one is real and the other is not. At the To Keung School of Midwifery at Canton, Brave Orchid is at the top of her class. With the skill and aplomb of Fa Mu Lan, she exorcises a "Sitting Ghost" from a "haunted" room in the women's dormitory. Back in her native village, she battled epidemics, delivered babies in pigsties, and straightened the bones of cripples.

When her husband bids her to join him in the Bronx fifteen years after he left China, Brave Orchid becomes baffled in an alien world of "Taxi Ghosts, Bus Ghosts, Police Ghosts, Fire Ghosts, Meter Reader Ghosts, Tree Trimming Ghosts, Five-and-Dime Ghosts." Hot work in the family laundry and then in the field picking tomatoes has battered her heroic spirit and given her varicose veins. "This is terrible ghost country," she laments, "where a human being works her life away. . . . Even the ghosts work, no time for acrobatics." Yet the same speed that confounds her mother in American society seems to energize Kingston. The final scene, Kingston at her parents' home on one of her yearly visits, shows at once the pain and the necessity of adult children establishing a life independent of their parents, yet maintaining an enduring, vital bond. Kingston muses, "Before we can leave our parents, they stuff our heads like the suitcases which they jam-pack with homemade underwear." The connection and the separation are both uncomfortable and satisfying.

The fourth chapter, "At the Western Palace," conveys connection on a different level—that between Brave Orchid and her sister Moon Orchid, who reunite in the United States after a thirty-year separation. Moon Orchid is timid and complacent; Brave Orchid, by comparison, seems powerful, having achieved a functional degree of identity in her new world. They work side by side in the family laundry as Brave Orchid aggressively fuels Moon Orchid's negligible curiosity to look up her husband in Los Angeles. Though Moon Orchid lacks nerve, Brave Orchid has enough for both of them. They discover that the husband is a successful brain surgeon who has remarried and fathered three children; though he has been sending Moon Orchid money in China all along, now that he sees her face to face he tells her that her provincial Chinese ways no longer fit into his new American life-style. Moon Orchid—rebuffed, paranoid, and very sad—goes quietly mad. She has not been able to synchronize her Chinese reality with her American situation.

In the final section, "Song for a Barbarian Reed Pipe," Kingston's childhood in the United States seems to mirror the silence and confusion of Moon Orchid's dotage. The culture clash that she experiences beginning as a kindergartner is portrayed symbolically when the author imagines her Chinese mother cutting her tongue so that she is unable to speak properly. American teachers do not understand her. While Kingston proudly covers her drawings with black paint, pleased with the "possibilities" that she has depicted, the teachers perceive only the unintelligible products of a deluded and depressed mind.

During class recitations, her voice seems to her "a crippled animal running on broken legs . . . bones rubbing jagged against one another." Eventually, she earns top grades in school, but her mother wishes that she would develop social skills instead. Kingston stores up resentments against her mother and against an education that failed to impart to her early and thoroughly the cultural and linguistic savvy that she needed. At the end of the book, she is still trying to sort out "what's just my childhood, just my imagination, just my family, just the village, just movies, just living." She concludes that she must make a trip to China, to find out for herself "what's a cheat story and what's not."

Critical Evaluation

The Woman Warrior is both a coming-of-age story and a tale of cultural assimilation. Kingston's life, from kindergarten to adulthood, is told in a nonlinear form. Rather than an extended narrative strand littered with time lines, dates, and chronological events, the autobiography is more creative, focusing selectively on the important, shaping influences from the author's female ancestors. A product of immigrant parents, Kingston's childhood and adolescence is compounded with difficult issues of identity. She celebrates her Chinese heritage—the source of imagery, inspiration, and vision—at the same time that she finds it an impediment to fitting into American society. Kingston thinks that her books are much more "American" than they are "Chinese." She wants her readers to realize how American her generation became. In chapters such as "At the Western Palace," in which Kingston and her siblings, in humorous contrast to Moon Orchid's expectations, not only spurn Chinese culture but also are ignorant of it, that message is unmistakable.

The book is very much a feminist document, portraying strong women who take control of their lives in the face of immense challenges. The Chinese phrase for storytelling is "talking-story," orally conveying in real or mythical illustration, often to a younger generation, some important truth. This is Kingston's rhetorical method. *The Woman Warrior* begins and ends with Kingston's mother talking-story, which in a sense defines their relationship: "The beginning is hers, the ending, mine." Their relationship and the composition process is complicated by the fact that Brave Orchid sometimes tells truths, sometimes lies. Part of Kingston's problem with separating from her mother and achieving her own identity is trying to discern the difference between the truth and the lies. Yet she implies that discovering which things are lies and which are truths is not, in itself, as important as the reason that they are lies. In fact, part of what Kingston tells readers is not the literal truth, either. She concocts several scenarios about the motivation for her aunt taking a lover in "No Name Woman." She reconstructs the story of Fa Mu Lan to make it her personal legend. She revises her mother's young adulthood to give the reader history beyond the facts that her mother provides. Simply studying the photograph of her mother's medical school graduation class inspires Kingston to talk story about, for one thing, the differences between her mother and her father.

The story of her father and her male ancestors, in fact, is the subject of her second book, *China Men* (1980), written at roughly the same time. Originally conceived as a single volume, *The Warrior Woman* and *China Men* together form Kingston's complete autobiography. She chose to publish them separately because she believed that the men's stories began to interfere with and intrude on those of the women, weakening the feminist point of view. The story of her forefathers, Kingston believes, is really the story of China's immigration to the United States. The women were largely left behind in China, some joining their husbands years later when the men had established themselves on the "Gold Mountain."

China Men is a story about the building of the transcontinental railroad and about the growth of private enterprise and the labor movement in this new world. It is set in a sweep from Hawaii to Alaska, from New York to California. A strong and very public story, Kingston reveals that it was more difficult for her to achieve than the more intimate story of her female ancestors, who tell largely an internal story. Because her father was a different gender from her and did not have a primary bond with her in the sense that her mother did, Kingston did not feel as great an immediate, personal access to his stories. Furthermore, Chinese men simply did not talk story. Instead, their communication, particularly to women, was characterized by angry screams, by rude and derogatory curses, and, above all, by silence. Kingston is separate and distant from her male ancestors. In fact, the kinship between the various male consciousnesses in the book emerges as a far greater bond than that between Kingston and her father.

Kingston did make good the resolve to visit China that she put forth at the end of *The Warrior Woman*, but not until she had completed both books. She said she wanted to write about Chinese myth, specifically, as it had affected her life so strongly, and meanwhile did not want a new set of impressions to get in the way. Together, *The Woman Warrior* and *China Men* allow Kingston to explore the full scope of her identity within herself and outside herself. In discovering both parents with language in her writing, she is discovering herself. Both books won the National Book Critics Circle Award in nonfiction. *The Woman Warrior* was also named one of the top ten nonfiction works of the decade by *Time* magazine in 1979. In 1980, Kingston was named a "living treasure" of Hawaii.

THE WORKS OF JONATHAN EDWARDS

Type of work: Essays and sermons
Author: Jonathan Edwards (1703-1758)
First published: 1731-1758 (*The Works of President Edwards*, 1808-1809)

Jonathan Edwards, a Calvinist preacher, was America's first eminent philosopher. Metaphysically, he was an idealist like George Berkeley, but his primary concern was not with the traditional problems of philosophy but with theological issues that had a direct bearing on the religious practices of his time. He used his philosophy to assert the absolute sovereignty of God and to reaffirm the doctrine of Original Sin. He argued that reason and natural goodness are not enough to make one virtuous: Humans need revelation and disinterested benevolence if they are to be worthwhile as religious people. Showing the influence of John Locke and Sir Isaac Newton, Edwards argued that every event has a cause; he then went on to maintain that humans are free, nevertheless, because they can do as they will and are therefore responsible for their actions.

The effect of Edwards' work was a strong revival of idealism and Calvinistic pietism. His own congregation responded with a surprising number of conversions, as he reports in his essay "A Narrative of Many Surprising Conversions in Northampton and Vicinity" (1736). Edwards attributed what he called the "awakening" to God's influence, but it is clear that his efforts were at least instrumental. The Puritan revival grew to such proportions that the phrase the "Great Awakening" was devised to describe the period between 1740 and 1742.

Edwards' earliest philosophical efforts are preserved in his "Notes on the Mind," an early product of his reading of Locke's *An Essay Concerning Human Understanding* (1690). Edwards went beyond Locke in much the same critical manner as Berkeley, pointing out that the primary qualities of extension, motion, and figure are as much dependent on the senses as are the secondary qualities of color, taste, sound, and odor. Like Berkeley, Edwards decided that objects are combinations of ideas and that the "Substance of all Bodies, is the infinitely exact, and precise, and perfectly stable Idea, in God's mind. . . ." Edwards identified perceptions with ideas and attributed all ideas to the influence of God. Like later idealists, he defined truth as the consistency of ideas with themselves: To know that a proposition is true, one correctly perceives the relations between ideas, but to have a false idea is to suppose that certain relations prevail among the ideas that actually do not so prevail. The essay also

presented an analysis of value in terms of "the inclination and disposition of the mind." In "Notes on the Mind," one also finds the claim that "all Virtue, which is the Excellency of minds, is resolved into *Love to Being*," an idea that was later developed in more detail in the essay entitled "A Dissertation on the Nature of True Virtue."

In the essay on true virtue, written in 1755, Edwards wrote that "true virtue"—by which he meant actual, as distinguished from merely apparent, moral excellence—"consists in benevolence to Being general. Or perhaps to speak more accurately, it is that consent, propensity and union of heart to Being in general, that is immediately exercised in a general good will." Edwards argued that all sin is the result of self-love that resists the directives of the "natural conscience." True virtue is the actual consent to Being, the acceptance of God, and must be distinguished from the natural conscience that approves of true virtue, although it is not itself the virtuous response to Being.

For many outside Edwards' faith, the problem has always been that of reconciling the idea of God's sovereignty with the idea that God, as Being, should be the object of disinterested benevolence, or love. In his sermon "Sinners in the Hands of an Angry God" (1741), for example, Edwards spoke from the pulpit of the imminence of hell for the wicked: "There is nothing that keeps wicked men at any one moment out of hell, but the mere pleasure of God. By the mere pleasure of God, I mean his sovereign pleasure, his arbitrary will, restrained by no obligation. . . ." He went on to warn that "natural men are held in the hand of God over the pit of hell; they have deserved the fiery pit, and are already sentenced to it." He declared that the wrath of God is "everlasting" and that the torments of hell will continue for "millions and millions of ages. . . ." Finally, he concluded that "it would be a wonder if some that are now present should not be in hell in a very short time, before this year is out. And it would be no wonder if some persons, that now sit here in some seats of this meeting-house in health, and quiet and secure, should be there before tomorrow morning."

In his "Personal Narrative" (1765), Edwards wrote that the doctrine of God's sovereignty "used to appear like a horrible doctrine to me," but he had come to regard the doctrine as "exceeding pleasant, bright, and sweet." For a man who had learned to consent to Being, the change of attitude was inevitable. Yet one may ask how Edwards was to reconcile for his congregation the idea of a sovereign God whose nature and grace are beyond discovery with the idea of a God worthy of love. To understand the answer to this question, one must consider, in turn, two such famous sermons as "God Glorified in Man's Dependence," delivered in 1731, and "A Divine and Supernatural Light, Immediately Imparted to the Soul by the Spirit of God, Shown to be Both a Scriptural and Rational Doctrine," delivered in 1734.

The former sermon was enthusiastically received by Calvinist ministers who sought, through its publication, to defend their faith from attack. In his sermon, Edwards argued that the redeemed are absolutely dependent on God, that His grace is entirely free, that all good is in God, and that the fact of humanity's dependence glorifies God. To have any hope of an eternal life, a man should "abase himself, and reflect on his own exceeding unworthiness of such a favor, and to exalt God alone." Although Edwards insisted that the redeemed have spiritual joy because of their dependence, the emphasis was more on the fact of dependence and on God's glory than on the satisfaction of being redeemed.

In the sermon "A Divine and Supernatural Light," Edwards used the psychology that he had learned from reading Locke to emphasize his claim that there is no natural way of coming to know and love God. The blessedness of some people, their spiritual happiness, resulted from God's having given them a spiritual light whereby they could come to be convinced of God's reality and excellence. Such a spiritual light cannot be explained in any of the ways by which one understands natural faculties of the understanding and will; it must be imparted by the Spirit of God. Edwards offered the doctrine as both scriptural and "rational." The sermon concluded with a reassuring statement of the value of the spiritual light: "It draws forth the heart in a sincere love to God, which is the only principle of a true, gracious, and universal obedience; and it convinces of the reality of those glorious rewards that God has promised to them that obey him."

By alternatively emphasizing the sovereignty of God and the joy of loving Him, Edwards achieved a balance between the harsh and the comforting aspects of his Calvinistic views.

Of his essays, the most famous is the essay on the freedom of the will, a book-length study entitled "A Careful and Strict Inquiry into the Modern Prevailing Notions of that Freedom of the Will, Which Is Supposed to be Essential to Moral Agency, Virtue and Vice, Reward and Punishment, Praise and Blame." The will is quickly and simply defined as the power to choose. Edwards then agreed that Locke was correct in distinguishing between will and desire, the latter being restricted to what is absent, but Edwards argued that the distinction was not important in the problem of free will. The will is determined, he wrote, because a choice is made in consequence of some influence. The will is always determined by the strongest motive, that is, by the prevailing inclination. Whether one considers natural or moral necessity, in either case one is considering the connection of cause and effect. By freedom is meant the power to do as one pleases or wills. Thus, even if the will is determined by the strongest motive, there is no contradiction involved in saying that people are free if they can do what they will. Even if the will is determined by cause, people are free if they can do as they choose.

Edwards would have rejected the question of the freedom or determination of the will. For him, the answer was that the will is both determined and free: It is determined in that it acts from causes, and it is free provided that the person who wills is able to act as he or she wills.

Edwards concluded that, whenever an act results from the exercise of a person's will, the agent is morally responsible for this act. By his philosophical resolution of the problem of free will, Edwards was able to relate moral necessity to God's necessarily choosing the best. He rejected Arminian criticisms that attempted to support a conception of liberty as "indifferent," that is, a conception of the will as capable of acting entirely without determination.

Other important essays by Edwards are "The Great Christian Doctrine of Original Sin Defended" (1758), "True Grace" (1753), "A Dissertation Concerning the End for which God Created the World" (1755), and "A Treatise Concerning Religious Affections" (1746).

Edwards brought all of his philosophical powers to bear on the issues that kept Calvinism in the midst of religious controversy, and although few modern philosophical critics would grant that he in any way proved his case, it is generally conceded that he played a major role in the "Great Awakening" and gave American philosophy an initial impetus and influence that continued until realistic and pragmatic ideas effectively displaced religious idealism.

THE WORLD ACCORDING TO GARP

Type of work: Novel
Author: John Irving (1942-   )
Type of plot: Dark domestic comedy
Time of plot: Mid-twentieth century
Locale: New England and Europe
First published: 1978

With its roots in the traditional novel and its style and sensibility set in postmodern fiction, The World According to Garp *marked Irving's emergence as a major figure in American literature. His depiction of an athlete and artist attempting to develop a strategy for survival in a world of random violence, vicious and psychotic behavior, social chaos, and individual uncertainty is a humane exploration of the exigencies of the human condition in the second half of the twentieth century.*

Principal Characters

T. S. Garp, an aspiring writer driven by a desire to protect his family from what he regards as a lethal universe. He is determined to follow the course of creativity outlined by his artistic abilities and inclinations. Reared by a very focused single mother who becomes a mythic heroine for a version of feminist philosophy, Garp experiences a series of devastating personal losses that he tries to handle through his relationships with the family that he loves, the work to which he is committed, and the comic and horrific "world" that fascinates and frightens him.

Jenny Fields, Garp's mother. The daughter of a prominent New England manufacturing executive, she rejects the pampered, privileged life for which she has been prepared. Instead, she becomes a nurse, engineers her sole pregnancy through no conventional contact with Garp's biological father, writes a book that becomes a feminist manifesto and projects her into the status of a goddess or protector to her gender, and sets an example of caring that inspires and daunts Garp.

Helen Holm, Garp's wife and the mother of Duncan, Walt, and Jenny, their children. The daughter of Ernie Holm, the wrestling coach at the Steering Academy where

Jenny Fields is head nurse, she is a professor of literature, Garp's friend and lover, and an intelligent woman whose warmth, insight, and understanding are crucial components in the psychic survival of the Garp family.

Duncan Garp, the first child born to Garp and Helen Holm. He is a wry, decent, and damaged boy whose solidity of character and sense of comic dislocation permit him to pursue a successful career as a painter in spite of his physical limitations. He carries in his tolerance and enthusiasm the spirit of his father's quests.

Roberta Muldoon, a transsexual former athlete who forgoes a successful career as a professional football player to become a supporter and bodyguard for Jenny Fields and a close friend of Garp.

John Wolf, a literary agent who realizes the worth and commercial appeal of Jenny Fields's manuscript for *A Sexual Suspect.* He is an editor in the classic tradition, understanding and appreciating literature while realizing the pressures of commercial publishing. He assists Garp by trying to act as a barrier between Garp's intense reactions to everything and the public and critical responses to his books.

The Story

Jenny Fields was born in 1920, the only daughter of a family prominent in New England as shoe manufacturers. She was not interested in following the course of social development outlined by her parents, and she dropped out of Wellesley College to attend nursing school.

Determined to live independently, she arranged a single sexual experience with a wounded soldier in Boston Mercy Hospital, where she worked in the intensive care ward. Technical Sergeant Garp was a ball turret gunner who was mentally disabled by a shard of flak on his thirty-fifth mission, and his condition deteriorated steadily, leading to his death shortly before Jenny gave birth to T. S. Garp, their son, who learned about his father from his mother's accounts.

Anxious to provide a proper intellectual environment for her son, Jenny Fields accepted a position at the Steering Academy, the relatively exclusive preparatory school that her father had attended. While working as a nurse there (later becoming the head nurse), Jenny attended classes to determine which ones would suit Garp best, and she read through the entire library shelf in literature, supplementing these books with others that she purchased and used to stock a private collection in the infirmary. Jenny Fields remained relatively distant from the faculty, but young Garp grew up within the world of the school, "aloof but eternally watchful," and found his métier and his mentor when he discovered Ernie Holm, the wrestling coach, in the wrestling room "padded against pain." Aside from several minor mishaps and some volatile encounters with the Percy family that ran the school, Garp discovered his vocation at Steering—he wrote one short story every month while he was a student—and, influenced by Helen Holm, Coach Holm's daughter, Garp decided to go to Europe with his mother after graduation.

In Europe, he continued his education on the streets, in restaurants, and in pensions in Vienna, trying to write but primarily observing the city and its inhabitants, including an older courtesan named Charlotte with whom he had a brief, poignant affair. His mother was working steadily on a memoir, her first writing experience, and Garp's temporary difficulty in completing his first published work, "The Pension Grillparzer," was overcome when Charlotte's death and inquiring letters from Helen Holm concentrated his intentions. He sent the manuscript to Helen as a proposal of sorts, and when he and his mother returned to the United States, Garp and Helen were married. His mother's massive memoir was recognized by an urbane, professional editor named John Wolf as a potential commercial blockbuster, and when it was published, Jenny Fields became an instant celebrity and a heroine for many women who shared her ideas and, admired her forthright and forceful pattern of expression.

Garp and Helen began to rear a family, with Helen working as a professor of literature and Garp staying home to write and care for their sons, Duncan and Walt. Their lives were complicated by a double affair with a colleague of Helen and his wife, which became the subject of an almost literally autobiographical novel, *Second Wind of a Cuckold*, a "serious" book that was as un-noticed as Garp's first novel, *Procrastination*. Aside from the familiar tensions inherent in many families, and Garp's obsessive concern about his family's safety even in the absence of any threats to their well-being, Helen and Garp were managing moderately well with their work and their marriage until Helen began an insignificant affair with a supercilious graduate student. Garp's discovery of this situation was very unsettling to him, in spite of his own occasional minor infidelities. Then, a tragic automobile accident, essentially caused by both Garp and Helen's foolishness, totally obliterated any sense of well-being, injuring everyone and causing Walt's death.

With the assistance of Jenny Fields, who was then administering a refuge for injured women at her old family mansion on the New Hampshire coast, the Garp family gradually recovered. Garp wrote about the shattering effect of the accident in a graphic, violent novel, *The World According to Bensenhaver*, and Jenny Garp was born. The Garp family visited Europe, continuing the healing process, but upon their return, the dreaded "Under Toad," a symbol of death, struck again: Jenny Fields was assassinated by the husband of a woman who refused to accept abusive behavior. Accompanied by his best friend, Roberta Muldoon, a former football player who has undergone a sex-change operation, Garp attended the first Feminist Funeral in disguise; he then attended the funeral of Stewart Percy, the former head of Steering, and Ernie Holm, again disguised. Unable to write, Garp became a wrestling coach for "something to *do.*" The Garp family bought the old Steering mansion, Helen began to teach again at the school, and Garp served on the board of the Fields Foundation, a trust set up by the Fields legacy to support projects proposed by women. Thus, the Garps began a kind of extended period of convalescence and waiting.

Garp was drawn back to his writing by his anger at self-righteous, self-pitying absolutists and began work on *My Father's Illusions*, an imaginative projection of his ancestry. Just as his life became somewhat stable and coherent again, he was murdered by another deranged zealot who blamed him for her unhappiness. Garp died content that his life had not been wasted, and that his family could stay strong through his enduring gifts of energy, decency, and unconditional love. The novel concludes with an extended epilogue that summarizes the circumstances of the lives of all the central characters in the story. While each brief sketch ends in death, it is the spirit of the distinctive life that each character exhibited that stands as a tribute and testament to Garp's heroic efforts to make a world in and of his art.

Critical Evaluation

In a characteristically contrarian gesture, John Irving wrote *The World According to Garp* in an attempt to use the means of a traditional novel on the largest scale at a time when minimalist fiction was being temporarily celebrated as the truest voice of the age. Working with the kind of sprawling structure that novelists such as Theodore Dreiser or Frank Norris employed to link the destiny of a family with the dynamics of social change across several generations, Irving begins with the world in which Garp's mother is born, follows Garp's growth toward maturity in the turmoil of the 1960's, and assesses the consequences of Garp's life as a projection of his impact on a generation living into a future beyond the publication date of the book.

Within this framework, Irving fashions a distinctly postmodern sensibility to examine, through the development of the artistic consciousness of his protagonists, a world in which the concept of the absurd is no longer relevant because everything that happens seems to be an expression of random, entropic forces. Almost nothing is predictable or controllable, eruptions of violence are commonplace, solipsism is pervasive, and the psychic instability engendered by this condition has driven almost all the characters in the novel into defensive extremes that make supportive emotional relationships very difficult to establish and maintain. Garp's mother, Jenny Fields, recognizes the emptiness of the dependent, ornamental role for which she is being prepared, and she tries to chart a course for herself that will be useful and satisfying. Her fierce independence, however, becomes a form of denial. Garp appreciates her resolution and shares her anger at mendacity and narcissism, but he is practically pulsating with a kind of energy that prohibits a controlled, sensible analysis of everything. The essential theme of the novel is Garp's quest for a life pattern that will enable him to direct this energy toward other people without smothering them (as in a wrestler's pinning hold). Irving adopts another nearly timeless motif, the power of art to clarify and occasionally console, as a vehicle for this quest.

The action-taking hero of Ernest Hemingway's fiction and the cerebral protagonist of Saul Bellow or J. D. Salinger are fused in a brash amalgam as Garp is keenly aware of both his body and his mind. He is prepared to use both faculties in his struggles with a dangerous and often actively hostile environment, and he draws his force from the most basic unit of strength, the family. In his case, however, the family is a nontraditional, isolated construct. Because the tight enclosure of love is so im-

portant to him, Garp tends to be wildly overprotective about it, but his concern is justified by the fractured families to which he is close and by the larger collapse of institutional structures everywhere. The process of his development as a writer parallels and reflects his strategies for shaping the self as an instrument of defensive action against the madness existing in the world. It is as if Garp is trying to build, in his fiction and in his world, a "family" sufficiently stable and resilient to withstand assault on all levels.

His initial reaction, like his mother's, is primarily against the "world according to Fat Stew," the reign at the Steering Academy of a wealthy, obtuse family with undeserved privilege and no perception. This family is Irving's symbol for the failure of mid-twentieth century American culture, a failure that includes a war demolishing Garp's father and that puts the country's Stewart Percys—with their old money, stupidity, arrogance, and intolerance—in charge of American political power. Garp's dismissal of this repugnant vestige of ancient hierarchy is fundamental, but the void left by this demolition is not easy to fill, especially because the field is being contested by an assortment of zealots and fanatics, "self-righteous" and full of "monstrous self-pity." The Ellen Jamesians, who practice self-mutilation to protest rape, and various cruel men, who are enraged because their scapegoats are in rebellion, represent opposite but allied poles of blindness and rigidity. Jenny Fields's answer is a world of "absolute clarity" that Garp admires, but his world is already too complex, too full of distinctions, for him to accept it totally. On his first trip to Europe, when he writes his first successful story, "The Pension Grillparzer," he is already aware of the complications and contradictions of life in which evil is prevalent and often inexplicable. His story is an attempt to handle the world with a kind of artistic and philosophical distance, but the automobile accident that surpasses his worst nightmares indicates that his art must grow from involvement, not containment.

Garp's understandable initial response to his loss is to use art as therapy. He writes *The World According to Bensenhaver* as an attempt to manage "overwhelming grief" and to objectify his anger, projecting the contesting forces of his psyche into the two central characters of the long opening chapter, Hope vs. Rath (wrath). He conceives Alden Bensenhaver as a "hovering angel," an "armed uncle" protecting a wounded family, but the elderly, well-meaning law officer is a symbol of suffocation, "more menace than protector" who threatens to drive everyone into caution and paranoia—another version of a life-denying extremism. The book is a gripping demonstration of the power of literal description, but the shock that it engenders carries no useful, resonant message for the human soul. Its composition does permit Garp to tangle with some hidden psychic demons, and its completion is a kind of exorcism, leaving him artistically exhausted but prepared for a personal healing through the love of his family.

This "family" is joined by spiritual affinity and defined by a tolerance for singularity stemming from a shared recognition that individual idiosyncrasy and personal desire can be reconciled with communal cooperation. It includes Roberta Muldoon, the transsexual former athlete who is "more feminine than anyone" with a body like "a highly trained rock"; Ellen James, whose mutilation has not crushed her aesthetic sensitivity; John Wolf, the elegant editor of Garp's work whose sophisticated sense of the publishing trade has not eroded his love for literary accomplishment; as well as Garp's blood kin. When Garp has recovered sufficiently to write again, his last book, *My Father's Illusions*, is an imaginative leap beyond the prison of the self to try to offer a life to the man he never knew; it is an empathetic act in which Garp attempts to give his father a personality beyond the tale of

his sexual presence. Garp's last work is never completed because he is murdered in his sanctuary (the wrestling room where "inexplicable closeness is possible") by the deranged Pooh Percy, the last member of the deteriorating old order, but the book has been conceived as an act of optimism. It is a document that determines the coordinates of Garp's world, and it remains as a part of his spiritual and artistic legacy to its inhabitants.

Irving's last chapter, "Life After Garp," is a map of his sphere. Its worldview grows from Garp's flinty integrity, and as Irving extends the novel into the fifth generation of the Fields and Garp family, an ethos of deep sentiment is generated, the moment of feeling that only an almost epochal work can achieve. When *The World According to Garp* was published, the bizarre wit, manic invention, and striking narration of the book immediately captivated many readers. The considerations of feminine realities from the perspective of an actively heterosexual and genuinely sympathetic male seemed timely, as did Irving's oblique incorporation of the devastating political murders of the 1960's. The passage of time has not dimmed the fire of Irving's style, while his feeling for essential human needs and the consolations of art has ensured that the novel will not depend on its brilliant use of the momentarily topical for its appeal.

YOU CAN'T GO HOME AGAIN

Type of work: Novel
Author: Thomas Wolfe (1900-1938)
Type of plot: Impressionistic realism
Time of plot: 1929-1936
Locale: New York, England, and Germany
First published: 1940

The ability to present real scenes and real people is a rare gift in the most mature writers, but Wolfe exhibited these talents while still in his thirties. His youth showed itself clearly in his four novels, including You Can't Go Home Again, *in his overexuberant desire to help humanity in spite of itself and in his lyric enthusiasm for the American Dream.*

Principal Characters

George Webber, a young writer in the first flush of success as a novelist. He learns that success creates enemies and that it is sometimes empty of meaning. His great aim in life, idealist that he is, is to write the truth, to portray people as they are—the great and small, the rich and poor. He faces disillusionment at every turn. He finds that people are greedy after the world's goods; he finds, too, that they do not relish his truthful portrayal of them. George again visits Germany, a place that he loves, only to find that country filled with fear and persecution in the 1930's, during the Nazi regime. He returns home to the United States to preach in new novels against selfishness and greed, hoping that he can awaken the people of his own land to arise and defeat the forces that are threatening the freedom of humankind.

Foxhall Edwards, an editor for a publishing house who becomes George Webber's friend and trusted adviser for a time. He is a genius at encouraging young writers to find themselves and to win the confidence that they need to produce literary art. He is also a skeptical person who believes that, if humans are not destined for

freedom, then they must accept this fact. Edwards' fatalism is at odds with George's idealistic desire to better the lot of humankind by working to change conditions. These divergent attitudes cause a break in the friendship between the two men.

Lloyd McHarg, a successful American novelist who has won worldwide fame based upon a number of excellent novels. He has found fame to be empty and searches for something else, he knows not what. McHarg's disillusionment is a bitter lesson for young, idealistic George Webber, for whom McHarg has been a symbol of greatness.

Esther Jack, an older woman who has been George's mistress in the past and becomes so again for a time after he has achieved success. He leaves her a second time when he decides that, in order to find himself, he must abandon Esther's sophisticated set and get to know the common people of the world.

Else von Kohler, a beautiful, intelligent young German woman with whom George has a tender romance while revisiting Germany during the 1930's.

The Story

As George Webber looked out of his New York apartment window that spring day in 1929, he was filled with happiness. The bitter despair of the previous year had been lost somewhere in the riotous time that he had spent in Europe, and it was good to be back in New York with the feeling that he knew where he was going. His book had been accepted by a great publishing firm, and Foxhall Edwards, the best editor of the house, had been assigned to help him with the corrections and revisions.

George had also resumed his old love affair with Esther Jack, who, married and the mother of a grown daughter, nevertheless returned his love with tenderness and passion. This love, however, was a flaw in George's otherwise great content, for he and Esther seemed to be pulling different ways. She was a famous stage designer who mingled with a sophisticated artistic set. George thought that he could find himself completely only if he lived among and understood the little people of the world.

Before George's book was published, he tried for the first time to go home again. Home was Libya Hill, a small city in the mountains of Old Catawba. When the aunt who had reared George died, he went back to Libya Hill for her funeral. There he learned that he could never really go home again, for home was no longer the quiet town of his boyhood but a growing city of money-crazy speculators who were concerned only with making huge paper fortunes out of real estate.

George found some satisfaction in the small excitement that he created because he had written a book that was soon to be published. Yet even that pleasure was not to last long. For when he returned to New York and the book was published, almost every citizen in Libya Hill wrote him letters filled with threats and curses. George had written of Libya Hill and the people he knew there. His only motive had been to tell the truth as he saw it, but his old friends and relatives in Libya Hill seemed to think that he had spied on them through his boyhood in order to gossip about them in later years. Even the small fame that he received in New York, where his book was favorably reviewed by the critics, could not atone for the abusive letters from Libya Hill. He believed that he could redeem himself only by working feverishly on his new book.

George moved to Brooklyn, first telling Esther good-bye. This severance from Esther was difficult, but George could not live a lie himself and attempt to write the truth. In Brooklyn, he did learn to know and love the little people—the derelicts, the prostitutes, the petty criminals—and he learned that they, like the so-called good men and women, were all representative of the United States. His only real friend was Foxhall Edwards, who had become like a father to George. Edwards was a great man, a genius among editors and a genius at understanding and encouraging those who, like George, found it difficult to believe in anything during the Great Depression years. Edwards, too, knew that only through truth could the United States and the world be saved from destruction. Unlike George, however, he believed that the truth cannot be thrust suddenly upon people; he calmly accepted conditions as they existed. George raged at his friend's skepticism.

After four years in Brooklyn, George finished the first draft of his new book. Tired of New York, he thought that he might find in Europe the atmosphere that he needed to complete his manuscript. In London, he met Lloyd McHarg, the embodiment of all that George wanted to be. George yearned for fame in that period of his life. Because his book had brought him temporary fame, quickly extinguished, he envied McHarg his world repu-

tation as a novelist. George was disillusioned when he learned that McHarg thought fame an empty thing. He had held the world in his hand for a time, but nothing had happened. Now he was living feverishly, looking for something that he could not name.

When his manuscript was ready for publication, George returned to New York, made the corrections that Edwards suggested, and then sailed again for Europe. He went to Germany, a country that he had not visited since 1928. In 1936, he was more saddened by the change in the German people than he had been by anything else in his life. He had always felt a kinship with the Germans, but they were no longer the people he had known. Persecution and fear tinged every life in that once-proud country, and George, sickened, wondered if there were any place in the world where truth and freedom still lived.

There were, however, two bright horizons in his visit to Germany. The first was the fame that greeted him on his arrival there. His first book had been well received, and his second, now published, was a great success. For a time, he basked in that glory, but soon, he, like McHarg, found fame an elusive thing that brought no real reward. His other great experience was his love for Else von Kohler. That was also an elusive joy, for her roots were deep in Germany, and George knew that he must return to the United States to cry out to his own people that they must live the truth and so save them from the world's ruin.

Before he left Germany, George saw more examples of the horror and tyranny under which the people existed, and he left with a heavy heart. He realized once more that one can never go home again.

Back in New York, he knew that he must break at last his ties with Foxhall Edwards. He wrote to Edwards, telling him why they could no longer travel the same path. First, he reviewed the story of his own life, through which he wove the story of his desire to make the American people awake to the great need for truth so that they might keep their freedom. He told Edwards, too, that in his youth he had wanted fame and love above all else. Having had both, he had learned that they were not enough. Slowly he had learned humility, and he knew that he wanted to speak the truth to the downtrodden, to all humanity. Because George knew he had to try to awaken the slumbering conscience of the United States, he was saying farewell to his friend. Edwards believed that, if the end of freedom was to be the lot of humanity, then fighting against that end was useless.

Sometimes George feared that the battle was lost, but he would never stop fighting as long as there was hope that his country would find itself. He knew at last the real enemy in American society. It was selfishness and greed, disguised as a friend of humankind. He thought that, if he could only get help from the little people, then he could defeat the enemy. Through George, the United States might go home again.

Critical Evaluation

In May, 1938, having broken with his first editor and mentor Maxwell Perkins ("Foxhall Edwards" in the novel), Thomas Wolfe deposited an unfinished manuscript of perhaps a million words on the desk of his new editor, Edward C. Aswell of Harper and Brothers, and left for a tour of the West. In Vancouver, he contracted pneumonia; in Seattle, it worsened. Finally, after Wolfe had been moved to Johns Hopkins in Baltimore, it was found that the illness had triggered the release of previously latent tuberculosis bacteria in his lungs that had gone to the brain; he died on September 15, 1938.

Thus, it was left to Aswell to assemble, organize, and edit Wolfe's admittedly unfinished material into publishable fictions. The major results of Aswell's efforts were the two massive novels that chronicle the life and artistic development of George Webber, *The Web and the Rock* (1939) and *You Can't Go Home Again*. Consequently, the episodic, fragmentary, sometimes even arbitrary structure of these books and the unevenness and occasional excessiveness of the writing must in part be the result of the compositional problems—though these flaws also exist in his two prior works. There is no way of knowing what the final form of the novels would have been had Wolfe lived to complete them to his own satisfaction.

It has been said that Wolfe wrote only one book during his career: a thinly disguised autobiography. In a sense this is true, but, like Walt Whitman, the American author who seems most like him in artistic intention and attitude, Wolfe saw his own experience as the focal point for the experience of a nation in the process of becoming. Thus, as the major character in Wolfe's novels strives for experience, personal meaning, and a means of artistic expression, he is also trying to seize and formalize the nature and direction of nothing less than American society itself.

You Can't Go Home Again is the most external and social of Wolfe's four major novels. The title sets the theme and action line of the novel. George cannot go "home" to any of the old places, experiences, or ideas that have formed him, because every time he attempts to do so he either finds a corruption that has destroyed the thing to which he would return or finds that he has gone beyond that particular experience and has neither the need nor the desire to repeat it. Metaphorically, "home" is the naïve, idealized vision of the United States and of his potential place in it that he had held as a young man, but now learns no longer exists and perhaps never did.

When George returns to his home town of Libya Hill to attend his aunt's funeral, he finds the old rural values gone and a new corrupt speculative fever running rampant. Then he sees the collapse of this greedy dream in the beginnings of the Great Depression. He cannot go back to his physical home because it no longer exists, and he is repelled by what has replaced it. Yet Libya Hill is only a microcosm, a foreshadowing of what he is to encounter. As the country enters into the Great Depression, George comes into painful contact with the results of the American economic and social system as he intimately observes its victims and its victimizers—and he seeks to disassociate himself from both.

It is Europe and especially Germany, however, that brings George to his final understanding. The notion that artistic success and fame will bring him satisfaction is destroyed by his meeting with the famous novelist Lloyd McHarg (a fictionalized Sinclair Lewis), who finds only bitterness, loneliness, and alcohol in his success. George then completes his education in Germany when he is exposed to the horror of the newly powerful Nazi regime. The Nazi horror, thus, is the logical extension and end result of the greed and corruption George has observed in American society, perhaps even the society of the not too distant future.

Yet *You Can't Go Home Again* is not a despairing book. It ends with an exhortation. For all the evil and pessimism that he has encountered in his education, George continues to believe that humankind in general and the United States in particular still have the potential to assert their positive capacities and to realize the ideals that they once possessed. That is where, as an artist in Whitman's tradition, George sees his place to be—as a spokesperson for that vision.

TITLE INDEX

AUTHOR INDEX